Seat Ibiza

Owners Workshop Manual

Mark Storey

Models covered *(6451 - 432)*

Ibiza 'Mk 4' 3-door Hatchback (SC), 5-door Hatchback & Estate (ST)

Petrol: 1.0 litre (999cc) 'MPI' & 'TSI', 1.2 litre 4-cyl 'TSI' (1197cc) & 1.4 litre 'MPI' (1390cc)
Turbo-diesel: 1.6 litre (1598cc)

Does NOT cover 1.2 litre 3-cylinder ('MPI'), 1.4 litre 'TSI', 1.6 litre, 1.8 litre or 2.0 litre petrol engines
Does NOT cover 1.2 litre, 1.4 litre, 1.9 litre or 2.0 litre diesels
Does NOT cover FR or Cupra models, or new 'Mk 5' Ibiza range introduced July 2017

ABCDE
FGHIJ
KLMNO
PQRST

A book in the **Haynes Owners Workshop Manual Series**

ISBN **978 1 78521 451 6**

British Library Cataloguing in Publication Data
A catalogue record for this book is available from the British Library.

Printed in Malaysia

Haynes Publishing
Sparkford, Yeovil, Somerset BA22 7JJ, England

Haynes North America, Inc
859 Lawrence Drive, Newbury Park, California 91320, USA

Printed using NORBRITE BOOK 48.8gsm (CODE: 40N6533) from NORPAC; procurement system certified under Sustainable Forestry Initiative standard. Paper produced is certified to the SFI Certified Fiber Sourcing Standard (CERT - 0094271)

Contents

Contents

REPAIRS AND OVERHAUL

Engine and associated systems

Transmission

Brakes and Suspension

Body equipment

REFERENCE

Index

The Seat Ibiza models covered by this manual were manufactured between May 2008 and June 2017. Commonly know as the 'Mk 4' and designated type 6J (up to the 2016 face lift) and type 6P until the end of production by Seat.

A wide variety of engines were fitted to the Seat Ibiza, however this manual only covers the most popular 1.0 litre 3-cylinder engine, the 1.2 litre 4-cylinder engine, the 1.4 litre 4-cylinder petrol engines. Diesel engine coverage is limited to the ever popular 1.6 CR engine. All the engines are of a well-proven design and, provided regular maintenance is carried out, are unlikely to give trouble.

Seat Ibiza models are available in 3- and 5-door Hatchback and 5-door Estate body styles. The estate model is referred to as the 'ST' by Seat.

Fully-independent front suspension is fitted, with the components attached to a subframe assembly; the rear suspension is semi-independent, with a torsion beam and trailing arms.

Transmission is provided by a five or six-speed manual gearbox with 7 speed DSG automatic gearbox also available.

A wide range of standard and optional equipment is available within the model range to suit most tastes, including anti-lock braking, traction control and air conditioning.

For the home mechanic, Seat Ibiza models are straightforward vehicles to maintain, and most of the items requiring frequent attention are easily accessible.

Your Seat Ibiza Manual

The aim of this manual is to help you get the best value from your vehicle. It can do so in several ways. It can help you decide what work must be done (even should you choose to get it done by a garage). It will also provide information on routine maintenance and servicing, and give a logical course of action and diagnosis when random faults occur. However, it is hoped that you will use the manual by tackling the work yourself. On simpler jobs it may even be quicker than booking the car into a garage and going there twice, to leave and collect it. Perhaps most important, a lot of money can be saved by avoiding the costs a garage must charge to cover its labour and overheads.

The manual has drawings and descriptions to show the function of the various components so that their layout can be understood. Tasks are described and photographed in a clear step-by-step sequence.

References to the 'left' and 'right' of the vehicle are in the sense of a person in the driver's seat facing forward.

Acknowledgements

Thanks are due to Draper Tools Limited and AST tools, who provided some of the workshop tools, and to all those people at Sparkford who helped in the production of this manual.

Working on your car can be dangerous. This page shows just some of the potential risks and hazards, with the aim of creating a safety-conscious attitude.

General hazards

Scalding

• Don't remove the radiator or expansion tank cap while the engine is hot.

• Engine oil, transmission fluid or power steering fluid may also be dangerously hot if the engine has recently been running.

Burning

• Beware of burns from the exhaust system and from any part of the engine. Brake discs and drums can also be extremely hot immediately after use.

Crushing

• When working under or near a raised vehicle, always supplement the jack with axle stands, or use drive-on ramps.

Never venture under a car which is only supported by a jack.

• Take care if loosening or tightening high-torque nuts when the vehicle is on stands. Initial loosening and final tightening should be done with the wheels on the ground.

Fire

• Fuel is highly flammable; fuel vapour is explosive.

• Don't let fuel spill onto a hot engine.

• Do not smoke or allow naked lights (including pilot lights) anywhere near a vehicle being worked on. Also beware of creating sparks (electrically or by use of tools).

• Fuel vapour is heavier than air, so don't work on the fuel system with the vehicle over an inspection pit.

• Another cause of fire is an electrical overload or short-circuit. Take care when repairing or modifying the vehicle wiring.

• Keep a fire extinguisher handy, of a type suitable for use on fuel and electrical fires.

Electric shock

• Ignition HT and Xenon headlight voltages can be dangerous, especially to people with heart problems or a pacemaker. Don't work on or near these systems with the engine running or the ignition switched on.

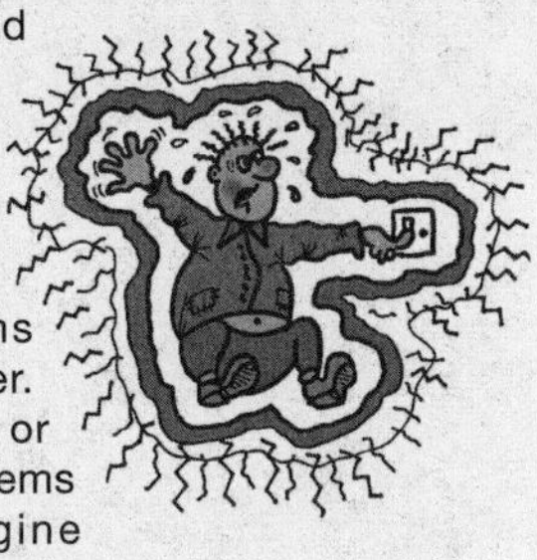

• Mains voltage is also dangerous. Make sure that any mains-operated equipment is correctly earthed. Mains power points should be protected by a residual current device (RCD) circuit breaker.

Fume or gas intoxication

• Exhaust fumes are poisonous; they can contain carbon monoxide, which is rapidly fatal if inhaled. Never run the engine in a confined space such as a garage with the doors shut.

• Fuel vapour is also poisonous, as are the vapours from some cleaning solvents and paint thinners.

Poisonous or irritant substances

• Avoid skin contact with battery acid and with any fuel, fluid or lubricant, especially antifreeze, brake hydraulic fluid and Diesel fuel. Don't syphon them by mouth. If such a substance is swallowed or gets into the eyes, seek medical advice.

• Prolonged contact with used engine oil can cause skin cancer. Wear gloves or use a barrier cream if necessary. Change out of oil-soaked clothes and do not keep oily rags in your pocket.

• Air conditioning refrigerant forms a poisonous gas if exposed to a naked flame (including a cigarette). It can also cause skin burns on contact.

Asbestos

• Asbestos dust can cause cancer if inhaled or swallowed. Asbestos may be found in gaskets and in brake and clutch linings. When dealing with such components it is safest to assume that they contain asbestos.

Special hazards

Hydrofluoric acid

• This extremely corrosive acid is formed when certain types of synthetic rubber, found in some O-rings, oil seals, fuel hoses etc, are exposed to temperatures above 4000C. The rubber changes into a charred or sticky substance containing the acid. *Once formed, the acid remains dangerous for years. If it gets onto the skin, it may be necessary to amputate the limb concerned.*

• When dealing with a vehicle which has suffered a fire, or with components salvaged from such a vehicle, wear protective gloves and discard them after use.

The battery

• Batteries contain sulphuric acid, which attacks clothing, eyes and skin. Take care when topping-up or carrying the battery.

• The hydrogen gas given off by the battery is highly explosive. Never cause a spark or allow a naked light nearby. Be careful when connecting and disconnecting battery chargers or jump leads.

Air bags

• Air bags can cause injury if they go off accidentally. Take care when removing the steering wheel and trim panels. Special storage instructions may apply.

Diesel injection equipment

• Diesel injection pumps supply fuel at very high pressure. Take care when working on the fuel injectors and fuel pipes.

Warning: Never expose the hands, face or any other part of the body to injector spray; the fuel can penetrate the skin with potentially fatal results.

Remember...

DO

• Do use eye protection when using power tools, and when working under the vehicle.

• Do wear gloves or use barrier cream to protect your hands when necessary.

• Do get someone to check periodically that all is well when working alone on the vehicle.

• Do keep loose clothing and long hair well out of the way of moving mechanical parts.

• Do remove rings, wristwatch etc, before working on the vehicle – especially the electrical system.

• Do ensure that any lifting or jacking equipment has a safe working load rating adequate for the job.

DON'T

• Don't attempt to lift a heavy component which may be beyond your capability – get assistance.

• Don't rush to finish a job, or take unverified short cuts.

• Don't use ill-fitting tools which may slip and cause injury.

• Don't leave tools or parts lying around where someone can trip over them. Mop up oil and fuel spills at once.

• Don't allow children or pets to play in or near a vehicle being worked on.

The following pages are intended to help in dealing with common roadside emergencies and breakdowns. You will find more detailed fault finding information at the back of the manual, and repair information in the main chapters.

If your car won't start and the starter motor doesn't turn

☐ If it's a model with automatic transmission, make sure the selector is in the P or N position.

☐ Open the bonnet and make sure that the battery terminals are clean and tight.

☐ Switch on the headlights and try to start the engine. If the headlights go very dim when you're trying to start, the battery is probably flat. Get out of trouble by jump starting using a friend's car.

If your car won't start even though the starter motor turns as normal

☐ Is there fuel in the tank?

☐ Is there moisture on electrical components under the bonnet? Switch off the ignition, and then wipe off any obvious dampness with a dry cloth. Spray a water-repellent aerosol product (WD-40 or equivalent) on ignition and fuel system electrical connectors like those shown in the photos. (Note that diesel engines don't usually suffer from damp).

A Check the condition and security of the battery connections

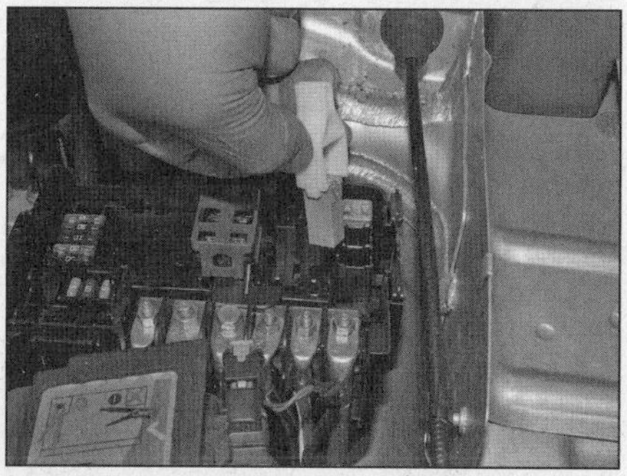

B Check the fuses and fusible links in the fusebox located next to the battery

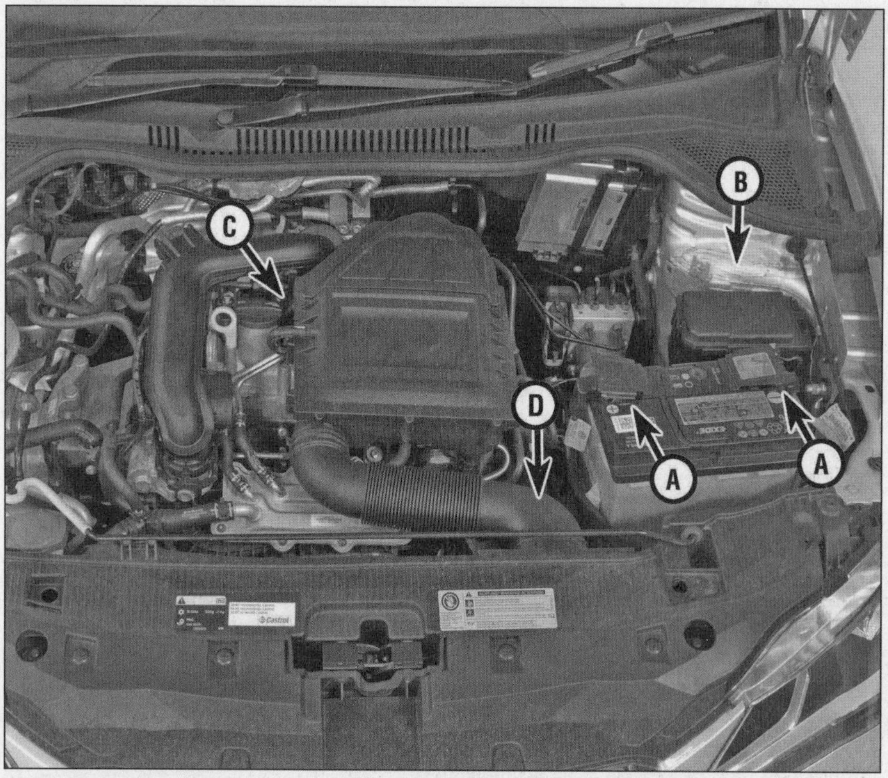

Check that electrical connections are secure (with the ignition switched off) and spray them with a water-dispersant spray like WD-40 if you suspect a problem due to damp.

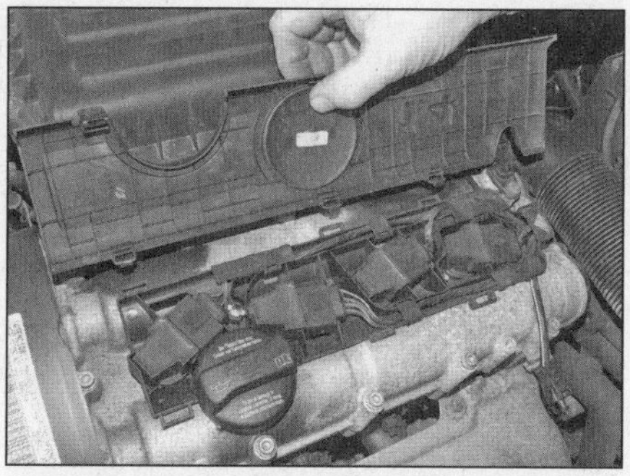

C Where possible check the wiring to the ignition coils (1.4 litre model shown)

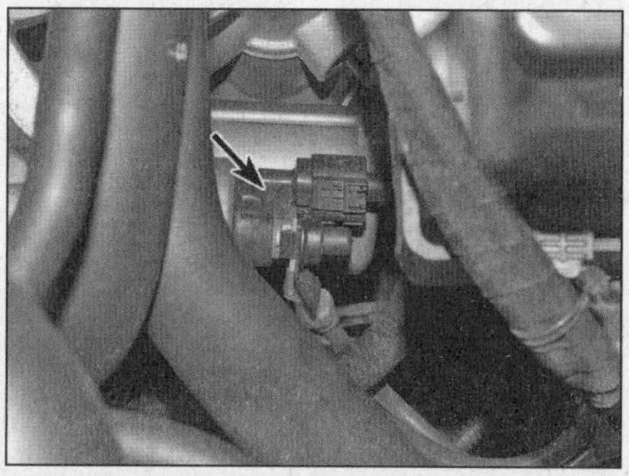

D Check that the starter motor wiring is secure

Jump starting

HAYNES HiNT *Jump starting will get you out of trouble, but you must correct whatever made the battery go flat in the first place. There are three possibilities:*

***1** The battery has been drained by repeated attempts to start, or by leaving the lights on.*

***2** The charging system is not working properly (alternator drivebelt slack or broken, alternator wiring fault or alternator itself faulty).*

***3** The battery itself is at fault (electrolyte low, or battery worn out).*

When jump-starting a car, observe the following precautions:

Caution: Remove the key in case the central locking engages when the jump leads are connected.

- ✔ Before connecting the booster battery, make sure that the ignition is switched off.
- ✔ Ensure that all electrical equipment (lights, heater, wipers, etc) is switched off.
- ✔ Take note of any special precautions printed on the battery case.
- ✔ Make sure that the booster battery is the same voltage as the discharged one in the vehicle.
- ✔ If the battery is being jump-started from the battery in another vehicle, the two vehicles MUST NOT TOUCH each other.
- ✔ Make sure that the transmission is in neutral (or P, in the case of automatic transmission).

HAYNES HiNT ***Budget jump leads can be a false economy, as they often do not pass enough current to start large capacity or diesel engines. They can also get hot.***

1 Connect one end of the red jump lead to the positive (+) terminal of the flat battery.

2 Connect the other end of the red lead to the positive (+) terminal of the booster battery.

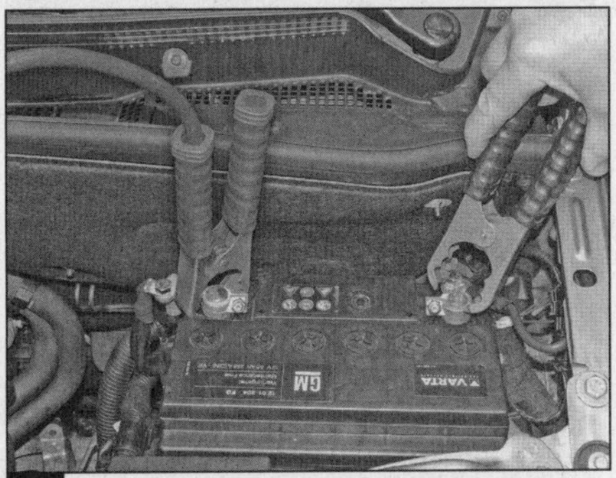

3 Connect one end of the black jump lead to the negative (-) terminal of the booster battery.

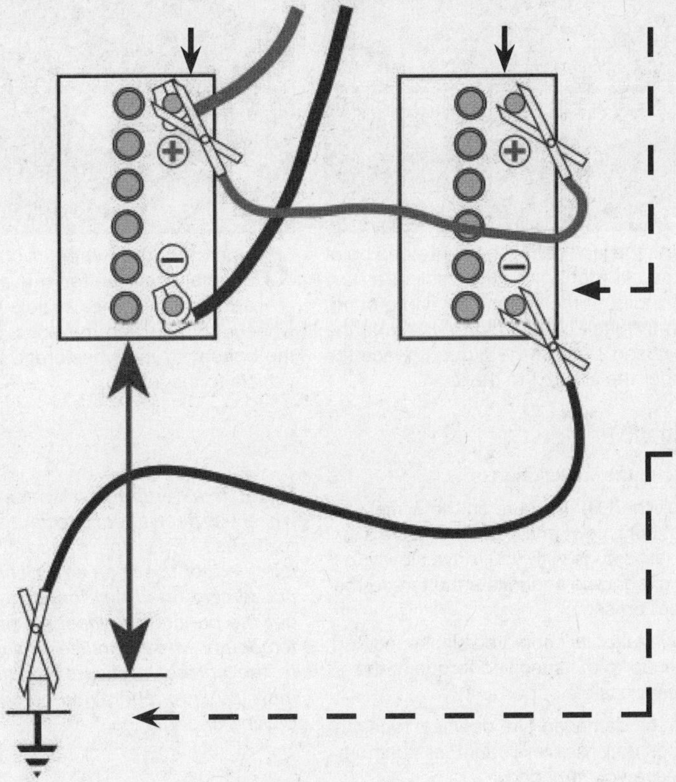

4 Connect the other end of the black jump lead to a suitable metal part of the engine on the vehicle to be started.

5 Make sure that the jump leads will not come into contact with the fan, drive-belts or other moving parts of the engine.

6 Start the engine using the booster battery and run it at idle speed. Switch on the lights, rear window demister and heater blower motor, then disconnect the jump leads in the reverse order of connection. Turn off the lights etc.

Wheel changing

Warning: Do not change a wheel in a situation where you risk being hit by other traffic. On busy roads, try to stop in a lay-by or a gateway. Be wary of passing traffic while changing the wheel – it is easy to become distracted by the job in hand.

Preparation

- ☐ When a puncture occurs, stop as soon as it is safe to do so.
- ☐ Park on firm level ground, if possible, and well out of the way of other traffic.
- ☐ Use hazard warning lights if necessary.
- ☐ If you have one, use a warning triangle to alert other drivers of your presence.
- ☐ Apply the handbrake and engage first or reverse gear (or P on models with automatic transmission).
- ☐ Chock the wheel diagonally opposite the one being removed – a couple of large stones will do for this.
- ☐ If the ground is soft, use a flat piece of wood to spread the load under the jack.
- ☐ Where fitted the spare wheel is located in the floor beneath the load area. Lift up the cover to access the wheel and tool kit.

Changing the wheel

1 The spare wheel and tools are stored in the luggage compartment. Lift out the jack and wheel changing tools from the centre of the spare wheel.

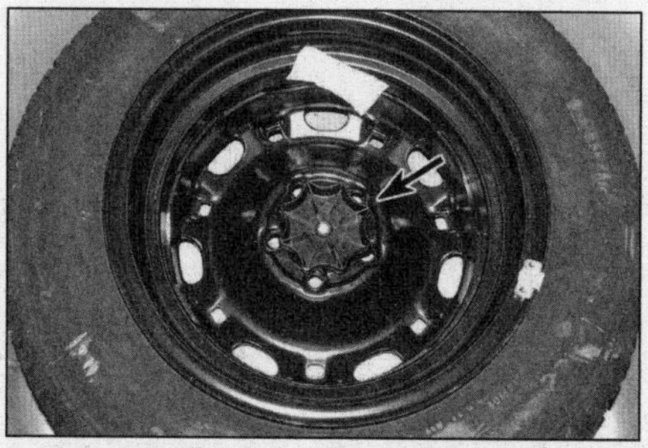

2 Unscrew the retainer and lift out the wheel.

3 Use the wire hook to remove the wheel trim if fitted. Where applicable, use the puller from the tool kit to remove the wheel bolt covers. On models with anti-theft wheel bolts the special socket will be needed.

4 Slacken each wheel bolt by half a turn (using the special adaptor for the anti-theft bolt).

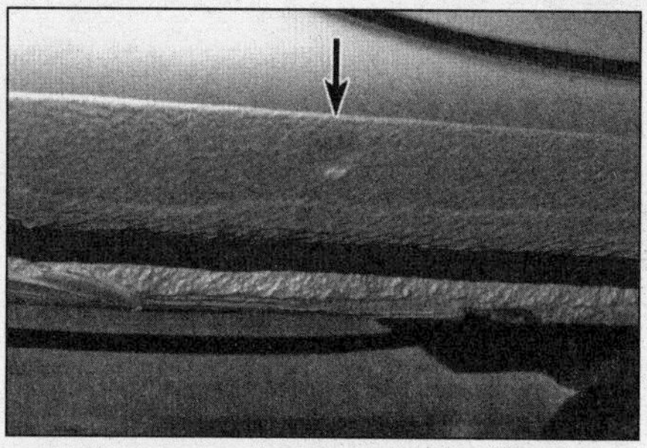

5 Locate the jack below the reinforced point on the sill (don't jack the vehicle at any other point of the sill) and on firm ground, then turn the jack handle clockwise until the wheel is raised clear of the ground. Place the spare under the sill next to the jack.

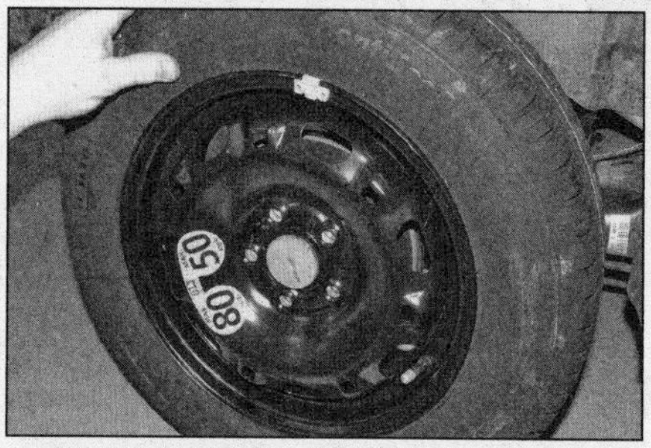

6 Unscrew the wheel bolts (using the special adaptor for the anti-theft bolt) and remove the wheel. Fit the spare wheel, and screw in the bolts. Lightly tighten the bolts with the wheelbrace then lower the vehicle to theground.

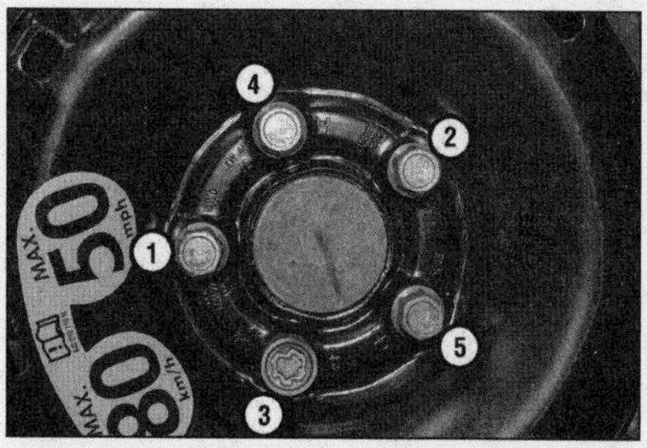

7 Securely tighten the wheel bolts in the sequence shown then refit the wheel trim/ hub cap. Stow the punctured wheel back in the spare wheel well.

Finally...

- ☐ Remove the wheel chocks.
- ☐ Check the tyre pressure on the wheel just fitted. If it is low, or if you don't have a pressure gauge with you, drive slowly to the next garage and inflate the tyre to the correct pressure.
- ☐ The wheel bolts should be slackened and tightened to the specified torque at the earliest possible opportunity.
- ☐ Have the damaged tyre or wheel repaired as soon as possible, or another puncture will leave you stranded.

Note: *If a temporary 'space-saver' spare wheel has been fitted, special conditions apply to its use. This type of spare wheel is only intended for use in an emergency, and should not remain fitted any longer than it takes to get the punctured wheel repaired. While the temporary wheel is in use, ensure it is inflated to the correct pressure, do not exceed 50 mph (80 kph), and avoid harsh acceleration, braking or cornering.*

Identifying leaks

Puddles on the garage floor or drive, or obvious wetness under the bonnet or underneath the car, suggest a leak that needs investigating. It can sometimes be difficult to decide where the leak is coming from, especially if an engine undershield is fitted. Leaking oil or fluid can also be blown rearwards by the passage of air under the car, giving a false impression of where the problem lies.

Warning: Most automotive oils and fluids are poisonous. Wash them off skin, and change out of contaminated clothing, without delay.

HAYNES HiNT *The smell of a fluid leaking from the car may provide a clue to what's leaking. Some fluids are distinctively coloured. It may help to remove the engine undershield, clean the car carefully and to park it over some clean paper overnight as an aid to locating the source of the leak. Remember that some leaks may only occur while the engine is running.*

Sump oil

Engine oil may leak from the drain plug...

Oil from filter

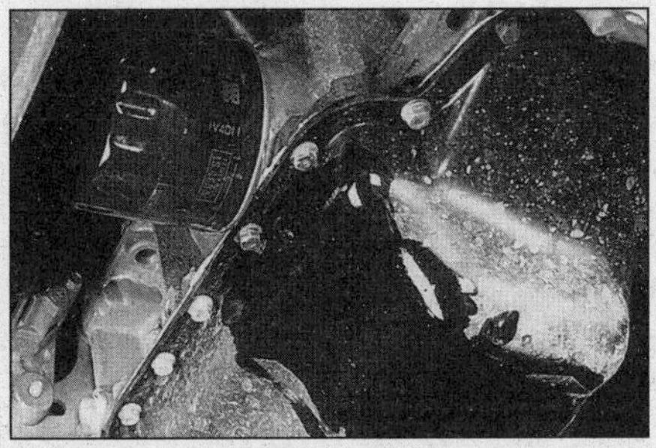

...or from the base of the oil filter.

Gearbox oil

Gearbox oil can leak from the seals at the inboard ends of the driveshafts.

Antifreeze

Leaking antifreeze often leaves a crystalline deposit like this.

Brake fluid

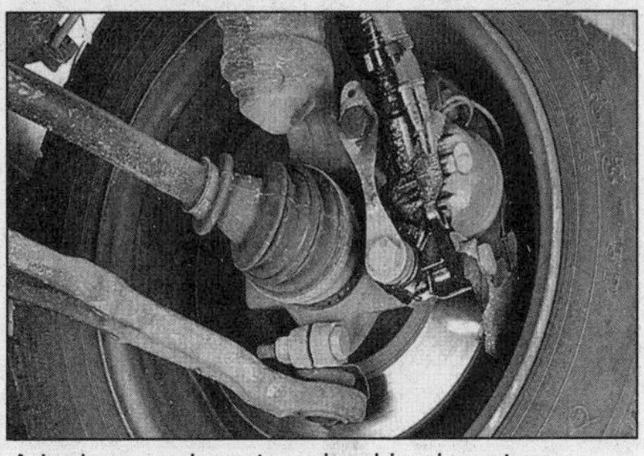

A leak occurring at a wheel is almost certainly brake fluid.

Towing

When all else fails, you may find yourself having to get a tow home – or of course you may be helping somebody else. Long-distance recovery should only be done by a garage or breakdown service. For shorter distances, DIY towing using another car is easy enough, but observe the following points:

Use a proper tow-rope – they are not expensive. The vehicle being towed must display an ON TOW sign in its rear window.

Always turn the ignition key to the 'On' position when the vehicle is being towed, so that the steering lock is released, and the direction indicator and brake lights work.

Only attach the tow-rope to the towing eyes provided. The front towing eye is located in the tool kit, and is screwed into position behind the vent/cover on the right-hand side of the front bumper **(see illustrations)**. The eye has a left-hand thread. The rear towing eye is located beneath the right-hand side of the rear bumper.

Before being towed, release the handbrake and select neutral on the transmission. On models with automatic transmission, do not exceed 30 mph (50 kph) and do not tow for more than 30 miles (50 km). If in doubt, do not tow, or transmission damage may result.

Note that greater-than-usual pedal pressure will be required to operate the brakes, since the vacuum servo unit is only operational with the engine running.

Because the power steering will not be operational, greater-than-usual steering effort will be required.

The driver of the car being towed must keep the tow-rope taut at all times to avoid snatching.

Make sure that both drivers know the route before setting off.

Only drive at moderate speeds and keep the distance towed to a minimum. Drive smoothly and allow plenty of time for slowing down at junctions.

Open the cover with the screwdriver from the tool kit...

...and screw in the towing eye. Tighten fully with the wheel brace.

Introduction

There are some very simple checks which need only take a few minutes to carry out, but which could save you a lot of inconvenience and expense.

These checks require no great skill or special tools, and the small amount of time they take to perform could prove to be very well spent, for example:

☐ Keeping an eye on tyre condition and pressures, will not only help to stop them wearing out prematurely, but could also save your life.

☐ Many breakdowns are caused by electrical problems. Battery-related faults are particularly common, and a quick check on a regular basis will often prevent the majority of these.

☐ If your car develops a brake fluid leak, the first time you might know about it is when your brakes don't work properly. Checking the level regularly will give advance warning of this kind of problem.

☐ If the oil or coolant levels run low, the cost of repairing any engine damage will be far greater than fixing the leak, for example.

Underbonnet check points

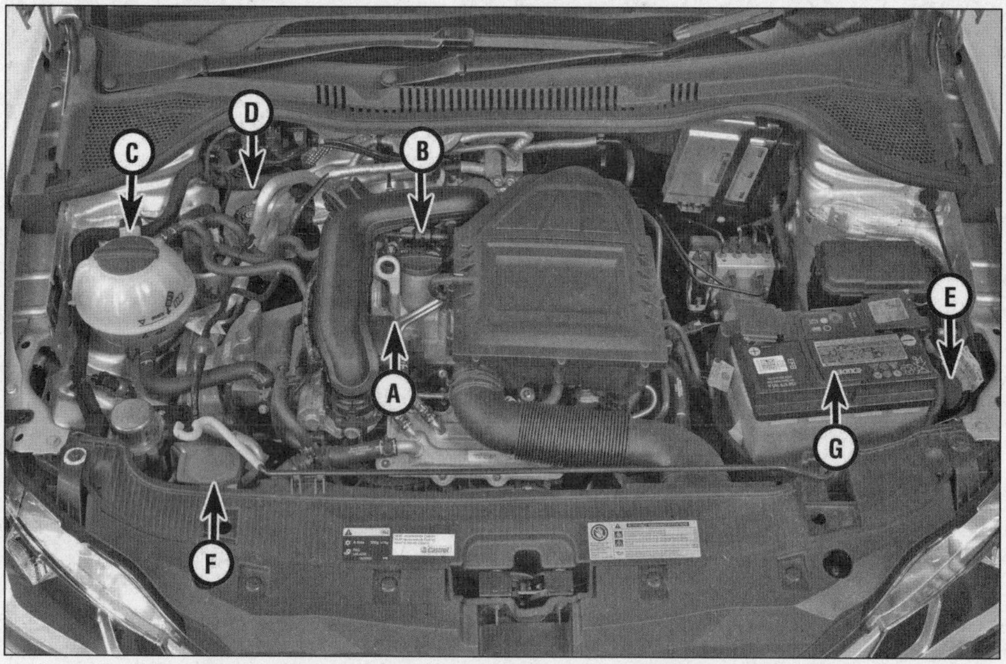

◀ 1.0 litre petrol TSI

A *Engine oil level dipstick*
B *Engine oil filler cap*
C *Coolant expansion tank*
D *Brake (and clutch) fluid reservoir*
E *Power steering fluid reservoir (where fitted)*
F *Screen washer fluid reservoir (on the left-hand side close to the battery on older models)*
G *Battery*

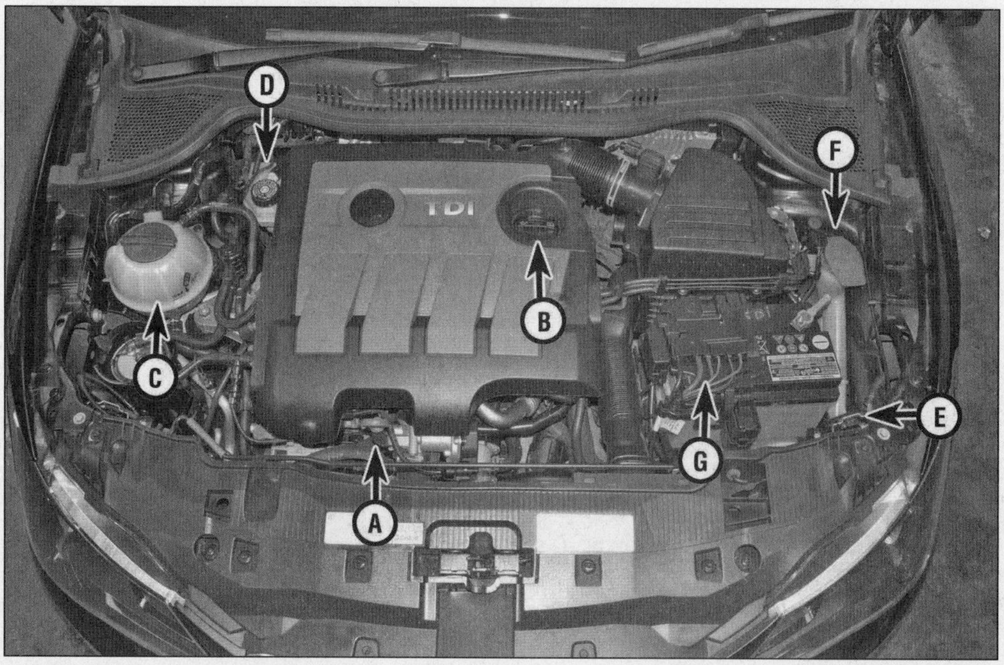

◀ 1.6 litre diesel

A *Engine oil level dipstick*
B *Engine oil filler cap*
C *Coolant expansion tank*
D *Brake (and clutch) fluid reservoir*
E *Power steering fluid reservoir*
F *Screen washer fluid reservoir*
G *Battery*

Engine oil level

Before you start

✔ Make sure that the car is on level ground.
✔ Check the oil level before the car is driven, or at least 5 minutes after the engine has been switched off.

> **HAYNES HiNT** ***If the oil is checked immediately after driving the vehicle, some of the oil will remain in the upper engine components, resulting in an inaccurate reading on the dipstick.***

The correct oil

Modern engines place great demands on their oil. It is very important that the correct oil for your car is used (see *Lubricants and fluids*).

Car care

- If you have to add oil frequently, you should check whether you have any oil leaks. Place some clean paper under the car overnight, and check for stains in the morning. If there are no leaks, then the engine may be burning oil.
- Always maintain the level between the upper and lower dipstick marks. If the level is too low, severe engine damage may occur. Oil seal failure may result if the engine is overfilled by adding too much oil.

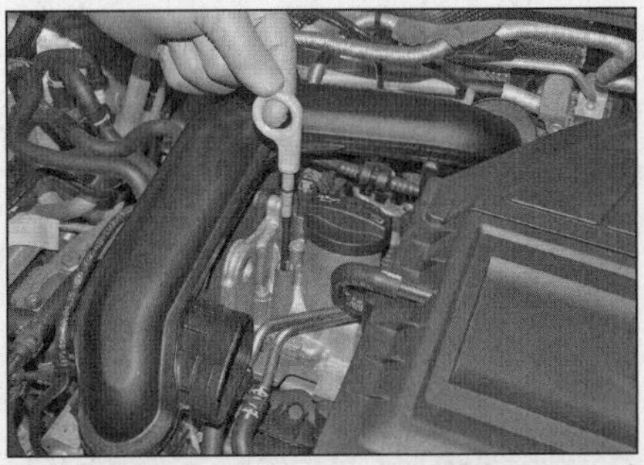

1 The dipstick is often brightly coloured for easy identification (see *Underbonnet check points* for exact location depending on model). Withdraw the dipstick, then use a clean rag or paper towel to wipe the oil from it. Insert the clean dipstick into the tube as far as it will go, then withdraw it again.

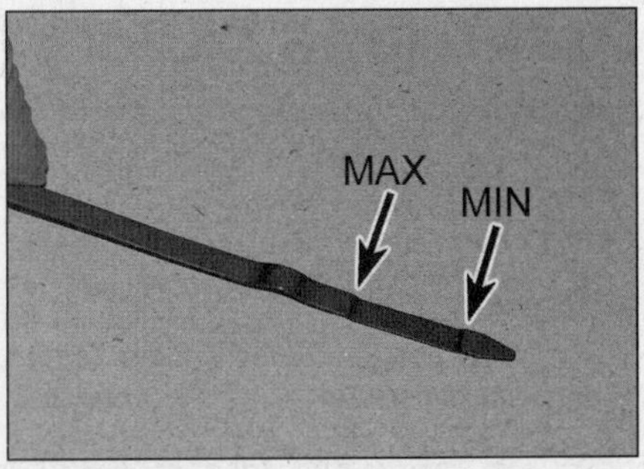

2 Note the level on the end of the dipstick, which should be between the upper (MAX) and lower (MIN) mark. Note: There are different dipsticks used, depending on engine. The one shown is from the 1.0 litre petrol engine.

3 Oil is added through the filler cap aperture. Unscrew the cap.

4 Top-up the oil level, using a funnel may help to reduce spillage. Add the oil slowly, checking the level on the dipstick frequently. Avoid overfilling (see *Car care*). Place some cloth rags around the filler cap aperture, if necessary, before topping up.

Coolant level

> ***Warning: Do not attempt to remove the expansion tank pressure cap when the engine is hot, as there is a very great risk of scalding. Do not leave open containers of coolant about, as it is poisonous.***

Car care

- With a sealed-type cooling system, adding coolant should not be necessary on a regular basis. If frequent topping-up is required, it is likely there is a leak. Check the radiator, all hoses and joint faces for signs of staining or wetness, and rectify as necessary.
- It is important that antifreeze is used in the cooling system all year round, not just during the winter months. Don't top up with water alone, as the antifreeze will become diluted.

1 The coolant level varies with the temperature of the engine. When the engine is cold, the coolant level should bebetween the MIN and MAX marks.

2 If topping-up is necessary, wait until the engine is cold. Slowly unscrew the cap to release any pressure present in the cooling system, and remove the cap.

3 Add a mixture of water and the specified antifreeze (see *Lubricants and fluids*) to the expansion tank until thecoolant level is halfway between the level marks. Refit the cap and tighten it securely.

Brake (and clutch) fluid level

Note: *On manual transmission models, the fluid reservoir also supplies the clutch master cylinder with fluid*

Warning: Brake fluid can harm your eyes and damage painted surfaces, so use extreme caution when handling and pouring it.

Warning: Do not use fluid that has been standing open for some time, as it absorbs moisture from the air, which can cause a dangerous loss of braking effectiveness.

Before you start

✔ Make sure that your car is on level ground.

✔ Cleanliness is of great importance when dealing with the braking system, so take care to clean around the reservoir cap before topping-up. Use only clean brake fluid.

Safety first!

- If the reservoir requires repeated topping-up this is an indication of a fluid leak somewhere in the system, which should be investigated immediately.
- If a leak is suspected, the car should not be driven until the braking system has been checked. Never take any risks where brakes are concerned.

1 The MIN and MAX marks are indicated on the reservoir. The fluid level must be kept between the marks at all times.Note that the level will drop naturally as the brake pad linings wear, but must never be allowed to fall below the MIN mark.

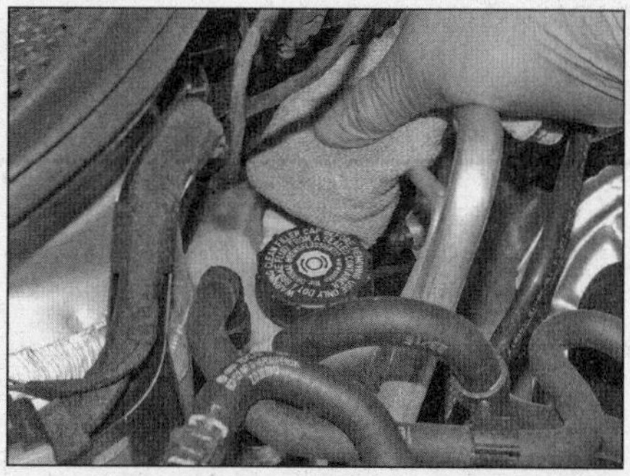

2 If topping-up is necessary, first wipe clean the area around the filler cap to prevent dirt entering the hydraulic system.

3 Unscrew and remove the reservoir cap.

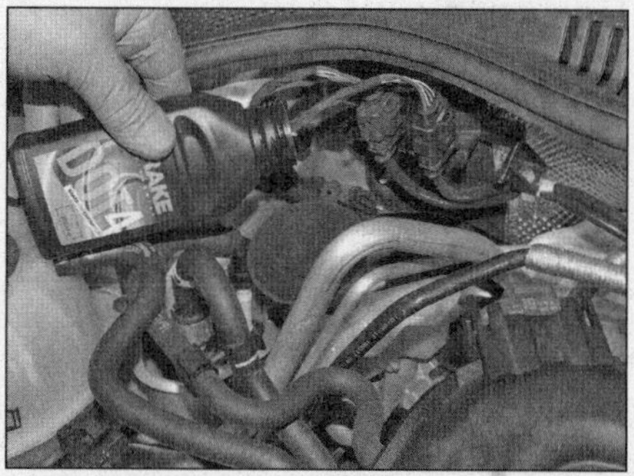

4 Carefully add fluid, taking care not to spill it onto the surrounding components (a funnel may help) Use only the specified fluid (see *Lubricants and fluids*); mixing different types can cause damage to the system. On completion, securely refit the cap and wipeaway any spilt fluid.

Screen washer fluid level

- Screenwash additives not only keep the windscreen clean during bad weather, they also prevent the washer system freezing in cold weather – which is when you are likely to need it most. Don't top-up using plain water, as the screenwash will become diluted, and will freeze in cold weather.

Warning: On no account use engine coolant antifreeze in the screen washer system – this may damage the paintwork.

1 The screen washer fluid reservoir is located either on the right-hand front side of the engine compartment, (close to the headlight) or the left-hand side behind the battery. Pull up the filler cap to release it from the reservoir.

2 When topping-up the reservoir, a screenwash additive should be added in the quantities recommended on the bottle.

Tyre condition and pressure

It is very important that tyres are in good condition, and at the correct pressure - having a tyre failure at any speed is highly dangerous.
Tyre wear is influenced by driving style - harsh braking and acceleration, or fast cornering, will all produce more rapid tyre wear. As a general rule, the front tyres wear out faster than the rears. Interchanging the tyres from front to rear ("rotating" the tyres) may result in more even wear. However, if this is completely effective, you may have the expense of replacing all four tyres at once!
Remove any nails or stones embedded in the tread before they penetrate the tyre to cause deflation. If removal of a nail does reveal that the tyre has been punctured, refit the nail so that its point of penetration is marked. Then immediately change the wheel, and have the tyre repaired by a tyre dealer.
Regularly check the tyres for damage in the form of cuts or bulges, especially in the sidewalls. Periodically remove the wheels, and clean any dirt or mud from the inside and outside surfaces. Examine the wheel rims for signs of rusting, corrosion or other damage. Light alloy wheels are easily damaged by "kerbing" whilst parking; steel wheels may also become dented or buckled. A new wheel is very often the only way to overcome severe damage.
New tyres should be balanced when they are fitted, but it may become necessary to re-balance them as they wear, or if the balance weights fitted to the wheel rim should fall off. Unbalanced tyres will wear more quickly, as will the steering and suspension components. Wheel imbalance is normally signified by vibration, particularly at a certain speed (typically around 50 mph). If this vibration is felt only through the steering, then it is likely that just the front wheels need balancing. If, however, the vibration is felt through the whole car, the rear wheels could be out of balance. Wheel balancing should be carried out by a tyre dealer or garage.

1 ***Tread Depth - visual check***
The original tyres have tread wear safety bands (B), which will appear when the tread depth reaches approximately 1.6 mm. The band positions are indicated by a triangular mark on the tyre sidewall (A).

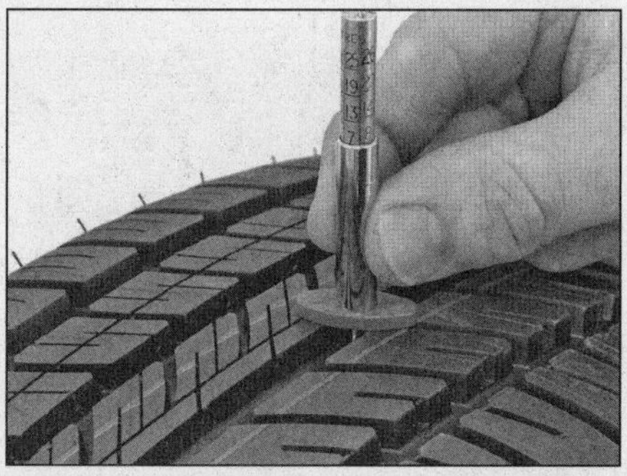

2 ***Tread Depth - manual check***
Alternatively, tread wear can be monitored with a simple, inexpensive device known as a tread depth indicator gauge.

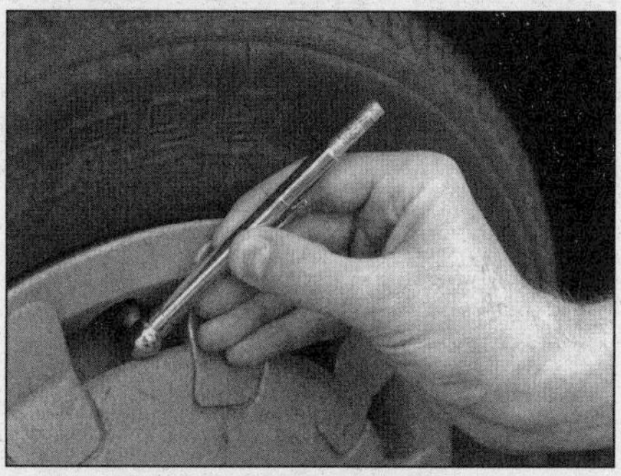

3 ***Tyre Pressure Check***
Check the tyre pressures regularly with the tyres cold. Do not adjust the tyre pressures immediately after the vehicle has been used, or an inaccurate setting will result.

Tyre tread wear patterns

Shoulder Wear

Underinflation (wear on both sides)
Under-inflation will cause overheating of the tyre, because the tyre will flex too much, and the tread will not sit correctly on the road surface. This will cause a loss of grip and excessive wear, not to mention the danger of sudden tyre failure due to heat build-up.
Check and adjust pressures
Incorrect wheel camber (wear on one side)
Repair or renew suspension parts
Hard cornering
Reduce speed!

Centre Wear

Overinflation
Over-inflation will cause rapid wear of the centre part of the tyre tread, coupled with reduced grip, harsher ride, and the danger of shock damage occurring in the tyre casing.
Check and adjust pressures

If you sometimes have to inflate your car's tyres to the higher pressures specified for maximum load or sustained high speed, don't forget to reduce the pressures to normal afterwards.

Uneven Wear

Front tyres may wear unevenly as a result of wheel misalignment. Most tyre dealers and garages can check and adjust the wheel alignment (or "tracking") for a modest charge.
Incorrect camber or castor
Repair or renew suspension parts
Malfunctioning suspension
Repair or renew suspension parts
Unbalanced wheel
Balance tyres
Incorrect toe setting
Adjust front wheel alignment
Note: *The feathered edge of the tread which typifies toe wear is best checked by feel.*

Battery

Caution: Before carrying out any work on the vehicle battery, read the precautions given in 'Safety first!' at the start of this manual.

✔ Make sure that the battery tray is in good condition, and that the clamp is tight. Corrosion on the tray, retaining clamp and the battery itself can be removed with a solution of water and baking soda. Thoroughly rinse all cleaned areas with water. Any metal parts damaged by corrosion should be covered with a zinc-based primer, then painted.

✔ Periodically (approximately every three months), check the charge condition of the battery as described in Chapter 5A Section 2.

✔ If the battery is flat, and you need to jump start your vehicle, see *Roadside repairs*.

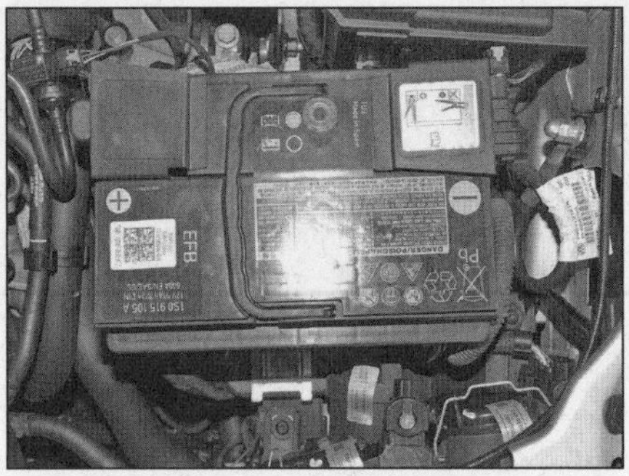

1 The battery is located in the front left hand corner of the engine compartment. Remove the covers, to gain access to the battery terminals.

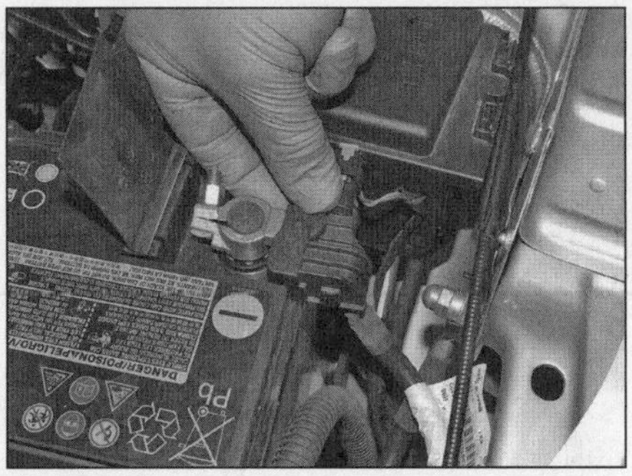

2 Check the security and condition of all the battery and fuse connections. The exterior of the battery should be inspected periodically for damage such as a cracked case or cover.

3 If corrosion (white, fluffy deposits) is evident, remove the cables from the battery terminals, clean them with a small wire brush, then refit them. Automotive stores sell a tool for cleaning the battery post...

4 ... as well as the battery cable clamps. **Note:** *Seat specifically prohibit the use of grease on the battery terminals.*

Electrical systems

✔ Check all external lights and the horn. Refer to Chapter 12 for details if any of the circuits are found to be inoperative.

✔ Visually check all accessible wiring connectors, harnesses and retaining clips for security, and for signs of chafing or damage.

HAYNES HiNT ***If you need to check your brake lights and indicators unaided, back up to a wall or garage door and operate the lights. The reflected light should show if they are working properly.***

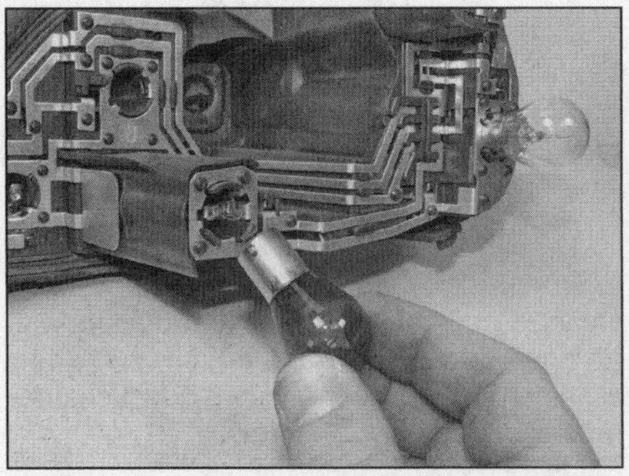

1 If a single indicator light, brake light or headlight has failed, it is likely that a bulb has blown and will need to be renewed. Refer to Chapter 12 for details. If both brake lights have failed, it is possible that the brake light switch operated by the brake pedal has failed. Refer to Chapter 9 for details.

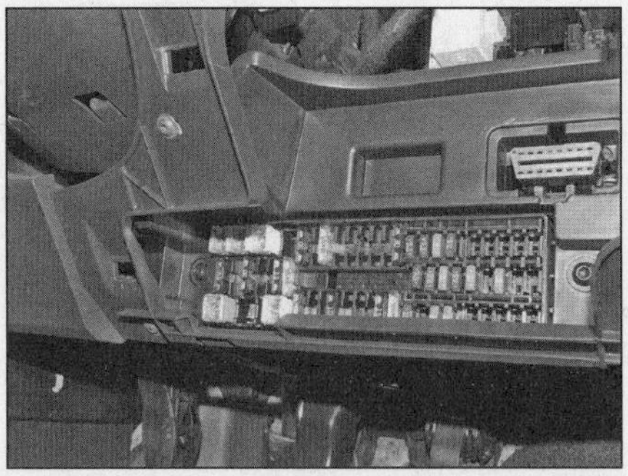

2 If more than one indicator light or headlight has failed, it is likely that either a fuse has blown or that there is a fault in the circuit. The main fuses are in the fusebox beneath a cover on the right-hand end of the facia panel. Unclip the cover. To renew a blown fuse, pull it from its location in the fusebox, using the plastic pliers provided.

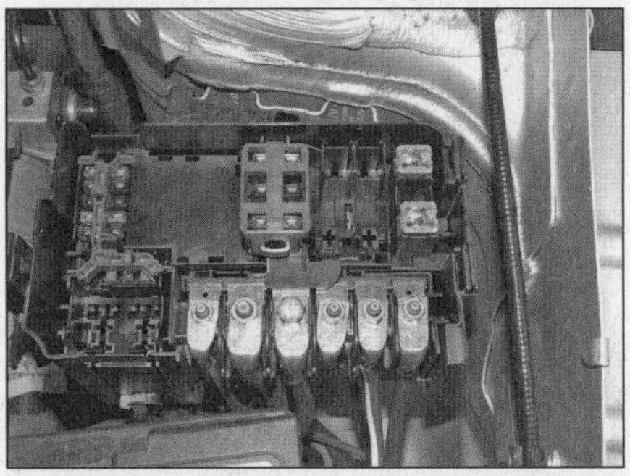

3 Additional heavy duty fuses and fusible links are in the fusebox located next to the battery. Always fit a new fuse of the same rating, available from car accessory shops. It is important that you find the reason that the fuse blew (see *Electrical fault finding* in Chapter 12).

Wiper blades

1 Check the condition of the wiper blades: if they are cracked or show signs of deterioration, or if the glass swept area is smeared, renew them. For maximum clarity of vision, wiper blades should be renewed annually.

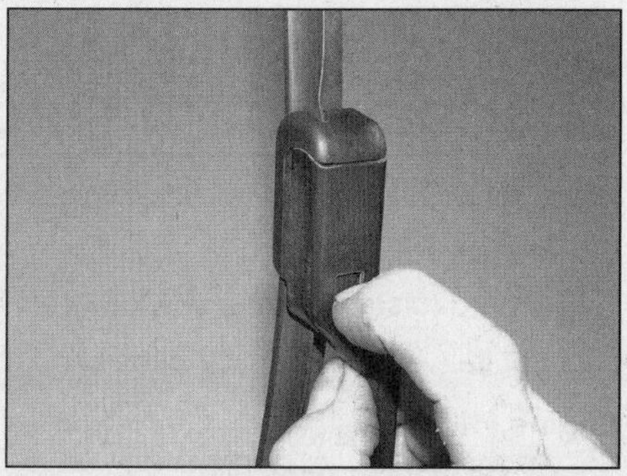

2 To remove a windscreen wiper blade, turn the ignition on, then turn the ignition off, and press the wiper switch stalk down once. This places the arms in the 'service' position. Lift the wiper from the screen and press the securing clip ...

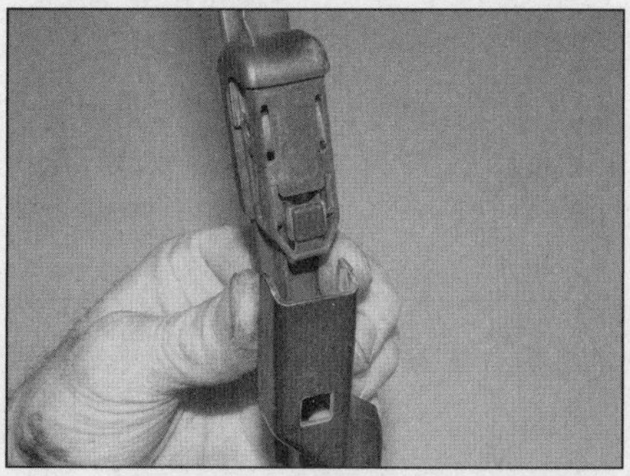

3 ... slide the blade upwards from the end of the wiper arm, taking care not to allow the wiper arm to spring back and damage the windscreen. When completed, return the blades to the park position by pressing the wiper switch stalk again.

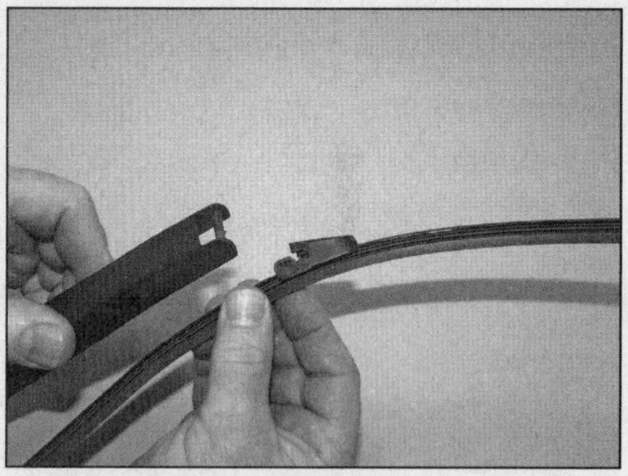

4 The rear wiper blade is remove in a similar manner to the front wiper blades.

Lubricants and fluids

Note: *Using lubricants and fluids that do not meet the Seat/VW standards may invalidate the warranty*

Engine (petrol):	
Standard (distance/time) service interval	VW 502 00 or VW 504 00
LongLife (variable) service interval	VW LongLife engine oil VW 504 00
Engine (diesel):	
Engines without particulate filter	VW 505 01, VW506 01 or VW 507 00
Engines with particulate filter	VW 507 00
Cooling system	VW additive which complies with specification TL-VW 774 G – antifreeze and corrosion protection
Manual transmission	VW G50 synthetic gear oil, viscosity SAE 75W/90 – G 052 512 A2
Automatic (DSG) transmission	G 052 145
Braking system	Hydraulic fluid to DOT 4 VW 501 14 (part no. B 000 750)
Power steering fluid	Hydraulic OIl – Pentosin CHF 11S / N 052 146 00 / TL 52 146 or Pentosin CHF 202 / N 052 146 01 / TL 52 146

Tyre pressures

Note: *The recommended tyre pressures for each vehicle are given on a sticker attached to the rear of the fuel filler flap* ***(see illustration)****. The pressures given are for the original equipment tyres – the recommended pressures may vary if any other make or type of tyre is fitted; check with the tyre manufacturer or supplier for latest recommendations. The following pressures are typical.*

All models	Front	Rear
Normal load	2.0 bars (29 psi)	2.2 bars (32 psi)
Full load	2.2 bars (32 psi)	2.8 bars (41 psi)
Space-saver spare wheel	4.2 bars (61 psi)	

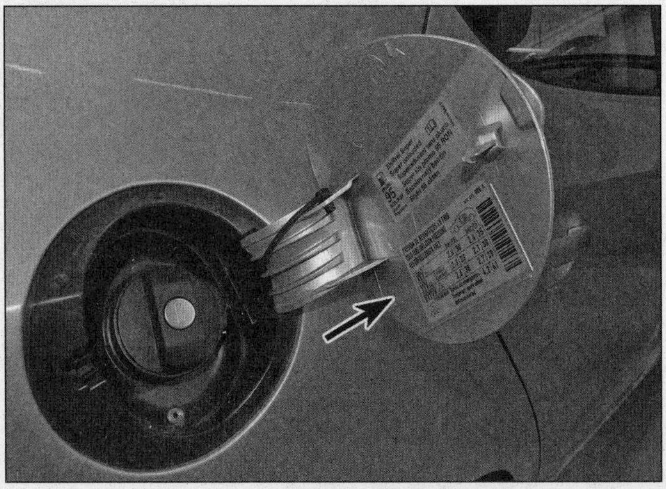

Tyre pressure label on inside of fuel flap

Chapter 1 Part A
Routine maintenance and servicing – petrol models

Contents

Degrees of difficulty

Easy, suitable for novice with little experience	Fairly easy, suitable for beginner with some experience	Fairly difficult, suitable for competent DIY mechanic	Difficult, suitable for experienced DIY mechanic	Very difficult, suitable for expert DIY or professional

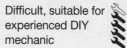

1 Servicing specifications – petrol models

Lubricants and fluids .... Refer to end of *Weekly checks* on page 0•16

Engine codes *

1.0 litre:	
MPI (DOHC)	CHYB
TSI (DOHC)	CHZC and CHZB
1.2 litre (All TSI):	
SOHC	CBZB
DOHC	CJZD and CJZC
1.4 litre (All MPI)	CGGB and BXW

**See 'Vehicle identification' at the end of this manual for the location of the engine code markings.*

Capacities

Engine oil – including filter (approximate):

1.0 litre (CHYB)	3.4 litres
1.0 litre (CHZB and CHZC)	4.0 litres
1.2 litre (CBZB):	
Up to 05/2011	3.6 litres
From 06/2011	3.9 litres
1.2 litre (CJZD and CJZC)	4.0 litres
1.4 litre	3.2 litres

Cooling system

1.0 litre (CHYB)	Not available
1.0 litre (CHZC and CHZB)	8.0 litres
1.2 and 1.4 litre	5.6 litres

Transmission

Manual transmission (type):	
0CF	1.1 litres
02Q/0DQ	2.2 litres
02U	2.1 litres
02T	2.0 litres

Fuel tank (approximate) .... 45 litres

Cooling system

Antifreeze mixture:	
40% antifreeze	Protection down to -25°C
50% antifreeze	Protection down to -35°C

Note: *Refer to antifreeze manufacturer for latest recommendations.*

Ignition system

Spark plugs:	Type	Electrode gap*
1.0 litre engines	NHK PKER7A8EGS	0.95 to 1.05 mm
1.2 litre engines (CBZB)	NGK 1ZFR6P7	0.7 to 0.8 mm
1.2 litre engines (CJZD and CJZC)	NGK PKER7A8EGS	0.7 to 0.8 mm
1.4 litre engines	NGK ZFR6T-11G	0.9 mm

** All spark plugs are supplied pre-gapped. No attempt should be made to adjust the gap*

Brakes

Brake pad/shoe minimum thickness:	Front pads	Rear pads / shoes
Including backing plate	14.0 mm	11.5 mm / 5.4 mm
Friction lining only:	2.0 mm	2.0mm / 1.5 mm

Torque wrench settings

	Nm	lbf ft
Manual transmission 02T:		
Filler/level and drain plug:		
Multi-splined (12-point) plug	25	18
Hexagon (Allen key) plug	32	23
Oil filter housing cap	25	18
Oil filter (spin on type)	20	15
Roadwheel bolts	120	89
Spark plugs:		
1.0 litre engine (CHYB)	22	16
1.0 litre (CHZB and CHZC)	25	18
1.2 litre engines (CBZB)	25	18
1.2 litre engines (CJZD and CJZC)	22	16
1.4 litre engines	30	22
Sump drain plug	30	22

2 Maintenance schedule – petrol models

Maintenance schedule

The maintenance intervals in this manual are provided with the assumption that you, not the dealer, will be carrying out the work. These are the minimum intervals recommended by us for cars driven daily. If you wish to keep your car in peak condition at all times, you may wish to perform some of these procedures more often. We encourage frequent maintenance, since it enhances the efficiency, performance and resale value of your car.

When the vehicle is new, it should be serviced by a dealer service department (or other workshop recognised by the vehicle manufacturer as providing the same standard of service) in order to preserve the warranty. The vehicle manufacturer may reject warranty claims if you are unable to prove that servicing has been carried out as and when specified, using only original equipment parts or parts certified to be of equivalent quality.

Longlife service schedule

All Seat models are equipped with a service interval display indicator in the instrument panel. Every time the engine is started the panel will illuminate for approximately 20 seconds with service information. With the standard fixed interval display, the service intervals are in accordance with specific distances and time periods. With the LongLife display, the service interval is variable. Once the service interval has been reached, the display will flash 'OIL service' for an oil change service or 'INSP service' for an inspection service.

For models using the LongLife schedule, the occurrence of either service reminder on the display unit will depend on how the car is being used (number of starts, length of journeys, vehicle speeds, brake pad wear, bonnet opening frequency, fuel consumption, oil level and oil temperature). For example, if a vehicle is being used under extreme driving conditions, the service may occur at 10 000 miles, whereas, if the vehicle is being used under moderate driving conditions, it may occur at 20 000 miles, although the maximum length of time between INSP services is 2 years. It is important to realise that this system is completely variable according to how the vehicle is being used, and therefore the service should be carried out when indicated on the display. **Note:** *Models with the variable service interval system are equipped with an engine oil level sensor, brake pad wear indicator, and a variable service indicator.*

The LongLife variable service intervals are only applicable to models with a PR number of QG1 (up to 2013) or QI6 (2013 on). This number is shown in the vehicle Service Schedule booklet, on a service interval plate next to the spare wheel well. With the variable (LongLife) service interval on models with these PR numbers, the engine must **only** be filled with the recommended LongLife engine oil (see *Lubricants and fluids*).

After completing a service, Seat technicians use a diagnostic too to reset the service display to the next service interval, and a print-out is put in the vehicle service record. The display can be reset by the owner as described in Section 8, but note that for models using the LongLife interval, the procedure will automatically reset the schedule to an amended LongLife interval, in which oil renewal and brake pad checks are based on distance/time while every other system remains LongLife. To have the display reset to the full LongLife schedule, it is necessary to take the car to a Seat dealer. Note that it is also possible to change (using the diagnostic tool) to fixed interval servicing.

Every 250 miles or weekly

- ☐ Refer to *Weekly checks*

'OIL service' on display

- ☐ Renew the engine oil and filter (Section 6)

Note: *Frequent oil and filter changes are good for the engine. We recommend changing the oil at least once a year.*

- ☐ Check the front and rear brake pad thickness (Section 7)
- ☐ Reset the service interval display (Section 8)

'INSP service' on display

Note: *In addition to the items given above.*

- ☐ Check the condition of the exhaust system and its mountings (Section 9)
- ☐ Check all underbonnet components and hoses for fluid and oil leaks (Section 10)
- ☐ Check the condition of the auxiliary drivebelt (Section 11 and Section 28)
- ☐ Check the coolant antifreeze concentration (Section 12)
- ☐ Check the brake hydraulic circuit for leaks and damage (Section 13)
- ☐ Check the headlight beam adjustment (Section 14)
- ☐ Renew the pollen filter element (Section 15)
- ☐ Check the manual transmission oil level (Section 16)
- ☐ Check the underbody protection for damage (Section 17)
- ☐ Check the condition of the driveshafts (Section 18)
- ☐ Check the steering and suspension components for condition and security (Section 19)
- ☐ Check the battery condition and (Section 20)
- ☐ Lubricate all hinges and locks (Section 21)
- ☐ Check the condition of the airbag unit(s) (Section 22)

'INSP service' on display (continued)

- ☐ Check the operation of the windscreen/tailgate/headlight washer system(s) (as applicable) (Section 23)
- ☐ Check the engine management self-diagnosis memory for faults (Section 24)
- ☐ Carry out a road test and check exhaust emissions (Section 25)

Every 40 000 miles or 4 years, whichever comes first

Note: *Many dealers perform these tasks at every second INSP service.*

- ☐ Renew the air filter element (Section 26)
- ☐ Renew the spark plugs (Section 27)
- ☐ Check the condition of the auxiliary drivebelt (Section 11 and Section 28)
- ☐ Check the power steering hydraulic fluid level (Section 29)
- ☐ Renew the timing belt and tensioner. (Section 30).

Note: *Seat specify timing belt inspection after the first 55 000 miles and then every 20 000 miles, but does not have a renewal interval time. However, if the car is used mainly for short journeys, we recommend that the timing belt be renewed at 55 000 miles when the first Inspection takes place. The belt renewal interval is very much up to the individual owner, bearing in mind that severe engine damage will result if the belt breaks in use. 1.2 litre CBZB engines have a maintenance-free timing chain fitted.*

Every 2 years

- ☐ Renew the brake (and clutch) fluid (Section 31)
- ☐ Renew the coolant (Section 32).

Note: *Renewing the coolant isn't included in the Seat schedule, and should not be required if the recommended Seat G12 LongLife coolant anti-freeze is used.*

3 Component location – petrol models

Underbonnet view – 1.0 litre TSI model

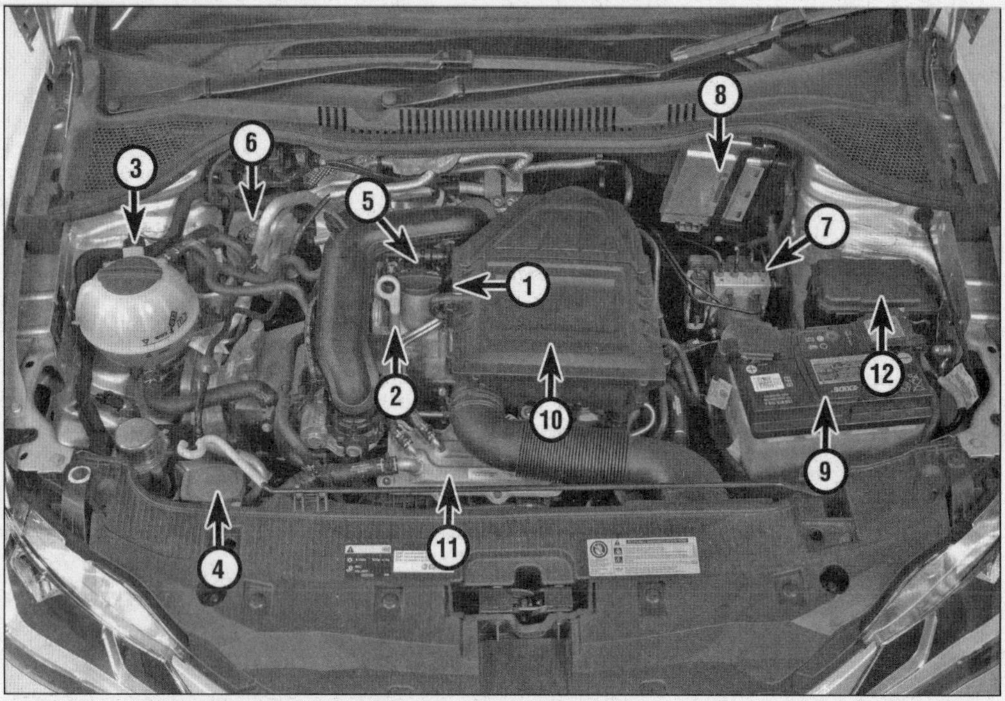

1. *Engine oil filler cap*
2. *Engine oil dipstick*
3. *Coolant expansion tank*
4. *Windscreen/headlight washer fluid reservoir*
5. *Spark plugs (below air filter housing)*
6. *Brake master cylinder fluid reservoir*
7. *Brake ABS unit*
8. *Engine management ECU*
9. *Battery*
10. *Air filter housing*
11. *Inlet manifold intercooler*
12. *Fuesebox*

Front underbody view – 1.0 litre TSI model

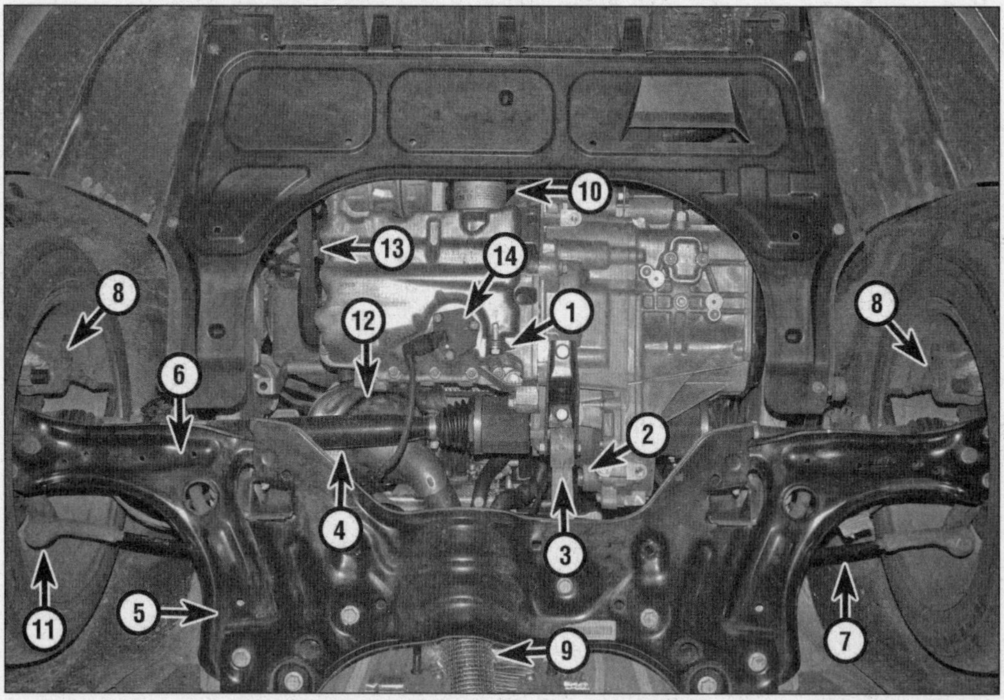

1. *Sump drain plug*
2. *Transmission oil drain plug*
3. *Rear engine mounting/link*
4. *Driveshaft*
5. *Front suspension subframe*
6. *Front suspension lower arm*
7. *Steering track rod*
8. *Front brake caliper*
9. *Exhaust flexible front pipe*
10. *Oil filter*
11. *Track rod end*
12. *Catalytic converter*
13. *Auxiliary drivebelt*
14. *Oil level/quality sensor*

Rear underbody view – 1.0 litre TSI model

1. *Fuel tank*
2. *Rear axle assembly*
3. *Rear suspension coil spring*
4. *Rear shock absorber*
5. *Exhaust rear silencer*
6. *Rear axle assembly front mountings*
7. *Handbrake cables*
8. *Fuel tank filler neck*
9. *Fuel filter*
10. *Spare wheel well*

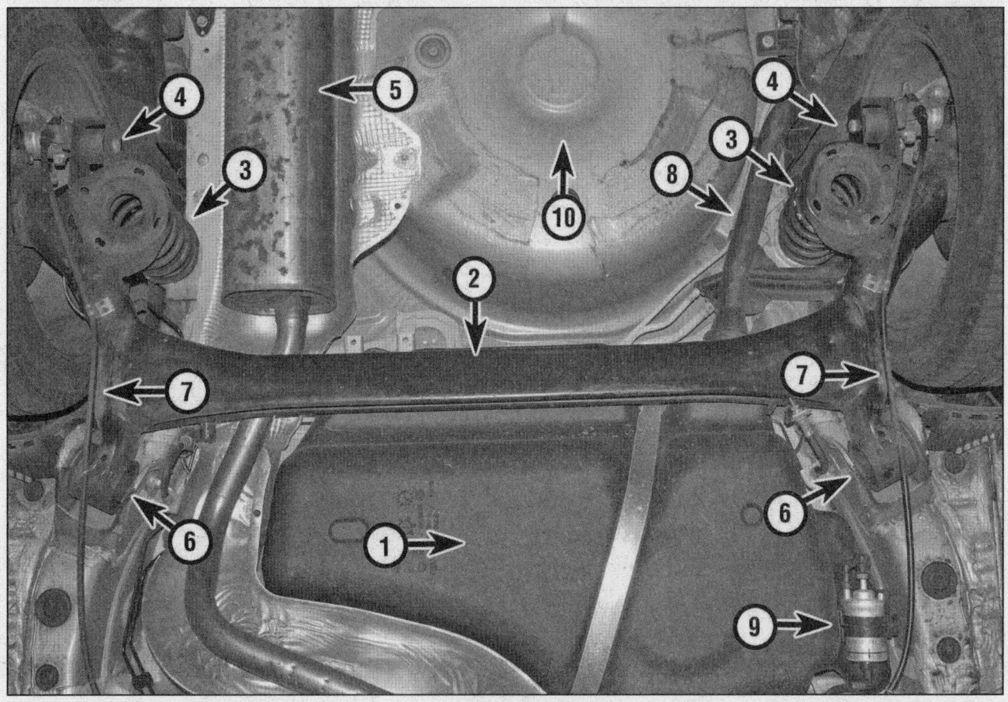

Under bonnet view – 1.4 Litre MPI model

1. *Engine oil filler cap*
2. *Engine oil dipstick*
3. *Coolant expansion tank*
4. *Windscreen/headlight washer fluid reservoir*
5. *Spark plugs (below cover)*
6. *Brake master cylinder fluid reservoir*
7. *Brake ABS unit*
8. *Engine management ECU*
9. *Battery*
10. *Air filter housing*
11. *Exhaust manifold*
12. *AC charge port*

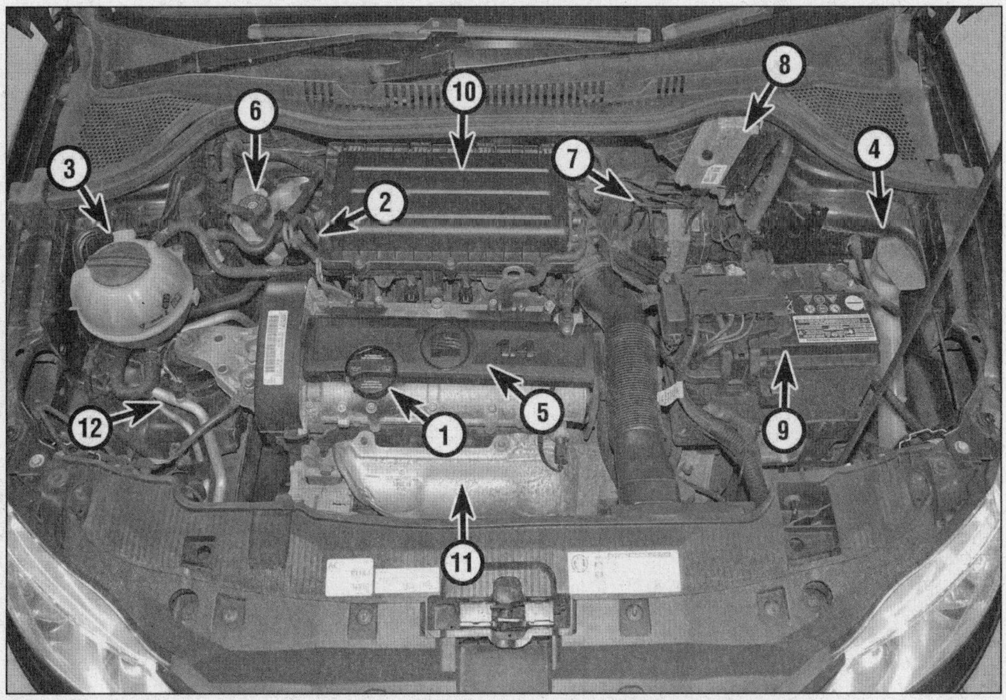

Front underbody view – 1.4 litre MPI model

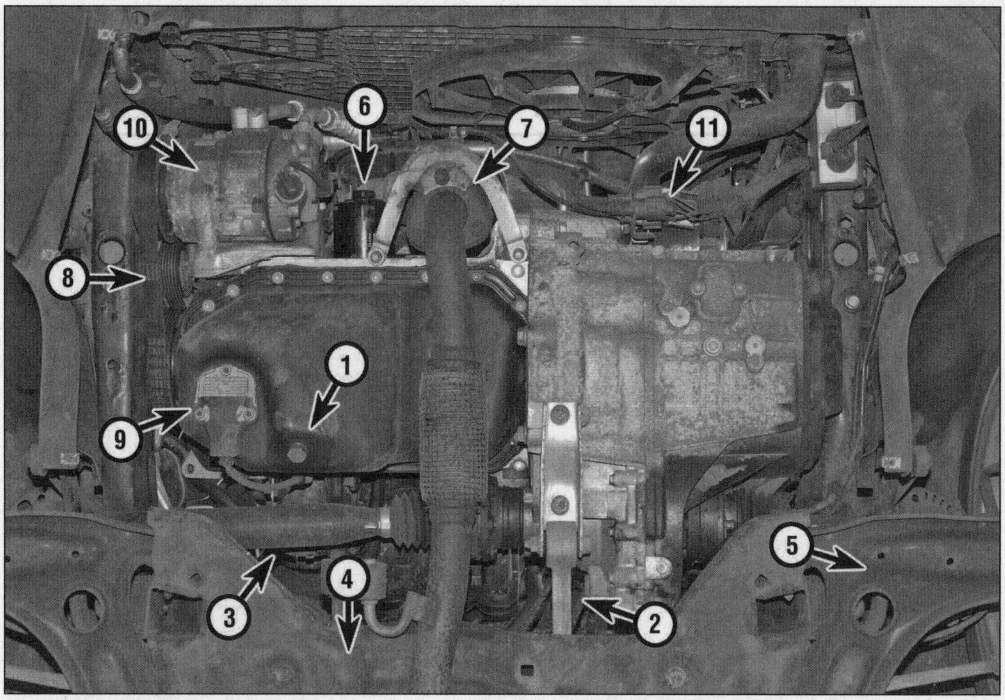

1 *Sump drain plug*
2 *Rear engine mounting/link*
3 *Driveshaft*
4 *Front suspension subframe*
5 *Front suspension lower arm*
6 *Oil filter*
7 *Catalytic converter*
8 *Auxiliary drivebelt*
9 *Oil level/quality sensor*
10 *AC Compressor*
11 *Starter motor*

4 Introduction

1 This Chapter is designed to help the home mechanic maintain his/her car for safety, economy, long life and peak performance.
2 The Chapter contains a master maintenance schedule, followed by Sections dealing specifically with each task in the schedule. Visual checks, adjustments, component renewal and other helpful items are included. Refer to the accompanying illustrations of the engine compartment and the underside of the car for the locations of the various components.
3 Servicing your car will provide a planned maintenance programme, which should result in a long and reliable service life. This is a comprehensive plan, so maintaining some items, but not others, will not produce the same results.
4 As you service your car, you will discover that many of the procedures can – and should – be grouped together, because of the particular procedure being performed, or because of the proximity of two otherwise unrelated components to one another. For example, if the car is raised for any reason, the exhaust can be inspected at the same time as the suspension and steering components.
5 The first step in this maintenance programme is to prepare yourself before the actual work begins. Read through all the Sections relevant to the work to be carried out, then make a list and gather all the parts and tools required. If a problem is encountered, seek advice from a parts specialist, or a dealer service department.

5 Regular maintenance

1 If, from the time the car is new, the routine maintenance schedule is followed closely, and frequent checks are made of fluid levels and high-wear items, as suggested throughout this manual, the engine will be kept in relatively good running condition, and the need for additional work will be minimised.
2 It is possible that there will be times when the engine is running poorly due to the lack of regular maintenance. This is even more likely if a used car, which has not received regular and frequent maintenance checks, is purchased. In such cases, additional work may need to be carried out, outside of the regular maintenance intervals.
3 If engine wear is suspected, a compression test (refer to Chapter 2A Section 2, Chapter 2B Section 2, Chapter 2C Section 2 or Chapter 2D Section 2) will provide valuable information regarding the overall performance of the main internal components. Such a test can be used as a basis to decide on the extent of the work to be carried out. If, for example, a compression test indicates serious internal engine wear, conventional maintenance as described in this Chapter will not greatly improve the performance of the engine, and may prove a waste of time and money, unless extensive overhaul work is carried out first.
4 The following series of operations are those most often required to improve the performance of a generally poor-running engine:

Primary operations

a) Clean, inspect and test the battery (See Section 20).
b) Check all the engine-related fluids (See 'Weekly checks').
c) Check the condition and tension of the auxiliary drivebelt (Section 11).
d) Renew the spark plugs (Section 27).
e) Check the condition of the air filter, and renew if necessary (Section 26).
f) Check the condition of all hoses, and check for fluid leaks (Section 10).

5 If the above operations do not prove fully effective, carry out the following secondary operations:

Secondary operations

6 All items listed under *Primary operations*, plus the following:
a) Check the charging system (see Chapter 5A Section 4).
b) Check the ignition system (see Chapter 5B Section 2).
c) Check the fuel system (see Chapter 4A)

6 Engine oil and filter renewal – petrol models

1 Frequent oil and filter changes are the most important maintenance procedures, which can be undertaken by the DIY owner. As engine oil ages, it becomes diluted and contaminated, which leads to premature engine wear.

2 Before starting this procedure, gather all the necessary tools and materials. Also make sure that you have plenty of clean rags and newspapers handy, to mop-up any spills. Ideally, the engine oil should be warm, as it will drain better, and more built-up sludge will be removed with it. Take care, however, not to touch the exhaust or any other hot parts of the engine when working under the car. To avoid any possibility of scalding, and to protect yourself from possible skin irritants and other harmful contaminants in used engine oils, it is advisable to wear gloves when carrying out this work. Access to the underside of the car will be greatly improved if it can be raised on a lift, driven onto ramps, or jacked up and supported on axle stands (see *Jacking and vehicle support*). Whichever method is chosen, make sure that the car remains level, or if it is at an angle, that the drain plug is at the lowest point. Where necessary, undo the retaining screws and remove the engine undershield(s), then also remove the engine top cover where applicable.

3 Using a socket and wrench or a ring spanner, slacken the drain plug about half a turn **(see illustrations)**. Position the draining container under the drain plug, and then remove the plug completely. Recover the sealing washer from the drain plug (the sealing ring may be part of the drain plug, and cannot be renewed separately).

4 Allow some time for the old oil to drain, noting that it may be necessary to reposition the container as the oil flow slows to a trickle.

5 After all the oil has drained, wipe off the drain plug with a clean rag, and fit a new sealing washer (or fit a complete new drain plug with sealing washer). Clean the area around the drain plug opening, and refit the plug. Tighten the plug to the specified torque.

6.3a Oil drain plug location on the sump – 1.4 litre engine

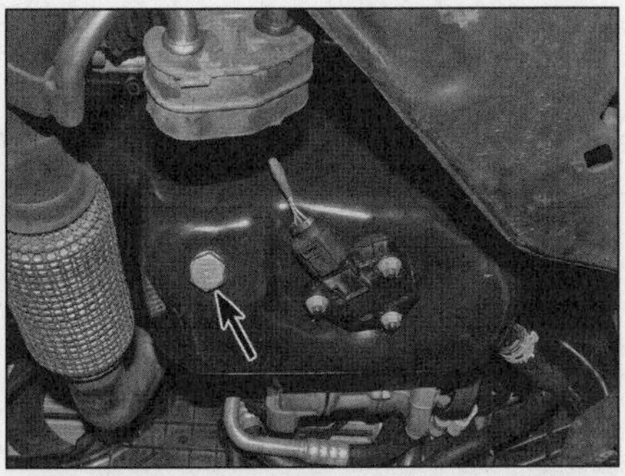

6.3b Oil drain plug location on the sump – 1.2 litre engine

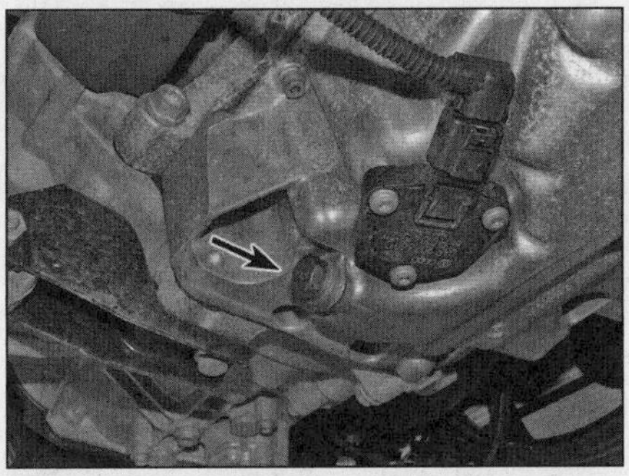

6.3c Oil drain plug location on the sump – 1.0 litre engine

6.3d The sealing washer may be integral with the plug

6 Move the container into position under the oil filter. On 1.0 litre engines, the filter is located at the front lower left-hand end of the engine. On 1.2 litre engines, the filter is located on the front right-hand end of the engine. On 1.4 litre engines, the filter is located on the front of the cylinder block **(see illustrations)**.

7 Using an oil filter removal tool (if necessary) slacken the filter initially, then unscrew it by hand the rest of the way **(see illustrations)**.

6.6a Oil filter location – 1.0 litre engine

6.6b Oil filter location – 1.2 litre engine

6.6c Oil filter location – 1.4 litre engines

6.7a Use a tool to initially slacken the filter and...

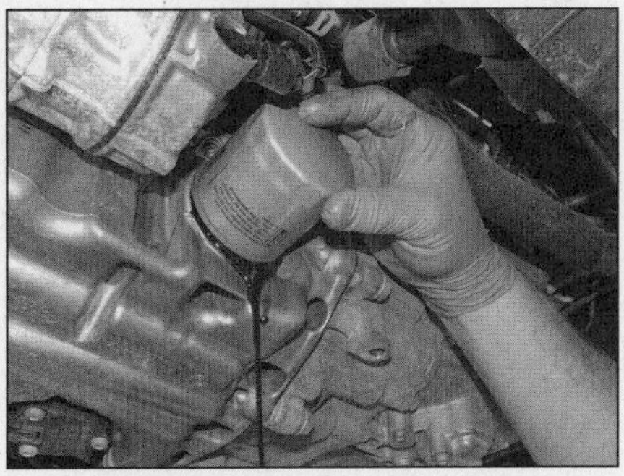

6.7b ...then spin it off by hand

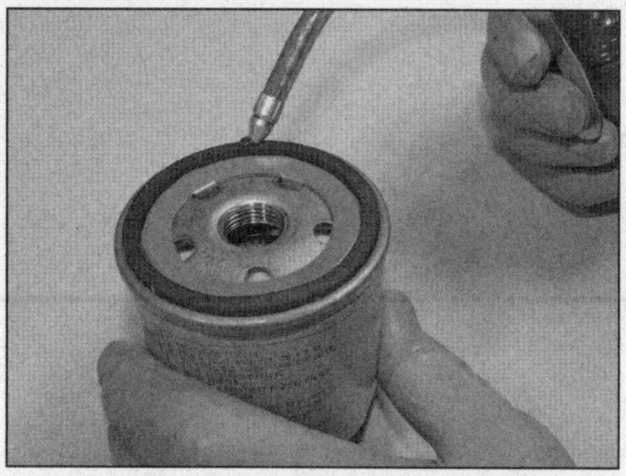

6.9 Lubricate the sealing ring

Hold the oil filter in an upright position as it is being removed, then empty the remaining oil from inside the filter into the container. Check the old filter to make sure that its rubber sealing ring has not stuck to the engine. If it has, carefully remove it.

8 Use a clean rag to remove all oil, dirt and sludge from the filter sealing area on the cylinder block (as applicable).

9 Apply a light coating of clean engine oil to the sealing ring on the new filter **(see illustration)**, and then screw it into position on the engine. Tighten the filter firmly by hand and then fully tighten with a torque wrench to the specified torque

10 Remove the dipstick, and then unscrew the oil filler cap from the cylinder head cover. Fill the engine, using the correct grade and type of oil (see *Lubricants and fluids)*. An oil can spout or funnel may help to reduce spillage **(see illustration)**. Pour in half the specified quantity of oil first, and then wait a few minutes for the oil to run to the sump. Continue adding oil a small quantity at a time until the level is mid way between the maximum and minimum marks. Do not overfill at this stage as the front of the vehicle is still raised and this will affect the dip stick reading. Refit the filler cap.

11 Start the engine and run it for a few minutes; check for leaks around the oil filter seal and the sump drain plug. Note that there may be a few seconds delay before the oil pressure warning light goes out when the engine is started, as the oil circulates through the engine oil galleries and the new oil filter before the pressure builds up.

7.1 The outer brake pads can be observed through the holes in the wheels

6.10 Use a funnel to reduce spillage when adding engine oil

12 Refit the engine undershield and lower the vehicle to the ground

13 Switch off the engine, and wait a few minutes for the oil to settle in the sump once more. With the new oil circulated and the filter completely full, recheck the level on the dipstick, and add more oil as necessary.

14 Dispose of the used engine oil and filter safely.

7 Brake pad/lining check

Front and rear disc brakes

1 The outer brake pads can be checked without removing the wheels; by observing the brake pads through the holes in the wheels **(see illustration)**. On models with steel wheels, remove the wheel trim. The thickness of the pad lining must not be less than the dimension given in the Section 1.

2 If the outer pads are worn near their limits, it is worthwhile checking the inner pads as well. Jack up car and support it on axle stands (see *Jacking and vehicle support)*. Remove the roadwheels.

3 Use a steel rule to check the thickness of the brake pads, and compare with the minimum thickness given in the Specifications **(see illustration)**.

4 For a comprehensive check, the brake pads should be removed and cleaned. The operation of the caliper can then also be checked, and the condition of the brake disc itself can be fully examined on both sides. Refer to Chapter 9.

7.3 A low cost pad thickness checking tool makes checking the pads easy

5 If any pad's friction material is worn to the specified minimum thickness or less, all four pads at the front or rear, as applicable, must be renewed as a set. Never renew the pads on just one wheel, as uneven braking will result.

6 On completion of the check, refit the roadwheels and lower the car to the ground.

Rear drum brakes

7 Chock the front wheels, then jack up the rear of the car and support it on axle stands (see *Jacking and vehicle support)*.

8 For a quick check, the thickness of friction material remaining on one of the brake shoes can be observed through a hole in the brake backplate, which is exposed by prising out the rubber sealing grommet. If a rod of the same diameter as the specified minimum friction material thickness is placed against the shoe friction material, the amount of wear can be assessed. A torch or inspection light will probably be required. If the friction material on any shoe is worn down to the specified minimum thickness or less, all four shoes must be renewed as a set.

9 For a comprehensive check, the brake drum should be removed and cleaned. This will allow the wheel cylinders to be checked, and the condition of the brake drum itself to be fully examined (see Chapter 9).

10 On completion of the check, refit the roadwheels where removed, and lower the car to the ground.

8 Resetting the service interval display

1 After all necessary maintenance work has been completed; the service interval display must be reset. Seat technicians use a special dedicated instrument to do this, and a printout is then put in the vehicle service record. It is possible for the owner on some models to reset the display as described in the following paragraphs, but note that the procedure will automatically reset the display to a 10 000 mile interval. To continue with the 'variable' intervals which take into consideration the number of starts, length of journeys, vehicle speeds, brake pad wear, bonnet opening frequency, fuel consumption, oil level and oil temperature, the display must be reset by a Seat dealership using the special dedicated instrument.

2 To reset the display, follow the procedures below **(see illustration)** :

a) Switch off the ignition.
b) Press and hold down the trip reset button '0.0/SET' beneath the speedometer
c) Switch the ignition on.
d) Release the reset button '0.0/SET'.
e) Then briefly press the clock setting

button beneath the rev counter (within 20 seconds).

f) The display will then switch back to its original display.

3 Where it is not possible to reset the display using the above procedure then most garages will have the equipment to reset the service interval display. The home mechanic who intends to keep the vehicle for a reasonable length of time may wish to invest in one of the low cost diagnostic tools now available in the aftermarket.

9 Exhaust system check

1 With the engine cold (at least an hour after the car has been driven), check the complete exhaust system from the engine to the end of the tailpipe. The exhaust system is most easily checked with the car raised on a hoist, or supported on axle stands, so that the exhaust components are readily visible and accessible (see *Jacking and vehicle support)*.

2 Check the exhaust pipes and connections for evidence of leaks, severe corrosion and damage. Make sure that all brackets and rubber mountings are in good condition, and that all relevant nuts and bolts are tight. Leakage at any of the joints or in other parts of the system will usually show up as a black sooty stain in the vicinity of the leak.

3 Rattles and other noises can often be traced to the exhaust system, especially the brackets and mountings. Try to move the pipes and silencers. If the components are able to come into contact with the body or suspension parts, secure the system with new mountings. Otherwise slacken the clamps and separate the joints (if possible), and then twist the pipes as necessary to provide additional clearance.

10 Hose and fluid leak check

1 Visually inspect the engine joint faces, gaskets and seals for any signs of water or oil leaks. Pay particular attention to the areas around the camshaft cover, cylinder head, oil filter and sump joint faces. Bear in mind that, over a period of time, some very slight seepage from these areas is to be expected – what you are really looking for is any indication of a serious leak. Should a leak be found, renew the offending gasket or oil seal by referring to the appropriate Chapters in this manual.

2 Also check the security and condition of all the engine-related pipes and hoses. Ensure that all cable-ties or securing clips are in place and in good condition. Clips that are broken or missing can lead to chafing of the hoses, pipes or wiring, which could cause more serious problems in the future.

3 Carefully check the radiator hoses and heater hoses along their entire length. Renew any hose that is cracked, swollen or deteriorated. Cracks will show up better if the hose is squeezed. Pay close attention to the hose clips that secure the hoses to the cooling system components. Hose clips can pinch and puncture hoses, resulting in cooling system leaks.

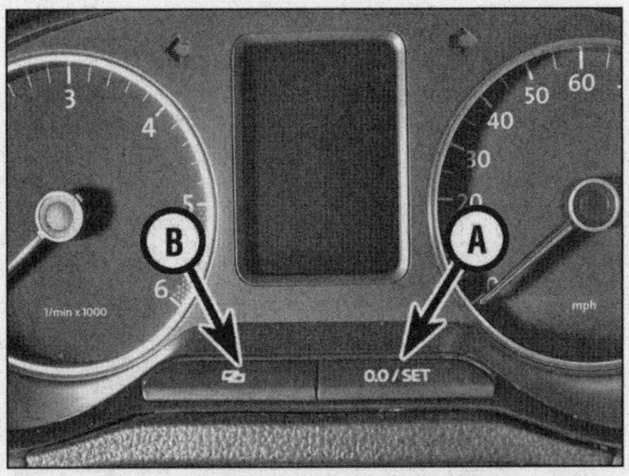

8.2 Press reset button (A) and then clock setting button (B)

4 Inspect all the cooling system components (hoses, joint faces, etc) for leaks **(see Haynes Hint)**. Where any problems of this nature are found on system components, renew the component or gasket with reference to Chapter 3.

5 With the car raised, inspect the petrol tank and filler neck for punctures, cracks and other damage. The connection between the filler neck and tank is especially critical. Sometimes a rubber filler neck or connecting hose will leak due to loose retaining clamps or deteriorated rubber.

6 Carefully check all rubber hoses and metal fuel lines leading away from the petrol tank. Check for loose connections, deteriorated hoses, crimped lines, and other damage. Pay particular attention to the vent pipes and hoses, which often loop up around the filler neck and can become blocked or crimped. Follow the lines to the front of the car, carefully inspecting them all the way. Renew damaged sections as necessary.

7 From within the engine compartment, check the security of all fuel hose attachments and pipe unions, and inspect the fuel hoses and vacuum hoses for kinks, chafing and deterioration.

8 Check the condition of the power steering fluid hoses and pipes.

HAYNES HiNT

A leak in the cooling system will usually show up as white – or rust-coloured deposits on the area adjoining the leak.

11 Auxiliary drivebelt check

1 Apply the handbrake, and then jack up the front of the car and support it on axle stands (see *Jacking and vehicle support)*.

2 Using a socket on the crankshaft pulley bolt, turn the engine slowly clockwise so that the full length of the auxiliary drivebelt can be examined. Look for cracks, splitting and fraying on the surface of the belt; check also for signs of glazing (shiny patches) and separation of the belt plies. Use a mirror to check the underside of the drivebelt **(see illustration)**. If damage or wear is visible, or if there are traces of oil or grease on it, the belt should be renewed (see Section 28).

12 Antifreeze check

1 The cooling system should be filled with the recommended antifreeze and corrosion protection fluid – **do not** mix this antifreeze with any other type. Over a period of time, the concentration of fluid may be reduced due to topping-up (this can be avoided by topping-up with the correct antifreeze mixture – see Specifications) or fluid loss. If loss of coolant has been evident, it is important to make the necessary repair before adding fresh fluid.

2 With the engine **cold**, carefully remove the cap from the expansion tank. If the engine is not completely cold, place a cloth rag over the cap before removing it, and remove it slowly to allow any pressure to escape.

3 Antifreeze checkers (hydrometers) are available from car accessory shops. Draw some coolant from the expansion tank and observe how many plastic balls are floating in the checker. Usually, 2 or 3 balls must be floating for the correct concentration of antifreeze, but follow the tool manufacturer's instructions.

11.2 Checking the underside of the auxiliary drivebelt with a mirror

4 If the concentration is incorrect, it will be necessary to either withdraw some coolant and add antifreeze, or alternatively drain the old coolant and add fresh coolant of the correct concentration (see Section 32).

13 Brake hydraulic circuit check

1 Check the entire brake hydraulic circuit for leaks and damage. Start by checking the master cylinder in the engine compartment. At the same time, check the vacuum servo unit and ABS units for signs of fluid leakage.
2 Raise the front and rear of the car and support it on axle stands (see *Jacking and vehicle support)*. Check the rigid hydraulic brake lines for corrosion and damage.
3 Check that the flexible hydraulic hoses to the front brake calipers are not twisted or chafing on any of the surrounding suspension components. To carry out this check, turn the steering fully to both sides to make this check. Also check that the hoses are not brittle or cracked **(see illustration)**.
4 Lower the car to the ground after making the checks.

14 Headlight beam adjustment

1 Accurate adjustment of the headlight beam is only possible using optical beam-setting

13.3 Twist the hoses and check for cracks or perishing

equipment, and this work should therefore be carried out by a Seat dealer or service station with the necessary facilities. All MOT stations have the necessary equipment.
2 Basic adjustments can be carried out in an emergency, and further details are given in Chapter 12 Section 10.

15 Pollen filter element renewal

1 The pollen filter is located on the heater assembly, and is removed into the passenger footwell.
2 Reach under the glovebox, and slide the two retaining catches on the pollen filter lower cover towards each other, to release and remove the cover **(see illustrations)**.
3 Withdraw the filter downwards from the heater assembly, and remove from inside the car **(see illustration)**.
4 Where fitted, separate the filter from the frame, noting the fitted direction of the air flow arrows which should point to the drivers side **(see illustration)**.
5 Fit the new filter to the frame (where applicable), with the airflow arrows pointing in the direction noted on removal. Insert the pollen into the heater assembly, and then refit the lower cover. Slide the two catches apart, to secure the cover to the housing.

16 Manual transmission oil level check – petrol models

1 Park the car on a level surface. For improved access to the filler/level plug, apply the handbrake, and then jack up the front of the car and support it on axle stands (see *Jacking and vehicle support)*, but note that the rear of the car should also be raised to ensure an accurate level check. The oil level must be checked before the car is driven, or at least 5 minutes after the engine has been switched off. If the oil is checked immediately after driving the car, some of the oil will remain distributed around the transmission components, resulting in an inaccurate level reading.
2 As applicable, undo the retaining screws and remove the engine undershield. Wipe clean the area around the transmission filler/level plug, which is situated on the rear, inner face of the transmission, above the engine rear mounting/torque link **(see illustration)**.
3 There are two types of filler/drain plugs fitted to the transmissions; if the multi-splined plug is fitted a special tool will be required (Seat tool T30023, though alternatives may be available). Since the plug will almost certainly be very tight, badly fitting substitute tools are unlikely to work, and damage may be caused to the plug's splines.
4 The oil level should reach the lower edge of the filler/level hole. A certain amount of oil will have gathered behind the filler/level plug, and will trickle out when it is removed; this does **not** necessarily indicate that the level is correct. To ensure that a true level is

15.2a Slide the catches towards each other...

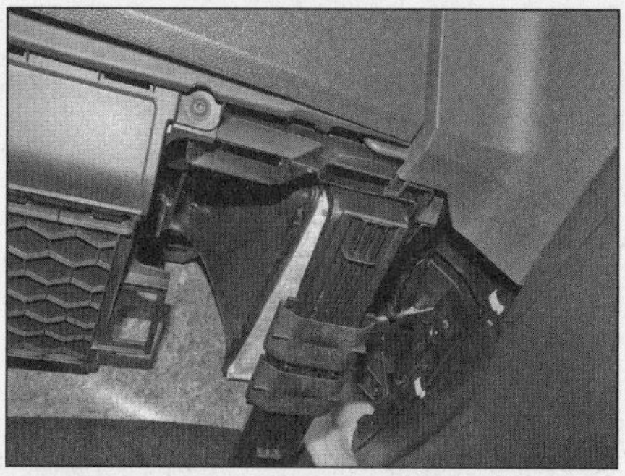

15.2b ...and remove the pollen filter lower cover

15.3 Withdraw the pollen filter into the passenger footwell

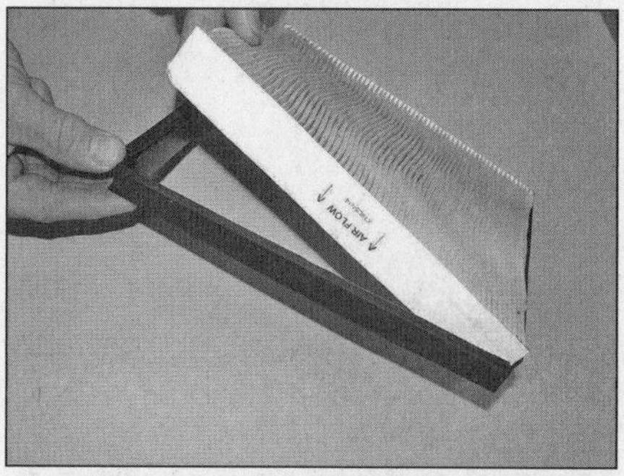

15.4 Remove the filter from the frame (where fitted)

16.2 Filler/level plug location – 02R transmission

established, wait until the initial trickle has stopped, and then add oil as necessary until a trickle of new oil can be seen emerging. The level will be correct when the flow ceases; use only good-quality oil of the specified type.

5 If the transmission has been overfilled so that oil flows out when the filler/level plug is removed, check that the car is completely level (front-to-rear and side-to-side), and allow the surplus to drain off into a suitable container.

6 When the oil level is correct, refit the filler/level plug and tighten it to the specified torque. Wipe off any spilt oil then refit the engine undershield(s), tighten the retaining screws securely, and lower the car to the ground.

17 Underbody protection check

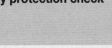

1 Raise and support the car on axle stands (see *Jacking and vehicle support)*. Using a torch or lead light, inspect the entire underside of the car, paying particular attention to the wheel arches. Look for any damage to the flexible underbody coating, which may crack or flake off with age, leading to corrosion (note, however, that there are plastic underbody panels to protect the underside of the vehicle). Also check that the wheel arch liners are securely attached with any clips provided – if they come loose, dirt may get in behind the liners and defeat their purpose. If there is any damage to the underseal, or any corrosion, it should be repaired before the damage gets too serious.

18 Driveshaft check

1 With the car raised and securely supported on stands, slowly rotate the roadwheel. Inspect the condition of the outer constant velocity (CV) joint rubber gaiters, squeezing the gaiters to open out the folds. Check for signs of cracking, splits or deterioration of the rubber, which may allow the grease to escape, and lead to water and grit entry into the joint. Also check the security and condition of the retaining clips. Repeat these checks on the inner joints **(see illustration)**. If any damage or deterioration is found, the gaiters should be renewed (see Chapter 8 Section 3).

2 At the same time, check the general condition of the CV joints themselves by first holding the driveshaft and attempting to rotate the wheel. Repeat this check by holding the inner joint and attempting to rotate the driveshaft. Any appreciable movement indicates wear in the joints, wear in the driveshaft splines, or a loose driveshaft retaining bolt.

19 Steering and suspension check

1 Raise the front and rear of the car, and securely support it on axle stands (see *Jacking and vehicle support)*.

2 Visually inspect the track rod end balljoint dust cover, the lower front suspension balljoint dust cover, and the steering rack-and-pinion gaiters for splits, chafing or deterioration. Any wear of these components will cause loss of lubricant, together with dirt and water entry, resulting in rapid deterioration of the balljoints or steering gear.

3 Check the power steering fluid hoses for chafing or deterioration, and the pipe and hose unions for fluid leaks. Also check for signs of fluid leakage under pressure from the steering gear rubber gaiters, which would indicate failed fluid seals within the steering gear.

4 Grasp the roadwheel at the 12 o'clock and 6 o'clock positions, and try to rock it **(see illustration)**. Very slight free play may be felt, but if the movement is appreciable, further investigation is necessary to determine the source. Continue rocking the wheel while an assistant depresses the footbrake. If the movement is now eliminated or significantly reduced, it is likely that the hub bearings are at fault. If the free play is still evident with the footbrake depressed, then there is wear in the suspension joints or mountings.

5 Now grasp the wheel at the 9 o'clock and 3 o'clock positions, and try to rock it as before. Any movement felt now may again be caused by wear in the hub bearings or the steering track rod balljoints. If the inner or outer balljoint is worn, the visual movement will be obvious **(see illustration)**.

6 Using a large screwdriver or flat bar, check for wear in the suspension mounting bushes by levering between the relevant suspension component and its attachment point. Some movement is to be expected as the mountings are made of rubber, but excessive wear should be obvious. Also check the condition of any visible rubber bushes, looking for splits, cracks or contamination of the rubber.

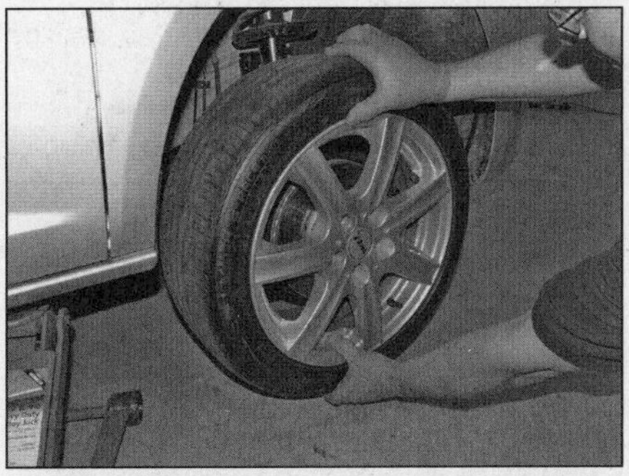

19.4 Check for wear in the hub bearings by grasping the wheel and trying to rock it

18.1 Check the condition of the driveshaft gaiter

7 With the car standing on its wheels, have an assistant turn the steering wheel back-and-forth about an eighth of a turn each way. There should be very little, if any, lost movement between the steering wheel and roadwheels. If this is not the case, closely observe the joints and mountings previously described, but in addition check the steering column universal joints for wear, and the rack-and-pinion steering gear itself.

8 Check for any signs of fluid leakage around the front suspension struts and rear shock absorber. Should any fluid be noticed, the suspension strut or shock absorber is defective internally, and should be renewed. **Note:** *Suspension struts/shock absorbers should always be renewed in pairs on the same axle to ensure correct vehicle handling*.

9 The efficiency of the suspension strut/shock absorber may be checked by bouncing the car at each corner. Generally speaking, the body will return to its normal position and stop after being depressed. If it rises and returns on a rebound, the suspension strut/shock absorber is probably suspect. Examine also the suspension strut/shock absorber upper and lower mountings for any signs of wear.

20 Battery check

1 The battery is located in the front, left-hand corner of the engine compartment. Release

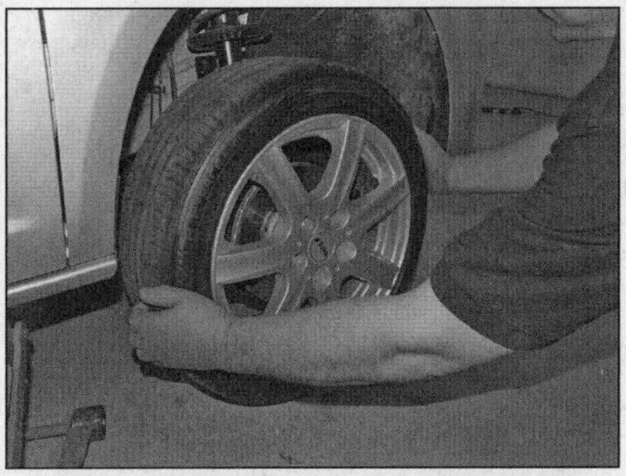

19.5 Grasping the wheel at the 3 o'clock and the 9 o'clock position will highlight steering problems

20.1 Unclip the plastic cover

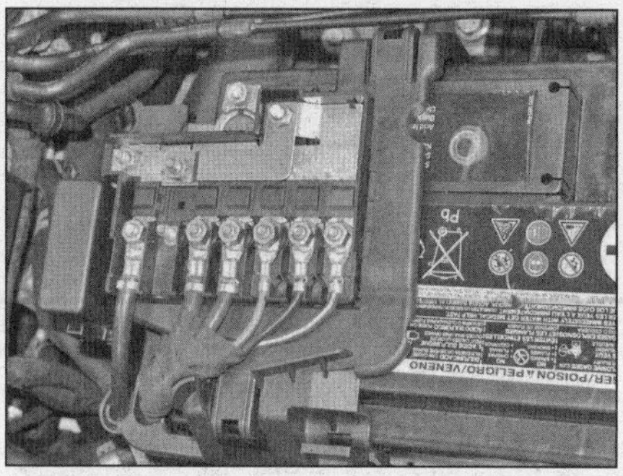

20.4 Fused links on top of the battery

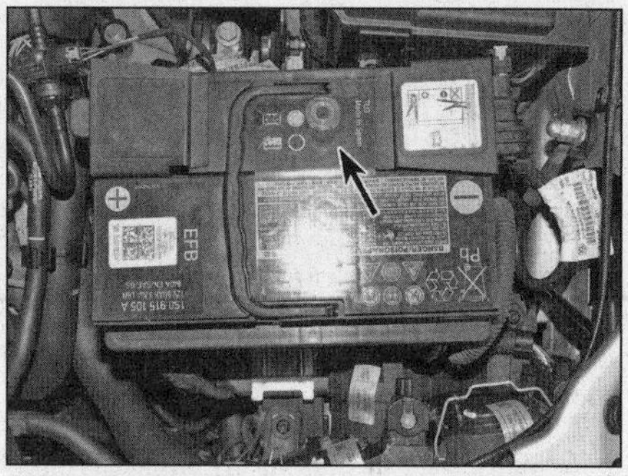

20.6 Window (eye) to check battery condition

the clip at the back, and then hinge the plastic cover forwards to gain access to the battery positive (+) terminal **(see illustration)**. Note that on later models no cover is fitted.

2 Where necessary, open the fuse holder plastic cover (squeeze together the locking lugs to release the cover) to gain access to the battery positive (+) terminal and fuse holder connections.

3 Check that both battery terminals and all the fuse holder connections are securely attached and are free from corrosion.

4 Release the retaining clips at the front of the plastic cover to access the wiring terminals on the top of the battery (where fitted) **(see illustration)**.

5 Check the battery casing for signs of damage or cracking and check the battery retaining clamp bolt is securely tightened. If the battery casing is damaged in any way the battery must be renewed (see Section).

6 Some models are fitted with a battery with a small window ('magic eye') that shows the state of the battery electrolyte. The window ('magic eye') is located on the top of the battery **(see illustration)** near the negative terminal. If the eye is green, the battery is in good condition and charged up. If the eye is black, the battery is flat and should be charged. If the eye is colourless or yellow, the electrolyte is in a critical condition. If charging the battery does not return the eye to green, the battery should be scrapped.

7 On completion of the check, clip the cover securely back onto the fuse holder and close up the insulator cover (where fitted).

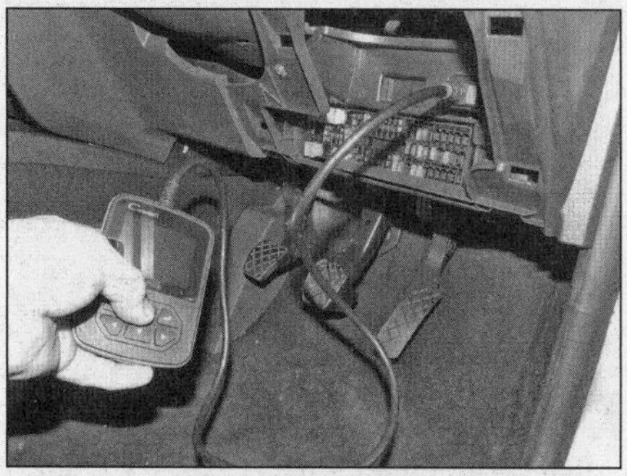

24.1 Checking for fault codes with a basic fault code reader

21 Hinge and lock lubrication

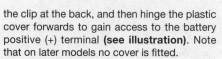

1 Lubricate the hinges of the bonnet, doors and tailgate with a light general-purpose oil. Similarly, lubricate all latches, locks and lock strikers. At the same time, check the security and operation of all the locks, adjusting them if necessary (see Chapter 11 Section 14).

2 Lightly lubricate the bonnet release mechanism and cable with suitable grease.

22 Airbag unit check

1 Inspect the exterior condition of the airbag(s) for signs of damage or deterioration. If an airbag shows signs of damage, it must be renewed (see Chapter 12 Section 24). Note that it is not permissible to attach any stickers to the surface of the airbag, as this may affect the deployment of the unit.

23 Windscreen/tailgate/ headlight washer system check

1 Check that each of the washer jet nozzles are clear and that each nozzle provides a strong jet of washer fluid.

2 The tailgate jet should be aimed to spray at the centre of the screen, using a pin.

3 The windscreen washer nozzles can be adjusted up and down as required.

4 Especially during the winter months, make sure that the washer fluid concentration is sufficient to avoid freezing.

24 Engine management self-diagnosis memory fault check

1 A Seat dealer or a specialist using diagnostic equipment should carry out this work. However low cost basic diagnostic machines are increasingly available. They do not have the functionality of professional equipment, but all are capable of reading the mandatory emissions related fault codes. The diagnostic socket is located beneath the driver's side of the facia, above the fusebox **(see illustration)**.

25 Road test and exhaust emissions check

Instruments and electrical equipment

1 Check the operation of all instruments and electrical equipment, including the air conditioning system, where applicable.

2 Make sure that all instruments read correctly, and switch on all electrical equipment in turn, to check that it functions properly.

Steering and suspension

3 Check for any abnormalities in the steering, suspension, handling or road 'feel'.

4 Drive the car, and check that there are no unusual vibrations or noises that may indicate wear in the driveshafts, wheel bearings, etc.

5 Check that the steering feels positive, with no excessive 'sloppiness', or roughness, and check for any suspension noises when cornering and driving over bumps.

Drivetrain

6 Check the performance of the engine, clutch, gearbox/transmission and driveshafts.

7 Listen for any unusual noises from the engine, clutch and gearbox/transmission.

8 Make sure the engine runs smoothly at idle, and there is no hesitation on accelerating.

9 Check that, where applicable, the clutch action is smooth and progressive, that the drive is taken up smoothly, and that the pedal travel is not excessive. Also listen for any noises when the clutch pedal is depressed.

10 Check that all gears can be engaged smoothly without noise, and that the gear lever action is smooth and not abnormally vague or 'notchy'.

11 Listen for a metallic clicking sound from the front of the car, as the car is driven slowly in a circle with the steering on full-lock. Carry out this check in both directions. If a clicking noise is heard, this indicates wear in a driveshaft joint, in which case renew the joint if necessary.

26.1a Release the rear and...

26.1b ...front hose clips

26.2 Remove the bolt

Braking system

12 Make sure that the car does not pull to one side when braking, and that the wheels do not lock when braking hard.
13 Check that there is no vibration through the steering when braking.
14 Check that the handbrake operates correctly without excessive movement of the lever, and that it holds the car stationary on a slope.
15 Test the operation of the brake servo unit as follows. With the engine off, depress the footbrake four or five times to exhaust the vacuum. Hold the brake pedal depressed, and then start the engine. As the engine starts, there should be a noticeable 'give' in the brake pedal as vacuum builds up. Allow the engine to run for at least two minutes, and then switch it off. If the brake pedal is depressed now, it should be possible to detect a hiss from the servo as the pedal is depressed. After about four or five applications, no further hissing should be heard, and the pedal should feel considerably harder.
16 Under controlled emergency braking, the pulsing of the ABS unit must be felt at the footbrake pedal.

Exhaust emissions check

17 Although not part of the manufacturer's maintenance schedule, this check will normally be carried out on a regular basis according to the country the car is operated in. Currently in the UK, exhaust emissions testing is included as part of the annual MOT test after the car is 3 years old.

26.3a Remove the breather hose...

26.3b ...unclip the wiring loom and lift off the housing

26 Air filter element renewal – petrol models

1.0 litre engines

1 Release the hose clips at the front and rear **(see illustrations)**.
2 Remove the front fixing **(see illustration)**.
3 Disconnect the breather hose, unclip the wiring loom and lift off the housing **(see illustrations)**.
4 Turn over the housing, remove the mounting screws and lift out the filter **(see illustrations)**.
5 Remove any debris and wipe clean the interior of the housing.
6 Fit the new air filter element in position, ensuring that the edges are securely seated.
7 Refit the cover and secure with the screws and refit the air filter housing using a reversal of the removal procedure.

1.2 litre engines (SOHC models)

Note: *On the single overhead camshaft models the filter is located behind the battery. The shape of the air filter housing is slightly different on later models, but removal and refitting is essentially the same for all versions.*

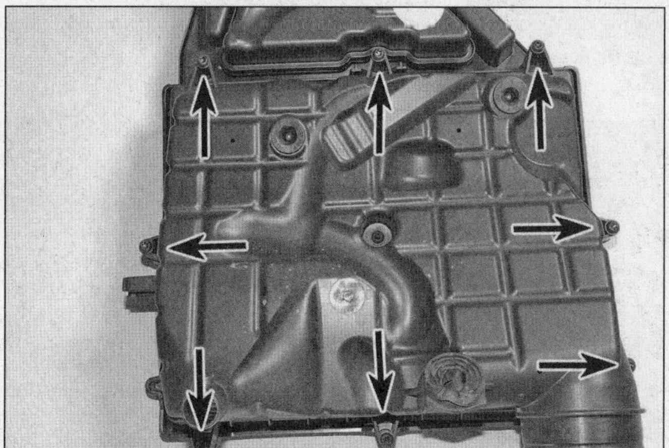

26.4a Remove the screws and...

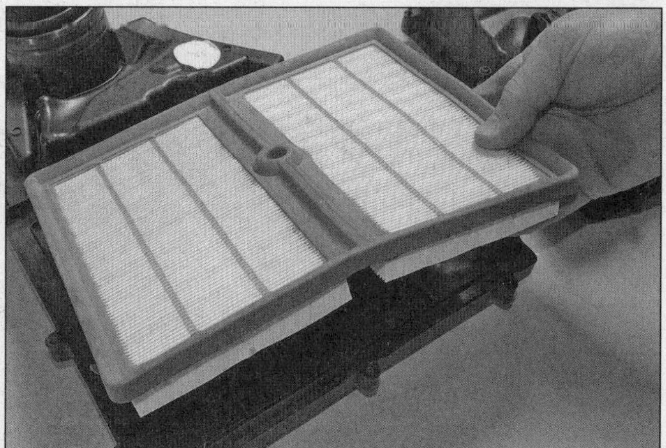

26.4b ...lift off the cover and remove the filter

26.13a Release the inlet duct...

26.13b ...the breather hose...

26.13c ...and the outlet duct

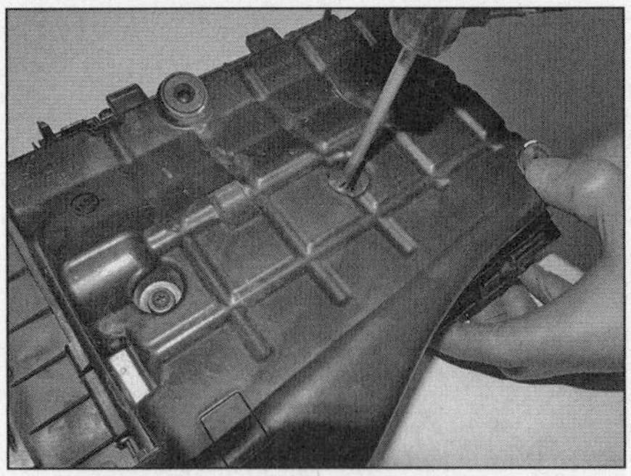

26.15a Remove the screws

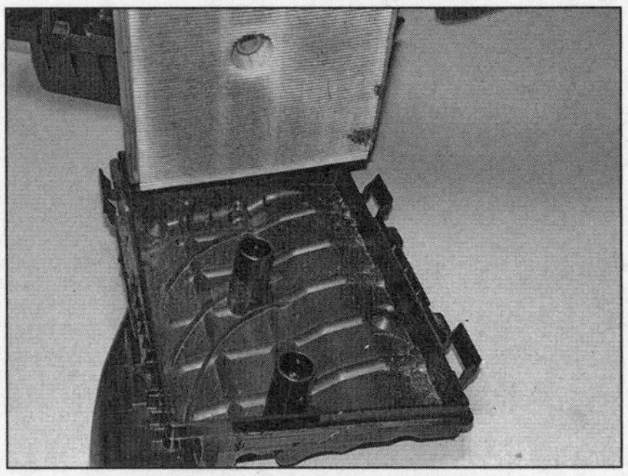

26.15b ...unclip the cover and remove the filter

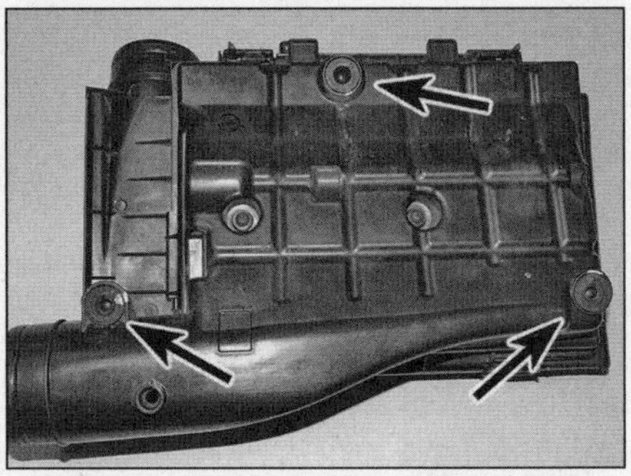

26.16 Lubricate the mounting points

8 Undo the screws and lift the cover from the air filter housing located on the left-hand rear corner of the engine compartment. If required, release the retaining clip and disconnect the air intake hose from the upper cover.

26.17a Remove the breather hose

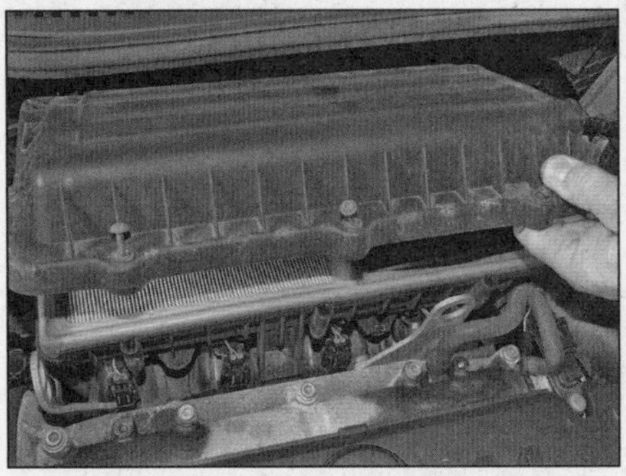

26.17c ...and lift the cover from place

9 Note how the element is fitted, then remove it.

10 Remove any debris and wipe clean the interior of the housing.

11 Fit the new air filter element in position, ensuring that the edges are securely seated.

26.17b Remove the air filter cover screws...

26.18 Remove the air filter element

12 Refit the cover and secure with the screws. If removed, secure the air intake hose to the upper cover with the retaining clip.

1.2 litre engines (DOHC models)

13 Compress and slide back the hose clips from the air inlet and outlet ducts **(see illustrations)**.

14 Pull up the complete air filter housing from the ball headed pegs.

15 On the bench turn over the housing and remove the screws. Release the clips and lift off the cover. Remove the air filter **(see illustrations)**.

16 Fit the new filter element using a reversal of the removal procedure. Lubricate the the locating pegs on the cover/housing with silicone grease or petroleum jelly **(see illustration)**.

1.4 litre engines

Note: *Some versions use the same air filter housing as the 1.2 litre single overhead camshaft engines.*

17 Disconnect the breather pipe from the left-hand side of the upper cover. Remove the fixing screws from the front of the housing, lift up the cover and remove the filter **(see illustrations)**.

18 Note its fitted position, then lift the element from the housing **(see illustration)**.

19 Remove any debris and wipe clean the interior of the housing.

20 Fit the new filter element in position.

21 Refit the cover and tighten the screws securely. Refit the breather pipe.

27.2 Remove the cover (1.4 litre engine shown)

27.4a Disconnect the wiring plugs

27.4b Remove the coil mounting bolts where fitted

27 Spark plug renewal

1 The correct functioning of the spark plugs is vital for the correct running and efficiency of the engine. It is essential that the plugs fitted are appropriate for the engine (see Specifications at the start of this Chapter). If this type is used and the engine is in good condition, the spark plugs should not need attention between scheduled renewal intervals. Spark plug cleaning should never be attempted. The days of adjusting and cleaning spark plugs are long gone. Check the gap by all means, but if in any doubt as to the condition and function of the spark plugs they should always be replaced.

2 Remove the engine cover (where fitted) and the air filter housing where required **(see illustration)**. On 1.0 litre TSI engines, unclip and place the turbocharger-to-throttle body pipe to one side.

3 All engines covered by this manual use an ignition coil for each cylinder except 1.2 litre engine where conventional HT leads are used.

4 Disconnect the wiring plugs from the coils. Where required remove the mounting bolts from the coils and unbolt the earth connector from the cylinder head cover – some models only **(see illustrations)**.

5 The HT coils must be pulled from the tops of the spark plugs. Seat technicians use a special tool for this as the coils can be very tight in their holders, however, a length of strong welding rod or similar, bent at right-angles at one end, will do the task. Hook the rod under the wiring connector/HT coil then pull directly upwards **(see illustrations)**.

27.5a Use a bent metal rod to release the HT coils...

27.5b ...or a cable tie wrapped around the coil

6 On 1.2 litre engines, the HT leads must now be pulled from the tops of the spark plugs. Seat technicians use a special tool (T10112A) to do this as the leads are very tight fit on top of the spark plugs, however, a length of strong welding rod or similar, bent at right-angles at one end, will do the task. Hook the rod under the connector/HT lead, then pull directly upwards **(see illustrations)**.

27.5c One version of the special tool expands in the mounting bolt hole to pull off the coil (1.0 litre engine)

27.5d A different version is required for models with no coil mounting bolt (1.4 litre engine)

27.5e Remove the coils from the cylinder head

27.6a Use a bent metal rod to release the HT leads...

27.6b...then remove them from the spark plug

27.8 Using a deep socket to remove the spark plugs

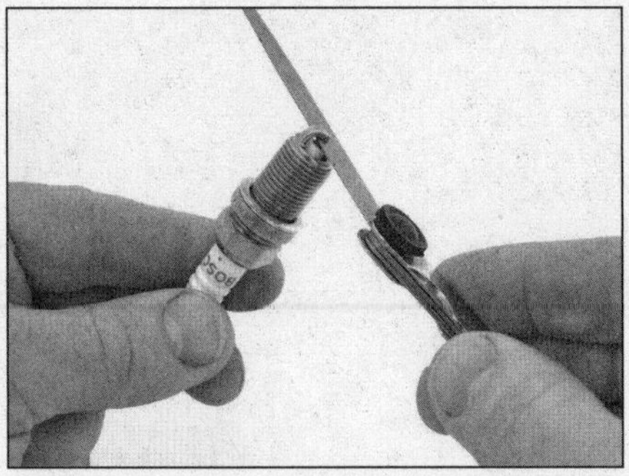

27.13a Check the electrode gap using a feeler gauge...

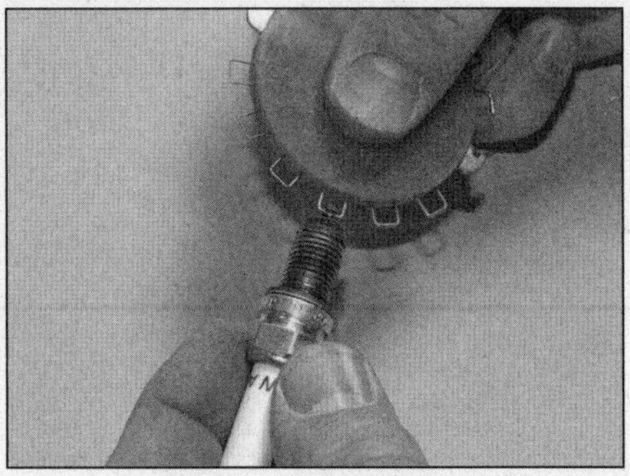

27.13b ...or a wire gauge

27.14 Using a piece of rubber hose to avoid cross threading the spark plugs

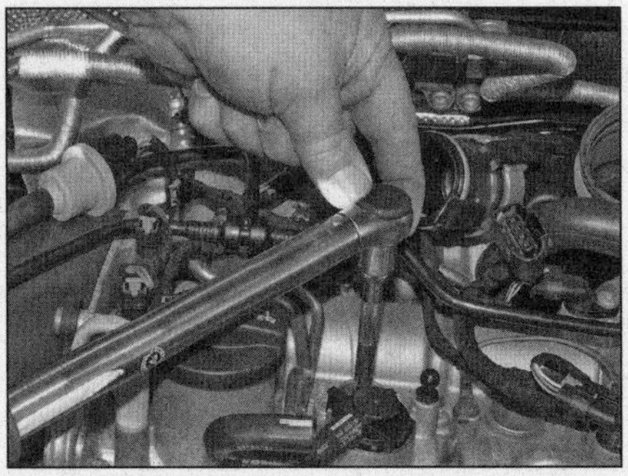

27.15 Tighten the spark plugs with a torque wrench

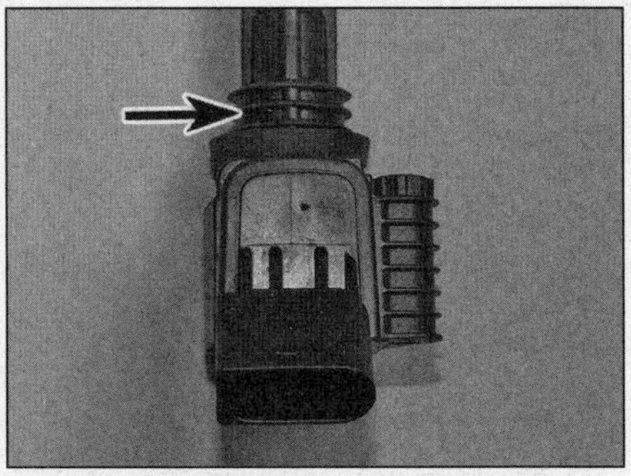

27.16 Align the boot correctly

7 It is advisable to remove the dirt from the spark plug recesses using a clean brush, vacuum cleaner or compressed air before removing the plugs, to prevent dirt dropping into the cylinders.

8 Unscrew the plugs using a spark plug spanner, suitable box spanner or a deep socket and extension bar **(see illustration)**. Keep the socket aligned with the spark plug – if it is forcibly moved to one side, the ceramic insulator may be broken off. The use of a universal joint socket will be helpful. As each plug is removed, examine it as follows.

9 Examination of the spark plugs will give a good indication of the condition of the engine. If the insulator nose of the spark plug is clean and white, with no deposits, this is indicative of a weak mixture or too hot a plug (a hot plug transfers heat away from the electrode slowly, a cold plug transfers heat away quickly).

10 If the tip and insulator nose are covered with hard black-looking deposits, then this is indicative that the mixture is too rich. Should the plug be black and oily, and then it is likely that the engine is fairly worn, as well as the mixture being too rich.

11 If the insulator nose is covered with light tan to greyish-brown deposits, then the mixture is correct and it is likely that the engine is in good condition.

12 The spark plug electrode gap is of considerable importance as, if it is too large or too small, the size of the spark and its efficiency will be seriously impaired.

13 The gap on single electrode plugs can be checked by measuring it with a feeler blade or special tool and checked against the specifications **(see illustrations)**. Do not attempt to adjust the gap. If the plug gap is outside the specifications it should be replaced. Note that replacement spark plugs are supplied correctly set.

14 Before fitting the spark plugs, check that the threaded connector sleeves are tight, and that the plug exterior surfaces and threads are clean. It's often difficult to screw in new spark plugs without cross-threading them – this can be avoided using a piece of rubber hose **(see illustration)**.

15 Remove the rubber hose (if used), and tighten the plug to the specified torque using the spark plug socket and a torque wrench **(see illustration)**. Refit the remaining spark plugs in the same manner.

16 Reconnect the ignition coils/HT leads (as applicable), using a reversal of the removal procedure. Where vent holes are provided on the spark plug boot section of the coil, these should be in line with the wiring plug connector **(see illustration)**. Rotate the boot as required.

17 Refit the air filter housing or engine cover as required.

28 Auxiliary drivebelt check and renewal

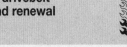

1 The multi-vee drivebelt drives the alternator and where fitted, the air conditioning compressor. On 1.2 litre engines it also drives the coolant pump.

2 On all engines, the drivebelt tension is adjusted automatically by a spring-tensioned idler. Removal and refitting is essentially the same for all engines covered in this manual.

Checking

3 See Section 11 for information on checking the condition of the drivebelt. When the belt is removed, check all pulleys are free from any damage and are secure. Also check that the alternator and air-conditioning compressor are mounted securely.

Renewal

4 For improved access, apply the handbrake, and then jack up the front of the vehicle and support it on axle stands (see *Jacking and vehicle support*). Remove the right-hand front roadwheel, and then remove the inner wheel arch liner. Note that it is possible to remove the belt from above with the vehicle on the ground, but care must be taken to align the belt around the crankshaft pulley as it is difficult to see from above.

5 If the drivebelt is to be re-used, mark it for clockwise direction to ensure it is refitted the same way round **(see illustration)**.

6 Either from above or below turn the tensioner pulley against the tension spring **(see illustrations)**. If necessary, the tensioner may be retained with a 4mm metal rod (drill bit) inserted through the hole in the pulley arm and body, to lock it in position.

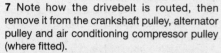

28.5 Mark the direction of rotation

7 Note how the drivebelt is routed, then remove it from the crankshaft pulley, alternator pulley and air conditioning compressor pulley (where fitted).

8 Locate the new drivebelt around the pulleys, then by holding the pressure of the tensioner with a spanner, remove the locking pin. Slowly release the pressure on the spanner, so that the tensioner takes up the slack in the belt. Check that the belt is located correctly in the multi-grooves in the pulleys **(see illustration)**.

9 Start the engine and check that the drivebelt runs, as it should over the pulleys. Make sure that all tools and hands are kept clear of the drivebelt with the engine running.

10 With the engine stopped, refit the inner wheel arch liner and roadwheel, and then lower the vehicle to the ground.

29 Power steering hydraulic fluid level check

1 Turn the front roadwheels to the straight-ahead position without starting the engine. If the car has been left standing for an hour or more, the power steering fluid will be cold (below 50°C), and the 'cold' level markings must be used. If, however, the engine is at normal temperature (above 50°C), the fluid will be hot, and the 'hot' level markings must be used.

Note: *On some models with a high capacity battery (larger in size), the battery and possibly the battery tray must be removed, in order to access the reservoir filler cap.*

29.2 Unscrew the cap from the hydraulic fluid reservoir

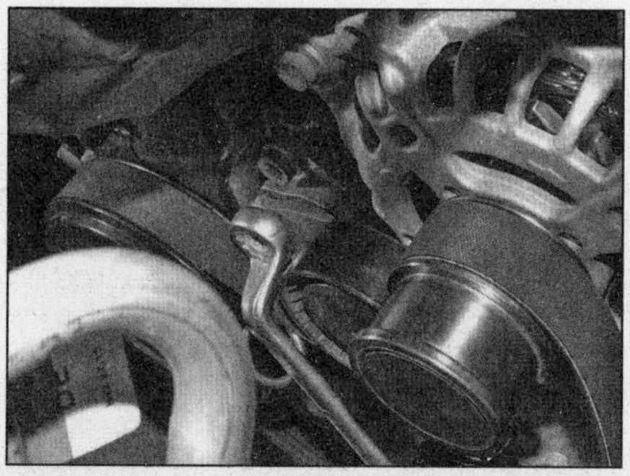

28.6a Turn the tensioner and release the auxiliary drivebelt (1.0 litre engines)

28.6c Use a spanner on the bolt (some 1.2 litre engines)

2 The reservoir for the Electrically Powered Hydraulic Steering (EPHS) is located on the front left-hand corner of the engine compartment. The fluid level is checked with the dipstick attached to the reservoir filler cap. Unscrew the cap from the hydraulic fluid reservoir, and wipe clean the integral dipstick with a clean cloth **(see illustration)**.

3 Screw on the cap hand-tight then unscrew it again and check the fluid level on the dipstick. The fluid level must be between the MIN (or lower) and MAX (or upper) marks **(see illustrations)**. If the fluid is cold (below 50°C), it must be at least above the lower level mark or MIN. If the fluid is hot (above 50°C), it must not be above the upper level mark or MAX.

4 If the level is above the maximum level mark, syphon off the excess amount. If it is below the minimum level mark, add the specified fluid as necessary *(see Lubricants and fluids)*, but in this case also check the system for leaks. On completion, screw on the cap and tighten. Refit the battery and tray where removed.

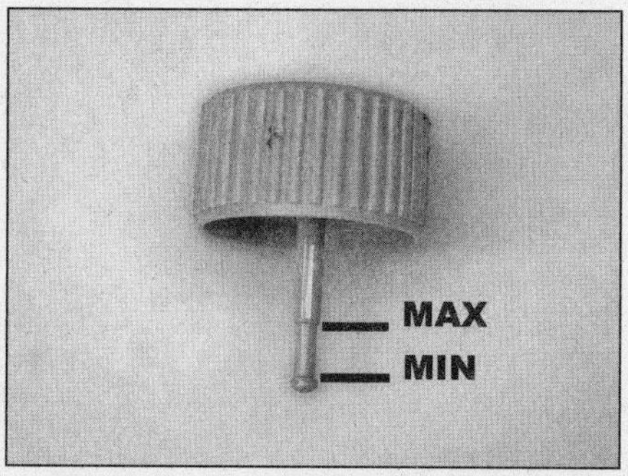

29.3a The power steering fluid level must be between the upper and lower marks

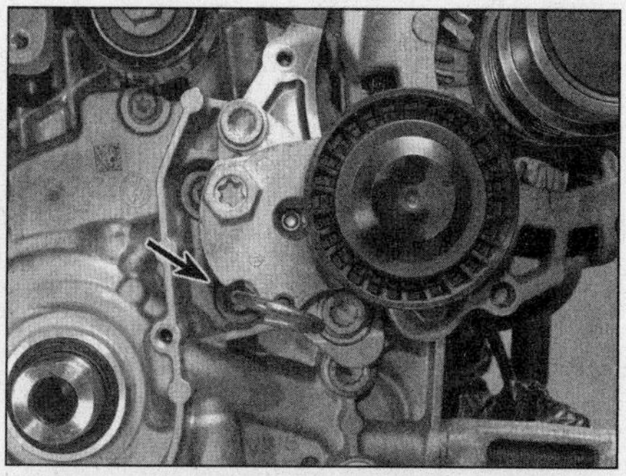

28.6b The tensioner locked in position (1.0 litre engines)

28.8 Make sure the multi-grooves locate correctly with the pulleys

30 Timing belt and tensioner renewal

1 Refer to Chapter 2A Section 6, Chapter 2C Section 7 or Chapter 2D Section 6 for renewal.

31 Brake (and clutch) fluid renewal

Warning: Brake hydraulic fluid can harm your eyes and damage painted surfaces, so use extreme

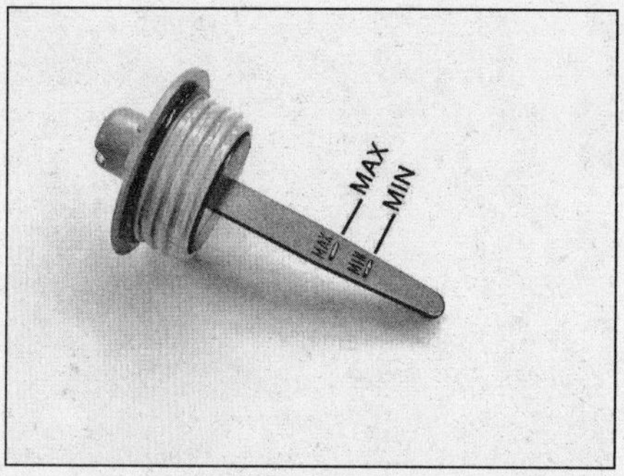

29.3b Alternative power steering cap markings

31.3 MAX and MIN levels on reservoir

caution when handling and pouring it. Do not use fluid that has been standing open for some time, as it absorbs moisture from the air. Excess moisture can cause a dangerous loss of braking effectiveness.

1 The procedure is similar to that for the bleeding of the hydraulic system as described in Chapter 6A Section 2, except that the brake fluid reservoir should be emptied by syphoning, using a clean poultry baster or similar before starting, and allowance should be made for the old fluid to be expelled when bleeding a section of the circuit. Since the clutch hydraulic system also uses fluid from the brake system reservoir, it should also be bled at the same time by referring to Chapter 6A Section 2.

2 Working as described in Chapter 9 Section 2, open the first bleed screw in the sequence, and pump the brake pedal gently until nearly all the old fluid has been emptied from the master cylinder reservoir.

3 Top-up to the MAX level with new fluid, and continue pumping until only the new fluid remains in the reservoir, and new fluid can be seen emerging from the bleed screw. Tighten the screw, and top the reservoir level up to the MAX level line **(see illustration)**.

4 Work through all the remaining bleed screws in the sequence until new fluid can be seen at all of them. Be careful to keep the master cylinder reservoir topped-up to above the MIN level at all times, or air may enter the system and greatly increase the length of the task.

5 When the operation is complete, check that all bleed screws are securely tightened, and that their dust caps are refitted. Wash off all traces of spilt fluid, and recheck the master cylinder reservoir fluid level.

6 Once the brake fluid has been changed the clutch fluid should also be renewed. Referring to Chapter 6A Section 2, bleed the clutch until new fluid is seen to be emerging from the slave cylinder bleed screw, keeping the master cylinder fluid level above the MIN level line at all times to prevent air entering the system. Once the new fluid emerges, securely tighten the bleed screw then disconnect and remove the bleeding equipment. Securely refit the dust cap then wash off all traces of spilt fluid.

7 Ensure the master cylinder fluid level is correct (see *Weekly checks)* and thoroughly check the operation of the brakes and (where necessary) clutch before taking the car on the road.

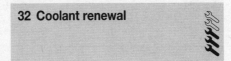

32 Coolant renewal

Note: *This work is not included in the Seat schedule, and should not be required if the recommended LongLife coolant anti-freeze/inhibitor is used. However, if standard antifreeze/inhibitor is used, the work should be carried out at the recommended interval.*

Warning: Wait until the engine is cold before starting this procedure. Do not allow antifreeze to come in contact with your skin, or with the car's painted surfaces. Rinse off spills immediately with plenty of water. Never leave antifreeze lying around in an open container, or in a puddle in the driveway or on the garage floor. Children and pets are attracted by its sweet smell, but antifreeze can be fatal if ingested.

Cooling system draining

1 With the engine completely cold, unscrew the expansion tank cap.

2 Firmly apply the handbrake then jack up the front of the car and support it on axle stands (see *Jacking and vehicle support*). Undo the retaining screws and remove the engine under shield to gain access to the base of the radiator.

3 Position a suitable container beneath the bottom hose fitting to the left-hand end of the radiator. Remove the spring type hose clip and disconnect the bottom hose from the radiator to drain the coolant **(see illustration)**.

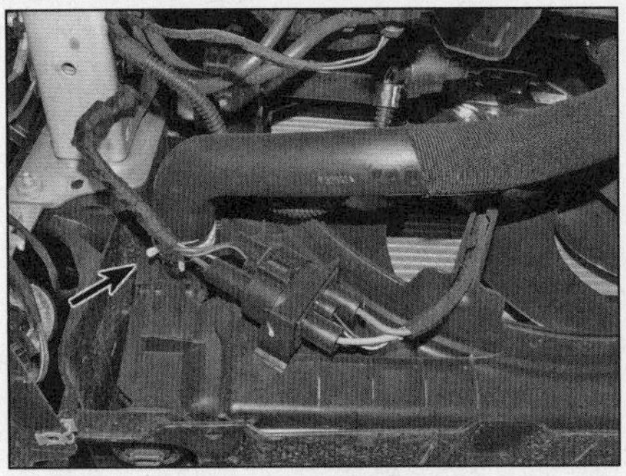

32.3 Remove the hose

32.5 Remove lower the hose to drain the coolant

4 On engines with an oil cooler, to fully drain the system, also disconnect one of the coolant hoses from the oil cooler which is located at the front of the cylinder block.

5 On 1.0 and 1.2 litre TSI models, there are two parts to the cooling systems. Both parts of the system will require draining. There is a second radiator below the main radiator **(see illustration)**, which feeds the charge air cooler inside the intake manifold. Disconnect the hose from the lower (charge air cooler) radiator to drain coolant.

6 If the coolant has been drained for a reason other than renewal then, provided it is clean, it can be re-used.

7 Once all the coolant has drained, securely tighten the radiator drain plug or reconnect the bottom hose to the radiator (as applicable). Where necessary, also reconnect the coolant hose to the oil cooler and secure it in position with the retaining clip. Refit the undershield(s), tighten the retaining screws securely.

Cooling system flushing

8 If the recommended Seat coolant has not been used and coolant renewal has been neglected, or if the antifreeze mixture has become diluted, the cooling system may gradually lose efficiency, as the coolant passages become restricted due to rust, scale deposits, and other sediment. The cooling system efficiency can be restored by flushing the system clean.

9 The radiator should be flushed separately from the engine, to avoid excess contamination.

Radiator flushing

10 To flush the radiator first tighten the radiator drain plug (where applicable).

11 Disconnect the top and bottom hoses and any other relevant hoses from the radiator.

12 Insert a garden hose into the radiator top inlet. Direct a flow of clean water through the radiator, and continue flushing until clean water emerges from the radiator bottom outlet.

13 If after a reasonable period the water still does not run clear, the radiator can be flushed with a good proprietary cleaning agent. It is important that the manufacturer's instructions are followed carefully. If the contamination is particularly bad, insert the hose in the radiator bottom outlet, and reverse-flush the radiator.

Engine flushing

14 To flush the engine, remove the thermostat (see Chapter 3 Section 4).

15 With the bottom hose disconnected from the radiator, insert a garden hose into the thermostat housing. Direct a clean flow of water through the engine, and continue flushing until clean water emerges from the radiator bottom hose.

16 When flushing is complete, refit the thermostat and reconnect the hoses.

Cooling system filling

17 Before attempting to fill the cooling system, ensure that all hoses are securely connected and their retaining clips are in good condition. If the recommended Seat coolant is not being used, ensure that a suitable antifreeze mixture is used all year round, to prevent corrosion of the engine components (see following sub-Section). **Note:** *Seat recommend that only distilled water should be used.*

18 Seat recommend the use of a vacuum tool to refill the cooling system. Suitable machines are widely available in the aftermarket **(see illustration)**. Follow the filling instructions supplied by the manufacturer.

19 When the engine has cooled, check the coolant level with reference to *Weekly checks*. Top-up the level if necessary, and refit the expansion tank cap.

Antifreeze mixture

20 If the recommended Seat coolant is not being used, the antifreeze should always be renewed at the specified intervals. This is necessary not only to maintain the antifreeze properties, but also to prevent corrosion, which would otherwise occur as the corrosion inhibitors become progressively less effective.

21 Always use an ethylene glycol based antifreeze that is suitable for use in mixed-metal cooling systems. The quantity of antifreeze and levels of protection are indicated in the Specifications.

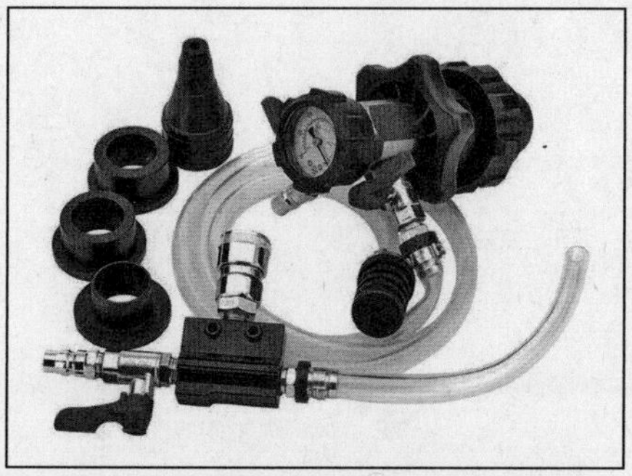

32.18 A suitable coolant filling tool from Draper tools

22 Before adding antifreeze, the cooling system should be completely drained, preferably flushed, and all hoses checked for condition and security.

23 After filling with antifreeze, a label should be attached to the expansion tank, stating the type and concentration of antifreeze used, and the date installed. Any subsequent topping-up should be made with the same type and concentration of antifreeze.

24 Do not use engine antifreeze in the windscreen/tailgate washer system, as it will damage the paintwork. A screen wash additive should be added to the washer system in the quantities stated on the bottle.

Airlocks

25 If, after draining and refilling the system, symptoms of overheating are found which did not occur previously, then the fault is almost certainly due to trapped air at some point in the system, causing an airlock and restricting the flow of coolant; usually, the air is trapped because the system was refilled too quickly.

26 If an airlock is suspected, first try gently squeezing all visible coolant hoses. A coolant hose, which is full of air, feels quite different to one full of coolant, when squeezed. After refilling the system, most airlocks will clear once the system has cooled, and been topped up.

27 While the engine is running at operating temperature, switch on the heater and heater fan, and check for heat output. Provided there is sufficient coolant in the system, any lack of heat output could be due to an airlock in the system.

28 Airlocks can have more serious effects than simply reducing heater output – a severe airlock could reduce coolant flow around the engine. Check that the radiator top hose is hot when the engine is at operating temperature – a top hose that stays cold could be the result of an airlock (or a non-opening thermostat).

29 If the problem persists, stop the engine and allow it to cool down **completely**, before unscrewing the expansion tank filler cap or loosening the hose clips and squeezing the hoses to bleed out the trapped air. In the worst case, the system will have to be at least partially drained (this time, the coolant can be saved for re-use) and flushed to clear the problem.

Chapter 1 Part B
Routine maintenance and servicing – diesel models

Contents

Degrees of difficulty

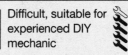

Easy, suitable for novice with little experience	Fairly easy, suitable for beginner with some experience	Fairly difficult, suitable for competent DIY mechanic	Difficult, suitable for experienced DIY mechanic	Very difficult, suitable for expert DIY or professional

1 Servicing specifications – diesel models

Lubricants and fluids .... Refer to end of *Weekly checks* on page 0•16

Engine codes *

1.6 litre engines	CLNA and CAYC

**See 'Vehicle identification' at the end of this manual for the location of the engine code markings.*

Capacities

Engine oil (including filter)	
1.6 litre engines	4.3 litres
Cooling system	
1.6 litre engines	8.0 litres
Transmission	
Manual transmission:	
Type 02T and 02R	2.0 litres
Fuel tank (approximate)	45 litres

Cooling system

Antifreeze mixture:	
40% antifreeze	Protection down to -25°C
50% antifreeze	Protection down to -35°C

Note: *Refer to antifreeze manufacturer for latest recommendations.*

Brakes

Brake pad minimum thickness: *	
Front	14.0 mm
Rear	11.5 mm
Friction lining only:	
Front and rear	2.0 mm
Rear brake shoe friction material minimum thickness	1.5 mm

**Including backing plate*

Torque wrench settings

	Nm	lbf ft
Alternator mounting bolt	20	15
Manual transmission 02R:		
Filler/level plug	30	22
Manual transmission 02T:		
Filler/level plug		
Multi-splined (12-point) plug	24	18
Hexagon (Allen key) plug	32	23
Oil filter cap	25	18
Roadwheel bolts	120	89
Sump drain plug	30	22

2 Maintenance schedule – diesel models

Maintenance schedule

The maintenance intervals in this manual are provided with the assumption that you, not the dealer, will be carrying out the work. These are the minimum intervals recommended by us for vehicles driven daily. If you wish to keep your vehicle in peak condition at all times, you may wish to perform some of these procedures more often. We encourage frequent maintenance, since it enhances the efficiency, performance and resale value of your vehicle.

When the vehicle is new, it should be serviced by a dealer service department (or other workshop recognised by the vehicle manufacturer as providing the same standard of service) in order to preserve the warranty. The vehicle manufacturer may reject warranty claims if you are unable to prove that servicing has been carried out as and when specified, using only original equipment parts or parts certified to be of equivalent quality.

Longlife service schedule

All Seat models are equipped with a service interval display indicator in the instrument panel. Every time the engine is started the panel will illuminate for approximately 20 seconds with service information. With the standard fixed interval display, the service intervals are in accordance with specific distances and time periods. With the LongLife display, the service interval is variable. Once the service interval has been reached, the display will flash 'OIL service' for an oil change service or 'INSP service' for an inspection service.

For models using the LongLife schedule, the occurrence of either service reminder on the display unit will depend on how the vehicle is being used (number of starts, length of journeys, vehicle speeds, brake pad wear, bonnet opening frequency, fuel consumption, oil level and oil temperature). For example, if a vehicle is being used under extreme driving conditions, the service may occur at 10 000 miles, whereas, if the vehicle is being used under moderate driving conditions, it may occur at 20 000 miles, although the maximum length of time between INSP services is 2 years. It is important to realise that this system is completely variable according to how the vehicle is being used, and therefore the service should be carried out when indicated on the display. Note: *Models with the variable service interval system are equipped with an engine oil level sensor, brake pad wear indicator, battery with a 'magic eye' charge indicator, and a variable service indicator.*

The LongLife variable service intervals are only applicable to models with a PR number of QG1 (up to 2013) or QI6 (2013 on). This number is shown in the vehicle Service Schedule booklet, on a service interval plate next to the spare wheel well. With the variable (LongLife) service interval on models with these PR numbers, the engine must **only** be filled with the recommended **LongLife** engine oil (see *Lubricants and fluids*).

After completing a service, Seat technicians use a diagnostic too to reset the service display to the next service interval, and a print-out is put in the vehicle service record. The display can be reset by the owner as described in Section 9, but note that for models using the LongLife interval, the procedure will automatically reset the schedule to an amended LongLife interval, in which oil renewal and brake pad checks are based on distance/time while every other system remains LongLife. To have the display reset to the full LongLife schedule, it is necessary to take the car to a Seat dealer. Note that it is also possible to change (using the diagnostic tool) to fixed interval servicing.

Every 250 miles or weekly

☐ Refer to *Weekly checks*

'OIL service' on display

☐ Renew the engine oil and filter (Section 7)

Note: *Frequent oil and filter changes are good for the engine. We recommend changing the oil at least once a year.*

☐ Check the front and rear brake pad thickness (Section 8)

☐ Reset the service interval display (Section 9)

'INSP service' on display

In addition to the items listed above, carry out the following:

☐ Check the condition of the exhaust system and its mountings (Section 10)

☐ Check all underbonnet components and hoses for fluid and oil leaks (Section 11)

☐ Renew the fuel filter (Section 28)

☐ Check the condition of the auxiliary drivebelt (Section 12)

☐ Check the coolant antifreeze concentration (Section 13)

☐ Check the brake hydraulic circuit for leaks and damage (Section 14)

☐ Check the headlight beam adjustment (Section 15)

☐ Renew the pollen filter element (Section 16)

☐ Check the manual transmission oil level (Section 17)

☐ Check the underbody protection for damage (Section 18)

☐ Check the condition of the driveshafts (Section 19)

☐ Check the steering and suspension components for condition and security (Section 20)

'INSP service' on display (continued)

☐ Check the battery condition and security (Section 21)

☐ Lubricate all hinges and locks (Section 22)

☐ Check the condition of the airbag unit(s) (Section 23)

☐ Check the operation of the windscreen/tailgate/ headlight washer system(s) (as applicable) (Section 24)

☐ Check the engine management self-diagnosis memory for faults (Section 25)

☐ Carry out a road test and check exhaust emissions (Section 26)

Every 40 000 miles or 4 years, whichever comes first

Note: *Many dealers perform these tasks with every second INSP service.*

☐ Renew the air filter element (Section 27)

☐ Check the condition of the auxiliary drivebelt (Section 12)

☐ Check the power steering hydraulic fluid level (Section 30)

Every 80 000 miles

☐ Renew the timing belt and tensioner roller (Section 31)

Every 2 years

☐ Renew the brake (and clutch) fluid (Section 32)

☐ Renew the coolant.

Note: *Renewing the coolant isn't included in the Seat schedule, and should not be required if the recommended Seat G12 LongLife coolant anti-freeze is used.*

3 Component location – diesel models

Underbonnet view of a 1.6 litre model (engine cover removed)

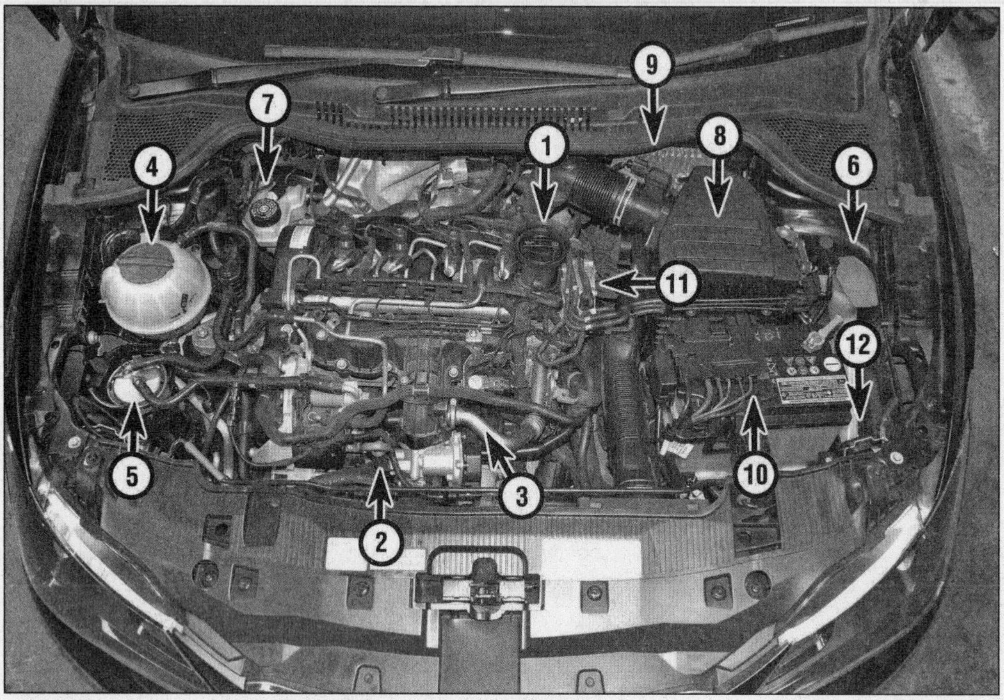

1. *Engine oil filler cap*
2. *Engine oil dipstick*
3. *Oil filter*
4. *Coolant expansion tank*
5. *Fuel filter*
6. *Windscreen/headlight washer fluid reservoir*
7. *Master cylinder brake fluid reservoir*
8. *Air filter housing*
9. *Engine management ECU*
10. *Battery*
11. *Brake vacuum pump*
12. *Power steering fluid reservoir (hidden by battery)*

Front underbody view of a 1.6 litre model

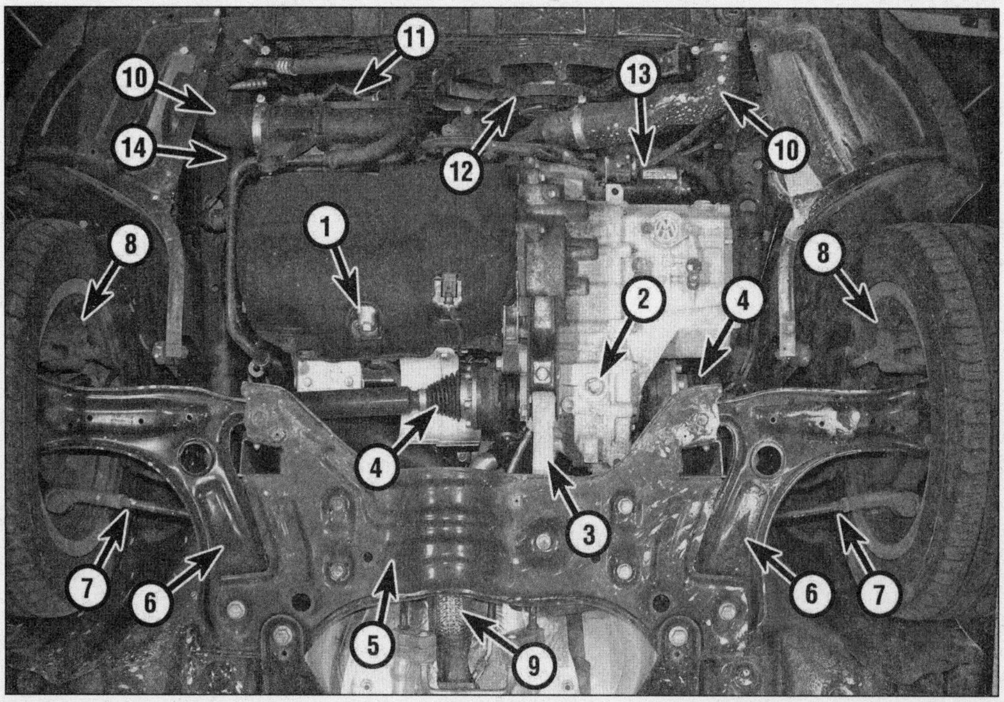

1. *Sump drain plug*
2. *Manual transmission drain plug*
3. *Engine rear mounting/link*
4. *Driveshaft*
5. *Front suspension subframe*
6. *Front suspension lower arm*
7. *Steering track rod*
8. *Front brake caliper*
9. *Front exhaust flexible pipe*
10. *Intercooler hoses*
11. *Air conditioning compressor*
12. *Radiator electric cooling fan*
13. *Starter motor*
14. *Auxiliary belt*

Rear underbody view of a 1.6 litre model

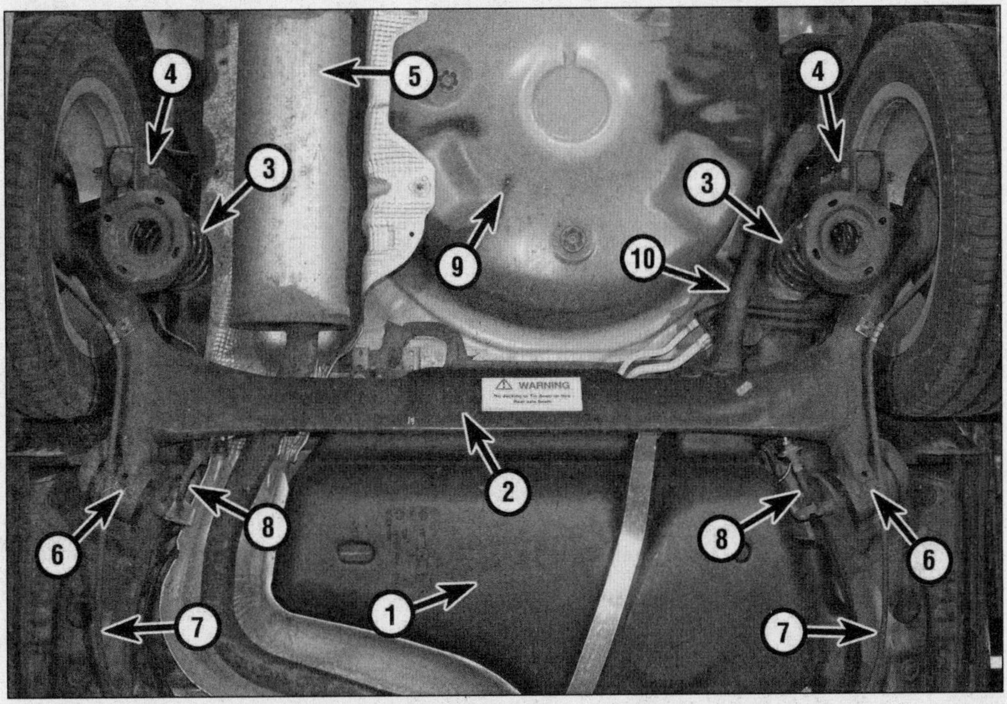

1 *Fuel tank*
2 *Rear axle assembly*
3 *Rear suspension coil spring*
4 *Rear shock absorber*
5 *Exhaust rear silencer*
6 *Rear axle assembly front mountings*
7 *Handbrake cables*
8 *Hydraulic brake line*
9 *Spare wheel well*
10 *Fuel tank filler neck*

4 Introduction

1 This Chapter is designed to help the home mechanic maintain his/her vehicle for safety, economy, long life and peak performance.
2 The Chapter contains a master maintenance schedule, followed by Sections dealing specifically with each task in the schedule. Visual checks, adjustments, component renewal and other helpful items are included. Refer to the accompanying illustrations of the engine compartment and the underside of the vehicle for the locations of the various components.
3 Servicing your vehicle will provide a planned maintenance programme, which should result in a long and reliable service life. This is a comprehensive plan, so maintaining some items but not others will not produce the same results.
4 As you service your vehicle, you will discover that many of the procedures can – and should – be grouped together, because of the particular procedure being performed, or because of the proximity of two otherwise unrelated components to one another. For example, if the vehicle is raised for any reason, the exhaust can be inspected at the same time as the suspension and steering components.
5 The first step in this maintenance programme is to prepare yourself before the actual work begins. Read through all the Sections relevant to the work to be carried out, then make a list and gather all the parts and tools required. If a problem is encountered, seek advice from a parts specialist, or a dealer service department.

5 Regular maintenance

1 If, from the time the vehicle is new, the routine maintenance schedule is followed closely, and frequent checks are made of fluid levels and high-wear items, as suggested throughout this manual, the engine will be kept in relatively good running condition, and the need for additional work will be minimised.
2 It is possible that there will be times when the engine is running poorly due to the lack of regular maintenance. This is even more likely if a used vehicle, which has not received regular and frequent maintenance checks, is purchased. In such cases, additional work may need to be carried out, outside of the regular maintenance intervals.
3 If engine wear is suspected, a compression test (refer to the Chapter 2E Section 2) will provide valuable information regarding the overall performance of the main internal components. Such a test can be used as a basis to decide on the extent of the work to be carried out. If, for example, a compression test indicates serious internal engine wear, conventional maintenance as described in this Chapter will not greatly improve the performance of the engine, and may prove a waste of time and money, unless extensive overhaul work is carried out first.
4 The following series of operations are those most often required to improve the perfor-mance of a generally poor-running engine:

Primary operations

a) Clean, inspect and test the battery (See 'Weekly checks').
b) Check all the engine-related fluids (See 'Weekly checks').
c) Check the condition and tension of the auxiliary drivebelt (Section 12).
d) Check the condition of the air filter, and renew if necessary (Section 27).
e) Check the condition of all hoses, and check for fluid leaks (Section 11).

5 If the above operations do not prove fully effective, carry out the following secondary operations:

Secondary operations

6 All items listed under Primary operations, plus the following:
a) Check the charging system (see Chapter 5A Section 4).
b) Check the preheating system (see Chapter 5C Section 2).
c) Renew the fuel filter and check the fuel system (see Chapter 4B).

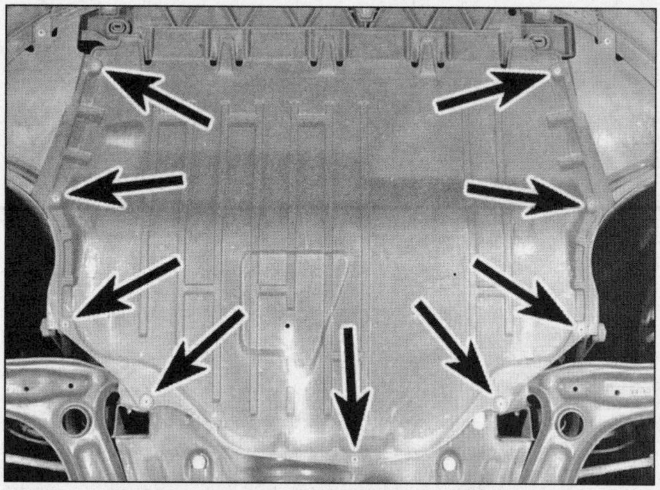

7.2a Remove the undershield screws...

7.2b ...and the engine cover

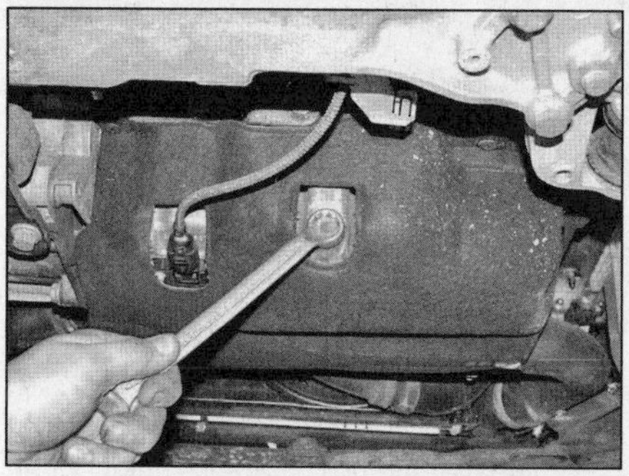

7.3a Undo the sump drain plug

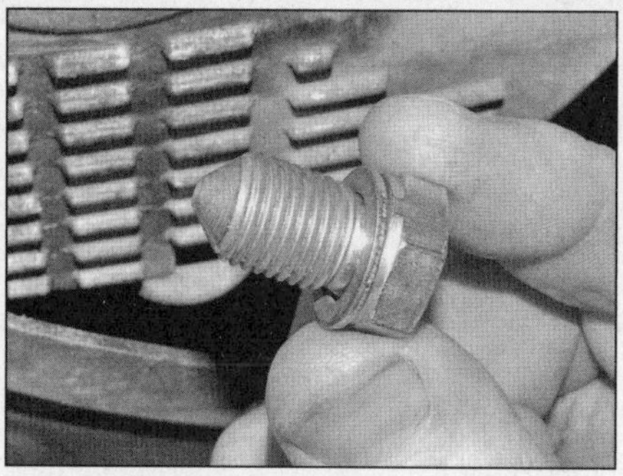

7.3b The seal is integral with the plug

HAYNES HiNT

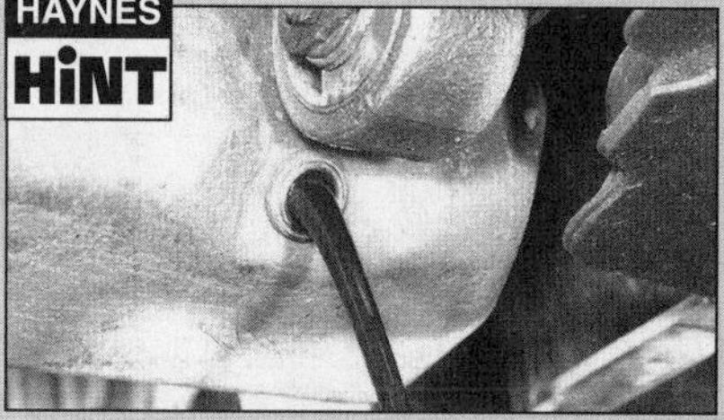

Keep the drain plug pressed into the sump while unscrewing it by hand the last couple of turns. As the plug releases, move it away sharply so the stream of oil issuing from the sump runs into the container, not up your sleeve.

6 'OIL service' on display

1 Renew the engine oil and filter (Section 7)
Note: *Frequent oil and filter changes are good for the engine. We recommend changing the oil at least once a year.*
2 Check the front and rear brake pad thickness (Section 8)
3 Reset the service interval display (Section 9)

7 Engine oil and filter renewal – diesel models

1 Frequent oil and filter changes are the most important preventative maintenance procedures, which can be undertaken by the DIY owner. As engine oil ages, it becomes diluted and contaminated, which leads to premature engine wear.
2 Before starting this procedure, gather all the necessary tools and materials. Also make sure that you have plenty of clean rags and newspapers handy, to mop-up any spills. Ideally, the engine oil should be warm, as it will drain better, and more built-up sludge will be removed with it. Take care, however, not to touch the exhaust or any other hot parts of the engine when working under the vehicle. To avoid any possibility of scalding, and to protect yourself from possible skin irritants and other harmful contaminants in used engine oils, it is advisable to wear gloves when carrying out this work. Access to the underside of the vehicle will be greatly improved if it can be raised on a lift, driven onto ramps, or jacked up and supported on axle stands (see *Jacking and vehicle support*). Whichever method is chosen, make sure that the vehicle remains level, or if it is at an angle, that the drain plug is at the lowest point. Undo the retaining screws and remove the engine undertray, then also remove the engine top cover **(see illustrations)**.

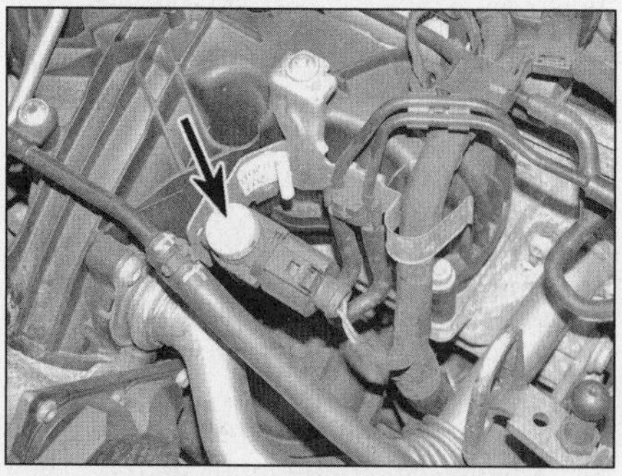

7.6 Remove the solenoid

3 Slacken the sump drain plug about half a turn. Position the draining container under the drain plug, and then remove the plug completely **(see illustrations** and **Haynes Hint)**. To drain all oil from the engine, loosen the cap from the top of the oil filter housing using a socket or spanner – this will allow the oil to drain from the filter housing into the sump.
4 Allow some time for the old oil to drain, noting that it may be necessary to reposition the container as the oil flow slows to a trickle.
5 After all the oil has drained, wipe off the drain plug with a clean rag, and fit a new sealing washer. Clean the area around the drain plug opening, and refit the plug. Tighten the plug securely. **Note:** *On some engines, the sealing washer is integral with the drain plug. On these engines, the drain plug must be renewed.*
6 Place absorbent cloths around the oil filter housing to catch any spilt oil. Unbolt the bracket and unclip the solenoid valve from above the oil filter **(see illustration)**.
7 Fully unscrew the cap from the top of the oil filter and remove it together with the filter element. Recover the large sealing ring from

7.7a Use a 32mm socket to unscrew the filter cap...

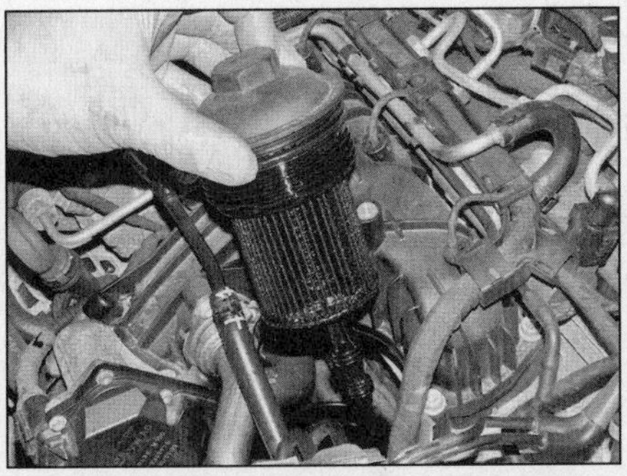
7.7b ...and withdraw the filter and cap...

7.7c ...then slide the old filter from the cap

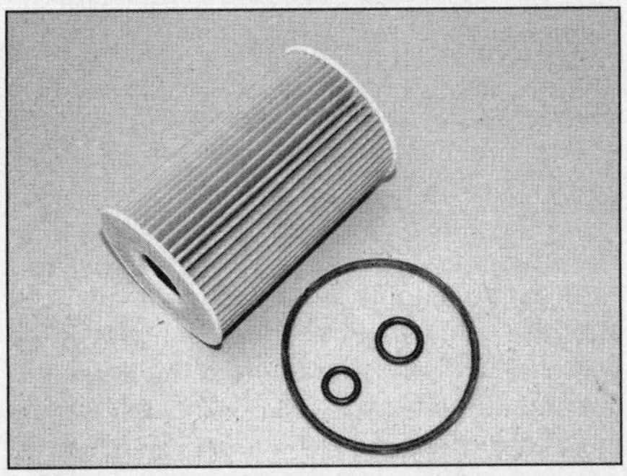
7.9a The new filter comes with three O-ring seals

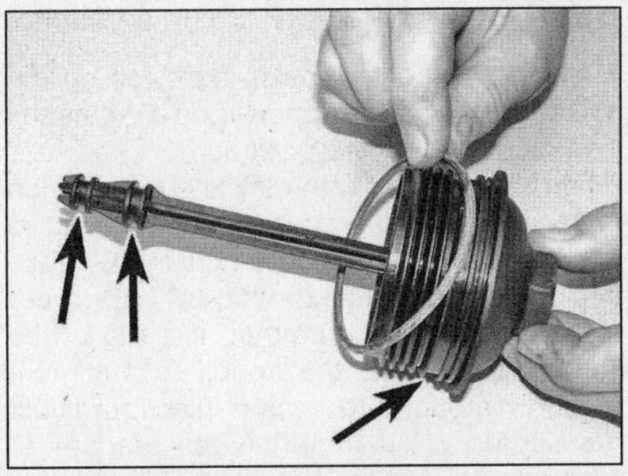
7.9b Fit the three seals to the oil filter cap in the positions shown...

7.9c ...then slide the new filter to the cap...

the cap, and the small sealing ring from the centre rod. Unclip the filter element from the cap and dispose of it **(see illustrations)**.

8 Using a clean rag, wipe all oil and sludge from the inside of the filter housing and cap.

9 Fit new sealing rings, then refit the assembly and tighten to the specified torque. Make sure the filter element is engaged with the cap and the correct way up **(see illustrations)**. Wipe up any spilt oil before refitting the engine top cover.

10 Remove the dipstick, and then unscrew the oil filler cap from the cylinder head cover. Fill the engine, using the correct grade and type of oil (see *Lubricants and fluids)*. An oil can spout or funnel may help to reduce spillage. Pour in half the specified quantity of oil first **(see illustration)**, then wait a few minutes for the oil to run to the sump (see *Weekly checks)*. Continue adding oil a small quantity at a time until the level is mid way between the maximum and minimum marks to the maximum mark on the dipstick. Refit the filler cap.

11 Start the engine and run it for a few minutes; check for leaks around the oil filter cap and the sump drain plug. Note that there may be a few seconds delay before the oil pressure warning light goes out when the engine is started, as the oil circulates through the engine oil galleries and the new oil filter before the pressure builds-up.

Warning: Do not increase the engine speed above idling while the oil pressure light is illuminated, as considerable damage can be caused to the turbocharger.

12 Remove the old oil and all tools from under the car then refit the undertray and lower the car to the ground. Also refit the engine top cover.

13 Switch off the engine, and wait a few minutes for the oil to settle in the sump once more. With the new oil circulated and the filter completely full, recheck the level on the dipstick, and add more oil as necessary.

14 Dispose of the used engine oil and filter safely.

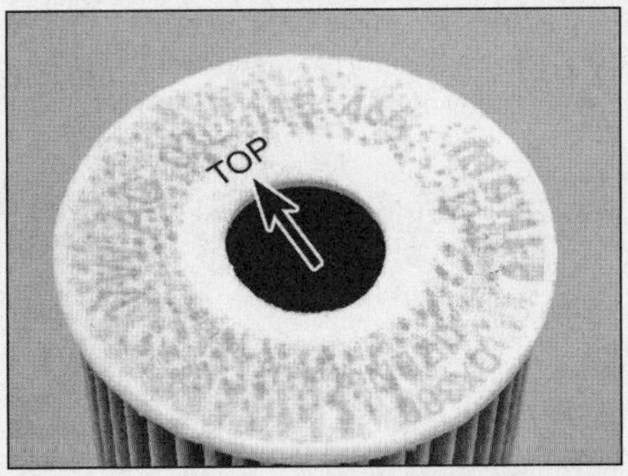

7.9d ...noting 'TOP' on the filter for correct fitting

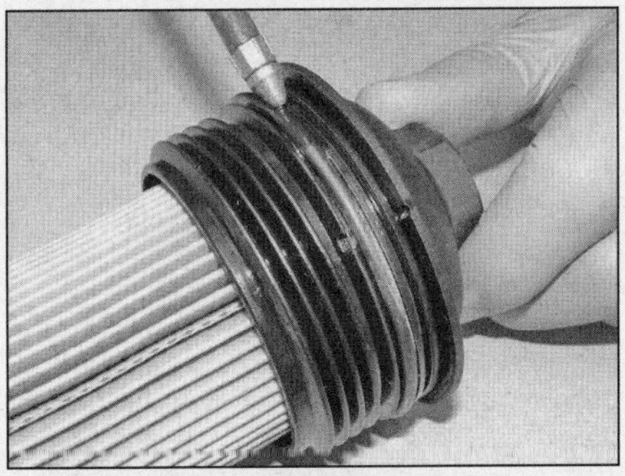
7.9e Lubricate the O-ring seals with clean engine oil...

7.9f ...then refit to the oil filter housing. Tighten the filter cap to the specified torque

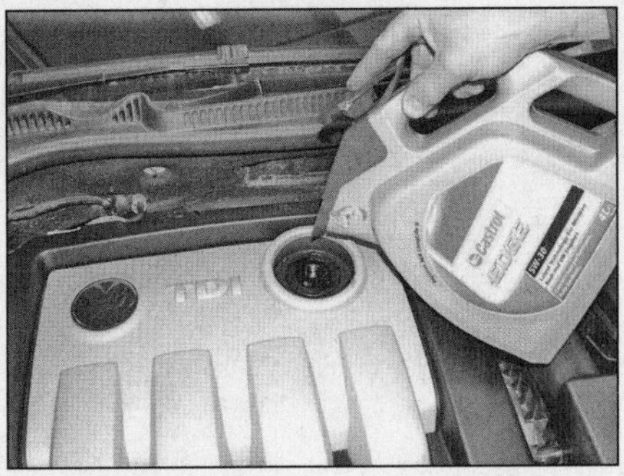

7.10 Pour in half the specified quantity of oil first, wait, then add the rest

8.1 The outer brake pads can be observed through the holes in the wheels

8 Brake pad/lining check

Front and rear disc brakes

1 The outer brake pads can be checked without removing the wheels; by observing the brake pads through the holes in the wheels **(see illustration)**. On models with steel wheels, remove the wheel trim. The thickness of the pad lining must not be less than the dimension given in the Section 1.

2 If the outer pads are worn near their limits, it is worthwhile checking the inner pads as well. Jack up car and support it on axle stands (see *Jacking and vehicle support)*. Remove the roadwheels.

3 Use a steel rule to check the thickness of the brake pads, and compare with the minimum thickness given in the Specifications **(see illustration)**.

4 For a comprehensive check, the brake pads should be removed and cleaned. The operation of the caliper can then also be checked, and the condition of the brake disc itself can be fully examined on both sides. Refer to Chapter 9.

5 If any pad's friction material is worn to the specified minimum thickness or less, all four pads at the front or rear, as applicable, must be renewed as a set. Never renew the pads on just one wheel, as uneven braking will result.

6 On completion of the check, refit the roadwheels and lower the car to the ground.

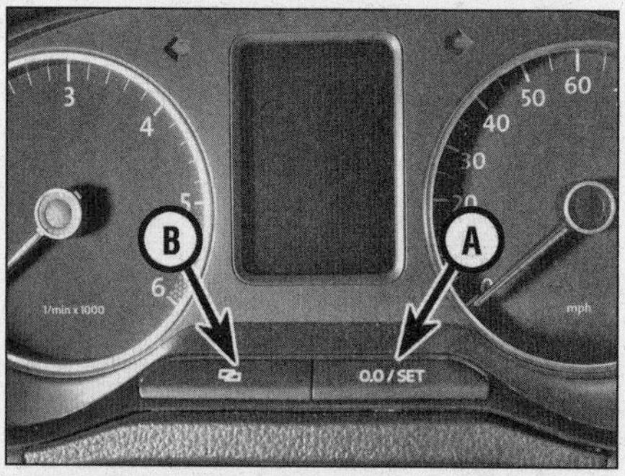

9.2 Press reset button (A) and then clock setting button (B)

8.3 A low cost pad thickness checking tool makes checking the pads easy

Rear drum brakes

7 Chock the front wheels, then jack up the rear of the car and support it on axle stands (see *Jacking and vehicle support)*.

8 For a quick check, the thickness of friction material remaining on one of the brake shoes can be observed through a hole in the brake backplate, which is exposed by prising out the rubber sealing grommet. If a rod of the same diameter as the specified minimum friction material thickness is placed against the shoe friction material, the amount of wear can be assessed. A torch or inspection light will probably be required. If the friction material on any shoe is worn down to the specified minimum thickness or less, all four shoes must be renewed as a set.

9 For a comprehensive check, the brake drum should be removed and cleaned. This will allow the wheel cylinders to be checked, and the condition of the brake drum itself to be fully examined (see Chapter 9).

10 On completion of the check, refit the roadwheels where removed, and lower the car to the ground.

9 Resetting the service interval display

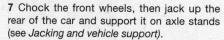

1 After all necessary maintenance work has been completed; the service interval display must be reset. Seat technicians use a special dedicated instrument to do this, and a printout is then put in the vehicle service record. It is possible for the owner on some models to reset the display as described in the following paragraphs, but note that the procedure will automatically reset the display to a 10 000 mile interval. To continue with the 'variable' intervals which take into consideration the number of starts, length of journeys, vehicle speeds, brake pad wear, bonnet opening frequency, fuel consumption, oil level and oil temperature, the display must be reset by a Seat dealership using the special dedicated instrument.

2 To reset the display, follow the procedures below **(see illustration)** :

a) Switch off the ignition.

b) Press and hold down the trip reset button '0.0/SET' beneath the speedometer

c) Switch the ignition on.

d) Release the reset button '0.0/SET'.

e) Then briefly press the clock setting button beneath the rev counter (within 20 seconds).

f) The display will then switch back to its original display.

3 Where it is not possible to reset the display using the above procedure then most garages will have the equipment to reset the service interval display. The home mechanic who intends to keep the vehicle for a reasonable length of time may wish to invest in one of the low cost diagnostic tools now available in the aftermarket.

10 Exhaust system check

1 With the engine cold (at least an hour after the vehicle has been driven), check the complete exhaust system from the engine to the end of the tailpipe. The exhaust system is most easily checked with the vehicle raised on a hoist, or supported on axle stands, so that the exhaust components are readily visible and accessible (see *Jacking and vehicle support*).

2 Check the exhaust pipes and connections for evidence of leaks, severe corrosion and damage. Make sure that all brackets and mountings are in good condition, and that all relevant nuts and bolts are tight. Leakage at any of the joints or in other parts of the system will usually show up as a black sooty stain in the vicinity of the leak.

3 Rattles and other noises can often be traced to the exhaust system, especially the brackets and mountings. Try to move the pipes and silencers. If the components are able to come into contact with the body or suspension parts, secure the system with new mountings. Otherwise separate the joints (if possible) and twist the pipes as necessary to provide additional clearance.

11 Hose and fluid leak check

1 Visually inspect the engine joint faces, gaskets and seals for any signs of water or oil leaks. Pay particular attention to the areas around the camshaft cover, cylinder head, oil filter and sump joint faces. Bear in mind that, over a period of time, some very slight seepage from these areas is to be expected – what you are really looking for is any indication of a serious leak. Should a leak be found, renew the offending gasket or oil seal by referring to the appropriate Chapters in this manual.

2 Also check the security and condition of all the engine-related pipes and hoses. Ensure that all cable-ties or securing clips are in place and in good condition. Clips which are broken or missing can lead to chafing of the hoses, pipes or wiring, which could cause more serious problems in the future.
3 Carefully check the radiator hoses and heater hoses along their entire length. Renew any hose which is cracked, swollen or deteriorated. Cracks will show up better if the hose is squeezed. Pay close attention to the hose clips that secure the hoses to the cooling system components. Hose clips can pinch and puncture hoses, resulting in cooling system leaks.
4 Inspect all the cooling system components (hoses, joint faces, etc) for leaks **(see Haynes Hint)**. Where any problems of this nature are found on system components, renew the component or gasket with reference to Chapter 3.
5 With the vehicle raised, inspect the petrol tank and filler neck for punctures, cracks and other damage. The connection between the filler neck and tank is especially critical. Sometimes a rubber filler neck or connecting hose will leak due to loose retaining clamps or deteriorated rubber.
6 Carefully check all rubber hoses and metal fuel lines leading away from the petrol tank. Check for loose connections, deteriorated hoses, crimped lines, and other damage. Pay particular attention to the vent pipes and hoses, which often loop up around the filler neck and can become blocked or crimped. Follow the lines to the front of the vehicle, carefully inspecting them all the way. Renew damaged sections as necessary.
7 From within the engine compartment, check the security of all fuel hose attachments and pipe unions, and inspect the fuel hoses and vacuum hoses for kinks, chafing and deterioration.
8 Check the condition of the power steering fluid hoses and pipes.

12 Auxiliary drivebelt check

1 Apply the handbrake, then jack up the front of the vehicle and support it on axle stands (see Chapter 13, Section 5).
2 Using a socket on the crankshaft pulley bolt, turn the engine slowly clockwise so that the full length of the auxiliary drivebelt can be examined. Look for cracks, splitting and fraying on the surface of the belt; check also for signs of glazing (shiny patches) and separation of the belt plies. Use a mirror to check the underside of the drivebelt **(see illustration)**. If damage or wear is visible, or if there are traces of oil or grease on it, the belt should be renewed (see Section 29).

HAYNES HiNT

A leak in the cooling system will usually show up as white- or rust-coloured deposits on the area adjoining the leak.

13 Antifreeze check

1 The cooling system should be filled with the recommended G12 antifreeze and corrosion protection fluid – do not mix this antifreeze with any other type. Over a period of time, the concentration of fluid may be reduced due to topping-up (this can be avoided by topping-up with the correct antifreeze mixture – see Specifications) or fluid loss. If loss of coolant has been evident, it is important to make the necessary repair before adding fresh fluid.
2 With the engine **cold**, carefully remove the cap from the expansion tank. If the engine is not completely cold, place a cloth rag over the cap before removing it, and remove it slowly to allow any pressure to escape.
3 Antifreeze checkers are available from car accessory shops. Draw some coolant from the expansion tank and observe how many plastic balls are floating in the checker. Usually, 2 or 3 balls must be floating for the correct concentration of antifreeze, but follow the manufacturer's instructions.
4 If the concentration is incorrect, it will be necessary to either withdraw some coolant and add antifreeze, or alternatively drain the old coolant and add fresh coolant of the correct concentration (see Section 33).

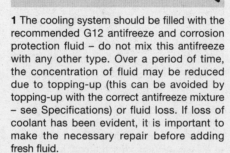

12.2 Checking the underside of the auxiliary drivebelt with a mirror

14 Brake hydraulic circuit check

1 Check the entire brake hydraulic circuit for leaks and damage. Start by checking the master cylinder in the engine compartment. At the same time, check the vacuum servo unit and ABS units for signs of fluid leakage.
2 Raise the front and rear of the vehicle and support it on axle stands (see *Jacking and vehicle support*). Check the rigid hydraulic brake lines for corrosion and damage.
3 At the front of the vehicle, check that the flexible hydraulic hoses to the calipers are not twisted or chafing on any of the surrounding suspension components. Turn the steering on full lock to make this check. Also check that the hoses are not brittle or cracked **(see illustration)**.
4 Lower the vehicle to the ground after making the checks.

15 Headlight beam adjustment

1 Accurate adjustment of the headlight beam is only possible using optical beam-setting equipment, and this work should therefore be carried out by a Seat dealer or service station with the necessary facilities.
2 Basic adjustments can be carried out in an emergency, and further details are given in Chapter 12 Section 10.

16 Pollen filter renewal

1 The pollen filter is located on the heater assembly, and is removed into the passenger footwell.
2 Reach under the glovebox, and slide the two retaining catches on the pollen filter lower cover towards each other, to release and remove the cover **(see illustrations)**.
3 Withdraw the filter downwards from the heater assembly, and remove from inside the car **(see illustration)**.

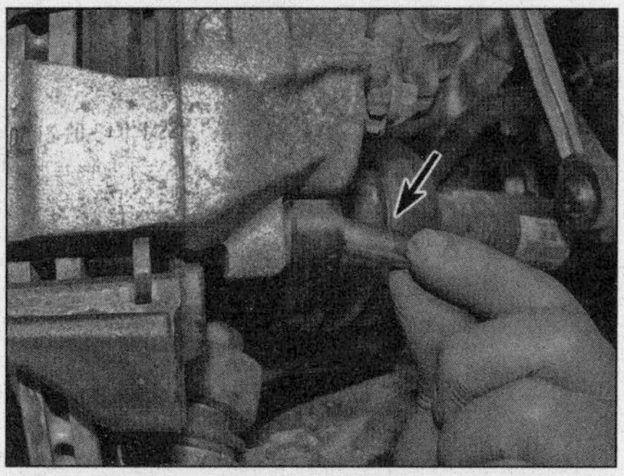

14.3 Twist the hoses and check for cracks or perishing

16.2a Slide the catches towards each other...

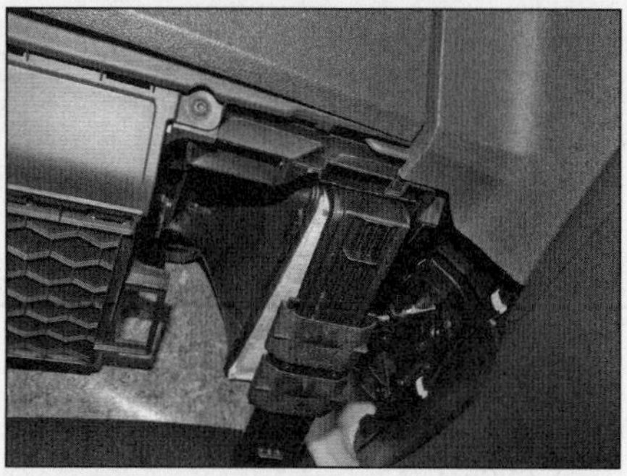

16.2b ...and remove the pollen filter lower cover

16.3 Withdraw the pollen filter into the passenger footwell

16.4 Remove the filter from the frame (where fitted)

4 Where fitted, separate the filter from the frame, noting the fitted direction of the air flow arrows which should point to the drivers side **(see illustration)**.

5 Fit the new filter to the frame (where applicable), with the airflow arrows pointing in the direction noted on removal. Insert the pollen into the heater assembly, and then refit the lower cover. Slide the two catches apart, to secure the cover to the housing.

17 Manual transmission oil level check – diesel models

1 Park the car on a level surface. For improved access to the filler/level plug, apply the handbrake, and then jack up the front of the car and support it on axle stands (see *Jacking and vehicle support)*, but note that the rear of the car should also be raised to ensure an accurate level check. The oil level must be checked before the car is driven, or at least 5 minutes after the engine has been switched off. If the oil is checked immediately after driving the car, some of the oil will remain distributed around the transmission components, resulting in an inaccurate level reading.

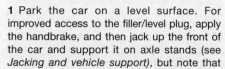

2 As applicable, undo the retaining screws and remove the engine undershield. Wipe clean the area around the transmission filler/level plug, which is situated on the rear, inner face of the transmission, above the engine rear mounting/torque link **(see illustration)**.

3 There are two types of filler/drain plugs fitted to the transmissions; if the multi-splined plug is fitted a special tool will be required (Seat tool T30023, though alternatives may be available). Since the plug will almost certainly be very tight, badly fitting substitute tools are unlikely to work, and damage may be caused to the plug's splines.

17.2 Filler/level plug location – 02R transmission

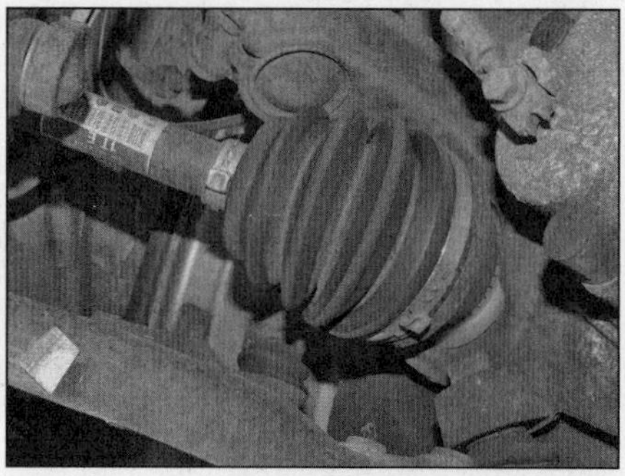

19.1 Check the condition of the driveshaft gaiters

4 The oil level should reach the lower edge of the filler/level hole. A certain amount of oil will have gathered behind the filler/level plug, and will trickle out when it is removed; this does **not** necessarily indicate that the level is correct. To ensure that a true level is established, wait until the initial trickle has stopped, and then add oil as necessary until a trickle of new oil can be seen emerging. The level will be correct when the flow ceases; use only good-quality oil of the specified type.

5 If the transmission has been overfilled so that oil flows out when the filler/level plug is removed, check that the car is completely level (front-to-rear and side-to-side), and allow the surplus to drain off into a suitable container.

6 When the oil level is correct, refit the filler/level plug and tighten it to the specified torque. Wipe off any spilt oil then refit the engine undershield(s), tighten the retaining screws securely, and lower the car to the ground.

18 Underbody protection check

1 Raise and support the vehicle on axle stands (see Chapter 13, Section 5). Using an electric torch or lead light, inspect the entire underside of the vehicle, paying particular attention to the wheel arches. Look for any damage to the flexible underbody coating, which may crack or flake off with age, leading to corrosion. Also check that the wheel arch liners are securely attached with any clips provided – if they come loose, dirt may get in behind the liners and defeat their purpose. If there is any damage to the underseal, or any corrosion, it should be repaired before the damage gets too serious.

19 Driveshaft check

1 With the vehicle raised and securely supported on stands, slowly rotate the roadwheel. Inspect the condition of the outer constant velocity (CV) joint rubber gaiters, squeezing the gaiters to open out the folds. Check for signs of cracking, splits or deterioration of the rubber, which may allow the grease to escape, and lead to water and grit entry into the joint. Also check the security and condition of the retaining clips. Repeat these checks on the inner joints**(see illustration)**. If any damage or deterioration is found, the gaiters should be renewed (see Chapter 8 Section 3).

2 At the same time, check the general condition of the CV joints themselves by first holding the driveshaft and attempting to rotate the wheel. Repeat this check by holding the inner joint and attempting to rotate the driveshaft. Any appreciable movement indicates wear in the joints, wear in the driveshaft splines, or a loose driveshaft retaining nut.

20 Steering and suspension check

1 Raise the front and rear of the car, and securely support it on axle stands (see *Jacking and vehicle support)*.

2 Visually inspect the track rod end balljoint dust cover, the lower front suspension balljoint dust cover, and the steering rack-and-pinion gaiters for splits, chafing or deterioration. Any wear of these components will cause loss of lubricant, together with dirt and water entry, resulting in rapid deterioration of the balljoints or steering gear.

3 Check the power steering fluid hoses for chafing or deterioration, and the pipe and hose unions for fluid leaks. Also check for signs of fluid leakage under pressure from the steering gear rubber gaiters, which would indicate failed fluid seals within the steering gear.

4 Grasp the roadwheel at the 12 o'clock and 6 o'clock positions, and try to rock it **(see illustration)**. Very slight free play may be felt, but if the movement is appreciable, further investigation is necessary to determine the source. Continue rocking the wheel while an assistant depresses the footbrake. If the movement is now eliminated or significantly reduced, it is likely that the hub bearings are at fault. If the free play is still evident with the footbrake depressed, then there is wear in the suspension joints or mountings.

5 Now grasp the wheel at the 9 o'clock and 3 o'clock positions, and try to rock it as before. Any movement felt now may again be caused by wear in the hub bearings or the steering track rod balljoints. If the inner or outer balljoint is worn, the visual movement will be obvious **(see illustration)**.

6 Using a large screwdriver or flat bar, check for wear in the suspension mounting bushes by levering between the relevant suspension

20.4 Check for wear in the hub bearings by grasping the wheel and trying to rock it

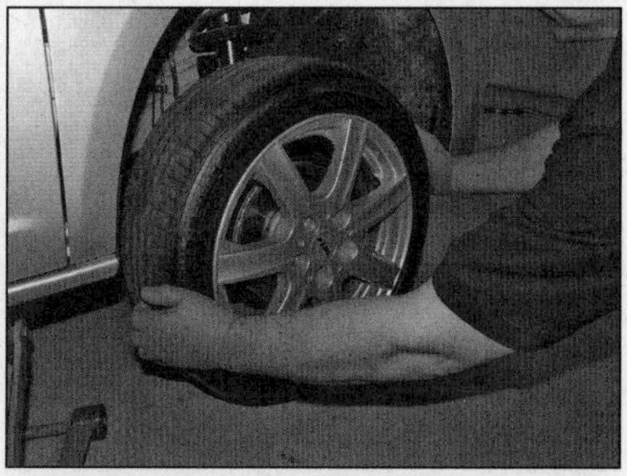

20.5 Grasping the wheel at the 3 o'clock and the 9 o'clock position will highlight steering problems

component and its attachment point. Some movement is to be expected as the mountings are made of rubber, but excessive wear should be obvious. Also check the condition of any visible rubber bushes, looking for splits, cracks or contamination of the rubber.

7 With the car standing on its wheels, have an assistant turn the steering wheel back-and-forth about an eighth of a turn each way. There should be very little, if any, lost movement between the steering wheel and roadwheels. If this is not the case, closely observe the joints and mountings previously described, but in addition check the steering column universal joints for wear, and the rack-and-pinion steering gear itself.

8 Check for any signs of fluid leakage around the front suspension struts and rear shock absorber. Should any fluid be noticed, the suspension strut or shock absorber is defective internally, and should be renewed.

Note: *Suspension struts/shock absorbers should always be renewed in pairs on the same axle to ensure correct vehicle handling.*

9 The efficiency of the suspension strut/shock absorber may be checked by bouncing the car at each corner. Generally speaking, the body will return to its normal position and stop after being depressed. If it rises and returns on a rebound, the suspension strut/shock absorber is probably suspect. Examine also the suspension strut/shock absorber upper and lower mountings for any signs of wear.

21 Battery check

1 The battery is located in the front, left-hand corner of the engine compartment. Release the clip at the back, and then hinge the plastic cover forwards to gain access to the battery positive (+) terminal **(see illustration)**. Note that on later models no cover is fitted.

2 Where necessary, open the fuse holder plastic cover (squeeze together the locking lugs to release the cover) to gain access to the battery positive (+) terminal and fuse holder connections.

3 Check that both battery terminals and all the fuse holder connections are securely attached and are free from corrosion.

4 Release the retaining clips at the front of the plastic cover to access the wiring terminals on the top of the battery (where fitted) **(see illustration)**.

5 Check the battery casing for signs of damage or cracking and check the battery retaining clamp bolt is securely tightened. If the battery casing is damaged in any way the battery must be renewed (see Section).

6 All models are fitted with a battery with a small window that shows the state of the battery electrolyte. The window is located on the top of the battery **(see illustration)** near the negative terminal. If the eye is green, the battery is in good condition and charged up. If the eye is black, the battery is flat and

21.1 Unclip the plastic cover

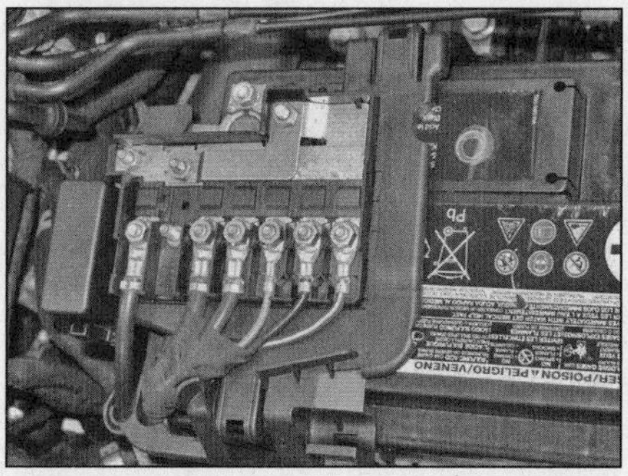

21.4 Fused links on top of the battery

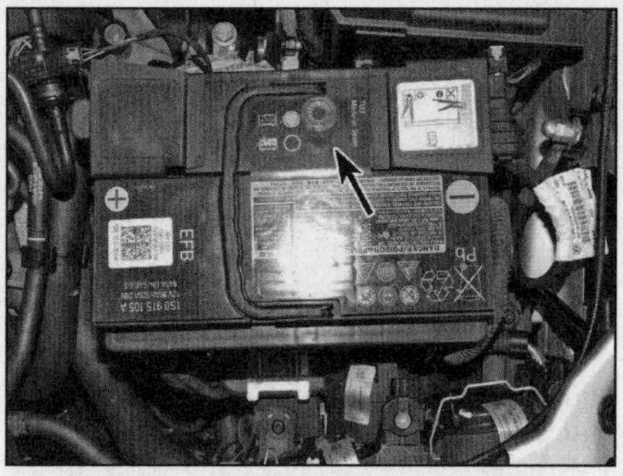

21.6 Window (eye) to check battery condition

should be charged. If the eye is colourless or yellow, the electrolyte is in a critical condition. If charging the battery does not return the eye to green, the battery should be scrapped.
7 On completion of the check, clip the cover securely back onto the fuse holder and close up the insulator cover (where fitted).

22 Hinge and lock lubrication

1 Lubricate the hinges of the bonnet, doors and tailgate with a light general-purpose oil. Similarly, lubricate all latches, locks and lock strikers. At the same time, check the security and operation of all the locks, adjusting them if necessary (see Chapter 11 Section 14).
2 Lightly lubricate the bonnet release mechanism and cable with a suitable grease.

23 Airbag unit check

1 Inspect the exterior condition of the airbag(s) for signs of damage or deterioration. If an airbag shows signs of damage, it must be renewed (see Chapter 12 Section 24). Note that it is not permissible to attach any stickers to the surface of the airbag, as this may affect the deployment of the unit.

24 Windscreen/tailgate/headlight washer system check

1 Check that each of the washer jet nozzles is clear and that each nozzle provides a strong jet of washer fluid.
2 The tailgate jet should be aimed to spray at the centre of the screen, using a pin.
3 The windscreen washer jet nozzles are preset by the manufacturer and cannot be adjusted.
4 Especially during the winter months, make sure that the washer fluid frost concentration is sufficient.

25 Engine management self-diagnosis memory fault check

1 A Seat dealer or a specialist using diagnostic equipment should carry out this work. However low cost basic diagnostic machines are increasingly available. They do not have the functionality of professional equipment, but all are capable of reading the mandatory emissions related fault codes. The diagnostic socket is located beneath the driver's side of the facia, above the fusebox **(see illustration)**.

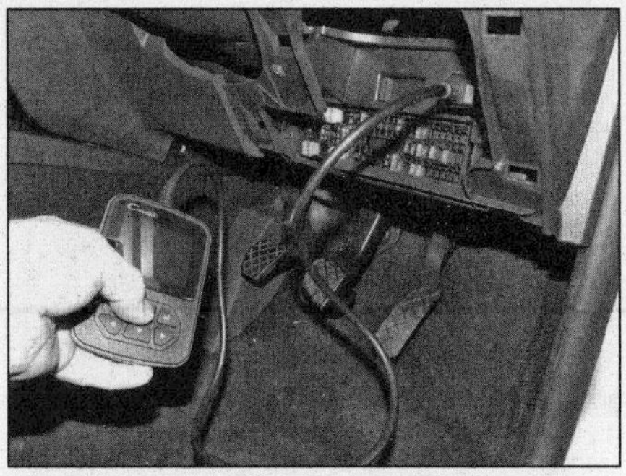

25.1 Checking for fault codes with a basic fault code reader

26 Road test and exhaust emissions check

Instruments and electrical equipment

1 Check the operation of all instruments and electrical equipment including the air conditioning system.
2 Make sure that all instruments read correctly, and switch on all electrical equipment in turn, to check that it functions properly.

Steering and suspension

3 Check for any abnormalities in the steering, suspension, handling or road 'feel'.
4 Drive the vehicle, and check that there are no unusual vibrations or noises which may indicate wear in the driveshafts, wheel bearings, etc.
5 Check that the steering feels positive, with no excessive 'sloppiness', or roughness, and check for any suspension noises when cornering and driving over bumps.

Drivetrain

6 Check the performance of the engine, clutch, gearbox/transmission and driveshafts.
7 Listen for any unusual noises from the engine, clutch and gearbox/transmission.
8 Make sure the engine runs smoothly at idle, and there is no hesitation on accelerating.
9 Check that the clutch action is smooth and progressive, that the drive is taken up smoothly, and that the pedal travel is not excessive. Also listen for any noises when the clutch pedal is depressed.
10 Check that all gears can be engaged smoothly without noise, and that the gear lever action is smooth and not abnormally vague or 'notchy'.
11 Listen for a metallic clicking sound from the front of the vehicle, as the vehicle is driven slowly in a circle with the steering on full-lock. Carry out this check in both directions. If a clicking noise is heard, this indicates wear in a driveshaft joint, in which case renew the joint if necessary.

Braking system

12 Make sure that the vehicle does not pull to one side when braking, and that the wheels do not lock when braking hard.
13 Check that there is no vibration through the steering when braking.
14 Check that the handbrake operates correctly without excessive movement of the lever, and that it holds the vehicle stationary on a slope.
15 Test the operation of the brake servo unit as follows. With the engine off, depress the footbrake four or five times to exhaust the vacuum. Hold the brake pedal depressed, then start the engine. As the engine starts, there should be a noticeable 'give' in the brake pedal as vacuum builds-up. Allow the engine to run for at least two minutes, and then switch it off. If the brake pedal is depressed now, it should be possible to detect a hiss from the servo as the pedal is depressed. After about four or five applications, no further hissing should be heard, and the pedal should feel considerably harder.
16 Under controlled emergency braking, the pulsing of the ABS unit must be felt at the footbrake pedal.

Exhaust emissions check

17 Although not part of the manufacturer's maintenance schedule, this check will normally be carried out on a regular basis according to the country the vehicle is operated in. Currently in the UK, exhaust emissions testing is included as part of the annual MOT test after the vehicle is 3 years old.

27.2a Unclip the vacuum pipes

27 Air filter element renewal – diesel models

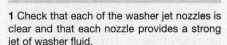

1 The air filter is housed in the air cleaner, which is situated on the left-hand side of the inner wing, behind the battery.
2 Where the vacuum pipes are mounted on the top half of the housing unclip them. Undo the six retaining screws and lift the cover from the top of the air cleaner body **(see illustrations)**.
3 If required, disconnect the wiring connector

from the air mass meter, then release the retaining clip and disconnect the air intake hose from the upper cover **(see illustration).**

4 Release the air filter element from the upper cover.

5 Remove any debris that may have collected inside the air cleaner housing. Make sure the O-ring is in position in the lower part of the housing **(see illustration)**, before refitting the new filter element.

6 Fit a new air filter element in position, ensuring that it is located correctly.

7 Refit the air cleaner upper cover and secure in position with the six retaining screws.

27.2b Remove the screws and...

27.2c ...remove the cover

27.3 Disconnect wiring plug, if required

27.5 Make sure the O-ring seal is fitted correctly

28 Fuel filter renewal

1 The fuel filter is mounted on the right-hand inner wing (right as seen from the driver's seat) **(see illustration).** Position a container underneath the filter unit and pad the surrounding area with rags to absorb any fuel that may be spilt.

Caution: Be prepared for an amount of fuel loss.

2 Disconnect the quick-release couplings (or spring clips) from the top of the fuel filter and move the two fuel hoses to one side, noting their fitted position for refitting.

3 Release the securing clips from around the upper edge of the fuel filter, and then withdraw it upwards from the filter mounting bracket.

4 Fit the new fuel filter into the mounting bracket, making sure the filter is fitted in the position noted on removal and the clips are secure around the upper edge of the filter.

5 Reconnect the fuel supply hose (from the fuel tank) to the inlet side of the filter, then fit a vacuum pump to the other side of the fuel filter and draw the fuel up into the filter. When the filter has been filled with fuel, refit the outlet fuel hose (to the fuel rail) back to the filter **(see illustrations)**. Remove the collecting container and rags from around the filter.

6 Start and run the engine at idle, and then check around the fuel filter for fuel leaks. **Note:** *It may take a few seconds of cranking before the engine starts.*

7 Raise the engine speed to about 2000 rpm several times, and then allow the engine to idle again. Observe the fuel flow through the transparent hose leading to the fuel injection pump and check that it is free of air bubbles.

29 Auxiliary drivebelt check and renewal

Checking

1 See Section 12 for information on checking the condition of the drivebelt. When the belt is removed, check all pulleys are free from any damage and are secure. Also check that the alternator and air-conditioning compressor are mounted securely.

2 There are two different types of tensioner fitted; the routing of the belt is the same, although the procedure for belt renewal is different (see the renewal procedure below).

Renewal

3 For improved access, apply the handbrake, and then jack up the front of the vehicle and support it on axle stands (see *Jacking and vehicle support*). Where fitted, remove the engine cover and engine undertray.

4 Remove the right-hand front roadwheel, then remove the access panel from the inner wheel arch.

5 To make access easier, depending on model, it will be necessary to slacken the retaining clips and move the charge air pipe to one side.

With automatic tensioner

6 Use a spanner on the centre bolt and turn the tensioner clockwise. Lock the tensioner in its released position by inserting a locking pin

28.1 Location of the fuel filter

28.5a Using a rubber bulb with one way valve to draw fuel...

28.5b ...or using a vacuum pump

29.6a Turn the tensioner clockwise...

29.6b ...and lock the tensioner in position

29.7 Note the fitted position of the belt before removal

29.8 With the locking pin removed, slowly take up the slack in the belt

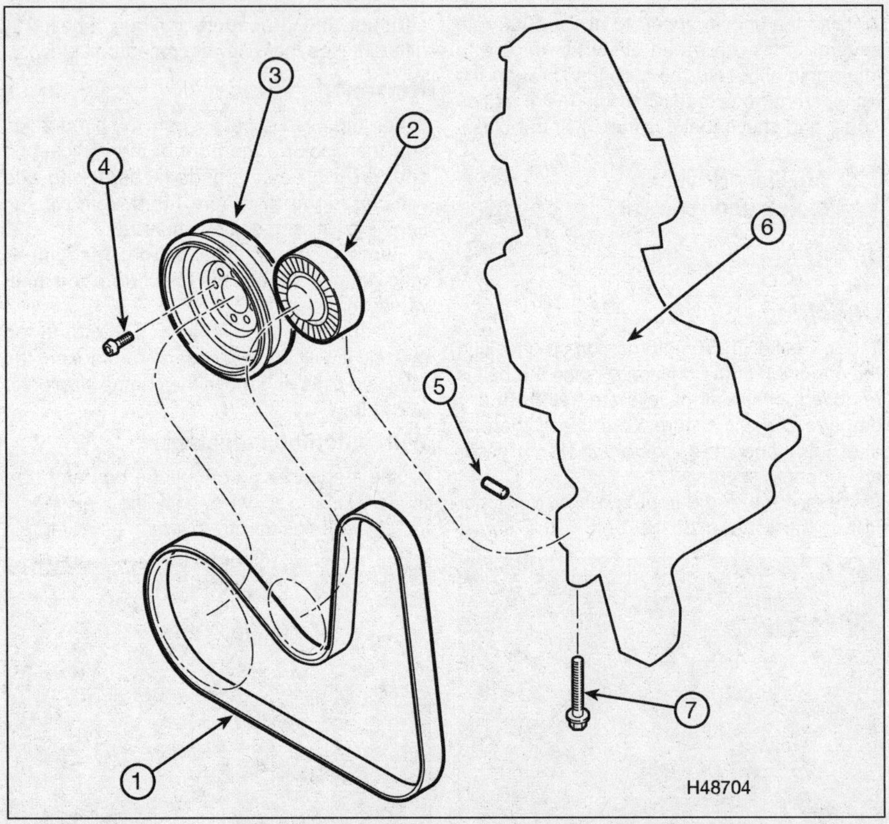

29.11 Auxiliary drivebelt with tensioner roller

1 Auxiliary belt
2 Tensioning roller
3 Crankshaft pulley
4 Securing bolt
5 Dowel
6 Mounting bracket
7 Tensioning roller securing bolt

(Allen key or similar) through the lug into the tensioner body **(see illustrations)**.

7 Note how the drivebelt is routed (and direction of rotation, if being reused), then remove it from the crankshaft pulley **(see illustration)**, alternator pulley, and air conditioning compressor pulley (as applicable).

8 Locate the new drivebelt on the pulleys, then by holding the pressure of the tensioner with a spanner, remove the locking pin. Slowly release the pressure on the spanner **(see illustration)**, so that the tensioner takes up the slack in the belt. Check that the belt is located correctly in the multi-grooves in the pulleys.

9 Start the engine and check that the drivebelt runs, as it should over the pulleys. Make sure that all tools and hands are kept clear of the drivebelt with the engine running.

10 With the engine stopped, refit the access panel and roadwheel, and then lower the vehicle to the ground. Refit the engine top cover and undertray, if removed.

With tensioner roller

11 Undo the tensioner roller retaining bolt, and remove the tensioner roller from the engine. Note the retaining bolt is below the tensioner roller, and goes up through the mounting bracket in a vertical direction **(see illustration)**. Discard the retaining bolt, as a new one will be required for refitting. To access the bolt it will necessary to undo the retaining bolts from the coolant pipe bracket and move them to one side.

12 Note how the drivebelt is routed, then remove it from the crankshaft pulley, alternator pulley, and air-conditioning compressor pulley (as applicable).

13 Locate the new drivebelt on the pulleys, then fit the tensioner roller, making sure its guide pin is located correctly in the mounting bracket.

14 Fit the new retaining bolt, and then tighten to the following five stages:

a) Tighten bolt by hand at this point.
b) Tighten bolt until it reaches stop.
c) Turn the bolt back through 90°
d) Tighten bolt to 30Nm.
e) Tighten a further 90°

15 When tensioner roller is fitted and the belt is tensioned, check the tensioner retaining bolt. The part of the bolt that has protruded out through the upper end of the mounting bracket (behind the tensioner roller) must not protrude more than 2.5mm higher than the outer surface of the tensioner roller. This ensures that the bolt has been tightened to its end stop.

16 Start the engine and check that the drivebelt runs, as it should over the pulleys. Make sure that all tools and hands are kept clear of the drivebelt with the engine running.

17 With the engine stopped, refit the access panel and roadwheel, and then lower the vehicle to the ground. Refit the engine top cover and undertray, if removed.

30.2 Unscrew the cap from the hydraulic fluid reservoir

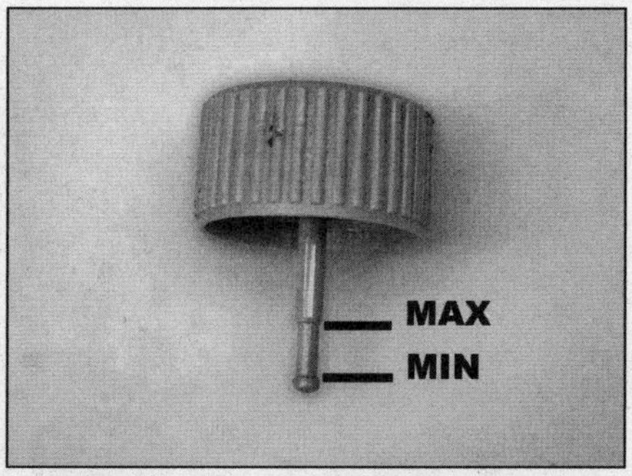

30.3a The power steering fluid level must be between the upper and lower marks

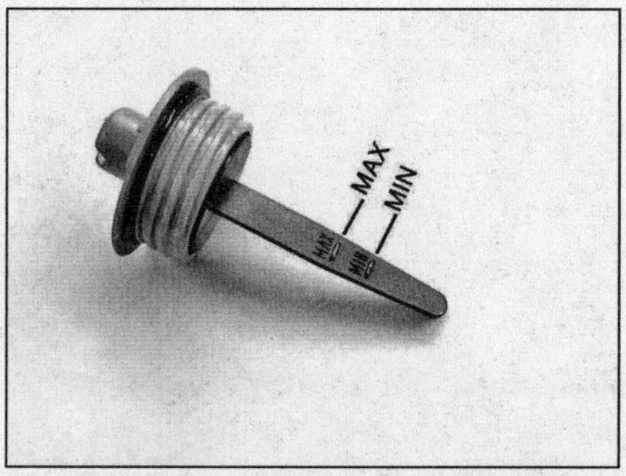

30.3b Alternative power steering cap markings

30 Power steering hydraulic fluid level check

1 Turn the front roadwheels to the straight-ahead position without starting the engine. If the car has been left standing for an hour or more, the power steering fluid will be cold (below 50°C), and the 'cold' level markings must be used. If, however, the engine is at normal temperature (above 50°C), the fluid will be hot, and the 'hot' level markings must be used.

Note: *On some models with a high capacity battery (larger in size), the battery and possibly the battery tray must be removed, in order to access the reservoir filler cap.*

2 The reservoir for the Electrically Powered Hydraulic Steering (EPHS) is located on the front left-hand corner of the engine compartment. The fluid level is checked with the dipstick attached to the reservoir filler cap. Unscrew the cap from the hydraulic fluid reservoir, and wipe clean the integral dipstick with a clean cloth **(see illustration)**.

3 Screw on the cap hand-tight then unscrew it again and check the fluid level on the dipstick. The fluid level must be between the MIN (or lower) and MAX (or upper) marks **(see illustrations)**. If the fluid is cold (below 50°C), it must be at least above the lower level mark or MIN. If the fluid is hot (above 50°C), it must not be above the upper level mark or MAX.

4 If the level is above the maximum level mark, syphon off the excess amount. If it is below the minimum level mark, add the specified fluid as necessary *(see Lubricants and fluids)*, but in this case also check the system for leaks. On completion, screw on the cap and tighten. Refit the battery and tray where removed.

31 Timing belt and tensioner renewal

1 Renewal of the timing belt and tensioner is covered in Chapter 2E Section 7.

32 Brake (and clutch) fluid renewal

Warning: Brake hydraulic fluid can harm your eyes and damage painted surfaces, so use extreme caution when handling and pouring it. Do not use fluid that has been standing open for some time, as it absorbs moisture from the air. Excess moisture can cause a dangerous loss of braking effectiveness.

1 The procedure is similar to that for the bleeding of the hydraulic system as described in Chapter 9 Section 2, except that the brake fluid reservoir should be emptied by syphoning, using a clean poultry baster or similar before starting, and allowance should be made for the old fluid to be expelled when bleeding a section of the circuit. Since the clutch hydraulic system also uses fluid from the brake system reservoir, it should also be bled at the same time by referring to Chapter 6A Section 2.

2 Working as described in Chapter 9 Section 2, open the first bleed screw in the sequence, and pump the brake pedal gently until nearly all the old fluid has been emptied from the master cylinder reservoir.

3 Top-up to the MAX level with new fluid, and continue pumping until only the new fluid remains in the reservoir, and new fluid can be seen emerging from the bleed screw. Tighten the screw, and top the reservoir level up to the MAX level line **(see illustration)**.

32.3 Top up the fluid to the MAX level

4 Work through all the remaining bleed screws in the sequence until new fluid can be seen at all of them. Be careful to keep the master cylinder reservoir topped-up to above the MIN level at all times, or air may enter the system and greatly increase the length of the task.

5 When the operation is complete, check that all bleed screws are securely tightened, and that their dust caps are refitted. Wash off all traces of spilt fluid, and recheck the master cylinder reservoir fluid level.

6 Once the brake fluid has been changed the clutch fluid should also be renewed. Referring to Chapter 6A Section 2, bleed the clutch until new fluid is seen to be emerging from the slave cylinder bleed screw, keeping the master cylinder fluid level above the MIN level line at all times to prevent air entering the system. Once the new fluid emerges, securely tighten the bleed screw then disconnect and remove the bleeding equipment. Securely refit the dust cap then wash off all traces of spilt fluid.

7 Ensure the master cylinder fluid level is correct (see *Weekly checks*) and thoroughly check the operation of the brakes and clutch before taking the car on the road.

33 Coolant renewal – diesel models

Note: *This work is not included in the Seat schedule, and should not be required if the recommended VW G12 LongLife coolant antifreeze/inhibitor is used. However, if standard antifreeze/inhibitor is used, the work should be carried out at the recommended interval.*

Warning: Wait until the engine is cold before starting this procedure. Do not allow antifreeze to come in contact with your skin, or with the car's painted surfaces. Rinse off spills immediately with plenty of water. Never leave antifreeze lying around in an open container, or in a puddle in the driveway or on the garage floor. Children and pets are attracted by its sweet smell, but antifreeze can be fatal if ingested.

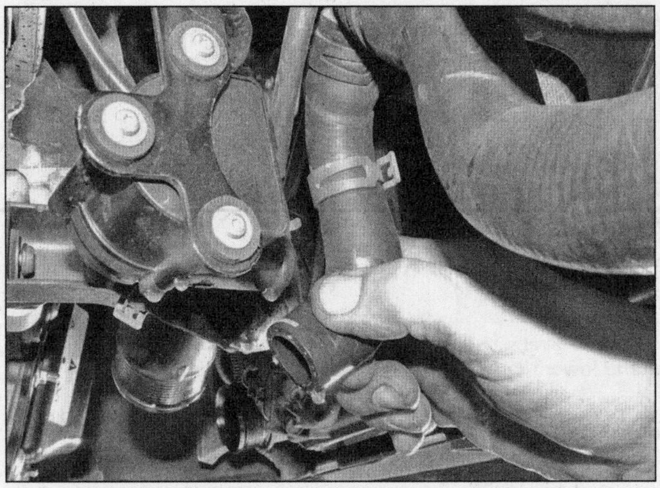

33.3 Disconnect the hose from the circulation pump

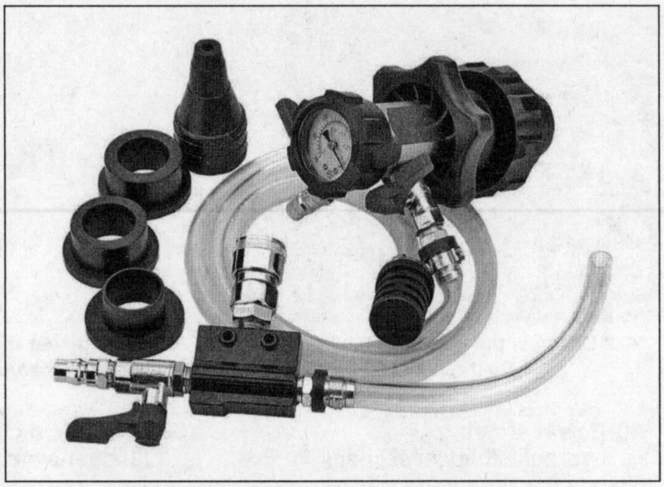

33.17 A suitable coolant filling tool from Draper tools

Cooling system draining

1 With the engine completely cold, unscrew the expansion tank cap.

2 Firmly apply the handbrake then jack up the front of the car and support it on axle stands (see *Jacking and vehicle support)*. Undo the retaining screws and remove the engine under shield to gain access to the base of the radiator.

3 Position a suitable container beneath the bottom hose fitting to the left-hand end of the radiator. Remove the retaining clip and disconnect the bottom hose from the radiator and the coolant hose to the auxiliary electric pump, to drain the coolant **(see illustration)**.

4 On engines with an oil cooler, to fully drain the system, also disconnect one of the coolant hoses from the oil cooler which is located at the front of the cylinder block.

5 If the coolant has been drained for a reason other than renewal then, provided it is clean, it can be re-used.

6 Once all the coolant has drained, securely tighten the radiator drain plug or reconnect the bottom hose to the radiator (as applicable). Where necessary, also reconnect the coolant hose to the oil cooler and secure it in position with the retaining clip. Refit the undershield(s), tighten the retaining screws securely.

Cooling system flushing

7 If the recommended Seat coolant has not been used and coolant renewal has been neglected, or if the antifreeze mixture has become diluted, the cooling system may gradually lose efficiency, as the coolant passages become restricted due to rust, scale deposits, and other sediment. The cooling system efficiency can be restored by flushing the system clean.

8 The radiator should be flushed separately from the engine, to avoid excess contamination.

Radiator flushing

9 To flush the radiator first tighten the radiator drain plug (where applicable).

10 Disconnect the top and bottom hoses and any other relevant hoses from the radiator.

11 Insert a garden hose into the radiator top inlet. Direct a flow of clean water through the radiator, and continue flushing until clean water emerges from the radiator bottom outlet.

12 If after a reasonable period, the water still does not run clear, the radiator can be flushed with a good proprietary cleaning agent. It is important that the manufacturer's instructions are followed carefully. If the contamination is particularly bad, insert the hose in the radiator bottom outlet, and reverse-flush the radiator.

Engine flushing

13 To flush the engine, remove the thermostat (see Chapter 3 Section 4).

14 With the bottom hose disconnected from the radiator, insert a garden hose into the thermostat housing. Direct a clean flow of water through the engine, and continue flushing until clean water emerges from the radiator bottom hose.

15 When flushing is complete, refit the thermostat and reconnect the hoses.

Cooling system filling

16 Before attempting to fill the cooling system, ensure that all hoses are securely connected and their retaining clips are in good condition. If the recommended Seat coolant is not being used, ensure that a suitable antifreeze mixture is used all year round, to prevent corrosion of the engine components (see following sub-Section). **Note:** *Seat recommend that only distilled water should be used.*

17 Seat recommend the use of a vacuum tool, to refill the cooling system. Suitable machines are widely available in the aftermarket **(see illustration)**. Follow the filling instructions supplied by the manufacturer.

18 When the engine has cooled, check the coolant level with reference to *Weekly checks.* Top-up the level if necessary, and refit the expansion tank cap.

Antifreeze mixture

19 If the recommended Seat/VW coolant is not being used, the antifreeze should always be renewed at the specified intervals. This is necessary not only to maintain the antifreeze properties, but also to prevent corrosion that would otherwise occur as the corrosion inhibitors become progressively less effective.

20 Always use an ethylene glycol based antifreeze, which is suitable for use in mixed-metal cooling systems. The quantity of antifreeze and levels of protection are indicated in the Specifications.

21 Before adding antifreeze, the cooling system should be completely drained, preferably flushed, and all hoses checked for condition and security.

22 After filling with antifreeze, a label should be attached to the expansion tank, stating the type and concentration of antifreeze used, and the date installed. Any subsequent topping-up should be made with the same type and concentration of antifreeze.

23 Do not use engine antifreeze in the windscreen/tailgate washer system, as it will damage the paintwork. A screen wash additive should be added to the washer system in the quantities stated on the bottle.

Airlocks

24 If, after draining and refilling the system, symptoms of overheating are found which did not occur previously, then the fault is almost certainly due to trapped air at some point in the system, causing an airlock and restricting the flow of coolant; usually, the air is trapped because the system was refilled too quickly.

25 If an airlock is suspected, first try gently squeezing all visible coolant hoses. A coolant hose, which is full of air, feels quite different to one full of coolant, when squeezed. After refilling the system, most airlocks will clear once the system has cooled, and been topped up.

26 While the engine is running at operating temperature, switch on the heater and heater fan, and check for heat output. Provided there is sufficient coolant in the system, any lack of heat output could be due to an airlock in the system.

27 Airlocks can have more serious effects than simply reducing heater output – a severe airlock could reduce coolant flow around the engine. Check that the radiator top hose is hot when the engine is at operating temperature – a top hose that stays cold could be the result of an airlock (or a non-opening thermostat).

28 If the problem persists, stop the engine and allow it to cool down **completely**, before unscrewing the expansion tank filler cap or loosening the hose clips and squeezing the hoses to bleed out the trapped air. In the worst case, the system will have to be at least partially drained (this time, the coolant can be saved for re-use) and flushed to clear the problem.

34 Particulate filter check

1 Eventually, the amount of ash deposited in the particle filter by the filtration process will cause a blockage, and engine running problems. Seat state that the maximum amount of ash is 60g. At this point, the particle filter must be renewed. Unfortunately, the mass of the ash can only be established using dedicated Seat (VAG group) diagnostic equipment, connected to the vehicle through the diagnostic plug under the drivers side of the facia. Consequently, we recommend this task is entrusted to a Seat dealer or suitably equipped specialist.

Chapter 2 Part A
1.0 litre (3-cylinder) petrol engine in-car repair procedures

Contents

Degrees of difficulty

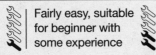

Easy, suitable for novice with little experience	Fairly easy, suitable for beginner with some experience	Fairly difficult, suitable for competent DIY mechanic	Difficult, suitable for experienced DIY mechanic	Very difficult, suitable for expert DIY or professional

Specifications

General

Type	Three-cylinder in-line, belt-driven double (DOHC) overhead camshaft, four-stroke, liquid-cooled	
Cubic capacity	999 cc	
Manufacturer's engine codes*:		
1.0 litre MPi	CHYB	
1.0 litre TSi	CHZC and CHZB	
Maximum power and torque output:	**Power**	**Torque**
CHYB	55 kW at 6200 rpm	95 Nm at 4000 rpm
CHZC	81 kW at 5500 rpm	200 Nm at 1500 to 3500 rpm
CHZB	70 kW at 5500 rpm	160 Nm at 1500 to 3500 rpm
Bore	74.5 mm	
Stroke	76.4 mm	
Compression ratio	10.5 : 1	
Compression pressures (oil temperature 30°C minimum):		
New	10.0 to 15.0 bars	
Minimum	7.0 bars	
Maximum difference between cylinders	3.0 bars	
Firing order	1 – 2 – 3	
No 1 cylinder location	Crankshaft pulley end	
Direction of crankshaft rotation	Clockwise (when viewed from right-hand side of car)	

**See 'Vehicle identification' at the end of this manual for the location of the engine code markings.*

Lubrication system

Oil pump type	Direct drive from crankshaft
Oil pressure switch pressure	0.3 to 0.6 bar
Oil pressure (Oil temperature at 80°C) :	
At idle	0.3 to 0.6 bar
At 2000 rpm	2.0 bar (minimum)
Above 2000 rpm	7.0 bar (maximum)

Camshaft

Camshaft endfloat (maximum)	0.25 mm

Torque wrench settings

	Nm	lbf ft
Air conditioning compressor	25	18
Auxiliary drivebelt tensioner bolt*	20	15
Camshaft housing bolts: *		
Stage 1	10	7
Stage 2	Angle-tighten a further 180°	
Camshaft position sensor	8	6
Camshaft sprocket (coolant pump drive): *		
Stage 1	20	15
Stage 2	Angle-tighten a further 90°	
Camshaft sprocket bolts: *		
MPI engines:		
Stage 1	50	37
Stage 2	Angle-tighten a further 90°	
TSI engines:		
Stage 1	50	37
Stage 2	Angle-tighten a further 135°	
Camshaft sprocket cover bolts (exhaust): *		
Stage 1	8	6
Stage 2	Angle-tighten a further 45°	
Camshaft sprocket blanking plug (inlet)	20	15
Coolant pump pulley	22	16
Connecting rod bolts: *		
Stage 1	30	22
Stage 2	Angle-tighten a further 90°	
Crankshaft main bearing bolts	Do not remove!	
Crankshaft pulley bolt: *		
Stage 1	150	110
Stage 2	Angle-tighten a further 180°	
Cylinder head bolts: *		
Stage 1	40	30
Stage 2	Angle-tighten a further 90°	
Stage 3	Angle-tighten a further 90°	
Stage 4	Angle-tighten a further 90°	
Engine mountings:		
Left-hand mounting:		
Mounting to body (upper bolt): *		
Stage 1	50	37
Stage 2	Angle-tighten a further 90°	
Mounting to body lower bolts: *		
Stage 1	50	37
Stage 2	Angle-tighten a further 90°	
Mounting to transmission bracket: *		
Stage 1	40	30
Stage 2	Angle-tighten a further 90°	
Bracket to transmission: *		
Stage 1	40	30
Stage 2	Angle-tighten a further 90°	
Right-hand mounting:		
Mounting to body bolts: *		
Stage 1	20	15
Stage 2	Angle-tighten a further 90°	
Mounting to engine bracket: *		
Stage 1	30	22
Stage 2	Angle-tighten a further 90°	
Earth strap nut	20	15
Bracket to engine block bolts: *		
Stage 1	7	5
Stage 2	40	30
Stage 3	Angle-tighten a further 90°	
Lower mounting (pendulum mount): *		
Bracket to engine/transmission:		
Stage 1	30	22
Stage 2	Angle-tighten a further 90°	
Pendulum to bracket bolt	Do not remove	
Pendulum mount to subframe: *		
Stage 1	40	30
Stage 2	Angle-tighten a further 90°	

Torque wrench settings (conitnued)

	Nm	lbf ft
Flywheel bolts: *		
Stage 1	60	44
Stage 2	Angle-tighten a further 90°	
Oil cooler bolts: *		
Stage 1	8	6
Stage 2	Angle-tighten a further 90°	
Oil filter	20	15
Oil level and temperature sender	9	7
Oil pressure control valve	8	6
Oil pressure switch (Do not re-use):*		
Stage 1	10	7
Stage 2	Angle-tighten a further 45°	
Oil pump bolts:		
Stage 1 (all bolts)	8	6
Stage 2 (upper 6 bolts only)	Angle-tighten a further 90°	
Stage 3 (front 2 spline bolts only – see text)	20	15
Oil pump suction pipe	6	4
Piston cooling jet valve/bolt	27	20
Sump bolts: *		
Stage 1	Screw in hand tight	
Stage 2	12	9
Sump oil drain plug	30	22
Timing belt cover (upper and lower bolts)	8	6
Timing belt tensioner bolt	25	18
Timing belt idler pulley bolt	45	33

**Do not re-use*

1 General Information

How to use this Chapter

1 This Part of Chapter 2 describes those repair procedures that can reasonably be carried out on the engine while it remains in the vehicle. If the engine has been removed from the vehicle and is being dismantled as described in Part F, any preliminary dismantling procedures can be ignored.

2 Note that while it may be possible physically to overhaul certain items while the engine is in the vehicle, such tasks are not usually carried out as separate operations, and usually require the execution of several additional procedures (not to mention the cleaning of components and of oilways); for this reason, all such tasks are classed as major overhaul procedures, and are described in Part F of this Chapter.

Engine description

3 Throughout this Chapter, engines are identified by the manufacturer's code letters. A listing of all engines covered, together with their code letters, is given in the Specifications.

4 The engines covered in this Part of Chapter 2 are of water-cooled, double-overhead camshaft (DOHC), in-line three-cylinder design. The engine family is designated EA211 by VAG (Volkswagen Audi Group). The engines have an aluminium alloy cylinder block fitted with grey cast-iron cylinder liners, and an aluminium alloy cylinder head. The exhaust manifold is integrated into the cylinder head. The engine is transversely mounted at the front of the vehicle, with the transmission unit on its left-hand end.

5 The crankshaft is of five-bearing type, but note that the crankshaft must not be removed due to the design of the bearing pedestals. Removing the bearing caps will distort the pedestals and damage the bearings.

6 The camshafts are mounted in a modular camshaft carrier and are driven by a toothed timing belt from the crankshaft sprocket. Variable Valve Timing (VVT) is fitted to the inlet and exhaust camshafts on all engines except those with engine code CHYB. On these models VVT is only fitted to the inlet camshaft. Repair to the camshafts is not possible. If a fault develops the entire camshaft housing (module) must be replaced.

7 The valves are closed by coil springs, and the valves run in guides pressed into the cylinder head. The camshafts actuate the valves by roller rocker fingers supported by hydraulic tappets.

8 The oil pump is a 'duocentric' oil pump driven directly by the crankshaft. Oil is drawn from the sump through a strainer, and then forced through an externally-mounted, renewable filter. From there, it is distributed to the cylinder head, where it lubricates the camshaft journals and hydraulic tappets, and also to the crankcase, where it lubricates the main bearings, connecting rod big-ends, gudgeon pins and cylinder bores. A coolant-fed oil cooler is fitted to all engines.

9 Engine coolant is circulated by a coolant pump, driven by a belt mounted to a sprocket on the left-hand end of the exhaust camshaft. TSI engines (codes CHZC and CHZB) also have an electric coolant pump fitted. For details of the cooling system, refer to Chapter 3 Section 7.

Operations with engine in car

10 The following operations can be performed without removing the engine:

a) *Compression pressure – testing.*
b) *Camshaft cover – removal and refitting.*
c) *Crankshaft pulley – removal and refitting.*
d) *Timing belt covers – removal and refitting.*
e) *Timing belt – removal, refitting and adjustment.*
f) *Timing belt tensioner and sprockets – removal and refitting.*
g) *Camshaft oil seal – renewal.*
h) *Camshaft and hydraulic tappets – removal, inspection and refitting.*
i) *Cylinder head – removal and refitting.*
j) *Cylinder head and pistons – decarbonising.*
k) *Sump – removal and refitting.*
l) *Oil pump – removal, overhaul and refitting.*
m) *Crankshaft oil seals – renewal.*
n) *Engine/transmission mountings – inspection and renewal.*
o) *Flywheel/driveplate – removal, inspection and refitting.*

Note: *It is possible to remove the pistons and connecting rods (after removing the cylinder head and sump) without removing the engine. However, this is not recommended. Work of this nature is more easily and thoroughly completed with the engine on the bench, as described in Chapter 2F.*

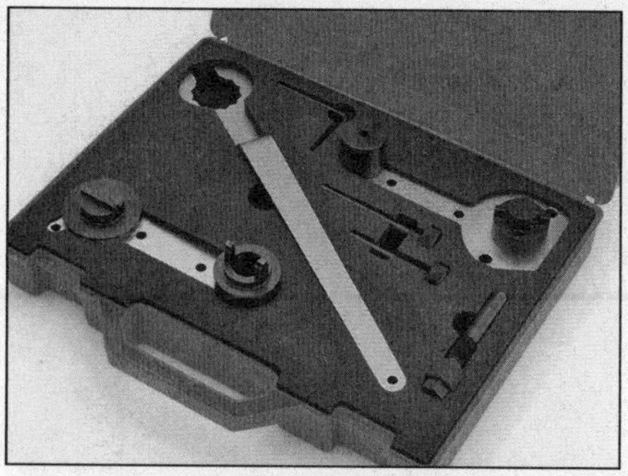

3.3 A set of suitable timing tools from AST tools. Note that T10476A will also be needed

2 Compression test – description and interpretation

1 When engine performance is down, or if misfiring occurs which cannot be attributed to the ignition or fuel systems, a compression test can provide diagnostic clues as to the engine's condition. If the test is performed regularly, it can give warning of trouble before any other symptoms become apparent.

2 The engine must be fully warmed-up to normal operating temperature, the battery must be fully charged, and the spark plugs must be removed (Chapter 1A Section 27). The aid of an assistant will also be required.

3 Disable the ignition system by unplugging the wiring plug from the ignition coil module or HT coils. Also, disconnect the wiring from the fuel injectors. **Note:** *This may generate a fault code in the engine management memory, and it will be necessary to have this code erased by a Seat dealer or diagnostic specialist on completion of the test.*

4 Fit a compression tester to the No 1 cylinder spark plug hole – the type of tester which screws into the plug thread is to be preferred.

5 Have the assistant hold the throttle wide open and crank the engine on the starter motor; after one or two revolutions, the compression pressure should build-up to a maximum figure and then stabilise. Record the highest reading obtained.

6 Repeat the test on the remaining cylinders, recording the pressure in each.

3.6 Unbolt the thermostat housing

7 All cylinders should produce very similar pressures, of the order of 10 to 15 bars. Any one cylinder reading below 10 bars, or a difference of more than 3 bars between cylinders, suggests a fault.

8 Note that the compression should build-up quickly in a healthy engine; low compression on the first stroke, followed by gradually increasing pressure on successive strokes, indicates worn piston rings.

9 A low compression reading on the first stroke, which does not build-up during successive strokes, indicates leaking valves or a blown head gasket (a cracked head could also be the cause).

10 If the pressure in any cylinder is reduced to 10 bars or less, carry out the following test to isolate the cause. Introduce a teaspoonful of clean oil into that cylinder through its spark plug hole and repeat the test.

11 If the addition of oil temporarily improves the compression pressure, this indicates that bore or piston wear is responsible for the pressure loss. No improvement suggests that leaking or burnt valves, or a blown head gasket, may be to blame.

12 A low reading from two adjacent cylinders is almost certainly due to the head gasket having blown between them; the presence of coolant in the engine oil will confirm this.

13 If one cylinder is about 20 percent lower than the others and the engine has a slightly rough idle; a worn camshaft lobe could be the cause.

14 On completion of the test, refit the spark plugs and reconnect the ignition system. Refit the fuel injector wiring. Have any fault code (see paragraph 3) erased by a Seat dealer or diagnostic specialist.

3 Engine assembly and valve timing marks – general information and usage

1 Top dead centre (TDC) is the highest point in its travel up-and-down its cylinder bore that each piston reaches as the crankshaft rotates. While each piston reaches TDC both at the top of the compression stroke and again at the top of the exhaust stroke, for the purpose of timing the engine, TDC refers to the No 1 piston position at the top of its compression stroke.

2 No 1 piston and cylinder are at the right-hand end of the engine. Note that the crankshaft rotates clockwise when viewed from the right-hand side of the car.

3 Disconnect the battery negative lead (refer to Chapter 5A Section 3). Remove all the spark plugs as described in Chapter 1A Section 27.

Note: *Seat/VW TDC setting tools T10494 and T10340 will be required for TSI engines (CHZC and CHZB engine codes) and setting tools T10340 and T10477 will be required for MPI engines (engine code CHYB). If further work is required then sprocket locking tool T10476A will also be required. These tools are available in the aftermarket* **(see illustration)**. Note that on TSI engines, very fine adjustment of the valve timing is possible with the Seat special tool VAS 611 007. This is a digital tool linked to the factory diagnostic tool and will require a Seat dealership to perform the adjustment.

TSI engines

4 Drain the coolant as described in Chapter 1A Section 32. There is no need to completely drain the system, the coolant level only needs to be lower than the thermostat housing.

5 Remove the air filter housing and the air intake from the throttle body as described in Chapter 4A Section 3.

6 Unbolt and move the thermostat housing to the side **(see illustration)**. There is no need to remove it completely.

7 Disconnect the EVAP hose from the crankcase breather hose and then unbolt the breather hose **(see illustrations)**.

3.7a Remove the EVAP hose...

3.7b ...then unbolt the breather hose...

3.7c ...and remove it

3.8 Release the wiring loom

3.9 Access to the bolt is difficult

3.10 Remove the cover

3.11 Remove the blanking cap

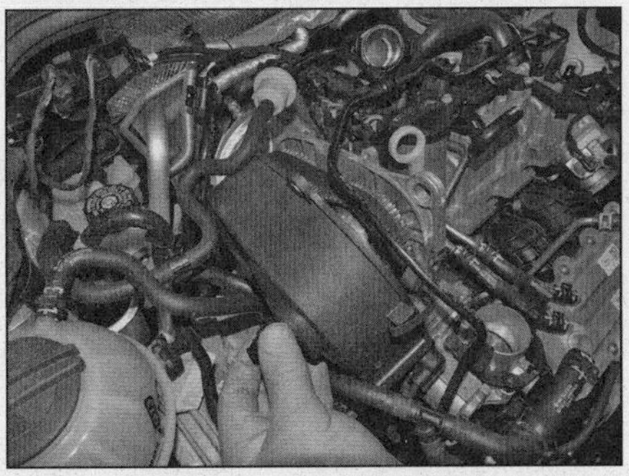

3.12 Remove the cover

3.15 The marks must align

8 At the rear of the engine, unclip the wiring loom from the coolant pump belt cover **(see illustration)**.

9 Release the coolant hose from the inlet duct (where fitted) and then (with difficulty) unbolt the inlet duct from the rear of the engine **(see illustration)**. Note that Seat list a special ball end Torx socket for this purpose (T10405). Pull out the ducting and move it away from the coolant pump belt cover.

10 Unbolt and remove the coolant pump belt cover **(see illustration)**.

11 Undo the bolts and remove the cap from the end of the inlet camshaft **(see illustration)**.

12 At the timing belt end of the engine unclip the fuel/coolant hoses and then remove the upper timing belt cover **(see illustration)**.

13 Jack up and support the front of the vehicle – see *Jacking and vehicle support*.

14 Remove the engine undershield and the right-hand wing liner to gain access to the crankshaft pulley

15 Using a socket on the crankshaft pulley bolt, rotate the crankshaft until the mark on the pulley aligns with the 'OT' mark on the timing belt lower cover **(see illustration)**. Highlight the pulley and the notch in the lower cover with paint or a marker pen if necessary.

16 The slots on the inlet and exhaust camshaft (at the transmission end of the engine) should be above an imaginary horizontal line draw through the centre line of the camshafts **(see illustration)**. If the slots are below the line rotate the crankshaft one revolution and check again. Trial fit the locking tool (T10494) at the transmission end of the engine.

17 The tool should slot easily into position. If necessary slight pressure can be applied to the timing belt between the inlet and exhaust sprockets. Seat list a special tool (T10487) for this purpose, but thumb pressure or the use of the handle of a hammer are just as effective **(see illustrations)**. Note the engine must remain at TDC – check the marks at the crankshaft pulley again after fitting the locking tool.

18 If the timing was set to TDC for further work (timing belt replacement for example) then the crankshaft can be locked in position using the timing pin (T10340) and following the procedure below for the 1.0 litre MPI engine. Note however that because the TSI version has a timing mark on the crankshaft pulley using a screwdriver in the number one spark plug hole is not required as the mark on the pulley can be brought to 90 degrees before TDC and the locking pin then fitted. Rotate the engine to TDC and the crankshaft will lock in position at TDC with the 'OT' and the pulley mark aligned.

19 Refitting is a reversal of removal.

3.16 The slots must be above the horizontal

3.17a The tool should slide easily into place

3.17b Slight adjustment of the camshafts is possible by pressing down on the belt

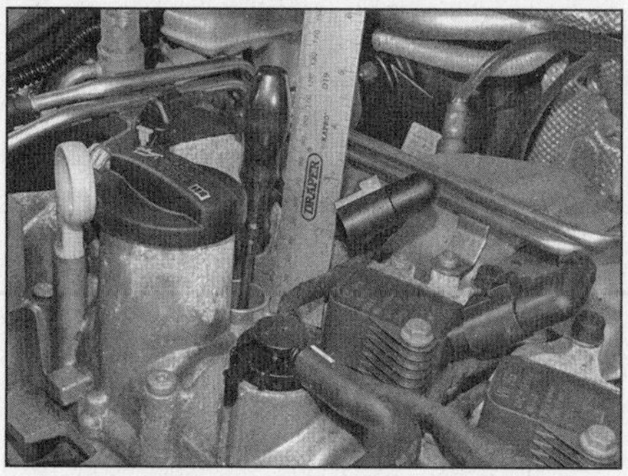

3.27 Raise the piston 30 mm

3.29a Fit the locking pin

3.29b When correctly fitted the pin locks against the crankshaft web (shown with the sump removed for clarity)

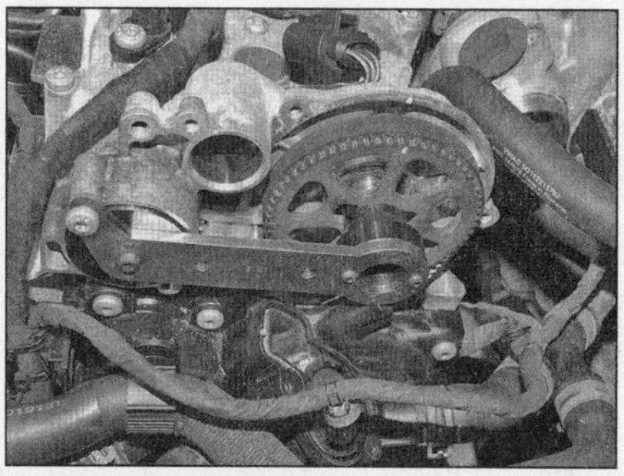

3.31 Slide the camshaft positioning tool into position

MPI engines

Note: *Setting the engine to TDC on MPI engines is similar to TSI engines, but there are important differences.*

20 Remove the air filter housing as described in Chapter 4A Section 3.

21 Depressurise the fuel system – see Chapter 4A Section 8. Anticipating some fuel spillage, disconnect the fuel lines at the inner wing and seal them.

22 Unclip the fuel lines from the timing belt upper cover and then remove the cover.

23 At the transmission end of the engine, unclip the coolant hose from the coolant pump belt cover and then remove the cover. Remove the blanking plate from the end of the inlet camshaft **(see illustrations 3.8 and 3.10)**.

24 If not already done so, remove the spark plug from number one cylinder and insert a screwdriver into the cylinder. The screwdriver must have a shank of at least 250 mm.

25 Jack up and support the front of the vehicle – see *Jacking and vehicle support*.

26 Remove the engine undershield and the right-hand wing liner to gain access to the crankshaft pulley

Caution: Follow the instruction closely, as it is possible to lock the engine in more than one position.

27 Using a socket on the crankshaft pulley rotate the engine in the normal direction (clockwise looking at the crankshaft pulley) until the number one piston is at BDC (Bottom Dead Centre). The screwdriver (and the piston) will now be at the lowest point. Using a suitable reference point rotate the engine further until the screwdriver rises up 30 mm **(see illustration)**.

28 Working under the vehicle, remove the blanking plug from the rear right-hand side of the engine block. If improved access is required, remove the driveshaft as described in Chapter 8, Section 2.

29 Insert the locking pin (T10340). Tighten the pin. Note that if the locking pin will not tighten fully if the engine is not set at TDC. If this is the case then remove the pin and turn the engine a further 90 degrees (in the normal direction). Refit the pin and then turn the engine another 90 degrees in the normal direction of rotation until the crankshaft is locked in position by the pin **(see illustrations)**.

30 Check that the engine is correctly position at TDC by checking the alignment of the camshaft sprockets. The marks on both sprockets will be in the 12 o'clock position and aligned with the marks on the camshaft housing if all is correct. A further check can be made by inserting the camshaft positioning tool (T10476A) between the sprockets. Note that when the camshaft positioning tool is fitted the marks on the sprocket (at the 3 o'clock and 9 o'clock position) will slightly offset.

31 The slots on the inlet and exhaust camshaft (at the transmission end of the engine) should be above an imaginary horizontal line draw through the centre line of the camshafts **(see illustration)**. Trial fit the locking tool (T10477) at the transmission end of the engine – it should slide easily into position.

32 If all is well refit the removed components in reverse order to removal. Start the engine and check carefully for fuel leaks.

4 Crankshaft pulley – removal and refitting

Removal

Note: *Whilst not strictly necessary, setting the engine at TDC (as described in Section 3) before removing the pulley is highly recommended. DO NOT slacken the pulley with the timing belt removed unless absolutely essential.*

1 Mark the auxiliary drivebelt for normal rotation to ensure correct refitting. Remove the auxilliary drivebelt as described in Chapter 1A Section 28.

2 Jack up and support the front of the vehicle (see *Jacking and vehicle support*). Where required remove the engine undershield and the right-hand wing liner. **Note:** *Releasing the pulley bolt by engaging 4th gear and having an assistant hold their foot on the brake is NOT recommended (or approved by Seat).*

3 A suitable crankshaft pulley locking tool will be required to hold the pulley stationary. A tool can be fabricated or a universal peg spanner type tool can be used **(see illustrations)**. The

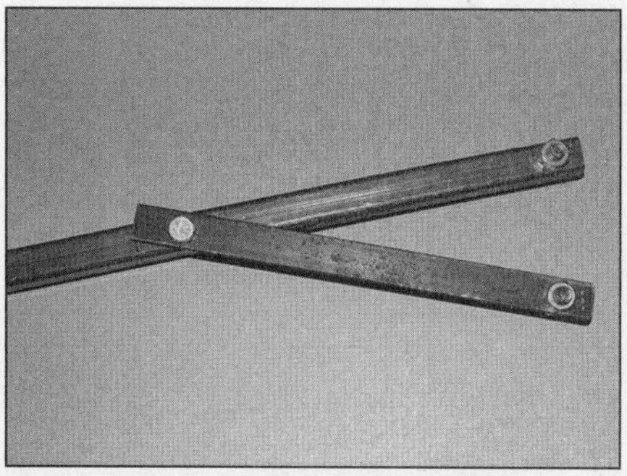

4.3a A home fabricated tool

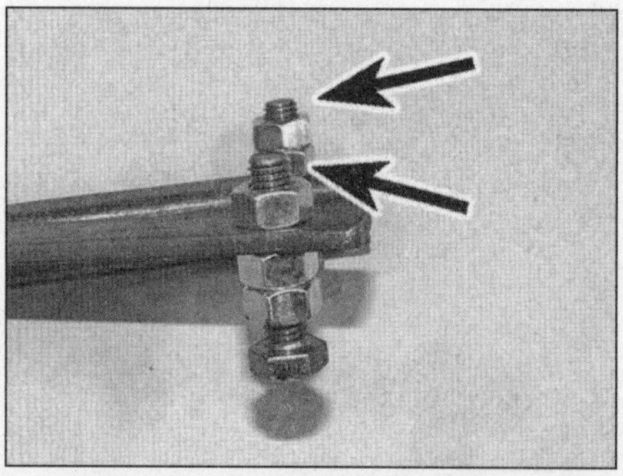

4.3b The tool will need adapting to fit the shallow slots in the crankshaft pulley

official factory tool (T10475) is also available from Seat dealers and the aftermarket (AST5144 with AST4939 for example). Due to the shallow depth of the slots in the pulley use of the correct tool is highly recommended.

4 Locate the pegs of the tool in the slots of the pulley and using a socket on a long knuckle bar release the pulley bolt **(see illustration)**. Remove the pulley.

Refitting

5 Lubricate the bolt threads with clean engine oil, locate the pulley and new bolt on the end of the crankshaft, then tighten it to the specified torque and angle while holding it stationary with the holding tool.

6 Refit the auxilliary drivebelt as described in Chapter 1A Section 28.

4.4 Removing the crankshaft pulley with the correct tool

5 Timing belt covers – removal and refitting

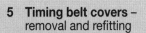

Removal

1 Remove the air cleaner/air inlet pipe as applicable.

2 Unclip the fuel pipe and EVAP pipe from the top cover and secure them to one side.

3 Remove the single bolt, release the clips at the side and remove the top cover **(see illustrations)**.

4 Apply the handbrake, then jack up the front of the car and support it on axle stands (see *Jacking and vehicle support*). Remove the right-hand front road wheel. For improved access, remove the right-hand front wheel arch liner and where necessary the engine undershield.

5 Mark the auxiliary drivebelt for direction of rotation to ensure correct refitting and then remove the belt as described in Chapter 1A Section 28 **(see illustration)**.

6 On MPI engines (CHYB engine code) remove the alternator upper mounting bolt, slacken the lower bolt and pivot the alternator away from the engine **(see illustration)**.

7 Remove the crankshaft pulley as described in Section 4.

8 Unbolt and remove the lower timing belt cover **(see illustrations)**.

9 The centre cover forms part of the engine mounting bracket and the engine must be supported from below if the cover is to be removed. Remove the engine mounting as described in Section 20 and then unbolt the centre cover/support bracket. Note that removal of the centre cover is not required for timing belt replacement, but on MPI engines removal is straight forward. On TSI engines removal is awkward because access to the mounting bolts of the heat shield of the catalytic converter is limited.

Refitting

10 Refitting is a reversal of removal. If the fuel lines were disconnected then check carefully for fuel leaks before driving the vehicle.

6 Timing belt – removal and refitting

Note: *Timing belt replacement is possible with the engine mounting bracket in position. On MPI engines once the engine is supported from below removal is relatively straightforward. On TSI engines because of the catalytic converter, removal (while not impossible) is hampered by the mounting of the catalytic converter and heat shield.*

Caution: The timing tools are alignment tools, they are not designed to hold the crankshaft or camshafts in position whilst the sprocket and pulley bolts are removed. Always use a counterhold tool to release and tighten the sprocket bolts and crankshaft pulley bolt.

5.3a Remove the bolt, release the clips...

5.3b ...and remove the cover

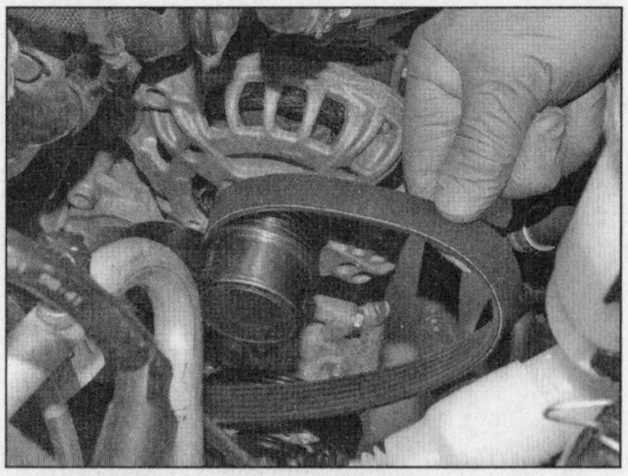

5.5 Remove the auxiliary drivebelt

5.6 Remove the upper mounting bolt

5.8a Unbolt and...

5.8b ...remove the lower cover

6.8 Remove the tensioner

6.10 Lower the bracket out of the engine bay

6.11a The index marks on the inlet camshaft sprocket...

6.11b ...and on the exhaust sprocket

Removal

1 Remove the timing belt upper cover, with reference to Section 5.

2 Jack up and support the front of the vehicle (see *Jacking and vehicle support*). Remove the wheel, the wing liner and where required the engine undershield.

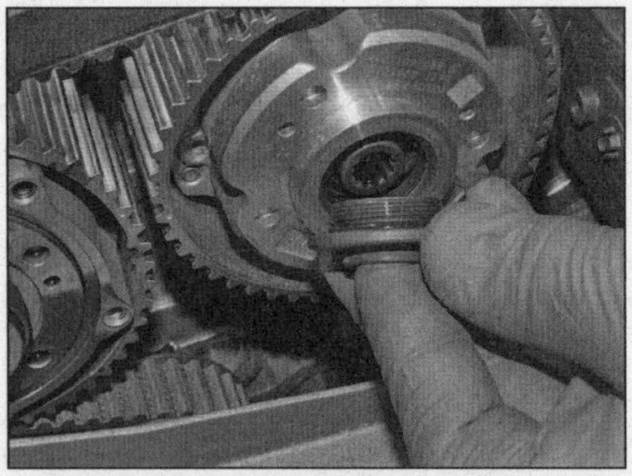

6.12a Remove the blanking plug...

6.12b ...and then slacken the sprocket bolt

6.12c On the exhaust camshaft remove the cover (TSI engines only)

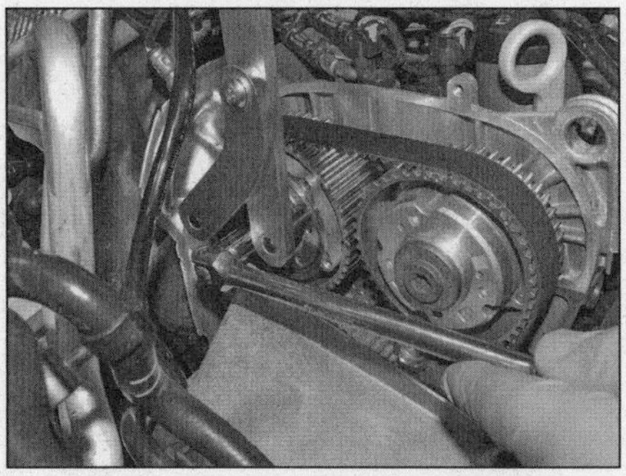

6.12d Slacken the exhaust camshaft sprocket

3 Slacken the crankshaft pulley bolt as described in Section 4. **Do not** remove the bolt at this stage.

4 Set the engine to TDC as described in Section 3 and install the timing tools. The crankshaft locking tool (T10340) should be fitted.

5 Remove the crankshaft pulley, with reference to Section 4. Before finally removing the pulley, check that No 1 piston is still positioned at TDC (Section 3).

6 Remove the timing belt lower cover as described in Section 5.

7 If the mounting bracket is to be removed, place a jack under the engine sump and (using a bock of wood to spread the load) support the engine. Unbolt the right-hand engine mounting from the engine bracket and inner wing as described in Section 20.

8 Unbolt and remove the auxiliary drivebelt tensioner **(see illustration)**.

9 Slacken the lower alternator mounting bolt, remove the upper bolt and then pivot the alternator away from the engine bracket **(see illustration 5.6)**.

10 Remove the support bracket from the main bracket (MPI engines) and then unbolt and remove the engine bracket from the engine block – 3 bolts. Lower the bracket from the engine, raising and lowering the engine on the jack as required to allow the bracket to pass down and out of the engine bay **(see illustration)**.

11 With the timing tool in position at transmission end of the camshafts, check that the marks on the camshaft sprockets are alighned with the index marks on the camshaft housing **(see illustrations)**.

12 Using an adjustable peg spanner (or the factory tool T10172) counterhold the inlet sprocket and remove the blanking plug. Next slacken (but do not remove) the sprocket retaining bolt **(see illustrations)**. On models with VVT on the exhaust camshaft, remove the cover (5 bolts). On all engines (whilst counterholding the sprocket), slacken (but do not remove) the exhaust camshaft sprocket retaining bolt. The sprockets must be free to turn, but not loose.

13 If the timing belt is to be refitted, mark its running direction. Note refitting a used timing belt is not recommended given the amount of work involved in removing it.

14 Loosen the timing belt tensioner securing bolt to release the tensioner. If the belt is being replaced with the engine mounting bracket in position, then the special tool (T10499 or aftermarket equivalent) will be required. If the bracket has been removed then once the bolt has been slackened the tensioner can be moved back with a 30 mm spanner or slip joint (water pump) pliers. Push back the tensioner and tighten the locking bolt. Remove the timing belt from the sprockets **(see illustrations)**.

15 If further work is anticipated, turn the crankshaft a quarter-turn (90°) anti-

6.14a Slacken the tensioner with a spanner and the special tool

6.14b Remove the timing belt

6.17 The tang on the tensioner must engage correctly in the cylinder head

6.19 Note that on TSI engines the horizontal index marks are offset

6.24a Over-tighten the tensioner by 10 mm...

clockwise to lower the pistons down their bores from the TDC position. This will eliminate any risk of piston-to-valve contact if the camshafts are turned whilst the timing belt is removed.

Refitting

16 Although not mandatory the fitting of a new tensioner and idler is highly recommended. If they are not to be replaced, they should be turned by hand and checked for play and abnormal noise.

17 Fit the new tensioner and idler pulley (see Section 7) ensuring that the tab on the rear of the tensioner fits into the slot on the cylinder head **(see illustration)**. Fit a new idler pulley.

18 Check that the camshaft locking tool is correctly fitted. If the pistons were lowered, then turn the crankshaft a quarter-turn (90°) clockwise to re-position the engine at TDC (the TDC timing pin should be in place).

19 Fit new bolts to the camshaft sprockets and tighten the bolts just enough to allow the sprockets to rotate freely but without any play. The vertical index marks must be aligned **(see illustrations 11a and 11b)** and the camshaft sprocket locking tool must be fitted **(see illustration)**.

20 Remove the crankshaft sprocket and clean the mounting surface. Refit the sprocket and install the new belt onto the crankshaft sprocket. Refit the lower timing belt cover and then refit the crankshaft pulley. Oil the threads of the new crankshaft pulley bolt before fitting it. If the factory tool is available fit the new bolt and tighten the new bolt fully to the specifies torque and angle. If a home fabricated tool is being used to hold the pulley then do not fully tighten the new bolt until the timing belt has been fitted and correctly tensioned.

21 On MPI engines, fit the timing belt around the tensioner, the camshaft exhaust sprocket, the inlet camshaft sprocket and the idler pulley. If the engine support bracket is in place feed the new belt up to the top of the engine though the bracket. Note that it may be necessary to temporarily remove the camshaft sprocket locking tool to fit the belt.

22 On TSI engines fit the belt over the idler pulley, the tensioner pulley and then around the camshaft sprockets. Note that it may be necessary to temporarily remove the camshaft sprocket locking tool to fit the belt.

23 Remove the camshaft sprocket locking tool (T10476A) and then tension the timing belt as follows:

24 Using a 30 mm spanner (or the special spanner) turn the tensioner so that the indicator is 10 mm to the right of the adjustment window. Next turn the tensioner back, so that it lies in the middle of the adjustment window **(see illustrations)**.

25 Hold the tensioner in this position and tighten the locking nut to the specified torque. If the belt is being replaced with the engine support bracket in position then the extended torque value must now be calculated. A suitable calculator is available on line (and for download) from Norbar.com (https://www.norbar.com/en-gb/Home/Torque-Wrench-Extension-Calculator). Alternatively the value can be calculated **(see illustrations)**.

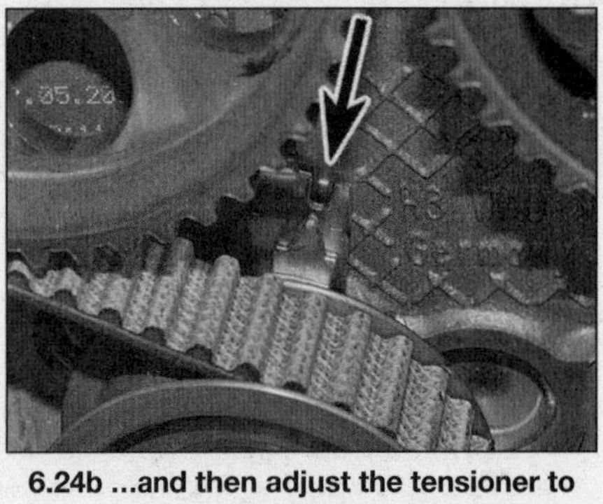

6.24b ...and then adjust the tensioner to the correct central position

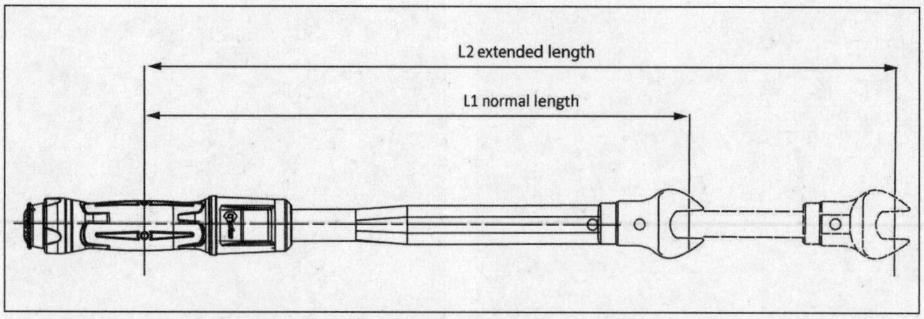

6.25a The formula M1 (the indicated torque wrench setting) = M2 (the actual torque at the nut) x L1/L2 (Illustration copyright of Norbar Torque Tools Ltd and used with their kind permission)

6.25b Tighten the tensioner to the calculated torque

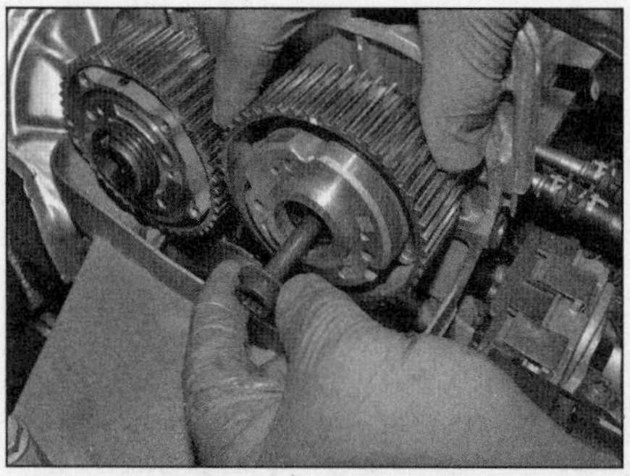

7.2a Remove the bolt...

7.2b ...remove the sprocket

7.2c ...and recover the sleeve

26 Using the peg spanner to counterhold the camshaft sprockets, tighten the new bolts to first stage torque (50 Nm).

27 Remove the timing tools from the crankshaft and the transmission end of the camshafts. If the crankshaft pulley was not fully tightened, then tighten the new bolt to the specified torque and angle.

28 Turn the crankshaft two revolutions in the normal direction of rotation and refit the timing tools as described in Section 3. Slightly depressing the new belt between the camshaft sprockets is permissible if the camshaft locking tool does not fit easily. If the tool does not fit the timing is incorrect and the installation procedure must be repeated.

29 Using the counterhold, tighten the camshaft sprockets to the second stage of the tightening procedure. Note that the final angle tightening is different depending on the engine – see the Section at the start of this Chapter.

7.3 Removing the exhaust camshaft sprocket on TSI engines is only possible after removing the engine support bracket

30 Fit a new blanking plug and seal to the inlet camshaft. On models with VVT on the exhaust camshaft, fit new bolts (and seal) to the cover and tighten the bolts to the specified torque.

31 Where removed, refit the engine bracket, alternator bolts, auxiliary belt tensioner, auxiliary belt and the engine mounting.

32 Fit the remaining components in reverse order to removal.

7 Timing belt tensioner and sprockets – removal and refitting

Camshaft sprockets

Removal

1 Remove the timing belt as described in Section 6. Removal of the timing belt requires the slackening of the sprocket bolts.

7.8 Remove the crankshaft sprocket

2 Unscrew the inlet camshaft sprocket bolt fully and then remove the sprocket from the end of the camshaft **(see illustrations)**.

3 On TSI engines removal of the exhaust camshaft sprocket is not possible with the engine support bracket in place. Remove the bracket and then remove the sprocket **(see illustration)**.

4 Discard the bolts as new ones must be used.

Refitting

5 Prior to refitting, check the camshaft oil seals for signs of leakage, and if necessary renew the seal as described in Section 8.

6 Follow the timing belt replacement procedure as described in Section 6 and then tighten the sprocket bolt to the specified torque. Prevent the sprocket from turning using the method used on removal. Note that there are different angle settings depending on the engine code (see Section).

Crankshaft sprocket

Removal

7 Remove the crankshaft pulley (Section 4) and the timing belt as described in Section 6.

8 Lift the crankshaft sprocket off the crankshaft **(see illustration)**.

Refitting

Warning: Do not turn the crankshaft, as the pistons may hit the valves.

9 Clean both surfaces of the sprocket and refit it.

10 Refit the timing belt as described in Section 6.

11 Clean the front surface of the sprocket again and the rear surface of the crankshaft pulley. Due to the unique design of the sprocket and crankshaft pulley it is essential that both mounting surfaces are thoroughly cleaned before installation.

12 Refit the remaining components in reverse order.

Tensioner assembly

Removal

13 Remove the timing belt as described in Section 6.

14 If the engine mounting bracket is in place, then remove the inlet camshaft sprocket and (taking care not to drop the bolt) unbolt and then lift the tensioner up and out.

15 Unscrew the bolt and then withdraw the tensioner assembly from the engine.

Refitting

16 Offer the tensioner assembly into, ensuring that the tang on the tensioner backplate engages with the corresponding cut-out in the cylinder head **(see illustration)**.

17 Refit the bolt, but do not fully tighten the nut at this stage.

18 Refit and tension the timing belt as described in Section 6.

Idler pulley

Removal

19 Remove the timing belt as described in Section 6.

20 Slacken the bolt and remove the tensioner as a complete assembly **(see illustration)**. Note that on some models the bolt is held captive in the idler by an O-ring seal.

Refitting

21 Refitting is a reversal of removal.

8 Camshaft oil seals – renewal

Note: *The oil seals are a PTFE (Teflon) type and are fitted dry, without using any grease or oil. These have a wider sealing lip and have been introduced instead of the coil spring type oil seal.*

7.16 The tang must engage with the cylinder head

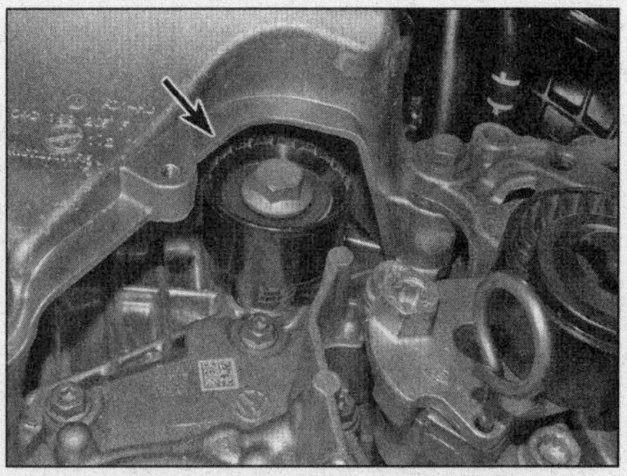

7.20 Remove the idler (from below)

Note: *Special Seat tools are available that enable the camshaft oil seals (and all the other oil seals) to be removed without fear of damaging the machined surfaces. These tools are relatively inexpensive and their use is highly recommended* ***(see illustration)***.

1 Remove the timing belt as described in Section 6.

2 Remove the camshaft sprocket as described in Section 7. Note that there is also a seal behind the coolant pump sprocket. This is replaced using the same method as for the camshaft oil seals.

3 Protect the cylinder head and lever out the seal using the special tool or a pick **(see illustrations)**.

4 Clean out the seal housing and the sealing surface of the camshaft by wiping it with a lint-free cloth. Remove any swarf or burrs that may cause the seal to leak.

5 Carefully push the seal over the camshaft until it is positioned above its housing **(see illustration)**.

6 Using a hammer and a socket of suitable diameter, drive the seal squarely into its housing **(see illustration)**. **Note:** *Select a socket that bears only on the hard outer surface of the seal, not the inner lip which can easily be damaged.*

7 Refit the camshaft sprocket with reference to Section 7.

8 Refit and tension the timing belt as described in Section 6.

9 Camshaft housing – removal and refitting

Note: *The camshafts are housed in a single combined valve cover and camshaft carrier. The camshafts can not be removed from the*

8.0 The working end of the special camshaft seal removal tool (T20143/1)

8.3a Use a pick or...

8.3b ...the special tool to lever out the seal

8.5 Fit the new seal

8.6 Drive the seal home with a suitable socket

9.7a Unbolt the inlet elbow from the turbocharger

9.7b Unbolt (and move to the side) the coolant pipes

9.9a Disconnect the wiring plug from the VVT control solenoid(s) and...

9.9b ...unbolt the ground wire

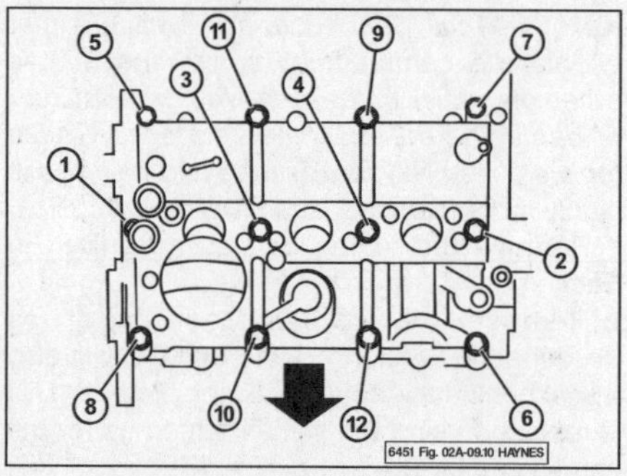

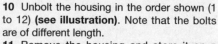

9.10 Slacken the bolts in the order shown

housing. If there is a fault with the camshafts (such as worn lobes, or excessive end float for example) then the complete housing and camshafts must be replaced.

Removal

1 Drain the coolant (Chapter 1A Section 32) and then remove the coolant pump as described in Chapter 3 Section 7.

2 Remove the air filter housing/air inlet duct as described in Chapter 4A Section 3.

3 Remove the ignition coils as described in Chapter 5B Section 3 and pull out the oil level dipstick.

4 Remove the timing belt from the camshaft sprockets as described in Section 6 – there is no need to completely remove the timing belt at this stage. Remove the camshaft sprockets.

5 If not still in position, fit the camshaft locking tool to the coolant pump sprocket and the inlet camshaft (as described in Section 3). Fitting the tool will lock the camshafts in position.

6 On TSI engines, disconnect the wiring plug and fuel lines from the high pressure fuel pump (Chapter 4A Section 4).

7 On TSI engines, remove the inlet duct from the rear of the engine and then remove the turbocharger coolant hoses **(see illustrations)**.

8 Disconnect the wiring plug from the EVAP control solenoid, disconnect the vapour hoses and move them to the side. Seal the hoses with blanking plugs.

9 Disconnect the wiring plugs from the camshaft position sensors and the VVT control valve(s). Unbolt the ground wire **(see illustrations)**. Release (and unbolt) the wiring loom from the retaining brackets and the camshaft position sensors. Move the wiring loom to the side.

10 Unbolt the housing in the order shown (1 to 12) **(see illustration)**. Note that the bolts are of different length.

11 Remove the housing and store it on a clean surface **(see illustration)**. Recover the gasket.

Refitting

12 Thoroughly clean the mating surfaces of the camshaft housing and the cylinder head.

13 Fit a new gasket, check that the cam followers are all correctly located and then lower the housing into position **(see illustrations)**.

14 Tighten the new bolts progressively in reverse order (12-1) to the specified torque in sequence **(see illustration 9.10)**.

15 The remainder of refitting is a reversal of removal, but consider fitting a new timing belt and always fit a new coolant pump belt. Rotate the engine at least twice in the normal direction to check the valve timing. Refill the coolant as described in Chapter 1A Section 32.

10 Camshafts – inspection

Note: *Due to the method of construction, the camshafts can not be removed from the camshaft housing. The camshafts are removed with the camshaft housing as described in Section 9.*

Inspection

1 Visually inspect the camshaft for evidence of wear on the surfaces of the lobes and journals

9.11 Lift off the camshaft housing

9.13a Fit the new gasket over the dowels

9.13b Lower the camshaft housing into position

(see illustration). Normally their surfaces should be smooth and have a dull shine; look for scoring, erosion or pitting and areas that appear highly polished, indicating excessive wear. Accelerated wear will occur once the hardened exterior of the camshaft has been damaged, so always renew worn items. **Note:** *If these symptoms are visible on the tips of the camshaft lobes, check the corresponding tappet/rocker finger, as it may be worn as well.*

2 If the machined surfaces of the camshaft appear discoloured or blued, it is likely that it has been overheated at some point, probably due to inadequate lubrication.

3 If there are any faults found with the camshafts the complete camshaft housing assembly must be replaced.

11 Hydraulic tappets/roller rocker fingers – removal, inspection and refitting

Removal

1 Remove the camshaft housing, as described in Section 9.

2 As the components are removed, keep them in strict order, so that they can be refitted in their original locations. Accelerated wear leading to early failure will result if the tappets and rocker fingers are interchanged.

3 Note the fitted position, then lift out the rocker finger complete with the hydraulic tappets **(see illustration)**.

4 Carefully unclip the tappets from the rocker fingers. It is advisable to store the tappets (in the correct order) upright in an oil bath whilst they are removed from the engine. Make a note of the position of each tappet, as they must be refitted in their original locations on reassembly.

Inspection

5 Check the cylinder head bore contact surfaces and the hydraulic tappets for signs of scoring or damage. Also, check that the oil holes in the tappets are free from obstructions. If significant scoring or damage is found, it may be necessary to renew the cylinder head and the complete set of tappets.

6 Check the valve, tappet and camshaft contact faces of the rockers for wear or damage, and also check the rockers for

10.1 Inspect the lobes of the camshafts

any signs of cracking. Renew any worn or damaged rockers.

7 Inspect the camshaft, as described in Section 10.

Refitting

8 Smear some clean engine oil onto the sides of the hydraulic tappets, and offer them into position in their original bores in the cylinder head. Push them down until they are seated correctly and lubricate the upper surface of the tappet.

9 Oil the rocker contact faces of the tappets, and the tops of the valve stems, then refit the rockers to their original locations, ensuring that the rockers are securely clipped onto the tappets.

10 Lubricate the camshaft lobe contact surfaces and refit the camshaft housing as described in Section 9.

12 Cylinder head – removal, inspection and refitting

Note: *The cylinder head must be removed with the engine cold. New cylinder head bolts and a new cylinder head gasket will be required on refitting.*

Removal

1 Disconnect the battery as described in Chapter 5A Section 3.

2 Drain the cooling system as described in Chapter 1A Section 32 and then remove the coolant hoses from the coolant pump.

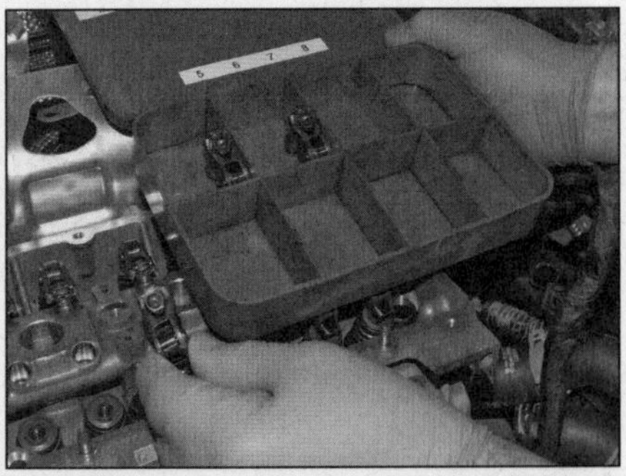

11.3 Lift out the tappets and rocker fingers

3 Remove the timing belt from the camshaft sprockets as described in Section 6. There is no need to completely remove the belt at this point, so the engine mounting bracket can be left in place, however the single bracket to cylinder head bolt must be removed **(see illustration)**.

4 Remove the camshaft housing as described in Section 9 and then remove the hydraulic tappets and rocker fingers. Store them in the correct cylinder order.

5 On MPI engines, remove the inlet manifold complete with the fuel injectors as described in Chapter 4A Section 9. On TSI engines remove the manifold, but the fuel rail can be left on the cylinder head (or removed).

6 Disconnect the wiring plugs from the fuel injectors, the fuel pressure sensor and the oil pressure sensor. If the cylinder head is to reworked, then remove the fuel rail and injectors at this point (TSI engines only). Alternatively remove the cylinder head complete with the fuel rail and fuel pump.

7 Jack up and support the front of the vehicle (see *Jacking and vehicle support*).

8 On MPI models remove the catalytic converter support bracket, remove the nuts securing the converter to the cylinder head and pull the converter off the studs.

9 On TSI models, release the clamp from the catalytic converter, remove the converter support bracket and separate the converter from the turbocharger. The turbocharger can be removed with the cylinder head if required. Secure the converter to the bulkhead with cable ties and remove the heat shield **(see illustrations)**.

12.3 Remove the bolt

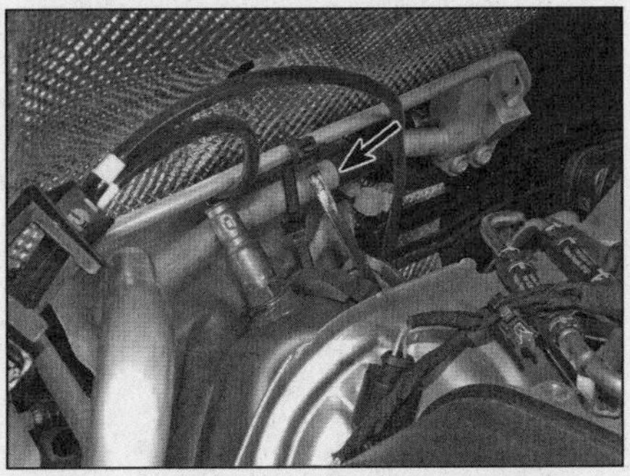

12.9a Secure the converter to the bulkhead...

12.9b ...and remove the heat shield

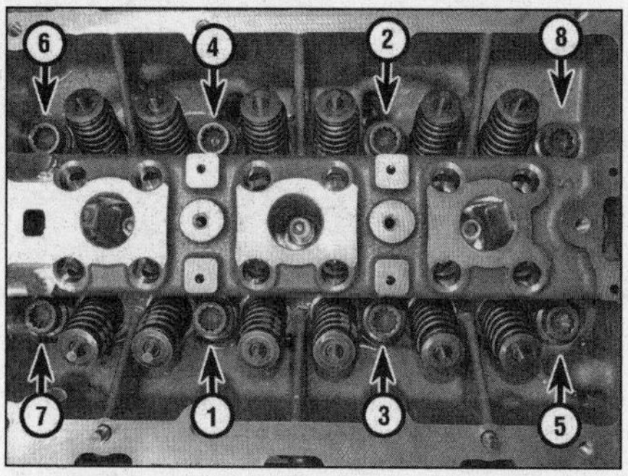

12.27 Tighten the bolts in sequence

10 Anticipating some oil spillage, disconnect the oil supply and oil return pipes from the turbocharger.

11 Disconnect the wiring plugs from the turbocharger control module (TSI engines) and from the coolant temperature sensor.

12 Progressively slacken the cylinder head bolts, by one turn at a time, in the reverse order to that shown **(see illustration 12.27)**. Remove the cylinder head bolts and dispose of them – new bolts must be fitted.

13 With all the bolts removed, lift the cylinder head from the block, together with the turbocharger (where fitted or if not removed). If the cylinder head is stuck, tap it with a soft-faced mallet to break the joint. **Do not** insert a lever into the gasket joint.

14 Lift the cylinder head gasket from the block.

Inspection

15 Dismantling and inspection of the cylinder head is covered in Chapter 2F Section 6.

Refitting

16 The mating faces of the cylinder head and block must be perfectly clean before refitting the head.

17 Use a scraper to remove all traces of gasket and carbon, also clean the tops of the pistons. Take particular care with the aluminium surfaces, as the soft metal is easily damaged.

18 Make sure that debris is not allowed to enter the oil and water passages – this is particularly important for the oil circuit, as carbon could block the oil supply to the camshaft and crankshaft bearings. Using adhesive tape and paper, seal the water, oil and bolt holes in the cylinder block. To prevent carbon entering the gap between the pistons and bores, smear a little grease in the gap. After cleaning a piston, rotate the crankshaft so that the piston moves down the bore, then wipe out the grease and carbon with a cloth rag. Clean the other piston crowns in the same way.

19 Check the head and block for nicks, deep scratches and other damage. If slight, they may be removed carefully with a file. More serious damage may be repaired by machining, but this is a specialist job.

20 If warpage of the cylinder head is suspected, use a straight-edge to check it for distortion, as described in Part F of this Chapter.

21 Ensure that the cylinder head bolt holes in the crankcase are clean and free of oil. Syringe or soak up any oil left in the bolt holes. This is most important in order that the correct bolt tightening torque can be applied, and to prevent the possibility of the block being cracked by hydraulic pressure when the bolts are tightened.

22 Ensure that the crankshaft has been turned to position Nos 1 and 4 pistons slightly down their bores from the TDC position (refer to timing belt refitting in Section 6). This will eliminate any risk of piston-to-valve contact as the cylinder head is refitted.

23 Where applicable, refit the turbocharger to the cylinder head with reference to Chapter 4C Section 6.

24 Ensure that the cylinder head locating dowels are in place in the cylinder block, then fit a new cylinder head gasket over the dowels, ensuring that the part number is uppermost. Where applicable, the OBEN/TOP marking should also be uppermost. Note that Seat recommend that the gasket is only removed from its packaging immediately prior to fitting.

25 Lower the cylinder head into position on the gasket, ensuring that it engages correctly over the dowels.

26 Fit the new cylinder head bolts, and screw them in as far as possible by hand.

27 Working progressively, in sequence, tighten all the cylinder head bolts to the specified Stage 1 torque **(see illustration)**.

28 Again working progressively, in sequence, tighten all the cylinder head bolts through the specified Stage 2 angle.

29 Tighten all the cylinder head bolts through the specified Stage 3 angle.

30 Finally, tighten all the cylinder head bolts, in sequence, through the specified Stage 4 angle.

31 Refit the camshaft housing as described in Section 9.

32 Refit and tension the timing belt as described in Section 7. The replacement of the timing belt is highly recommended.

33 Refit the auxiliary drivebelt as described in Chapter 1A Section 28.

34 If the fuel pump was removed (TSI models only), install the cam follower (tappet), fit a new O-ring seal and then refit the pump using new bolts (Chapter 4A Section 4). Fit a new high pressure pipe between the high pressure pump and the fuel rail.

35 On TSI engines, if the fuel rail and injectors have been removed, fit new seals to the injectors (Chapter 4A Section 4) and then refit the the fuel rail

36 Refit the inlet manifold as described in Chapter 4A Section 9.

37 On TSI engines, fill the turbocharger with fresh oil though the oil supply pipe. Reconnect the turbocharger supply pipe and return line using new seals.

38 Reconnect the catalytic converter using a new gasket and clamp (Chapter 4C Section 7).

39 Refit the spark plugs and ignition coils.

40 Reconnect all wiring plugs and coolant hoses. Secure the loom and coolant hoses to the retaining clips and brackets.

41 Refill the cooling system as described in Chapter 1A Section 32.

42 Follow the procedure described in Chapter 2F Section 19 before starting the engine.

13 Sump – removal and refitting

Note: *VAG sealant (D 176 404 A2 or equivalent) will be required to seal the sump on refitting.*

Removal

1 Apply the handbrake, then jack up the front of the vehicle and support securely on axle stands (see *Jacking and vehicle support*).

2 Where required, remove the securing screws and withdraw the engine undertray(s).

3 Drain the engine oil and remove the oil filter as described in Chapter 1A Section 6.

4 Disconnect the wiring connector from the oil level/temperature sender in the sump **(see illustration)**.

5 Unscrew and remove the bolts securing the sump to the transmission and then remove the main sump bolts. Special Seat tool T10058 (or equivalent) is essential to enable removal of the two bolts hidden inside the transmission bell housing. This tool is a long 5 mm ball end hex key **(see illustrations)** that

13.4 Disconnect the wiring connector from the oil level/temperature sender

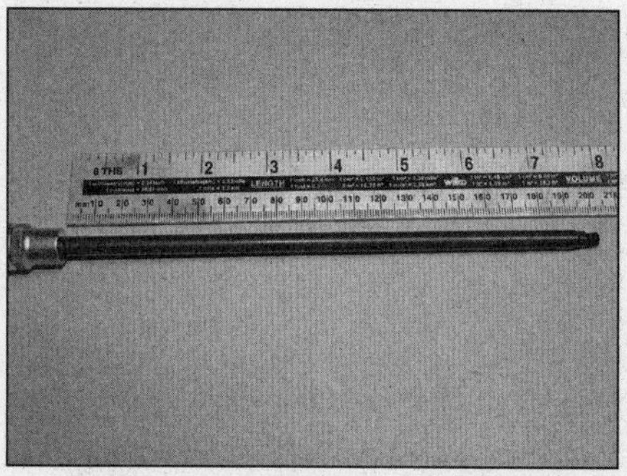

13.5a The special hex key required to...

13.5b ...access the hidden bolts (shown with transmission removed)

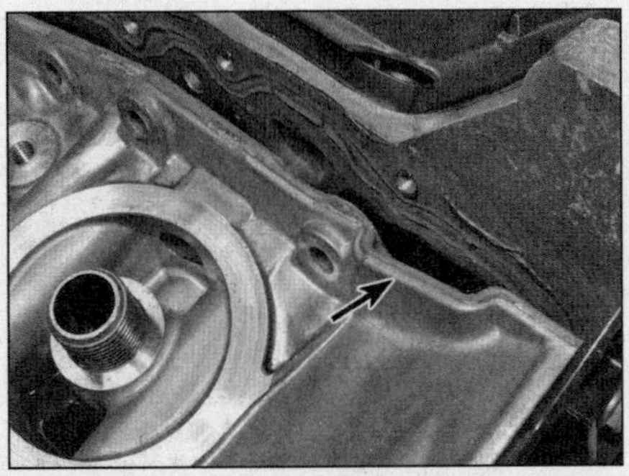

13.7 Gently prise the sump free

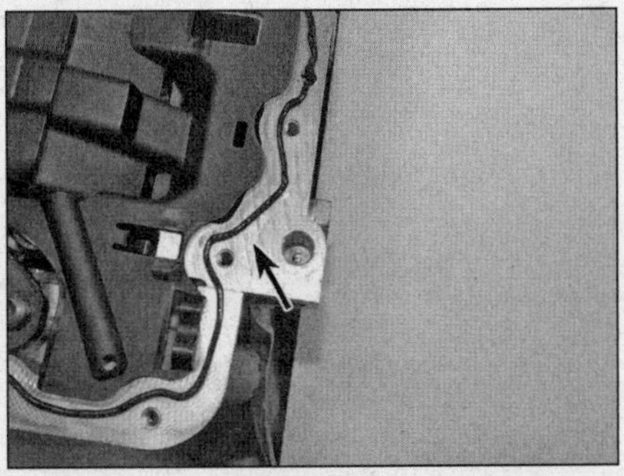

13.9 Apply the sealant around the inside of the bolt holes

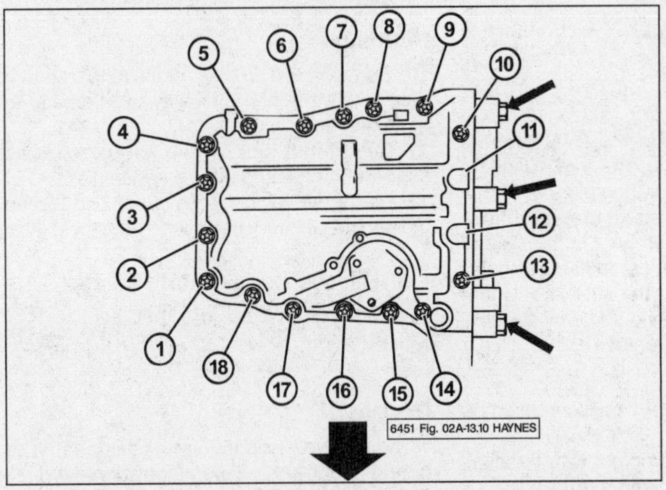

13.10 Tighten the bolts in order and then tighten the transmission to sump bolts (arrowed)

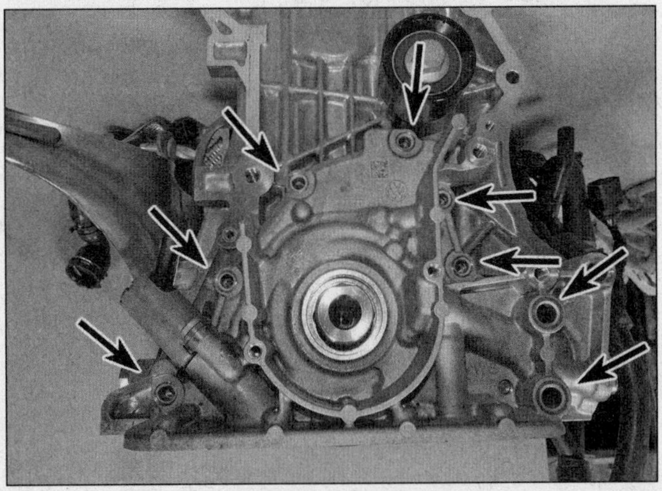

14.6 Remove the bolts

must be angled through the sump to access the partially hidden bolts.

6 The sump is bonded to the engine block with a liquid gasket. Removal can be difficult due to the adhesive nature of the sealant.

7 A levering point is provided at the rear of the engine block and this should be used to partially release the sump **(see illustration)**. As soon as comes free at any point a sharp knife can be used to further release the sealant.

Refitting

8 Begin refitting by thoroughly cleaning the mating faces of the sump and cylinder block. Ensure that all traces of old sealant are removed.

9 Ensure that the cylinder block mating face of the sump is free from all traces of old sealant, oil and grease, and then apply a 2.0 to 3.0 mm thick bead of silicone sealant (VAG D 176 404 A2 or equivalent) to the sump **(see illustration)**. Note that the sealant should be run around the inside of the bolt holes in the sump. The sump must be fitted within 5 minutes of applying the sealant.

10 If working on the sump with the engine installed, fit guide studs to the to the opposite corners of the block and then offer the sump up to the block. Fit the new bolts and tighten the bolts in sequence until contact is made **(see illustration)**. Fully tighten the bolts to the specified torque and the second stage angle setting.

11 Refit the sump to bell housing bolts, and tighten them to the specified torque.

12 Refit the wiring connector to the oil level/temperature sender, then refit the engine undertray(s), and lower the vehicle to the ground.

13 Allow at least 30 minutes from the time of refitting the sump for the sealant to dry, then refill the engine with oil, with reference to Chapter 1A Section 6.

14 Oil pump – removal and refitting

Note: *Individual parts are not available for the oil pumps. If they are worn or faulty they must be replaced as a complete assembly.*

Removal

1 Remove the timing belt as described in Section 6.

2 Remove the sump as described in Section 13.

3 Unbolt and remove the auxiliary belt tensioner.

4 Remove the alternator as described in Chapter 5A Section 5.

5 Remove the crankshaft oil seal as described in Section 18.

6 Anticipate some oil spillage by placing shop towels below the pump. Remove the oil pump mounting bolts **(see illustration)** and pull the oil pump off the dowel pins. Slide the pump off the crankshaft nose and remove it.

7 Recover the gasket **(see illustration)**.

Refitting

8 Clean and inspect the mounting surface and then fit a new gasket. Locate the gasket over the dowel pins.

9 Rotate the pump, so that the notches in the

14.7 Remove the gasket

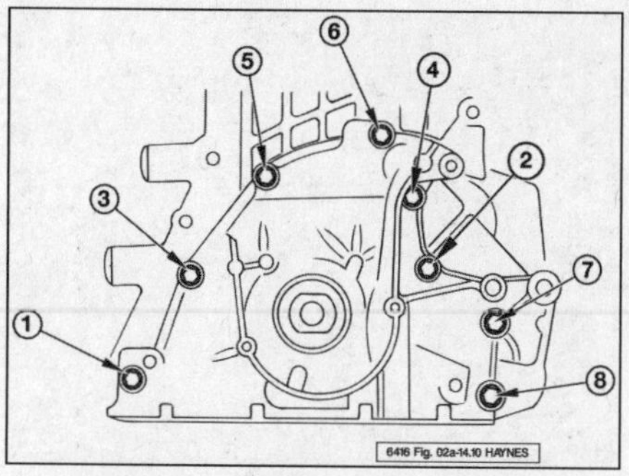

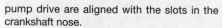

14.10 Tighten the bolts 1-6 to the specified torque and angle and then tighten bolts 7 and 8 to the specified torque

pump drive are aligned with the slots in the crankshaft nose.

10 Fit the pump and secure it in place with new bolts.Tighten the bolts in the correct order to the specified torque. Note that the outer spline head bolts have a torque and angle setting and must be replaced **(see illustration)**.

11 Fit a new crankshaft oil seal as described in Section 18. Do not be tempted to fit the oil seal with the pump off the engine. It will be damaged when refitted due to the lip on the crankshaft nose.

12 Install the sump (Section 13) and the alternator (Chapter 5A Section 5) and then fit the remaining components in the reverse order to removal.

15 Oil pressure switch and oil pressure control valve – removal and refitting

Note: *MPI engines have a pressure regulating valve in the oil pump. The valve is not replaceable. Pressure is constantly regulated to 3.5 Bar. TSI engines have variable oil pressure, adaptable according to engine load and speed. Both engines have a single oil pressure switch fitted below the inlet manifold. TSI engines have an oil pressure regulating valve mounted low on the rear of the engine block.*

Note: *Seat insist that the oil pressure switches must be replaced if removed.*

16.1 Oil level/temperature sender – located in the base of the sump

15.2 Oil pressure switch (shown with inlet manifold removed)

Oil pressure switch and control valve

Removal

1 On MPI engines unclip the EVAP control solenoid from the side of the inlet manifold and then disconnect the wiring plug.

2 On TSI engines remove the alternator as described in Chapter 5A Section 5 and disconnect the wiring plug **(see illustration)**.

3 On MPI engines cover the alternator with a shop towel and anticipating some oil spillage, unscrew the switch and remove it.

Refitting

4 Dispose of the switch – a new one must be fitted.

5 Fit the new switch, complete with the seal, and tighten it to the specified torque.

6 Reconnect the wiring and refit the other components. If raised, lower the vehicle, then check and top-up the engine oil if required.

Oil pressure control valve

Note: *Only fitted to TSI engines.*

Removal

7 Jack up and support the front of the vehicle – see *Jacking and vehicle support*.

8 Remove the engine undershield (where fitted) and then unbolt the catalytic converter support bracket.

9 Disconnect the wiring plug and remove the fixing bolt **(see illustration)**. Anticipating some oil spillage pull the valve from the housing in the engine block.

17.3 Remove the bolts

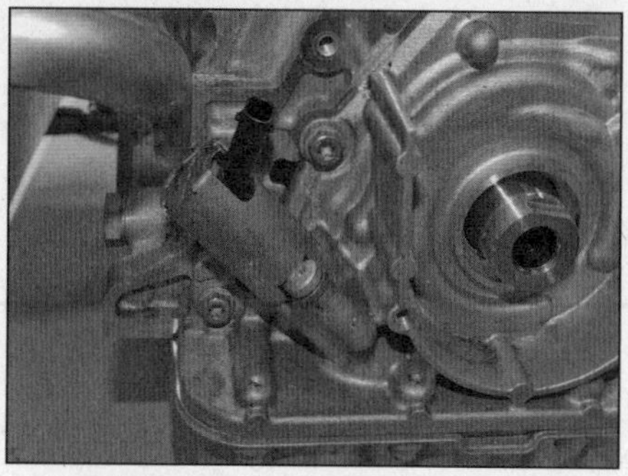

15.9 The oil pressure control valve

Refitting

10 Remove the O-ring seals and replace them. Refit the control valve and tighten the mounting bolt.

11 Reconnect the wiring plug, refit the support bracket and engine undershield.

12 Lower the vehicle, then check and top-up the engine oil if required.

16 Oil level/temperature sender – removal and refitting

Removal

1 The oil level/temperature sender is fitted to bottom of the sump **(see illustration)**.

2 Drain the engine oil as described in Chapter 1A Section 6.

3 Disconnect the wiring connector and wipe clean the area around the sender.

4 Undo the three retaining bolts and remove the sender.

Refitting

5 Examine the sealing washer for signs of damage or deterioration and if necessary renew.

6 Refit the sender and tighten the retaining bolts to the specified torque.

7 Securely reconnect the wiring connector then refill the engine with oil, with reference to Chapter 1A Section 6.

8 On completion, check and, if necessary, top-up the engine oil as described in *Weekly checks*.

17 Engine oil cooler – removal and refitting

Removal

1 Where fitted the oil cooler is mounted at the front of the engine block, hidden by the inlet manifold.

2 Drain the coolant and remove the inlet manifold as described in Chapter 4A Section 9.

3 Anticipating some spillage, remove the bolts **(see illustration)** and lift off the oil cooler. Recover the O-ring seals.

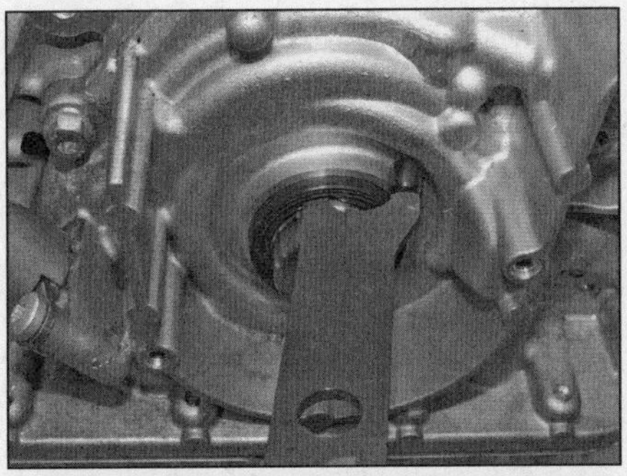

18.2 Remove the seal with the special tool

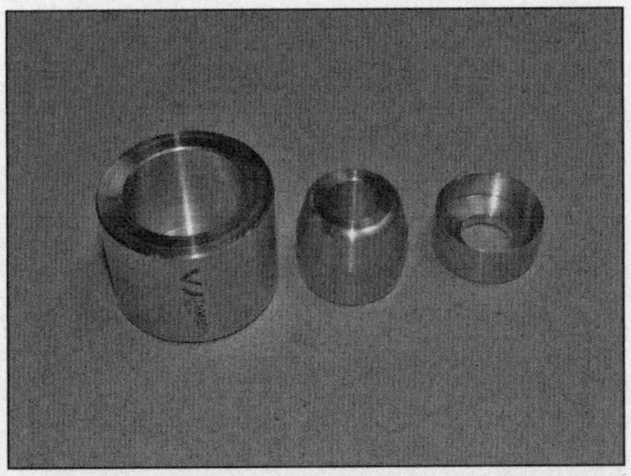

18.4a The component parts of the special tool

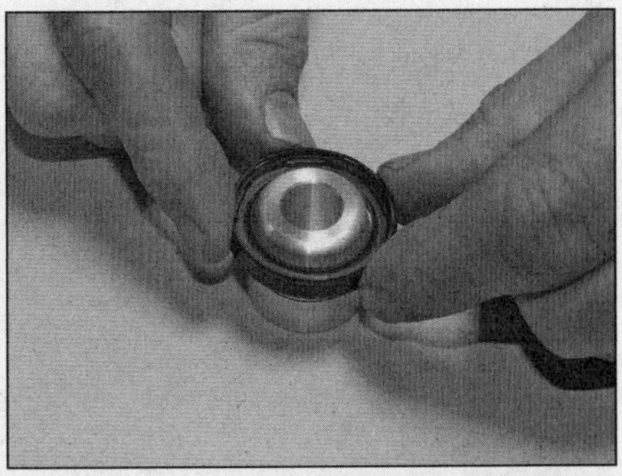

18.4b Fit the new seal onto the assembly sleeve...

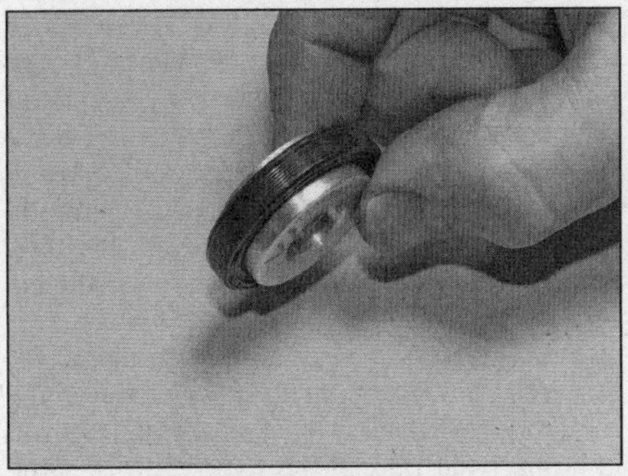

18.4c ...and slide it onto the installation sleeve

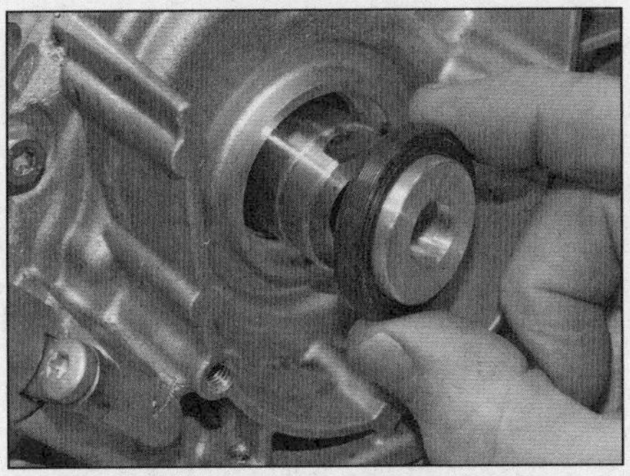

18.4d Fit the sleeve to the crankshaft nose...

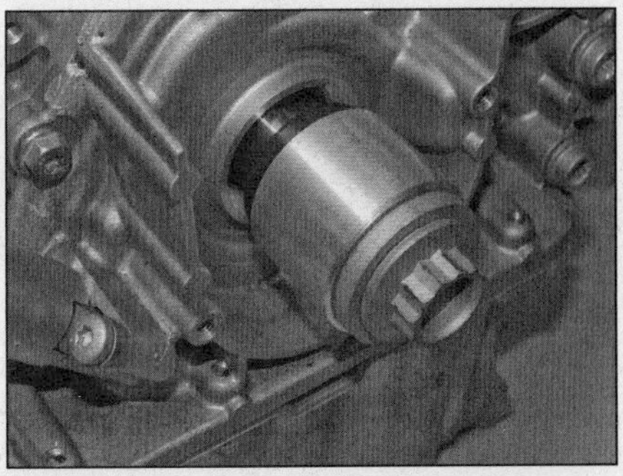

18.4e ...and install the thrust sleeve using the old crankshaft pulley bolt. Push the new seal onto the crankshaft by tightening the bolt

Refitting

4 Refitting is a reversal of removal, bearing in mind the following points:

a) Use new seals.
b) Use new bolts.

18 Crankshaft oil seals – renewal

Note: *The oil seals are a PTFE (Teflon) type and are fitted dry, without using any grease or oil. These have a wider sealing lip and have been introduced instead of the coil spring type oil seal.*

Timing belt end oil seal

Note: *The seal is a teflon type seal and must be installed dry. Do not oil the seal or crankshaft nose before installing.*

1 Remove the timing belt as described in Section 7, and the crankshaft sprocket with reference to Section 7.

2 The seal must be removed using the special Seat tool (T21043/1) or equivalent **(see illustration and see illustration 8.0a)**. Using any other may damage the nose of the crankshaft and is not recommended.

3 Thoroughly clean the oil seal seating in the housing or oil pump.

4 Note that Seat list a seal installer tool (T10485) and (because of the sharp lip on the crankshaft nose) this should be used **(see illustrations)**.

5 Note that the special tool will align the new seal correctly and set to the correct deopth.

6 Refit the crankshaft sprocket, timing belt and crankshaft pulley.

Flywheel end oil seal

Note: *In these engines, the seal, sealing flange and sender wheel are a complete unit. Special tools are required to refit the sealing flange, and press the sender wheel onto the end of the crankshaft. It is not possible to accurately fit these parts without the tools, which are available from Seat (part no. T10134) and may be available from aftermarket automotive tool specialists. E.g. Draper or AST tools.*

7 Remove the flywheel as described in Section 19, then prise the intermediate plate from the locating dowels on the cylinder block and unhook it from behind the top of the seal housing **(see illustrations)**.

8 Undo the bolt securing the crankshaft speed sensor and remove it from the seal housing, then undo the bolts securing the sealing flange to the cylinder block **(see illustrations)**.

18.7a Remove the intermediate plate from the dowels ...

18.7b ... and from behind the top of the crankshaft seal housing

18.8a Undo the crankshaft speed sensor retaining bolt

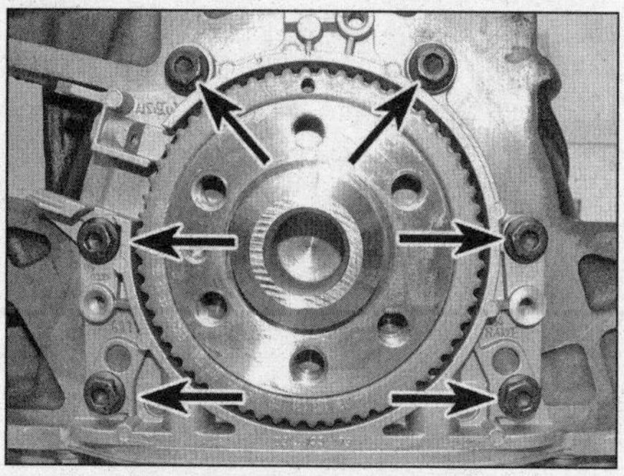

18.8b Sealing flange bolts

18.9a Screw in three 6 x 35 mm bolts ...

18.9b ...and draw the sealing flange and sender wheel from place

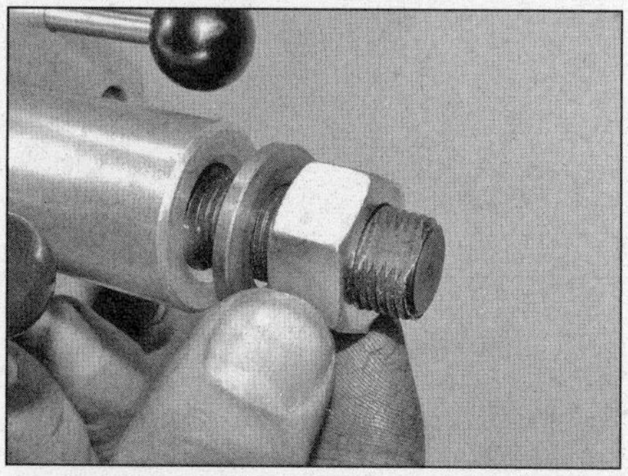

18.11a Rotate the nut until its level with the end of the flat clamping surface...

18.11b ...then clamp it in a vice

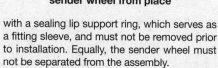

9 Insert three 6 x 35 mm bolts into the threaded holes in the sealing flange. Tighten the bolts gradually and evenly, and press the sealing flange, and sender wheel from the crankshaft/cylinder block **(see illustrations)**. The seal, sender wheel and sealing flange are supplied as a complete unit.

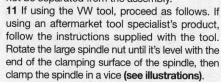

10 Ensure the mating face of the cylinder block is clean and free from debris. The new sealing flange/seal/sender wheel assembly is supplied with a sealing lip support ring, which serves as a fitting sleeve, and must not be removed prior to installation. Equally, the sender wheel must not be separated from the assembly.

11 If using the VW tool, proceed as follows. If using an aftermarket tool specialist's product, follow the instructions supplied with the tool. Rotate the large spindle nut until it's level with the end of the clamping surface of the spindle, then clamp the spindle in a vice **(see illustrations)**.

12 Press the tool housing downwards until it rests on the nut and washer. Rotate the nut until the inner part of the tool is at the same height as the housing **(see illustrations)**.

13 Remove the seal securing clip. The hole on the sender wheel must align with the marking on the sealing flange **(see illustrations)**.

14 Place the flange outer side down on a clean, flat surface, then press the seal guide fitting sleeve (supplied ready fitted), housing, and sender wheel downwards until all the

18.12a Rotate the nut until the inner part of the tool ...

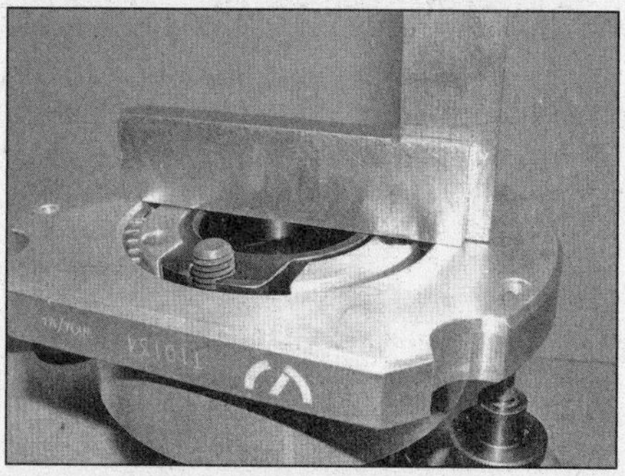

18.12b ...is flush with the flat surface of the housing

18.13a Remove the securing clip ...

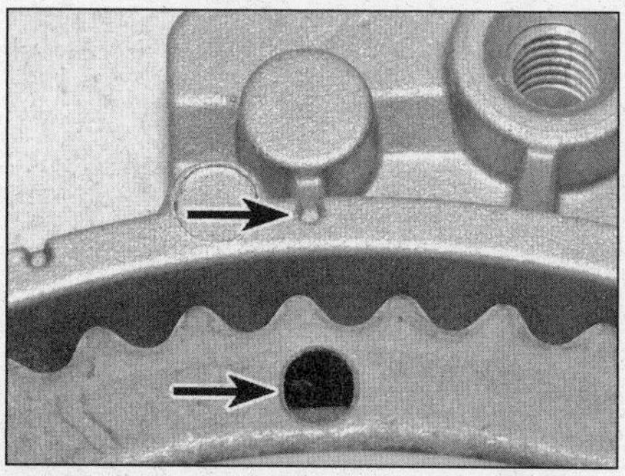

18.13b ...the hole in the sender wheel should align with the marking on the flange

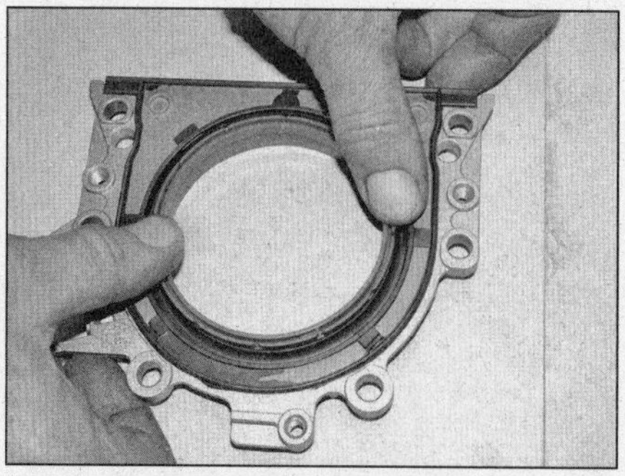

18.14a Press the assembly downwards on a clean, flat surface...

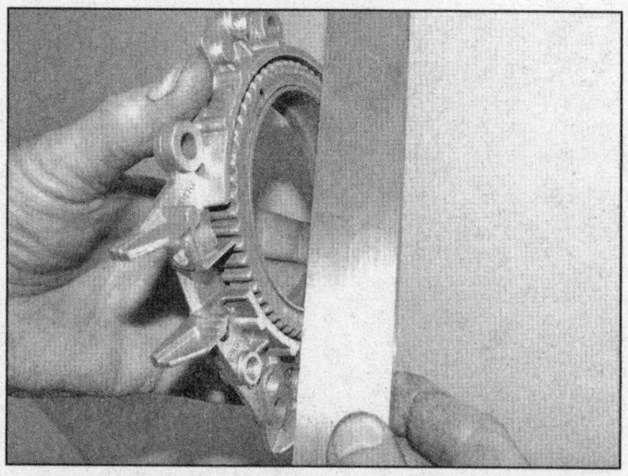

18.14b ...so the upper edge of the sender wheel is level with the edge of the flange

components are flat on the surface. In this position the upper edge of the sender wheel should be level with the edge of the sealing flange **(see illustrations)**.

15 Place the sealing flange on the assembly tool, so the pin locates in the hole in the sender wheel **(see illustration)**.

16 Push the sealing flange and guide fitting sleeve against the tool whilst tightening the 3 knurled screws. Ensure the pin is still located in the sender wheel **(see illustration)**.

17 Ensure the end of the crankshaft is clean, and is locked at TDC on No. 1 cylinder as described in Section 3.

18 Unscrew the large nut to the end of the spindle threads, then press the spindle inwards as far as possible **(see illustrations)**.

19 Align the flat side of the assembly with the sump flange, then secure the tool to the crankshaft using the integral Allen bolts **(see illustration)**. Only hand tighten the bolts.

20 Insert two M7x 35 mm bolts to guide the sealing flange to the cylinder block **(see illustration)**.

21 Using hand pressure alone, push the tool assembly onto the crankshaft until the seal guide fitting sleeve contacts the crankshaft flange, then push the guide pin (black knob) into the hole in the crankshaft. This is to ensure the sender wheel reaches its correct installation position **(see illustration)**.

22 Rotate the large nut until it makes contact with the tool housing, then tighten it to 35 Nm. After tightening this nut, a small air gap must still be present between the sealing flange and cylinder block **(see illustrations)**.

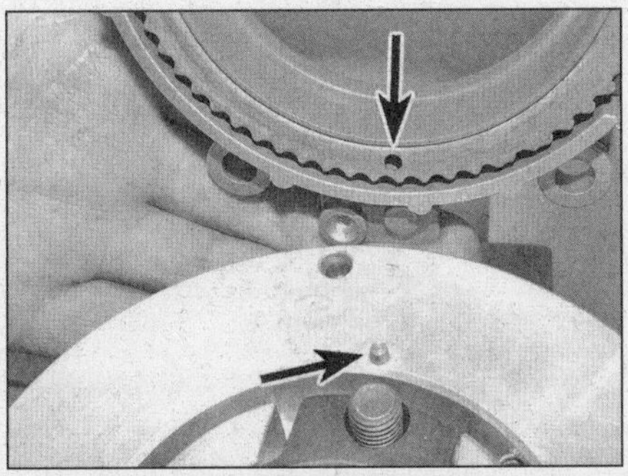

18.15 Fit the flange to the tool, ensuring the pin locates in the hole

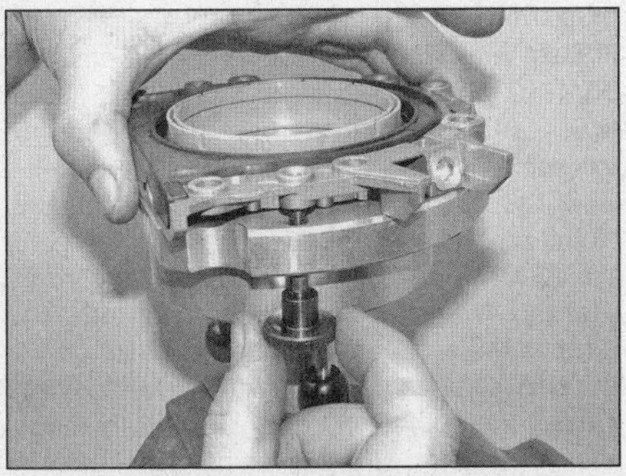

18.16 With the pin engaged in the hole, tighten the 3 knurled screws to secure the flange to the tool

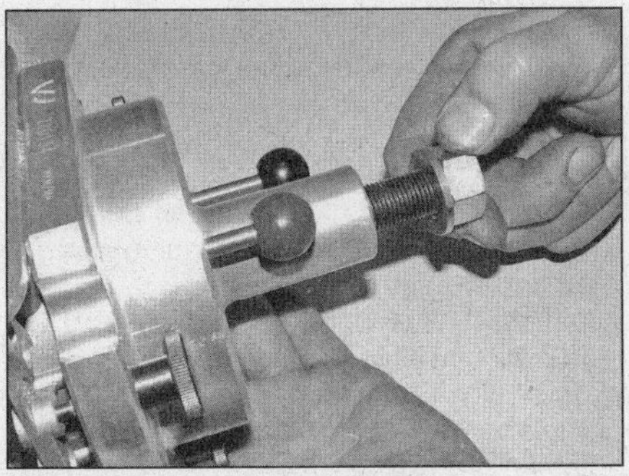

18.18a Unscrew the nut to the end of the thread ...

18.18b ...and push the spindle in as far as possible

23 Unscrew the large nut; the two M7 x 35mm screws, the three knurled screws and the Allen bolts securing the tool to the crankshaft. Remove the tool, and pull the seal guide fitting sleeve from place (if it didn't come out with the tool) **(see illustration)**.

24 Use a vernier caliper or feeler gauge to measure the fitted depth of the sender wheel

18.19 Hand-tighten the hex bolts to secure the tool to the crankshaft

18.20 Use two M7 x 35 mm bolts to guide the sealing flange

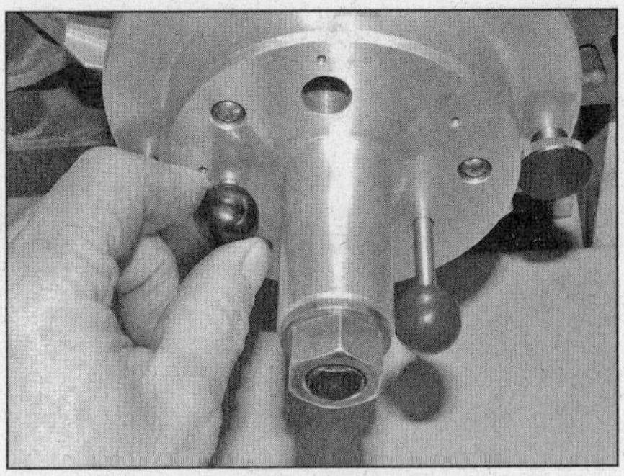

18.21 Push the black knob into the hole in the crankshaft

18.22a After tightening the spindle nut to 35 Nm ...

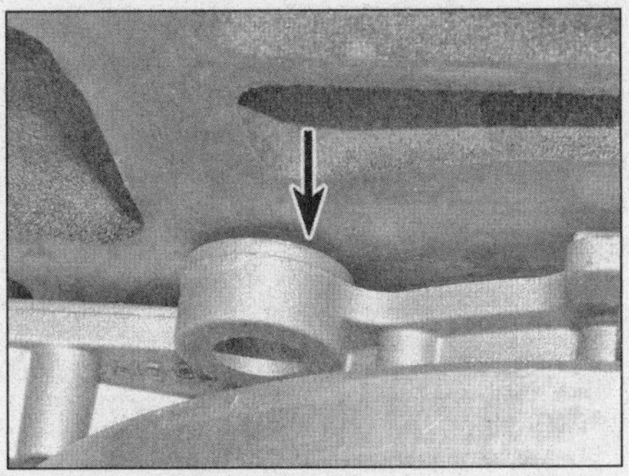

18.22b ...there should be an air gap between the sealing flange and the cylinder block

18.23 Remove the tool and seal fitting guide sleeve

in relation to the crankshaft flange **(see illustration)**. The correct depth is 0.5 mm.

25 If the gap is correct, fit the sealing flange bolts and tighten them to the specified torque.

26 If the gap is too small, re-attach the tool to the sealing flange and crankshaft, then refit the two M7 x 35 mm screws to the flange. Tighten the large spindle nut to 40 Nm, remove the tool and re-measure the air gap. If the gap is still too small, re-attach the tool and tighten the spindle nut to 45 Nm. Re-measure the gap. When the gap is correct, refit the flange retaining bolts, and tighten them to the specified torque.

27 The remainder of refitting is a reversal of removal.

18.24 Measure the fitted depth of the sender wheel in relation to the end of the crankshaft

19 Flywheel – removal, inspection and refitting

Note: *New flywheel securing bolts will be required on refitting.*

Removal

1 Remove the gearbox (see Chapter 7A Section 3 or Chapter 7B Section 2) and where fitted the clutch (Chapter 6A Section 6).

2 The flywheel bolts are offset to ensure correct fitment. Unscrew the bolts while holding the flywheel stationary. Temporarily insert a bolt in the cylinder block, and use a screwdriver to hold the flywheel or make up a holding tool **(see illustrations)**.

3 Lift the flywheel from the crankshaft **(see illustration)**.

Inspection

4 Check the flywheel for wear and damage. Examine the starter ring gear for excessive wear to the teeth. If any wear is found the complete flywheel must be replaced. If the clutch friction face is discoloured or scored excessively, it may be possible to regrind it, but this work should also be entrusted to an automotive machine shop.

5 Where a dual mass flywheel is fitted the following guidelines may help decide if replacement is required. If in doubt, a professional inspection is recommended. The dual-mass flywheel should be checked as follows:

Warpage

6 Place a straight edge across the face of the drive surface, and check by trying to insert a feeler gauge between the straight edge and the drive surface **(see illustration)**. The flywheel will normally warp like a bowl – ie. Higher on the outer edge. If the warpage is more than 0.40 mm, the flywheel may need replacing.

Free rotational movement

7 This is the distance the drive surface of the flywheel can be turned independently of the flywheel primary element, using finger effort alone. Move the drive surface in one direction and make a mark where the locating pin aligns with the flywheel edge. Move the drive surface in the other direction (finger pressure only) and make another mark **(see illustration)**. The total of free movement should not exceed 20.0 mm. If it's more, the flywheel may need replacing.

Total rotational movement

8 This is the total distance the drive surface can be turned independently of the flywheel primary element. Insert two bolts into the clutch pressure plate/damper unit mounting holes, and with the crankshaft/flywheel held stationary, use a lever/pry bar between the bolts and use some effort to move the drive surface fully in one direction – make a mark where the locating pin aligns with the flywheel edge. Now force the drive surface fully in the opposite direction, and make another mark. The total rotational movement should not exceed 44.00 mm. If it does, have the flywheel professionally inspected.

Lateral movement

9 The lateral movement (up and down) of the drive surface in relation to the primary element of the flywheel, should not exceed 2.0 mm. If it does, the flywheel may need replacing. This can be checked by pressing the drive surface down on one side into the flywheel (flywheel horizontal) and making an alignment mark between the drive surface and the inner edge of the primary element. Now press down on the opposite side of the drive surface, and make another mark above the original one. The difference between the two marks is the lateral movement **(see illustration)**.

19.2a Tool used to hold the flywheel stationary

19.2b Unscrew the securing bolts (dual mass version shown)...

19.3 ...and remove the flywheel

19.6 Flywheel warpage check – see text

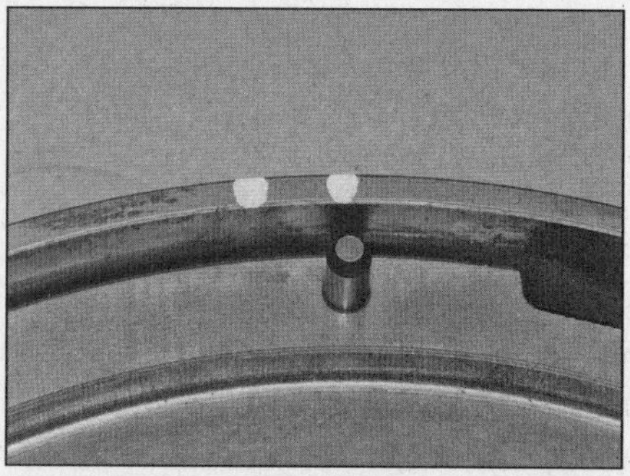

19.7 Flywheel free rotational movement check alignment marks – see text

10 There should be no cracks in the drive surface of the flywheel. If cracks are evident, the flywheel will need replacing.

Refitting

11 Refitting is a reversal of removal, bearing in mind the following points.
a) Ensure that the engine to transmission plate is in place before fitting the flywheel.
b) Use new bolts when refitting the flywheel and coat the threads of the bolts with locking fluid before inserting them. Tighten the securing bolts to the specified torque.

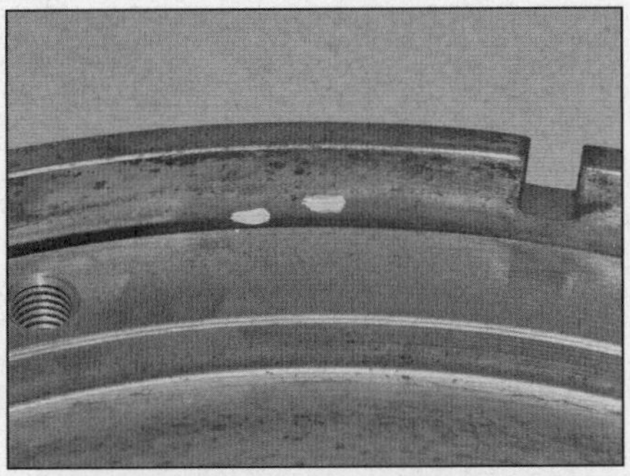

19.9 Flywheel lateral movement check marks – see text

20 Engine mountings – inspection and renewal

Inspection

1 If improved access is required, jack up the front of the vehicle, and support it securely on axle stands (see *Jacking and vehicle support*). Where fitted, remove the engine undershield.

2 Check the mounting rubbers to see if they are cracked, hardened or separated from the metal at any point; renew the mounting if any such damage or deterioration is evident.

3 Check that all the mountings are securely tightened; use a torque wrench to check if possible.

4 Using a large screwdriver or a crowbar, check for wear in the mounting by carefully levering against it to check for free play. Where this is not possible, enlist the aid of an assistant to move the engine/transmission back-and-forth, or from side-to-side, whilst you observe the mounting. While some free play is to be expected, even from new components, excessive wear should be obvious. If excessive free play is found, check first that the fasteners are correctly secured, then renew any worn components as described in the following paragraphs.

Renewal

Right-hand mounting

Note: *Two versions of the right-hand mount are fitted, Removal and refitting is essentially the same for both versions.*

5 Support the engine on a trolley jack under the sump. Use a block of wood between the sump and the head of the jack, to prevent any damage to the sump.

6 On MPI engines remove the air filter housing as described in Chapter 4A Section 3.

7 Where required, unclip the fuel lines from the coolant reservoir/timing belt cover. There is no need to disconnect the fuel lines.

8 Disconnect the level sensor wiring plug and remove the screws from the coolant reservoir **(see illustration)**.

9 Unbolt the coolant reservoir and move it to one side.

Note: *On models fitted with a single central nut holding the mounting together DO NOT remove the nut. The mounting must be removed as a complete assembly.*

10 Where fitted unbolt the earth cable and then unscrew the bolts securing the mounting to the body. Unscrew the bolts securing the mounting to the engine bracket. Withdraw the mounting from the engine compartment **(see illustrations)**.

11 Refitting is a reversal of removal, bearing in mind the following points.
a) Use new bolts.
b) Align the mounting so that it is not twisted. On mounts with a single central nut centralise the mounting with the holes in the bodywork.
c) Tighten all fixings to the specified torque.

Left-hand mounting

Note: *New mounting bolts will be required on refitting.*

12 Support the transmission on a trolley jack with a block of wood placed between the head of the jack and the transmission to spread the load.

13 Disconnect the battery, remove the battery and battery tray as described in Chapter 5A Section 3.

14 Where required, release the wiring loom and move it to the side to gain access to the mounting bolts.

15 Remove the mounting to body bolts and then remove the bolts securing the mounting to the transmission bracket **(see illustration)**.

16 Lift out the mounting and then where required, unbolt and remove the bracket from the transmission **(see illustration)**. Removal of the bracket is essential for transmission removal.

17 Refitting is a reversal of removal, bearing in mind the following points:
a) Use new mounting bolts.
b) Tighten all fixings to the specified torque.

20.8 Disconnect the level sensor wiring plug and remove the screws

20.10a Remove the earth cable

20.10b Remove the bolts and lift out the mounting

20.15 Remove the bolts

20.16 Remove the bracket from the transmission

20.19 Remove the bolts

20.20 Remove the mounting

Rear mounting (torque arm)

Note: *The bolt between the bracket (at the transmission) and the pendulum mount should not be removed*.

18 Apply the handbrake, then jack up the front of the vehicle and support securely on axle stands (see *Jacking and vehicle support*). Where fitted remove the engine undershield.

19 Working under the vehicle, unscrew and remove the bolts securing the mounting to the transmission **(see illustration)**.

20 Unscrew the bolt securing the mounting to the subframe. Remove the mounting from under the vehicle **(see illustration)**.

21 Refitting is a reversal of removal, but use new mounting securing bolts, and tighten all fixings to the specified torque.

Chapter 2 Part B
1.2 litre (SOHC) petrol engine in-car repair procedures

Contents

Degrees of difficulty

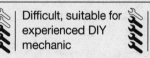

Easy, suitable for novice with little experience	Fairly easy, suitable for beginner with some experience	Fairly difficult, suitable for competent DIY mechanic	Difficult, suitable for experienced DIY mechanic	Very difficult, suitable for expert DIY or professional

Specifications

General

Type	Four-cylinder in-line, chain-driven single overhead camshaft (SOHC), four stroke, 8-valve, liquid-cooled
Cubic capacity	1197 cc
Manufacturer's engine code*	CBZB
Maximum power output	77 kW @ 5000 rpm
Maximum torque output	175 Nm @ 1550-4100 rpm
Bore	71.0 mm
Stroke	75.6 mm
Compression ratio	10 : 1
Compression pressures (oil temperature 30°C minimum):	
New	10.0 to 15.0 bars
Minimum	7.0 bars
Maximum difference between cylinders	3.0 bars
Firing order	1 – 3 – 4 – 2
No 1 cylinder location	Crankshaft pulley end
Direction of crankshaft rotation	Clockwise (when viewed from right-hand side of car)

**See 'Vehicle identification' at the end of this manual for the location of the engine code markings.*

Camshafts

Camshaft endfloat (maximum)	0.4 mm
Camshaft bearing running clearance	No figure specified
Camshaft run-out	No figure specified

Lubrication system

Oil pump type	Gear type, driven by chain from the crankshaft
Oil pressure (oil temperature 80°C):	
Minimum @ idling	0.3 to 0.7 bar
Minimum @ 2000 rpm	2.0 bar
Maximum @ high rpm	7.0 bar

Torque wrench settings	Nm	lbf ft
Air conditioning compressor bolts	25	18
Alternator	25	18
Ancillary (alternator, etc) bracket mounting bolts	25	18
Auxiliary drivebelt guide pulley bolt	40	30
Auxiliary drivebelt tensioner securing bolt:		
Stage 1	40	30
Stage 2	Angle-tighten a further 90°	
Big-end bearing caps bolts*:		
Stage 1	30	22
Stage 2	Angle-tighten a further 90°	
Camshaft bearing frame screws	8	5
Camshaft carrier-to cylinder head bolts*:		
Stage 1	8	5
Stage 2	Angle-tighten a further 90°	
Camshaft sprocket bolt*:		
Stage 1	50	37
Stage 2	Angle-tighten a further 90°	
Coolant pump bolts	9	7
Coolant pump pulley bolts	20	15
Crankcase breather (oil separator) bolts	10	7
Crankshaft oil seal housing bolts	12	9
Crankshaft pulley/sprocket bolt*:		
Stage 1	150	111
Stage 2	Angle-tighten a further 180°	
Cylinder block screw plug	30	22
Cylinder head bolts*:		
Stage 1	40	30
Stage 2	Angle-tighten a further 90°	
Stage 3	Angle-tighten a further 90°	
Engine/transmission left-hand mounting to transmission*:		
Stage 1	40	30
Stage 2	Angle-tighten a further 90°	
Engine/transmission left-hand mounting to body*:		
Stage 1	50	37
Stage 2	Angle-tighten a further 90°	
Engine/transmission rear mounting bracket to transmission*:		
Stage 1	30	22
Stage 2	Angle-tighten a further 90°	
Engine/transmission rear mounting link to subframe*:		
Stage 1	40	30
Stage 2	Angle-tighten a further 90°	
Engine/transmission right-hand mounting to engine*:		
Stage 1	30	22
Stage 2	Angle-tighten a further 90°	
Engine/transmission right-hand mounting to body*:		
Stage 1	20	15
Stage 2	Angle-tighten a further 90°	
Engine-to-transmission bolts:		
M10 bolts	40	30
M12 bolts	80	59
Exhaust manifold nuts	25	18
Exhaust pipe-to-manifold nuts	25	18
Flywheel/driveplate bolts*:		
Stage 1	60	44
Stage 2	Angle-tighten a further 90°	
Knock sensor	20	15
Oil cooler securing nut	25	18
Oil drain plug	30	22
Oil level/temperature sensor-to-sump bolts	10	7
Oil pick-up pipe securing bolts	10	7
Oil pressure warning light switch	20	15
Oil pump securing bolts*:		
Stage 1	14	11
Stage 2	Angle-tighten a further 90°	
Oil pump sprocket securing bolt:		
Stage 1	20	15
Stage 2	Angle-tighten a further 90°	

Torque wrench settings (continued)

	Nm	lbf ft
Sump:		
Sump-to-cylinder block	13	10
Sump-to-transmission bolts	40	30
Timing chain guide rail bolts	18	13
Timing chain lower (aluminium) cover bolts:		
Stage 1	5	3
Stage 2	Angle-tighten a further 30°	
Timing chain upper (plastic) cover bolts:		
Stage 1	5	3
Stage 2	8	5
Timing chain tensioner	60	44

**Use new fasteners*

1 General Information

Using this Chapter

1 This Part of Chapter 2 describes those repair procedures that can reasonably be carried out on the engine while it remains in the car. If the engine has been removed from the car and is being dismantled as described in Part F, any preliminary dismantling procedures can be ignored.

2 Note that while it may be possible physically to overhaul items such as the piston/connecting rod assemblies while the engine is in the car, such tasks are not usually carried out as separate operations, and usually require the execution of several additional procedures (not to mention the cleaning of components and of oil ways); for this reason, all such tasks are classed as major overhaul procedures, and are described in Part F of this Chapter.

Caution: The crankshaft must not be removed on these engines. If the crankshaft or main bearing surfaces are worn or damaged, the complete crankshaft/cylinder block assembly must be renewed.

3 Part H describes the removal of the engine/transmission from the car and the full overhaul procedures that can then be carried out.

Engine description

4 The engine is a water-cooled, single overhead camshaft (SOHC), in-line four-cylinder unit, with an aluminium-alloy cylinder block and cylinder head. It is mounted transversely at the front of the car, with the transmission bolted to the left-hand side of the engine.

5 The crankshaft is of five-bearing type, and thrustwashers are fitted to the centre main bearing to control crankshaft endfloat. The crankshaft and main bearings are matched to the alloy cylinder block, and it is not possible to reassemble the crankshaft and cylinder block once the components have been separated. If the crankshaft or bearings are worn, the complete cylinder block/crankshaft assembly must be renewed.

6 The camshaft is driven by a chain from the crankshaft sprocket, and is located in a camshaft carrier, which is bolted to the top of the cylinder head.

7 The valves are closed by coil springs, and run in guides pressed into the cylinder head; the camshafts actuate the valves by roller rockers and hydraulic tappets. There are two valves per cylinder, one inlet valve and one exhaust valve.

8 The oil pump is driven from the end of the crankshaft by a chain. Oil is drawn from the sump through a strainer, and then forced through an externally mounted, renewable filter. From there, it is distributed to the cylinder head, where it lubricates the camshaft journals and hydraulic tappets, and also to the crankcase, where it lubricates the main bearings, connecting rod big-ends, gudgeon pins and cylinder bores.

9 Engine coolant is circulated by a pump, driven by the auxiliary belt. For details of the cooling system, refer to Chapter 3.

Repairs with engine in car

10 The following operations can be performed without removing the engine:

a) Compression pressure – testing.
b) Camshaft carrier – removal and refitting.
c) Crankshaft pulley – removal and refitting.
d) Timing chain covers – removal and refitting.
e) Timing chain – removal, refitting and adjustment.
f) Timing chain guides and sprocket – removal and refitting.
g) Camshaft oil seal(s) – renewal.
h) Camshaft and hydraulic tappets – removal, inspection and refitting.
i) Cylinder head – removal and refitting.*
j) Sump – removal and refitting.
k) Oil pump – removal, overhaul and refitting.
l) Crankshaft oil seals – renewal.
m) Engine/transmission mountings – inspection and renewal.
n) Flywheel – removal, inspection and refitting.

Note: ** Cylinder head dismantling procedures are detailed in Chapter 2F Section 6.*

2 Compression test – description and interpretation

1 When engine performance is down, or if misfiring occurs which cannot be attributed to the ignition or fuel systems, a compression test can provide diagnostic clues as to the engine's condition. If the test is performed regularly, it can give warning of trouble before any other symptoms become apparent.

2 The engine must be fully warmed-up to normal operating temperature, the battery must be fully charged and the spark plugs must be removed. The aid of an assistant will be required.

3 Disable the ignition system by disconnecting the wiring plug from the ignition coil.

4 Fit a compression tester to the No 1 cylinder spark plug hole. The type of tester that screws into the plug thread is preferred.

5 Have the assistant hold the throttle wide open and crank the engine for several seconds on the starter motor. **Note:** *The throttle will not operate until the ignition is switched on. After one or two revolutions, the compression pressure should build up to a maximum figure and then stabilise. Record the highest reading obtained.*

6 Repeat the test on the remaining cylinders, recording the pressure in each.

7 All cylinders should produce very similar pressures. Any difference greater than that specified indicates the existence of a fault. Note that the compression should build-up quickly in a healthy engine. Low compression on the first stroke, followed by gradually increasing pressure on successive strokes, indicates worn piston rings. A low compression reading on the first stroke, which does not build-up during successive strokes, indicates leaking valves or a blown head gasket (a cracked head could also be the cause). Deposits on the undersides of the valve heads can also cause low compression.

8 If the pressure in any cylinder is reduced to the specified minimum or less, carry out the following test to isolate the cause. Introduce

AST timing kit

3.8 Remove the bracket

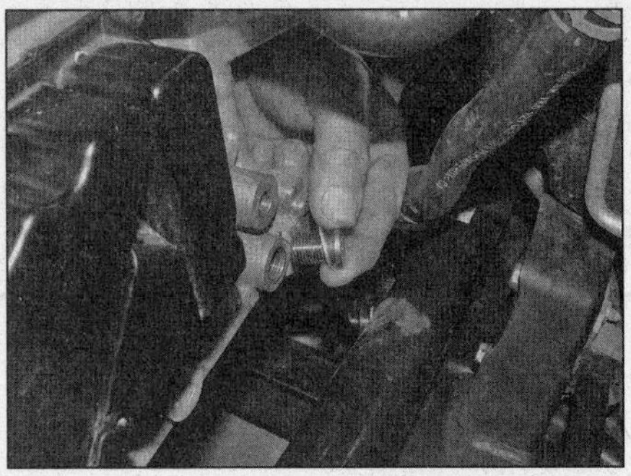
3.9a Remove the plug...

3.9b ...screw in the tool...

3.9c ...until it is fully fitted

a teaspoonful of clean oil into that cylinder through its spark plug hole and repeat the test.

9 If the addition of oil temporarily improves the compression pressure, this indicates that bore or piston wear is responsible for the pressure loss. No improvement suggests that leaking or burnt valves, or a blown head gasket, may be to blame.

10 A low reading from two adjacent cylinders is almost certainly due to the head gasket having blown between them and the presence of coolant in the engine oil will confirm this.

11 If one cylinder is about 20 percent lower than the others and the engine has a slightly rough idle; a worn camshaft lobe could be the cause.

12 On completion of the test, refit the spark plugs and reconnect the ignition wiring.

3 Engine assembly and setting the timing – general information and usage

General information

1 TDC is the highest point in the cylinder that each piston reaches as it travels up and down when the crankshaft turns. Each piston reaches TDC at the end of the compression stroke and again at the end of the exhaust stroke, but TDC generally refers to piston position on the compression stroke. No 1 piston is at the timing chain end of the engine.

2 Positioning No 1 piston at TDC is an essential part of many procedures, such as timing chain removal and camshaft removal.

3 The design of the engines covered in this Chapter is such that piston-to-valve contact may occur if the camshaft or crankshaft is turned with the timing chain removed. For this reason, it is important to ensure that the camshaft and crankshaft do not move in relation to each other once the timing chain has been removed from the engine.

Setting the timing

Note: *Locking pins will be required to lock the camshaft sprockets in position during this procedure. Seat tools T10340 and T10414 are used to lock the crankshaft and camshaft in position. Other company's such as AST can supply a timing kit for this engine **(see illustration)**.*

4 Before starting work, make sure that the battery negative lead is disconnected as described in Chapter 5A Section 3.

5 To make the engine easier to turn, remove all of the spark plugs as described in Chapter 1A Section 27

6 Apply the handbrake, then jack up the front of the car and support on axle stands (see *Jacking and vehicle support*).

7 Remove the right-hand front roadwheel, then remove the securing screws and/or clips, and remove the appropriate engine undershields to enable access to the crankshaft pulley.

8 Working down the right-hand rear of the engine, undo the retaining bolts and remove the coolant hose bracket from the cylinder block **(see illustration)**.

9 Slacken and remove the screw plug from the rear of the cylinder block. Seat special tool (T10340) can be fitted into the cylinder block until it is fully in place. If the special tool does not screw fully into place, remove tool and turn the engine through 90° in direction of engine rotation. Then refit the Seat special tool (T10340) again so that it can be screwed fully into the cylinder block, then tighten to 30Nm **(see illustrations)**.

10 Turn the crankshaft in the direction of engine rotation until the crankshaft comes to a stop, against the Seat special tool **(see illustration)**.

11 Working at the left-hand end of the cylinder head, disconnect the hose, undo the retaining bolt and remove the valve from the end of the camshaft cover **(see illustrations)**.

12 With the engine in this position, the Seat

3.10 Crankshaft stops against special tool

3.11a Disconnect the hose...

3.11b ...undo the screw and remove the valve

3.12a Fit the tool into the camshaft...

3.12b ...and tighten the bolt

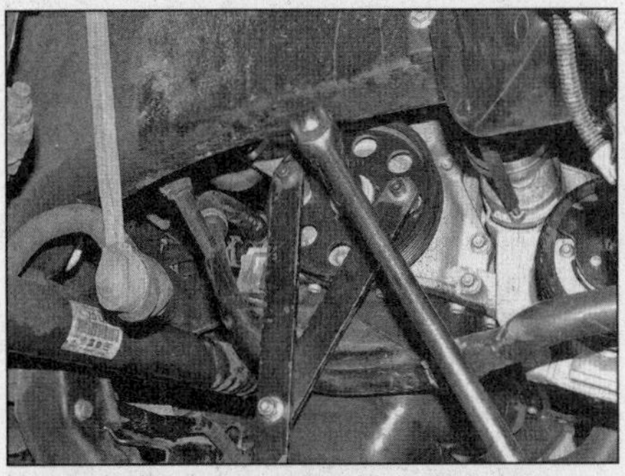

4.6 Counterhold the crankshaft pulley using a tool similar to that shown

4.8a Removing the bolt...

4.8b ...and pulley

special tool (T10414) can be bolted into the end of the camshaft cover and locate with the slot in the end of the camshaft**(see illustrations)**.

13 If tool T10414 cannot be positioned correctly in the camshaft cover, then check that tool T10340 in the rear of the cylinder block is fitted correctly, as described previously. If tool T10414 still does not fit correctly, then the timing is out, and the timing chain will need to be checked.

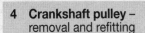

4 Crankshaft pulley – removal and refitting

Removal

1 Disconnect the battery negative lead as described in Chapter 5A Section 3.

2 For improved access, jack up the front of the car, and support securely on axle stands (see *Jacking and vehicle support*). Remove the right-hand front roadwheel.

3 Remove the securing screws and/or release the clips, and withdraw the relevant engine undershield(s) to enable access to the crankshaft pulley.

4 If necessary (for any later work to be carried out), set the timing as described in the previous Section 3.

5 Remove the auxiliary drivebelt, as described in Chapter 1A Section 28.

6 To prevent the crankshaft from turning as the pulley bolt is slackened, a tool similar to that shown can be used. Engage the tool with two of the slots in the pulley **(see illustration)**.

7 Counterhold the pulley, and slacken the pulley bolt (take care – the bolt is very tight) using a socket and a suitable extension.

8 Unscrew the bolt, and remove the pulley **(see illustrations)**.

Refitting

9 Make sure the pulley is clean, and refit to the end of the crankshaft. Fit the new pulley securing bolt, then prevent the crankshaft from turning as during removal. Tighten to the specified torque, in the two stages given in the Specifications.

10 Refit the auxiliary drivebelt as described in Chapter 1A Section 28.

11 Refit the engine undershield and roadwheel, then lower the car to the ground, and reconnect the battery negative lead.

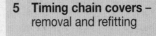

5 Timing chain covers – removal and refitting

Note: *Seat recommend that sealant D 189 500 A1 and D 154 103 A1 are used when refitting the covers.*

Upper outer cover

1 Drain the cooling system, as described in Chapter 1A Section 32.

2 Release the securing clips, and disconnect the hoses from the coolant pipes. Unclip the hoses from across the front of the upper timing chain cover, and move them to one side **(see illustrations)**.

3 Undo the retaining bolts and carefully lever the cover from the cylinder head **(see**

5.2a Release the securing clips arrowed...

5.2b ...and move the hoses to one side

5.3a Carefully lever the cover...

5.3b ...from the cylinder head

5.4a Guide pins

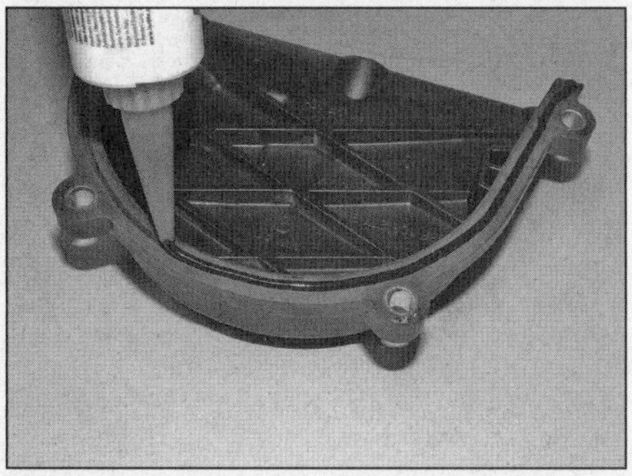

5.4b Apply 3mm bead of sealant around the cover

5.4c Slide the cover into position

illustrations). The cover is bonded to the cylinder head with sealant and can be difficult to remove. Take care not to damage the cover or mating surface of the cylinder head on removal.

4 Refitting is a reversal of removal, noting the following points: -

a) Make sure all the old sealant is removed from the cover and the mating surface on the cylinder head, using sealant remover.

*b) Seat recommend that two guide pins are screwed into the cylinder head, to slide the cover into place **(see illustrations)**. Two lengths of threaded rod can be used for this procedure.*

*c) Apply Seat recommended sealant around the outer edge of the cover – approx. 3mm diameter bead **(see illustration)**. Apply slightly more sealant where the camshaft cover meets the cylinder head, to make sure there is a good seal. The sealant begins to harden after 6 minutes, so cover will need to be in place and torqued up within this time.*

d) Tighten the bolts in two stages (see specifications at the beginning of this Chapter), starting from the lower bolts and working up to the top of the cover.

e) After refitting the coolant hoses, refill the cooling system as described in Chapter 1A Section 32

Lower outer cover

5 Remove the crankshaft pulley, as described in Section 4.

6 Unclip the plastic cover, undo the retaining bolt and remove the guide pulley from the alternator mounting bracket **(see illustrations)**.

7 Undo the retaining bolts and remove the auxiliary belt pulley from the coolant pump **(see illustrations)**. Using a length of flat metal with a hole drilled in the end, hold the pulley in place to slacken the retaining bolts.

8 Remove the sump (oil pan) as described in Section 11

9 To make access easier, support the engine then remove the right-hand engine mounting as described in Section 17

10 Undo the three mounting bolts and remove the mounting bracket from the end of the cylinder head **(see illustration)**.

11 Undo the retaining bolts and discard, as new ones will be required for refitting. Carefully lever the cover from the cylinder block **(see illustrations)**. The cover is bonded to the cylinder block with sealant and can be difficult to remove. Take care not to damage the cover or mating surface of the cylinder block on removal. Note there are two locating dowels in the cylinder block which can become tight in the cover.

5.6a Unclip the plastic cover...

5.6b ...and remove the guide pulley

5.7a Hold the pulley to slacken the bolts...

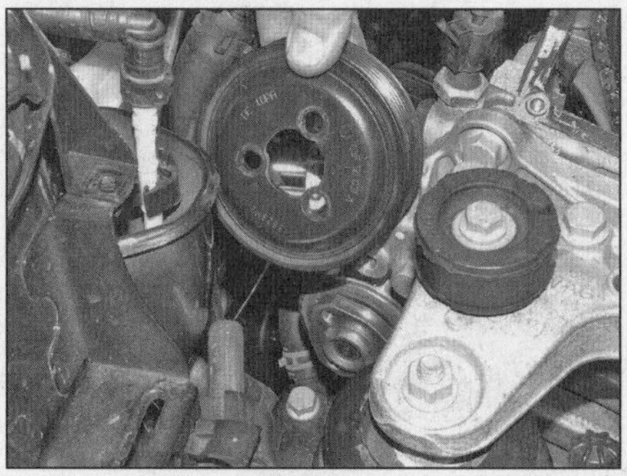

5.7b ...then remove the pulley

12 Refitting is a reversal of removal, noting the following points:

a) *Make sure all the old sealant is removed from the cover and the mating surface on the cylinder block, using chemical sealant remover.*

b) *Seat recommend that a special guide tool/ sleeve (T10417/1) should be fitted over the end of the crankshaft **(see illustration)** before refitting the cover, as damage to the seal will occur. Clean the dowels in the cylinder block, before guiding the cover on to them.*

c) *Apply Seat recommended sealant around the outer edge of the cover – approx. 3mm diameter bead **(see illustration)**. Apply sealant around all bolt holes. The sealant begins to harden after 6 minutes, so cover will need to be in place and bolts torqued up within this time.*

d) *Take care when sliding the cover into place over the end of the crankshaft, as the seal can easily be damaged. Keep the cover square to the cylinder block as it is aligned with the dowels.*

e) *Fit new bolts and tighten in two stages (see specifications at the beginning of this Chapter), starting from the lower bolt on the right-hand side of the cover and working anti-clockwise around the cover.*

f) *Remove the Seat special tool/sleeve (T10417/1) and refit the crankshaft pulley with reference to Section 4.*

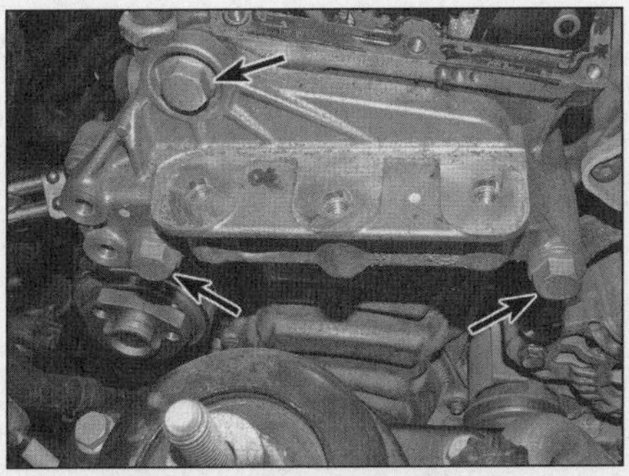

5.10 Mounting bracket bolts

5.11a Position of upper locating dowel...

5.11b ...and lower locating dowel

5.11c Remove lower cover

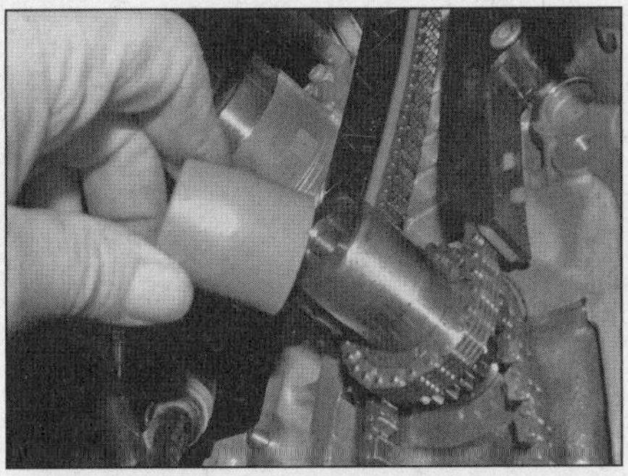

5.12a Fit tool/sleeve (T10417/1) over the end of the crankshaft

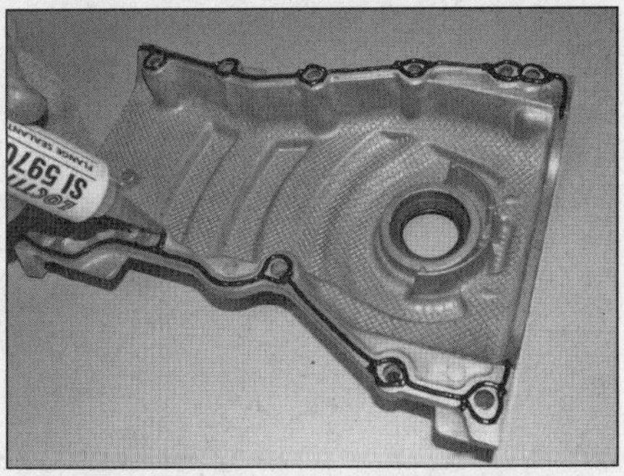

5.12b Apply sealant around the cover...

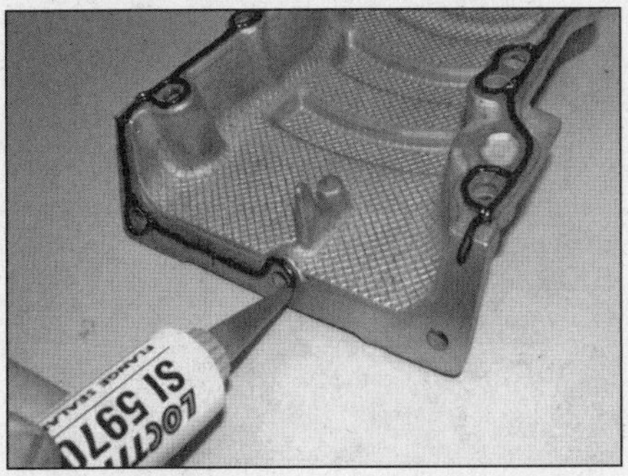

5.12c ...and along the upper edge

5.12d Once in place remove tool/sleeve from crankshaft

6 Timing chain and oil pump drive chain – removal and refitting

Removal

Timing chain

1 Disconnect the battery negative lead as described in Chapter 5A Section 3.

2 Remove the upper timing chain cover as described in Section 5.

3 Turn the crankshaft and set the timing, as described in Section 3. Temporarily refit the crankshaft pulley, so that the engine can be rotated using the securing bolt.

4 Remove the lower timing chain cover as described in Section 5

5 If not already done, remove the complete engine right-hand mounting assembly, as described in Section 17. Also, unbolt the mounting bracket from the cylinder block.

6 If the timing chain is to be refitted, mark the running direction to ensure correct refitting.

7 Slacken and remove the timing chain tensioner at the rear of the cylinder head **(see illustration)**.

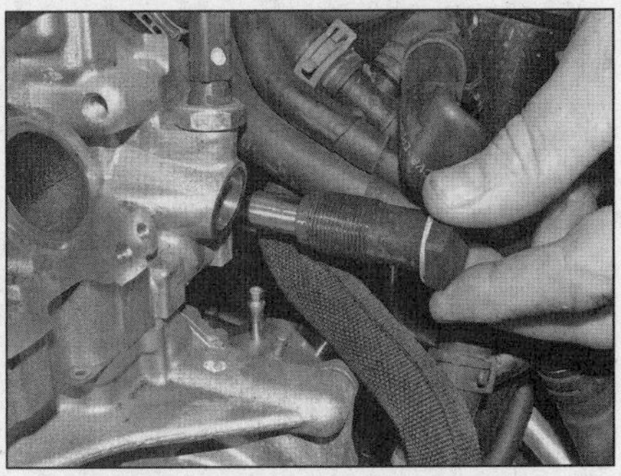

6.7 Remove the chain tensioner

6.8 Hold the sprocket while slackening the bolt

6.9a Remove the camshaft sprocket

6.9b Release the chain from around the crankshaft sprocket

8 Using a tool to hold the camshaft sprocket in position, slacken the camshaft sprocket securing bolt **(see illustration)**.

9 Remove the securing bolt, and then release the chain from the sprocket and lower it down through the cylinder head. Noting the fitted position of the chain, release it from around the crankshaft sprocket and remove it from the engine **(see illustrations)**.

Oil pump drive chain

10 Once the timing chain has been removed, to remove the oil pump drive chain, proceed as follows.

11 Using a flat bladed screwdriver, carefully release the retaining clips and remove the plastic cover from over the oil pump sprocket and drive chain **(see illustration)**.

12 If the oil pump drive chain is to be refitted, mark the running direction to ensure correct refitting.

13 Undo the oil pump retaining bolts and remove the pump **(see illustration)**. Disengage the pump sprocket from the drive chain as it is removed.

14 Noting the fitted position of the chain, release it from around the crankshaft gear and remove it from the engine

Refitting

Oil pump drive chain

15 Place the drive chain around the crankshaft inner gear, making sure it is fitted in the same running direction as noted on removal.

16 Locate the oil pump sprocket into the lower part of the chain and fit the three oil pump securing bolts. Tighten the new bolts to the torque specified in the specifications at the beginning of this Chapter.

17 Refit the plastic cover over the oil pump sprocket and drive chain.

Timing chain

18 Where applicable, ensure that the oil pump drive chain has been refitted.

19 Make sure the camshaft and crankshaft timing is still set in the correct position, as described in Section 3.

20 Fit the timing chain around the crankshaft gear and pass it up through the end of the cylinder head, guiding it upwards between the sliding rail and tensioning rail. If the original chain is being refitted, observe the running direction as noted on removal. An Allen key or similar can be used to hold the chain in position, until the camshaft sprocket is fitted **(see illustrations)**.

21 Insert the camshaft sprocket into the timing chain and with the chain sitting inside the guide rails correctly, fit the retaining bolt to the sprocket and only tighten hand tight at this time **(see illustrations)**.

6.11 Remove the plastic cover

6.13 Oil pump retaining bolts

6.20a Hold the timing chain onto the crankshaft gear...

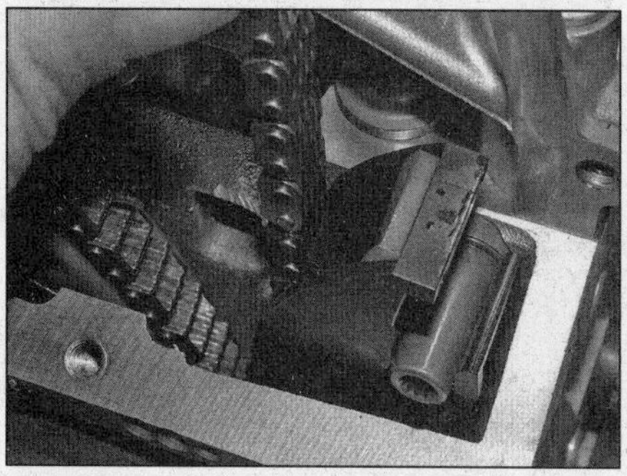
6.20b ...pass the chain between the guides...

6.20c ...and hold it in position

6.21a Insert sprocket into chain...

22 Refit the timing chain tensioner to the rear of the cylinder head, and then tighten to the specified torque.

23 Hold the camshaft sprocket in position with the holding tool (as used on removal) and tighten the camshaft sprocket retaining bolt to the stage one of the specified torque setting **(see illustration)**. **Note:** *The stage two torque setting is only completed once the timing is set in the correct position.*

24 Remove the timing setting pins from the cylinder block at the rear of the engine and the left-hand end of the camshaft cover.

25 Refit the crankshaft pulley and using a spanner on the bolt, turn the engine through two complete turns in the normal direction of rotation, then once again insert the timing pins to check the timing is set correctly, as described in Section 3.

26 If the timing pins cannot be fitted in the correct position, remove the timing chain tensioner and slacken the camshaft sprocket bolt, then insert the timing pins in the correct position. The refitting procedure for fitting the tensioner and tightening camshaft sprocket will need to be repeated.

27 When the chain tension is correct, and the timing pins are aligned the camshaft sprocket bolt can now be tightened to the stage two torque setting. Hold the camshaft sprocket in position with the holding tool, and then tighten the securing bolt to the stage two torque setting.

28 Refit the lower timing chain cover, with reference to Section 5 if necessary.

29 Refit the crankshaft pulley as described in Section 4.

30 Refit the upper timing chain cover.

7 Camshaft carrier – removal and refitting

Note: *On early models, Seat recommend that sealant D 189 500 A1 and D 154 103 A1 are used when refitting the camshaft carrier. On vehicles from 06/2011 it has been updated and a coated metal gasket is fitted.*

Removal

1 Disconnect the battery negative lead as described in Chapter 5A Section 3.

7.6 ...and remove air intake pipe

6.21b ...and tighten hand tight (at this time)

2 Remove the upper timing chain cover, as described in Section 5.

3 Turn the crankshaft and set the timing, as described in Section 3.

4 Slacken and remove the timing chain tensioner at the rear of the cylinder head, as described in previous section. Using a tool to hold the camshaft sprocket in position, slacken the camshaft sprocket securing bolt. Remove the securing bolt, and then position the camshaft sprocket complete with cahin away from the end of the camshaft. The sprocket can rest on the lug in the cylinder head, so will not drop down **(see illustration)**.

5 Disconnect the wiring connector from the sensor on the air intake pipe **(see illustration)**.

6 Undo the two retaining bolts, release the retaining clips and remove the air intake pipe from over the cylinder head cover **(see illustration)**.

7.4 Rest the sprocket in position

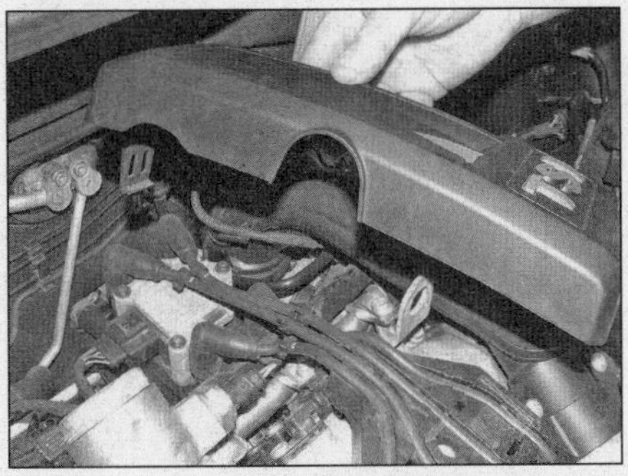

7.7 Unclip the cover

6.23 Holding the camshaft sprocket in position with the holding tool

7 Unclip the trim cover from over the HT leads **(see illustration)**.

8 Disconnect the HT leads from the top of the spark plugs (see Chapter 1A Section 27), then undo the retaining bolt and remove the HT leads and guide from the top of the cylinder head cover and move them to the rear of the engine **(see illustration)**.

9 Disconnect the camshaft position sensor wiring connector **(see illustration)**.

10 Remove the high pressure fuel pump and fuel rail from the top of the cylinder head cover, as described in Chapter 4A Section 4

11 Remove the exhaust manifold/turbocharger from the front of the engine, as described in Chapter 4C Section 6

12 If not already done, remove the oil level dipstick from the front of the cylinder head cover.

13 Working progressively from the outside to the centre, in a diagonal sequence, slacken

7.5 Disconnect the sensor wiring connector...

7.8 Undo bolt

7.9 Disconnect sensor wiring connector

7.13 Removing the camshaft carrier

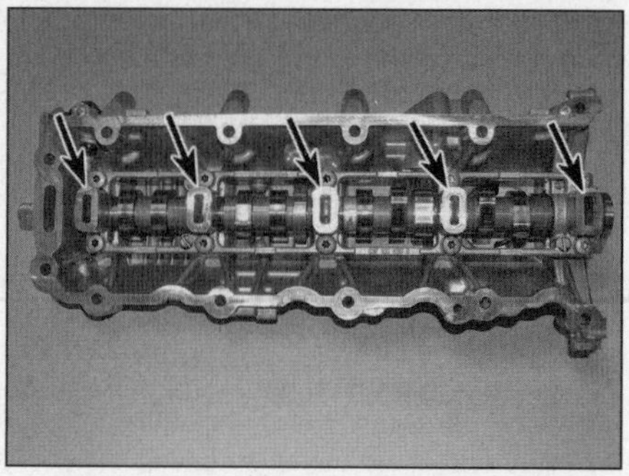
7.18 Apply a thin layer of sealant to the mating faces

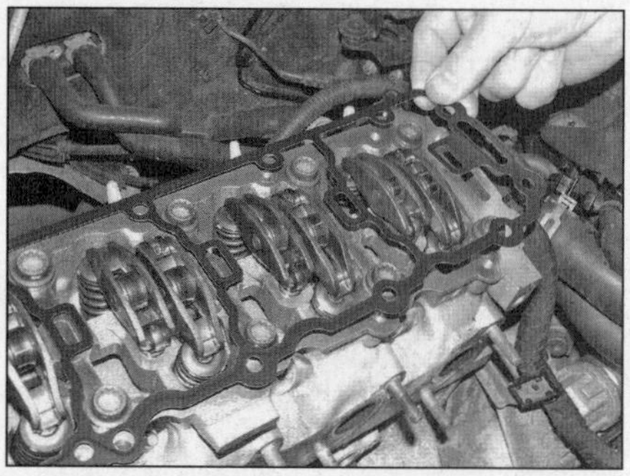
7.19 Fit a new gasket

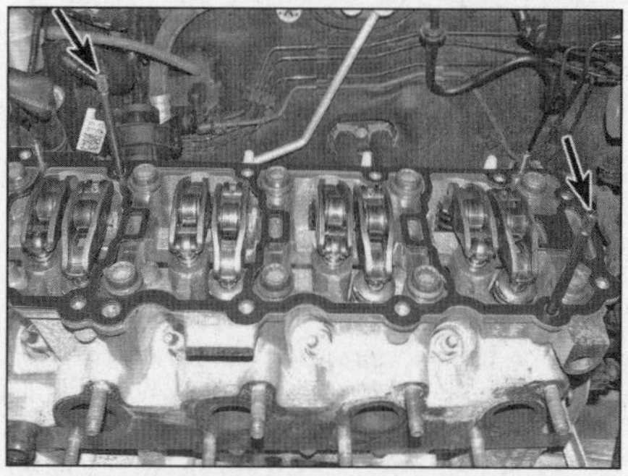
7.20a Guide pins arrowed

7.20b Carefully lower the camshaft carrier

and remove the camshaft carrier securing bolts. Carefully lift the camshaft carrier from the cylinder head, taking care not to disturb the hydraulic rocker arms **(see illustration)**. Discard the gasket, as a new one will be required for refitting.

14 The camshaft can be removed from the carrier, as described in Section 8.

Refitting

15 Commence refitting by thoroughly cleaning all traces of old sealant/gasket, and all traces of oil and grease, from the mating faces of the cylinder head and camshaft carrier. Ensure that no debris enters the cylinder head or camshaft carrier.

16 Ensure that the crankshaft is still positioned correctly and has not been moved from the set position, and that the camshaft is locked in position with the locking tool, as described in Section 3.

7.22 Remove the guide pins

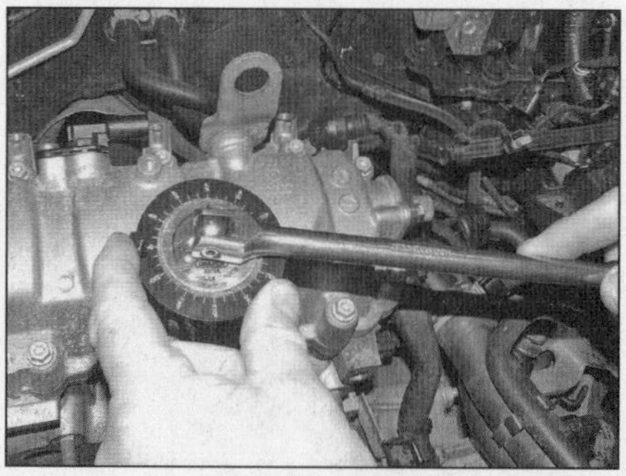
7.23 Tightening the bolts through the specified Stage 2 angle

17 Check that the valve rockers are correctly located on the valves, and securely clipped into position on the hydraulic tappets.

18 On early models, apply sealant (Seat D 189 500 A1, or equivalent) to the camshaft carrier to cylinder head mating face (apporx. 2-3mm thick) and around all the bolt holes. Then apply a thin layer of sealant (Seat D 154 103 A1) evenly around the five mating surfaces below the camshaft bearing journals inside the carrier **(see illustration)**. Do not apply the sealant too thickly, as excess sealant may enter and block the oilways, causing engine damage.

19 On vehicles from 06/2011, fit a new coated metal gasket to the cylinder head **(see illustration)**. Seat recommend that the gasket should be kept in its wrapping until it is being fitted, as any damage to the gasket will result in a leak.

20 Carefully lower the camshaft carrier onto the cylinder head, until the camshafts rest on the rockers. Note that the camshaft carrier locates on dowels in the cylinder head. Seat recommend that two guide pins are fitted to the cylinder head, to make fitting easier **(see illustration)**. If the guide pins are not available, two guide pins can be made up as follows:

a) *Cut the heads off two M6 bolts, then cut slots in the top of each bolt to enable the bolt to be unscrewed using a flat-bladed screwdriver.*
b) *Screw one bolt into each of the camshaft carrier bolt locations at opposite corners of the cylinder head (front left and rear right).*
c) *Lower the camshaft carrier over the bolts/pins to guide it into position on the cylinder head* **(see illustration)**.

21 Fit new camshaft carrier securing bolts, and tighten them progressively, working from the centre out, in a diagonal sequence (i.e. tighten all bolts through one turn, then tighten all bolts through a further turn, and so on). Ensure that the camshaft carrier sits squarely on the cylinder head as the bolts are tightened, and make sure that the carrier engages with the cylinder head dowels.

22 Once the camshaft carrier contacts the surface of the cylinder head, where applicable, unscrew the two guide studs **(see illustration)**, and fit the two remaining new camshaft carrier securing bolts in their place.

23 Tighten the camshaft carrier securing bolts to the specified torque, in the two stages given in the Specifications **(see illustration)**.

24 Leave the camshaft carrier sealant to dry for approximately 10 minutes before carrying out any further work on the cylinder head or camshaft carrier.
25 Once the sealant has been allowed to dry, clean the area around the cylinder head cover, making sure that there is no sealant protruding at the ends of the camshaft carrier, where the upper timing chain cover is fitted.
26 Refit the timing chain and set the timing, as described in Section 6
27 Refit the upper timing chain cover, as described in Section 5
28 Refit the exhaust manifold/turbocharger, as described in Chapter 4C Section 6.
29 Refit the high pressure fuel pump and fuel rail, as described in Chapter 4A Section 4
30 Reconnect the camshaft position sensor wiring connector.
31 Refit the cable guide and reconnect the ignition coils to the spark plugs. Clip cover back into place over the HT leads.
32 Refit the air intake pipe across the top of the cylinder head cover, tighten the retaining bolts and reconnect the sensor wiring connector.
33 Reconnect the battery negative lead.

8 Camshaft – removal, inspection and refitting

Removal

1 Remove the camshaft carrier as described in Section 7.
2 Place the camshaft carrier upside down on a clean workbench, and then slacken the camshaft bearing frame retaining screws. Working progressively from the outside to the centre, in a diagonal sequence, slacken and remove the camshaft bearing frame screws **(see illustration)**.
3 Carefully remove the camshaft from the camshaft carrier, taking care not to damage the bearing surfaces of the camshaft and housing as it is removed.

Inspection

4 Visually inspect the camshaft for evidence of wear on the surfaces of the lobes and journals. Normally their surfaces should be smooth and have a dull shine; look for scoring, erosion or pitting and areas that appear highly polished, indicating excessive wear. Accelerated wear will occur once the hardened exterior of the camshaft has been damaged, so always renew worn items. **Note:** *If these symptoms are visible on the tips of the camshaft lobes, check the corresponding rocker, as it will probably be worn as well.*
5 If the machined surfaces of the camshaft appear discoloured or blue, it is likely that it has been overheated at some point, probably due to inadequate lubrication. This may have distorted the shaft, so check the run-out as follows: place the camshaft between two

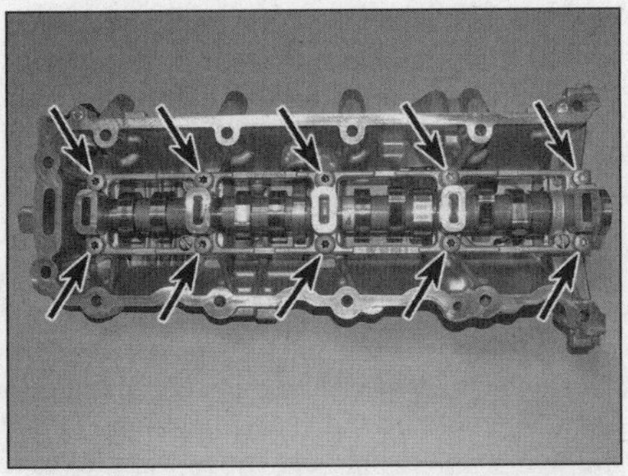

8.2 Camshaft bearing frame retaining screws

V-blocks and using a DTI gauge, measure the run-out at the centre journal. No maximum run-out figure is quoted by the manufacturers, but it should be obvious if the camshaft is excessively distorted.
6 To measure camshaft endfloat, temporarily refit the relevant camshaft to the camshaft carrier, and refit the camshaft sealing plate to the rear of the camshaft carrier. Anchor a DTI gauge to the timing belt end of the camshaft carrier and align the gauge probe with the camshaft axis. Push the camshaft to one end of the camshaft carrier as far as it will travel, then rest the DTI gauge probe on the end of the camshaft, and zero the gauge display. Push the camshaft as far as it will go to the other end of the camshaft carrier, and record the gauge reading. Verify the reading by pushing the camshaft back to its original position and checking that the gauge indicates zero again.
7 Check that the camshaft endfloat measurement is within the limit listed in the Specifications. Wear outside of this limit may be cured by renewing the relevant camshaft carrier endplate, although wear is unlikely to be confined to any one component, so renewal of the camshafts and camshaft carrier must be considered.

Refitting

8 Refitting is a reversal of removal, bearing in mind the following points:

a) Lubricate the bearing surfaces in the camshaft carrier, and the camshaft lobes before refitting the camshaft.
b) When fitting the bearing frame, make sure it is located correctly on the centering pins inside the camshaft carrier.
c) Working progressively from the inside to the outside, in a diagonal sequence, tighten the bearing frame securing screws to the correct torque setting
d) Refit the camshaft carrier as described in Section 7.

9 Rockers and hydraulic tappets – removal, inspection and refitting

Removal

1 Remove the camshaft carrier, as described in Section 7.
2 As the components are removed, keep them in strict order, so that they can be refitted in their original locations.
3 Carefully lift the hydraulic tappets and rocker from their bores in the cylinder head **(see illustration)**. It is advisable to store the tappets (in order) upright in an oil bath whilst they are removed from the engine.
4 If required, unclip the rockers from the hydraulic tappets, then store the tappets (in order) upright in an oil bath whilst they are removed from the engine.

Inspection

5 Check the tappet bores in the cylinder head for signs of scoring or damage. If significant scoring or damage is found, it may be necessary to renew the cylinder head and the complete set of tappets.
6 Inspect the hydraulic tappets for obvious signs of wear or damage, and renew if necessary. Check that the oil holes in the tappets are free from obstructions.
7 Check the valve, tappet, and camshaft contact faces of the rockers for wear or damage, and also check the rockers for any signs of cracking. Renew any worn or damaged rockers.
8 Inspect the camshaft lobes, as described in Section 8.

Refitting

9 Oil the tappet bores in the cylinder head, and the hydraulic tappets themselves, then carefully slide the tappets into their original bores **(see illustration)**.

9.3 Removing a hydraulic tappet/rocker

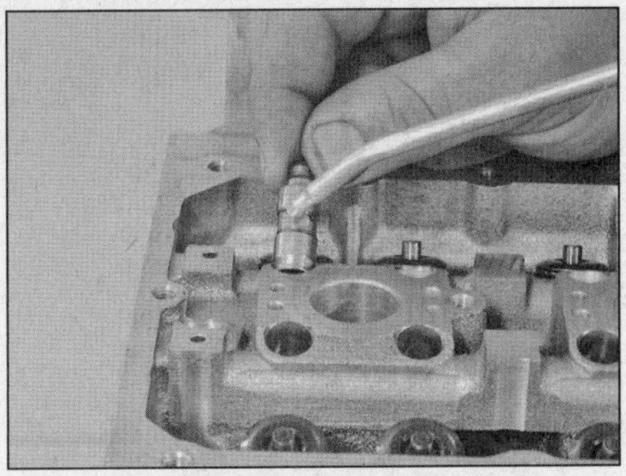

9.9 Oil the tappets before fitting

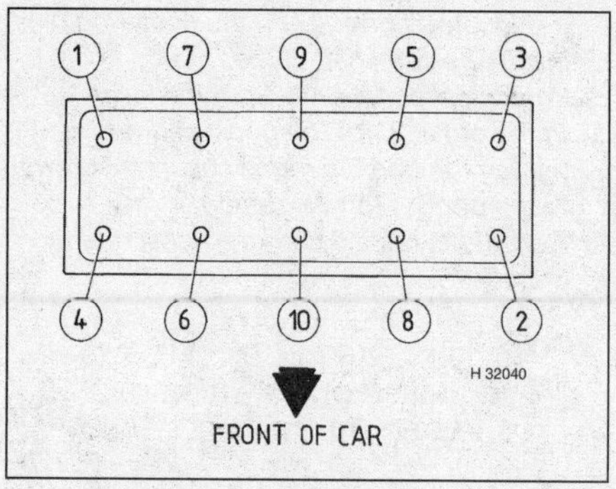

10.12 Cylinder head bolt slackening sequence

10 Oil the rocker contact faces of the tappets, and the tops of the valve stems, then refit the rockers to their original locations, ensuring that the rockers are securely clipped onto the tappets.

11 Check the endfloat of each camshaft, as described in Section 8, then refit the camshaft carrier as described in Section 7.

10 Cylinder head – removal, inspection and refitting

Note: *The cylinder head must be removed with the engine cold.*

Removal

1 Disconnect the battery negative lead as described in Chapter 5A Section 3.

2 Drain the cooling system, as described in Chapter 1A Section 32

3 Remove the timing chain, as described in Section 6.

4 If the engine is currently supported using a hoist attached to the engine lifting brackets bolted to the cylinder head, it will now be necessary to attach a suitable bracket to the cylinder block, so that the engine can still be supported as the cylinder head is removed.

5 Support the engine from underneath using a jack and a block of wood, and then (where applicable) transfer the lifting tackle from the bracket on the cylinder head to the bracket bolted to the cylinder block.

6 Release the hose clips, and disconnect the two radiator hoses from the coolant housing at the transmission end of the cylinder head. Similarly, release the hose clips and disconnect the remaining three small coolant hoses from the rear of the coolant housing.

7 Remove the inlet manifold from the rear of the cylinder head, as described in Chapter 4A Section 9

8 Disconnect the wiring plug from the coolant temperature sensor, located in the coolant housing at the transmission end of the cylinder head, then unclip the wiring harnesses from the coolant housing, and move them to one side.

9 Remove the exhaust manifold/turbocharger from the front of the cylinder head, with reference to Chapter 4C Section 6.

10 Remove the camshaft carrier, with reference to Section 7.

11 Remove the rockers and hydraulic tappets, as described in Section 9

12 Progressively slacken the cylinder head bolts in order, then unscrew and remove the bolts **(see illustration)**.

13 With all the bolts removed, lift the cylinder head from the block. If the cylinder head is stuck, tap it with a soft-faced mallet to break the joint. **Do not** insert a lever into the gasket joint.

14 Lift the old cylinder head gasket from the block and discard, as a new one will be required for refitting.

Inspection

15 Dismantling and inspection of the cylinder head is covered in Part F of this Chapter. Additionally, check the condition of the coolant pump pipe-to-thermostat housing O-ring, and renew if necessary.

Refitting

16 The mating faces of the cylinder head and block must be perfectly clean before refitting the head. Use a scraper to remove all traces of gasket and carbon, also clean the tops of the pistons. Take particular care with the aluminium surfaces, as the soft metal is easily damaged. Make sure that debris is not allowed to enter the oil and water passages – this is particularly important for the oil circuit, as carbon could block the oil supply to the camshaft and crankshaft bearings. Using adhesive tape and paper, seal the water, oil and bolt holes in the cylinder block. To prevent carbon entering the gap between the pistons and bores, smear a little grease in the gap. After cleaning a piston, rotate the crankshaft to that the piston moves down the bore, and then wipe out the grease and carbon with a cloth rag. Clean the other piston crowns in the same way.

17 Check the head and block for nicks, deep scratches and other damage. If slight, they may be removed carefully with a file. More serious damage may be repaired by machining, but this is a specialist job.

18 If warpage of the cylinder head is suspected, use a straight-edge to check it for distortion, as described in.

19 Ensure that the cylinder head bolt holes in the crankcase are clean and free of oil. Syringe or soak up any oil left in the bolt holes. This is most important in order that the correct bolt tightening torque can be applied, and to prevent the possibility of the block being cracked by hydraulic pressure when the bolts are tightened.

20 Ensure that the crankshaft has been turned to position No's 1 and 4 pistons slightly down their bores from the TDC position (see Section 6). This will eliminate any risk of piston-to-valve contact as the cylinder head is refitted. Also ensure that the camshaft is locked in the TDC position using the locking tool, as described in Section 3.

21 Ensure that the cylinder head locating dowels are in place in the cylinder block, and then fit a new cylinder head gasket over the dowels, ensuring that the part number is uppermost. Where applicable, the OBEN/TOP marking should also be uppermost **(see illustrations)**. Note that Seat recommend that the gasket is only removed from its packaging immediately prior to fitting.

22 Lower the cylinder head into position on the gasket, ensuring that it engages correctly over the dowels. As the cylinder head is lowered into position, ensure that the coolant pump pipe engages with the thermostat housing (use a new O-ring if necessary).

23 Fit the new cylinder head bolts, and screw them in as far as possible by hand.

24 Working progressively, in sequence, tighten all the cylinder head bolts to the specified Stage 1 torque **(see illustration)**.

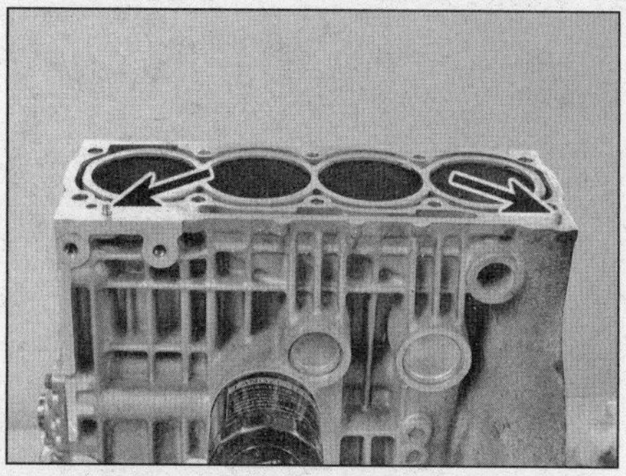

10.21a Ensure that the dowels are in place in the cylinder block...

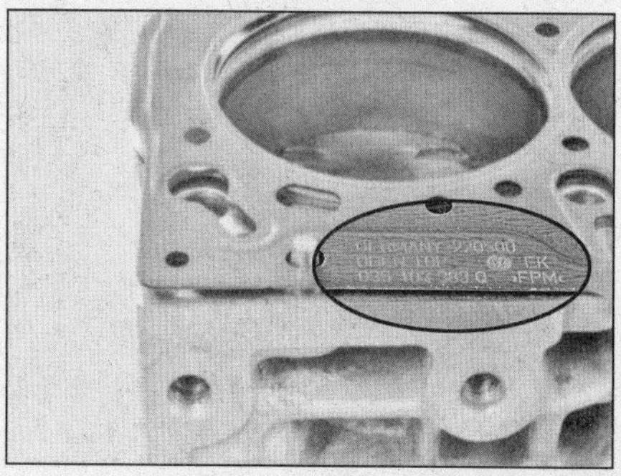

10.21b ...and the gasket part number and OBEN/TOP markings are uppermost

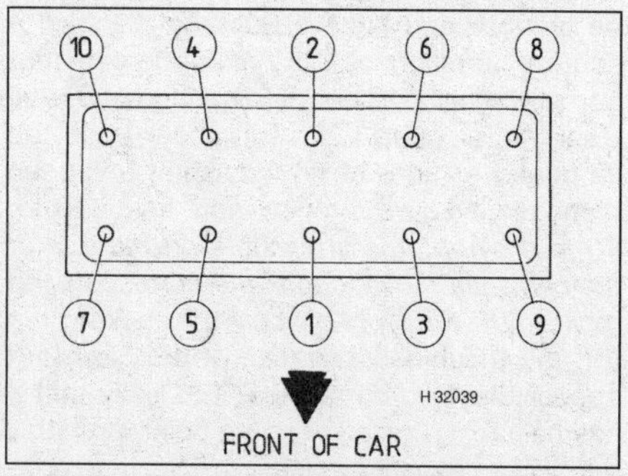

10.24 Cylinder head bolt tightening sequence

25 Again working progressively, in sequence, tighten all the cylinder head bolts through the specified Stage 2 angle.
26 Finally, tighten all the cylinder head bolts, in sequence, to the specified Stage 3 torque.
27 Where applicable, reconnect the lifting tackle to the engine right-hand lifting bracket on the cylinder head, then adjust the lifting tackle to support the engine. Once the engine is adequately supported using the cylinder head bracket, disconnect the lifting tackle from the bracket bolted to the cylinder block, and unbolt the improvised engine lifting bracket from the cylinder block. Alternatively, remove the trolley jack and block of wood from under the engine.
28 Refit the rockers and hydraulic tappets, as described in Section 9.
29 Refit the camshaft carrier as described in Section 7.
30 Further refitting is a reversal of removal, bearing in mind the following points:

a) Refit the exhaust manifold/turbocharger, as described in Chapter 4C Section 6.
b) Refit the inlet manifold, as described in Chapter 4A Section 9.
c) Refit the timing chain, as described in Section 6.
d) Ensure that all wires, pipes and hoses are correctly reconnected and routed, as noted before removal.
e) Tighten all fixings to the specified torque, where applicable.
f) On completion, refill the cooling system as described in Chapter 1A Section 32.

11 Sump – removal and refitting

Removal

1 Disconnect the battery negative lead as described in Chapter 5A Section 3.
2 Chock the rear wheels and apply the handbrake, then jack up the front of the car and support it on axle stands (see *Jacking and vehicle support*). Where fitted, remove the engine undertray.
3 Drain the engine oil, then clean and refit the engine oil drain plug, tightening it to the specified torque wrench setting. If the engine is nearing the service interval when the oil and filter are due for renewal, it is recommended that the filter is also removed and a new one fitted. After reassembly, the engine can then be replenished with fresh engine oil. Refer to Chapter 1A Section 6, for further information.
4 Remove the exhaust front pipe with reference to Chapter 4C Section 7.
5 Disconnect the wiring from the oil level/ temperature sender **(see illustration)**.
6 Undo the securing bolts and remove the metal plate from the transmission **(see illustration)**.
7 Undo the retaining bolt and disconnect the coolant hose from the end of the sump **(see illustration)**.

11.5 Oil level/temp sender

11.6 Remove transmission plate

11.7 Undo the coolant pipe securing bolt

11.8 Two bolts at the transmission end of the sump

8 Progressively unscrew and remove the sump retaining bolts, noting the position of the two bolts, which are partially hidden, at the transmission end of the sump **(see illustration)**.
9 Break the joint by striking the sump with a rubber-headed hammer, then lower the sump away from the engine and withdraw it.
10 While the sump is removed, take the opportunity to clean the oil pump pick-up/ strainer pipe mesh using a suitable solvent. Inspect the strainer mesh for signs of clogging or splitting and renew if necessary, referring to Section 12, for further information.

Refitting

11 Thoroughly clean all traces of sealant and oil from the mating surfaces of the cylinder block/crankcase and sump, and then use a clean rag to wipe out the sump and the engine's interior.

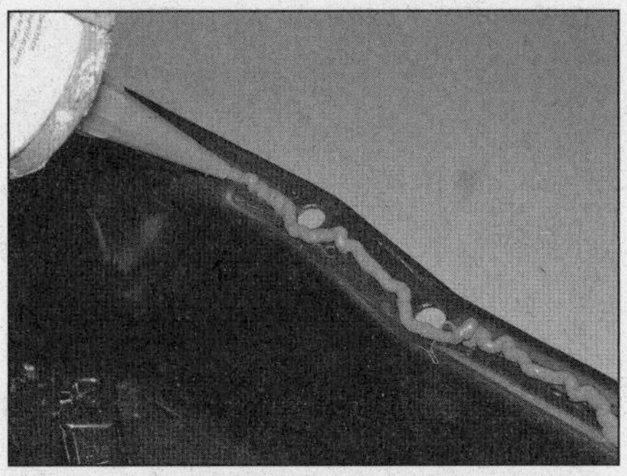

11.12 Apply a bead of sealant

12 Apply a 2.0 to 3.0 mm diameter bead of sealant to the sump mating flange, making sure that the bead is around the inner edges of the bolt holes **(see illustration)**. The bead must not exceed 3.0 mm diameter. **Note:** *The sump must be refitted within 5 minutes of applying the sealant.*
13 When refitting the sump, to guide the sump into position on the cylinder block mating face, two guide studs can be improvised by cutting the heads off two M6 bolts, and cutting slots in the ends of the bolts so that they can later by unscrewed using a flat-bladed screwdriver. Screw the guide studs into two diagonally opposite sump securing bolt holes.
14 Offer the sump into position, then refit the sump bolts and tighten them to the specified torque. Once the sump is held securely in position, unscrew the guide studs, and refit the remaining two sump securing bolts.
15 Refit the metal plate at the transmission end of the sump.
16 Refit the coolant pipe mounting bracket to the end of the sump and tighten the securing bolt.
17 Reconnect the wiring to the oil level/ temperature sender.
18 Refit the exhaust front pipe with reference to Chapter 4C Section 7.
19 Refit the engine undertray and lower the car to the ground.
20 Reconnect the battery negative lead.
21 Refill the engine with oil as described in Chapter 1A Section 6.

12.2 Remove the sprocket cover

12.3 Oil pump securing bolts

14.2 Disconnecting the oil pressure switch wiring connector

12 Oil pump – removal and refitting

Note: *No spare parts are available for the oil pump, and if worn or faulty the complete pump must be renewed.*

Removal

1 Remove the sump as described in Section 11.

2 Using a flat bladed screwdriver, carefully unclip the plastic cover from over the oil pump sprocket and drive chain **(see illustration)**.

3 Unscrew the securing bolts, noting their locations to ensure correct refitting, and remove the oil pump from the drive chain **(see illustration)**.

Refitting

4 Locate the oil pump sprocket into the lower part of the chain and fit the three oil pump securing bolts. Tighten the new bolts to the torque specified in the specifications at the beginning of this Chapter.

5 Refit the plastic cover over the sprocket and drive chain.

6 Refit the sump as described in Section 11.

13 Oil pressure relief valve – removal, inspection and refitting

1 The oil pressure relief valve is an integral part of the oil pump. The valve piston and spring are located to the side of the oil pump rotors and can be inspected once the oil pump has been removed from the engine and the rear cover has been removed (see Section 12). If any sign of wear or damage is found the oil pump assembly will have to be renewed; the relief valve piston and spring are not available separately.

14 Oil pressure warning light switch – removal and refitting

Removal

1 The oil pressure warning light switch is fitted to the rear right-hand end of the cylinder head, above the timing chain tensioner.

2 Disconnect the wiring connector and wipe clean the area around the switch **(see illustration)**.

3 Unscrew the switch from the cylinder head and remove it along with its sealing washer. If the switch is to be left removed from the engine for any length of time, plug the hole in the cylinder head.

Refitting

4 Examine the sealing washer for signs of damage or deterioration and if necessary renew.

5 Refit the switch, complete with washer, and tighten it to the specified torque.

6 Securely reconnect the wiring connector to the pressure switch. Check and, if necessary, top-up the engine oil as described in *Weekly checks*.

15.6a Remove the intermediate plate from the dowels...

15.6b ...and from behind the top of the crankshaft seal housing

15 Crankshaft oil seals – renewal

Timing chain end oil seal

1 Remove the crankshaft pulley, as described in Section 4, then note the fitted depth of the oil seal in the timing cover.

2 Carefully lever the old seal out of the timing cover using a suitable flat-bladed screwdriver, taking great care not to damage the cover or crankshaft. Alternatively, punch or drill two small holes opposite each other in the seal, then screw a self-tapping screw into each and pull on the screws with pliers to extract the seal.

3 Thoroughly clean the cover where the oil seal is seated.

4 Note that the new oil seal must not be oiled or greased, and the contact surfaces of the timing cover must be completely dry. New oil seals are provided with a fitting adapter. Locate the adapter and new seal over the crankshaft and onto the timing cover, and press it into position until it is at the fitted depth previously noted. If necessary, the seal can be tapped into position using a suitable tubular drift, such as a socket, which bears only on the hard outer edge of the seal. Note that the sealing lips must face inwards.

5 Refit the crankshaft pulley with reference to Section 4

Flywheel end oil seal

Note: *In these engines, the seal, sealing flange and sender wheel are a complete unit. Special tools are required to refit the sealing flange, and press the sender wheel onto the end of the crankshaft. It is not possible to accurately fit these parts without the tools, which may be available from Seat (part no. T10134) and are available from aftermarket automotive tool specialists. E.g. Laser tools).*

6 Remove the flywheel as described in Section, then prise the intermediate plate from the locating dowels on the cylinder block and unhook it from behind the top of the seal housing **(see illustrations)**.

15.7a Undo the crankshaft speed sensor retaining bolt

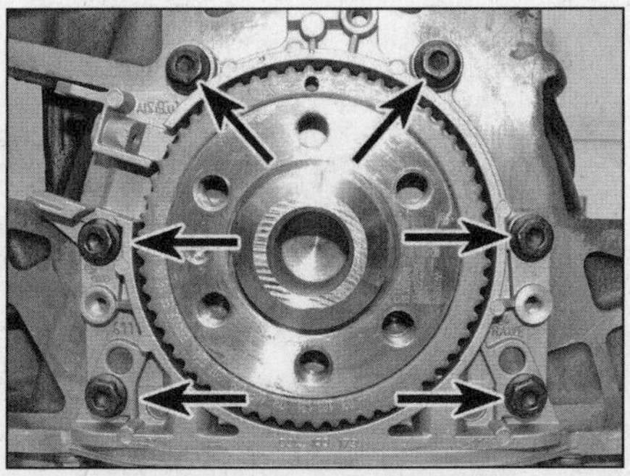

15.7b Sealing flange bolts

15.8a Screw in three 6 x 35 mm bolts...

15.8b ...and draw the sealing flange and sender wheel from place

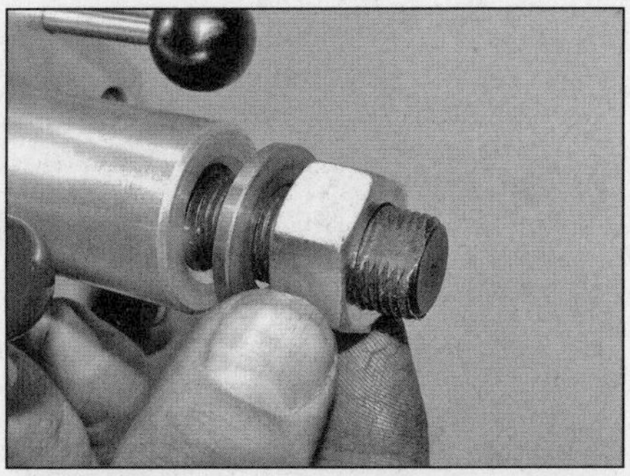

15.10a Rotate the nut until it's level with the end of the flat clamping surface...

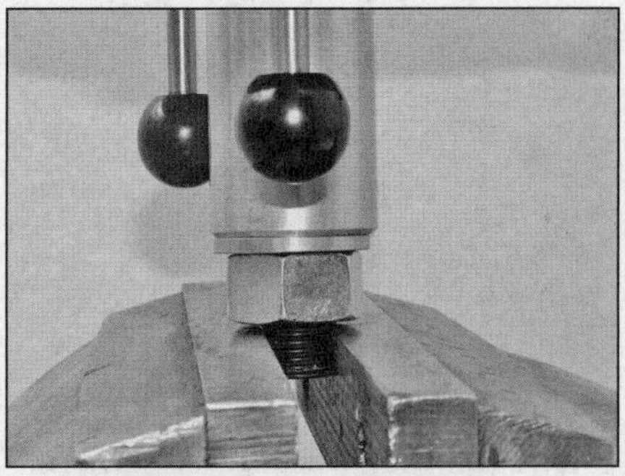

15.10b ...then clamp it in a vice

7 Undo the bolt securing the crankshaft speed sensor and remove it from the seal housing, then undo the bolts securing the sealing flange to the cylinder block **(see illustrations)**.

8 Insert three 6 x 35 mm bolts into the threaded holes in the sealing flange. Tighten the bolts gradually and evenly, and press the sealing flange, and sender wheel from the crankshaft/cylinder block **(see illustrations)**. The seal, sender wheel and sealing flange are supplied as a complete unit.

9 Ensure the mating face of the cylinder block is clean and free from debris. The new sealing flange/seal/sender wheel assembly is supplied with a sealing lip support ring, which serves as a fitting sleeve, and must not be removed prior to installation. Equally, the sender wheel must not be separated from the assembly.

10 If using the Seat tool, proceed as follows. If using an aftermarket tool specialist's product, follow the instructions supplied with the tool. Rotate the large spindle nut until it's level with the end of the clamping surface of the spindle, then clamp the spindle in a vice **(see illustrations)**.

11 Press the tool housing downwards until it rests on the nut and washer. Rotate the nut until the inner part of the tool is at the same height as the housing **(see illustrations)**.

12 Remove the seal securing clip. The hole on the sender wheel must align with the marking on the sealing flange **(see illustrations)**.

13 Place the flange outer side down on a clean, flat surface, then press the seal guide fitting sleeve (supplied ready fitted), housing, and sender wheel downwards until all the components are flat on the surface. In this position the upper edge of the sender wheel should be level with the edge of the sealing flange **(see illustrations)**.

14 Place the sealing flange on the assembly

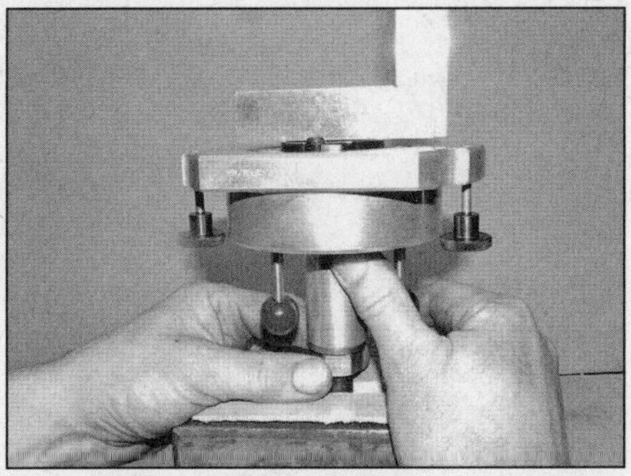

15.11a Rotate the nut until the inner part of the tool...

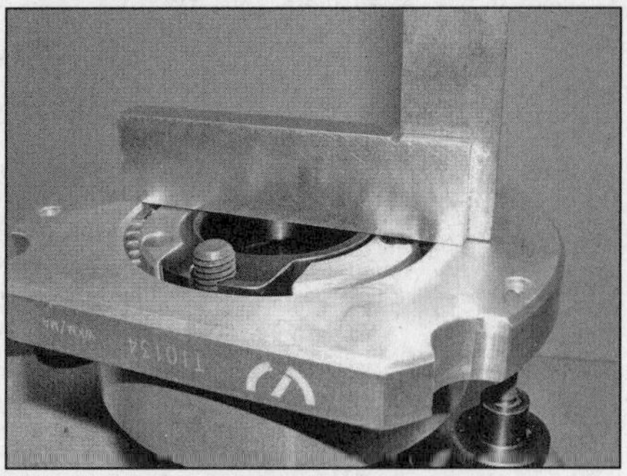

15.11b ...is flush with the flat surface of the housing

15.12a Remove the securing clip...

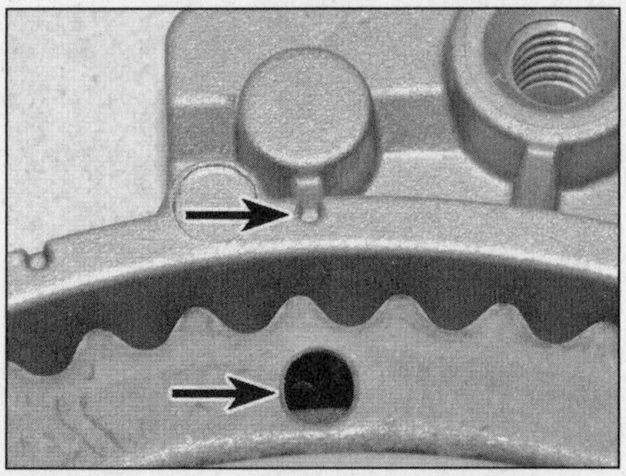

15.12b ...the hole in the sender wheel should align with the marking on the flange

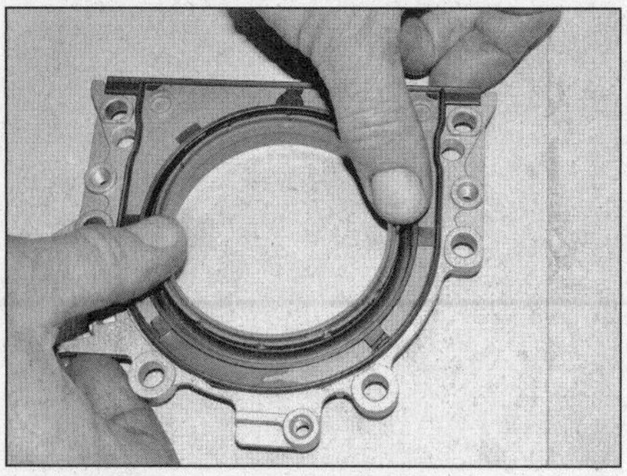

15.13a Press the assembly downwards on a clean, flat surface...

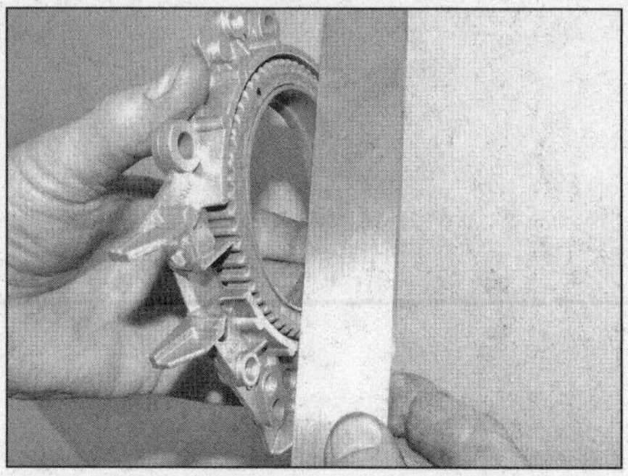

15.13b ...so the upper edge of the sender wheel is level with the edge of the flange

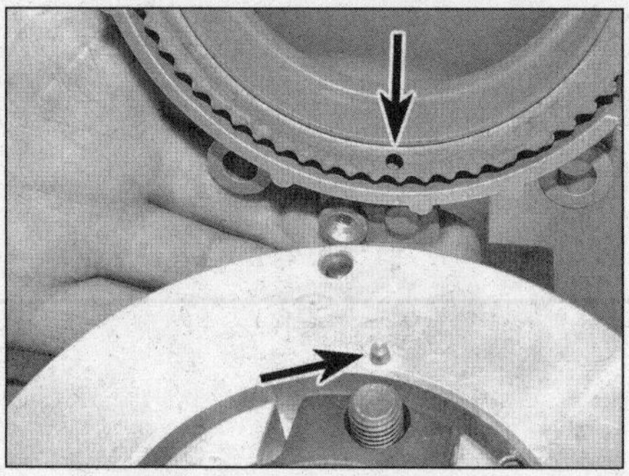

15.14 Fit the flange to the tool, ensuring the pin locates in the hole

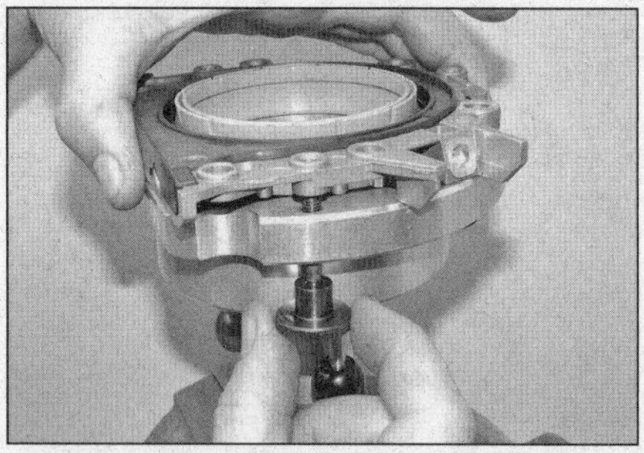

15.15 With the pin engaged in the hole, tighten the 3 knurled screws to secure the flange to the tool

15.17a Unscrew the nut to the end of the thread...

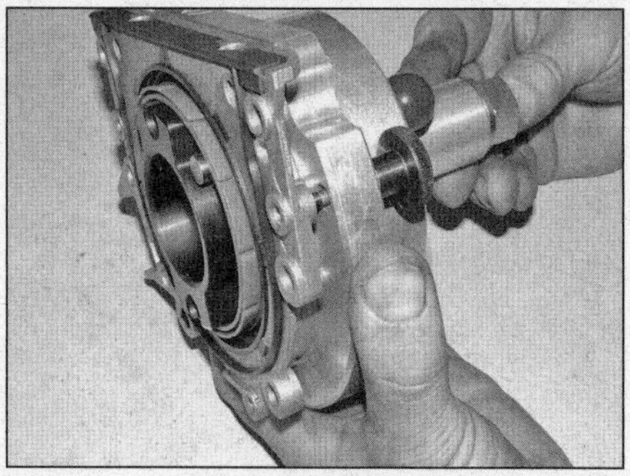

15.17b ...and push the spindle in as far as possible

tool, so the pin locates in the hole in the sender wheel **(see illustration)**.

15 Push the sealing flange and guide fitting sleeve against the tool whilst tightening the 3 knurled screws. Ensure the pin is still located in the sender wheel **(see illustration)**.

16 Ensure the end of the crankshaft is clean, and is locked at TDC on No. 1 cylinder as described in Section 3.

17 Unscrew the large nut to the end of the spindle threads, then press the spindle inwards as far as possible **(see illustrations)**.

18 Align the flat side of the assembly with the sump flange, then secure the tool to the crankshaft using the integral Allen bolts **(see illustration)**. Only hand tighten the bolts.

19 Insert two M7x 35 mm bolts to guide the sealing flange to the cylinder block **(see illustration)**.

20 Using hand pressure alone, push the tool assembly onto the crankshaft until the seal guide fitting sleeve contacts the crankshaft flange, then push the guide pin (black knob) into the hole in the crankshaft. This is to ensure the sender wheel reaches its correct installation position **(see illustration)**.

21 Rotate the large nut until it makes contact with the tool housing, then tighten it to 35 Nm. After tightening this nut, a small air gap must still be present between the sealing flange and cylinder block **(see illustrations)**.

15.18 Hand-tighten the Allen bolts to secure the tool to the crankshaft

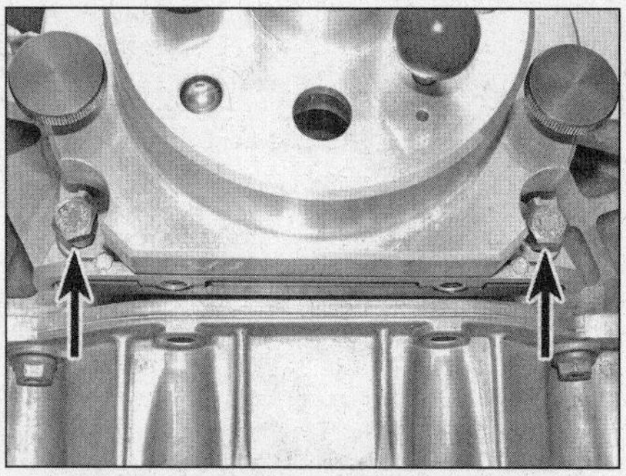

15.19 Use two M7 x 35 mm bolts to guide the sealing flange

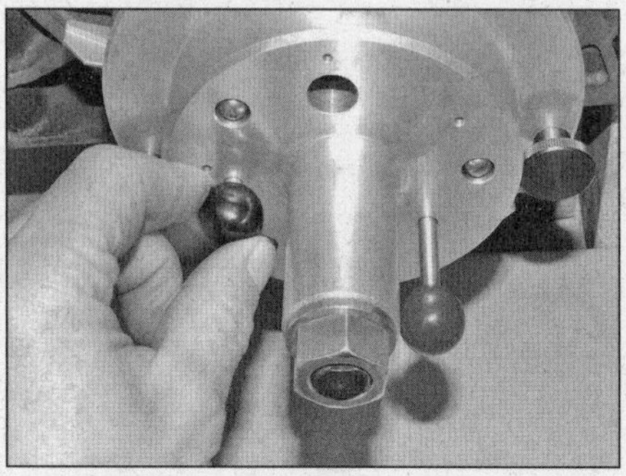

15.20 Push the black knob into the hole in the crankshaft

15.21a After tightening the spindle nut to 35 Nm...

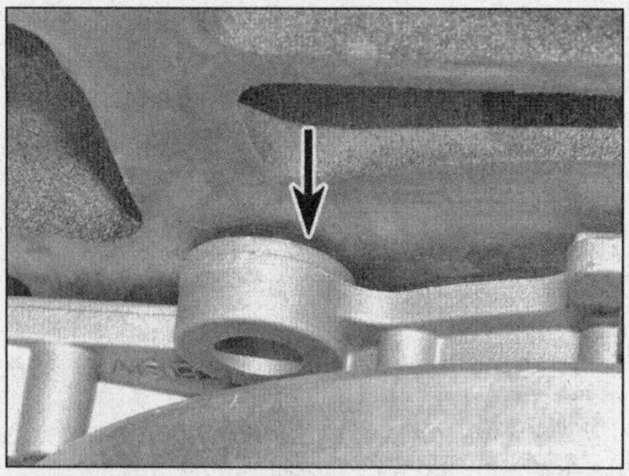

15.21b ...there should be an air gap between the sealing flange and the cylinder block

22 Unscrew the large nut; the two M7 x 35 mm screws, the three knurled screws and the Allen bolts securing the tool to the crankshaft. Remove the tool, and pull the seal guide fitting sleeve from place (if it didn't come out with the tool) **(see illustration)**.

23 Use a vernier caliper or feeler gauge to measure the fitted depth of the sender wheel in relation to the crankshaft flange **(see illustration)**. The correct depth is 0.5 mm.

24 If the gap is correct, fit the sealing flange bolts and tighten them to the specified torque.

25 If the gap is too small, re-attach the tool to the sealing flange and crankshaft, then refit the two M7 x 35 mm guide bolts to the flange. Tighten the large spindle nut to 40 Nm, remove the tool and re-measure the air gap. If the gap is still too small, re-attach the tool and tighten the spindle nut to 45 Nm. Re-measure the gap. When the gap is correct, refit the flange retaining bolts, and tighten them to the specified torque.

26 The remainder of refitting is a reversal of removal.

16 Flywheel – removal, inspection and refitting

Removal

1 Remove the transmission (see Chapter 7A Section 3 or Chapter 7B Section 2) and on manual transmissions the clutch (see Chapter 6A Section 6).

2 The flywheel can only be fitted in one position due to the offset of the flywheel mounting holes in the end of the crankshaft.

3 On dual-mass flywheels, rotate the outside of the flywheel so that the bolts align with the holes (if necessary).

4 Unscrew the bolts and remove the flywheel. Using a locking tool, counter-hold the flywheel to prevent it from turning **(see illustration)**. Discard the bolts, as new ones must be fitted.

Inspection

5 Check the flywheel for wear and damage. Examine the starter ring gear for excessive wear to the teeth. If the driveplate or its ring gear are damaged, the complete driveplate must be renewed. If the clutch friction face is discoloured or scored excessively, it may be possible to regrind it, but this work should also be entrusted to a specialist.

6 There should be no cracks in the drive surface of the flywheel. If cracks are evident, the flywheel may need replacing.

Dual-mass flywheels

7 The following are guidelines only, but should indicate whether professional inspection is necessary, check as follows:

8 Warpage: Place a straight edge across the face of the drive surface, and check by trying to insert a feeler gauge between the straight edge and the drive surface **(see illustration)**. The flywheel will normally warp like a bowl – ie. Higher on the outer edge. If the warpage is more than 0.40 mm, the flywheel may need replacing.

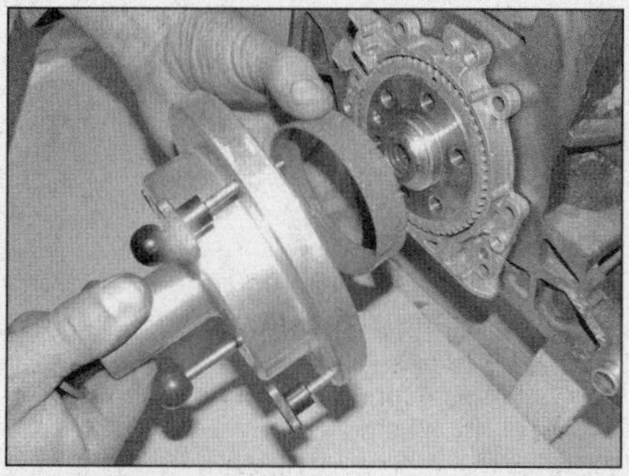

15.22 Remove the tool and seal fitting guide sleeve

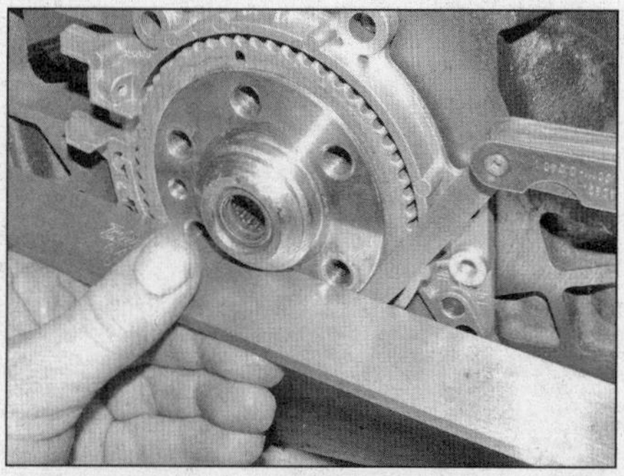

15.23 Measure the fitted depth of the sender wheel in relation to the end of the crankshaft

9 Free rotational movement: This is the distance the drive surface of the flywheel can be turned independently of the flywheel primary element, using finger effort alone. Move the drive surface in one direction and make a mark where the locating pin aligns with the flywheel edge. Move the drive surface in the other direction (finger pressure only) and make another mark **(see illustration)**. The total of free movement should not exceed 20.0 mm. If it's more, the flywheel may need replacing.

10 Total rotational movement: This is the total distance the drive surface can be turned independently of the flywheel primary element. Insert two bolts into the clutch pressure plate/damper unit mounting holes, and with the crankshaft/flywheel held stationary, use a lever/pry bar between the bolts and use some effort to move the drive surface fully in one direction – make a mark where the locating pin aligns with the flywheel edge. Now force the drive surface fully in the opposite direction, and make another mark. The total rotational movement should not exceed 44.00 mm. If it does, have the flywheel professionally inspected.

11 Lateral movement: The lateral movement (up and down) of the drive surface in relation to the primary element of the flywheel, should not exceed 2.0 mm. If it does, the flywheel may need replacing. This can be checked by pressing the drive surface down on one side into the flywheel (flywheel horizontal) and making an alignment mark between the drive surface and the inner edge of the primary element. Now press down on the opposite side of the drive surface, and make another mark above the original one. The difference between the two marks is the lateral movement **(see illustration)**.

16.4 Use a locking tool to counterhold the flywheel

16.8 Flywheel warpage check – see text

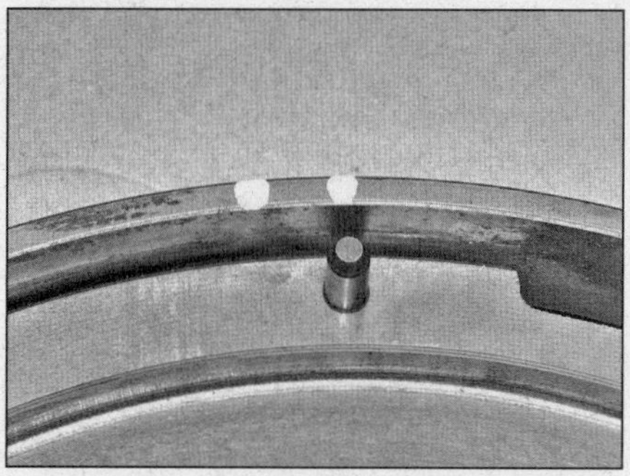

16.9 Flywheel free rotational movement check alignment marks – see text

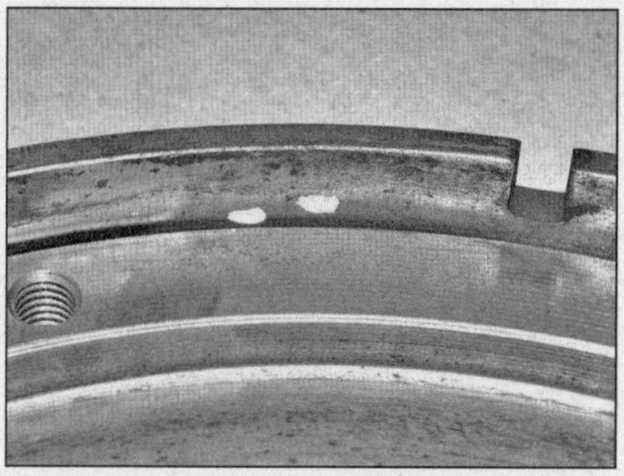

16.11 Flywheel lateral movement check marks – see text

16.12 Use new bolts when refitting

Refitting

12 Refitting is a reversal of removal. Use new bolts when refitting the flywheel or driveplate **(see illustration)**, and coat the threads of the bolts (if not already coated with locking compound) with locking fluid before inserting them. Tighten them to the specified torque.

17 Engine/transmission mountings – inspection and renewal

Inspection

1 If improved access is required, jack up the front of the car, and support it securely on axle stands (see *Jacking and vehicle support*). Remove the securing screws and remove the engine under shield.

2 Check the mounting rubbers to see if they are cracked, hardened or separated from the metal at any point; renew the mounting if any such damage or deterioration is evident.

3 Check that all the mountings are securely tightened; use a torque wrench to check if possible.

4 Using a large screwdriver or lever, check for wear in the mounting by carefully levering against it to check for free play. Where this is not possible, enlist the aid of an assistant to move the engine/transmission back-and-forth, or from side-to-side, whilst you observe the mounting. While some free play is to be expected, even from new components, excessive wear should be obvious. If excessive free play is found, check first that the fasteners are correctly secured, and then renew any worn components as described in the following paragraphs.

Caution: Do NOT undo the centre bolt, securing the bracket to the flexible mounting.

5 When working on the right-hand mounting and rear lower mounting (torque arm), remove the mounting as a complete unit. Seat state that the mounting bracket-to-flexible mounting nut/bolt should not be slackened, see following procedures for each individual mounting.

Renewal

6 The engine mountings on the 1.2 litre, petrol engines, are similar to those fitted on the 1.0 litre, 3-cylinder petrol models, see Chapter 2A Section 20, for the removal and refitting procedures of the engine mountings.

Chapter 2 Part C
1.2 litre (DOHC) petrol engine in-car repair procedures

Contents

Degrees of difficulty

Easy, suitable for novice with little experience	Fairly easy, suitable for beginner with some experience	Fairly difficult, suitable for competent DIY mechanic	Difficult, suitable for experienced DIY mechanic	Very difficult, suitable for expert DIY or professional

Specifications

General

Manufacturers engine codes*	CJZD and CJZC
Maximum power output:	
Engine code CJZD	81 kW at 4600 to 5600 rpm
Engine code CJZC	66 kW at 4400 to 5400 rpm
Maximum torque output:	
Engine code CJZD	175 Nm at 1400 to 4000 rpm
Engine code CJZC	160 Nm at 1400 to 3500 rpm
Bore	71.0 mm
Stroke	75.6 mm
Compression ratio	10.5 : 1
Compression pressure:	
Minimum compression pressure	Approximately 7.0 bar
Maximum difference between cylinders	Approximately 3.0 bar
Firing order	1 -3 -4 -2
Number 1 cylinder location	Timing belt end

**See 'Vehicle identification' at the end of this manual for the location of the engine code markings.*

Lubrication system

Oil pump type	Direct drive from, crankshaft
Oil pressure (oil temperature 80°C):	
At idle	0.6 bar (minimum)
At 2000 rpm	1.5 bar (minimum)
At 4500 rpm	2.8 bar (minimum)

Torque wrench settings

	Nm	lbf ft
Ancillary (alternator, etc) bracket mounting bolts	45	33
Auxiliary drivebelt tensioner securing bolt: *		
Stage 1	20	15
Stage 2	Angle-tighten a further 90°	
Big-end bearing cap bolts: *		
Stage 1	30	22
Stage 2	Angle-tighten a further 90°	
Camshaft cover bolts: *		
Stage 1	10	7
Stage 2	Angle-tighten a further 180°	
Camshaft sprocket bolts*:		
Exhaust sprocket:		
Stage 1	50	37
Stage 2	Angle-tighten a further 90°	
Inlet sprocket bolt: *		
Stage 1	50	37
Stage 2	Angle-tighten a further 135°	
Camshaft sprocket plug (Inlet)*	20	15
Coolant pump bolts:		
Stage 1	10	7
Stage 2	Loosen one revolution	
Stage 3	10	7
Stage 4	12	9
Coolant pump sprocket bolt*:		
Stage 1	20	15
Stage 2	Angle-tighten a further 90°	
Crankshaft oil seal/ oil pump housing bolts: *		
Stage 1 (upper 6 bolts)	8	6
Stage 2	Angle-tighten a further 90°	
Lower bolts (bottom right)	20	15
Crankshaft position sensor wheel-to-crankshaft bolts	10	7
Crankshaft sprocket bolt: *		
Stage 1	150	110
Stage 2	Angle-tighten a further 180°	
Cylinder head bolts: *		
Stage 1	40	30
Stage 2	Angle-tighten a further 90°	
Stage 3	Angle-tighten a further 90°	
Stage 4	Angle-tighten a further 90°	
Engine mountings:		
RH engine mounting*:		
Mounting to engine bracket:		
Stage 1	60	44
Stage 2	Angle-tighten a further 90°	
Mounting to body:		
Stage 1	40	30
Stage 2	Angle-tighten a further 90°	
Mounting to body (horizontal bolt):		
Stage 1	20	15
Stage 2	Angle-tighten a further 90°	
Bracket to engine:		
Stage 1	7	5
Stage 2	40	30
Stage 3	Angle-tighten a further 90°	
LH engine mounting*:		
Mounting to body:		
Stage 1	50	37
Stage 2	Angle-tighten a further 90°	
Mounting to transmission:		
Stage 1	60	44
Stage 2	Angle-tighten a further 90°	
Rear pendulum mounting*:		
To transmission:		
Stage 1	50	37
Stage 2	Angle-tighten a further 90°	
To subframe:		
Stage 1	130	96
Stage 2	Angle-tighten a further 90°	

Torque wrench settings (continued)	Nm	lbf ft
Flywheel*:		
Stage 1	60	44
Stage 2	Angle-tighten a further 90°	
Inlet manifold to head	8	6
Oil cooler bolts: *		
Stage 1	8	6
Stage 2	Angle-tighten a further 90°	
Oil drain plug	30	22
Oil level/temperature sender bolts	8	6
Oil pick-up pipe-to-oil pump bolts	8	6
Oil pressure switch	20	15
Oil spray jet/pressure relief valve bolts	27	20
Roadwheel bolts	120	89
Sump bolts: *		
Stage 1	8	6
Stage 2	Angle-tighten a further 90°	
Thermostat cover bolts (large cooling circuit)	8	6
Thermostat cover (to coolant pump)	8	6
Timing belt outer cover bolts	8	6
Timing belt rear cover bolts:		
Small bolts	10	7
Large bolt	23	17
Timing belt tensioner bolt	25	18
Timing belt idler pulley bolt	45	33
Timing TDC pin blanking plug	30	22
Turbocharger to cylinder head nuts*	14	10
Turbocharger heat shield bolts (main bolts)	25	18

**Do not re-use*

1 General Information

How to use this Chapter

1 This Part of Chapter 2 describes those repair procedures that can reasonably be carried out on the engine while it remains in the vehicle. If the engine has been removed from the vehicle and is being dismantled as described in Part F, any preliminary dismantling procedures can be ignored.

2 Note that while it may be possible physically to overhaul certain items while the engine is in the vehicle, such tasks are not usually carried out as separate operations, and usually require the execution of several additional procedures (not to mention the cleaning of components and of oilways); for this reason, all such tasks are classed as major overhaul procedures, and are described in Part F of this Chapter.

Engine description

3 Throughout this Chapter, engines are identified by the manufacturer's code letters. A listing of all engines covered, together with their code letters, is given in the Specifications.

4 The engines covered in this Part of the Chapter are of water-cooled, double-overhead camshaft (DOHC), in-line four-cylinder design. The engine family is designated EA211 by VAG (Volkswagen Audi Group). The engines have an aluminium alloy cylinder block fitted with grey cast-iron cylinder liners, and an aluminium alloy cylinder head. The exhaust manifold is integrated into the cylinder head. The engine is transversely mounted at the front of the vehicle, with the transmission unit on its left-hand end.

5 The crankshaft is of five-bearing type, but note that the crankshaft must not be removed due to the design of the bearing pedestals. Removing the bearing caps will distort the pedestals and damage the bearings.

6 The camshafts are mounted in a modular camshaft carrier and are driven by a toothed timing belt from the crankshaft sprocket. Variable Valve Timing (VVT) is fitted to the inlet camshaft on all versions. Repair to the camshafts is not possible. If a fault develops the entire housing (module) is replaced.

7 The valves are closed by coil springs, and the valves run in guides pressed into the cylinder head. The camshafts actuate the valves by roller rocker fingers supported by hydraulic tappets.

8 All engines have a 'duocentric' oil pump driven directly by the crankshaft. Oil is drawn from the sump through a strainer, and then forced through an externally-mounted, renewable filter. From there, it is distributed to the cylinder head, where it lubricates the camshaft journals and hydraulic tappets, and also to the crankcase, where it lubricates the main bearings, connecting rod big-ends, gudgeon pins and cylinder bores. A coolant-fed oil cooler is fitted to all engines.

9 Engine coolant is circulated by a pump, driven by the timing belt. For details of the cooling system, refer to Chapter 3.

Operations with engine in car

10 The following operations can be performed without removing the engine:

a) Compression pressure – testing.
b) Camshaft cover – removal and refitting.
c) Crankshaft pulley – removal and refitting.
d) Timing belt covers – removal and refitting.
e) Timing belt – removal, refitting and adjustment.
f) Timing belt tensioner and sprockets – removal and refitting.
g) Camshaft oil seal – renewal.
h) Camshaft and hydraulic tappets – removal, inspection and refitting.
i) Cylinder head – removal and refitting.
j) Cylinder head and pistons – decarbonising.
k) Sump – removal and refitting.
l) Oil pump – removal, overhaul and refitting.
m) Crankshaft oil seals – renewal.
n) Engine/transmission mountings – inspection and renewal.
o) Flywheel/driveplate – removal, inspection and refitting.

Note: *It is possible to remove the pistons and connecting rods (after removing the cylinder head and sump) without removing the engine. However, this is not recommended. Work of this nature is more easily and thoroughly completed with the engine on the bench, as described in Chapter 2F.*

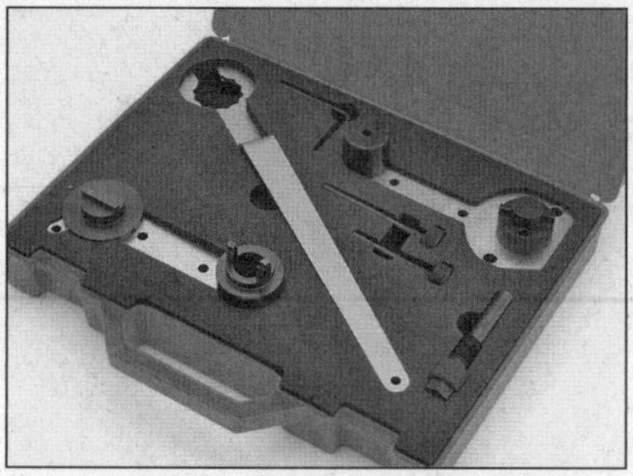

3.0 A full set of aftermarket timing tools from AST tools

3.6 Remove the charge air and inlet air ducts

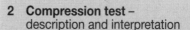

2 Compression test – description and interpretation

Caution: The following work may insert fault codes in the engine management ECU. These fault codes must be cleared by a Seat dealer or suitably equipped repairer.

Note: *A suitable compression tester will be required for this test.*

1 When engine performance is down, or if misfiring occurs which cannot be attributed to the ignition or fuel systems, a compression test can provide diagnostic clues as to the engine's condition. If the test is performed regularly it can give warning of trouble before any other symptoms become apparent.

2 The engine must be fully warmed-up to normal operating temperature, the battery must be fully-charged and the spark plugs must be removed (Chapter 1A Section 27). The aid of an assistant will be required.

3 Disable the ignition system either by disconnecting the wiring plugs from the coils (see Chapter 5B Section 3) or install a remote starter switch to the starter motor.

4 Referring to Chapter 4A Section 4, disconnect the wiring from the fuel injectors.

5 Fit a compression tester to the No 1 cylinder spark plug hole. The type of tester which screws into the plug thread is preferred.

6 Have the assistant hold the throttle wide open and crank the engine for several seconds on the starter motor. **Note:** *The throttle will not operate until the ignition is switched on.* After one or two revolutions, the compression pressure should build-up to a maximum figure and then stabilise. Record the highest reading obtained.

7 Repeat the test on the remaining cylinders, recording the pressure in each.

8 All cylinders should produce very similar pressures. Any difference greater than that specified indicates the existence of a fault. Note that the compression should build-up quickly in a healthy engine. Low compression on the first stroke, followed by gradually increasing pressure on successive strokes, indicates worn piston rings. A low compression reading on the first stroke, which does not build-up during successive strokes, indicates leaking valves or a blown head gasket (a cracked head could also be the cause). Deposits on the undersides of the valve heads can also cause low compression.

9 If the pressure in any cylinder is reduced to the specified minimum or less, carry out the following test to isolate the cause. Introduce a teaspoonful of clean oil into that cylinder through its spark plug hole and repeat the test.

10 If the addition of oil temporarily improves the compression pressure, this indicates that bore or piston wear is responsible for the pressure loss. No improvement suggests that leaking or burnt valves, or a blown head gasket, may be to blame.

11 A low reading from two adjacent cylinders is almost certainly due to the head gasket having blown between them and the presence of coolant in the engine oil will confirm this.

3.7a Disconnect the EVAP hose and...

3.7b ...then remove the breather hose

12 If one cylinder is about 20 percent lower than the others and the engine has a slightly rough idle, a worn camshaft lobe could be the cause.

13 If the compression reading is unusually high, the combustion chambers are probably coated with carbon deposits. If this is the case, the cylinder head should be removed and decarbonised.

14 On completion of the test, refit the spark plugs, and reconnect the ignition coils.

15 Have any fault codes cleared by a Seat dealer or suitably equipped garage.

3 Engine assembly and valve timing marks – general information and usage

Note: *A set of specific timing tools will be required to set the engine at TDC (Top Dead Centre). These are available in the aftermarket* ***(see illustration)*** *or directly from Seat.*

General information

1 TDC is the highest point in the cylinder that each piston reaches as it travels up and down when the crankshaft turns. Each piston reaches TDC at the end of the compression stroke and again at the end of the exhaust stroke, but TDC generally refers to piston position on the compression stroke. No 1 piston is at the timing belt end of the engine.

2 Positioning No 1 piston at TDC is an essential part of many procedures, such as timing belt removal and camshaft removal.

3 The design of the engines covered in this Chapter is such that piston-to-valve contact may occur if the camshaft or crankshaft is turned with the timing belt removed. For this reason, it is important to ensure that the camshaft and crankshaft do not move in relation to each other once the timing belt has been removed from the engine.

Setting No 1 cylinder to TDC and checking the timing

4 Jack up and support the front of the vehicle (see *Jacking and vehicle support*), remove the engine undershield and then drain the coolant as described in Chapter 1A Section 32. Note that there is no need to completely drain the coolant, the level only requires lowering to below the coolant pump.

5 Remove the air filter housing as described in Chapter 4A Section 3.

6 Remove the air inlet pipes from the transmission end of the engine **(see illustration)**.

7 Disconnect the evaporative emissions (EVAP) hose and then remove the crankcase breather hose from the left-hand end of the engine **(see illustrations)**.

8 Remove the coolant hose and air inlet duct. Where required disconnect the wiring plugs from the coolant temperature sensor and the charge air (boost pressure) sensor.

9 Unclip the wiring loom from the coolant pump drivebelt sprocket and then remove the coolant pump drivebelt cover **(see illustrations)**.

10 Unscrew the bolts and remove the cover from the inlet camshaft **(see illustration)**.

11 Remove the spark plug from cylinder number 1. If desired, to make the engine easier to turn, remove all of the spark plugs as described in Chapter 1A Section 27.

12 Insert a long screwdriver into the spark plug hole of number 1 cylinder and then rotate the engine (via the crankshaft pulley bolt) in the normal direction, until the the piston is at the bottom of the stroke (BDC – Bottom Dead Centre).

13 Turn the crankshaft in the normal direction of rotation (clockwise when looking at the crankshaft pulley) until the screwdriver has risen by 30 mm **(see illustration)**.

14 Remove the blanking plug from the right-hand rear of the cylinder block and insert the crankshaft locking tool T10340 (or equivalent) into the block **(see illustration)**. Slowly rotate the crankshaft in the normal direction until it stops against the locking pin.

15 Note that if the pin can cannot be fully inserted, remove it and rotate the engine another 90 degrees in the normal direction and refit the pin. Turn the engine further clockwise until the crankshaft stops against the pin.

16 Next check the position of the camshaft sprockets. Looking through the exhaust camshaft sprocket, check the the grooves directly behind the sprocket are level and above and imaginary line drawn through the centre of the sprocket.

17 Next check the position of the inlet camshaft grooves, again they should be just above the horizontal. **Note:** *If the camshafts are not aligned as shown, then the engine is set at TDC on number 4 cylinder. Remove the crankshaft timing pin, rotate the engine one revolution and repeat the alignment procedure*.

18 This is the basic check of the correct timing. The timing can be verified by fitting the timing tool (T10494) to the inlet and exhaust camshafts **(see illustration)**. If the tool can not be fitted it is permissible to slightly depress the timing belt (using special tool T10487 or an equivalent) between the inlet and exhaust camshaft sprockets to correct any minor alignment issues. The timing belt upper cover must be removed as described in Section 6 first.

19 Remove the timing tools on completion and then refit the removed components. Refill the cooling system as described in Chapter 1A Section 32.

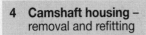

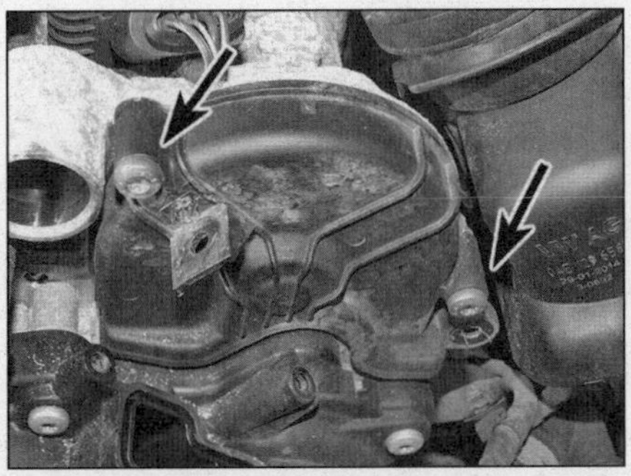

3.9a Remove the screws and...

3.9b ...lift off the cover

3.10 Remove the cover

3.13 Raise the piston by 30 mm

3.14 Remove the blanking plug

3.18 Fit the camshaft setting tool

4 Camshaft housing – removal and refitting

Note: *The camshafts are housed in a single combined valve cover and camshaft carrier. The camshafts can not be removed from the housing. If there is a fault with the camshafts (such as worn lobes, or excessive end float for example) then the complete housing and camshafts must be replaced.*

Removal

1 Drain the coolant (Chapter 1A Section 32) and then remove the coolant pump as described in Chapter 3 Section 7.

2 Remove the air filter housing as described in Chapter 4A Section 3.

3 Remove the ignition coils as described in Chapter 5B Section 3.

4 Remove the timing belt from the camshaft sprockets as described in Section 7 – there is no need to completely remove the timing belt at this stage.

5 Fit the camshaft locking tool to the coolant pump sprocket and the inlet camshaft (as described in Section 3). Fitting the tool will lock the camshafts in position.

6 Disconnect the wiring plug and fuel lines from the high pressure fuel pump (Chapter 4A Section 4).

7 Remove the inlet duct from the rear of the engine and then remove the turbocharger coolant hoses **(see illustrations)**.

4.7a Unbolt the inlet elbow from the turbocharger

4.7b Unbolt (and move to the side) the coolant pipes

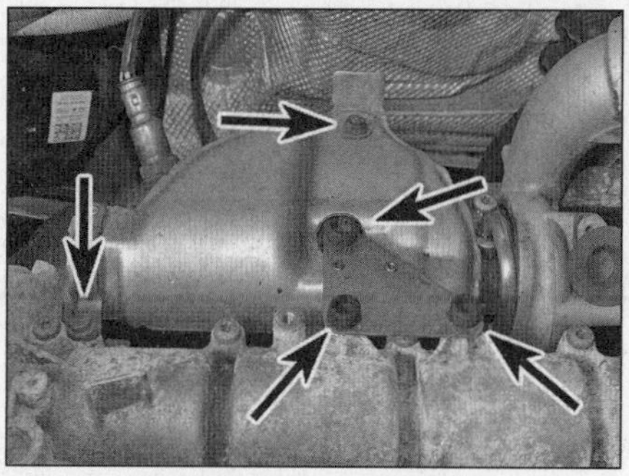

4.8a Unbolt and then…

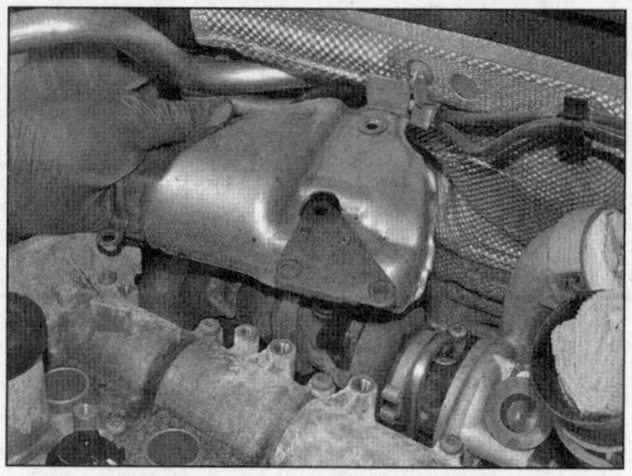

4.8b …remove the heat shield

4.9a Disconnect the wiring plug from the VVT control solenoid and…

4.9b …unbolt the ground wire

8 Unbolt and remove the heat shield from the top of the turbocharger **(see illustrations)**.

9 Disconnect the wiring plugs from the camshaft position sensor and the VVT control valve. Unbolt the ground wire **(see illustrations)**. Release (and unbolt) the wiring loom from the retaining brackets and then move the wiring loom to the side.

4.11a Remove the camshaft housing and…

4.11b …then recover the gasket

4.13 Fit guide studs to the cylinder head

4.14 Lower the new gasket over the studs

10 Remove the dipstick and then unbolt the housing in the reverse order (15 to 1) to that shown **(see illustration 4.15)**.

11 Remove the housing and store it on a clean surface. Recover the gasket **(see illustrations)**.

Refitting

12 Thoroughly clean the mating surfaces of the camshaft housing and the cylinder head.

13 Fit guide studs to the cylinder head. These can be fabricated from bolts with their heads cut off and a slot filed into the end of the stud for removal **(see illustration)**.

14 Fit a new gasket **(see illustration)**, check that the cam followers are all correctly located and then lower the housing into position.

15 Tighten the new bolts progressively to the specified torque in sequence **(see illustration)**.

16 The remainder of refitting is a reversal of removal, but consider fitting a new timing belt and always fit a new coolant pump belt. Rotate the engine at least twice in the normal direction to check the valve timing. Refill the coolant as described in Chapter 1A Section 32.

5 Crankshaft pulley – removal and refitting

Removal

1 Raise the front right-hand side of the vehicle, and support the vehicle securely on axle stands (see *Jacking and vehicle support*). Remove the road wheel.

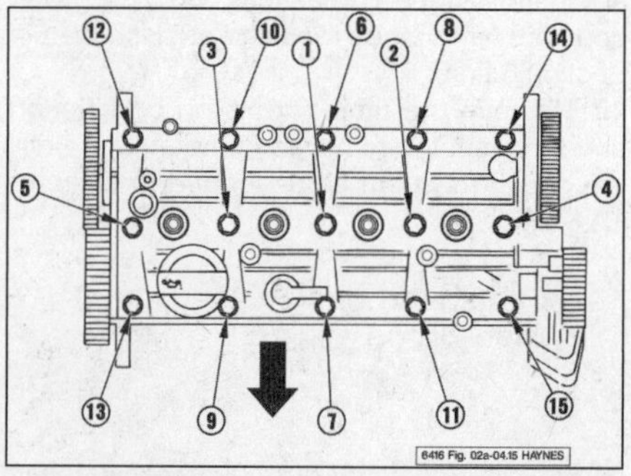

4.15 Tighten the bolts in the order shown

2 Remove the wing liner **(see illustration)**.
3 If necessary (for any later work to be carried out), turn the crankshaft using a socket or spanner on the crankshaft sprocket bolt until the relevant timing marks align (see Section 3).
4 Remove the auxiliary drivebelt as described in Chapter 1A Section 28.
Caution: The bolt is difficult to release, due to the high torque and angle setting required. A home made tool can be fabricated, but the use of the correct tool (AST 5144 for example) is highly recommended.
5 Use a large peg wrench (or the special tool T10475) to counterhold the pulley and then remove the bolt **(see illustrations)**. Dispose of the bolt, a new one will be required for refitting.

Refitting

6 Clean the mounting surface of both the pulley and the crankshaft. Refit the pulley to the sprocket, lubricate the new bolt and fit it.
7 Tighten the new bolt to the specified torque.
8 The refitting of the remaining components is a reversal of removal.

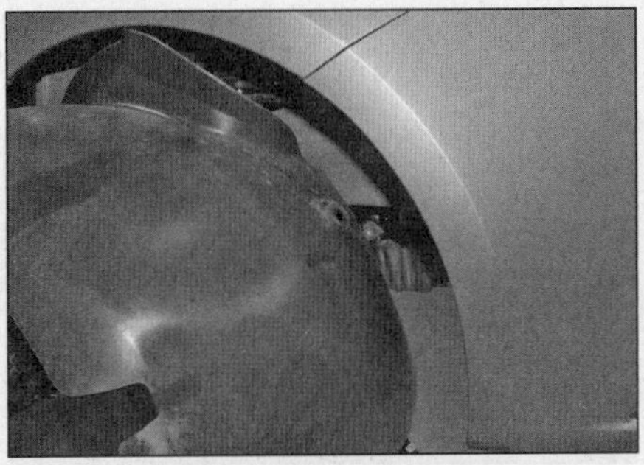

5.2 Remove the wing liner

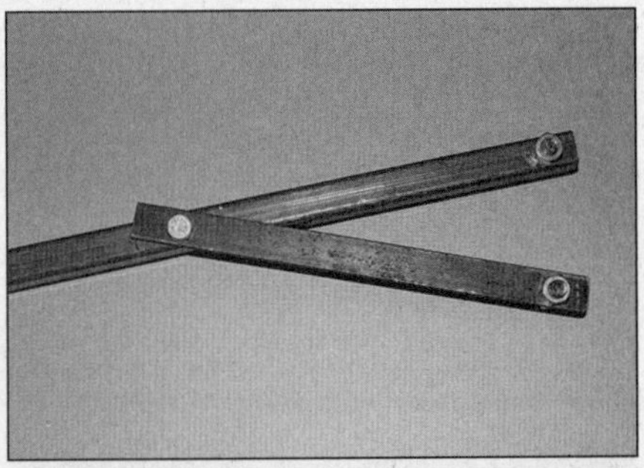

5.5a A large adjustable peg wrench will be required to counterhold the pulley

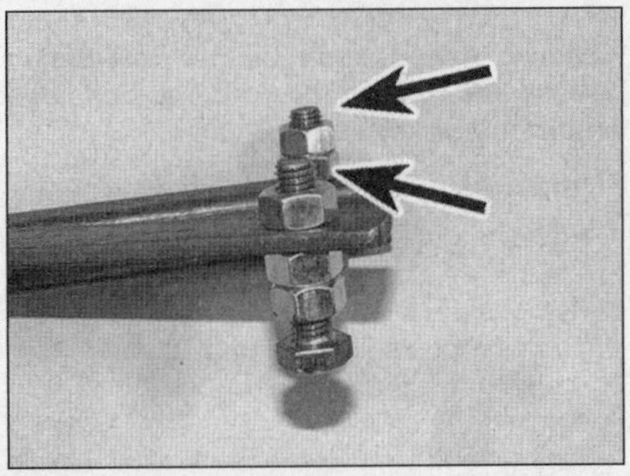

5.5b Adapt the tool, so that the bolts engage with the shallow slots in the pulley

5.5c Counterhold the pulley with the tool and slacken the bolt

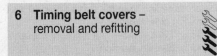

6 Timing belt covers – removal and refitting

Note: *The centre cover is the engine support bracket. Removal is described in Section 7.*

Upper cover

Removal

1 Unclip the fuel lines from the cover and move them to the side **(see illustration)**.
2 Remove the bolt from the coolant pipe bracket, release the retaining clips and lift off the cover **(see illustrations)**.

Refitting

3 Refitting is a reversal of removal.

Lower cover

Removal

4 Remove the crankshaft pulley (see Section 5).
5 Unscrew the securing bolts, and withdraw the cover from the front of the engine **(see illustrations)**.

6.1 Unclip the fuel lines

6.2a Release the front clip...

6.2b ...the rear clip...

6.2c ...and lift off the cover

6.5a Remove the bolts...

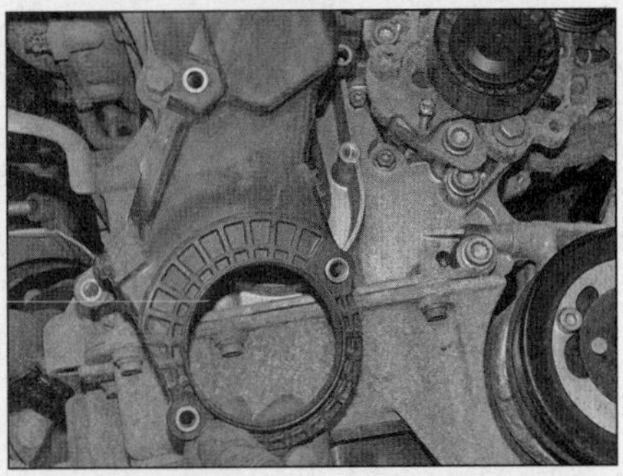

6.5b ...and remove the lower the cover

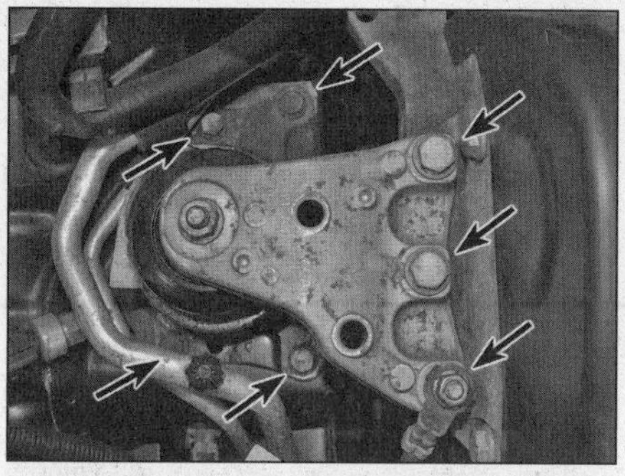

7.9 Remove the engine mounting. Do not remove the centre bolt

7.10 Remove the tensioner

7.11 Remove the upper bolt and pivot the alternator away from the engine bracket

Refitting

6 Refitting is a reversal of removal.

7 Timing belt – removal and refitting

Note: *Timing belt replacement is possible with the engine mounting bracket in position. However without the special torque wrench adapter, tightening the tensioner to the correct torque is not possible. If the tensioner is to be replaced at the same time (as recommended) then removal of the bracket is required anyway. The procedure described below includes removal of the engine mounting bracket.*

Caution: The timing tools are alignment tools, they are not designed to hold the crankshaft or camshafts in position whilst the sprocket and pulley bolts are removed. Always use a counterhold tool to release and tighten the sprocket bolts and crankshaft pulley bolt.

Removal

1 Remove the air filter housing as described in Chapter 4A Section 3.

2 Remove the inlet and outlet pipes from the turbocharger **(see illustration 3.6)**.

3 Remove the timing belt upper cover, with reference to Section 6.

4 Jack up and support the front of the vehicle (see *Jacking and vehicle support*). Remove the wheel and then the lower section of the right-hand wing liner.

5 Slacken the crankshaft pulley bolt as described in Section 5. **Do not** remove the bolt at this stage.

6 Turn the crankshaft to position No 1 piston at TDC, as described in Section 3 and install the timing tools.

7 Remove the crankshaft pulley, with reference to Section 5. Before finally removing the pulley, check that No 1 piston is still positioned at TDC (Section 5).

8 Remove the timing belt lower cover as described in Section 6.

9 Using a block of wood (to spread the load) place a jack under the engine sump and support the engine. Unbolt the right-hand engine mounting from the engine bracket and inner wing **(see illustration)**.

10 Unbolt and remove the auxiliary drivebelt tensioner **(see illustration)**.

11 Slacken the lower alternator mounting bolt, remove the upper bolt and then pivot the alternator away from the engine bracket **(see illustration)**.

12 Unbolt and remove the engine bracket from the engine block – 3 bolts. Lower the bracket from the engine, raising and lowering the engine on the jack as required to allow the bracket to pass down and out of the engine bay **(see illustrations)**.

13 Using an adjustable peg spanner (or the factory tool T10172) counterhold the inlet sprocket and remove the blanking plug. Next slacken (but do not remove) the sprocket retaining bolt **(see illustrations)**. On models with VVT on the exhaust camshaft, remove the cover (5 bolts). On all engines (whilst counterholding the sprocket), slacken (but do not remove) the exhaust camshaft sprocket retaining bolt.

14 If the timing belt is to be refitted, mark its running direction.

15 Loosen the timing belt tensioner securing

7.12a Unbolt the coolant hose

7.12b Lower the bracket out of the engine bay

7.13a Remove the blanking plug...

7.13b ...and then slacken the sprocket bolt

7.13c Repeat the procedure on the exhaust camshaft sprocket

nut to release the tensioner. Push back the tensioner and tighten the locking nut. Remove the timing belt from the sprockets.

16 If further work is anticipated, turn the crankshaft a quarter-turn (90°) anti-clockwise to position Nos 1 and 4 pistons slightly down their bores from the TDC position. This will eliminate any risk of piston-to-valve contact if the crankshaft or camshaft is turned whilst the timing belt is removed.

Refitting

17 Although not mandatory the fitting of a new tensioner and idler is highly recommended. If they are not to be replaced, they should be turned by hand and checked for play and abnormal noise.

18 Fit the new tensioner, checking that the tab on the rear fits into the slot on the cylinder head **(see illustration)**. Fit a new idler pulley.

19 Check that the camshaft locking tool is correctly fitted. If the crankshaft was lowered, then turn the crankshaft a quarter-turn (90°) clockwise to reposition the engine at TDC (the TDC timing pin should be in place).

20 Fit new bolts to the camshaft sprockets and tighten the bolts, so that the sprockets rotate freely without any play.

21 Remove the crankshaft sprocket and clean the mounting surface. Refit the sprocket.

22 Fit the timing belt around the crankshaft sprocket, the idler, the tensioner and the camshaft sprockets **(see illustration)**.

23 The timing belt must now be tensioned as follows.

24 Using a 30 mm spanner turn the tensioner so that the indicator is 10 mm to the right of the adjustment window. Next turn the tensioner back, so that it lies in the middle of the adjustment window **(see illustrations)**.

25 Hold the tensioner in this position and tighten the locking nut to the specified torque.

26 Using the peg spanner to counterhold the camshaft sprockets, tighten the new bolts to 50 Nm.

27 Remove the timing tools from the crankshaft and the camshafts.

28 Fit the lower timing belt cover and tighten the bolts.

29 Clean the mounting surface of both the crankshaft pulley and the crankshaft sprocket. Fit the crankshaft sprocket with the new bolt and tighten the bolt using the counterhold tool and socket to the specified torque.

30 Turn the crankshaft two revolutions in the normal direction of rotation and refit the timing tools as described in Section 3. Slightly depressing the new belt between the camshaft sprockets is is permissible if the camshaft locking tool does not fit easily. If the tool does not fit the timing is incorrect and the installation procedure must be repeated.

31 Using the counterhold, tighten the camshaft sprockets to the second stage of the tightening procedure. Note that the final angle tightening is different for the inlet and exhaust camshafts.

7.18 The tang on the tensioner must engage correctly in the cylinder head

7.22 Fit the new belt

7.24a Over-tighten the tensioner by 10 mm...

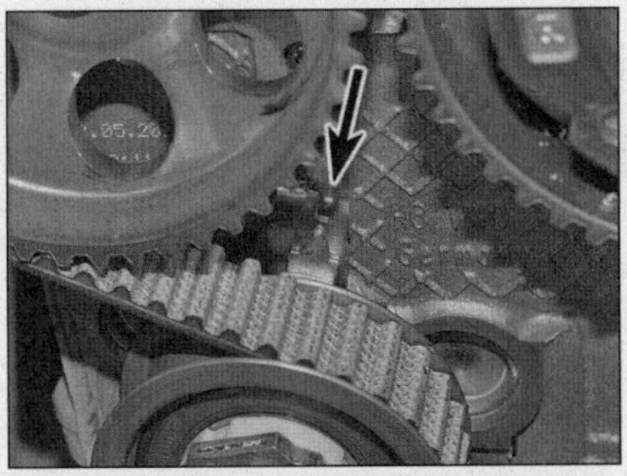

7.24b ...and then adjust the tensioner to the correct central position

32 Fit a new blanking plug and seal to the inlet camshaft.

33 Refit the engine bracket, alternator bolts and the engine mounting.

34 Fit the remaining components in reverse order to removal.

8 Timing belt tensioner and sprockets – removal and refitting

Camshaft sprockets

Removal

1 Remove the timing belt as described in Section 7.

2 The camshaft must be held stationary as the sprocket bolt is slackened. This can be achieved by making up a tool, and using it to hold the sprocket stationary by means of the holes in the sprocket face. The tool fits easily into the exhaust camshaft sprocket. On the inlet camshaft the only location points are shallow holes in the face of the VVT hub. A factory tool is available to overcome this problem (T10172) but is also possible to fabricate a similar tool **(see illustrations)**. If a home made tool is used an assistant will be required to keep the tool locked in place, whilst the bolt is slackened.

3 Unscrew the sprocket bolt and withdraw it, then withdraw the sprocket from the end of the camshaft **(see illustrations)**.

4 Repeat the procedure for the other sprocket. Discard the bolts as new ones must be used.

Refitting

5 Prior to refitting, check the camshaft oil

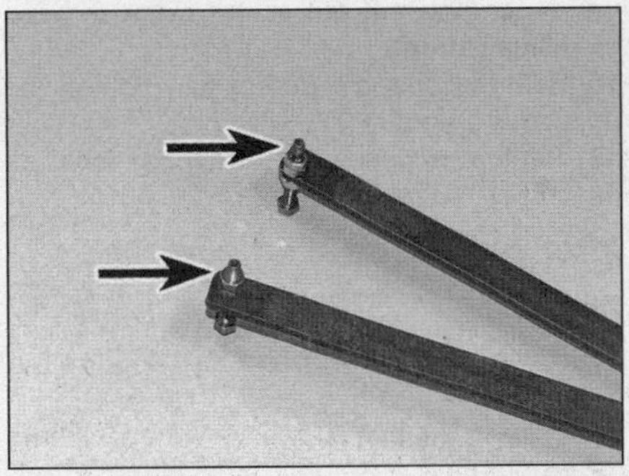

8.2a Adjust the depth of the bolts and file them as required to ensure a snug fit

8.2b Use the tool to counterhold the sprocket

8.3a Remove the bolt and...

8.3b ...remove the sprocket

8.15 The tang must engage with the cylinder head

8.19 Remove the idler

seals for signs of leakage, and if necessary renew the seal as described in Section 11.

6 Follow the timing belt replacement procedure as described in Section 7 and then tighten the sprocket bolt to the specified torque. Prevent the sprocket from turning using the method used on removal.

Crankshaft sprocket

Removal

7 Remove the crankshaft pulley (Section 5) and the timing belt as described in Section 7.

8 Slide the crankshaft sprocket off the crankshaft.

Refitting

Warning: Do not turn the crankshaft, as the pistons may hit the valves.

9 Clean both surfaces of the sprocket and refit it.

10.3 Lift out the tappets and rocker fingers

10 Refit the timing belt as described in Section 7.

11 Clean the front surface of the sprocket again and the rear surface of the crankshaft pulley. Due to the unique design of the sprocket and crankshaft pulley it is essential that both mounting surfaces are thoroughly cleaned before installation.

12 Refit the remaining components in reverse order.

Tensioner assembly

Removal

13 Remove the timing belt (see Section 7).

14 Unscrew the bolt and then withdraw the tensioner assembly from the engine.

Refitting

15 Offer the tensioner assembly into position over the mounting stud, ensuring that the tang on the tensioner backplate engages with the corresponding cut-out in the cylinder head **(see illustration)**.

16 Refit the bolt, but do not fully tighten the nut at this stage.

17 Refit and tension the timing belt as described in Section 7.

Idler pulley

Removal

18 Remove the timing belt as described in Section 7.

19 Slacken the bolt and remove the tensioner as a complete assembly **(see illustration)**. Note that on some models the bolt is held captive in the idler by an O-ring seal.

Refitting

20 Refitting is a reversal of removal.

9 Camshafts – inspection

Note: *Due to the method of construction, the camshafts can not be removed from the camshaft housing. The camshafts are removed with the camshaft housing as described in Section 4.*

Inspection

1 Visually inspect the camshaft for evidence of wear on the surfaces of the lobes and journals. Normally their surfaces should be smooth and have a dull shine; look for scoring, erosion or pitting and areas that appear highly polished, indicating excessive wear. Accelerated wear will occur once the hardened exterior of the camshaft has been damaged, so always renew worn items. **Note:** *If these symptoms are visible on the tips of the camshaft lobes, check the corresponding tappet/rocker finger, as it may be worn as well.*

2 If the machined surfaces of the camshaft appear discoloured or blued, it is likely that it has been overheated at some point, probably due to inadequate lubrication.

3 If there are any faults found with the camshafts the complete camshaft housing assembly must be replaced.

10 Hydraulic tappets/roller rocker fingers – removal, inspection and refitting

Removal

1 Remove the camshaft housing, as described in Section 4.

2 As the components are removed, keep them in strict order, so that they can be refitted in their original locations. Accelerated wear leading to early failure will result if the tappets and rocker fingers are interchanged.

3 Note the fitted position, then lift out the rocker finger complete with the hydraulic tappets **(see illustration)**.

4 Carefully unclip the tappets from the rocker fingers. It is advisable to store the tappets (in the correct order) upright in an oil bath whilst they are removed from the engine. Make a note of the position of each tappet, as they must be refitted in their original locations on reassembly.

Inspection

5 Check the cylinder head bore contact surfaces and the hydraulic tappets for signs of scoring or damage. Also, check that the oil holes in the tappets are free from obstructions. If significant scoring or damage is found, it may be necessary to renew the cylinder head and the complete set of tappets.

11.4 Lever out the seal

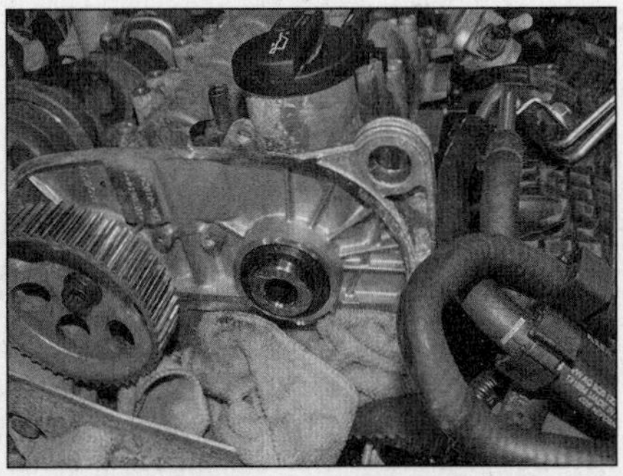

11.6 Fit the new seal

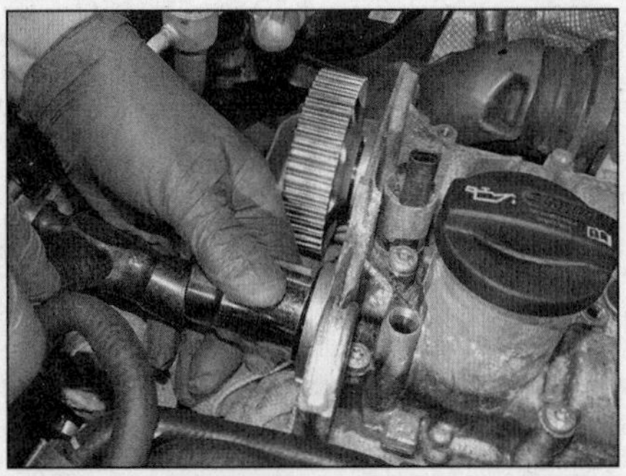

11.7 Drive the seal home with a suitable socket

6 Check the valve, tappet and camshaft contact faces of the rockers for wear or damage, and also check the rockers for any signs of cracking. Renew any worn or damaged rockers.
7 Inspect the camshaft, as described in Section 9.

Refitting

8 Smear some clean engine oil onto the sides of the hydraulic tappets, and offer them into position in their original bores in the cylinder head. Push them down until they are seated correctly and lubricate the upper surface of the tappet.
9 Oil the rocker contact faces of the tappets, and the tops of the valve stems, then refit the rockers to their original locations, ensuring that the rockers are securely clipped onto the tappets.
10 Lubricate the camshaft lobe contact surfaces and refit the camshaft housing as described in Section 4.

11 Camshaft oil seals – renewal

Note: *The oil seals are a PTFE (Teflon) type and are fitted dry, without using any grease or oil. These have a wider sealing lip and have been introduced instead of the coil spring type oil seal.*
1 Remove the timing belt as described in Section 7.
2 Remove the camshaft sprocket as described in Section 8. Note that there is also a seal behind the coolant pump sprocket. This is replaced using the same method as for the camshaft oil seals.
3 Drill two small holes into the existing oil seal, diagonally opposite each other. Take great care to avoid drilling through into the seal housing or camshaft sealing surface. Thread two self-tapping screws into the holes and, using a pair of pliers, pull on the heads of the screws to extract the oil seal.
4 Alternatively (and where possible) protect the cylinder head and lever out the seal **(see illustration)**.
5 Clean out the seal housing and the sealing surface of the camshaft by wiping it with a lint-free cloth. Remove any swarf or burrs that may cause the seal to leak.
6 Carefully push the seal over the camshaft until it is positioned above its housing **(see illustration)**.
7 Using a hammer and a socket of suitable diameter, drive the seal squarely into its housing **(see illustration)**. **Note:** *Select a socket that bears only on the hard outer surface of the seal, not the inner lip which can easily be damaged.* Remove the adhesive tape from the end of the camshaft after the seal has been located correctly.
8 Refit the camshaft sprocket with reference to Section 8.
9 Refit and tension the timing belt as described in Section 7.

12 Cylinder head – removal, inspection and refitting

Note: *The cylinder head must be removed with the engine cold. New cylinder head bolts and a new cylinder head gasket will be required on refitting.*

Removal

1 Disconnect the battery as described in Chapter 5A Section 3.
2 Drain the cooling system as described in Chapter 1A Section 32 and then remove the coolant hoses from the coolant pump.
3 Remove the timing belt from the camshaft sprockets as described in Section 7. There is no need to completely remove the belt at this point, so the engine mounting bracket can be left in place.

12.8 Remove the heat shield

4 Remove the camshaft housing as described in Section 4 and then remove the hydraulic tappets and rocker fingers. Store them in the correct cylinder order.
5 Remove the inlet manifold as described in Chapter 4A Section 9.
6 Disconnect the wiring plugs from the fuel injectors, the fuel pressure sensor and the oil pressure sensor. If the cylinder head is to reworked, then remove the fuel rail and injectors at this point. Alternatively remove the cylinder head complete with the fuel rail and fuel pump.
7 Jack up and support the front of the vehicle (see *Jacking and vehicle support*).
8 Remove the heat shield from above the right-hand driveshaft **(see illustration)**.
9 Release the clamp from the catalytic converter, remove the converter support bracket and seperate the convertor from the turbocharger. Secure the converter to the bulkhead with cable ties.
10 Anticipating some oil spillage, disconnect the oil supply and oil return pipes from the turbocharger.
11 Disconnect the wiring plugs from the turbocharger control module and from the coolant temperature sensor.
12 Remove the upper rear bolt from the engine support bracket. Support the engine on a jack (using a block of wood to spread the load) and remove the engine mounting to improve access. Refit the mounting after the bolt is removed. Remove the jack from the sump.
13 Progressively slacken the cylinder head bolts, by one turn at a time, in the reverse order to that shown **(see illustration 12.28)**. Remove the cylinder head bolts and dispose of them – new bolts must be fitted.
14 With all the bolts removed, lift the cylinder head from the block, together with the turbocharger. If the cylinder head is stuck, tap it with a soft-faced mallet to break the joint. **Do not** insert a lever into the gasket joint.
15 Lift the cylinder head gasket from the block.

Inspection

16 Dismantling and inspection of the cylinder head is covered in Chapter 2F Section 6.

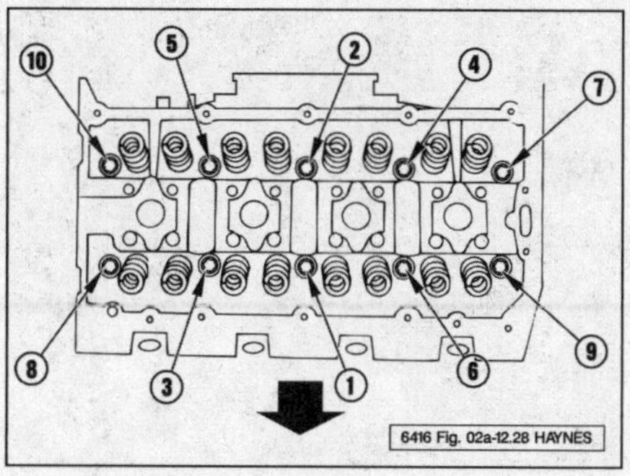

12.28 Tighten the bolts in sequence

Refitting

17 The mating faces of the cylinder head and block must be perfectly clean before refitting the head.

18 Use a scraper to remove all traces of gasket and carbon, also clean the tops of the pistons. Take particular care with the aluminium surfaces, as the soft metal is easily damaged.

19 Make sure that debris is not allowed to enter the oil and water passages – this is particularly important for the oil circuit, as carbon could block the oil supply to the camshaft and crankshaft bearings. Using adhesive tape and paper, seal the water, oil and bolt holes in the cylinder block. To prevent carbon entering the gap between the pistons and bores, smear a little grease in the gap. After cleaning a piston, rotate the crankshaft so that the piston moves down the bore, then wipe out the grease and carbon with a cloth rag. Clean the other piston crowns in the same way.

20 Check the head and block for nicks, deep scratches and other damage. If slight, they may be removed carefully with a file. More serious damage may be repaired by machining, but this is a specialist job.

21 If warpage of the cylinder head is suspected, use a straight-edge to check it for distortion, as described in Part D of this Chapter.

22 Ensure that the cylinder head bolt holes in the crankcase are clean and free of oil. Syringe or soak up any oil left in the bolt holes. This is most important in order that the correct bolt tightening torque can be applied, and to prevent the possibility of the block being cracked by hydraulic pressure when the bolts are tightened.

23 Ensure that the crankshaft has been turned to position Nos 1 and 4 pistons slightly down their bores from the TDC position (refer to timing belt refitting in Section 7). This will eliminate any risk of piston-to-valve contact as the cylinder head is refitted.

24 Where applicable, refit the turbocharger to the cylinder head with reference to Chapter 4C Section 6.

25 Ensure that the cylinder head locating dowels are in place in the cylinder block, then fit a new cylinder head gasket over the dowels, ensuring that the part number is uppermost. Where applicable, the OBEN/TOP marking should also be uppermost. Note that Seat recommend that the gasket is only removed from its packaging immediately prior to fitting.

26 Lower the cylinder head into position on the gasket, ensuring that it engages correctly over the dowels.

27 Fit the new cylinder head bolts, and screw them in as far as possible by hand.

28 Working progressively, in sequence, tighten all the cylinder head bolts to the specified Stage 1 torque **(see illustration)**.

29 Again working progressively, in sequence, tighten all the cylinder head bolts through the specified Stage 2 angle.

30 Tighten all the cylinder head bolts through the specified Stage 3 angle.

31 Finally, tighten all the cylinder head bolts, in sequence, through the specified Stage 4 angle.

32 Refit the camshaft housing as described in Section 4.

33 Refit and tension the timing belt as described in Section 7. The replacement of the timing belt is highly recommended.

34 Refit the auxiliary drivebelt as described in Chapter 1A Section 28.

35 If the fuel pump was removed, install the cam follower (tappet), fit a new O-ring seal and then refit the pump using new bolts (Chapter 4A Section 4).

36 If the fuel rail and injectors have been removed, fit new seals to the injectors (Chapter 4A Section 4) and then refit the the fuel rail

37 Refit the inlet manifold as described in Chapter 4A Section 9.

38 Fill the turbocharger with fresh oil though the oil supply pipe. Reconnect the turbocharger supply pipe and return line using new seals.

39 Reconnect the catalytic converter using a new gasket and clamp (Chapter 4C Section 7).

40 Refit the spark plugs and ignition coils.

41 Reconnect all wiring plugs. Secure the loom to the retaining clips and brackets.

42 Refill the cooling system as described in Chapter 1A Section 32.

13 Sump – removal and refitting

Note: *Seat special tool (T10058) will be required to access the bolts hidden by the transmission. The tool is a long reach ball end 5 mm hex key and without it the transmission will have to be removed to access the bolts* ***(see illustration)****.*

Note: *VAG sealant (D 176 404 A2 or equivalent) will be required to seal the sump on refitting.*

Removal

1 Apply the handbrake, then jack up the front of the vehicle and support securely on axle stands (see *Jacking and vehicle support*).

2 Remove the securing screws and withdraw the engine undertray(s).

3 Drain the engine oil and remove the oil filter as described in Chapter 1A Section 6.

4 Disconnect the wiring connector from the oil level/temperature sender in the sump **(see illustration)**.

5 Unscrew and remove the bolts securing the sump to the cylinder block/upper sump. Remove the bolts securing the sump to the bell housing. The sump is bonded to the engine block with a liquid gasket. Removal can be difficult due to the adhesive nature of the sealant.

6 A levering point is provided at the rear of the engine block **(see illustration)** and this should be used to partially release the sump.

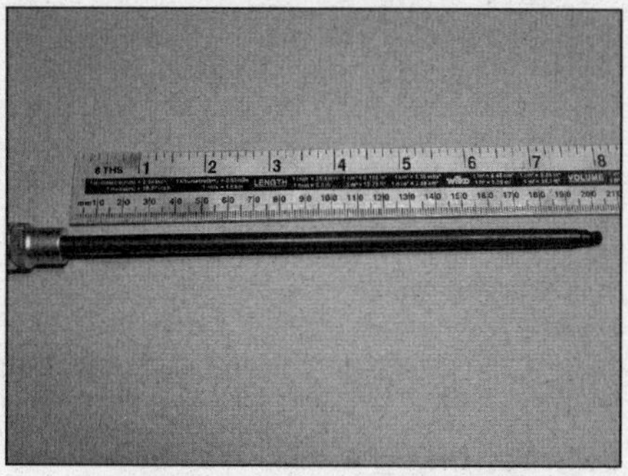

13.0 Seat special tool T10058

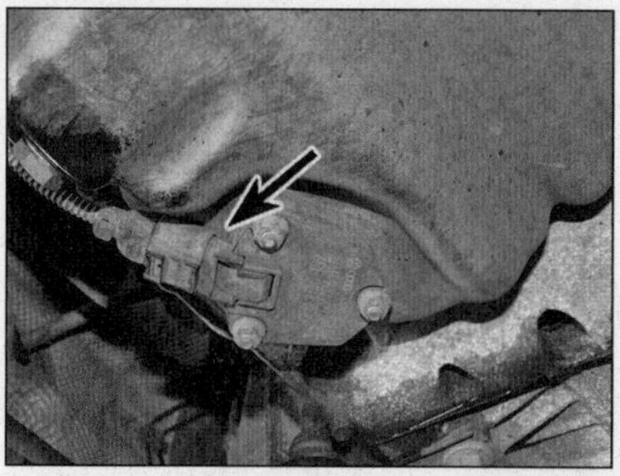

13.4 Disconnect the wiring connector from the oil level/temperature sender

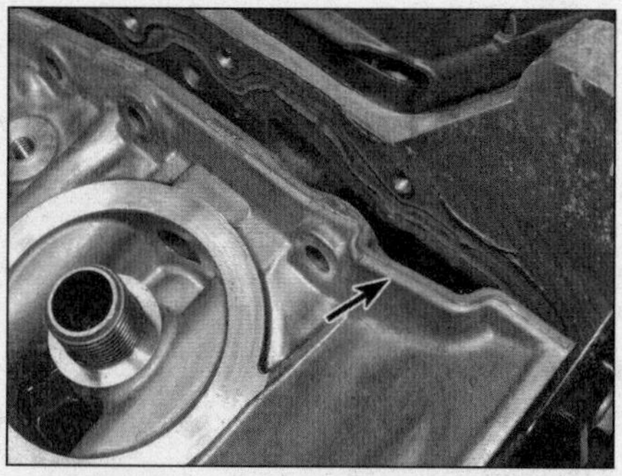

13.6 A levering point is provided

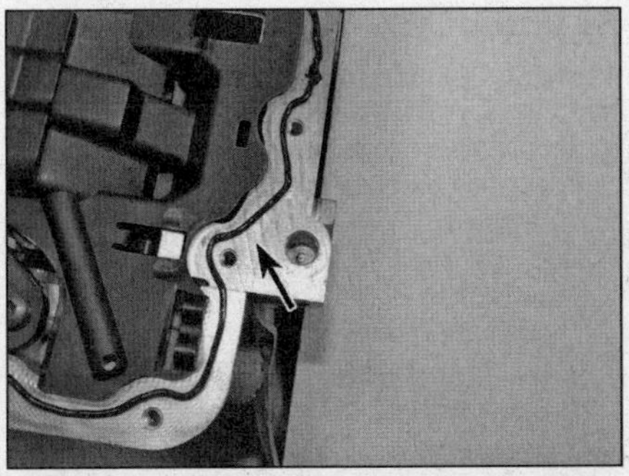

13.8 Apply the sealant around the inside of the bolt holes

As soon as the sump comes free at any point a sharp knife can be used to further release the sealant. Seat list a special knife tool (T10561) for this purpose.

Refitting

7 Begin refitting by thoroughly cleaning the mating faces of the sump and cylinder block. Ensure that all traces of old sealant are removed.

8 Ensure that the cylinder block mating face of the sump is free from all traces of old sealant, oil and grease, and then apply a 2.0 to 3.0 mm thick bead of silicone sealant (VAG D 176 404 A2 or equivalent) to the sump **(see illustration)**. Note that the sealant should be run around the inside of the bolt holes in the sump. The sump must be fitted within 5 minutes of applying the sealant.

9 Fit guide studs to the to the opposite corners of the and then offer the sump up to the block. Fit the new bolts and tighten the bolts in sequence until contact is made **(see illustrations)**. Fully tighten the bolts to the specified torque and then tighten the bolts to the second stage angle setting.

10 Refit the sump to bell housing bolts, and tighten them to the specified torque.

11 Refit the wiring connector to the oil level/ temperature sender, then refit the engine undertray(s), and lower the vehicle to the ground.

12 Allow at least 30 minutes from the time of refitting the sump for the sealant to dry, then refill the engine with oil, with reference to Chapter 1A Section 6.

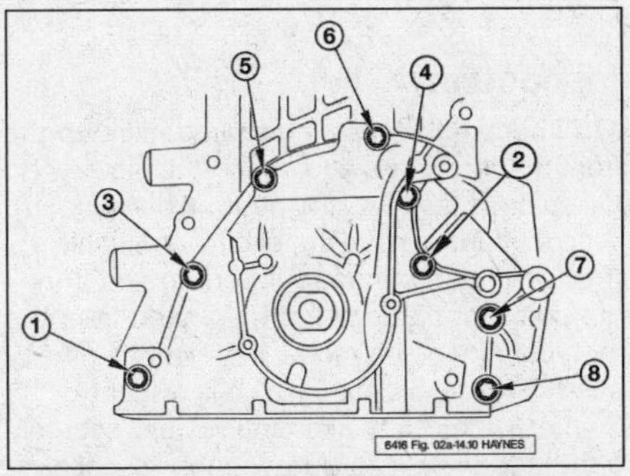

14.10 Tighten the bolts 1-6 to the specified torque and angle and then tighten bolts 7 and 8 to the specified torque

13.9a Fit guide studs to the engine

14 Oil pump – removal and refitting

Note: *Individual parts are not available for the oil pumps. If they are worn or faulty they must be replaced as a complete assembly.*

Removal

1 Remove the timing belt as described in Section 7.

2 Remove the sump as described in Section 13.

3 Unbolt and remove the auxiliary belt tensioner.

4 Remove the alternator as described in Chapter 5A Section 5.

5 Remove the crankshaft oil seal as described in Section 16.

6 Anticipate some oil spillage by placing shop towels below the pump. Remove the oil pump mounting bolts and pull the oil pump off the dowel pins. Slide the pump off the crankshaft nose and remove it.

7 Remove the gasket.

Refitting

8 Clean and inspect the mounting surface and then fit a new gasket. Locate the gasket over the dowel pins.

9 Rotate the pump, so that the notches in the pump drive are aligned with the slots in the crankshaft nose.

10 Fit the pump and secure it in place with new bolts.Tighten the bolts in the correct order to the specified torque. Note that the upper bolts have a torque and angle setting and must be replaced **(see illustration)**.

11 Fit a new crankshaft oil seal as described in Section 16.

12 Install the sump (Section 13) and the alternator (Chapter 5A Section 5) and then fit the remaining components in the reverse order to removal.

15.2a Tool used to hold the flywheel stationary

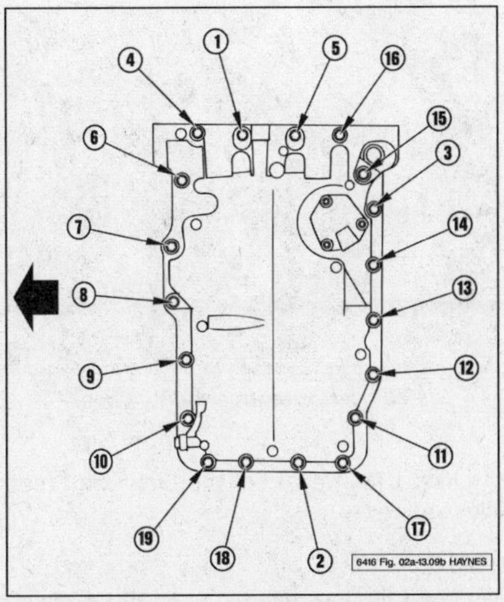

13.9b Tighten the bolts in sequence

15 Flywheel – removal, inspection and refitting

Note: *New flywheel securing bolts will be required on refitting.*

Removal

1 Remove the gearbox (see Chapter 7A Section 3 or Chapter 7B Section 2) and where fitted the clutch (Chapter 6A Section 6).

2 The flywheel bolts are offset to ensure correct fitment. Unscrew the bolts while holding the flywheel stationary. Temporarily insert a bolt in the cylinder block, and use a screwdriver to hold the flywheel or make up a holding tool **(see illustrations)**.

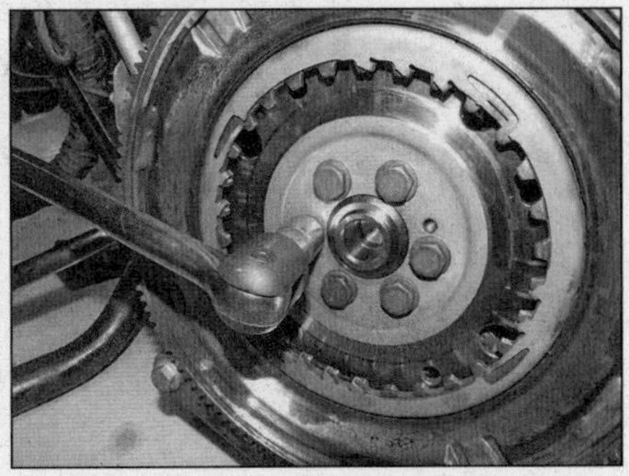

15.2b Unscrew the securing bolts...

15.3 ...and remove the flywheel

3 Lift the flywheel from the crankshaft **(see illustration)**.

Inspection

4 Check the flywheel for wear and damage. Examine the starter ring gear for excessive wear to the teeth. If any wear is found the complete flywheel must be replaced. If the clutch friction face is discoloured or scored excessively, it may be possible to regrind it, but this work should also be entrusted to an automotive machine shop.

5 Where a dual mass flywheel is fitted the following guidelines may help decide if replacement is required. If in doubt, a professional inspection is recommended. The dual-mass flywheel should be checked as follows:

Warpage

6 Place a straight edge across the face of the drive surface, and check by trying to insert a feeler gauge between the straight edge and the drive surface **(see illustration)**. The flywheel will normally warp like a bowl – ie. Higher on the outer edge. If the warpage is more than 0.40 mm, the flywheel may need replacing.

Free rotational movement

7 This is the distance the drive surface of the flywheel can be turned independently of the flywheel primary element, using finger effort alone. Move the drive surface in one direction and make a mark where the locating pin aligns with the flywheel edge. Move the drive surface in the other direction (finger pressure only) and make another mark **(see illustration)**. The total of free movement should not exceed 20.0 mm. If it's more, the flywheel may need replacing.

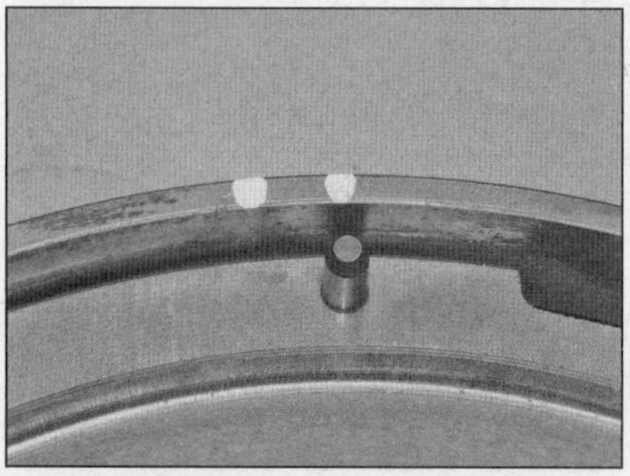

15.7 Flywheel free rotational movement check alignment marks – see text

15.6 Flywheel warpage check – see text

Total rotational movement

8 This is the total distance the drive surface can be turned independently of the flywheel primary element. Insert two bolts into the clutch pressure plate/damper unit mounting holes, and with the crankshaft/flywheel held stationary, use a lever/pry bar between the bolts and use some effort to move the drive surface fully in one direction – make a mark where the locating pin aligns with the flywheel edge. Now force the drive surface fully in the opposite direction, and make another mark. The total rotational movement should not exceed 44.00 mm. If it does, have the flywheel professionally inspected.

Lateral movement

9 The lateral movement (up and down) of the drive surface in relation to the primary element of the flywheel, should not exceed 2.0 mm. If it does, the flywheel may need replacing. This can be checked by pressing the drive surface down on one side into the flywheel (flywheel horizontal) and making an alignment mark between the drive surface and the inner edge of the primary element. Now press down on the opposite side of the drive surface, and make another mark above the original one. The difference between the two marks is the lateral movement **(see illustration)**.

10 There should be no cracks in the drive surface of the flywheel. If cracks are evident, the flywheel will need replacing.

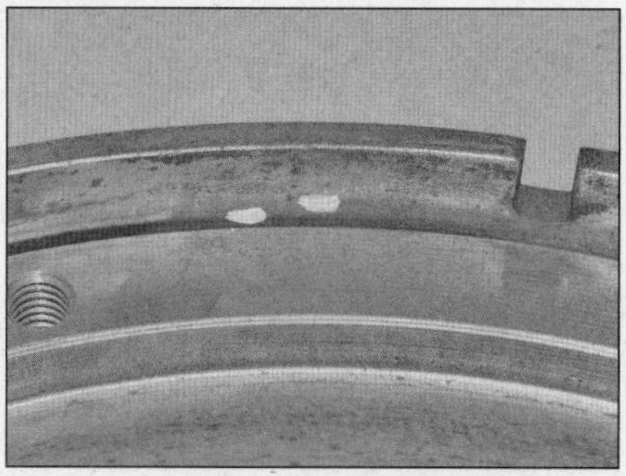

15.9 Flywheel lateral movement check marks – see text

Refitting

11 Refitting is a reversal of removal, bearing in mind the following points.

a) *Ensure that the engine to transmission plate is in place before fitting the flywheel.*
b) *Use new bolts when refitting the flywheel and coat the threads of the bolts with locking fluid before inserting them. Tighten the securing bolts to the specified torque.*

16 Crankshaft oil seals – renewal

Note: *The oil seals are a PTFE (Teflon) type and are fitted dry, without using any grease or oil. These have a wider sealing lip and have been introduced instead of the coil spring type oil seal.*

Timing belt end oil seal

Note: *If the oil seal housing/oil pump is removed, VAG sealant (D 176 404 A2, or equivalent) will be required to seal the housing on refitting.*

1 Remove the timing belt as described in Section 7, and the crankshaft sprocket with reference to Section 8.

2 Oil seal replacement is identical to that shown in Chapter 2A. Follow the procedure described in the Chapter 2A Section 18.

Flywheel end oil seal

Note: *In these engines, the seal, sealing flange and sender wheel are a complete unit. Special tools are required to refit the sealing flange, and press the sender wheel onto the end of the crankshaft. It is not possible to accurately fit these parts without the tools, which is be available from Seat (part no. T10134) and are available from aftermarket automotive tool specialists. E.g. Draper tools).*

3 The seal is identical to the seal fitted to the 1.2 litre SOHC engine. Follow the instructions given in Chapter 2B Section 15 to replace the seal.

17 Engine mountings – inspection and renewal

Inspection

1 If improved access is required, jack up the front of the vehicle, and support it securely on axle stands (see *Jacking and vehicle support*). Where fitted, remove the engine undershield.

2 Check the mounting rubbers to see if they are cracked, hardened or separated from the metal at any point; renew the mounting if any such damage or deterioration is evident.

3 Check that all the mountings are securely tightened; use a torque wrench to check if possible.

4 Using a large screwdriver or a crowbar, check for wear in the mounting by carefully

17.8 Disconnect the level sensor wiring plug and remove the screws

17.10a Remove the earth cable

17.10b Remove the bolts and lift out the mounting

levering against it to check for free play. Where this is not possible, enlist the aid of an assistant to move the engine/transmission back-and-forth, or from side-to-side, whilst you observe the mounting. While some free play is to be expected, even from new components, excessive wear should be obvious. If excessive free play is found, check first that the fasteners are correctly secured, then renew any worn components as described in the following paragraphs.

Renewal

Right-hand mounting

Note: *Two versions of the right-hand mount are fitted, Removal and refitting is essentially the same for both versions*.

5 Support the engine on a trolley jack under the sump. Use a block of wood between the sump and the head of the jack, to prevent any damage to the sump.

6 On MPI engines remove the air filter housing as described in Chapter 4A Section 3.

7 Where required, unclip the fuel lines from the coolant reservoir/timing belt cover. There is no need to disconnect the fuel lines.

8 Disconnect the level sensor wiring plug and remove the screws from the coolant reservoir **(see illustration)**.

9 Unbolt the coolant reservoir and move it to one side.

Note: *On models fitted with a single central nut holding the mounting together DO NOT remove the nut. The mounting must be removed as a complete assembly*.

10 Where fitted unbolt the earth cable and then unscrew the bolts securing the mounting to the body. Unscrew the bolts securing the mounting to the engine bracket. Withdraw the mounting from the engine compartment **(see illustrations)**.

11 Refitting is a reversal of removal, bearing in mind the following points.

a) Use new bolts.
b) Align the mounting so that it is not twisted. On mounts with a single central nut centralise the mounting with the holes in the bodywork.
c) Tighten all fixings to the specified torque.

Left-hand mounting

Note: *New mounting bolts will be required on refitting*.

12 Support the transmission on a trolley jack with a block of wood placed between the head of the jack and the transmission to spread the load.

13 Disconnect the battery, remove the battery and battery tray as described in Chapter 5A Section 3.

14 Where required, release the wiring loom and move it to the side to gain access to the mounting bolts.

15 Remove the mounting to body bolts and then remove the bolts securing the mounting to the transmission bracket **(see illustration)**.

16 Lift out the mounting and then where required, unbolt and remove the bracket from the transmission **(see illustration)**. Removal of the bracket is essential for transmission removal.

17 Refitting is a reversal of removal, bearing in mind the following points:

a) Use new mounting bolts.
b) Tighten all fixings to the specified torque.

Rear mounting (torque arm)

Note: *The bolt between the bracket (at the transmission) and the pendulum mount should not be removed*.

18 Apply the handbrake, then jack up the front of the vehicle and support securely on axle stands (see *Jacking and vehicle support*). Where fitted remove the engine undershield.

19 Working under the vehicle, unscrew and remove the bolts securing the mounting to the transmission **(see illustration)**.

20 Unscrew the bolt securing the mounting to the subframe. Remove the mounting from under the vehicle **(see illustration)**.

21 Refitting is a reversal of removal, but use new mounting securing bolts, and tighten all fixings to the specified torque.

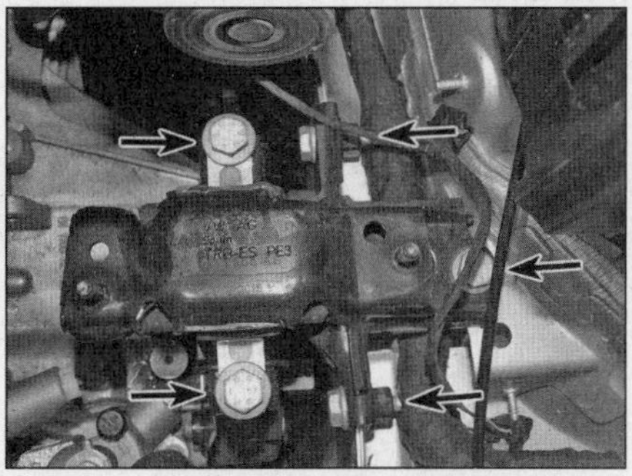

17.15 Remove the bolts

17.16 Remove the bracket from the transmission

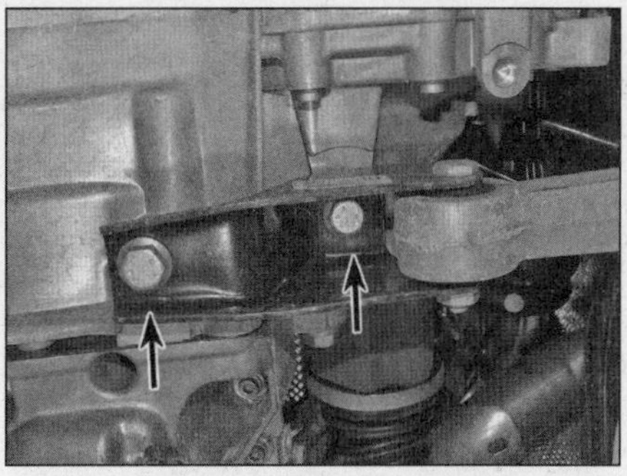

17.19 Remove the bolts

17.20 Remove the mounting

18.3 Remove the bolts

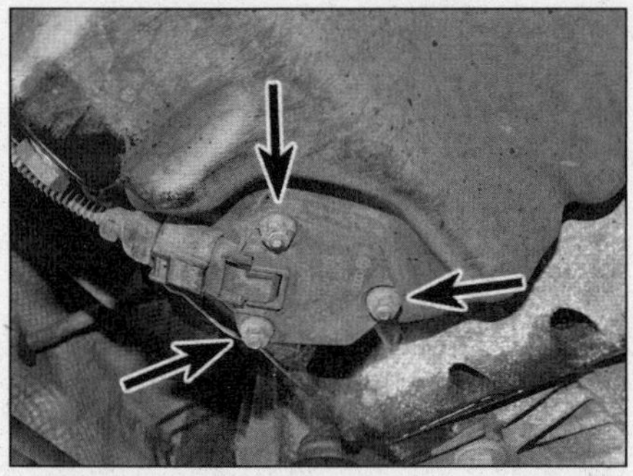

20.1 Oil level/temperature sender – located in the base of the sump

18 Engine oil cooler – removal and refitting

Removal

1 The oil cooler is mounted at the front of the engine block, hidden by the inlet manifold.

19.1 Oil pressure switch (shown with inlet manifold removed)

2 Drain the coolant and remove the inlet manifold as described in Chapter 1A Section 32.

3 Anticipating some spillage, remove the bolts **(see illustration)** and lift of the oil cooler. Recover the O-ring seals.

Refitting

4 Refitting is a reversal of removal, bearing in mind the following points:

a) Use new seals.

b) Use new bolts.

19 Oil pressure warning light switch – removal and refitting

Note: *Seat insist that the oil pressure switches must be replaced if removed.*

Removal

1 Unclip the EVAP control solenoid from the side of the inlet manifold and then disconnect the wiring plug **(see illustration)**.

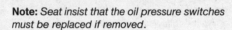

2 Anticipating some oil spillage, unscrew the switch and remove it.

Refitting

3 Dispose of the switch – a new one must be fitted.

4 Fit the new switch, complete with the seal, and tighten it to the specified torque.

5 Reconnect the wiring and refit the other components. Check and top-up the engine oil if required.

20 Oil level/temperature sender – removal and refitting

Removal

1 The oil level/temperature sender is fitted to bottom of the sump **(see illustration)**.

2 Drain the engine oil as described in Chapter 1A Section 6.

3 Disconnect the wiring connector and wipe clean the area around the sender.

4 Undo the three retaining bolts and remove the sender.

Refitting

5 Examine the sealing washer for signs of damage or deterioration and if necessary renew.

6 Refit the sender and tighten the retaining bolts to the specified torque.

7 Securely reconnect the wiring connector then refill the engine with oil, with reference to Chapter 1A Section 6.

8 On completion, check and, if necessary, top-up the engine oil as described in *Weekly checks*.

Chapter 2 Part D
1.4 litre petrol engine in-car repair procedures

Contents

Degrees of difficulty

Easy, suitable for novice with little experience	Fairly easy, suitable for beginner with some experience	Fairly difficult, suitable for competent DIY mechanic	Difficult, suitable for experienced DIY mechanic	Very difficult, suitable for expert DIY or professional

Specifications

General

Type	Four-cylinder in-line, belt-driven double overhead camshaft (DOHC), four stroke, 16-valve, liquid-cooled
Cubic capacity	1390 cc
Manufacturer's engine code*	CGGB and BXW
Maximum power output	63 kW @ 5000 rpm
Maximum torque output	132 Nm @ 3800 rpm
Bore	76.5 mm
Stroke	75.6 mm
Compression ratio	10.5 : 1
Compression pressures (oil temperature 30°C minimum):	
New	10.0 to 15.0 bars
Minimum	7.0 bars
Maximum difference between cylinders	3.0 bars
Firing order	1 – 3 – 4 – 2
No 1 cylinder location	Crankshaft pulley end
Direction of crankshaft rotation	Clockwise (when viewed from right-hand side of car)

**See 'Vehicle identification' at the end of this manual for the location of the engine code markings.*

Camshafts

Camshaft endfloat (maximum)	0.15 mm
Camshaft bearing running clearance	No figure specified
Camshaft run-out	No figure specified

Lubrication system

Oil pump type	Gear type, driven directly from front of crankshaft
Oil pressure (oil temperature 80°C):	
Minimum @ idling	0.3 to 0.7 bar
Minimum @ 2000 rpm	2.0 bar
Maximum @ high rpm	7.0 bar

Torque wrench settings

	Nm	lbf ft
Alternator	20	15
Ancillary (alternator, etc) bracket mounting bolts	50	37
Auxiliary drivebelt tensioner securing bolt:		
M8 bolt:		
Stage 1	20	15
Stage 2	Angle-tighten a further 90°	
M10 bolt	45	33
Big-end bearing caps bolts*:		
Stage 1	30	22
Stage 2	Angle-tighten a further 90°	
Camshaft carrier bolts*:		
Stage 1	10	7
Stage 2	Angle-tighten a further 90°	
Camshaft left-hand endplate bolts	10	7
Camshaft sprocket bolts*:		
Stage 1	20	15
Stage 2	Angle-tighten a further 90°	
Clutch pressure plate mounting bolts*:		
Stage 1	60	44
Stage 2	Angle-tighten a further 90°	
Coolant pump bolts	20	15
Crankcase breather (oil separator) bolts	10	7
Crankshaft oil seal housing bolts	12	9
Crankshaft pulley/sprocket bolt*:		
Stage 1	90	66
Stage 2	Angle-tighten a further 90°	
Cylinder head bolts*:		
Stage 1	30	22
Stage 2	Angle-tighten a further 90°	
Stage 3	Angle-tighten a further 90°	
Engine/transmission left-hand mounting to transmission*:		
Stage 1	40	30
Stage 2	Angle-tighten a further 90°	
Engine/transmission left-hand mounting to body*:		
Stage 1	50	37
Stage 2	Angle-tighten a further 90°	
Engine/transmission rear mounting bracket to transmission*:		
Stage 1	30	22
Stage 2	Angle-tighten a further 90°	
Engine/transmission rear mounting link to subframe*:		
Stage 1	40	30
Stage 2	Angle-tighten a further 90°	
Engine/transmission right-hand mounting to engine*:		
Stage 1	20	15
Stage 2	Angle-tighten a further 90°	
Engine/transmission right-hand mounting to body*:		
Stage 1	30	22
Stage 2	Angle-tighten a further 90°	
Engine-to-automatic transmission bolts:		
M12 bolts	80	59
M10 cylinder block-to-transmission bolts	60	44
M10 sump-to-transmission bolts	25	18
Engine-to-manual transmission bolts	80	59
Engine-to-manual transmission cover plate bolts	10	7
Exhaust manifold nuts	25	18
Exhaust pipe-to-manifold nuts	40	30
Flywheel/driveplate bolts*:		
Stage 1	60	44
Stage 2	Angle-tighten a further 90°	
Knock sensor	20	15
Oil cooler securing nut	25	18
Oil drain plug	30	22
Oil level/temperature sensor-to-sump bolts	10	7
Oil pick-up pipe securing bolts	10	7
Oil pressure warning light switch	25	18
Oil pump securing bolts*	12	9

Torque wrench settings (continued)

	Nm	lbf ft
Sump:		
Sump-to-cylinder block bolts:		
Metal sump	15	11
Aluminium sump	13	10
Sump-to-transmission bolts	45	33
Timing belt idler pulley bolt	50	37
Timing belt outer cover bolts:		
Small bolts	10	7
Large bolts	20	15
Timing belt rear cover bolts:		
Small bolts	10	7
Large bolt (coolant pump bolts)	20	15
Timing belt tensioner:		
Main timing belt tensioner bolt	20	15
Secondary timing belt tensioner bolt	20	15

*Use new fasteners

1 General Information

Using this Chapter

1 This Part of Chapter 2 describes those repair procedures that can reasonably be carried out on the engine while it remains in the car. If the engine has been removed from the car and is being dismantled as described in Part F, any preliminary dismantling procedures can be ignored.

2 Note that while it may be possible physically to overhaul items such as the piston/connecting rod assemblies while the engine is in the car, such tasks are not usually carried out as separate operations, and usually require the execution of several additional procedures (not to mention the cleaning of components and of oil ways); for this reason, all such tasks are classed as major overhaul procedures, and are described in Part F of this Chapter.

Caution: The crankshaft must not be removed on these engines. If the crankshaft or main bearing surfaces are worn or damaged, the complete crankshaft/cylinder block assembly must be renewed.

3 Part F describes the removal of the engine/transmission from the car and the full overhaul procedures that can then be carried out.

Engine description

4 The engine is a water-cooled, double overhead camshaft, in-line four-cylinder unit, with an aluminium-alloy cylinder block and cylinder head. It is mounted transversely at the front of the car, with the transmission bolted to the left-hand side of the engine.

5 The crankshaft is of five-bearing type, and thrustwashers are fitted to the centre main bearing to control crankshaft endfloat. The crankshaft and main bearings are matched to the alloy cylinder block, and it is not possible to reassemble the crankshaft and cylinder block once the components have been separated. If the crankshaft or bearings are worn, the complete cylinder block/crankshaft assembly must be renewed.

6 The inlet camshaft is driven by a toothed belt from the crankshaft sprocket, and the exhaust camshaft is driven from the inlet camshaft by a second toothed belt. The camshafts are located in a camshaft carrier, which is bolted to the top of the cylinder head.

7 The valves are closed by coil springs, and run in guides pressed into the cylinder head; the camshafts actuate the valves by roller rockers and hydraulic tappets. There are four valves per cylinder, two inlet valves and two exhaust valves.

8 The oil pump is driven directly from the end of the crankshaft. Oil is drawn from the sump through a strainer, and then forced through an externally mounted, renewable filter. From there, it is distributed to the cylinder head, where it lubricates the camshaft journals and hydraulic tappets, and also to the crankcase, where it lubricates the main bearings, connecting rod big-ends, gudgeon pins and cylinder bores.

9 Engine coolant is circulated by a pump, driven by the main timing belt. For details of the cooling system, refer to Chapter 3.

Repairs with engine in car

10 The following operations can be performed without removing the engine:

a) Compression pressure – testing.
b) Camshaft carrier – removal and refitting.
c) Crankshaft pulley – removal and refitting.
d) Timing belt covers – removal and refitting.
e) Timing belt(s) – removal, refitting and adjustment.
f) Timing belt tensioner and sprockets – removal and refitting.
g) Camshaft oil seal(s) – renewal.
h) Camshafts and hydraulic tappets – removal, inspection and refitting.
i) Cylinder head – removal and refitting.*
j) Sump – removal and refitting.
k) Oil pump – removal, overhaul and refitting.
l) Crankshaft oil seals – renewal.
m) Engine/transmission mountings – inspection and renewal.
n) Flywheel – removal, inspection and refitting.

Note: * *Cylinder head dismantling procedures are detailed in Chapter 2F Section 6.*

Note: *It is possible to remove the pistons and connecting rods (after removing the cylinder head and sump) without removing the engine. However, this is not recommended. Work of this nature is more easily and thoroughly completed with the engine on the bench, as described in Chapter 2F Section 9.*

2 Compression test – description and interpretation

1 When engine performance is down, or if misfiring occurs which cannot be attributed to the ignition or fuel systems, a compression test can provide diagnostic clues as to the engine's condition. If the test is performed regularly, it can give warning of trouble before any other symptoms become apparent.

2 The engine must be fully warmed-up to normal operating temperature, the battery must be fully charged and the spark plugs must be removed. The aid of an assistant will be required.

3 Disable the ignition system by disconnecting the wiring plug from the ignition coils.

4 Fit a compression tester to the No 1 cylinder spark plug hole. The type of tester that screws into the plug thread is preferred.

5 Have the assistant hold the throttle wide open and crank the engine for several seconds on the starter motor. **Note:** *The throttle will not operate until the ignition is switched on.* After one or two revolutions, the compression pressure should build up to a maximum figure and then stabilise. Record the highest reading obtained.

6 Repeat the test on the remaining cylinders, recording the pressure in each.

7 All cylinders should produce very similar pressures. Any difference greater than that specified indicates the existence of a fault. Note that the compression should build-up quickly in a healthy engine. Low compression on the first stroke, followed by gradually increasing pressure on successive strokes, indicates worn piston rings. A low

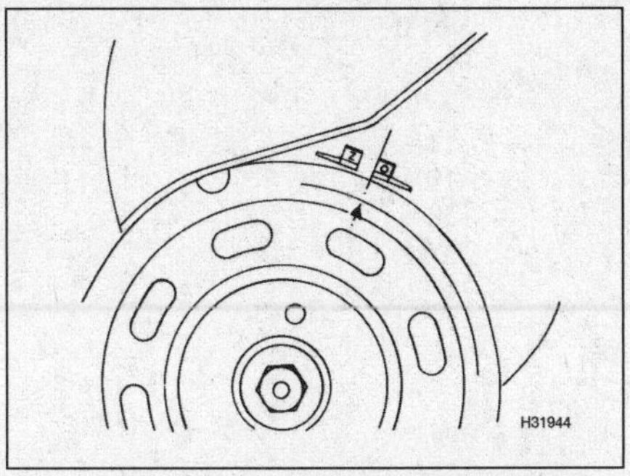

3.4a Crankshaft pulley timing mark aligned with TDC mark on timing belt cover

3.4b Timing mark scribed on inner flange of pulley aligned with TDC mark on timing belt cover

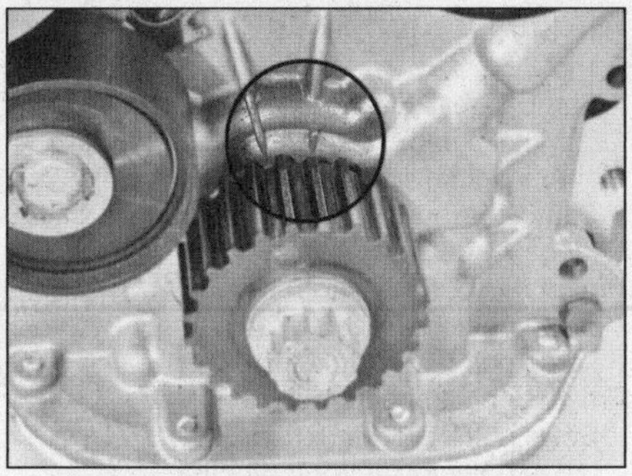

3.5 Crankshaft sprocket tooth with chamfered edge aligns with cast arrow on oil pump

compression reading on the first stroke, which does not build-up during successive strokes, indicates leaking valves or a blown head gasket (a cracked head could also be the cause). Deposits on the undersides of the valve heads can also cause low compression.

8 If the pressure in any cylinder is reduced to the specified minimum or less, carry out the following test to isolate the cause. Introduce a teaspoonful of clean oil into that cylinder through its spark plug hole and repeat the test.

9 If the addition of oil temporarily improves the compression pressure, this indicates that bore or piston wear is responsible for the pressure loss. No improvement suggests that leaking or burnt valves, or a blown head gasket, may be to blame.

10 A low reading from two adjacent cylinders is almost certainly due to the head gasket having blown between them and the presence of coolant in the engine oil will confirm this.

11 If one cylinder is about 20 percent lower than the others and the engine has a slightly rough idle; a worn camshaft lobe could be the cause.

12 On completion of the test, refit the spark plugs and reconnect the ignition wiring.

3 Engine assembly and valve timing marks – general information and usage

General information

1 TDC is the highest point in the cylinder that each piston reaches as it travels up and down when the crankshaft turns. Each piston reaches TDC at the end of the compression stroke and again at the end of the exhaust stroke, but TDC generally refers to piston position on the compression stroke. No 1 piston is at the timing belt end of the engine.

2 Positioning No 1 piston at TDC is an essential part of many procedures, such as timing belt removal and camshaft removal.

3 The design of the engines covered in this Chapter is such that piston-to-valve contact may occur if the camshaft or crankshaft is turned with the timing belt removed. For this reason, it is important to ensure that the camshaft and crankshaft do not move in relation to each other once the timing belt has been removed from the engine.

4 The crankshaft pulley has a marking which, when aligned with a corresponding reference marking on the timing belt cover, indicates that No 1 piston (and hence also No 4 piston) is at TDC. Note that on some models, the crankshaft pulley timing mark is located on the outer flange of the pulley. In order to make alignment of the timing marks easier, it is advisable to remove the pulley (see Section 4) and, using a set-square, scribe a corresponding mark on the inner flange of the pulley **(see illustrations)**.

5 Note that there is also a timing mark that can be used with the crankshaft sprocket – this is useful if the crankshaft pulley and timing belt have been removed. When No 1 piston is at TDC, the crankshaft sprocket tooth with the chamfered inner edge aligns with a cast arrow on the oil pump **(see illustration)**.

6 The camshaft sprockets are equipped with TDC positioning holes. When the positioning holes are aligned with the corresponding holes in the camshaft carrier, No 1 piston is at TDC on the compression stroke **(see illustration)**.

7 Additionally, on some models, the flywheel/driveplate has a TDC marking, which can be observed by unscrewing a protective plastic cover from the transmission bellhousing. The mark takes the form of a notch in the edge of the flywheel on manual transmission models, or an O marking on automatic transmission models. Note that it is not possible to use these marks on all models due to the limited access available to view the marks.

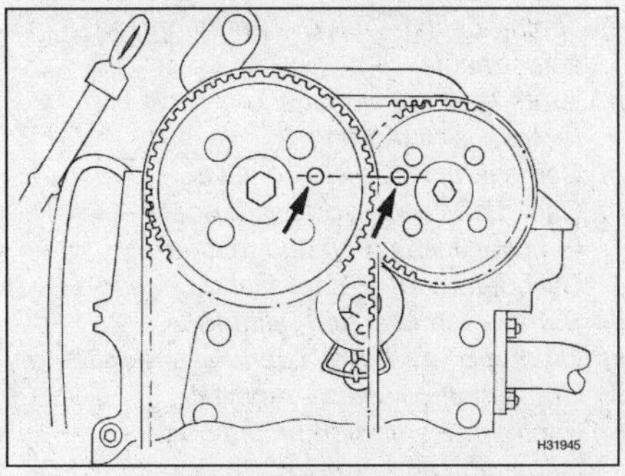

3.6 Camshaft sprocket positioning holes (arrowed) aligned

Setting No 1 cylinder to TDC

Note: *Suitable locking pins will be required to lock the camshaft sprockets in position during this procedure. On some engines, it may be necessary to use a small engineer's mirror to view the timing marks from under the wheel arch.*

8 Before starting work, make sure that the ignition is switched off (ideally, the battery negative lead should be disconnected as described in Chapter 5A Section 3).

9 Remove the air cleaner assembly as described in Chapter 4A Section 3.

10 If desired, to make the engine easier to turn, remove all of the spark plugs as described in Chapter 1A Section 27.

11 Apply the handbrake, then jack up the front of the car and support on axle stands (see Chapter 13 Section 5).

12 Remove the right-hand front roadwheel, then remove the securing screws and/or clips, and remove the appropriate engine undershields to enable access to the crankshaft pulley.

13 Remove the upper timing belt cover as described in Section 5.

14 Turn the engine clockwise, using a spanner on the crankshaft pulley bolt, until the TDC mark on the crankshaft pulley or flywheel/driveplate is aligned with the corresponding mark on the timing belt cover or transmission casing, and the locking pin holes in the camshaft sprockets are aligned with the corresponding holes in the camshaft carrier.

15 If necessary, to give sufficient clearance for the camshaft locking tool to be engaged with the camshaft sprockets, unbolt the air cleaner support bracket from the engine mounting. Similarly, if necessary, unbolt the power steering fluid reservoir and move it to one side, leaving the fluid hoses connected.

16 A suitable tool will now be required to lock the camshaft sprockets in the TDC position. A special Seat tool is available for this purpose, but a suitable tool can be improvised using two M8 bolts and nuts, and a short length of steel bar. With the camshaft sprocket positioned as described in paragraph 14, measure the distance between the locking pin hole centres, and drill two corresponding 8 mm holes in the length of steel bar. Slide the M8 bolts through the holes in the bar, and secure them using the nuts.

17 Slide the tool into position in the holes in the camshaft sprockets, ensuring that the pins (or bolts) engage with the holes in the camshaft carrier **(see illustration)**. The engine is now locked in position, with No 1 piston at TDC on the compression stroke.

4 Crankshaft pulley – removal and refitting

Removal

1 Disconnect the battery negative lead as described in Chapter 5A Section 3.

2 For improved access, jack up the front of the car, and support securely on axle stands (see *Jacking and vehicle support*). Remove the right-hand front roadwheel. Also remove the engine top cover and where necessary disconnect the ventilation hose.

3 Remove the securing screws and/or release the clips, and withdraw the relevant engine undershield(s) to enable access to the crankshaft pulley.

4 If necessary (for any later work to be carried out), turn the crankshaft using a socket or spanner on the crankshaft pulley bolt, until the relevant timing marks align (see Section 3).

5 Remove the auxiliary drivebelt, as described in Chapter 1A Section 28.

6 To prevent the crankshaft from turning as the pulley bolt is slackened, a tool similar to that shown can be used. Engage the tool with

3.17 Tool used to lock camshaft sprockets at TDC (engine and timing belt removed)

two of the slots in the pulley **(see illustration)**.

7 Counterhold the pulley, and slacken the pulley bolt (take care – the bolt is very tight) using a socket and a suitable extension.

8 Unscrew the bolt, and remove the pulley **(see illustration)**.

9 Refit the crankshaft pulley securing bolt, with a spacer washer positioned under its head, to retain the crankshaft sprocket.

Refitting

10 Unscrew the crankshaft pulley/sprocket bolt used to retain the sprocket, and remove the spacer washer, then refit the pulley to the sprocket. Ensure that the locating pin on the sprocket engages with the corresponding hole in the pulley.

11 Oil the threads of the new crankshaft pulley bolt. Prevent the crankshaft from turning as during removal, then fit the new pulley securing bolt, and tighten it to the specified torque, in the two stages given in the Specifications.

12 Refit the auxiliary drivebelt as described in Chapter 1A Section 28.

13 Refit the engine undershield(s) and top cover.

14 Refit the roadwheel, lower the car to the ground, and reconnect the battery negative lead.

5 Timing belt covers – removal and refitting

Upper outer cover

1 Remove the air cleaner assembly as described in Chapter 4A Section 3. Also remove the engine top cover and, where necessary, disconnect the ventilation hose.

2 Release the two securing clips, and lift the cover from the engine **(see illustration)**.

3 Refitting is a reversal of removal.

Lower outer cover

4 Remove the crankshaft pulley, as described in Section 4.

5 Release the two cover securing clips, located at the rear of the engine, then unscrew the two lower securing bolts, and the single bolt securing the cover to the engine mounting bracket. Withdraw the cover downwards from the engine **(see illustrations)**.

6 Refitting is a reversal of removal, but refit the crankshaft pulley with reference to Section 4.

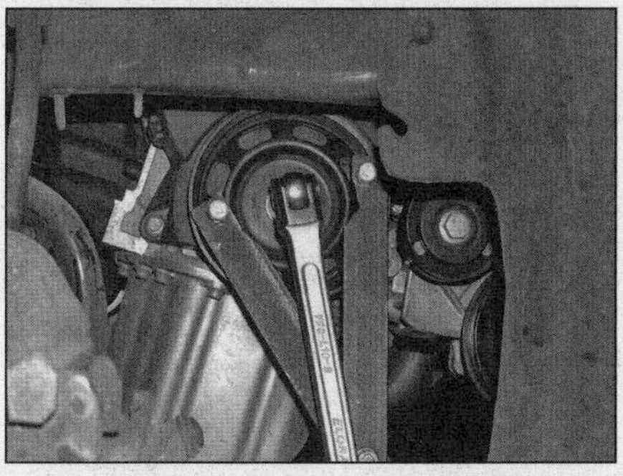

4.6 Counterhold the crankshaft pulley using a tool similar to that shown

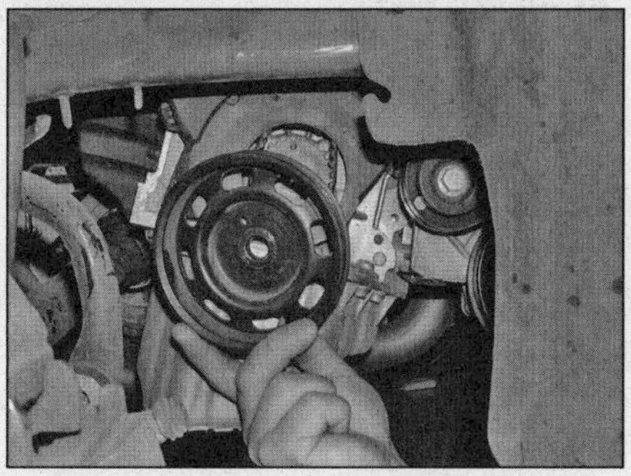

4.8 Removing the crankshaft pulley

5.2 Removing the upper outer timing belt cover

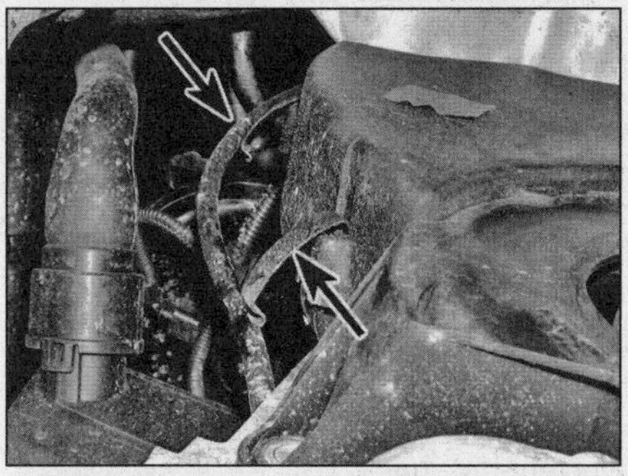

5.5a Release the two securing clips...

5.5b ...then unscrew the two lower securing bolts...

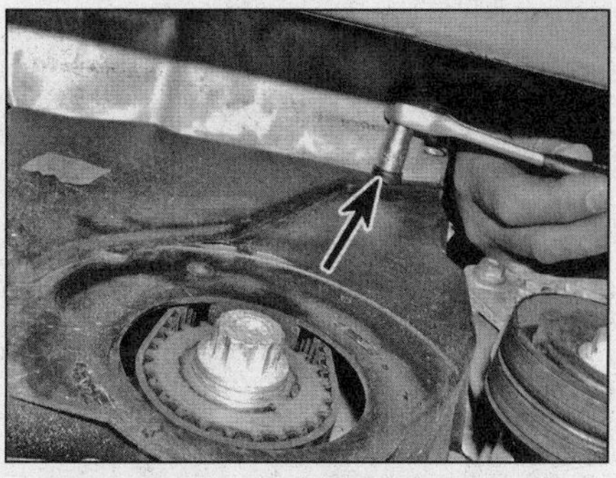

5.5c ...and the single bolt securing the cover to the engine mounting bracket...

5.5d ...and withdraw the lower timing belt cover

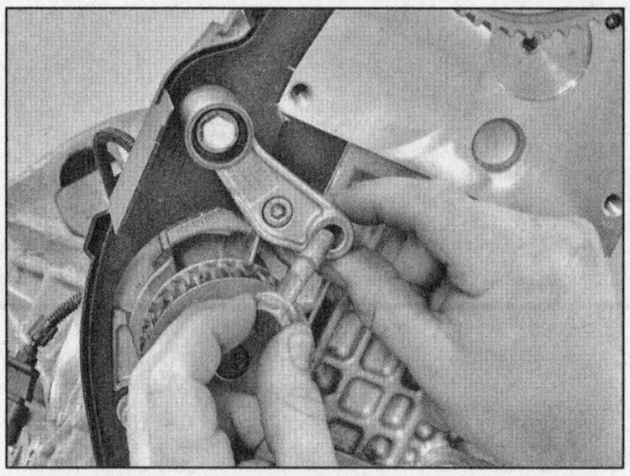

5.8 Removing the idler pulley/bracket assembly (viewed with engine removed)

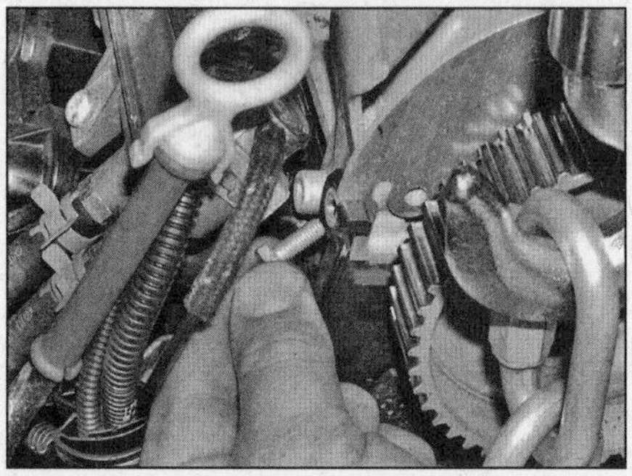

5.9 Unscrew rear timing belt cover bolt next to engine right-hand lifting eye

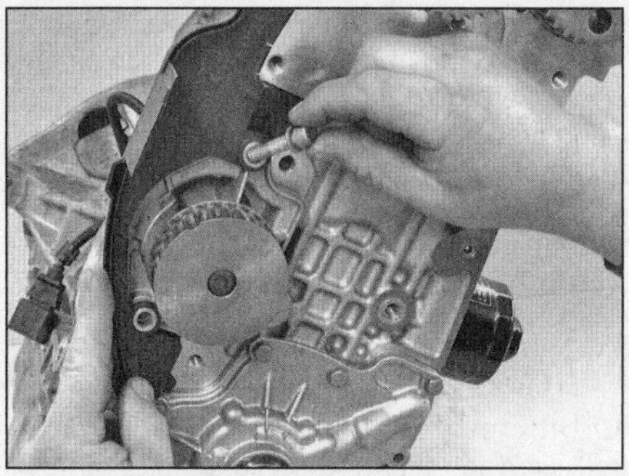

5.10 Removing the rear timing belt cover (viewed with engine removed)

Rear timing belt cover

Note: *As the rear timing belt cover securing bolts also secure the coolant pump, it is advisable to drain the cooling system (see Chapter 1A Section 32) before starting this procedure, and to renew the coolant pump seal/gasket (see Chapter 3 Section 7) before refitting the cover. Refill the cooling system with reference to Chapter 1A Section 32.*

7 Remove the timing belt as described in Section 6.

8 Unbolt the timing belt idler pulley/bracket assembly **(see illustration)**.

9 Unscrew the rear timing belt cover securing bolt located next to the engine right-hand lifting eye **(see illustration)**.

10 Unscrew the two securing bolts, and remove the rear timing belt cover. Note that the bolts also secure the coolant pump **(see illustration)**.

11 Refitting is a reversal of removal, but tighten the timing belt idler pulley/bracket bolt to the specified torque, and refit the timing belt as described in Section 6.

6 Timing belt(s) – removal and refitting

Removal

1 These engines have two timing belts; the main timing belt drives the inlet camshaft from the crankshaft, and the secondary timing belt drives the exhaust camshaft from the inlet camshaft.

Main timing belt

2 Disconnect the battery negative lead as described in Chapter 5A Section 3.

3 Remove the air cleaner assembly as described in Chapter 4A Section 3. Also remove the engine top cover and, where necessary, disconnect the ventilation hose.

4 Remove the upper and lower timing belt covers as described in Section 5.

5 Refit the crankshaft pulley securing bolt, with a spacer washer positioned under its head, to retain the crankshaft sprocket.

6 Turn the crankshaft to position No 1 piston at TDC on the compression stroke, and lock the camshaft sprockets in position, as described in Section 3.

7 Unscrew the securing screw, and move the power steering fluid reservoir clear of the working area, leaving the fluid hoses connected. Where necessary, unclip the charcoal canister hose from the reservoir.

8 Where applicable, on models with air conditioning, unscrew the securing bolt, and remove the auxiliary drivebelt idler pulley.

9 Attach a hoist and lifting tackle to the right-hand (timing belt end) engine lifting bracket, and raise the hoist to just take the weight of the engine.

10 Remove the complete engine right-hand mounting assembly, as described in Section 19. Also, unbolt the mounting bracket from the cylinder block.

11 Unscrew the four securing bolts, and remove the engine right-hand mounting bracket from the engine.

12 If either of the timing belts are to be refitted, mark their running directions to ensure correct refitting.

13 Engage a suitable Allen key with the hole in the main timing belt tensioner plate, then slacken the tensioner bolt, lever the tensioner anti-clockwise using the Allen key (to release the tension on the belt), and retighten the tensioner bolt **(see illustration)**.

14 Temporarily remove the camshaft sprocket locking tool, then slide the main timing belt from the sprockets, noting it's routing **(see illustration)**. Refit the camshaft sprocket locking tool once the timing belt has been removed.

15 Turn the crankshaft a quarter-turn (90°) anti-clockwise to position No's 1 and 4 pistons slightly down their bores from the TDC position. This will eliminate any risk of piston-to-valve contact if the crankshaft or camshaft is turned whilst the timing belt is removed.

Secondary timing belt

16 Once the main timing belt has been removed, to remove the secondary timing belt, proceed as follows.

17 Engage a suitable Allen key with the hole in the secondary timing belt tensioner plate, then slacken the tensioner bolt, and lever the tensioner clockwise using the Allen key (to release the tension on the belt). Unscrew the securing bolt, and remove the secondary timing belt tensioner **(see illustrations)**.

18 Temporarily remove the camshaft sprocket locking tool, and slide the

6.13 Slacken the tensioner bolt, lever the tensioner anti-clockwise, then retighten

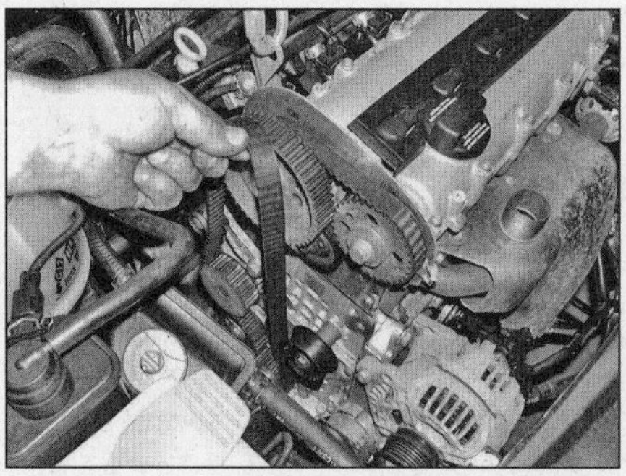

6.14 Removing the main timing belt

6.17a Slacken the tensioner bolt, and lever the tensioner clockwise...

6.17b ...then unscrew the bolt and remove the tensioner

6.18 Removing the secondary timing belt

secondary timing belt from the sprockets **(see illustration)**. Refit the sprocket locking tool once the belt has been removed.

Refitting

Secondary timing belt

19 Check that the camshaft sprockets are still locked in position by the locking pins **(see illustration)**.

20 Temporarily remove the camshaft sprocket locking tool, and fit the secondary timing belt around the camshaft sprockets. Make sure that the belt is as tight as possible on its top run between the sprockets (but note that there will be some slack in the belt). If the original belt is being refitted, observe the running direction markings. Refit the camshaft sprocket locking tool once the belt has been fitted to the sprockets.

21 Check that the secondary timing belt tensioner pointer is positioned on the far right of the tensioner backplate.

22 Lift the lower run of the secondary timing belt using the tensioner, and fit the tensioner securing bolt (if necessary turn the tensioner with an Allen key until the bolt hole in the tensioner aligns with the bolt hole in the cylinder head). Make sure that the lug on the tensioner backplate engages with the core plug hole in the cylinder head **(see illustration)**.

23 Use the Allen key to turn the tensioner anti-clockwise until the tensioner pointer aligns with the lug on the tensioner backplate, with the lug positioned against the left-hand stop in the core plug hole **(see illustration)**. Tighten the tensioner bolt to the specified torque.

24 Turn the crankshaft a quarter-turn (90°) clockwise to reposition No's 1 and 4 pistons at TDC. Ensure that the crankshaft sprocket tooth with the chamfered inner edge is aligned with the corresponding mark on the oil pump housing.

Main timing belt

25 Where applicable, ensure that the secondary drivebelt has been refitted and tensioned, then again temporarily remove the camshaft sprocket locking tool, and fit the main timing belt around the sprockets. If the original belt is being refitted, observe the running direction markings. Work in an anti-clockwise direction, starting at the coolant pump sprocket, followed by the tensioner roller, crankshaft sprocket, idler pulley, inlet camshaft sprocket and the second idler pulley. Once the belt has been refitted, refit the camshaft sprocket locking tool.

26 Ensure that the tensioner bolt is slack, then engage an Allen key with the hole in the tensioner plate, and turn the plate clockwise until the tension indicator pointer is aligned with the centre of the cut-out in the backplate. Tighten the tensioner securing bolt to the specified torque.

27 Remove the camshaft sprocket locking tool.

28 Using a spanner or socket on the crankshaft pulley bolt, turn the engine through two complete turns in the normal direction of rotation, until the crankshaft sprocket tooth with the chamfered inner edge is aligned with the corresponding mark on the oil pump housing **(see illustration 6.19)**. Check that the locking tool can again be fitted to lock the camshaft sprockets in position – if not, one or both of the timing belts may have been incorrectly fitted.

29 With the crankshaft timing marks aligned, and the camshaft sprockets locked in position, check the tension of the timing belts. The secondary and main belt tension indicators should be positioned as described in paragraphs 23 and 25 respectively – if not, repeat the appropriate tensioning procedure, then recheck the tension.

30 When the belt tension is correct, refit the engine right-hand mounting bracket, and tighten the securing bolts to the specified torque.

31 Disconnect the hoist and lifting tackle from the engine lifting bracket.

32 Where applicable, refit the auxiliary drivebelt idler pulley.

33 Refit the lower outer timing belt cover, with reference to Section 5 if necessary.

34 Refit the crankshaft pulley as described in Section 4.

35 Refit the upper outer timing belt cover.

36 Refit the air cleaner assembly, and reconnect the battery negative lead.

6.19 Crankshaft sprocket tooth with chamfered edge aligned with cast arrow on oil pump

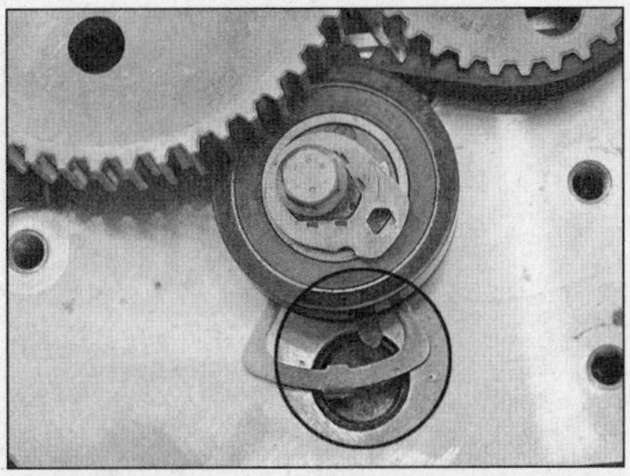

6.22 Ensure the backplate lug engages correctly with the core plug hole

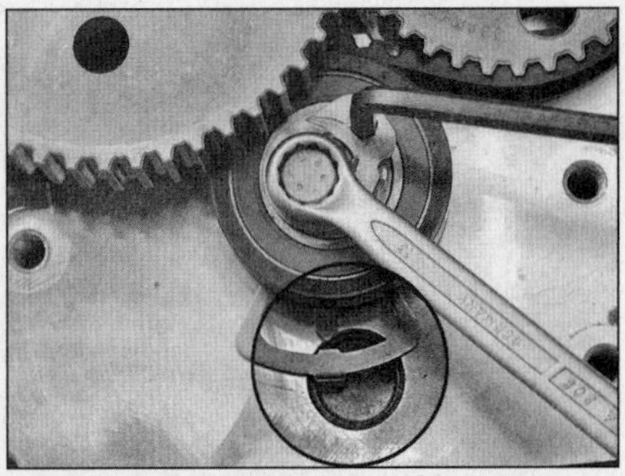

6.23 Turn the tensioner anti-clockwise to align the tensioner pointer and the lug

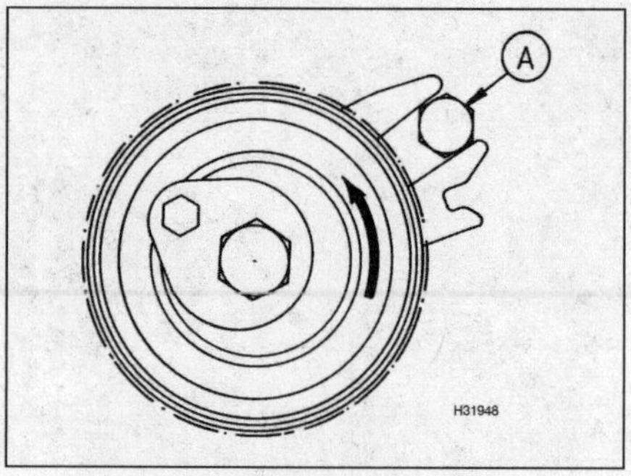

7.3 Turn tensioner anti-clockwise to position shown before fitting. Cut-out engages with bolt (A)

7.8a Removing the smaller...

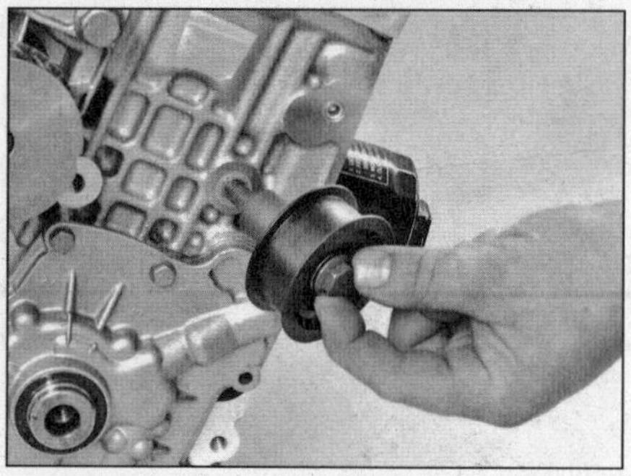

7.8b ...and larger timing belt idler pulleys

7 Timing belt tensioner and sprockets – removal, inspection and refitting

Tensioner

Main timing belt

1 Remove the main timing belt as described in Section 6.

2 Unscrew the main timing belt tensioner bolt, and remove the tensioner from the engine.

3 Engage an Allen key with the hole in the tensioner plate, and turn the tensioner anti-clockwise to the position shown **(see illustration)**.

4 Refit the tensioner to the engine, ensuring that the cut-out in the tensioner backplate engages with the bolt on the cylinder block **(refer to illustration 7.3)**. Refit the tensioner securing bolt, and tighten by hand.

5 Refit and tension the main timing belt as described in Section 6.

Secondary timing belt

6 Removal and refitting of the tensioner is described as part of the timing belt removal procedure in Section 6.

Main timing belt idler pulleys

7 Remove the timing belt as described in Section 6.

8 Unscrew the securing bolt and remove the relevant idler pulley. Note that the smaller pulley (the idler pulley nearest the inlet manifold side of the engine) can be removed complete with its mounting bracket (unbolt the mounting bracket bolt, leaving the pulley attached to the bracket) **(see illustrations)**.

9 Refit the relevant idler pulley and tighten the securing bolt to the specified torque. Note that if the smaller idler pulley has been removed complete with its bracket; ensure that the bracket locates over the rear timing belt cover bolt on refitting.

10 Refit and tension the main timing belt as described in Section 6.

Crankshaft sprocket

11 Remove the main timing belt as described in Section 6.

12 Unscrew the crankshaft pulley, and the washer used to retain the sprocket, and withdraw the sprocket from the crankshaft.

13 Commence refitting by positioning the sprocket on the end of the crankshaft, noting that the pulley locating pin must be outermost **(see illustration)**. Temporarily refit the pulley securing bolt and washer to retain the sprocket.

14 Refit the main timing belt as described in Section 6.

Camshaft sprockets

15 Remove the main and secondary timing belts as described in Section 6. Ensure that the crankshaft has been turned a quarter-turn (90°) anti-clockwise to position No's 1 and 4 pistons slightly down their bores from the TDC position. This will eliminate any risk of piston-to-valve contact if the crankshaft or camshaft is turned whilst the timing belt is removed.

16 The relevant camshaft sprocket bolt must now be slackened. The camshaft must be prevented from turning as the sprocket bolt is unscrewed – **do not** rely solely on the sprocket locking tool for this. To hold the sprocket, make up a tool, and use it to hold the sprocket stationary by means of the holes in the sprocket **(refer to illustration 7.19)**.

17 Unscrew the camshaft sprocket bolt, and withdraw the sprocket from the end of the camshaft, noting which way round it is fitted.

18 Commence refitting by offering the sprocket up to the camshaft, ensuring that lug on the sprocket engages with the notch in the end of the camshaft. If both camshaft sprockets have been removed, note that the double sprocket (for the main and secondary timing belts) should be fitted to the inlet camshaft, and note that the exhaust camshaft sprocket must be fitted first **(see illustration)**.

19 Fit a new sprocket securing bolt, then use the tool to hold the sprocket stationary, as during removal, and tighten the bolt to the specified torque, in the two stages given in the Specifications **(see illustration)**.

20 Refit the secondary and main timing belts as described in Section 6.

Coolant pump sprocket

21 The coolant pump sprocket is integral with the coolant pump. Refer to Chapter 3 Section 7, for details of coolant pump removal.

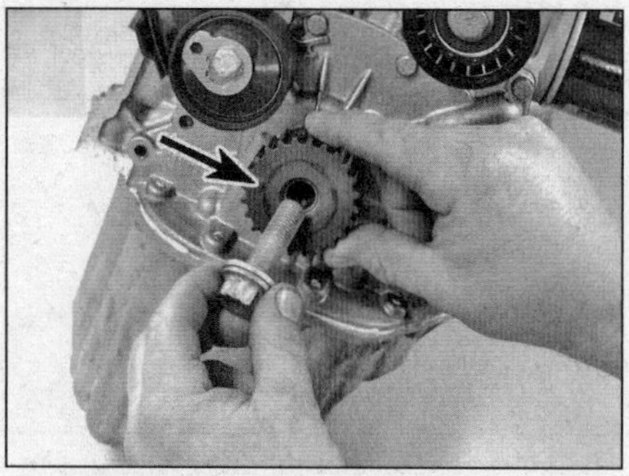

7.13 Refitting the crankshaft sprocket. The pulley locating pin must be outermost

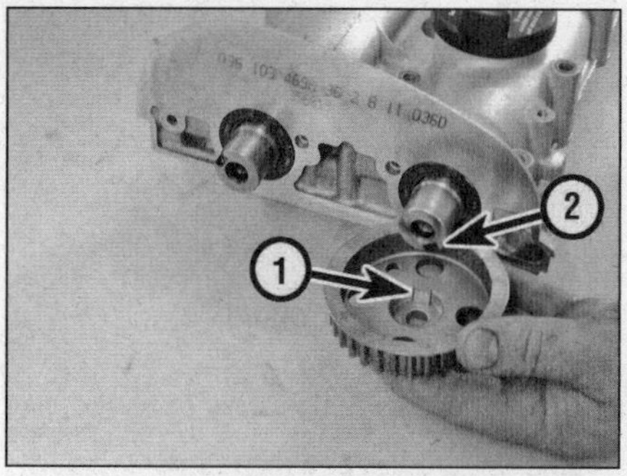

7.18 Ensure sprocket lug (1) engages with camshaft notch (2)

7.19 Tighten the sprocket securing bolt using a suitable tool to hold the sprocket stationary

8 Camshaft carrier – removal and refitting

Removal

1 Disconnect the battery negative lead as described in Chapter 5A Section 3.

2 Remove the main and secondary timing belts, as described in Section 6.

3 Disconnect the wiring and remove the ignition coils from the spark plugs (see Chapter 1A Section 27), then remove the cable guide.

4 Disconnect the inlet camshaft position sensor wiring connector **(see illustration)**.

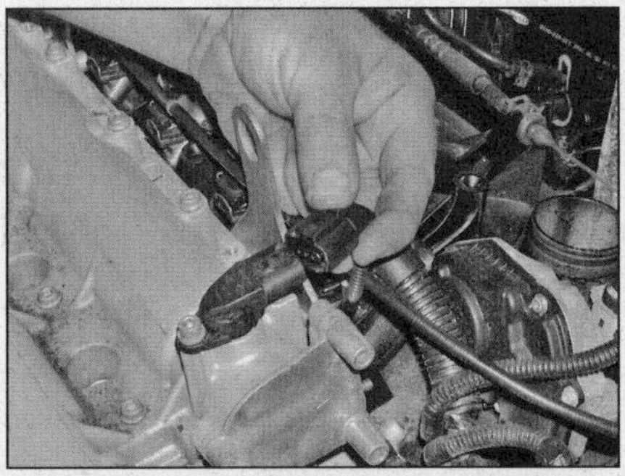

8.4 Disconnect the wiring connector from the inlet camshaft position sensor

5 Where fitted, unscrew the bolt securing the exhaust gas recirculation solenoid valve to the end of the camshaft carrier **(see illustration)**. Move the valve to one side.

8.5 Unbolt the exhaust gas recirculation solenoid valve from the camshaft carrier

6 Disconnect the wiring plug from the oil pressure warning light switch, located at the front left-hand corner of the camshaft carrier. Release the wiring harness from the clip on the end of the camshaft carrier, and move the wiring to one side **(see illustrations)**.

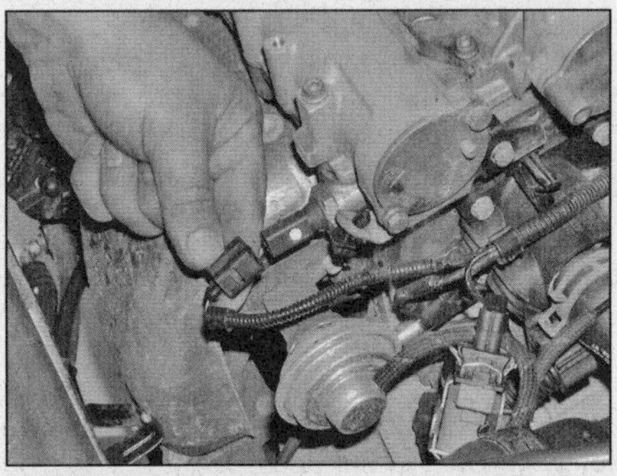

8.6a Disconnect the oil pressure warning light switch wiring plug...

8.6b ...then release the wiring from the clip on the end of the camshaft carrier

7 Remove the rear timing belt cover securing bolt, located next to the engine right-hand lifting eye **(see illustration)**.

8 Working progressively from the centre out, in a diagonal sequence, slacken and remove the camshaft carrier securing bolts **(see illustration)**.

9 Carefully lift the camshaft carrier from the cylinder head. The camshafts can be removed from the carrier, as described in Section 9.

Refitting

10 Commence refitting by thoroughly cleaning all traces of old sealant, and all traces of oil and grease, from the mating faces of the cylinder head and camshaft carrier. Ensure that no debris enters the cylinder head or camshaft carrier.

11 Ensure that the crankshaft is still positioned a quarter-turn (90°) anti-clockwise from the TDC position, and that the camshafts are locked in position with the locking tool, as described in Section 3.

12 Check that the valve rockers are correctly located on the valves, and securely clipped into position on the hydraulic tappets.

13 Apply a thin, even coat of sealant (Seat AMV 188 003, or equivalent) to the cylinder head mating face of the camshaft carrier **(see illustration)**. Do not apply the sealant too thickly, as excess sealant may enter and block the oilways, causing engine damage.

14 Carefully lower the camshaft carrier onto the cylinder head, until the camshafts rest on the rockers. Note that the camshaft carrier locates on dowels in the cylinder head; if desired, to make fitting easier, two guide studs can be made up as follows:

a) *Cut the heads off two M6 bolts, then cut slots in the top of each bolt to enable the bolt to be unscrewed using a flat-bladed screwdriver.*
b) *Screw one bolt into each of the camshaft carrier bolt locations at opposite corners of the cylinder head.*
c) *Lower the camshaft carrier over the bolts to guide it into position on the cylinder head.*

15 Fit new camshaft carrier securing bolts, and tighten them progressively, working from the centre out, in a diagonal sequence (i.e. tighten all bolts through one turn, then tighten all bolts through a further turn, and so on). Ensure that the camshaft carrier sits squarely on the cylinder head as the bolts are tightened, and make sure that the carrier engages with the cylinder head dowels. Where applicable, once the camshaft carrier contacts the surface of the cylinder head, unscrew the two guide studs, and fit the two remaining new camshaft carrier securing bolts in their place.

16 Tighten the camshaft carrier securing

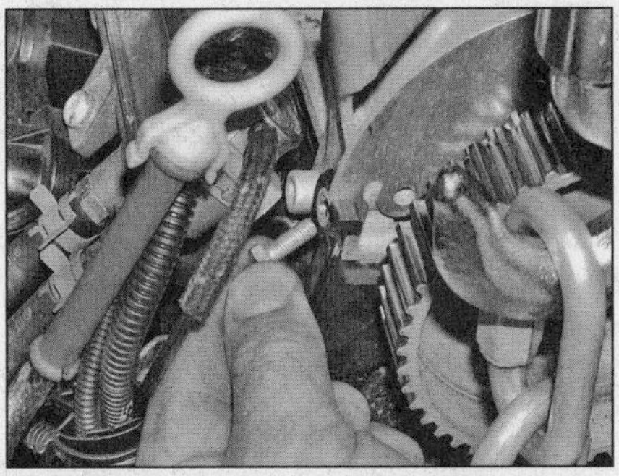

8.7 Remove the timing belt rear cover bolt next to the engine right-hand lifting eye

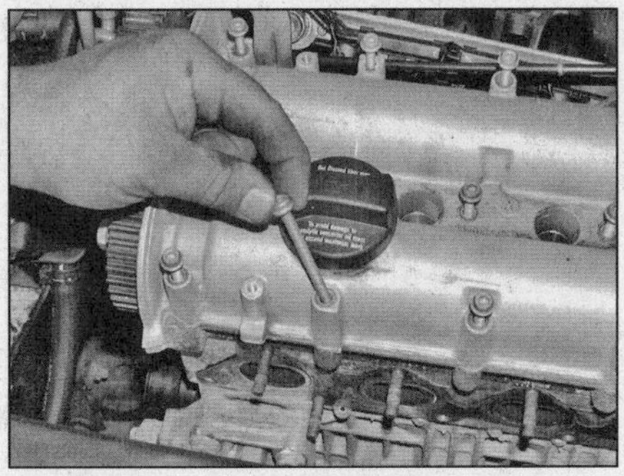

8.8 Removing the camshaft carrier securing bolts

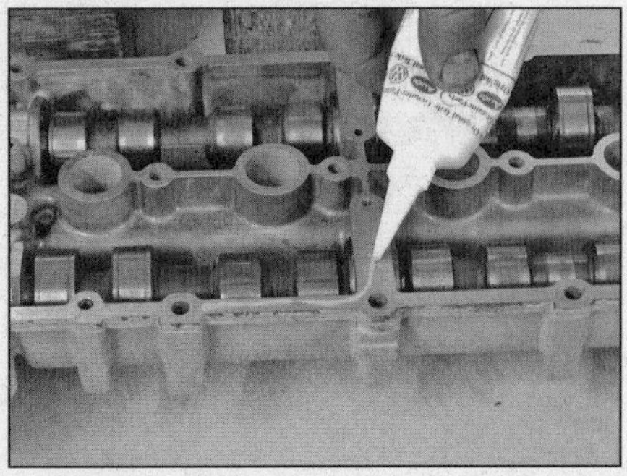

8.13 Spread sealant on the camshaft carrier's cylinder head mating face

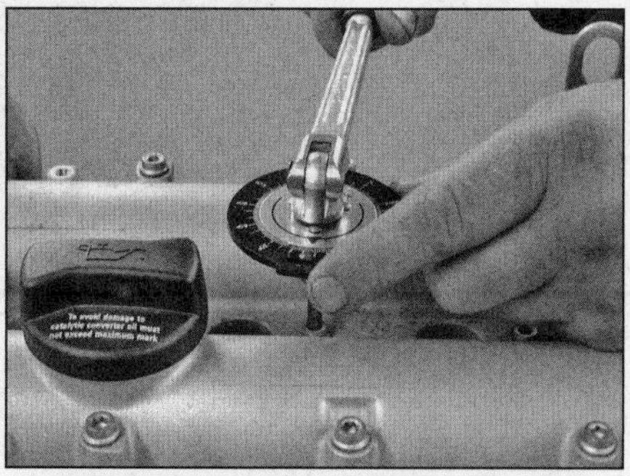

8.16 Tightening a camshaft carrier bolt through the specified Stage 2 angle

bolts to the specified torque, in the two stages given in the Specifications **(see illustration)**.

17 Leave the camshaft carrier sealant to dry for approximately 30 minutes before carrying out any further work on the cylinder head or camshaft carrier.

18 Once the sealant has been allowed to dry, refit the rear timing belt cover bolt.

19 Reconnect the oil pressure warning light switch wiring plug, and clip the wiring into position on the end of the camshaft carrier.

20 Refit the exhaust gas recirculation solenoid valve bracket to the camshaft carrier, and tighten the securing bolt. Make sure that the lug on the camshaft carrier endplate engages with the corresponding hole in the solenoid valve bracket.

21 Reconnect the camshaft position sensor wiring connector.

22 Refit the cable guide and reconnect the ignition coils to the spark plugs.

23 Refit the secondary and main timing belts, as described in Section 6.

24 Reconnect the battery negative lead.

9 Camshafts – removal, inspection and refitting

Removal

1 Remove the camshaft carrier as described in Section 8.

2 Remove the camshaft sprockets, with reference to Section 7 if necessary.

3 If the inlet camshaft is to be removed, unscrew the securing bolt, and remove the inlet camshaft position sensor **(see illustration)**.

4 Remove the relevant camshaft carrier endplate **(see illustration)**.

5 Carefully withdraw the relevant camshaft from the endplate end of the camshaft carrier, taking care not to damage the bearing surfaces of the camshaft and housing as the camshaft is withdrawn **(see illustration)**.

Inspection

6 Visually inspect the camshafts for evidence of wear on the surfaces of the lobes and journals. Normally their surfaces should be smooth and have a dull shine; look for scoring, erosion or pitting and areas that appear highly polished, indicating excessive wear. Accelerated wear will occur once the hardened exterior of the camshaft has been damaged, so always renew worn items. **Note:** *If these symptoms are visible on the tips of the camshaft lobes, check the corresponding rocker, as it will probably be worn as well.*

7 If the machined surfaces of the camshaft appear discoloured or blue, it is likely that it has been overheated at some point, probably due to inadequate lubrication. This may have distorted the shaft, so check the run-out as follows: place the camshaft between two V-blocks and using a DTI gauge, measure the run-out at the centre journal. No maximum run-out figure is quoted by the manufacturers, but it should be obvious if the camshaft is excessively distorted.

8 To measure camshaft endfloat, temporarily refit the relevant camshaft to the camshaft carrier, and refit the camshaft sealing plate to the rear of the camshaft carrier. Anchor a DTI gauge to the timing belt end of the camshaft carrier and align the gauge probe with the camshaft axis. Push the camshaft to one end of the camshaft carrier as far as it will travel, then rest the DTI gauge probe on the end of the camshaft, and zero the gauge display. Push the camshaft as far as it will go to the other end of the camshaft carrier, and record the gauge reading. Verify the reading by pushing the camshaft back to its original position and checking that the gauge indicates zero again.

9 Check that the camshaft endfloat measurement is within the limit listed in the Specifications. Wear outside of this limit may be cured by renewing the relevant camshaft carrier endplate, although wear is unlikely to be confined to any one component, so renewal of the camshafts and camshaft carrier must be considered.

Refitting

10 Refitting is a reversal of removal, bearing in mind the following points:

a) *Before refitting the camshaft, renew the camshaft oil seals, with reference to Section 11.*

b) *Lubricate the bearing surfaces in the camshaft carrier, and the camshaft lobes before refitting the camshaft(s).*

c) *Refit the camshaft sprocket(s) with reference to Section 7, noting that if both sprockets have been removed, the exhaust camshaft sprocket must be fitted first.*

d) *Refit the camshaft carrier as described in Section 8.*

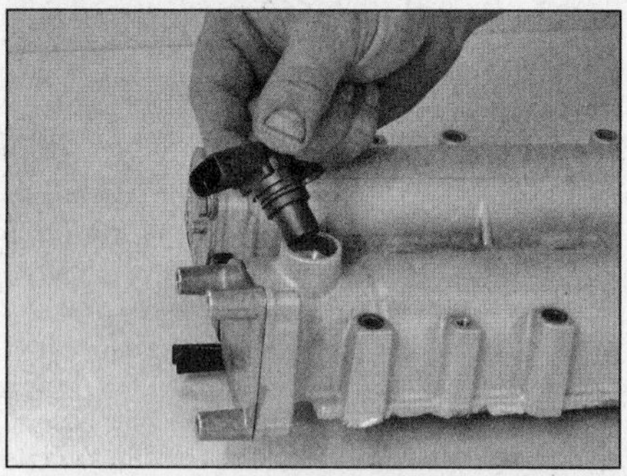

9.3 Remove the inlet camshaft position sensor

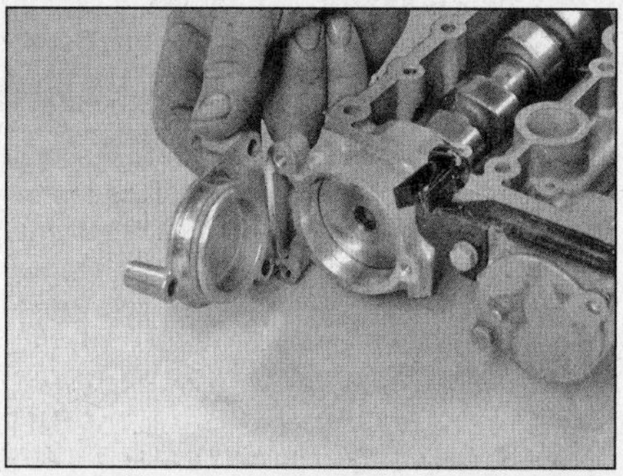

9.4 Remove the camshaft carrier endplate

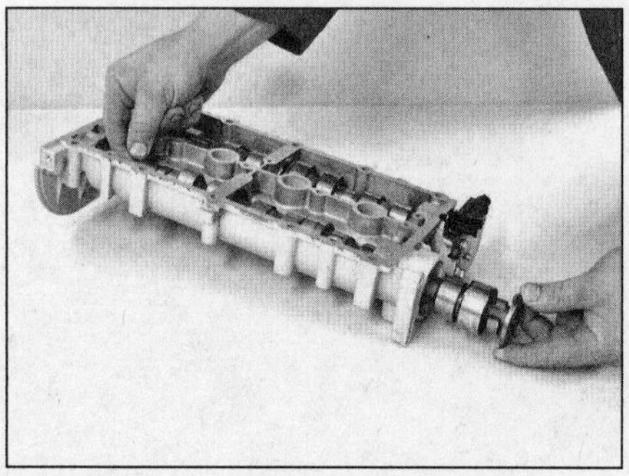

9.5 Withdraw the camshaft from the camshaft carrier

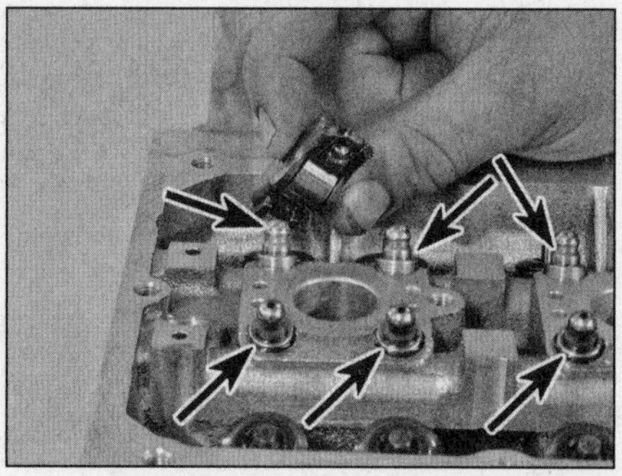

10.3 Removing a rocker. Note the tappets

10 Rockers and hydraulic tappets – removal, inspection and refitting

Removal

1 Remove the camshaft carrier, as described in Section 8.

2 As the components are removed, keep them in strict order, so that they can be refitted in their original locations.

3 Unclip the rockers from the hydraulic tappets, and lift them from the cylinder head **(see illustration)**.

4 Carefully lift the hydraulic tappets from their bores in the cylinder head. It is advisable to store the tappets (in order) upright in an oil bath whilst they are removed from the engine.

Inspection

5 Check the tappet bores in the cylinder head for signs of scoring or damage. If significant scoring or damage is found, it may be necessary to renew the cylinder head and the complete set of tappets.
6 Inspect the hydraulic tappets for obvious signs of wear or damage, and renew if necessary. Check that the oil holes in the tappets are free from obstructions.
7 Check the valve, tappet, and camshaft contact faces of the rockers for wear or damage, and also check the rockers for any signs of cracking. Renew any worn or damaged rockers.
8 Inspect the camshaft lobes, as described in Section 9.

Refitting

9 Oil the tappet bores in the cylinder head, and the hydraulic tappets themselves, then carefully slide the tappets into their original bores **(see illustration)**.
10 Oil the rocker contact faces of the tappets, and the tops of the valve stems, then refit the rockers to their original locations, ensuring that the rockers are securely clipped onto the tappets.
11 Check the endfloat of each camshaft, as described in Section 9, then refit the camshaft carrier as described in Section 8.

11 Camshaft oil seals – renewal

Right-hand oil seals

1 Remove the main and secondary timing belts as described in Section 6.
2 Remove the relevant camshaft sprocket as described in Section 7.
3 Drill two small holes into the existing oil seal, diagonally opposite each other. Take great care to avoid drilling through into the seal housing or camshaft sealing surface. Thread two self-tapping screws into the holes, and using a pair of pliers, pull on the heads of the screws to extract the oil seal.
4 Clean out the seal housing and the sealing surface of the camshaft by wiping it with a lint-free cloth. Remove any swarf or burrs that may cause the seal to leak.
5 Lubricate the lip and outer edge of the new oil seal with clean engine oil, and push it over the camshaft until it is positioned above its housing. To prevent damage to the sealing lips, wrap some adhesive tape around the end of the camshaft.
6 Using a hammer and a socket of suitable diameter, drive the seal squarely into its housing. **Note:** *Select a socket that bears only on the hard outer surface of the seal, not the inner lip that can easily be damaged.*

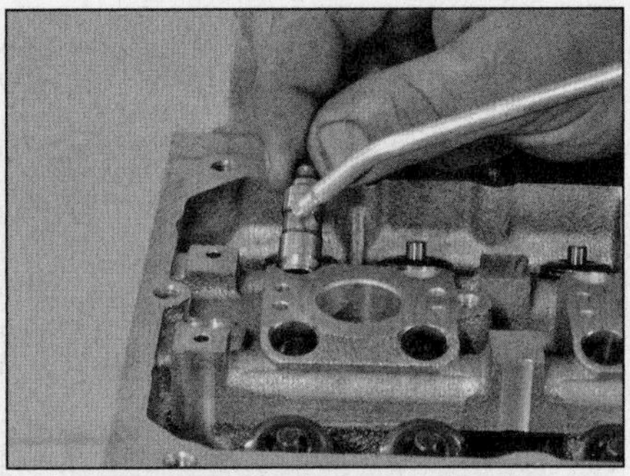

10.9 Oil the tappets before fitting

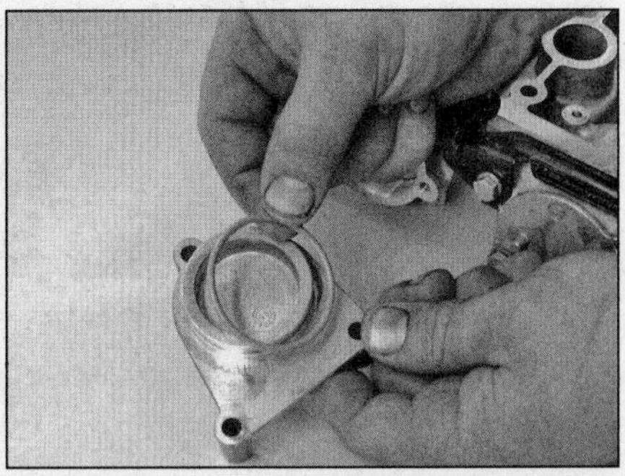

11.12 Renew the camshaft carrier endplate O-ring

7 Refit the relevant camshaft sprocket with reference to Section 7.
8 Refit and tension the secondary and main timing belts as described in Section 6.

Left-hand oil seals

9 The camshaft left-hand oil seals take the form of O-rings located in the grooves in the camshaft carrier endplates.
10 Unscrew the securing bolts, and remove the relevant camshaft endplate.
11 Prise the old O-ring from the groove in the endplate.
12 Lightly oil the new O-ring, and carefully locate it in the groove in the endplate **(see illustration)**.
13 Refit the endplate, and tighten the securing bolts to the specified torque.

12 Cylinder head – removal, inspection and refitting

Note: *The cylinder head must be removed with the engine cold.*

Removal

1 Disconnect the battery negative lead as described in Chapter 5A Section 3.
2 Drain the cooling system as described in Chapter 1A Section 32.
3 Remove the main and secondary timing belts as described in Section 6.
4 As the engine is currently supported using a hoist attached to the engine lifting brackets bolted to the cylinder head, it is now necessary to attach a suitable bracket to the cylinder block, so that the engine can still be supported as the cylinder head is removed.
5 A suitable bracket can be bolted to the cylinder block using spacers, and a long bolt screwed into the hole located next to the coolant pump **(see illustration)**. Ideally, attach a second set of lifting tackle to the hoist, adjust the lifting tackle to support the engine using the bracket attached to the cylinder block, and then disconnect the lifting tackle attached to the bracket on the cylinder head. Alternatively, temporarily support the engine under the sump using a jack and a block of wood, and then transfer the lifting tackle from the bracket on the cylinder head to the bracket bolted to the cylinder block.
6 Release the hose clips, and disconnect the two radiator hoses from the coolant housing at the transmission end of the cylinder head **(see illustration)**. Similarly, release the hose clips and disconnect the remaining three small coolant hoses from the rear of the coolant housing.
7 Remove the air cleaner assembly, complete with the air trunking, as described in Chapter 4A Section 3.
8 Unscrew the bolt securing the oil level dipstick tube bracket to the cylinder head, then lift the dipstick tube, and turn it to

12.5 Home-made engine lifting bracket fitted next to the coolant pump

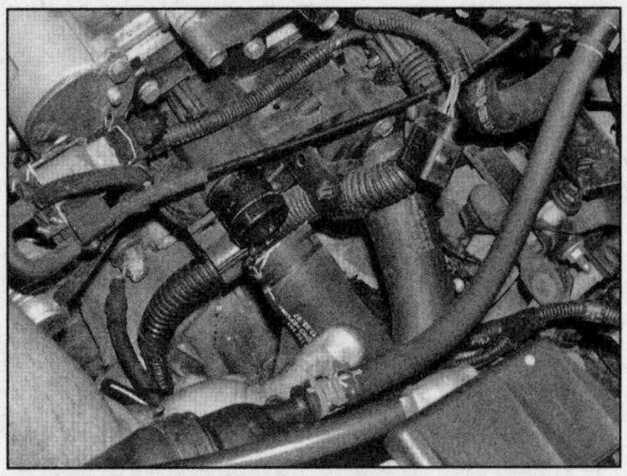

12.6 Disconnect the radiator hoses from the cylinder head coolant housing

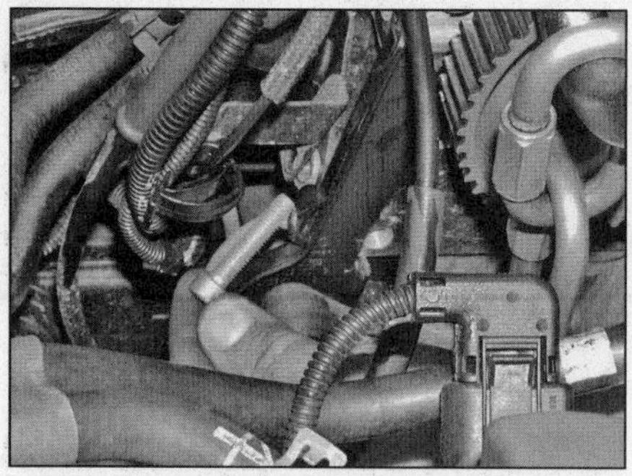

12.8 Unscrew the dipstick tube bracket bolt from the cylinder head

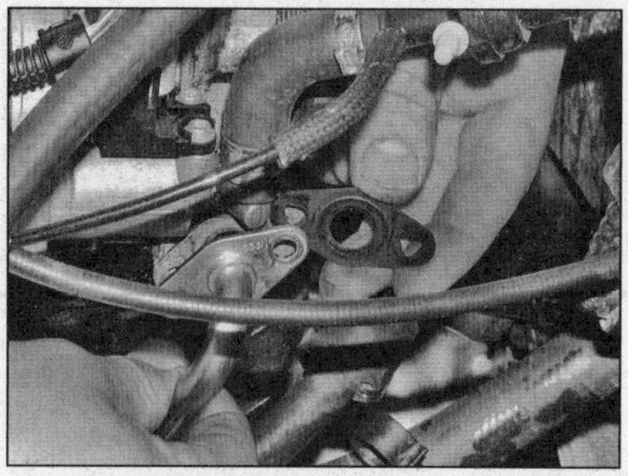

12.9 Disconnect the EGR pipe from the throttle body and recover the gasket

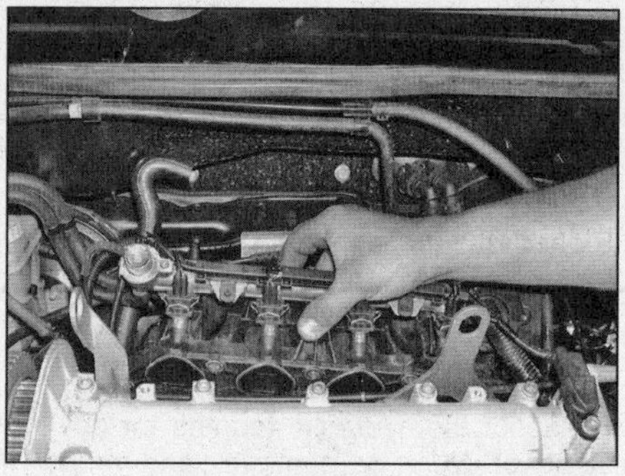

12.10 Lift the inlet manifold back from the engine

one side, to clear the working area **(see illustration)**. Release the wiring harnesses from the clip on the dipstick tube bracket. Note that the dipstick tube bracket bolt also secures the inlet manifold.

9 Where fitted, unscrew the two securing bolts and disconnect the exhaust gas recirculation (EGR) pipe from the throttle body and recover the gasket **(see illustration)**. Also unscrew the bolt securing the EGR pipe bracket to the coolant housing.

10 Unscrew the six securing bolts (three upper and three lower) and lift the inlet manifold back from the engine **(see illustration)**. Ensure that the inlet manifold is adequately supported in the engine compartment, and take care not to strain any wires, cables or hoses. Recover the O-rings if they are loose.

11 Unbolt the wiring connector bracket from the right-hand rear corner of the cylinder head **(see illustration)**.

12 Disconnect the wiring plug from the coolant temperature sensor, located in the coolant housing at the transmission end of the cylinder head, then unclip the wiring harnesses from the coolant housing, and move them to one side **(see illustrations)**.

13 Disconnect the vacuum hose from the exhaust gas recirculation (EGR) valve (where applicable).

14 Unclip the wiring from the bracket attached to the exhaust heat shield, then unscrew the securing bolts (two upper bolts and one lower bolt), and remove the heat shield **(see illustrations)**.

15 Disconnect the exhaust front section from the manifold with reference to Chapter 4C Section 8. If desired, the exhaust manifold can be removed as follows:

a) Unscrew the union nut securing the EGR pipe to the exhaust manifold, and remove the EGR pipe (where applicable).

b) Unscrew the exhaust manifold securing nuts, then lift off the manifold and recover the gasket.

16 Remove the camshaft carrier, with reference to Section 8.

17 Pull out the metal clip securing the plastic coolant pipe to the coolant housing at the left-hand rear corner of the cylinder head **(see illustration)**.

18 Progressively slacken the cylinder head bolts in order, then unscrew and remove the bolts **(see illustration)**.

19 With all the bolts removed, lift the cylinder head from the block. If the cylinder head is stuck, tap it with a soft-faced mallet to break the joint. **Do not** insert a lever into the gasket joint. As the cylinder head is lifted off, release the coolant pump pipe from the thermostat housing on the cylinder head.

20 Lift the cylinder head gasket from the block.

12.11 Unbolt the wiring bracket from the cylinder head right rear corner

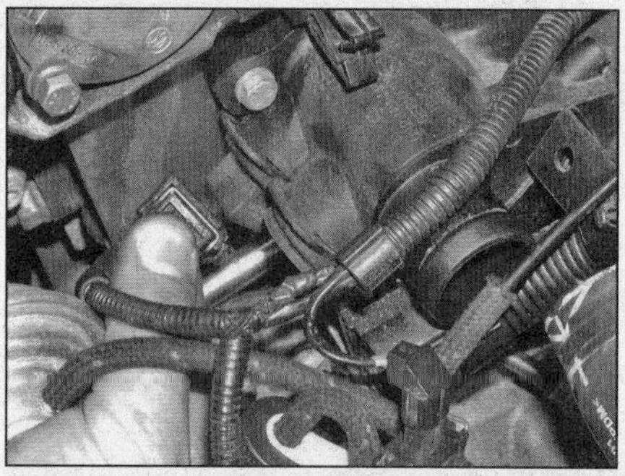

12.12a Disconnect the coolant temperature sensor wiring plug...

12.12b ...then unclip the wiring harnesses and move them to one side

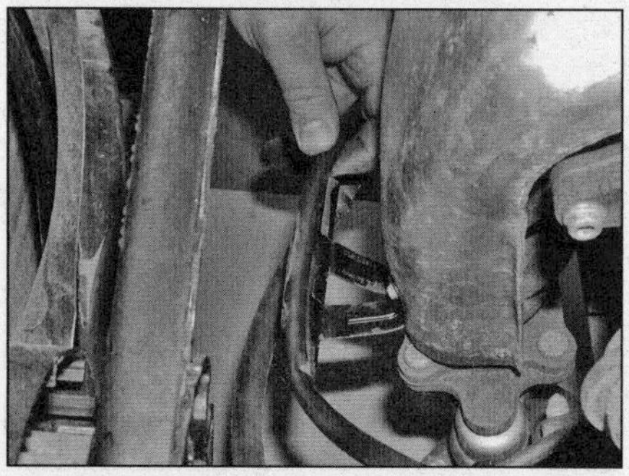

12.14a Unclip the wiring from the bracket on the exhaust heat shield...

12.14b ...then remove the heat shield

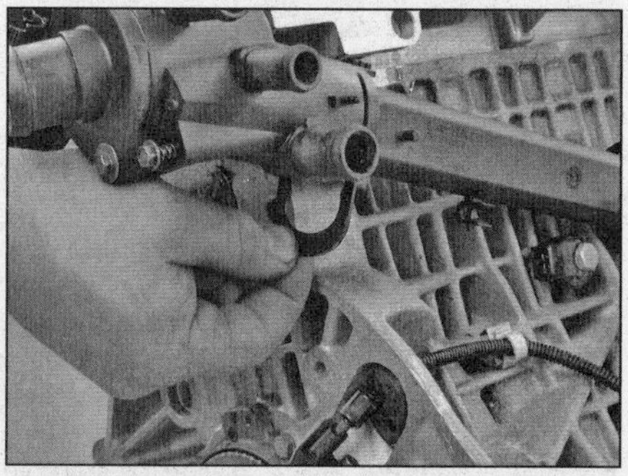

12.17 Pull out the coolant pipe-to-housing metal clip (engine removed for clarity)

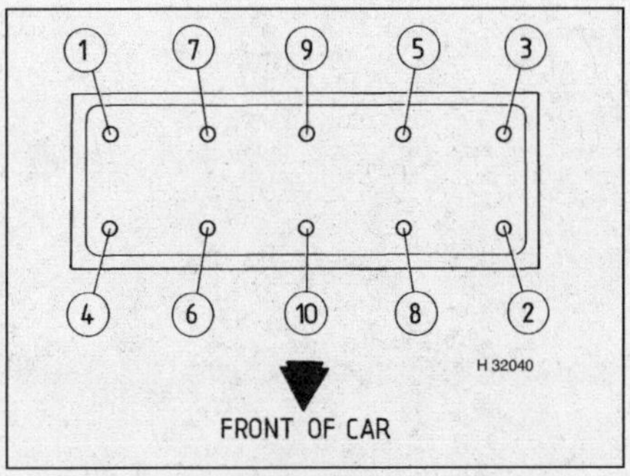

12.18 Cylinder head bolt slackening sequence

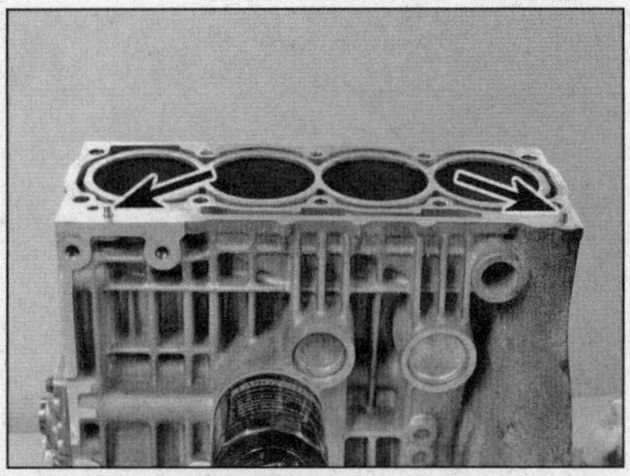

12.27a Ensure that the dowels are in place in the cylinder block…

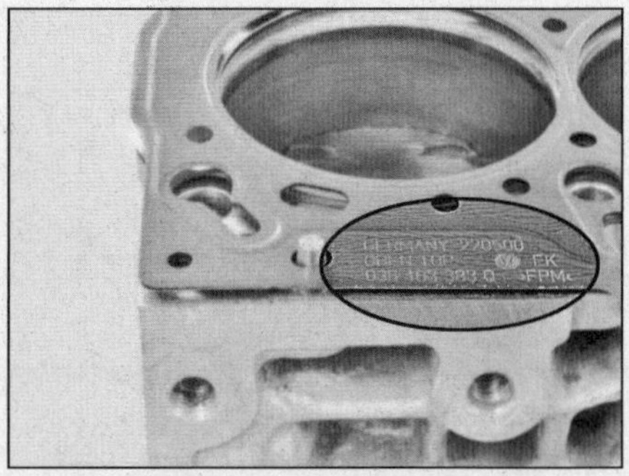

12.27b …and the gasket part number and OBEN/TOP markings are uppermost

Inspection

21 Dismantling and inspection of the cylinder head is covered in Part H of this Chapter. Additionally, check the condition of the coolant pump pipe-to-thermostat housing O-ring, and renew if necessary.

Refitting

22 The mating faces of the cylinder head and block must be perfectly clean before refitting the head. Use a scraper to remove all traces of gasket and carbon, also clean the tops of the pistons. Take particular care with the aluminium surfaces, as the soft metal is easily damaged. Make sure that debris is not allowed to enter the oil and water passages – this is particularly important for the oil circuit, as carbon could block the oil supply to the camshaft and crankshaft bearings. Using adhesive tape and paper, seal the water, oil and bolt holes in the cylinder block. To prevent carbon entering the gap between the pistons and bores, smear a little grease in the gap. After cleaning a piston, rotate the crankshaft to that the piston moves down the bore, and then wipe out the grease and carbon with a cloth rag. Clean the other piston crowns in the same way.

23 Check the head and block for nicks, deep scratches and other damage. If slight, they may be removed carefully with a file. More serious damage may be repaired by machining, but this is a specialist job.

24 If warpage of the cylinder head is suspected, use a straight-edge to check it for distortion, as described in Part F of this Chapter.

25 Ensure that the cylinder head bolt holes in the crankcase are clean and free of oil. Syringe or soak up any oil left in the bolt holes. This is most important in order that the correct bolt tightening torque can be applied, and to prevent the possibility of the block being cracked by hydraulic pressure when the bolts are tightened.

26 Ensure that the crankshaft has been turned to position No's 1 and 4 pistons slightly down their bores from the TDC position (see Section 6). This will eliminate any risk of piston-to-valve contact as the cylinder head is refitted. Also ensure that the camshaft sprockets are locked in the TDC position using the locking tool, as described in Section 3.

27 Ensure that the cylinder head locating dowels are in place in the cylinder block, and then fit a new cylinder head gasket over the dowels, ensuring that the part number is uppermost. Where applicable, the OBEN/ TOP marking should also be uppermost **(see illustrations)**. Note that Seat recommend that the gasket is only removed from its packaging immediately prior to fitting.

28 Lower the cylinder head into position on the gasket, ensuring that it engages correctly over the dowels. As the cylinder head is lowered into position, ensure that the coolant pump pipe engages with the thermostat housing (use a new O-ring if necessary).

29 Fit the new cylinder head bolts, and screw them in as far as possible by hand.

30 Working progressively, in sequence, tighten all the cylinder head bolts to the specified Stage 1 torque **(see illustration)**.

31 Again working progressively, in sequence, tighten all the cylinder head bolts through the specified Stage 2 angle.

32 Finally, tighten all the cylinder head bolts, in sequence, to the specified Stage 3 torque.

33 Reconnect the lifting tackle to the engine right-hand lifting bracket on the cylinder head, then adjust the lifting tackle to support the engine. Once the engine is adequately supported using the cylinder head bracket, disconnect the lifting tackle from the bracket bolted to the cylinder block, and unbolt the improvised engine lifting bracket from the cylinder block. Alternatively, remove the trolley jack and block of wood from under the sump.

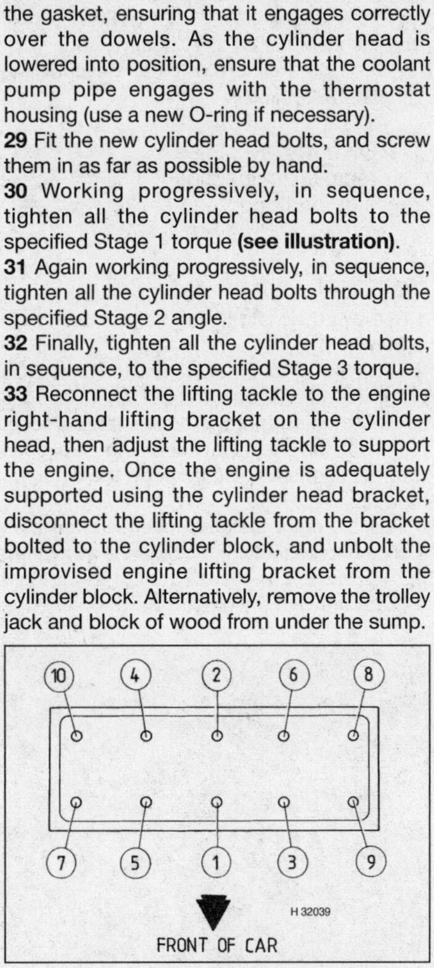

12.30 Cylinder head bolt tightening sequence

34 Refit the clip securing the plastic coolant pipe to the coolant housing.

35 Refit the camshaft carrier as described in Section 8.

36 Further refitting is a reversal of removal, bearing in mind the following points:

a) Refit the exhaust manifold and reconnect the EGR pipe, and/or reconnect the exhaust front section to the manifold, as described in Chapter 4C Section 8.

b) Refit the inlet manifold using new O-rings.

c) Reconnect the EGR pipe (where applicable) to the throttle body using a new gasket.

d) Refit the secondary and main timing belts as described in Section 6.

e) Ensure that all wires, pipes and hoses are correctly reconnected and routed, as noted before removal.

f) Tighten all fixings to the specified torque, where applicable.

g) On completion, refill the cooling system as described in Chapter 1A Section 32.

13 Sump – removal and refitting

Removal

1 Disconnect the battery negative lead (as described in Section).

2 Chock the rear wheels and apply the handbrake, then jack up the front of the car and support it on axle stands (see Chapter 13 Section 5). Remove the engine undertray.

3 Drain the engine oil, then clean and refit the engine oil drain plug, tightening it to the specified torque wrench setting. If the engine is nearing the service interval when the oil and filter are due for renewal, it is recommended that the filter is also removed and a new one fitted. After reassembly, the engine can then be replenished with fresh engine oil. Refer to Chapter 1A Section 6, for further information.

4 Remove the exhaust front pipe with reference to Chapter 4C Section 8.

5 Disconnect the wiring from the oil level/ temperature sender.

6 Unscrew the two bolts securing the sump rear flange to the transmission.

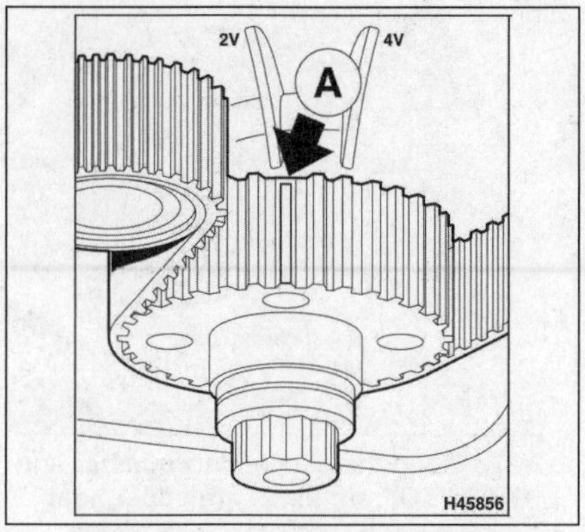

14.3 Position chamfered tooth (A) as shown

14.8 Removing the oil pump

14.10 Lifting off the oil pump rear cover

7 Progressively unscrew and remove the sump retaining bolts.

8 Break the joint by striking the sump with the palm of the hand, then lower the sump away from the engine and withdraw it.

9 While the sump is removed, take the opportunity to clean the oil pump pick-up/strainer pipe mesh using a suitable solvent. Inspect the strainer mesh for signs of clogging or splitting and renew if necessary, referring to Section 14, for further information.

Refitting

10 Thoroughly clean all traces of sealant and oil from the mating surfaces of the cylinder block/crankcase and sump, and then use a clean rag to wipe out the sump and the engine's interior.

11 Apply a 2.0 to 3.0 mm diameter bead of sealant to the sump mating flange, making sure that the bead is around the inner edges of the bolt holes. The bead must not exceed 3.0 mm diameter. **Note:** *The sump must be refitted within 5 minutes of applying the sealant.*

12 When refitting the sump, to guide the sump into position on the cylinder block mating face, two guide studs can be improvised by cutting the heads off two M6 bolts, and cutting slots in the ends of the bolts so that they can later by unscrewed using a flat-bladed screwdriver. Screw the guide studs into two diagonally opposite sump securing bolt holes.

13 Offer the sump into position, then refit the sump bolts and tighten them to the specified torque. Once the sump is held securely in position, unscrew the guide studs, and refit the remaining two sump securing bolts.

14 Insert the two rear flange bolts and tighten them to the specified torque.

15 Reconnect the wiring to the oil level/temperature sender.

16 Refit the exhaust front pipe with reference to Chapter 4C Section 8.

17 Refit the engine undertray and lower the car to the ground.

18 Reconnect the battery negative lead.

19 Refill the engine with oil as described in Chapter 1A Section 6.

14 Oil pump – removal, inspection and refitting

Removal

1 Remove the main timing belt as described in Section 6.

2 Turn the crankshaft a quarter-turn (90°) clockwise to reposition No's 1 and 4 pistons at TDC. Ensure that the crankshaft sprocket tooth with the chamfered inner edge is aligned with the corresponding mark on the oil pump housing.

3 Turn the crankshaft to move the crankshaft sprocket three teeth anti-clockwise away from the TDC position. The third tooth to the right of the tooth with the ground-down outer edge must align with the corresponding mark on the oil pump housing **(see illustration)**. This procedure positions the crankshaft correctly to enable oil pump refitting.

4 Remove the timing belt tensioner as described in Section 7.

5 Remove the sump as described in Section 13.

6 Unscrew the securing bolts and remove the oil pick-up pipe from the oil pump. Recover the gasket.

7 Remove the crankshaft sprocket; noting which way round it is fitted.

8 Unscrew the securing bolts, noting their locations to ensure correct refitting, and remove the oil pump **(see illustration)**. Recover the gasket.

Inspection

9 No spare parts are available for the oil pump, and if worn or faulty the complete pump must be renewed.

10 To inspect the oil pump rotors, remove the securing screws, and lift off the oil pump rear cover **(see illustration)**.

11 Note that the rotors fit with the punched dots on the edges of the rotors facing the oil pump cover **(see illustration)**.

12 Lift out the rotors, and inspect them for wear and damage. If there are any signs of wear or damage, the complete oil pump assembly must be renewed.

13 Lubricate the contact faces of the rotors with clean engine oil, then refit the rotors to the pump, ensuring that the punched dots on the edges of the rotors face the pump cover.

14 Refit the pump cover, and tighten the screws securely.

15 Using a flat-bladed screwdriver, prise the crankshaft oil seal from the oil pump, and discard it **(see illustration)**.

16 Thoroughly clean the oil seal seat in the oil pump.

17 Press or drive a new oil seal into position in the oil pump, using a socket or tube of suitable diameter **(see illustration)**. Ensure that the seal seats squarely in the oil pump. Ensure that the socket or tube bears only on the hard outer ring of the seal, and take care not to damage the seal lips. Press or drive the seal into position until it is seated on the shoulder in the housing. Make sure that the closed end of the seal is facing outwards.

14.11 Note that the rotors fit with the punched dots facing the oil pump cover

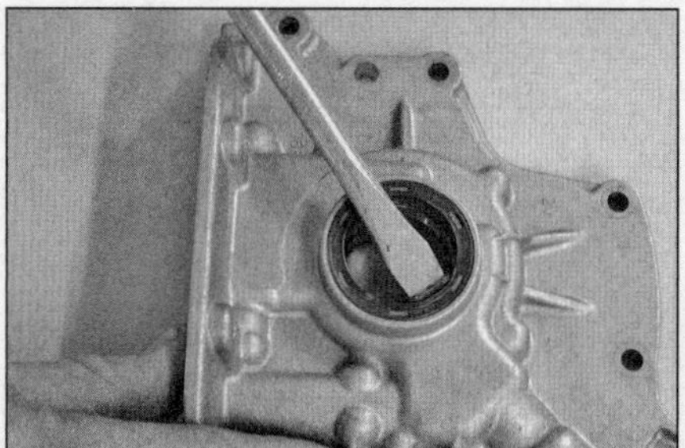

14.15 Prise the crankshaft oil seal from the oil pump

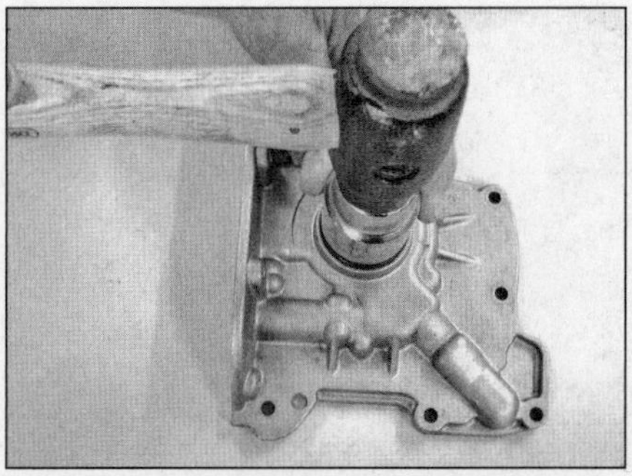

14.17 Driving a new oil seal into the oil pump using a socket

14.20 Fit a new gasket over the dowels in the cylinder block

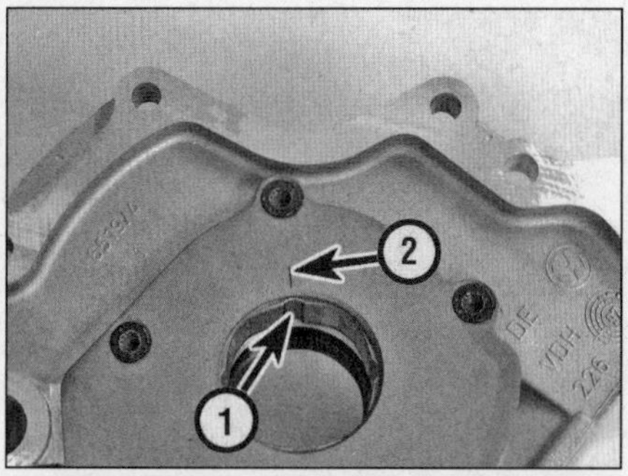

14.21 Align one of the rotor drive cut-outs (1) with the oil pump rear cover mark (2)

14.24 Slide the oil pump over the crankshaft. Note the tape used to protect the oil seal

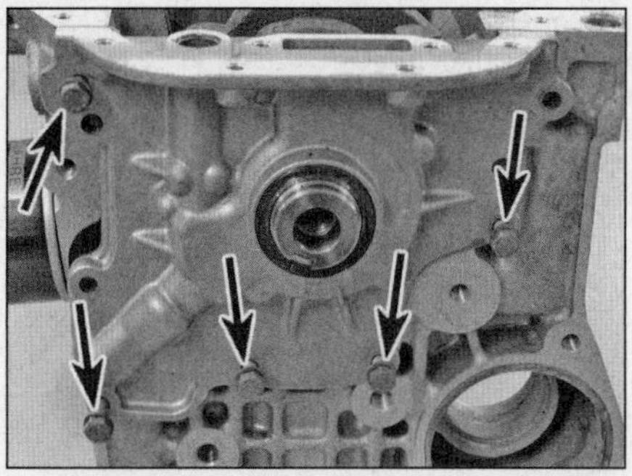

14.25 Fit the new oil pump securing bolts to the locations noted before removal

14.27 Fit a new oil pick-up pipe gasket

Refitting

18 Commence refitting by cleaning all traces of old gasket and sealant from the mating faces of the cylinder block and oil pump.

19 Wind a length of tape around the end of the crankshaft to protect the oil seal lips as the oil pump is slid into position.

20 Fit a new oil pump gasket over the dowels in the cylinder block **(see illustration)**.

21 Turn the inner oil pump rotor to align one of the drive cut-outs in the edge of the inner rotor with the line mark on the oil pump rear cover **(see illustration)**.

22 Lightly oil the four tips of the oil pump drive cam on the end of the crankshaft.

23 Coat the lips of the crankshaft oil seal with a thin film of clean engine oil.

24 Slide the oil pump into position over the end of the crankshaft until it engages with the dowels, taking care not to damage the oil seal, and ensuring that the inner rotor engages with the drive cam on the crankshaft **(see illustration)**.

25 Fit new oil pump securing bolts to the locations noted before removal, and tighten them to the specified torque **(see illustration)**.

26 Remove the tape from the end of the crankshaft, then refit the crankshaft sprocket, noting that the pulley locating pin must be outermost. Temporarily refit the securing bolt and washer to retain the sprocket.

27 Refit the oil pick-up pipe, using a new gasket, and tighten the securing bolts to the specified torque **(see illustration)**.

28 Refit the sump as described in Section 13.

29 Refit the timing belt tensioner as described in Section 7.

30 Refit the main timing belt as described in Section 6.

15 Oil pressure relief valve – removal, inspection and refitting

1 The oil pressure relief valve is an integral part of the oil pump. The valve piston and spring are located to the side of the oil pump rotors and can be inspected once the oil pump has been removed from the engine and the rear cover has been removed (see Section 14). If any sign of wear or damage is found the oil pump assembly will have to be renewed; the relief valve piston and spring are not available separately.

16 Oil pressure warning light switch – removal and refitting

Removal

1 The oil pressure warning light switch is fitted to the left-hand end of the cylinder head. To gain access to the switch, remove the air cleaner as described in Chapter 4A Section 3.

2 Disconnect the wiring connector and wipe clean the area around the switch **(see illustration)**.

3 Unscrew the switch from the cylinder head and remove it along with its sealing washer. If the switch is to be left removed from the engine for any length of time, plug the hole in the cylinder head.

Refitting

4 Examine the sealing washer for signs of damage or deterioration and if necessary renew.

5 Refit the switch, complete with washer, and tighten it to the specified torque.

6 Securely reconnect the wiring connector then refit the air cleaner. Check and, if necessary, top-up the engine oil as described in *Weekly checks*.

17 Crankshaft oil seals – renewal

Right-hand oil seal

1 Remove the main timing belt as described in Section 6, and the crankshaft sprocket with reference to Section 7.

16.2 Disconnecting the oil pressure switch wiring connector

18.2a Tool used to hold the flywheel stationary

18.2b Unscrew the securing bolts...

18.3 ...and remove the flywheel

2 To remove the seal without removing the oil pump, drill two small holes diagonally opposite each other, insert self-tapping screws, and pull on the heads of the screws with pliers.

3 Alternatively, the oil seal can be removed with the oil pump (see Section 14).

4 Thoroughly clean the oil seal seating in the oil pump.

5 Wind a length of tape around the end of the crankshaft to protect the oil seal lips as the seal is fitted.

6 Fit a new oil seal to the oil pump, pressing or driving it into position using a socket or tube of suitable diameter. Ensure that the socket or tube bears only on the hard outer ring of the seal, and take care not to damage the seal lips. Press or drive the seal into position until it is seated on the shoulder in the oil pump. Make sure that the closed end of the seal is facing outwards.

7 Refit the crankshaft sprocket with reference to Section 7, and the main timing belt as described in Section 6.

Left-hand oil seal

8 The crankshaft left-hand oil seal is integral with the housing, and must be renewed as an assembly, complete with the crankshaft speed/position sensor wheel. The sensor wheel is attached to the oil seal/housing assembly, and is a press-fit on the crankshaft flange. Seat special tool T10134 is required to fit this assembly. There is no locating key, and there are no alignment marks and if the sensor wheel is not precisely aligned on the crankshaft, the crankshaft speed/position sensor will send incorrect TDC signals to the engine management ECU, and the engine will not run correctly if at all

9 Replacement of the seal is described in Chapter 2A Section 18.

18 Flywheel – removal, inspection and refitting

Note: *New flywheel securing bolts will be required on refitting.*

Removal

1 Remove the gearbox (see Chapter 7A Section 3 or Chapter 7B Section 2) and where fitted the clutch (Chapter 6A Section 6).

2 The flywheel/driveplate bolts are offset to ensure correct fitment. Unscrew the bolts while holding the flywheel stationary. Temporarily insert a bolt in the cylinder block, and use a screwdriver to hold the flywheel or make up a holding tool **(see illustrations)**.

3 Lift the flywheel from the crankshaft **(see illustration)**.

Inspection

4 Check the flywheel for wear and damage. Examine the starter ring gear for excessive wear to the teeth. If any wear is found the complete flywheel must be replaced. If the clutch friction face is discoloured or scored excessively, it may be possible to regrind it, but this work should also be entrusted to an automotive machine shop.

5 Where a dual mass flywheel is fitted the following guidelines may help decide if replacement is required. If in doubt, a professional inspection is recommended. The dual-mass flywheel should be checked as follows:

18.6 Flywheel warpage check – see text

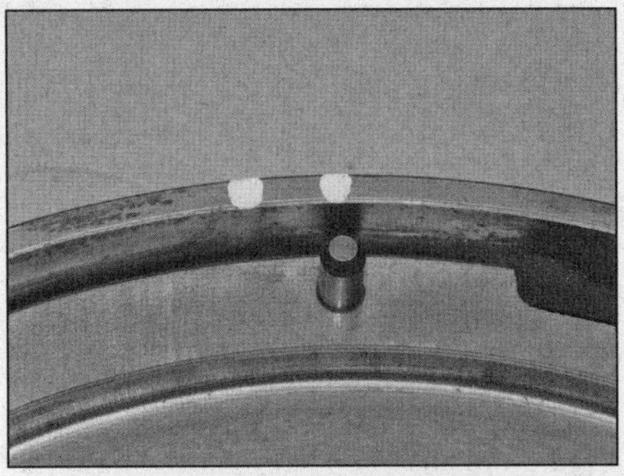
18.7 Flywheel free rotational movement check alignment marks – see text

Warpage

6 Place a straight edge across the face of the drive surface, and check by trying to insert a feeler gauge between the straight edge and the drive surface **(see illustration)**. The flywheel will normally warp like a bowl – ie. Higher on the outer edge. If the warpage is more than 0.40 mm, the flywheel may need replacing.

Free rotational movement

7 This is the distance the drive surface of the flywheel can be turned independently of the flywheel primary element, using finger effort alone. Move the drive surface in one direction and make a mark where the locating pin aligns with the flywheel edge. Move the drive surface in the other direction (finger pressure only) and make another mark **(see illustration)**. The total of free movement should not exceed 20.0 mm. If it's more, the flywheel may need replacing.

Total rotational movement

8 This is the total distance the drive surface can be turned independently of the flywheel primary element. Insert two bolts into the clutch pressure plate/damper unit mounting holes, and with the crankshaft/flywheel held stationary, use a lever/pry bar between the bolts and use some effort to move the drive surface fully in one direction – make a mark where the locating pin aligns with the flywheel edge. Now force the drive surface fully in the opposite direction, and make another mark. The total rotational movement should not exceed 44.00 mm. If it does, have the flywheel professionally inspected.

Lateral movement

9 The lateral movement (up and down) of the drive surface in relation to the primary element of the flywheel, should not exceed 2.0 mm. If it does, the flywheel may need replacing. This can be checked by pressing the drive surface down on one side into the flywheel (flywheel horizontal) and making an alignment mark between the drive surface and the inner edge of the primary element. Now press down on the opposite side of the drive surface, and make another mark above the original one. The difference between the two marks is the lateral movement **(see illustration)**.

10 There should be no cracks in the drive surface of the flywheel. If cracks are evident, the flywheel will need replacing.

Refitting

11 Refitting is a reversal of removal, bearing in mind the following points.

a) Ensure that the engine to transmission plate is in place before fitting the flywheel.

b) Use new bolts when refitting the flywheel and coat the threads of the bolts with locking fluid before inserting them. Tighten the securing bolts to the specified torque.

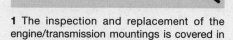

19 Engine/transmission mountings – inspection and renewal

1 The inspection and replacement of the engine/transmission mountings is covered in Chapter 2A Section 20.

18.9 Flywheel lateral movement check marks – see text

Notes

Chapter 2 Part E
1.6 litre diesel engine in-car repair procedures

Contents

Degrees of difficulty

Easy, suitable for novice with little experience	Fairly easy, suitable for beginner with some experience	Fairly difficult, suitable for competent DIY mechanic	Difficult, suitable for experienced DIY mechanic	Very difficult, suitable for expert DIY or professional

Specifications

General

Type	Four-cylinder in-line, belt-driven double overhead camshaft (DOHC), four stroke, 16-valve, liquid-cooled
Cubic capacity	1598 cc
Manufacturer's engine codes*	CAYA and CLNA
Maximum power output:	
CAYC	77 kW at 4400 rpm
CLNA	77 kW at 4400 rpm
Maximum torque output:	
CAYC	250 Nm at 1500 to 2500 rpm
CLNA	250 Nm at 1500 to 2500 rpm
Bore	79.5 mm
Stroke	80.5 mm
Compression ratio	16.5 : 1
Compression pressures (oil temperature 80°C minimum):	
New	25.0 to 31.0 bars
Minimum	19.0 bars
#Maximum difference between cylinders	5.0 bars
Firing order	1 – 3 – 4 – 2
No.1 cylinder location	Timing belt end

**See 'Vehicle identification' at the end of this manual for the location of the engine code markings.*

Lubrication system

Oil pump type	Gear type, belt-driven from crankshaft
Oil pressure switch (green)	0.5 bar
Oil pressure (oil temperature 80°C):	
Minimum @ idling	0.6 bar
Minimum @ 2000 rpm	1.0 bar
Maximum @ high rpm	5.0 bar

Torque wrench settings

	Nm	lbf ft
Ancillary (alternator, etc) bracket mounting bolts*:		
Stage 1 (all six bolts)	40	30
Stage 2 (for two lower bolts)	Angle-tighten a further 45°	
Stage 2 (for four upper bolts)	Angle-tighten a further 90°	
Auxiliary drivebelt tensioner securing bolt:		
Stage 1	20	15
Stage 2	Angle-tighten a further 180°	
Big-end bearing caps bolts*:		
Stage 1	30	22
Stage 2	Angle-tighten a further 90°	
Camshaft retaining frame bolts	10	7
Camshaft cover bolts	10	7
Camshaft sprocket hub centre bolt	100	74
Camshaft sprocket-to-hub bolts*:		
Stage 1	20	15
Stage 2	Angle-tighten a further 45°	
Common rail bolts	22	16
Coolant pump bolts	15	11
Crankshaft oil seal housing bolts	15	11
Crankshaft pulley-to-sprocket bolts*:		
Stage 1	10	7
Stage 2	Angle-tighten a further 90°	
Crankshaft sprocket bolt*:		
Stage 1	120	89
Stage 2	Angle-tighten a further 90°	
Cylinder head bolts*:		
Stage 1	30	22
Stage 2	60	44
Stage 3	Angle-tighten a further 90°	
Stage 4	Angle-tighten a further 90°	
Engine mountings:		
RH engine mounting*:		
Mounting bracket to engine:		
Stage 1	40	30
Stage 2	Angle-tighten a further 180°	
Mounting to body:		
Stage 1	40	30
Stage 2	Angle-tighten a further 90°	
Mounting to bracket:		
Stage 1	60	44
Stage 2	Angle-tighten a further 90°	
LH engine/transmission mounting*:		
Mounting to body:		
Stage 1	40	30
Stage 2	Angle-tighten a further 90°	
Mounting to bracket on transmission:		
Stage 1	60	44
Stage 2	Angle-tighten a further 90°	
Rear mounting link*:		
Link-to-transmission:		
Short (front) bolt:		
Stage 1	40	30
Stage 2	Angle-tighten a further 90°	
Long (rear) bolt:		
Stage 1	60	44
Stage 2	Angle-tighten a further 90°	
Link-to-subframe:		
Stage 1	100	74
Stage 2	Angle-tighten a further 90°	
Flywheel*:		
Stage 1	60	44
Stage 2	Angle-tighten a further 90°	
Fuel pump hub nut	95	70
Fuel pump sprocket bolts*	20	15
Main bearing cap bolts*:		
Stage 1	65	48
Stage 2	Angle-tighten a further 90°	

Torque wrench settings (continued)	Nm	lbf ft
Oil cooler screws	11	7
Oil drain plug*	30	22
Oil filter housing-to-cylinder block bolts*:		
Stage 1	14	10
Stage 2	Angle-tighten a further 180°	
Oil filter cover	25	18
Oil level/temperature sensor-to-sump bolts	9	7
Oil pick-up pipe securing bolts	9	7
Oil pressure warning light switch	22	16
Oil pump securing bolts	16	11
Piston oil spray jet bolt	27	19
Sump-to-cylinder block bolts	13	9
Sump-to-transmission bolts	40	30
Thermostat housing	15	11
Timing belt outer cover bolts	10	7
Timing belt tensioner roller securing nut:		
Stage 1	20	15
Stage 2	Angle-tighten a further 45°	
Timing belt idler pulleys:		
Lower idler roller nut	20	15
Upper idler roller (small) bolt	15	11
Upper idler roller (large) bolt*:		
Stage 1	50	37
Stage 2	Angle-tighten a further 90°	

**Do not re-use*

1 General Information

How to use this Chapter

1 This Part of Chapter 2 describes those repair procedures that can reasonably be carried out on the engine while it remains in the vehicle. If the engine has been removed from the vehicle and is being dismantled as described in Part F, any preliminary dismantling procedures can be ignored.

2 Note that while it may be possible physically to overhaul certain items while the engine is in the vehicle, such tasks are not usually carried out as separate operations, and usually require the execution of several additional procedures (not to mention the cleaning of components and of oilways); for this reason, all such tasks are classed as major overhaul procedures, and are described in Part F of this Chapter.

Engine description

3 Throughout this Chapter, engines are referred to by type, and are identified and referred to by the manufacturer's code letters. A listing of all engines covered, together with their code letters, is given in the Specifications at the start of this Chapter.

4 The engines are water-cooled, double overhead camshafts (DOHC), in-line four-cylinder units, with cast-iron cylinder blocks and aluminium-silicone alloy cylinder heads. All are mounted transversely at the front of the vehicle, with the transmission bolted to the left-hand end of the engine.

5 The crankshaft is of five-bearing type, and thrustwashers are fitted to the centre main bearing (No.3) to control crankshaft endfloat.

6 Drive for the exhaust camshaft is by a toothed timing belt from the crankshaft, with the intake camshaft driven by interlocking gears at the left-hand end of both camshafts. The gears incorporate a toothed backlash compensator element. Each camshaft is mounted at the top of the cylinder head, and is secured by a bearing frame/ladder.

7 The valves are closed by coil springs, and run in guides pressed into the cylinder head. The valves are operated by roller rocker arms incorporating hydraulic tappets.

8 The gear-type oil pump is driven by a belt from the right-hand (timing belt) end of the crankshaft. Oil is drawn from the sump through a strainer, and then forced through an externally mounted, renewable filter. From there, it is distributed to the cylinder head, where it lubricates the camshaft journals and hydraulic tappets, and also to the crankcase, where it lubricates the main bearings, connecting rod big-ends, gudgeon pins and cylinder bores. A coolant-fed oil cooler is fitted to the oil filter housing on all engines. Oil jets are fitted to the base of each cylinder – these spray oil onto the underside of the pistons, to improve cooling.

9 All engines are fitted with a combined brake servo vacuum pump, driven by the camshaft on the transmission end of the cylinder head.

10 On all engines, engine coolant is circulated by a pump, driven by the timing belt. For details of the cooling system, refer to Chapter 3.

Operations with engine in car

11 The following operations can be performed without removing the engine:

a) Compression pressure – testing.
b) Camshaft cover – removal and refitting.
c) Crankshaft pulley – removal and refitting.
d) Timing belt covers – removal and refitting.
e) Timing belt – removal, refitting and adjustment.
f) Timing belt tensioner and sprockets – removal and refitting.
g) Camshaft oil seals – renewal.
h) Camshafts and hydraulic tappets – removal, inspection and refitting.
i) Cylinder head – removal and refitting.
j) Cylinder head and pistons – decarbonising.
k) Sump – removal and refitting.
l) Oil pump – removal, overhaul and refitting
m) Crankshaft oil seals – renewal.
n) Engine/transmission mountings – inspection and renewal.
o) Flywheel/driveplate – removal, inspection and refitting.

Note: *It is possible to remove the pistons and connecting rods (after removing the cylinder head and sump) without removing the engine. However, this is not recommended. Work of this nature is more easily and thoroughly completed with the engine on the bench.*

2 Compression and leakdown tests – description and interpretation

Compression test

Note: *A compression tester suitable for use with diesel engines will be required for this test.*

1 When engine performance is down, or if misfiring occurs which cannot be attributed to the ignition or fuel systems, a compression test can provide diagnostic clues as to the engine's condition. If the test is performed regularly, it can give warning of trouble before any other symptoms become apparent.

3.8 The alignment mark on the crankshaft sprocket should be almost vertical

2 The engine must be fully warmed-up to normal operating temperature, the battery must be fully charged, and you will require the aid of an assistant.

3 Remove the glow plugs as described in Chapter 5C Section 2, and then fit a compression tester to the No.1 cylinder glow plug hole. The type of tester that screws into the plug thread is preferred. **Note:** *Part of the glow plug removal procedure is to disconnect the fuel injector wiring plugs. As a result of the plugs being disconnected and the engine cranked, faults may be stored in the ECU memory. These must be erased after the compression test.*

4 Have your assistant crank the engine for several seconds on the starter motor. After one or two revolutions, the compression pressure should build-up to a maximum figure and then stabilise. Record the highest reading obtained.

5 Repeat the test on the remaining cylinders, recording the pressure in each.

6 The cause of poor compression is less easy to establish on a diesel engine than on a petrol engine. The effect of introducing oil into the cylinders (wet testing) is not conclusive, because there is a risk that the oil will sit in the recess on the piston crown, instead of passing to the rings. However, the following can be used as a rough guide to diagnosis.

7 All cylinders should produce very similar pressures. Any difference greater than that specified indicates the existence of a fault. Note that the compression should build-up quickly in a healthy engine. Low compression on the first stroke, followed by gradually increasing pressure on successive strokes, indicates worn piston rings. A low compression reading on the first stroke, which does not build-up during successive strokes, indicates leaking valves or a blown head gasket (a cracked head could also be the cause).

8 A low reading from two adjacent cylinders is almost certainly due to the head gasket having blown between them and the presence of coolant in the engine oil will confirm this.

9 On completion, remove the compression tester, and refit the glow plugs.

10 Reconnect the wiring to the injector solenoids. Finally, have a Seat dealer or suitably equipped specialist erase any fault codes from the ECU memory.

Leakdown test

11 A leakdown test measures the rate at which compressed air fed into the cylinder is lost. It is an alternative to a compression test, and in many ways it is better, since the escaping air provides easy identification of where pressure loss is occurring (piston rings, valves or head gasket).

12 The equipment required for leakdown testing is unlikely to be available to the home mechanic. If poor compression is suspected, have the test performed by a suitably equipped garage.

3.9a Fit the tool to the hole in the oil seal housing...

3.9b ...so the marks on the tool and sprocket align

3.9c Insert a 6 mm locking tool into the camshaft hub...

3.9d ...with the arrow almost at the 12 o'clock position

3 Engine assembly and valve timing marks – general information and usage

General information

1 TDC is the highest point in the cylinder that each piston reaches as it travels up-and-down when the crankshaft turns. Each piston reaches TDC at the end of the compression stroke and again at the end of the exhaust stroke, but TDC generally refers to piston position on the compression stroke. No 1 piston is at the timing belt end of the engine.

2 Positioning No 1 piston at TDC is an essential part of many procedures, such as timing belt removal and camshaft removal.

3 The design of the engines covered in this Chapter is such that piston-to-valve contact may occur if the camshaft or crankshaft is turned with the timing belt removed. For this reason, it is important to ensure that the camshaft and crankshaft do not move in relation to each other once the timing belt has been removed from the engine.

Setting TDC on No 1 cylinder

Note: *Special tool T10050 is required to lock the crankshaft sprocket in the TDC position. Alternatively obtain a tool from automotive tool specialists. Try asttools.co.uk.*

4 Raise the front of the vehicle and support it securely on axle stands (see *Jacking and vehicle support*). Remove the front right-hand road wheel, then release the fasteners and remove the lower section of the wheelarch liner.

5 Remove the auxiliary drivebelt as described in Chapter 1B Section 29.

6 Remove the crankshaft pulley/vibration damper as described in Section 5.

7 Remove the timing belt outer covers as described in Section 6.

8 Using a spanner or socket on the crankshaft sprocket bolt, turn the crankshaft in the normal direction of rotation (clockwise) until the alignment mark on the face of the sprocket is almost vertical, and the hole in the camshaft sprocket hub aligns with the hole in the cylinder head **(see illustration).**

9 While in this position it should be possible to insert the special tool T10050 to lock the crankshaft, and a 6 mm diameter rod/drill bit to lock the camshafts **(see illustrations). Note:** *The mark on the crankshaft sprocket and the mark on the special tool must align, whilst at the same time the shaft of tool must engage in the drilling in the crankshaft oil seal housing.*

10 The engine is now set to TDC on No.1 cylinder.

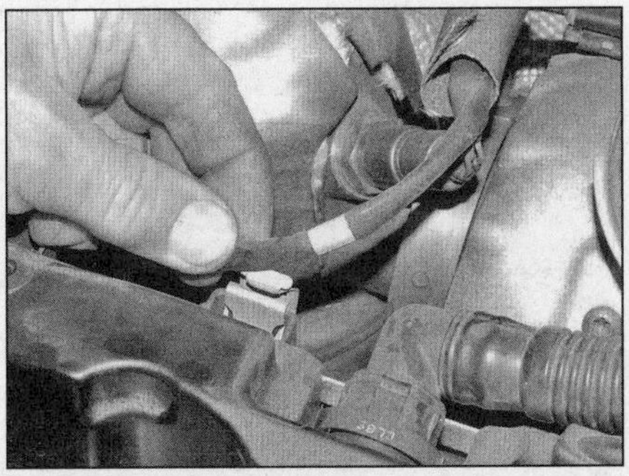

4.3 Unclip the wiring from the retaining clips

4.4 Squeeze together the sides of the collar to disconnect the breather hose

4.5 Undo the bolts and lift away the camshaft cover

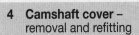

4 Camshaft cover – removal and refitting

Removal

1 Remove the fuel injectors (Chapter 4B Section 5) and fuel rail (Chapter 4B Section 12).
2 Remove the timing belt upper cover as described in Section 6.
3 Note their fitted positions, then disconnect the vacuum hoses from the camshaft cover, and release them, and the wiring loom from the retaining clips at the rear of the cover **(see illustration)**.
4 Squeeze together the sides of the collar, and disconnect the breather hose from the camshaft cover **(see illustration)**.
5 Release the wiring from the clips at the rear of the cover, then unscrew the camshaft cover retaining bolts and lift the cover away. If the cover sticks, do not attempt to lever it off – instead free it by working around the cover and tapping it lightly with a soft-faced mallet **(see illustration)**.
6 Recover the camshaft cover gasket. Inspect the gasket carefully, and renew it if damage or deterioration is evident – note that the retaining bolts and seals must be pushed fully through the cover **(see illustrations)**.
7 Clean the mating surfaces of the cylinder head and camshaft cover thoroughly, removing all traces of oil – take care to avoid damaging the surfaces as you do this.

Refitting

8 Refit the camshaft cover by following the removal procedure in reverse, tightening the cover retaining bolts to the specified torque, starting with the centre bolts and working outwards.

5 Crankshaft pulley – removal and refitting

Removal

1 Switch off the ignition and all electrical consumers and remove the ignition key.

4.6a Renew the cover seal if necessary

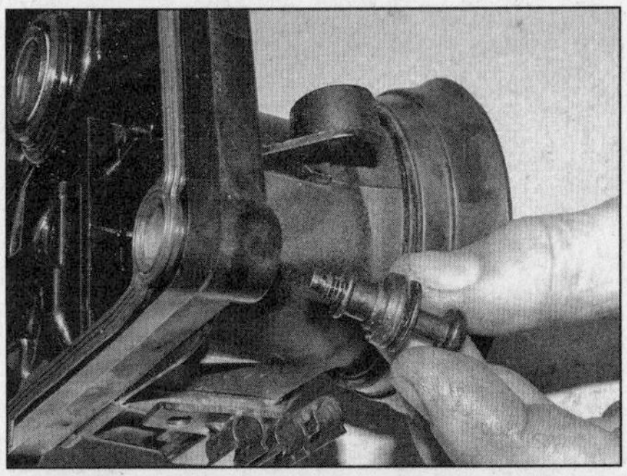

4.6b Bolts and seals must be pushed fully through the cover before fitting the gasket

2 Raise the front right-hand side of the vehicle, and support securely on axle stands (see *Jacking and vehicle support*). Remove the roadwheel.
3 Remove the securing fasteners and withdraw the lower section of the front wheel arch liner.
4 Slacken the bolts securing the crankshaft pulley to the sprocket **(see illustration)**. If necessary, the pulley can be prevented from turning by counterholding with a spanner or socket on the crankshaft sprocket bolt.
5 Remove the auxiliary drivebelt, as described in Chapter 1B Section 29.
6 Unscrew the bolts securing the pulley to the sprocket, and remove the pulley. Discard the bolts – new ones must be fitted.

Refitting

7 Refit the pulley over the locating peg on the crankshaft sprocket, then fit the new pulley securing bolts.
8 Refit and tension the auxiliary drivebelt.
9 Prevent the crankshaft from turning as during removal, then fit the pulley securing bolts, and tighten to the specified torque.
10 Refit the wheel arch liner.
11 Refit the roadwheel and lower the vehicle to the ground.

6 Timing belt covers – removal and refitting

Upper outer cover

1 Pull the engine top cover upwards to release the mountings **(see illustration)**.
2 Release the hoses from the retaining

5.4 Undo the pulley bolts, counterholding it with a socket on the centre sprocket bolt

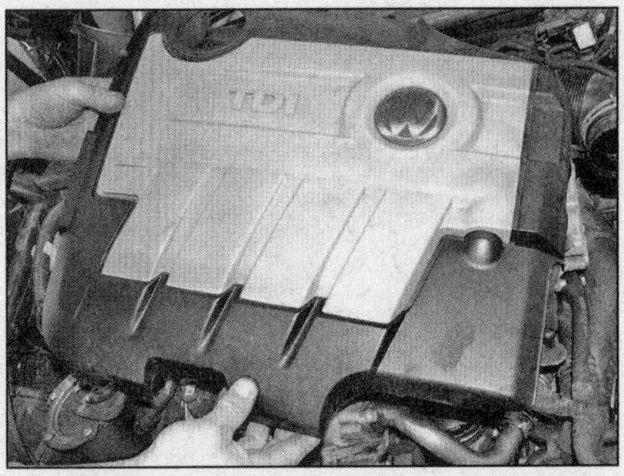

6.1 Pull the plastic cover upwards from the mountings

6.2 Unclip the hoses from the retaining clips

6.3a Disconnect the wiring connector...

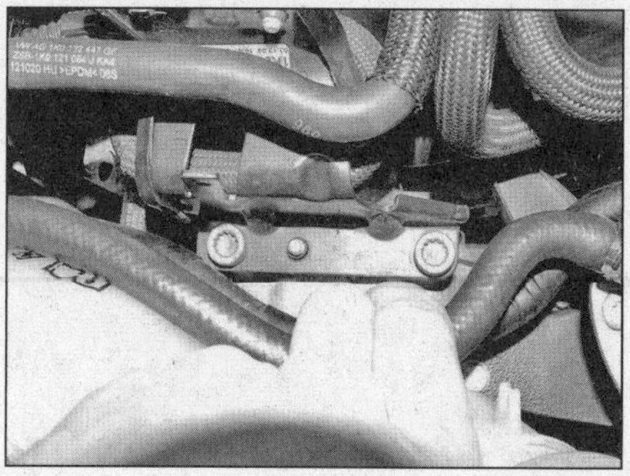

6.3b ...undo the two retaining bolts...

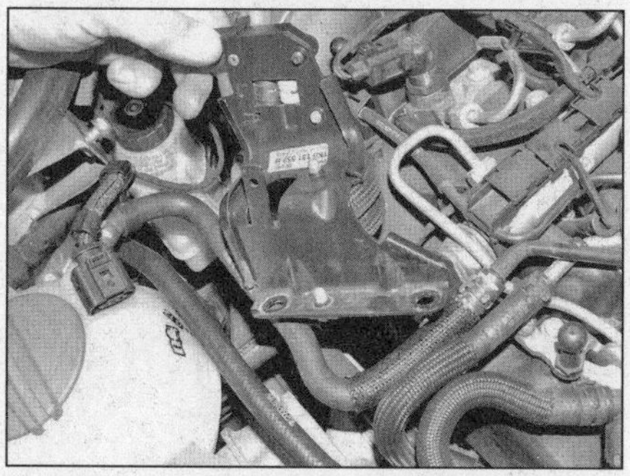

6.3c ...and withdraw the mounting bracket

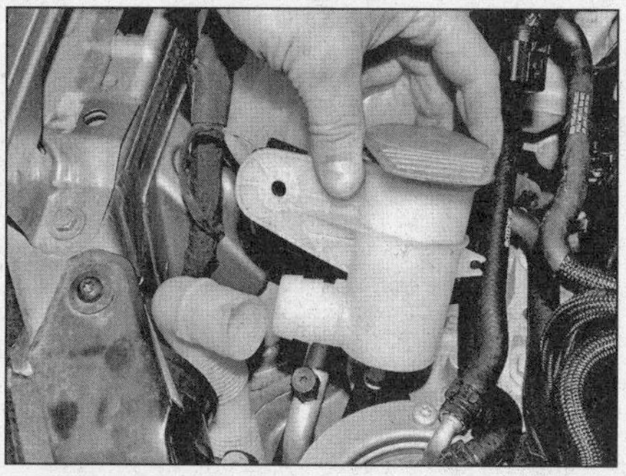

6.4 Remove the washer reservoir filler neck

clips on the right-hand side of the cylinder head and move them to one side **(see illustration)**.

3 Disconnect the wiring plug, undo the retaining bolts, and remove the pressure differential sender (for particulate filter) including bracket from the top of the engine mounting and move it to one side **(see illustrations)**.

4 Undo the retaining bolt, then twist the washer reservoir filler neck to remove it from engine compartment **(see illustration)**.

5 Undo the retaining bolts and nut, then remove the fuel filter from the engine mounting and move it to one side **(see illustrations)**. The fuel hoses do not need to be disconnected from the filter.

6 To make access easier, undo the retaining bolt, disconnect the wiring connector and move the coolant reservoir to one side **(see illustration)**.

7 Disconnect the radiator outlet temperature sensor wiring plug **(see illustration)**.

8 Release the 3 clips and remove the timing belt upper cover **(see illustrations)**.

9 Refitting is a reversal of removal, noting that the lower edge of the upper cover engages with the lower cover.

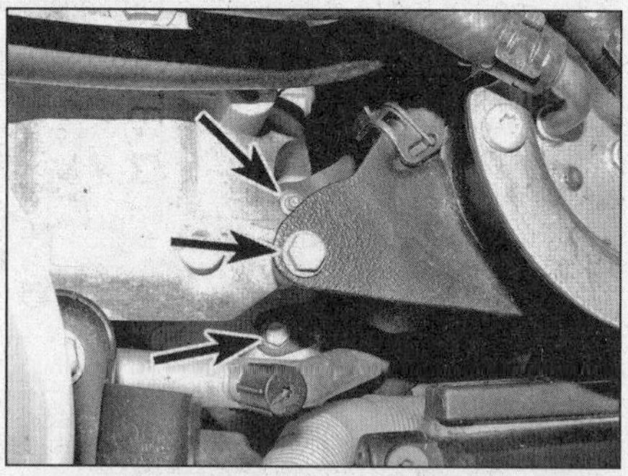

6.5a Undo the filter retaining bolts/nut...

6.5b ...and release the fuel pipe retaining clip

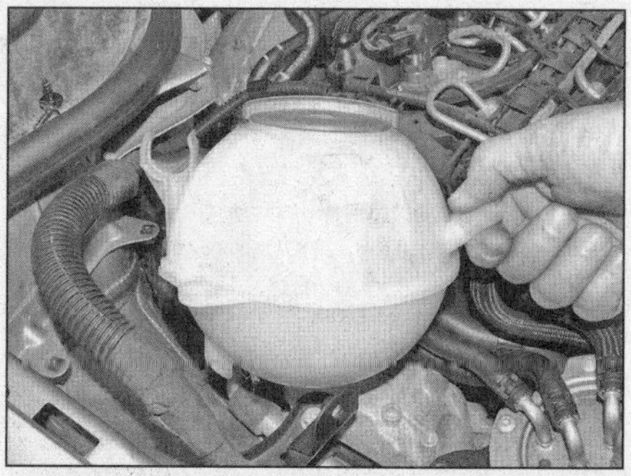

6.6 Move the coolant reservoir to one side

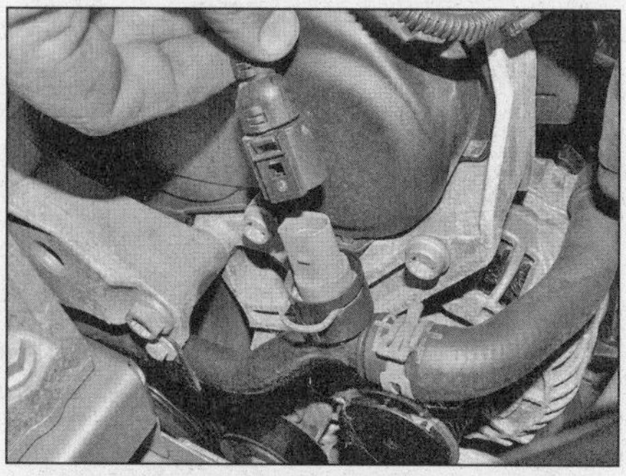

6.7 Disconnect the temperature sensor wiring connector

6.8a Release the rear lower clip...

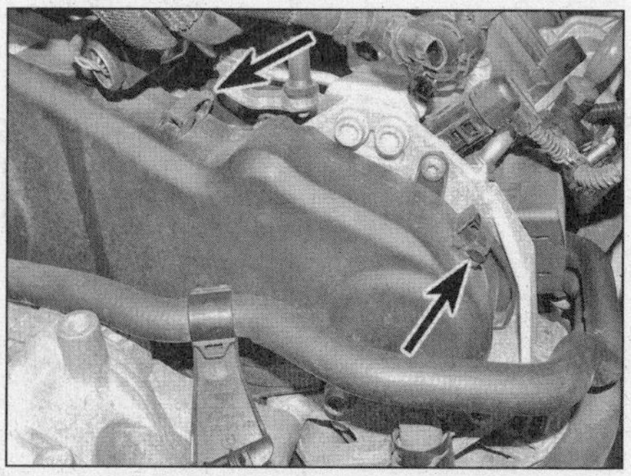

6.8b ...the two upper front clips...

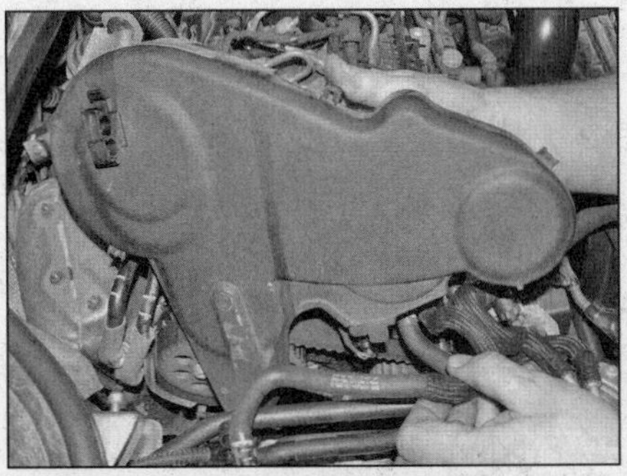

6.8c ...and manoeuvre the upper cover from place

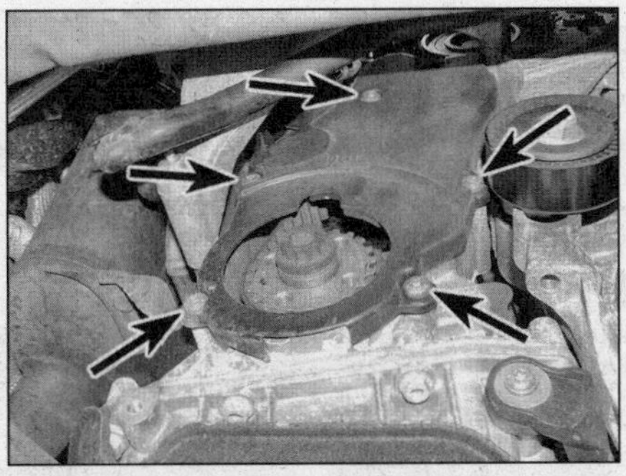

6.12a Undo the lower cover retaining bolts

6.12b ...and manoeuvre the lower cover from place

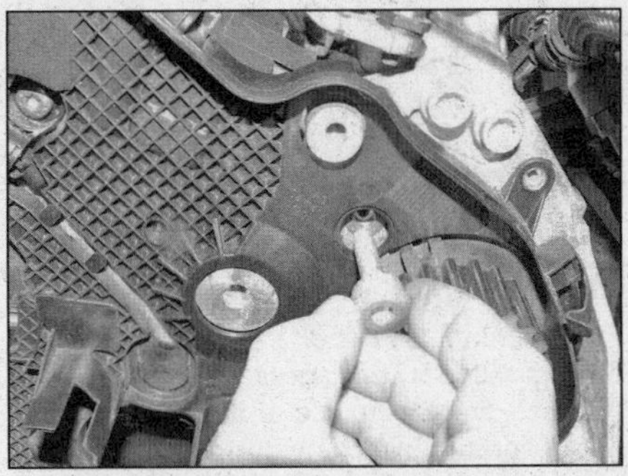

6.16a Remove the retaining bolts...

6.16b ...and remove the rear cover

Lower outer cover

10 Remove the upper cover as described previously.

11 If not already done, remove the crankshaft pulley as described in Section 5.

12 Unscrew the five bolts securing the lower cover, and remove it **(see illustrations)**.

13 Refitting is a reversal of removal; noting that the upper edge of the lower cover engages with the upper cover.

Rear cover

14 Remove the timing belt, tensioner and sprockets as described in Section 7 and Section 8.

15 Undo the retaining bolt and remove the rear hub cover from the end of the camshaft.

16 Slacken and withdraw the retaining bolts and lift the timing belt inner cover from the studs on the end of the engine, and remove it from the engine compartment **(see illustrations)**. It may be required to remove the coolant pump (Chapter 3 Section 7), before the rear cover can be removed.

17 Refitting is a reversal of removal.

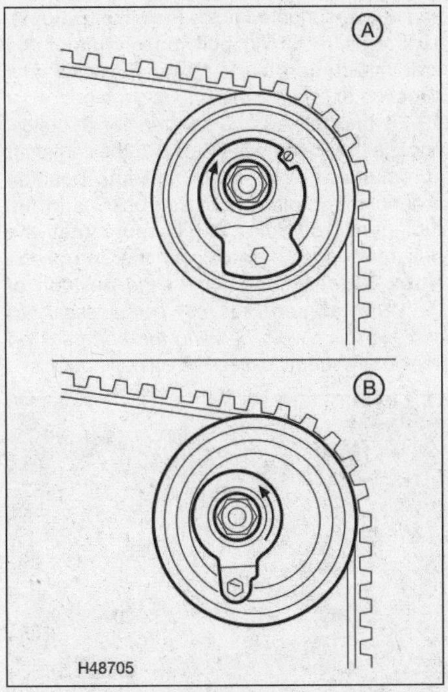

7.0a Two types of tensioner Type (A) and type (B)

A Roller tensions clockwise
B Roller tensions anti-clockwise

7 Timing belt – removal, inspection and refitting

Note: *There are two types of tensioner fitted to this engine and they are not interchangeable* ***(see illustration)****. Check to see which type is fitted before removing the timing belt. Type A tensioner requires a locking pin for installation and it tensions the belt by rotating clockwise. Type B tensioner does not require a locking pin for installation and it tensions the belt by rotating anti-clockwise. See text.*

7.4 Slacken the sprocket-to-hub bolts

Removal

1 The primary function of the toothed timing belt is to drive the camshaft, but it also drives the coolant pump and high-pressure fuel pump. Should the belt slip or break in service, the valve timing will be disturbed and piston-to-valve contact may occur, resulting in serious engine damage. For this reason, it is important that the timing belt is tensioned correctly, and inspected regularly for signs of wear or deterioration.

2 Switch off the ignition and all electrical consumers and remove the ignition key.

3 Set the engine to TDC on No. 1 cylinder as described in Section 3.

4 Slacken the three bolts securing the sprocket to the camshaft hub by 90° **(see illustration)**.

5 Slacken the three bolts securing the sprocket to the high-pressure fuel pump by 90° **(see illustration)**.

7.5 Slacken the high-pressure fuel pump sprocket bolts

7.6 Insert an Allen key, slacken the nut, and rotate the hub anti-clockwise until a 2 mm rod/drill bit can be inserted to lock the hub to the pulley

7.7 Rotate the tensioner hub clockwise until it hits the stop

Type A tensioner

6 Insert a suitable Allen key into the tensioner hub, then slacken the retaining nut and rotate the tensioner hub anti-clockwise until it can be locked in place using a 2.0 m pin/drill bit **(see illustration)**.

7 Leaving the pin in place, now rotate the tensioner hub clockwise to the stop, and hand-tighten the retaining nut **(see illustration)**.

Type B tensioner

8 Insert a suitable Allen key into the tensioner hub, then slacken the retaining nut and rotate the tensioner hub clockwise, until the tensioner hub is loosened. When in position hand-tighten the retaining nut.

All engines

9 If the original timing belt is to be refitted, mark the running direction of the belt, to ensure correct refitting.

Caution: If the belt appears to be in good condition and can be re-used, it is essential that it is refitted the same way around, otherwise accelerated wear will result, leading to premature failure.

10 Slide the belt from the sprockets, taking care not to twist or kink the belt excessively if it is to be re-used.

Inspection

11 Examine the belt for evidence of contamination by coolant or lubricant. If this is the case, find the source of the contamination before progressing any further. Check the belt for signs of wear or damage, particularly around the leading edges of the belt teeth. Renew the belt if its condition is in doubt; the cost of belt renewal is negligible compared with potential cost of the engine repairs, should the belt fail in service. The belt must be renewed if it has covered the mileage given in Chapter 1B Section 31, however, if it has covered less, it is prudent to renew it regardless of condition, as a precautionary measure.

12 If the timing belt is not going to be refitted for some time, it is a wise precaution to hang a warning label on the steering wheel, to remind yourself (and others) not to attempt to start the engine. Have the battery disconnected to prevent any engine damage.

13 If the tensioner roller is to be renewed, the engine mounting will need to be removed, as described in Section 16. Then the tensioner removed as described in Section 8.

Refitting

14 Ensure that the crankshaft and camshaft are still set to TDC on No 1 cylinder, as described in Section 3. The camshaft sprocket bolts should be renewed, and slackened at this point.

15 Renew the high-pressure fuel pump sprocket bolts one at a time. They should also be slackened.

16 Using a screwdriver on the bolts heads, rotate the high-pressure fuel pump clockwise until a 6.0 mm locking pin/drill bit can be inserted into the housing adjacent to the sprocket, locking the pump in place **(see illustration)**.

17 Rotate the camshaft sprocket and high-pressure fuel pump sprocket fully clockwise so that the securing bolts are at the end of the elongated holes **(see illustrations)**.

18 Loop the timing belt loosely under the crankshaft sprocket. **Note:** *Observe any direction of rotation markings on the belt.*

19 Fit the belt around the tensioner pulley, engage the timing belt teeth with the camshaft sprockets, then manoeuvre it into position around the coolant pump sprocket and the fuel pump sprocket. Make sure that the belt teeth seat correctly on the sprockets. **Note:** *Slight adjustment to the position of the camshaft sprocket may be necessary to achieve this. Avoid bending the belt back on itself or twisting it excessively as you do this.*

7.16 Rotate the high-pressure fuel pump clockwise until a 6 mm drill bit/rod can be inserted into the housing and hub

7.17a Rotate the sprockets fully clockwise until the fuel pump sprocket...

7.17b ...and camshaft sprocket bolts are at the end of the elongated holes

7.20 Timing belt routing

7.21a Rotate the tensioner clockwise...

20 Finally, fit the belt around the idler roller **(see illustration)**. Ensure that any slack in the belt is in the section of belt that passes over the tensioner roller.

Type A tensioner

21 Loosen the timing belt tensioner securing nut, and pull out the tensioner locking pin. Turn the tensioner clockwise with an Allen key until the pointer is just past the middle of the gap in the tensioner base plate **(see illustrations)**. With the tensioner held in this position, tighten the securing nut to the specified torque and angle.

Type B tensioner

22 Loosen the timing belt tensioner securing nut, and turn the tensioner anti-clockwise with an Allen key until the pointer is just past the middle of the gap in the tensioner base plate **(see illustration)**. With the tensioner held in this position, tighten the securing nut to the specified torque and angle.

All engines

23 Counterhold the camshaft sprocket and fuel pump sprocket with a home made tool to prevent any rotation, and then tighten the camshaft sprocket and fuel pump sprocket bolts to 20 Nm **(see illustrations)**.
24 Remove the sprockets' locking tools and the crankshaft locking tool **(see illustrations)**.
25 Using a spanner or wrench and socket on the crankshaft pulley centre bolt, rotate the crankshaft clockwise through two complete revolutions. Reset the engine to TDC on No.1 cylinder, with reference to Section 3 and refit the crankshaft locking tool.
26 Check that the tensioner roller indicator arm is centred, or within a maximum of 5 mm to the right of the notch in the base plate **(see illustration)**. If not, hold the tensioner hub stationary with an Allen key, slacken the retaining nut and position the arm in the centre of the notch. Tighten the retaining nut to the specified torque. Remove the Allen key.
27 Check that the camshaft sprocket locking pin can still be inserted. **Note:** *It's very difficult*

7.21b ...until the pointer is just past the gap in the base plate

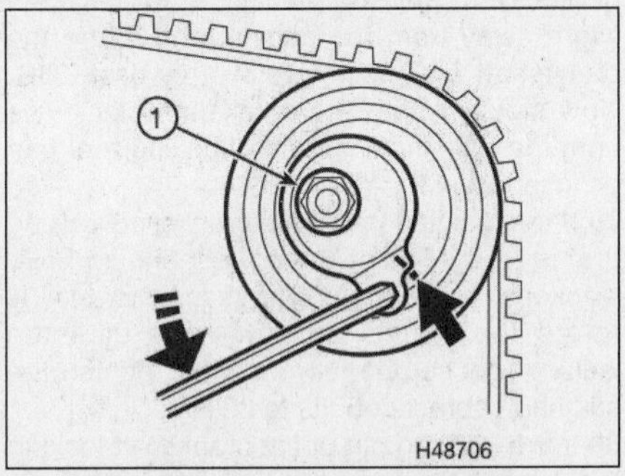

7.22 Turn the tensioner anti-clockwise and secure the retaining nut

7.23a Counterhold the camshaft sprocket...

7.23b ...and the pump sprocket, while the bolts are tightened

7.24a Remove the upper locking pins...

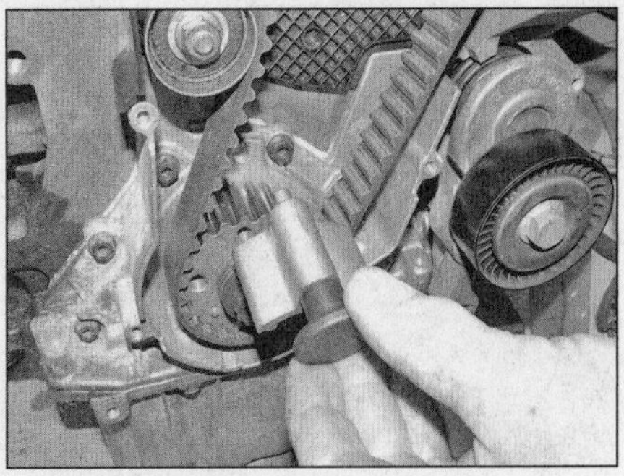

7.24b ...and crankshaft locking tool

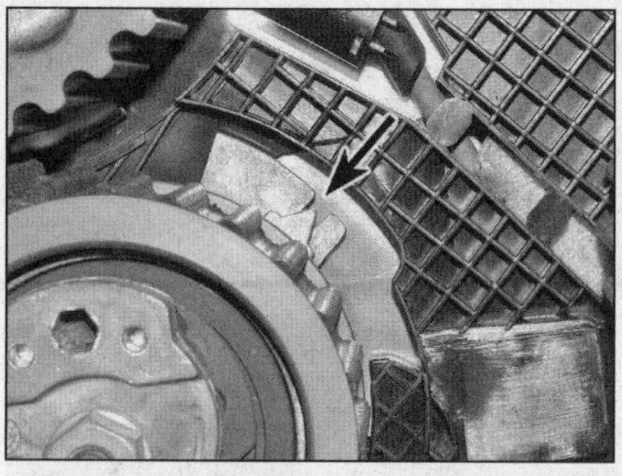

7.26 Check the pointer is centred or within 5mm to the right of the gap in the base plate

to align the locking point of the fuel pump hub again **(see illustration)**. *However, a slight misalignment of holes will not affect engine performance.*

28 If the camshaft sprocket locking pin cannot be inserted, pull the crankshaft locking tool slight away from the engine, and rotate the crankshaft *anti-clockwise* slightly past TDC. Now slowly rotate the crankshaft clockwise until the camshaft sprocket locking tool can be inserted.

29 If the locating pin of the crankshaft locking tool is to the left of the corresponding hole, slacken the camshaft sprocket bolts, slowly rotate the crankshaft clockwise until the locking tool can be fully inserted. Tighten the camshaft sprocket bolts to 20 Nm.

30 If the locating pin of the crankshaft locking tool is to the right of the corresponding hole, slacken the camshaft sprocket bolts, rotate

8.4 Coolant pipe upper mounting bolt and lower mounting nut

7.27 Slight misalignment of the pump sprocket timing hole is acceptable

the crankshaft anti-clockwise slightly until the pin is to the left of the hole, then slowly rotate it clockwise until the lock tool can be fully inserted. Tighten the camshaft sprocket bolts to 20 Nm.

31 Remove the crankshaft and camshaft locking tools, then rotate the crankshaft 2 complete revolutions clockwise and check the locking tools can be reinserted. If necessary, repeat the adjustment procedure described previously.

32 Tighten the camshaft and fuel pump sprocket bolts to the specified torque.

33 The remainder of refitting is a reversal of removal.

8 Timing belt tensioner and sprockets – removal and refitting

Timing belt tensioner

Removal

1 In order to remove the timing belt tensioner, then engine mounting bracket must first be removed. Either support the engine from above using a crossbeam or an engine hoist or support if from underneath with a trolley jack and block of wood.

2 Remove the timing belt as described in Section 7.

3 Undo the bolts and remove the right-hand engine mounting.

4 Undo the bolt securing the coolant pipe to the mounting bracket **(see illustration)**.

5 Working in the wheelarch area, undo the nut securing the lower end of the coolant pipe.

6 Undo the 3 retaining bolts and remove the engine mounting bracket **(see illustration)**.

7 Unscrew the timing belt tensioner nut, and remove the tensioner from the engine.

Refitting

8 When refitting the tensioner to the engine, ensure that the lug on the tensioner backplate engages with the corresponding cut-out in the rear timing belt cover, then refit the tensioner nut **(see illustration)**.

9 The remainder of refitting is a reversal of removal.

Idler pulleys

Removal

10 Remove the timing belt as described in Section 7.

11 Unscrew the relevant idler pulley/roller securing bolt/nut, and then withdraw the pulley **(see illustration)**.

Refitting

12 Refit the pulley and tighten the securing bolt or nut to the specified torque. **Note:** *Renew the large roller/pulley retaining bolt (where applicable).*

13 Refit and tension the timing belt as described in Section 7.

Crankshaft sprocket

Note: *A new crankshaft sprocket securing bolt must be used on refitting.*

Removal

14 Remove the timing belt as described in Section 7.

15 The sprocket securing bolt must now be slackened, and the crankshaft must be prevented from turning as the sprocket bolt is unscrewed. To hold the sprocket, make up a suitable tool, and screw it to the sprocket using two bolts screwed into two of the crankshaft pulley bolt holes.

16 Hold the sprocket using the tool, then slacken the sprocket securing bolt. Take care, as the bolt is very tight. Do not allow the crankshaft to turn as the bolt is slackened.

17 Unscrew the bolt, and slide the sprocket from the end of the crankshaft, noting which way round the sprocket's raised boss is fitted. If required, use a puller to withdraw the

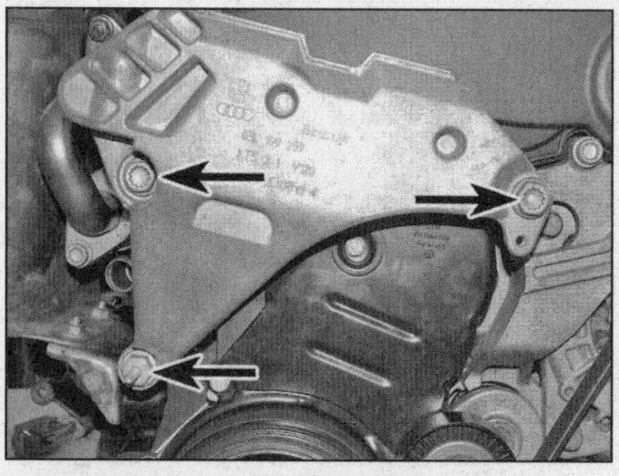

8.6 Engine mounting bracket bolts

8.8 Ensure the lug on the backplate engages with the cut-out in the timing belt cover

8.11 Timing belt idler pulleys

sprocket from the end of the crankshaft **(see illustration)**.

Refitting

18 Commence refitting by positioning the sprocket on the end of the crankshaft.

19 Fit a new sprocket securing bolt, then counterhold the sprocket using the method employed on removal, and tighten the bolt to the specified torque in the two stages given in the Specifications.

20 Refit the timing belt as described in Section 7.

Camshaft sprocket

Removal

21 Remove the timing belt as described in Section 7, then rotate the crankshaft 90° anti-clockwise to prevent any accidental piston-to-valve contact.

22 Unscrew and remove the three retaining bolts and remove the camshaft sprocket from the camshaft hub.

Refitting

23 Refit the sprocket ensuring that it is fitted the correct way round, as noted before removal, then insert the new sprocket bolts, and tighten by hand only at this stage.

24 If the crankshaft has been turned, turn the crankshaft clockwise 90° back to TDC.

25 Refit and tension the timing belt as described in Section 7.

Camshaft hub

Note: *Seat technicians use special tool T10051 to counterhold the hub, however it is possible to fabricate a suitable alternative.*

Removal

26 Remove the camshaft sprocket as described previously in this Section.

27 Engage special tool T10051 with the three locating holes in the face of the hub to prevent the hub from turning. If this tool is not available, fabricate a suitable alternative. Whilst holding the tool, undo the central hub retaining bolt about two turns **(see illustration)**.

28 Slide the hub from the camshaft. If necessary, attach Seat tool T10052 (or a similar three-legged puller) to the hub, and evenly tighten the puller until the hub is free of the camshaft taper **(see illustration)**.

Refitting

29 Ensure that the camshaft taper and the hub centre is clean and dry, locate the hub on the taper, noting that the built-in key in the hub taper must align with the keyway in the camshaft taper **(see illustration)**.

30 Hold the hub in this position with tool T10051 (or similar home-made tool), and tighten the central bolt to the specified torque.

31 Refit the camshaft sprocket as described previously in this Section.

Coolant pump sprocket

32 The coolant pump sprocket is integral with the coolant pump. Refer to Chapter 3 Section 7 for details of coolant pump removal.

8.17 Using a puller to remove the crankshaft sprocket

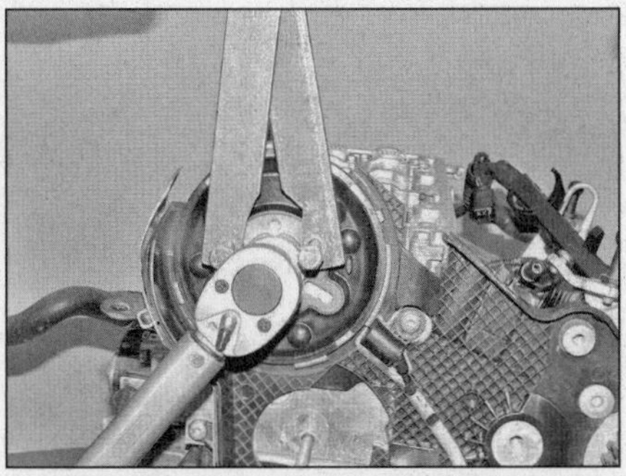

8.27 Fabricate a home made tool to counterhold the hub. Undo the bolt...

8.28 ...and slide the hub from the camshaft

8.29 Ensure the integral key aligns with the keyway in the camshaft

9 Camshaft and hydraulic tappets – removal, inspection and refitting

Note: *A new camshaft oil seal(s) will be required on refitting. Seat removal tool T40094 (or similar tool) will be required to refit the camshafts – this is necessary to prevent damage to the retaining frame and cylinder head as the camshafts are refitted.*

Removal

1 With the timing set at TDC, remove the camshaft hub (see Section 8).

2 Remove the camshaft cover (see Section 4).

3 Remove the brake vacuum pump as described in Chapter 9 Section 24.

4 If the camshafts are not going to be renewed, use two flat pieces of metal flat bar and cable ties and secure the two camshafts to the retaining frame **(see illustrations)**. Progressively unscrew the camshaft retaining frame bolts in the reverse of the sequence shown in illustration 9.29, and carefully remove the retaining frame, complete with camshafts. Remove the oil seal from the end of the camshaft and discard it – a new one will be required for refitting.

5 If the camshafts are going to be renewed, progressively unscrew the camshaft retaining frame bolts in the reverse of the sequence shown in illustration 9.27, and carefully remove the retaining frame. Then carefully lift the camshafts from the cylinder head, keeping them identified for location. Remove the oil seal from the end of the camshaft and discard it – a new one will be required for refitting.

6 Lift the rocker arms and hydraulic tappets from place. Store the rockers and tappets in

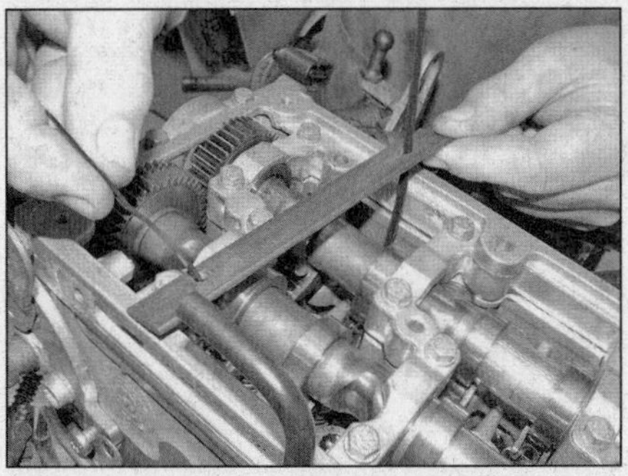

9.4a Using flat metal bar and cable ties to secure the camshafts...

9.4b ...to the upper ladder frame for removal

9.7 Make alignment marks for the position of the sprockets

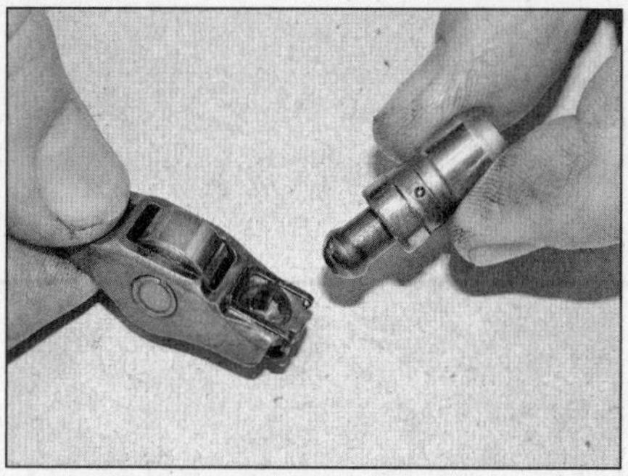
9.10 Check the tappets for wear

a container with numbered compartments to ensure they are refitted to their correct locations. It is recommended that the tappets are kept immersed in oil for the period they are removed from the cylinder head.

Inspection

7 If the camshafts are still secured to the retaining frame, mark the two sprockets in relation with each other, then cut the cable ties to remove them from the frame **(see illustration)**. With the camshafts removed, examine the retaining frame and the bearing locations in the cylinder head for signs of obvious wear or pitting. If evident, a new cylinder head will probably be required. Also check that the oil supply holes in the cylinder head are free from obstructions.

8 Visually inspect the camshafts for evidence of wear on the surfaces of the lobes and journals. Normally their surfaces should be smooth and have a dull shine; look for scoring, erosion or pitting and areas that appear highly polished, indicating excessive wear. Accelerated wear will occur once the hardened exterior of the camshaft has been damaged, so always renew worn items. **Note:** *If these symptoms are visible on the tips of the camshaft lobes, check the corresponding rocker arm, as it will probably be worn as well.*

9 If the machined surfaces of the camshaft appear discoloured or blued, it is likely that it has been overheated at some point, probably due to inadequate lubrication. This may have distorted the shaft, so have the camshaft runout and endfloat checked by an automotive engine reconditioning specialist.

10 Inspect the hydraulic tappets for obvious signs of wear or damage **(see illustration)**, and renew if necessary. Check that the oil holes in the tappets are free from obstructions.

Refitting

11 Oil the rocker arms and hydraulic tappets, and then refit them to their original positions.

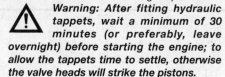

Warning: After fitting hydraulic tappets, wait a minimum of 30 minutes (or preferably, leave overnight) before starting the engine; to allow the tappets time to settle, otherwise the valve heads will strike the pistons.

Using Seat special tool No.T40094

12 If the camshafts were removed from the retaining frame, use the Seat special tool No.T40094, as shown in the following procedures **(see illustration)**.

13 Position the inlet camshaft as shown with the cylinder head bolt indents facing outwards, then slide the end support into the slot in the end of the camshaft **(see illustrations)**.

14 Position the exhaust camshaft on the supports, again with the cylinder head bolt indents facing outwards, and then fit the locating clamp into the slot in the end of the camshaft **(see illustrations)**.

15 Fit the Seat clamping tool No.T40096 to the double gear on the exhaust camshaft, tightening the knurled thumb wheel until the faces of the gear teeth are in alignment **(see illustration)**. Note some camshafts only have a single sprocket, so will not require this procedure.

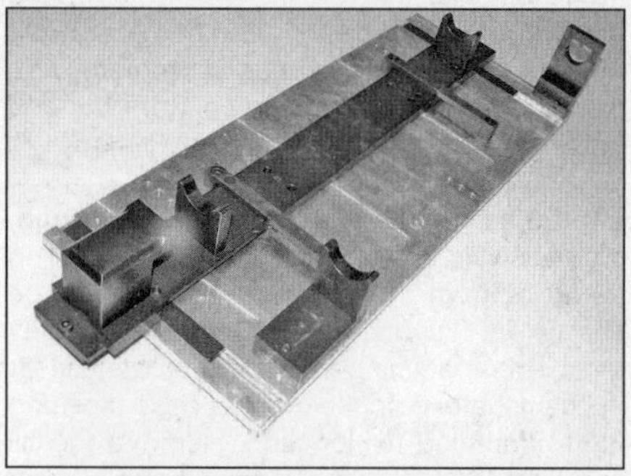
9.12 Seat special tool no. T40094 shown

9.13a Position the inlet camshaft on the tool with the head bolt indent facing outwards...

9.13b ...then slide the end of the special tool, in to the slot in the end of the camshaft

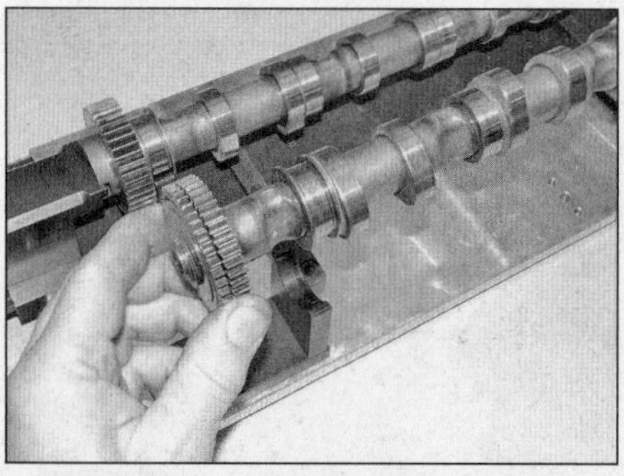
9.14a Position the exhaust camshaft on the tool with the head bolt indent facing outwards...

9.14b ...then fit special tool clamp into the slot in the end of the exhaust camshaft

9.15 Tighten the thumbwheel to align the gear teeth. Ensure the clamping jaw with the arrow is seated on the wider gear

9.16 Slide the exhaust camshaft to the inlet camshaft until the teeth are in mesh

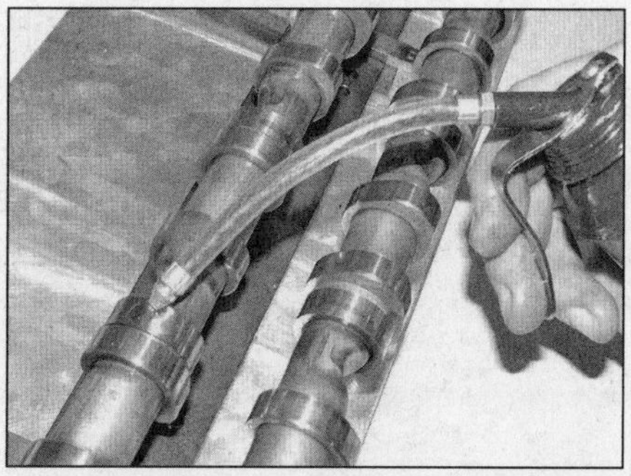

9.17a Lubricate the bearing mountings...

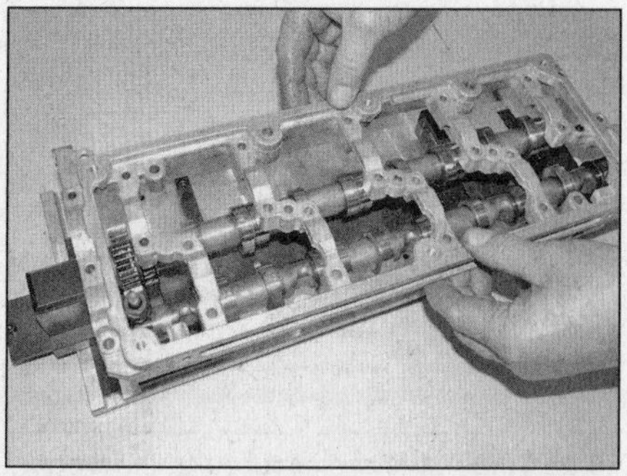

9.17b ...and fit the upper ladder frame to the camshafts

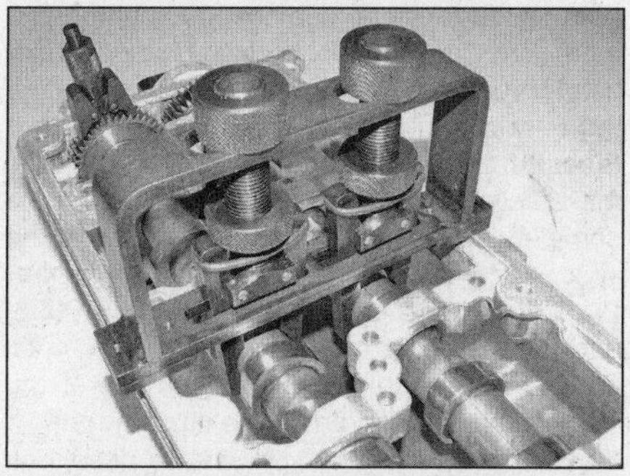

9.18 Secure the camshafts in place in the frame using tool No. T40095

9.19a Slide the locking tool out from the end of the inlet camshaft...

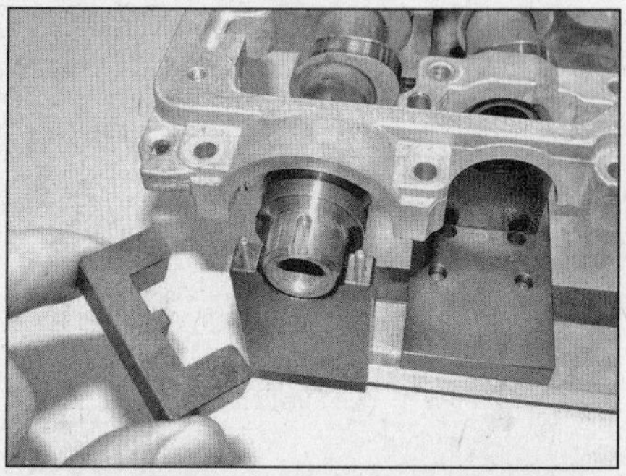

9.19b ...and remove the locking clamp from the end of the exhaust camshaft

16 Slide the exhaust camshaft towards the inlet camshaft until the gear teeth engage **(see illustration)**.

17 Ensure the gasket faces of the retaining frame are clean, then apply a smear of clean engine oil to the bearing surfaces and lower the frame into position over the camshafts **(see illustrations)**. Ensure the bearing surfaces locate correctly on the camshafts.

18 Fit the clamping tool No.T40095 over the camshafts and frame, and tighten the thumbwheels to hold the camshafts in position in the frame **(see illustration)**.

19 Slide out locking clamps from each end of the camshafts **(see illustrations)**, and then lift the camshafts, retaining frame and clamping tool from the Seat special tool no. 40094.

Without the Seat special tool

20 Ensure the gasket faces of the retaining frame are clean, then apply a smear of clean engine oil to the bearing surfaces and turn it upside down on a clean surface.

21 Position the camshafts on the retaining frame with the cylinder head bolt indents facing outwards. Align the marks made on the camshaft sprockets on removal **(see illustration 9.7)**.

22 If a double gear is fitted to the exhaust camshaft, fit the Seat clamping tool No.T40096 (or similar) to align the faces of the teeth. If the clamping tool is not available use two flat bladed screwdrivers and a pair of pliers, this will need an assistant to keep firm pressure on the camshafts to make sure they locate in the retaining frame correctly **(see illustrations)**. Note some camshafts only have a single sprocket, so will not require this procedure.

23 With the marks on the sprockets aligned and the cylinder head bolt indents facing outwards, the slot in the end of the inlet camshaft (that drives the vacuum pump) should be horizontal and the slot in the end of the exhaust camshaft (that locates the timing belt sprocket) should be at the top when fitted **(see illustrations)**.

9.22a Special tool for aligning teeth on sprocket

9.22b Using two flat bladed screwdrivers and a pair of pliers to align teeth

9.23a The inlet camshaft slot needs to be horizontal

9.23b Slot in end of exhaust camshaft should be at the 12 o'clock position

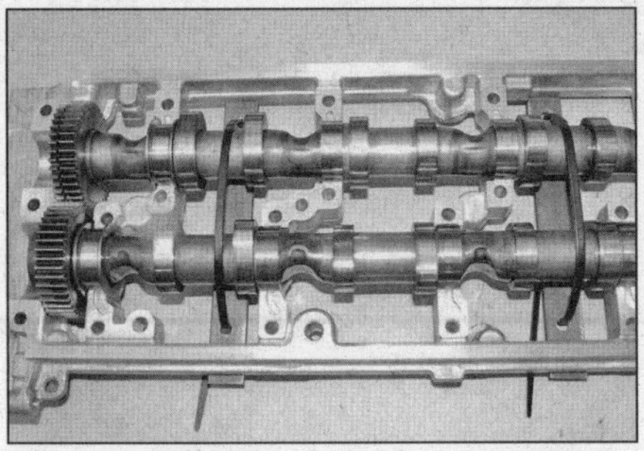

9.24 Camshafts are secured to the ladder frame with two pieces of flat bar and cable ties

9.25a Apply a 2.0 mm thick bead of sealant...

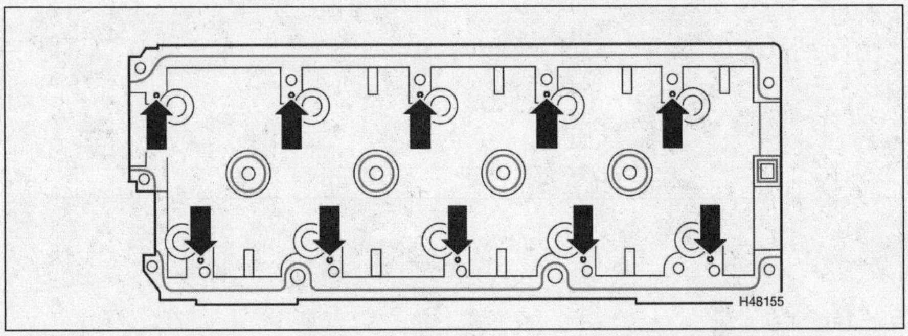

9.25b ...to the area shown by the thick, black line, taking care not to block the oil holes

24 With the camshafts correctly in position, ensuring the camshafts locate correctly in the bearing surfaces on the retaining frame, use two flat pieces of metal flat bar and cable ties to secure them in position **(see illustration)**. ***Caution: Make sure the camshafts are located correctly in the bearing surfaces on the retaining frame, otherwise damage can occur, and this could damage the retaining frame when tightening down onto the cylinder head. The retaining frame is matched to the cylinder head and can only be purchased with a new cylinder head. If there is any doubt, then the Seat special tool should be used, see previous refitting procedure.***

All

25 Ensure the sealing surfaces of the cylinder head are clean, and then apply a 2.0 mm wide bead of sealant (D 176 501 A1 or equivalent) as shown. Take care not to apply too much sealant, ensuring the oil holes supply holes are not blocked **(see illustrations)**.

26 Fit a new sealing cap to the timing belt end of the cylinder head and make sure the locating dowels are fitted to the cylinder head **(see illustrations)**.

27 Apply a smear of clean engine oil to the bearing surfaces and place the camshafts, frame and clamping tool in place on the cylinder head. Progressively, carefully, hand tighten the frame retaining bolts in the sequence shown **(see illustration)**, until the retaining frame makes contact with the cylinder head over the complete surface, then tighten the bolts to the specified torque, again in the correct sequence.

28 Remove the gear aligning tool (T40096) and the clamping tool (T40095), or the metal flat bars and cable ties from the top of the camshaft retaining frame **(see illustration)**.

29 Renew the camshaft oil seal as described in Section 10.

30 The remainder of refitting is a reversal of removal.

10 Camshaft oil seals – renewal

Right-hand oil seal

1 Remove the camshaft sprocket and hub, as described in Section 8.

2 Drill two small holes into the existing oil seal, diagonally opposite each other. Take great care to avoid drilling through into the seal housing or camshaft sealing surface. Thread two self-tapping screws into the holes, and using a pair of pliers, pull on the heads of the screws to extract the oil seal **(see illustration)**.

3 Clean out the seal housing and the sealing surface of the camshaft by wiping it with a lint-free cloth. Remove any swarf or burrs that may cause the seal to leak.

9.26a Fit a new seal/end cap to the cylinder head

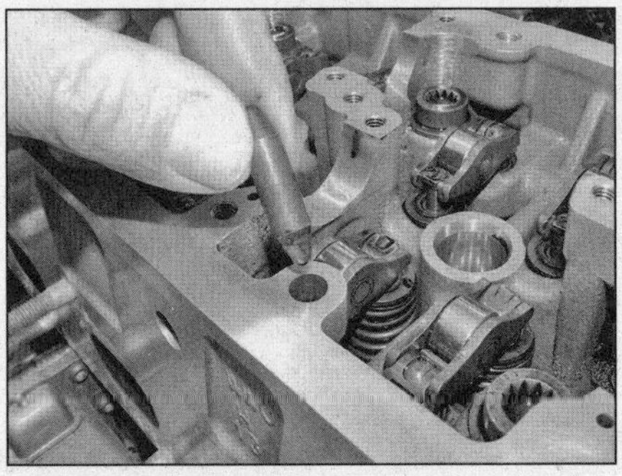

9.26b Check that the locating dowels are in place

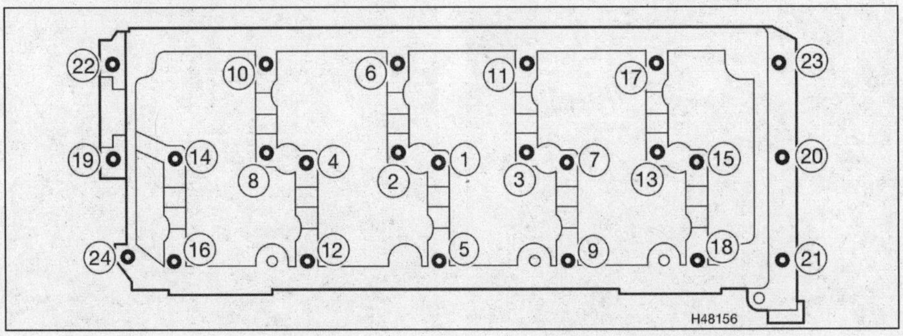

9.27 Camshaft retaining frame bolt tightening sequence

9.28 Remove the cable ties and flat bar from the top of the ladder frame

10.2 Screw-in a self-tapping screw, then pull the screw and seal from place

10.4 Using a plastic sleeve to slide seal over end of camshaft

10.5 Note some seals have 'OUTSIDE' marked on them

4 Do not lubricate the lip and outer edge of the new oil seal, push it over the camshaft until it is positioned in place above it's housing. To prevent damage to the sealing lips, wrap some adhesive tape around the end of the camshaft **(see illustration)**.

5 Using a hammer and a socket of suitable diameter, drive the seal squarely into its housing. Make sure the seal is fitted the correct way around, some have 'OUTSIDE' stamped on the seal **(see illustration)**. **Note:** *Select a socket that bears only on the hard outer surface of the seal, not the inner lip that can easily be damaged.*

6 Refit the camshaft sprocket and its hub, as described in Section 8.

Left-hand oil seal

7 The left-hand camshaft oil seal is formed by the brake vacuum pump seal. Refer to Chapter 9 Section 24, for details of brake vacuum pump removal and refitting.

11 Cylinder head – removal, inspection and refitting

Note: *The cylinder head must be removed with the engine cold. New cylinder head bolts and a new cylinder head gasket will be required on refitting, and suitable studs will be required to guide the cylinder head into position – see text.*

Removal

1 Remove the battery and battery tray, as described in Chapter 5A Section 3.

2 Drain the cooling system and engine oil (see Chapter 1B).

3 Pull the plastic cover on the top of the engine upwards to release it from its mountings.

4 Remove the air filter housing as described in Chapter 4B Section 3.

5 Remove the radiator cooling fan(s) and shroud as described in Chapter 3 Section 3.

6 Undo the bolts and remove the air hose/duct from the intercooler to the turbocharger. Release the wiring looms from the clips as necessary to enable the duct to be manoeuvred from place.

7 Remove the camshaft cover as described in Section 4.

8 Remove the camshaft sprocket and hub as described in Section 8.

9 Remove the inlet manifold as described in Chapter 4B Section 6.

10 Undo the retaining bolts, and remove the charge air pipe from the turbocharger **(see illustration)**.

11 Remove the EGR pipes from the cylinder head.

12 Remove the exhaust manifold/turbocharger, as described in Chapter 4D Section 5.

13 There is no need to completely remove the front pipe/particulate filter from the vehicle. Slacken the Allen bolt and release the clamp securing the diesel particulate filter/catalytic converter to the turbocharger, then undo the bolts/nuts securing the brackets to the cylinder block/head and lay the filter/converter to one side.

14 Apply a little lubrication spray to the rubber sleeve, pull up the pipe from the vacuum pump, then undo the 4 retaining bolts and remove the vacuum pump from the left-hand end of the cylinder head **(see illustration)**. Renew the pump-to-cylinder head seal/gasket (Chapter 9 Section 24).

15 Disconnect the coolant temperature sensor wiring plug at the left-hand end of the cylinder head, and release the wiring loom from any retaining clips.

16 Disconnect the gearchange cables from the levers on the manual transmission as described in Chapter 7A Section 2.

17 Undo the bolts/nut, securing the gearchange bracket to the top of the transmission. Move the bracket and cables to one side.

18 Note their fitted locations, then release the clamps and disconnect the various coolant hoses from the cylinder head.

19 Disconnect the wiring connector from the oil pressure switch, undo the bolt securing the pipe bracket at the left-hand end of the cylinder head **(see illustrations)**, and the bolt securing the lifting bracket on the rear of the head.

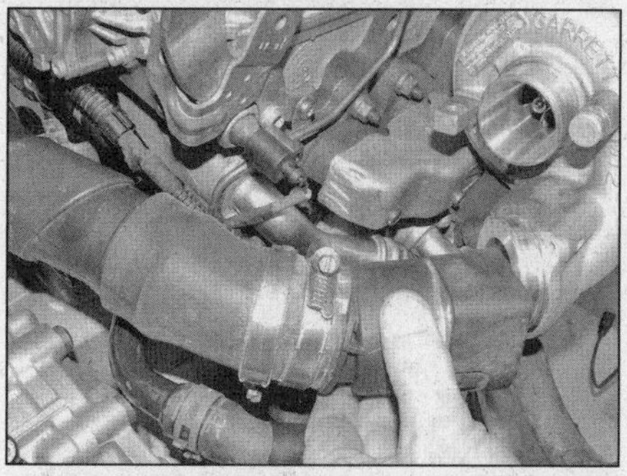

11.10 Remove the charge air pipe from the turbocharger

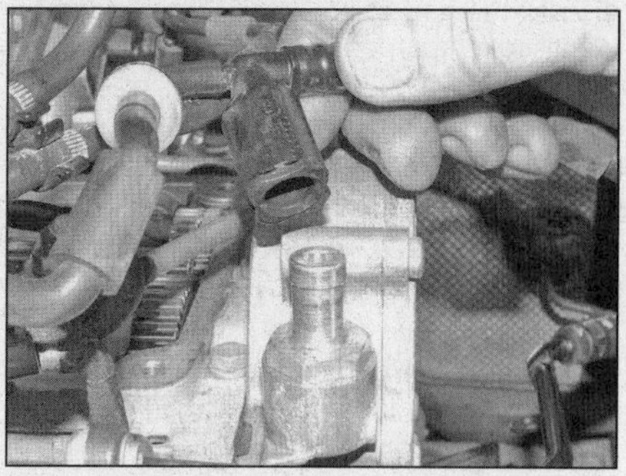

11.14 Disconnect the vacuum pipe

11.19a Disconnect the oil pressure switch wiring connector

11.19b Undo the retaining bolt/screw and remove the lifting bracket

11.20 Undo the bolt securing the timing belt guard

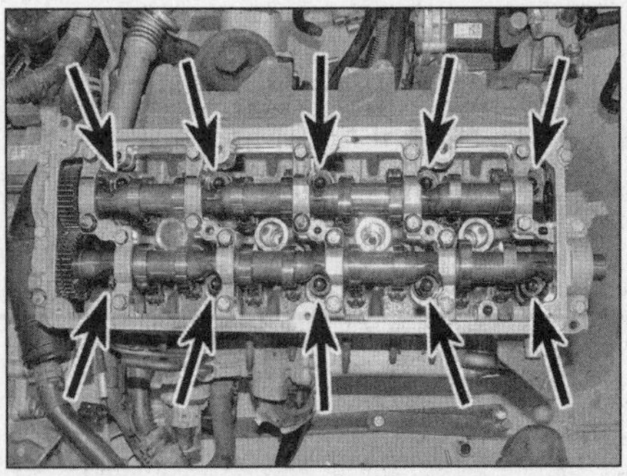

11.21 Undo the cylinder head bolts using a M12 multi-splined (12 pointed star) tool

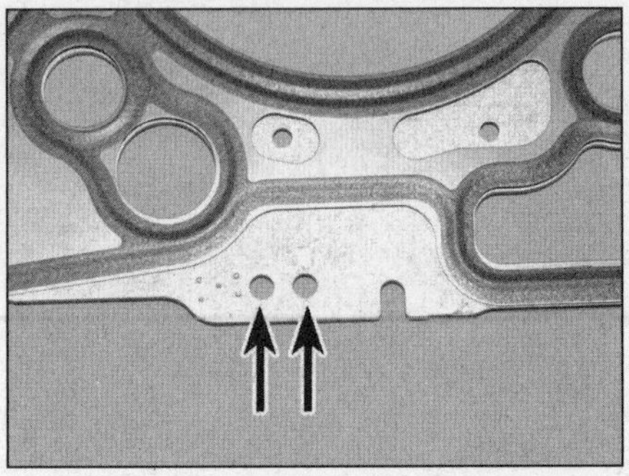

11.24 The holes identify the thickness of the cylinder head gasket

20 Undo the bolt securing the timing belt guard adjacent to the timing belt tensioner, and the bolt securing the camshaft position sensor, then remove the tensioner retaining nut **(see illustration)**.

21 Using an M12 multi-splined tool (12 pointed star), undo the cylinder head bolts, working from the outside-in, evenly and gradually **(see illustration)**. Remove the bolts and recover the washers. Check that nothing remains connected, and starting at the gearbox side, lift the cylinder head from the engine block, sliding the belt tensioner from the mounting stud as the cylinder head is removed. Seek assistance if possible, as it is a heavy assembly, especially as it is being removed complete with the manifolds.

22 Remove the gasket from the top of the block, noting the locating dowels. If the dowels are a loose fit, remove them and store them with the head for safekeeping. Do not discard the gasket yet – it will be needed for identification purposes.

Inspection

23 Dismantling and inspection of the cylinder head is covered in Part 2F.

Cylinder head gasket selection

Note: *A dial test indicator (DTI) will be required for this operation.*

24 Examine the old cylinder head gasket for manufacturer's identification markings **(see illustration)**. These will be in the form of holes, and a part number on the edge of the gasket. Unless new pistons have been fitted, the new cylinder head gasket must be of the same type as the old one.

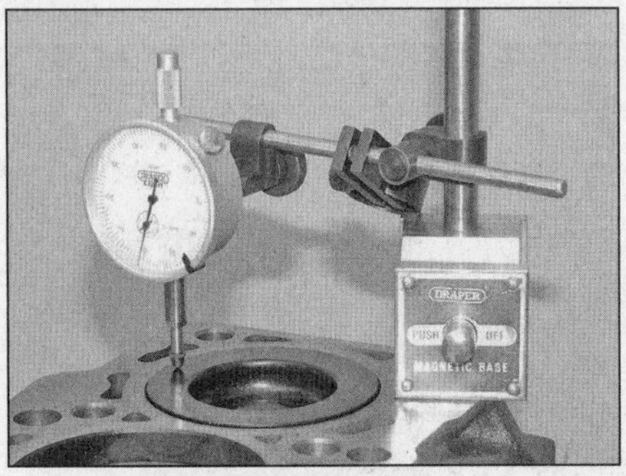

11.27 Measure the piston protrusion using a DTI gauge

25 If new piston assemblies have been fitted as part of an engine overhaul, or if a new short engine is to be fitted, the projection of the piston crowns above the cylinder head mating face of the cylinder block at TDC must be measured. This measurement is used to determine the thickness of the new cylinder head gasket required.

26 Anchor a dial test indicator (DTI) to the top face (cylinder head gasket mating face) of the cylinder block, and zero the gauge on the gasket mating face.

27 Rest the gauge probe on No 1 piston crown, and turn the crankshaft slowly by hand until the piston reaches TDC. Measure and record the maximum piston projection at TDC **(see illustration)**.

28 Repeat the measurement for the remaining pistons, and record the results.

29 If the measurements differ from piston-to-piston, take the highest figure, and use this to determine the thickness of the head gasket required as follows.

Piston projection	Gasket identification (number of holes)
0.91 to 1.00 mm	*1*
1.01 to 1.10 mm	*2*
1.11 to 1.20 mm	*3*

30 Purchase a new gasket according to the results of the measurements.

Refitting

31 The mating faces of the cylinder head and block must be perfectly clean before refitting the head. Use a scraper to remove all traces of gasket and carbon, also clean the tops of the pistons. Take particular care with the aluminium surfaces, as the soft metal is easily damaged.

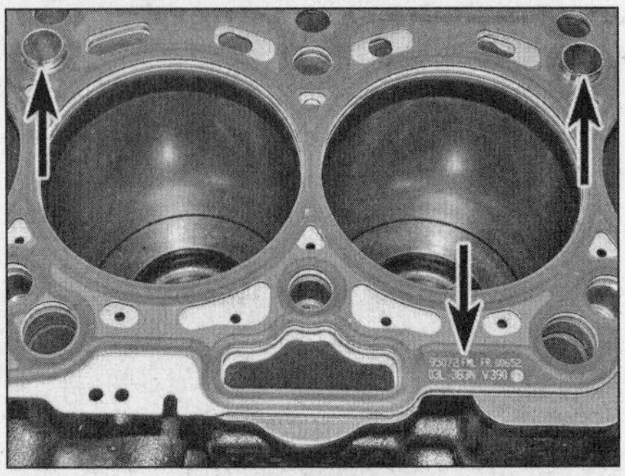

11.39 Ensure the dowels are in place, then fit the new gasket with the part number uppermost

32 Make sure that debris is not allowed to enter the oil and water passages – this is particularly important for the oil circuit, as carbon could block the oil supply to the camshaft and crankshaft bearings. Using adhesive tape and paper, seal the water, oil and bolt holes in the cylinder block.

33 To prevent carbon entering the gap between the pistons and bores, smear a little grease in the gap. After cleaning a piston, rotate the crankshaft to that the piston moves down the bore, and then wipe out the grease and carbon with a cloth rag. Clean the other piston crowns in the same way.

34 Check the head and block for nicks, deep scratches and other damage. If slight, they may be removed carefully with a file. More serious damage may be repaired by machining, but this is a specialist job.

35 If warpage of the cylinder head is suspected, use a straight-edge to check it for distortion, as described in Chapter 2F Section 7.

36 Ensure that the cylinder head bolt holes in the crankcase are clean and free of oil. Syringe or soak up any oil left in the bolt holes. This is most important in order that the correct bolt tightening torque can be applied, and to prevent the possibility of the block being cracked by hydraulic pressure when the bolts are tightened.

37 Turn the crankshaft anti-clockwise all the pistons at an equal height, approximately half-way down their bores from the TDC position (see Section 3). This will eliminate any risk of piston-to-valve contact as the cylinder head is refitted.

38 Where applicable, refit the manifolds.

39 Ensure that the cylinder head locating dowels are in place in the cylinder block, and then fit the new cylinder head gasket over the dowels, ensuring that the part number is uppermost **(see illustration)**. Note that Seat recommend that the gasket is only removed from its packaging immediately prior to fitting.

40 Lower the cylinder head into position on the gasket, ensuring that it engages correctly over the dowels. Refit the timing belt tensioner as the cylinder head is refitted.

41 Fit the washers in place then fit the new cylinder head bolts to the locations, and screw them in as far as possible by hand. Do not oil the bolt threads.

42 Working progressively, in sequence, tighten all the cylinder head bolts to the specified Stage 1 torque **(see illustration)**.

43 Again working progressively, in sequence, tighten all the cylinder head bolts to the specified Stage 2 torque.

44 Tighten all the cylinder head bolts, in sequence, through the specified Stage 3 angle.

45 Finally, tighten all the cylinder head bolts, in sequence, through the specified Stage 4 angle.

46 The remainder of the refitting procedure is a reversal of the removal procedure, noting the following points:

a) Tighten all fasteners to their specified torque where given.
b) Renew all seals and gaskets.
c) Refill the cooling system.
d) Refill the engine oil.
e) Ensure all wiring is correctly routed.
f) Run the vehicle and make sure the cooling fans operate when the engine gets up to temperature.

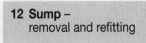

12 Sump – removal and refitting

Removal

1 Apply the handbrake, then jack up the front of the vehicle and support securely on axle stands (see *Jacking and vehicle support)*.

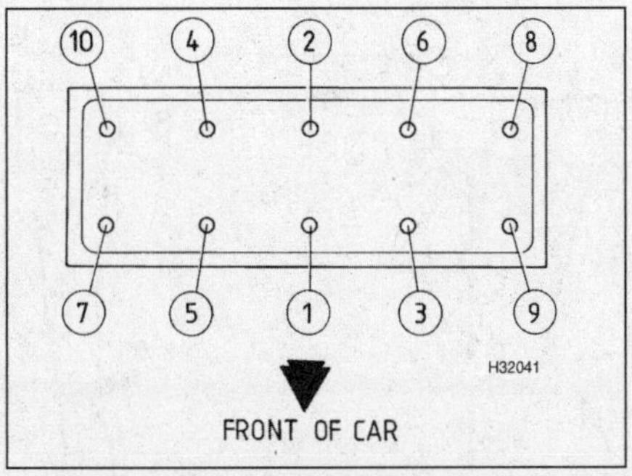

11.42 Cylinder head bolt tightening sequence

2 Remove the securing screws and withdraw the engine undershield.

3 Drain the engine oil as described in Chapter 1B Section 7.

4 Release the retaining clips and remove the air hose from the intercooler outlet to the charge air pipe **(see illustration)**.

5 Undo the retaining bolts, release the clamp and move the charger air pipe from the front of the cylinder block **(see illustrations)**. Disconnect the charger air pressure sensor wiring plug.

6 Disconnect the wiring connector from the oil level/temperature sender in the sump.

7 Release the retaining clips and remove the sump insulation cover from the sump **(see illustrations)**.

8 Unscrew and remove the bolts securing the sump to the cylinder block, and the bolts securing the sump to the transmission casing, then withdraw the sump **(see illustrations)**. If necessary, release the sump by tapping with a soft-faced hammer.

Refitting

9 Begin refitting by thoroughly cleaning the

12.4 Slacken the two retaining clips

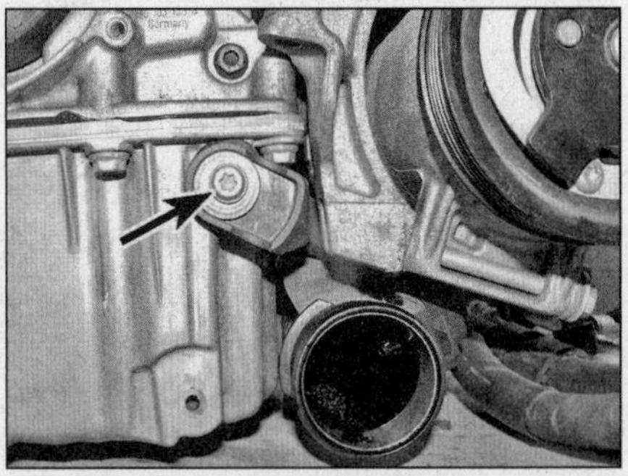

12.5a Undo the retaining bolt on the end of the sump...

12.5b ...and the bolt on the front of the cylinder block...

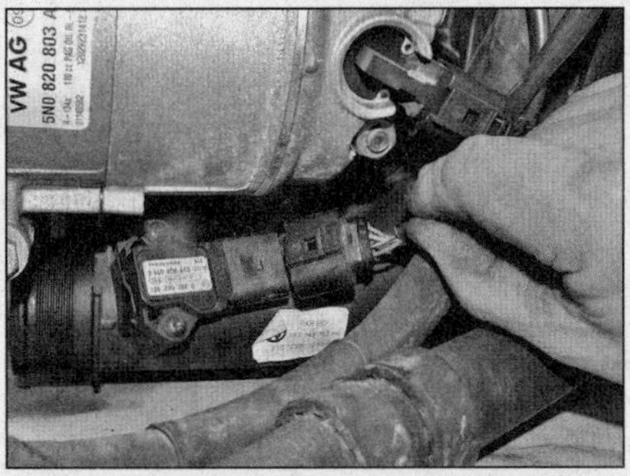

12.5c ...then disconnect the pressure switch wiring connector

12.7a Release the two clips at the rear of the sump

12.7b At the front, prise down the centre pin and pull the clip downwards

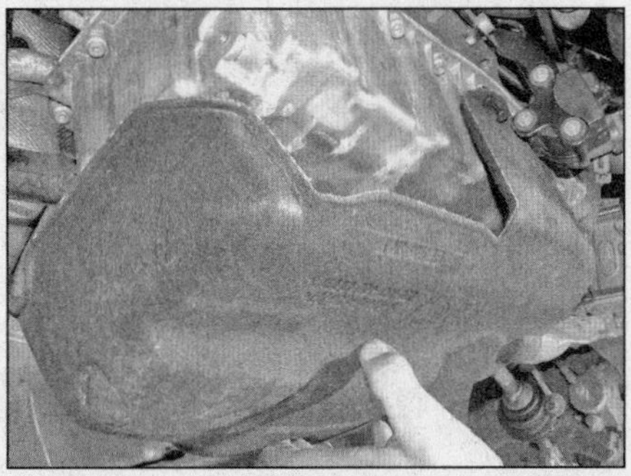

12.7c Remove the insulation cover from around the sump

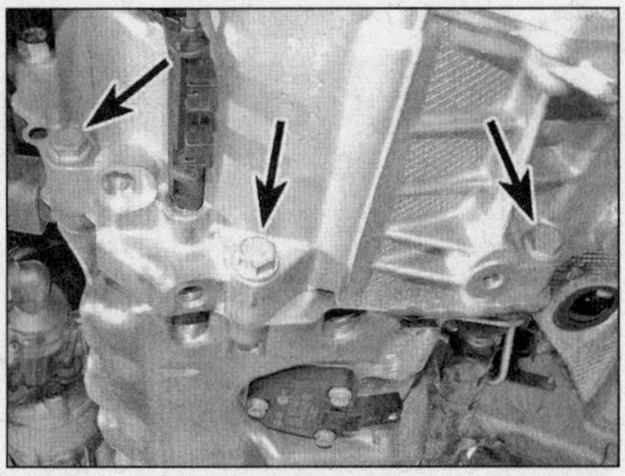

12.8a Undo the three transmission to sump bolts...

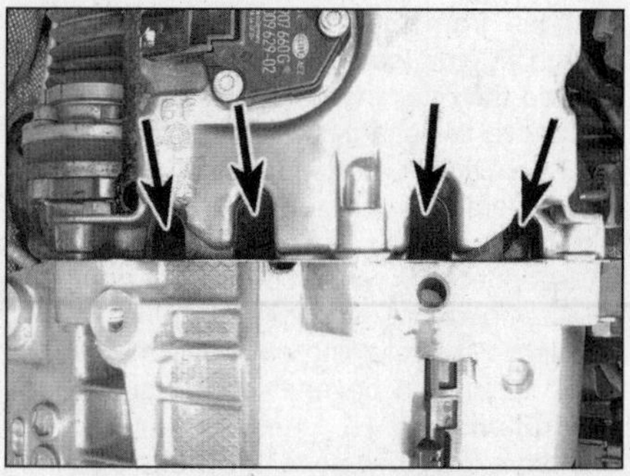

12.8b ...and also the four bolts at the transmission end of the sump

mating faces of the sump and cylinder block. Ensure that all traces of old sealant are removed.

10 Ensure that the cylinder block mating face of the sump is free from all traces of old sealant, oil and grease, and then apply a 2.0 to 3.0 mm thick bead of silicone sealant (Seat/VW D 176 404 A2 or equivalent) to the sump **(see illustration)**. Note that the sealant should be run around the inside of the bolt holes in the sump. The sump must be fitted within 5 minutes of applying the sealant.

11 Offer the sump up to the cylinder block, then refit the sump-to-cylinder block bolts, and lightly tighten them by hand, working progressively in a diagonal sequence. **Note:** *If the sump is being refitted with the engine and transmission separated, make sure that the sump is flush with the flywheel end of the cylinder block.*

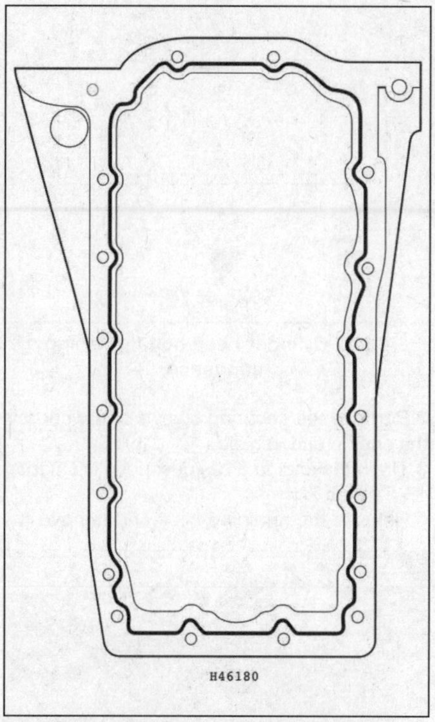

12.10 Apply a bead of sealant to the around the inside of the bolt holes

12 Refit the sump-to-transmission casing bolts, and tighten them lightly, using a socket.

13 Again working in a diagonal sequence, lightly tighten the sump-to-cylinder block bolts, using a socket.

13.2 Remove the oil pick-up pipe/filter

13.3 Remove the oil baffle plate bolt (which is also one of the oil pump mounting bolts)

13.4 Oil pump mounting bolts

13.11 Fit a new seal to the end of the oil pick-up pipe

14 Tighten the sump-to-transmission casing bolts to the specified torque.

15 Working in a diagonal sequence, progressively tighten the sump-to-cylinder block bolts to the specified torque.

16 The remainder of refitting is a reversal of removal, noting to allow at least 30 minutes from the time of refitting the sump for the sealant to dry, then refill the engine with oil.

13 Oil pump and drive belt – removal, inspection and refitting

Oil pump removal

1 Remove the sump as described in Section 12.

2 Unscrew the flange bolts and remove the oil pick-up pipe/filter from the oil pump **(see illustration)**. Recover the O-ring seal and discard, as a new one will be required for refitting.

3 Unscrew the securing bolt, and remove the oil baffle from the cylinder block **(see illustration)**.

4 Unscrew and remove the mounting bolts, and release the oil pump from the dowels in the crankcase **(see illustration)**. Unhook the oil pump drive sprocket from the belt and withdraw the oil pump and oil pick-up pipe from the engine. Note, the bolt holding the baffle plate is also one of the pump mounting bolts.

Oil pump inspection

5 Clean the pump thoroughly, and inspect for signs of damage or wear. If evident, renew the oil pump.

Oil pump refitting

6 Prime the pump with oil by pouring oil into the pick-up pipe aperture while turning the driveshaft.

7 If the drive belt and crankshaft sprocket have been removed, delay refitting them until after the oil pump has been mounted on the cylinder block.

8 Engage the oil pump sprocket with the drive belt, and then locate the oil pump on the dowels. Refit and tighten the mounting bolts to the specified torque.

9 Where applicable, refit the drive belt and crankshaft sprocket using a reversal of the removal procedure.

10 Refit the oil baffle plate, and tighten the securing bolt.

11 Refit the pick-up pipe to the oil pump, using a new O-ring seal, and tighten the securing bolts **(see illustration)**.

12 Refit the sump as described in Section 12.

Oil pump drive belt and sprockets

Note: *Seat/VW sealant (D 176 404 A2 or equivalent) will be required to seal the crankshaft oil seal housing on refitting, and it is advisable to fit a new crankshaft oil seal.*

14.4 Use a locking tool to counterhold the flywheel

14.7 Flywheel warpage check – see text

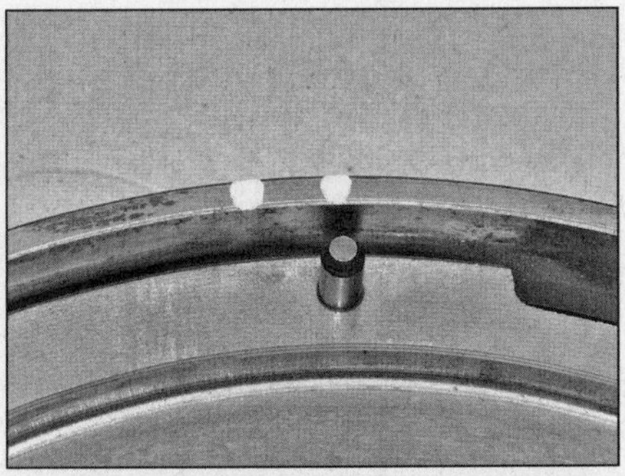

14.8 Flywheel free rotational movement check alignment marks – see text

Removal

13 Proceed as described in paragraphs 1 and 2.

14 To remove the belt, remove the timing belt as described in Section 7, then unbolt the crankshaft oil seal housing from the cylinder block, as described in Section 15. Unhook the belt from the sprocket on the end of the crankshaft.

15 The oil pump drive sprocket is a press-fit on the crankshaft, and cannot easily be removed. Consult a Seat dealer for advice if the sprocket is worn or damaged.

Inspection

16 It is wise to renew the belt in any case if the engine is to be overhauled, If there is any doubt as to the condition of the belt, renew it.

Refitting

17 If the oil pump has been removed, refit the oil pump as described previously in this Section before refitting the belt and sprocket.

18 Engage the oil pump sprocket with the belt, then engage the belt with the crankshaft sprocket.

19 Fit a new crankshaft oil seal to the housing, and refit the housing as described in Section 15.

20 Where applicable, refit the oil baffle and pick-up pipe, and tighten the securing bolts.

21 Refit the sump as described in Section 12.

14 Flywheel – removal, inspection and refitting

Removal

1 On manual transmission models, remove the gearbox (see Chapter 7A Section 3) and clutch (see Chapter 6A Section 6).

2 The flywheel can only be fitted in one position due to the offset of the flywheel mounting holes in the end of the crankshaft. Note, manual models are fitted with a dual-mass flywheel.

3 Rotate the outside of the dual-mass flywheel so that the bolts align with the holes (if necessary).

4 Unscrew the bolts and remove the flywheel. Using a locking tool, counter-hold the flywheel to prevent it from turning **(see illustration)**. Discard the bolts, as new ones must be fitted. **Note:** *In order not to damage the flywheel, do not allow the bolt heads to make contact with the flywheel during the unscrewing procedure.*

Inspection

5 Check the dual-mass flywheel for wear and damage. Examine the starter ring gear for excessive wear to the teeth. If the driveplate or its ring gear are damaged, the complete driveplate must be renewed. The flywheel ring gear, however, may be renewed separately from the flywheel, but the work should be entrusted to a Seat dealer.

6 The following are guidelines only, but should indicate whether professional inspection is necessary. The dual-mass flywheel should be checked as follows:

7 Warpage: Place a straight edge across the face of the drive surface, and check by trying to insert a feeler gauge between the straight edge and the drive surface **(see illustration)**. The flywheel will normally warp like a bowl – ie. Higher on the outer edge. If the warpage is more than 0.40 mm, the flywheel may need replacing.

8 Free rotational movement: This is the distance the drive surface of the flywheel can be turned independently of the flywheel primary element, using finger effort alone. Move the drive surface in one direction and make a mark where the locating pin aligns with the flywheel edge. Move the drive surface in the other direction (finger pressure only) and make another mark **(see illustration)**. The total of free movement should not exceed 20.0 mm. If it's more, the flywheel may need replacing.

9 Total rotational movement: This is the total distance the drive surface can be turned independently of the flywheel primary element. Insert two bolts into the clutch pressure plate/damper unit mounting holes, and with the crankshaft/flywheel held stationary, use a lever/pry bar between the bolts and use some effort to move the drive surface fully in one direction – make a mark where the locating pin aligns with the flywheel edge. Now force the drive surface fully in the opposite direction, and make another mark. The total rotational movement should not exceed 44.00 mm. If it does, have the flywheel professionally inspected.

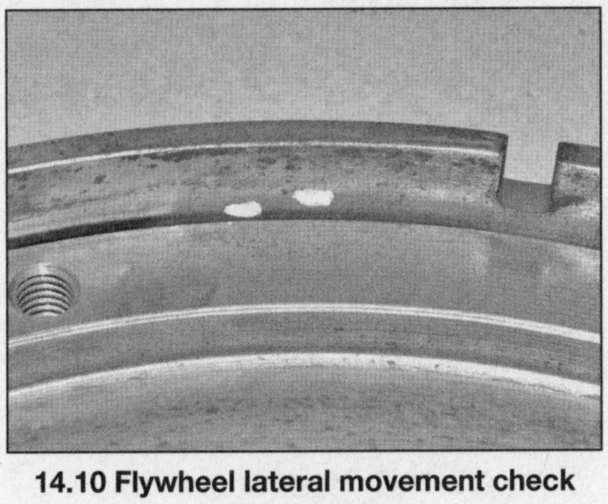

14.10 Flywheel lateral movement check marks – see text

10 Lateral movement: The lateral movement (up and down) of the drive surface in relation to the primary element of the flywheel, should not exceed 2.0 mm. If it does, the flywheel may need replacing. This can be checked by pressing the drive surface down on one side into the flywheel (flywheel horizontal) and making an alignment mark between the drive surface and the inner edge of the primary element. Now press down on the opposite side of the drive surface, and make another mark above the original one. The difference between the two marks is the lateral movement **(see illustration)**.

11 There should be no cracks in the drive surface of the flywheel. If cracks are evident, the flywheel may need replacing.

Refitting

12 Refitting is a reversal of removal. Use new bolts when refitting the flywheel or driveplate **(see illustration)**, and coat the threads of the bolts (if not already coated with locking compound) with locking fluid before inserting them. Tighten them to the specified torque.

14.12 Use new bolts when refitting

15.2 Pull the screw and seal from place using pliers

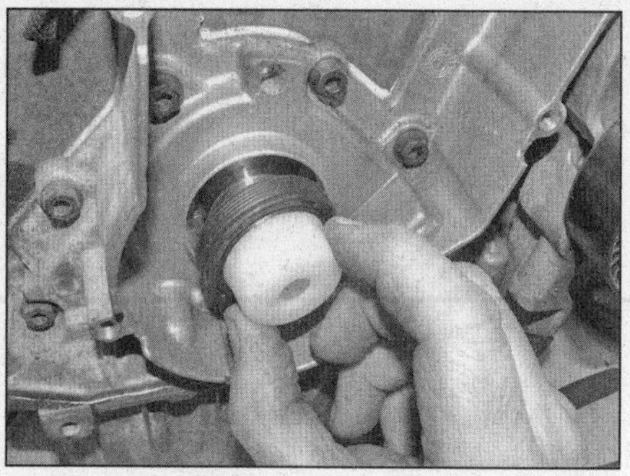

15.5 Using a plastic sleeve to slide the seal over the end of the crankshaft

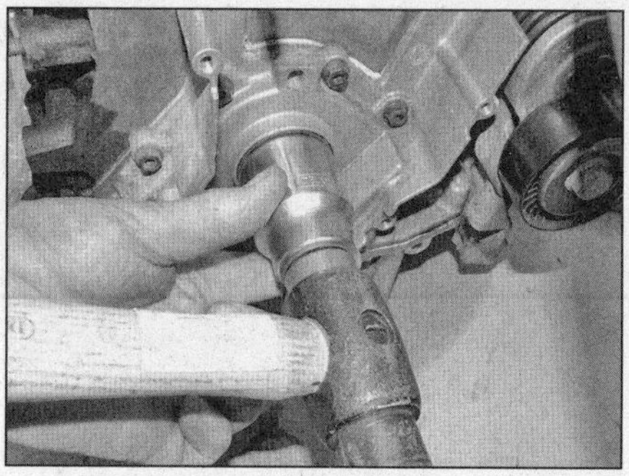

15.6 Carefully tap the seal into position

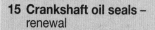

15 Crankshaft oil seals – renewal

Note: *The oil seals are a PTFE (Teflon) type and are fitted dry, without using any grease or oil. These have a wider sealing lip and have been introduced instead of the coil spring type oil seal.*

Timing belt end oil seal

1 Remove the timing belt as described in Section 7, and the crankshaft sprocket with reference to Section 8.

2 To remove the seal without removing the housing, drill two small holes diagonally opposite each other, insert self-tapping screws, and pull on the heads of the screws with pliers **(see illustration)**.

3 Alternatively, to remove the oil seal complete with its housing, proceed as follows.

a) *Remove the sump as described in Section 12. This is necessary to ensure a satisfactory seal between the sump and oil seal housing on refitting.*

b) *Unbolt and remove the oil seal housing.*

c) *Working on the bench, lever the oil seal from the housing using a suitable screwdriver. Take care not to damage the seal seating in the housing.*

4 Thoroughly clean the oil seal seating in the housing.

5 Wind a length of tape around the end of the crankshaft (or a plastic sleeve) to protect the oil seal lips as the seal (and housing, where applicable) is fitted **(see illustration)**.

6 Fit a new oil seal to the housing, pressing or driving it into position using a socket or tube of suitable diameter. Ensure that the socket or tube bears only on the hard outer ring of the seal, and take care not to damage the seal lips. Press or drive the seal into position until it is seated on the shoulder in the housing **(see illustration)**. Make sure that the closed end of the seal is facing outwards.

7 If the oil seal housing has been removed, proceed as follows, otherwise proceed to paragraph 11.

8 Clean all traces of old sealant from the crankshaft oil seal housing and the cylinder block, then coat the cylinder block mating faces of the oil seal housing with a 2.0 to 3.0 mm thick bead of silicone sealant (Seat/VW D 176 404 A2, or equivalent). Note that the seal housing must be refitted within 5 minutes of applying the sealant.

Caution: DO NOT put excessive amounts of sealant onto the housing as it may get into the sump and block the oil pick-up pipe.

9 Refit the oil seal housing, and tighten the bolts progressively to the specified torque.

10 Refit the sump as described in Section 12.

11 Refit the crankshaft sprocket with reference to Section 8, and the timing belt as described in Section 7.

Flywheel end oil seal

Note: *In these engines, the seal, sealing flange and sender wheel are a complete unit. Special tools are required to refit the sealing flange, and press the sender wheel onto the end of the crankshaft. It is not possible to accurately fit these parts without the tools, which are be available from Seat/VW (part no. T10134) and maybe available from aftermarket automotive tool specialists.*

12 Remove the flywheel as described in Section 14, then prise the intermediate plate from the locating dowels on the cylinder block and unhook it from behind the top of the seal housing **(see illustrations)**.

13 Undo the bolt securing the crankshaft speed sensor and remove it from the seal housing, then undo the bolts securing the sealing flange to the cylinder block **(see illustrations)**.

14 Insert three 6 x 35 mm bolts into the threaded holes in the sealing flange. Tighten the bolts gradually and evenly, and press the sealing flange, and sender wheel from the crankshaft/cylinder block **(see illustrations)**. The seal, sender wheel and sealing flange are supplied as a complete unit.

15.12a Remove the intermediate plate from the dowels...

15.12b ...and from behind the top of the crankshaft seal housing

15.13a Undo the crankshaft speed sensor retaining bolt

15.13b Sealing flange bolts

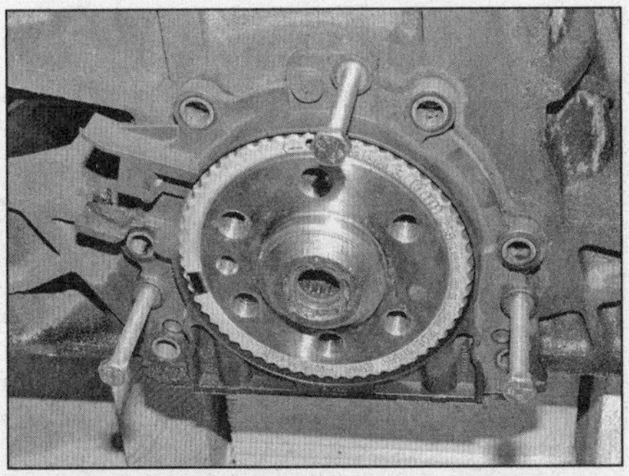

15.14a Screw in three 6 x 35 mm bolts...

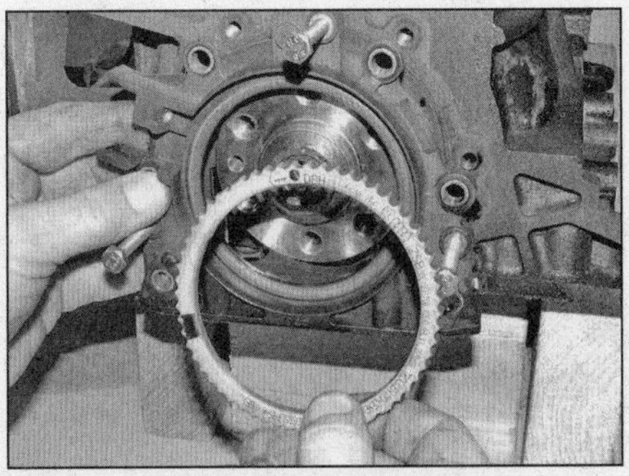

15.14b ...and draw the sealing flange and sender wheel from place

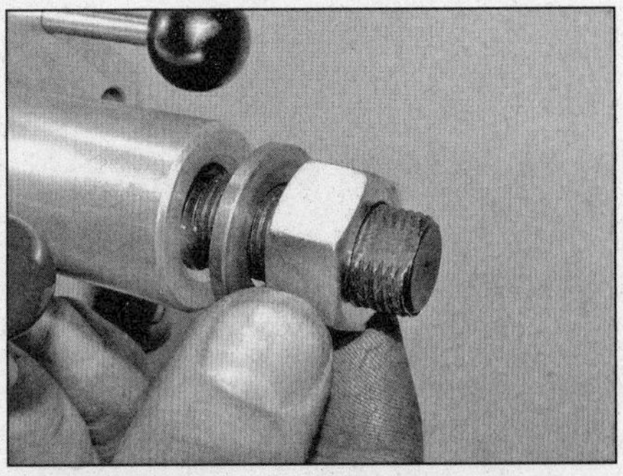

15.16a Rotate the nut until its level with the end of the flat clamping surface...

15.16b ...then clamp it in a vice

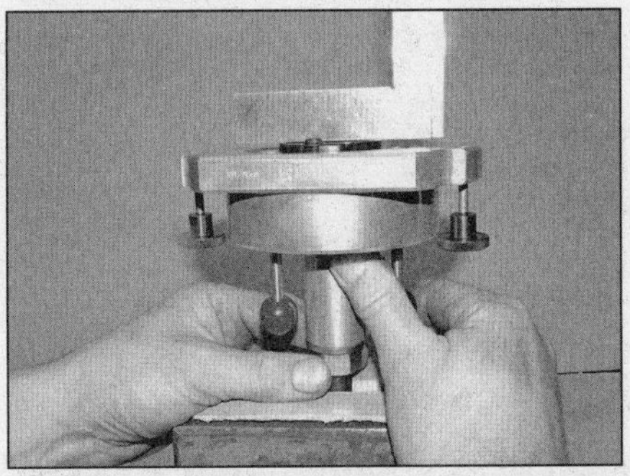

15.17a Rotate the nut until the inner part of the tool...

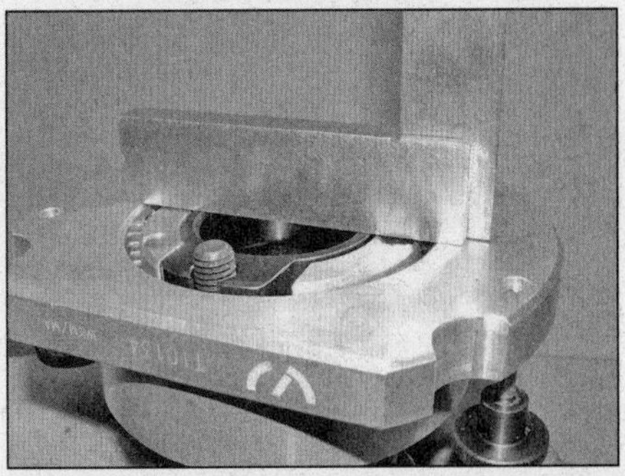

15.17b ...is flush with the flat surface of the housing

15 Ensure the mating face of the cylinder block is clean and free from debris. The new sealing flange/seal/sender wheel assembly is supplied with a sealing lip support ring, which serves as a fitting sleeve, and must not be removed prior to installation. Equally, the sender wheel must not be separated from the assembly.

16 If using the Seat tool, proceed as follows. If using an aftermarket tool specialist's product, follow the instructions supplied with the tool. Rotate the large spindle nut until it's level with the end of the clamping surface of the spindle, then clamp the spindle in a vice **(see illustrations)**.

17 Press the tool housing downwards until it rests on the nut and washer. Rotate the nut until the inner part of the tool is at the same height as the housing **(see illustrations)**.

18 Remove the seal securing clip. The hole on the sender wheel must align with the marking on the sealing flange **(see illustrations)**.

19 Place the flange outer side down on a clean, flat surface, then press the seal guide fitting sleeve (supplied ready fitted), housing, and sender wheel downwards until all the components are flat on the surface. In this position the upper edge of the sender wheel should be level with the edge of the sealing flange **(see illustrations)**.

20 Place the sealing flange on the assembly tool, so the pin locates in the hole in the sender wheel **(see illustration)**.

21 Push the sealing flange and guide fitting

15.18a Remove the securing clip...

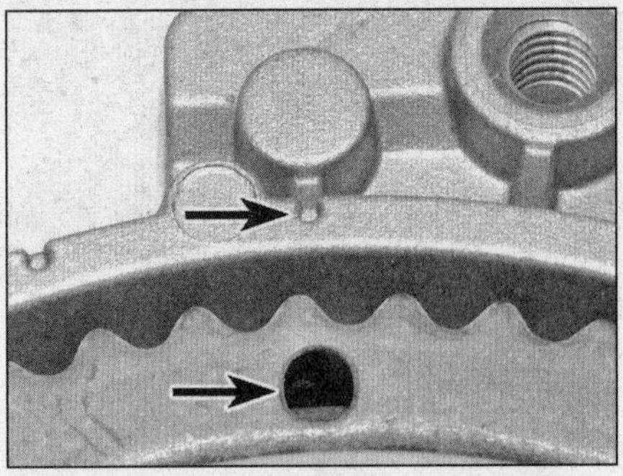

15.18b ...the hole in the sender wheel should align with the marking on the flange

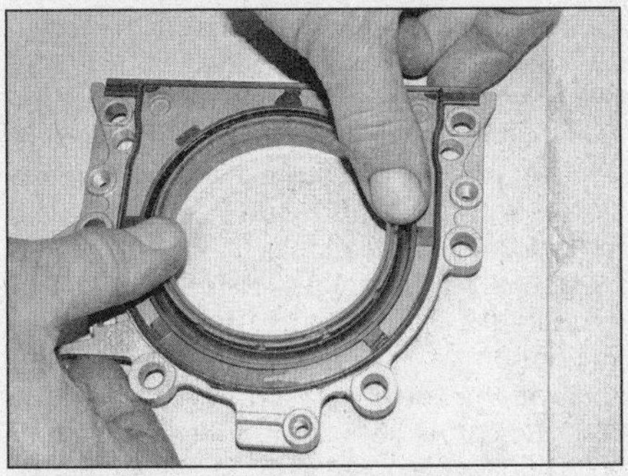

15.19a Press the assembly downwards on a clean, flat surface...

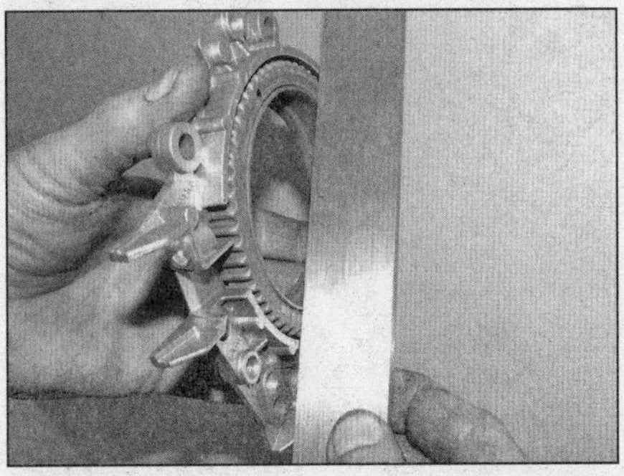

15.19b ...so the upper edge of the sender wheel is level with the edge of the flange

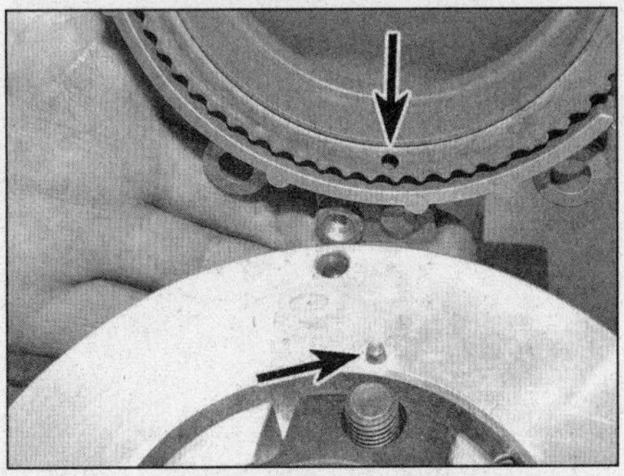

15.20 Fit the flange to the tool, ensuring the pin locates in the hole

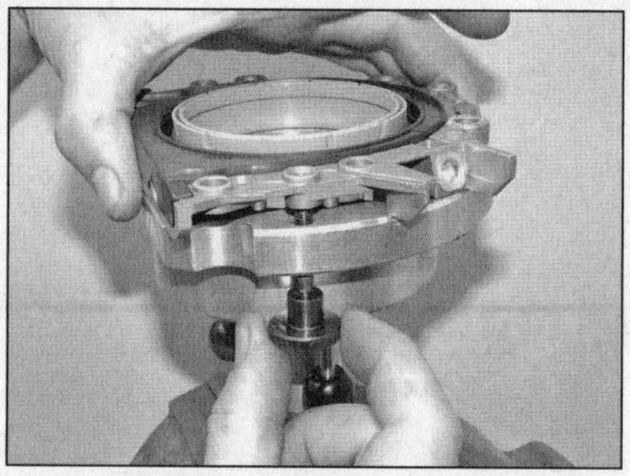

15.21 With the pin engaged in the hole, tighten the 3 knurled screws to secure the flange to the tool

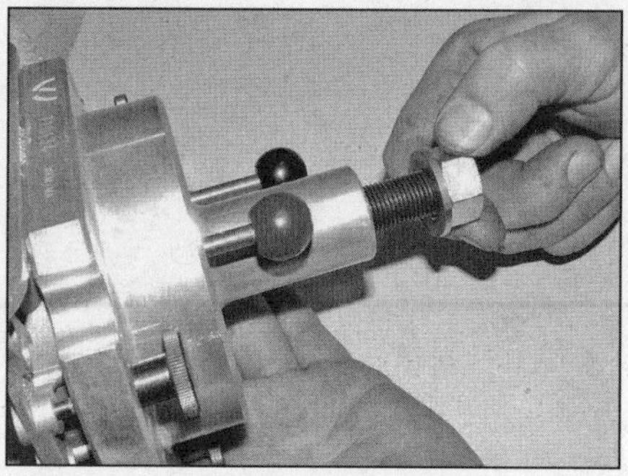

15.23a Unscrew the nut to the end of the thread...

15.23b ...and push the spindle in as far as possible

15.24 Hand-tighten the Allen bolts to secure the tool to the crankshaft

15.25 Use two M7 x 35 mm bolts to guide the sealing flange

15.26 Push the black knob into the hole in the crankshaft

sleeve against the tool whilst tightening the 3 knurled screws. Ensure the pin is still located in the sender wheel **(see illustration)**.

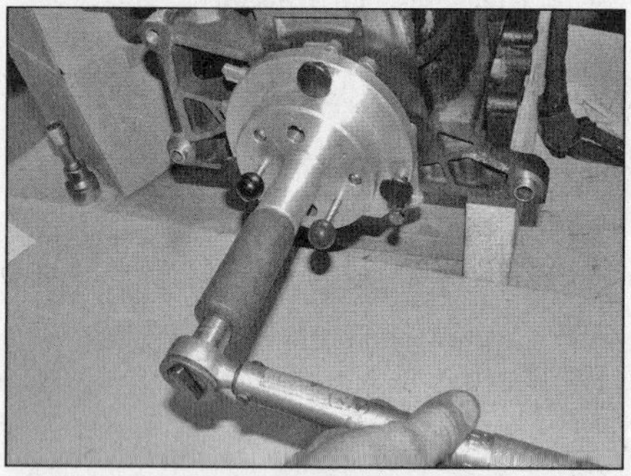

15.27a After tightening the spindle nut to 35 Nm...

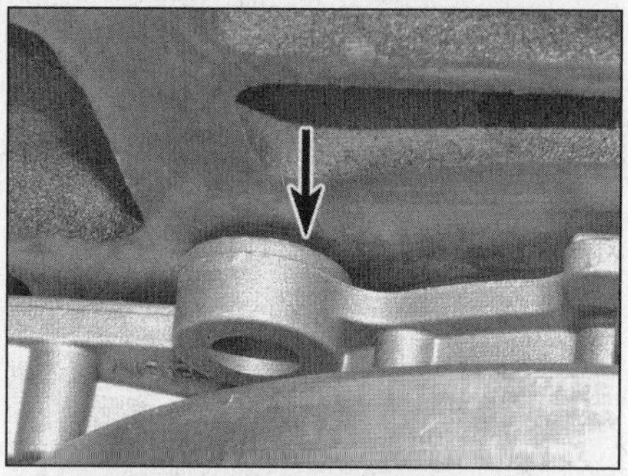

15.27b ...there should be an air gap between the sealing flange and the cylinder block (arrowed)

15.28 Remove the tool and seal fitting guide sleeve

15.29 Measure the fitted depth of the sender wheel in relation to the end of the crankshaft

22 Ensure the end of the crankshaft is clean, and is locked at TDC on No. 1 cylinder as described in Section 3.

23 Unscrew the large nut to the end of the spindle threads, then press the spindle inwards as far as possible **(see illustrations)**.

24 Align the flat side of the assembly with the sump flange, then secure the tool to the crankshaft using the integral Allen bolts **(see illustration)**. Only hand tighten the bolts.

25 Insert two M7x 35 mm bolts to guide the sealing flange to the cylinder block **(see illustration)**.

26 Using hand pressure alone, push the tool assembly onto the crankshaft until the seal guide fitting sleeve contacts the crankshaft flange, then push the guide pin (black knob) into the hole in the crankshaft. This is to ensure the sender wheel reaches its correct installation position **(see illustration)**.

27 Rotate the large nut until it makes contact with the tool housing, then tighten it to 35 Nm. After tightening this nut, a small air gap must still be present between the sealing flange and cylinder block **(see illustrations)**.

28 Unscrew the large nut; the two M7 x 35 Nm screws, the three knurled screws and the Allen bolts securing the tool to the crankshaft. Remove the tool, and pull the seal guide fitting sleeve from place (if it didn't come out with the tool) **(see illustration)**.

29 Use a vernier caliper or feeler gauge to measure the fitted depth of the sender wheel in relation to the crankshaft flange **(see illustration)**. The correct depth is 0.5 mm.

30 If the gap is correct, fit the sealing flange bolts and tighten them to the specified torque.

31 If the gap is too small, re-attach the tool to the sealing flange and crankshaft, then

17.4a Undo the engine oil cooler retaining screws

17.4b Renew the seals/gaskets

17.5a Disconnect the coolant hoses...

17.5b ...release the oil dipstick guide tube retaining clip...

17.5c ...and undo the filter housing retaining bolts

17.6 Renew the seals/gaskets

refit the two M7 x 35 mm guide bolts to the flange. Tighten the large spindle nut to 40 Nm, remove the tool and re-measure the air gap. If the gap is still too small, re-attach the tool and tighten the spindle nut to 45 Nm. Re-measure the gap. When the gap is correct, refit the flange retaining bolts, and tighten them to the specified torque.

32 The remainder of refitting is a reversal of removal.

16 Engine/transmission mountings – inspection and renewal

Inspection

1 If improved access is required, jack up the front of the vehicle, and support it securely on axle stands (see *Jacking and vehicle support*). Remove the engine top cover that also incorporates the air filter, and then remove the engine undershield(s).

2 Check the mounting rubbers to see if they are cracked, hardened or separated from the metal at any point; renew the mounting if any such damage or deterioration is evident.

3 Check that all the mountings are securely tightened; use a torque wrench to check if possible.

4 Using a large screwdriver or a crowbar, check for wear in the mounting by carefully levering against it to check for free play. Where this is not possible, enlist the aid of an assistant to move the engine/transmission back-and-forth, or from side-to-side, whilst you observe the mounting. While some free play is to be expected, even from new components, excessive wear should be obvious. If excessive free play is found, check first that the fasteners are correctly secured, and then renew any worn components as described in the following paragraphs.

Caution: Do NOT undo the centre bolt, securing the bracket to the flexible mounting.

5 When working on the right-hand mounting and rear lower mounting (torque arm), remove the mounting as a complete unit. Seat state that the mounting bracket-to-flexible mounting nut/bolt should not be slackened, see following procedures for each individual mounting.

Renewal

6 The engine mountings on the 1.6 litre engine are similar to those fitted on the 1.0 litre petrol model, see Chapter 2A Section 20, for the removal and refitting procedures of the engine mountings.

17 Engine oil cooler/ filter housing – removal and refitting

Removal

1 The oil cooler is mounted on the lower part of the oil filter housing on the front of the cylinder block.

2 Position a container beneath the oil filter housing to catch escaping oil and coolant.

3 Clamp the oil cooler coolant hoses to minimise coolant spillage, or drain the cooling system as described in Chapter 1B Section 33.

4 Unscrew the oil cooler retaining screws and remove the oil cooler from the front of the oil filter housing **(see illustrations)**. Recover the O-rings from between the cooler and the oil filter housing, new ones will be required for refitting.

5 If required, disconnect the coolant hose, unclip the dipstick from the side of the housing, then undo the retaining bolts and remove the oil filter housing from the cylinder block **(see illustrations)**.

Refitting

6 Refitting is a reversal of removal, bearing in mind the following points:

*a) Use new oil cooler and housing O-rings **(see illustration)**.*

b) Tighten the oil cooler and filter housing bolts to the correct torque.

c) On completion, check and if necessary top-up the oil and coolant levels.

18 Oil pressure warning light switch – removal and refitting

Removal

1 The oil pressure warning light switch is fitted to the left-hand rear of the cylinder head **(see illustration)**. Remove the engine top cover to gain access to the switch.

2 Slacken the retraining clips and remove the

18.1 Oil pressure warning light switch location

air intake hose from the turbocharger to the air cleaner housing.

3 Disconnect the wiring connector and wipe clean the area around the switch.

4 Unscrew the switch and remove it, along with its sealing washer (where fitted). If the switch is to be left removed from the engine for any length of time, plug the aperture in the cylinder head.

Refitting

5 Examine the sealing washer for signs of damage or deterioration and if necessary renew.

6 Refit the switch, complete with washer (where fitted), and tighten it to the specified torque.

7 Securely reconnect the wiring connector, refit the air intake hose and then, if necessary, top-up the engine oil as described in *Weekly checks*. On completion, refit the engine top cover.

19 Oil level/temperature sender – removal and refitting

Removal

1 The oil level/temperature sender is fitted to bottom of the sump **(see illustration)**.

2 Drain the engine oil as described in Chapter 1B Section 7.

3 Disconnect the wiring connector from the sender.

4 Release the retaining clips and remove the insulation cover from the sump **(see illustration 12.7)**.

5 Wipe clean the area around the sender, then undo the three retaining bolts and remove the sender.

19.1 Oil level/temperature sensor location

Refitting

6 Examine the sealing washer for signs of damage or deterioration and if necessary renew.

7 Refit the switch and tighten the retaining bolts to the specified torque.

8 Refit the insulation cover, then reconnect the wiring connector and refill the engine with oil (refer to Chapter 1B Section 7).

9 On completion, check and, if necessary, top-up the engine oil as described in *Weekly checks*.

Chapter 2 Part F
Engine removal and overhaul procedures

Contents

Degrees of difficulty

Easy, suitable for novice with little experience	Fairly easy, suitable for beginner with some experience	Fairly difficult, suitable for competent DIY mechanic	Difficult, suitable for experienced DIY mechanic	Very difficult, suitable for expert DIY or professional

Specifications

Engine codes*

1.0 litre engines	CHYB, CHZC and CHZB
1.2 litre petrol engines:	
SOHC	CBZB
DOHC	CJZD and CJZC
1.4 litre petrol engine	BXW and CGGB
1.6 litre diesel engine	CAYC and CLNA

**See 'Vehicle identification' at the end of this manual for the location of the engine code markings.*

Cylinder head

Minimum permissible dimension between the top of the valve stem and the top surface of the cylinder head:	
1.0 litre engines	N/A
1.2 litre engines	N/A
1.4 litre engines:	
Inlet valves	7.6 mm
Exhaust valves	7.6 mm
Minimum cylinder head height:	
Petrol engines:	
1.0 litre engines	N/A
1.2 litre engines	N/A
1.4 litre engines	108.25 mm
Diesel engines	No reworking permitted
Maximum cylinder head gasket face distortion:	
Petrol engines	0.05 mm
Diesel engines	0.10 mm

Valves

Valve stem diameter:	**Inlet**	**Exhaust**
Petrol engines:		
1.0 litre	4.973 mm	4.963 mm
1.2 litre:		
Engine code CJZD and CJZC	4.973 mm	4.963 mm
Engine code CBZB	5.98 mm	5.96 mm
1.4 litre	5.973 mm	5.953 mm
Diesel engines	5.968 to 5.982 mm	5.958 to 5.972 mm
Valve head diameter:		
Petrol engines:		
1.0 litre	28.5 mm	25.0 mm
1.2 litre:		
Engine code CJZD and CJZC	26.5 mm	23.5 mm
Engine code CBZB	35.5 mm	30.0 mm
1.4 litre	29.5 mm	26.0 mm
Diesel engines	26.50 to 26.70 mm	24.40 to 24.60 mm
Valve length:		
Petrol engines:		
1.0 litre	110.25 mm	110.09 mm
1.2 litre:		
Engine code CJZD and CJZC	110.25 mm	110.09 mm
Engine code CBZB	98.67 mm	98.36 mm
1.4 litre	100.9 mm	100.5 mm
Diesel engines	99.30 mm	99.10 mm
Valve seat angle 1.0 litre engines	45°	30°
Valve seat angle 1.2 litre engines (CJZD and CJZC)	45°	30°
Valve seat angle 1.2 litre engines (CBZB)	44°50'	44°50'
Valve seat angle (all other engines)	45°	45°

Camshaft

Petrol engines:	
Endfloat (axial clearance) – maximum wear limit	0.20 mm
Diesel engines:	
Endfloat (axial clearance):	
New	0.048 to 0.118 mm
Wear limit	0.17 mm
Bearing running (radial) clearances	0.035 to 0.085 mm

Crankshaft

Petrol engines	See Note in Section 2
Diesel engines:	
Main journal diameter	54.00 mm (Nominal)
Big-end journal diameter	47.80 mm (Nominal)
Endfloat (axial clearance):	
New	0.07 to 0.17 mm
Wear limit	0.37 mm
Main bearing running (radial) clearances:	
New	0.03 to 0.08 mm
Wear limit	0.17 mm
Big-end bearing running (radial) clearance	0.03 to 0.08 mm

Pistons/connecting rods

Connecting rod side-play on crankshaft journal:	**New**	**Wear limit**
Petrol engines:		
1.0 and 1.2 litre	See Note in Section 2	
1.4 litre	0.10 to 0.35 mm	0.40 mm
Diesel engines	N/A	0.37 mm
Piston and cylinder bore diameters	**Piston**	**Cylinder bore**
Petrol engines:		
1.0 litre	74.454 mm	74.505 mm
1.2 litre	See Note in Section 2	
1.4 litre:		
Standard	76.470 mm	76.510 mm
1st oversize	76.720 mm	76.760 mm
2nd oversize	76.970 mm	77.010 mm
Diesel engines:		
1.6 litre (Standard)	79.455 mm	79.50 mm

Piston rings

	New	Wear limit
End gaps:		
Petrol engines:		
1.0 litre:		
Top compression ring	0.20 to 0.35 mm	1.0 mm
Lower compression ring	0.40 to 0.60 mm	1.0 mm
Oil scraper ring	0.20 mm to 0.90 mm	N/A
1.2 litre	See Note in Section 2	
1.4 litre:		
Top compression ring	0.20 to 0.50 mm	1.0 mm
Lower compression ring	0.40 to 0.70 mm	1.0 mm
Oil scraper ring	0.40 to 1.40 mm	N/A
Diesel engines:		
Compression rings	0.20 to 0.40 mm	1.0 mm
Oil scraper ring	0.25 to 0.50 mm	1.0 mm
Ring-to-groove clearance:		
Petrol engines:		
1.0 litre:		
Top compression ring	0.04 to 0.08 mm	0.15 mm
Lower compression ring	0.02 to 0.06 mm	0.15 mm
Oil scraper ring	Not measurable	
1.2 litre	See Note in Section 2	
1.4 litre:		
Compression rings	0.04 to 0.08 mm	0.15 mm
Oil scraper ring	N/A	N/A
Diesel engines:		
1st compression ring	0.06 to 0.09 mm	0.25 mm
2nd compression ring	0.05 to 0.08 mm	0.25 mm
Oil scraper ring	0.03 to 0.06 mm	0.15 mm

Torque wrench settings

Refer to Chapter 2A, 2B, 2C, 2D or 2E as applicable.

1 General Information

1 Included in this Part of Chapter 2 are details of removing the engine from the car and general overhaul procedures for the cylinder head, cylinder block and all other engine internal components.

2 The information given ranges from advice concerning preparation for an overhaul and the purchase of new parts, to detailed step-by-step procedures covering removal, inspection, renovation and refitting of engine internal components.

3 After Section 6, all instructions are based on the assumption that the engine has been removed from the car. For information concerning in-car engine repair, as well as the removal and refitting of those external components necessary for full overhaul, refer to the relevant in-car repair procedure section in the appropriate Chapter and to Section 6 of this Chapter. Ignore any preliminary dismantling operations described in the relevant in-car repair sections that are no longer relevant once the engine has been removed from the car.

4 Apart from torque wrench settings, which are given at the beginning of the relevant in-car repair procedure in Chapter, all specifications relating to engine overhaul are given at the beginning of this part of Chapter 2.

2 Engine overhaul – general information

1 On all petrol engines, the crankshaft must not be removed. Loosening the main bearing cap bolts will cause deformation of the cylinder block. If the crankshaft or main bearing surfaces are worn or damaged, the complete crankshaft/cylinder block assembly must be renewed.

2 It is not always easy to determine when, or if, an engine should be completely overhauled, as a number of factors must be considered.

3 High mileage is not necessarily an indication that an overhaul is needed, while low mileage does not preclude the need for an overhaul. Frequency of servicing is probably the most important consideration. An engine, which has had regular and frequent oil and filter changes, as well as other required maintenance, should give many thousands of miles of reliable service. Conversely, a neglected engine may require an overhaul very early in its life.

4 Excessive oil consumption is an indication that piston rings, valve seals and/or valve guides are in need of attention. Make sure that oil leaks are not responsible before deciding that the rings and/or guides are worn. Perform a compression (or leakdown) test, as described in Chapter 2A Section 2, Chapter 2B Section 2, Chapter 2C Section 2, Chapter 2D Section 2 or Chapter 2E Section 2 (as applicable), to determine the likely cause of the problem.

5 Check the oil pressure with a gauge fitted in place of the oil pressure switch, and compare it with that specified. If it's extremely low, the main and big-end bearings, and/or the oil pump, are probably worn.

6 Loss of power, rough running, knocking or metallic engine noises, excessive valve gear noise, and high fuel consumption may also point to the need for an overhaul, especially if they are all present at the same time. If a complete service does not remedy the situation, major mechanical work is the only solution.

7 An engine overhaul involves restoring all internal parts to the specification of a new engine. During an overhaul, the pistons and the piston rings are renewed. New main and big-end bearings are generally fitted (where possible); if necessary, the crankshaft may be renewed to restore the journals. The valves are also serviced as well, since they are usually in less-than-perfect condition at this point. While the engine is being overhauled, other components, such as the starter and alternator, can be overhauled as well. The end result should be an as-new engine that will give many trouble-free miles. **Note:** *Critical cooling system components such as the hoses, thermostat and coolant pump should be renewed when an engine is overhauled. The radiator should be checked carefully, to ensure that it is not clogged or leaking. Also, it* *is a good idea to renew the oil pump whenever the engine is overhauled.*

8 Before beginning the engine overhaul, read through the entire procedure, to familiarise yourself with the scope and requirements of the job. Overhauling an engine is not difficult if you follow carefully all of the instructions, have the necessary tools and equipment, and pay close attention to all specifications. It can, however, be time-consuming. Plan on the car being off the road for a minimum of two weeks, especially if parts must be taken to an engineering works for repair or reconditioning. Check on the availability of parts and make sure that any necessary special tools and equipment are obtained in advance. Most work can be done with typical hand tools, although a number of precision measuring tools are required for inspecting parts to determine if they must be renewed. Often an engineering works will handle the inspection of parts and offer advice concerning reconditioning and renewal. **Note:** *Always wait until the engine has been completely dismantled, and until all components (especially the cylinder block and the crankshaft) have been inspected, before deciding what service and repair operations must be performed by an engineering works. The condition of these components will be the major factor to consider when determining whether to overhaul the original engine, or to buy a reconditioned unit. Do not, therefore, purchase parts or have overhaul work done on other components until they have been thoroughly inspected.* As a general rule, time is the primary cost of an overhaul, so it does not pay to fit worn or sub-standard parts.

9 As a final note, to ensure maximum life and minimum trouble from a reconditioned engine, everything must be assembled with care, in a spotlessly clean environment.

3 Engine/transmission removal – preparation and precautions

1 If you have decided that the engine must be removed for overhaul or major repair work, several preliminary steps should be taken.

2 Locating a suitable place to work is extremely important. Adequate workspace, along with storage space for the vehicle, will be needed. If a workshop or garage is not available, at the very least a solid, level, clean work surface is required.

3 If possible, clear some shelving close to the work area and use it to store the engine components and ancillaries as they are removed and dismantled. In this manner, the components stand a better chance of staying clean and undamaged during the overhaul. Laying out components in groups, together with their fixings bolts, screws, etc, will save time and avoid confusion when the engine is refitted.

4 Clean the engine compartment and engine before beginning the removal procedure; this will help visibility and help to keep tools clean.

5 The help of an assistant is essential; there are certain instances when one person cannot safely perform all of the operations required to remove the engine from the vehicle. Safety is of primary importance, considering the potential hazards involved in this kind of operation. A second person should always be in attendance to offer help in an emergency. If this is the first time you have removed an engine, advice and aid from someone more experienced would also be beneficial.

6 Plan the operation ahead of time. Before starting work, obtain (or arrange for the hire of) all of the tools and equipment you will need. Access to the following items will allow the task of removing and refitting the engine to be completed safely and with relative ease: a hoist and lifting tackle – rated in excess of the weight of the engine, complete sets of spanners and sockets as described at the rear of this manual, wooden blocks, and plenty of rags and cleaning solvent for mopping-up spilled oil, coolant and fuel. A selection of different-sized plastic storage bins will also prove useful for keeping dismantled components grouped together. If any of the equipment must be hired, make sure that you arrange for it in advance, and perform all of the operations possible without it beforehand; this may save you time and money.

7 Plan on the vehicle being out of use for quite a while, especially if you intend to carry out an engine overhaul. Read through the whole of this Section and work out a strategy based on your own experience, and the tools, time and workspace available to you. Some of the overhaul processes may have to be carried out by a Seat dealer or an engineering works – these establishments often have busy schedules, so it would be prudent to consult them before removing or dismantling the engine, to get an idea of the amount of time required to carry out the work.

8 When removing the engine from the vehicle, be methodical about the disconnection of external components. Labelling cables and hoses as they are removed will greatly assist the refitting process.

9 Always be extremely careful when lifting the engine from the engine compartment. Serious injury can result from careless actions. If help is required, it is better to wait until it is available rather than risk personal injury and/or damage to components by continuing alone. By planning ahead and taking your time, a job of this nature, although major, can be accomplished successfully and without incident.

4 Engine and transmission – removal and refitting

Removal

1 For the home mechanic the easiest way to remove the engine and transmission assembly is by completely removing the front lock carrier panel and dragging the assembly out of the front of the engine bay. On models with air conditioning the AC system must be de-gassed (by an air conditioning specialist) before removing the panel. Alternatively the engine and transmission can be removed by lowering it from the engine bay. However this approach still requires the lock carrier moving to the service position (as described in Chapter 11 Section 8), so it may as well be removed completely.

2 Remove the battery and battery tray, as described in Chapter 5A Section 3.

3 Remove the engine top cover and air filter assembly (Chapter 4A Section 3 or Chapter 4B Section 3) and all associated air ducting.

4 Apply the handbrake, then jack up the front of the vehicle and support it on axle stands (see *Jacking and vehicle support*). Remove both front roadwheels.

5 Drain the cooling system as described in Chapter 1A Section 32 or Chapter 1B Section 33.

6 Remove the front bumper, as described in Chapter 11 Section 6.

7 Remove the lock carrier as described in Chapter 11 Section 8.

Caution: Have the air conditioning system discharged by a suitably qualified specialist. It is a criminal offence to knowingly discharge the refrigerant to the atmosphere.

8 Noting their locations, disconnect all wiring, coolant hoses, vacuum hoses and fuel lines from the engine/transmission, with reference to the relevant Chapters of this Manual. Alternatively, the engine wiring loom may remain on the engine by disconnecting it from the left-hand side rear of the engine compartment, and removing the engine management ECU (Chapter 4A Section 4 or Chapter 4B Section 4) located on the bulkhead. Tape over or plug fuel lines to prevent entry of dust and dirt.

9 Remove the front exhaust pipe with reference to Chapter 4C Section 8 or Chapter 4D Section 9. On models where the catalytic converter is close to the turbocharger, disconnect the converter for the turbocharger and leave the converter (and exhaust system) in place.

10 Unbolt the rear engine pendulum arm from the transmission **(see illustration)**.

4.10 Remove the rear mounting

11 Disconnect the gearchange mechanism with reference to Chapter 7A Section 2 (manual transmission) or Chapter 7B Section 4 (DSG transmission) **(see illustration)**.

12 On manual transmission models, remove the clutch slave cylinder. **Note:** *Do not depress the clutch pedal once the slave cylinder has been removed.*

13 If the lock carrier panel is to be left in place then unbolt the AC compressor (refer to Chapter 3 Section 10) from the front of the engine, without disconnecting the refrigerant lines. Suspend the compressor to one side of the engine compartment.

14 Refer to Chapter 8 Section 2, and disconnect the driveshafts from the transmission drive flanges. Suspend them from the underbody **(see illustration)**. Alternatively remove them completely.

15 Also unbolt the coolant expansion tank and place to one side.

16 Connect a hoist and lifting tackle to the engine lifting brackets on the cylinder head **(see illustration)**, and raise the hoist to just take the weight of the engine/transmission.

17 Unbolt the right- and left-hand engine mountings with reference to Chapter 2A Section 20, Chapter 2B Section 17, Section, Chapter 2D Section 19 or Chapter 2E Section 16.

18 Make a final check to ensure that all relevant wiring, hoses and pipes have been disconnected, then carefully swivel the engine/transmission assembly away from the sides of the engine compartment, lift it upwards or lower it and withdraw forwards from the front of the car.

Separation

Engine and manual transmission

19 Remove the starter motor (Chapter 5A Section 8).

20 Where applicable, unscrew the bolt securing the small engine-to-transmission plate to the transmission.

21 Ensure that both engine and transmission are adequately supported, and then unscrew the remaining engine-to-transmission bolts, noting the location of each bolt, and the locations of any brackets secured by the bolts.

22 Carefully withdraw the transmission from the engine, ensuring that the weight of the transmission is not allowed to hang on the input shaft while it is engaged with the clutch friction disc. Recover the engine-to-transmission plate.

Engine and DSG (dual clutch) transmission

23 Remove the starter motor (Chapter 5A Section 8).

24 Disconnect the coolant hoses from the gearbox oil cooler. Plug the openings to prevent contamination.

25 Disconnect the wiring harness between the engine and gearbox, and move to one side.

26 Ensure that both engine and transmission are adequately supported, and then unscrew the engine-to-transmission bolts, noting the location of each bolt, and the locations of any brackets secured by the bolts.

4.11 Disconnect the gearchange cables

27 Carefully withdraw the transmission from the engine (take care – the transmission is heavy).

Reconnection and refitting

Engine and manual transmission

28 Reconnection and refitting are a reversal of removal, bearing in mind the following points:

a) *Smear the splines of the transmission input shaft with a little high melting-point grease.*
b) *Ensure that any brackets noted before removal are in place on the engine-to-transmission bolts.*
c) *Tighten all fixings to the specified torque, where given.*
d) *Where applicable, have the air conditioning system recharged with refrigerant by a suitably qualified professional.*
e) *Ensure that all wiring, hoses and pipes are correctly reconnected and routed as noted before removal.*
f) *Ensure that the fuel lines are correctly reconnected.*
g) *On completion, refill the cooling system as described in Chapter 1A Section 32 or Chapter 1B Section 33.*
h) *Have the engine management system checked for fault codes by a Seat dealer.*

Engine and DSG (dual clutch) transmission

29 Reconnection and refitting are a reversal of removal, bearing in mind the following points:

4.16 The engine and transmission securely supported on the lifting eyes

4.14 Suspend the driveshafts clear of the transmission

a) *When fitting the torque converter (where applicable), make sure that both the drive pins engage with the transmission fluid pump.*
b) *On completion, check and if necessary top-up the transmission fluid level as described in Chapter 7B Section 6.*

5 Engine overhaul – preliminary information

1 It is much easier to dismantle and work on the engine if it is mounted on a portable engine stand. These stands can often be hired from a tool hire shop. Before the engine is mounted on a stand, the flywheel should be removed, so that the stand bolts can be tightened into the end of the cylinder block/crankcase. **Note:** *Do not measure cylinder bore dimensions with the engine mounted on this type of stand.*

2 If a stand is not available, it is possible to dismantle the engine with it blocked up on a sturdy workbench, or on the floor. Be very careful not to tip or drop the engine when working without a stand.

3 If you intend to obtain a reconditioned engine, all ancillaries must be removed first, to be transferred to the new engine (just as they will if you are doing a complete engine overhaul yourself). These components include the following (it may be necessary to transfer additional components, such as the oil level dipstick/tube assembly, oil filter housing, etc, depending on which components are supplied with the reconditioned engine:

Petrol engines

a) *Alternator (including mounting brackets) and starter motor (Chapter 5A).*
b) *The ignition system components including all sensors and spark plugs (Chapter 1A Section 27 and Chapter 5B).*
c) *The fuel injection system components (Chapter 4A Section 4).*
d) *All electrical switches, actuators and sensors, and the engine wiring harness (Chapter 4A Section 4).*
e) *Inlet and exhaust manifolds (Chapter 4A Section 9 and Chapter 4C Section 6).*

f) Engine mountings (Chapter 2A Section 20, Chapter 2B Section 17, Section or Chapter 2D Section 19).
g) Clutch components (Chapter 6A Section 6).
h) Oil separator (where applicable).

Diesel engines

a) Alternator (including mounting brackets) and starter motor (Chapter 5A).
b) The glow plug/preheating system components (Chapter 5C).
c) All fuel system components, including the fuel injection pump, fuel injectors, all sensors and actuators (Chapter 4B).
d) The brake vacuum/tandem pump (Chapter 9 Section 24).
e) All electrical switches, actuators and sensors, and the engine wiring harness (Chapter 4B Section 4).
f) Inlet and exhaust manifolds, and turbocharger (Chapter 4B Section 6 and Chapter 4D Section 5).
g) Engine mountings (Chapter 2E Section 16).
h) Clutch components (Chapter 6A Section 6).

All engines

Note: *When removing the external components from the engine, pay close attention to details that may be helpful or important during refitting. Note the fitted position of gaskets, seals, spacers, pins, washers, bolts, and other small components.*

4 If you are obtaining a short engine (the engine cylinder block/crankcase, crankshaft, pistons and connecting rods, all fully assembled), then the cylinder head, sump, oil pump, timing belt(s) and chain (as applicable – together with tensioner(s) and covers), auxiliary drivebelt (together with its tensioner), coolant pump, thermostat housing, coolant outlet elbows, oil filter housing and where applicable oil cooler will also have to be removed.

5 If you are planning a full overhaul, the engine can be dismantled in the order given below:

a) Inlet and exhaust manifolds (see the relevant parts of Chapter 4A or Chapter 4B)
b) Timing chain/belt(s), sprockets and tensioner(s) (see Chapter 2A Section 6, Chapter 2B Section 6, Chapter 2C Section 7, Chapter 2D Section 6 or Chapter 2E Section 7).
c) Cylinder head (see Chapter 2A Section 12, Chapter 2B Section 10, Chapter 2C Section 12, Chapter 2D Section 12 or Chapter 2E Section 11).
d) Flywheel/driveplate (see Chapter 2A Section 19, Chapter 2B Section 16, Chapter 2C Section 15, Chapter 2D Section 18 or Chapter 2E Section 14).
e) Sump (see Chapter 2A Section 13, Chapter 2B Section 11, Chapter 2C Section 13, Chapter 2D Section 13 or Chapter 2E Section 12).
f) Oil pump (see Chapter 2A Section 14, Chapter 2B Section 12, Chapter 2C Section 14, Chapter 2D Section 14 or Chapter 2E Section 13).
g) Piston/connecting rod assemblies (see Section 9).
h) Crankshaft (see Section 10).

6 Cylinder head – dismantling

Note: *A valve spring compressor tool will be required for this operation.*

Petrol engines

1 With the cylinder head removed (as described in the relevant part of Chapter 2A Section 12, Chapter 2B Section 10, Chapter 2C Section 12 or Chapter 2D Section 12) proceed as follows.

2 Remove the inlet and exhaust manifolds as described in Chapter 4A Section 9 and Chapter 4C Section 7 or Chapter 4C Section 6.

3 Remove the camshaft(s) and hydraulic tappets/roller rocker fingers as described in Chapter 2A, Chapter 2B, Chapter 2C or Chapter 2D.

4 If desired, unbolt the coolant housing from the rear of the cylinder head, and recover the seal.

5 Where applicable, remove the camshaft position sensor, with reference to Chapter 4A Section 4.

6 Where applicable, unscrew the securing nut, and recover the washer, and remove the timing belt tensioner pulley from the stud on the cylinder head.

7 Unbolt any remaining auxiliary brackets and/or engine lifting brackets from the cylinder head as necessary, noting their locations to aid refitting. Where applicable, unscrew the securing bolt and remove the secondary timing belt tensioner from the timing belt end of the cylinder head.

8 Turn the cylinder head over, and rest it on one side.

9 Using a valve spring compressor, compress each valve spring in turn, until the split collets can be removed. Release the compressor, and lift off the spring cap and spring. If, when the valve spring compressor is screwed down, the spring cap refuses to free and expose the split collets, gently tap the top of the tool, directly over the spring cap, with a light hammer. This will free the retainer **(see illustrations)**.

10 Using a pair of pliers, or a removal tool, carefully extract the valve stem oil seal from the top of the valve guide **(see illustrations)**.

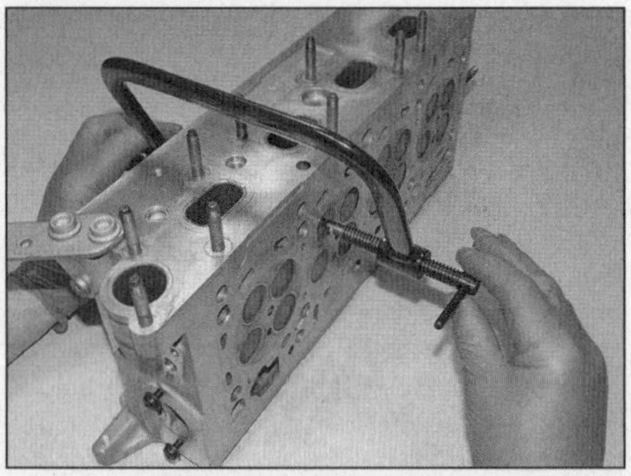

6.9a Compress a valve spring with a compressor tool

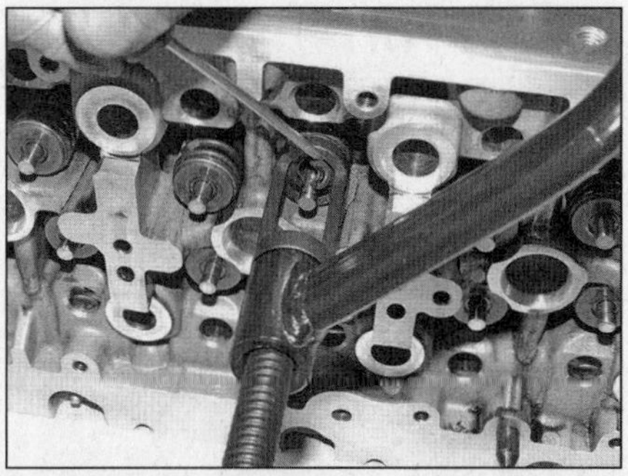

6.9b Remove the collets and release the spring compressor

6.9c Remove the spring cap...

6.9d ...and valve spring

6.10a The valve guide oil seals are removed...

11 Withdraw the valve from the gasket side of the cylinder head **(see illustration)**.

12 It is essential that each valve is stored together with its collets, cap, spring and spring seat. The valves should be kept in their correct sequences, unless they are so badly worn that they are to be renewed.

> **HAYNES HiNT** *If they are going to be kept and used again, place each valve assembly in a labelled polythene bag or similar small container. Label each bag, noting that No 1 valve is nearest to the timing belt/chain end of the cylinder head.*

Diesel engines

13 With the cylinder head removed as described in Chapter 2E Section 11, proceed as follows.

14 Remove the inlet and exhaust manifolds (and turbocharger, where applicable) as described in Chapter 4B Section 6 and Chapter 4D Section 5.

15 Remove the camshaft and hydraulic tappets, as described in Chapter 2E Section 9.

16 Remove the glow plugs, with reference to Chapter 5C Section 2.

17 Remove the fuel injectors, with reference to Chapter 4B Section 5.

18 Unscrew the nut and remove the timing belt tensioner pulley from the stud on the timing belt end of the cylinder head.

19 Unbolt any remaining auxiliary brackets and/or engine lifting brackets from the cylinder head as necessary, noting their locations to aid refitting.

20 Proceed as described in paragraphs 8 to 12.

7 Cylinder head and valves – cleaning and inspection

1 Thorough cleaning of the cylinder head and valve components, followed by a detailed inspection, will enable you to decide how much valve service work must be carried out during engine overhaul. **Note:** *If the engine has been severely overheated, it is best to assume that the cylinder head is warped – check carefully for signs of this.*

Cleaning

2 Using a suitable degreasing agent, remove all traces of oil deposits from the cylinder head, paying particular attention to the camshaft bearing surfaces, hydraulic tappet bores, valve guides and oilways. Scrape off any traces of old gasket from the mating surfaces, taking care not to score or gouge them. If using emery paper, do not use a grade of less than 100. Turn the head over and, using a blunt blade, scrape any carbon deposits from the combustion chambers and ports. Finally, wash the entire head

6.10b ...with special pliers

casting with a suitable solvent to remove the remaining debris.

3 Clean the valve heads and stems using a fine wire brush (or a power-operated wire brush). If the valve is covered with heavy carbon deposits, scrape off the majority of the deposits with a blunt blade first, then use the wire brush.

4 Thoroughly clean the remainder of the components using solvent and allow them to dry completely. Discard the oil seals, as new ones must be fitted when the cylinder head is reassembled.

Inspection

Cylinder head

Note: *If the valve seats are to be reground, ensure that the maximum permissible reworking dimension is not exceeded (the maximum dimension will only allow minimal reworking to produce a perfect seal between valve and seat). If the maximum dimension is exceeded, the function of the hydraulic tappets cannot be guaranteed, and the cylinder head must be renewed. Refer to paragraph 6 for details of how to calculate the maximum permissible reworking dimension.*

5 Examine the head casting closely to identify any damage or cracks that may have developed. Cracks can often be identified from evidence of coolant or oil leakage. Pay particular attention to the areas around the valve seats and spark plug/fuel injector holes. If cracking is discovered in this area, Seat state that, on diesel engines, the cylinder head may be re-used, provided the cracks

6.11 Removing a valve

are no larger than 0.5 mm wide. More serious damage will mean the renewal of the cylinder head casting.

6 Moderately pitted and scorched valve seats can be repaired by lapping the valves in during reassembly, as described later in this Chapter, however the maximum permissible reworking dimension **must** not be exceeded, which will only allow minimal reworking (see note at beginning of paragraph 5). Note that dimensions are only available for the 1.4 litre petrol engine. To calculate the maximum permissible reworking dimension, proceed as follows **(see illustration)** :

a) *If a new valve is to be fitted, use the new valve for the following calculation.*
b) *Insert the valve into its guide in the cylinder head, and push the valve firmly on to its seat.*
c) *Measure the distance between the top face of the valve stem, and either the top surface of the cylinder head or spring seat surface (as applicable). Record the measurement obtained.*
d) *Consult the Specifications, and compare the measured distance with that given in the Specifications.*

7 Measure any distortion of the gasket surfaces using a straight-edge and a set of feeler blades. Take one measurement longitudinally on the manifold mating surface(s). Take several measurements across the head gasket surface, to assess the level of distortion in all planes **(see illustration)**. Compare the measurements with the figures in the Specifications.

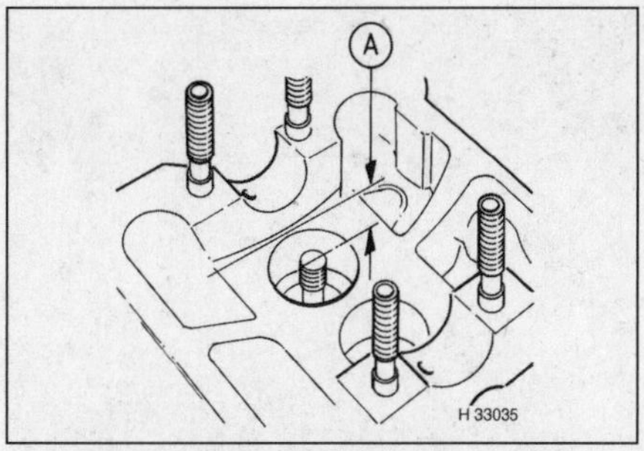

7.6 Measure the distance (A) between the top face of the valve stem and the top surface of the cylinder head

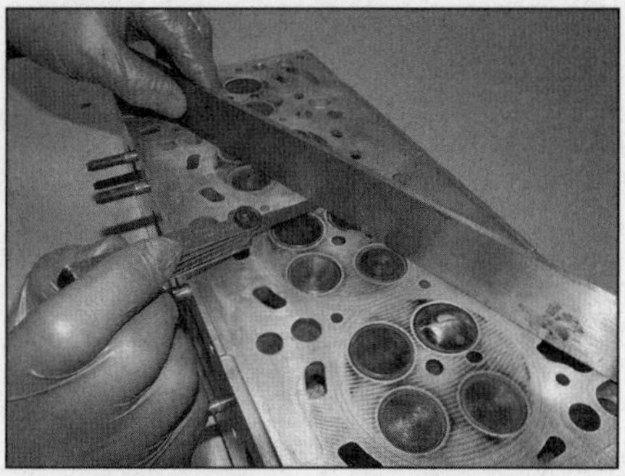

7.7 Measure the distortion of the cylinder head gasket surface

7.10 Measure the diameter of the valve stems using a micrometer

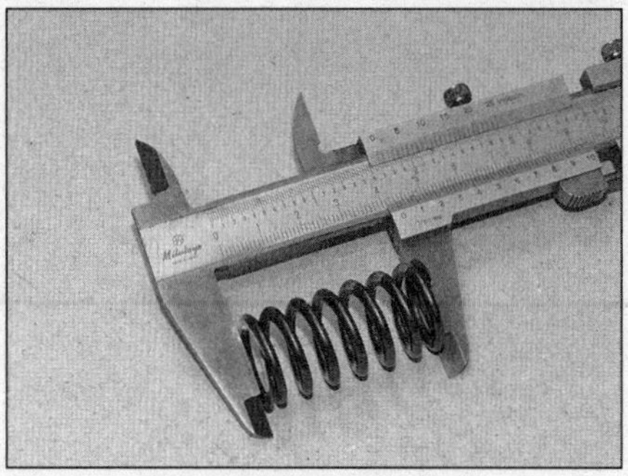

7.13 Measure the free length of each valve spring

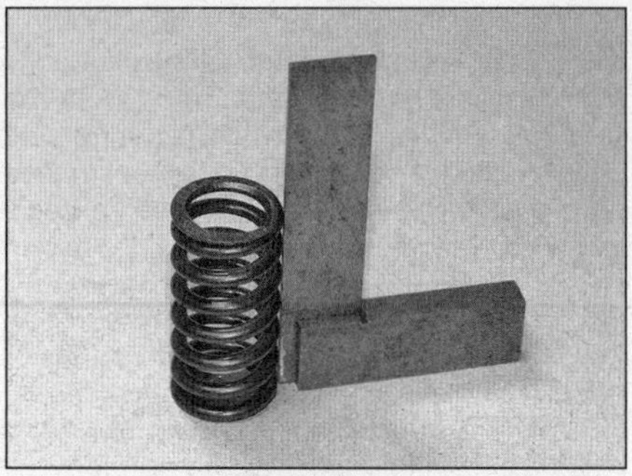

7.14 Check the squareness of a valve spring

8 On petrol engines, if the head is distorted beyond the specified limit, it may be possible to have it machined by an engineering works, provided that the minimum permissible cylinder head height is maintained.

9 On diesel engines, if the head is distorted beyond the specified limit, the head must be renewed.

Valves and associated components

Note: *On all engines, the valve heads cannot be recut, although they may be lapped in.*

10 Examine each valve closely for signs of wear. Inspect the valve stems for wear ridges, scoring or variations in diameter; measure their diameters at several points along their lengths with a micrometer, and compare with the figures given in the Specifications **(see illustration)**.

11 The valve heads should not be cracked, badly pitted or charred. Note that light pitting of the valve head can be rectified by lapping-in the valves during reassembly, as described in Section 8.

12 Check that the valve stem end face is free from excessive pitting or indentation; this could be caused by defective hydraulic tappets.

13 Using vernier calipers, measure the free length of each of the valve springs. As a manufacturer's figure is not quoted, the only way to check the length of the springs is by comparison with a new component. Note that valve springs are usually renewed during a major engine overhaul **(see illustration)**.

14 Stand each spring on its end on a flat surface, against an engineer's square **(see illustration)**. Check the squareness of the spring visually, and renew it if it appears distorted.

15 Renew the valve stem oil seals regardless of their apparent condition.

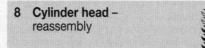

8 Cylinder head – reassembly

Note: *A valve spring compressor tool will be required for this operation.*

1 To achieve a gas-tight seal between the valves and their seats, it will be necessary to lap-in (or grind-in) the valves. To complete this process you will need a quantity of fine/coarse grinding paste and a grinding tool – this can either be of the rubber sucker type, or the automatic type which is driven by a rotary power tool.

2 Smear a small quantity of *fine* grinding paste on the sealing face of the valve head. Turn the cylinder head over so that the combustion chambers are facing upwards and insert the valve into the correct guide. Attach the grinding tool to the valve head and using a backward/forward rotary action, grind the valve head into its seat. Periodically lift the valve and rotate it to redistribute the grinding paste **(see illustration)**.

3 Continue this process until the contact between valve and seat produces an unbroken, matt grey ring of uniform width, on both faces. Repeat the operation on the remaining valves.

4 If the valves and seats are so badly pitted that coarse grinding paste must be used, bear in that there is a maximum permissible reworking dimension for the valves and seats. Refer to the Specifications at the beginning of this Chapter for the limits, and note that if exceeded due to excessive lapping-in, the hydraulic tappets may not operate correctly, and the cylinder head must be renewed.

5 Assuming the repair is feasible, work as described previously, but use coarse grinding paste initially, to achieve a dull finish on the valve face and seat. Wash off the coarse paste with solvent and repeat the process using fine grinding paste to obtain the correct finish.

6 When all the valves have been ground in, remove all traces of grinding paste from the cylinder head and valves using solvent, and allow the head and valves to dry completely.

7 Turn the cylinder head on its side.

8 Working on one valve at a time, lubricate the valve stem with clean engine oil, and insert the valve into its guide. Fit one of the protective plastic sleeves supplied with the new valve stem oil seals over the end of the valve stem – this will protect the oil seal as it is being fitted **(see illustrations)**.

9 Dip a new valve stem seal in clean engine oil, and carefully push it over the valve stem and onto the top of the valve guide – take care not to damage the stem seal as it is fitted. Use a suitable long-reach socket or a suitable valve stem seal fitting tool to press the seal firmly into position **(see illustration)**. Remove the protective sleeve from the valve stem.

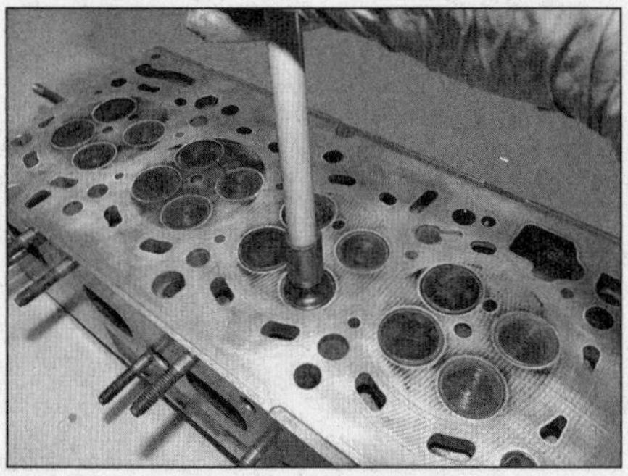

8.2 Grinding-in a valve

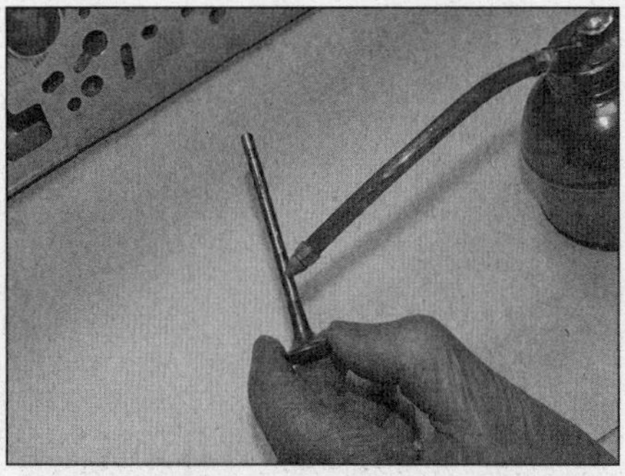

8.8a Lubricate the valve stem with clean engine oil

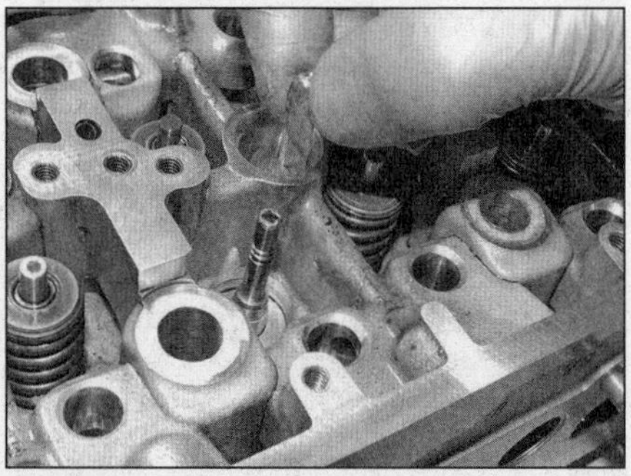

8.8b Fit a protective sleeve over the valve stem before fitting the stem seal

8.9 Use a long-reach socket to fit a valve stem oil seal

8.10 Fit a valve spring...

8.11a ...and upper spring seat ...

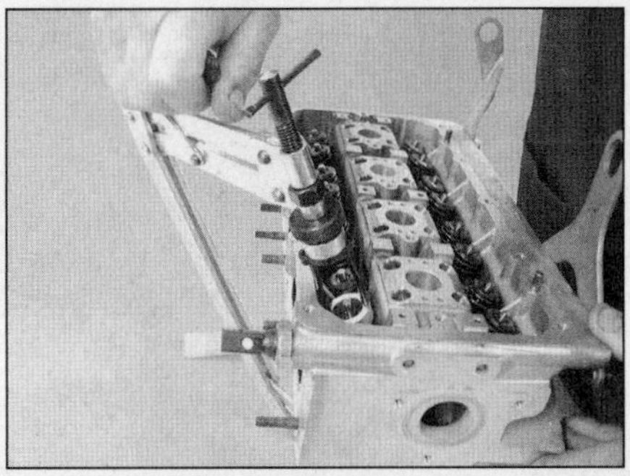

8.11b ... then compress a valve spring using a compressor tool

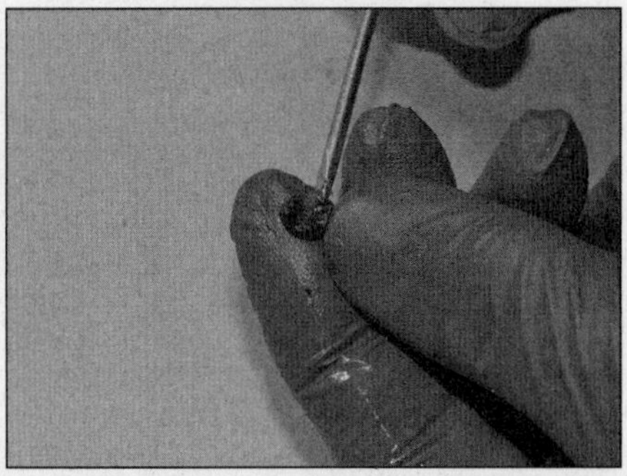

8.11c Use grease to hold the split collets in the groove

10 Locate the valve spring over the valve stem, ensuring that the lower end of the spring seats correctly on the cylinder head **(see illustration)**.

11 Fit the upper spring seat over the top of the spring then, using a valve spring compressor, compress the spring until the upper seat is pushed beyond the collet grooves in the valve stem. Refit the split collets. Gradually release the spring compressor, checking that the collets remain correctly seated as the spring extends. When correctly seated, the upper spring seat should force the collets securely into the grooves in the end of the valve stem **(see illustrations)**.

> **HAYNES HiNT** ***Use a little dab of grease to hold the collets in position on the valve stem while the spring compressor is released.***

12 Repeat this process for the remaining sets of valve components, ensuring that all components are refitted to their original locations. To settle the components after installation, strike the end of each valve stem with a mallet, using a block of wood to protect the stem from damage. Check before progressing any further that the split collets remain firmly seated in the grooves in the end of the valve stem.

Petrol engines

13 Refit the brackets previously removed, and also where applicable refit the secondary timing belt tensioner.

14 Where applicable, refit the timing belt tensioner pulley on the stud, and loosely refit the securing nut and washer.

15 Where applicable, refit the camshaft position sensor, with reference to Chapter 4A Section 4.

16 If removed, refit the coolant housing to the cylinder head, together with a new seal, and tighten the mounting bolts.

17 Refit the camshaft(s) and hydraulic tappets/roller rocker fingers with reference to Chapter 2A Section 9, Chapter 2B Section 8, Chapter 2C Section 4 or Chapter 2D Section 9.

18 Refit the inlet and exhaust manifolds with reference to Chapter 4A Section 9 and Chapter 4C Section 6.

Diesel engines

19 Refit the brackets previously removed, then refit the timing belt tensioner pulley on the stud, and loosely refit the securing nut and washer.

20 Refit the fuel injectors, with reference to Chapter 4B Section 5.

21 Refit the glow plugs, with reference to Chapter 5C Section 2.

22 Refit the camshaft and hydraulic tappets, with reference to Chapter 2E Section 9.

23 Refit the inlet and exhaust manifolds (and turbocharger, where applicable) with reference to Chapter 4B Section 6 and Chapter 4D Section 5.

9 Piston/connecting rod assemblies – removal

1 Remove the cylinder head, sump, oil baffle and oil pump pick-up pipe, as applicable, with reference to Chapter 2A, Chapter 2B, Chapter 2C, Chapter 2D or Chapter 2E.

2 Inspect the tops of the cylinder bores for ridges at the point where the pistons reach top dead centre. These must be removed otherwise, the pistons may be damaged when they are pushed out of their bores. Use a scraper or ridge reamer to remove the ridges. Such a ridge indicates excessive wear of the cylinder bore.

3 Check the connecting rods and big-end caps for identification markings. Both connecting rods and caps should be marked with the cylinder number on one side of each assembly. Note that No 1 cylinder is at the timing belt end of the engine. If no marks are present, using a hammer and centre-punch, paint or similar, mark each connecting rod and big-end bearing cap with its respective cylinder number – note on which side of the connecting rods and caps the marks are made **(see illustration)**.

4 Similarly, check the piston crowns for direction markings. An arrow on each piston crown should point towards the timing belt end of the engine. On some engines, this mark may be obscured by carbon build-up, in which case the piston crown should be cleaned to check for a mark. In some cases, the direction arrow may have worn off, in which case a suitable mark should be made on the piston crown using a scriber – do not

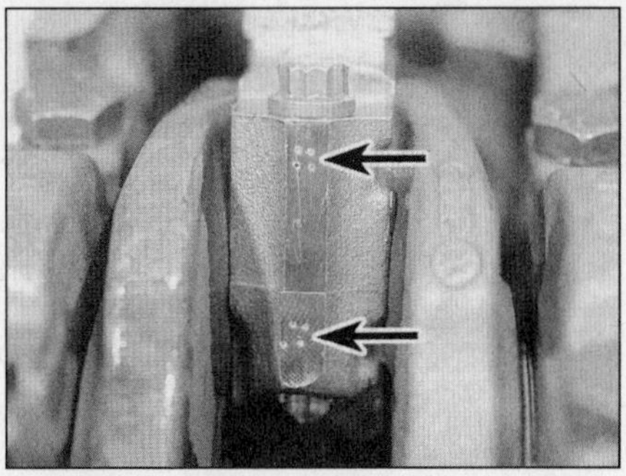

9.3 Mark the big-end caps and connecting rods with their cylinder numbers

9.6a Unscrew the big-end bearing cap bolts...

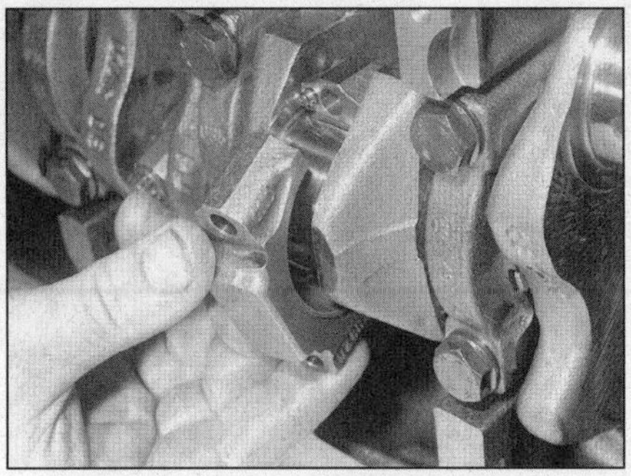

9.6b ...and remove the cap

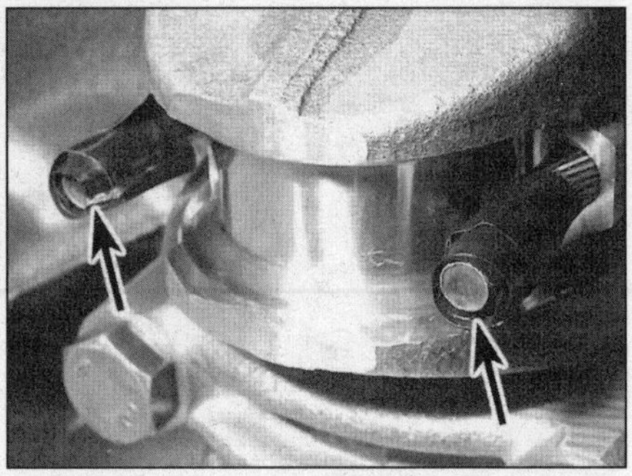

9.7 Wrap the threaded ends of the bolts with tape

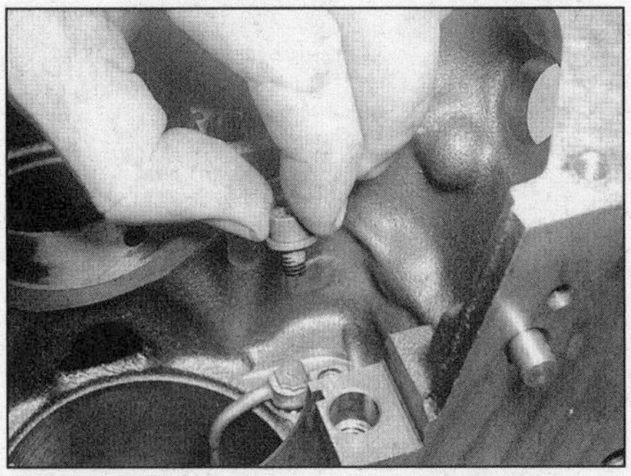

9.12a Remove the securing bolts...

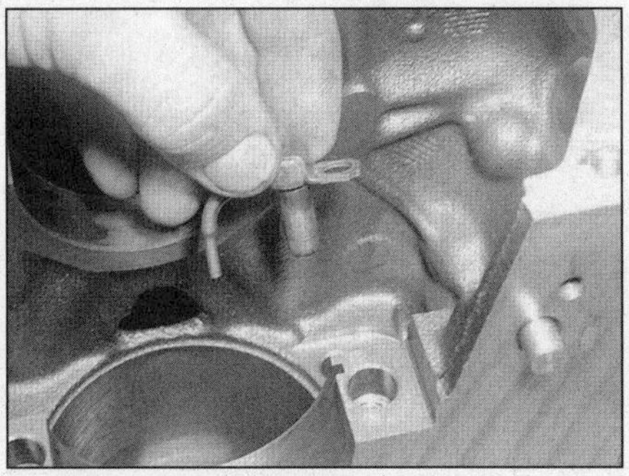

9.12b ...and withdraw the piston cooling oil spray jets

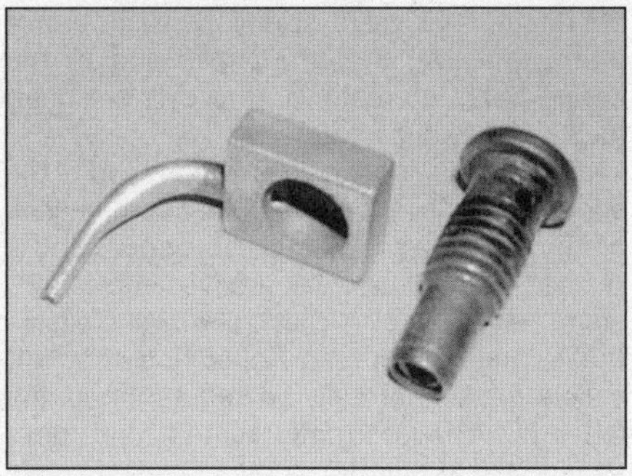

9.12c Piston cooling spray jet and retainer

deeply score the piston crown, but ensure that the mark is easily visible.

5 Turn the crankshaft to bring No 1 piston to bottom dead centre (on 4-cylinder engines, No 4 piston will also be at BDC).

6 Unscrew the bolts or nuts, as applicable, from No 1 piston big-end bearing cap. Lift off the cap, and recover the bottom half bearing shell. If the bearing shells are to be re-used, tape the cap and bearing shell together. Note that if the bearing shells are to be re-used, they must be fitted to the original connecting rod and cap **(see illustrations)**.

7 Where the bearing caps are secured with nuts, wrap the threaded ends of the bolts with insulating tape to prevent them scratching the crankpins and bores when the pistons are removed **(see illustration)**.

8 Using a hammer handle, push the piston up through the bore, and remove it from the top of the cylinder block. Where applicable, take care not to damage the piston cooling oil spray jets in the cylinder block as the piston/connecting rod assembly is removed. Recover the upper bearing shell, and tape it to the connecting rod for safe-keeping.

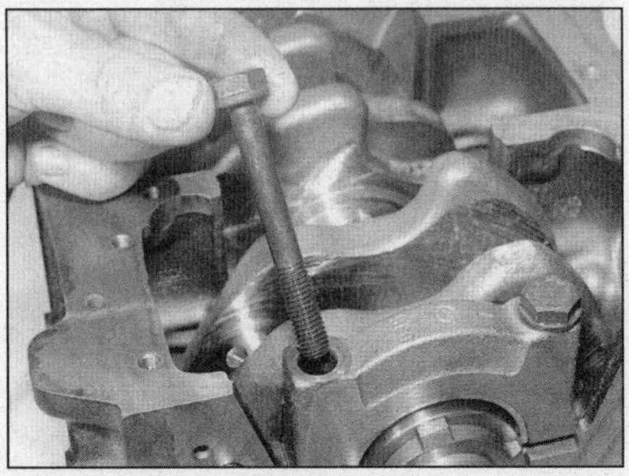

10.5 Slacken and remove the main bearing cap bolts

9 Loosely refit the big-end cap to the connecting rod, and secure with the bolts or nuts, as applicable – this will help to keep the components in their correct order.

10 On 4-cylinder engines, remove No 4 piston assembly in the same way.

11 Turn the crankshaft as necessary to bring No 2 piston to bottom dead centre, and remove them in the same way (on 4-cylinder engines, No 3 piston will also be at BDC).

12 Where applicable, remove the securing bolts, and withdraw the piston cooling oil spray jets from the bottom of the cylinder block **(see illustrations)**.

10 Crankshaft (diesel engines) – removal

Caution: On petrol engines, the crankshaft must not be removed. Loosening the main bearing cap bolts will cause deformation of the cylinder block. On these engines, if the crankshaft or main bearing surfaces are worn or damaged, the complete crankshaft/cylinder block assembly must be renewed. The following procedure only applies to diesel engines.

Note: *If no work is to be done on the pistons and connecting rods, there is no need to remove the cylinder head and push the pistons out of the cylinder bores. The pistons should just be pushed far enough up the bores so that they are positioned clear of the crankshaft journals.*

1 Remove the timing belt and crankshaft sprocket, sump and oil baffle plate, oil pump and pick-up pipe, flywheel, and the crankshaft oil seal housings, as described in Chapter 2E.

2 Remove the pistons and connecting rods, or disconnect them from the crankshaft, as described in Section 9.

3 Check the crankshaft endfloat as described in Section 13, then proceed as follows.

4 The main bearing caps should be numbered 1 to 5 from the timing belt end of the engine. If the bearing caps are not marked, mark them accordingly using a centre-punch. Note the orientation of the markings to ensure correct refitting.

5 Slacken and remove the main bearing cap bolts, and lift off each cap. If the caps appear to be stuck, tap them with a soft-faced mallet to free them from the cylinder block **(see illustration)**. Recover the lower bearing shells, and tape them to their caps for safe-keeping.

6 Lift the crankshaft from the cylinder block. Take care, as the crankshaft is heavy. On engines with a crankshaft speed/position sensor fitted, lay the crankshaft on wooden blocks – **do not** rest the crankshaft on the sensor wheel.

7 Recover the upper bearing shells from the cylinder block, and tape them to their respective caps for safe-keeping. Similarly, recover the upper crankshaft endfloat control thrustwasher halves from either side of No 3 main bearing, noting their orientation.

8 On engines with a crankshaft speed/position sensor wheel fitted, unscrew the securing bolts, and remove the sensor wheel, noting which way round it is fitted.

11 Cylinder block/crankcase – cleaning and inspection

Cleaning

1 Remove all external components and electrical switches/sensors from the block, including mounting brackets, the coolant pump, the oil filter/cooler housing, etc. For complete cleaning, the core plugs should ideally be removed. Drill a small hole in the plugs, and then insert a self-tapping screw into the hole. Extract the plugs by pulling on the screw with a pair of grips, or by using a slide hammer.

2 Scrape all traces of gasket and sealant from the cylinder block/crankcase, taking care not to damage the sealing surfaces.

3 Remove all oil gallery plugs (where fitted). The plugs are usually very tight – they may have to be drilled out, and the holes re-tapped. Use new plugs when the engine is reassembled.

4 If the casting is extremely dirty, it should be steam-cleaned. After this, clean all oil holes and galleries one more time. Flush all internal passages with warm water until the water runs clear. Dry thoroughly, and apply a light film of oil to all mating surfaces and cylinder bores, to prevent rusting. If you have access to compressed air, use it to speed up the drying process, and to blow out all the oil holes and galleries.

Warning: Wear eye protection when using compressed air.

5 If the castings are not very dirty, you can do an adequate cleaning job with hot, soapy water and a stiff brush. Take plenty of time, and do a thorough job. Regardless of the cleaning method used, be sure to clean all oil holes and galleries very thoroughly, and to dry all components well. Protect the cylinder bores as described above, to prevent rusting.

6 Where applicable, check the piston cooling oil spray jets for damage, and renew if necessary. Check the oil spray hole and the oil passages for blockage.

7 All threaded holes must be clean, to ensure accurate torque readings during reassembly. To clean the threads, run the correct-size tap into each of the holes to remove rust, corrosion, thread sealant or sludge, and to restore damaged threads **(see illustration)**. If possible, use compressed air to clear the holes free of debris produced by this operation. **Note:** *Take extra care to exclude all cleaning liquid from blind tapped holes, as the casting may be cracked by hydraulic action if a bolt is threaded into a hole containing liquid.*

HAYNES HiNT ***A good alternative is to inject aerosol-applied water dispersant lubricant into each hole, using the long spout usually supplied.***

8 After coating the mating surfaces of the new core plugs with suitable sealant, fit them to the cylinder block. Make sure that they are driven in straight and seated correctly, or leakage could result.

HAYNES HiNT ***A large socket with an outside diameter which will just fit into the core plug can be used to drive the core plug into position.***

9 Apply suitable sealant to the new oil gallery plugs, and insert them into the holes in the block. Tighten them securely.

10 If the engine is not going to be reassembled immediately, cover it with a large plastic bag to keep it clean; protect all mating surfaces and the cylinder bores, to prevent rusting.

Inspection

11 Visually check the castings for cracks and corrosion. Look for stripped threads in the threaded holes. If there has been any history of internal coolant leakage, it may be worthwhile having an engine overhaul specialist check the cylinder block/crankcase for cracks with special equipment. If defects are found, have them repaired, if possible, or renew the assembly.

12 Check each cylinder bore for scuffing and scoring.

13 If in any doubt as the condition of the cylinder block have the block/bores inspected and measured by an engine reconditioning specialist. They will be able to advise on whether the block is serviceable, whether a rebore is necessary, and supply the appropriate pistons and rings.

14 If the bores are in reasonably good condition and not excessively worn, then it may only be necessary to renew the piston rings.

15 If this is the case, the bores should be honed, to allow the new rings to bed-in correctly and provide the best possible seal. Consult an engine reconditioning specialist.

16 On diesel engines, if the oil filter/cooler housing was removed, it can be refitted at this stage if wished. Use a new gasket, and before fully tightening the bolts, align the housing faces with those of the engine block.

17 The cylinder block/crankcase should now be completely clean and dry, with all components checked for wear or damage, and repaired or overhauled as necessary.

18 Apply a light coating of engine oil to the mating surfaces and cylinder bores to prevent rust forming.

19 Refit as many ancillary components as possible, for safe-keeping. If reassembly is not to start immediately, cover the block with a large plastic bag to keep it clean, and protect the machined surfaces as described above to prevent rusting.

11.7 To clean the cylinder block threads, run a correct-size tap into the holes

12 Piston/connecting rod assemblies – cleaning and inspection

Cleaning

1 Before the inspection process can begin, the piston/connecting rod assemblies must be cleaned, and the original piston rings removed from the pistons.

2 The rings should have smooth, polished working surfaces, with no dull or carbon-coated sections (showing that the ring is not sealing correctly against the bore wall, so allowing combustion gases to blow-by) and no traces of wear on their top and bottom surfaces. The end gaps should be clear of carbon, but not polished (indicating a too-small end gap), and all the rings (including the elements of the oil control ring) should be free to rotate in their grooves, but without excessive up-and-down movement. If the rings appear to be in good condition, they are probably fit for further use; check the end gaps (in an unworn part of the bore) as described in Section 16.

3 If any of the rings appears to be worn or damaged, or has an end gap significantly different from the specified value, the usual course of action is to renew all of them as a set. **Note:** *While it is usual to renew piston rings when an engine is overhauled, they may be re-used if in acceptable condition. If re-using the rings, make sure that each ring is marked during removal to ensure that it is refitted correctly.*

4 Carefully expand the old rings over the top of the pistons. The use of two or three old feeler blades will be helpful in preventing the rings dropping into empty grooves **(see illustration)**. Be careful not to scratch the piston with the ends of the ring. The rings are brittle, and will snap if they are spread too far. They are also very sharp – protect your hands and fingers. Note that the third ring incorporates an expander. Keep each set of

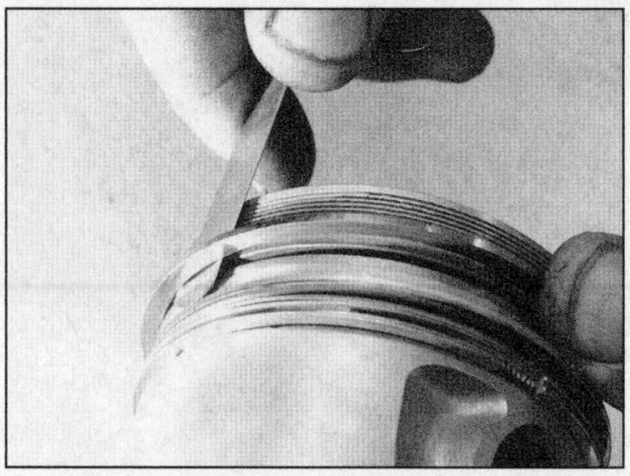

12.4 Old feeler blades can be used to prevent piston rings from dropping into empty grooves

rings with its piston if the old rings are to be re-used. Note which way up each ring is fitted to ensure correct refitting.

5 Scrape away all traces of carbon from the top of the piston. A hand-held wire brush (or a piece of fine emery cloth) can be used, once the majority of the deposits have been scraped away.

6 Remove the carbon from the ring grooves in the piston, using an old ring. Break the ring in half to do this (be careful not to cut your fingers – piston rings are sharp). Be careful to remove only the carbon deposits – do not remove any metal, and do not nick or scratch the sides of the ring grooves.

7 Once the deposits have been removed, clean the piston/connecting rod assembly with paraffin or a suitable solvent, and dry thoroughly. Make sure that the oil return holes in the ring grooves are clear.

Inspection

8 If the pistons and cylinder bores are not damaged or worn excessively, and if the cylinder block does not need to be rebored, the original pistons can be refitted.

9 Using a micrometer, measure the diameter of all four pistons at a point 10 mm from the bottom of the skirt, at right-angles to the gudgeon pin axis **(see illustration)**. Compare the measurements with those listed in the Specifications. Note that the piston size grades are stamped on the piston crowns.

10 If the piston diameter is incorrect for its particular size, then it must be renewed. **Note:** *If the cylinder block was rebored during a previous overhaul, oversize pistons may already have been fitted.* Record all of the measurements and use them to check the piston clearances against the cylinder bore measurements made in Section 11.

11 Normal piston wear shows up as even vertical wear on the piston thrust surfaces, and slight looseness of the top ring in its groove. New piston rings should always be used when the engine is reassembled.

12 Carefully inspect each piston for cracks around the skirt, around the gudgeon pin holes, and at the piston ring 'lands' (between the ring grooves).

13 Look for scoring and scuffing on the piston skirt, holes in the piston crown, and burned areas at the edge of the crown. If the skirt is scored or scuffed, the engine may have been suffering from overheating, and/or abnormal combustion that caused excessively high operating temperatures. The cooling and lubrication systems should be checked thoroughly.

14 Scorch marks on the sides of the pistons show that blow-by has occurred.

15 A hole in the piston crown, or burned areas at the edge of the piston crown, indicates that abnormal combustion (pre-ignition, knocking, or detonation) has been occurring.

16 If any of the above problems exist, the causes must be investigated and corrected, or the damage will occur again. The causes may include incorrect ignition/injection pump timing, inlet air leaks or incorrect air/fuel mixture (petrol engines), or a faulty fuel injector (diesel engines).

17 Corrosion of the piston, in the form of pitting, indicates that coolant has been leaking into the combustion chamber and/or the crankcase. Again, the cause must be corrected, or the problem may persist in the rebuilt engine.

18 Locate a new piston ring in the appropriate groove and measure the ring-to-groove clearance using a feeler blade **(see illustration)**. Note that the rings are of different widths, so use the correct ring for the groove. Compare the measurements with those listed; if the clearances are outside of the tolerance band, then the piston must be renewed. Confirm this by checking the width of the piston ring with a micrometer.

19 New pistons can be purchased from a Seat dealer.

20 Examine each connecting rod carefully for signs of damage, such as cracks around the big-end and small-end bearings. Check that the rod is not bent or distorted. Damage is highly unlikely, unless the engine has been seized or badly overheated. Detailed checking of the connecting rod assembly can only be carried out by a Seat dealer or engine repair specialist with the necessary equipment.

21 The gudgeon pins are of the floating type, secured in position by two circlips. The pistons and connecting rods can be separated as follows.

22 Using a small flat-bladed screwdriver, prise out the circlips, and push out the gudgeon pin **(see illustrations)**. Hand pressure should be sufficient to remove the pin. Identify the piston and rod to ensure correct reassembly. Discard the circlips – new ones *must* be used on refitting. If the gudgeon pin proves difficult to remove, heat the piston to 60°C with hot water – the resulting expansion will then allow the two components to be separated.

23 Examine the gudgeon pin and connecting rod small-end bearing for signs of wear or damage. It should be possible to push the gudgeon pin through the connecting rod bush by hand, without noticeable play. Wear can be cured by renewing both the pin and bush. Bush renewal, however, is a specialist job – press facilities are required, and the new bush must be reamed accurately.

24 Examine all components, and obtain any new parts from your Seat dealer. If new pistons are purchased, they will be supplied

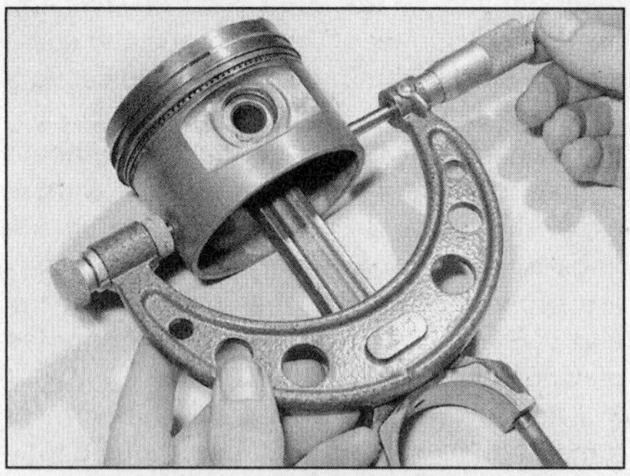

12.9 Using a micrometer to measure the diameter of a piston

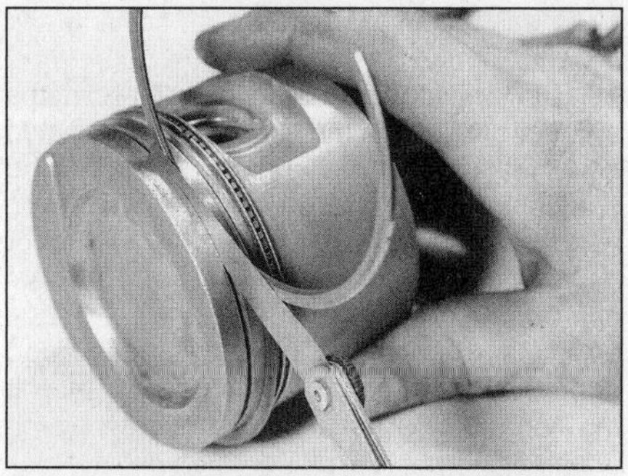

12.18 Measure the piston ring-to-groove clearance using a feeler blade

12.22a Use a small flat-bladed screwdriver to prise out the circlip...

12.22b ...then push out the gudgeon pin and separate the piston and connecting rod

complete with gudgeon pins and circlips. Circlips can also be purchased individually.

25 The orientation of the piston with respect to the connecting rod must be correct when the two are reassembled. The piston crown is marked with an arrow (which may be obscured by carbon deposits). The arrow must point towards the timing belt end of the engine when the piston is installed. The connecting rod and its bearing cap both have recesses machined into them on one side, close to their mating surfaces – these recesses must both face the same way as the arrow on the piston crown when correctly installed. Reassemble the two components to satisfy this requirement **(see illustrations)**.

12.25a The piston crown is marked with an arrow which must point towards the timing belt/chain end of the engine

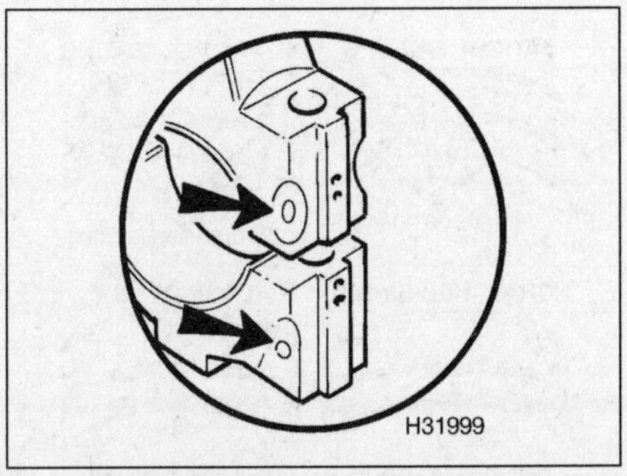

12.25b The recesses in the connecting rod and bearing cap must face the timing belt/chain end of the engine

26 Apply a smear of clean engine oil to the gudgeon pin. Slide it into the piston and through the connecting rod small-end. Check that the piston pivots freely on the rod, then secure the gudgeon pin in position with two new circlips. Ensure that each circlip is correctly located in its groove in the piston.

27 Repeat the cleaning and inspection process for the remaining pistons and connecting rods.

13 Crankshaft (diesel engines) – checking endfloat and inspection

Checking endfloat

1 If the crankshaft endfloat is to be checked, this must be done when the crankshaft is still installed in the cylinder block/crankcase, but is free to move (see Section 10).

2 Check the endfloat using a dial gauge in contact with the end of the crankshaft. Push the crankshaft fully one way, and then zero the gauge. Push the crankshaft fully the other way, and check the endfloat. The result can be compared with the specified amount, and will give an indication as to whether new thrustwasher halves are required **(see illustration)**. Note that all thrustwashers must be of the same thickness.

3 If a dial gauge is not available, feeler blades can be used. First push the crankshaft fully towards the flywheel end of the engine, and then use feeler blades to measure the gap between the web of No 3 crankpin and the thrustwasher halves **(see illustration)**.

13.2 Measure crankshaft endfloat using a dial gauge

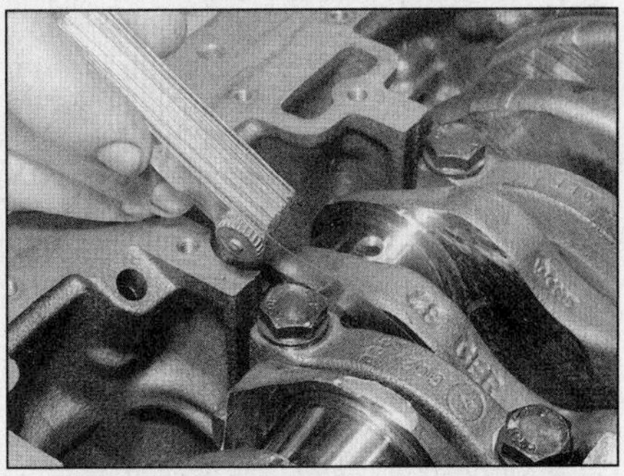

13.3 Measure crankshaft endfloat using feeler blades

Inspection

4 Clean the crankshaft using paraffin or a suitable solvent, and dry it, preferably with compressed air if available. Be sure to clean the oil holes with a pipe cleaner or similar probe, to ensure that they are not obstructed. ***Warning: Wear eye protection when using compressed air.***

5 Check the main and big-end bearing journals for uneven wear, scoring, pitting and cracking.

6 Big-end bearing wear is accompanied by distinct metallic knocking when the engine is running (particularly noticeable when the engine is pulling from low speed) and some loss of oil pressure.

7 Main bearing wear is accompanied by severe engine vibration and rumble – getting progressively worse as engine speed increases – and again by loss of oil pressure.

8 Check the bearing journal for roughness by running a finger lightly over the bearing surface. Any roughness (which will be accompanied by obvious bearing wear) indicates that the crankshaft requires regrinding (where possible) or renewal.

9 If the crankshaft has been reground, check for burrs around the crankshaft oil holes (the holes are usually chamfered, so burrs should not be a problem unless regrinding has been carried out carelessly). Remove any burrs with a fine file or scraper, and thoroughly clean the oil holes as described previously.

10 Using a micrometer, measure the diameter of the main and big-end bearing journals, and compare the results with the Specifications, where given. By measuring the diameter at a number of points around each journal's circumference, you will be able to determine whether or not the journal is out-of-round. Take the measurement at each end of the journal, near the webs, to determine if the journal is tapered.

11 Check the oil seal contact surfaces at each end of the crankshaft for wear and damage. If the seal has worn a deep groove in the surface of the crankshaft, consult an engine overhaul specialist; repair may be possible, but otherwise a new crankshaft will be required.

12 If the crankshaft journals have not already been reground, it may be possible to have the crankshaft reconditioned, and to fit oversize shells (see Section 17). If no oversize shells are available and the crankshaft has worn beyond the specified limits, it will have to be renewed. Consult your Seat dealer or engine specialist for further information on parts availability.

14 Main and big-end bearings – inspection

Inspection

1 Even though the main and big-end bearings should be renewed during the engine overhaul, the old bearings should be retained for close examination, as they may reveal valuable information about the condition of the engine **(see illustration)**.

2 Bearing failure can occur due to lack of lubrication, the presence of dirt or other foreign particles, overloading the engine, or corrosion. Regardless of the cause of bearing failure, the cause must be corrected before the engine is reassembled, to prevent it from happening again.

3 When examining the bearing shells, remove them from the cylinder block/crankcase, the main bearing caps, the connecting rods

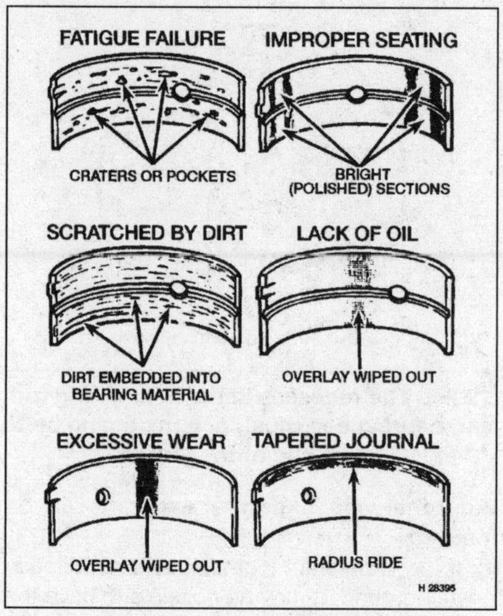

14.1 Typical bearing failures

and the connecting rod big-end bearing caps. Lay them out on a clean surface in the same general position as their location in the engine. This will enable you to match any bearing problems with the corresponding crankshaft journal. Do not touch any shell's internal bearing surface with your fingers while checking it, or the delicate surface may be scratched.

4 Dirt and other foreign matter get into the engine in a variety of ways. It may be left in the engine during assembly, or it may pass through filters or the crankcase ventilation system. It may get into the oil, and from there into the bearings. Metal chips from machining operations and normal engine wear are often present. Abrasives are sometimes left in engine components after reconditioning, especially when parts are not thoroughly cleaned using the proper cleaning methods. Whatever the source, these foreign objects often end up embedded in the soft bearing material, and are easily recognised. Large particles will not embed in the bearing, but will score or gouge the bearing and journal. The best prevention for this cause of bearing failure is to clean all parts thoroughly, and keep everything spotlessly clean during engine assembly. Frequent and regular engine oil and filter changes are also recommended.

5 Lack of lubrication (or lubrication breakdown) has a number of interrelated causes. Excessive heat (which thins the oil), overloading (which squeezes the oil from the bearing face) and oil leakage (from excessive bearing clearances, worn oil pump or high engine speeds) all contribute to lubrication breakdown. Blocked oil passages, which usually are the result of misaligned oil holes in a bearing shell, will also oil-starve a bearing, and destroy it. When lack of lubrication is the cause of bearing failure, the bearing material is wiped or extruded from the steel backing of the bearing. Temperatures may increase to the point where the steel backing turns blue from overheating.

6 Driving habits can have a definite effect on bearing life. Full-throttle, low-speed operation (labouring the engine) puts very high loads on bearings, tending to squeeze out the oil film. These loads cause the bearings to flex, which produces fine cracks in the bearing face (fatigue failure). Eventually, the bearing material will loosen in pieces, and tear away from the steel backing.

7 Short-distance driving leads to corrosion of bearings, because insufficient engine heat is produced to drive off the condensed water and corrosive gases. These products collect in the engine oil, forming acid and sludge. As the oil is carried to the engine bearings, the acid attacks and corrodes the bearing material.

8 Incorrect bearing installation during engine assembly will lead to bearing failure as well. Tight-fitting bearings leave insufficient bearing running clearance, and will result in oil starvation. Dirt or foreign particles trapped behind a bearing shell result in high spots on the bearing, which lead to failure.

9 Do not touch any shell's internal bearing surface with your fingers during reassembly, as there is a risk of scratching the delicate surface, or of depositing particles of dirt on it.

10 As mentioned at the beginning of this Section, the bearing shells should be renewed as a matter of course during engine overhaul. To do otherwise is false economy.

Bearings selection

11 Main and big-end bearings for the engines described in this Chapter are available in standard sizes and a range of undersizes to suit reground crankshafts.

12 The running clearances will need to be checked when the crankshaft is refitted with its new bearings (see Section 17 and Section 18).

15 Engine overhaul – reassembly sequence

1 Before reassembly begins, ensure that all new parts have been obtained, and that all necessary tools are available. Read through the entire procedure to familiarise yourself with the work involved, and to ensure that all items necessary for reassembly of the engine are at hand. In addition to all normal tools and materials, thread-locking compound will be needed. A suitable tube of liquid sealant will also be required for the joint faces that are fitted without gaskets.

2 In order to save time and avoid problems, engine reassembly can be carried out in the following order, referring to Part A, B, C, D or E of this Chapter. Where applicable, use new gaskets and seals when refitting the various components.

a) Crankshaft (Section 17).
b) Piston/connecting rod assemblies (Section 18).
c) Oil pump.
d) Sump.
e) Flywheel/driveplate.
f) Cylinder head.
g) Timing chain/belt(s), tensioner and sprockets.
h) Inlet and exhaust manifolds.
i) Engine external components.

3 At this stage, all engine components should be absolutely clean and dry, with all faults repaired. The components should be laid out (or in individual containers) on a completely clean work surface.

16 Piston rings – refitting

1 Before fitting new piston rings, the ring end gaps must be checked as follows.

2 Lay out the piston/connecting rod assemblies and the new piston ring sets, so that the ring sets will be matched with the same piston and cylinder during the end gap measurement and subsequent engine reassembly.

3 Insert the top ring into the first cylinder, and push it down the bore using the top of the piston. This will ensure that the ring remains square with the cylinder walls. Position the ring approximately 15.0 mm the bottom of the cylinder bore, at the lower limit of ring travel. Note that the top and second compression rings are different.

4 Measure the end gap using feeler blades, and compare the measurements with the figures given in the Specifications **(see illustration)**.

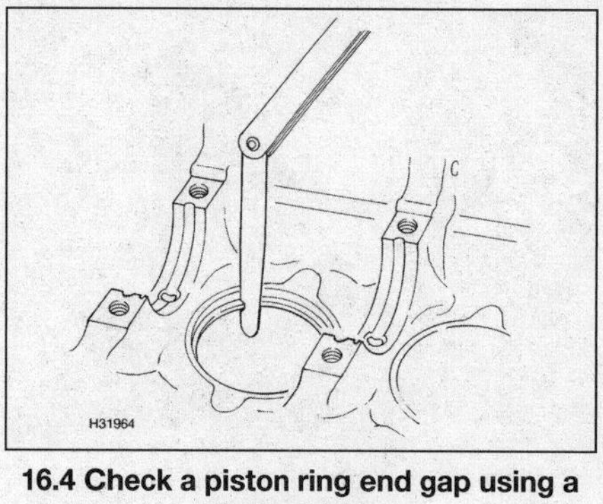

16.4 Check a piston ring end gap using a feeler blade

5 If the gap is too small (unlikely if genuine Seat parts are used), it must be enlarged, or the ring ends may contact each other during engine operation, causing serious damage. Ideally, new piston rings providing the correct end gap should be fitted. As a last resort, the end gap can be increased by filing the ring ends very carefully with a fine file. Mount the file in a vice equipped with soft jaws, slip the ring over the file with the ends contacting the file face, and slowly move the ring to remove material from the ends. Take care, as piston rings are sharp, and are easily broken.

6 With new piston rings, it is unlikely that the end gap will be too large. If the gaps are too large, check that you have the correct rings for your engine and for the particular cylinder bore size.

7 Repeat the checking procedure for each ring in the first cylinder, and then for the rings in the remaining cylinders. Remember to keep rings, pistons and cylinders matched up.

8 Once the ring end gaps have been checked and if necessary corrected, the rings can be fitted to the pistons.

9 Fit the piston rings using the same technique as for removal. Fit the bottom (oil control) ring first, and work up. Note that a two- or three-section oil control ring may be fitted; where a two-section ring is fitted, first insert the wire expander, then fit the ring. Ensure that the rings are fitted the correct way up – the top surface of the rings is normally marked TOP **(see illustration)**. Offset the piston ring gaps by 120° from each other. **Note:** *Always follow any instructions supplied with the new piston ring sets – different manufacturers may specify different procedures. Do not mix up the top and second compression rings, as they have different cross-sections.*

17 Crankshaft (diesel engines) – refitting and main bearing clearance check

Main bearing clearance check

1 The running clearance check can be carried out using the original bearing shells. However, it is preferable to use a new set, since the results obtained will be more conclusive. If new shells are being fitted, ensure that all traces of the protective grease are cleaned off using paraffin.

2 If still fitted, carefully lift the crankshaft out of the cylinder block, and wipe off the surfaces of the bearing shells in the crankcase and bearing cap(s).

3 Clean the backs of the bearing shells, and the bearing locations in both the cylinder block/crankcase and the main bearing cap(s).

4 With the cylinder block positioned on a clean work surface, with the crankcase uppermost, press the bearing shells into their locations, ensuring that the tab on each shell engages in the notch in the cylinder block or bearing cap, and that the oil holes in the cylinder block and bearing shell are aligned **(see illustration)**. Take care not to touch any shell's bearing surface with your fingers. If the original bearing shells are being used for the check, ensure that they are refitted in their original locations.

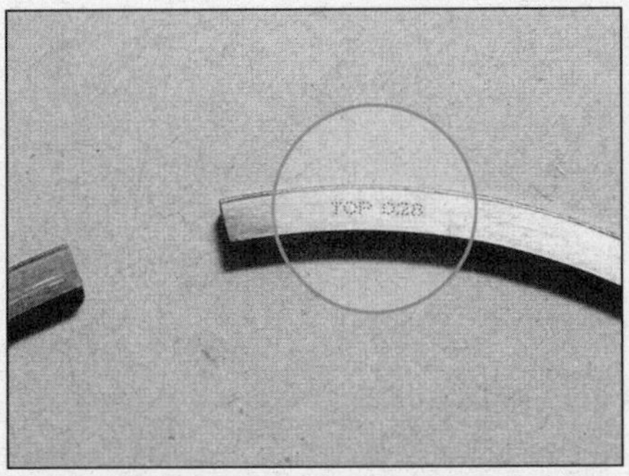

16.9 Piston ring TOP marking

5 Fit the crankshaft endfloat control thrustwasher halves either side of the No 3 main bearing location. Use a small quantity of grease to hold them in place. Ensure that the thrustwashers are seated correctly in the machined recesses, with the oil grooves facing outwards.

6 The running clearance can be checked, although this will be difficult to achieve without a range of internal micrometers or internal/external expanding calipers. Refit the main bearing cap(s) to the cylinder block/crankcase, with bearing shells in place. With the original cap retaining bolts tightened to the specified torque, measure the internal diameter of each assembled pair of bearing shells. If the diameter of each corresponding crankshaft journal is measured and then subtracted from the bearing internal diameter, the result will be the main bearing running clearance.

Final crankshaft refitting

7 Where applicable, refit the speed/position sensor wheel to the crankshaft, and tighten the securing bolts to the specified torque. Make sure that the sensor wheel is correctly orientated as noted before removal.

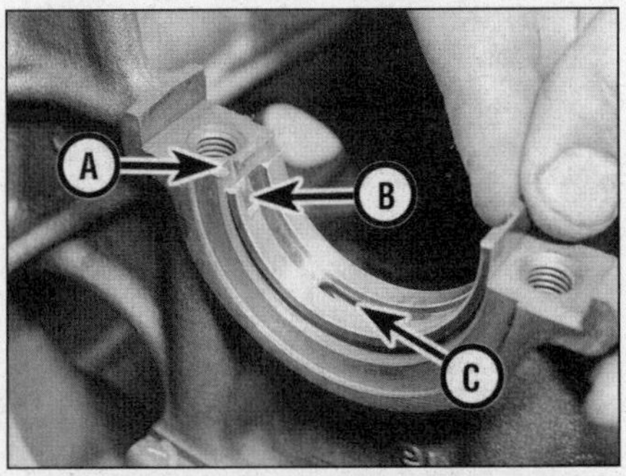

17.4 Bearing shell correctly refitted

A Recess in cylinder block
B Lug on bearing shell
C Oil hole

8 Liberally coat the bearing shells in the crankcase with clean engine oil of the appropriate grade **(see illustration)**. Make sure that the bearing shells are still correctly seated in their locations.

9 Lower the crankshaft into position so that No 1 cylinder crankpin is at BDC, ready for fitting No 1 piston. Ensure that the crankshaft endfloat control thrustwasher halves, either side of the No 3 main bearing location, remain in position. Where applicable, take care not to damage the crankshaft speed/position sensor wheel as the crankshaft is lowered into position.

10 Lubricate the lower bearing shells in the main bearing caps with clean engine oil. Make sure that the crankshaft endfloat control thrustwasher halves are still correctly seated either side of No 3 bearing cap **(see illustrations)**.

11 Fit the main bearing cap(s) in the correct location and orientation – where applicable, No 1 bearing cap must be at the timing end of the engine and the bearing shell tab locating recesses in the crankcase and bearing caps must be adjacent to each other **(see illustration)**. Insert the bearing cap bolts (using new bolts where necessary – see Torque wrench settings in the Specifications), and hand-tighten them only.

12 Working from the centre bearing cap outwards, tighten the bearing cap bolts to their specified torque. On diesel engines where two Stages are given for the torque,

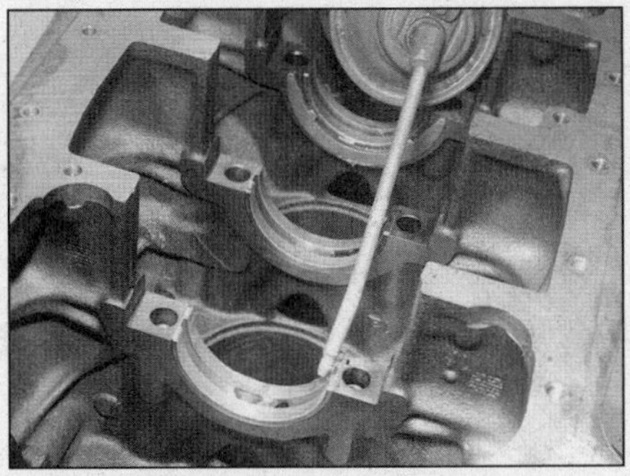

17.8 Lubricate the upper bearing shells

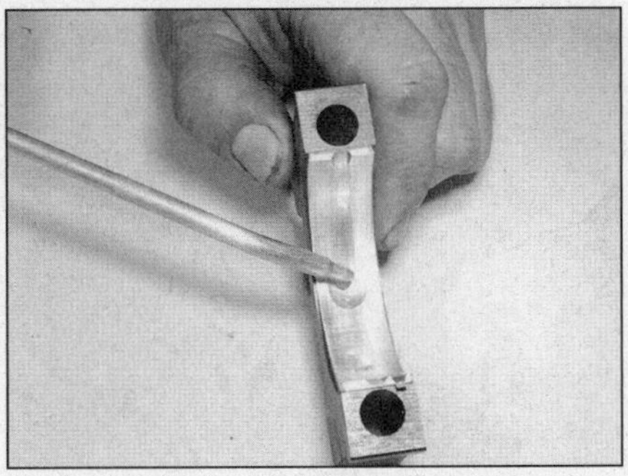

17.10a Lubricate the lower bearing shells...

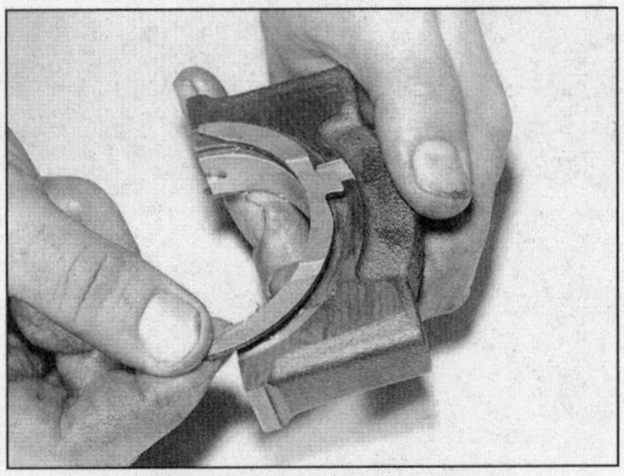

17.10b...and make sure that the thrustwashers are correctly seated

17.11 Fitting No 1 main bearing cap

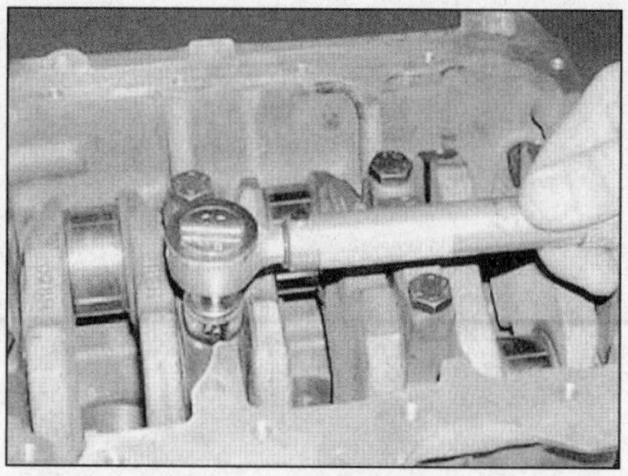
17.12a Tighten the main bearing cap bolts to the specified torque...

17.12b ...then through the specified angle

tighten all bolts to the Stage 1 torque, then go round again, and tighten all bolts through the Stage 2 angle **(see illustrations)**.

13 Check that the crankshaft rotates freely by turning it by hand. If resistance is felt, recheck the bearing running clearances, as described previously.

14 Check the crankshaft endfloat as described at the beginning of Section 13. If the thrust surfaces of the crankshaft have been checked and new thrustwashers have been fitted, then the endfloat should be within specification.

15 Refit the pistons and connecting rods or reconnect them to the crankshaft as described in Section 18.

16 Refit the crankshaft oil seal housings, flywheel, oil pump and pick-up pipe, sump and oil baffle plate, crankshaft sprocket and timing belt as described in Chapter 2E.

18 Piston/connecting rod assemblies – refitting and big-end bearing clearance check

Note: *A piston ring compressor tool will be required for this operation.*

Big-end bearing clearance check

1 The running clearance check can be carried out using the original bearing shells. However, it is preferable to use a new set, since the results obtained will be more conclusive.

2 Clean the backs of the bearing shells, and the bearing locations in both the connecting rods and the big-end bearing caps.

3 Press the bearing shells into their locations, ensuring that the tab on each shell engages in the notch in the connecting rod or cap. Take care not to touch any shell's bearing surface with your fingers. If the original bearing shells are being used for the check, ensure that they are refitted in their original locations.

4 The running clearance can be checked, although this will be difficult to achieve without a range of internal micrometers or internal/external expanding calipers. Refit the big-end bearing cap to the connecting rod, using the marks made or noted on removal to ensure that they are fitted the correct way around, with the bearing shells in place. With the original cap retaining bolts or nuts (as applicable) correctly tightened, use an internal micrometer or vernier caliper to measure the internal diameter of each assembled pair of bearing shells. If the diameter of each corresponding crankshaft journal is measured, and then subtracted from the bearing internal diameter, the result will be the big-end bearing running clearance.

Piston/connecting rods refitting

5 Note that the following procedure assumes that the crankshaft main bearing caps are in place.

6 Where applicable, refit the piston cooling oil spray jets to the bottom of the cylinder block, and tighten the securing bolts to the specified torque.

7 On engines where the big-end bearing caps are secured by nuts, renew the bolts/studs in the connecting rods. Tap the old bolts/studs out of the connecting rods using a soft-faced mallet, and tap the new bolts/studs into position. On engines where the caps are secured by bolts, renew the bolts.

8 Ensure that the bearing shells are correctly fitted, as described at the beginning of this Section. If new shells are being fitted, ensure that all traces of the protective grease are cleaned off using paraffin. Wipe dry the shells and connecting rods with a lint-free cloth.

9 Lubricate the cylinder bores, the pistons, piston rings and upper bearing shells with clean engine oil **(see illustrations)**. Lay out each piston/connecting rod assembly in order on a clean work surface. Where the bearing caps are secured with nuts, pad the threaded ends of the bolts with insulating tape to prevent them scratching the crankpins and bores when the pistons are refitted.

10 Start with piston/connecting rod assembly No 1. Make sure that the piston rings are still spaced as described in Section 16, then clamp them in position with a piston ring compressor tool.

11 Insert the piston/connecting rod assembly into the top of No 1 cylinder. Lower the big-end in first, guiding it to protect the cylinder bores. Where oil jets are located at the bottoms of the bores, take particular care not to damage them when guiding the connecting rods onto the crankpins.

12 Ensure that the orientation of the piston in its cylinder is correct – refer to Section 12 for details.

13 Using a block of wood or hammer handle against the piston crown, tap the assembly into the cylinder until the piston crown is flush with the top of the cylinder **(see illustration)**.

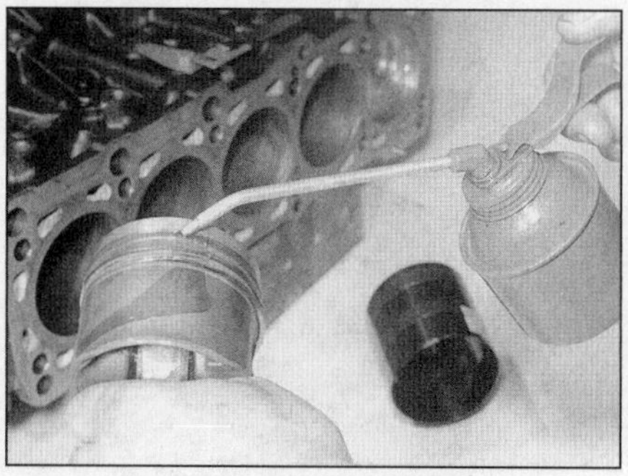
18.9a Lubricate the pistons...

18.9b ...and big-end upper bearing shells with clean engine oil

18.13 Using a hammer handle to tap the piston into its bore

14 Ensure that the bearing shell is still correctly installed in the connecting rod, and then liberally lubricate the crankpin and both bearing shells with clean engine oil.
15 Taking care not to mark the cylinder bores; tap the piston/connecting rod assembly down the bore and onto the crankpin. On engines where the big-end caps are secured by nuts, remove the insulating tape from the threaded ends of the connecting rod bolts. Oil the bolt threads, and on engines where the big-end caps are secured by bolts, oil the undersides of the bolt heads.
16 Fit the big-end bearing cap, tightening its new retaining nuts or bolts (as applicable) finger-tight at first. On diesel engines, the connecting rod and its bearing cap both have recesses machined into them on one side, close to their mating surfaces – these recesses must both face the same way as the arrow on the piston crown (i.e. towards the timing belt end of the engine) when correctly installed. Reassemble the two components to satisfy this requirement.
17 Tighten the retaining bolts or nuts to the specified torque and angle as given in the Specifications **(see illustrations)**.
18 Refit the remaining piston/connecting rod assemblies in the same way.
19 Rotate the crankshaft by hand. Check that it turns freely; some stiffness is to be expected if new parts have been fitted, but there should be no binding or tight spots.
20 On diesel engines, if new pistons have been fitted, or if a new short engine has been fitted, the projection of the piston crowns above the cylinder head mating face of the cylinder block at TDC must be measured. This measurement is used to determine the thickness of the new cylinder head gasket required. This procedure is described as part of the Cylinder head – removal, inspection and refitting procedure in Chapter 2E Section 11.
21 Proceed as follows according to engine type:
a) *Refit the oil pump pick-up pipe and oil baffle, the sump and the cylinder head as described in Chapter 2A, Chapter 2B, Chapter 2C, Chapter 2D or Chapter 2E.*

18.17a Tighten the big-end bearing cap bolts/nuts to the specified torque...

18.17b ...then through the specified angle

19 Engine – initial start-up after overhaul and reassembly

1 Refit the remainder of the engine components in the order listed in Section 5 of this Chapter. Refit the engine to the vehicle as described in Section 4 of this Chapter. Double-check the engine oil and coolant levels, and make a final check that everything has been reconnected. Make sure that there are no tools or rags left in the engine compartment.
2 Reconnect the battery negative lead (refer to *Disconnecting the battery* in the *Reference* Chapter at the end of this manual).

Petrol models

3 Remove the spark plugs, referring to Chapter 1A Section 27, for details.
4 The engine must be immobilised such that it can be turned over using the starter motor, without starting – refer to Chapter 2A Section 2, Chapter 2B Section 2, Chapter 2C Section 3, Chapter 2D Section 2 or Chapter 2E Section 2. Also, disable the fuel pump by unplugging the fuel pump power relay from the relay board with reference to Chapter 12 Section 3.
Caution: To prevent damage to the catalytic converter, it is important to disable the fuel system.
5 Turn the engine using the starter motor until the oil pressure warning light goes out. If the light fails to extinguish after several seconds of cranking, check the engine oil level and oil filter security. Assuming these are correct, check the security of the oil pressure switch wiring – do not progress any further until you are satisfied that oil is being pumped around the engine at sufficient pressure.
6 Refit the spark plugs, and reconnect the ignition and fuel pump wiring.

Diesel models

7 Disconnect the injector solenoids by disconnecting the connector at the end of the cylinder head. **Note:** *As a result of the wiring being disconnected, faults will be stored in the ECU memory. These must be erased after starting the engine.*
8 Turn the engine using the starter motor until the oil pressure warning light goes out.
9 If the light fails to extinguish after several seconds of cranking, check the engine oil level and oil filter security. Assuming these are correct, check the security of the oil pressure switch cabling – do not progress any further until you are satisfied that oil is being pumped around the engine at sufficient pressure.
10 Reconnect the wiring as applicable.

All models

11 Start the engine, but be aware that as fuel system components have been disturbed, the cranking time may be a little longer than usual.
12 While the engine is idling, check for fuel, water and oil leaks. Don't be alarmed if there are some odd smells and the occasional plume of smoke as components heat up and burn off oil deposits.
13 Assuming all is well; keep the engine idling until hot water is felt circulating through the top hose.
14 After a few minutes, stop the engine then recheck the oil and coolant levels, and top-up as necessary.
15 There is no need to retighten the cylinder head bolts once the engine has been run following reassembly.
16 If new pistons, rings or crankshaft bearings have been fitted, the engine must be treated as new, and run-in for the first 600 miles (1000 km). Do not operate the engine at full-throttle, or allow it to labour at low engine speeds in any gear. It is recommended that the engine oil and filter be changed at the end of this period.

Chapter 3
Cooling, heating and ventilation systems

Contents

Degrees of difficulty

Easy, suitable for novice with little experience	Fairly easy, suitable for beginner with some experience	Fairly difficult, suitable for competent DIY mechanic	Difficult, suitable for experienced DIY mechanic	Very difficult, suitable for expert DIY or professional

Specifications

Cooling system pressure cap

Opening pressure:	
Black cap	1.6 to 1.8 bar
Blue cap	1.4 bar

Thermostat

Petrol engines

1.0 litre engines:	
Primary thermostat opens at	80°C
Secondary thermostat opens at	105°C
1.2 litre engines:	
Begins to open	87°C
Fully open	105°C
1.4 litre engines:	
Begins to open	84°C
Fully open	98°C

Diesel engines

Begins to open	92°C
Fully open	107°C

Cooling fan

Fan speeds:	
1st speed cut-in	92 to 97°C
1st speed cut-out	91 to 84°C
2nd speed cut-in	99 to 105°C
2nd speed cut-out	98 to 91°C

Coolant temperature sensor

Resistances:	
At 30°C	1500 to 2000 ohms
At 80°C	275 to 375 ohms

Air-conditioning

Refrigerant:	
Capacity	500 ± 15g
Type	R134a
Compressor make/type:	
Delphi	6CVC 140
Denso	6SEU14
Sanden	6PXE14 or 7PXE16
Refrigerant oil type / oil capacity for replacement compressor:	
Delphi 6CVC 140	G 052 300 A2 or G 052 154 A2 / 110cm^3 ± 10cm^3
Denso 6SEU14	G 052 300 A2 / 85cm^3 ± 10cm^3
Sanden 6PXE14 & 7PXE16	G 052 154 A2 / 110cm^3 ± 10cm^3

Torque wrench settings	Nm	lbf ft
Air conditioning condenser	5	4
Coolant pump:		
1.0 and 1.2 litre DOHC petrol engines:		
Stage 1	10	7
Stage 2	Slacken 360°	
Stage 3	10	7
Stage 4	12	8
1.2 litre SOHC petrol engines	24	18
1.4 litre petrol engines	20	15
Diesel engines	15	11
Coolant pump pulley (1.2 litre petrol engines)	22	16
Distribution housing (diesel engines)	10	7
Radiator	5	4
Radiator cooling fan shroud bolts	10	7
Radiator cooling fan thermo-switch	35	26
Thermostat cover (diesel engines)	15	11
Thermostat/distribution housing:		
1.2 litre petrol engines	8	6
1.4 litre petrol engines	10	7

1 General information and precautions

1 On all models a pressurised cooling system is used, with a coolant pump, a crossflow radiator and one (or two) electric cooling fans. All models have a thermostat and a heater matrix, as well as the interconnecting hoses. 1.0 and 1.2 litre petrol engines have dual thermostats.

2 The system functions as follows. Coolant is circulated through the cylinder block and head passages by the coolant pump. On diesel engines and 1.4 litre petrol engines the pump is driven by the timing belt. On 1.0 and 1.2 DOHC petrol engines the pump is driven by an auxiliary belt attached to the exhaust camshaft at the transmission end of the cylinder head. On 1.2 SOHC engines (engine code CBZB) the coolant pump is driven by the auxiliary drivebelt. Models with liquid intercoolers also have an additional electrically operated coolant pump fitted.

3 As the coolant temperature increase the thermostat opens and coolant passes through the radiator (where it is cooled) and back to the engine. As the temperature increases further the electric radiator cooling fan will be brought into operation to assist with cooling.

1.0 and 1.2 (DOHC) petrol engine cooling system

4 The thermostats and coolant pump are integrated into a single unit. The larger thermostat (closest to the cylinder head) opens at 87°C or 80°C depending on the year of production. This thermostat controls the flow coolant from the radiator to the cylinder head. The second smaller thermostat controls the flow of coolant between the radiator and the engine block and opens at 105°C. Both thermostats are available as parts.

5 A separate cooling circuit, with it's own electric coolant pump controls the flow of coolant between the charge air cooler (part of the inlet manifold) and the charge air cooler radiator (intercooler). Turbocharger cooling is integrated into this circuit. The charge air cooler and the engine cooling circuit share the same coolant expansion tank with coolant for the charge air cooler being tapped off via a Tee junction and one way check valve **(see illustration)**. In the event of an unexplained coolant loss both coolant circuits should be checked for leaks.

Diesel engine cooling system

6 The coolant pump in the diesel engines is shut off at start up – there is no coolant flow around the engine block. Cabin heating and EGR cooling is provided by a separate electric cooling pump directly connected to the cylinder head. As soon as the engine warms up the coolant pump engages and coolant flows through the engine block, oil cooler and throttle body. When the engine temperature increases further the thermostat opens and coolant flows through the radiator.

7 The charge air cooler is a separate circuit with it's own electric coolant pump. Cooling is controlled by the engine management ECU independently of the main cooling circuit. Both circuits share the same coolant reservoir.

Air conditioning

8 Refer to Section 11 for information on the air conditioning system.

Precautions

Warning: Do not attempt to remove the expansion tank filler cap or disturb any part of the cooling system while the engine is hot, as there is a high risk of scalding. If the expansion tank filler cap must be removed before the engine and radiator have fully cooled (even though this is not recommended) the pressure in the cooling system must first be relieved. Cover the cap with a thick layer of cloth, to avoid scalding, and slowly unscrew the filler cap until a hissing sound can be heard. When the hissing has stopped, indicating that the pressure has reduced, slowly unscrew the filler cap until it can be removed; if more hissing sounds are heard, wait until they have stopped before unscrewing the cap completely. At all times keep well away from the filler cap opening.

Warning: Do not allow antifreeze to come into contact with skin or painted surfaces of the vehicle. Rinse off spills immediately with

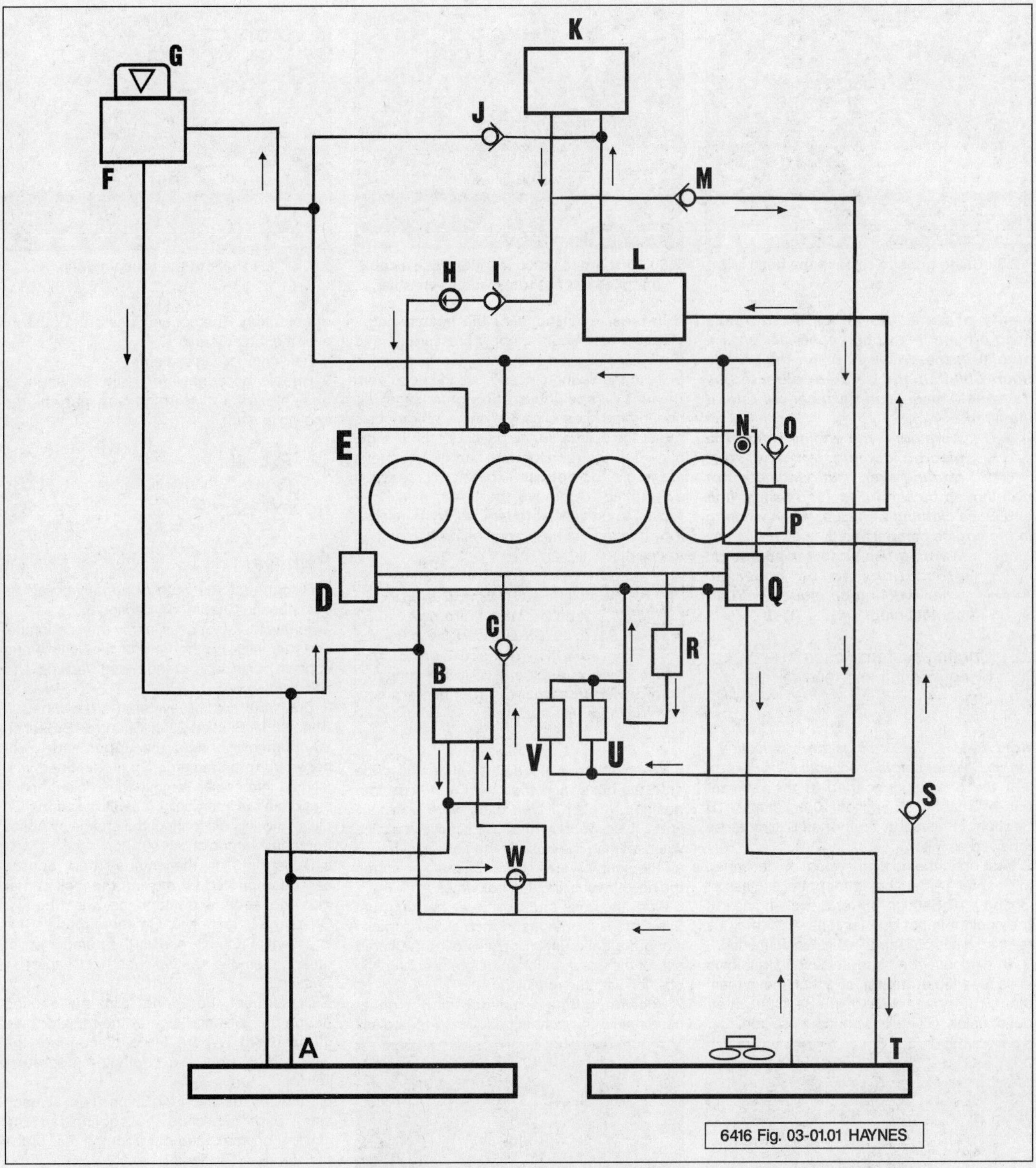

1.5 Schematic of the cooling system (typical)

A Intercooler radiator
B Charge air cooler (in inlet manifold)
C Check valve
D Coolant pump
E Engine
F Coolant reservoir
G Reservoir cap
H Electric coolant pump (for cabin heating)
I Check valve
J Check valve (some vehicles)
K Heater matrix (cabin heating)
L EGR cooler
M Check valve
N Coolant temperature sensor
O Check valve
P Coolant distribution housing
Q Thermostat
R Oil cooler
S Check valve
T Radiator
U Throttle body
V EGR control motor
W Charge air cooling pump

2.3a Using grips to release the hose clip or...

2.3b ...in hard to reach locations use a cable operated release tool (widely available)

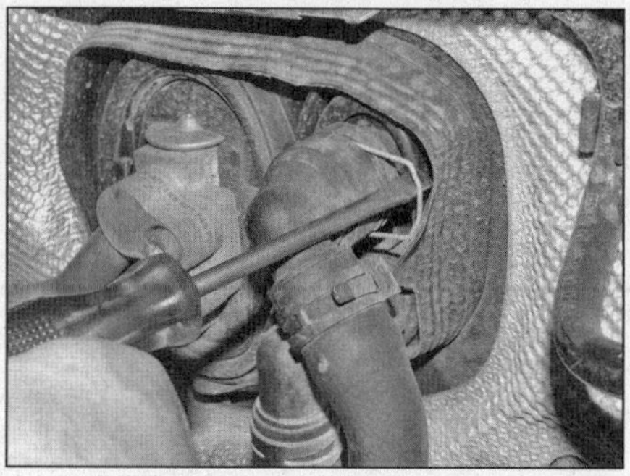

2.4 Pull out the retaining clip

plenty of water. Never leave antifreeze lying around in an open container or in a puddle in the driveway or on the garage floor. Children and pets are attracted by its sweet smell. Antifreeze can be fatal if ingested.

Warning: If the engine is hot, the electric cooling fan may start rotating even if the engine is not running, so be careful to keep hands, hair and loose clothing well clear when working in the engine compartment.

Warning: Refer to for additional precautions to be observed when working on models with air conditioning.

2 Cooling system hoses – disconnection and renewal

Note: *Refer to the warnings given in Section 1 of this Chapter before proceeding.*

1 If the checks described in the relevant part of Chapter 1A Section 10 or Chapter 1B Section 11 reveal a faulty hose, it must be renewed as follows.

2 First drain the cooling system as described in Chapter 1A Section 32 for petrol engines or Chapter 1B Section 33 for diesel engines. If the coolant is not due for renewal, it may be re-used if it is collected in a clean container.

3 To disconnect a hose, release its retaining clips **(see illustrations)**, and then move them along the hose, clear of the relevant inlet/outlet union. Carefully work the hose free.

4 In order to disconnect the heater matrix inlet and outlet hoses, apply pressure to hold the hose on to the relevant union then either, pull out the spring clip and pull the hose from the union **(see illustration)**or release the spring type hose clips. On some later models rotate the collars on the bayonet type fittings. Note that the radiator inlet and outlet unions are fragile; do not use excessive force when attempting to remove the hoses. If a hose proves to be difficult to remove, try to release it by rotating the hose ends before attempting to free it.

HAYNES HiNT

If all else fails, cut the hose with a sharp knife, then slit it so that it can be peeled off in two pieces. Although this may prove expensive if the hose is otherwise undamaged, it is preferable to buying a new radiator.

5 When fitting a hose, first slide the clips onto the hose, and then work the hose into position. If clamp type clips were originally fitted, it is a good idea to use screw-type clips when refitting the hose. If the hose is stiff, use a little soapy water as a lubricant, or soften the hose by soaking it in hot water.

6 Work the hose into position, checking that it is correctly routed, and then slide each clip along the hose until it passes over the flared end of the relevant union, before securing it in position with the retaining clip.

7 Prior to refitting a radiator inlet or outlet hose renew the connection O-ring regardless of condition. The connections are a push-fit over the radiator unions.

8 Refill the cooling system.

9 Check thoroughly for leaks as soon as possible after disturbing any part of the cooling system.

3 Radiator – removal, inspection and refitting

Removal

1 Disconnect the battery negative lead as described in Chapter 5A Section 3.

2 To give better access, apply the handbrake, and then jack up the front of the vehicle and support it on axle stands (see *Jacking and vehicle support)*.

3 Drain the cooling system as described in Chapter 1A Section 32 or Chapter 1B Section 33, then disconnect the upper and lower hoses from the radiator. On model fitted with a liquid intercooler, remove the coolant hoses and drain the intercooler **(see illustration)**. On diesel models disconnect the charge air hoses from the intercooler.

4 Depending on the engine fitted, access can be improved by moving the lock carrier into the service position as described in Chapter 11 Section 8. On some models this is essential. On all models the bumper cover must be removed as described in Chapter 11 Section 6.

5 Disconnect the wiring from the cooling fan on the left-hand side of the radiator **(see illustration)**. Where fitted disconnect the wiring plug from the coolant temperature sensor

6 Release the securing clips (two at each side), and then slide the cooling fan and cowling upwards and out from the rear of the radiator (See Section 5).

7 Working at the front of the panel **(see illustration)**, undo the retaining screws and carefully tilt the radiator backwards.

Models with air-conditioning

8 With the radiator tilted back, undo the retaining screw that secures the air-conditioning pipe mounting bracket to the right-hand lower side of the radiator **(see**

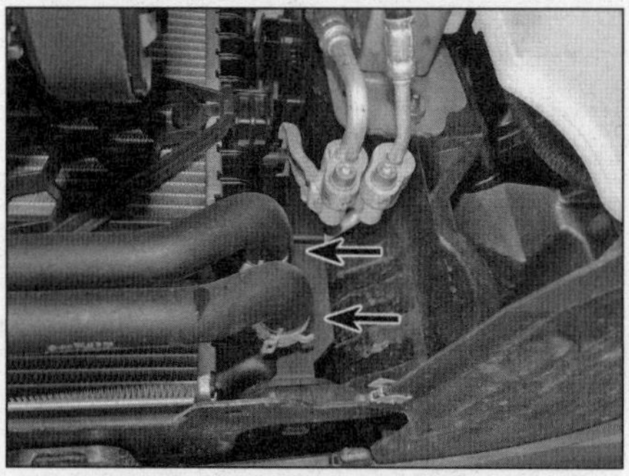

3.3 Remove both hoses from the intercooler (where fitted)

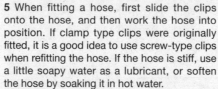

3.5 Disconnect the cooling fan wiring plug

3.7 Undo the radiator mounting screws (one side shown)

3.8a Undo the mounting bracket securing screw (diesel models)

3.8b On some engines the bracket screws are accessed from the side (1.0 litre petrol engine shown)

3.9a Undo the lower securing screws (one side shown)...

3.9b ...and upper securing screws (one side shown)...

3.10 Remove the radiator, complete with the intercooler

illustrations). Where required unclip the refrigerant pipes from the inner wing. DO NOT disconnect the refrigerant pipes.

9 Undo the four screws at the front of the condenser that secure it to the radiator, then using cable ties (or similar) secure the condenser to the front cross panel **(see illustrations)**.

All models

10 The radiator can now be removed from inside the front of the engine compartment. On turbo charged diesel engines, the intercooler is attached across the lower part of the radiator; lift the radiator complete with intercooler out from the front panel. On turbo charged petrol engines, the charge air cooler radiator is attached across the lower part of the main radiator; lift the radiator complete with charge air cooler out from the front panel **(see illustration)**.

11 With the radiator on the bench, separate the intercooler form the radiator **(see illustration)**.

Inspection

12 If the radiator has been removed due to suspected blockage, reverse flush it.

13 Clean dirt and debris from the radiator fins, using an air-line (in which case, wear eye protection) or a soft brush. Be careful, as the fins are sharp and easily damaged.

14 If necessary, a radiator specialist can perform a 'flow test' on the radiator, to establish whether an internal blockage exists.

15 A leaking radiator must be referred to a specialist for permanent repair. Do not attempt to weld or solder a leaking radiator, as damage may result.

16 If the radiator is to be sent for repair or renewed, remove the cooling fan and thermo-switch.

Refitting

17 Refitting is a reversal of removal, but check the condition of the mounting rubbers and renew if necessary **(see illustration)**. On completion, refill the cooling system as described in Chapter 1A Section 32 or Chapter 1B Section 33, using the correct type of antifreeze.

4 Thermostat – removal, testing and refitting

1 As the thermostat ages, it will become slower to react to changes in water temperature ('lazy'). Ultimately, the unit may stick in the open or closed position, and this causes problems. A thermostat that is stuck open will result in a very slow warm-up; a thermostat, which is stuck shut, will lead to rapid overheating.

2 Before assuming the thermostat is to blame for a cooling system problem, check the coolant level. If the system is draining due to a leak, or has not been properly filled, there may be an airlock in the system (refer to the coolant renewal procedure).

3 If the engine seems to be taking a long time to warm up (based on heater output), the thermostat could be stuck open. Don't necessarily believe the temperature gauge reading – some gauges never seem to register very high in normal driving.

4 A lengthy warm-up period might suggest that the thermostat is missing – it may have been removed or inadvertently omitted by a previous owner or mechanic. Don't drive the car without a thermostat – the engine

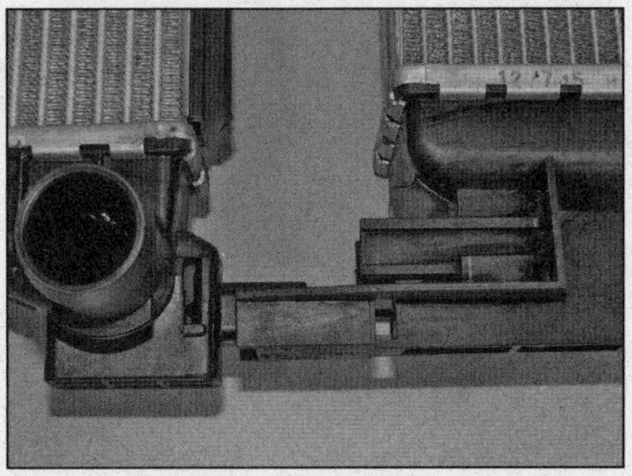
3.11 Unclip the intercooler from the radiator

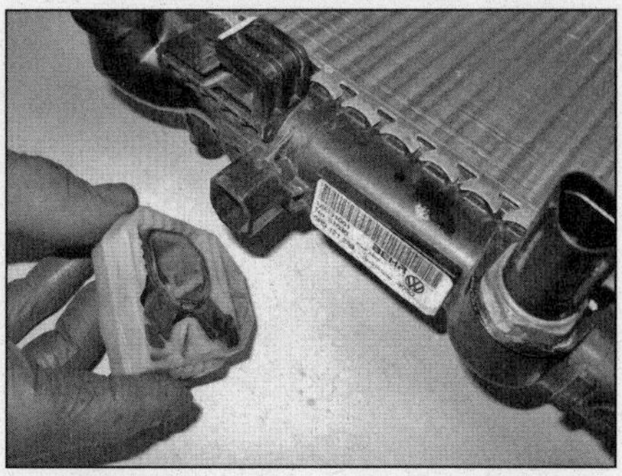
3.17 Check the radiator mounting rubbers

4.20a Remove the coolant hoses

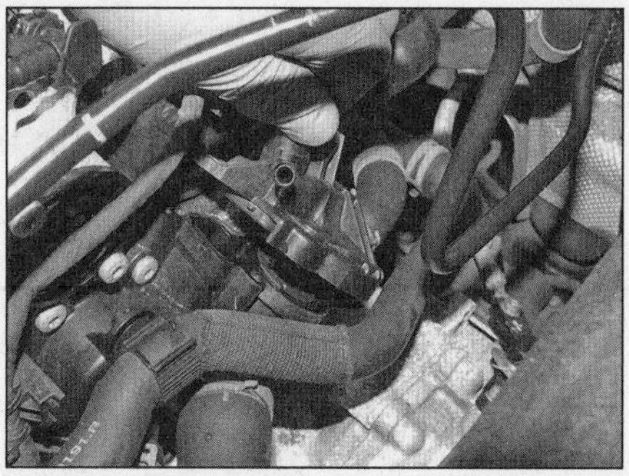
4.20b Remove the cover

4.20c The large cooling circuit thermostat

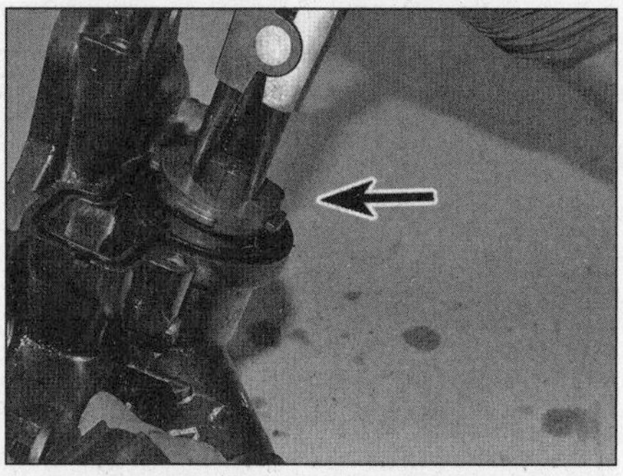
4.21 Remove the thermostat

management system's ECU will then stay in warm-up mode for longer than necessary, causing emissions and fuel economy to suffer.

5 If the engine runs hot, use your hand to check the temperature of the radiator top hose. If the hose isn't hot, but the engine clearly is, the thermostat is probably stuck closed, preventing the coolant inside the engine from escaping to the radiator – renew the thermostat. Again, this problem may also be due to an airlock (refer to the coolant renewal procedure).

6 If the radiator top hose is hot, it means that the coolant is flowing (at least as far as the radiator) and the thermostat is open. Consult the *Fault diagnosis* section at the end of this manual to assist in tracing possible cooling system faults, but a lack of heater output would now definitely suggest an airlock or a blockage.

7 To gain a rough idea of whether the thermostat is working properly when the engine is warming up, without dismantling the system, proceed as follows.

8 With the engine completely cold, start the engine and let it idle, while checking the temperature of the radiator top hose. Periodically check the temperature indicated on the coolant temperature gauge – if overheating is indicated, switch the engine off immediately.

9 The top hose should feel cold for some time as the engine warms up, and should then get warm quite quickly as the thermostat opens.

10 The above is not a precise or definitive test of thermostat operation, but if the system does not perform as described, remove and test the thermostat as described below.

Removal

1.2 litre SOHC Petrol engines

Note: *The thermostat is part of the housing. It can not be removed. If faulty the complete housing must be replaced.*

11 The thermostat is located at the left-hand end of the cylinder head.

12 Drain the cooling system as described in Chapter 1A Section 32.

13 Remove the air filter housing (Chapter 4A Section 3) and disconnect the battery as described in Chapter 5A Section 3.

14 Release the spring type hose clips and remove the coolant hoses.

15 Disconnect the wiring plug from the coolant temperature sensor and then at the rear of the housing remove the horse shoe clip from the rear coolant pipe.

16 Remove the thermostat housing bolts and pull the housing off the rear coolant pipe. Remove the O-ring seal from the pipe and the gasket from the housing.

17 Remove the coolant hose from the rear transfer pipe and pull the pipe from the back of the coolant pump. Remove the O-ring seal (both seals should be replaced).

1.0 and 1.2 DOHC Petrol engines

18 Drain the cooling system as described in Chapter 1A Section 32.

Large cooling circuit thermostat

19 Remove the air filter housing and the charge air pipe.

20 The the thermostat for the large cooling circuit is fitted behind the top cover of the coolant pump/thermostat housing. Remove the coolant hose (or hoses) from the cover. Remove the screws and then remove the cover to expose the thermostat **(see illustrations)**.

21 Seat list a special socket (T10508) to aid removal of the large circuit thermostat, but this tool is not essential. The thermostat can be removed with long nose pliers or circlip pliers. Hold the thermostat with the pliers, push down slightly and rotate the thermostat to remove it **(see illustration)**.

Small cooling circuit thermostat

22 Remove the coolant pump as described in Section 7.

23 Remove the coolant pump from the thermostat housing **(see illustrations)**.

24 Lift out the thermostat noting the orientation **(see illustration)**.

4.23a Remove the bolts in the order shown

4.23b Lift the coolant pump from the thermostat housing

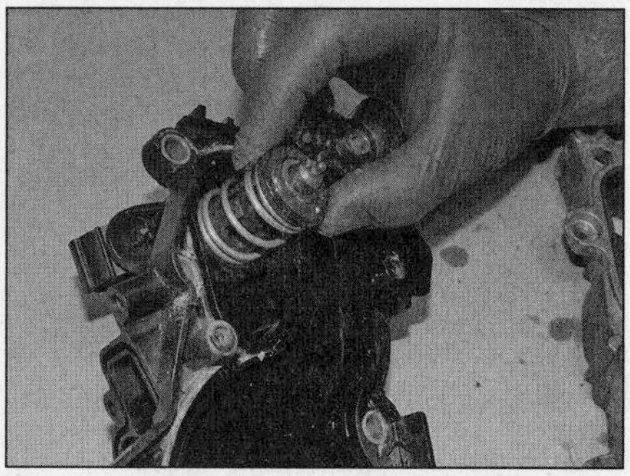
4.24 Remove the thermostat

4.27 Disconnect the coolant hose

4.28 Remove and discard the seal

4.29 Remove the thermostat

1.4 litre Petrol engines

25 Drain the cooling system as described in Chapter 1A Section 32.

26 The thermostat is located on the left-hand end of the cylinder head.

27 Release the retaining clip and disconnect the coolant radiator bottom hose from the thermostat cover **(see illustration)**.

28 Unscrew the retaining bolts and remove the thermostat housing cover and sealing ring from the engine. Discard the seal; a new one must be used on refitting **(see illustration)**.

29 Remove the thermostat from the housing **(see illustration)**. Note that the thermostat is only available together with its spring housing.

Diesel engines

30 The thermostat is located behind the alternator at the front right-hand side of the engine cylinder block. There are two types of thermostat fitted to diesel models:

a) *Single hose to the thermostat cover, and the thermostat can be renewed separately*
b) *Four hoses to the thermostat housing, the thermostat is part of the housing and can only be renewed as a complete assembly.*

31 Drain the cooling system as described in Chapter 1B Section 33. If the coolant is not due for renewal, it may be re-used if it is collected in a clean container.

32 Slacken the retaining clips and remove the rubber hose from the intercooler and charge air ducting to the throttle housing/inlet manifold.

33 Undo the bolt on the right-hand end of the engine, and disconnect the wiring connector from the charge pressure/temperature sensor on the charge air ducting.

34 Slacken the clip securing the charge air ducting to the throttle housing/inlet manifold, then undo the bolt at the rear of the air-conditioning compressor and withdraw the ducting out from the front of the engine.

35 To make access easier, remove the alternator as described in Chapter 5A Section 5.

36 Release the securing clip(s) and disconnect the coolant hose(s) from the thermostat cover/housing **(see illustrations)**.

37 Unscrew the two securing bolts, and remove the thermostat cover/housing complete with the thermostat. Note the locations of any brackets secured by the bolts. Recover the O-ring if it is loose **(see illustrations)**. **Note:** *On thermostat housing with four hose connections, there is a collar that fits into the cylinder block, which is a tight fit, and will need to be rotated from side to side to release it. Damage may occur, so a new one will be required for refitting.*

38 On models with one hose connections to the thermostat cover, remove the thermostat by twisting the thermostat 90° clockwise, and then pull it from the cover.

39 On models with three (or four) hose connections to the thermostat housing, the thermostat cannot be removed, renew the complete unit.

Testing

Note: *If there is any question about the operation of the thermostat, it's best to renew it – they are not expensive items. Testing involves heating in, or over, an open pan of boiling water, which carries with it the risk of scalding. A thermostat that has seen more than five years' service may well be past its best already.*

40 If the thermostat remains in the open position at room temperature, it is faulty, and must be renewed as a matter of course.

41 Check to see if there's an open temperature marking stamped on the thermostat.

42 Using a thermometer and container of water, heat the water until the temperature corresponds with the temperature marking stamped on the thermostat. If no marking is found, start the test with the water hot, and heat slowly until it boils.

43 Suspend the (closed) thermostat on a length of string in the water, and check that maximum opening occurs before the water boils.

44 Remove the thermostat and allow it to cool down, check that it closes fully.

4.36a Release the hose securing clip(s)...

4.36b ...there could be up to four hoses depending on model

4.37a Undo the retaining bolts (four hose fitment)...

4.37b ...and remove the thermostat housing – single hose fitment

4.46a Renew the O-ring seal – single hose fitment

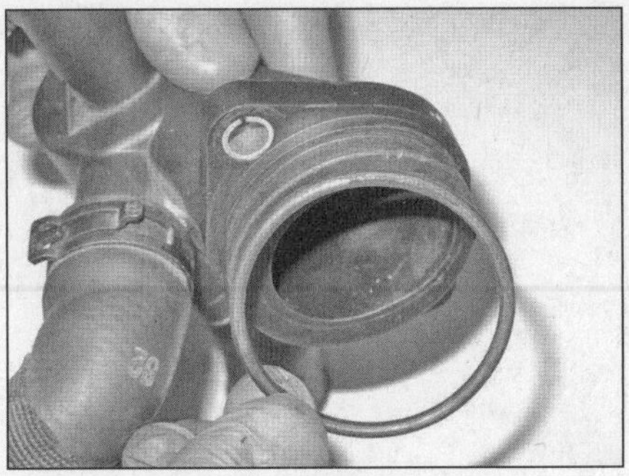

4.46b Renew the O-ring seal – four hose fitment

4.46c Always fit a new gasket

45 If the thermostat does not open and close as described, or if it sticks in either position, it must be renewed.

Refitting

46 Refitting is a reversal of removal, bearing in mind the following points:

a) Refit the thermostat using a new O-ring ***(see illustrations)****.*

b) Always fit a new gasket where applicable ***(see illustrations)****.*

c) Insert the thermostat into the cover and twist 90° anti-clockwise (diesel engines).

d) Ensure that any brackets are in place on the thermostat cover bolts as noted before removal.

e) Refit the alternator (where applicable).

f) Refill the cooling system with the correct type and quantity of coolant.

5 Electric cooling fan – testing, removal and refitting

Testing

1 The cooling fan is supplied with current through the ignition switch, cooling fan control unit (where applicable), the relay(s) and fuses/fusible link. The circuit is completed by the cooling fan thermostatic switch, which is mounted in the left-hand end of the radiator. The cooling fan has two speed settings; the thermostatic switch actually contains two switches, one for the stage 1 fan speed setting and another for the stage 2 fan speed setting. Testing of the cooling fan circuit is as follows, noting that the following check should be carried out on both the stage 1 speed circuit and speed 2 circuit (see wiring diagrams in Chapter 14).

2 If the fan does not appear to work, first check the fuses/fusible links. If they are good, run the engine until normal operating temperature is reached, then allow it to idle. If the fan does not cut in within a few minutes, switch off the ignition and disconnect the wiring plug from the cooling fan switch. Bridge the relevant two contacts in the wiring plug using a length of spare wire, and switch on the ignition. If the fan now operates, the switch is probably faulty and should be renewed.

3 If the switch appears to work, the motor can be checked by disconnecting the motor wiring connector and connecting a 12-volt supply directly to the motor terminals. If the motor is faulty, it must be renewed, as no spares are available.

4 If the fan still fails to operate, check the cooling fan circuit wiring. Check each wire for continuity and ensure that all connections are clean and free of corrosion.

5 On models with a cooling fan control unit, if no fault can be found with the fuses/fusible links, wiring, fan switch, or fan motor, then it is likely that the cooling fan control unit is faulty. Testing of the unit should be entrusted to a Seat dealer or specialist; if the unit is faulty it must be renewed.

5.7 Removing the air ducting panel

5.9 Unclip the wiring connector from the cowling

5.10a Release the retaining clips

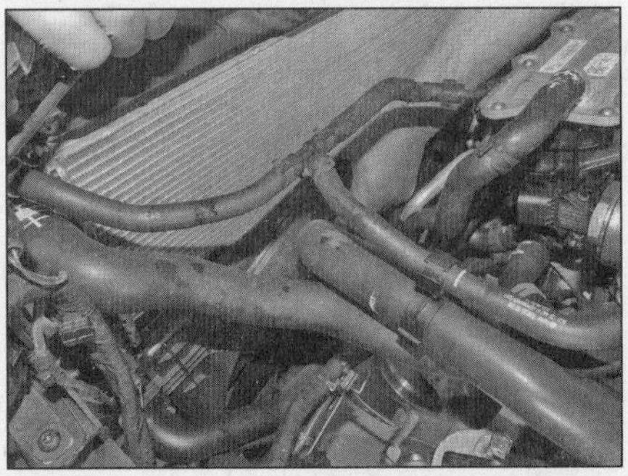

5.10b The fan and shroud are lowered from the engine bay on the 1.0 litre TSI engines

Removal and refitting

6 Disconnect the battery negative lead as described in Chapter 5A Section 3.

7 Where applicable, undo the retaining screws and disconnect the air intake duct from the bonnet slam panel **(see illustration)**.

8 On diesel models disconnect the charge air pipes from the intercooler.

9 Disconnect the wiring plug from the cooling fan motor, and slide the connector from the retaining bracket **(see illustration)**. where required unclip the coolant hose from the shroud.

10 Release the retaining clips (two at each side) and remove the cooling fan and shroud away from the radiator. The fan and shroud can either be lowered or lifted from the engine bay, depending on the model **(see illustrations)**. Take care not to damage the radiator fins as the fan assembly is removed.

11 If required, undo the nuts securing the fan to the radiator shroud, and withdraw the fan **(see illustration)**.
12 Refitting is a reversal of removal.

6 Cooling system electrical switches and sensors – testing, removal and refitting

Cooling fan thermostatic switch

Note: *Some models do not have a thermostatic switch fitted in the radiator.*

Testing

1 Testing of the switch is described in Section 5, as part of the electric cooling fan test procedure.

Removal

2 The thermo-switch is located in the left-hand side of the radiator (where fitted). The engine and radiator must be cold before removing the switch.
3 Disconnect the battery negative lead as described in Chapter 5A Section 3.
4 Either drain the radiator to below the level of the switch, or have ready a suitable plug which can be used to plug the switch aperture in the radiator whilst the switch is removed. If a plug is used, take great care not to damage the radiator, and do not use anything that will allow foreign matter to enter the radiator.
5 Disconnect the wiring plug from the thermo-switch.
6 Carefully unscrew the thermo-switch from the radiator **(see illustration)**.

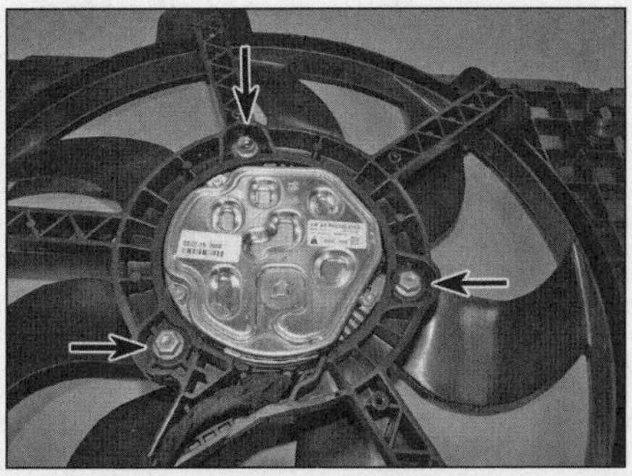

5.11 Remove the nuts

Refitting

7 Refitting is a reversal of removal, but apply a smear of suitable grease to the threads of the switch and tighten it to the specified torque. On completion, refill the cooling system with the correct type and quantity of coolant, or top-up as described in *Weekly checks.*
8 Start the engine and run it until it reaches normal operating temperature, then continue to run the engine and check that the cooling fan cuts in and functions correctly.

Coolant temperature sensors

Testing

9 On 1.0 and 1.2 litre DOHC engines the coolant temperature sensor is located at the left-hand rear of the cylinder head **(see illustration)**.
10 On 1.2 SOHC and 1.4 litre petrol engines the coolant temperature sensor is located n the coolant distribution housing on the left-hand end of the cylinder head **(see illustration)**.
11 On diesel engines the sensor is at the left-hand side of the cylinder head **(see illustration)**.
12 The sensor contains a thermistor, which consists of an electronic component whose electrical resistance decreases at a predetermined rate as its temperature rises. When the coolant is cold, the sensor resistance is high, current flow through the gauge is reduced, and the gauge needle points towards the 'cold' end of the scale. Typical resistances are given in the Specifications; however, the sensor can also be checked by a Seat dealer, or specialist using diagnostic equipment. If the sensor is faulty, it must be renewed.

Removal and refitting

13 Disconnect the wiring plug from the relevant temperature sensor. Partially drain the cooling system to below the level of the sensor (as described in Chapter 1A Section 32 or Chapter 1B Section 33).
14 Either remove the fixing bolt and pull out the sensor or carefully withdraw the retaining clip and pull the sensor from the housing **(see illustrations)**. Recover the O-ring.
15 Refitting is a reversal of removal, bearing in mind the following points:

a) Refit the sensor with a new O-ring.
b) Refill the cooling system, or top-up as described in 'Weekly checks'.

6.6 Unscrew the thermo-switch

6.9 Coolant temperature sensor – 1.0 litre petrol models

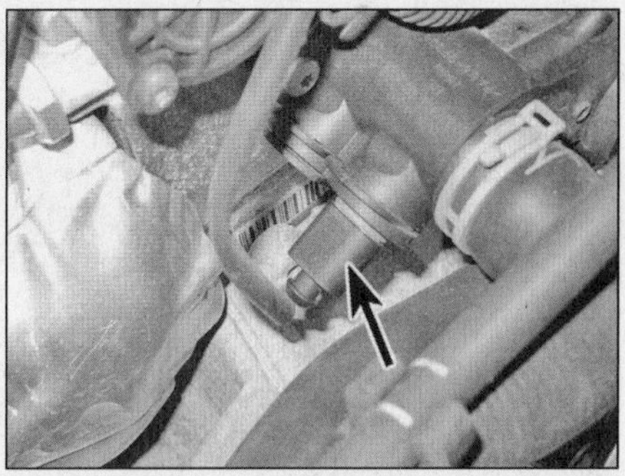

6.10 Coolant temperature sensor – 1.4 litre petrol models

6.11 Coolant temperature sensor – diesel models

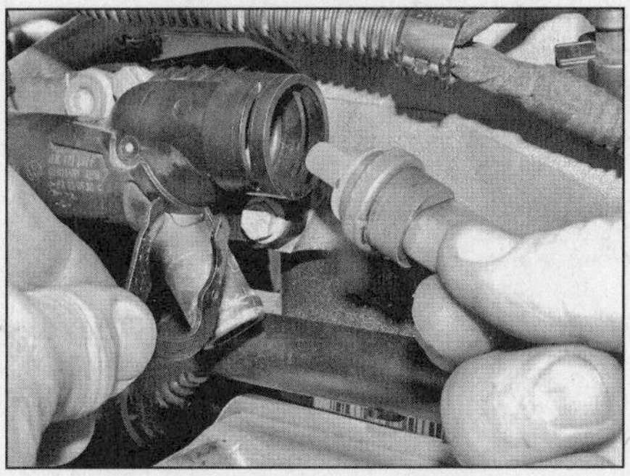

6.14a Pull out the clip and sensor...

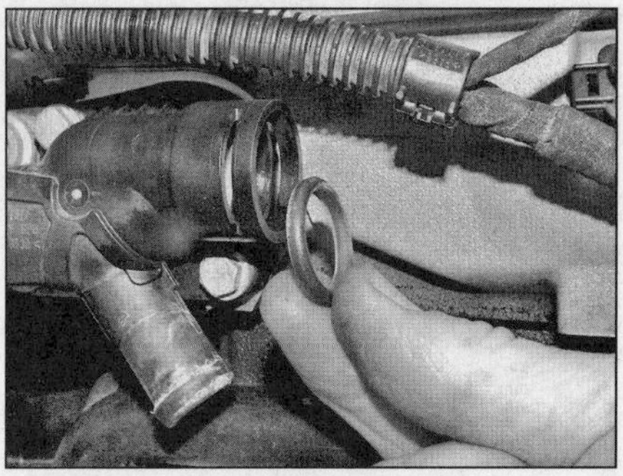

6.14b ...and recover the sealing ring – diesel model shown

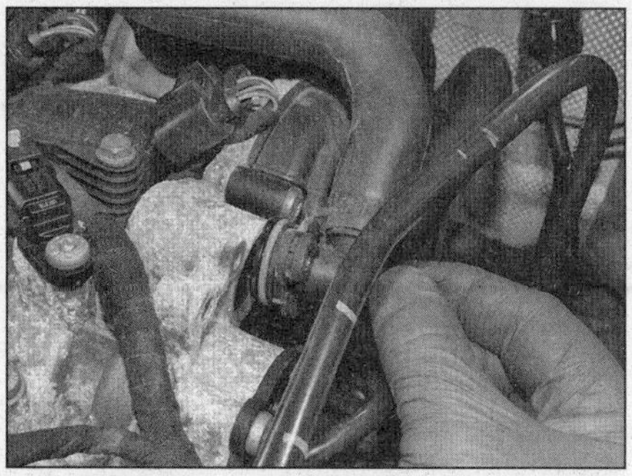
7.4 Remove the breather hose

7.5 Remove the screw with difficulty

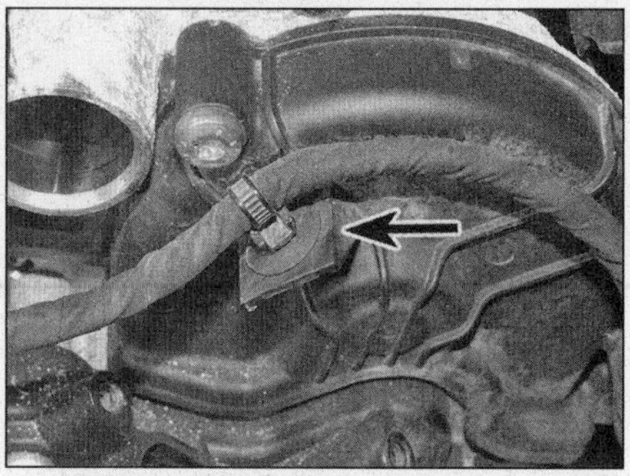
7.6a Unclip the wiring loom...

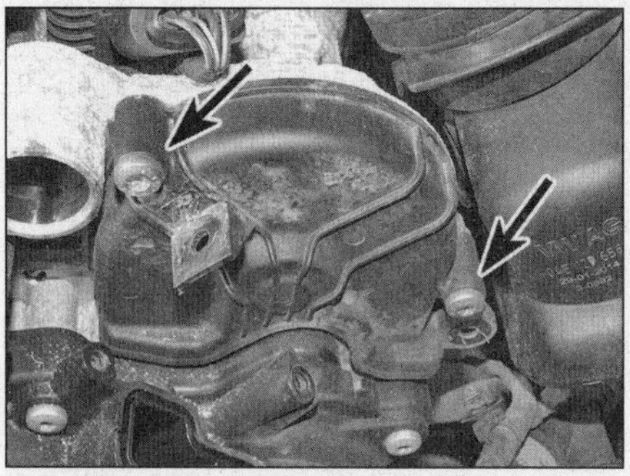
7.6b ...remove the bolts...

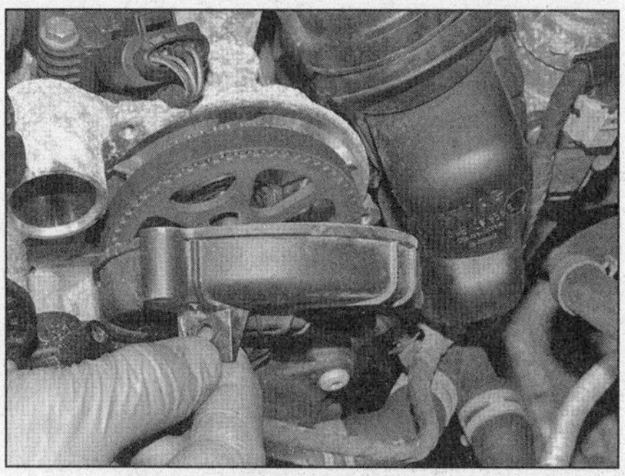
7.6c ...and lift off the cover

7.9a Always fit a new gasket

7 Coolant pump – removal and refitting

1.0 and 1.2 DOHC petrol engines

Removal

1 Drain the cooling system as described in Chapter 1A Section 32.

2 Remove the air filter housing and charge air hose as described in Chapter 4A Section 3.

3 Remove the battery and battery tray as described in Chapter 5A Section 3.

4 Remove the breather hose from the top of the valve cover **(see illustration).** Where fitted remove the EVAP hose from the breather hose.

5 On TSI engines remove the turbocharger inlet duct. Note that the screw is difficult to access **(see illustration)**. See Chapter 2A Section 3 for further details.

6 Release the wiring loom clip from the coolant pump drivebelt cover and then remove the cover **(see illustrations)**.

7 Remove the coolant hoses from the pump. where required disconnect the gear selector cables from the transmission (as described in Chapter 7A Section 2).

8 Working in the sequence shown **(see illustration 7.9d)** unbolt the pump and remove it with complete with the drivebelt.

Refitting

9 Refitting is a reversal of removal, noting the following:

*a) Fit a new gasket **(see illustration)**.*
b) The drivebelt must be replaced.
*c) Lubricate the new seal with coolant, then install the pump and hand-tighten the bolts in order **(see illustration)**.*
d) Tighten the bolts in order to 10 Nm, then slacken the bolts by one full turn.
e) An assistant will be required to complete the next stage.
*f) Using the hex hole provided **(see illustration)** on the pump fit a torque wrench, set at 30 Nm and turn the pump with the wrench so that the belt is tensioned to 30 Nm.*
g) With the aid of an assistant (and whilst still holding the torque wrench at 30 Nm) tighten the bolts 2, 1 and 5 to the third stage torque.
h) Remove the torque wrench and tighten the bolts to the fourth stage torque.

The remainder of refitting is a reversal of removal.

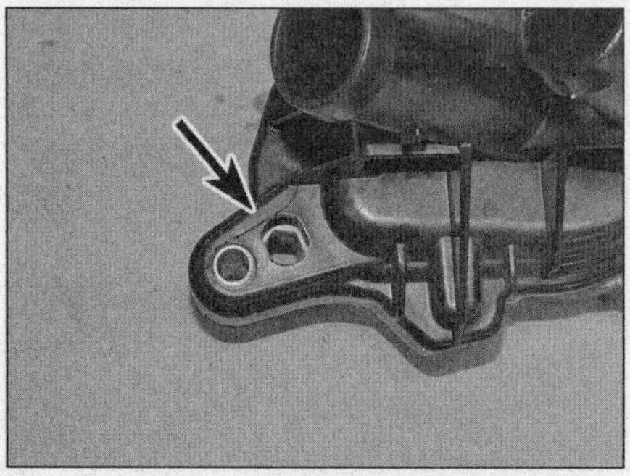
7.9b The hex hole in the pump for belt tensioning

7.9c Tension the pump with a torque wrench

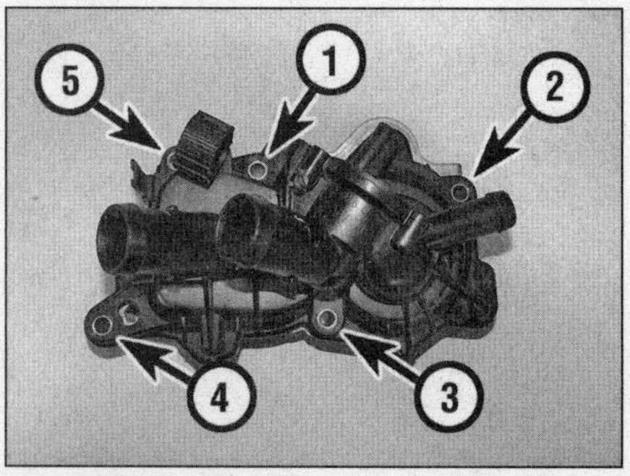

7.9d Tighten the bolts in the order shown

7.13 Remove the bracket

7.14a Using a metal bar to hold the pulley in position – if required

7.14b Removing the coolant pump pulley

1.2 litre SOHC petrol engines

Note: *The gasket is part of the coolant pump and cannot be separated, if there is any damage to the seal and a leak occurs, the coolant pump will need to be renewed complete with gasket.*

Removal

10 Drain the cooling system as described in Chapter 1A Section 32.

11 Before removing the auxiliary drivebelt, slacken the coolant pump pulley mounting bolts (do not remove at this point).

12 Remove the auxiliary drivebelt as described in Chapter 1A Section 28.

13 Where applicable, undo the retaining bolts and remove the bracket from the rear of the cylinder head **(see illustration)**.

14 Fully unscrew the bolts and remove the pulley from the coolant pump **(see illustrations)**.

15 Where fitted, disconnect the vacuum hose from the top of the coolant pump **(see illustration)**.

16 Unscrew the coolant pump retaining bolts, and withdraw the pump from the engine block. If the pump or gasket are faulty, then the complete coolant pump must be renewed **(see illustration)**.

Refitting

17 Refitting is a reversal of removal, bearing in mind the following points:

a) *Clean the surface of the engine block before refitting the pump.*
b) *Refit the coolant pump and torque bolts as specified.*
c) *On 1.2 litre, 3-cyl. engine, apply suitable sealant to the threads of the front retaining bolt.*
d) *On 1.2 litre, 4-cyl. engines, reconnect the vacuum hose to the top of the coolant pump*
e) *Refill the cooling system.*

1.4 litre petrol engines

Note: *The gasket is part of the coolant pump and cannot be separated, if there is any damage to the seal and a leak occurs, the coolant pump will need to be renewed complete with gasket.*

Removal

18 Drain the cooling system as described in Chapter 1A Section 32. **Note:** *The coolant pump is driven by the timing belt on 1.4 litre petrol engines.*

7.15 Remove the vacuum hose

7.16 Removing the coolant pump

19 Remove the main timing belt as described in Chapter 2D Section 6. If the belt is to be re-used, note the direction of rotation.

20 Remove the timing belt idler roller, and rear timing belt cover.

21 Before removing the coolant pump, place a rag below it to prevent any spillage over the timing belt and gears, as applicable.

22 Unscrew the coolant pump retaining bolts, and withdraw the pump from the engine block. Note the gasket is integral with the pump and must not be removed. If faulty, the pump must be renewed **(see illustration)**.

Refitting

23 Refitting is a reversal of removal, bearing in mind the following points:

a) *Clean the surface of the engine block before refitting the pump.*
b) *Refit the coolant pump and torque bolts as specified.*
c) *Refill the cooling system.*

Diesel engines

Note: *The coolant pump is driven by the timing belt on all diesel engines.*

24 Drain the cooling system as described in Chapter 1B Section 33.

25 Remove the timing belt as described in Chapter 2E Section 7.

26 Unscrew the coolant pump retaining bolts, and remove the pump from the engine block. Recover the O-ring seal from the groove in the pump. If the pump is faulty, it must be renewed **(see illustrations)**.

27 Refitting is a reversal of removal, bearing in mind the following points.

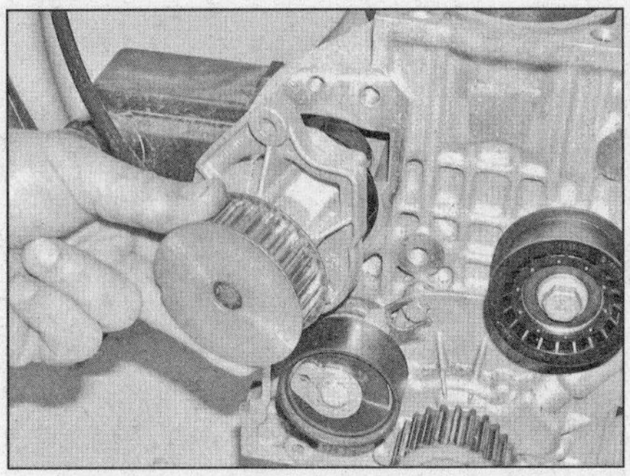

7.22 Withdraw the coolant pump

7.26a Undo the coolant pump bolts...

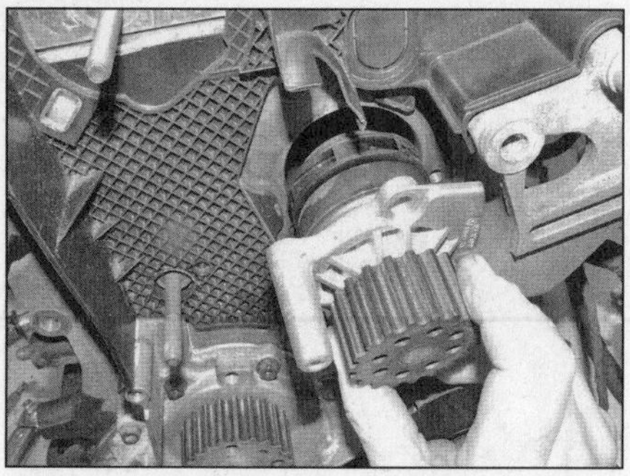

7.26b ...remove it from the cylinder block...

7.26c ...and recover the sealing ring

a) Fit the coolant pump with a new O-ring.
b) Lubricate the O-ring with coolant.
c) Refill the cooling system.

Electric circulation pump

28 Raise the front of the vehicle and support is securely on axle stands (see *Jacking and vehicle support*). Undo the fasteners and remove the engine undertray.

29 There is an electric circulation pump fitted to the following models **(see illustrations)**:

a) On 1.0 litre DOHC, TSI petrol engines, the pump is fitted to the front of the engine block.
b) On 1.2 litre SOHC, TSI engines the pump is fitted to the rear of the engine block
c) On 1.2 litre DOHC, TSI petrol engines, the pump is fitted to front of the engine block.
d) On 1.6 litre diesel engines the pump is fitted to the front of the sump.

30 Disconnect the wiring plug connector to the pump **(see illustration)**.

31 Fit hose clamps to the coolant hoses connected to the pump, and release the clips and disconnect the hoses from the pump **(see illustration)**. Be prepared for some loss of coolant.

32 Undo the retaining bolt and remove the pump **(see illustration)**.

33 Refitting is a reversal of removal. Refill the cooling system, or top-up as described in *Weekly checks*.

8 Heating and ventilation system – general information

Heating system

1 The heating/ventilation system consists of a four-speed blower motor (housed in the passenger compartment), face-level vents in the centre and at each end of the facia, and air ducts to the front and rear footwells.

2 The control unit is located in the facia, and the controls operate flap valves to deflect and mix the air flowing through the various parts of the heating/ventilation system. The flap valves are contained in the air distribution housing, which acts as a central distribution unit, passing air to the various ducts and vents.

3 Cold air enters the system through the grille at the rear of the engine compartment. A pollen filter is fitted in the heater assembly to filter out dust, soot, pollen and spores from the air entering the car.

4 If warm air is required, the cold air is passed over the heater matrix, which is effectively a small radiator, with engine coolant flowing through it. Diesel models are fitted with an additional electric heating element below the matrix, to ensure quick heater output – this heating element only operates when the coolant temperature is below 80°C.

5 The airflow, which can be boosted by the blower, then flows through the various ducts, according to the settings of the controls. Stale air is expelled through ducts below the rear window.

6 If necessary, the outside air supply can be closed off, allowing the air inside the car to be recirculated. This can be useful to prevent unpleasant odours entering from outside the car, but should only be used briefly, as the recirculated air inside the car will soon deteriorate.

9 Heating and ventilation system components – removal and refitting

Heater control panel

1 On late models unclip the lower switch panel to expose the fixing screws **(see illustration)**.

2 On early models remove the screws **(see illustration)**.

3 Remove the trim panel and then remove the screws (late models). On early models release the complete panel and surround **(see illustrations)**.

7.29a Electric circulation pump – 1.0 litre TSI petrol engines

7.29b Electric circulation pump – 1.2 litre TSI petrol engines

7.30 Disconnect the wiring connector

7.31 Disconnect the coolant hoses (1.6 litre diesel shown)

7.32 Undo the mounting bracket securing bolt

9.1 Release the switch panel

9.2 Remove the screws

9.3a Undo the two retaining screws

9.3b Release the complete control panel (early model with climate control shown)

9.4a Lower the panel down and out through the lower opening

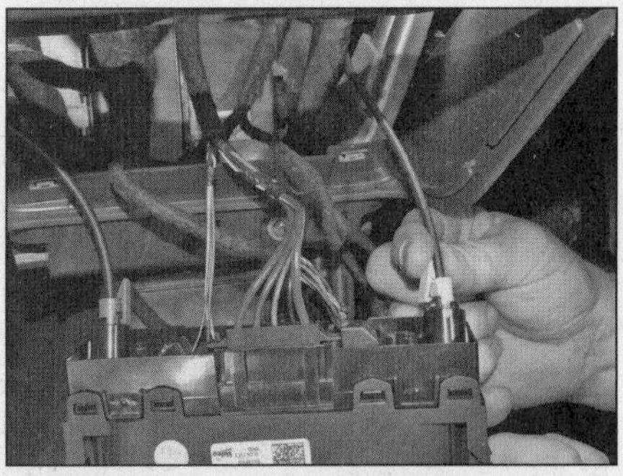

9.4b Release the bowden cables...

4 Pull the panel forward and disconnect the wiring plugs. On models with manual heater controls unclip the bowden cables **(illustrations)**.

5 Refitting is a reversal of removal, ensuring that the wiring connectors are connected securely.

Heater matrix

Note: *If the matrix is being replaced, always drain the system and replace the coolant (see Chapter 1A Section 32 or Chapter 1B Section 33).*

6 At the rear of the engine compartment, gain access to the heater hoses.

7 Using hose clamps, clamp the heater matrix inlet and return hoses located on the bulkhead at the rear of the engine compartment. Place a container beneath the hoses, then release the retaining clips and disconnect them. Note the location of the hoses for correct refitting. Alternatively drain the cooling system as described in Chapter 1A Section 32 or Chapter 1B Section 33.

8 With the hoses disconnected, remove the coolant from the matrix by blowing air into the inlet tube; preferably using an airline, then the coolant can be caught coming out of the outlet tube using a container.

Caution: Always use eye protection when using an airline.

9 Remove the centre console, as described in Chapter 11 Section 27.

10 Unclip the rubber sleeve from the air vent on the heater lower housing **(see illustration)**. On models fitted with a supplementary electric heater disconnect the wiring plugs form the heater and move the loom to the side.

11 To improve access remove the airbag control module from below the housing. Disconnect the battery before proceeding (as described in Chapter 5A Section 3), then disconnect the wiring plug, unbolt and remove the module **(see illustrations)**.

12 Release the clips that hold the lower

9.4c ...and disconnect the wiring plugs

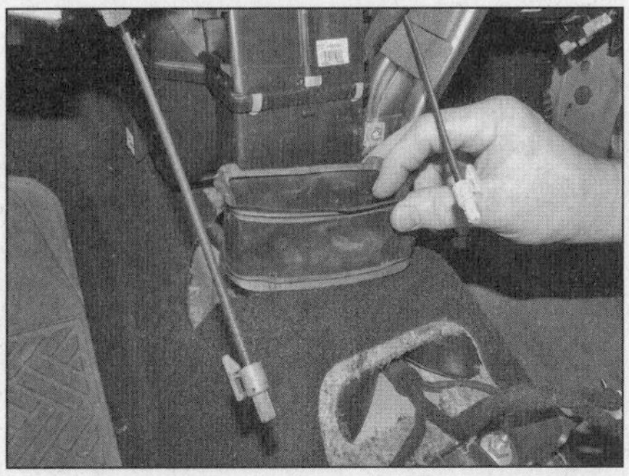

9.10 Remove the rubber air vent sleeve

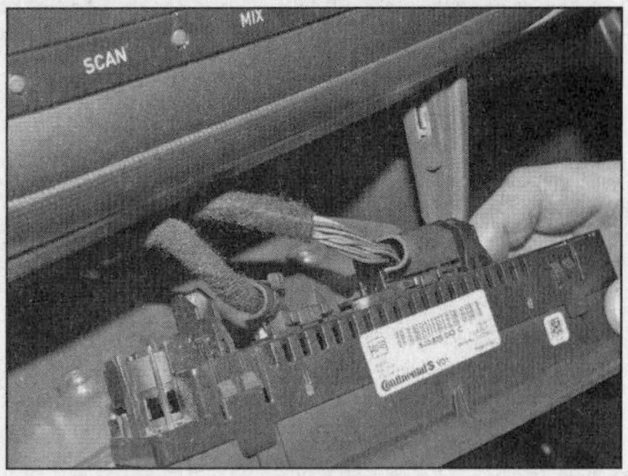

9.4d Cables are not used on models with climate control

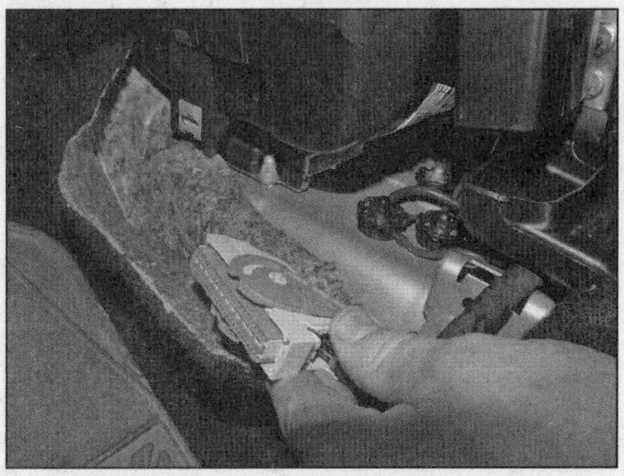

9.11a Disconnect the wiring plug...

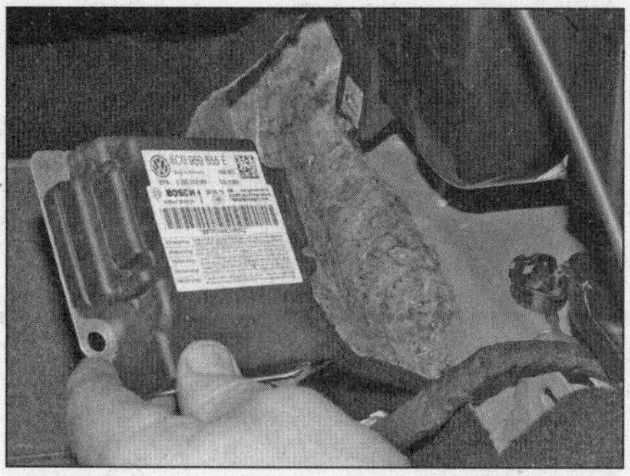

9.11b ...and remove the module

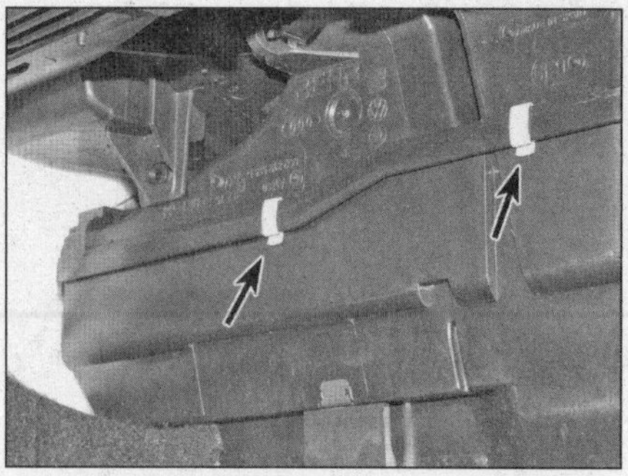

9.12 Release the clips (one side shown)

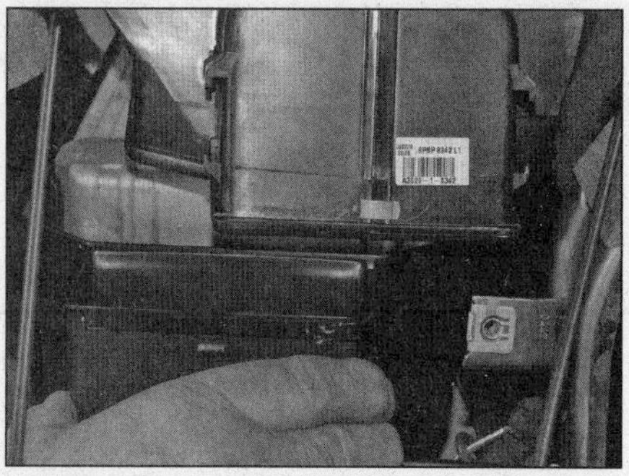

9.13a Lower the matrix and housing...

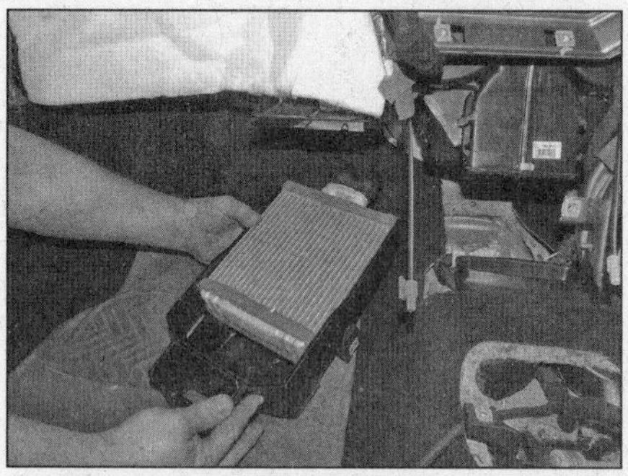

9.13b ...into the passenger footwell

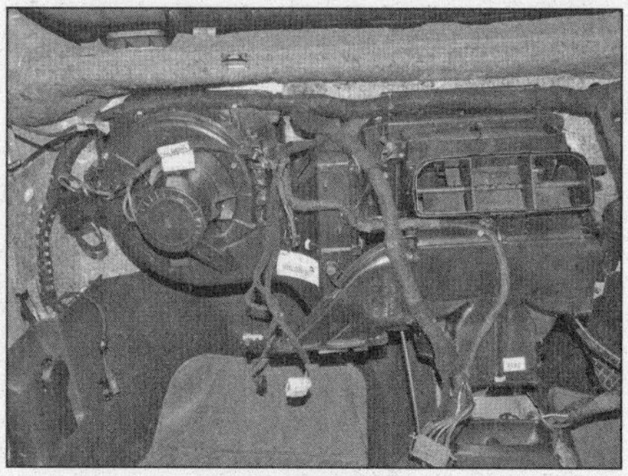

9.16 The heater housing with the crossmember removed

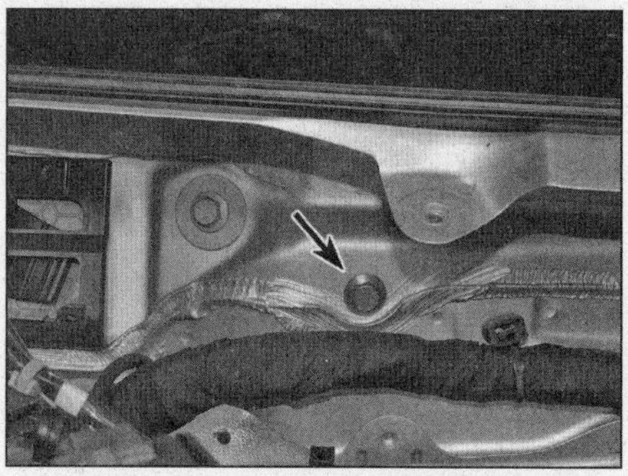

9.17 Remove the mounting bolts (one shown)

section of the heater housing to the main body **(see illustration)**.

13 Withdraw the lower part of the housing complete with heater matrix from inside the passenger compartment **(see illustrations)**. Take care not to damage the pipes, as they are withdrawn from the bulkhead grommet. Place cloth rags or similar on the floor beneath the heater matrix to catch any coolant that may be lost, as the heater matrix is removed.

14 Refitting is a reversal of removal, noting the following.

a) Make sure the foam seal is fitted correctly around the perimeter of the matrix.

b) Make sure the matrix is located correctly in the housing.

c) Check that the coolant pipes locate correctly in the rubber grommet in the bulkhead

d) Refill the cooling system and top-up the coolant level with reference to 'Weekly checks' at the beginning of this Manual.

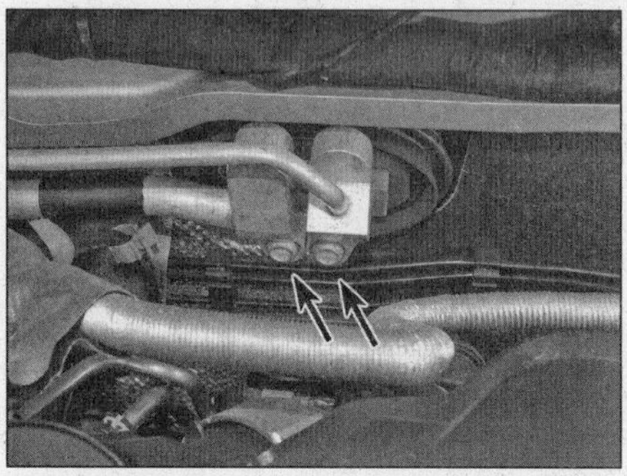

9.20 Unbolt the refrigerant lines from the evaporator expansion valve

Heater housing

Warning: Refer to the precautions given in Section 11.

15 It is not possible to remove the housing without opening the refrigerant circuit to the air-conditioning evaporator; therefore this task must be entrusted to a Seat dealer or an air conditioning specialist, before removal of the heater housing.

Caution: The air conditioning compressor is driven permanently by the auxiliary drivebelt, and is not fitted with a magnetic clutch. It is not recommended that the engine is started without refrigerant being present in the system, as the compressor may overheat causing internal damage. Note also that if the refrigerant circuit is not opened within 10 minutes of evacuation, slight pressure may develop due to re-evaporation.

16 Remove the facia panel and crossmember as described in Chapter 11 Section 28 and Chapter 11 Section 29 **(see illustration)**.

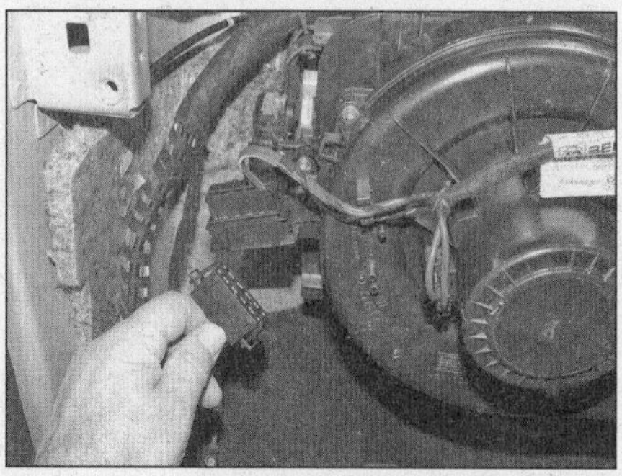

9.22a Disconnect the wiring plug

17 Remove the wiper motor (as described in Chapter 12 Section 16) to gain access to the heater housing bolts **(see illustration)**.

18 Using hose clamps, clamp the heater matrix inlet and return hoses located on the bulkhead at the rear of the engine compartment. Place a container beneath the hoses, then pull out the clips and disconnect them. Note the location of the hoses for correct refitting.

19 With the hoses disconnected, remove the coolant from the matrix by blowing air into the inlet tube; preferably using an airline, then the coolant can be caught coming out of the outlet tube using a container.

Caution: Always use eye protection when using an airline.

20 With the refrigerant evacuated, unscrew the bolts securing the refrigerant lines to the evaporator on the bulkhead at the rear of the engine compartment, and detach them. Recover the seals and plug the lines and evaporator openings to prevent entry of foreign matter and water vapour. Discard the seals, as new ones must be used on refitting **(see illustration)**.

21 Inside the car, place cloth rags or similar on the floor beneath the heater unit.

22 Note the location and routing of the wiring loom and then disconnect and unclip it from the housing **(see illustrations)**.

23 Carefully pull the heater unit from the bulkhead, taking care not to damage the matrix tubes on the bulkhead **(see illustration)**. The help of an assistant may be

9.22b Cut the cable ties as required

9.23 Remove the housing

9.31 The temperature sensor (shown with the housing removed)

required. Be prepared for coolant spillage as the assembly is removed from inside the car. As the heater unit assembly is removed, check to see if there is any wiring still attached to the housing.

24 If necessary, the heater may be further dismantled on the bench.

25 Refitting is a reversal of removal, but refill the cooling system and top-up the coolant with reference to *Weekly checks* at the beginning of this Manual. Have the air-conditioning system refilled by a Seat dealer or an air conditioning specialist, when finished.

Fresh air/recirculating/ temperature/ flap positioning servomotors

Note: *Depending on model, there may be up to five air flap servomotors fitted.*

26 On the model being worked on, there are two air flap motors to the left-hand side of the heater housing and one on the right.

27 To access the servo motors, remove the facia panel and crossmember, as described in Chapter 11 Section 28.

28 Disconnect the wiring, undo the motor retaining bolt(s), then remove it from its mountings, and where applicable, separate it from the air flap lever. Note the position of the drive/gear on the rear of the servomotor, as it needs to be re-aligned when refitting. If the drive/gear is not aligned correctly, the flaps will not operate correctly.

29 Refitting is a reversal of removal. Note that if the motor is renewed, its basic settings may need to be reprogrammed by a dealer using specialist equipment.

Evaporator core temperature sensor

30 Remove the facia as described in Chapter 11 Section 28.

31 Reach around the rear of the heater housing and disconnect the wiring plug. Pull the sensor form the housing **(see illustration)**.

Heater blower motor

32 Remove the glovebox as described in Chapter 11 Section 26.

33 Move the insulation material covering the heater blower housing. It can be tucked up behind the housing.

34 Remove the screws and remove the lower facia strut **(see illustration)**.

35 Disconnect the wiring plug from the blower motor, unclip the wiring loom from the housing and release the cable tie and wiring from the top right-hand side of the blower housing.

36 Undo the retaining screws from around the outside of the housing and remove the blower motor **(see illustrations)**.

37 Refitting is a reversal of removal. Secure the wiring loom with new cable ties as required.

Heater blower motor series resistor

38 Remove the glovebox as described in Chapter 11 Section 26.

39 Fold the insulation material up and out of the way.

Caution: The resistor may be very hot if the heater has recently been in use.

9.34 Remove the support strut

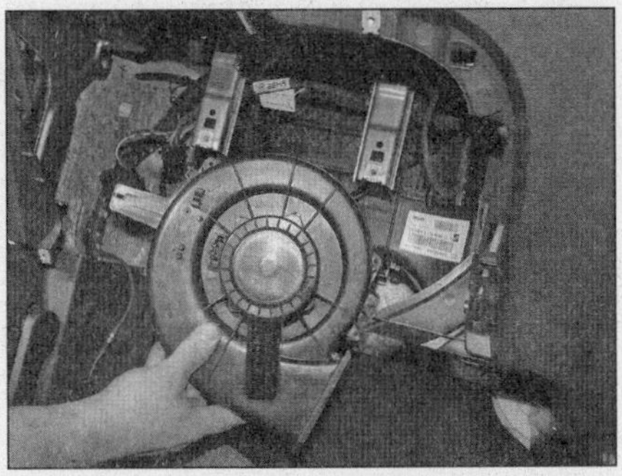

9.36b Lower the motor and remove it

40 Reach up to the right-hand side of the blower motor and rotate the resister to release it from the heater housing. Lower the resistor and disconnect the wiring plug.

41 Refitting is the reverse of removal.

Auxiliary heater

42 Some diesel engine models are equipped with an auxiliary electrically powered heating element within the heating unit, below the heater matrix. In order to remove the element, gain access to the heater matrix, as described previously. Note there is no need to drain the coolant – the heater matrix will remain in place.

43 Disconnect the wiring plugs and then unclip the lower section of the heater housing.

44 Withdraw the auxiliary heater out from the lower housing, noting its fitted position **(see illustration)**.

45 Refitting is a reversal of removal.

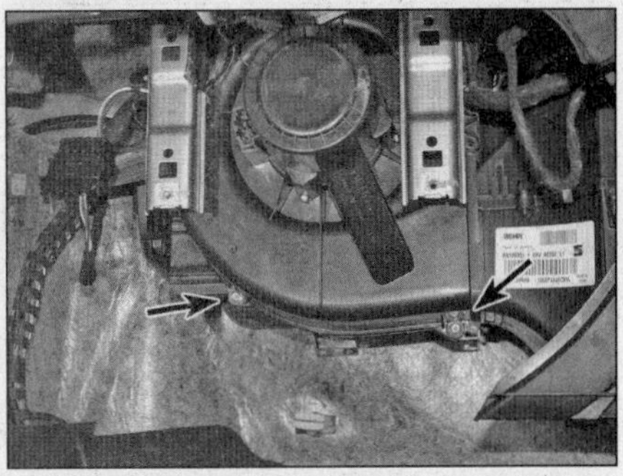

9.36a Remove the screws (two shown, but more hidden at the sides and top)

9.44 Remove the auxiliary heater from the lower housing

10.4a Work around the heater housing removing the screws...

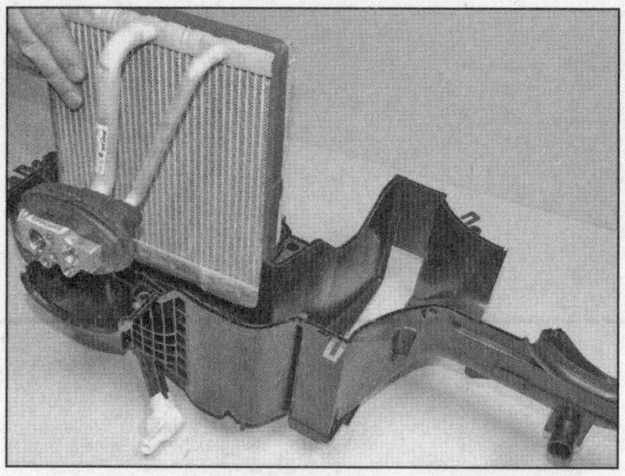

10.4b ...until the evaporator can be removed

10.7 Disconnect the refrigerant lines to the condenser

10 Air conditioning system components – removal and refitting

Warning: Refer to the precautions given in Section 11, before working on the air-conditioning system.

1 Before working on any components in the air-conditioning system, have the refrigerant evacuated from the air conditioning system by a dealer or refrigeration specialist.

Warning: It is a criminal offence to knowingly discharge refrigerant to the atmosphere.

Caution: The air conditioning compressor is driven permanently by the auxiliary drivebelt, and is not fitted with a magnetic clutch. It is not recommended that the engine be started without refrigerant being present in the system, as the compressor may overheat causing internal damage. Note also that if the refrigerant circuit is not opened within 10 minutes of evacuation, slight pressure may develop due to re-evaporation.

Evaporator

2 Remove the heater housing and heater matrix, as described earlier in Section 9.

3 Remove the rubber gaiter and foam cushion from around the refrigerant pipes.

4 Working your way around the housing, undo the retaining screws and release the securing clips and split the housing, then withdraw the evaporator from the housing **(see illustrations)**.

5 Refitting is a reversal of removal, fit new seals and have the system recharged by a Seat dealer or refrigeration specialist.

10.14a Refrigerant lines to the compressor

10.14b Seal the lines and the openings in the compressor

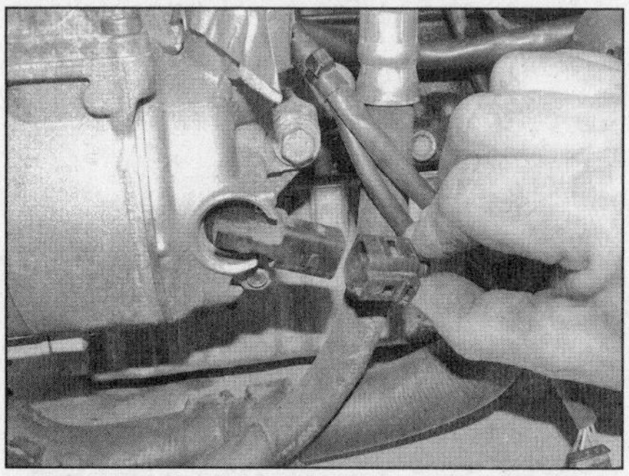

10.15 Disconnect the wiring connector

10.16 Unscrew the compressor mounting bolts (Delphi compressor shown)

Condenser

6 Have the refrigerant evacuated from the air conditioning system by a Seat dealer or refrigeration specialist.

7 Undo the two bolts securing the refrigerant lines to the condenser **(see illustration)**. As the pipes are disconnected, recover the seals and plug the lines and condenser openings to prevent entry of foreign matter and water vapour.

8 Remove the radiator (and intercooler where fitted) as described in Section 3 of this Chapter. There is no need to separate the condenser from the radiator in the vehicle as both can be removed together.

9 With the radiator and condenser removed from the engine compartment, undo the retaining screws and split the condenser from the radiator, taking care not to damage its fins.

10 Refitting is a reversal of removal, but fit new seals, and have the system recharged by a Seat dealer or refrigeration specialist.

Compressor

11 Have the refrigerant evacuated from the air conditioning system by a Seat dealer or refrigeration specialist.

12 Remove the auxiliary drivebelt as described in Chapter 1A Section 28 or Chapter 1B Section 29.

13 On diesel engines remove the charge air pipe.

14 Unscrew the retaining bolts and disconnect the refrigerant lines from the compressor **(see illustrations)**. Remove the O-ring seals and renew them if necessary. Plug the open pipes and ports to prevent the ingress of moisture.

15 Disconnect the wiring plug connector from the rear of the compressor **(see illustration)**.

16 Undo the retaining bolts **(see illustration)**, and withdraw the compressor from the mounting bracket.

17 Refitting is a reversal of the removal procedure, ensure that all the fixings are tightened to the specified torque settings, where given. On completion, fit new O-rings to the refrigerant lines, and then have the system recharged by a Seat dealer or refrigeration specialist.

Receiver/drier

Note: *Check for the availability of parts before removal, there are different makes of receiver/drier and some cannot be renewed separately from the condenser.*

18 The receiver/drier is attached to the left-hand side of the condenser.

19 Remove the condenser, as described above.

20 Unscrew the cap (with a T50 torx socket) from the top of the receiver/drier **(see illustration)**.

Caution: DO NOT remove this cap if the system has not been evacuated, as it will be under high pressure.

21 Push downwards slightly on sealing cover and extract the retaining circlip from inside the end of the condenser. Pull the receiver/drier filter element from place.

22 Refitting is a reversal of the removal procedure, ensure that all the fixings are tightened to the specified torque settings, where given. On completion, fit new O-rings and then have the system recharged by a Seat dealer or refrigeration specialist.

11 Air conditioning system – general information and precautions

General information

1 Air conditioning is fitted as standard to most models, and is available as manually operated (Climatic) or automatically-operated (Climatronic). The Climatronic system works in conjunction with the heating and air conditioning systems to maintain a selected vehicle interior temperature fully automatically.

2 The air conditioning system enables the temperature of incoming air to be lowered, and dehumidifies the air, which makes for rapid demisting and increased comfort. The cooling side of the system works in the same way as a domestic refrigerator. Refrigerant gas is drawn into a belt-driven compressor and passes into a condenser mounted in front of the radiator, where it loses heat and becomes liquid. The liquid passes through an expansion valve to an evaporator, where it changes from liquid under high pressure to gas under low pressure. This change is accompanied by a drop in temperature, which in turn cools the evaporator. The refrigerant returns to the compressor and the cycle begins again.

10.20 Remove the cap

3 Air blown through the evaporator passes to the air distribution unit, where it is mixed with hot air blown through the heater matrix to achieve the desired temperature in the passenger compartment.

4 The operation of the system is controlled electronically by coolant temperature switches, and pressure switches which are screwed into the compressor high-pressure line. Any problems with the system should be referred to a Seat dealer or an air conditioning specialist.

5 The only operation that can be carried out easily without discharging the refrigerant is the renewal of the compressor drivebelt, which is covered in the relevant part of Chapter 1A Section 28 or Chapter 1B Section 29. Removal of the evaporator and condenser requires the evacuation of the refrigerant **(see illustration)**. If necessary the compressor can be unbolted and moved aside, without disconnecting its flexible hoses, after removing the drivebelt.

11.5 Service ports for the recovery of the refrigerant. Shown connected to the recovery machine

Precautions

6 When an air conditioning system is fitted, it is necessary to observe special precautions whenever dealing with any part of the system, its associated components and any items which require disconnection of the system. If for any reason the system must be disconnected, entrust this task to yourSeat dealer or an air conditioning specialist.

Warning: The refrigeration circuit contains a refrigerant and it is therefore dangerous to disconnect any part of the system without specialised knowledge and equipment. The refrigerant is potentially dangerous and should only be handled by qualified persons. If it is splashed onto the skin it can cause frostbite. It is not itself poisonous, but in the presence of a naked flame (including a cigarette) it forms a poisonous gas. Uncontrolled discharging of the refrigerant is dangerous and potentially damaging to the environment.

7 Do not operate the air conditioning system if it is known to be short of refrigerant, as this may damage the compressor.

Chapter 4 Part A
Petrol engine fuel systems

Contents

Degrees of difficulty

Easy, suitable for novice with little experience	Fairly easy, suitable for beginner with some experience	Fairly difficult, suitable for competent DIY mechanic	Difficult, suitable for experienced DIY mechanic	Very difficult, suitable for expert DIY or professional

Specifications

Engine codes *

1.0 litre	CHYB, CHZC and CHZB
1.2 litre:	
SOHC	CBZB
DOHC	CJZD and CJZC
1.4 litre	BXW and CGGB

**See 'Vehicle identification' at the end of this manual for the location of the engine code markings.*

System type

1.0 litre engines	Bosch Motronic ME 17.5 UDS
1.2 litre engines:	
#Engine codes CBZB	Siemans Simos 10 UDS
Engine code CJZD and CJZC	Bosch Motronic MED 17.525 UDS
1.4 litre engines	Magneti Marelli 4HV

Fuel system

Recommended fuel minimum octane rating:	
All models	95 RON unleaded (91 RON unleaded may be used, but with reduced performance)
Fuel pump type	Electric, immersed in fuel tank
Fuel pump delivery rate:	
1.0 litre engines	1000 cc/60 sec (minimum battery voltage: 10.5 V)
1.2 litre engines	1500 cc/60 sec (minimum battery voltage: 10.5 V)
1.4 litre engines	540 cc/30 secs (battery voltage of 10.5 V)
Regulated fuel pressure	4.0 bar minimum to 7.0 bar maximum
Engine idle speed (non-adjustable, electronically controlled)	650 to 850 rpm
Idle CO content (non-adjustable, electronically controlled)	0.5 % max
Injector electrical resistance (typical)	12 to 17 ohms

Torque wrench settings	Nm	lbf ft
Camshaft position sensor	8	6
Fuel rail mounting bolts	10	7
Fuel tank strap securing bolts	25	18
Fuel sender unit/pump retaining ring	80	58
Inlet air temperature/pressure sensor	3	2
Inlet manifold:		
1.0 and 1.2 litre engines	8	6
1.4 litre engines	20	15
Knock sensor(s)	20	15
Oxygen sensor(s)	50	37
Throttle body	7	6
High pressure fuel pump (TSI and FSI engines):		
Fuel pump bolts	20	15
Union nuts	25	18

1 General information and precautions

General information

1 The systems described in this Chapter are all self-contained engine management systems, which control both the fuel injection and ignition. This Chapter deals with the fuel system components only – see Chapter 4C for information on the exhaust and emission control systems, and to Chapter 5B for details of the ignition system.

2 The fuel injection system comprises a fuel tank, an electric fuel pump/level sender unit, a fuel filter, fuel supply and return lines, a throttle valve control unit, a fuel rail, four electronic fuel injectors, and an Electronic Control Unit (ECU) together with its associated sensors, actuators and wiring. All the fuel systems used operate in the same manner, but there are some detail differences. The electronic power control system (EPC) is completely electronic, and no accelerator cable is fitted. The position of the accelerator pedal is signalled from the pedal control unit by two variable resistors, and the throttle valve is then activated by an electric motor in the throttle valve control unit on the inlet manifold. With the engine stopped, the position of the throttle valve is directly comparable to the position of the accelerator pedal, however, when the engine is running the engine control unit opens and closes the throttle valve independently according to the prevailing conditions. This may mean, for example, that the throttle valve may be fully open even though the accelerator pedal is only half open. The engine electronic control unit (ECU) determines the best position for the throttle valve in the interests of exhaust gas emission and fuel consumption. In the event of a fault in the system, the EPC warning light will illuminate on the instrument panel and the fault will be stored in the fault memory. The system then switches to its emergency settings and the engine speed is increased to allow the driver to take the car to a Seat dealer, however, the accelerator pedal position senders are no longer operational.

3 The fuel pump is immersed in the fuel inside the tank, and delivers a constant supply of fuel through a cartridge filter to the fuel rail. The pressure regulator is integral with the fuel filter located next to the fuel tank, and the return line is taken from the filter to the fuel tank. The fuel pressure regulator maintains a constant fuel pressure to the fuel injectors, and returns excess fuel to the tank through the return line. This constant flow system also helps to reduce fuel temperature, and prevents vaporisation.

4 The fuel injectors are opened and closed by the Electronic Control Unit (ECU), which calculates the injection timing and duration according to engine speed, crankshaft/camshaft position, throttle position and rate of opening, inlet manifold depression, inlet air temperature, coolant temperature and exhaust gas oxygen content information, received from sensors mounted on and around the engine.

5 Inlet air is drawn into the engine through the air cleaner, which contains a renewable paper filter element. On all engines, the inlet air temperature is regulated by a valve mounted in the air cleaner inlet trunking, which blends air at ambient temperature with hot air, drawn from over the exhaust manifold.

6 The temperature and pressure of the air entering the engine is measured by a sensor located on the inlet manifold. This information is used by the ECU to fine-tune the fuelling requirements for different operating conditions.

7 Idle speed is determined by the ECU, and manual adjustment of the engine idle speed is not necessary or possible.

8 The exhaust gas oxygen content is constantly monitored by the ECU through two oxygen sensors (also known as lambda sensors). One is fitted before the catalytic converter, and the other after – this improves sensor response time and accuracy, and the ECU compares the signals from each sensor to confirm that the converter is working correctly. The ECU uses the information from the sensors to modify the injection timing and duration to maintain the optimum air/fuel ratio – a result of this is that manual adjustment of the idle exhaust CO content is not necessary or possible.

9 On all engines, the ECU controls the operation of the activated charcoal filter evaporative loss system.

10 It should be noted that fault diagnosis of all the engine management systems described in this Chapter is only possible with dedicated electronic test equipment. Simple low cost hand held (or smart phone) fault code readers are available in the aftermarket, however they will not display all the engine fault codes. As a general rule they will only list the mandatory emissions related fault codes. Some tools may be capable of displaying faults from all vehicle systems as well as showing actual live data from the engine management control unit. More complex issues will require access to professional level equipment or the manufacturers own diagnostic tool. Once the fault has been identified, the removal/refitting sequences detailed in the following Sections will then allow the appropriate component(s) to be renewed as required. **Note:** *The engine code will be found on the vehicle data sticker, close to (or inside) the spare wheel well, or on the plate fixed to the right-hand inner wing* ***(see illustrations)***.

1.10a Vehicle information label in luggage compartment ...

1.10b ...and fixed to the right-hand inner wing

Precautions

Warning: Petrol is extremely flammable – great care must be taken when working on any part of the fuel system.

Caution: Do not smoke, or allow any naked flames or uncovered light bulbs near the work area. Note that gas-powered domestic appliances with pilot flames, such as heaters boilers and tumble-dryers, also present a fire hazard – bear this in mind if you are working in an area where such appliances are present. Always keep a suitable fire extinguisher close to the work area, and familiarise yourself with its operation before starting work. Wear eye protection when working on fuel systems, and wash off any fuel spilt on bare skin immediately with soap and water. Note that fuel vapour is just as dangerous as liquid fuel – possibly more so; a vessel that has been emptied of liquid fuel will still contain vapour, and can be potentially explosive.

Caution: Many of the operations described in this Chapter involve the disconnection of fuel lines, which may cause an amount of fuel spillage. Before commencing work, refer to the above 'Warning' and the information in 'Safety first!' at the beginning of this manual.

Caution: Residual fuel pressure always remains in the fuel system; long after the engine has been switched off. This pressure must be relieved in a controlled manner before work can commence on any component in the fuel system – refer to Section 8 for details.

Caution: When working with fuel system components, pay particular attention to cleanliness – dirt entering the fuel system may cause blockages, which will lead to poor running.

Caution: In the interests of personal safety and equipment protection, many of the procedures in this Chapter suggest that the negative lead be removed from the

battery terminal. This firstly eliminates the possibility of accidental short-circuits being caused as the car is being worked upon, and secondly prevents damage to electronic components (e.g. sensors, actuators, ECUs) which are particularly sensitive to the power surges caused by disconnection or reconnection of the wiring harness whilst they are still 'live'. Refer to 'Disconnecting the battery' at the rear of this manual.

2 Fuel pipes and connections

1 Disconnect the battery as described in Chapter 5A Section 3.
2 The fuel supply pipe connects the fuel pump in the fuel tank to the high pressure fuel pump on the engine.
3 Whenever you're working under the vehicle, be sure to inspect all fuel and evaporative emission pipes for leaks, kinks, dents and other damage. Always replace a damaged fuel pipe immediately.
4 If you find signs of dirt in the pipes during disassembly, disconnect all pipes and blow them out with compressed air. Inspect the fuel strainer on the fuel pump pick-up unit for damage and deterioration.

Steel tubing

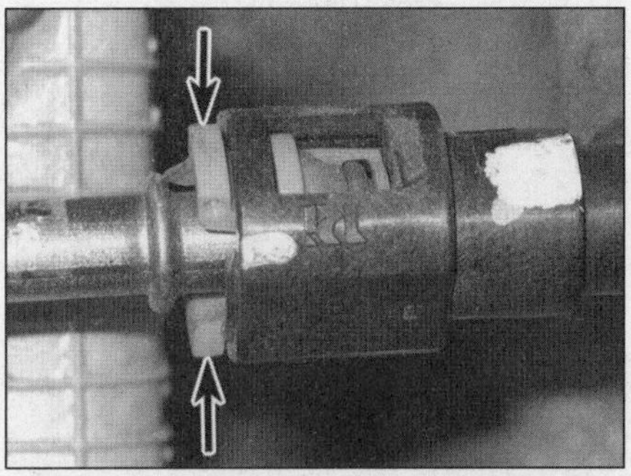

2.10a Two-tab type fitting; depress both tabs with your fingers, then pull the fuel pipe and the fitting apart

5 It is critical that the fuel pipes be replaced with pipes of equivalent type and specification.
6 Some steel fuel pipes have threaded fittings. When loosening these fittings, hold the stationary fitting with a spanner while turning the union nut.

Plastic tubing

⚠ ***Warning: When removing or installing plastic fuel tubing, be careful not to bend or twist it too much, which can damage it. Also, plastic fuel tubing is NOT heat resistant, so keep it away from excessive heat.***

7 When replacing fuel system plastic tubing, use only original equipment replacement plastic tubing.

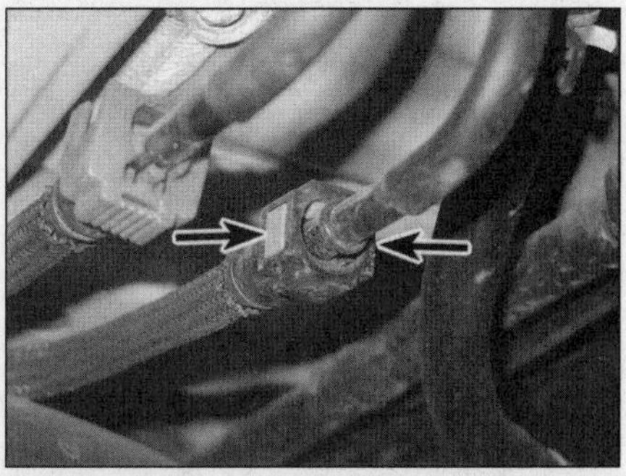

2.10b On this type of fitting, depress the two buttons on opposite sides of the fitting, then pull it off the fuel pipe

Flexible hoses

8 When replacing fuel system flexible hoses, use original equipment replacements, or hose to the same specification.
9 Don't route fuel hoses (or metal pipes) within 100 mm of the exhaust system or within 280 mm of the catalytic converter. Make sure that no rubber hoses are installed directly against the vehicle, particularly in places where there is any vibration. If allowed to touch some vibrating part of the vehicle, a hose can easily become chafed and it might start leaking. A good rule of thumb is to maintain a minimum of 8.0 mm clearance around a hose (or metal pipe) to prevent contact with the vehicle underbody.

Disconnecting Fuel pipe Fittings

10 Typical fuel pipe fittings:

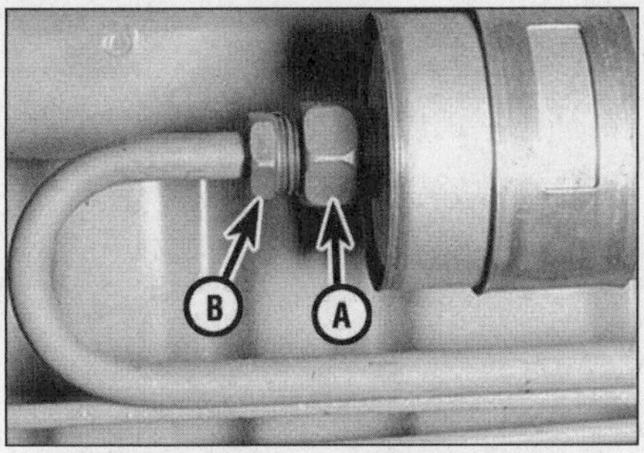

2.10c Threaded fuel pipe fitting; hold the stationary portion of the pipe or component (A) while loosening the union nut (B) with a flare-nut spanner

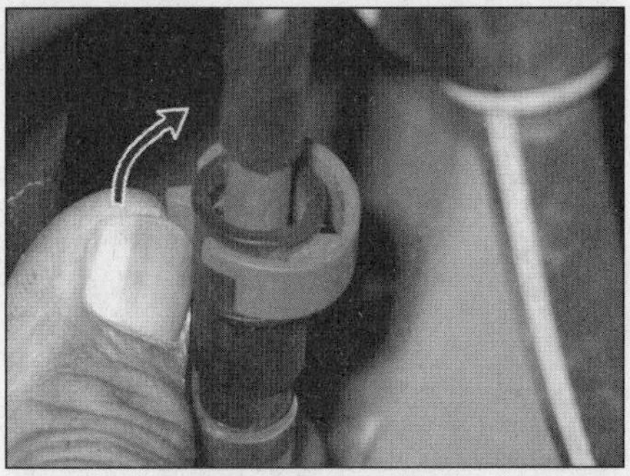

2.10d Plastic collar-type fitting; rotate the outer part of the fitting

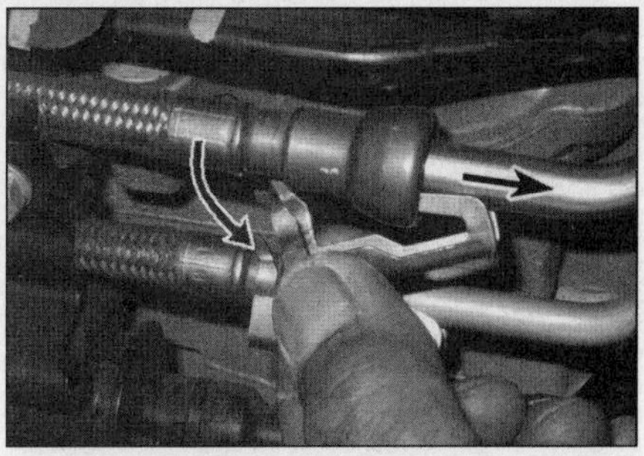

2.10e Metal collar quick-connect fitting; pull the end of the retainer off the fuel pipe and disengage the other end from the female side of the fitting...

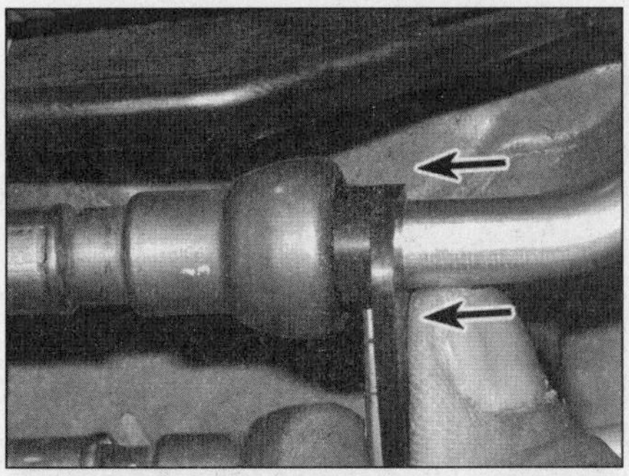

2.10f ...insert a fuel pipe separator tool into the female side of the fitting, push it into the fitting and pull the fuel pipe off the pipe

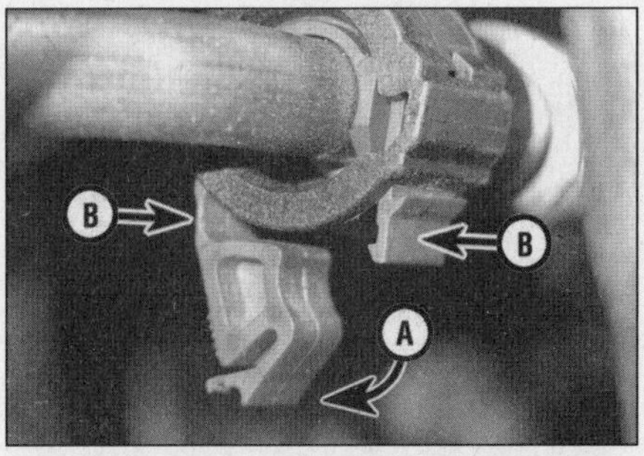

2.10g Some fittings are secured by lock tabs. Release the lock tab (A) and rotate it to the fully-opened position, squeeze the two smaller lock tabs (B)...

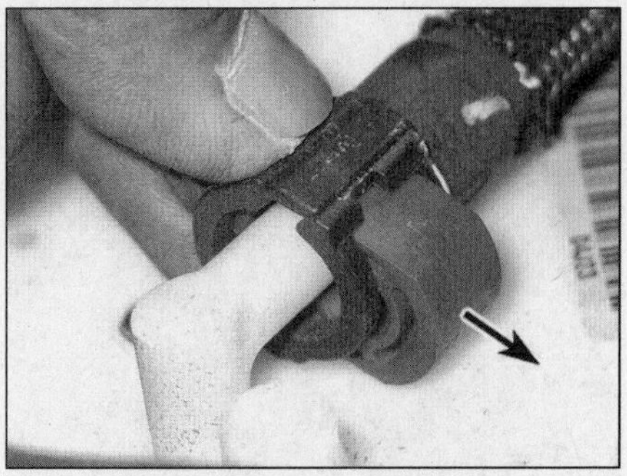

2.10h ...then push the retainer out and pull the fuel pipe off the pipe

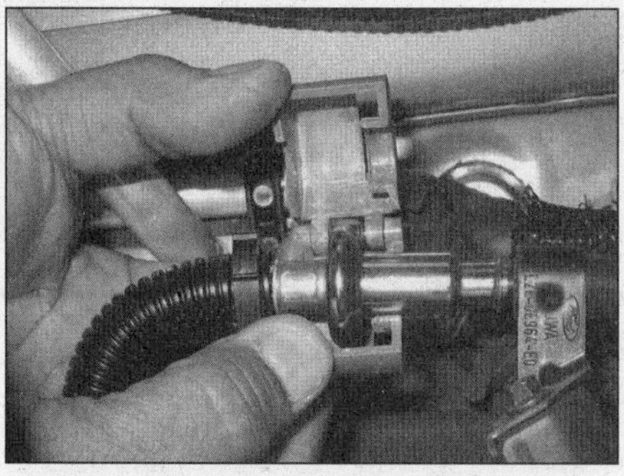

2.10i Spring-lock coupling; remove the safety cover, install a coupling release tool and close the tool around the coupling...

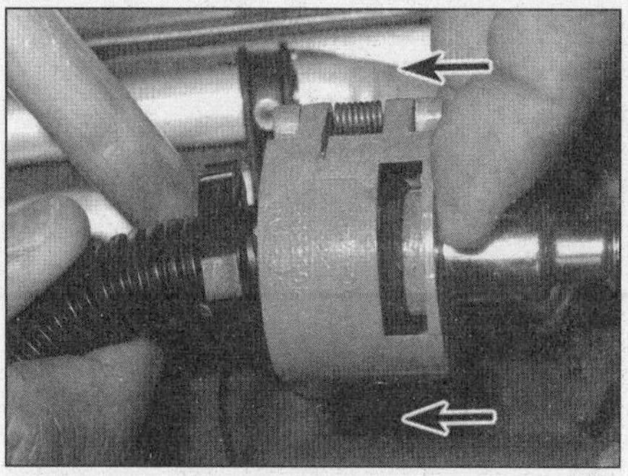

2.10j ...push the tool into the fitting, then pull the two pipes apart

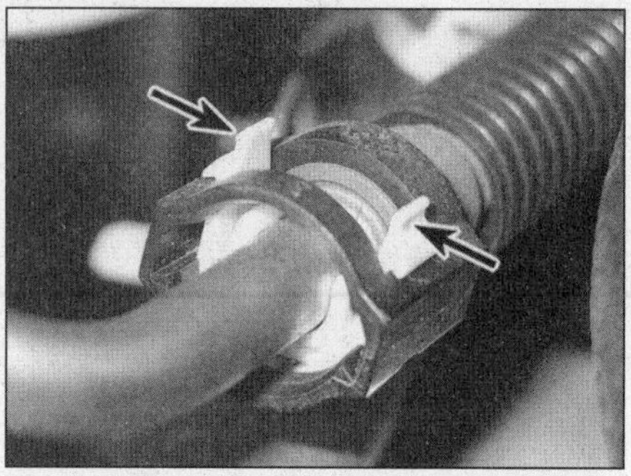

2.10k Hairpin clip type fitting: push the legs of the retainer clip together, then push the clip down all the way until it stops and pull the fuel pipe off the pipe

3 Air filter housing and inlet system – removal and refitting

Removal

1.0 litre engine (TSI versions)

1 At the front of the housing slacken the spring type hose clip and remove the hose **(see illustration)**.

2 Slacken and remove the single bolt at the front of the housing **(see illustration)**.

3 At the left-hand side of the housing unclip the vacuum hose and then prise off the breather hose from the right-hand side **(see illustration)**.

4 At the rear of the housing release the spring type hose clip and pull the housing off the turbocharger **(see illustrations)**.

5 Unclip the vacuum lines from the bottom of the housing and remove it.

6 If required the inlet duct from the turbocharger to the throttle bod can be removed.

7 Disconnect the wiring plug from the boost pressure sensor and unclip the EVAP and vacuum hoses **(see illustration)**.

8 Release the clips at the turbocharger and the throttle body and remove the duct **(see illustrations)**.

1.0 litre engine (MPI versions)

9 Prise off the breather hose from the right-hand side of the housing.

10 Pull up the housing at the rear to release it from the mounting studs and then pull it up at the front. Move it to the right to release the inlet duct from the mounting and then remove the complete assembly from the vehicle.

1.2 litre engine (SOHC)

11 Unbolt the inlet duct from the bonnet slam panel. Release the duct from the turbocharger inlet by either releasing the spring type hose clip or by removing the bolts.

12 Remove the vacuum hose from the duct and then remove the single bolt from the housing.

13 Pull up the housing to release it from the rubber mountings and remove it.

3.1 Release the spring clip

3.2 Remove the bolt

3.3 Remove the breather hose

3.4a Remove the rear spring clip...

3.4b ...and lift off the housing

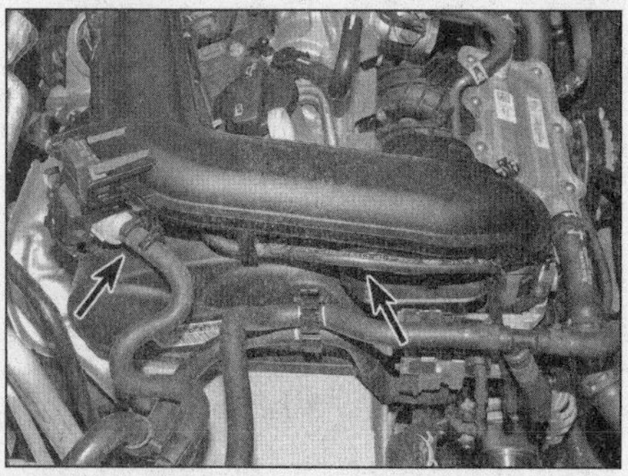

3.7 Unclip the hoses

3.8a Release the clips and...

3.8b Remove the charge air pipe

3.14a Release the spring type clamp. Note the special tool

3.14b Remove the inlet duct

3.15a Remove the breather hose

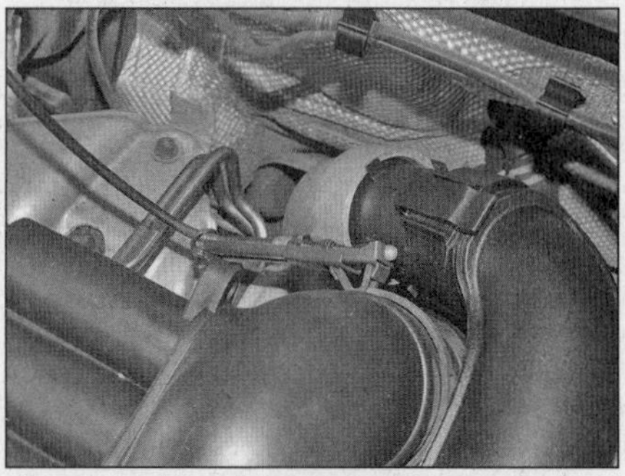

3.15b Release the duct at the turbocharger...

1.2 litre engine (DOHC)

14 Release the spring hose clip from the air inlet duct **(see illustrations)**.

15 Pull off the breather hose and then release the outlet duct at the air filter or the turbocharger **(see illustrations)**.

16 Remove the housing by pulling it straight up off the mounting rubbers **(see illustration)**.

17 If required the charge air pipe (turbocharger to throttle body) can now be removed.

18 Disconnect the wiring plug from the airflow sensor and then release the spring clips from the throttle body and inlet manifold **(see illustrations)**. Remove the duct.

19 The air filter inlet duct can also be removed if required.

1.4 litre engine

20 Remove the air filter element as described in Chapter 1A Section 26.

21 Release the catches, and disconnect the hose from the intake duct at the slam panel.

22 Pull the hose from the non-return valve at the left-hand side of the air cleaner, and pull the vacuum hose and valve from the rear corner.

23 Pull the air cleaner assembly upwards from the locating pins. Unclip the fuel hose, as the assembly is withdrawn.

3.15c ...or the air filter housing

3.16 Remove the air filter housing

3.18a Disconnect the wiring plug...

3.18b ...and release the clips at the throttle body

3.18c Release the duct at the turbocharger

Refitting

24 Refitting is a reversal of removal in all cases, but check that the all the rubber sockets are correctly orientated in their housings before pushing the air filter housing fully home.

4 Fuel system components – removal and refitting

Note: *Observe the precautions in Section 1 before working on any component in the fuel system. Information on the engine management system sensors which are more directly related to the ignition system will be found in Chapter 5B. After fitting any of the components in this Section, have the engine management ECU's fault memory interrogated and any resident faults erased by a Seat dealer or suitably-equipped specialist.*

Throttle valve control unit

Caution: If the throttle valve control unit is renewed, it will be necessary to program the new unit to the car before it can be used – this will need to be carried out by a Seat dealer or specialist.

1 The throttle valve is removed in a similar way on all the engines covered in this manual.

2 On 1.0 litre MPI engines (engine code CHYB) and all 1.4 litre engines remove the air filter housing as described in Section 3.

3 On 1.0 litre TSI engines and 1.2 litre engines disconnect the boost pressure sensor and then remove the air intake hose **(see illustrations)**.

4 On all engines disconnect the wiring plug from the throttle valve **(see illustration)**.

5 Where required remove the crankcase breather hose and then unbolt the throttle valve. Recover the seal **(see illustrations)**.

4.3a Disconnect the boost pressure wiring plug

4.3b Release the securing clips...

4.3c ...and remove the air intake pipe

4.4 Disconnect the wiring plug

4.5a Remove the screws (1.2 litre shown)...

4.5b ...and where fitted remove the bracket

4.5c Remove the throttle valve and...

4.5d ...recover the seal

4.5e The throttle body is removed in the same way on the 1.0 litre TSI engine. Remove the bolts...

4.5f ...lift off the throttle body...

4.5g ...and recover the seal

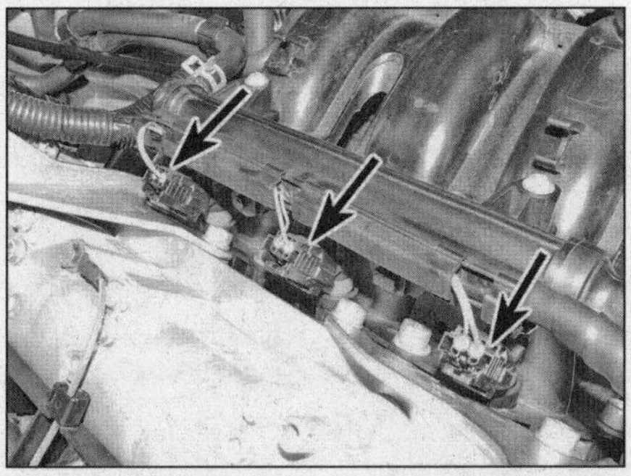

4.9 Fuel injector wiring and fuel rail

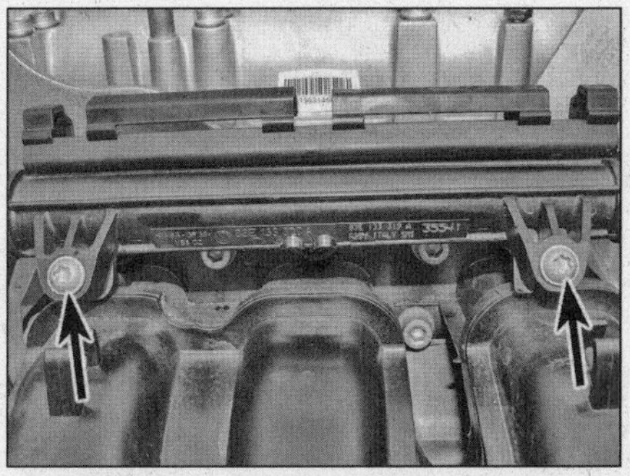

4.12a Unscrew the mounting bolts...

6 Refitting is a reversal of removal, noting the following:

a) Discard the seal – a new one must be fitted.

b) Clean the faces of the inlet manifold and throttle valve.

Fuel injectors and fuel rail

Note: *If a faulty injector is suspected, before removing the injectors, it is worth trying the effect of one of the proprietary injector-cleaning treatments. These can be added to the petrol in the tank, and are intended to clean the injectors as you drive.*

1.0 and 1.4 litre MPI engines

7 Disconnect the battery as described in Chapter 5A Section 3.

8 On 1.0 litre engines remove the air filter housing as described in Section 3.

9 Unplug the injector harness connectors, labelling them to aid correct refitting later **(see illustration)**. On 1.0 litre models disconnect the wiring plug from the EVAP control solenoid. Release the wiring harness clips from the top of the fuel rail, and lay the harness to one side.

10 Refer to Section 8 and depressurise the fuel system.

11 Squeeze the catch on the quick-release fitting(s), and disconnect the fuel supply and return hoses from the bulkhead. Where required release the fuel lines from the retaining clips.

12 Unscrew and remove the fuel rail mounting bolts, then carefully lift the rail away from the inlet manifold, together with the injectors. Recover the injector lower O-ring seals as they emerge from the manifold **(see illustrations)**.

13 The injectors can be removed individually from the fuel rail by extracting the relevant metal clip and easing the injector out of the rail. Recover the injector upper O-ring seals **(see illustrations)**.

14 Check the electrical resistance of the injectors using a multi-meter, and compare it with the Specifications.

15 Refit the injectors and fuel rail by following the removal procedure in reverse, noting the following points:

a) Renew the injector O-ring seals if they appear worn or damaged. Apply a little engine oil to the seals to assist their refitting **(see illustration)**.

b) Ensure that the injector retaining clips are securely seated.

c) Check that all electrical connections are remade correctly.

d) On 1.4 litre engines, purge air from the fuel rail by loosening the vent valve and temporarily switching on the ignition in order to operate the fuel pump. Tighten the vent valve when the fuel is free of air bubbles.

e) On completion, check for fuel leaks before bringing the car back into service.

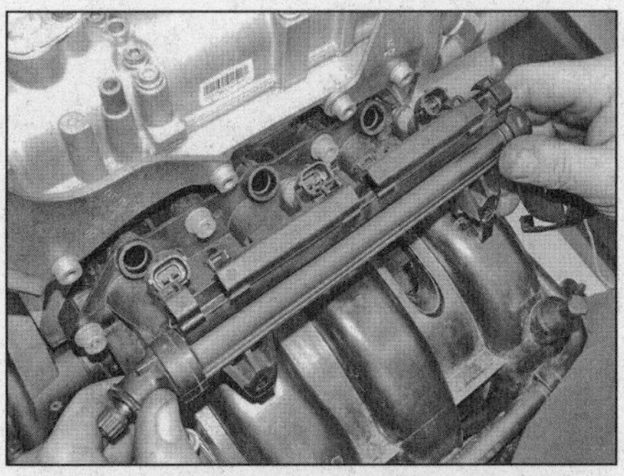

4.12b ...and lift the fuel rail with injectors from the inlet manifold...

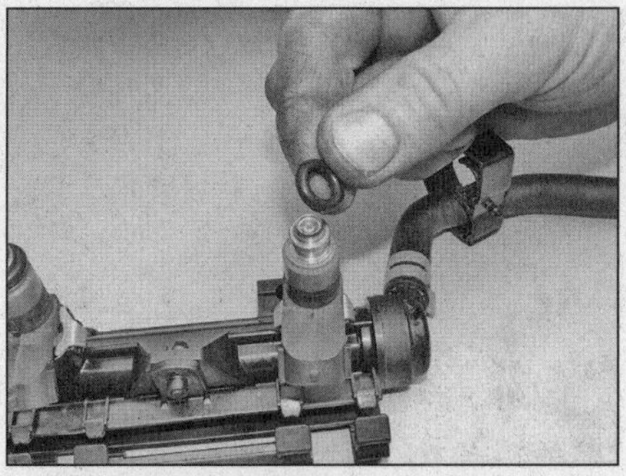

4.12c ...then recover the injector lower O-ring seals

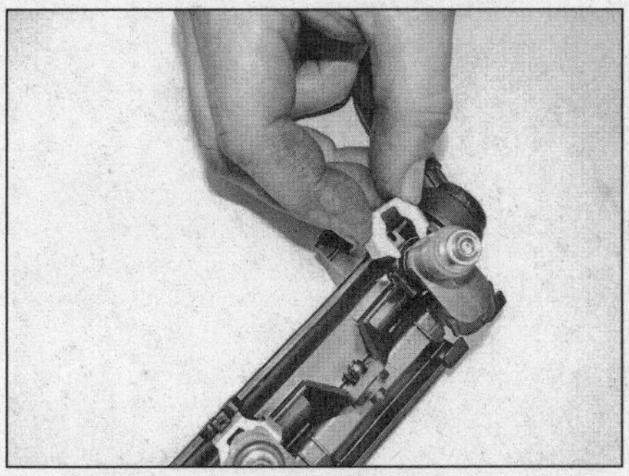

4.13a Extract the metal clip...

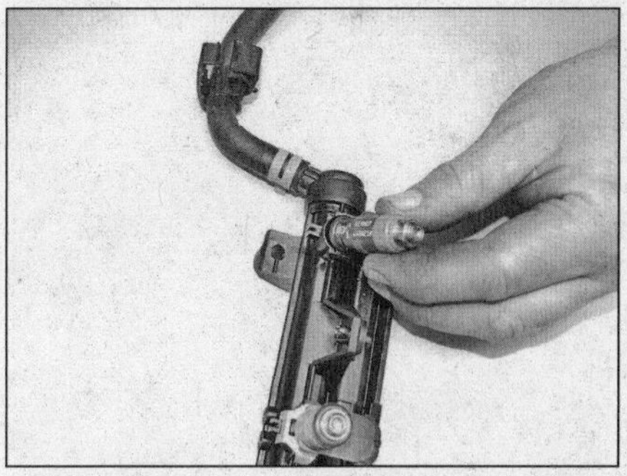

4.13b ...withdraw the injector from the fuel rail...

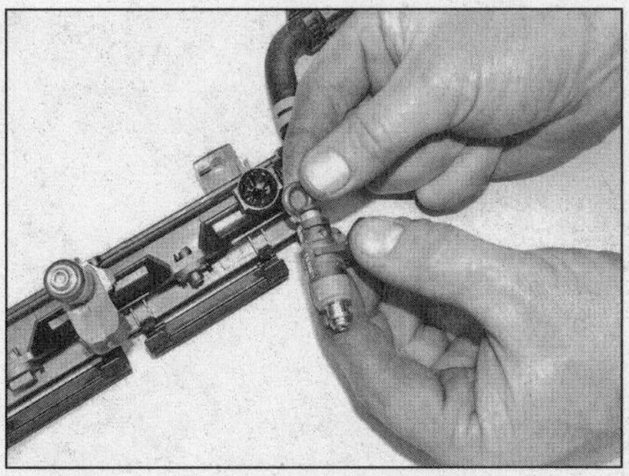

4.13c ...and recover the injector upper O-ring seal

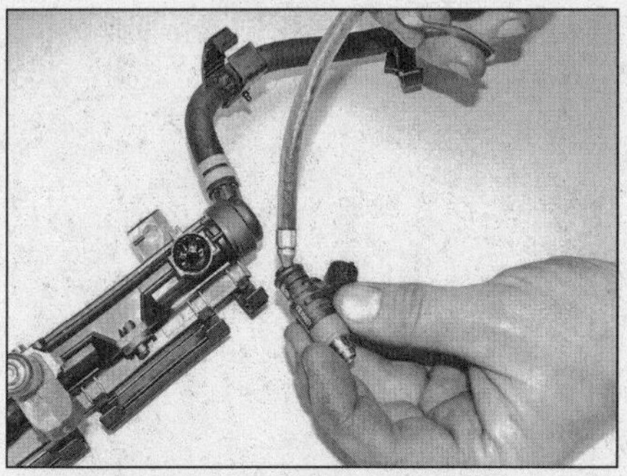

4.15 Apply a little engine oil to the O-ring seals to assist their refitting

4.17 Disconnect the wiring plug

4.18 Seal the fuel rail

4.19a Remove the bolts and...

4.19b ...lift off the fuel rail

4.20 Disconnect the wiring plugs from the injectors

1.0 and 1.2 litre TSI engines

Note: *Observe the precautions in Section 1 before working on any component in the fuel system. If a faulty injector is suspected, before removing the injectors, it is worth trying the effect of one of the proprietary injector-cleaning treatments. These can be added to the petrol in the tank, and are intended to clean the injectors as you drive. Note that Seat technicians use tool T10133C to remove the injectors and fit the new injector seals – although the tool may not be required to remove the injectors, tools T10133/5 and T10133/6 (part of the kit) it will be required to fit the new seals.*

Warning: The fuel injection system operates at high pressure and must be depressurised before starting work as described in Section 8.

16 Remove the inlet manifold as described in Section 9.

17 Disconnect the wiring plug from the pressure sensor **(see illustration)**.

18 Place shop towels below the fuel rail to absorb any escaping fuel. Unbolt the high pressure fuel supply pipe from the rail. Seal the rail **(see illustration)**.

19 Remove the mounting bolts from the fuel rail and pull the rail of the injectors **(see illustrations)**. The injectors may come out with the fuel rail, if this is the case disconnect the wiring plug from the injector(s) as the fuel rail is removed.

20 Disconnect the wiring plugs from the fuel injectors **(see illustration)**.

21 Remove the injector support ring and seal from the cylinder head **(see illustrations)**.

22 Where the special tool is available, instal the impact sleeve over the injector and gently tap each injector in turn to break the seal. Where the tool is not available use a suitable drift or bolt **(see illustration)**. Do not uses excessive force or the injector will be damaged.

23 At this stage Seat technicians use the puller tool from the tool kit to extract the injector. Note that earlier version of the special tool have a slide hammer as part of the tool kit. Where available this can also be used **(see illustrations)**.

4.21a Remove the support rings...

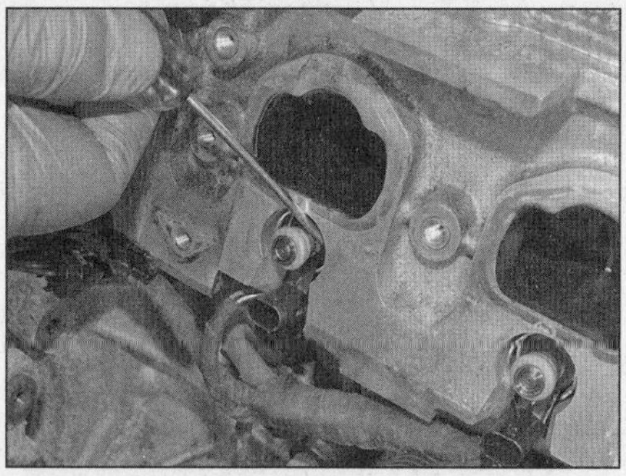

4.21b ...and seals from each injector

4.22 Gently tap the injector

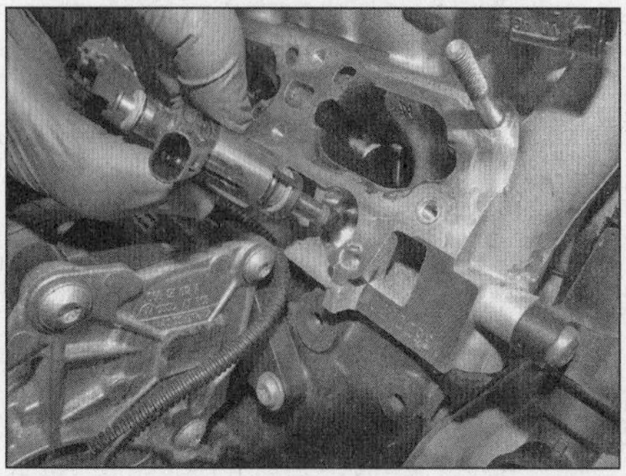

4.23a Always try to pull out the injectors by hand first

4.23b Using the slide hammer to remove the injector

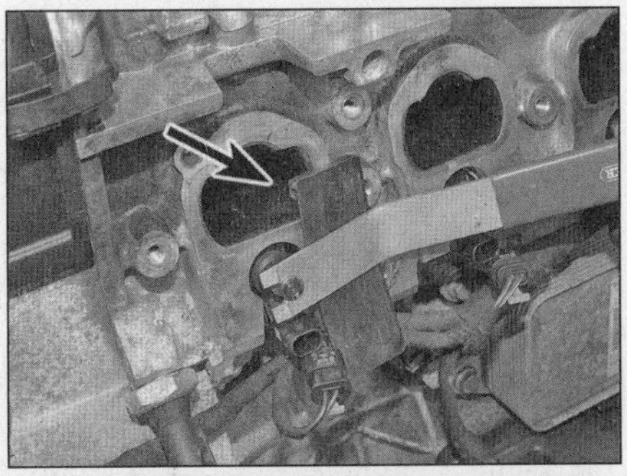

4.24 Provide a fulcrum and lever out the injector

24 Where the correct tool is not available is also possible to remove the injectors by carefully prising them from the cylinder head. Use a block of wood or similar soft material as the fulcrum to avoid damage to the cylinder head **(see illustration)**. Where this is not possible the fuel injectors must be removed with the correct tool.

4.26a Thoroughly clean the injector seatings in the cylinder head

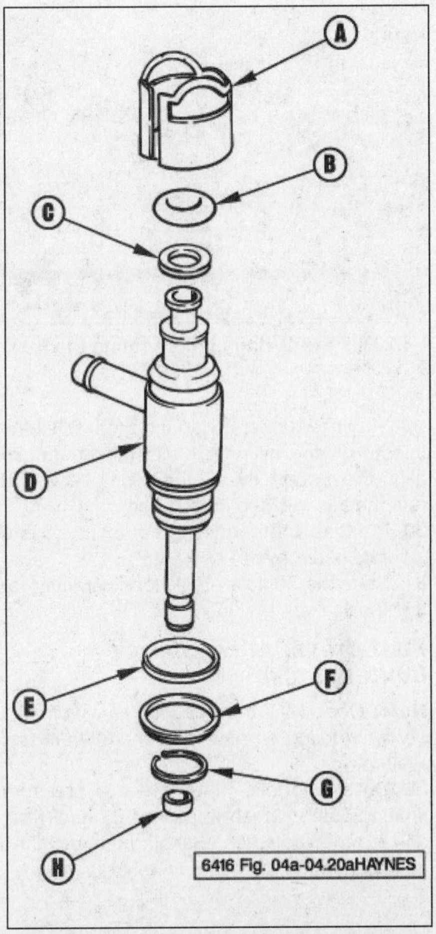

4.25 1.0 and 1.2 litre engine fuel injector details

A Support ring
B O-ring seal
C Spacer
D Injector
E Upper seal
F Lower seal
G Circlip
H Teflon seal

Injector seals

25 The injectors fitted to the 1.0 and 1.2 litre engines are the same **(see illustration)**.

26 Refitting is a reversal of removal, but thoroughly clean the cylinder head seatings, and fit new injector seals **(see illustrations)**. On all engine codes the seals are made of Teflon, and the special VAG tool will be required to compress the seals before fitting the injectors to the cylinder head. **Do not** grease or oil the seals.

27 With the new seal in position the tool can be used to compress the seal fully into the groove. Leaving the injector for a reasonable time period will also help the seal contract around the groove in the injector.

28 Fit a new support ring and then fit a new O-ring seal to the top of the injector **(see illustration)**. Fit new lower lower seals and a new circlip on 1.2 and 1.4 litre engines. On 2.0 litre engines fit a new lower seal.

4.26b Cut off the old seal with a sharp knife

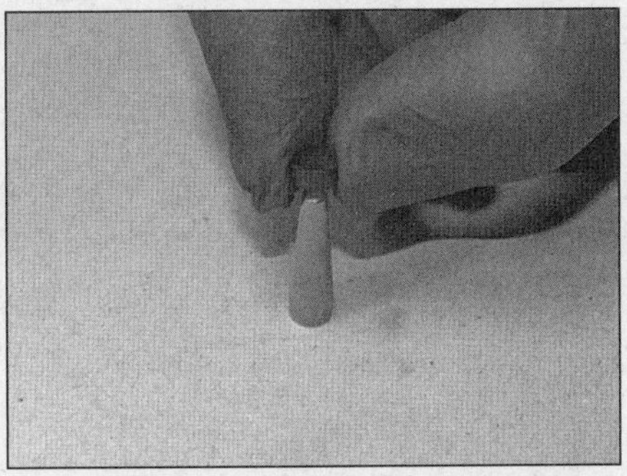

4.26c Fit the new seal onto the assembly taper

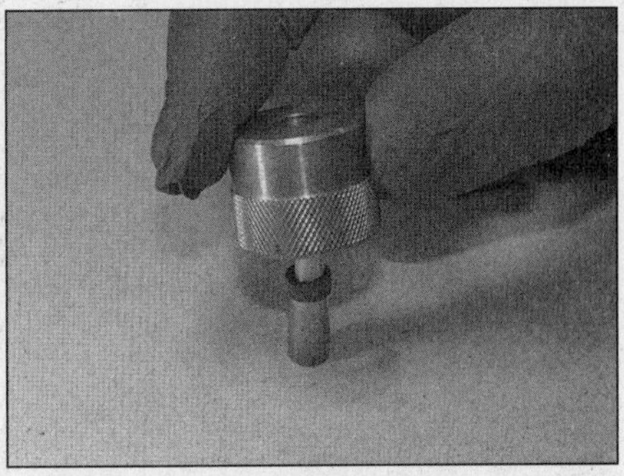

4.26d Push the seal down on the taper with the sleeve tool

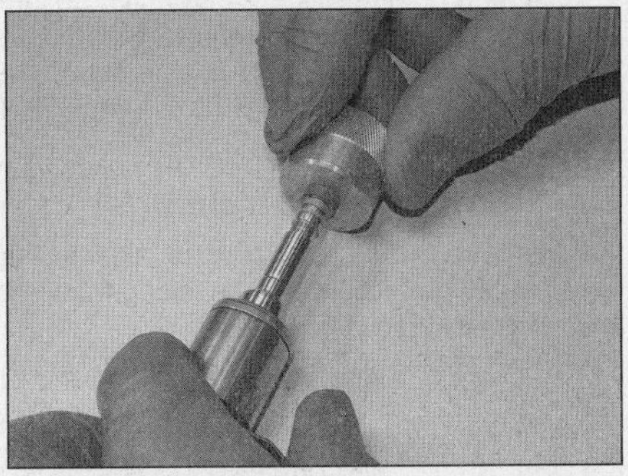

4.26e Fit the taper to the injector, invert the sleeve and push the seal onto the injector

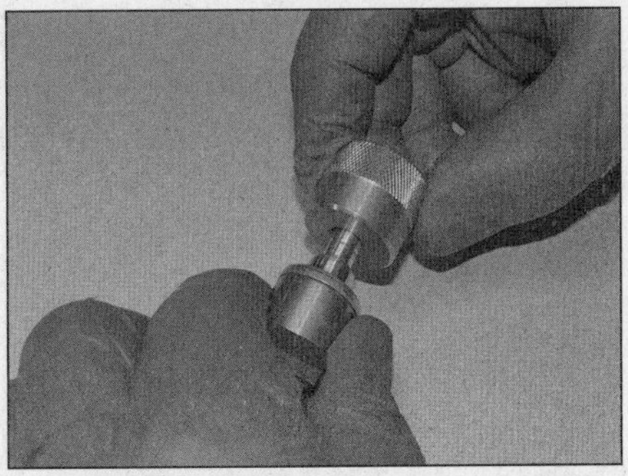

4.26f Rotate the sleeve as the seal is pushed into the groove

4.28 Fit a new seal and support ring. Note the orientation of the support ring

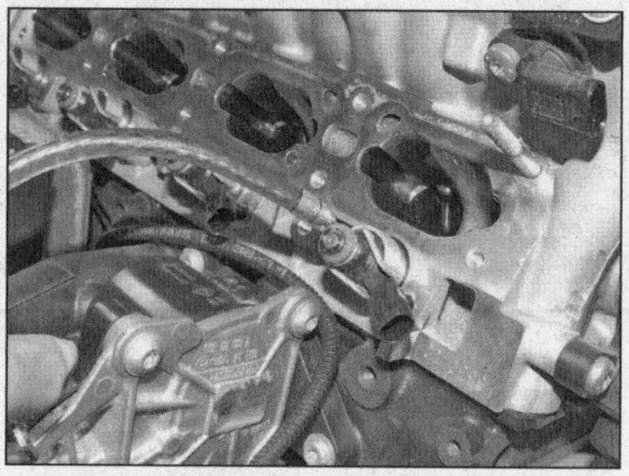

4.29 Oil the O-rings before fitting the fuel rail

4.40 The sensor on the 1.0 litre TSI engine (shown with the transmission removed)

29 Fit a new upper collar and then install the injector in the cylinder head, taking care to align them correctly. Oil the O-ring seals and refit the fuel rail **(see illustration)**.

30 Refitting the remaining components is a reversal of removal.

31 Start the vehicle and check carefully for any fuel leaks.

Fuel pressure regulator/ limiting valve

Note: *Observe the precautions in Section 1 before working on any component in the fuel system*.

32 On all models, there is a fuel pressure limiting valve, which is part of the fuel filter and is renewed when changing the fuel filter, as described in Section 5.

Fuel pressure sensor

33 Refer to Section 8 and de-pressurise the fuel system.

34 The fuel pressure sensor is fitted to the end of the fuel rail on TSI engines. Disconnect the wiring connector and unscrew the pressure sensor **(see illustration 4.17)**.

Engine speed sensor (TDC sensor)

35 The engine speed sensor is mounted at the left-hand rear of the cylinder block, next to the transmission bellhousing. Access is very difficult. Where necessary, prise out the rubber bung for access to the sensor.

36 On 1.0 litre and 1.4 litre MPI engines jack up and support the front of the vehicle. Remove the engine undershield (where fitted) and then remove the pendulum engine mounting as described in Chapter 2A Section 20. To improve access pivot the sump to the rear by using a strap and pull the sump towards the subframe.

37 On 1.0 litre TSI engines remove the inlet manifold as described in Section 9.

38 On 1.0 and 1.2 litre TSI engines disconnect the wiring plug, unbolt and then move the electric charge air cooling pimp to the side.

39 Trace the wiring back from the sensor, and unplug the harness connector.

40 Unscrew the retaining bolt and withdraw the sensor from the cylinder block/ transmission **(see illustration)**.

41 Refitting is a reversal of removal.

Inlet air temperature/ pressure sensor

42 The combined inlet air temperature and pressure sensor is located on the inlet manifold.

43 Disconnect the wiring from the sensor **(see illustration)**.

44 The sensor is ether clipped to the manifold or screwed in place. Unclip or unscrew the sensor and remove it. Recover the O-ring seal(s). If the clips brake, then it can be screwed into position with the holes provided.

45 Refitting is a reversal of removal, but renew the O-ring(s) and guide plate if necessary.

Knock sensor

46 The knock sensor is located on the rear of the cylinder block on 1.0 litre engines engines and at the front on 1.2 and 1.4 litre engines. Access is difficult **(see illustrations)**.

47 Apply the handbrake then jack up the front of the car and support it on axle stands (see *Jacking and vehicle support)*, and then remove the engine undershield (where fitted).

48 On 1.2 litre engines, remove the auxiliary drivebelt as described in Chapter 1A Section 28 and then (where fitted) unbolt the AC compressor and secure it to the side (see Chapter 3 Section 10). DO NOT disconnect the refrigerant lines.

49 On 1.0 engines remove the catalytic converter support bracket from the rear of the engine. Unbolt the heat shield to access the sensor.

50 On all engines, disconnect the wiring plug from the sensor. Unscrew the mounting bolt and remove the sensor from the cylinder block.

51 Refitting is the reverse of removal. Ensure the mating surfaces of the sensor and cylinder block are clean and dry, and ensure the mounting bolt is tightened to the specified torque to ensure correct operation.

Camshaft position sensor(s)

52 Remove the air inlet pipe or air filter as applicable and disconnect the wiring from the sensor **(see illustration)**.

53 Unscrew the mounting bolt, and remove the sensor.

54 Refitting is a reversal of removal.

Coolant temperature sensor

55 Refer to Chapter 3 Section 6.

4.43 Disconnect the wiring connector – 1.2 litre shown

4.46a The knock sensor is located on the rear of the cylinder block (1.0 litre engine)

4.46b The knock sensor on the 1.2 litre engine

4.52 The camshaft position sensors on the 1.0 litre TSI engine

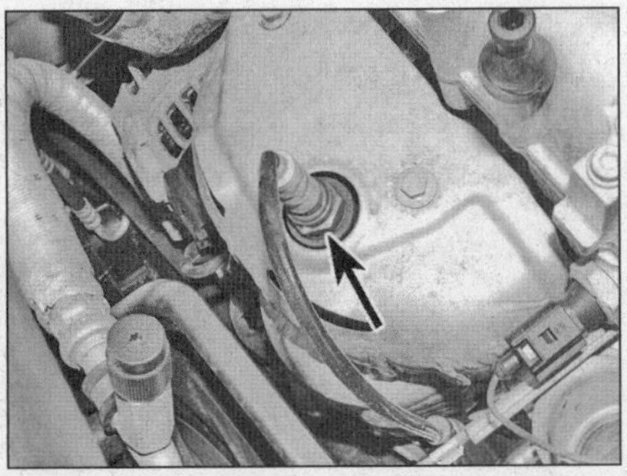

4.56a Oxygen (lambda) sensor on the exhaust manifold

4.56b The upstream sensor on 1.0 litre TSI engine

4.56c Oxygen (lambda) sensor upstream of catalytic converter – 1.2 litre shown

Oxygen (lambda) sensor(s)

56 All engines have one oxygen sensor fitted before the catalytic converter and one sensor fitted after the catalytic converter **(see illustrations)**. Access to the upstream sensor is from above, and to the downstream sensor from below.

⚠ ***Warning: Working on the sensor(s) is only advisable with the engine (and therefore the exhaust system) completely cold. The catalytic converter in particular will be very hot for some time after the engine has been switched off.***

57 Working from the sensor, trace the wiring harness from the oxygen sensor back to the connector, and disconnect it **(see illustration)**.

58 Release the sensor wiring from any retaining clips, noting how it is routed.

59 Slacken and withdraw the sensor, taking care to avoid damaging the sensor probe as it is removed. **Note:** *As a flying lead remains connected to the sensor after it has been disconnected,if the correct-size spanner is not available, a slotted socket will be required to remove the sensor***(see illustrations)**.

60 Apply a little high-temperature anti-seize grease to the sensor threads – avoid contaminating the probe tip.

61 Refit the sensor, tightening it to the correct torque. Restore the harness connection.

Throttle pedal/position sensor

62 Release the securing clip and disconnect the wiring connector from the top of the accelerator pedal **(see illustration)**.

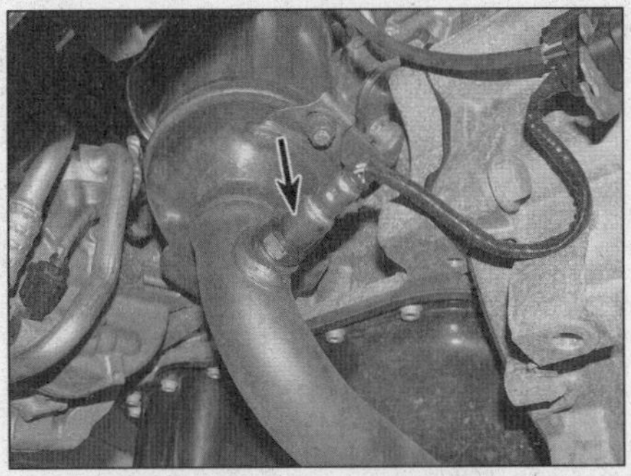

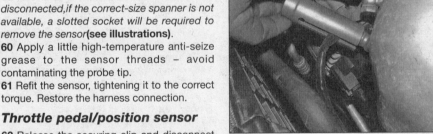

4.56d Oxygen (lambda) sensor downstream of catalytic converter – 1.2 litre shown

63 Undo the retaining nuts and remove the throttle pedal from the mounting bracket **(see illustration)**.

64 Refitting is a reversal of removal.

4.59a Using a slotted socket to loosen the oxygen (lambda) sensor

4.57 Disconnect the sensor wiring connectors

Clutch pedal switch

65 The clutch switch is mounted on top of the clutch pedal bracket, and sends a signal to the ECU **(see illustration)**. The purpose of

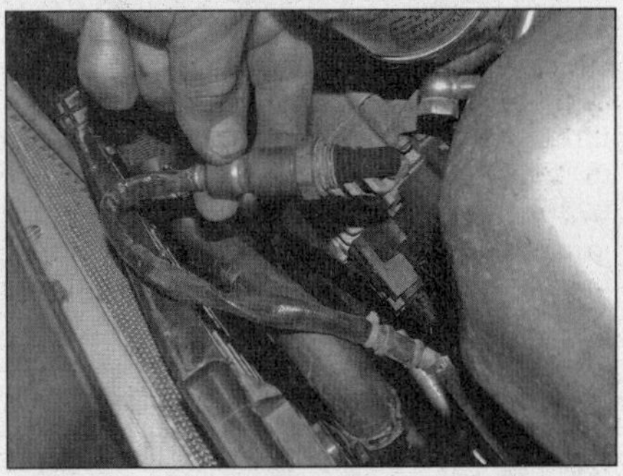

4.59b Removing the oxygen (lambda) sensor from the exhaust front pipe

4.62 Disconnect the wiring connector

4.63 Undo the pedal retaining nuts

4.65 Clutch pedal switch

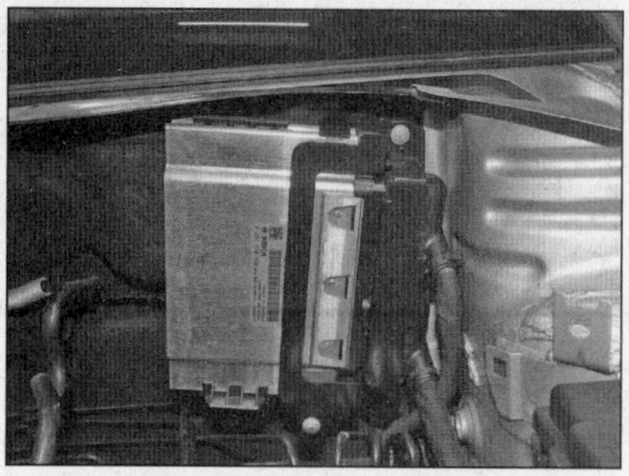

4.70 The location of the ECU

4.72 Remove the security bracket shear bolts

4.73a Unclip the ECU from the mounting bracket

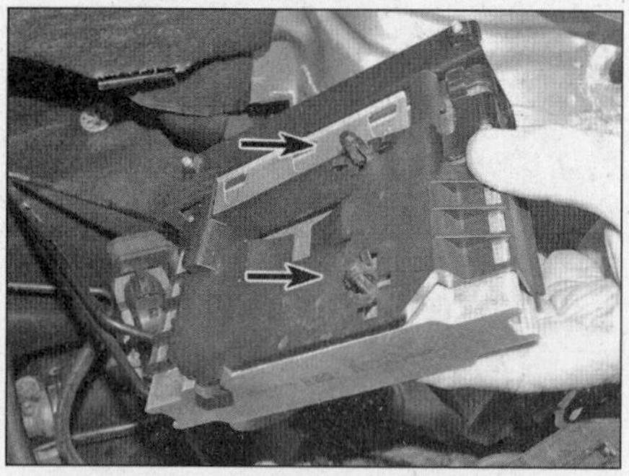

4.73b On later models the ECU can easily be removed, but not disconnected

4.74 Disconnecting the wiring plug

4.75 The mounting bracket screws

the switch is to avoid engine over-revving and load change jolts when the clutch is released. The switch also deactivates the cruise control system (where fitted) when the pedal is pressed.

66 To remove the switch, first remove the facia lower trim panel on the driver's side, as described in Chapter 11 Section 28.

67 Locate the switch wiring plug in front of the clutch pedal, and disconnect it.

68 Rotate the switch anti-clockwise and remove it.

69 When refitting the switch, first extend the switch plunger to its fullest extent, and then hold the clutch pedal depressed when offering it into position. Once the switch has been clipped into place, release the pedal – this sets the switch adjustment. Further refitting is a reversal of removal.

Electronic control unit (ECU)

Caution: Always wait at least 30 seconds after switching off the ignition before disconnecting the wiring from the ECU. When the wiring is disconnected, all the learned values are erased, although any contents of the fault memory are retained. After reconnecting the wiring, the basic settings must be reinstated by a Seat dealer using a special test instrument. Note also that if the ECU is renewed, the identification of the new ECU must be transferred to the immobiliser control unit by a Seat dealer.

70 The ECU is located on the engine compartment bulkhead, behind the air cleaner assembly **(see illustration)**. Remove the air cleaner assembly, as described in Section 3.

71 Disconnect the battery negative lead and position it away from the terminal (Refer to Chapter 5A Section 3).

72 The wiring connectors on the ECU have a security bracket **(see illustration)**, either drill out the shear bolts that are holding the security cover together, or cut a slot in them and unscrew them with a screwdriver. New shear bolts will be required for refitting.

73 Release the retaining clips and remove the ECU from the mounting bracket on the bulkhead. On later models once the plenum chamber cover is removed (see Chapter 12 Section 16) the ECU bracket can be unclipped from the plenum chamber and the complete assembly moved to the side. This improves access to the shear bolts **(see illustrations)**.

74 Disconnect the wiring plugs from the ECU by sliding the locking levers outwards, then release them from the ECU **(see illustration)**. Remove the ECU from the vehicle.

75 If required remove the screws (where fitted) and remove the mounting bracket **(see illustration)**.

76 Refitting is a reversal of removal. Bear in mind the comments made in the Caution above – the ECU will not work correctly until it has been electronically coded.

High-pressure fuel pump (TSI engines only)

Caution: The system must be depressurised before the pump is removed – see Section 8.

77 Where required, remove the air filter housing as described in Section 3.

78 Place shop towels beneath the pump and then remove the fuel supply hose and the high pressure fuel line **(see illustration)**.

79 Disconnect the wiring plug and unbolt the pump **(see illustration)**.

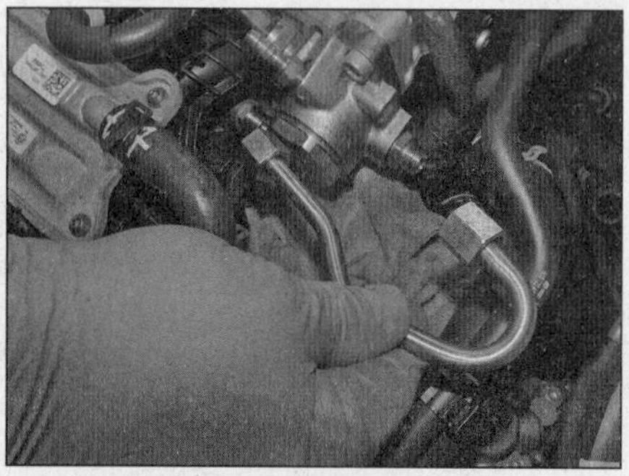

4.78 Remove the fuel lines

4.79 Remove the pump...

4.80 ...and recover the bucket tappet

80 Extract the bucket tappet/push rod from the housing **(see illustration)**.

81 Refitting is a reversal of removal, noting the following:

a) Clean the mating faces of the pump and camshaft housing.

b) Lubricate the bucket tappet/push rod with clean engine oil, then insert it in the camshaft housing.

c) Smear clean engine oil on the new O-ring seal, then refit the fuel pump together with the O-ring seal. Insert the mounting bolts and tighten to the specified torque.

d) Reconnect the wiring, then reconnect the fuel lines and tighten the union nut(s) to the specified torque. To ensure correct seating, the pump bolts must be progressively tightened to their specified torque.

e) Where removed, refit the air filter housing as described in Section 3.

5 Fuel filter – renewal

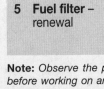

Note: *Observe the precautions in Section 1 before working on any component in the fuel system.*

1 Depressurise the fuel system as described in Section 8. Remember, however, that this procedure merely relieves the fuel pressure, reducing the risk of fuel spraying when the connections are disturbed – fuel will still be spilt during filter renewal, so take precautions accordingly.

2 The fuel filter is located under the vehicle, to the front right-hand side of the fuel tank **(see illustration)**.

3 Jack up the right-hand rear of the car, and support it on an axle stand (see *Jacking and vehicle support*). When positioning the axle stand, ensure that it will not inhibit access to the filter.

4 To further improve access, if necessary, unhook the handbrake cable from the adjacent wire clip.

5 Disconnect the fuel hoses at either end of the filter, noting their locations for refitting **(see illustrations)**. There are two hoses, a feed hose coloured black and a return hose coloured blue at one end, and there is one hose at the engine/fuel rail end of the filter which is coloured black. The connections are of quick-release type, disconnected by squeezing the catch on each. It may be necessary to release the hoses from the clips on the underside of the car, to allow greater movement.

6 Before removing the filter, look for an arrow marking **(see illustration)**, which points in the direction of fuel flow – in this case, towards the front of the car/engine. The new filter must be fitted the same way round.

7 The filter sits in a support collar – undo the retaining screw and release the collar by carefully pulling the retaining arm off the peg on the filter body, and slide the filter out **(see illustration)**. Try to keep it as level as possible, to reduce fuel spillage. Dispose of the old filter carefully – even if the fuel inside is tipped out, the filter element will still be soaked in fuel, and will be highly flammable.

8 Offer the new filter into position, ensuring that the direction-of-flow arrow is pointing towards the front of the car. Turn the filter so that the peg can be engaged with the retaining arm, and push the arm onto the peg to secure. Ensure that the filter is securely mounted on the car **(see illustration)**.

9 Connect the fuel hoses to each end of the filter, in the same positions as noted on removal. Push the hoses fully onto the filter stubs and, if necessary, clip them back to the underside of the car. Hook the handbrake cable back in place, if it was disturbed.

10 Switch on the ignition to activate the fuel pump. Check for signs of fuel leakage at both ends of the filter.

11 If all is well, lower the car to the ground, and then start the engine. Check under the car for signs of fuel leaks from the filter.

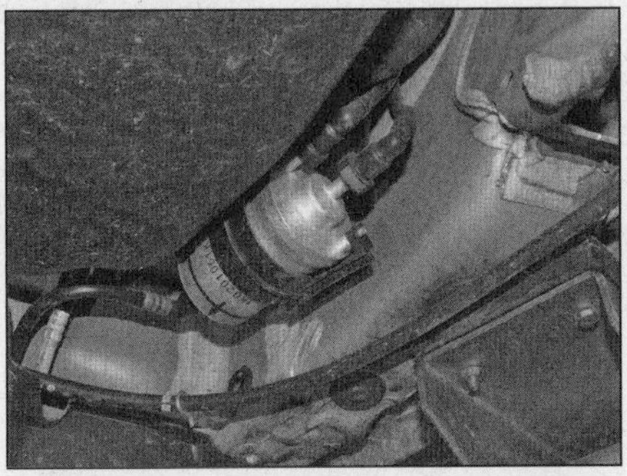

5.2 Fuel filter location next to fuel tank

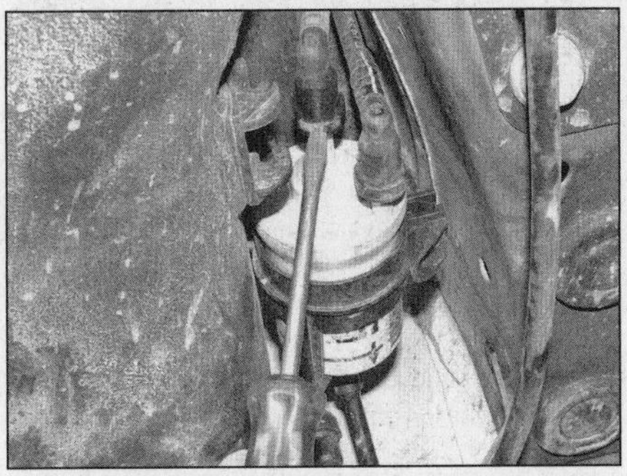

5.5a Release the locking clips...

5.5b ...and disconnect the fuel lines

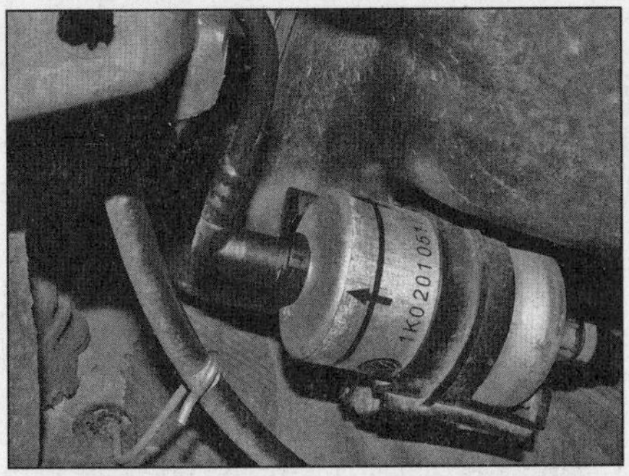

5.6 Note the direction of flow markings

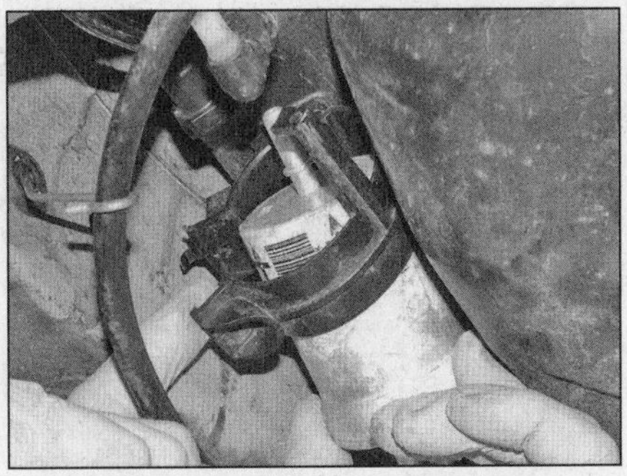

5.7 Slide the filter from the bracket

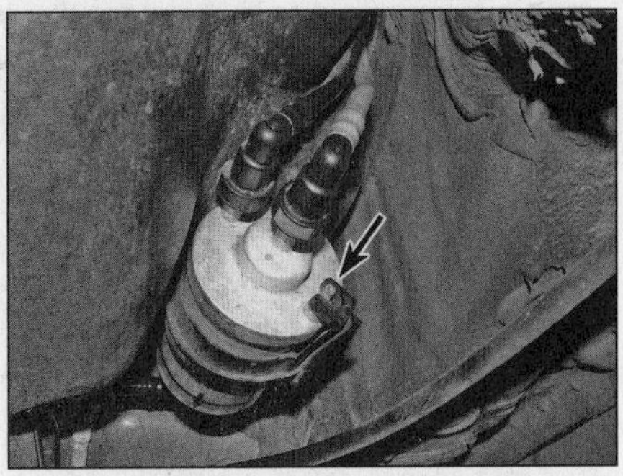

5.8 Peg locates in the bracket

6.5 Lift the fuel pump access hatch...

6.7 Note the location of the connections for refitting

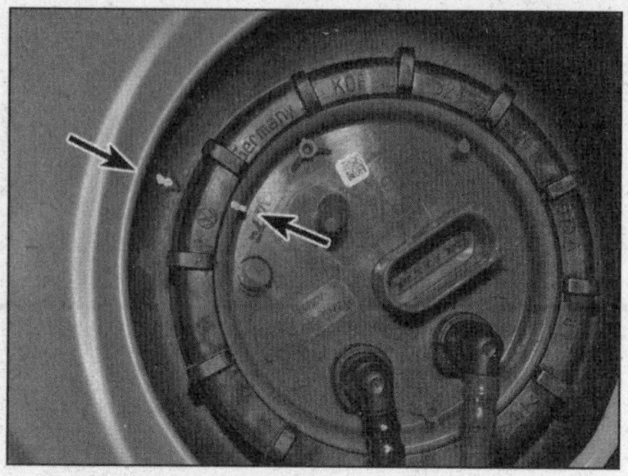

6.8a Note the alignment marks...

6.8b ...then unscrew the plastic securing ring

6.9 Lift out the pump/sender unit and recover the flange seal

6 Fuel pump and gauge sender unit – removal and refitting

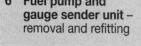

Note: *Observe the precautions in Section 1 before working on any component in the fuel system.*

Warning: Avoid direct skin contact with fuel – wear protective clothing and gloves when handling fuel system components. Ensure that the work area is well ventilated to prevent the build-up of fuel vapour.

General information

1 The fuel pump and gauge sender unit are combined in one assembly, which is mounted in the top of the fuel tank. Access is through a hatch provided in the load space floor.

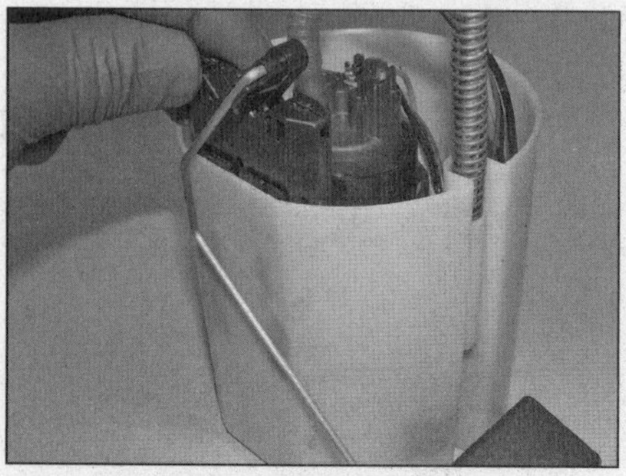

6.14a Unclip the sender...

Caution: Removal of the sender unit involves exposing the contents of the fuel tank to the atmosphere.

Removal

2 Depressurise the fuel system as described in Section 8.

3 Ensure that the car is parked on a level surface, and then disconnect the battery negative lead as described in Chapter 5A Section 3.

4 Fold the rear seat cushion forwards, and lift the carpet section from the load space floor.

5 Unclip the access panel, and lift the hatch away from the floorpan, noting its fitted position **(see illustration)**.

6 Unplug the wiring harness connector from the pump/sender unit.

7 Pad the area around the supply and return fuel hoses with rags to absorb any spilt fuel, then squeeze the catch to release the hose clips and disconnect them from the ports at the sender unit **(see illustration)**. Observe the supply and return arrow markings on the ports – label the fuel hoses accordingly to ensure correct refitting later. The supply pipe is black, and may have white markings, while the return pipe is blue, or has blue markings. Depending on model there may be two or three fuel pipes connected to the sender unit.

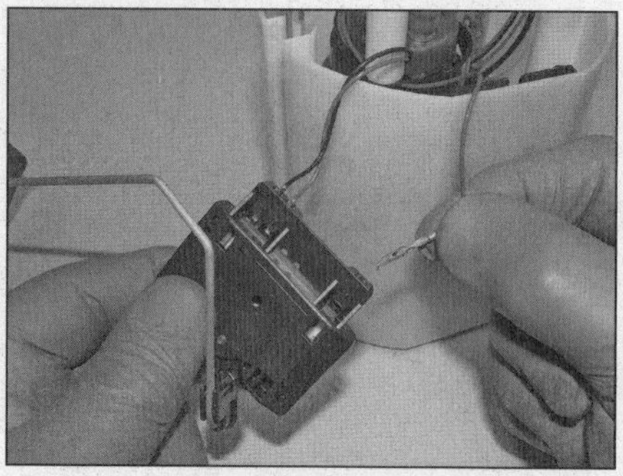

6.14b ...and disconnect the wiring

8 Note the position of the alignment marks, then unscrew the plastic securing ring and remove it. Use a pair of water pump pliers or a suitable tool to grip and rotate the plastic securing ring, if necessary **(see illustrations)**.

9 Lift out the pump/sender unit, holding it above the level of the fuel in the tank until the excess fuel has drained out. Recover the flange seal **(see illustration)**.

10 Remove the pump/sender unit from the car, and lay it on an absorbent card or rag. Inspect the float at the end of the sender unit swinging arm for punctures and fuel ingress – renew the unit if it appears damaged.

11 The fuel pick-up incorporated in the assembly is spring-loaded to ensure that it always draws fuel from the lowest part of the tank. Check that the pick-up is free to move under spring tension with respect to the sender unit body.

12 Inspect the rubber seal from the fuel tank aperture for signs of fatigue – renew it if necessary.

13 Inspect the sender unit wiper and track; clean off any dirt and debris that may have accumulated, and look for breaks in the track.

14 If required, the sender unit can be separated from the assembly, release the retaining clips and slide the unit out from the housing, then disconnect the small wires, noting their fitted positions **(see illustrations)**.

15 Connect a hand-held multi-meter to the brown and black wires terminals in the sender/pump unit socket. With the float arm at its lower stop position (tank empty) the resistance should be approx 50 ohms. With the float arm at its upper stop position (tank full) the resistance should be 290 ohms **(see illustrations)**. There are five terminals inside the connector socket, the outer terminals are for the pump and are larger. Use the two smaller outer terminals of the three in the centre, terminals 2 and 4.

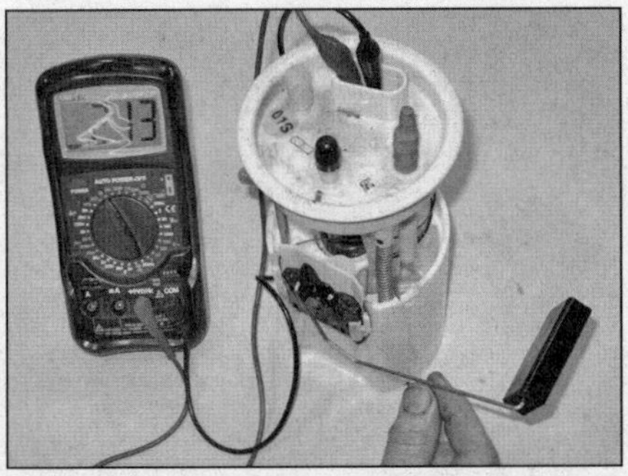

6.15a Checking the resistance of the sender unit...

6.15b ...across terminals 2 and 4

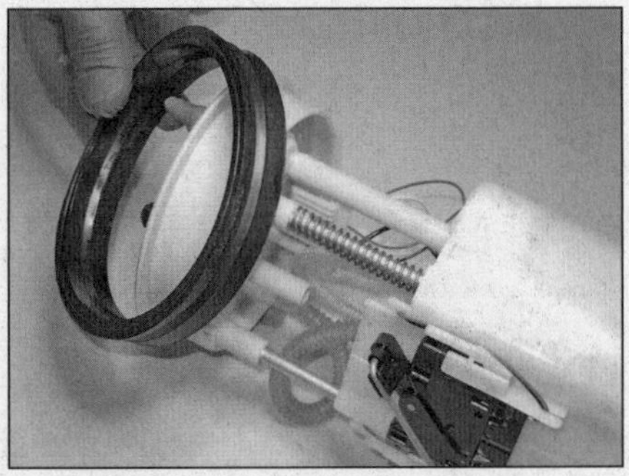

6.16 Fit the new seal to the fuel pump

Refitting

16 Refit the pump/sender unit by following the removal procedure in reverse, noting the following points:

a) *Smear the outside of tank aperture rubber seal with clean fuel or lubricating spray, to ease fitting. Unless a new seal is required, the seal should be left on the pump unit before fitting* **(see illustration)**. *When the unit is almost fully in place, slide the seal down and locate it on the rim of the tank aperture, then slide the unit fully home.*
b) *Take care not to bend the float arm as the unit is refitted.*
c) *The arrow markings on the sender unit body and the access aperture must be aligned.*
d) *Reconnect the fuel hoses to the correct ports – observe the direction-of-flow arrow markings, and refer to paragraph 7.*
e) *On completion, check that all associated pipes are securely clipped to the tank.*
f) *Before refitting the access hatch and rear seat, run the engine and check for fuel leaks.*

7 Fuel tank – removal and refitting

Note: *Observe the precautions in Section 1 before working on any component in the fuel system.*

Removal

1 Before the tank can be removed, it must be drained of as much fuel as possible. As no drain plug is provided, it is preferable to carry out this operation with the tank almost empty.

2 Open the fuel filler flap, and unscrew the fuel filler cap – leave the cap loosely in place.

3 Disconnect the battery negative lead as described in Chapter 5A Section 3. Using a hand pump or syphon, remove any remaining fuel from the bottom of the tank.

4 Gain access to the top of the fuel pump/sender unit as described in Section 6, and disconnect the wiring harness from the top of the pump/sender unit at the multi-plug connector.

5 Loosen the right-hand rear wheel bolts, then jack up the rear of the car and remove the right-hand rear wheel.

6 Remove the right-hand rear wheel arch liner.

7 Remove the activated charcoal (evaporative) filter from its location behind the filler tube under the right-hand rear wheel arch.

8 Open the fuel filler flap and unscrew the retaining screw (on the side opposite the flap hinge), then ease the flap unit out of position in the wing panel. Recover the rubber seal that fits around the filler neck.

9 Working back under the wheel arch, undo the screw securing the filler tube to the body.

10 On some models, the fuel tank is protected from below by plastic covers, undo the fasteners and remove the covers.

11 If necessary, unbolt the exhaust rear silencer mounting, and carefully lower the rear section of the exhaust system. Given that the rear axle assembly has to be removed (or at least lowered) to allow the tank to be removed, it is preferable to remove the rear section of the exhaust system completely.

12 Refer to Chapter 10 Section 13, and remove the rear axle assembly. Alternatively, it is possible to just lower the axle out of position, rather than completely removing it.

13 Depressurise the fuel system as described in Section 8.

14 Remove the fuel filter from the side of the fuel tank, as described in Section 5, or alternatively disconnect the single outlet hose from the engine side of the filter.

15 Unscrew and remove the retaining bolts and detach the tensioning strap from under the centre of the tank **(see illustration)**.

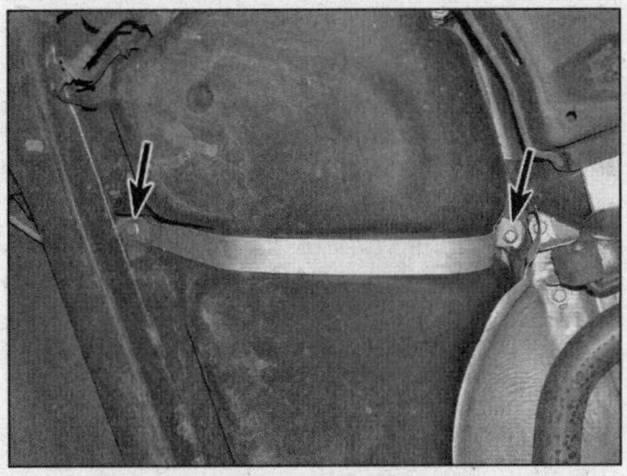

7.15 Fuel tank tensioning strap bolts

16 Position a trolley jack under the centre of the tank. Insert a flat block of wood between the jack head and the tank to prevent damage to the tank surface. Raise the jack to support the weight of the tank.

17 Unscrew and remove the tank mounting bolts **(see illustration)**.

18 Lower the tank from the underside of the car. If necessary, detach the various pipes and hoses from the tank, and remove the fuel pump and gauge sender unit with reference to Section 6.

19 If the tank is contaminated with sediment or water, swill the tank out with clean fuel. The tank is injection-moulded from a synthetic material and, if damaged, should be renewed. However, in certain cases it may be possible to have small leaks or minor damage repaired. Seek the advice of a suitable specialist before attempting to repair the fuel tank.

Refitting

20 Refitting is the reverse of the removal procedure, noting the following points:

a) *When lifting the tank back into position, take care to ensure none of the hoses get trapped between the tank and vehicle body.*
b) *Ensure that all pipes and hoses are correctly routed, are not kinked, and are securely held in position with their retaining clips.*
c) *Tighten the tank strap retaining bolts to the specified torque.*
d) *On completion, refill the tank with fuel, and check for signs of leakage prior to taking the car out on the road.*

7.17 One of the bolts securing the fuel tank

9.13 Unclip the vacuum hose

9.16a Remove the manifold...

9.16b ...and remove the seals

8 Fuel injection system – depressurisation

Note: *Observe the precautions in Section 1 before working on any component in the fuel system.*

Warning: The following procedure will merely relieve the pressure in the fuel system – remember that fuel will still be present in the system components and take precautions accordingly before disconnecting any of them.

1 The fuel system referred to in this Section is defined as the tank-mounted fuel pump, the fuel filter, the fuel injectors, and the metal pipes and flexible hoses of the fuel lines between these components. All these contain fuel, which will be under pressure while the engine is running and/or while the ignition is switched on. The pressure will remain for some time after the ignition has been switched off, and must be relieved before any of these components are disturbed for servicing work. Ideally, the engine should be allowed to cool completely before work commences.

2 Place a suitable container beneath the relevant connection/union to be disconnected, and then wrap clean cloth around it. Where a union connection is fitted, loosen it slightly before wrapping the cloth around.

3 Slowly open the connection to avoid a sudden release of pressure. Once the pressure has been released, disconnect the fuel line. Insert plugs to minimise fuel loss and prevent the entry of dirt into the fuel system.

9 Inlet manifold – removal and refitting

Note: *Observe the precautions in Section 1 before working on any component in the fuel system.*

Removal

1 First, disconnect the battery negative lead (as described in Chapter 5A Section 3).

2 Remove the air filter housing and inlet ducting as described in Section 3.

1.0 litre and 1.4 litre MPI engines

3 The inlet manifold is fitted to the rear of the cylinder head on 1.4 litre engines and to the front on 1.0 litre engines.

4 If the manifold is to be replaced remove the throttle control valve as described in Section 4. If the manifold is being removed for access tot he cylinder head the throttle valve can be left in place.

5 Disconnect the vacuum hose for the brake vacuum servo and unclip the wiring loom from the manifold.

6 To allow the manifold to be removed completely, and to improve access to the manifold mounting bolts, remove the fuel rail and injectors as described in Section 4. However, if the manifold is being removed as part of another procedure (such as cylinder head or engine removal), the fuel rail can be left in place.

7 Disconnect the wiring plug from the inlet air temperature/pressure sensor, referring if necessary to Section 4 for more details. Alternatively, remove it completely.

8 Remove the single lower bolt and then progressively loosen the main upper manifold to cylinder head bolts. Withdraw the manifold from the cylinder head. Recover the O-ring seals – all should be renewed when refitting the manifold.

1.0 litre and 1.2 litre TSI engines

9 Drain the coolant as described in Chapter 1A Section 32.

10 On 1.2 litre DOHC engines depressurise the fuel system as described in Section 8 and then (anticipating some fuel spillage) remove the fuel line from the manifold.

11 Disconnect the wiring plugs from the boost pressure sensor, throttle control valve and the EVAP control solenoid. On 1.2 DOHC engines disconnect the wiring plug from the fuel pressure sensor.

12 If the manifold is to be replaced, remove the throttle control valve as described in Section 4. If the manifold is being removed for access to the cylinder head, then the valve can be left on the inlet manifold.

13 Remove the coolant hoses from the manifold and disconnect the vacuum hose **(see illustration)**.

14 On 1.2 litre SOHC engines disconnect the wiring plug from the coil pack, unbolt the coil pack it and move it to the side.

15 Where required release the coolant hose from the support bracket on the side of the manifold.

16 Remove the bolts and lift out the inlet manifold. Recover the seals/gaskets as required **(see illustrations)**.

Refitting

17 Refitting is a reversal of removal. Use a new gasket or seals, as applicable, and tighten the retaining bolts/nuts to the specified torque. Refill the coolant system as described in Chapter 1A Section 32 and check for coolant leaks

10 Fuel injection system – testing and adjustment

1 If a fault appears in the fuel injection system, first ensure that all the system wiring connectors are securely connected and free of corrosion. Then ensure that the fault is not due to poor maintenance; i.e. check that the air cleaner filter element is clean, the spark plugs are in good condition and correctly gapped, the cylinder compression pressures are correct, the ignition system wiring is in good condition and securely connected, and the engine breather hoses are clear and undamaged.

2 If these checks fail to reveal the cause of the problem, the car should be taken to a suitably equipped Seat dealer for testing. A diagnostic connector is incorporated in the engine management system wiring harness, into which dedicated electronic test equipment can be plugged (the purple-coloured connector is located at the lower end of the facia, behind a trim panel on the drivers side of the vehicle) **(see illustrations)**. The test equipment is capable of 'interrogating' the engine management system ECU electronically and accessing its internal fault log (reading fault codes).

3 Fault codes can only be extracted from the ECU using a dedicated fault code reader. A Seat dealer will obviously have such a reader, but they are also available from other suppliers. Low cost tools are now widely available, but they will lack the in depth coverage of the professional aftermarket tools or the official factory tool **(see illustrations)**.

4 Using this equipment, faults can be pinpointed quickly. Testing all the system components individually in an attempt to locate the fault by elimination is a time-consuming operation that is unlikely to be fruitful (particularly if the fault occurs dynamically), and carries a high risk of damage to the ECU's internal components. However it is important to note that whilst the test equipment can point to a faulty component, further testing will be required to confirm the component is faulty. For example a fault might be recorded for the coolant temperature sensor, but is the sensor faulty or is there a wiring issue?

10.2a Remove the panel to access the fusebox and diagnostic port

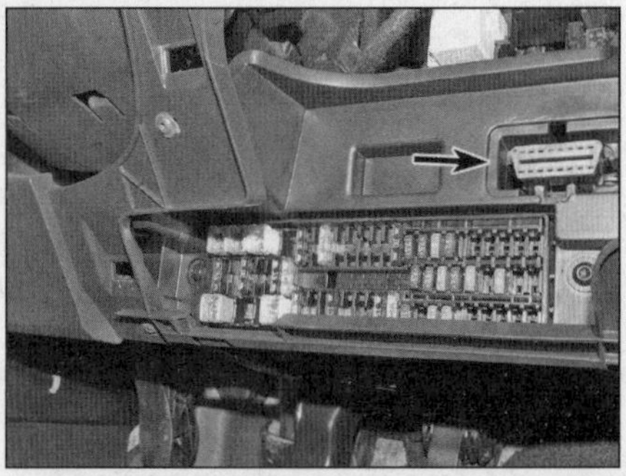

10.2b The diagnostic connector above the fusebox

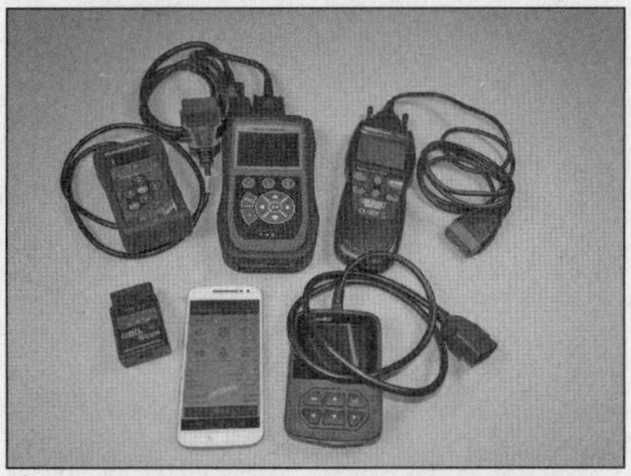

10.3a A selection of low cost diagnostic tools. All are capable of displaying the mandatory emissions related fault codes

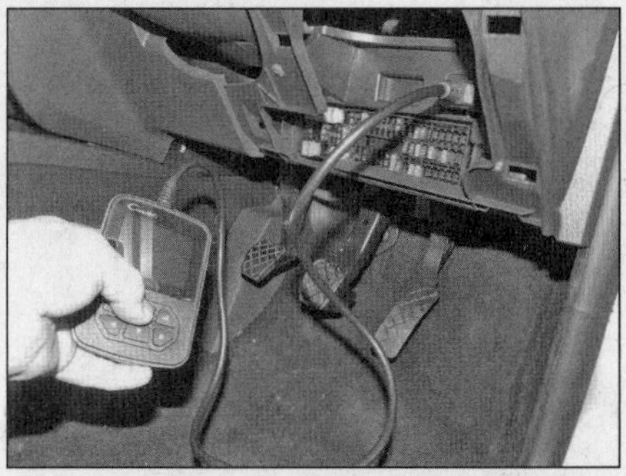

10.3b Checking for fault codes

11 Cruise control system – general information

1 Certain models may be equipped with a cruise control system, in which the driver can set a chosen speed, which the system will then try to maintain regardless of gradients, etc.

2 Once the desired speed has been set, the system is entirely under the control of the engine management ECU, which regulates the speed via the throttle valve control unit.

3 The system refers to signals from the engine speed sensor (see Section 4) and roadspeed sensor (on the transmission).

4 The system is deactivated if the clutch or brake pedals are pressed, signalled by the clutch pedal switch (Section 4) or the brake stop-light switch (Chapter 9 Section 21).

5 The cruise control switch is part of the steering column combination switch assembly, which can be removed as described in Chapter 12 Section 5.

6 Any problems with the system which are not caused by wiring faults or failure of the components mentioned in this Section should be referred to a Seat dealer. In the event of a problem occurring, it is advisable to first take the car to a suitably equipped dealer for electronic fault diagnosis, using a fault code reader – refer to Section 10.

Chapter 4 Part B
Diesel engine fuel systems

Contents

Degrees of difficulty

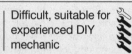

Easy, suitable for novice with little experience	Fairly easy, suitable for beginner with some experience	Fairly difficult, suitable for competent DIY mechanic	Difficult, suitable for experienced DIY mechanic	Very difficult, suitable for expert DIY or professional

Specifications

Engine codes*

1.6 litre	CAYC and CLNA

**See 'Vehicle identification' at the end of this manual for the location of the engine code markings.*

General

Fuel injection system	Electronic, direct, common rail injection
Firing order	1-3-4-2
Maximum engine speed	N/A (ECU controlled)
Engine fast idle speed	N/A (ECU controlled)
Turbocharger type	Garrett or KKK

Torque wrench settings

Torque wrench settings	Nm	lbf ft
Camshaft position sensor (Hall sender)	10	7
EGR pipe flange-to-inlet manifold bolts	8	6
Engine speed/TDC sender	5	4
Flap motor housing	10	7
Fuel pressure regulating valve (left-hand end of fuel rail)	80	59
Fuel pressure sender (right-hand end of fuel rail)	100	74
Fuel pump bolts*:		
Two lower bolts (long):		
Stage 1	20	15
Stage 2	Angle-tighten a further 180°	
One upper bolt (short):		
Stage 1	20	15
Stage 2	Angle-tighten a further 45°	
Fuel rail	22	16
High-pressure fuel pipe unions	28	20
Injector clamp/cover mounting:		
Clamp bolt*:		
Stage 1	8	6
Stage 2	Angle-tighten a further 180°	
Inlet manifold to cylinder head	8	6
Oxygen (Lambda probe) sensor	50	37
Toothed belt pulley on high-pressure pump bolts*	20	15

**Do not re-use*

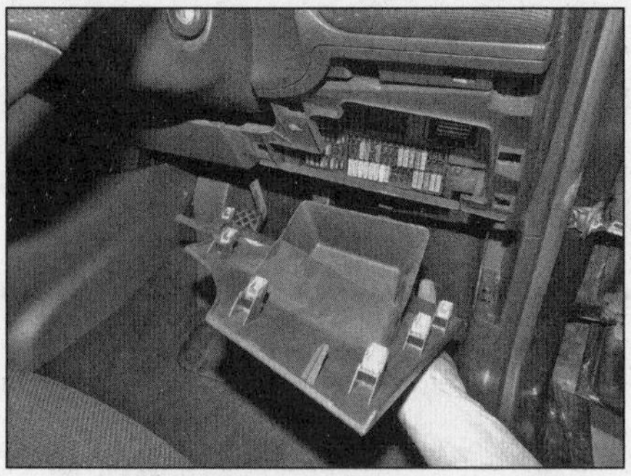

1.5a Remove the panel to access the fusebox and diagnostic port

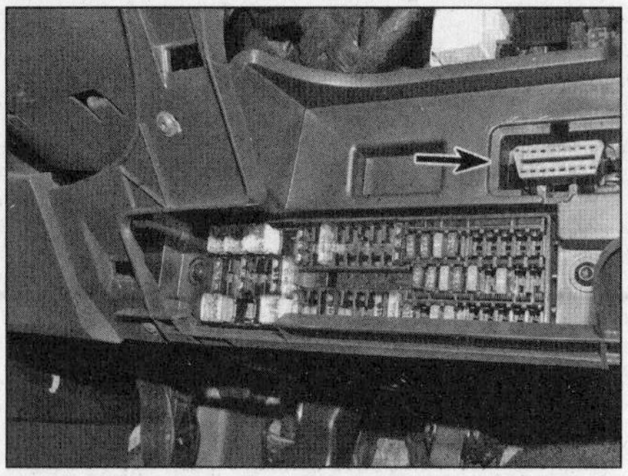

1.5b The diagnostic connector above the fusebox

1 General information and precautions

General information

1 All engines covered by this Manual are fitted with a direct-injection fuelling system, incorporating a fuel tank, an engine-bay mounted fuel filter with an integral water separator, fuel supply and return lines and four fuel injectors. Also there is a second fuel filter with an integral fuel pressure regulator, located under the vehicle, to the right-hand side front of the fuel tank.

2 The fuel system is the familiar Common Rail system, where fuel is supplied from a timing belt-driven high-pressure pump to a common fuel rail (or reservoir). The injectors are fitted into the cylinder head and are connected to the fuel rail by rigid metal pipes. The precise timing of the pre-, main, and post-injections are controlled by the engine management ECM and an electrically operated Piezo crystal incorporated into the injector design. All engines are fitted with a turbocharger.

3 The direct-injection fuelling system is controlled electronically by a diesel engine management system, comprising an Electronic Control Module (ECM) and its associated sensors, actuators and wiring. In addition, the ECM manages the operation of the Exhaust Gas Recirculation (EGR) emission control system (), the turbocharger boost pressure control system and the glow plug control system (Chapter 5C Section 2).

1.5c A selection of low cost diagnostic tools. All are capable of displaying the mandatory emissions related fault codes

4 A flap valve/throttle valve module fitted to the intake manifold is closed by the ECM for 3 seconds as the engine is switched off, to minimise the air intake as the engine shuts down. This minimises the vibration felt as the pistons come up against the volume of highly compressed air present in the combustion chambers.

5 A dedicated diagnostic port is fitted to all models that allows access to any recorded fault codes. Fault codes can only be extracted from the ECU using a dedicated fault code reader. A Seat dealer will obviously have such a reader, but they are also available from other suppliers. Low cost tools are now widely available, but they will lack the in depth coverage of the professional aftermarket tools or the official factory tool **(see illustrations)**.

Precautions

Many of the operations described in this Chapter involve the disconnection of fuel lines, which may cause an amount of fuel spillage. Before commencing work, refer to the warnings below and the information in '*Safety first!*' at the beginning of this manual.

⚠ ***Warning: When working on any part of the fuel system, avoid direct contact skin contact with diesel fuel – wear protective clothing and gloves when handling fuel system components. Ensure that the work area is well ventilated to prevent the build-up of diesel fuel vapour.***

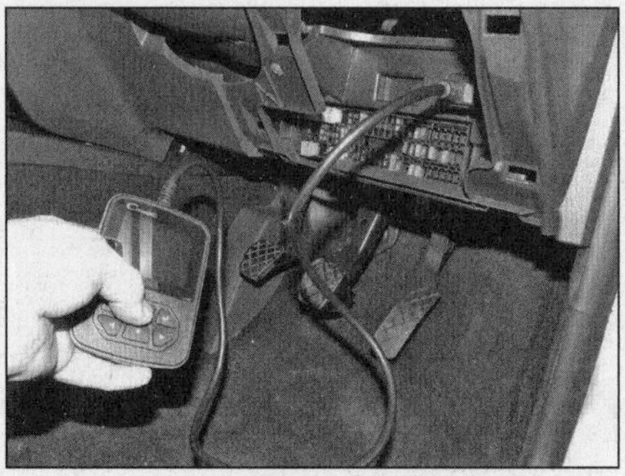

1.5d Checking for fault codes

- ***Fuel injectors operate at extremely high pressures and the jet of fuel produced at the nozzle is capable of piercing skin, with potentially fatal results. When working with pressurised injectors, take care to avoid exposing any part of the body to the fuel spray. It is recommended that a diesel fuel systems specialist should carry out any pressure testing of the fuel system components.***
- ***Under no circumstances should diesel fuel be allowed to come into contact with coolant hoses – wipe off accidental spillage immediately. Hoses that have been contaminated with fuel for an extended period should be renewed.***
- ***Diesel fuel systems are particularly sensitive to contamination from dirt, air and water. Pay particular attention to cleanliness when working on any part of the fuel system, to prevent the ingress of dirt. Thoroughly clean the area around fuel unions before disconnecting them. Only use lint-free cloths and clean fuel for component cleansing.***
- ***Store dismantled components in sealed containers to prevent contamination and the formation of condensation.***

2 Fuel pipe and connectors

1 Disconnect the battery as described in Chapter 5A Section 3 before proceeding.

2 The fuel supply pipe connects the fuel pump in the fuel tank to the fuel filter on the engine.

3 Whenever you're working under the vehicle, be sure to inspect all fuel and evaporative emission pipes for leaks, kinks, dents and other damage. Always replace a damaged fuel pipe immediately.

4 If you find signs of dirt in the pipes during disassembly, disconnect all pipes and blow them out with compressed air. Inspect the fuel strainer on the fuel pump pick-up unit for damage and deterioration.

Steel tubing

5 It is critical that the fuel pipes be replaced with pipes of equivalent type and specification.

6 Some steel fuel pipes have threaded fittings. When loosening these fittings, hold the stationary fitting with a spanner while turning the union nut.

Plastic tubing

⚠ ***Warning: When removing or installing plastic fuel tubing, be careful not to bend or twist it too much, which can damage it. Also, plastic fuel tubing is NOT heat resistant, so keep it away from excessive heat.***

7 When replacing fuel system plastic tubing, use only original equipment replacement plastic tubing.

Flexible hoses

8 When replacing fuel system flexible hoses, use original equipment replacements, or hose to the same specification.

9 Don't route fuel hoses (or metal pipes) within 100 mm of the exhaust system or within 280 mm of the catalytic converter. Make sure that no rubber hoses are installed directly against the vehicle, particularly in places where there is any vibration. If allowed to touch some vibrating part of the vehicle, a hose can easily become chafed and it might start leaking. A good rule of thumb is to maintain a minimum of 8.0 mm clearance around a hose (or metal pipe) to prevent contact with the vehicle underbody.

Disconnecting Fuel pipe Fittings

10 Refer to Chapter 4A, Section 2 for typical fuel pipe fittings:

3 Air cleaner assembly – removal and refitting

Removal

1 Disconnect the wiring plug from the air mass meter.

2 Loosen the clip and disconnect the air duct from the air mass meter **(see illustration)**.

3 Unclip the vacuum hoses from across the front of the filter housing **(see illustration)**.

4 Disconnect the pre-heating hose from the side of the air filter housing (only fitted to vehicles in cold climate zones).

5 Undo the retaining bolt at the front left-hand side of the housing and lift the air cleaner assembly upwards to release it from the locating pegs **(see illustration)**.

6 Unclip the plastic air ducting from the front crossmember **(see illustration)**, and as the air cleaner assembly is removed, withdraw the air ducting from under the side of the battery.

Refitting

7 Refit the air cleaner by following the removal procedure in reverse. Make sure the assembly is located correctly on the lower mounting pegs.

4 Diesel engine management system – component removal and refitting

Throttle valve housing/module

1 Remove the engine upper trim cover **(see illustrations)**.

2 Slacken the retaining clips and remove the air intake rubber hose from the throttle housing **(see illustration)**. If required, undo the bolts securing the air intake plastic hose from the intercooler to the throttle housing, this will allow easier removal of the intake rubber hose.

3.2 Disconnect the wiring connector (A) and securing clip (B)

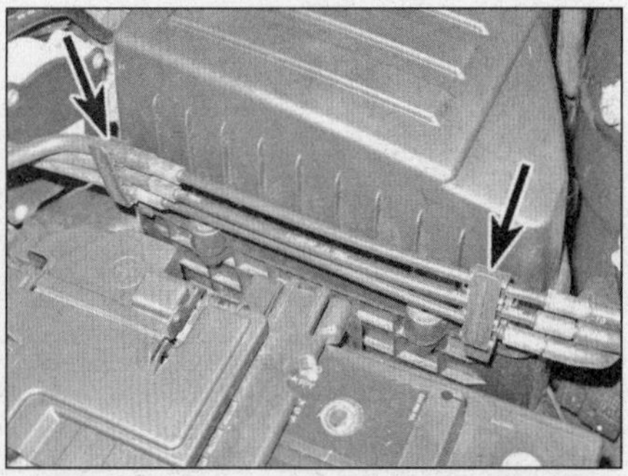

3.3 Release the vacuum hose securing clips

3.5 Undo the mounting bolt

3.6 Release the air ducting

3 Disconnect the wiring plug connector, from the throttle housing/module **(see illustration)**.

4 Undo the retaining bolt and disconnect the dipstick guide tube from the throttle housing **(see illustration)**.

5 Unscrew and remove the retaining bolts, then lift the throttle housing/module away from the inlet manifold **(see illustration)**. Recover the O-ring seal; a new one will be required for refitting.

4.1a Remove the engine upper trim cover...

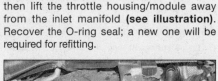

4.1b ...and the insulation cover (where fitted)

4.2 Slacken the two retaining clips

4.3 Disconnect the wiring connector

4.4 Undo the dipstick tube retaining bolt

4.5 Undo the throttle housing retaining bolts

4.6 Fit a new seal to housing on refitting

6 Refitting is a reversal of removal, noting the following:

a) *Use a new throttle housing-to-inlet manifold seal* ***(see illustration).***
b) *Tighten the throttle housing bolts evenly to the specified torque.*
c) *Ensure that all hoses and electrical connectors are refitted securely.*

Inlet manifold flap motor

Note: *On some engines there is an electrically operated flap motor located on the inlet manifold, this is not fitted to all models.*

7 Although the manifold flap motor is bolted to the end of the inlet manifold, Seat do not recommend that it is removed, check with your local dealer before removing any components.

Air mass meter

8 The air mass meter is located in the outlet from the air cleaner assembly on the left-hand side of the engine compartment.

9 Disconnect the wiring plug connector from the air mass meter.

10 Slacken the retaining clip and disconnect the air intake ducting from the air mass meter **(see illustration 2.2)**.

11 Undo the retaining screws securing the meter to the air cleaner upper housing. Withdraw the meter and recover the O-ring seal.

Caution: Handle the air mass meter carefully – its internal components are easily damaged.

12 Refitting is a reversal of removal. Renew the O-ring seal if it appears damaged.

Charge air pressure/ temperature sensor

13 The sensor is located in the air ducting just below the air-conditioning compressor, at the front of the engine **(see illustration)**. To access the sensor, jack up the front of the vehicle and support it on axle stands (see *Jacking and vehicle support*), and then remove the engine undertray.

4.13 Sensor location

4.16 Fuel pressure regulator valve

4.17 Disconnect the fuel hose

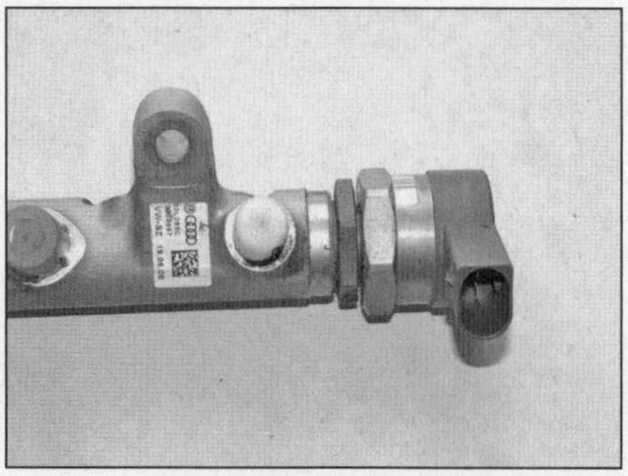

4.21 Pressure regulator valve fitted to the left-hand end of the fuel rail

14 Disconnect the wiring then undo the two retaining screws and remove the sensor from the intake ducting.

15 Refit the sensor by reversing the removal procedure, using a new O-ring seal.

Fuel pressure regulating valve

16 The fuel pressure regulating valve is fitted to the left-hand end of the fuel rail **(see illustration)**. If the valve is removed from the fuel rail, then it will need to be renewed, as it has a deformable sealing lip as part of the valve.

17 To check the operation of the regulating valve, first disconnect the fuel return hose from the fuel rail and plug the end **(see illustration)**. Then fit a piece of hose from the fuel rail and the other end into a container.

18 There are three checks that can be made, the first two with the engine running and the third if the vehicle will not start:

a) *Start the engine and run at idle for 30 seconds, there should be approx. 75ml of fuel in the container.*
b) *Start engine and increase engine speed to 2000rpm, there should be NO fuel in the container (a few droplets of fuel are allowed).*
c) *On vehicles that will not run, turn the ignition key and crank the engine, there should be 0ml of fuel in the container (allow for a few droplets of fuel).*

19 If any of these readings are not attained, renew the regulating valve.

20 To renew the valve, remove the fuel rail as described in Section 12.

21 Clean around the valve, then slacken the valve from the end of the fuel rail **(see illustration)** ; counter hold the fuel rail using the flats on the housing. Plug the end of the rail to prevent dirt from entering.

22 Refit the new valve by reversing the removal procedure, making sure that the threads are all clean before refitting. Check the deformable seal on the new valve, before refitting, to check it is not damaged. Apply a small amount of Molybdenum grease to seal and threads.

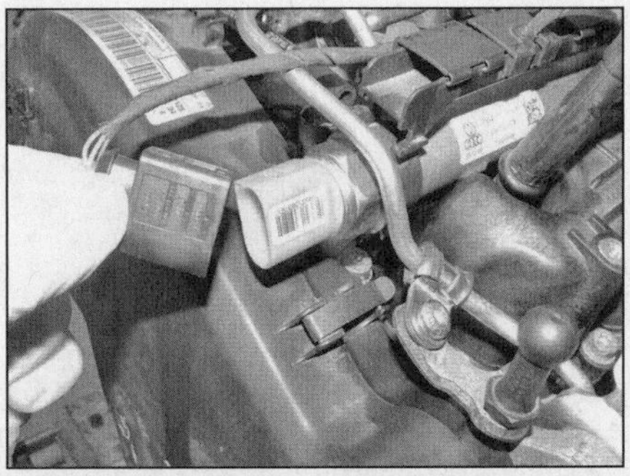
4.24 Disconnect the wiring connector from the fuel pressure sensor

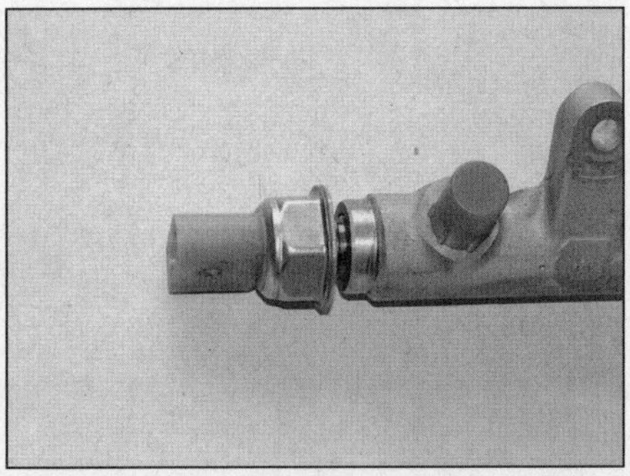
4.25 The fuel pressure sensor is fitted to the right-hand end of the fuel rail

4.27a Fuel temperature sensor...

4.27b ...or in fuel line

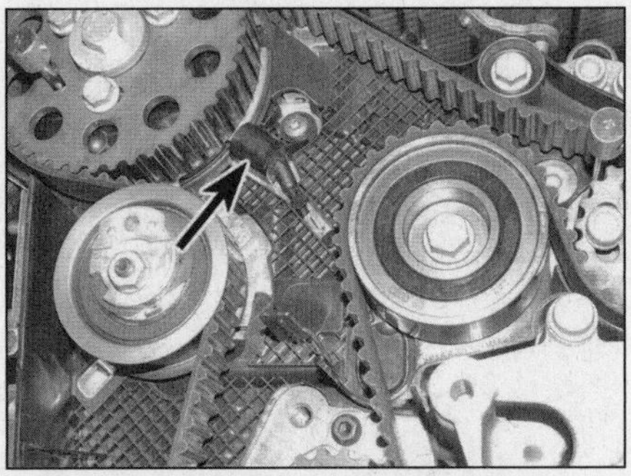
4.31 Camshaft position sensor

4.33 Disconnect the sensor wiring connector

Fuel pressure sensor

23 The fuel pressure sensor is fitted to the right-hand end of the fuel rail. If the engine will not start, disconnect the sensor wiring connector and see if the engine will start. If the engine starts, the fuel pressure switch is faulty. With the connector removed a value is taken from the control unit, so that the engine will start, in this mode the maximum engine speed is limited to 3000rpm.

24 To renew the sensor, first disconnect the wiring plug connector **(see illustration)**.

25 Clean around the sensor, then slacken it from the end of the fuel rail **(see illustration)**; plug the end of the rail to prevent dirt from entering.

26 Refit the pressure sensor by reversing the removal procedure, making sure that the threads are all clean before refitting. The sensor has a deformable seal, check for damage. Keep the threads free of oil and grease.

Fuel temperature sensor

27 The fuel temperature sensor is located in the fuel supply line at the top of the high-pressure fuel pump **(see illustrations)**, or in the fuel line, depending on model.

28 First, disconnect the wiring connector, then release the securing clips and disconnect the hoses from the sensor assembly.

29 Refit the fuel temperature sensor by reversing the removal procedure.

Coolant temperature sensors

30 Refer to Chapter 3 Section 6.

Camshaft position sensor

31 The camshaft position sensor (Hall sender) is located behind the timing belt cover, below the camshaft sprocket **(see illustration)**.

32 Remove the timing belt, as described in Chapter 2E Section 7.

33 Disconnect the sensor wiring plug connector, located at the rear of the oil filter housing against the cylinder block **(see illustration)**.

34 To make access easier undo the retaining bolt and remove the timing belt idler pulley **(see illustration)**.

35 Using a screwdriver prise out the aperture cover in the rear plastic cover, then withdraw the wiring plug through the cover, unhooking it from the rear cover **(see illustration)**.

36 Undo the retaining bolt and remove the camshaft sensor from the cylinder head.

37 Refitting is a reversal of removal, but tighten the bolt to the specified torque setting and fit rubber plugs to the aperture for the wiring in the rear plastic cover.

Engine speed/TDC sensor

38 The engine speed/TDC sensor is mounted on the front cylinder block, adjacent to the mating surface of the block and transmission bellhousing **(see illustration)**.

4.34 Unbolt the idler pulley

4.35 Prise up the aperture cover

4.38 Crankshaft position speed sensor

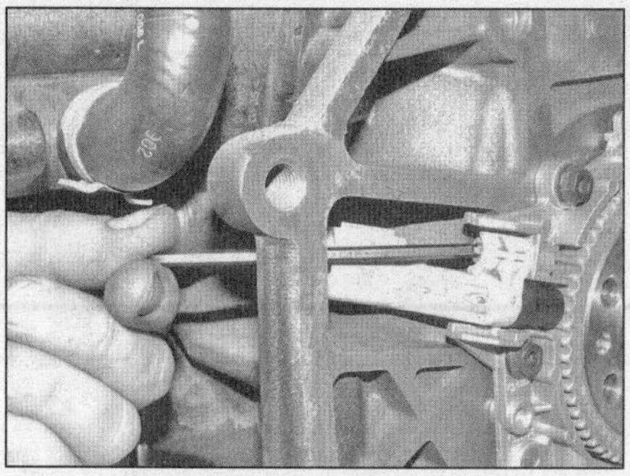

4.40a Undo the retaining bolt...

4.40b ...and withdraw the sensor

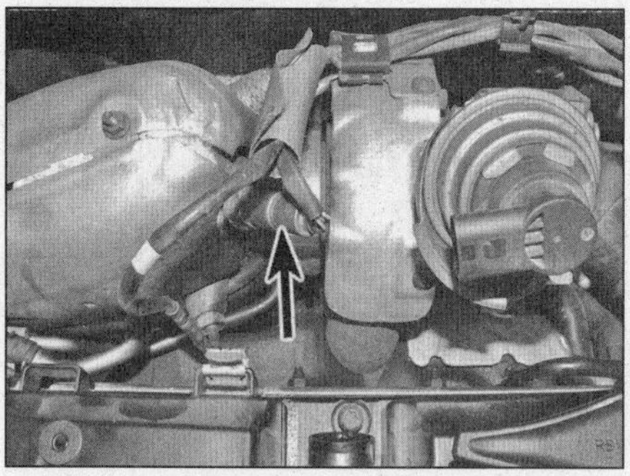

4.42a Oxygen sensor

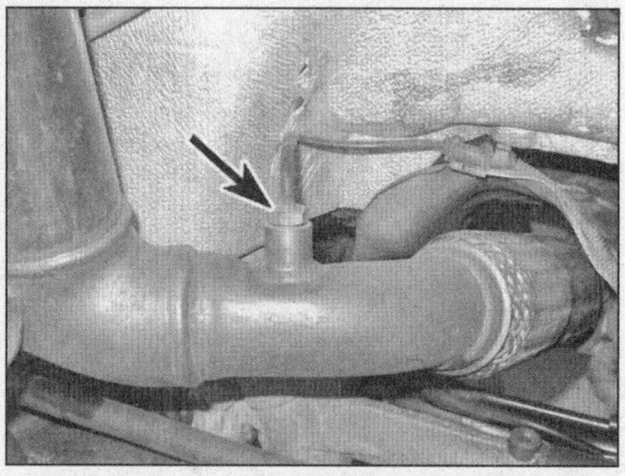

4.42b Gas sensor fitted to models with a particulate filter

39 Access is from beneath the engine compartment. Apply the handbrake, and then jack up the front of the vehicle and support it on axle stands (see *Jacking and vehicle support*). Remove the engine undertray.

40 Remove the retaining screw and withdraw the sensor from the cylinder block **(see illustrations)**.

41 Refit the sensor by reversing the removal procedure.

Oxygen (lambda probe) sensor

Warning: Working on the sensors is only advisable with the engine (and therefore the exhaust system) completely cold. The catalytic converter in particular will be very hot for some time after the engine has been switched off.

42 All models have a sensor threaded into the top of the catalytic converter/particulate filter **(see illustrations)**. Note, on some models there may be a second sensor in the front pipe after the catalytic converter/particulate filter. **Note:** *Do not confuse exhaust gas sensors fitted to the exhaust system; these are only fitted to models with a particulate filter.*

43 Working from the sensor, trace the wiring harness from the oxygen sensor back to the connector, and disconnect it. Unclip the sensor wiring from any retaining clips, noting how it is routed.

44 Access to the upstream sensor is possible on some models from above, while the downstream sensor (where fitted) is only accessible from below.

45 Unscrew and remove the sensor, taking care to avoid damaging the sensor probe as it is removed. **Note:** *As a flying lead remains connected to the sensor after it has been disconnected, if the correct-size spanner is not available, a slotted socket will be required to remove the sensor.*

46 Apply a little high-temperature anti-seize grease to the sensor threads – avoid contaminating the probe tip.

47 Refit the sensor, tightening it to the correct torque. Reconnect the wiring; making sure that the wiring loom is secured in its retaining clips.

Throttle pedal/position sensor

48 Release the securing clip and disconnect the wiring connector from the top of the accelerator pedal **(see illustration)**.

49 Undo the retaining nuts and remove the throttle pedal from the mounting bracket **(see illustration)**.

50 Refitting is a reversal of removal.

Clutch pedal switch

51 The clutch switch is mounted on the clutch pedal bracket, and sends a signal to the ECU **(see illustration)**. The purpose of the switch is to avoid engine over-revving and load change jolts when the clutch is released. The switch also deactivates the cruise control system (where fitted) when the pedal is pressed.

52 To remove the switch, first remove the facia lower trim panel on the driver's side, as described in Chapter 11 Section 28.

53 Locate the switch wiring plug in front of the clutch pedal, and disconnect it.

54 Rotate the switch anti-clockwise and remove it.

55 When refitting the switch, first extend the switch plunger to its fullest extent, and then hold the clutch pedal depressed when offering it into position. Once the switch has been clipped into place, release the pedal – this sets the switch adjustment. Further refitting is a reversal of removal.

Electronic control unit (ECU)

Caution: Always wait at least 30 seconds after switching off the ignition before disconnecting the wiring from the ECU. When the wiring is disconnected, all the learned values are erased, although any contents of the fault memory are retained. After reconnecting the wiring, the basic settings must be reinstated by a Seat dealer using a special test instrument. Note also that if the ECU is renewed, the identification of the new ECU must be

4.48 Release the wiring connector

4.49 Undo the pedal mounting nuts

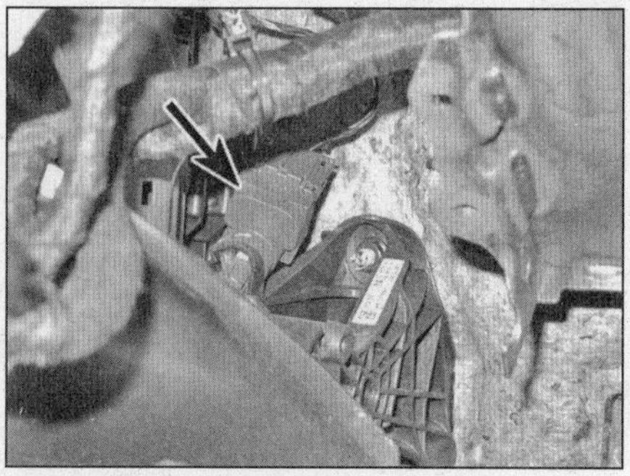

4.51 Clutch pedal switch

transferred to the immobiliser control unit by a Seat dealer.

56 The ECU is located on the engine compartment bulkhead, behind the air cleaner assembly **(see illustration)**. Remove the air cleaner assembly, as described in Section 3.

57 Disconnect the battery negative lead and position it away from the terminal as described in Chapter 5A Section 3.

58 Release the retaining clips and remove the ECU from the mounting bracket on the bulkhead **(see illustration)**.

59 Disconnect the wiring plugs from the ECU by sliding the locking levers outwards, then release them from the ECU **(see illustration)**. Remove the ECU from the vehicle.

60 If required release the securing clips at the rear of the bulkhead panel, to remove the mounting bracket **(see illustration)**.

61 Refitting is a reversal of removal. Bear in mind the comments made in the Caution above – the ECU will not work correctly until it has been electronically coded.

5 Injectors – general information, removal and refitting

Warning: Exercise extreme caution when working on the fuel injectors. Never expose the hands or any part of the body to injector spray, as the high pressure can cause the fuel to penetrate the skin, with possibly fatal results. You are strongly advised to have any work, which involves testing the injectors under pressure carried out, by a dealer or fuel injection specialist. Refer to the precautions given in Section 1 of this Chapter before proceeding.

General information

1 Injectors do deteriorate with prolonged use, and it is reasonable to expect them to need reconditioning or renewal after 60,000 miles (100,000 km) or so. Accurate testing, overhaul and calibration of the injectors must be left to a specialist.

Removal

Note: *Take care not to allow dirt into the injectors or fuel pipes during this procedure. Do not drop the injectors or allow the needles at their tips to become damaged. The injectors are precision-made to fine limits, and must not be handled roughly. Keep the injectors identified for position to ensure correct refitting.*

2 Pull the plastic cover over the engine upwards from its' mountings. Where fitted, remove the foam insulation over the injectors **(see illustrations 4.1a & 4.1b)**

3 Ensure the area around the injectors and the pipes/return hoses is clean and free from debris. The use of a vacuum cleaner is recommended. Plug all fuel lines when they have been disconnected to prevent any dirt ingress **(see illustration)**.

4.56 Location of ECU

4.58 Unclip the control unit from the mounting bracket

4.59 Pull out the locking slides to disconnect the wiring

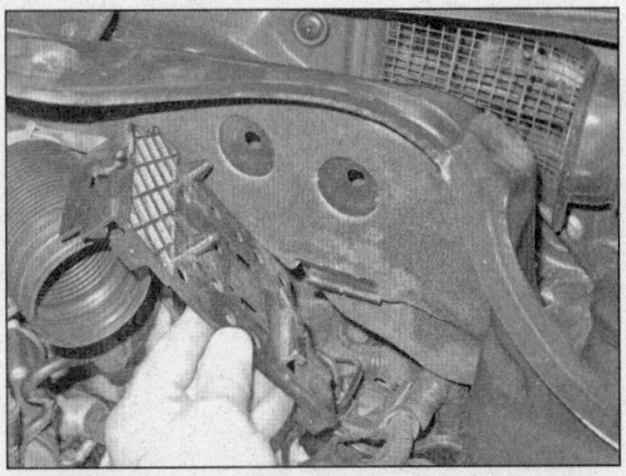
4.60 Unclip the mounting bracket from the bulkhead

4 Disconnect the injector wiring plug connectors **(see illustration)**.

5 Using a pair of long-nose pliers, withdraw the retaining clip from the side of the injector and remove the fuel return hose **(see illustrations)**. Discard the o-ring seals, as new ones will be required for refitting.

6 Counterhold the injector with an open-ended spanner when releasing the pipe union. Undo the unions and

5.3 Fit sealing caps to prevent dirt ingress

5.4 Disconnect the wiring plugs from the injectors

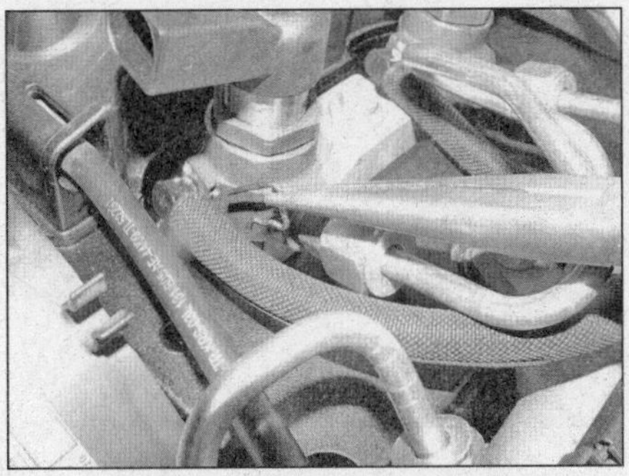
5.5a Remove the retaining clips...

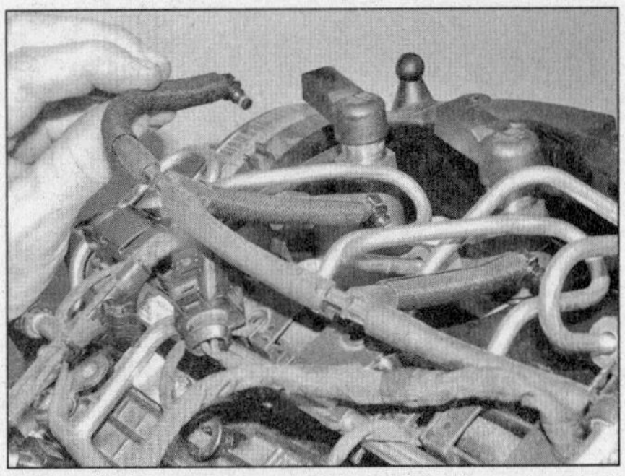
5.5b ...and disconnect the fuel return pipes

5.6a Use two spanners to counterhold the fuel pipe to the injector...

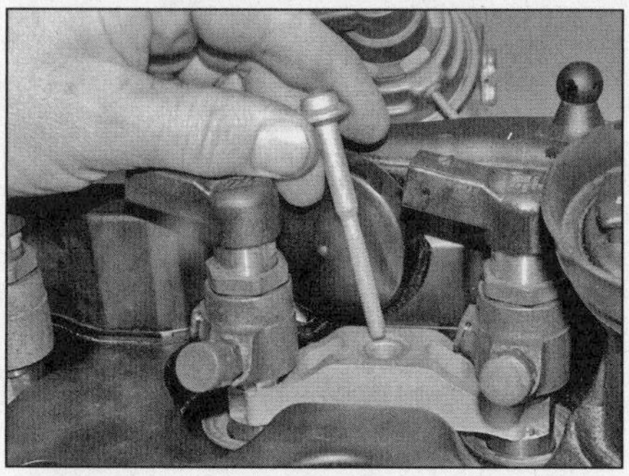

5.7 Remove the injector clamp retaining bolts

remove the high-pressure pipes from between the fuel rail and the injectors **(see illustrations)**. Plug the openings to prevent contamination.

7 Undo the bolt securing the injector clamp

5.6b ...and remove the high pressure fuel pipes

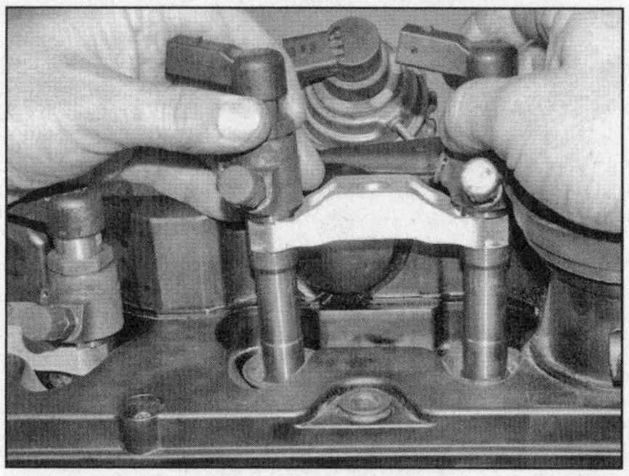

5.9 Remove two injectors at a time with retaining clamp

(see illustration), note that one clamp secures two injectors in place.

8 Seat technicians use a slide hammer (tool T10055) and adapter (T10402) to pull the injector from the cylinder head. If this tool is not available, it may be possible to fabricate an equivalent tool to pull the injector out of the cylinder head.

9 Two injectors will need to be removed together, as the clamping piece is slotted into both injectors. Recover the copper seal and O-rings and discard. New ones must be used for refitting **(see illustration)**. **Note:** *The injectors can only be refitted to their original positions. Mark the injectors to avoid confusion if refitting the original injectors.*

Refitting

10 If required, renew the injector seals in the top of the camshaft cover. Using a screwdriver, prise the seal out from the cover; the new seal can then be pressed firmly into the cover **(see illustrations)**. There are different size seals depending on engine code, make sure the correct seals are supplied. Also make sure the spring on the inside lip of the seal does not drop into the camshaft cover.

11 Ensure the areas around the injector locations in the cylinder head are clean and free from debris. Use a vacuum cleaner if available. Clean any carbon deposits from the injector and sealing surfaces with a cloth soaked in clean engine oil or rust-releasing spray.

12 To remove the copper sealing washer, spray rust-releasing spray around the injector nozzle, then clamp the seal in a vice, and use a twisting motion to pull the injector from the seal. Push the new copper seal into place **(see illustrations)**. Do not touch the very end of the injector, or you could block up the nozzle.

13 Apply a little clean engine oil to the return pipe connection, and fit the new O-ring **(see illustration)**.

5.10a Carefully prise out the seal...

5.10b ...and fit the new seal...

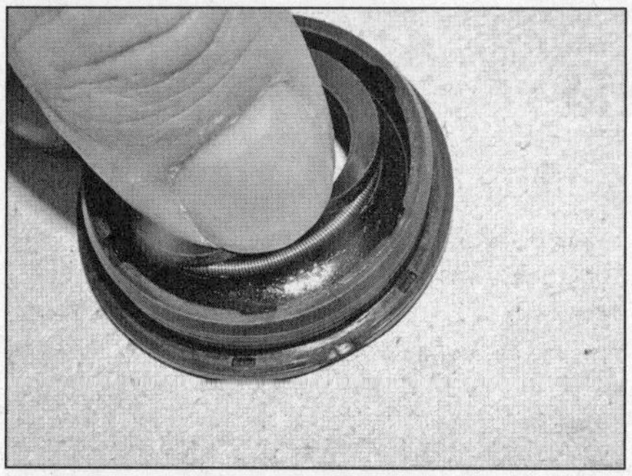

5.10c ...making sure the spring does not fall into the cover

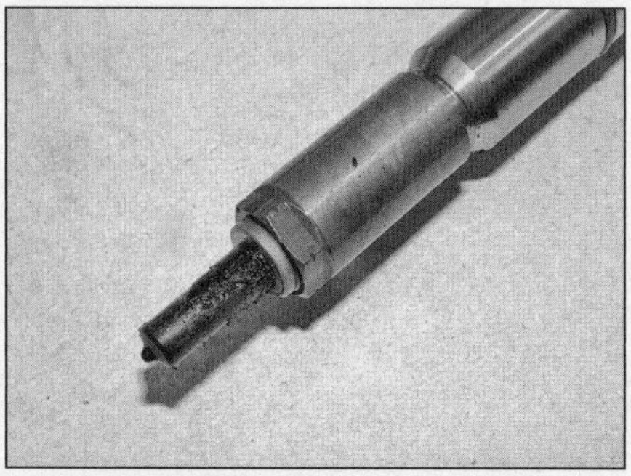

5.12a Clean off the carbon around the end of the injector...

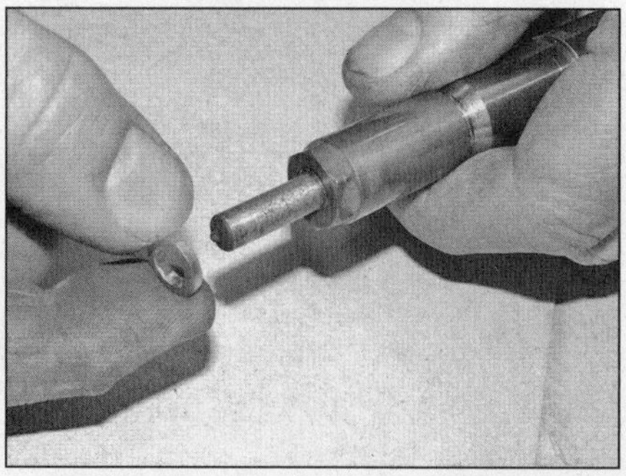

5.12b ...and fit a new sealing washer

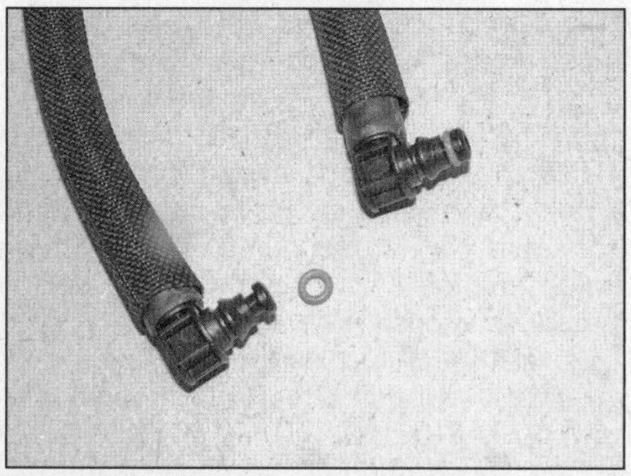

5.13 Fit new O-ring seals to the fuel return lines

14 To renew the main injector O-ring seal, Seat specify the use of tool no. T10377. This tool allows the O-ring to slide over the end of the injector without twisting. With care, the seals can be fitted without the tool **(see illustration)**.

15 Apply a smear of clean engine oil to the main O-ring seal, and insert the injector into place in the cylinder head **(see illustrations)**. Note that if the original injectors are being refitted, they must go into their original positions. Tighten the injector clamping bolt/nut to the specified torque.

16 Refit the high-pressure fuel pipes and tighten the unions to the specified torque. Note that the pipes may be re-used providing the tapered seats are undamaged; the pipes are not deformed, constricted or corroded. Counterhold the injector with an open-ended spanner when tightening the pipe union.

17 Use new securing clips when fitting the return hoses to the sides of the injector **(see illustration)**.

18 The remainder of refitting is a reversal of removal, noting the following:

a) If one or more injectors have been renewed, the 'injector delivery calibration values' and 'injector voltage calibration values' must be entered into the ECM using Seat/VW diagnostic equipment. Entrust this task to a Seat dealer or suitably equipped specialist.

b) After completion of the work, the fuel system must be bled as described in Section 11.

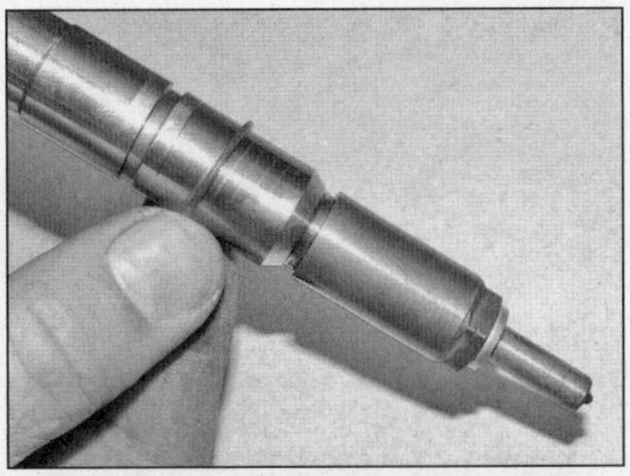

5.14 Fit a new main O-ring seal without twisting it

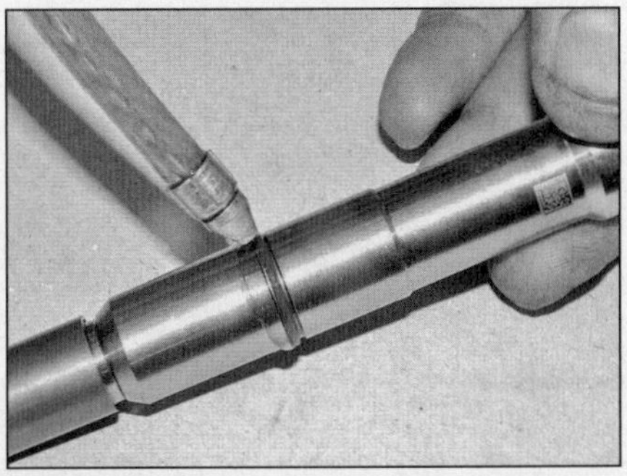

5.15a Lubricate the seal with some clean oil...

5.15b ...and then fit the injectors

5.17 Fit new clips to secure the fuel return lines

6 Inlet manifold – removal and refitting

Removal

1 Remove the throttle housing, as described in Section 4 of this Chapter.

2 Remove the fuel rail from the top of the inlet manifold, as described in Section 12 of this Chapter.

3 Undo the retaining screw(s) and move the coolant return pipe to one side **(see illustration)**.

4 Undo the two retaining screws and move the fuel return pipe to one side **(see illustration)**.

5 Where fitted, disconnect the wiring plug connector from the manifold flap motor **(see illustration)**.

6 Undo the retaining screw and remove the EGR cooler changeover valve from the manifold **(see illustration)**.

7 Slacken the retaining clamp and disconnect the EGR pipe **(see illustration)**.

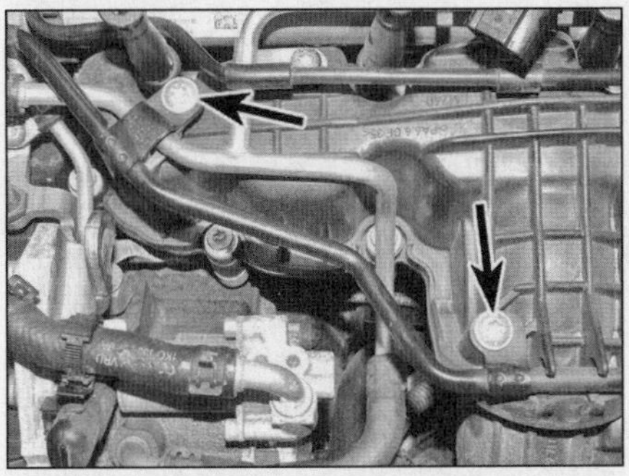

6.3 Undo the coolant pipe retaining screws

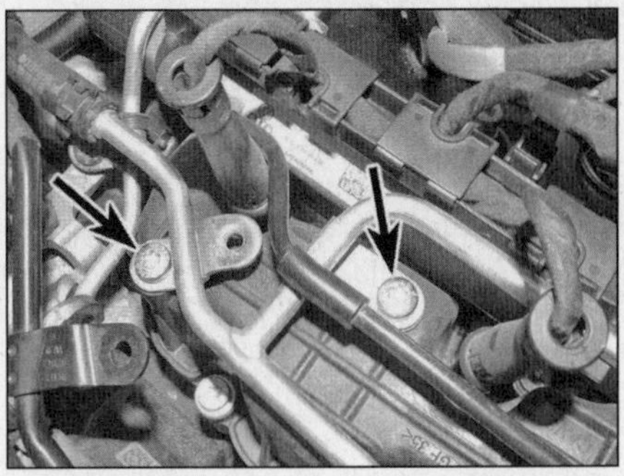

6.4 Undo the fuel line retaining screws

6.5 Disconnect the wiring connector

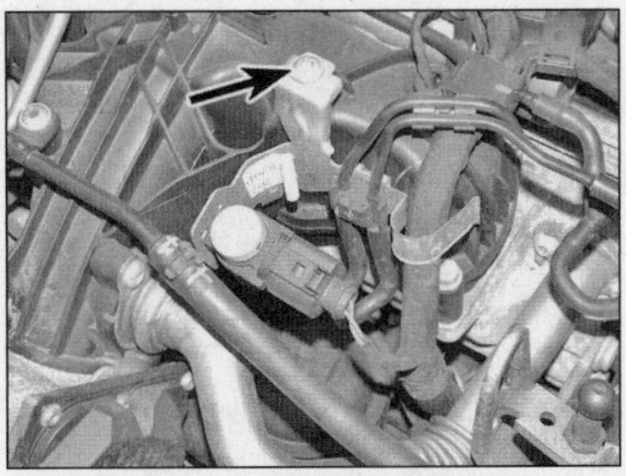

6.6 Undo the mounting bracket securing bolt

6.7 Slacken the EGR pipe retaining clamp

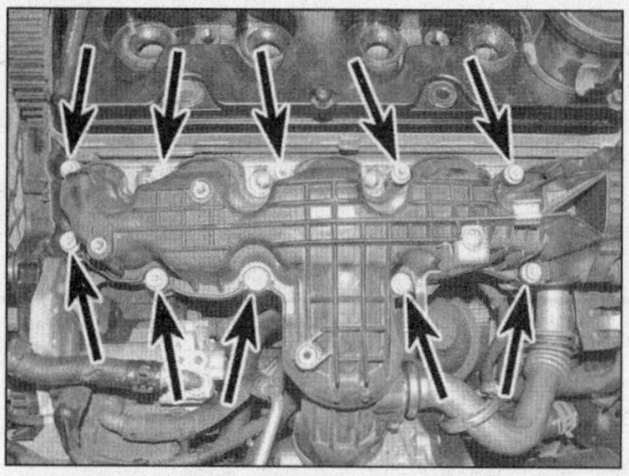

6.8a Undo the retaining bolts...

6.8b ...and remove the inlet manifold

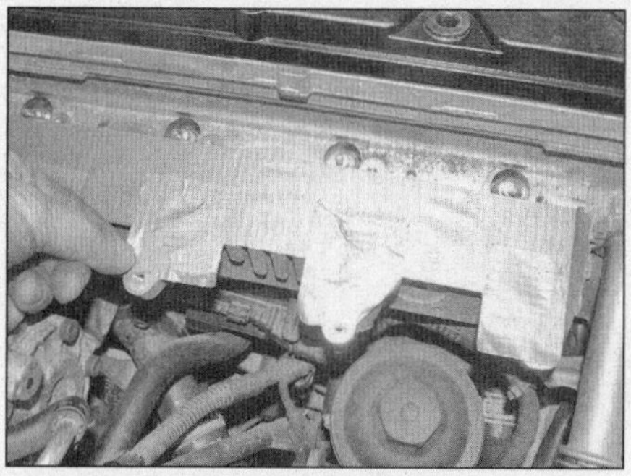

6.8c Cover the inlet manifold recess with tape

6.9 Refit new seals and gaskets

8 Undo the manifold retaining bolts, starting from the outside and working inwards in a diagonal sequence **(see illustrations)**. Lift the manifold from the cylinder head and retrieve the gasket seals; discard, as new ones will be required for refitting.

Refitting

9 Refitting is a reversal of removal, using new seals and gaskets **(see illustration)**. Remember to renew any self-locking nuts. Tighten the manifold retaining bolts to the specified torque setting, starting from the inside and working outwards in a diagonal sequence.

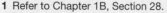

7 Fuel filter – renewal

1 Refer to Chapter 1B, Section 28.

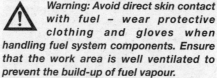

8 Fuel gauge sender unit – removal and refitting

Note: *Observe the precautions in Section 1 before working on any component in the fuel system.*

Warning: Avoid direct skin contact with fuel – wear protective clothing and gloves when handling fuel system components. Ensure that the work area is well ventilated to prevent the build-up of fuel vapour.

1 The fuel gauge sender unit is mounted in the top of the fuel tank. Access is beneath a cover in the load space floor. The unit protrudes into the fuel tank, and its removal involves exposing the contents of the tank to the atmosphere.

2 Refer to the procedures in Chapter 4A Section 6, for removal and refitting procedures.

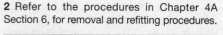

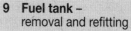

9 Fuel tank – removal and refitting

Note: *Observe the precautions in Section 1 before working on any component in the fuel system.*

1 Refer to the procedures in Chapter 4A Section 7, for the removal of the fuel tank, as the procedure is the same as petrol models.

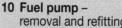

10 Fuel pump – removal and refitting

Removal

1 Remove the timing belt and pump sprocket as described in Chapter 2E Section 7.

2 Disconnect the wiring connector from the fuel metering valve on top of the fuel pump **(see illustration)**.

3 Undo the two retaining screws and move the coolant return pipe to one side.

4 Undo the two retaining screws and move the fuel return pipe to one side.

5 Undo the pipe retaining bracket screw and the two retaining bolts, then remove the lifting eye from the front of the engine **(see illustration)**.

6 Slacken the fuel pipe unions and remove the high-pressure pipe from the pump to the fuel rail **(see illustration)**.

7 Release the retaining clips and disconnect the two fuel hoses from the top of the fuel pump **(see illustration)**.

8 Counterhold the pump hub using Seat/VW tool T10051, and undo the pump hub nut. In the absence of this special tool, counterhold the hub using something to lock the sprocket, whilst the centre nut is slackened **(see illustration)**.

9 Using a suitable two-legged puller (or Seat/VW tool T40064) and two bolts, remove the hub complete with sprocket from the pump shaft.

10 Undo the 3 retaining bolts and remove the pump **(see illustration)**.

10.2 Disconnect the pump wiring connector

10.5 Remove the lifting bracket from above the fuel pump

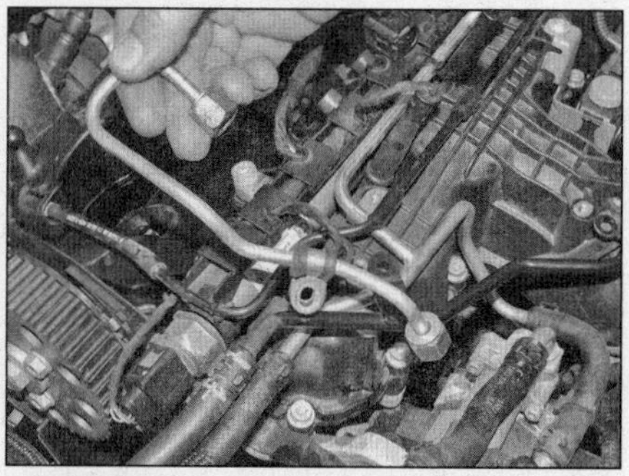

10.6 Remove the high pressure fuel line from the pump

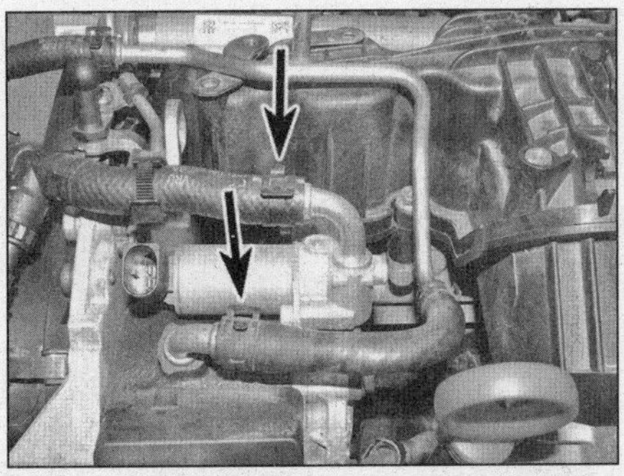

10.7 Disconnect the fuel hoses from the pump

10.8 Remove the fuel pump center hub nut

10.10 Fuel pump mounting bolts

Refitting

11 Refitting is a reversal of removal, noting the following points:

a) Ensure all fuel pipes/hose connections are clean and free from debris.

b) The high-pressure fuel pipe from the pump to the common rail maybe re-used providing it's not been damaged.

c) Tighten all fasteners to their specified torque where given.

d) Fill the pump with clean fuel through the fuel supply pipe aperture prior to starting.

e) Bleed the fuel system as described in Section 11.

11 Fuel system bleeding

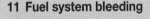

1 Prime the high pressure fuel pump by filling it with clean diesel through the fuel supply aperture, then operate the starter for shorts bursts (no more than 10 seconds at a time) until the engine starts. Operate the engine at a fast idle (approx 2000 rpm) for several minutes before allowing it to return to its normal idle speed.

2 If the engine fails to start, it must be filled/bled using Seat/VW diagnostic equipment (or alternative aftermarket diagnostic equipment. Using this equipment operates the electric fuel pumps for 3 minutes.

3 Once the engine has been started, test-drive the vehicle over a distance of at least 15 miles with at least one period of full acceleration. If there is any air left in the fuel system, the engine management ECU may switch to 'limp home' mode, and store a fault code. Have the fault code cleared and road test the vehicle again.

12 Fuel rail – removal and refitting

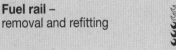

Note: *Observe the precautions in Section 1 before working on any component in the fuel system.*

Removal

1 Pull the plastic cover on the top of the engine upwards from its' mountings and remove the foam insulation (where fitted) **(see illustrations 4.1a and 4.1b)**. Ensure the area around the fuel rail and pipes is clean and free from debris. If available, use a vacuum cleaner.

2 Disconnect the wiring connectors from the fuel injectors.

3 Counterhold the injector with an open-ended spanner when releasing the pipe union. Undo the unions and remove the high-pressure pipes from between the fuel rail and the injectors **(see illustrations)**. Plug the openings to prevent contamination.

4 Release the retaining clips and disconnect the fuel return hose from the fuel rail **(see illustrations)**.

5 Undo the retaining bolts, disconnect the coolant return hose from the expansion tank, and move the coolant pipe/hose to one side.

6 Slacken the fuel pipe unions and remove the high-pressure pipe from the pump to the fuel rail **(see illustration 10.6)**.

7 Disconnect the wiring plugs from the glow plugs, fuel pressure regulating valve, and the fuel pressure sensor at each end of the fuel rail. Unclip the wiring loom retaining bracket from the top of the fuel rail and move it to one side **(see illustration)**.

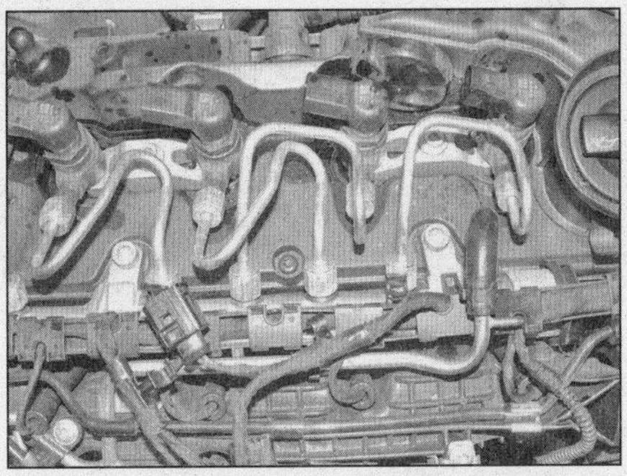

12.3a Remove the high pressure pipes from the rail and injectors...

12.3b ...and fit sealing caps to prevent dirt ingress

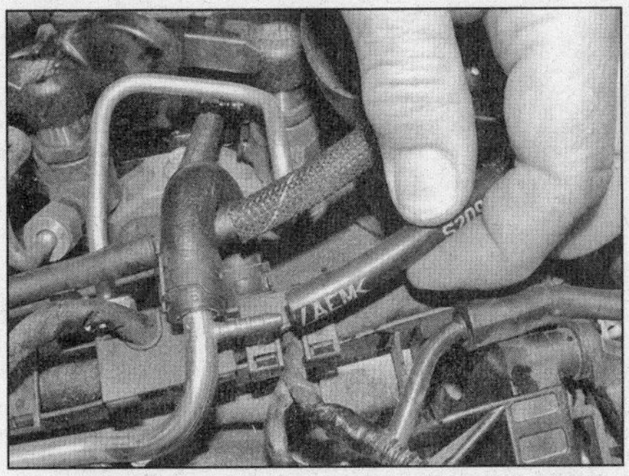

12.4a Disconnect the hose from the return pipe...

12.4b ...and the return pipe from the fuel rail

12.7 Lift the wiring loom over and place to one side

12.8 Undo the fuel rail mounting bolts

8 Undo the multi-spline retaining bolts and remove the fuel rail **(see illustration)**.

9 If required, note their fitted positions, then unscrew the fuel pressure sensor and pressure regulating valve from the fuel rail, as described in Section 4. **Note:** *Seat insist that once removed, the pressure regulating valve cannot be re-used*.

Refitting

10 Where applicable, refit the fuel pressure sensor and the new regulating valve to the fuel rail, and tighten them to the specified torque. Note that the threads of the sensors must be clean and free from oil and grease.

11 The remainder of refitting is a reversal of removal, noting the following points:

a) Refit the high-pressure fuel pipes and tighten the unions to the specified torque. Note that the high-pressure fuel pipes may be re-used providing the tapered seats are undamaged; the pipes are not deformed, constricted or corroded.

b) After completion of the work, the fuel system must be bled as described in Section 11.

Chapter 4 Part C
Emission control and exhaust systems – petrol engines

Contents

Degrees of difficulty

Easy, suitable for novice with little experience	Fairly easy, suitable for beginner with some experience	Fairly difficult, suitable for competent DIY mechanic	Difficult, suitable for experienced DIY mechanic	Very difficult, suitable for expert DIY or professional

Specifications

Engine codes *

1.0 litre engines	CHYB, CHZC and CHZB
1.2 litre engines:	
SOHC	CBZB
DOHC	CJZD and CJZC
1.4 litre engines	CGGB and BXW

See 'Vehicle identification' at the end of this manual for the location of the engine code markings.

Emission control applications

1.0 litre and 1.2 litre	Catalytic converter complete with exhaust front pipe, pre-cat oxygen sensor in top of front pipe, after-cat sensor behind cat in exhaust front pipe, No EGR system. Exhaust manifold complete with turbocharger.
1.4 litre engines	Pre-Catalytic converter complete with exhaust manifold, main catalytic converter in exhaust front pipe. Pre-cat oxygen sensor in top of exhaust manifold, after-cat sensor in the rear of the intermediate/flexible pipe. No EGR system.

Torque wrench settings

	Nm	lbf ft
Catalytic converter support bracket to engine bolts:		
1.0 litre MPI engine (CHYB)	23	17
1.0 litre TSI engine (CHZC and CHZB)	20	15
1.2 litre (SOHC) engine	25	18
1.2 litre engine (DOHC)	20	15
Catalytic converter to turbocharger clamp (all TSI engines)	15	12
Catalytic converter to exhaust pipe clamp (all engines)	23	17
Exhaust manifold nuts*		
1.0 litre MPI engines	23	17
1.4 litre MPI engines	25	18
Exhaust front flexible pipe-to-catalytic converter:		
1.2 litre (SOHC engines) exhaust nuts*	40	30
1.2 litre, 3-cylinder (DOHC engines) exhaust nuts*	25	18
1.4 litre engines:		
Bolts	20	15
Nuts*	40	30
Exhaust manifold-to-catalytic converter nuts (1.2 litre, 4-cyl engines)	25	18
Exhaust pipe clamp bolts	25	18
Exhaust mounting bracket bolts	25	18
Oxygen (Lambda probe) sensors:		
1.2 litre engines	50	37
1.4 litre engines:		
Oxygen sensor before catalytic converter	50	37
Oxygen sensor after catalytic converter	55	41
Turbocharger to cylinder head nuts: *		
1.0 litre (TSI) engines	25	18
1.2 litre (SOHC)	18	13
1.2 litre (DOHC) engine	14	11

Do not re-use

1 General Information

Emission control systems

1 All petrol models are designed to use unleaded petrol, and are controlled by engine management systems that are programmed to give the best compromise between driveability, fuel consumption and exhaust emission production. In addition, a number of systems are fitted that help to minimise other harmful emissions. A crankcase emission control system is fitted, which reduces the release of pollutants from the engine's lubrication system, and a catalytic converter is fitted which reduces exhaust gas pollutant. An evaporative loss emission control system is fitted which reduces the release of gaseous hydrocarbons from the fuel tank.

Crankcase emission control

2 To reduce the emission of unburned hydrocarbons from the crankcase into the atmosphere, the engine is sealed and the blow-by gases and oil vapour are drawn from inside the crankcase, through a wire-mesh oil separator, into the inlet tract to be burned by the engine during normal combustion.

3 Under conditions of high manifold depression, the gases will be sucked positively out of the crankcase. Under conditions of low manifold depression, the gases are forced out of the crankcase by the (relatively) higher crankcase pressure. If the engine is worn, the raised crankcase pressure (due to increased blow-by) will cause some of the flow to return under all manifold conditions.

Exhaust emission control

4 To minimise the amount of pollutants that escape into the atmosphere, all petrol models are fitted with one (1.0 and 1.2 litre engines) or two (1.4 litre engine) catalytic converters in the exhaust system. The fuelling system is of the closed-loop type, in which an oxygen (lambda) sensor in the exhaust system provides the engine management system ECU with constant feedback, enabling the ECU to adjust the air/fuel mixture to optimise combustion.

5 The oxygen sensor has a built-in heating element, controlled by the ECU through the oxygen sensor relay, to quickly bring the sensor's tip to its optimum operating temperature. The sensor's tip is sensitive to oxygen, and sends a voltage signal to the ECU that varies according to the amount of oxygen in the exhaust gas. If the inlet air/fuel mixture is too rich, the exhaust gases are low in oxygen so the sensor sends a low-voltage signal, the voltage rising as the mixture weakens and the amount of oxygen rises in the exhaust gases. Peak conversion efficiency of all major pollutants occurs if the inlet air/fuel mixture is maintained at the chemically correct ratio for the complete combustion of petrol of 14.7 parts (by weight) of air to 1 part of fuel (the stoichiometric ratio). The sensor output voltage alters in a large step at this point, the ECU using the signal change as a reference point and correcting the inlet air/fuel mixture accordingly by altering the fuel injector pulse width.

6 All models covered in this manual have two oxygen (lambda probe) sensors, one before and one after the catalytic converter(s). This enables more efficient monitoring of the exhaust gas, allowing a faster response time. The overall efficiency of the converter itself can also be checked. Details of the oxygen (lambda probe) sensor removal and refitting are given in Chapter 4A Section 4.

Evaporative emission control

7 To minimise the escape of unburned hydrocarbons into the atmosphere, an evaporative loss emission control system is fitted to all petrol models. The fuel tank filler cap is sealed and a charcoal canister is mounted under the right-hand rear wing panel next to the fuel filler neck, this collects the petrol vapours released from the fuel contained in the fuel tank. It stores them until they can be drawn from the canister (under the control of the fuel injection/ignition system ECU) via the purge valve(s) into the inlet tract, where the engine then burns them during normal combustion.

8 To ensure that the engine runs correctly when it is cold and/or idling and to protect the catalytic converter from the effects of an over-rich mixture, the purge control valve(s) are not opened by the ECU until the engine has warmed-up, and the engine is under load; the valve solenoid is then modulated on and off to allow the stored vapour to pass into the inlet tract.

Exhaust systems

9 On most models, the exhaust system is

the exhaust manifold (or combined manifold and turbocharger), front pipe(s), intermediate pipe and silencer, and tailpipe and silencer. The systems fitted differ in detail depending on the engine fitted. On 1.4 litre engines, there are two catalytic converters, one is part of the exhaust manifold and the second one is part of the middle section of exhaust, fitted behind the front flexible pipe.

10 The system is supported by various metal brackets screwed to the vehicle floor, with rubber vibration dampers fitted to suppress noise, refer to Section 8, of this Chapter.

2 Evaporative loss emission control system – information and component renewal

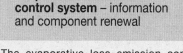

1 The evaporative loss emission control system consists of the purge valve, the activated charcoal filter canister and connecting vacuum hoses.

2 The location of the purge (or solenoid) valve varies according to the engine fitted. The charcoal canister is located near the fuel tank behind the right-hand rear wheel arch liner.

3 To remove the purge valve, check that the ignition is switched off, then disconnect the wiring plug and the two hoses **(see illustration)**.

4 To remove the canister, chock the front wheels, and then jack up the rear of the car and support it on axle stands (*see Jacking and vehicle support*). Remove the right-hand rear roadwheel and the wheel arch liner. Disconnect the hose leading to the solenoid valve from the top of the adapter, and then disconnect the hose from the fuel tank from the side of the adapter. Unscrew the mounting bolt and lower the canister from the body **(see illustrations)**.

5 Refitting is a reversal of removal.

2.3 The purge valve on the 1.0 litre TSI engine

2.4a Remove the wing liner

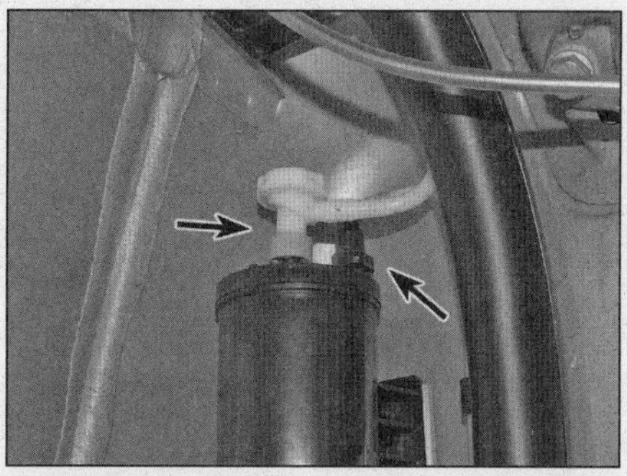

2.4b Remove the breather and vent hoses

2.4c Remove the bolt, slide up and then lower the canister from the vehicle

3 Crankcase emission system – general information

1 The crankcase emission control system consists of hoses connecting the crankcase to the air cleaner or inlet manifold. Oil separator units are fitted to some petrol engines, usually at the back of the engine **(see illustration)**.

2 The system requires no attention other than to check at regular intervals that the hoses, valve and oil separator are free of blockages and in good condition.

4 Turbocharger – general information and precautions

General information

1 A turbocharger is fitted to all 1.0 litre and 1.2 litre TSI engines, and is integral with the exhaust manifold Section 6.

2 The turbocharger increases engine efficiency by raising the pressure in the inlet manifold above atmospheric pressure. Instead of the air simply being sucked into the cylinders, it is forced in.

3 Energy for the operation of the turbocharger comes from the exhaust gas. The gas flows through a specially-shaped housing (the turbine housing) and in so doing, spins the turbine wheel. The turbine wheel is attached to a shaft, at the end of which is another vaned wheel, known as the compressor wheel. The compressor wheel spins in its own housing, and compresses the inducted air on the way to the inlet manifold.

4 The compressed air passes through a charge air cooler, which is fitted in the inlet manifold. There is a secondary radiator (charge air cooler) fitted below the engine radiator at the front of the engine compartment. The coolant is circulated around the charge air cooler system by an electric recirculation pump fitted at the rear of the engine below the inlet manifold. The purpose of the charge air cooler is to remove from the inducted air some of the heat gained in being compressed. Because cooler air is denser, removal of this heat further increases engine efficiency.

3.1 Oil separator (1.2 litre SOHC)

5 Boost pressure (the pressure in the inlet manifold) is limited by a wastegate, which diverts the exhaust gas away from the turbine wheel in response to a pressure-sensitive actuator.

6 The turbo shaft is pressure-lubricated by an oil feed pipe from the engine oil filter mounting. The shaft 'floats' on a cushion of oil. Oil is returned to the sump through a return pipe that connects to the sump.

Precautions

7 The turbocharger operates at extremely high speeds and temperatures. Certain precautions must be observed to avoid premature failure of the turbo, or injury to the operator.

8 Do not operate the turbo with any parts exposed – foreign objects falling onto the rotating vanes could cause excessive damage and (if ejected) personal injury.

9 Cover the turbocharger air inlet ducts to prevent debris entering, and clean using lint-free cloths only.

10 Do not race the engine immediately after start-up, especially if it is cold. Give the oil a few seconds to circulate.

11 Observe the recommended intervals for oil and filter changing, and use a reputable oil of the specified quality. Neglect of oil changing,

5.3 Electric recirculation pump (1.2 SOHC)

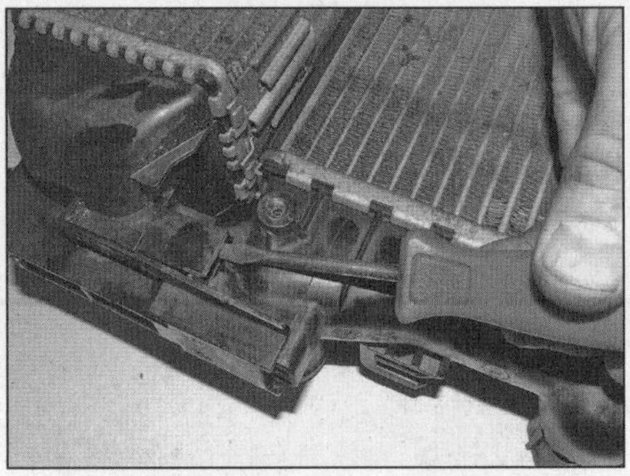

5.6a Release the retaining clip...

5.6b ...and disconnect the charge air cooler

or use of inferior oil, can cause carbon formation on the turbo shaft and subsequent failure. Thoroughly clean the area around all oil pipe unions before disconnecting them, to prevent the ingress of dirt. Store dismantled components in a sealed container to prevent contamination.

5 Charge air cooler – general information, removal and refitting

Note: *A charge air cooler system is fitted to all TSI engines. This is a secondary cooling system which circulates coolant through a charge air cooler (radiator), which is fitted below the engine radiator, through hoses to a smaller charge air cooler (radiator) which fits inside the inlet manifold.*

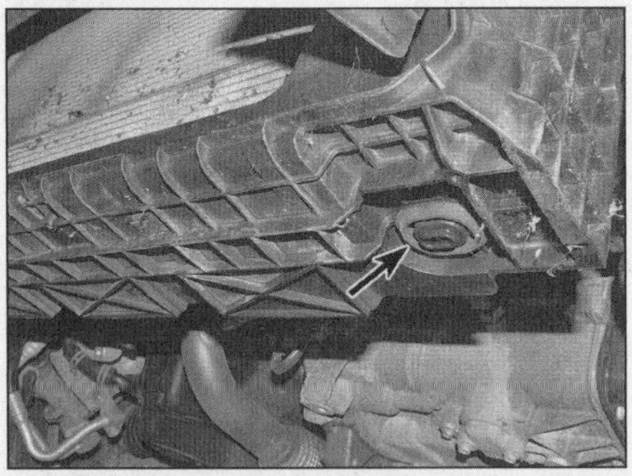

5.7 Check the rubber grommets in the crossmember

5.9 Move the HT coil to one side (1.2 SOHC engines)

General information

1 The charge air cooler is effectively a secondary radiator, used to cool the pressurised inlet air that enters the engine. Removal and refitting is essentially the same for all TSI engines.

2 When the turbocharger compresses the inlet air, one side effect is that the air is heated, causing the air to expand. If the inlet air can be cooled, a greater effective volume of air will be inducted, and the engine will produce more power.

3 The compressed air from the turbocharger, which is fed straight into the inlet manifold, is cooled by an air cooler which is fitted inside the inlet manifold. A secondary radiator is located below the engine radiator at the front of the engine compartment. The coolant is then circulated around the charge air cooler system by means of an electric recirculation pump **(see illustration)**, which is fitted to the rear of the engine below the inlet manifold.

5.8 Remove the lower hose

5.10 Disconnect coolant hoses

4 There is a charge air pressure/temperature sensor fitted to the air inlet ducting from the turbcharger to the inlet manifold.

Charge air cooler (below engine radiator)

Removal

5 The charge air cooler radiator is attached to the lower part of the engine radiator on the lock carrier (the crossmember incorporating the radiator grille and air-conditioning condenser). Remove the engine radiator as described in Chapter 3 Section 3, for access to the charge air cooler radiator.

6 Release the retaining clips and disconnect the charge air cooler radiator from the lower part of the radiator **(see illustrations)**.

Refitting

7 Refitting is a reversal of removal, noting the following points:

a) *Check the rubber grommets are still located in the lower crossmember* **(see illustration)**.
b) *Refer to Chapter 3, when refitting the radiator.*
c) *Ensure that the hose clips are securely refitted, to prevent any leaks.*

Charge air cooler (in inlet manifold)

Removal

8 The charge air cooler fitted inside the inlet manifold. Drain the coolant from the charge air cooling circuit by removing the lower hose from the charge air cooler, below the engine radiator at the front of the vehicle **(see illustration)**.

9 On 1.2 litre SOHC engines, undo the retaining screws, disconnect the wiring connector and move the ignition coil to one side **(see illustration)**.

10 Slacken the retaining clips and disconnect the two coolant hoses from the charge air cooler **(see illustration)**. If required, clamp the two coolant hoses to prevent any further coolant spillage.

11 Slacken and remove the retaining screws, then withdraw the charge air cooler from the inlet manifold **(see illustrations)**. Discard the gasket/seal, as a new one will be required for refitting.

5.11a Undo the retaining screws (manifold removed for clarity)...

5.11b ...and withdraw the charge air cooler

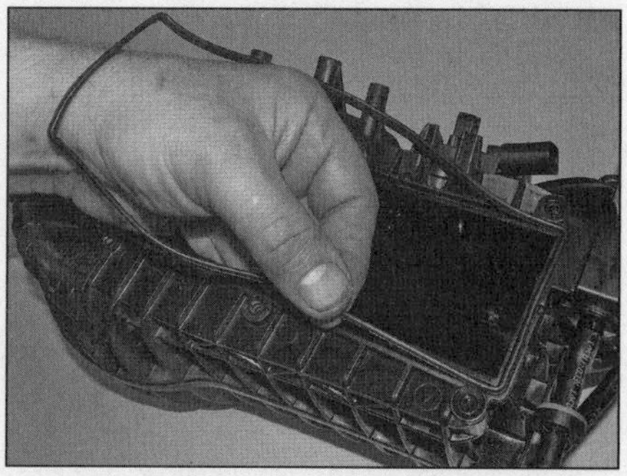

5.12 Fit new gasket/seal

Refitting

12 Refitting is a reversal of removal, noting the following points:

a) *Fit a new gasket/seal to the manifold, before refitting the charge air cooler* ***(see illustration)****.*
b) *Refill the cooling system as described in Chapter 1A Section 32.*
c) *On 1.2 litre SOHC engines, make sure the ignition coil wiring connector is secure*

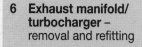

6 Exhaust manifold/ turbocharger – removal and refitting

Note: *The turbocharger cannot be removed from the exhaust manifold on 1.2 SOHC engines. On 1.0 litre and 1.2 DOHC engines the turbocharger bolts directly to the cylinder head – the exhaust manifold is integrated into the cylinder head on these engines.*

1 Apply the handbrake, then jack up the front of the vehicle and support it on axle stands (see *Jacking and vehicle support*). Disconnect the battery negative terminal as described in Chapter 5A Section 3.

1.2 litre SOHC engines

Removal

2 The exhaust manifold/turbocharger is located on the front of the engine on 1.2 SOHC engines and at the rear on all other engines.

3 Drain the cooling system as described in Chapter 1A Section 32

4 Undo the retaining screws, disconnect the wiring connector from the charge pressure/ temperature sensor and unclip the air charge air pipe from the throttle valve control unit and the turbocharger **(see illustration)**.

5 Disconnect the wiring connector from the turbocharger unit **(see illustration)**.

6 Release the retaining clip and disconnect the air intake hose from the air filter housing to the turbocharger.

7 Disconnect the HT leads from the spark plugs and move them to the rear of the cylinder head cover.

8 Slacken and remove the banjo bolt from the pipe going into the oil filter housing **(see illustration)**. Retrieve the washers and discard, as new ones will be required for refitting. **Note:** *Place a rag over the alternator to prevent any oil getting into the alternator.*

9 Remove the upper oxygen sensor from the front pipe **(see illustration)**.

10 Undo the retaining bolts and remove the heat shield from over the exhaust manifold/ turbocharger. It will be necessary to remove the cable guide bracket on the lower bolts **(see illustrations)**.

6.4 Remove the charge air pipe

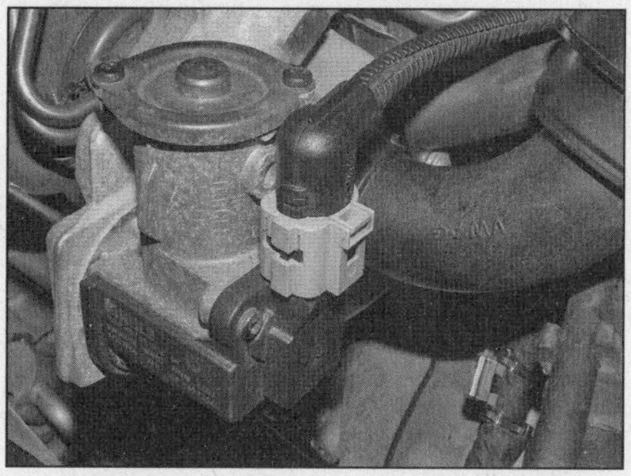

6.5 Disconnect the wiring connector

6.8 The oil pipe banjo bolt

6.9 Remove the oxygen sensor

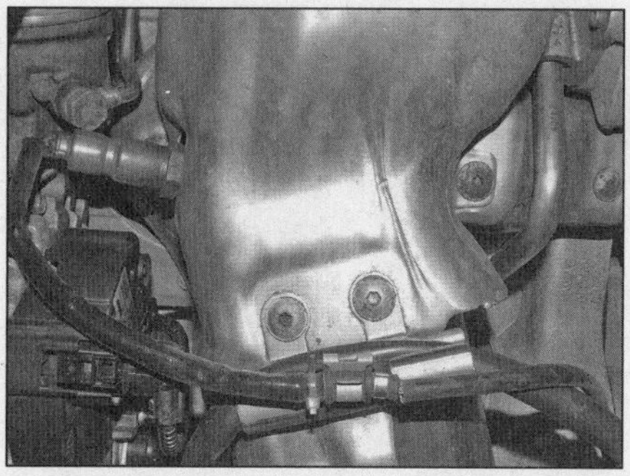

6.10a Cable guide bracket lower mounting bolts

6.10b Remove the heat shield

6.11 Disconnect the sensor wiring connectors

6.12a Disconnect the front pipe from the middle section

6.12b Undo the four nuts to the manifold

6.13 Remove the oil feed pipe

11 Trace the wiring back from the oxygen sensors, to the front of the transmission, and then disconnect the wiring plug connectors **(see illustration)**. Release the wiring from its retaining clips, noting its routing and fitted position.

12 Working under the vehicle, unbolt the exhaust front pipe/catalytic converter to middle pipe bolts/nuts. Undo the front pipe to manifold nuts, lower the front pipe and recover the gasket; a new one will be required on refitting **(see illustrations)**.

Caution: Handle the flexible, braided section of the front pipe carefully, and do not bend it excessively, if it is bent more than 10° it could get damaged.

13 Undo the upper banjo bolt on the turbocharger and remove the oil feed pipe **(see illustration)**. Retrieve the washers and discard, as new ones will be required for refitting.

14 Disconnect the coolant hoses, then undo the retaining bolts and remove the metal coolant pipes from across the top of the manifold **(see illustration)**.

15 Undo the retaining bolt and remove the oil return pipe from under the turbocharger **(see illustration)**.

16 Undo the retraining bolt and remove the heat shield from the lower part of the turbocharger **(see illustration)**.

17 Undo the retaining bolt that holds the turbocharger upper brace to the top of the cylinder head **(see illustration)**.

18 Unscrew the nuts and withdraw the exhaust manifold/turbocharger from the cylinder head. Discard the nuts, as new ones must be used on refitting. Also, recover the gasket and discard **(see illustration)**.

Refitting

19 Refitting is a reversal of the removal procedure but note the following:

a) *Fit a new gasket* **(see illustrations)** *and tighten all nuts and bolts to the specified torque where given.*
b) *Fit a new seal between the turbocharger and the catalytic converter.*
c) *If the turbocharger is being replaced due*

6.14 Remove the metal coolant pipes

6.15 The oil return pipe

6.16 Remove the lower heat shield

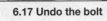

6.17 Undo the bolt

6.18 Unbolt and remove the exhaust manifold

6.19a The new gasket has the heat shield attached

6.19b Use new special nuts

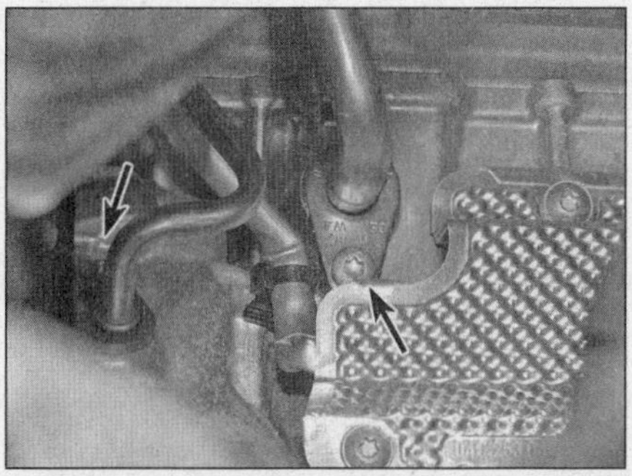
6.22 Remove the oil supply and drain lines

6.23a Release the turbocharger to catalytic converter clamp

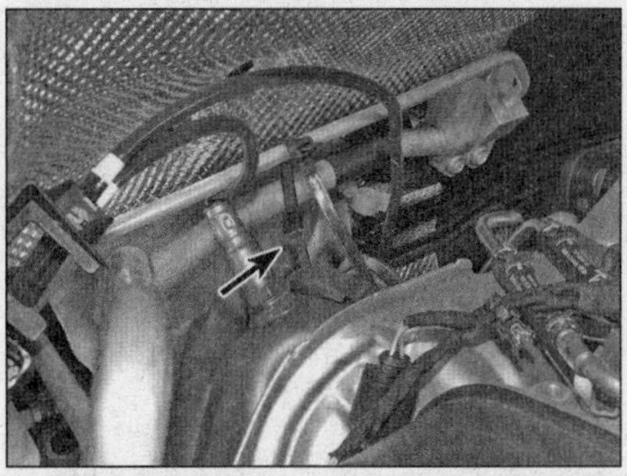
6.23b Secure the converter with cable ties

6.25 Remove the breather hose

6.26 Remove the inlet elbow

to internal damage it is essential that all charge air and exhaust passages are checked for debris before installing the new turbocharger.

d) *Fill the turbocharger (and oil lines) with fresh oil before starting the engine.*

e) *DO NOT run the engine above idle until the oil has fully circulated around the turbocharger.*

1.0 and 1.2 litre DOHC engines

Removal

20 Drain the cooling system as described in Chapter 1A Section 32.

21 Where fitted, remove the heat shield from the above the driveshaft.

22 Disconnect the wiring plug from the oil pressure switch and then (with difficulty) remove the the oil supply and return lines **(see illustration)**. Anticipate some loss of engine oil as the lines are removed.

23 Unbolt the catalytic converter from the turbocharger. Use cable ties and secure the converter to the side **(see illustrations)**.

24 Remove the air inlet ducting as described in Section 4A Section 3.

25 Protect the coolant pump and then remove the EVAP hose and the crankcase breather hose **(see illustration)**.

26 Unbolt the inlet elbow from the turbocharger **(see illustration)**. Access to the fixing is difficult.

27 Disconnect the coolant hoses and move them to the side **(see illustration)**.

28 Unbolt and remove the heat shield from the turbocharger.

29 Unbolt and remove the turbocharger **(see illustrations)**.

Refitting

30 Refitting is a reversal of removal but note the following:

a) *Use new gasket and nuts to secure the turbocharger to the cylinder head.*

b) *Fit a new seal between the turbocharger and the catalytic converter.*

c) *If the turbocharger is being replaced due to internal damage it is essential that*

6.27 Remove the coolant hoses

6.29a Working from below remove the nuts

6.29b Remove the upper support bracket...

6.29c ...and then remove the turbocharger

7.10 Disconnect the sensor plugs and remove them from the bracket

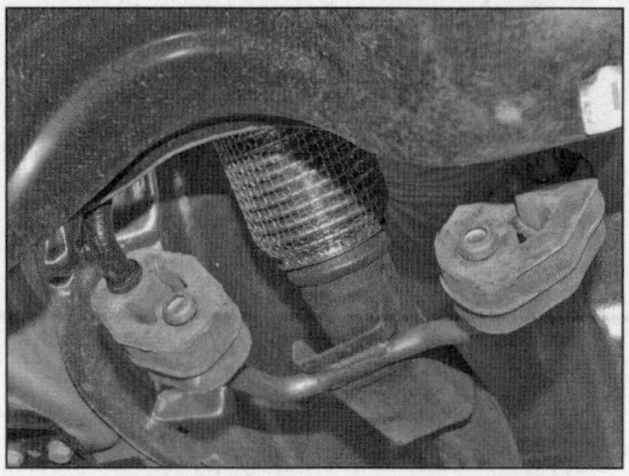

7.13 Remove the mounting rubbers

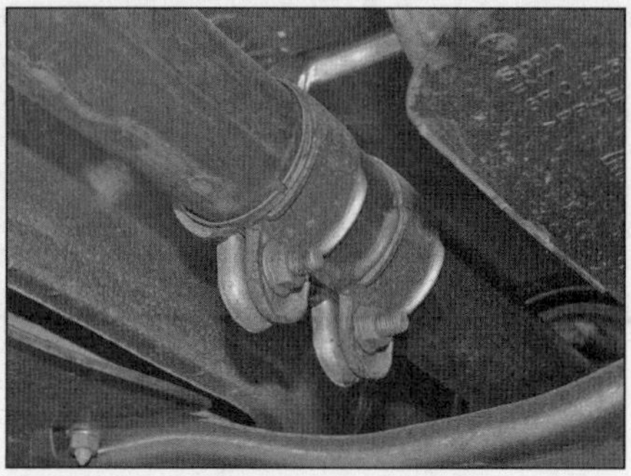

7.14 Slacken the clamp

all charge air and exhaust passages are checked for debris before installing the new turbocharger.

d) *Fill the turbocharger (and oil lines) with fresh oil before starting the engine.*

e) *DO NOT run the engine above idle until the oil has fully circulated around the turbocharger.*

7 Exhaust manifold/ catalytic converter – removal and refitting

Note: *On the 1.0 litre engine (CHYB) and the 1.2 litre SOHC engine (CBZB) the exhaust manifold is integrated into the cylinder head, with only a very short section of exhaust manifold before the catalytic converter or turbocharger. On the 1.0 litre TSI and 1.2 litre DOHC engines (CJZD and CJZC) the turbocharger bolts directly to the cylinder head. On the 1.4 litre engine a more traditional manifold and catalytic converter are fitted. The catalytic converter cannot be removed from the exhaust manifold.*

1.0 litre MPI engines

Removal

Note: *Only applies to MPI models. Engine code CHYB.*

1 At the rear of the engine disconnect the wiring plugs from the Oxygen sensors. Release the plugs from the bracket.

2 Jack up and support the front of the vehicle (see *Jacking and vehicle support*).

3 At the junction with the main exhaust system slacken the joining sleeve bolts and separate the exhaust from the catalytic converter.

4 Remove the catalytic converter support bracket.

5 Unbolt the converter from the cylinder head.

6 Pull the converter off the mounting studs and then release it from the flexible mountings.

Refitting

7 Always fit an new gasket and tighten the bracket and mounting nuts in the sequenced described below:

a) *Fit the bracket to the engine block and tighten to 23 Nm.*

b) *Slacken the mounting bolts on the upper section of the bracket.*

c) *Fit the new gasket and tighten the mounting bolts to 23 Nm.*

d) *Fit the bolt to the bracket and through the catalytic converter and tighten to 23 Nm.*

e) *Tighten the upper section of the mounting bracket to the lower section of the bracket to 23 Nm.*

8 The remainder of refitting is a reversal of removal.

1.0 and 1.2 DOHC TSI engines

Note: *On these engines the turbocharger bolts directly to the cylinder head and the catalytic converter is then clamped directly to the turbocharger*

Removal

9 Separate the catalytic converter from the turbocharger as described in Section 6.

10 Disconnect the oxygen sensor wiring plugs **(see illustration)** and then remove both sensors – see Section 6.

11 Jack up and support the front of the vehicle (see *Jacking and vehicle support*) and then remove the engine undershield.

12 Working form below remove the converter mounting nuts from the support bracket.

13 Release the exhaust pipe from the mounting rubbers at the rear of the front subframe **(see illustration)**.

14 Slacken the exhaust clamp and slide it along the exhaust system **(see illustration)**.

15 Manoeuvre the catalytic converter down and past the subframe and remove it from the vehicle.

Refitting

16 Always fit an new gasket and tighten the bracket and mounting nuts in the sequenced described below:

a) *Fit the catalytic converter to the turbocharger (with a new gasket) and fit the clamp – do not fully tighten the clamp.*

b) *Fit the nuts to the bracket and tighten by hand – it should still be possible to move the converter.*

c) *Tighten the clamp to 15 Nm.*

d) *Tighten the inside nut (closest to the transmission) to 20 Nm.*

e) *Tighten the outside nut (at the rear of the bracket) to 20 Nm.*

f) *Tighten the outside nut to 20 Nm.*

1.4 litre engines

Removal

17 Apply the handbrake, then jack up the front of the vehicle and support it on axle stands (see *Jacking and vehicle support*).

18 The exhaust manifold/catalytic converter is located on the front of the engine. To make access easier, first move the lock carrier/ front cross member assembly to its service position.

19 Undo the retaining bolts and remove the heat shield from over the exhaust manifold. On some models, it may be necessary to remove the cable guide bracket on the lower bolts **(see illustration)**.

20 Working under the vehicle, unbolt the exhaust front pipe/catalytic converter to front flexible flange bolts/nuts **(see illustration)**.

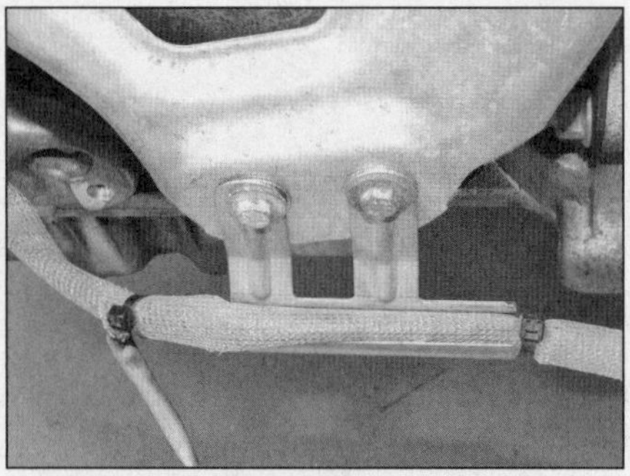

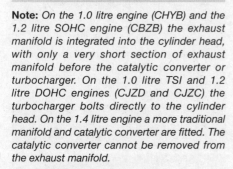

7.19 Cable guide bracket on the heat shield lower mounting bolts

7.20 Front pipe flange with mounting bracket – 1.4 litre engine

Lower the front pipe and recover the gasket; a new one will be required on refitting.

Caution: Caution: Handle the flexible, braided section of the front pipe carefully, and do not bend it excessively, if it is bent more than 10° it could get damaged.

21 Trace the wiring back from the oxygen sensor, located above the catalytic converter on the manifold, and then disconnect the wiring plug connector. Release the wiring from its retaining clips, noting its routing and fitted position.

22 Unscrew the nuts and withdraw the exhaust manifold from the cylinder head. Discard the nuts, as new ones must be used on refitting. Also, recover the gasket and discard **(see illustrations)**.

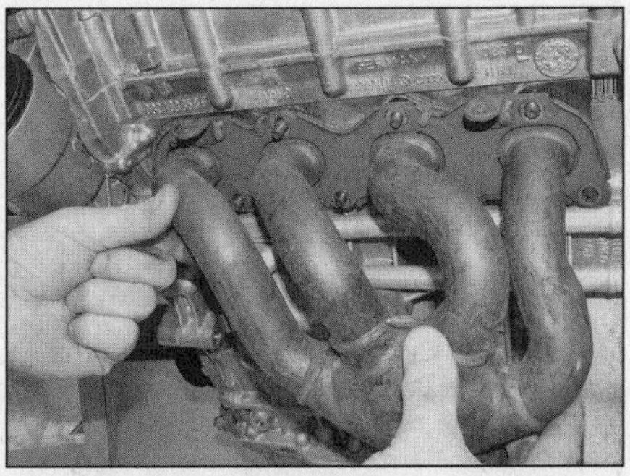

7.22a Unbolt and remove the exhaust manifold...

7.22b ...and recover the gasket

Refitting

23 Refitting is a reversal of the removal procedure, but fit new gaskets and tighten all nuts and bolts to the specified torque where given.

8 Exhaust system – component renewal

Warning: Allow ample time for the exhaust system to cool before starting work. In particular, note that the catalytic converter runs at very high temperatures. If there is any chance that the system may still be hot, wear suitable gloves. When removing the exhaust sections, take care not to damage the oxygen sensors if they are not removed from their locations.

Note: *The removal of the front section of the exhaust (complete with the catalytic converter) is covered in Section 7.*

Removal

1 The original Seat exhaust system fitted in the factory is in two sections on all models covered in this manual. The front section on all models except 1.4 litre engines also contains the catalytic converter and a flexible section with 1.2 DOHC models also having an expansion box fitted behind the flexible section.

2 All models have two silencers fitted in the exhaust after the catalytic converter/front pipe. The original factory assemble is a single part, but cut marks are provides to allow the exhaust to be cut so that separate mid and tail silencers can be fitted when required.

3 To remove part of the system, first jack up the front or rear of the car and support it on axle stands (see *Jacking and vehicle support*). Alternatively, position the car over an inspection pit or on car ramps.

Factory exhaust system

4 Not the position and angle of the joining sleeve before slackening the bolts **(see illustration)**.

5 Slide the sleeve towards the engine and then (where required) unbolt and remove the transmission tunnel cross member.

6 Release the exhaust system from the mounting rubbers and lower it to the ground.

Rear pipe and silencer(s)

7 If the factory-fitted Seat rear section is being worked on, examine the pipe just in front of the rear axle for three pairs of punch marks, or three line markings. The centre marking indicates the point at which to cut the pipe, while the outer marks indicate the position for the ends of the new clamp required when refitting. Cut through the pipe using the centre mark as a guide, making the cut as square to the pipe as possible if either section is to be re-used.

8 If the factory-fitted rear section has already been renewed, loosen the nuts securing the clamp between the silencers so that the clamp can be moved.

Rear silencers

9 The rear silencers are supported by rubber mountings that locate on mounting brackets, which are bolted to the underside of the car **(see illustration)**.

10 Undo the clamp bolts at the front of the rear silencers and slide it along the pipe to release it from the centre section. Lower the silencers out of position and release the mounting(s) from the underside of the car.

Refitting

11 Each section is refitted by a reversal of the removal sequence, noting the following points:

8.4 Unbolt the joining sleeve

a) Ensure that all traces of corrosion have been removed from the flanges or pipe ends, and renew all necessary gaskets.
b) If necessary, renew the clamps, and use the markings on the pipes as a guide to the clamp's correct fitted position.
c) Inspect the mountings for signs of damage or deterioration, and renew as necessary.
d) If using exhaust assembly paste, make sure this is only applied to joints downstream of the catalyst.
e) Prior to tightening the exhaust system mountings and clamps, ensure that all rubber mountings are correctly located and that there is adequate clearance between the exhaust system and vehicle underbody. Try to ensure that no unnecessary twisting stresses are applied to the pipes – move the pipes relative to each other at the clamps to relieve this.

9 Catalytic converter – general information and precautions

1 The catalytic converter is a reliable and simple device which needs no maintenance in itself, but there are some facts of which an owner should be aware if the converter is to function properly for its full service life:

a) DO NOT use leaded or lead-replacement petrol in a car equipped with a catalytic converter – the lead (or other additives) will coat the precious metals, reducing their converting efficiency and will eventually destroy the converter.

8.9 Exhaust rubber mountings

b) Always keep the ignition and fuel systems well maintained in accordance with the manufacturer's schedule.

c) If the engine develops a misfire, do not drive the car at all (or at least as little as possible) until the fault is cured.

d) DO NOT push- or tow-start the car – this will soak the catalytic converter in unburned fuel, causing it to overheat when the engine does start.

e) DO NOT switch off the ignition at high engine speeds – i.e. do not 'blip' the throttle immediately before switching off the engine.

f) DO NOT use fuel or engine oil additives – these may contain substances harmful to the catalytic converter.

g) DO NOT continue to use the car if the engine burns oil to the extent of leaving a visible trail of blue smoke.

h) Remember that the catalytic converter operates at very high temperatures. DO NOT, therefore, park the car in dry undergrowth, over long grass or piles of dead leaves after a long run.

i) Remember that the catalytic converter is FRAGILE – do not strike it with tools during servicing work, and take care handling it when removing it from the car for any reason.

j) In some cases, a sulphurous smell (like that of rotten eggs) may be noticed from the exhaust. This is common to many catalytic converter-equipped cars, and has more to do with the sulphur content of the brand of fuel being used than the converter itself.

k) The catalytic converter, used on a well-maintained and well-driven car, should last for between 50,000 and 100,000 miles – if the converter is no longer effective, it must be renewed.

Chapter 4 Part D
Emission control and exhaust systems – diesel engines

Contents

Degrees of difficulty

Easy, suitable for novice with little experience	Fairly easy, suitable for beginner with some experience	Fairly difficult, suitable for competent DIY mechanic	Difficult, suitable for experienced DIY mechanic	Very difficult, suitable for expert DIY or professional

Specifications

Engine codes*

1.6 litre – common rail injection	CAYC and CLNA

**See 'Vehicle identification' at the end of this manual for the location of the engine code markings.*

Emission control applications

All engines	Particulate filter in the front downpipe with catalytic converter and oxygen (lambda probe) sensor. EGR system fitted, with exhaust gas temperature sensors and exhaust gas pressure sensor. Engine code CAYC has a DPF (Diesel Particulate Filter) fitted.

Torque wrench settings	Nm	lbf ft
Catalytic converter/particulate filter mounting bracket nuts/bolts	25	18
EGR cooler mounting bolts	9	6
EGR recirculation metal pipes:		
to-cooler bolts	9	6
to-cylinder head bolts	9	6
to-exhaust manifold nuts	24	18
to-inlet manifold clamp bolt	5	4
Exhaust clamp nuts	25	18
Exhaust gas temperature senders	45	33
Exhaust/turbo manifold to cylinder head	24	18
Turbocharger pulsation damper bolts	10	7
Turbocharger oil return pipe flange bolts*	17	13
Turbocharger oil return banjo bolt*	40	30
Turbocharger oil supply banjo bolt	30	22
Turbocharger-to-downpipe/catalytic converter clamp	7	5

**Do not re-use*

2.1 Disconnecting the breather hose

1 General Information

Emission control systems

1 All diesel-engined models have a crankcase emission control system, and in addition, are fitted with a catalytic converter. All diesel engines are fitted with an Exhaust Gas Recirculation (EGR) system to reduce exhaust emissions. Models with engine code CAYC have a diesel particulate filter fitted.

Crankcase emission control

2 To reduce the emission of unburned hydrocarbons from the crankcase into the atmosphere, the engine is sealed and the blow-by gases and oil vapour are drawn from inside the crankcase, through a wire mesh oil separator, into the inlet tract to be burned by the engine during normal combustion.

3 Under conditions of high manifold depression, the gases will be sucked positively out of the crankcase. Under conditions of low manifold depression, the gases are forced out of the crankcase by the (relatively) higher crankcase pressure. If the engine is worn, the raised crankcase pressure (due to increased blow-by) will cause some of the flow to return under all manifold conditions.

Exhaust emission control

4 An oxidation catalyst is fitted in the exhaust system of all diesel-engined models. This has the effect of removing a large proportion of the gaseous hydrocarbons, carbon monoxide and particulates present in the exhaust gas. Some models have a particulate filter, which is fitted behind the catalytic converter in order to filter out soot particles.

5 An Exhaust Gas Recirculation (EGR) system is fitted to all diesel-engined models. This reduces the level of nitrogen oxides produced during combustion by introducing a proportion of the exhaust gas back into the inlet manifold under certain engine operating conditions. The system is controlled electronically by the diesel engine management ECU.

6 Models with engine code CAYC have a particulate filter fitted. These are designed to collect and then burn off the captured soot particles. Pre and post DPF pressure sensors calculate the particulate level in the filter and when this level is reached the filter cleans itself (regenerates). The engine management system alters the fuelling of the engine in order to increase the temperature in the filter and burn off the accumulated particulates.

Exhaust systems

7 The exhaust system consists of the exhaust manifold, front flexible pipe with catalytic converter/particulate filter and rear pipe section including silencer. The turbocharger is integral with the exhaust manifold, and is driven by the exhaust gases.

8 The system is supported by various metal brackets screwed to the vehicle floor, with rubber vibration dampers fitted to suppress noise.

2 Crankcase emission system – general information

1 The crankcase emission control system consists of hoses connecting the crankcase to the air cleaner, cylinder head cover and/or inlet manifold **(see illustration)**.

2 The system requires no attention other than to check at regular intervals that the hoses and pressure-regulating valve are free of blockages and in good condition.

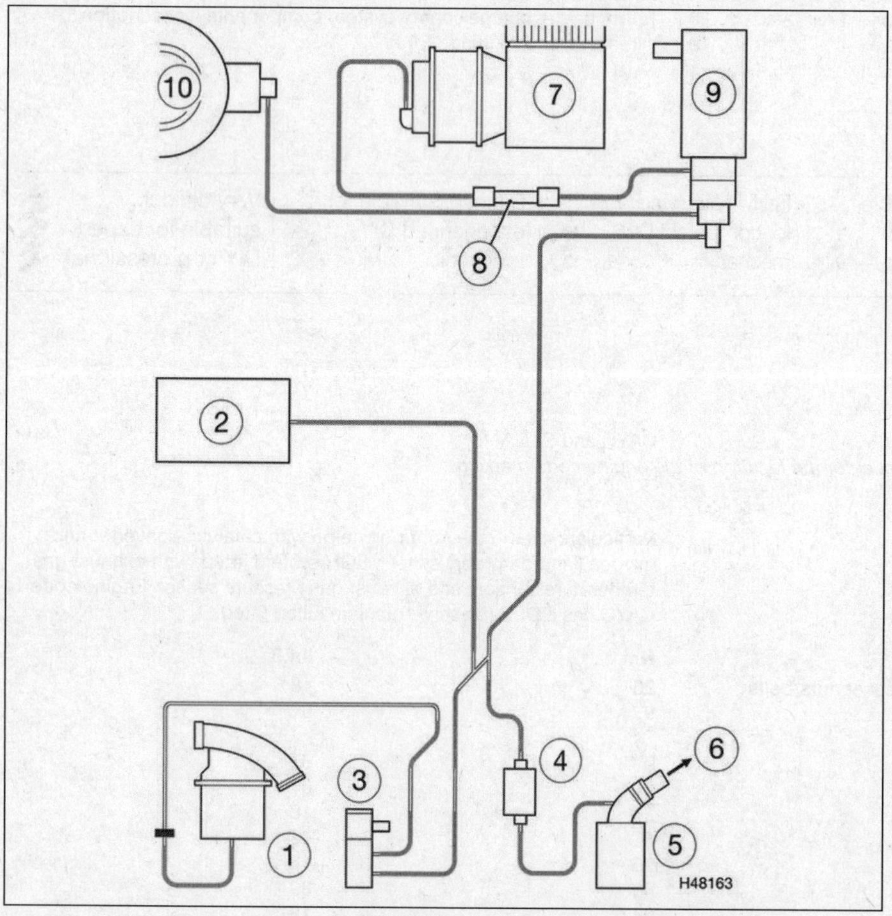

3.1 Vacuum hose layout – diesel engines

1 *EGR cooler change over vacuum unit*
2 *Cylinder head cover*
3 *EGR cooler change over valve*
4 *Non-return valve*
5 *Vacuum pump connection*
6 *To brake servo*
7 *Air filter*
8 *Silencer*
9 *Charge pressure control solenoid valve*
10 *Vacuum unit on turbocharger (with position sensor)*

3 Exhaust Gas Recirculation (EGR) system – component removal

1 The EGR system consists of the EGR valve, which directs exhaust gas from the exhaust manifold to the inlet manifold, and a control (change-over) valve that actuates the system according to engine load and speed **(see illustration)**. There is a vacuum-operated changeover unit, which is fitted on the EGR cooler for recirculating the exhaust gas. All this is connected by a series of vacuum hoses, and metal corrugated cooler pipes. There is also a recirculation potentiometer fitted to the EGR valve, this is controlled directly from the engine

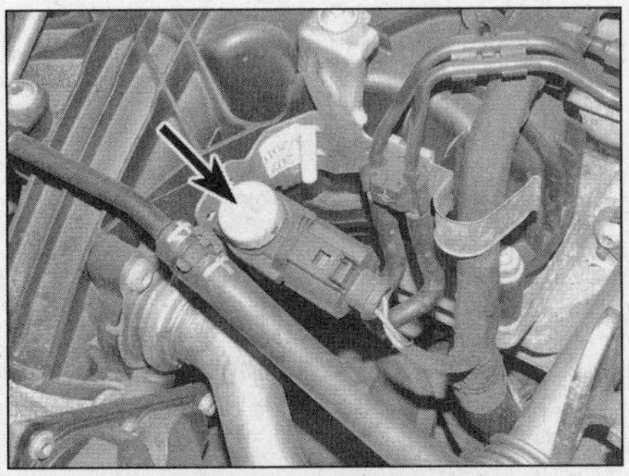
3.3 EGR cooler solenoid valve

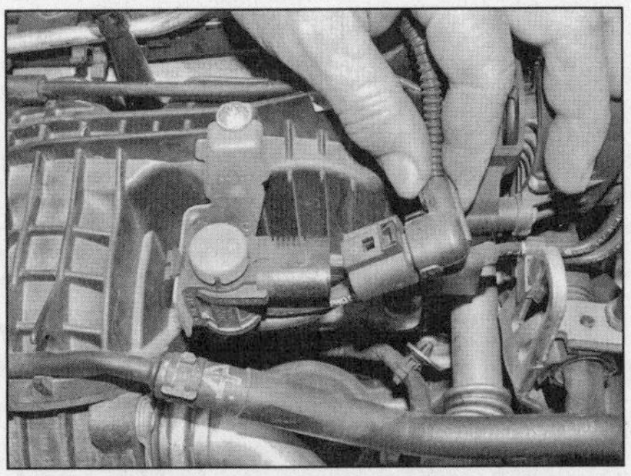
3.4 Disconnect the wiring connector...

3.5 ...then unclip the valve from the bracket

3.10a Disconnect the hoses...

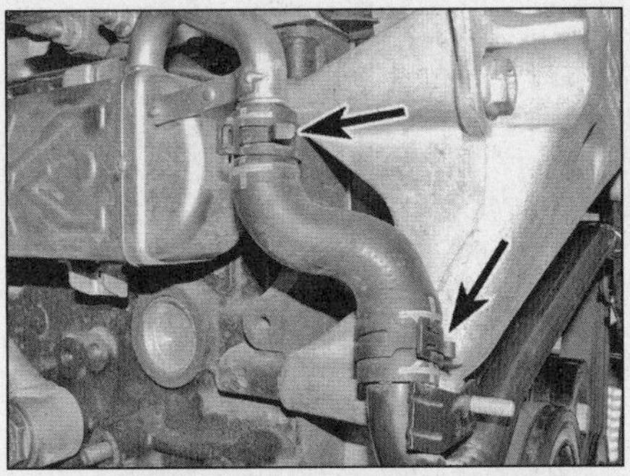
3.10b ...from the EGR cooler

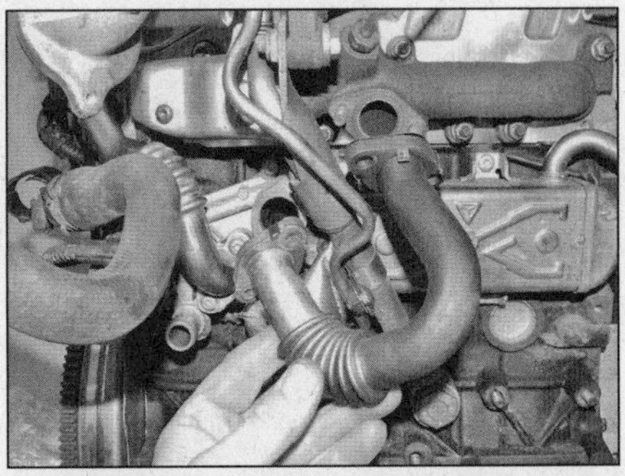
3.11 Remove the EGR pipe from the cooler to the manifold

management ECU, which then activates the control motor.

2 The EGR valve is integral with the exhaust gas cooler, which is bolted to the rear of the cylinder block. It is joined to the exhaust manifold and cylinder head, by flanged corrugated metal pipes. The system is activated by a solenoid valve mounted at the front of the inlet manifold, which is controlled by the ECU.

EGR cooler 'change-over' solenoid valve

3 The EGR vacuum-solenoid valve is mounted on the front of the inlet manifold **(see illustration)**. Do not confuse the EGR solenoid with the turbo charge pressure control solenoid, which is mounted on the bulkhead.

4 Disconnect the wiring plug from the solenoid valve **(see illustration)**.

5 Unclip the valve from the mounting bracket **(see illustration)**, then identify the vacuum hoses for refitting and disconnect them from the valve.

6 Refitting is a reversal of removal. Ensure that the hoses and wiring plug are reconnected securely and correctly.

EGR valve

7 The EGR valve is incorporated into the EGR cooler, remove the cooler as described in paragraphs 8 to 16. At the time of writing, it was not possible to separate the EGR valve from the cooler.

EGR cooler

8 Remove the exhaust front pipe/catalytic converter/ particulate filter as described in Section 8.

9 Drain the cooling system as described in Section. If required the coolant hoses can be clamped before removal, to save draining the complete system.

10 Release the retaining clips and disconnect the coolant hoses from each end of the EGR cooler **(see illustrations)**. Be prepared for coolant spillage.

11 Undo the two retaining screws from the cooler, the two retaining nuts from the exhaust manifold and remove the EGR metal connecting pipe **(see illustration)**.

12 Undo the two retaining screws from the cooler, the two retaining screws from the cylinder head and remove the EGR metal connecting pipe **(see illustrations)**.

13 Undo the upper bolts and lower banjo bolt and remove the turbocharger oil return pipe/support from the rear of the engine **(see illustrations)**.

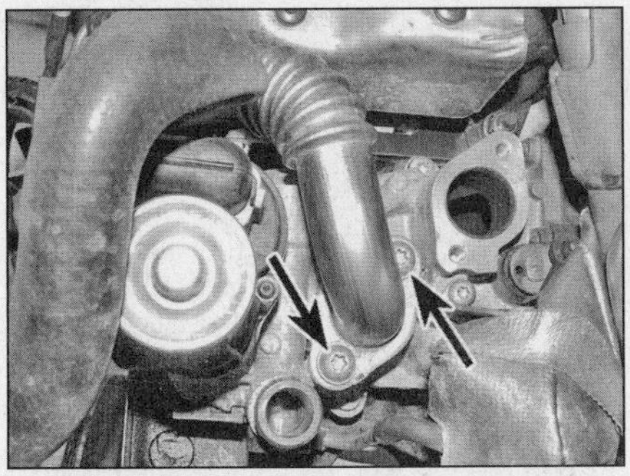
3.12a Undo the EGR pipe bolts to the cooler

3.12b Undo the EGR pipe bolts to the cylinder head

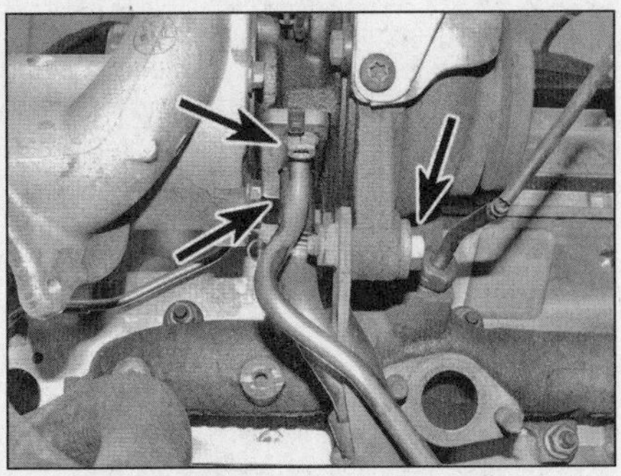
3.13a Undo the upper bolts...

3.13b ...and lower banjo bolts...

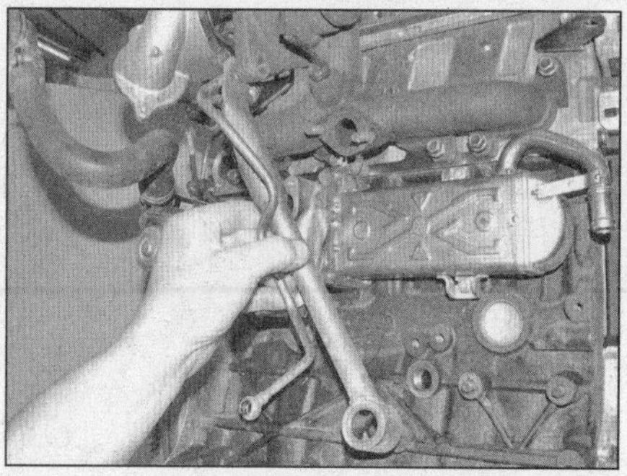

3.13c ...then remove the pipes and support bracket

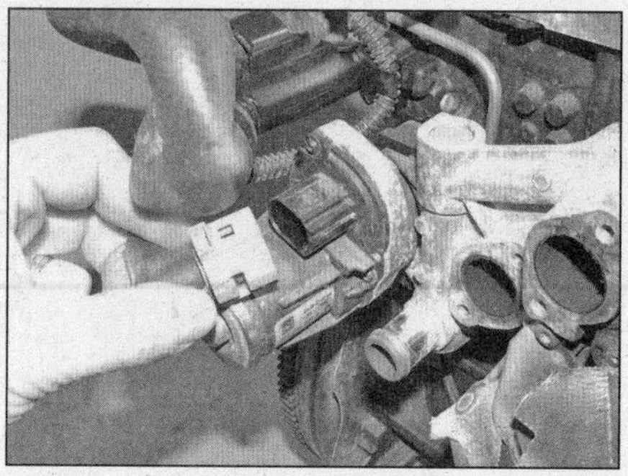

3.14 Disconnect the wiring connector from the EGR valve

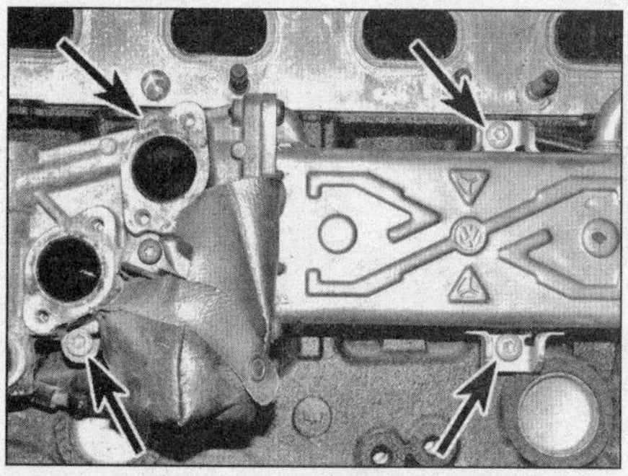

3.15 EGR cooler securing bolts

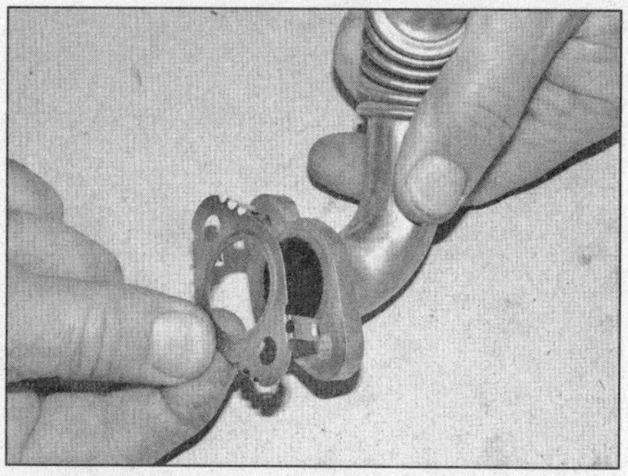

3.16 Fit new gaskets to the EGR pipes

14 Disconnect the wiring plug connector from the EGR valve **(see illustration)**.

15 Disconnect the vacuum hose from vacuum unit on the lower part of the cooler, then undo the four retaining bolts **(see illustration)**, and remove the cooler from the rear of the engine.

16 Refitting is a reversal of removal, using new gaskets **(see illustration)**, and tightening the retaining bolts to the specified torque.

4 Turbocharger – general information and precautions

General information

1 A turbocharger is fitted to all engines, and is integral with the exhaust manifold.

2 The turbocharger increases engine efficiency by raising the pressure in the inlet manifold above atmospheric pressure. Instead of the air simply being sucked into the cylinders, it is forced in.

3 Energy for the operation of the turbocharger comes from the exhaust gas. The gas flows through a specially shaped housing (the turbine housing) and in so doing, spins the turbine wheel. The turbine wheel is attached to a shaft, at the end of which is another vaned wheel, known as the compressor wheel. The compressor wheel spins in its own housing, and compresses the inducted air on the way to the inlet manifold.

4 Between the turbocharger and the inlet manifold, the compressed air passes through an intercooler (see Section 7 for details). The purpose of the intercooler is to remove from the inducted air some of the heat gained in being compressed. Because cooler air is denser, removal of this heat further increases engine efficiency.

5 Boost pressure (the pressure in the inlet manifold) is limited by a wastegate, which diverts the exhaust gas away from the turbine wheel in response to a pressure-sensitive actuator.

6 The turbo shaft is pressure-lubricated by an oil feed pipe from the engine oil filter mounting. The shaft 'floats' on a cushion of oil. Oil is returned to the sump through a return pipe that connects to the rear of the cylinder block.

Precautions

The turbocharger operates at extremely high speeds and temperatures. Certain precautions must be observed to avoid premature failure of the turbo, or injury to the operator.

- *Do not operate the turbo with any parts exposed – foreign objects falling onto the rotating vanes could cause excessive damage and (if ejected) personal injury.*
- *Cover the turbocharger air inlet ducts to prevent debris entering, and clean using lint-free cloths only.*
- *Do not race the engine immediately after start-up, especially if it is cold. Give the oil a few seconds to circulate.*
- *Observe the recommended intervals for oil and filter changing, and use a reputable oil of the specified quality. Neglect of oil changing, or use of inferior oil, can cause carbon formation on the turbo shaft and subsequent failure. Thoroughly clean the area around all oil pipe unions before disconnecting them, to prevent the ingress of dirt. Store dismantled components in a sealed container to prevent contamination.*

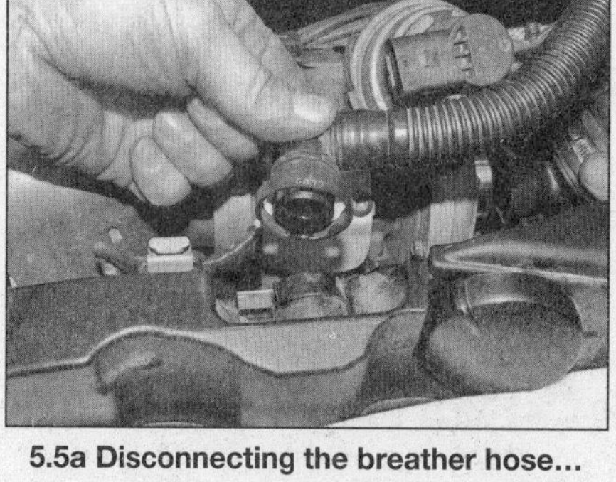

5.5a Disconnecting the breather hose...

5 Turbocharger and exhaust manifold – removal and refitting

Note: *This Section describes removal of the turbocharger together with the exhaust manifold. On all diesel engines covered in this Manual, the turbocharger cannot be removed from the exhaust manifold.*

Removal

1 Apply the handbrake, then jack up the front of the vehicle and support it on axle stands (see *Jacking and vehicle support*). Remove the engine compartment undertray and the engine top cover.

2 Remove the bulkhead panel from the rear of the engine compartment, as described in Chapter 12 Section 16 (wiper motor/linkage removal).

3 Remove the air cleaner assembly and ducting as described in Chapter 4B Section 3.

4 Undo the clamp securing the exhaust front pipe/catalytic converter/ particulate filter to the turbocharger and move front pipe to one side, refer to the information given in Section 8.

5 Undo the retaining bolt, unclip the breather pipe and disconnect the air intake hose from the turbocharger **(see illustrations)**.

5.5b ...undo the retaining screw...

5.5c ...and disconnect the air intake hose

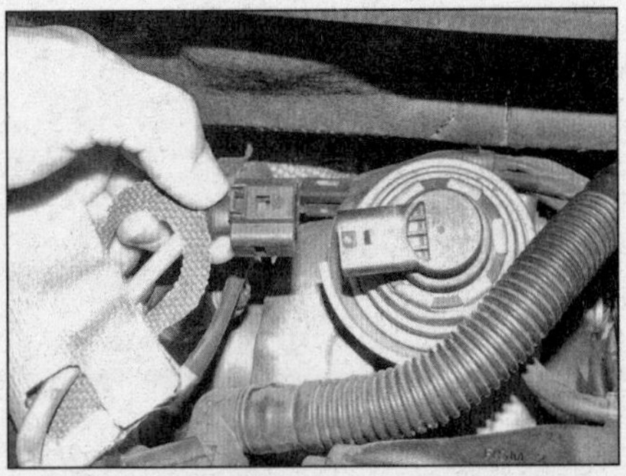

5.6a Disconnect the wiring connector...

5.6b ...and vacuum hose from the charge pressure valve

5.7 Trace the wiring back from the gas temperature sensor

5.8 Disconnect the charge air pipe/pulsation damper from the turbo

6 Disconnect the wiring connector and vacuum pipe from the charge pressure valve on top of the turbocharger **(see illustrations)**.

7 Located at the engine compartment bulkhead, disconnect the exhaust gas temperature sensor wiring plugs **(see illustration)**, and detach the connector from the bulkhead bracket. Note that there is one wiring connector behind the mounting plate on the bulkhead, trace the wiring back from the relevant sensor, noting its routing and releasing it from any retaining clips.

8 Slacken the retaining clips, undo the two retaining bolts and withdraw the pulsation damper from the charge air ducting to the turbo **(see illustration)**.

9 Undo the retaining screws and remove the EGR metal connecting pipes, with reference to Section 3.

10 Undo the two upper securing bolts and the lower banjo bolts for the oil supply and return for the turbocharger. Then remove the oil return pipe/support from the rear of the engine **(see illustrations 3.13a, 3.13b & 3.13c)**

11 Undo the two retaining screws and remove the heat shield from the manifold **(see illustration)**.

12 Check around the turbocharger/exhaust manifold and unclip any wiring or hoses still connected, noting their fitted position and the routing of all cables.

13 Undo the retaining nuts and manoeuvre the exhaust manifold/turbocharger assembly out from the engine compartment **(see illustration)**.

Refitting

14 Refit the turbocharger by following the removal procedure in reverse, noting the following points:

a) Renew exhaust manifold gaskets, sealing washers and O-rings ***(see illustration)****.*

b) Fit new gasket to the oil return pipe upper flange ***(see illustration)****.*

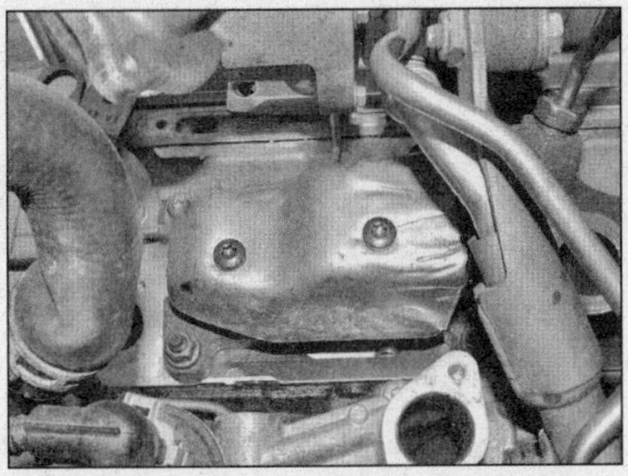

5.11 Undo the two retaining screws from the heat shield

5.13 Remove the turbocharger/manifold from the engine compartment

5.14a Fit the new exhaust manifold gasket...

5.14b ...oil return/supply pipe gasket...

5.14c ...oil return banjo bolt...

c) Fit new banjo bolt to oil return pipe ***(see illustration)****.*

d) Fit new sealing washers to the oil supply pipe ***(see illustration)****.*

e) Before reconnecting the oil supply pipe, fill the turbocharger with fresh oil using an oil can.

f) Tighten all nuts and bolts to the specified torque, where given.

g) Ensure that the air hose clips are securely tightened, to prevent air leaks.

h) When the engine is started after refitting, allow it to idle for approximately one minute to give the oil time to circulate around the turbine shaft bearings. Check for signs of oil or coolant leakage from the relevant unions.

6.2 Boost pressure solenoid valve

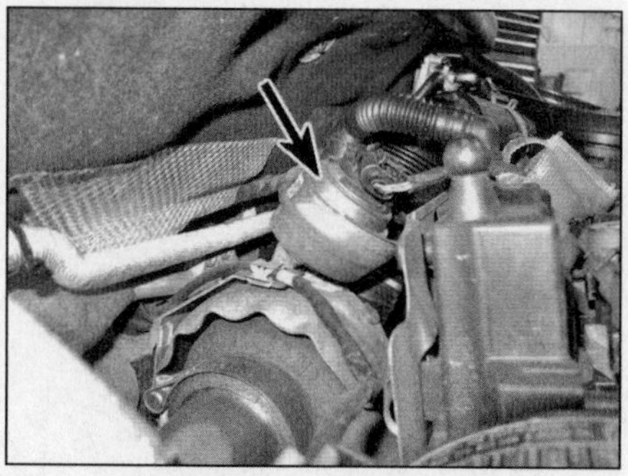

6.7 Charge pressure valve

5.14d ...and oil supply sealing washers

6 Turbocharger charge control system components – description, removal and refitting

Description

1 The turbocharger wastgate valve is operated by vacuum supplied by the brake vacuum pump mounted on the left-hand end of the cylinder head. The vacuum supply is controlled by an electrically operated solenoid valve activated by the engine management ECU. The solenoid valve is mounted on the left-hand inner wing panel at the side of the air cleaner houisng. The valve has three hoses connecting it to the air cleaner, turbocharger vacuum unit and vacuum pump. It is important that the hoses are connected correctly to the solenoid valve **(see illustration 3.1)**.

6.5 Disconnect the wiring connector and disconnect the vacuum hoses

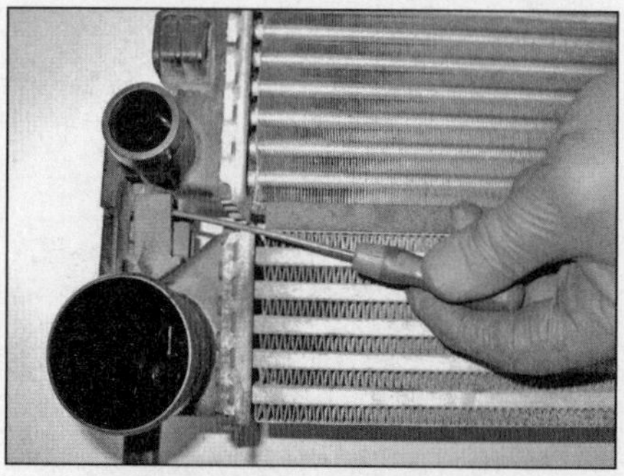

7.6a Release the retaining clip...

Charge pressure control solenoid valve

2 The charge pressure solenoid valve is mounted on the left-hand inner wing panel **(see illustration)**, at the rear of the battery.
3 Disconnect the wiring from the solenoid valve.
4 Undo the two retaining nuts and withdraw the solenoid valve away from the wing panel, unclipping the vacuum hoses from their retaining clips.
5 Remove the vacuum hoses from the ports on the control solenoid valve, noting their order of connection carefully as they need to be fitted in the correct position on refitting **(see illustration)**.
6 Refitting is a reversal of removal.

Charge pressure valve (wastegate)

7 The Charge pressure 'boost' valve is fitted to the top of the turbocharger and cannot be renewed separately as it is an integral part of the turbocharger **(see illustration)**.

7 Intercooler – general information, removal and refitting

General information

1 The intercooler is effectively an 'air radiator', used to cool the pressurised inlet air before it enters the engine.
2 When the turbocharger compresses the inlet air, one side effect is that the air is heated, causing the air to expand. If the inlet air can be cooled, a greater effective volume of air will be inducted, and the engine will produce more power.
3 The compressed air from the turbocharger, which would normally be fed straight into the inlet manifold, is instead ducted around the engine to the base of the intercooler. The intercooler is mounted at the front of the car, in the airflow. The heated air entering one side of the intercooler is cooled by the airflow over the intercooler fins, much as with the radiator.
4 There is a charge air pressure/temperature sensor fitted to the air inlet ducting from the intercooler to the inlet manifold. See Chapter 4B Section 4, for removal and refitting procedure.

Removal

5 The intercooler is attached to the lower part of the radiator on the lock carrier (the crossmember incorporating the radiator grille and air-conditioning condenser). Remove the radiator as described in Chapter 3 Section 3, for access to the intercooler. This procedure may include moving the lock carrier to its Service position, See Chapter 3 Section 3.
6 Release the retaining clips and disconnect the intercooler from the lower part of the radiator **(see illustrations)**.

Refitting

7 Refitting is a reversal of removal, noting the following points:

*a) Check the rubber grommets are still located in the lower crossmember **(see illustration)**.*

b) Refer to Chapter 3 Section 3, when refitting the radiator.

c) Ensure that the air hose clips are securely refitted, to prevent air leaks.

8 Catalytic converter/ particulate filter – removal and refitting

Warning: Warning: Allow ample time for the exhaust system to cool before starting work. In particular, note that the catalytic converter runs at very high temperatures. If there is any chance that the system may still be hot, wear suitable gloves.

Note: *This Section describes removal of the exhaust front flexible pipe/catalytic converter/particulate filter, which is one complete assembly. The subframe will need to be removed, to allow enough room for the assembly to be lowered out from under the rear of the engine.*

1 Disconnect the battery negative lead and position it away from the terminal as described in Chapter 5A Section 3.

2 Working at the engine compartment bulkhead, disconnect the wiring plugs for the oxygen sensor and exhaust gas temperature sensors.

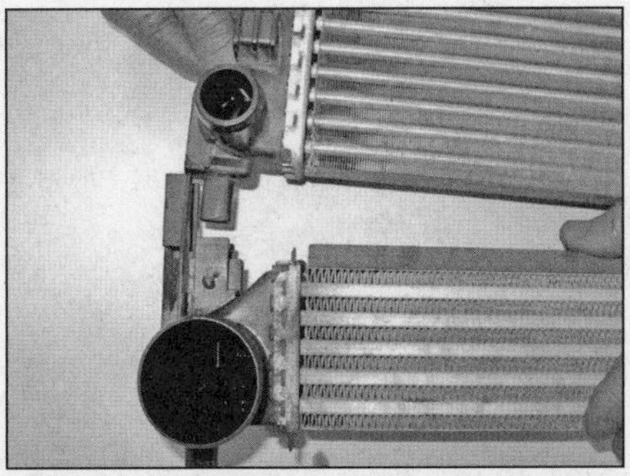

7.6b ...and disconnect the intercooler

3 Trace the wiring back from the sensors, noting their routing and release the wiring harness from the retaining clips **(see illustration)**. Note the sensors can stay fitted to the exhaust at this point, if a new catalytic converter/particulate is fitted, then the sensors can be swapped over with the system of the vehicle.

4 Slacken the retaining bolt to release the clamp between the turbocharger and the catalytic converter/particulate filter **(see illustration)**.

5 Release the hoses from the timing cover **(see illustration)**, release the retaining clip and disconnect the pressure hose from the exhaust to the differential pressure sender.

6 On models with particulate filter, slacken and remove the upper mounting bolt at the right-hand rear corner of the cylinder head, **(see illustration)**.

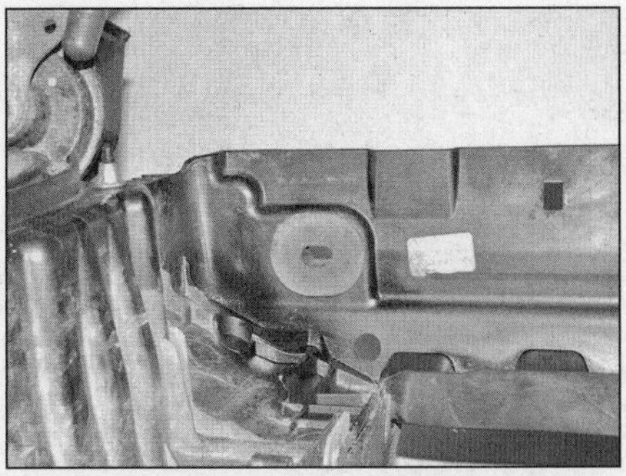

7.7 Check the rubber grommets in the crossmember

7 Apply the handbrake, then jack up the front of the vehicle and support it on axle stands (see *Jacking and vehicle support*). Remove the engine compartment undertray.

8 Where fitted, undo the two retaining bolts and remove the heat shield from above the right-hand drive shaft **(see illustration)**.

9 To prevent any damage to the front flexible pipe use a couple of pieces of metal bar and some retaining clips to prevent the flexible pipe from bending to far and getting damaged **(see illustration)**.

Caution: Handle the flexible, braided section of the front pipe carefully, and do not bend it excessively, if it is bent more than 10° it could get damaged.

10 Slacken the retaining bolts and slide the exhaust clamp to the rear of the vehicle, and disengage the exhaust front pipe rubber

8.3 Unclip the wiring loom

8.4 Undo the exhaust/turbo securing clamp

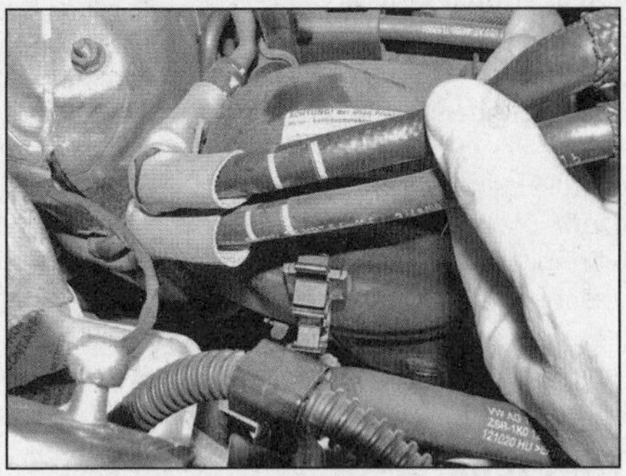

8.5 Unclip the hoses from the retaining clips on the timing cover

8.6 Undo the retaining bolt

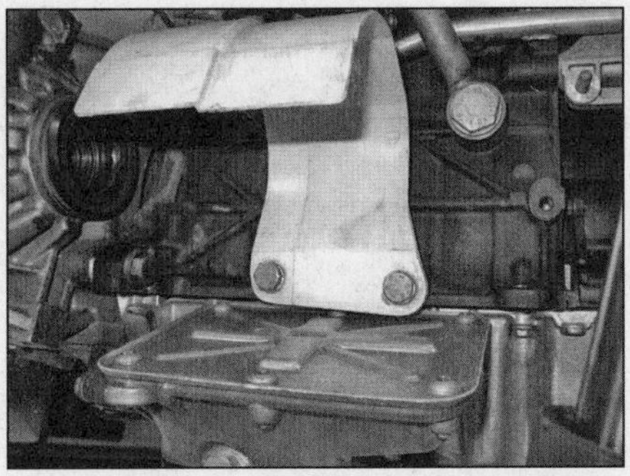

8.8 Remove the heat shield from the cylinder block

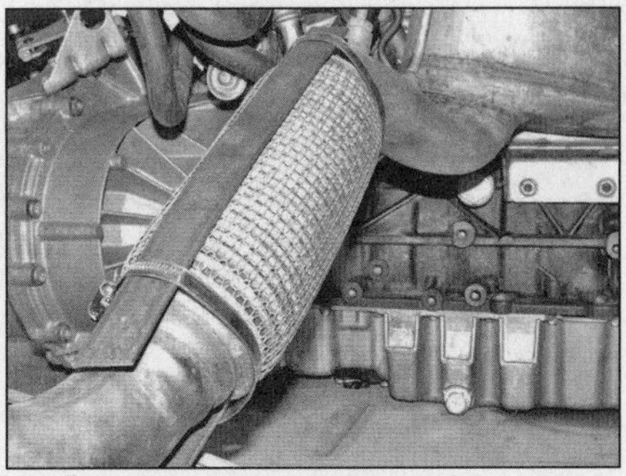

8.9 Support the flexible pipe with flat metal bar and securing clips

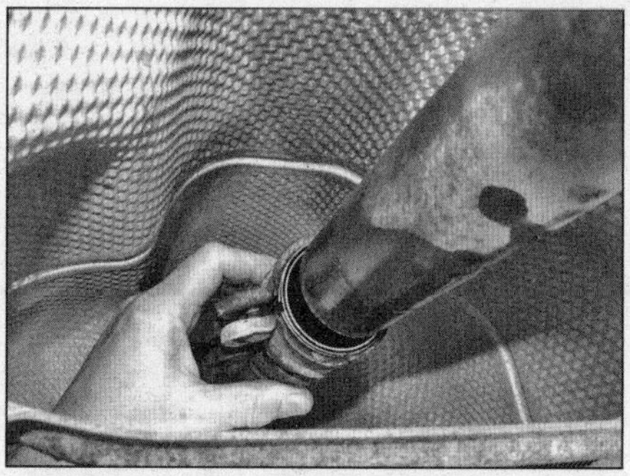

8.10a Slide the exhaust clamp along the exhaust...

8.10b ...and release the rubber mountings

8.11a Undo the upper securing nuts...

8.11b ...and lower securing nuts...

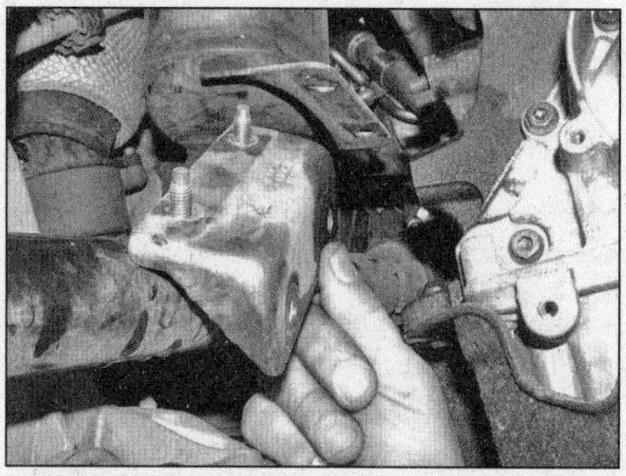

8.11c ...then remove the lower mounting bracket

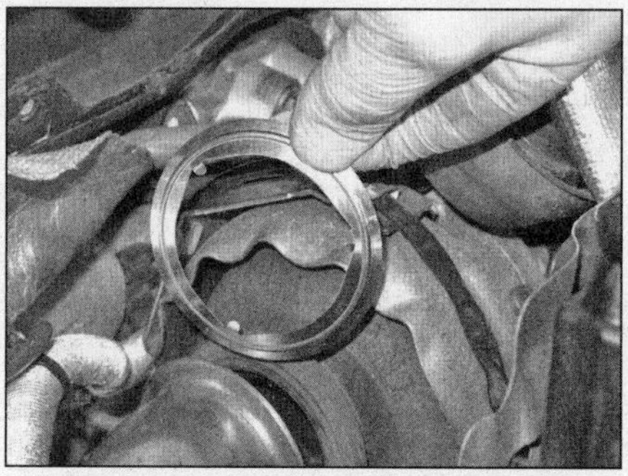

8.14 Renew the gasket between the particulate filter and the turbo

mountings from the rear of the subframe **(see illustrations)**.

11 Undo the nuts securing the catalytic converter/particulate filter lower support bracket to the cylinder block **(see illustrations)**.

12 Lower the front subframe, as described in Chapter 10 Section 18, when removing the steering gear assembly.

13 Carefully manoeuvre the catalytic converter/particulate filter downwards from place. Take care not to damage any wiring, making sure that all wiring has been disconnected and release from their retaining clips. Also take care not to bend the flexible section of the exhaust pipe at an angle of more than 10°.

Refitting

14 Refit the exhaust catalytic converter/particulate filter assembly by following the removal procedure in reverse, but renew all gaskets **(see illustration)** and tighten all nuts and bolts to the specified torque, where given.

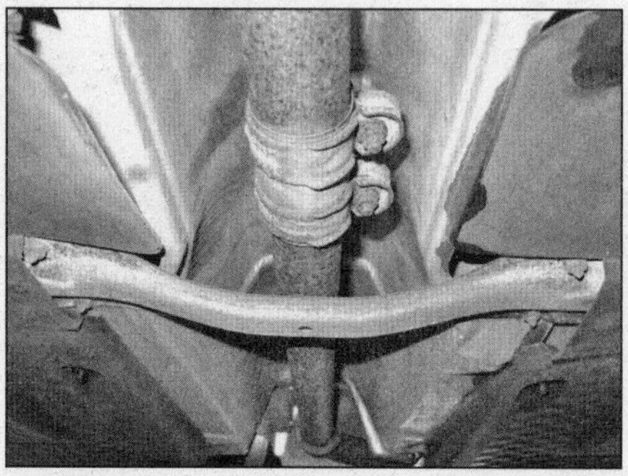

9.4 Slacken the bolts on the exhaust pipe clamp

9 Exhaust system – component renewal

Warning: Allow ample time for the exhaust system to cool before starting work. In particular, note that the catalytic converter runs at very high temperatures. If there is any chance that the system may still be hot, wear suitable gloves.

Removal

1 The original Seat system fitted in the factory is in two sections. The front section includes the catalytic converter (or 'catalyst'), and (where fitted) the particulate filter. The rear section, which connects to the front section under the centre of the vehicle, has a silencer fitted at the rear.

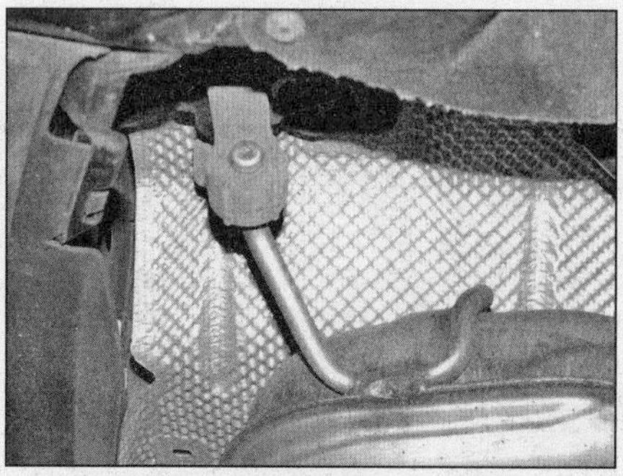

9.5a Rear silencer exhaust rubber mounting

2 To remove part of the system, first jack up the front or rear of the car and support it on axle stands (see *Jacking and vehicle support*). Alternatively, position the car over an inspection pit or on car ramps.

Front pipe (catalytic converter/ particulate filter)

Caution: Handle the flexible, braided section of the front pipe carefully, and do not bend it excessively, if it is bent more than 10° it could get damaged.

3 The front flexible pipe section is part of the catalytic converter/particulate filter, remove the front pipe assembly as described in Section 8.

Rear pipe and silencer

4 Unscrew the clamp bolt securing the rear section of exhaust to the front section **(see illustration)**.

5 Release the silencer from the rubber mountings, then twist it from the centre section and withdraw it from under the car **(see illustrations)**.

6 If required, undo the retaining bolts and remove the mounting brackets from across the exhaust tunnel, to make removal easier **(see illustration)**.

7 If the factory-fitted Seat rear section is being worked on, examine the pipe in front of the rear axle for three pairs of punch marks, or three line markings. The centre marking indicates the point at which to cut the pipe, while the outer marks indicate the position for the ends of the new clamp required when refitting. Cut through the pipe using the centre mark as a guide, making the cut as square to the pipe as possible if either resulting section is to be re-used.

8 If the factory-fitted rear section has already been renewed, unscrew the clamp bolts between the two sections, to remove individual sections.

Refitting

9 Each section is refitted by a reversal of the removal sequence, noting the following points:

a) Ensure that all traces of corrosion have been removed from the flanges or pipe ends, and renew all necessary gaskets.
b) The design of the clamps used between the exhaust sections means that they play a greater role in ensuring a gas-tight seal – fit new clamps if they are in less than perfect condition.
c) When fitting the clamps, use the markings on the pipes as a guide to the clamps correct fitted position.
d) Inspect the mountings for signs of damage or deterioration, and renew as necessary.
e) If using exhaust assembly paste, make sure this is only applied to joints downstream of the catalyst.
f) Prior to tightening the exhaust system mountings and clamps, ensure that all rubber mountings are correctly located and that there is adequate clearance between the exhaust system and vehicle underbody.

9.5b Rubber mounting on centre section of exhaust

9.6 Mounting bracket across exhaust tunnel

10 Catalytic converter – general information and precautions

1 The catalytic converter fitted to diesel models is simpler than that fitted to petrol models, but it still needs to be treated with respect to avoid problems. The converter is a reliable and simple device which needs no maintenance in itself, but there are some facts of which an owner should be aware if the converter is to function properly for its full service life:

a) DO NOT use fuel or engine oil additives – these may contain substances harmful to the catalytic converter.
b) DO NOT continue to use the car if the engine burns (engine) oil to the extent of leaving a visible trail of blue smoke.
c) Remember that the catalytic converter is FRAGILE – do not strike it with tools during servicing work, and take care handling it when removing it from the car for any reason.
d) The catalytic converter, used on a well-maintained and well-driven car, should last for between 50,000 and 100,000 miles – if the converter is no longer effective, it must be renewed

Chapter 5 Part A
Starting and charging systems

Contents

Degrees of difficulty

Easy, suitable for novice with little experience	Fairly easy, suitable for beginner with some experience	Fairly difficult, suitable for competent DIY mechanic	Difficult, suitable for experienced DIY mechanic	Very difficult, suitable for expert DIY or professional

Specifications

Engine codes *

Petrol engines	
1.0 litre engines	CHYB, CHZC and CHZB
1.2 litre:	
SOHC	CBZB
DOHC	CJZD and CJZC
1.4 litre	CGGB and BXW
Diesel engines	
1.6 litre	CAYC and CLNA

**See 'Vehicle identification' at the end of this manual for the location of the engine code markings.*

General

System type	12-volt, negative-earth

Starter motor

Rating:	
Petrol engines	12V, 1.1 kW
Diesel engines	12V, 2.0 kW

Battery

Ratings	36 to 72 Ah (depending on model and market)

Alternator

Rating	55, 60, 70 or 90 amp
Minimum brush length	5.0 mm

Torque wrench settings

	Nm	lbf ft
Alternator mounting bolts	25	18
Battery clamping plate bolt	20	15
Battery terminal clamp bolts	6	4
Battery tray	10	8
Starter motor mounting bolts:		
Long bolts (into engine block)	80	59
Short bolts (into transmission)	40	30

1 General information and precautions

General information

1 The engine electrical system consists mainly of the charging and starting systems. Because of their engine-related functions, these are covered separately from the body electrical devices such as the lights, instruments, etc (which are covered in Chapter 12). On petrol engine models refer to Chapter 5B for information on the ignition system, and on diesel models refer to Chapter 5C for information on the preheating system.

2 The electrical system is of the 12-volt negative-earth type.

3 The battery is of the low-maintenance or maintenance-free (sealed for life) type and is charged by the alternator, which is belt-driven from the crankshaft pulley.

4 The starter motor is of the pre-engaged type, with an integral solenoid. On starting, the solenoid moves the drive pinion into engagement with the flywheel ring gear before the starter motor is energised. Once the engine has started, a one-way clutch prevents the motor armature being driven by the engine until the pinion disengages from the flywheel.

5 Further details of the various systems are given in the relevant Sections of this Chapter. While some repair procedures are given, the usual course of action is to renew the component concerned.

Precautions

Warning: It is necessary to take extra care when working on the electrical system to avoid damage to semi-conductor devices (diodes and transistors), and to avoid the risk of personal injury. In addition to the precautions given in 'Safety first!' observe the following when working on the system:

a) Always remove rings, watches, etc, before working on the electrical system. Even with the battery disconnected, capacitive discharge could occur if a component's live terminal is earthed through a metal object. This could cause a shock or nasty burn.

b) Do not reverse the battery connections. Components such as the alternator, electronic control units, or any other components having semi-conductor circuitry could be irreparably damaged.

c) Never disconnect the battery terminals, the alternator, any electrical wiring or any test instruments when the engine is running.

d) Do not allow the engine to turn the alternator when the alternator is not connected.

e) Never test for alternator output by flashing the output lead to earth.

f) Always ensure that the battery negative lead is disconnected when working on the electrical system.

g) If the engine is being started using jump leads and a slave battery, connect the batteries positive-to-positive and negative-to-negative (see Jump starting at the beginning of the manual). This also applies when connecting a battery charger.

h) Before using electric-arc welding equipment on the car, disconnect the battery, alternator and components such as the electronic control units (where applicable) to protect them from the risk of damage.

Caution: Certain radios fitted as standard equipment by Seat have a built-in security code to deter thieves. If the power source to the unit is cut, the anti-theft system will activate. Even if the power source is immediately reconnected, the radio will not function until the correct security code has been entered. Therefore, if you do not know the correct security code for the radio do not disconnect the battery negative terminal or remove the radio/cassette unit from the car. Refer to your Seat dealer for further information on whether the unit fitted to your car has a security code.

2.4 Checking the battery voltage

2 Battery – testing and charging

Testing

1 All original equipment batteries are sealed for life maintenance-free batteries. These may be one of three types:

a) Standard lead acid. Sealed for life with a visual charge indicator fitted.

b) Absorbent Glass Mat (AGM) Lead acid battery with the electrolyte absorbed in a glass matrix. No visual indicator fitted.

c) Enhanced Flooded Battery (EFB). Visual indicator fitted. Used on some stop-start models.

2 Topping-up and testing of the electrolyte in each cell is not possible. The condition of the battery can therefore only be tested using a battery condition indicator or a voltmeter.

3 All models (except those with AGM batteries) are fitted with a maintenance-free battery with a built-in charge condition indicator. The indicator is located in the top of the battery casing, and indicates the condition of the battery from its colour. If the indicator shows green, then the battery is in a good state of charge. If the indicator turns darker, eventually to black, then the battery requires charging, as described later in this Section. If the indicator shows clear/yellow, then the electrolyte level in the battery is too low to allow further use, and the battery should be renewed. **Do not** attempt to charge, load or jump-start a battery when the indicator shows clear/yellow. **Note:** *From around 2009 Seat introduced batteries that only have a two colour visual indicator. If the indicator shows black there is sufficient electrolyte in the cell, if the indicator shows light yellow the electrolyte level is low and the battery must be replaced. Note that the indicator is only a guide to the electrolyte level on one cell and is not a guide to the state of charge.*

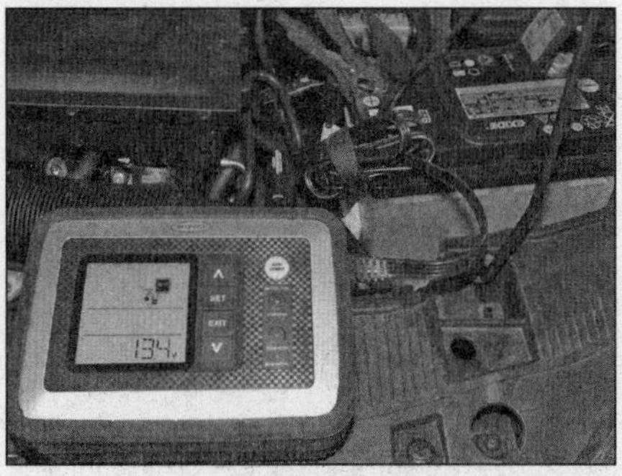

2.6 Modern battery chargers can often test battery capacity

4 If testing the battery using a voltmeter, connect the voltmeter across the battery and note the voltage **(see illustration)**. The test is only accurate if the battery has not been subjected to any kind of charge for the previous six hours. If this is not the case, switch on the headlights for 30 seconds, then wait four to five minutes before testing the battery after switching off the headlights. All other electrical circuits must be switched off, so check that the doors and tailgate are fully shut when making the test.

5 If the voltage reading is less than 12.2 volts, then the battery is discharged, whilst a reading of 12.2 to 12.4 volts indicates a partially discharged condition. The battery should be recharged as described later in this Section.

6 The preferable method of testing the battery is to use a digital battery analyser. Most garages (and battery supply specialists) will have one. These machines are capable of assessing the condition and performance of the battery without removing it from the vehicle or disconnecting the battery terminals. Note also that many modern battery chargers will also have some ability to test the battery **(see illustration)**.

Charging

Note: *The following is intended as a guide only. Always refer to the manufacturer's recommendations (often printed on a label attached to the battery) before charging a battery.*

7 If the battery is to be recharged, we recommend that you use an 'intelligent' charger. Where an AGM or EFB battery is fitted it is essential that the charger is specifically capable of charging these types of battery. Whilst some chargers are capable of safely charging the battery with the battery connected to the vehicle, if you are unsure, always disconnect the battery. If the battery is disconnected (e.g. if it is to be removed and recharged on the bench), note that certain 'learned' values will be lost from the engine management ECU memory, requiring the car to be driven over a short distance after refitting the battery. Also, when the battery is reconnected, the warning lights for the ESP and electro-mechanical steering will light up and stay on. They will extinguish if you drive briefly in a straight line at a speed of 9 to 13 mph.

3 Battery – disconnecting, reconnecting, removal and refitting

Disconnecting the battery

Warning: There are two methods of battery disconnection: If working on the airbag system then the battery must be disconnected and reconnected with the ignition ON. When working on all other systems the battery must be disconnected and connected with the ignition OFF.

1 Lower the drivers window and remove the key from the ignition. Note the warning above!

2 The battery is located on the left-hand side of the engine compartment. Where fitted, open the cover to gain access to the battery.

3 Loosen the clamp nut and disconnect the battery negative lead (-) **(see illustrations)**.

4 Move the negative (earth) lead away from the terminal. Cover the lead (or battery terminal) with a suitable insulator (a plastic bag is ideal) or simply secure it to the side with a cable tie.

Reconnecting the battery

5 Reconnect the negative lead. Push it down until it is flush with the battery terminal post and then tighten the nut to the specified torque.

6 Refit the battery cover and close the bonnet.

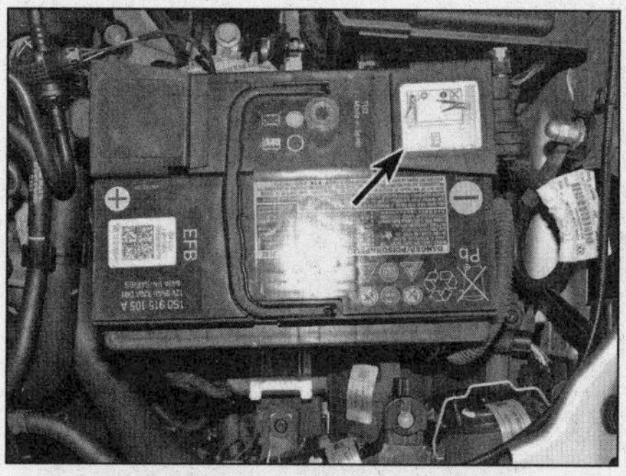

3.3a Open the terminal cover...

3.3b ...disconnect the battery negative terminal

7 Reach through the open drivers window and turn on the sidelights. Wait a minute or so to allow the on board computer systems to boot up and for the battery voltage to stabilise.

8 Start the vehicle (from the outside where possible) and then open and close all the power windows. Adjust the clock time and re-activate the audio unit by inserting the security code (where applicable).

9 To restore the electric window automatic opening/closing function (where fitted) power up the window and as soon as the window stops, hold the switch for 5 seconds. Repeat the procedure with the window powered down.

10 After reconnecting the battery and starting the vehicle the ESP (Electronic Stability Programme) the TCS (Traction Control System) and the power steering warning light will remain on until the vehicle is driven in a straight line at a speed of 10 mph or more.

Removal

11 Disconnect the battery negative cable as described above and then disconnect the battery positive cable **(see illustrations)**.

12 Where fitted, remove the insulated cover and then unscrew the retaining clamp bolt **(see illustrations)**. Lift the battery from the engine compartment.

13 If necessary the battery tray can now be removed. Remove the air filter housing as described in Chapter 4A Section 3 (petrol engines) or Chapter 4B Section 3 (diesel engines).Unclip the wiring loom and then unbolt and remove the battery tray **(see illustrations)**.

Refitting

14 Refitting is a reversal of removal.

3.11a Where the fusible links are fitted to the top of the battery, open the cover

3.11b Unbolt and disconnect the positive lead

3.12a Remove the retaining clamp bolt...

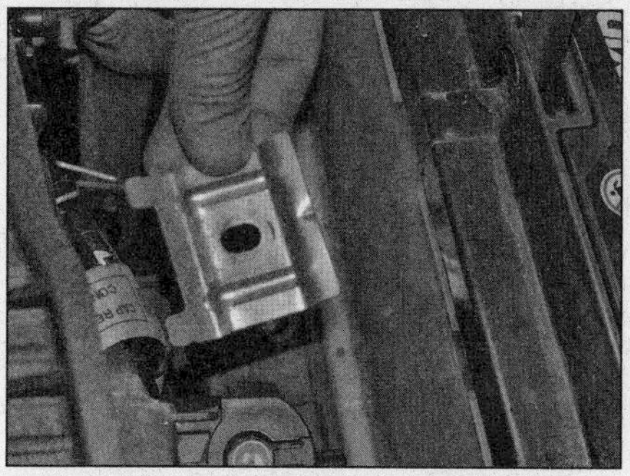

3.12b ...and remove the clamp

3.13a Remove the bolts...

3.13b ...and lift out the support tray

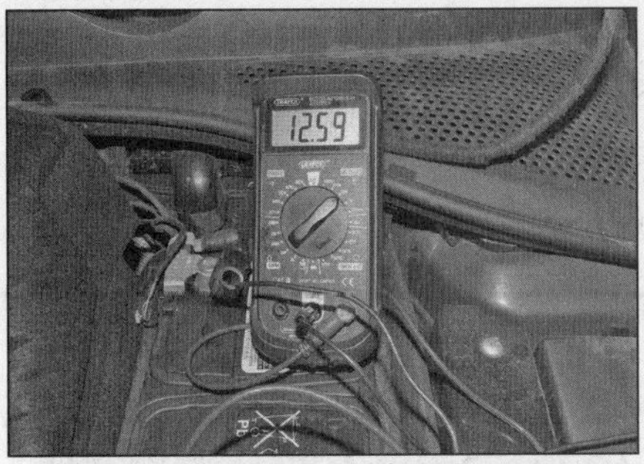

4.5 Nominal battery voltage (engine off)

4 Alternator/charging system – testing in car

Note: *Refer to Section 1 of this Chapter before starting work.*

1 If the charge warning light fails to illuminate when the ignition is switched on, first check the alternator wiring connections for security. If the light still fails to illuminate, check the continuity of the warning light feed wire from the alternator to the bulbholder. If all is satisfactory, the alternator is at fault and should be renewed or taken to an auto-electrician for testing and repair.

2 Similarly, if the charge warning light comes on with the ignition, but is then slow to go out when the engine is started, this may indicate an impending alternator problem. Check all the items listed in the preceding paragraph, and refer to an auto-electrical specialist if no obvious faults are found.

4.7 The full load output of the alternator

3 If the charge warning light illuminates when the engine is running, stop the engine and check that the auxiliary drivebelt is intact and correctly tensioned, and that the alternator connections are secure. If all is so far satisfactory, check the alternator brushes and slip-rings as described in Section 6. If the fault persists, the alternator should be renewed, or taken to an auto-electrician for testing and repair.

4 If the alternator output is suspect even though the warning light functions correctly, the regulated voltage may be checked as follows.

5 Connect a voltmeter across the battery terminals, and start the engine **(see illustration)**.

6 Increase the engine speed until the voltmeter reading remains steady; the reading should be approximately 12 to 13 volts, and no more than 14 volts.

7 Switch on as many electrical accessories (e.g. the headlights, heated rear window and heater blower) as possible, and check that the alternator maintains the regulated voltage at around 13 to 14 volts **(see illustration)**.

8 If the regulated voltage is not as stated, this may be due to worn brushes, weak brush springs, a faulty voltage regulator, a faulty diode, a severed phase winding or worn or damaged slip-rings. The brushes and slip-rings may be checked as described in Section 6, but if the fault persists, the alternator should be renewed or taken to an auto-electrician.

5 Alternator – removal and refitting

Removal

1 Disconnect the battery negative lead as described in Section 3.

2 To give better access (on some models), apply the handbrake, and then jack up the front of the vehicle and support it on axle stands (see *Jacking and vehicle support*).

3 Remove the auxiliary drivebelt from the alternator pulley (see Chapter 1A Section 28 or Chapter 1B Section 29). If you intend to remove the drivebelt completely, mark the drivebelt direction of rotation to ensure it is refitted correctly.

4 Depending on model, it may be necessary to unbolt the air conditioning compressor from below the alternator, and then suspend it to one side, making sure that the hoses are not damaged. Refer to Chapter 3 Section 10 for further information on removing the compressor.

5 Release the securing clip and disconnect the wiring connector from the alternator **(see illustration)**. Note that on some models it will be necessary to unbolt the top mount, slacken the lower bolt and pivot the alternator away from the engine to access the wiring plug(s)

6 Remove the protective cap (where fitted), unscrew and remove the nut and washers, then disconnect the battery positive cable from the alternator terminal **(see illustration)**.

7 Where applicable, unscrew the retaining nut and remove the cable guide **(see illustration)**.

8 Unscrew and remove the lower, then upper bolts, then lift the alternator away from its bracket **(see illustrations)**. On some models,

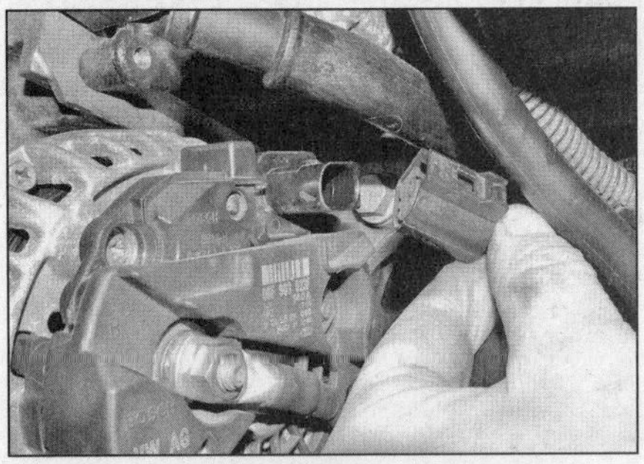
5.5 Unplug the wiring connector

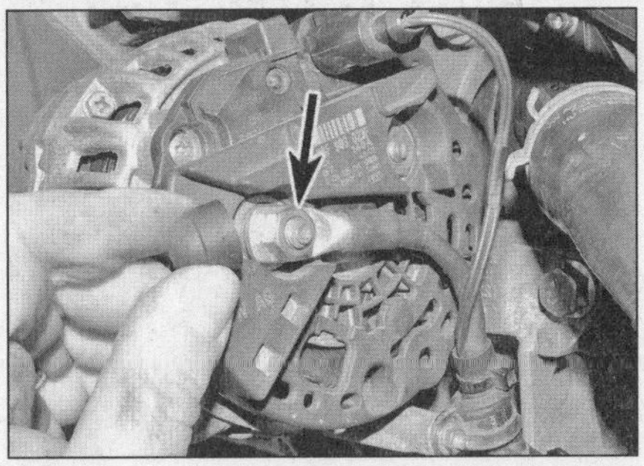
5.6 Disconnect the positive lead securing nut

5.7 Undo the cable guide retaining nut

5.8a Alternator mounting bolts – petrol engines

5.8b Alternator mounting bolts – diesel engines

it will be necessary to remove the auxiliary belt tensioner, to access the alternator mounting bolt.

Refitting

9 The alternator mounting bushes are self-centralising and should be carefully tapped back approximately 1.0 mm before refitting. Note that on some models the alternator bolts directly to the engine block.

10 Refitting is a reversal of removal. Refit the auxiliary drivebelt. Before fitting the alternator, it may be necessary to tap the sliding sleeve in the alternator housing back a couple of millimeters **(see illustration)**. So that it can be fitted back to the mounting bracket easier. Tighten the alternator mounting bolts to the specified torque.

6 Alternator – brush holder/regulator module renewal

Note: *The following procedure is for a Bosch type alternator, other makes will vary depending on model.*

1 Remove the alternator, as described in Section 5.

2 Place the alternator on a clean work surface, with the pulley facing down.

3 Undo the screw and the two retaining nuts, and lift away the outer plastic cover **(see illustration)**.

4 Undo the three screws, and remove the voltage regulator **(see illustrations)**.

5 Measure the free length of the brush contacts **(see illustration)**. Check the measurement with the Specifications; renew the module if the brushes are worn below the minimum limit.

6 Clean and inspect the surfaces of the slip-rings, at the end of the alternator shaft **(see illustration)**. If they are excessively worn, or damaged, the alternator must be renewed.

7 Before refitting the module, depress the brushes in their released position, and hold them there by pulling out the cap – with the module in position, press the cap to release the brushes. The remaining reassembly is a reversal of the dismantling procedure. On completion, refer to Section 5 and refit the alternator.

5.10 Tap the spacer down slightly to aid refitting

7 Starting system – testing

Note: *Refer to Section 1 of this Chapter before starting work.*

1 If the starter motor fails to operate when the ignition key is turned to the appropriate position, the following faults may be the cause:

a) The battery is faulty/flat.
b) The electrical connections between the switch, solenoid, battery and starter motor are somewhere failing to pass the necessary current from the battery through the starter to earth.
c) The solenoid is faulty.
d) The starter motor is mechanically or electrically defective.

2 To check the battery, switch on the headlights. If they dim after a few seconds, this indicates that the battery is discharged – recharge (see Section) or renew the battery. If the headlights glow brightly, operate the ignition switch and observe the lights. If they dim, then this indicates that current is reaching the starter motor; therefore the fault must lie in the starter motor. If the lights continue to glow brightly (and no clicking sound can be heard from the starter motor solenoid), this indicates that there is a fault in the circuit or solenoid – see following paragraphs. If the starter motor turns slowly when operated, but the battery is in good condition, then this indicates that either the starter motor is faulty, or there is considerable resistance somewhere in the circuit.

3 If a fault in the circuit is suspected, disconnect the battery leads, as described in Section 3. And then disconnect the earth connection to the body and the earth connection to the engine. Thoroughly clean the connections, and reconnect the leads and wiring. Repeat the procedure for the battery positive terminal at the starter main terminal. Use a voltmeter or test light to check that full battery voltage is available at the battery positive lead connection to the solenoid, and that the earth is sound.

4 If the battery and all connections are in good condition, check the circuit by disconnecting the wire from the solenoid blade terminal. Connect a voltmeter or test light between the wire end and a good earth (such as the battery negative terminal), and check that the wire is

6.3 On the Bosch type, remove the outer cover nuts/screw...

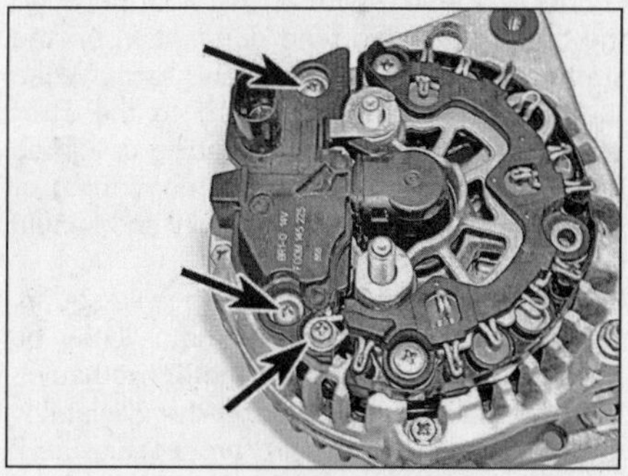

6.4a ...undo the screws...

6.4b ...and remove the brush holder/ regulator

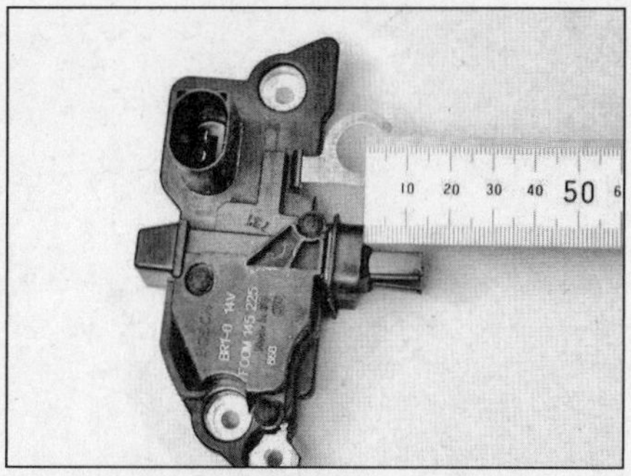

6.5 Measure the brush length

6.6 Clean and inspect the surfaces of the slip-rings

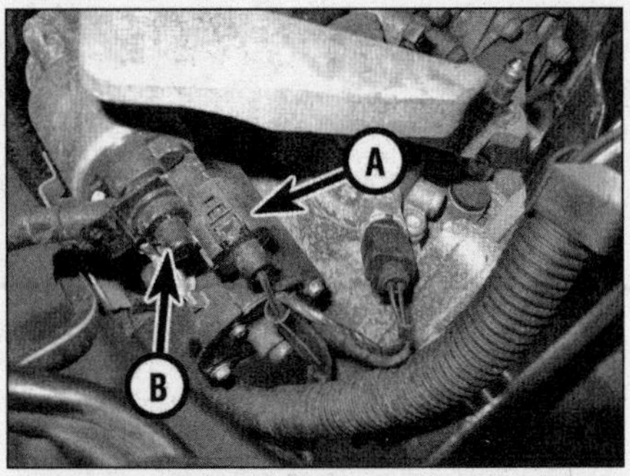

8.3 Starter wiring plug connector (A) – Battery positive cable (B)

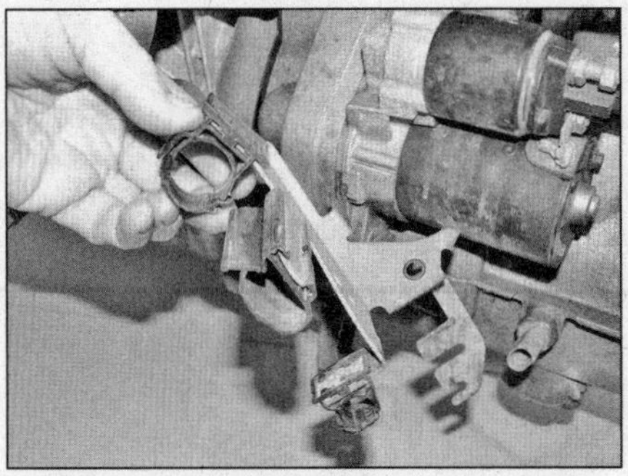
8.5 Removing the wiring loom support bracket

8.6 Remove the earth cable (where fitted)

8.7a The starter bolt also secures the transmission

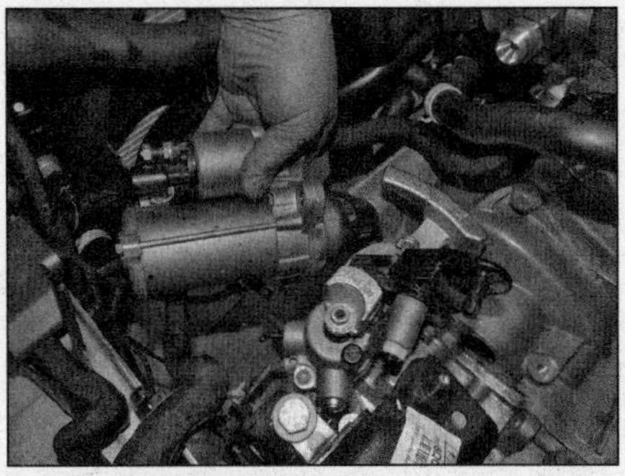
8.7b Remove the starter motor

live when the ignition switch is turned to the start position. If it is, then the circuit is sound, if not, the circuit wiring can be checked as described in Chapter 12.

5 The solenoid contacts can be checked by connecting a voltmeter or test light between the battery positive feed connection on the starter side of the solenoid, and earth. When the ignition switch is turned to the start position, there should be a reading or lighted bulb, as applicable. If there is no reading or lighted bulb, the solenoid is faulty and should be renewed.

6 If the circuit and solenoid are proved sound, the fault must lie in the starter motor. It may be possible to have the starter motor overhauled by a specialist, but check on the availability and cost of spares before proceeding, as it may prove more economical to obtain a new or exchange motor.

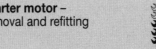

8 Starter motor – removal and refitting

Removal

1 Disconnect the battery negative lead as described in Section 3. Where fitted, remove the engine cover and then the air filter housing if required (see Chapter 4A Section 3 or Chapter 4B Section 3.

2 Remove the battery and battery tray with reference to Section 3 and where necessary unbolt the selector cables from the transmission as described in Chapter 7A Section 2.

3 Release the securing clip and disconnect the wiring plug from the starter **(see illustration)**.

4 Remove the protective cap, unscrew and remove the nut and washers **(see illustration 8.3)**, then disconnect the battery positive cable from the solenoid terminal.

5 Undo the retaining nut and disconnect the wiring bracket from the lower starter motor mounting bolt **(see illustration)**.

6 On some models, it may be necessary to undo the retaining nut and disconnect the earth cable from the upper starter motor mounting bolt **(see illustration)**.

7 Unscrew the two mounting bolts and withdraw the starter motor from the engine compartment **(see illustrations)**. Depending on model, it may be necessary to slacken the securing nut, and then lift the gearshift lever on top of the transmission, to completely remove the upper starter motor retaining bolt.

Refitting

8 Refit the starter motor by following the removal procedure in reverse. Tighten the mounting bolts to the specified torque.

9 Starter motor – testing and overhaul

1 If the starter motor is thought to be defective, it should be removed from the car and taken to an auto-electrician for assessment. In the majority of cases, new starter motor brushes can be fitted at a reasonable cost. However, check the cost of repairs first as it may prove more economical to purchase a new or exchange motor.

Chapter 5 Part B
Ignition system – petrol engines

Contents

Degrees of difficulty

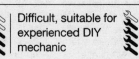

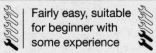

Easy, suitable for novice with little experience	Fairly easy, suitable for beginner with some experience	Fairly difficult, suitable for competent DIY mechanic	Difficult, suitable for experienced DIY mechanic	Very difficult, suitable for expert DIY or professional

Specifications

Engine codes *

1.0 litre engines	CHYB, CHZC and CHZB
1.2 litre engines	CBZB, CJZD and CJZC
1.4 litre engines	BXW and CGGB

**See 'Vehicle identification' at the end of this manual for the location of the engine code markings.*

System type

1.0 litre engine (all engines)	Bosch Motrornic ME17
1.2 litre:	
Engine code CBZB	Siemens Simos 10
Engine sodes CJZD and CJZC	Bosch Motronic MED 17.5.21
1.4 litre (all engines)	Magneti Marelli 4HV

Ignition coil

1.2 litre engine (SOHC)	Single DIS ignition coil with four HT leads, camshaft position sensor (in cylinder head cover), knock sensor fitted to the rear of the cylinder block
All other engines	Individual coil per cylinder (no HT leads), camshaft position sensor (in cylinder head), knock sensor fitted to the rear of the cylinder block

Spark plugs

See Chapter 1A Specifications

Torque wrench settings

Torque wrench settings	Nm	lbf ft
Camshaft position sensor mounting bolt:		
1.0 litre	8	6
1.2 litre	5	4
1.4 litre	10	7
Knock sensor mounting bolt (all engines)	20	15
Spark plugs:		
1.0 and 1.2 litre engines	22	16
1.4 litre engines	25	18

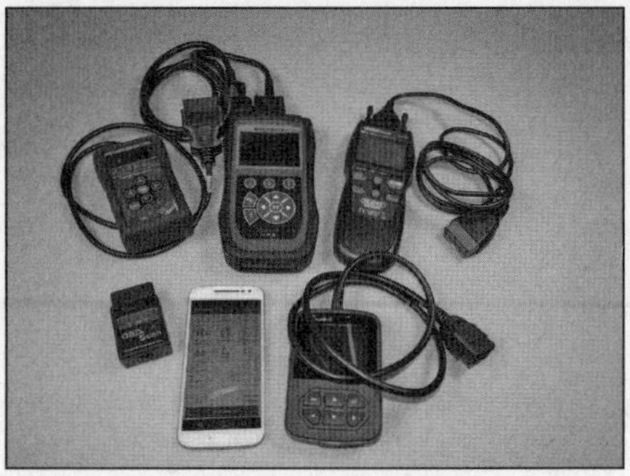

1.7 A wide range of low cost diagnostic tools are available

1 General Information

1 The Bosch, Siemens and Magneti-Marelli ignition systems described in this Chapter, are part of the self-contained engine management systems which control both the fuel injection and ignition. This Chapter deals with the ignition system components only – refer to Chapter 4A for details of the fuel system components.

2 The ignition system comprises the spark plugs, ignition coil(s), HT leads (where fitted) and the Electronic Control Unit (ECU) together with its associated sensors, actuators and wiring. The component layout varies from system to system but the basic operation is the same for all models.

3 The ECU supplies a voltage to the input stage of the ignition coil, which causes the primary windings in the coil to be energised. The supply voltage is periodically interrupted by the ECU and this results in the collapse of the primary magnetic field, which then induces a much larger voltage (called the HT voltage) in the secondary coil. This voltage is directed to the spark plug in the cylinder where the piston is currently at the end of its compression stroke. The spark plug electrodes form a gap small enough for the HT voltage to arc across, and the resulting spark ignites the fuel/air mixture in the cylinder. The timing of this sequence of events is critical and is regulated solely by the ECU.

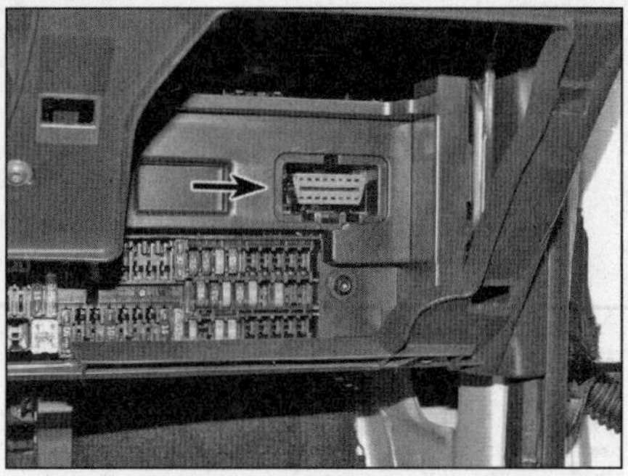

2.2 The location of diagnostic connector

4 The ECU calculates and controls the ignition timing primarily according to engine speed, crankshaft/camshaft position; throttle position and inlet air temperature, received from sensors mounted on and around the engine. Other parameters that affect ignition timing are coolant temperature and engine knock, these being monitored by sensors mounted on the engine.

5 The knock sensor is mounted on the cylinder block in order to detect engine pre-ignition (or 'pinking'). If pre-ignition occurs, the ECU retards the ignition timing in steps until the pre-ignition ceases. The ECU then advances the ignition timing in steps until it is restored to normal, or until pre-ignition occurs again.

6 Idle speed control is achieved partly by the electronic throttle valve positioning module, and partly by the ignition system, which gives fine control of the idle speed by altering the ignition timing. Manual adjustment of the engine idle speed or ignition timing is not necessary or possible.

7 It should be noted that fault diagnosis of all the engine management systems described in this Chapter is only possible with dedicated electronic test equipment. Simple low cost hand held (or smart phone) fault code readers are available in the aftermarket, however they will not display all the engine fault codes **(see illustration)**. As a general rule they will only list the mandatory emissions related fault codes. Some tools may be capable of displaying faults from all vehicle systems as well as showing actual live data from the engine management control unit. More complex issues will require access to professional level equipment or the manufacturers own diagnostic tool. Once the fault has been identified, the removal/refitting sequences detailed in the following Sections will then allow the appropriate component(s) to be renewed as required.

2 Ignition system – testing

Warning: Extreme care must be taken when working on the system with the ignition switched on; it is possible to get a substantial electric shock from a vehicle's ignition system. Persons with cardiac pacemaker devices should keep well clear of the ignition circuits, components and test equipment. Always switch off the ignition before disconnecting or connecting any component and when using a multi-meter to check resistances.

1 If a fault appears in the engine management (fuel injection/ignition) system which is thought to be ignition related, first ensure that the fault is not due to a poor electrical connection or poor maintenance; i.e. check that the air cleaner filter element is clean, the spark plugs are in good condition and correctly gapped, that the engine breather hoses are clear and undamaged. If the engine is running very roughly, check the compression pressures as described in relevant part of Chapter 2, depending on engine.

2 If these checks fail to reveal the cause of the problem the vehicle should be taken to a Seat dealer or suitable equipped garage for testing. Alternatively a basic fault code reader can be used (see Section 1). A diagnostic connector is incorporated in the engine management circuit into which a special electronic diagnostic tester can be plugged **(see illustration)**.

3 The only ignition system checks which can be carried out by the home mechanic are those described in Chapter 1A Section 27, relating to the spark plugs.

3 HT coil – removal and refitting

Engines with single DIS ignition coil

1 The ignition coil unit is mounted on top of the inlet manifold, at the rear of the engine.

2 Release the securing clips and remove the trim cover from over the HT leads **(see illustrations)**.

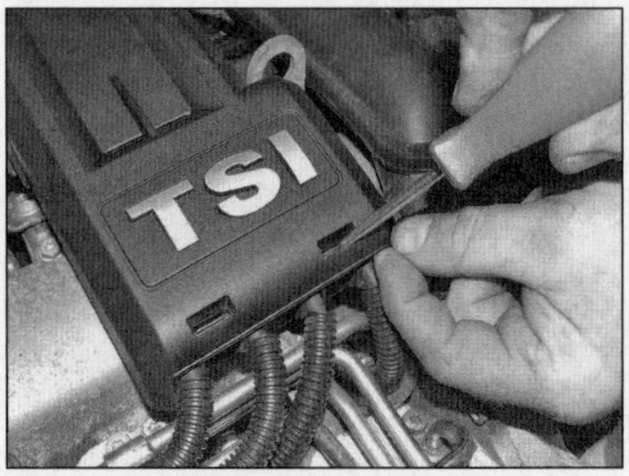

3.2a Release the clips...

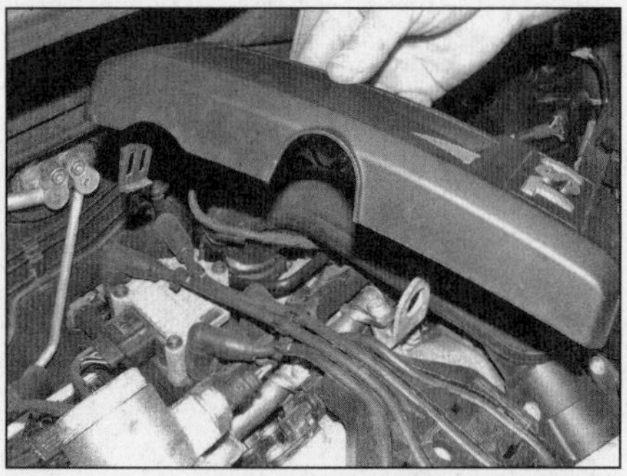

3.2b ...and remove the trim cover

3 Make sure the ignition is switched off, and then disconnect the wiring connector from the ignition coil **(see illustration)**.

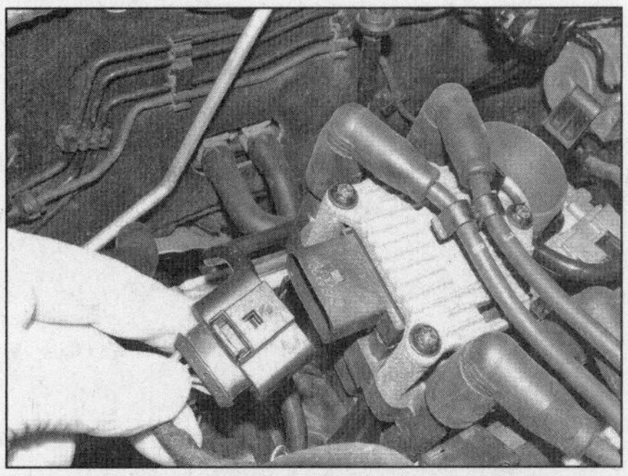

3.3 Disconnect the wiring connector

3.4 Remove the ignition coil

3.7 Ignition coils on the 1.4 litre engine

4 Undo the three retaining bolts and lift the coil from the inlet manifold **(see illustration)**.
5 Note the fitted position of the HT leads, and then pull them from the top of the ignition coil.
6 Refitting is a reversal of the relevant removal procedure.The HT leads are numbered, and will need to be fitted in the correct position when re-assembling.

Engines with one coil per spark plug

7 Removal of the ignition coils is covered in the spark plug renewal procedure in Chapter 1A Section 27, since the coils must be removed for access to the plugs **(see illustration)**.
8 Refitting is a reversal of the relevant removal procedure.

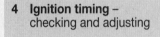

4 Ignition timing – checking and adjusting

1 The ignition timing is under the control of the engine management system ECU and is not manually adjustable without access to dedicated electronic test equipment. A basic setting cannot be quoted because the ignition timing is constantly being altered to control engine idle speed (see Section 1 for details).
2 The vehicle must be taken to a dealer if the timing requires checking or adjustment.

5.1a Knock sensor (1.4 litre engine)

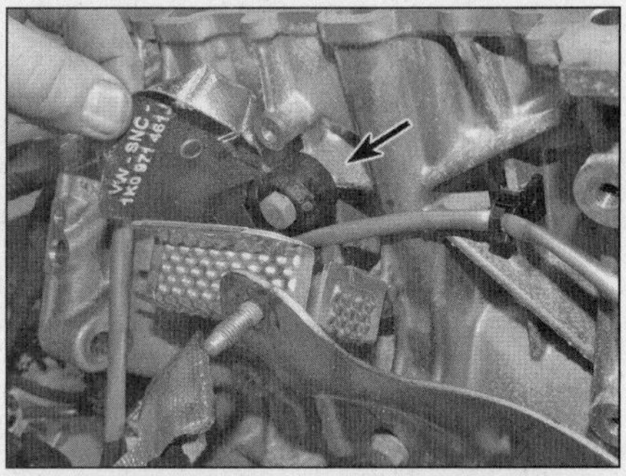

5.1b On turbocharged engines the sensor is hidden behind a heat shield

5 Knock sensor – removal and refitting

Removal

1 The knock sensor is located on the rear of the cylinder block **(see illustrations)**.
2 Remove the engine top cover (where fitted) to gain access to the sensor from above. Alternatively for access from below, apply the handbrake, then jack up the front of the vehicle and support it on axle stands (see *Jacking and vehicle support*). Access to the knock sensor is very awkward, and can only be improved by either removing the inlet manifold (see Chapter 4A Section 9) or removing the right-hand driveshaft (see Chapter 8 Section 2).
3 Disconnect the wiring from the sensor or trace the wiring back from the sensor and disconnect its wiring connector.
4 Unscrew the mounting bolt and remove the sensor from the cylinder block, noting its fitted position.

Refitting

5 Refitting is the reverse of removal. Ensure the mating surfaces of the sensor and cylinder block are clean and dry and ensure the mounting bolt is tightened to the specified torque to ensure correct operation.

Chapter 5 Part C
Pre-heating system – diesel engines

Contents

Degrees of difficulty

Easy, suitable for novice with little experience	Fairly easy, suitable for beginner with some experience	Fairly difficult, suitable for competent DIY mechanic	Difficult, suitable for experienced DIY mechanic	Very difficult, suitable for expert DIY or professional

Specifications

Torque wrench setting	Nm	lbf ft
Glow plug to cylinder head	18	13

1 General Information

1 To assist cold starting and to help control harmful emissions, diesel engine models are fitted with a preheating system, which consists of glow plugs, a glow plug control unit, a facia-mounted warning light and the associated electrical wiring. The glow plug control unit on some models, is incorporated in the ECU, other models have a control unit/relay located on the mounting bracket on the front of the battery.

2 The glow plugs are miniature electric heating elements, encapsulated in a metal case with a probe at one end and electrical connection at the other. Each inlet tract has a glow plug threaded into it, which is positioned directly in line with the incoming spray of fuel. When the glow plug is energised, the fuel passing over it is heated, allowing its optimum combustion temperature to be achieved more readily in the combustion chamber.

3 The duration of the preheating period is governed by the ECU, which monitors the temperature of the engine through the coolant temperature sensor and alters the preheating time to suit the conditions. Pre-heating only takes place at coolant temperature below 9°C.

4 The glow plugs also play an important role in emission control, especially on models fitted with a particulate filter.

5 A facia-mounted warning light informs the driver that preheating is taking place. The light extinguishes when sufficient preheating has taken place to allow the engine to be started, but power will still be supplied to the glow plugs for a further period until the engine is started. If no attempt is made to start the engine, the power supply to the glow plugs is switched off to prevent battery drain and glow plug burn-out. If the warning light flashes, or comes on during normal driving, this indicates a fault with the diesel engine management system, which should be investigated by a Seat dealer as soon as possible.

6 After the engine has been started, the glow plugs continue to operate for a further period of time. This helps to improve fuel combustion whilst the engine is warming-up, resulting in quieter, smoother running and reduced exhaust emissions.

2 Glow plugs – testing, removal and refitting

Warning: A correctly functioning glow plug will become red-hot in a very short time. This should be in mind when removing the glow plugs, if they have recently been in use. If a glow plug is dropped, it may be damaged internally, which could result in ceramic fragments entering the engine causing extensive damage. Do not fit a glow plug that has been dropped.

Testing

1 If the system malfunctions, testing is ultimately by substitution of known good units, but some preliminary checks may be made as described in the following paragraphs.

2 Before testing the system, use a multi-meter to check that the battery voltage is at least 11.5. Switch off the ignition.

3 Pull the engine upper trim cover upwards to remove it from the top of the engine.

4 Disconnect the wiring plug from the coolant temperature sender at the left-hand end of the engine **(see illustration)**. Disconnecting the sender in this way simulates a cold engine, which is a requirement for the glow plug system to activate.

5 Disconnect the wiring connector from the most convenient glow plug, and connect a suitable multimeter between the wiring connector and a good earth.

6 Have an assistant switch on the ignition for approximately 20 seconds.

7 Battery voltage should be displayed – note that the voltage will drop to zero when the preheating period ends.

8 If no supply voltage can be detected at the glow plug, then either the glow plug relay (where applicable) or the supply wiring must be faulty. Also check that the glow plug fuse or fusible link has not blown – if it has, this may indicate a serious wiring fault; consult a Seat dealer or diesel specialist for advice.

9 To locate a faulty glow plug, first disconnect the battery negative cable and position it away from the terminal.

10 Disconnect the wiring plug from the

2.4 Temperature sensor location

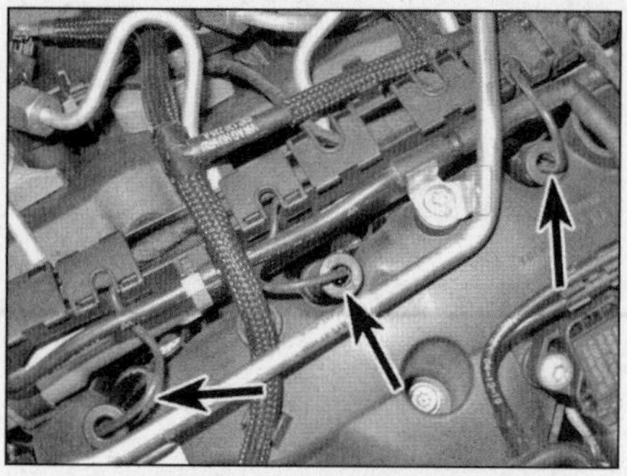
2.15a Glow plug wiring

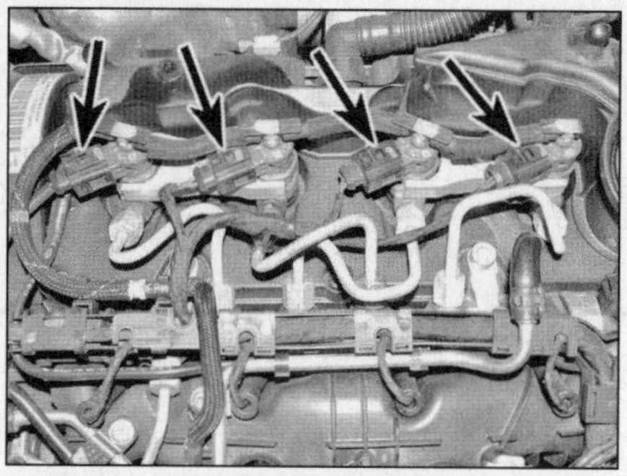
2.15b Disconnect the wiring plugs from the injectors

2.17 Disconnect the return hose from the fuel rail

2.18a Using long nose pliers...

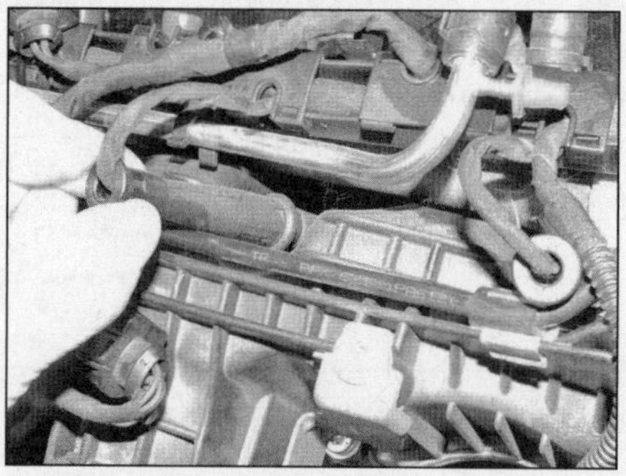
2.18b ...pull the connectors from the top of the glow plugs

3.1 Glow plug control unit location

glow plug terminal. Measure the electrical resistance between the glow plug terminal and the engine earth. At the time of writing, this information is not available – as a guide, a resistance of more than a few ohms indicates that the plug is defective.

11 If a suitable ammeter is available, connect it between the glow plug and its wiring connector, and measure the steady-state current consumption (ignore the initial current surge, which will be about 50% higher). As a guide, high current consumption (or no current draw at all) indicates a faulty glow plug.

12 As a final check, remove the glow plugs and inspect them visually, as described in the next sub-Section. A badly burned or charred stem may be an indication of a faulty fuel injector.

Removal

Note: *Refer to the Warning at the start of this Section before proceeding.*

13 Pull the plastic cover on the top of the engine upwards from its' mountings.

14 Where fitted, remove the noise insulation from above the injectors.

15 Due to the wiring loom to the glow plugs being short **(see illustrations)**, it may be necessary to disconnect the wiring plugs from the injectors, exhaust gas pressure sensor, and fuel rail pressure sensor, then when the loom is released and unclipped from the top of the cylinder head.

16 To remove the wiring loom upwards it will be necessary to undo the retaining bolts and detach the coolant pipe from the intake manifold, then move it to the front of the manifold.

17 Also release the retaining clips and disconnect the fuel return hose from the fuel rail and the fuel return pipe connectors from the top of the fuel rail **(see illustration)**. Plug the openings to prevent contamination. Move the entire fuel return pipe assembly to the one side, be prepared for fuel spillage.

18 Pull the connectors from the top of the glow plugs and move the wiring loom to one side. Be sure to only pull on the underside of the ridge at the top of the connectors **(see illustrations)**.

19 Clean the area around the glow plugs; use a vacuum cleaner if possible. Spray brake cleaner (or similar) around the glow plug opening, letting it penetrate briefly, and then blow out with compressed air.

Caution: Always wear protective goggles to protect your eyes, when using compressed air.

20 Using a universal joint, extension and a deep 10 mm socket, unscrew and remove the glow plug(s) from the cylinder head. Note that the plug must be kept 'straight' when being removed, as it can be easily damaged.

Refitting

21 Refitting is a reversal of removal, but tighten the glow plugs to the specified torque.

3 Glow plug control unit – removal and refitting

Note: *The glow plug control unit may be incorporated inside the engine management ECU. Follow the procedure below for models with separate glow plug control unit.*

Removal

1 The glow plug control unit (where applicable) is located on the fuse box in front of the battery **(see illustration)**.

2 Release the retaining clip and slide the control unit from the mounting bracket.

3 Disconnect the wiring connector and remove the control unit

Refitting

4 Refitting is a reversal of removal.

Chapter 6 Part A
Clutch – manual transmission

Contents

Degrees of difficulty

Easy, suitable for novice with little experience	Fairly easy, suitable for beginner with some experience	Fairly difficult, suitable for competent DIY mechanic	Difficult, suitable for experienced DIY mechanic	Very difficult, suitable for expert DIY or professional

Specifications

Engine codes *

Petrol engines

1.0 litre:	
DOHC (MPI)	CHYB
DOHC (TSI)	CHZB and CHZC
1.2 litre:	
SOHC (TSI)	CBZB
DOHC (TSI)	CJZD and CJZC
1.4 litre (MPI)	BXW and CGGB

Diesel engines

1.6 litre	CLNA and CAYC

**See 'Vehicle identification' at the end of this manual for the location of the engine code markings.*

General

Type	Single dry plate, diaphragm spring
Operation	Hydraulic with master and slave cylinders
Application:	
Petrol models:	
1.0 litre (CHYB)	5-speed transmission 0CF
1.0 litre (CHZC and CHZB)	5-speed transmission 0DF or 6-speed transmission 0DQ
1.2 litre (CBZB)	5-speed transmission 02T
1.2 litre (CJZD and CJZC)	5-speed transmission 02T or 6-speed transmission 02U
1.4 litre (BXW and CGGB)	5-speed transmission 02T
Diesel models:	
1.6 (CAYC and CLNA)	5-speed transmission 02T or 02R

Torque wrench settings	Nm	lbf ft
Clutch master cylinder mounting nuts*	28	21
Clutch pedal mounting bracket nuts*	28	21
Clutch pedal pivot nut*	25	18
Clutch pressure plate-to-flywheel bolts:		
M6 bolts	13	9
M7 bolts	20	15
Clutch slave cylinder mounting bolts	20	15
Guide tube-to-transmission bolts:		
02T transmission*:		
Stage 1	5	3
Stage 2	Angle-tighten a further 90°	

**Use new bolts/nuts*

2.5 The slave cylinder bleed screw

1 General Information

1 The clutch is of single dry plate type, incorporating a diaphragm spring pressure plate, and is hydraulically operated.

2 The pressure plate is bolted to the rear face of the flywheel, and the friction disc is located between the pressure plate and the flywheel friction surface. The friction disc hub is splined to the transmission input shaft and is free to slide along the splines. Friction lining material is riveted to each side of the disc, and the disc hub incorporates cushioning springs to absorb transmission shocks and ensure a smooth take-up of drive.

3 When the clutch pedal is depressed, the slave cylinder pushrod moves the top of the release lever towards the engine, and the lower end of the lever pivots on a ball-stud located in the transmission bellhousing. The release bearing is forced onto the pressure plate diaphragm spring fingers. As the centre of the diaphragm spring is pushed in, the outer part of the spring moves out and releases the pressure plate from the friction disc. Drive then ceases to be transmitted to the transmission.

4 When the clutch pedal is released, the diaphragm spring forces the pressure plate into contact with the linings on the friction disc, and at the same time pushes the disc slightly forward along the input shaft splines into engagement with the flywheel. The friction disc is now firmly sandwiched between the pressure plate and flywheel. This causes drive to be taken up.

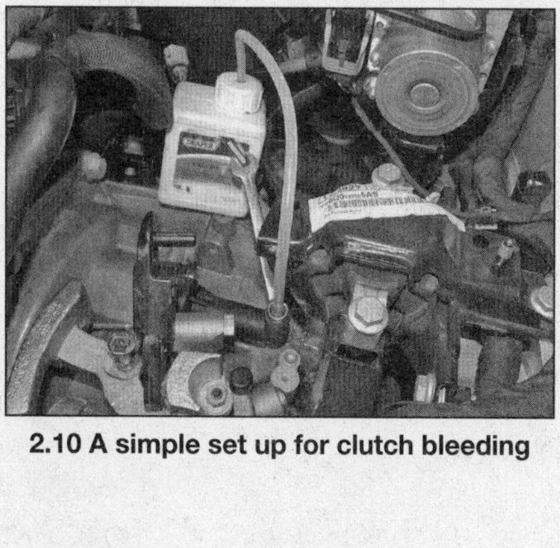

2.10 A simple set up for clutch bleeding

5 As the linings wear on the friction disc, the pressure plate rest position moves closer to the flywheel resulting in the 'rest' position of the diaphragm spring fingers being raised. The hydraulic system requires no adjustment since the quantity of hydraulic fluid in the circuit automatically compensates for wear every time the clutch pedal is operated.

2 Hydraulic system – bleeding

Warning: Hydraulic fluid is poisonous; thoroughly wash off spills from bare skin without delay. Seek immediate medical advice if any fluid is swallowed or gets into the eyes. Certain types of hydraulic fluid are inflammable and may ignite when brought into contact with hot components. Hydraulic fluid is also an effective paint stripper. If spillage occurs onto painted bodywork or fittings, it should be washed off immediately, using copious quantities of cold water. It is also hygroscopic (it absorbs moisture from the air) therefore old fluid should never be re-used.

1 The correct operation of any hydraulic system is only possible after removing all air from the components and circuit; this is achieved by bleeding the system.

2 During the bleeding procedure, add only clean, unused hydraulic fluid of the recommended type; never re-use fluid that has already been bled from the system. Ensure that sufficient fluid is available before starting work.

3 If there is any possibility of incorrect fluid being already in the system, the hydraulic circuit must be flushed completely with uncontaminated, correct fluid.

4 If hydraulic fluid has been lost from the system, or air has entered because of a leak, ensure that the fault is cured before continuing further.

5 The bleed screw is located on the slave cylinder located on the top of the transmission **(see illustration)**. Remove the air filter housing or ducting, as required to gain access.

6 Check that all pipes and hoses are secure, unions tight and the bleed screw is closed. Clean any dirt from around the bleed screw.

7 Unscrew the master cylinder fluid reservoir cap (the clutch shares the same fluid reservoir as the braking system), and top the master cylinder reservoir up to the upper (MAX) level line. Refit the cap loosely, and remember to maintain the fluid level at least above the lower (MIN) level line throughout the procedure, or there is a risk of further air entering the system.

8 There are a number of one-man, do-it-yourself bleeding kits currently available from motor accessory shops. It is recommended that one of these kits is used whenever possible, as they greatly simplify the bleeding operation, and reduce the risk of expelled air and fluid being drawn back into the system. If such a kit is not available, the basic (two-man) method must be used, which is described in detail below.

9 If a kit is to be used, prepare the vehicle as described previously, and follow the kit manufacturer's instructions, as the procedure may vary slightly according to the type being used; generally, they are as outlined below in the relevant sub-section.

Bleeding

Basic (two-man) method

10 Collect a clean glass jar, a suitable length of plastic or rubber tubing which is a tight fit over the bleed screw, and a ring spanner to fit the screw **(see illustration)**. The help of an assistant will also be required.

11 Remove the dust cap from the bleed screw. Fit the spanner and tube to the screw, place the other end of the tube in the jar, and pour in sufficient fluid to cover the end of the tube.

12 Ensure that the fluid level is maintained at least above the lower level line in the reservoir throughout the procedure.

13 Have the assistant fully depress the clutch pedal several times to build up pressure, and then maintain it on the final down stroke.

14 While pedal pressure is maintained, unscrew the bleed screw (approximately one turn) and allow the compressed fluid and air to flow into the jar. The assistant should maintain pedal pressure and should not release it until instructed to do so. When the flow stops, tighten the bleed screw again, have the assistant release the pedal slowly, and recheck the reservoir fluid level.

15 Repeat the steps given in paragraphs 13 and 14 until the fluid emerging from the bleed screw is free from air bubbles. If the master cylinder has been drained and refilled allow approximately five seconds between cycles for the master cylinder passages to refill.

16 When no more air bubbles appear, tighten the bleed screw securely, remove the tube and spanner, and refit the dust cap. Do not overtighten the bleed screw.

Using a one-way valve kit

17 As their name implies, these kits consist of a length of tubing with a one-way valve fitted, to prevent expelled air and fluid being drawn back into the system; some kits include a translucent container, which can be positioned so that the air bubbles can be more easily seen flowing from the end of the tube.

18 The kit is connected to the bleed screw, which is then opened. The user returns to the driver's seat, depresses the clutch pedal with a smooth, steady stroke, and slowly releases it; this is repeated until the expelled fluid is clear of air bubbles.

19 Note that these kits simplify work so much that it is easy to forget the fluid reservoir level; ensure that this is maintained at least above the lower level line at all times.

Using a pressure-bleeding kit

20 These kits are usually operated by the reservoir of pressurised air contained in the spare tyre. However, note that it will probably be necessary to reduce the pressure to a lower level than normal; refer to the instructions supplied with the kit.

21 By connecting a pressurised, fluid-filled container to the fluid reservoir, bleeding can be carried out simply by opening the bleed screw and allowing the fluid to flow out until no more air bubbles can be seen in the expelled fluid.

22 This method has the advantage that the large reservoir of fluid provides an additional safeguard against air being drawn into the system during bleeding.

All methods

23 When bleeding is complete, and correct pedal feel is restored, tighten the bleed screw securely and wash off any spilt fluid. Refit the dust cap to the bleed screw.

24 Check the hydraulic fluid level in the master cylinder reservoir, and top-up if necessary (see *Weekly checks)*.

25 Discard any hydraulic fluid that has been bled from the system; it will not be fit for re-use.

26 Check the operation of the clutch pedal. If the clutch is still not operating correctly, air must still be present in the system, and further bleeding is required. Failure to bleed satisfactorily after a reasonable repetition of the bleeding procedure may be due to worn master cylinder/release cylinder seals.

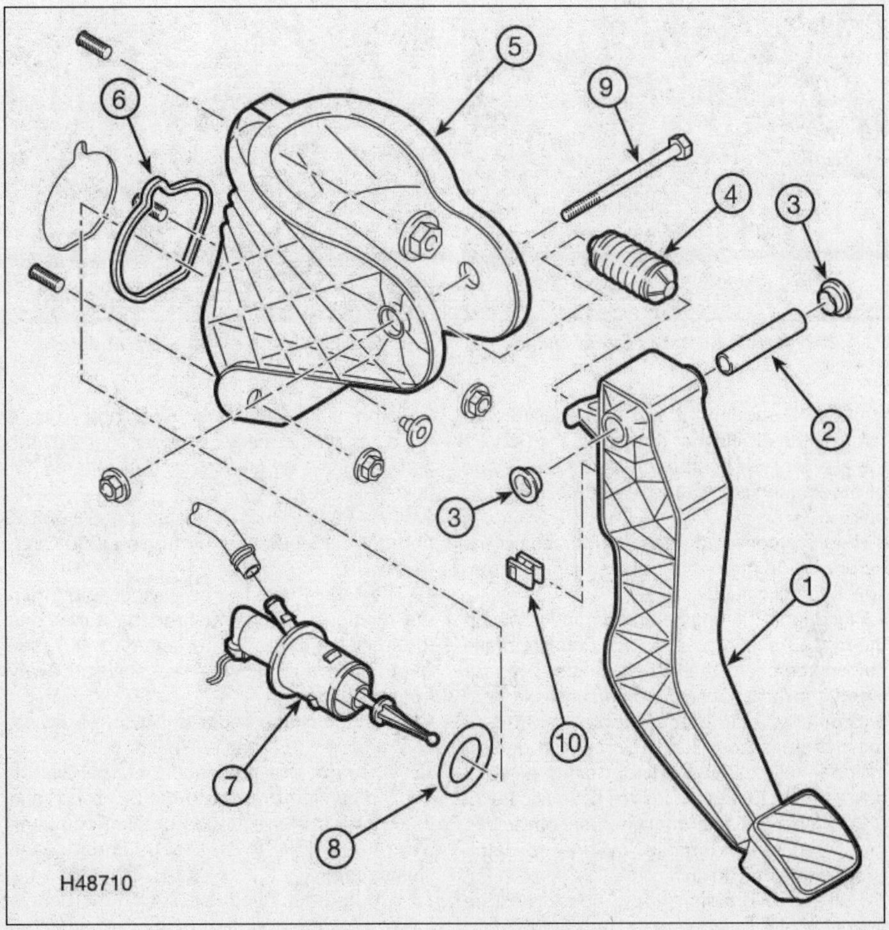

3.5 Clutch pedal assembly

1 *Clutch pedal*
2 *Pivot pin*
3 *Bearing bushes*
4 *Over centre spring*
5 *Mounting bracket*
6 *Seal*
7 *Master cylinder*
8 *Seal*
9 *Pivot bolt*
10 *Pedal securing clip*

3 Clutch pedal – removal and refitting

Removal

1 Move the driver's seat fully to the rear, and adjust the steering column to its highest position.

2 Disconnect the battery negative lead (as described in Chapter 5A Section 3) and position it away from the terminal.

3 Where fitted, remove the driver's side lower facia trim panel, with reference to Chapter 11 Section 28.

4 Where fitted, remove the crash bar from the pedal by unbolting it.

5 Undo the retaining nut and remove the pedal pivot bolt. On some models this will require a hex key (8 mm) and removing the pivot bolt will destroy the pivot – a new one must be fitted. Move the pedal downwards and withdraw the over-centre spring from inside the top of the mounting bracket **(see illustration)**. **Note:** *The clutch pedal will still be attached to the master cylinder operating-rod.*

6 Working at each side of the clutch pedal, release the retaining clip to disengage the master cylinder push-rod from the pedal **(see illustration)**. The pedal can now be removed from the mounting bracket.

7 If required, undo the three mounting nuts and remove the mounting bracket from the bulkhead. Discard the self-locking nuts, as new ones will be required for refitting

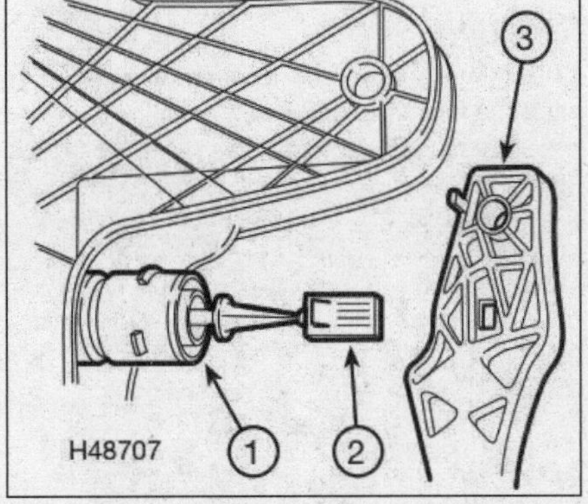

3.6 Master cylinder pushrod to pedal securing clip

1 *Master cylinder pushrod*
2 *Securing clip*
3 *Clutch pedal*

Refitting

8 Refitting is a reversal of removal, bearing in mind the following points:

a) *Press the pushrod retaining clip firmly into the pedal until it is heard to engage.*
b) *Tighten all fixings to the specified torque, where given.*
c) *On models fitted with single use pivot bolt, fit a new bolt.*
d) *On completion, check the brake/clutch fluid level, and top-up if necessary*

4 Master cylinder – removal, overhaul and refitting

Note: *Refer to the Warning at the beginning of Section 2.*

Removal

1 The clutch master cylinder is part of the clutch pedal assembly and is removed with the pedal assembly. Hydraulic fluid for the unit is supplied from the brake master cylinder reservoir.

4.4 Hydraulic hose to master cylinder

2 On LHD models, it will be necessary to remove the air cleaner assembly, then unclip the auxiliary relay carrier on the left-hand side of the engine compartment, and position it to one side.
3 Before proceeding, place cloth rags on the carpet inside the car to prevent damage from spilt hydraulic fluid.
4 Working in the engine compartment, clamp the hydraulic fluid hose leading from the brake fluid reservoir to the clutch master cylinder **(see illustration)**, using a brake hose clamp.
5 Similarly, clamp the rubber section of the hydraulic hose leading from the master cylinder to the slave cylinder using a brake hose clamp, to prevent loss of hydraulic fluid.
6 Position a suitable container, or some cloth rags, beneath the master cylinder to catch escaping hydraulic fluid.
7 Pull the hydraulic supply hose from the clutch master cylinder on the bulkhead.

5.6 Fluid pipe retaining clip

5.7a Slave cylinder mounting bolts

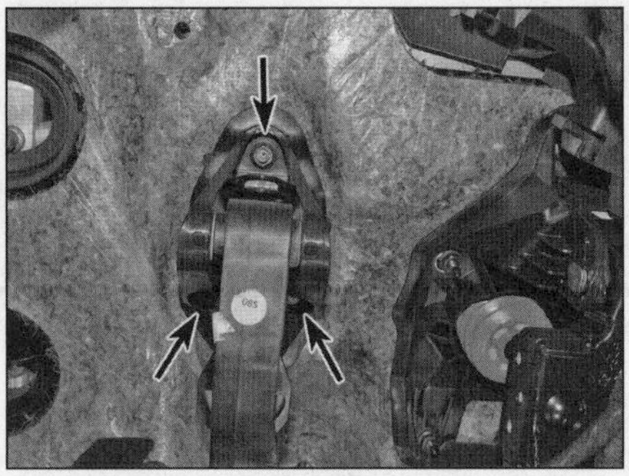

4.12 Undo the pedal bracket nuts

8 Pull the fluid outlet hose retaining clip from the union on the master cylinder, then pull the pipe from the union. Again, be prepared for fluid spillage.
9 Where fitted, remove the clutch pedal switch from the pedal bracket by turning it 90° anti-clockwise.
10 The pedal must now be disconnected from the master cylinder pushrod by squeezing together the tabs of the securing clip (see Section 3), and moving the pushrod away from the pedal.
11 Twist the clutch pedal stop anti-clockwise, and remove it from the bulkhead.
12 Unscrew the nuts securing the clutch pedal mounting bracket to the bulkhead, and then remove the mounting bracket complete with the pedal from the bulkhead **(see illustration)**.
13 With the mounting bracket on the bench, the over-centre spring must be disconnected and removed from the pedal – see Section 3.
14 With the over-centre spring removed, remove the spring seat from the pedal bracket. The seat must be renewed whenever removed.
15 Remove the master cylinder from the bracket.

Overhaul

16 No spare parts are available from Seat for the master cylinder. If the master cylinder is faulty or worn, the complete assembly must be renewed.

Refitting

17 Refitting is a reversal of removal, bearing in mind the following points:

5.7b Removing the clutch slave cylinder

a) Ensure that the pedal-to-master cylinder pushrod retaining clip is fitted to the master cylinder pushrod before attempting to reconnect the pushrod to the pedal.
b) Push the pedal onto the pushrod to engage the retaining clip. Make sure that the clip is securely engaged.
c) On completion, bleed the clutch hydraulic system as described in Section 2.

5 Slave cylinder – removal, overhaul and refitting

Note: *Refer to the Warning at the beginning of Section 2 regarding the hazards of working with hydraulic fluid.*

Removal

1 The slave cylinder is located on the top of the transmission casing. First remove the engine top cover.
2 Remove the battery and battery tray, as described in Chapter 5A Section 3.
3 Where necessary, remove the air cleaner and air ducting with reference to Chapter 4A Section 3, Chapter 4B Section 3.
4 If required, to make access to the slave cylinder easier, remove the gear change cables and mounting bracket from the top of the transmission housing, as described in Chapter 7A Section 2.
5 Clamp the rubber section of the hydraulic hose leading from the master cylinder to the slave cylinder using a brake hose clamp, to prevent loss of hydraulic fluid. Place a wad of clean rag beneath the fluid line connection on the slave cylinder to catch escaping fluid.
6 Pull the fluid pipe retaining clip from the union on the slave cylinder **(see illustration)**, then disconnect the pipe from the union. Release the fluid line from the bracket, and position it clear of the slave cylinder. Be prepared for fluid spillage.
7 Unscrew the two bolts securing the slave cylinder to the transmission casing, and withdraw the slave cylinder **(see illustrations)**.

Overhaul

8 No spare parts are available from Seat for the slave cylinder. If the slave cylinder is faulty or worn, the complete assembly must be renewed.

Refitting

9 Refitting is a reversal of removal, bearing in mind the following points:
a) Apply a little molybdenum sulphide-based grease to the end of the slave cylinder plunger.
b) Tighten the slave cylinder securing bolts to the specified torque.
c) On completion, bleed the clutch hydraulic system as described in Section 2.

6 Clutch friction disc and pressure plate – removal, inspection and refitting

Warning: Dust created by clutch wear and deposited on the clutch components may cause a health hazard. DO NOT blow it out with compressed air or inhale any of it. DO NOT use petrol or petroleum-based solvents to clean off the dust. Brake system cleaner or methylated spirit should be used to flush the dust into a suitable receptacle. After the clutch components are wiped clean with clean rags, dispose of the contaminated rags and cleaner in a sealed container.

Removal

1 Access to the clutch is obtained by removing the transmission as described in Chapter 7A Section 3.

2 Mark the clutch pressure plate and flywheel in relation to each other **(see illustration)**.

3 Hold the flywheel stationary, and then unscrew the clutch pressure plate bolts progressively in diagonal sequence. With the bolts unscrewed two or three turns, check that the pressure plate is not binding on the dowel pins. If necessary, use a screwdriver to release the pressure plate.

4 Remove all the bolts, then lift the clutch pressure plate and friction disc from the flywheel **(see illustration)**.

Inspection

5 Clean the pressure plate, disc and flywheel. Do not inhale the dust, as it may be dangerous to health.

6 Examine the fingers of the diaphragm spring for wear or scoring. If the depth of wear exceeds half the thickness of the fingers, a new pressure plate assembly must be fitted.

7 Examine the pressure plate for scoring, cracking and discoloration. Light scoring is acceptable, but if excessive, a new pressure plate assembly must be fitted.

8 Examine the friction disc linings for wear and cracking, and for contamination with oil or grease. The linings are worn excessively if they are worn down to, or near, the rivets. Check the disc hub and splines for wear, by temporarily fitting it on the transmission input shaft. Renew the friction disc as necessary.

9 Examine the flywheel friction surface for scoring, cracking and discoloration (caused by overheating). If excessive, it may be possible to have the flywheel machined by an engineering works, otherwise it should be renewed.

10 Ensure that all parts are clean, and free of oil or grease, before reassembling. Apply just a small amount of high-melting-point grease to the splines of the friction disc hub. Note that new pressure plates may be coated with protective grease. It is only permissible to clean the grease away from the friction disc lining contact area. Removal of the grease from other areas will shorten the service life of the clutch.

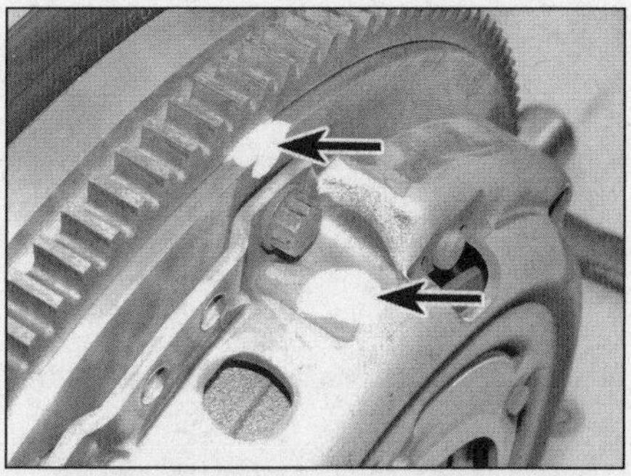

6.2 Mark the clutch pressure plate and flywheel in relation to each other

6.4 Lift the pressure plate and friction disc away from the flywheel

Refitting

11 Commence reassembly by locating the friction disc on the flywheel, with the raised, torsion spring side of the hub facing outwards. If necessary, the centralising tool (see paragraph 14) may be used to hold the disc on the flywheel at this stage **(see illustration)**.

12 Locate the clutch pressure plate on the disc, and fit it onto the location dowels **(see illustration)**. If refitting the original pressure plate, make sure that the previously-made marks are aligned.

13 Insert the bolts finger-tight to hold the pressure plate in position **(see illustration)**.

14 The friction disc must now be centralised, to ensure correct alignment of the transmission input shaft with the spigot bearing in the crankshaft. To do this, a proprietary tool may be used **(see illustration 6.11)**. Universal tools are increasingly popular as they don't rely on centralising the clutch on the central spigot bearing housing **(see illustration)**.

15 Tighten the pressure plate bolts progressively and in diagonal sequence, until the specified torque setting is achieved, and then the centralising tool can be removed.

16 Check the release bearing in the transmission bellhousing for smooth operation, and if necessary renew it with reference to Section 7.

17 Refit the transmission with reference to Chapter 7A Section 3.

7 Release bearing and lever – removal, inspection and refitting

Removal

1 First, remove the transmission as described

6.11 Locating the friction disc on the flywheel

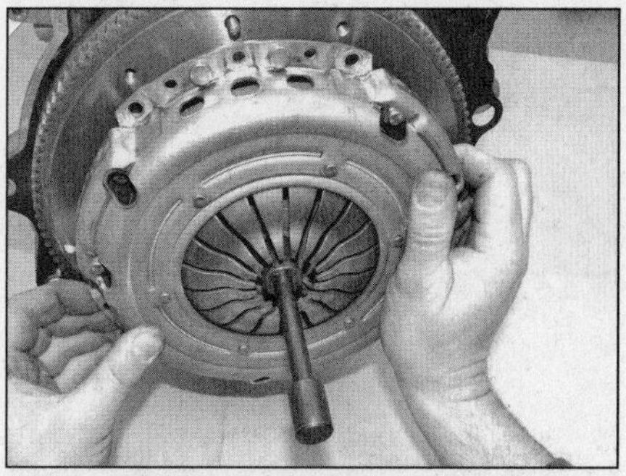

6.12 Locating the clutch pressure plate over the friction disc

6.13 Insert the bolts finger-tight initially

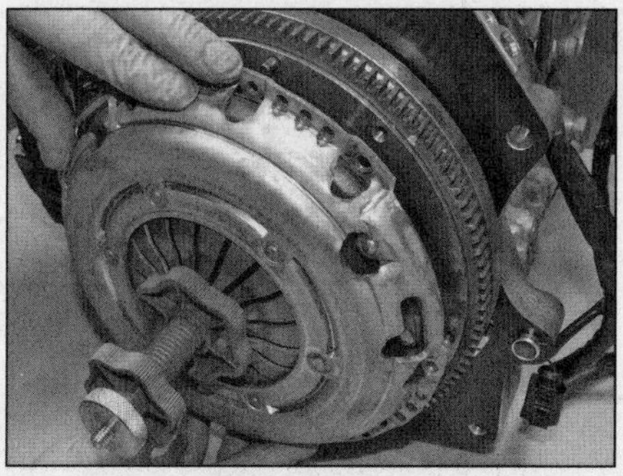

6.14 Using a universal tool to centralise the clutch assembly

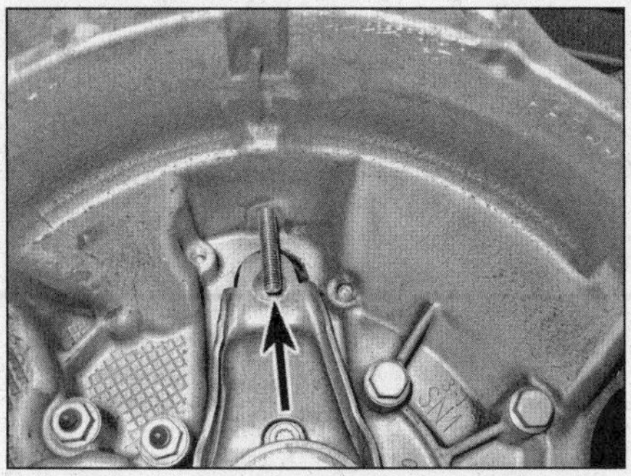

7.1 Bolt securing the release lever in position

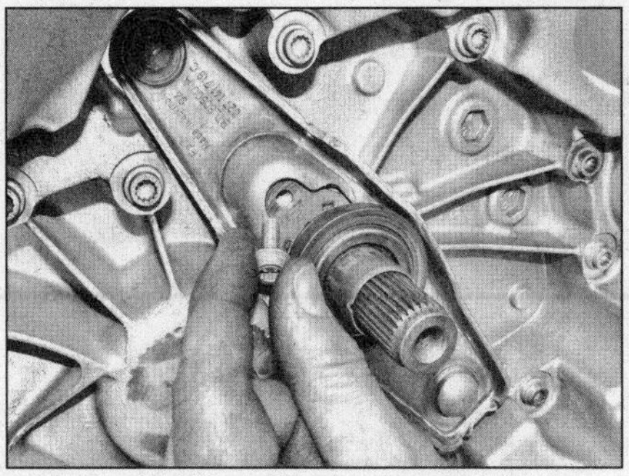

7.2 Unscrew the retaining bolts

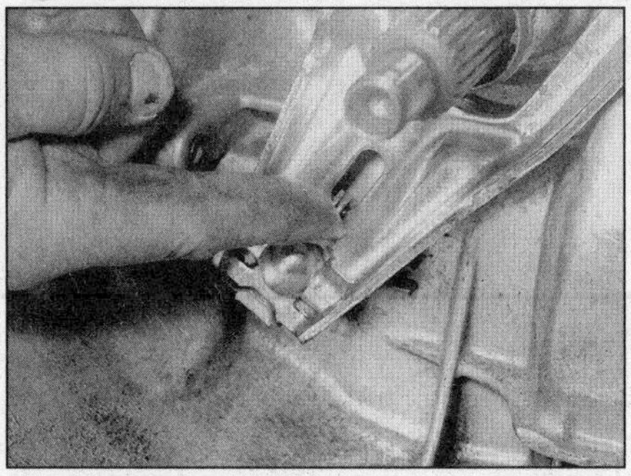

7.3 Push the spring clip to release the arm from the ball-stud

in Chapter 7A Section 3. If a long bolt was fitted through the top of the transmission to prevent the release lever from moving while the transmission was removed, it can now be removed **(see illustration)**.

2 On 02T transmissions, unscrew and remove the guide tube retaining bolts **(see illustration)**, on these transmissions the release bearing and lever are removed together with the guide tube, and then separated on the bench.

3 Prise the release lever from the ball-stud on the transmission housing, to do this, press the retaining spring through the release lever **(see illustration)**.

4 Slide the release lever and bearing (together with the guide tube on 02T transmissions), over the transmission input shaft.

5 On 02T transmissions, turn the guide tube 90° to align the tabs with the slots in the release bearing, and withdraw the tube **(see illustration)**.

6 Using a screwdriver, depress the clips and remove the bearing from the release lever **(see illustrations)**.

Inspection

7 Spin the release bearing by hand, and check it for smooth running. Any tendency to seize or run rough will necessitate renewal of the bearing. If the bearing is to be re-used, wipe it clean with a dry cloth; the bearing should not be washed in a liquid solvent, as this will remove the internal grease.

8 Clean the release lever, ball-stud and guide sleeve.

Refitting

9 Lubricate the ball-stud in the transmission bellhousing with molybdenum disulphide-based grease. Also smear a little grease on the release bearing surface which contacts the diaphragm spring fingers in the clutch cover.

10 If removed, refit the ball-stud spring to the release lever **(see illustrations)**.

11 Locate the bearing on the lever, and press until the clips engage.

12 On 02T transmissions, locate the guide tube on the bearing, align the tabs with the slots, then insert and turn through 90°.

13 Locate the release lever on the ball-stud, and press until the retaining spring holds it in position **(see illustration)**.

14 Slide the bearing and lever (and guide tube on 02T transmissions), over the input shaft and locate it in position.

15 On 02T transmissions, insert the guide tube retaining bolts and tighten to the specified torque.

16 Refit the transmission as described in Chapter 7A Section 3. If required, refit a long bolt through the top of the transmission to prevent the release lever from moving while the transmission is fitted **(see illustration 7.1)**. Remember to remove the bolt from the top of the transmission, before fitting the clutch slave cylinder.

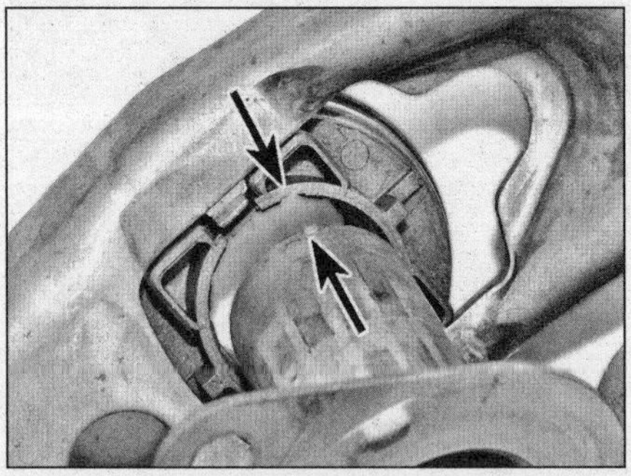

7.5 Removing the guide tube from the release bearing. Note the tab and slot (arrowed)

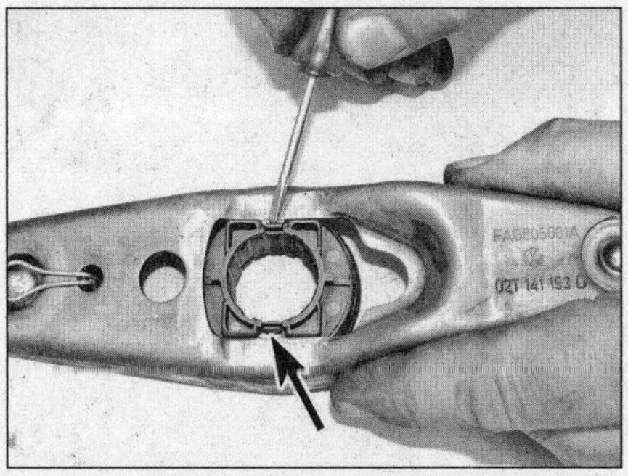

7.6a Depress the clips...

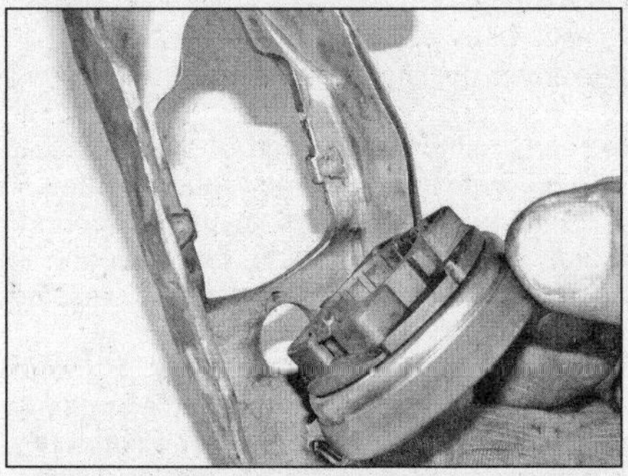

7.6b ...and remove the bearing from the release lever

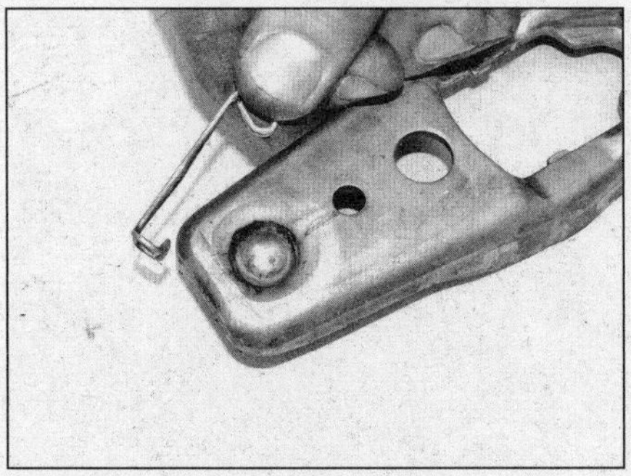

7.10a Hook the spring over the end of the lever...

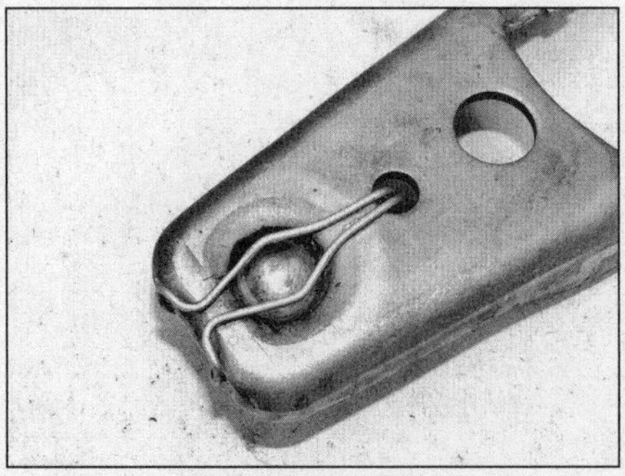

7.10b ...and press the other end into the hole

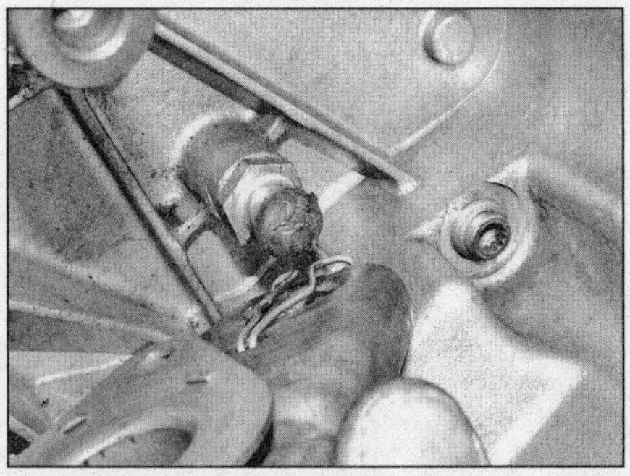

7.13 Locating the release lever and spring onto the ball-stud

Chapter 6 Part B
Clutch – DSG transmission

Contents

Degrees of difficulty

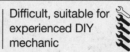

Easy, suitable for novice with little experience	Fairly easy, suitable for beginner with some experience	Fairly difficult, suitable for competent DIY mechanic	Difficult, suitable for experienced DIY mechanic	Very difficult, suitable for expert DIY or professional

Specifications

General

Type	7 speed transmission (OCW), Dual dry clutch assembly	

Torque wrench settings

Torque wrench settings	Nm	lbf ft
7 speed transmission:		
Release lever K2 bolts*:		
Stage 1	8	6
Stage 2	Angle-tighten a further 90°	

Use new bolts/nuts

1 General information

1 The seven speed transmission fitted to the Ibiza range of vehicles all have all have a 'dry' dual clutch fitted.

2 Before removing the transmission, it is vitally important that a full diagnostic code read is performed on the vehicle. This will require professional level diagnostic equipment. The factory diagnostic tool will be more than capable, but several aftermarket tools should also give access to not only the DSG fault codes (if there are any), but also the 'live data'. The 'live data is' the actual information coming live (as the vehicle is driven) from the engine management ECU. This information can help identify any potential, or real problems.

2 7 Speed transmission clutch – removal and refitting

Removal

1 Remove the transmission as described in Chapter 7B Section 2.

2 A set of special tools will be required from either a Seat dealer or the aftermarket **(see illustration)**. These tools are essential. Note that some of the available tools adopt a unique approach to both removing the clutch and calculating the required shims. These tools will be supplied with their own instructions.

3 If not done during removal of the transmission, remove the breather plugs from the transmission and mechatronic unit and seal the breathers. The mechatronic breather will likely be damaged during removal, so a new breather will be required on refitting.

4 Support the transmission in an upright position on the workbench.

5 Note the position of the central hub circlip and remove it **(see illustrations)**.

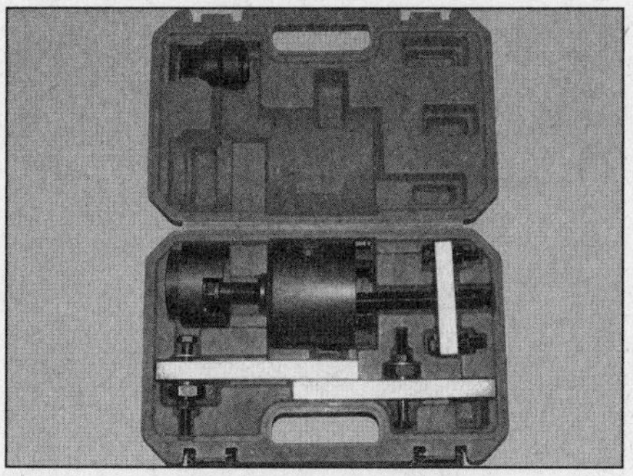

2.2 An aftermarket set of the essential clutch tools

2.5a Note the position of the circlip

2.5b Remove the circlip

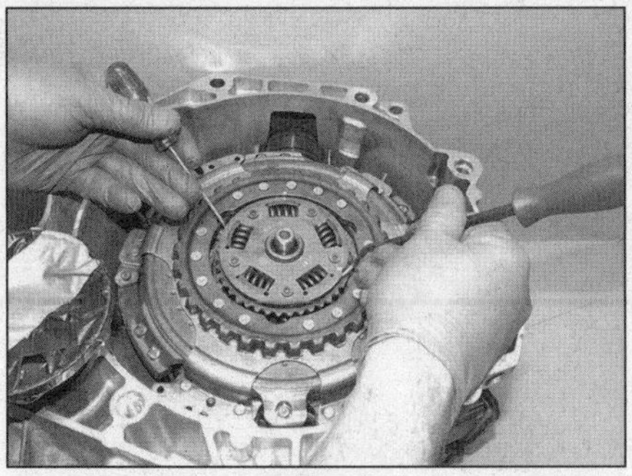
2.6a Lift up...

2.6b ...and remove the clutch hub

2.8a Install the tool and compress the clutch assembly

2.8b Remove the tool and remove the circlip

6 Lift out the central hub (clutch) using a hooked tool (fabricated from welding rod or similar) **(see illustrations)**.
7 If the clutch is to be replaced, then the position of the bearings should be measured now – see the adjustment Section.
8 Remove the now exposed circlip. If the circlip can not be released then fit the special tool (T10323) with the forcing screw and thrust plate across the bell housing and compress the clutch by tightening the screw by hand ONLY. Remove the special tool and remove the circlip **(see illustrations)**.
9 With the circlip removed, install the special tool and pull out the clutch **(see illustrations)**.
10 Recover the shims and bearing **(see illustrations)**.

Refitting

11 If any parts of the clutch assembly are replaced, then the adjustment procedure (detailed below) must be carried out.
12 Replace the shims, exactly as removed.
13 Refit the main clutch plate with the assembly tool and wind out the forcing screw to lower the clutch into position.
14 Refit the thrust piece, bridge and forcing screw. Feed in the forcing screw, whilst rocking the clutch slightly with one hand. The clutch will lose all play when the limit stop is reached, at this point, remove the special tool. Do not overtighten the forcing screw or the clutch will be damaged.
15 Remove the tool and fit the new circlip. The circlip must be fitted with the narrower face of the circlip on top.
16 Instal the puller (T10373A) from the special tool kit and (using the tool) pull up the clutch assembly with one hand, whilst pushing the clutch in the normal direction of rotation. The clutch should slide up into contact with the circlip. Note that the circlip may already be in contact with the clutch, so this procedure may not be strictly necessary.
17 Refit the central hub – it will only fit in one position. Fit the large circlip.
18 Check that the clutch is free to rotate. If the clutch does not turn freely then the clutch has been not installed correctly. If the clutch has been replaced, the correct shims may not have been fitted. Remove the clutch and refit it.
19 Refit the transmission as described in Chapter 7B Section 2.

Adjustment

20 If any parts of the clutch assembly have been replaced the adjustment procedure must be carried out.
21 With the clutch assembly removed, clean out the bellhousing using brake cleaner and then remove the operating arm ball pin. The

2.9a Instal the special tool and...

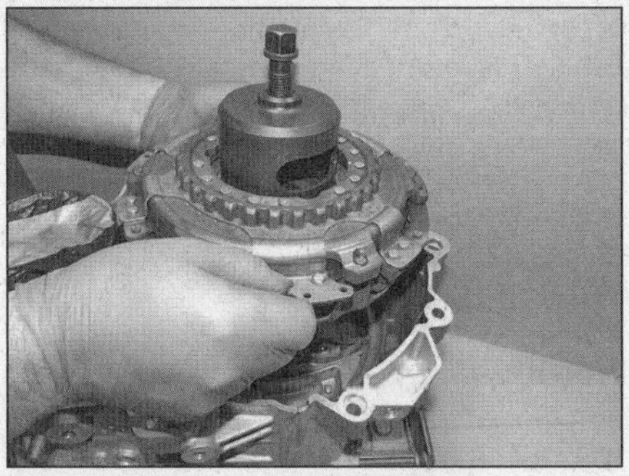
2.9b ... pull out the clutch

2.10a Remove the bearing...

2.10b ...the large shim (K1)...

2.10c ...and the small shim

2.22 A straight edge will be required

2.23 Measure the distance to the top of the outer input shaft

pin can be removed with pliers and must be replaced. Fit the new pin and tap it into position with a soft faced hammer or block of wood.

22 Instal the old circlip to the outer input shaft and then place a straight edge across the face of the bellhousing **(see illustration)**.

23 Using a depth gauge (a digital or mechanical vernier gauge is ideal) measure the distance to the top of the input outer shaft **(see illustration)**. Note down this number, or if using a digital gauge, then 'zero' the gauge. **Note:** *This measurement can also be taken with the clutch hub removed, but with the main clutch still installed.*

24 Next measure the distance to the top of the circlip and note down this number **(see illustration)**. Subtract the first number from the second and note this down. If a digital vernier is used simply note down the measurement. Repeat the procedure on the opposite side of the shaft.

25 To get the average height divide the measurements by two. Note down the number. The table below shows the method used to calculate the first stage of determining the shim thickness for clutch K1. Note that the numbers given in the table are arbitrary – they are not actual measurements.

Distance to circlip (X1)	*57.50mm*
Distance to top of outer shaft (X2)	*54.90mm*
Calculated dimension (X1 – X2 = T1)	*2.60mm*
*Distance to circlip (Y1)**	*57.45mm*
*Distance to to top of outer shaft (Y2)**	*54.84mm*
Calculated dimension (Y1 – Y2 = T2)	*2.61mm*
Average dimension (T1 + T2/2)	*2.605mm*

** Taken 180 degrees from the first measurements (X1 and X2)*

26 Remove the circlip and dispose of it – a new one will be required for refitting.

27 The procedure must now be repeated, but the second measurement is now taken to the top edge of the installed gauge block (T10466) This forms part of the special tool kit.

28 If removed, instal the large release arm with no shims **(see illustration)**. The arm must be correctly seated.

29 Instal the gauge block, press down on the block and rotate it to fully engage it.

30 Next measure the distance to the top of the gauge block and note down this number. Subtract the first number (derived from the average distance to the top of the circlip – T1 + T2 divided by 2 in our table example) from the second and note this down. If a digital vernier is used simply note down the measurement. Repeat the procedure on the opposite side of the shaft.

31 To get the average height divide the measurements by two. Note down the number.

32 The bearing tolerance can now be calculated. Subtract the first measurement noted down (paragraph 6) from the second (paragraph 13) to find the tolerance. Note down this number.

2.24 Measure the distance to the top of the circlip (X1 in the table)

2.28 Instal the large release arm

2.33 The K1 tolerance

33 On the new clutch read the tolerance value for the bearing 'K1' **(see illustration)**.
34 Take the calculated height of the bearing (the figure derived in paragraph 31) and add the tolerance value taken from the new clutch. Note that the value on the new clutch may be a minus figure and must be subtracted, not added.
35 This calculated figure is the thickness of the shim required. A total of eleven shims are available (see the table). Select the shim closest to the available size.

K1 Bearing – calculated shim thickness (in mm)	Available shim (in mm)
1.21 to 1.60	*1.50*
1.61 to 1.80	*1.70*
1.81 to 2.00	*2.10*
2.21 to 2.40	*2.30*
2.41 to 2.60	*2.50*
2.61 to 2.80	*2.70*
2.81 to 3.00	*2.90*
3.01 to 3.20	*3.10*
3.21 to 3.40	*3.30*
3.41 to 3.80	*3.50*

36 Remove the gauge block and the large engagement lever in preparation for calculating the shim for the smaller operating lever (K2 bearing).
37 The second shim thickness is calculated in a similar manner to the first. Instal the smaller release arm. Note that new release arms may be supplied with the guide sleeve in the unlocked position. Rotate it to lock it in place – the holes of the guide will be at 90 degrees to the major axis when the sleeve is correctly installed.

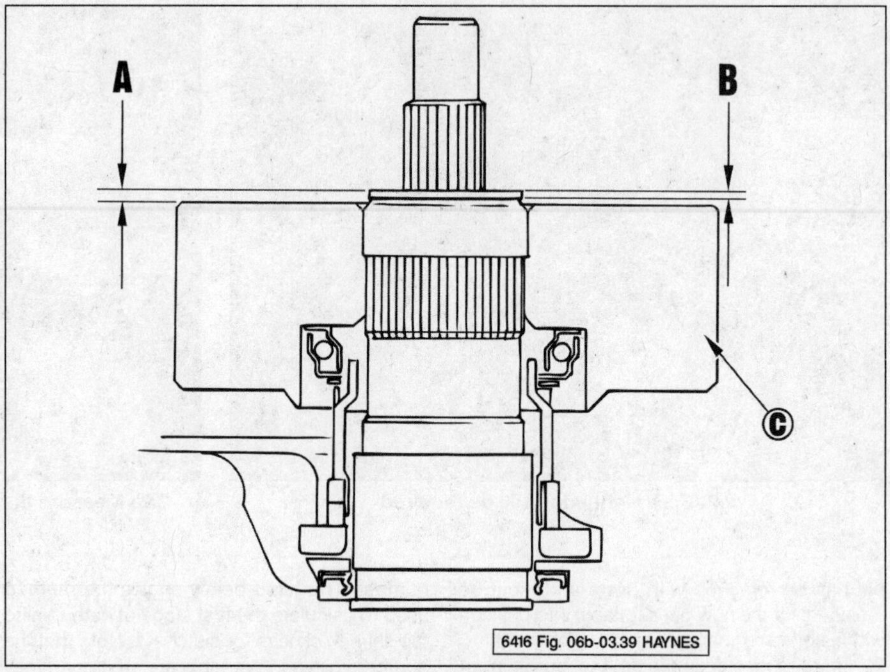

2.39 Calculating the shim for thickness for bearing K2.

A = Calculated height (see text) *B = Previously calculated height* *C = Gauge block*

38 Insert the new bolts and tighten them to the specific torque and then instal the gauge block (T10466). Rotate the gauge block to fully engage it.
39 Measure the height to the gauge block **(see illustration)**. Subtract the measured distance from the input shaft (T1 + T2 divided by 2 in our example table) from the measured distance to the gauge block and note down the measurement. On the illustration this is dimension A, minus dimension B.
40 Repeat the procedure on the opposite side and calculate the average by dividing by 2.
41 On the new clutch note the 'K2' tolerance and add it to the calculated tolerance. Note that the new clutch tolerance may be minus and so must be subtracted from the calculated tolerance.
42 Select the correct shim from the available ones (see the table).

K2 Bearing – calculated bearing thickness (in mm)	Available shims (in mm)
0.31 to 0.90	*0.80*
0.91 to 1.10	*1.00*
1.11 to 1.30	*1.20*
1.31 to 1.50	*1.40*
1.51 to 1.70	*1.60*
1.71 to 1.90	*1.80*
1.91 to 2.10	*2.00*
2.11 to 2.30	*2.20*
2.31 to 2.50	*2.40*
2.51 to 2.70	*2.60*
2.71 to 3.30	*2.80*

43 With both new shim thicknesses calculated the clutch assembly can be installed with the new shims as described above.

Chapter 7 Part A
Manual transmission

Contents

Degrees of difficulty

Easy, suitable for novice with little experience	Fairly easy, suitable for beginner with some experience	Fairly difficult, suitable for competent DIY mechanic	Difficult, suitable for experienced DIY mechanic	Very difficult, suitable for expert DIY or professional

Specifications

General

Type	Transversely mounted, front-wheel-drive layout with integral transaxle differential/final drive. Five forward speeds, one reverse.
Application:	
Petrol engines:	
1.0 litre (CHYB)	5-speed transmission 0CF
1.0 litre (CHZC)	6-speed transmission 0DQ
1.0 litre (CHZB)	5-speed transmission 0DF/02T
1.2 litre (CBZB)	5-speed transmission 02T
1.2 litre (CJZD)	6-speed transmission 02U/0DQ
1.2 litre (CJZC)	5-speed transmission 0DF/02T
1.4 litre (BXW and CGGB)	5-speed transmission 02T
Diesel engines:	
1.6 litre (CAYC and CLNA)	5-speed transmission 02R

Torque wrench settings

Torque wrench settings	Nm	lbf ft
Clutch slave cylinder bolts	20	15
Driveshaft flange bolt*	25	18
Guide sleeve (for clutch release bearing):		
02T/0DF/02U/0DQ transmission: *		
Stage 1	5	3
Stage 2	Angle-tighten a further 90°	
02R transmission	20	15
Reversing light switch	20	15
Filler/level and drain plug:		
02R transmission (diesel engines)	35	26
02T transmission (petrol engines):		
Multi-splined (12-point) plug	25	18
Hexagon (Allen key) plug	30	22
Mounting bracket to transmission:		
Stage 1	40	30
Stage 2	Angle-tighten a further 90°	
Small cover plate bolt	10	7
Transmission to engine:		
M12 bolts	80	59
M10 bolts	40	30

**Do not re-use*

1 General Information

1 The manual transmission is bolted directly to the left-hand end of the engine. This layout has the advantage of providing the shortest possible drive path to the front wheels, as well as locating the transmission in the airflow through the engine bay, optimising cooling. The unit is cased in aluminium alloy.

2 Drive from the crankshaft is transmitted by the clutch to the gearbox input shaft, which is splined to accept the clutch friction disc.

3 All forward gears are fitted with synchromesh. The floor-mounted gear lever is connected to the gearbox by selector and shift cables **(see illustration)**. This actuates selector forks inside the gearbox, which are slotted onto the synchromesh sleeves. The sleeves, which are locked to the gearbox shafts but can slide axially by means of splined hubs, press baulk rings into contact with the respective gear/pinion. The coned surfaces between the baulk rings and the pinion/gear act as a friction clutch, that progressively matches the speed of the synchromesh sleeve (and hence the gearbox shaft) with that of the gear/pinion. This allows gearchanges to be carried out smoothly.

4 Drive is transmitted to the differential crownwheel, which rotates the differential case and planetary gears, thus driving the sun gears and driveshafts. The rotation of the differential planetary gears on their shaft allows the inner roadwheel to rotate at a slower speed than the outer roadwheel during cornering.

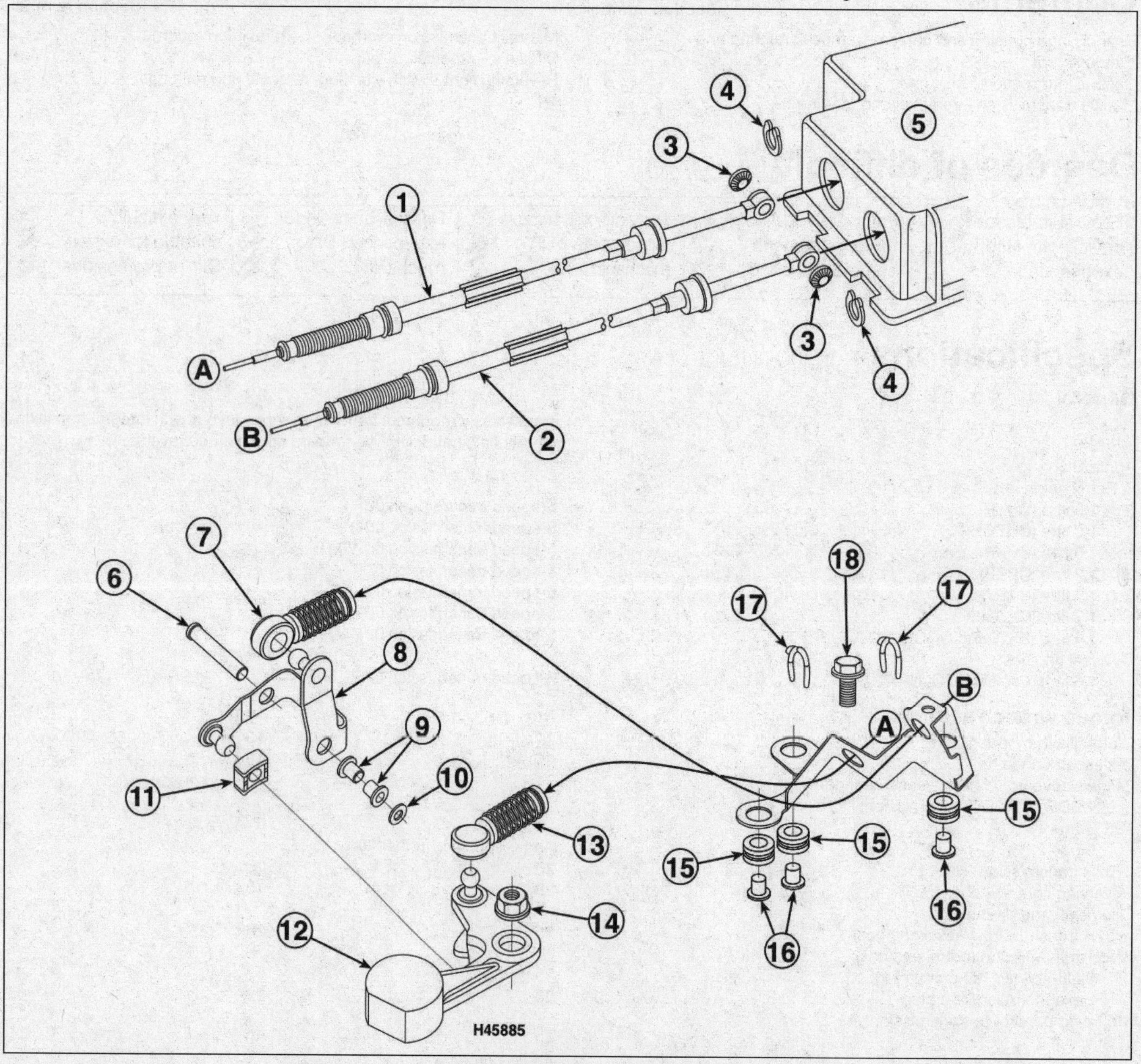

1.3 Gearchange cable components

1 Shift cable
2 Selector cable
3 Press-stud
4 Circlip
5 Shift housing
6 Pivot
7 Selector cable lock
8 Relay lever
9 Bushes
10 Circlip
11 Sliding shoe
12 Shift lever with weight
13 Shift cable lock
14 Nut
15 Grommet
16 Spacer
17 Circlip
18 Bolt

2.3a Release the locking clips...

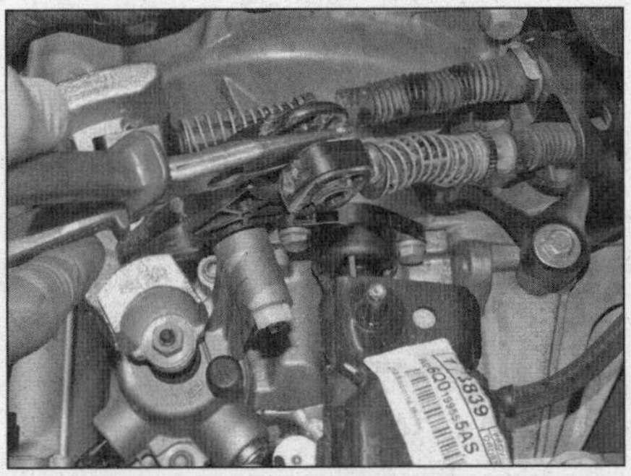

2.3b ...and prise off the inner cables ...

2.3c ...and outer cable securing clips

2 Gear change housing and cables – removal, refitting and adjustment

Removal

1 Remove the battery and battery tray as described in Chapter 5A Section 3.

2 Remove the air cleaner housing as described in Chapter 4A Section 3 (petrol) or Chapter 4B Section 3 (diesel).

3 Prise out the clips securing the inner cable to the lever on the transmission, and the outer cable to the support bracket **(see illustrations)**. Withdraw the cable from the support bracket and discard the clips – new ones must be fitted.

4 Working inside the vehicle, remove the centre console, as described in Chapter 11 Section 27.

5 Remove the insulation around the base of the gear change housing to access the mounting nuts **(see illustration)**.

6 Raise the front of the vehicle and support it securely on axle stands (see *Jacking and vehicle support*).

7 Remove the centre tunnel front heat shield from the underside of the vehicle to gain access to the base of the selector lever housing and cables **(see illustration)**. **Note:** *It may be necessary to separate the exhaust downpipe from the intermediate pipe to remove the housing.*

8 Working back inside the vehicle, undo the retaining nuts, then remove the bracket and lower the gear change housing downwards. Withdraw it complete with selector cables out from under the vehicle. It may be useful having the aid of an assistant at this point, to be under the vehicle when lowering the gear change housing.

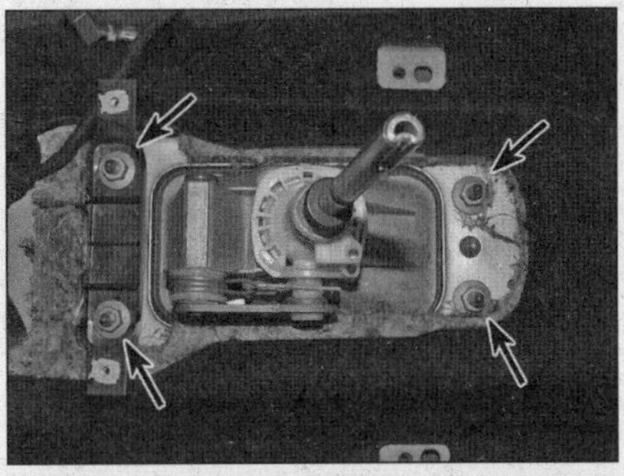

2.5 Gearchange housing mounting nuts

9 To remove the cables from the gear change housing, prise out the clips securing the inner cable to the lower part of the gear lever, and then withdraw the securing clips from the outer cable to the gear change housing **(see illustration 1.3)**. Withdraw the cables and discard the clips – new ones must be fitted.

Refitting

10 Refitting is the reversal of the removal procedure, noting the following points:

a) *Ensure that the cables are correctly routed and secured, as noted on removal.*
b) *Take care not to bend or kink the cables.*
c) *Carry out the cable adjustment procedure described below before reconnecting the cable at the transmission end.*
d) *When refitting the cables, use new clips.*

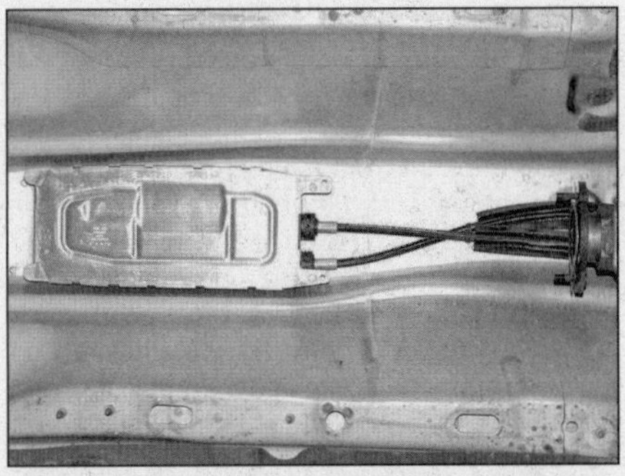

2.7 Lower section of gearchange housing, viewed from under the vehicle

Adjustment

11 If not already done remove the battery and battery tray, as described in Section. If required remove the air cleaner housing, and air ducting for better access to the top of the transmission.

12 With the gearchange set in the neutral position, push the two locking collars (one on each cable) forwards to compress the springs, turn them clockwise (looking from the driver's seat) to lock into position **(see illustration)**.

13 Press down on the selector shaft on the top of the transmission, and push the locking pin into the transmission while turning it clockwise 90°, until it engages and the selector shaft cannot move **(see illustrations)**.

2.12 Push the collar down and lock in position

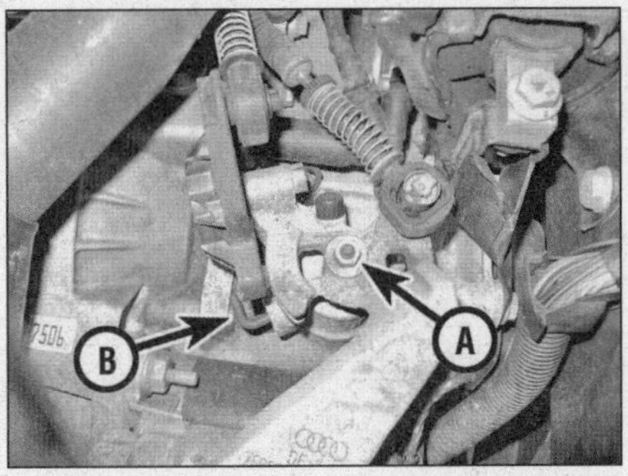

2.13a Press down on (A), then turn the angle lever (B) – 02R transmssion

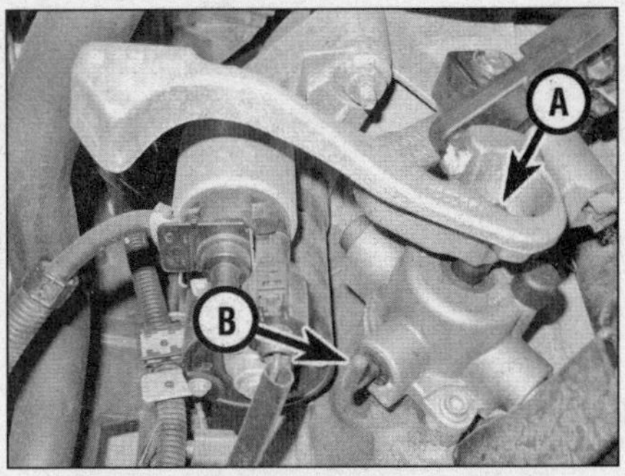

2.13b Press down on (A), then turn the angle lever (B) 02T transmssion

2.14 Locking the gear lever in position with a drill bit

2.15 Release the two locking collars

14 Working inside the vehicle, unclip the gear lever gaiter from the centre console and lift out the insulator. Still in the neutral position, move the gear lever as far to the left as possible and insert the locking pin (or drill bit) through the hole in the base of the gear lever and into the hole in the housing **(see illustration)**.

15 Working back in the engine bay, turn the two locking collars on the cables anti-clockwise (looking from the driver's seat) so that the springs will release them back into position and lock the cables **(see illustration)**.

16 With the cable adjustment set, the locking pin in the transmission housing, can now be turned anti-clockwise 90°, to its original position. Pointing upwards on 02T transmissions and pointing to the rear on 02R transmissions.

17 Inside the vehicle, remove the locking pin (or drill bit) from the gear lever, and then check the operation of the selector mechanism. When the gear lever is at rest in neutral, it should be central, ready to select 3rd or 4th. The gear lever gaiter and insulator can now be refitted to the centre console.

18 Refit the air ducting, engine top cover/air filter and battery/tray.

3 Manual transmission – removal and refitting

Removal

Note: *The official method of removing the transmission requires the engine to be supported from above using a support bar that extends across the top of the engine and locates on the inner wings close to the suspension tower. The support bar also requires additional brackets, not readily available to the home mechanic. The method described below involves supporting the engine from an engine crane and then removing the transmission. This does limit access, so ensure that any components that require removal from underneath are removed before installing the engine crane. An alternative method (and recommended if work on the engine is also required) is to remove the front lock carrier completely and pull the engine and transmission forward as a complete assembly. Note that on models fitted with AC, the refrigerant must be removed first as described in Chapter 3 Section 11.*

1 Select a solid, level surface to park the vehicle upon. Give yourself enough space to move around it easily. Apply the handbrake and chock the rear wheels.

2 Raise the front of the vehicle and support it securely on axle stands (see *Jacking and vehicle support*). Where fitted, remove the engine/transmission undertray sections. Position a suitable container beneath the transmission, then unscrew the drain plug and drain the transmission oil.

3 Remove the air cleaner housing as described in Chapter 4A Section 3, or Chapter 4B Section 3.

4 Remove the battery and battery tray with reference to Section 5A Section 3.

5 Where required either remove the radiator fan assembly (Chapter 3 Section 5) or move the front lock panel to the service position.

6 Release the retaining clips and disconnect the gear selector cables from the gear selector levers, as described in Section 2. Also, unbolt and remove the cable mounting bracket from the top of the transmission **(see illustration)**.

7 The clutch slave cylinder is on the top of the transmission, undo the retaining bolts and place the cylinder to one side, with reference to Chapter 6A Section 5.

Caution: Do not depress the clutch pedal with the slave cylinder removed or disconnected.

8 Insert a long bolt (approx. 60mm) through the bolt hole above the clutch slave cylinder aperture, this will prevent the clutch fork falling of into the bell housing, as the transmission is removed or refitted **(see illustration)**.

9 Unbolt the earth cable from the engine/transmission or subframe.

10 Unscrew and remove the upper bolts securing the transmission to the engine.

11 Disconnect the wiring from the reversing light switch, and where fitted, the neutral position switch on vehicles with a start/stop system.

12 With reference to Chapter 5A Section 8, remove the starter motor.

13 On models fitted with driveshafts that fit directly into the transmission, slacken the driveshaft hub bolts before raising the vehicle. Note that even on driveshafts that bolt to the transmission complete removal can make transmission removal slightly easier.

14 Raise the front of the vehicle and support it securely on axle stands (see *Jacking and vehicle support*). Where fitted, remove the engine/transmission undertray sections. Position a suitable container beneath the transmission, then unscrew the drain plug and drain the transmission oil.

15 Remove the lower left-hand wheel arch liner.

16 Where fitted, unbolt the shield from the rear of the cylinder block **(see illustration)**, which goes around the top of the right-hand driveshaft.

17 Slacken the clamp securing the exhaust intermediate pipe to the rear section and undo the front mounting bracket bolts. This will

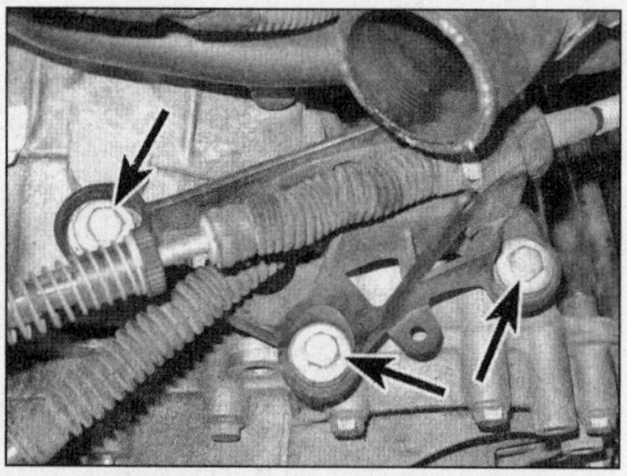

3.6 Mounting bracket bolts

3.8 Insert a bolt to secure the release lever

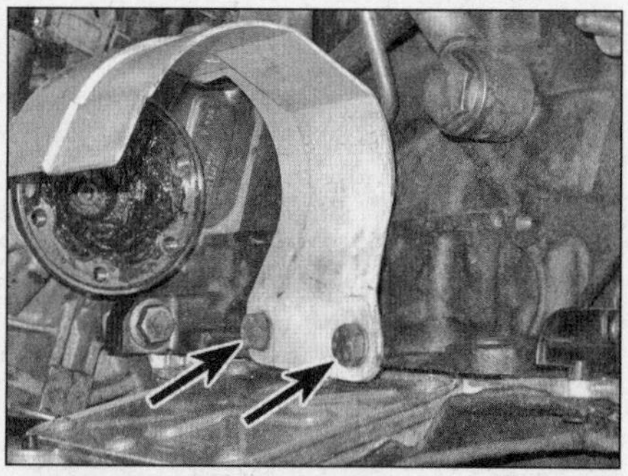

3.16 Undo the heat shield mounting bolts

allow the engine to be moved forwards and backwards during the transmission removal and alignment procedures. Consequently, there is no need to completely separate the exhaust pipe sections. Take care not to damage the front flexible pipe as the engine is being moved.

18 With reference to the Chapter 8 Section 2, unscrew and remove the bolts securing the driveshafts to the transmission output flanges. Tie the right-hand driveshaft to one side, and then tie the left-hand driveshaft to the suspension strut, so that the shaft is as high as possible. On models with direct fit driveshafts remove the driveshafts completely as described in Chapter 8 Section 2.

19 Unbolt the engine rear mounting torque arm from the bottom of the transmission **(see illustration)**. **Note:** *Do Not undo the centre bolt that goes through the rubber mounting, as this is set in position.*

20 Where applicable, unbolt the small flywheel cover plate from the rear of the transmission bellhousing **(see illustration)**. This is removed to allow the driveshaft flange to be able to clear the flywheel.

21 Using a suitable hoist, support the weight of the engine.

22 Unscrew the bolts securing the transmission mounting to the body. Also, unbolt the mounting bracket from the transmission **(see illustrations)**.

23 Lower the engine/transmission assembly slightly and, using a trolley jack, support the transmission. Position the jack so that it can be withdrawn from the left-hand side of the car. As the engine/transmission is moved, make sure any wiring or hoses are not damaged.

24 Unscrew and remove the remaining lower transmission-to-engine mounting bolts, including the bolt located on the left-hand rear of the engine **(see illustrations)**.

25 Carefully pull the transmission directly away from the engine, taking care not to allow its weight to rest on the clutch friction disc hub. A second person is helpful to pull the engine as far forwards as possible.

26 On models with driveshafts that have a bolted flange, it will be necessary to manouvre the right-hand driveshaft flange, from around the flywheel on removal. If required, hold the drive flange in position and undo the centre securing bolt, then the drive flange can be removed **(see illustration)**, as described in Section 6, to make removal of the transmission easier.

Warning: Support the transmission to ensure that it remains steady on the jack head. Keep the transmission level until the input shaft is fully withdrawn from the clutch friction disc.

27 When the transmission is clear of the locating dowels and clutch components, lower the transmission to the ground and withdraw from under the car.

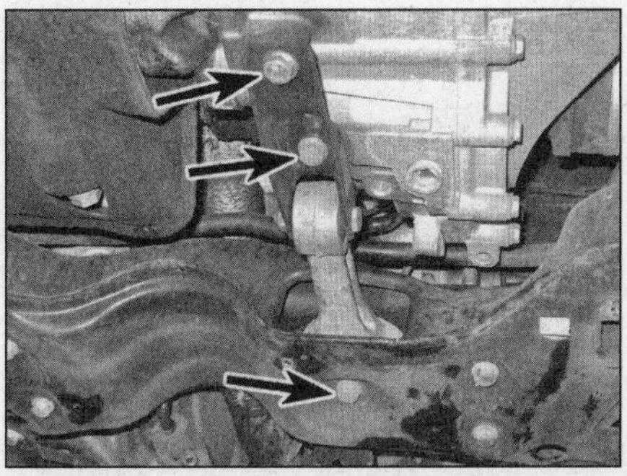

3.19 Undo the mounting bolts

3.20 Cover plate retaining bolt

3.22a Transmission mounting to body...

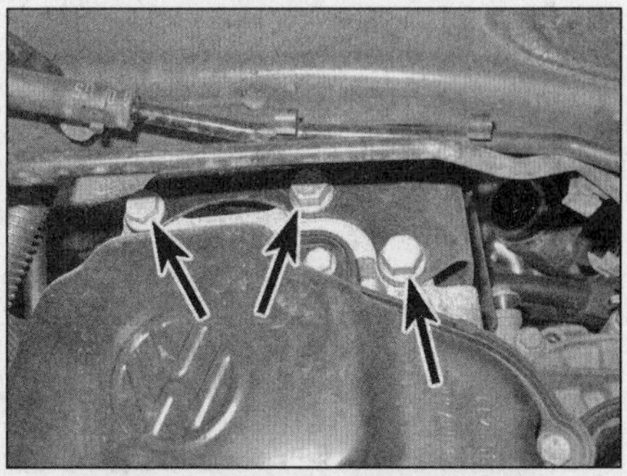

3.22b ...and mounting bracket to transmission bolts

Refitting

28 Refitting the transmission is essentially a reversal of the removal procedure, but note the following points:

a) Apply a smear of special grease (usually supplied with the clutch kit) to the clutch friction disc hub splines. Do not use high melting-point grease.

b) In order to align the transmission with the

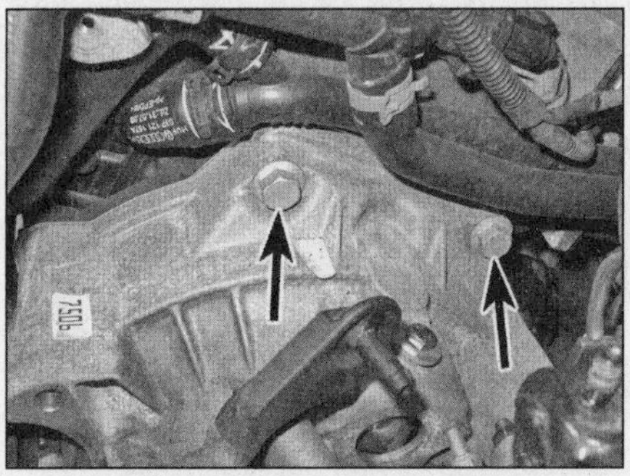

3.24a Upper transmission bolts...

3.24b ...lower transmission bolts...

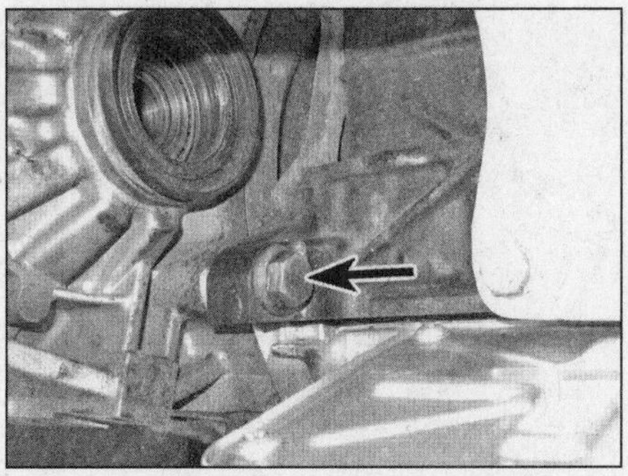

3.24c ...and rear transmission bolt

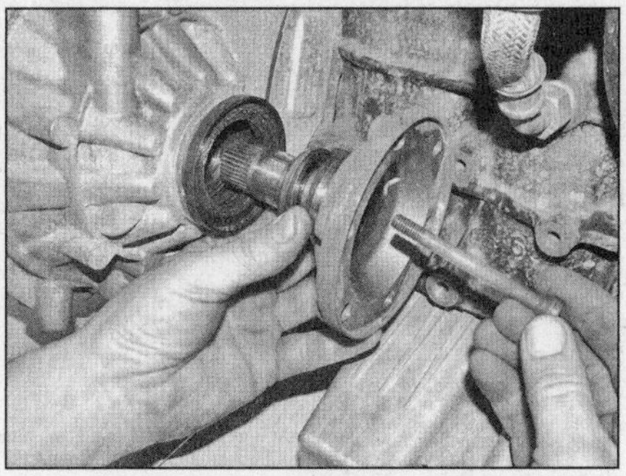

3.26 Removing the left-hand drive flange

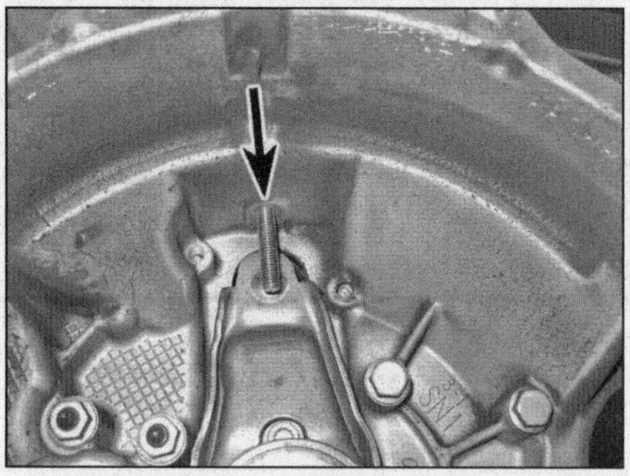

3.28 Remove the bolt securing the clutch fork

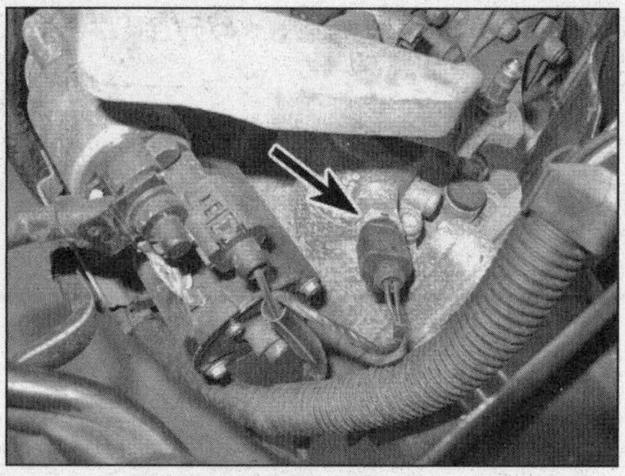

5.2a Reversing light switch – 02R transmission

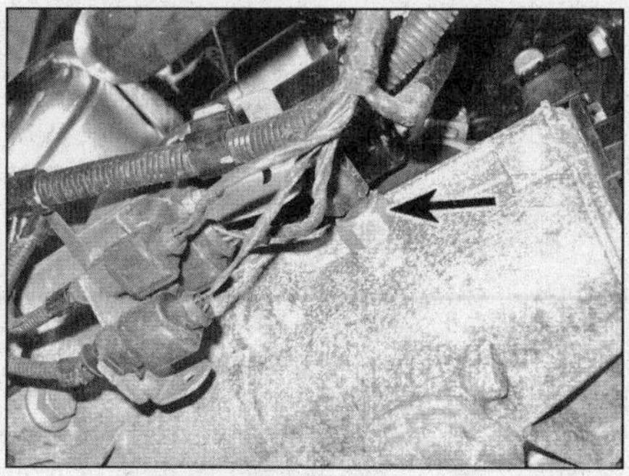

5.2b Reversing light switch – 02T and 0DF transmissions

flywheel; gently pull the engine forward as the transmission is manoeuvred into place.

c) *Tighten the transmission-to-engine bolts to the specified torque.*
d) *Remember to remove the bolt that was holding the clutch fork in position for refitting, once the transmission is bolted in place* ***(see illustration)***
e) *Refer to the relevant part of Chapter 2 and tighten the engine mounting bolts to the correct torque.*
f) *Refer to Chapter 8 Section 2, and then tighten the driveshaft bolts to the specified torque.*
g) *On completion, refer to Section 2 and check the gearchange linkage/cable adjustment.*
h) *Refill the transmission with the correct grade and quantity of oil. Refer to 'Lubricants and fluids' at the beginning of this Manual.*

4 Manual transmission overhaul – general information

1 The overhaul of the manual transmission is a complex and often expensive task for the DIY home mechanic to undertake, which requires access to specialist equipment. It involves dismantling and reassembly of many small components, measuring clearances precisely and, if necessary, adjusting them by selecting shims and spacers. Internal transmission components are also often difficult to obtain and in many instances, extremely expensive. Because of this, if the transmission develops a fault or becomes noisy, the best course of action is to have the unit overhauled by a specialist repairer or to obtain an exchange reconditioned unit.

2 Nevertheless, it is not impossible for the more experienced mechanic to overhaul the transmission if the special tools are available and the job is carried out in a deliberate step-by-step manner, to ensure nothing is overlooked.

3 The tools necessary for an overhaul include internal and external circlip pliers, bearing pullers, a slide hammer, a set of pin punches, a dial test indicator and possibly a hydraulic press. In addition, a large, sturdy workbench and a vice will be required.

4 During dismantling of the transmission, make careful notes of how each component is fitted to make reassembly easier and accurate.

5 Before dismantling the transmission, it will help if you have some idea of where the problem lies. Certain problems can be closely related to specific areas in the transmission, which can make component examination and renewal easier. Refer to the *Fault finding* Section in this manual for more information.

5 Reversing light switch – testing, removal and refitting

Testing

1 Ensure that the ignition switch is turned to the 'off' position.

2 Disconnect the wiring from the reversing light switch **(see illustrations)**. The switch is screwed into the front of the casing on 02T/0DF transmissions, and into the shift cover on the top of the 02R transmission.

3 Connect the probes of a continuity tester, or multimeter set to the resistance measurement function, across the terminals of the reversing light switch.

4 The switch contacts are open when any gear other than reverse is selected; the tester/meter should indicate an open circuit or infinite resistance. When reverse gear is selected, the switch contacts should close, causing the tester/meter to indicate continuity or zero resistance.

5 If the switch does not operate correctly, it should be renewed.

Removal

6 Ensure that the ignition switch is turned to the 'off' position.

7 Disconnect the wiring from the reversing light switch.

8 Unscrew and remove the switch from the casing. On the 02T and 0DF transmissions, recover the sealing ring.

Refitting

9 Refitting is a reversal of removal, but tighten the switch to the specified torque. On the 02T and 0DF transmissions, renew the sealing ring. On the 02R transmission, apply some molybdenum disulphide grease to the peg.

6 Oil seals – renewal

Driveshaft oil seals

1 Remove the appropriate driveshaft as described in Chapter 8 Section 2.

2 On models fitted with a bolt on driveshaft, undo the retaining bolt and remove the appropriate driveshaft flange from the transmission **(see illustrations)**.

3 Carefully prise the oil seal out of the transmission **(see illustration)**, using a large flat-bladed screwdriver, noting its fitted position.

4 Remove all traces of dirt from the area around the oil seal aperture, then apply a

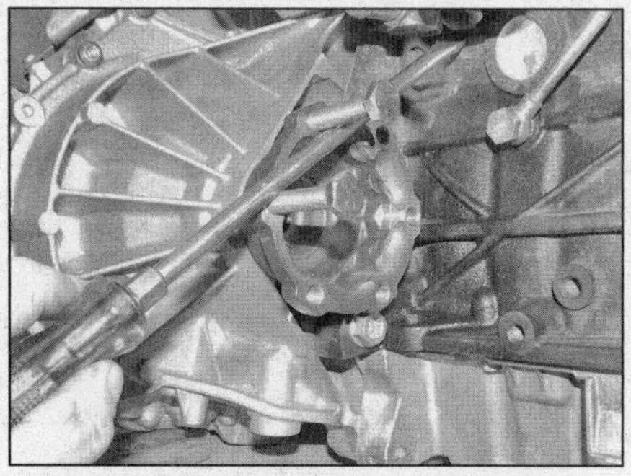

6.2a Hold the drive flange in position...

6.2b ...remove the centre bolt...

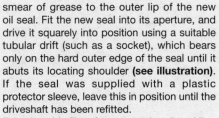

6.2c ...then slide the drive flange from the transmission

6.3 Remove the old oil seal

6.4 Drive the new oil seal into position

smear of grease to the outer lip of the new oil seal. Fit the new seal into its aperture, and drive it squarely into position using a suitable tubular drift (such as a socket), which bears only on the hard outer edge of the seal until it abuts its locating shoulder **(see illustration)**. If the seal was supplied with a plastic protector sleeve, leave this in position until the driveshaft has been refitted.

5 Apply a thin film of grease to the oil seal lip.

6 When refitting the driveshaft flange, pressure will need to be applied to the flange to compress the spring, when fitting the flange centre bolt. Tighten the bolt to the specified torque setting.

7 Refit the driveshaft as described in Chapter 8 Section 2.

Input shaft oil seal

Note: *On some transmissions, the oil seal appears to be integral with the guide sleeve. Check with your Seat parts specialist before removal.*

8 Remove the transmission as described in Section 3, and the clutch release mechanism as described in Chapter 6A Section 6.

9 Undo the bolts (two or three bolts, depending on model) securing the clutch release bearing guide sleeve in position, and slide the guide off the input shaft, along with its sealing ring or gasket (as applicable). Recover any shims or thrustwashers, which have stuck to the rear of the guide sleeve, and refit them to the input shaft.

10 Where applicable, carefully lever the oil seal out of the guide using a suitable flat-bladed screwdriver or remove the seal using a drift.

11 Before fitting a new seal, check the input shaft's seal rubbing surface for signs of burrs, scratches or other damage, which may have caused the seal to fail in the first place. It may be possible to polish away minor faults of this sort using fine abrasive paper; however, more serious defects will require the renewal of the input shaft. Ensure that the input shaft is clean and greased, to protect the seal lips on refitting.

12 Lubricate the lips of the seal before refitting to the transmission or guide tube.

13 Fit a new sealing ring or gasket (as applicable) to the rear of the guide sleeve, then carefully slide the sleeve into position over the input shaft. Refit the retaining bolts and tighten them to the specified torque setting.

14 Take the opportunity to inspect the clutch components if not already done (Chapter 6A Section 6). Finally, refit the transmission as described in Section 3.

Chapter 7 Part B
DSG semi-automatic transmission

Contents

Degrees of difficulty

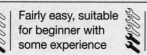

Easy, suitable for novice with little experience	Fairly easy, suitable for beginner with some experience	Fairly difficult, suitable for competent DIY mechanic	Difficult, suitable for experienced DIY mechanic	Very difficult, suitable for expert DIY or professional

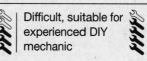

Specifications

General

Transmission type:	
0CW/0AM	7 speed. Dual dry clutch.
Transmission capacity:	
After draining (for general repair)	1.9 litres
After draining and extracting oil for removal of the control unit	2.1 litres
Mechatronic hydraulic oil	1.0 litre

Torque wrench settings

Torque wrench settings	Nm	lbf ft
Transmission-to-engine bolts:		
M10 bolts	40	30
M12 bolts	80	59
Transmission mounting bracket to transmission bolts*:		
Stage 1	40	30
Stage 2	Angle-tighten a further 90°	
Mounting to body bolts*:		
Stage 1	60	44
Stage 2	Angle-tighten a further 90°	
Pendulum mount*		
To transmission:		
Stage 1	50	37
Stage 2	Angle-tighten a further 90°	
To subframe:		
Stage 1	130	96
Stage 2	Angle-tighten a further 90°	
Drain plug (0CW transmission)	30	22

**Do not re-use*

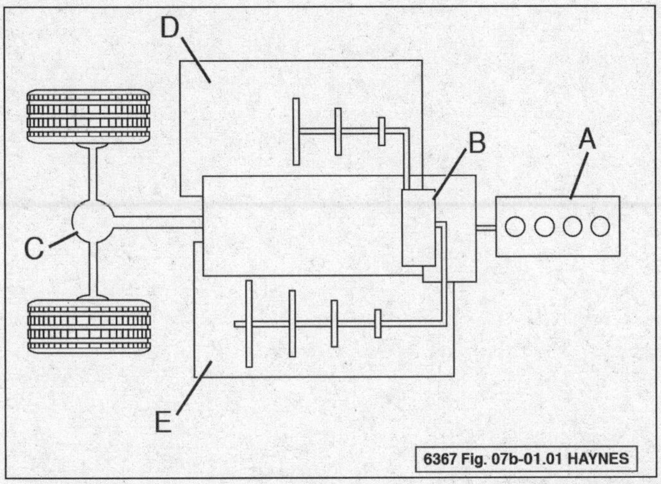

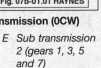

1.1 Schematic view of the seven speed transmission (0CW)

A Engine
B Dual clutch
C Final drive
D Sub transmission 1 (gears 2, 4, 6 and reverse)
E Sub transmission 2 (gears 1, 3, 5 and 7)

1.3 Clutch assembly – 0CW transmission

1 General Information

1 The Seat semi-automatic Direct Shift Gearbox (DSG) has seven-forward speeds (and one reverse). In contrast to traditional automatic transmissions where a fluid flywheel (torque converter) transmits the power from the engine to the gearbox, the seven spped DSG transmission has a twin-clutch **(see illustration)**. The main advantages of the DSG transmission, is near-instant gear changes, with seamless, highly efficient drive, resulting in less exhaust emissions and improved fuel consumption.

2 On the front of the transmission housing is a mechatronic unit, this is made up of mechanical and electronic components. The electronic part of the unit uses information from sensors (e.g. engine speed, road speed, driving mode etc.) to determine the optimum gear and shift commands, the mechanical part then selects the correct gear required. The mechatronic unit is a sealed unit, and is bolted to the front of the transmission.

3 On 7-speed transmissions, the clutch is of a dual-clutch dry plate type, which has two friction discs and a spring loaded centre hub **(see illustration)**. The clutch friction disc nearest the engine is operated by the larger outer release lever (K1) and operates 1st, 3rd, 5th & 7th gears. The clutch friction disc nearest the transmission is operated by the smaller inner release lever (K2) and operates 2nd, 4th, 6th & Reverse gears. With this system whilst 'K1' has a gear engaged, then 'K2' will pre-select the next gear ready to change gear. The clutch assembly can only be purchased as a complete unit, and if renewed, new release levers will also be needed.

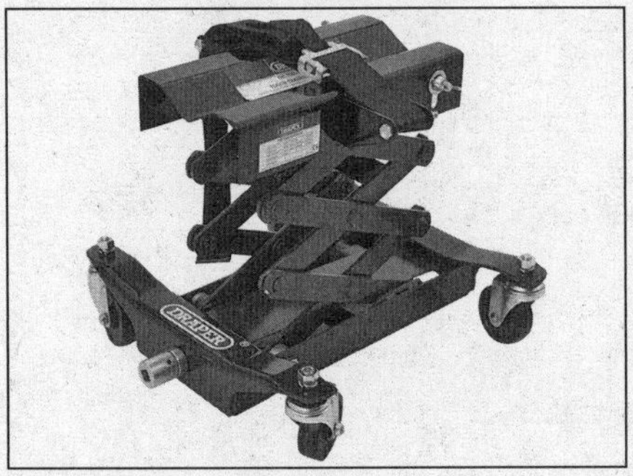

2.0 Transmission support jack

4 A fault diagnosis system is integrated into the control unit, but analysis can only be undertaken with specialised equipment. It is important that any transmission fault be identified and rectified at the earliest possible opportunity. A Seat dealer or suitably equipped specialist can 'interrogate' the ECM fault memory for stored fault codes, enabling him to pinpoint the fault quickly. Once the fault has been corrected and any fault codes have been cleared, normal transmission operation is restored.

5 Because of the need for special test equipment, the complexity of some of the parts, and the need for scrupulous cleanliness when these transmissions, the work which the owner can do is limited. Most major repairs and overhaul operations should be left to a Seat dealer or specialist, who will be equipped with the necessary equipment for fault diagnosis and repair. The information in this Chapter is therefore limited to a description of the removal and refitting of the transmission as a complete unit. The removal, refitting and adjustment of the selector cable is also described.

6 In the event of a transmission problem occurring, consult a Seat dealer or transmission specialist before removing the transmission from the vehicle, since the majority of fault diagnosis is best carried out with the transmission still in the vehicle.

2 Transmission – removal and refitting

Note: *A safe method of supporting the engine while the transmission is removed will be required. The recommended method of removing the transmission is to support both the engine and transmission with a support bar that fits across the engine bay. Support bars are readily available in the aftermarket, however the special extensions and fittings specified by Seat are not available. Where the correct support bar is not available the best alternative for the home mechanic is to support the engine with an engine crane (installed from the side) and then support the transmission with a trolley jack or ideally a transmission jack* ***(see illustration)****. Consideration should also be given to removing the complete transmission and engine as a single unit (as described in Chapter 2F Section 4) as removal of the DSG transmission requires the removal of the front subframe. Whichever method is used the aid of an assistant is essential.*

Warning: The mechatronic unit on the front of the 7-speed transmission is a sealed unit. If any oil is lost from this mechatronic unit, it will need to be renewed, as it cannot be refilled. Remove the breather cap from the top of the unit and cover with blanking plug, to prevent any loss of oil.

Removal

1 The transmission is removed downwards from the engine compartment. First, select a solid, level surface to park the vehicle upon. Give yourself enough space to move around it easily. Select P, apply the handbrake, and chock the rear wheels.

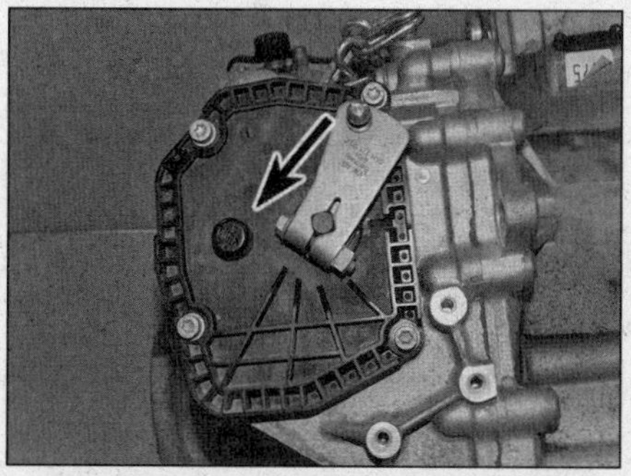

2.5 Fit a blanking plug to the breather

2.7 Remove the earth cable

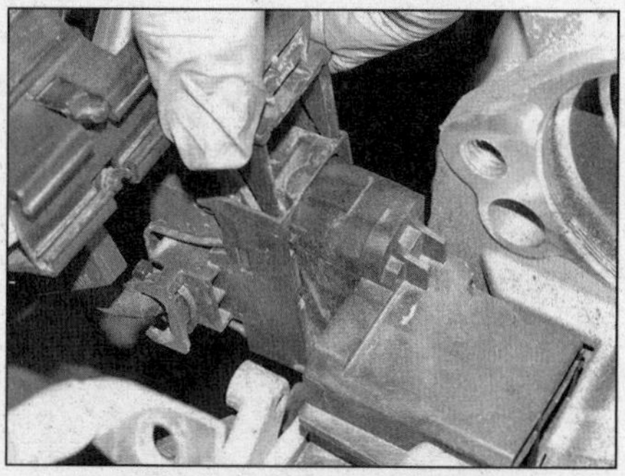

2.9 Slide up the locking collar

2 Loosen the front wheel bolts, and the driveshaft hub bolts. Do not undo the hub bolt more than 90° at this point; otherwise the wheel bearing could be damaged, whilst the weight is still on the wheels.

3 Raise the front of the vehicle and rest it securely on axle stands (see *Jacking and vehicle support*). Remove the front wheels. Allow a suitable working clearance underneath for the eventual withdrawal of the transmission. Undo the fasteners and remove the engine/transmission undershield.

4 Remove the air filter housing as described in Chapter 4A Section 3 (petrol engine) or Chapter 4B Section 3 (diesel engine) and then remove the battery and support tray Chapter 5A Section 3.

5 Where fitted remove the breather plug from the top of the transmission and fit a sealing plug **(see illustration)**. The vent plug will more than likely be damaged on removal, so a new one will be required for refitting. Note that some models have a vent hose and not a simple plug.

6 Undo the retaining clips and remove the turbocharger intake hose and charge air pipe to the intercooler or air filter as described in Chapter 4A Section 3 (petrol engines) or Chapter 4B Section 3 (diesel engines)

7 Remove the earth cable **(see illustration)** and then remove the starter motor as described in Chapter 5A Section 8. Not that some versions of the transmission have a bell housing (to engine) bolt fitted inside the starter motor housing.

8 Disconnect the selector cable from the selector shaft lever on the top of the transmission, as described in Section 4. Position the cable to one side.

9 Disconnect the wiring plug connectors from the front of the transmission. Slide the locking lever upwards to disconnect **(see illustration)**. Detach the wiring loom and remove the mounting brackets from the transmission.

10 Remove the upper engine to transmission mounting bolts.

11 Remove the radiator cooling fan assembly as described in Chapter 3 Section 5.

12 Undo the bolts and slide rearwards the exhaust pipe connecting piece between the front and rear sections of the exhaust system. Also undo the retaining bolts and remove the exhaust front mounting bracket **(see illustration). Note:** *On some models the exhaust must be detached at the turbocharger and removed.*

13 Where fitted, disconnect the wiring plug from the engine oil level/temperature sensor on the sump **(see illustration)**. This will prevent the sensor from damage when the engine moves forward.

14 With reference to Chapter 8 Section 2, unscrew and remove the bolts securing the driveshafts to the transmission output flanges. Tie the right-hand driveshaft to one side, and then tie the left-hand driveshaft to the suspension strut, so that the shaft is as high as possible **(see illustration)**. Alternatively, completely remove the driveshaft.

15 Remove the front subframe, complete with the track control arms as described in Chapter 10 Section 18. The steering rack can either be removed with the subframe or detatched from the subframe and left in place.

16 Support the engine with a hoist or (where available) with the factory support bar located on the suspension strut towers and inner wings. Depending on the engine, temporarily remove components as necessary to attach the hoist.

17 Position a trolley jack underneath the transmission, and raise it to just take the weight of the unit.

18 Undo and remove the bolts securing the left-hand transmission mounting. Lower the engine and transmission slightly and remove the bracket from the transmission **(see illustrations)**.

19 Where fitted, undo the retaining bolt and remove the small cover plate located above the right-hand driveshaft flange.

20 Lower the engine/transmission until there

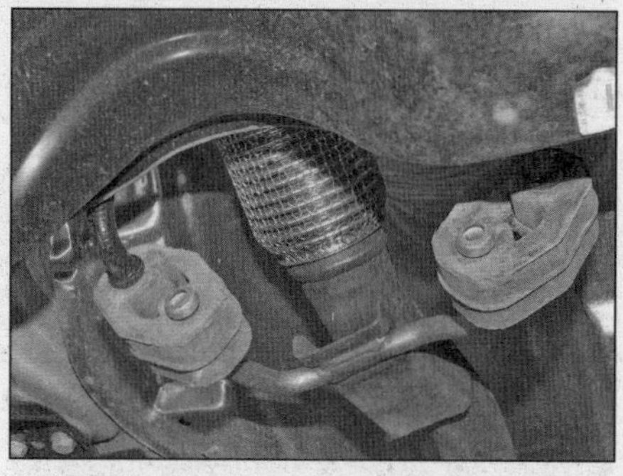

2.12 Release the exhaust system from the mountings

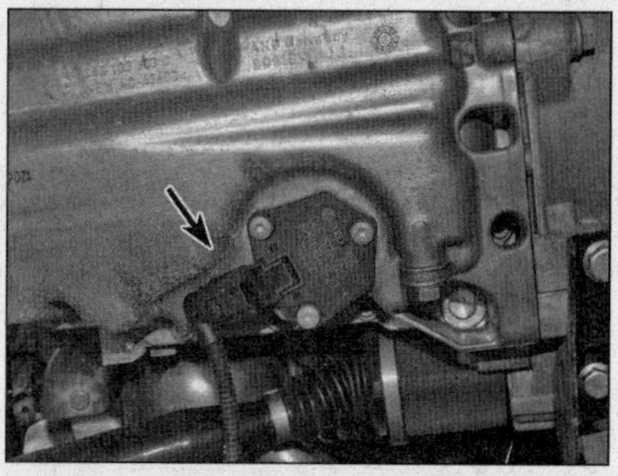

2.13 Disconnect the oil level/temperature sensor wiring connector

2.14 Fasten the driveshaft to one side

2.18a Remove the transmission mounting...

2.18b ...and then remove the bracket from the transmission

is sufficient clearance between the upper edge of the transmission and the left-hand chassis member.

21 Unscrew and remove the lower bolts securing the transmission to the engine, noting the bolt locations, as they are of different sizes and lengths.

22 Check that all the fixings and attachments are clear of the transmission. Enlist the aid of an assistant to help in guiding and supporting the transmission during its removal.

23 The transmission is located on engine alignment dowels, and if stuck on them, it may be necessary to carefully tap and prise the transmission free of the dowels to allow separation. Once the transmission is disconnected from the location dowels, swivel the unit out and lower it out of the vehicle. Note that the transmission must be turned to allow the driveshaft flange to clear the engine block. This is a difficult manoeuvre as the transmission must be supported at all times and not allowed to hang on the transmission input shaft.

> **Warning: *Support the transmission to ensure that it remains steady on the jack head.***

24 When the transmission is clear of the locating dowels and clutch components, lower the transmission to the ground and withdraw from under the car. Make sure that the transmission does not fall and lose any transmission oil. Also make sure that the clutch assembly comes away with the transmission, and stays inside the bell-housing.

Refitting

25 Refitting the transmission is essentially a reversal of the removal procedure, but note the following points:

a) *Always replace the spigot bearing as described in Section 7.*
b) *When reconnecting the transmission to the engine, ensure that the location dowels are in position, and that the transmission is correctly aligned with them before pushing it fully into engagement with the engine.*
c) *Tighten all retaining bolts to their specified torque wrench settings.*
d) *Be sure to guide the selector cable into the support bracket as the transmission is refitted – renew the retaining clips.*
e) *Adjust the selector cable, as described in Section 4.*
f) *Refer to Chapter 8 Section 2, and then tighten the driveshaft bolts to the specified torque.*
g) *On completion, check the coolant level.*
h) *If a new transmission unit has been fitted, it will be necessary to have the transmission ECM 'matched' to the engine management ECM electronically, to ensure correct operation – seek the advice of your VAG/Seat dealer or suitably equipped specialist.*
i) *Refill the transmission with the correct grade and quantity of oil, as described in Section 6.*

3 Transmission overhaul – general information

1 In the event of a fault occurring, it will be necessary to establish whether the fault is electrical, mechanical or hydraulic in nature, before repair work can be contemplated. Diagnosis requires detailed knowledge of the transmission's operation and construction, as well as access to specialised test equipment, and so is deemed to be beyond the scope of this manual. It is therefore essential that problems with the automatic transmission be referred to a Seat dealer or specialist for assessment.

2 Note that a faulty transmission should not be removed before the vehicle has been assessed by a dealer or specialist, as fault diagnosis is best carried out with the transmission still in the vehicle.

4 Selector lever housing and cable – removal, refitting and adjustment

Note: *The selector lever housing and cable should not be separated, remove the housing and cable as a complete unit.*

Removal

1 Move the selector lever to the P position, and remove the battery and battery tray as described in Chapter 5A Section 3.

2 Remove the air filter housing as described in Chapter 4A Section 3 (petrol engine) or Chapter 4B Section 3 (diesel engine).

3 Working inside the vehicle, remove the centre console and gear selector knob, as described in Chapter 11 Section 27.

4 Working inside the engine compartment, use a pair of long-nose pliers to release the cable end fitting from the ball head on the selector lever **(see illustration)**.

5 Prise out the clip securing the outer cable and withdraw the cable from the support bracket on the transmission **(see illustration)**. Discard the retaining clip – as a new one must be fitted.

6 Raise the front of the vehicle and support it securely on axle stands (see *Jacking and vehicle support*).

7 Remove the centre tunnel front heat shield from the underside of the vehicle to gain access to the base of the selector lever housing and cable. It may be necessary to separate the exhaust downpipe from the intermediate pipe.

8 Working inside the vehicle, undo the retaining nuts **(see illustrations)**, then remove the bracket and lower the gear selector housing downwards. Withdraw it complete with selector cable out from under the vehicle. It may be useful having the aid of an assistant at this point, to be under the vehicle when lowering the selector housing.

Refitting

9 Refitting is the reversal of the removal procedure, noting the following points:

a) *DO NOT grease the cable end fittings.*

4.4 Prise the inner cable from the ball joint

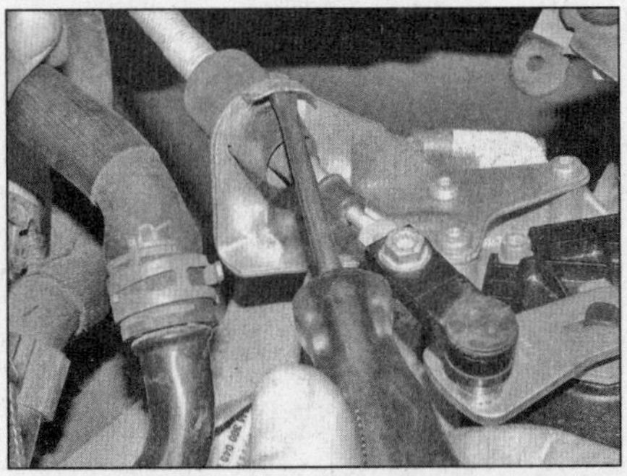

4.5 Release the outer cable securing clip

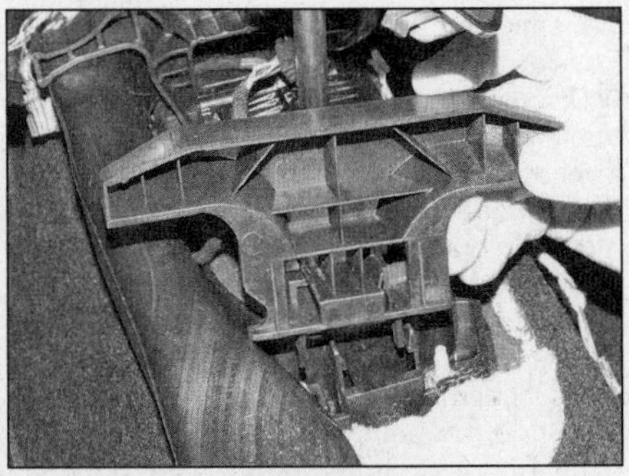

4.8a Remove the rear bracket (where fitted)...

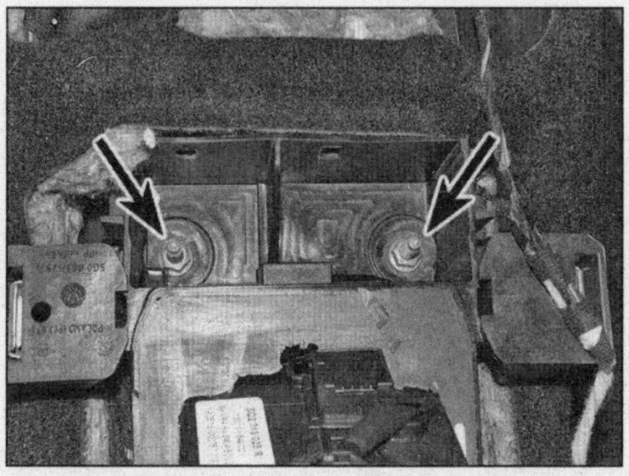

4.8b ...and then remove the front...

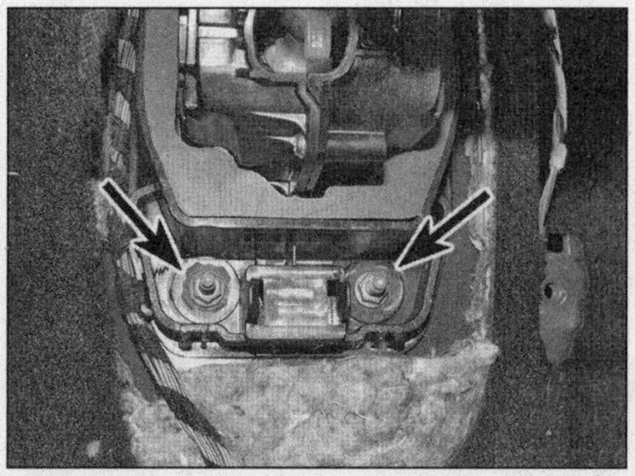

4.8c ...and rear mounting nuts

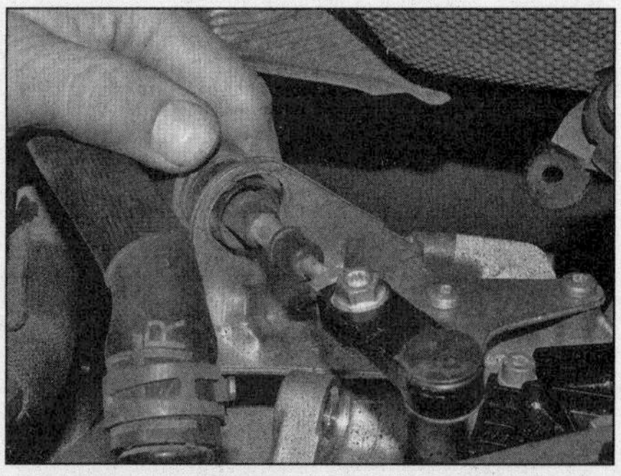

4.13a Secure the outer cable in the bracket ...

b) Ensure that the cable is correctly routed and secured, as noted on removal.
c) Take care not to bend or kink the cable.
d) Carry out the cable adjustment procedure described below before reconnecting the cable at the transmission end.
e) When refitting the outer cable to the support bracket, use new clips.

Adjustment

10 Inside the car, move the selector lever to the P position.
11 If not already done, disconnect the cable from the selector lever on the transmission.
12 Move the selector lever inside the vehicle from 'P' to 'S' and back, repeatedly, to check that everything moves easily. Seat recommend that you **do not** grease the cable.
13 Reconnect the cable to the lever at the transmission, and then slacken the cable adjusting bolt **(see illustrations)**.
14 Check that both the selector lever inside the car and the lever on the transmission are in their P positions. Gently rock the levers backwards and forwards to make sure the cable is settled. Do not move either lever out of the P position.
15 The transmission lever is in the P position when it is pushed back towards the selector cable mounting bracket **(see illustration)**.
16 When in position, tighten the cable adjusting bolt.
17 Verify the operation of the selector lever by shifting through all gear positions and checking that every gear can be selected smoothly and without delay.

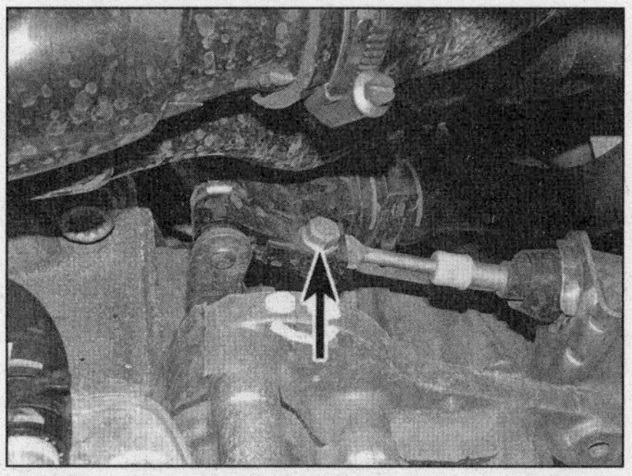

4.13b ...and slacken the cable adjustment screw

4.15 Push the lever in the direction show

5 Emergency release of selector lever

1 If the vehicles battery is disconnected or discharged, it is possible to release the selector lever from its locked position.
2 Carefully prise up the selector lever gaiter surround trim from the console and move it to one side **(see illustration)**.
3 Press the yellow plastic wedge downwards **(see illustration)**. It should now be possible to move the selector lever to the desired position.
4 Note that some very early models (up to 02/2009) do not have the integrated locking peg fitted. On these transmissions an electromagnet, magnetic switch is fitted and the switch must be pushed into position with a screwdriver **(see illustration)**.

6 Transmission oil renewal

Note: *The transmission oil is filled for life. There is no requirement to change the oil.*
1 Take the vehicle on a short journey to warm the transmission oil, and then park the car on

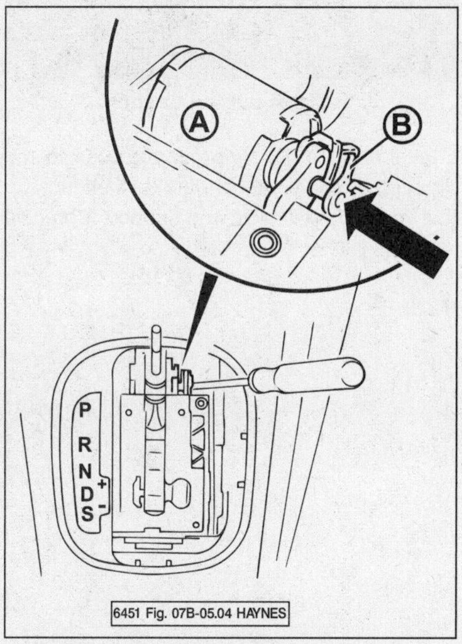

5.4 Push in the lever (B) on the switch (A). Hold in position and move the gear selector lever from the 'P' position

5.2 Prise up the selector lever gaiter surround trim

5.3 Press down the yellow plastic peg

6.2 Transmission oil drain plug

6.7 Breather cap on selector cover

7.2 Check the depth of the bearing before removal

7.3a Select the correct puller,...

7.3b ...pull out the bearing...

7.3c ... and remove it

a level surface. For improved access to the drain plug, apply the handbrake, then jack up the front of the vehicle and support it on axle stands (see *Jacking and vehicle support*), but note that the rear of the vehicle should also be raised to ensure all oil is drained.

2 Undo the retaining screws and remove the engine undertray. Wipe clean the area around the transmission drain plug, which is situated on the lower rear of the transmission **(see illustration)**.

3 Place a container under the transmission casing, then unscrew the drain plug from the base of the differential housing, and allow the oil to drain.

4 Remove the battery and battery tray as described in Chapter 5A Section 3.

5 Remove the air filter housing as described in Chapter 4A Section 3 (petrol engine) or Chapter 4B Section 3 (diesel engine).

6 When the oil has finished draining, clean the surrounding area, refit the drain plug and tighten it to the specified torque.

7 Unclip the breather cap from the selector cover plate on the top of the transmission casing **(see illustration)**.

8 Using a length of hose, and funnel, add 1.7 litres of new oil to the transmission. Only use the correct Seat oil, for the 7-speed transmissions.

9 Refit the breather cap, making sure that it is secure. Renew if damaged.

10 The remainder of refitting is a reversal of removal.

7 Spigot bearing – renewal

1 The spigot bearing must always be replaced on DSG transmissions.

2 As a reference measure the depth of the installed bearing before removal **(see illustration)**. The factory setting is 2.0 mm inside the end of the crankshaft.

3 An internal bearing puller and slide hammer are required to remove the bearing. Select a suitable expanding mandrel and pull out the bearing **(see illustrations)**.

4 Fit the new bearing by driving in into the crankshaft using a socket that bears only on the outer edge of the bearing. Check that the bearing is set to the correct depth and refit the transmission as described in Section 2.

Chapter 8
Driveshafts

Contents

Degrees of difficulty

Easy, suitable for novice with little experience	Fairly easy, suitable for beginner with some experience	Fairly difficult, suitable for competent DIY mechanic	Difficult, suitable for experienced DIY mechanic	Very difficult, suitable for expert DIY or professional

Specifications

General

Driveshaft type	Steel shafts with outer constant velocity joints and inner tripod or constant velocity joints (according to type).
Type code differences:	
VL 90, VL 100 or VL 107	CV joints each end, inner joint diameter 90mm, 100mm or 107 mm bolted to transmission drive flanges on each side
VL 107	CV joints at each end, with push fit inner CV joint
TS1800	CV outer joint, tripod inner joint push fit to transmission

Lubrication

Overhaul and repair	Use only special grease supplied in sachets with gaiter/overhaul kits
Joint grease type	Refer to a Seat dealer

Torque wrench settings

Torque wrench settings	Nm	lbf ft
Driveshaft-to-transmission flange bolts:		
Stage 1	10	7
Stage 2:		
M8 x 48 bolts* – (VL90 & VL100 type joint)	40	30
M10 x 52 bolts* – (VL107 type joint)	70	52
M10 x 23 bolts – (AAR 2000/108 type joint)	70	52
Driveshaft/Hub nut (12 point – 36mm): *		
Stage 1	50	37
Stage 2	Angle-tighten a further 45°	
Lower arm-to-balljoint nuts*	100	74
Lower rear mounting-to-transmission bolts: *		
Stage 1	50	37
Stage 2	Angle-tighten a further 90°	
Wheel bolts	120	89

**Use new bolts/nuts*

1 General Information

1 Drive is transmitted from the differential to the front wheels by means of two steel driveshafts of either solid or hollow construction (depending on model, and which side of the vehicle). Both driveshafts are splined at their outer ends, to accept the wheel hubs, and are secured to the hub by a large bolt/nut. The inner end of each driveshaft is either bolted to a transmission drive flange or splined directly onto the differential splined shaft.

2 The outer ends of each driveshaft are fitted with ball-bearing type constant velocity (CV) joints, to ensure the smooth and efficient transmission of drive at all the angles possible, as the roadwheels move up-and-down with the suspension, and as they turn from side to side under steering.

3 The inner ends of each driveshaft (except for the TS1800 type joint) are fitted with ball and cage type constant velocity (CV) joint. The TS1800 driveshaft has a triple roller type (tripod) joint fitted to the inner end of the driveshaft.

4 Hytrel (thermoplastic elastomer) gaiters are fitted over the CV joints with steel clips. These gaiters combine the flexibility of rubber with the strength and durability of thermoplastics. The gaiters contain the grease that lubricates the joints, and also protect the joints from the entry of dirt and debris.

2 Driveshafts – removal and refitting

Removal

1 Remove the wheel trim/centre cap (as applicable) then apply the handbrake, and partially unscrew the relevant hub bolt/nut with the vehicle resting on its wheels, by a maximum of 90° – note that it is very tight, and an extension bar will probably be required to aid unscrewing. Also slacken the road wheel securing bolts by half a turn. **Note:** *Do not loosen the bolt more than 90° with the vehicle standing on the ground, as the wheel bearings may be damaged.*

2.3 Remove the heat shield

2.4a Remove the driveshaft/hub nut

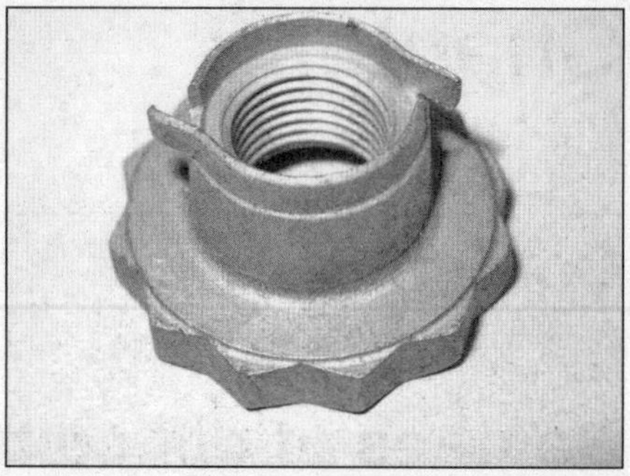

2.4b A new nut will be required for refitting

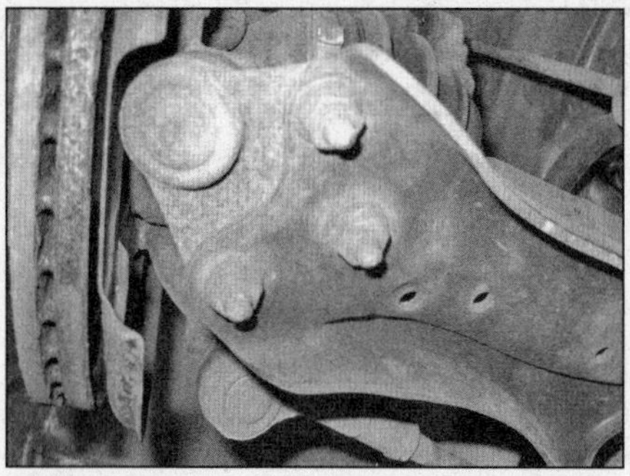

2.5 Undo the lower ball joint retaining nuts

2.6 Slide the driveshaft out from the hub assembly

2.7 Unbolt the pendulum mount

2 Jack up the front of the vehicle and support it on axle stands (see *Jacking and vehicle support*). Remove the appropriate front roadwheel.

3 Remove the retaining screws and/or clips, and remove the undershields from beneath the engine/transmission unit to gain access to the driveshafts. Where necessary, also unbolt the heat shield from the rear of the cylinder block to improve access to the right-hand driveshaft inner joint **(see illustration)**.

4 Unscrew and remove the driveshaft/hub nut **(see illustrations)**. **Note:** *Discard the nut and obtain a new one.*

5 Unscrew the three nuts securing the front suspension lower arm balljoint to the lower arm **(see illustration)**. Discard the nuts, as new ones must be used on refitting.

6 Lever the lower arm downwards to release it from the balljoint studs, then pull the hub carrier outwards, and at the same time withdraw the driveshaft outer constant velocity joint from the hub **(see illustration)**. If the joint splines are a tight fit in the hub, tap the joint out of the hub using a soft-faced mallet and drift. If this fails to free the driveshaft from the hub, the joint will have to be pressed out using a suitable tool bolted to the hub.

7 On some models, in order to gain the necessary clearance required to withdraw the left-hand driveshaft, it may be necessary to unbolt the rear engine transmission mounting **(see illustration)**, and move the engine slightly. Taking care not to damage the exhaust flexible front pipe. **Note:** ***Do Not*** *undo the centre bolt that goes through the rubber mounting, as this is set in position.*

8 Proceed as follows according to driveshaft type.

Caution: Support the driveshaft by suspending it with wire or string – do not allow it to hang under its own weight, or the joint may be damaged.

Inner joint with drive flange – VL90, VL100 and VL107

9 Mark the inner joint in relation to the drive flange for refitting. Using a multi-splined tool, unscrew and remove the six bolts securing the inner driveshaft joint to the transmission flange and, recover the retaining plates from underneath the bolts **(see illustrations)**.

10 On push fit VL107 drive shafts drain the transmission as described in Chapter and then lever the shaft from the differential housing with a pry bar. To avoid damage to the transmission use a block of wood as the fulcrum on the transmission casing **(see illustration)**.

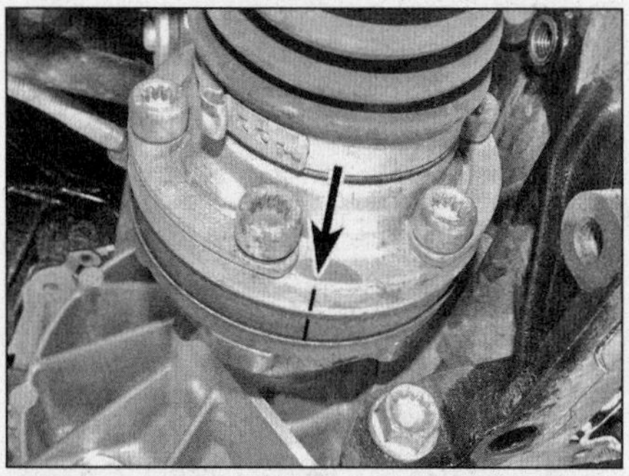

2.9a Make alignment marks...

2.9b ...and remove the drive flange bolts and plates

2.10 Lever out the driveshaft at the point shown

Inner joint triple roller (tripod) located in joint body – TS1800

11 Mark the inner joint body and driveshaft in relation to each other, as the tripod joint will need to be refitted in the joint body in the same position. Loosen the larger retaining clip, ease off the rubber gaiter, and pull the triple roller out of the joint body. It is also possible to remove the shaft as a complete assembly, or remove the inner tripod housing after removing the shaft. Use the method described in the previous paragraph.

All types

12 Manoeuvre the driveshaft out from underneath the vehicle and (where fitted) recover the gasket from the end of the inner constant velocity joint. **Note:** *Discard the gasket and obtain a new one.*

Caution: Do not allow the vehicle to rest on its wheels with one or both driveshaft(s) removed, as damage to the wheel bearings may result.

13 If moving the vehicle is unavoidable, temporarily insert the outer end of the driveshaft(s) in the hub(s), and tighten the driveshaft retaining bolt(s); in this case, the inner end(s) of the driveshaft(s) must be supported, for example by suspending with string from the vehicle underbody.

Refitting

14 Where applicable, check the condition of the circlip on the inner end of the driveshaft, and if necessary, renew it.

15 As applicable, clean the splines on each end of the driveshaft and in the hub and apply a little oil, and where applicable wipe clean the oil seal in the transmission casing. Check the oil seal and if necessary renew it as described in Chapter 7A Section 6. Smear a little oil on the lips of the oil seal before fitting the driveshaft.

Inner joint with bolted drive flange – VL90, VL100 and VL107

16 Ensure that the transmission flange and inner joint mating surfaces are clean and dry. Where necessary, fit a new gasket to the joint by peeling off its backing foil and sticking it in position **(see illustration)**.

17 Manoeuvre the driveshaft into position, aligning the previously made marks, and then align the inner joint holes with those on the transmission flange. Refit the new retaining bolts and locking plates, and then tighten the retaining bolts to the specified torque.

Inner joint triple roller (tripod) located in joint body – TS1800

18 Fill the inner joint with the specified quantity of grease, and then locate the driveshaft tripod into the joint body, aligning the previously made marks. Ease the gaiter onto the joint body, and secure the gaiter with a new retaining clip.

All types

19 With the lower arm levered downwards, engage the outer joint with the hub. Fit the new hub nut and use it to draw the joint fully into position.

20 Align the balljoint studs with the holes in the lower arm, then release the arm and fit the three new nuts. Tighten the nuts to the specified torque.

21 Where applicable, refit the lower rear mounting-to-transmission bolts, and then tighten the new bolts to the specified torque.

22 Tighten the driveshaft/hub nut to the Stage 1 torque setting. **Note:** *The nut must be tightened with the wheel clear of the ground.*

2.16 Locate a new gasket on the inner joint

23 Refit the roadwheel and lower the vehicle to the ground, then angle-tighten the driveshaft bolt through the Stage 2 angle (see Specifications).

24 Once the driveshaft bolt is correctly tightened, tighten the wheel bolts to the specified torque and refit the wheel trim/centre cap.

3 Driveshaft rubber gaiters – renewal

1 Remove the driveshaft from the car, as described in Section 2. Continue as described under the relevant sub-heading. Driveshafts with a tripod type inner joint can be identified by the shape of the inner CV joint; the driveshaft retaining bolt holes are in extensions from the joint, giving it a six-pointed star-shaped exterior, in contrast to the smooth, circular shape of the ball-and-cage joint **(see illustrations)**.

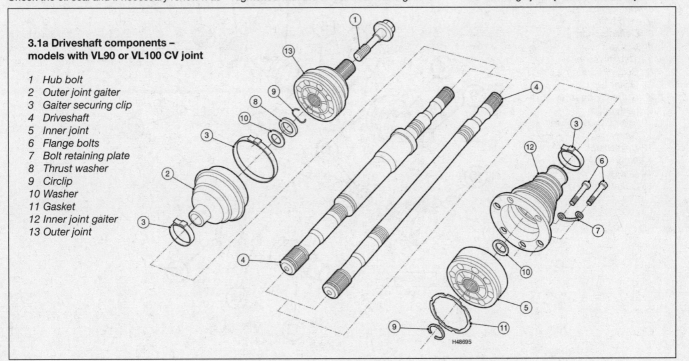

3.1a Driveshaft components – models with VL90 or VL100 CV joint

1 Hub bolt
2 Outer joint gaiter
3 Gaiter securing clip
4 Driveshaft
5 Inner joint
6 Flange bolts
7 Bolt retaining plate
8 Thrust washer
9 Circlip
10 Washer
11 Gasket
12 Inner joint gaiter
13 Outer joint

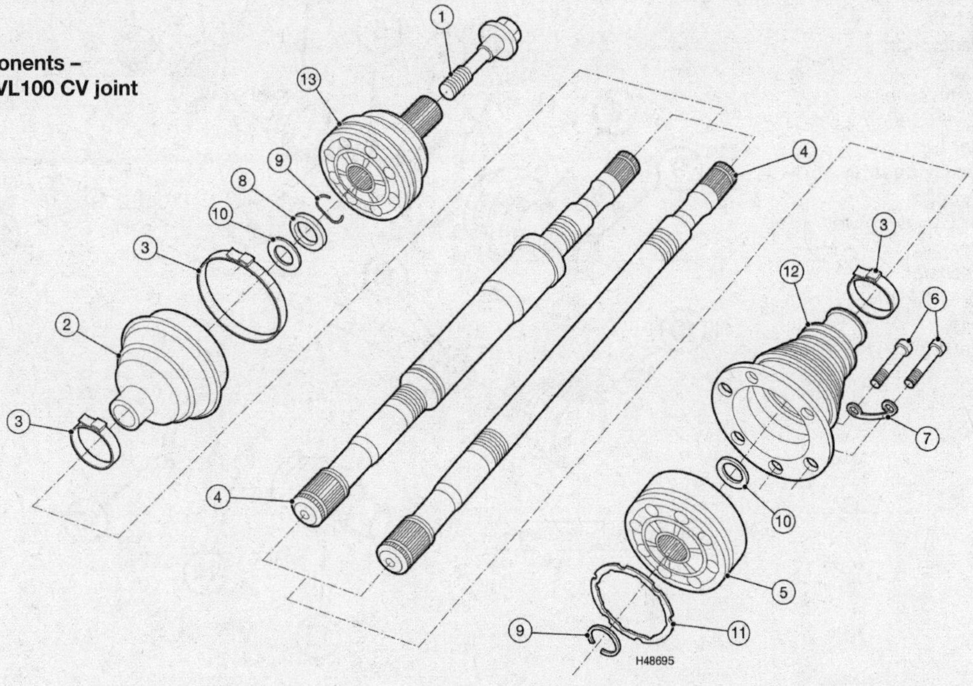

3.1b Driveshaft joint components – models with VL107 CV joint

1 Outer joint
2 Hub bolt
3 Circlip
4 Thrust washer
5 Washer
6 Gaiter securing clip
7 Outer joint gaiter
8 Driveshaft
9 Inner joint gaiter
10 Flange bolts
11 Bolt retaining plate
12 Metal cover
13 Inner 'bolt-on' joint
14 Gasket
15 Circlip
16 Metal end cover

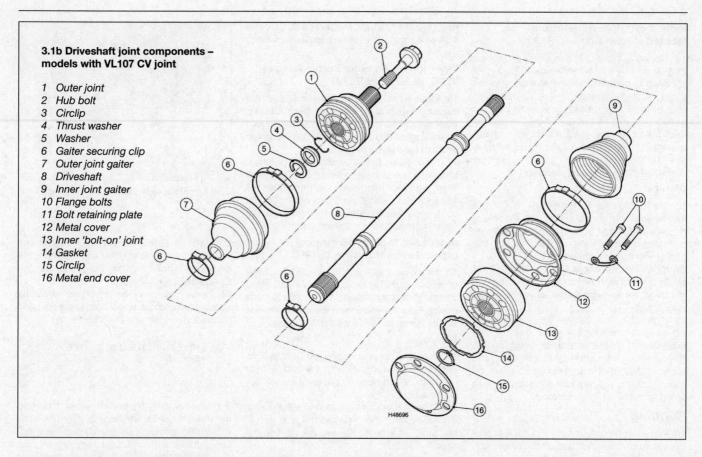

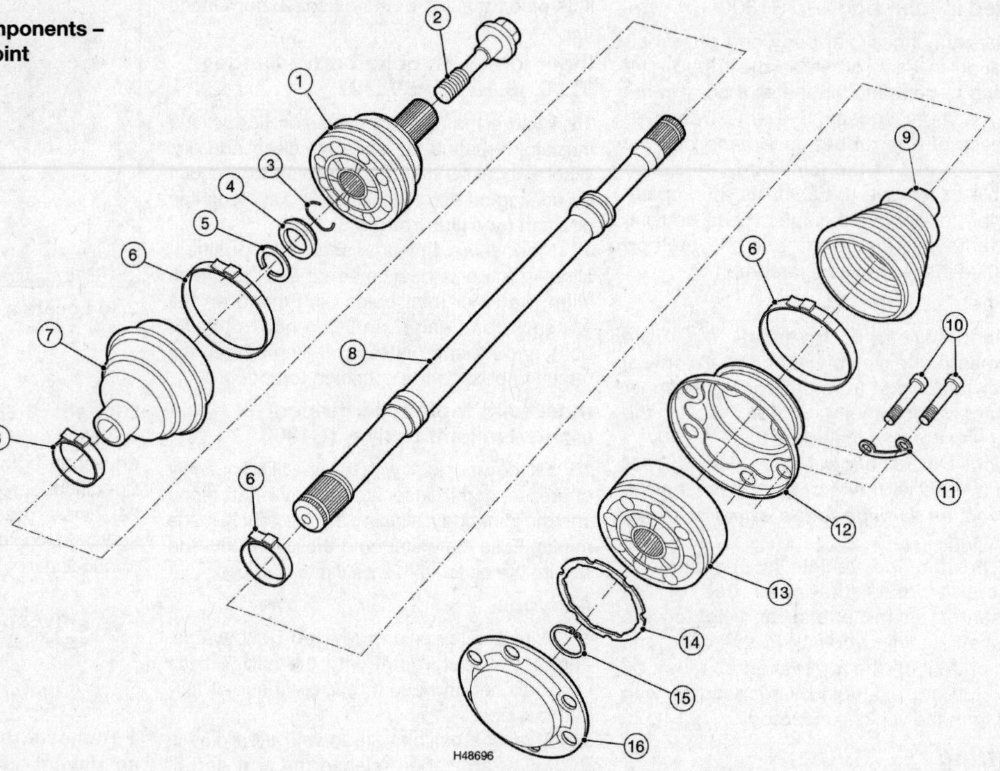

3.1c Driveshaft joint components – models with VL 107 push fit CV joint

1 Outer joint
2 Hub bolt
3 Deflector ring
4 Circlip
5 Thrust washer
6 Belleville spring
7 Gaiter clip
8 Outer CV boot
9 Gaiter clip
10 Inner CV joint gaiter
11 Gaiter clip
12 Driveshaft
13 Inner CV Joint
14 Circlip
15 Gaiter clip

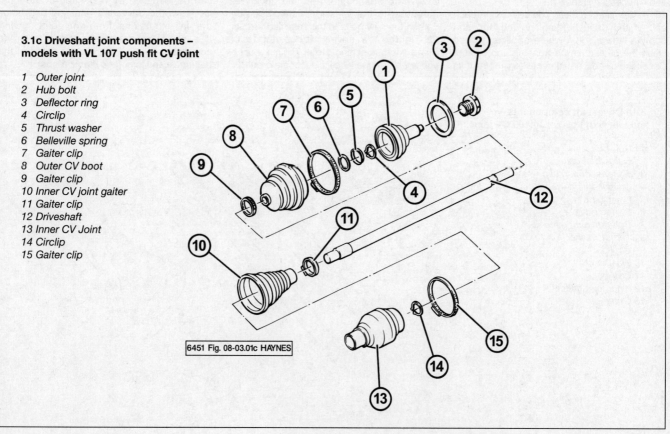

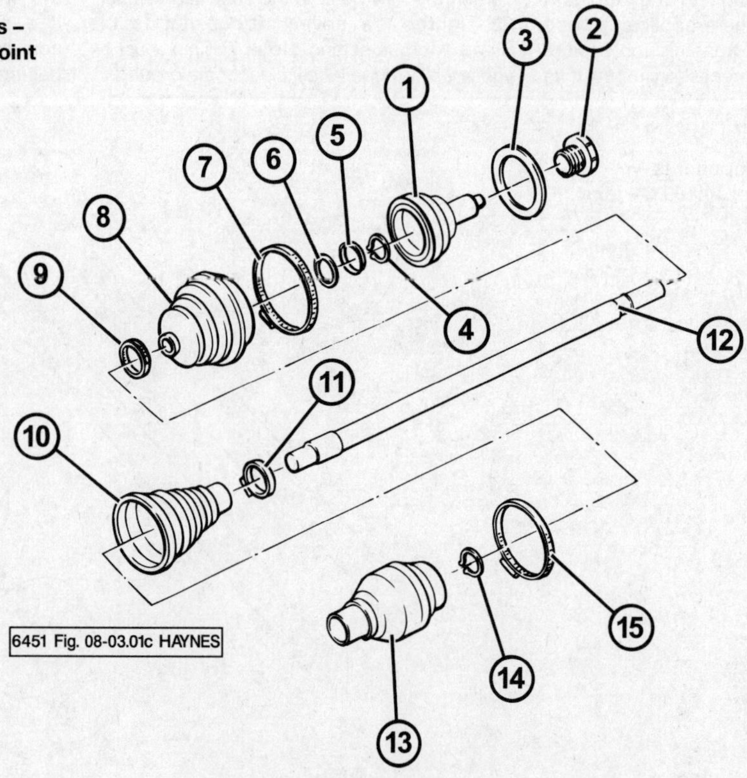

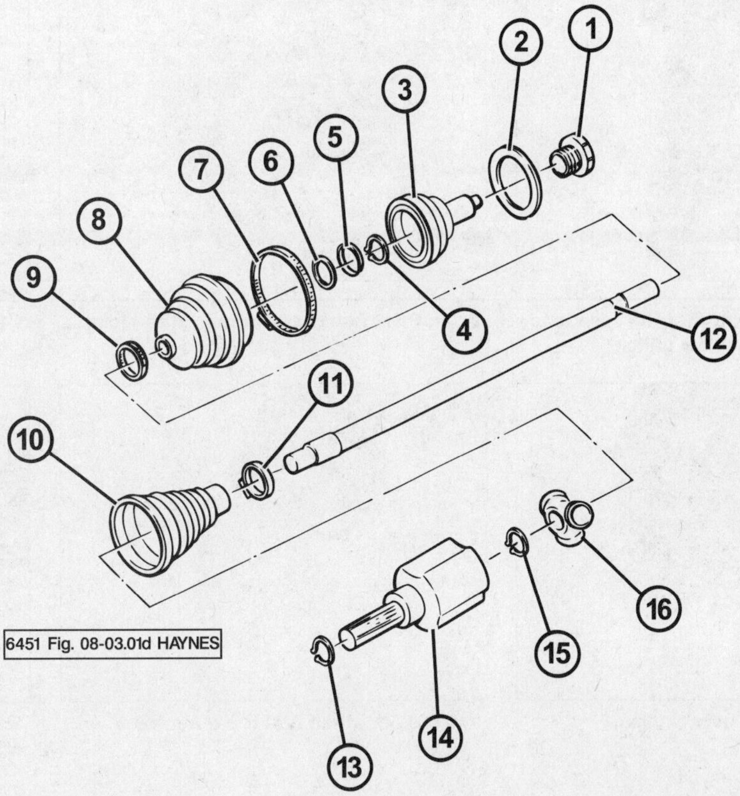

3.1d Driveshaft joint components – models with TS1800 CV joint

1 Hub bolt
2 Deflector ring
3 Outer CV joint
4 Circlip
5 Thrust washer
6 Belleville washer
7 Gaiter clip
8 CV gaiter
9 Gaiter clip
10 Inner CV gaiter
11 Gaiter circlip
12 Driveshaft
13 Circlip
14 Inner CV joint body
15 Circlip
16 Tripod roller joint
17 Gaiter clip

Outer CV joint gaiter – all types of driveshafts

2 Secure the driveshaft in a vice equipped with soft jaws, and release the two outer joint gaiter retaining clips **(see illustration)**. If necessary, the retaining clips can be cut to release them.

3 Slide the rubber gaiter down the shaft to expose the constant velocity joint, and scoop out excess grease **(see illustration)**.

4 Using a soft-faced mallet, tap the joint off the end of the driveshaft **(see illustration)**.

5 Remove the circlip from the driveshaft groove, and slide off the thrustwasher and dished washer, noting which way around it is fitted **(see illustration)**.

6 Slide the rubber gaiter off the driveshaft and discard it **(see illustration)**.

3.2 Release the outer joint gaiter clips...

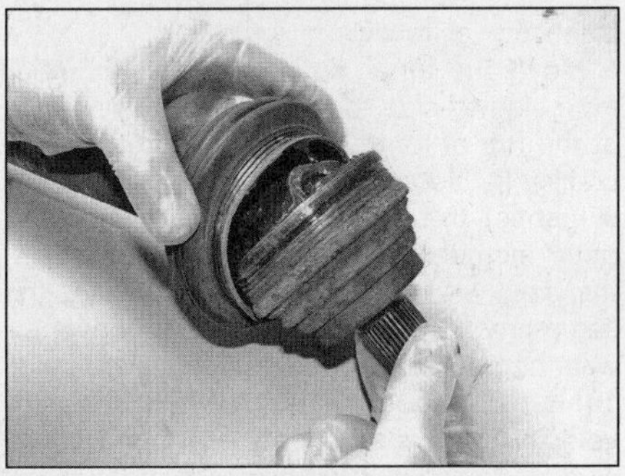

3.3 ...and slide the gaiter away from the joint

3.4 Use a mallet to drive the outer joint from the driveshaft

3.5 Removing the circlip, thrustwasher and dished washer

3.6 Removing the outer gaiter

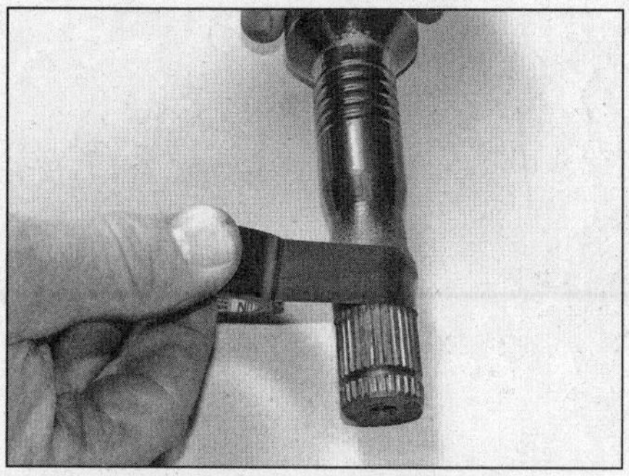

3.11 Temporarily tape over the splines to protect the new gaiter

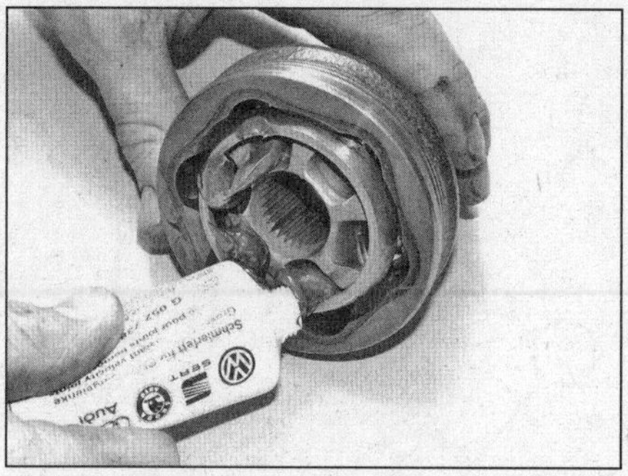

3.14a Pack half of the grease in the joint...

3.14b ...and the remaining half in the gaiter

3.15a Fit a new circlip...

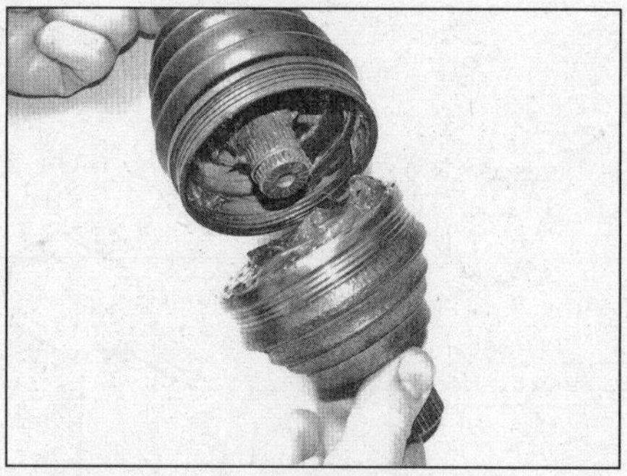

3.15b ...then refit the outer joint

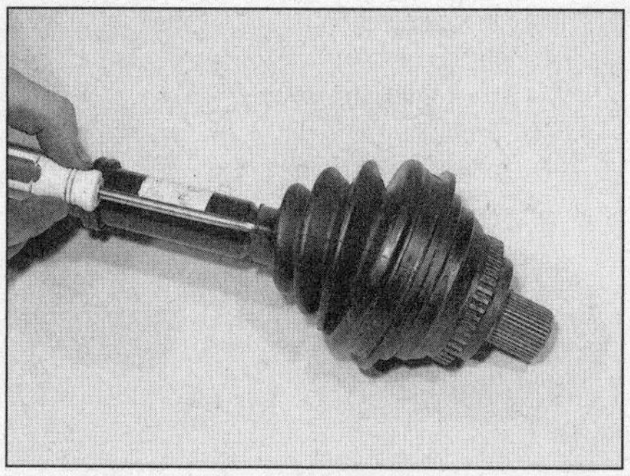

3.16 Seat the gaiter on the outer joint and driveshaft, then lift its inner lip to equalise the air pressure

7 Thoroughly clean the constant velocity joint(s) using paraffin, or a suitable solvent, and dry thoroughly. Carry out a visual inspection as follows.

8 Move the inner splined driving member from side-to-side to expose each ball in turn at the top of its track. Examine the balls for cracks, flat spots or signs of surface pitting.

9 Inspect the ball tracks on the inner and outer members. If the tracks have widened, the balls will no longer be a tight fit. At the same time, check the ball cage windows for wear or cracking between the windows.

10 If on inspection any of the constant velocity joint components are found to be worn or damaged, it will be necessary to renew the complete joint assembly. If the joint is in satisfactory condition, obtain a new gaiter and retaining clips, a constant velocity joint circlip and the correct type of grease. Grease is often supplied with the joint repair kit – if not, use good-quality molybdenum disulphide grease.

11 Tape over the splines on the end of the driveshaft, to protect the new gaiter as it is slid into place **(see illustration)**.

12 Slide the new gaiter onto the end of the driveshaft, then remove the protective tape from the driveshaft splines.

13 Slide on the dished washer, making sure its convex side is innermost, followed by the thrustwasher.

14 Pack the joint with half the quantity of the specified type of grease. Work the grease well into the bearing tracks whilst twisting the joint, and fill the rubber gaiter with the remaining half **(see illustrations)**.

15 Fit a new circlip to the driveshaft, then tap the joint onto the driveshaft until the circlip engages in its groove **(see illustrations)**. Make sure that the joint is securely retained by the circlip.

16 Ease the gaiter over the joint, and ensure that the gaiter lips are correctly located on both the driveshaft and constant velocity joint. Lift the outer sealing lip of the gaiter to equalise air pressure within the gaiter **(see illustration)**.

17 Fit the large metal retaining clip to the gaiter. Pull the clip as tight as possible, and locate the hooks on the clip in their slots. Remove any slack in the gaiter retaining clip by carefully compressing the raised section of the clip. In the absence of the special tool, a pair of side-cutters may be used, taking care not to cut the clip **(see illustrations)**. Secure the small retaining clip using the same procedure.

18 Check the constant velocity joint moves freely in all directions, then refit the driveshaft to the vehicle, as described in Section 2.

3.17a Fit the large metal retaining clip...

3.17b ...and use a suitable tool to tighten it

Inner gaiter with bolted drive flange – VL90, VL100 and VL107

19 Secure the driveshaft in a vice equipped with soft jaws, then release the gaiter small securing clip, securing the gaiter to the driveshaft **(see illustration)**.

20 Using a hammer and a small drift, carefully drive the gaiter metal ring from the joint outer member **(see illustration)**.

21 Slide the gaiter down the driveshaft to expose the constant velocity joint, and scoop out excess grease.

3.19 Release the gaiter small securing clip...

3.20 ...drive the metal ring from the joint outer member

3.22 Remove the circlip...

3.23a ...followed by the joint...

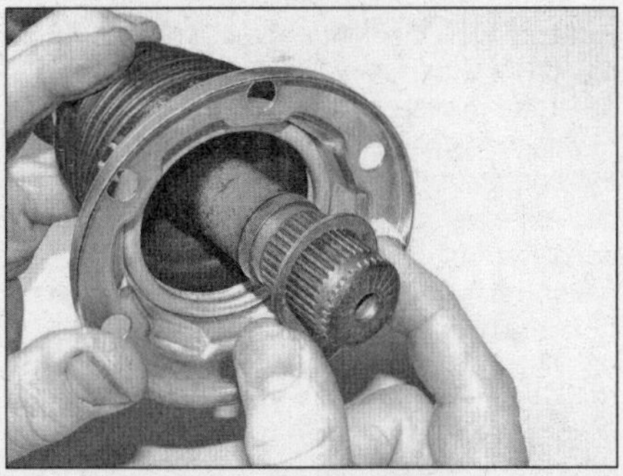
3.23b ...dished washer...

3.24 ...and gaiter

22 Remove the circlip from the end of the driveshaft using circlip pliers **(see illustration)**.

23 Press or drive the driveshaft from the joint, taking great care not to damage the joint. Recover the dished washer fitted between the constant velocity joint and the gaiter **(see illustrations)**.

24 Slide the gaiter from the end of the driveshaft **(see illustration)**.

25 Proceed as described previously in paragraphs 7 to 12 **(see illustrations)**.

26 Slide the dished washer onto the driveshaft, making sure its convex side is innermost.

27 Fit the joint to the end of the driveshaft, noting that the chamfered edge of the internal splines on the joint should face towards the driveshaft. Drive or press the joint into position until it contacts the shoulder on the driveshaft.

28 Fit a new circlip to retain the joint on the end of the driveshaft.

29 Pack the joint with the half the recommended quantity of grease (see Specifications), and then pack the gaiter with the remaining half **(see illustrations)**.

30 Slide the gaiter up the driveshaft, and press or drive the gaiter metal ring onto the joint outer member. To ensure the bolt holes are correctly positioned, temporarily fit a couple of flange bolts **(see illustrations)**.

31 If the left-hand driveshaft is being worked

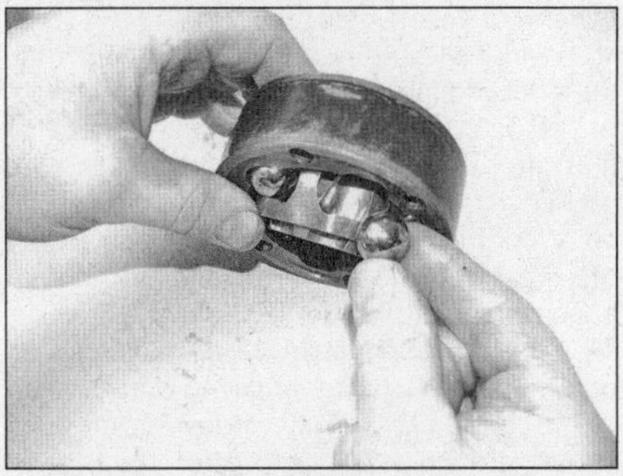
3.25a Tilt the splined hub and cage to remove the ball-bearings...

3.25b ...then separate the hub from the cage

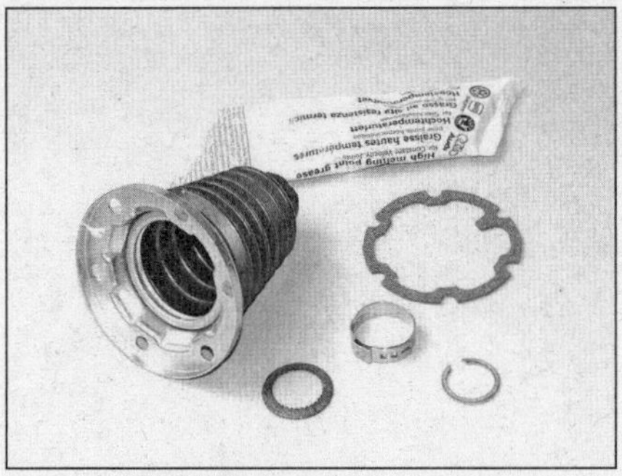
3.25c Inner CV joint gaiter repair kit

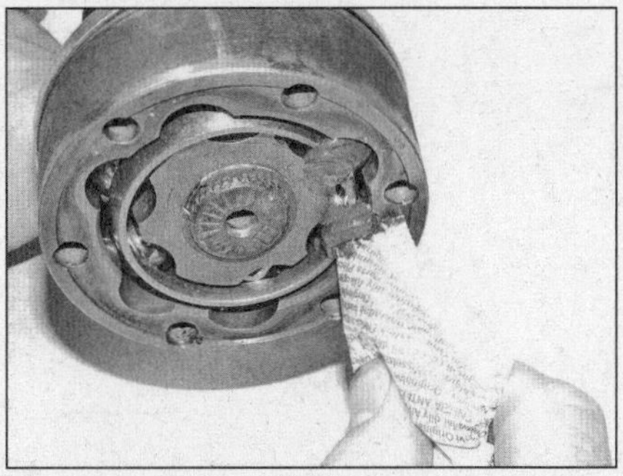
3.29a Pack the inner joint with half of the grease...

3.29b ...then pack the gaiter with the remaining half

3.30a Temporarily fit the flange bolts to ensure the bolt holes are correctly aligned...

3.30b ...then drive the metal ring onto the joint outer member

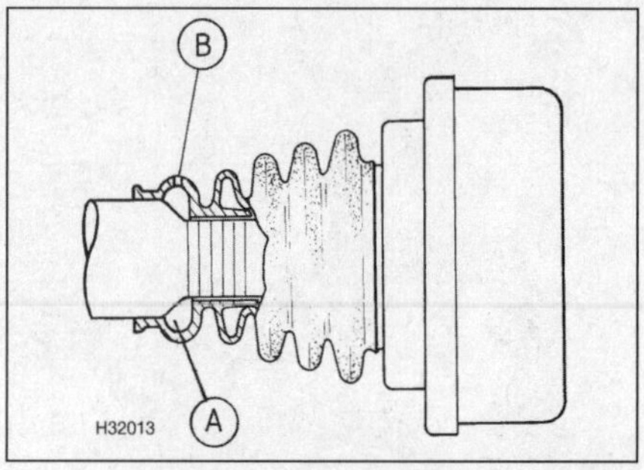

3.32 Installation position of inner joint gaiter on right-hand driveshaft

A Vent chamber in gaiter
B Vent hole

on, slide the outboard end of the gaiter into position using the mark made previously (see paragraph 29), then secure the outer gaiter securing clip in position as described in paragraph 17.

32 If the right-hand driveshaft is being worked on, slide the outboard end of the gaiter into position on the driveshaft, then secure the outer gaiter securing clip in position as described in paragraph 17 **(see illustration)**.

33 Check the driveshaft joint moves freely in all directions, then refit the driveshaft to the vehicle, as described in Section 2.

Inner gaiter with push fit joint – VL 107

34 The inner CV gaiter is removed and refitted exactly the same as the outer CV gaiter. See the above description for the outer gaiter removal procedure.

Inner gaiter with triple roller (tripod) joint – TS1800

35 Secure the driveshaft in a vice equipped with soft jaws, and clean out the old grease from around the triple roller joint and inside the gaiter.

36 Remove the circlip from the end of the driveshaft.

37 Press or drive the driveshaft from the tripod, taking great care not to damage the surfaces of the roller locating arms.

38 Slide the outer member and the rubber gaiter from the end of the driveshaft.

39 Thoroughly clean the joint components using paraffin, or a solvent, and dry thoroughly. Carry out a visual inspection as follows.

40 Inspect the tripod rollers and the joint outer member for signs of wear, pitting or scuffing on their mating surfaces **(see illustration)**. Check that the joint rollers rotate smoothly, with no traces of roughness.

41 If the rollers or outer member shown signs of wear or damage, it will be necessary to renew the complete driveshaft, since the joint is not available separately. If the joint is in satisfactory condition, obtain a repair kit, consisting of a new gaiter, retaining clips, circlip, and the correct type and quantity of grease.

42 Tape over the splines on the end of the driveshaft, to protect the new gaiter as it is slid into place, and then slide the new gaiter over the end of the driveshaft.

43 Press or drive the tripod onto the end of the driveshaft until it contacts the stop, ensuring that the marks made on the end of the driveshaft and the tripod before dismantling are aligned. Note that the chamfered edge of the internal splines on the tripod should face towards the driveshaft.

44 Fit the new circlip to retain the tripod on the end of the driveshaft.

45 Work half of the grease supplied with the repair kit into the inner end of the joint housing, then slide the housing over the tripod, ensuring that the marks made during dismantling are aligned, and clamp the housing in the vice.

46 Work the rest of the grease supplied with the repair kit into the outer end of the joint housing **(see illustration)**.

47 Slide the rubber gaiter along the driveshaft onto the joint housing, ensuring that the end of the gaiter seats in the groove in the joint housing, and secure with the large clip as described in paragraph 17.

48 Lift the gaiter outer end to equalise the air pressure in the gaiter (taking care not to damage the gaiter), then secure the outer gaiter securing clip in position using the same method used previously **(see illustration)**.

49 Check the driveshaft joint moves freely in all directions, then refit the driveshaft to the vehicle, as described in Section 2.

4 Driveshaft overhaul – general information

1 If any of the checks, reveal wear in any driveshaft joint, first remove the roadwheel trim or centre cap (as applicable) and check that the hub bolt is tight. If the bolt is loose, obtain a new one, and tighten it to the specified torque (see Section 2). If the bolt is tight, refit the centre cap/trim, and repeat the check on the other hub bolt.

2 Road test the vehicle, and listen for a metallic clicking from the front of the vehicle as the vehicle is driven slowly in a circle on full-lock. If a clicking noise is heard, this indicates wear in the outer constant velocity joint; this means that the joint must be renewed.

3 If vibration consistent with roadspeed is felt through the car when accelerating, there is a possibility of wear in the inner constant velocity joints.

4 To check the joints for wear, remove the driveshafts, then dismantle them as described in Section 3. If any wear or free play is found, the affected joint must be renewed. Refer to a Seat dealer for information on the availability of driveshaft components.

3.40 Check the tripod rollers and outer member for signs of wear

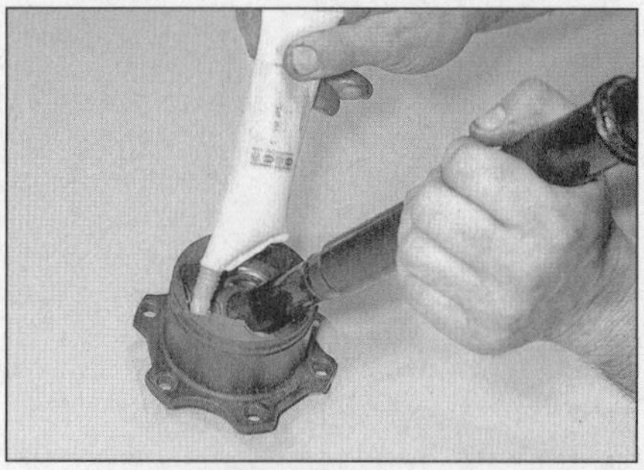

3.46 Work the grease into the joint outer housing

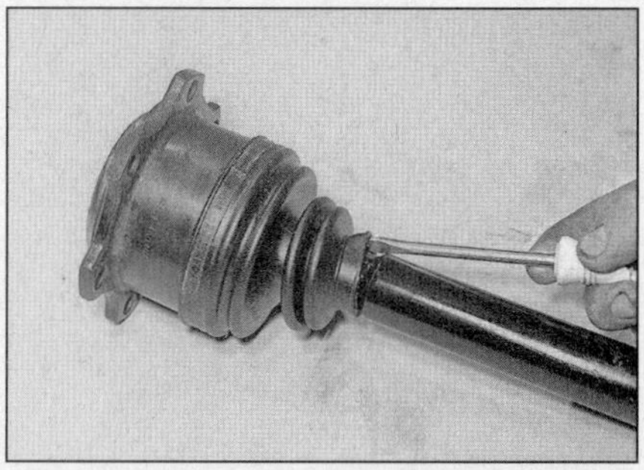

3.48 Lift the gaiter outer end to equalize the air pressure

Chapter 9
Braking system

Contents

Degrees of difficulty

Easy, suitable for novice with little experience	Fairly easy, suitable for beginner with some experience	Fairly difficult, suitable for competent DIY mechanic	Difficult, suitable for experienced DIY mechanic	Very difficult, suitable for expert DIY or professional

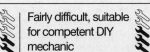

Specifications

Front brakes

Caliper types:	
Engine codes CLNA, CJZD and CAYC *	FN3
All other engine codes *	FSIII
Disc diameter:	
FSIII	256 mm
FN3	288 mm
Disc thickness:	
New:	
FSIII	22.0 mm
FN3	25.0 mm
Minimum permissible thickness:	
FSIII	19.0 mm
FN3	22.0 mm
Maximum disc run-out	0.1 mm
Brake pad minimum thickness (friction material only)	2.0 mm

**See 'Vehicle identification' at the end of this manual for the location of the engine code markings.*

Rear disc brakes

Caliper type	C 38
Disc diameter	230 mm
Disc thickness:	
New	9.0 mm
Minimum thickness	7.0 mm
Maximum disc run-out	0.1 mm
Brake pad minimum thickness (friction material only)	2.0 mm

Rear drum brakes

Drum diameter:	
New	200 mm
Maximum diameter	201.5 mm
Brake lining width	40 mm
Brake lining thickness:	
New	5 mm
Minimum	2.2 mm

Torque wrench settings	Nm	lbf ft
ABS control unit retaining bolts	8	6
ABS control unit mounting bracket nuts	20	15
ABS wheel sensor retaining bolts	8	6
Brake pedal pivot shaft nut*	25	18
Brake light switch	5	4
Brake disc shield bolts	12	9
Front brake caliper:		
Guide pins (FSIII calipers)	28	21
Guide pins (FN3 calipers)	30	22
Mounting bracket bolts (FN3 calipers)	125	92
Hydraulic brake line to caliper banjo bolt	35	26
Hydraulic brake line union nuts	14	10
Master cylinder mounting nuts*	50	36
Rear brake caliper:		
Guide pin bolts*	35	26
Mounting bracket bolts (multi-point socket head): *		
Stage 1	90	66
Stage 2	Angle-tighten a further 90°	
Roadwheel bolts	120	89
Servo unit mechanical vacuum pump (diesel models)	10	8
Servo unit mounting bolts	25	18

**Use new bolts*

1 General information and precautions

General information

1 The braking system is of servo-assisted, diagonal dual-circuit hydraulic type. The arrangement of the hydraulic system is such that each circuit operates one front and one rear brake from a tandem master cylinder. Under normal circumstances, both circuits operate in unison, but, if there is hydraulic failure in one circuit, full braking force will still be available at two wheels. On petrol engines with a manual transmission, vacuum for the servo unit is supplied from the inlet manifold. On diesel engines a combined fuel lift pump and vacuum pump is driven off the left-hand end of the camshaft.

2 All models covered by this manual are equipped with disc brakes at the front. Either rear drum brakes or rear disc brakes may be fitted depending on model. ABS is fitted as standard to all models (refer to Section 22 for further information on ABS operation).

3 The front disc brakes are actuated by single-piston sliding type calipers, which ensure that equal pressure is applied to each disc pad.

4 On models with rear drum brakes, the rear brakes incorporate leading and trailing shoes, which are actuated by twin-piston wheel cylinders. A self-adjust mechanism is incorporated, to compensate for brake shoe wear. The handbrake lever operates the rear shoes by two cables.

5 On models with rear disc brakes, the brakes are actuated by single-piston sliding calipers, which incorporate mechanical handbrake mechanisms.

Precautions

6 When servicing any part of the system, work carefully and methodically; also observe scrupulous cleanliness when overhauling any part of the hydraulic system. Always renew components in axle sets (where applicable) if in doubt about their condition, and use only genuine Seat parts, or at least those of known good quality. Note the warnings given in Section 2 and at relevant points in this Chapter concerning the dangers of brake dust and hydraulic fluid.

Warning: Brake fluid is poisonous. Take care to keep it off bare skin, and in particular not to get splashes in your eyes. The fluid also attacks paintwork and plastics – wash off spillages immediately with cold water. Finally, brake fluid is highly inflammable, and should be handled with the same care as petrol.

7 Make sure the ignition is off (take out the key) before disconnecting any braking system hydraulic union, and do not switch it on until after the hydraulic system has been bled. Failure to do this could lead to air entering the ABS hydraulic unit. If air enters the hydraulic unit pump, it will prove very difficult (in some cases impossible) to bleed the unit.

8 When servicing any part of the system, work carefully and methodically – do not take short cuts; also observe scrupulous cleanliness when overhauling any part of the hydraulic system.

9 Always renew components in axle sets, where applicable – this means replacing brake pads on BOTH sides, even if only one set of pads is worn, or one wheel cylinder is leaking (for example). In the instance of uneven brake wear, the cause should be investigated and fixed (on front brakes, sticking caliper pistons is a likely problem).

10 Although brake pads are asbestos-free, the dust created by wear of pads may cause a health hazard. Never blow it out with compressed air, and don't inhale any of it.

11 DO NOT use petroleum-based solvents to clean brake parts; use brake cleaner or methylated spirit only.

12 DO NOT allow any brake fluid, oil or grease to contact the brake pads or disc.

2 Hydraulic system – bleeding

Warning: Hydraulic fluid is poisonous; wash off immediately and thoroughly in the case of skin contact, and seek immediate medical advice if any fluid is swallowed or gets into the eyes. Certain types of hydraulic fluid are flammable, and may ignite when allowed into contact with hot components; when servicing any hydraulic system, it is safest to assume that the fluid is flammable, and to take precautions against the risk of fire as though it is petrol that is being handled. Hydraulic fluid is also an effective paint stripper, and will attack plastics; if any is spilt, it should be washed off immediately, using copious quantities of fresh water. Finally, it is hygroscopic (it absorbs moisture from the air) – old fluid may be contaminated and unfit for further use. When topping-up or renewing the fluid, always use the recommended type, and ensure that it comes from a freshly opened sealed container.

Note: *It is recommended that at least 0.25 litre of brake fluid should be expelled from each caliper.*

General

1 The correct operation of any hydraulic system is only possible after removing all air from the components and circuit; this is achieved by bleeding the system. Since the clutch hydraulic system also uses fluid from the brake system reservoir, it should also be bled at the same time by referring to Chapter 6A Section 2.

2 During the bleeding procedure, add only clean, unused hydraulic fluid of the recommended type; never re-use fluid that has already been bled from the system. Ensure that sufficient fluid is available before starting work.

3 If there is any possibility of incorrect fluid being already in the system, the brake components and circuit must be flushed completely with uncontaminated, correct fluid, and new seals should be fitted to the various components.

4 If hydraulic fluid has been lost from the system, or air has entered because of a leak, ensure that the fault is cured before continuing further.

5 Park the vehicle on level ground, then chock the wheels and release the handbrake.

6 Check that all pipes and hoses are secure, unions tight and bleed screws closed. Clean any dirt from around the bleed screws.

7 Unscrew the master cylinder reservoir cap, and top the reservoir up to the MAX level line; refit the cap loosely, and remember to maintain the fluid level at least above the MIN level line throughout the procedure, or there is a risk of further air entering the system.

8 There is a number of one-man, do-it-yourself brake bleeding kits currently available from motor accessory shops. It is recommended that one of these kits is used whenever possible, as they greatly simplify the bleeding operation, and reduce the risk of expelled air and fluid being drawn back into the system. If such a kit is not available, the basic (two-man) method must be used, which is described in detail below.

9 If a kit is to be used, prepare the vehicle as described previously, and follow the kit manufacturer's instructions, as the procedure may vary slightly according to the type being used; generally, they are as outlined below in the relevant sub-section.

10 Whichever method is used, the same sequence must be followed (paragraph 12) to ensure the removal of all air from the system.

Bleeding sequence

11 If the system has been only partially disconnected, and suitable precautions were taken to minimise fluid loss, it should be necessary only to bleed that part of the system.

12 If the complete system is to be bled, then it should be done working in the following sequence:

RHD models

a) Right-hand front brake.
b) Left-hand front brake.
c) Right-hand rear brake.
d) Left-hand rear brake.

LHD models

a) Left-hand front brake.
b) Right-hand front brake.
c) Left-hand rear brake.
d) Right-hand rear brake.

13 If the hydraulic fluid has run dry in either chamber of the reservoir, the system must be pre-bled as follows, before carrying out the bleeding sequence described above:

a) Bleed the front left and right brakes simultaneously.
b) Bleed the rear left and right brakes simultaneously.

Bleeding

Basic (two-man) method

14 Collect together a clean glass jar of reasonable size, a suitable length of plastic or rubber tubing which is a tight fit over the bleed screw, and a ring spanner to fit the screw. The help of an assistant will also be required.

15 Remove the dust cap from the first screw in the sequence **(see illustration)**. Fit the spanner and tube to the screw, place the other end of the tube in the jar, and pour in sufficient fluid to cover the end of the tube.

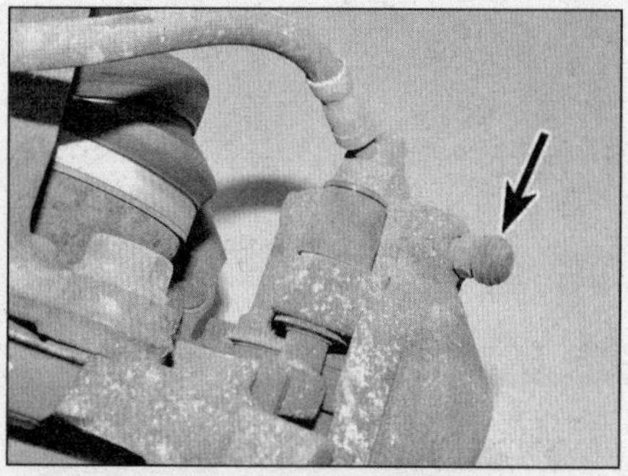

2.15 Remove the dust cap from the first bleed screw in the sequence

16 Ensure that the master cylinder reservoir fluid level is maintained at least above the MIN level line throughout the procedure.

17 Have the assistant fully depress the brake pedal several times to build-up pressure, and then maintain it on the final downstroke.

18 While pedal pressure is maintained, unscrew the bleed screw (approximately one turn) and allow the compressed fluid and air to flow into the jar. The assistant should maintain pedal pressure, following it down to the floor if necessary, and should not release it until instructed to do so. When the flow stops, tighten the bleed screw again, have the assistant release the pedal slowly, and recheck the reservoir fluid level.

19 Repeat the steps given in paragraphs 16 and 17 until the fluid emerging from the bleed screw is free from air bubbles. If the master cylinder has been drained and refilled, and air is being bled from the first screw in the sequence, allow approximately five seconds between cycles for the master cylinder passages to refill.

20 When no more air bubbles appear, tighten the bleed screw securely, remove the tube and spanner, and refit the dust cap. Do not overtighten the bleed screw.

21 Repeat the procedure on the remaining screws in the sequence, until all air is removed from the system and the brake pedal feels firm again.

Using a one-way valve kit

22 As their name implies, these kits consist of a length of tubing with a one-way valve fitted, to prevent expelled air and fluid being drawn back into the system; some kits include a translucent container, which can be positioned so that the air bubbles can be more easily seen flowing from the end of the tube.

23 The kit is connected to the bleed screw, which is then opened. The user returns to the driver's seat, depresses the brake pedal with a smooth, steady stroke, and slowly releases it; this is repeated until the expelled fluid is clear of air bubbles **(see illustration)**.

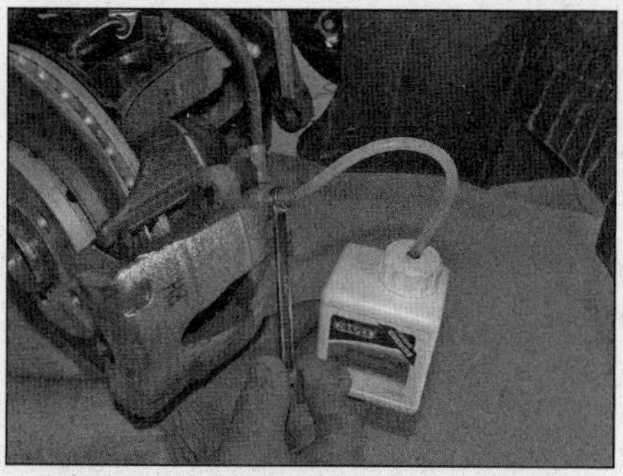

2.23 Bleeding a brake using a one-way valve kit

24 Note that these kits simplify work so much that it is easy to forget the master cylinder reservoir fluid level; ensure that this is maintained at least above the MIN level line at all times.

Using a pressure-bleeding kit

25 These kits are usually operated by the reservoir of pressurised air contained in the spare tyre. However, note that it will be probably necessary to reduce the pressure to less than 1.0 bar (14.5 psi); refer to the instructions supplied with the kit.

26 By connecting a pressurised, fluid-filled container to the master cylinder reservoir, bleeding can be carried out simply by opening each screw in turn (in the specified sequence), and allowing the fluid to flow out until no more air bubbles can be seen in the expelled fluid.

27 This method has the advantage that the large reservoir of fluid provides an additional safeguard against air being drawn into the system during bleeding.

28 Pressure-bleeding is particularly effective when bleeding 'difficult' systems, or when bleeding the complete system at the time of routine fluid renewal.

All methods

29 When bleeding is complete, and firm pedal feel is restored, wash off any spilt fluid, tighten the bleed screws securely, and refit their dust caps.

30 Check the hydraulic fluid level in the master cylinder reservoir, and top-up if necessary (see *Weekly checks*).

31 Discard any hydraulic fluid that has been bled from the system; it will not be fit for re-use.

3.6a Brake hose retaining clip in strut...

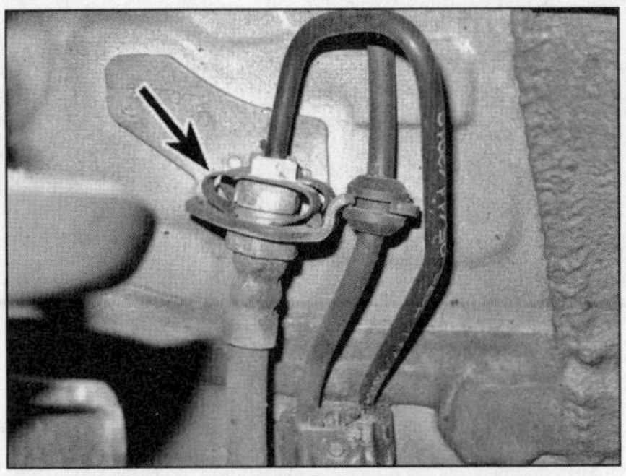

3.6b ...and on inner wing panel

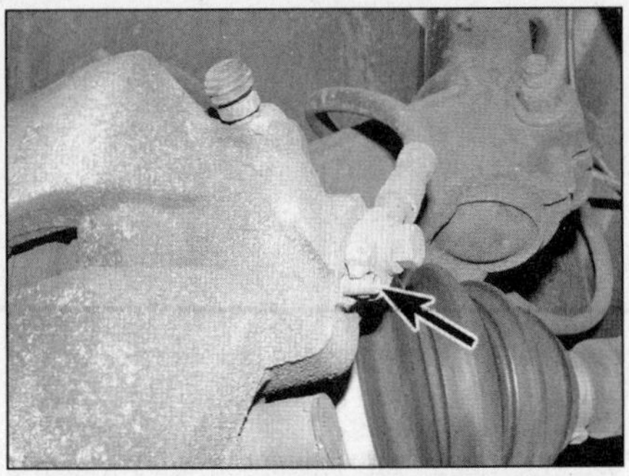

3.6c Locating peg for brake hose end fitting

32 Check the feel of the brake pedal. If it feels at all spongy, air must still be present in the system, and further bleeding is required. Failure to bleed satisfactorily after a reasonable repetition of the bleeding procedure may be due to worn master cylinder seals.

3 Hydraulic pipes and hoses – renewal

Note: *Refer to the note in Section 2 concerning the dangers of hydraulic fluid.*

1 If any pipe or hose is to be renewed, minimise fluid loss by first removing the master cylinder reservoir cap, then tightening it down onto a piece of polythene to obtain an airtight seal. Alternatively, flexible hoses can be sealed, if required, using a proprietary brake hose clamp; metal brake pipe unions can be plugged (if care is taken not to allow dirt into the system) or capped immediately they are disconnected. Place a wad of rag under any union that is to be disconnected, to catch any spilt fluid.

2 If a flexible hose is to be disconnected, where applicable unscrew the brake pipe union nut before removing the spring clip which secures the hose to its mounting bracket.

3 To unscrew the union nuts, it is preferable to obtain a brake pipe spanner of the correct size; these are available from most large motor accessory shops. Failing this, a close-fitting open-ended spanner will be required, though if the nuts are tight or corroded, their flats may be rounded-off if the spanner slips. In such a case, a self-locking wrench is often the only way to unscrew a stubborn union, but it follows that the pipe and the damaged nuts must be renewed on reassembly. Always clean a union and surrounding area before disconnecting it. If disconnecting a component with more than one union, make a careful note of the connections before disturbing any of them.

4 If a brake pipe is to be renewed, it can be obtained, cut to length and with the union nuts and end flares in place, from Seat dealers. All that is then necessary is to bend it to shape, following the line of the original, before fitting it to the car. Alternatively, most motor accessory shops can make up brake pipes from kits, but this requires very careful measurement of the original, to ensure that the new pipe is of the correct length. The safest answer is usually to take the original to the shop as a pattern.

5 On refitting, do not overtighten the union nuts. It is not necessary to exercise brute force to obtain a sound joint.

6 Ensure that the pipes and hoses are correctly routed, with no kinks, and that they are secured in the clips or brackets provided **(see illustrations)**. After fitting, remove the polythene from the reservoir, and bleed the hydraulic system as described in Section 2. Wash off any spilt fluid, and then check carefully for fluid leaks.

4 Front brake pads – renewal

Warning: Renew both sets of front brake pads at the same time – never renew the pads on only one wheel, as uneven braking may result. Note that the dust created by wear of the pads may contain asbestos, which is a health hazard. Never blow it out with compressed air, and don't inhale any of it. An approved filtering mask should be worn when working on the brakes. DO NOT use petrol or petroleum-based solvents to clean brake parts; use a proprietary brake cleaner only.

1 Two types of front caliper are fitted to the Ibiza range – see Specifications. There are minor differences, but removal and refitting of the brake pads is essentially the same for all types of caliper. Note however that FS III type brakes have an inner and outer brake pad with spring clips attached. FN type brake pads have a specific direction of rotation marked on them **(see illustrations)**.

2 Apply the handbrake, then slacken the front roadwheel nuts. Jack up the front of the vehicle and support it on axle stands. Remove both front roadwheels.

3 Follow the accompanying photos **(illustrations 4.3a to 4.3u)** for the actual pad renewal procedure. Be sure to stay in order and read the caption under each illustration, and note the following points:

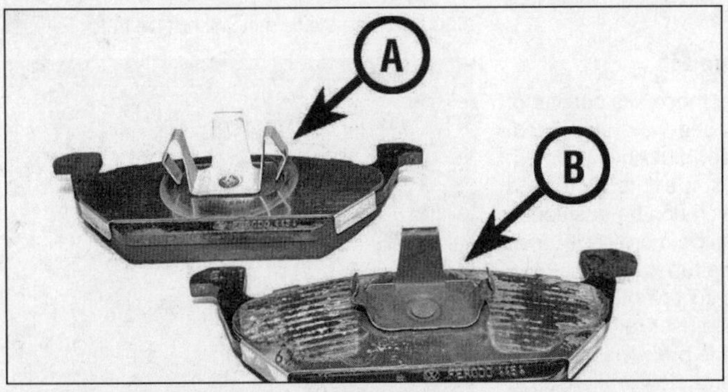

4.1a Note the that the brake pads have different spring clips and must be fitted correctly. A = Inner (piston side) pad and B = outer pad

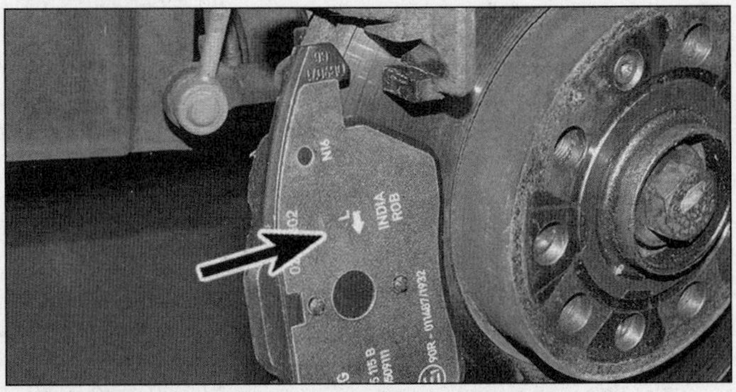

4.1b FN3 brake pads have the direction of rotation marked.

a) New pads may have an adhesive foil on the backplates. Remove this foil prior to installation.

b) Thoroughly clean the caliper guide surfaces, and apply a little brake assembly (polycarbamide) grease. DO NOT use a copper based grease.

c) When pushing the caliper piston back to accommodate new pads, keep a close eye on the fluid lever in the reservoir.

d) If there is any doubt as to the condition of the brake pads, always replace them.

4 Depress the brake pedal repeatedly, until the pads are pressed into firm contact with the brake disc, and normal (non-assisted) pedal pressure is restored.

5 Repeat the above procedure on the remaining front brake caliper.

6 Refit the roadwheels, then lower the vehicle to the ground and tighten the roadwheel nuts to the specified torque.

7 Check the hydraulic fluid level as described in *Weekly checks*.

Caution: New pads will not give full braking efficiency until they have bedded-in. Be prepared for this, and avoid hard braking as far as possible for the first hundred miles or so after pad renewal.

4.3a Where fitted disconnect the pad wear warning light wiring plug

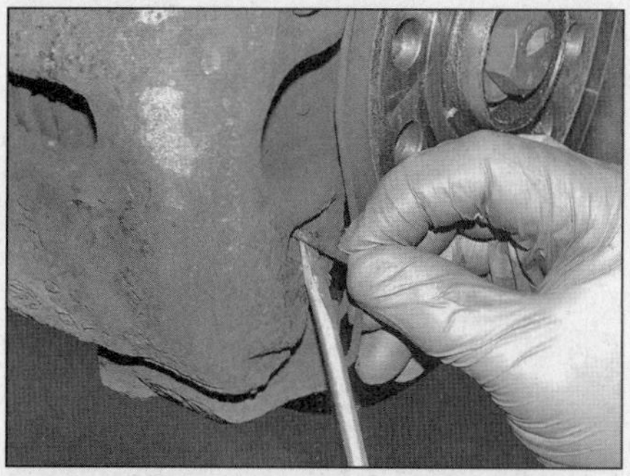

4.3b On FN3 type brakes remove the spring

4.3c Remove the upper and lower dust caps

4.3d Remove the upper guide pin bolt...

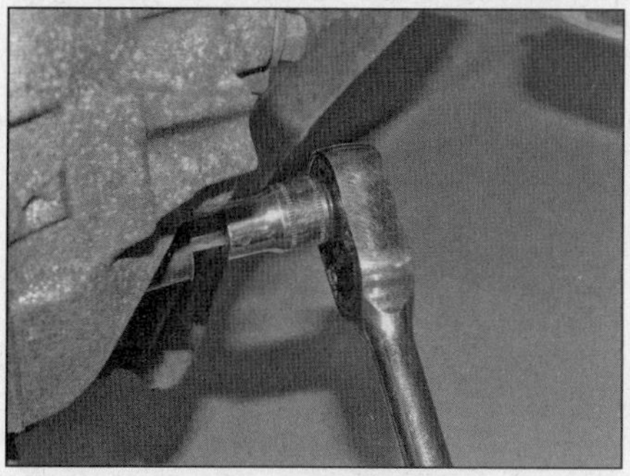

4.3e ...and the lower

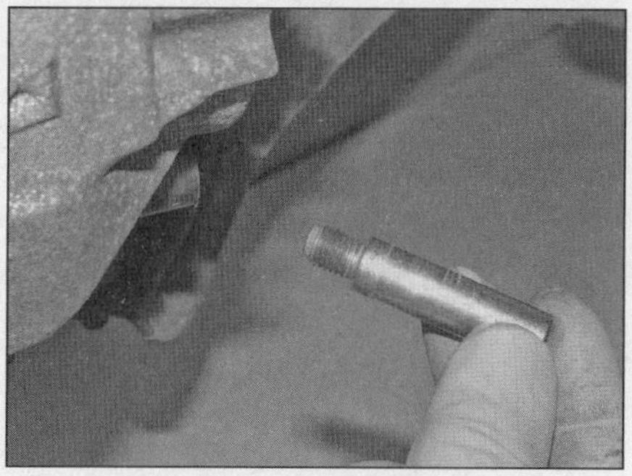

4.3f Pull out both guide pins

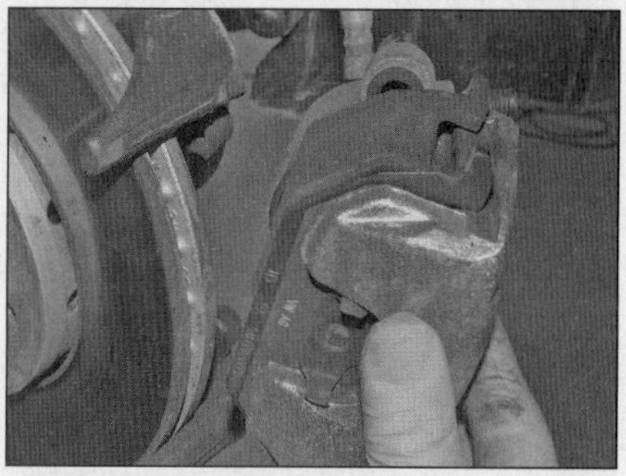

4.3g Lift off the caliper. Rocking the caliper as it is removed will help push the piston back, allowing the pads to clear the brake disc

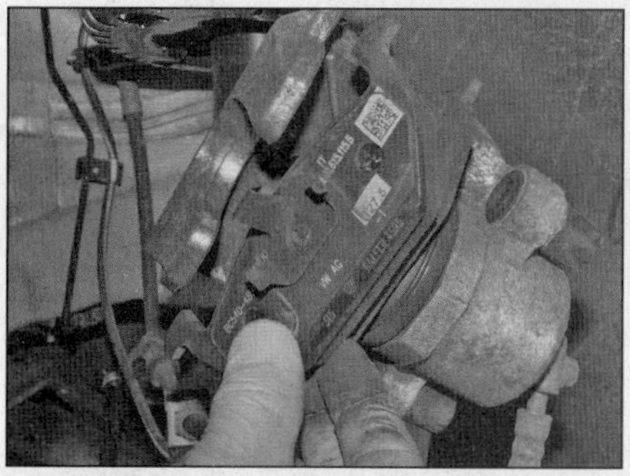

4.3h Remove the outer brake pad...

4.3i ...and then the inner

4.3j Use a wind back tool to push in the piston. Note that the caliper is supported from the coil spring to avoid straining the brake hose

4.3k A 'G' type clamp can also be used. Note the block of wood used to protect the face of the piston. Check the fluid level in the master cylinder. The level will rise as the piston is pushed back and it may be necessary to remove some fluid from the reservoir. Avoid spilling brake fluid and clean any spills immediately with shop towels and brake cleaner

4.3l Inspect the brake disc and then clean the brake pad mounting surfaces...

4.3m ...and the caliper. Use a proprietary brake cleaner

4.3n Inspect the piston dust seal and check that the guide pins slide freely in the caliper bracket

4.3o Fit the new brake pad to the piston (inboard) side of the caliper...

4.3p ...and to the outer side

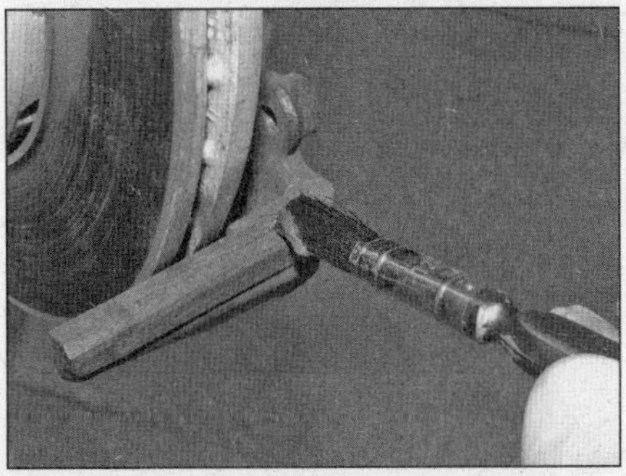

4.3q Apply a little brake lubricant ('cera-tec') grease to the pad mounting surfaces. DO NOT use a copper based grease

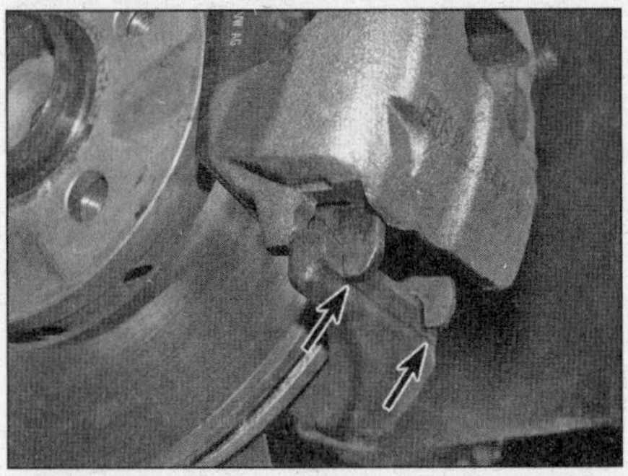

4.3r Fit the caliper, ensuring that the brake pads rest correctly on the bracket

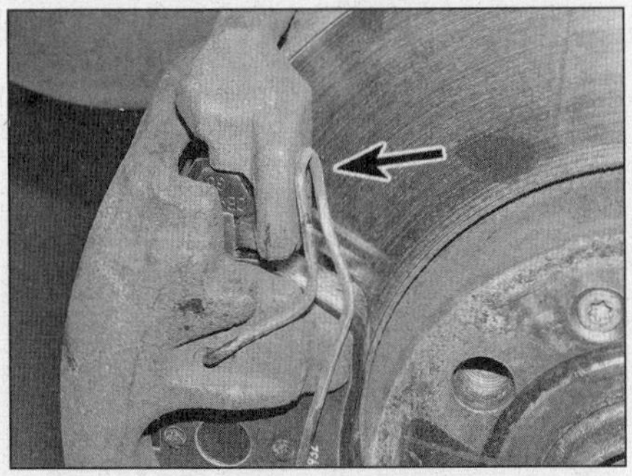

4.3s On FN3 brakes the spring must be refitted correctly

4.3t Fit the guide pins and tighten them to the specified torque

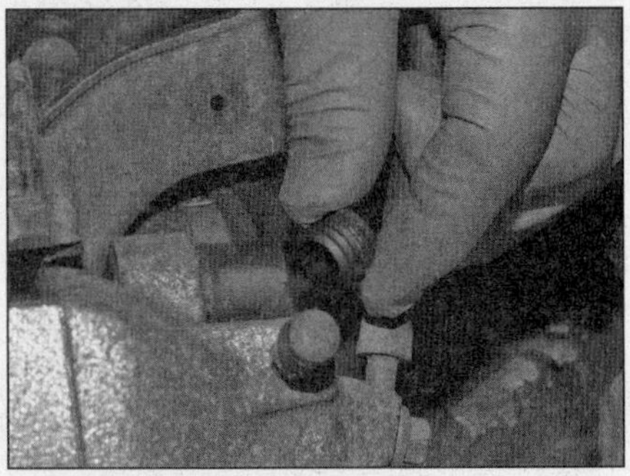

4.3u Refit the dust caps and (where fitted) connect the wiring plug for the brake pad wear warning light

5 Front brake caliper – removal, overhaul and refitting

Note: *Before starting work, refer to the note at the beginning of Section 2 concerning the dangers of hydraulic fluid, and to the warning at the beginning of Section concerning the dangers of asbestos dust.*

Removal

1 Apply the handbrake, then jack up the front of the vehicle and support it on axle stands (see *Jacking and vehicle support*). Remove the appropriate roadwheel.

2 Minimise fluid loss by first removing the master cylinder reservoir cap, and then tightening it down onto a piece of polythene, to obtain an airtight seal. Alternatively, use a brake hose clamp, a G-clamp or a similar tool to clamp the flexible hose.

3 Clean the area around the union, and then loosen the brake hose union nut.

4 Remove the brake pads as described in Section.

5 Unscrew the caliper from the end of the brake hose and remove it from the vehicle.

Overhaul

6 With the caliper on the bench, wipe away all traces of dust and dirt, but *avoid inhaling the dust, as it is injurious to health.*

7 Withdraw the partially ejected piston from the caliper body, and remove the dust seal.

8 Using a small screwdriver, extract the piston hydraulic seal, taking great care not to damage the caliper bore **(see illustration)**.

9 Thoroughly clean all components, using only methylated spirit, isopropyl alcohol or clean hydraulic fluid as a cleaning medium. Never use mineral-based solvents such as petrol or paraffin, as they will attack the hydraulic system rubber components. Dry the components immediately, using compressed air or a clean, lint-free cloth. Use compressed air to blow clear the fluid passages.

10 Check all components, and renew any that are worn or damaged. Check particularly the cylinder bore and piston; these should be renewed if they are scratched, worn or corroded in any way (note that this means the renewal of the complete caliper body assembly). Similarly check the condition of the spacers/guide pins and their bushes/bores (as applicable); both spacers/pins should be undamaged and (when cleaned) a reasonably tight sliding fit in their bores. If there is any doubt about the condition of any component, renew it.

11 If the assembly is fit for further use, obtain the appropriate repair kit; the components are available from Seat dealers in various combinations.

12 Renew all rubber seals, dust covers and caps disturbed on dismantling as a matter of course; these should never be re-used.

13 On reassembly, ensure that all components are clean and dry.

14 Thinly coat the piston and piston seal with brake fitting paste (Seat/VW part no G 052 150 A2). This should be included in the Seat caliper overhaul/repair kit.

15 Fit the new piston (fluid) seal, using only your fingers (no tools) to manipulate it into the cylinder bore groove. Fit the new dust seal to the piston, and refit the piston to the cylinder bore using a twisting motion; ensure that the piston enters squarely into the bore. Press the piston fully into the bore, then press the dust seal into the caliper body.

Refitting

16 Screw the caliper fully onto the flexible hose union.

17 Refit the brake pads as described in Section 4.

18 Securely tighten the brake pipe union nut.

19 Remove the brake hose clamp or polythene, as applicable, and bleed the hydraulic system as described in Section 2. Note that, providing the precautions described were taken to minimise brake fluid loss, it should only be necessary to bleed the relevant front brake.

20 Refit the roadwheel, then lower the vehicle to the ground and tighten the roadwheel bolts to the specified torque.

6 Brake disc – inspection, removal and refitting

Note: *Before starting work, refer to the note at the beginning of Section concerning the dangers of asbestos dust.*

Note: *If either disc requires renewal, BOTH should be renewed at the same time, to ensure even and consistent braking. New brake pads should also be fitted.*

Front brake disc

Inspection

1 Apply the handbrake, then jack up the front of the car and support it on axle stands (see *Jacking and vehicle support*). Remove the appropriate front roadwheel.

2 Slowly rotate the brake disc so that the full area of both sides can be checked; remove the brake pads if better access is required to

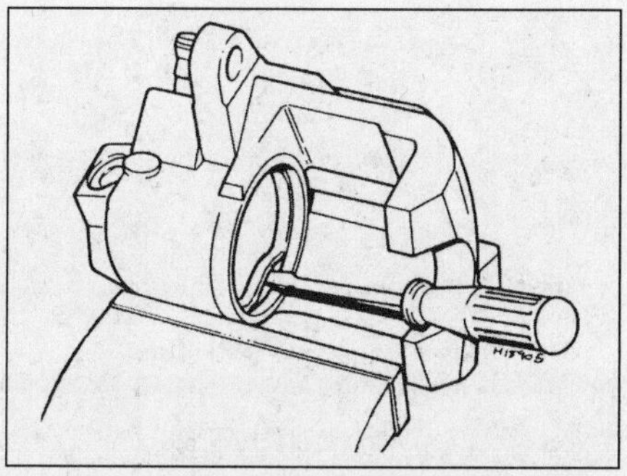

5.8 Use a small screwdriver to extract the caliper piston hydraulic seal

the inboard surface. Light scoring is normal in the area swept by the brake pads, but if heavy scoring or cracks are found, the disc must be renewed.

3 It is normal to find a lip of rust and brake dust around the perimeter of the disc; this can be scraped off if required. If, however, a lip has formed due to excessive wear of the brake pad swept area, then the disc thickness must be measured using a micrometer **(see illustration)**. Take measurements at several places around the disc, at the inside and outside of the pad swept area; if the disc has worn at any point to the specified minimum thickness or less, the disc must be renewed.

4 If the disc is thought to be warped, it can be checked for run-out. Either use a dial gauge mounted on any convenient fixed point, while the disc is slowly rotated, or use feeler blades to measure (at several points all around the disc) the clearance between the disc and a fixed point, such as the caliper mounting bracket. If the measurements obtained are at the specified maximum or beyond, the disc is excessively warped, and must be renewed; however, it is worth checking first that the hub bearings are in good condition. If the run-out is excessive, the disc must be renewed **(see illustration)**.

5 Check the disc for cracks, especially around the wheel bolt holes, and any other wear or damage, and renew if necessary.

Removal

6 Remove the brake pads as described in Section 4.

7 On models with FN3 front brake calipers, unscrew the two bolts securing the brake

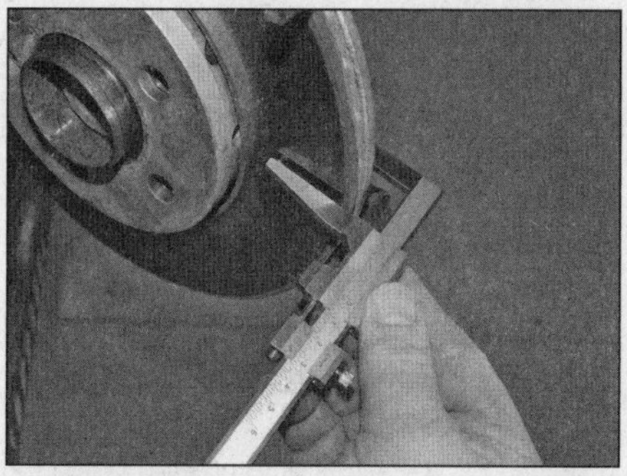

6.3 Specialist vernier gauges are available for checking the disc thickness

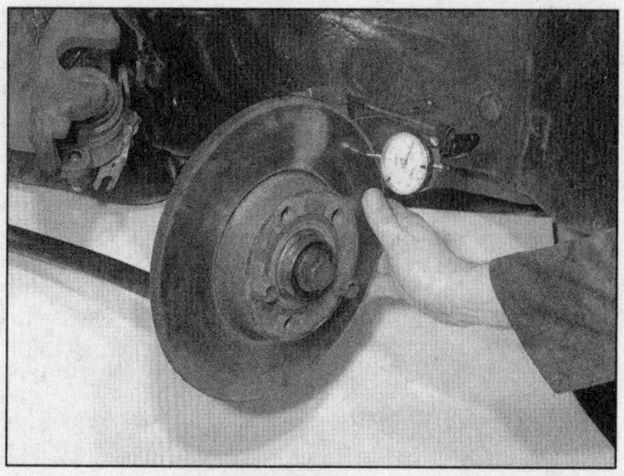

6.4 Using a DTI gauge to measure disc run-out

6.8 Undo the disc retaining screw

caliper mounting bracket to the hub carrier, then slide the caliper assembly off the disc. Using a piece of wire or string, tie the caliper to the front suspension coil spring, to avoid placing any strain on the brake hose.

8 Use chalk or paint to mark the relationship of the disc to the hub, then remove the screw securing the brake disc to the hub, and remove the disc **(see illustration)**. If it is tight, apply penetrating fluid, and tap its rear face gently with a hide or plastic mallet. The use of excessive force could cause the disc to be damaged.

Refitting

9 Refitting is the reverse of the removal procedure, noting the following points:

a) *Ensure that the mating surfaces of the disc and hub are clean and flat.*
b) *Align (if applicable) the marks made on removal, and securely tighten the disc retaining screw.*
c) *If a new disc has been fitted, use a suitable solvent to wipe any preservative coating from the disc, before refitting the caliper.*
d) *On models with FN3 brake calipers, slide the caliper into position over the disc, making sure the pads pass either side of the disc. Tighten the caliper bracket mounting bolts to the specified torque.*
e) *Fit the pads as described in Section 4.*
f) *Refit the roadwheel, then lower the vehicle to the ground and tighten the roadwheel bolts to the specified torque. On completion, repeatedly depress the brake pedal until normal (non-assisted) pedal pressure returns.*

6.13 Remove the rear brake disc

Rear brake disc

Inspection

10 Firmly chock the front wheels, then jack up the rear of the car and support it on axle stands. Remove the appropriate rear roadwheel.

11 Inspect the disc as described in paragraphs 1 to 5.

Removal

12 Unscrew the two bolts securing the brake caliper mounting bracket in position, then slide the caliper assembly off the disc. Using a piece of wire or string, tie the caliper to the rear suspension coil spring, to avoid placing any strain on the hydraulic brake hose.

13 Use chalk or paint to mark the relationship of the disc to the hub, then remove the screw securing the brake disc to the hub, and remove the disc **(see illustration)**. If it is tight, apply penetrating fluid, and tap its rear face gently with a hide or plastic mallet. The use of excessive force could cause the disc to be damaged.

Refitting

14 Refitting is a reversal of the removal procedure, noting the following points:

a) *Ensure that the mating surfaces of the disc and hub are clean and flat.*
b) *Align (if applicable) the marks made on removal, and securely tighten the disc retaining screw.*
c) *If a new disc has been fitted, use a suitable solvent to wipe any preservative coating from the disc, before refitting the caliper.*
d) *Slide the caliper into position over the disc, making sure the pads pass either side of the disc. Tighten the caliper bracket mounting bolts to the specified torque. If new discs have been fitted and there is insufficient clearance between the pads to accommodate the new, thicker disc, it may be necessary to push the piston back into the caliper body as described in Section 8.*
e) *Refit the roadwheel, then lower the vehicle to the ground and tighten the roadwheel bolts to the specified torque. On completion, repeatedly depress the brake pedal until normal (non-assisted) pedal pressure returns.*

7 Front brake disc shield – removal and refitting

Removal

1 Remove the brake disc as described in Section 6.

2 Unscrew the securing bolts, and remove the brake disc shield.

Refitting

3 Refitting is a reversal of removal. Tighten the shield retaining bolts to the specified torque. Refit the brake disc with reference to Section 6.

8 Rear brake pads – removal, inspection and refitting

Note: *Before starting work, refer to the note at the beginning of Section concerning the dangers of asbestos dust. New caliper mounting bolts will be required on refitting.*

Removal

1 Chock the front wheels, then jack up the rear of the vehicle and support it on axle stands (see *Jacking and vehicle support*). Remove the rear wheels.

2 Follow the accompanying photos **(illustrations 4.3a to 4.3q)** for the actual pad renewal procedure. Be sure to stay in order and read the caption under each illustration, and note the following points:

a) *New pads may have an adhesive foil on the backplates. Remove this foil prior to installation.*
b) *Thoroughly clean the caliper guide surfaces, and apply a little brake assembly (polycarbamide) grease. DO NOT use a copper based grease.*
c) *When pushing the caliper piston back to accommodate new pads, keep a close eye on the fluid lever in the reservoir.*
d) *If there is any doubt as to the condition of the brake pads, always replace them.*

3 Depress the brake pedal repeatedly, until the pads are pressed into firm contact with the brake disc, and normal (non-assisted) pedal pressure is restored.

4 Repeat the above procedure on the remaining rear brake caliper.

5 If necessary, adjust the handbrake as described in Section 17.

6 Refit the roadwheels, then lower the vehicle to the ground and tighten the roadwheel bolts to the specified torque setting.

7 Check the hydraulic fluid level as described in *Weekly checks*.

8 New pads will not give full braking efficiency until they have bedded-in. Be prepared for this, and avoid hard braking as far as possible for the first hundred miles or so after pad renewal.

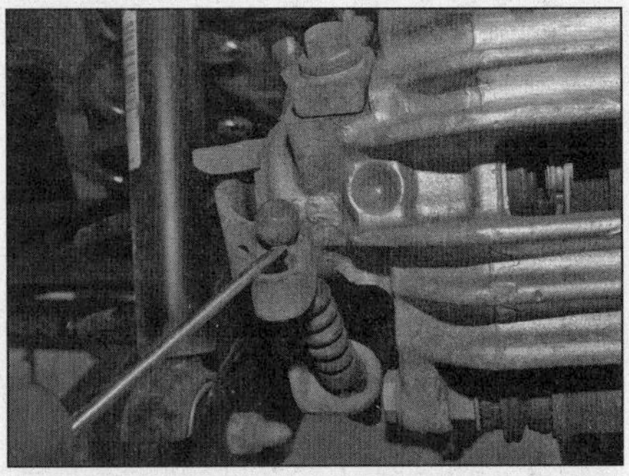

8.2a Unhook the brake cable. Note that it may be necessary to slacken the cable

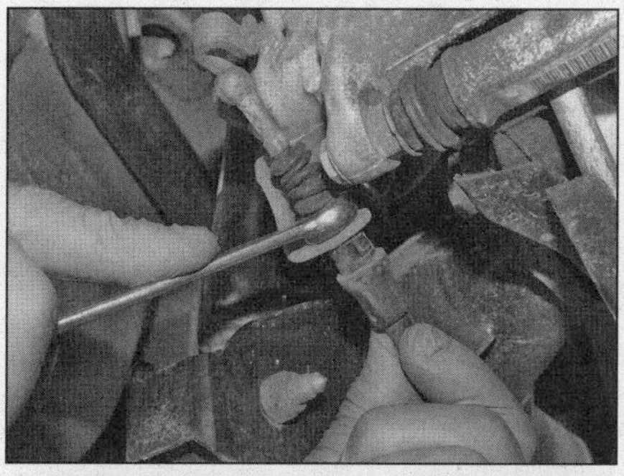

8.2b Release the outer cable from the bracket by using a spanner to compress the locking tabs. On some models lever out the metal circlip to release the cable

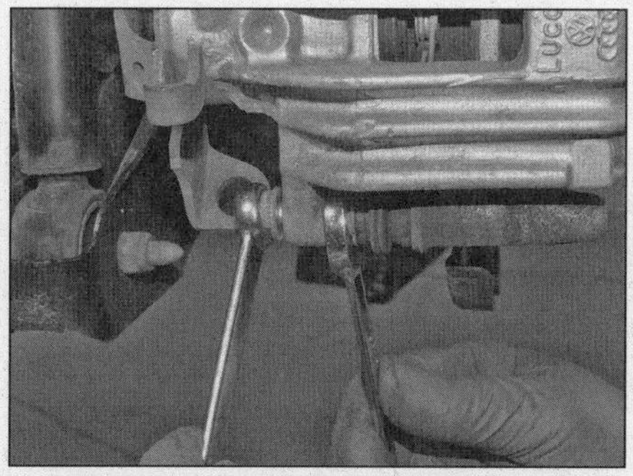

8.2c Use a spanner to counterhold the guide pin and remove the lower...

8.2d ...and then the upper guide pin bolts

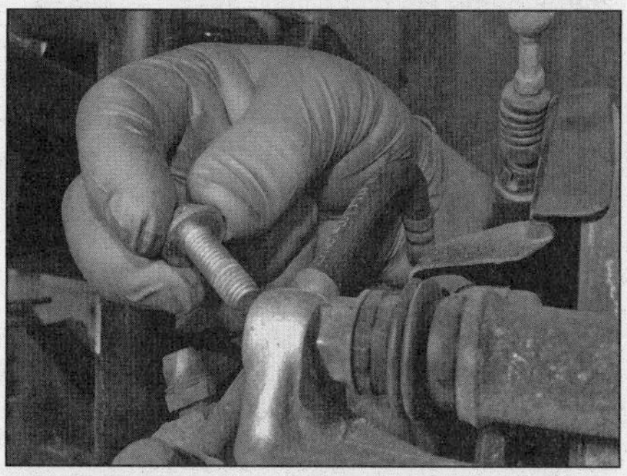

8.2e Remove both bolts and then...

8.2f ...remove the caliper. Rocking the caliper will push the piston back and will help it over the lip on the disc

8.2g Rest the caliper on the rear axle. Do not strain the brake flexible hose

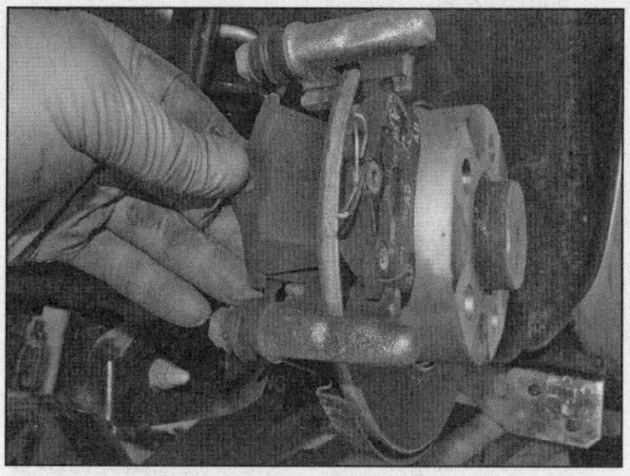

8.2h Remove the inner and...

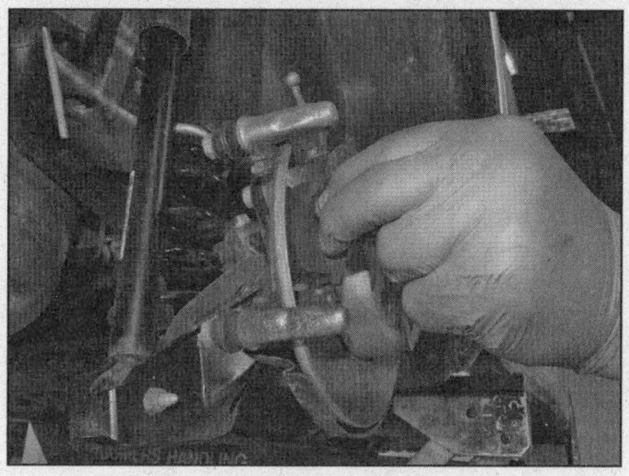

8.2i ...outer brake pads

8.2j Check that both guide pins move freely. Clean and lubricate if required. Note that the stepped pin fits in the top

8.2k Clean and inspect the caliper, bracket and brake disc. Use a proprietary brake cleaner and brush

8.2l Using a brake piston wind back tool, push the piston into the caliper. Note that the piston must rotate as it is pushed back or the handbrake mechanism will be damaged

8.2m Lightly lubricate the contact points on the brake pads. Use a brake specific lubricant. Do not use a copper based grease

8.2n Fit the brake pads and then...

8.2o ...refit the brake caliper. Note the position of the anti-rattle springs. They must be compressed to align the caliper with the guide pin bolt holes

8.2p Fit new bolts to the guide pins and tighten them to the specified torque

8.2q Refit the handbrake cable and check the operation of the handbrake

9 Rear brake caliper – removal, overhaul and refitting

Note: *Before starting work, refer to the note at the beginning of Section 2 concerning the dangers of hydraulic fluid, and to the warning at the beginning of Section concerning the dangers of asbestos dust.*

Removal

1 Chock the front wheels, then jack up the rear of the vehicle and support on axle stands (see *Jacking and vehicle support*). Remove the relevant rear wheel.

2 Minimise fluid loss by first removing the master cylinder reservoir cap, and then tightening it down onto a piece of polythene, to obtain an airtight seal. Alternatively, use a brake hose clamp, a G-clamp or a similar tool to clamp the flexible hose.

3 Clean the area around the union on the caliper, and then loosen the brake hose union nut.

4 Lift the caliper from the brake pads as described in Section 8.

5 Unscrew the caliper from the end of the flexible hose and remove it from the vehicle.

Overhaul

Note: *It is not possible to overhaul the brake caliper handbrake mechanism. If the mechanism is faulty, or fluid is leaking from the handbrake lever seal the caliper assembly must be renewed.*

6 With the caliper on the bench, wipe away all traces of dust and dirt, but avoid inhaling the dust, as it is injurious to health.

7 Using a small screwdriver, carefully prise out the dust seal from the caliper, taking care not to damage the piston.

8 Remove the piston from the caliper bore by rotating it in an anti-clockwise direction. This can be achieved using a suitable pair of circlip pliers engaged in the caliper piston slots. Once the piston turns freely but does not come out any further, the piston can be withdrawn by hand.

9 Using a small screwdriver, extract the piston hydraulic seal(s), taking care not to damage the caliper bore.

10 Withdraw the guide pins from the caliper, and remove the guide sleeve gaiters.

11 Thoroughly clean all components, using only methylated spirit, isopropyl alcohol or clean hydraulic fluid as a cleaning medium. Never use mineral-based solvents such as petrol or paraffin, as they will attack the hydraulic system rubber components. Dry the components immediately, using compressed air or a clean, lint-free cloth. Use compressed air to blow clear the fluid passages.

12 Check all components, and renew any that are worn or damaged. Check particularly the cylinder bore and piston; these should be renewed (note that this means the renewal of the complete caliper body assembly) if they are scratched, worn or corroded in any way. Similarly check the condition of the spacers/guide pins and their bushes/bores (as applicable); both spacers/pins should be undamaged and (when cleaned) a reasonably tight sliding fit in their bores. If there is any doubt about the condition of any component, renew it.

13 If the assembly is fit for further uses obtain the appropriate repair kit; the components are available from Seat dealers in various combinations.

14 Renew all rubber seals, dust covers and caps disturbed on dismantling as a matter of course; these should never be re-used.

15 On reassembly, ensure that all components are clean and dry.

16 Smear a thin coat of brake fitting paste (Seat/VW part no G 052 150 A2) on the piston, seal and caliper bore. This should be included in the overhaul/repair kit. Fit the new piston (fluid) seal, using only the fingers (no tools) to manipulate into the cylinder bore groove.

17 Fit the new dust seal to the piston groove, then refit the piston assembly. Turn the piston in a clockwise direction, using the method employed on dismantling, until it is fully retracted into the caliper bore.

18 Press the dust seal into position in the caliper housing.

19 Apply the grease supplied in the repair kit, or a copper-based brake grease or anti-seize compound, to the guide pins. Fit the new gaiters to the guide pins and fit the pins to the caliper ensuring that the gaiters are correctly located in the grooves on both the pins and caliper.

20 Prior to refitting, fill the caliper with fresh hydraulic fluid by slackening the bleed screw and pumping the fluid through the caliper until bubble-free fluid is expelled from the union hole.

Refitting

21 Screw the caliper fully onto the flexible hose union.

22 Refit the caliper over the brake pads as described in Section 8.

23 Securely tighten the brake pipe union nut.

24 Remove the brake hose clamp or remove the polythene from the fluid reservoir, as applicable, and bleed the hydraulic system as described in Section 2. Note that, providing the precautions described were taken to minimise brake fluid loss, it should only be necessary to bleed the relevant rear brake.

25 Connect the handbrake cable to the caliper, and adjust the handbrake as described in Section 17.

26 Refit the roadwheel, then lower the vehicle to the ground and tighten the roadwheel bolts to the specified torque. On completion, check the hydraulic fluid level as described in *Weekly checks*.

10 Rear brake drum – removal, inspection and refitting

Note: *Before starting work, refer to the warning at the beginning of Section concerning the dangers of asbestos dust.*

Removal

1 Remove the wheel trim (where applicable), then loosen the rear roadwheel bolts and chock the front wheels. Jack up the rear of the car, and support on axle stands positioned under the body side members (see *Jacking and vehicle support*). Remove the roadwheel.

2 Fully release the handbrake.

3 Extract the drum securing screw and remove the drum. The drum may be tight due to the brake shoes binding on the inner circumference of the drum. If this is the case, insert a screwdriver through one of the wheel bolt holes in the brake drum and hub, and lever up the wedge key in order to allow the brake shoes to retract fully. The wedge key is located beneath the front of the wheel cylinder **(see illustrations)**. The brake drum can now be withdrawn.

Inspection

Note: *If either drum requires renewal, BOTH should be renewed at the same time, to ensure even and consistent braking. New brake shoes should also be fitted.*

4 Brush the dust and dirt from the drum, taking care not to inhale it.

5 Examine the internal friction surface of the drum. If deeply scored, or so worn that the drum has become ridged to the width of the shoes, then both drums must be renewed.

6 Regrinding of the friction surface may be possible provided the maximum diameter given in the Specifications and on the drum itself is not exceeded.

Refitting

7 If a new brake drum is to be fitted, use a suitable solvent to remove any preservative coating that may have been applied to its interior. Prior to refitting the drum, fully retract the brake shoes by lifting up the wedge key.

8 Refit the brake drum and tighten the securing screw.

9 Adjust the brakes by operating the footbrake a number of times. A clicking noise will be heard at the drum as the automatic adjuster operates. When the clicking stops, adjustment is complete.

10 Refit the roadwheel and lower the car to the ground.

11 Repeat the above procedure on the remaining rear brake assembly, then check and, if necessary, adjust the handbrake cable (see Section 17).

12 On completion, refit the roadwheels, then lower the car to the ground and tighten the wheel bolts to the specified torque.

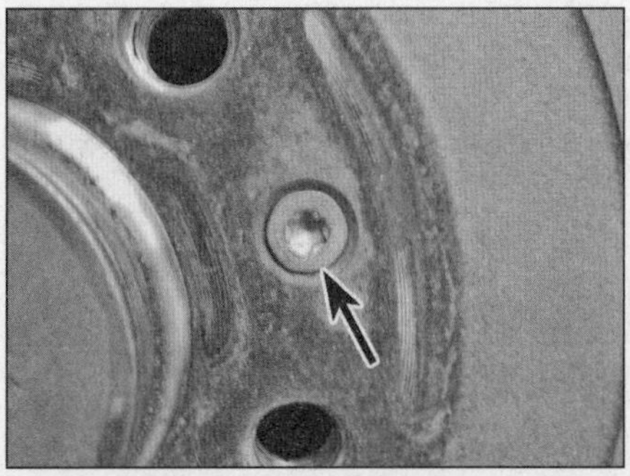

10.3a Rear brake drum securing screw

10.3b If the drum is tight, insert a screwdriver in through one of the wheel bolt holes...

10.3c ...and lever up on the wedge key to retract the brake shoes (drum removed for clarity)

10.3d Removing the rear brake drum

11 Rear brake shoes – removal, inspection and refitting

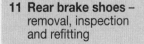

Note: *Refer to the warning at the start of Section before starting work.*

1 Remove the brake drum (see Section 10), then carefully remove all traces of brake dust from the brake drum, backplate and shoes.

2 Measure the thickness of the friction material of each brake shoe at several points; if either shoe is worn at any point to the specified minimum thickness or less, **all four** shoes must be renewed as a set. The shoes should also be renewed if any are fouled with oil or grease; there is no way of degreasing friction material, once contaminated.

3 If any of the brake shoes are worn unevenly, or fouled with oil or grease, trace and rectify the cause before reassembly.

4 To renew the brake shoes, continue as follows. If all is well, refit the brake drum as described in Section 10.

5 Note the position of the brake shoes and springs, and mark the webs of the shoes, if necessary, to aid refitting **(see illustration)**.

6 To facilitate easy removal and refitting of the brake shoes, we found it necessary to remove the hub/bearing assembly first (see Chapter 10 Section 9), although this may not be necessary on some models.

7 Using a pair of pliers, remove the shoe retainer spring cups by depressing and turning them through 90°. With the cups removed, lift off the springs and withdraw the retainer pins **(see illustration)**.

8 Ease the shoes out one at a time from the

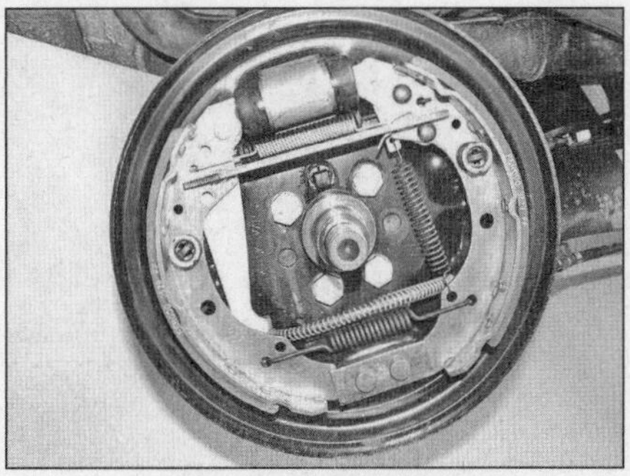

11.5 Note the position of the brake shoes before dismantling them

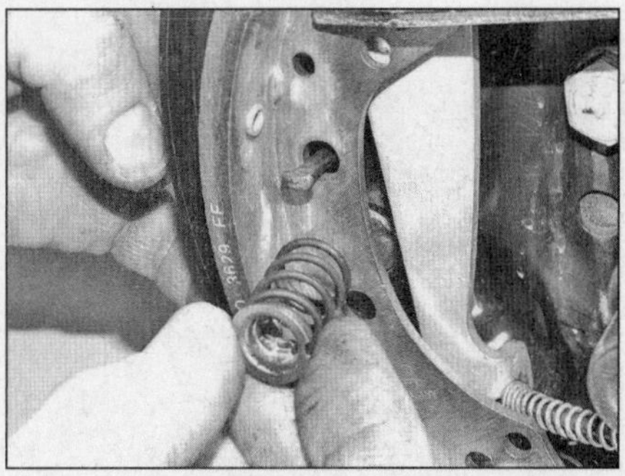

11.7 Removing the shoe retainer spring cup, spring and retainer pin

11.8a Ease the shoes out from the lower pivot point...

11.8b ...and detach the lower return spring

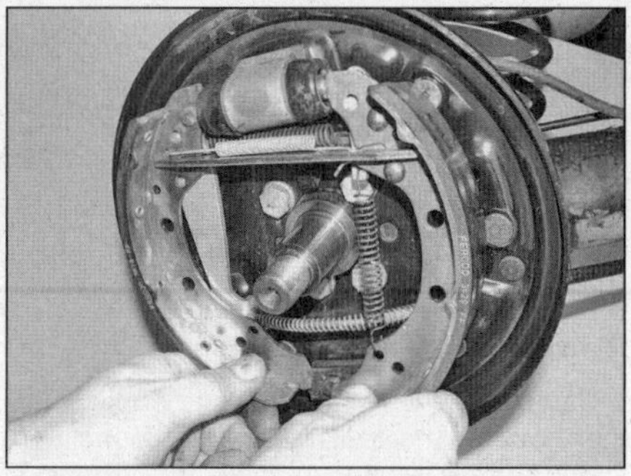
11.9a Ease the upper ends of the shoes from their wheel cylinder locations...

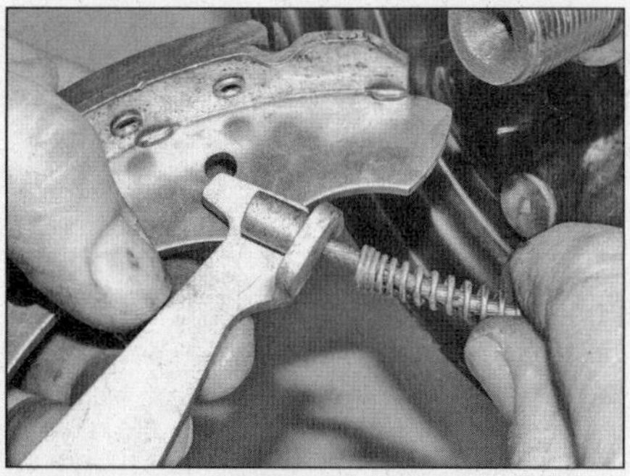
11.9b ...then disconnect the handbrake cable and remove the shoe assembly

11.9c Use a cable-tie or elastic band to retain the wheel cylinder pistons

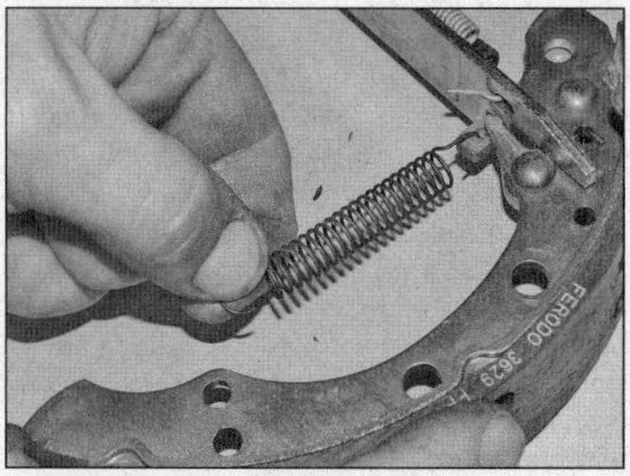
11.10 Unhook the adjuster wedge key spring and remove it

lower pivot point, to release the tension of the return spring, then disconnect the lower return spring from both shoes **(see illustrations)**.

9 Ease the upper end of both shoes out from their wheel cylinder locations, taking care not to damage the wheel cylinder seals, and disconnect the handbrake cable from the trailing shoe. The brake shoe assembly can then be manoeuvred out of position and away from the backplate. Do not depress the brake pedal until the brakes are reassembled; wrap a strong elastic band or fit a cable tie around the wheel cylinder pistons to retain them **(see illustrations)**.

10 Make a note of the correct fitted positions of all components, then unhook the spring, and disengage the wedge key spring **(see illustration)**.

11 Unhook the upper return spring and remove the trailing shoe from the leading shoe and strut. A length of bent welding rod may be used to unhook the spring **(see illustrations)**.

12 Withdraw the wedge key, noting which way around it is fitted, then ease the strut out from the leading shoe and detach the tensioning spring. If necessary, mount the strut in a vice, and use the length of bent welding rod to remove the spring **(see illustrations)**.

13 Examine all components for signs of wear or damage, and renew as necessary.

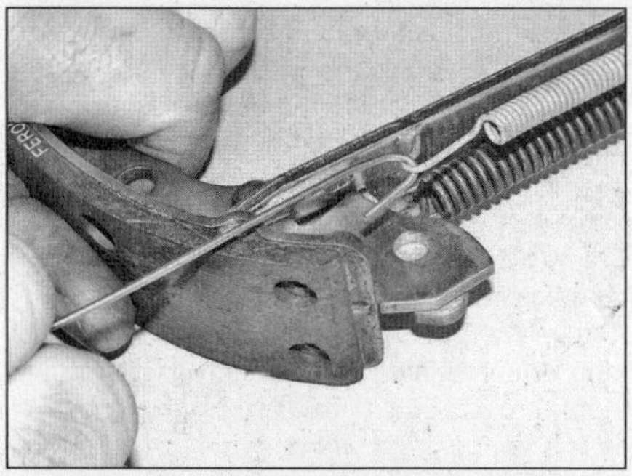
11.11a Using a length of bent welding rod to unhook the upper return spring

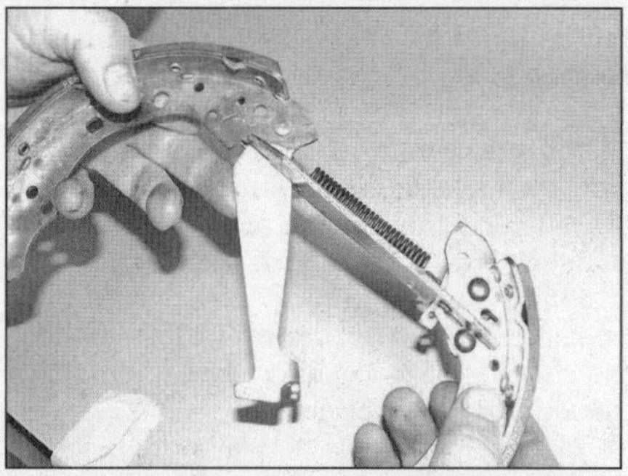
11.11b Remove the trailing shoe from the leading shoe and strut

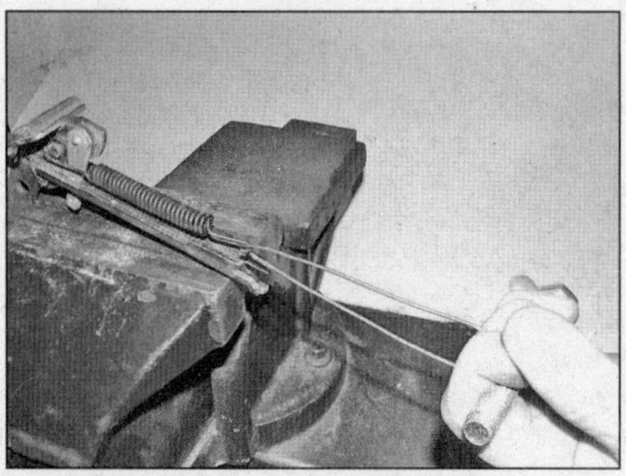
11.12a Mount the strut in a vice, and use welding rod to unhook the tensioning spring

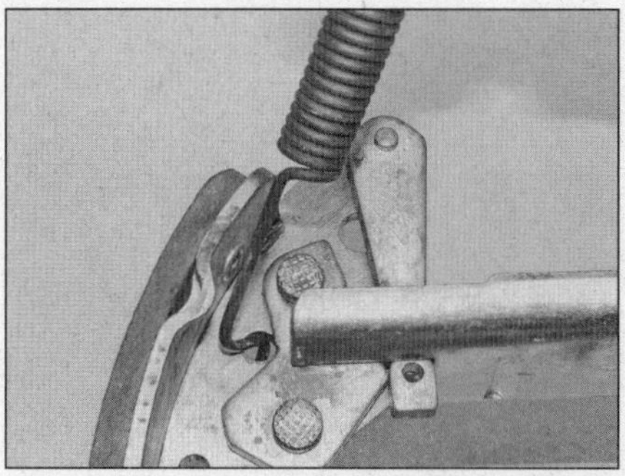
11.12b Remove the wedge key and unhook the spring...

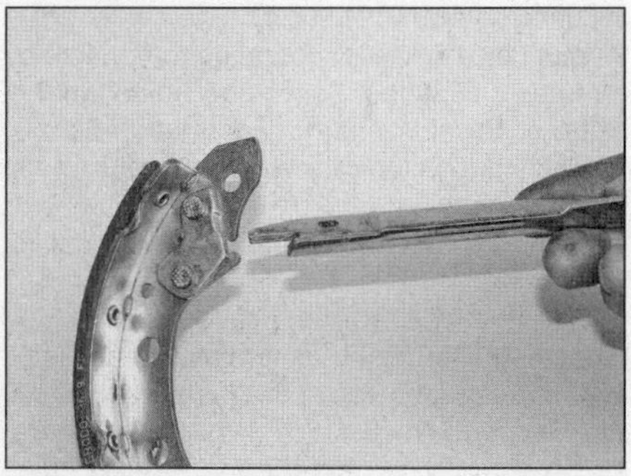
11.12c ...then separate the strut from the leading shoe

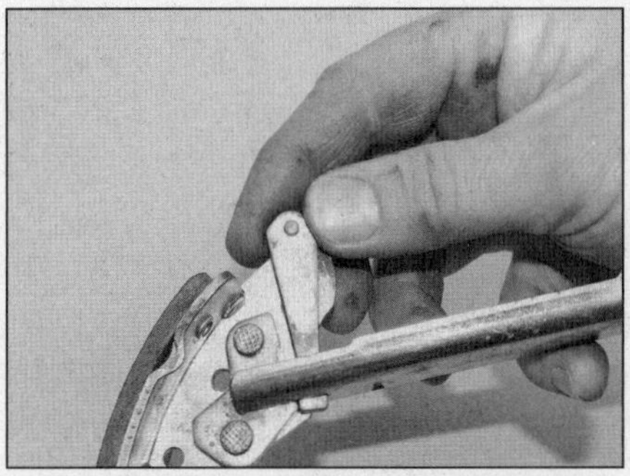

11.17 Insert the wedge key, ensuring its peg is facing away from the shoe

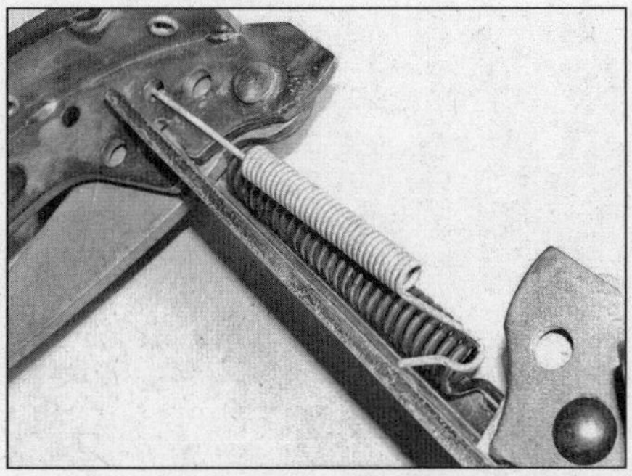

11.18 Refitting the upper return spring

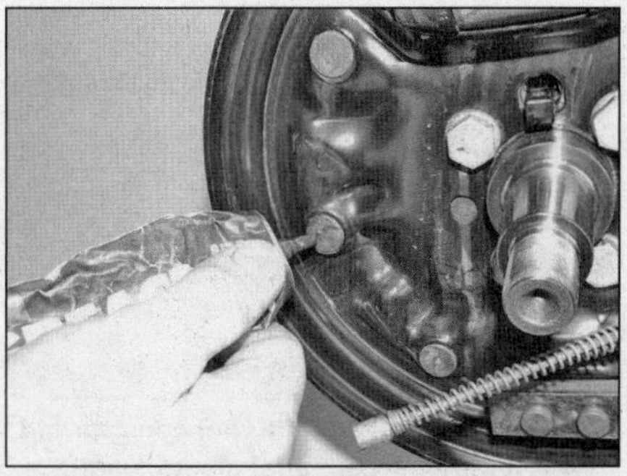

11.20 Apply high-temperature brake grease to the shoe contact areas on the backplate

14 Peel back the rubber protective caps, and check the wheel cylinder for fluid leaks or other damage; check that both cylinder pistons are free to move easily. Refer to Section 12, if necessary, for information on wheel cylinder overhaul.
15 Apply a little brake grease to the contact areas of the pushrod and handbrake lever.
16 Hook the tensioning spring into the leading shoe. Engage the strut with the opposite end of the spring, and pivot the strut into position into the leading shoe slot.
17 Insert the wedge key between the leading shoe and pushrod, making sure it is fitted the correct way around **(see illustration)**.
18 Fit the upper return spring to the leading shoe and engage the spring in its hole in the trailing shoe **(see illustration)**. Ensure the spring is correctly fitted then pivot the trailing shoe into position making sure both the shoe and handbrake lever are correctly engaged with the strut.
19 Fit the spring to the wedge key, and hook it onto the trailing shoe.
20 Prior to installation, clean the backplate, and apply a thin smear of high-temperature brake grease or anti-seize compound to the shoe contact areas **(see illustration)**, and to the wheel cylinder pistons and lower pivot point. Do not allow the lubricant to foul the friction material.
21 Remove the elastic band or cable tie fitted to the wheel cylinder, and offer up the shoe assembly.
22 Connect the handbrake cable to the handbrake lever, and locate the top of the shoes in the wheel cylinder piston slots.
23 Fit the lower return spring to the shoes, then lever the bottom of the shoes onto the bottom anchor.
24 Tap the shoes to centralise them with the backplate, then refit the shoe retainer pins and springs, and secure them in position with the spring cups.
25 Refit the hub as described in Chapter 10 Section 9, and then refit the brake drum as described in Section 10.
26 Repeat the above procedure on the remaining rear brake.
27 Once both sets of rear shoes have been renewed, adjust the lining-to-drum clearance by repeatedly depressing the brake pedal until normally (non-assisted) pedal pressure returns.
28 Check and, if necessary, adjust the handbrake as described in Section 17.
29 On completion, check the hydraulic fluid level as described in *Weekly checks*.

12 Rear wheel cylinder – Inspection, removal and refitting

Note: *Before starting work, refer to the note at the beginning of Section 2 concerning the dangers of hydraulic fluid, and to the warning at the beginning of the Section 1 concerning the dangers of asbestos dust.*

Inspection

1 Remove the brake drum as described in Section 10.
2 Pull back the dust seal and check for the presence of brake fluid. If traces of moisture are visible the cylinder should be replaced.

Removal

3 Using pliers, carefully unhook the upper brake shoe return spring, and remove it from both brake shoes. Pull the upper ends of the shoes away from the wheel cylinder to disengage them from the pistons.
4 Minimise fluid loss by first removing the master cylinder reservoir cap, and then tightening it down onto a piece of polythene, to obtain an airtight seal. Alternatively, use a brake hose clamp, a G-clamp or a similar tool to clamp the flexible hose at the nearest convenient point to the wheel cylinder.
5 Wipe away all traces of dirt around the brake pipe union at the rear of the wheel cylinder, and unscrew the union nut. Carefully ease the pipe out of the wheel cylinder, and plug or tape over its end to prevent dirt entry. Wipe off any spilt immediately.
6 Unscrew the two wheel cylinder retaining bolts from the rear of the backplate, and remove the cylinder, taking great care not to allow surplus hydraulic fluid to contaminate the brake shoe linings.

Refitting

7 Ensure that the backplate and wheel cylinder mating surfaces are clean, then spread the brake shoes and manoeuvre the wheel cylinder into position. Engage the brake pipe, and screw in the union nut two or three turns to ensure that the thread has started.
8 Insert the two wheel cylinder retaining bolts, and tighten them to the specified torque. Now fully tighten the brake pipe union nut.
9 Remove the clamp from the flexible brake hose, or the polythene from the master cylinder reservoir (as applicable).
10 Ensure that the brake shoes are correctly located in the cylinder pistons, and then refit the brake shoe upper return spring, using a screwdriver to stretch the spring into position.
11 Refit the brake drum (see Section 10).
12 Bleed the brake hydraulic system as described in Section 2. Providing suitable precautions were taken to minimise loss of fluid, it should only be necessary to bleed the relevant rear brake.

13 Brake pedal – removal and refitting

Removal

Note: *The brake pedal is removed with the accelerator pedal.*

1 Disconnect the battery negative lead as described in Chapter 5A Section 3.
2 Where fitted, remove the trim panel and air distribution duct from below the facia panel on the driver's side, across the top of the pedal assembly.
3 Disconnect the wiring plug form the accelerator pedal and then (where fitted) undo the mounting bolt/nut and remove the crash bar from above the brake pedal.
4 It is now necessary to release the brake pedal from the ball on the vacuum servo pushrod. To do this, a Seat special tool is available, but a suitable alternative can be improvised. Note that the plastic lugs in the pedal are very stiff, and it will not be possible to release them by hand. Depress and hold down the pedal, then, using the tool, release the securing lugs, and pull the pedal from the servo pushrod **(see illustrations)**.

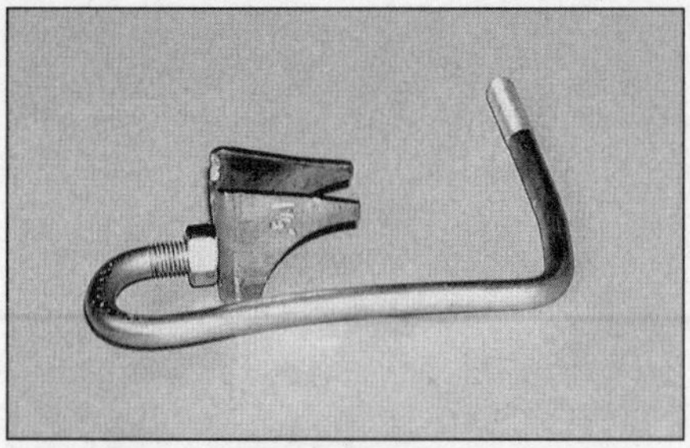

13.4a Improvised special tool constructed from a modified exhaust clamp, used to release the brake pedal from the servo pushrod

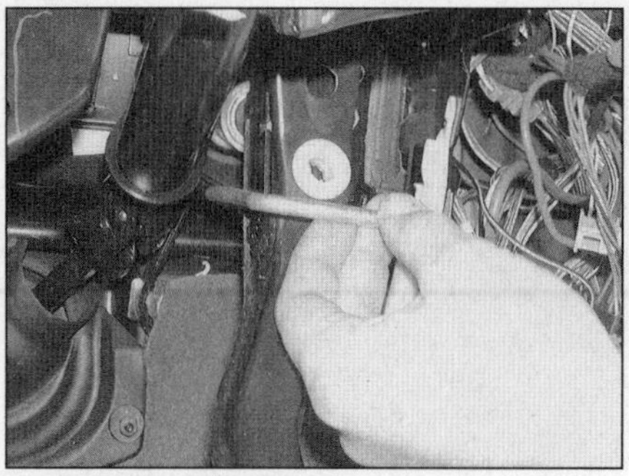

13.4b Using the tool to release the brake pedal from the servo pushrod

13.4c The plastic lugs securing the brake pedal to the servo pushrod

5 Remove the pedal assembly mounting nuts and withdraw the pedals from the vehicle.

6 Carefully clean all components, and renew any that are worn or damaged.

Refitting

7 Prior to refitting, apply a smear of multi-purpose grease to the pivot shaft and pedal bearing surfaces.

8 Hold the servo unit pushrod, and push the pedal back onto the pushrod ball. Make sure the pedal is securely fastened to the pushrod.

9 The remainder of the refitting procedure is the opposite of the removal.

14 Servo unit – testing, removal and refitting

Testing

1 To test the operation of the servo unit, depress the footbrake several times to exhaust the vacuum, then start the engine whilst keeping the pedal firmly depressed. As the engine starts, there should be a noticeable 'give' in the brake pedal as the vacuum builds-up. Allow the engine to run for at least two minutes, and then switch it off. If the brake pedal is now depressed, it should feel normal, but further applications should result in the pedal feeling firmer, with the pedal stroke decreasing with each application.

2 If the servo does not operate as described, first inspect the servo unit non-return valve as described in Section 15. On diesel models (and some petrol models), also check the operation of the vacuum pump as described in Section 24.

3 If the servo unit still fails to operate satisfactorily, the fault lies within the unit itself. Repairs to the unit are not possible – if faulty, the servo unit must be renewed.

Removal

4 The number of components requiring removal will depend on the engine fitted. Not all parts refereed to are fitted to all engines.

5 Remove the air filter housing and charge air ducting as required.

6 Jack up and support the vehicle as described in *Jacking and vehicle support*. Remove the engine undershield and (where fitted) the driveshaft heat shield.

7 Where applicable remove the heat shield from the servo, then carefully ease the vacuum valve out from the sealing grommet in the front of the servo. Where applicable, also disconnect the wiring from the servo vacuum sensor, then extract the retaining circlip with a screwdriver, and withdraw the sensor from the servo.

8 Remove the master cylinder as described in Section 16.

9 On LHD models with manual transmission, disconnect the gearchange cables from the levers on the transmission, then unbolt the gearchange support bracket and tie it to one side.

10 Release the brake pedal pushrod from the brake servo as described in Section 13 and then unbolt the brake pedal assembly.

11 Support the weight of the engine under the sump with a trolley jack. Using a block of wood to spread the load and then remove the right-hand engine mount and rear pendulum mount as described Chapter 2A Section 20 (1.0 litre engines), Chapter 2B Section 17 (1.2 SOHC engines), Section (1.2 DOHC engines), Chapter 2D Section 19 (1.4 litre engines) or Chapter 2E Section 16 (1.6 litre diesel engines).

12 Carefully lower and raise the engine (using the trolley jack) to create enough space to extract the brake servo. On some engines the engine must be pulled forward to make the space. Install an engine crane to take the weight of the engine if this is the case. Note that pulling the right-hand end of the engine forward may damage the exhaust system flexible mount. If this is the case disconnect the exhaust at the manifold/turbocharger.

15.1 Non-return valve and vacuum sensor in the brake servo vacuum pipe

13 Manoeuvre the servo unit out of position, and recover the gasket where fitted.

Refitting

14 Check the servo unit vacuum hose sealing grommet for signs of damage or deterioration, and renew if necessary.

15 Where applicable, fit a new gasket to the rear of the servo unit, and then reposition the unit in the engine compartment.

16 From inside the vehicle, ensure that the servo unit pushrod is correctly engaged with the brake pedal, and push the pedal onto the pushrod ball. Check the pushrod ball is securely engaged, then refit the servo unit mounting nuts and tighten them to the specified torque.

17 On LHD models with manual transmission, refit the gearchange cables and support bracket.

18 Carefully ease the vacuum hose back into position in the servo, taking great care not to displace the sealing grommet. Refit the heat shield to the servo and, where applicable, refit the vacuum sensor and wiring.

19 Refit the master cylinder as described in Section 16 of this Chapter.

20 On completion, start the engine and check for air leaks at the vacuum hose-to-servo unit connection; check the operation of the braking system.

15 Servo non-return valve – testing, removal and refitting

1 The non-return valve is located in the vacuum hose leading from the inlet manifold or vacuum pump to the brake servo. Some models also have a vacuum sensor fitted **(see illustration)**.

Removal

2 Ease the vacuum hose out of the servo unit, taking care not to displace the grommet.

3 Note the routing of the hose, then slacken the retaining clip(s) and disconnect the opposite end of the hose assembly from the manifold/vacuum pump **(see illustration)** and remove it from the car. Note that the check valve is supplied with the hose as a single assembly.

Testing

4 Examine the check valve and vacuum hose for signs of damage, and renew if necessary.
5 The valve may be tested by blowing through it in both directions; air should flow through the valve in one direction only; when blown through from the servo unit end of the valve. Renew the valve if this is not the case.
6 Examine the servo unit rubber sealing grommet for signs of damage or deterioration, and renew as necessary.

Refitting

7 Ensure that the sealing grommet is correctly fitted to the servo unit.
8 Ease the hose union into position in the servo, taking great care not to displace or damage the grommet.
9 Ensure that the hose is correctly routed, and connect it to the inlet manifold/vacuum pump, ensuring the hose is secured in the retaining clips.
10 On completion, start the engine and check the valve-to-servo unit connection for signs of air leaks.

15.3 Disconnect the hose from the vacuum pump (diesel engine shown)

16 Master cylinder – removal, overhaul and refitting

Note: *Before starting work, refer to the warning at the beginning of Section 2 concerning the dangers of hydraulic fluid. A new master cylinder O-ring will be required on refitting.*

Removal

1 Disconnect the battery negative lead as described in Chapter 5A Section 3. Remove the engine top cover and air inlet trunking as required.
2 On LHD models, remove the battery and tray.
3 Disconnect the wiring plug from the coolant reservoir, remove the screws and move the reservoir to the side.
4 On models with fuel lines connected close to the master cylinder depressurise the fuel system (Chapter 4A Section 8) and then disconnect the fuel lines. Seal the fuel lines.
5 Remove the master cylinder reservoir cap, disconnecting the wiring plug from the brake fluid level warning switch **(see illustration)**, and then syphon the hydraulic fluid from the reservoir. **Note:** *Do not syphon the fluid by mouth, as it is poisonous; use a syringe or an old antifreeze tester.*
6 Disconnect the wiring connector from the brake light switch **(see illustration 21.1)**, at the lower part of the master cylinder.
7 To remove the hydraulic fluid reservoir from the top of the master cylinder, undo the retaining bolt and pull the reservoir upwards from the rubber grommets **(see illustration)**. On manual transmission models, disconnect and plug the clutch master cylinder supply hose from the side of the brake fluid reservoir.
8 Wipe clean the area around the brake pipe unions on the side of the master cylinder, and place absorbent rags beneath the pipe unions to catch any leaking fluid. Make a note of the correct fitted positions of the unions, then unscrew the union nuts and carefully withdraw the pipes. Plug or tape over the pipe ends and master cylinder orifices, to minimise the loss of brake fluid, and to prevent the entry of dirt into the system. Wash off any spilt fluid immediately with cold water.
9 Unscrew and remove the two nuts and washers securing the master cylinder to the vacuum servo unit, remove the heat shield (where fitted), then withdraw the unit from the engine compartment **(see illustration)**. Remove the O-ring from the rear of the master cylinder, and check it for damage, renew if required.

Overhaul

10 If the master cylinder is faulty, it must be renewed. Repair kits are not available from Seat dealers, so the cylinder must be treated as a sealed unit.
11 The only items that can be renewed are the mounting seals for the fluid reservoir; if these show signs of deterioration, prise them out with a screwdriver. Lubricate the new seals with clean brake fluid, and press them into the master cylinder ports.

Refitting

12 Remove all traces of dirt from the master cylinder and servo unit mating surfaces, and fit a new O-ring to the groove on the master cylinder body.
13 Fit the master cylinder to the servo unit, ensuring that the servo unit pushrod enters the master cylinder bore centrally. Refit the heat shield (where applicable), and the master cylinder mounting nuts, and then tighten them to the specified torque.
14 Wipe clean the brake pipe unions, then refit them to the master cylinder ports and tighten them securely.
15 Refit the hydraulic fluid reservoir; making sure it is entered correctly in the rubber grommets.
16 On manual transmission models, reconnect the clutch master cylinder supply hose to the reservoir.
17 Refill the master cylinder reservoir with new fluid, and bleed the complete hydraulic system as described in Section 2.
18 Reconnect the wiring to the brake level sender unit and brake light switch as applicable.
19 On LHD models, refit the battery and tray.
20 Refit the engine cover and air trunking where necessary, and then reconnect the battery negative lead.

17 Handbrake – adjustment

1 To check the handbrake adjustment, first apply the footbrake firmly several times to establish correct shoe-to-drum/pad-to-disc clearance, then apply and release the handbrake three times.

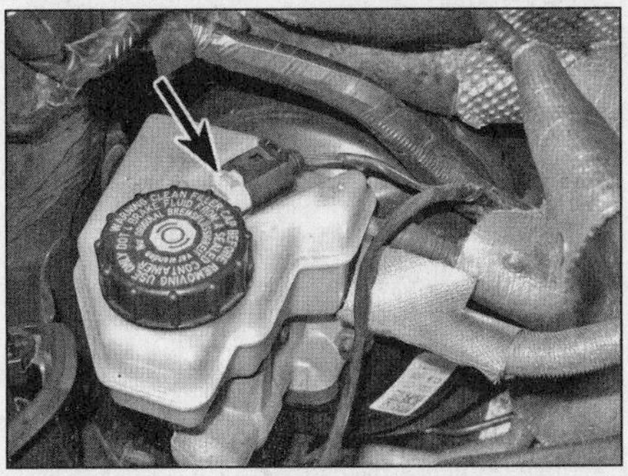

16.5 Brake fluid level warning switch

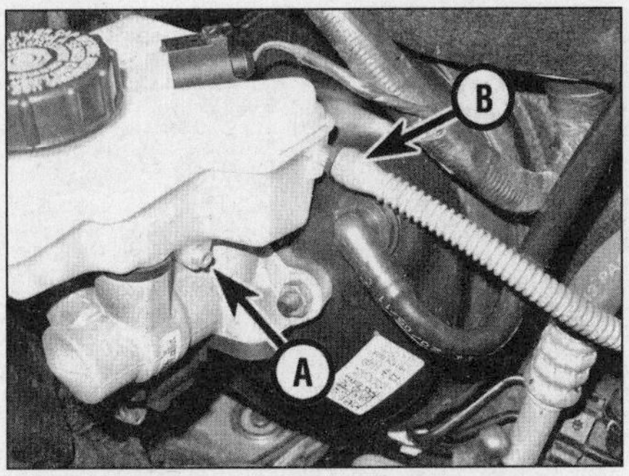

16.7 Reservoir retaining bolt (A) – clutch supply hose (B)

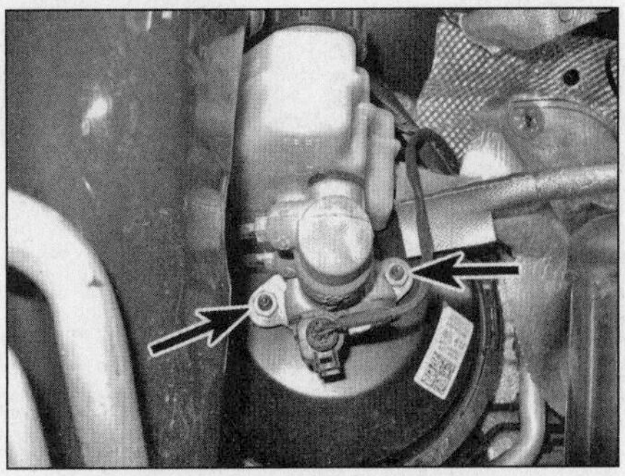

16.9 Master cylinder securing nuts

17.3 Handbrake cable adjuster nut

2 Applying normal moderate pressure, pull the handbrake lever to the fully applied position, counting the number of clicks emitted from the handbrake ratchet mechanism. If adjustment is correct, there should be approximately 4 clicks before the handbrake is fully applied. If there are more clicks, adjust as follows.

3 Depending on specification, it will be necessary to either remove the centre trim from the centre console or remove the armrest and then the centre trim. See Chapter 11 Section 27, as applicable, to gain access to the handbrake lever adjustment nut **(see illustration)**.

4 Chock the front wheels, then jack up the rear of the car and support it on axle stands. Continue as described under the relevant sub-heading.

Rear drum brake models

5 With the handbrake set on the 1st notch of the ratchet mechanism, turn the adjustment nut until it is just difficult to turn both rear wheels. Now release the handbrake lever, and check that the wheels rotate freely; if not, back off the adjustment nut. Apply the handbrake fully, and check that the handbrake is fully applied on the 4th notch.

6 Once adjustment is correct, refit the centre console upper rear section as described in Chapter 11 Section 27.

Rear disc brake models

Note: *Adjustment will normally only be require after replacing the handbrake cable, the brake disc or the caliper. Adjustment will not normally be require after changing the brake pads.*

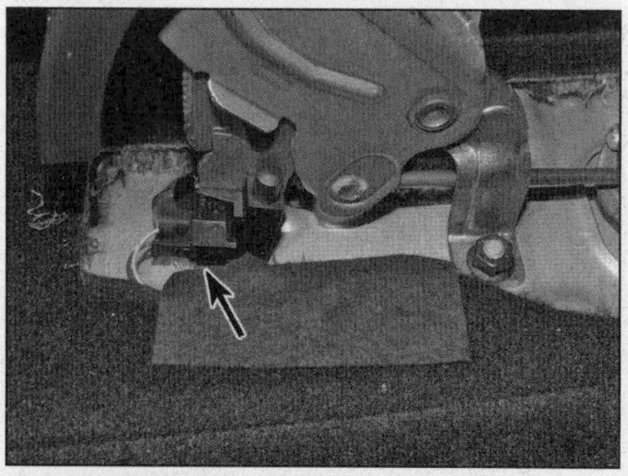

18.3 Handbrake warning light switch

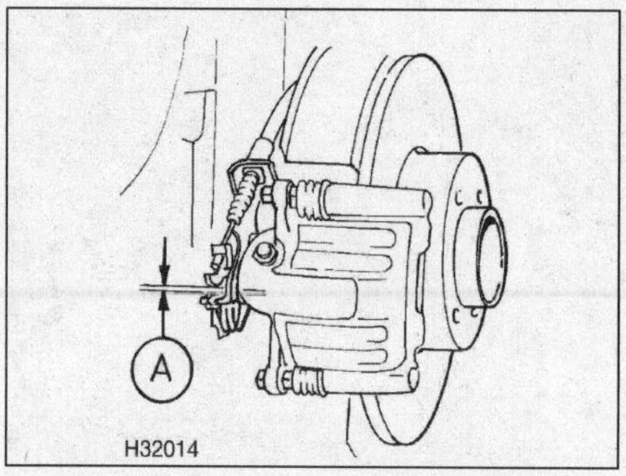

17.8 Turn the nut until a gap (A) of between 1.0 and 1.5 mm can be seen

7 With the handbrake fully released, slacken the adjustment nut until both the rear caliper handbrake levers are back against their stops.

8 Tighten the adjustment nut until both handbrake levers just move off the caliper stops. **Note:** *The nut is contoured to prevent it coming loose, and it is important that the adjustment is checked with the nut fully seated in the equaliser bar.* The gap between each caliper handbrake lever and its stop must be between 1.0 and 1.5 mm **(see illustration)**.

9 Fully apply the handbrake lever three times, then release it and check that both wheels still rotate freely. Check the adjustment by applying the handbrake fully, counting the clicks emitted from the handbrake ratchet. The handbrake must be fully applied on the 4th notch.

10 Once adjustment is correct, refit the centre console centre section as described in Chapter 11 Section 27.

18 Handbrake lever – removal and refitting

Removal

1 Remove the centre console as described in Chapter 11 Section 27.

2 If desired, remove the handbrake lever cover sleeve by depressing the locating tag with a screwdriver, then sliding the sleeve from the lever.

3 Disconnect the wiring connector from the handbrake 'on' warning light switch **(see illustration)**.

4 Loosen the handbrake cable adjuster nut sufficiently to allow the ends of the cables to be disengaged from the equaliser plate.

5 Unscrew the retaining nuts, and withdraw the lever.

Refitting

6 Refitting is a reversal of removal, bearing in mind the following points.

a) *Before refitting the handbrake lever cover, adjust the handbrake as described in Section 17.*

b) *Check the operation of the handbrake 'on' warning switch before refitting the centre console.*

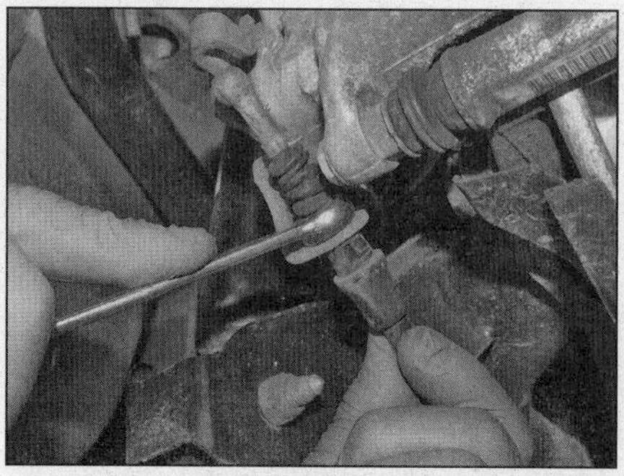

19.6 Release the cable inner from its lever and withdraw the cable from the caliper

19 Handbrake cables – removal and refitting

Removal

1 Remove the centre console as described in Chapter 11 Section 27, to gain access to the handbrake lever. The handbrake cable consists of two sections, a right- and a left-hand section, which are linked to the lever by an equaliser plate. Each section can be removed individually.

2 Loosen the handbrake cable adjuster nut sufficiently to allow the ends of the cables to be disengaged from the equaliser plate, see Section 18.

3 Chock the front wheels, then jack up the rear of the car and support it on axle stands (see *Jacking and vehicle support*).

4 Work back along the length of the cable, noting its correct routing, and free it from all the relevant guides and retaining clips.

5 On rear drum brake models, remove the brake shoes as described in Section 11, and then release the cable from the backplate.

6 On rear disc brake models, disengage the inner cable from the caliper handbrake lever, then remove the outer cable retaining clip and detach the cable from the caliper **(see illustration)**.

7 Withdraw the cable from beneath the car.

Refitting

8 Refitting is a reversal of removal, but adjust the handbrake as described in Section 17 before refitting the centre console.

20 Handbrake 'on' warning light switch – removal and refitting

Removal

1 Disconnect the battery negative lead as described in Chapter 5A Section 3.

2 Remove the centre console, with reference to Chapter 11 Section 27.

3 Disconnect the wiring plug from the switch.
4 Release the securing lugs, and remove the switch from the handbrake lever assembly **(see illustration)**.

Refitting

5 Refitting is a reversal of removal.

21 Brake light switch – removal and refitting

Removal

1 The brake light switch is located on the lower part of the master cylinder **(see illustration)**. Remove the engine cover (diesel engines) and where applicable, remove the air inlet trunking to improve access.
2 Disconnect the wiring from the switch.
3 Unscrew the mounting bolt, then pull the switch from the bottom of the master cylinder, and remove it from the locking lug at the top.

Refitting

4 Refitting is a reversal of removal, but tighten the mounting bolt to the specified torque.

22 Anti-lock braking system (ABS) – general information and precautions

1 The anti-lock braking system (ABS) fitted as standard to all models, prevents wheel lock-up under heavy braking, and not only optimises stopping distances, but also improves steering control. By electronically monitoring the speed of each roadwheel in relation to the other wheels, the system can detect when a wheel is about to lock-up, before control is actually lost. The brake fluid pressure applied to that wheel's brake caliper is then decreased and restored ('modulated') several times a second until control is regained. The system components are: four wheel-speed sensors, a hydraulic unit with integral Electronic Control Unit (ECU), brake lines and a dashboard-mounted warning light. The four wheel-speed sensors are mounted on the wheel hub carriers. Each wheel has a rotating toothed hub mounted on the driveshaft (front) or on the hub (rear). The wheel speed sensors are mounted in close proximity to these hubs. The teeth produce a voltage waveform whose frequency varies with the speed of the hubs. These waveforms are transmitted to the ECU, and used to calculate the rotational speed of each wheel. The ECU has a self-diagnostic facility, to inhibit the operation of the ABS if a fault is detected, lighting the dashboard-mounted warning light. The braking system will then revert to conventional, non-ABS operation. If the nature of the fault is not immediately obvious upon inspection, the vehicle should be taken to a Seat dealer or suitably equipped garage, who will have the diagnostic equipment required to interrogate the ABS ECU electronically and pin-point the problem.

20.4 Unclip the handbrake warning light switch

2 There are two ABS systems fitted to the models covered in this Manual.
3 One version includes a traction control system (TCS), which uses the basic ABS system, with an additional pump and valves fitted to the hydraulic actuator. If wheelspin is detected at a speed below 30 mph, one of the valves opens, to allow the pump to pressurise the relevant brake, until the spinning wheel slows to a rotational speed corresponding to the speed of the vehicle. This has the effect of transferring torque to the wheel with most traction. At the same time, the throttle plate is closed slightly, to reduce the torque from the engine.
4 The second version includes electronic differential locking (EDL) and an electronic stability programme (ESP). The EDL system applies the brake of the spinning wheel in order to transfer torque to the wheel with the better grip. On models with ESP, the system recognises critical driving conditions and stabilises the vehicle by individual wheel braking and by intervention in the engine control, which occurs independently of the position of the brake and accelerator pedals.
5 The operation of the ABS system is entirely dependent on electrical signals. To prevent the system responding to any inaccurate signals, a built-in safety circuit monitors all signals received by the ECU. If an inaccurate signal or low battery voltage is detected, the ABS system is automatically shut down, and the warning light on the instrument panel is illuminated, to inform the driver that the ABS system is not operational. Normal braking will still be available, however.

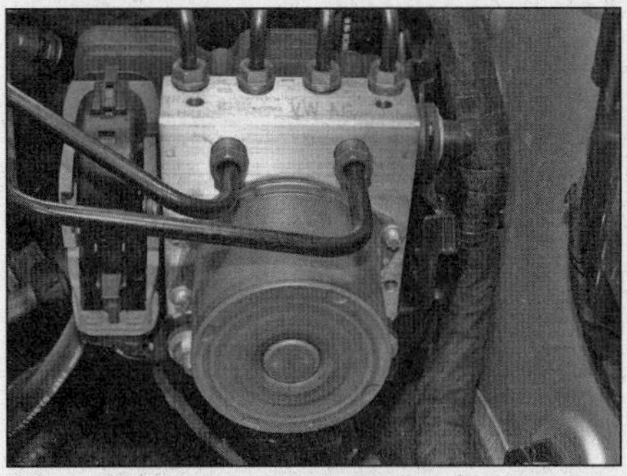

23.1 ABS hydraulic unit

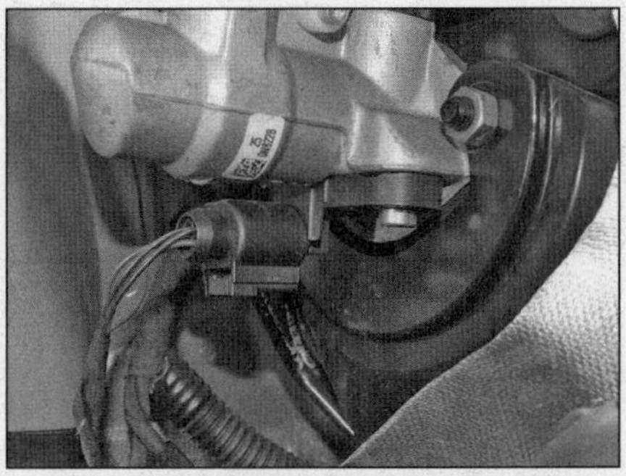

21.1 Brake light switch

6 If a fault does develop in the ABS system, the car must be taken to a Seat dealer for fault diagnosis and repair.

23 Anti-lock braking system (ABS) components – removal and refitting

Hydraulic unit

1 Removal and refitting of the hydraulic unit is best entrusted to a Seat dealer. It is positioned in the left-hand rear corner of the engine compartment, behind the battery **(see illustration)**. If the fluid is lost from the hydraulic unit, there is no guarantee that the unit can be sufficiently filled or the fluid bled through the unit. Also a fault diagnosis check must be performed on completion using specialist equipment.

Electronic control module (ECM)

2 The ECM is mounted at the rear of the hydraulic unit, secured by three Torx screws. Although it can be separated from the hydraulic unit, due to the delicacy of the components and the need for absolute cleanliness, it is recommended that the work be entrusted to a Seat dealer. See hydraulic unit information in paragraph 1.

Front wheel sensor

Removal

3 Chock the rear wheels, then firmly apply the handbrake, jack up the front of the car and support on axle stands (see *Jacking and vehicle support*). Remove the appropriate front roadwheel.
4 Disconnect the electrical connector from the sensor by carefully lifting up the retaining tag, and pulling the connector from the sensor **(see illustration)**.
5 Slacken and remove the hexagon socket-head bolt securing the sensor to the hub carrier, and remove the sensor from the car **(see illustration)**.

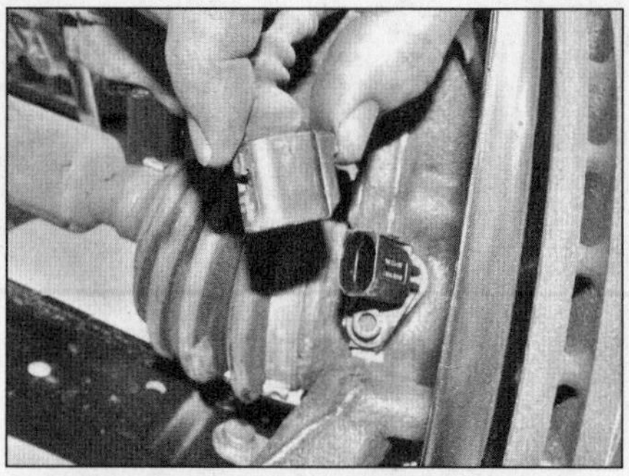

23.4 Disconnect the wiring connector...

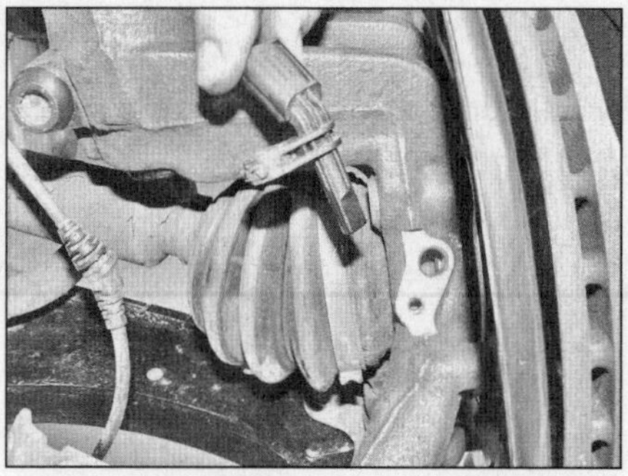

23.5 ...and unbolt the front wheel sensor

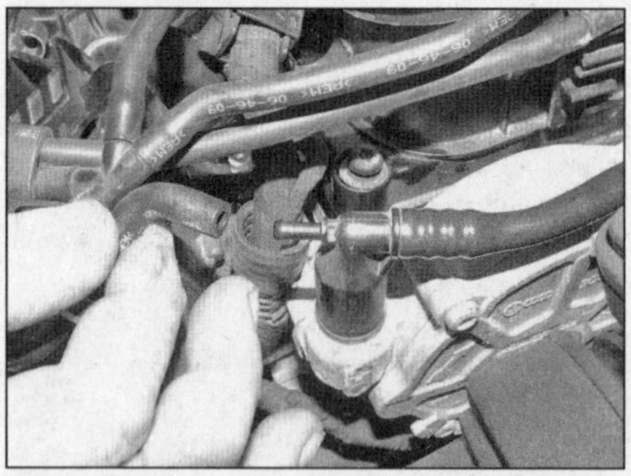

24.5 Disconnect the small vacuum pipe

24.7 Remove the vacuum hose and rubber seal

Refitting

6 Ensure that the sensor and hub carrier sealing faces are clean.

7 Apply a thin coat of multi-purpose grease to the mounting hole inner surface, then fit the sensor to the hub carrier. Refit the retaining bolt and tighten it to the specified torque.

8 Ensure that the sensor wiring is correctly routed and retained by all the necessary clips, and reconnect the wiring connector.

9 Refit the roadwheel, then lower the car to the ground and tighten the roadwheel bolts to the specified torque.

Rear wheel sensor

Removal

10 Chock the front wheels, then jack up the rear of the car and support it on axle stands (see *Jacking and vehicle support*). Remove the appropriate roadwheel.

11 Remove the sensor as described in paragraphs 4 and 5, for front wheel speed sensor.

Refitting

12 Refit the sensor as described above in paragraphs 6 to 9.

Reluctor rings

13 The reluctor rings are integral with the wheel bearings (front and rear), and can only be inspected after removal of the hub assembly. If faulty, the bearings must be renewed as described in Chapter 10 Section 3 (front) and Chapter 10 Section 9 (rear).

24 Vacuum pump – testing, removal and refitting

Note: *A vacuum pump is fitted to all diesel models and all 1.0 litre and 1.2 litre petrol models except the 1.2 SOHC engine (code CBZB). Repair is not possible on either type of pump, if faulty the pump must be replaced.*

24.8 Vacuum pump securing bolts

24.10 The petrol engine vacuum pump

Testing

1 The operation of the braking system vacuum pump can be checked using a vacuum gauge. First, remove the engine top cover to access the vacuum hose.

2 Disconnect the vacuum hose from the pump, and connect the gauge to the pump union using a suitable length of hose.

3 Start the engine and allow it to idle, and then measure the vacuum created by the pump. As a guide, after one minute, a minimum of approximately 500 mm Hg should be recorded. If the vacuum registered is significantly less than this, it is likely that the pump is faulty. However, seek the advice of a Seat dealer before condemning the pump.

4 Reconnect the vacuum hose. Overhaul of the vacuum pump is not possible, since no major components are available separately for it. If faulty, the complete pump assembly must be renewed.

Removal

Diesel engine

Note: *A new pump O-ring will be required on refitting.*

5 Disconnect the small vacuum pipe from the vacuum hose connector on the top of the vacuum pump **(see illustration)**.

6 Release the securing clips and remove the air intake hose from across the end of the cylinder head, to access the vacuum pump.

7 Pull the vacuum hose from the top of the pump, noting the rubber seal may stay on the vacuum pump outlet pipe **(see illustration)**.

8 Unscrew the four mounting bolts and withdraw the vacuum pump from the cylinder head **(see illustration)**. Recover the O-ring seal and discard, as a new one will be required for refitting.

Petrol engine

9 The pump is mounted behind the right-hand headlight. Disconnect the wiring plug.

10 Disconnect the vacuum line(s) and pull the pump straight up off the rubber mountings **(see illustration)**.

Refitting

Diesel engines

11 Fit the new O-ring seal to the vacuum pump, and apply a smear of oil to aid installation.

12 Manoeuvre the vacuum pump into position, making sure that the slot in the pump drive gear aligns with the slot on the pump driveshaft.

13 Refit the pump retaining bolts, and tighten to the specified torque.

14 Reconnect the vacuum hoses and secure with the retaining clip (where fitted). If the vacuum hose seal is still fitted to the outlet pipe on the vacuum pump, remove it and fit it inside the end of the vacuum hose before refitting.

15 Refit the air intake pipe and engine top cover.

Petrol engine

16 Refitting is a reversal of removal.

Chapter 10
Suspension and steering

Contents

Degrees of difficulty

Easy, suitable for novice with little experience	Fairly easy, suitable for beginner with some experience	Fairly difficult, suitable for competent DIY mechanic	Difficult, suitable for experienced DIY mechanic	Very difficult, suitable for expert DIY or professional

Specifications

Front suspension

Type	Independent, with MacPherson struts incorporating coil springs and telescopic shock absorbers. Anti-roll bar fitted to all models

Rear suspension

Type	Transverse torsion beam axle with trailing arms. Separate gas-filled telescopic shock absorbers and coil springs. Anti-roll bar fitted to all models

Steering

Type	Rack-and-pinion. Power assistance standard

Roadwheels

Type	Aluminium alloy

Tyres

Standard sizes	155/80R13, 165/70R14, 185/60R14, 185/55R15, 195/55R15 and 205/45R16
Pressures	See *Weekly checks*

Vehicle ride height

Front:	
Standard and sports running gear	369 mm
FR model running gear	364 mm
Rear:	
Standard and sports running gear	376 mm
FR model running gear	371 mm

Wheel alignment and steering angles*

Front wheel:	
Camber angle:	
Standard suspension	-39' ± 30'
Sports suspension	-39' ± 30'
Maximum difference between sides (all models)	30'
Castor angle:	
Standard suspension	5° 10' ± 30'
Sports suspension	5° 10' ± 30'
Maximum difference between sides (all models)	30'
Toe setting	+10' ± 10'
Toe-out on turns (20° left or right):	
Standard suspension	1° 19' ± 20'
Sports suspension	1° 19' ± 20'
Rear wheel:	
Camber angle	-1°30' ± 10'
Maximum difference between sides	30'
Toe in :	
Standard suspension	+26' ± 10'
Sports suspension	+26' ± 10'
Maximum difference between sides	20'

Note: * *Refer to a Seat dealer for the latest recommendations.*

Torque wrench settings	Nm	lbf ft
Front suspension		
Anti-roll bar:		
Drop link nuts	40	30
Mounting clamp bolts*:		
Stage 1	20	15
Stage 2	Angle-tighten a further 90°	
Driveshaft/Hub nut (12 point – 36mm)*:		
Stage 1	50	37
Stage 2	Angle-tighten a further 45°	
Engine rear mounting link:		
To transmission bolts*:		
Stage 1	30	22
Stage 2	Angle-tighten a further 90°	
To subframe bolt*:		
Stage 1	40	30
Stage 2	Angle-tighten a further 90°	
Lower arm:		
Front pivot bolt*:		
Stage 1	70	52
Stage 2	Angle-tighten a further 90°	
Lower arm mounting bracket rear plate:		
Small bolts*:		
Stage 1	20	15
Stage 2	Angle-tighten a further 90°	
Large bolt*:		
Stage 1	70	52
Stage 2	Angle-tighten a further 90°	
Balljoint-to-lower arm nuts*	100	74
Balljoint nut*:		
Stage 1	20	15
Stage 2	Angle-tighten a further 90°	
Subframe-to-underbody bolts*:		
Stage 1	70	52
Stage 2	Angle-tighten a further 90°	
Suspension strut:		
Bottom clamp bolt nut*:		
Stage 1	60	44
Stage 2	Angle-tighten a further 90°	
Piston rod nut*	60	44
Upper mounting-to-body nut*	60	44

**Do not re-use*

Torque wrench settings (continued)

Torque wrench settings (continued)	Nm	lbf ft
Rear suspension		
Axle mounting bolts and nuts*:		
Stage 1	45	33
Stage 2	Angle-tighten a further 90°	
Hub nut (12-point)*:		
Stage 1	70	52
Stage 2	Angle-tighten a further 30°	
Shock absorber:		
Lower mounting bolt and nut*:		
Stage 1	40	30
Stage 2	Angle-tighten a further 90°	
Upper mounting bracket-to-body bolts*:		
Stage 1	30	22
Stage 2	Angle-tighten a further 90°	
Upper mounting nut to bracket*	25	18
Stub axle/bearing hub bolts*:		
Stage 1	30	22
Stage 2	Angle-tighten a further 90°	
Vehicle level sender:		
Sender to underbody (pop-rivet screw)	8	6
Sender link to lower arm	6	4
Do not re-use		
Steering		
Power steering hose union to electric pump	30	22
Power steering hose union to steering gear:		
Supply (banjo bolt)	40	30
Return (union)	30	22
Steering column mounting bolts	23	17
Steering column lower universal joint clamp bolt*:		
Stage 1	20	15
Stage 2	Angle-tighten a further 180°	
Steering gear mounting bolts*:		
Stage 1	50	37
Stage 2	Angle-tighten a further 90°	
Steering wheel bolt*:		
Stage 1	30	22
Stage 2	Angle-tighten a further 90°	
Track rod balljoint nut*:		
Stage 1	20	15
Stage 2	Angle-tighten a further 90°	
Track rod balljoint locknut	50	37
Track rod inner balljoint to steering rack	80	59
Do not re-use		
Roadwheels		
Roadwheel bolts	120	89

1 General Information

1 The independent front suspension is of the MacPherson strut type, incorporating coil springs and integral telescopic shock absorbers. The struts are located by transverse lower suspension arms, which use rubber inner mounting bushes, and incorporate a balljoint at the outer ends. The front wheel bearing housings, which carry the wheel bearings, brake calipers and the hub/disc assemblies, are attached to the MacPherson struts by clamp bolts, and connected to the lower arms through the balljoints. A front anti-roll bar is fitted to all models. The anti-roll bar is rubber-mounted, and is connected to both lower suspension arms by short links.

2 The rear suspension consists of a torsion beam axle with telescopic shock absorbers and coil springs. An anti-roll bar is incorporated into the rear axle beam.

3 The safety steering column incorporates an intermediate shaft at its lower end. The intermediate shaft is connected to both the steering column and steering gear by universal joints, although the shaft is supplied as part of the column assembly and cannot be separated. Both the inner steering column and intermediate shaft have splined sections, which collapse during a major frontal impact. The outer column is also telescopic with two sections, to facilitate reach adjustment.

4 The steering gear is mounted onto the front subframe, and is connected by two track rods, with balljoints at their inner and outer ends, to the steering arms projecting rearwards from the wheel bearing housings. The track rod ends are threaded to the track rods in order to allow adjustment of the front wheel toe setting.

5 Electrically Powered Hydraulic Steering (EPHS) is fitted as standard on all early models. Later models have electric power steering, with the motor incorporated into the steering column. On EPHS models, the system electric pump and hydraulic fluid reservoir are located behind the front bumper, on the left-hand side.

6 All UK models are fitted with an Anti-lock Brake System (ABS), and most models can

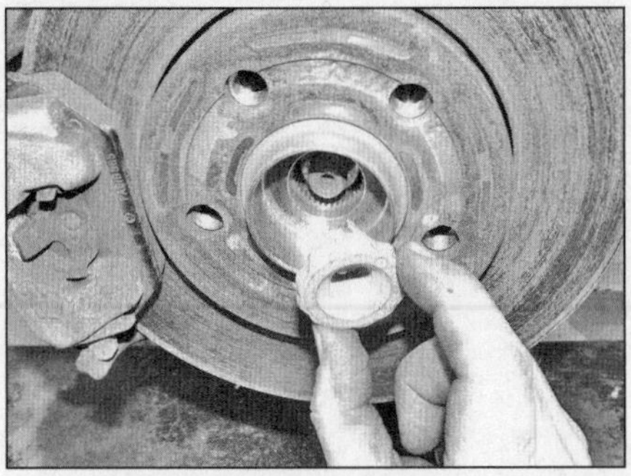

2.3 Removing the 12-point driveshaft retaining nut

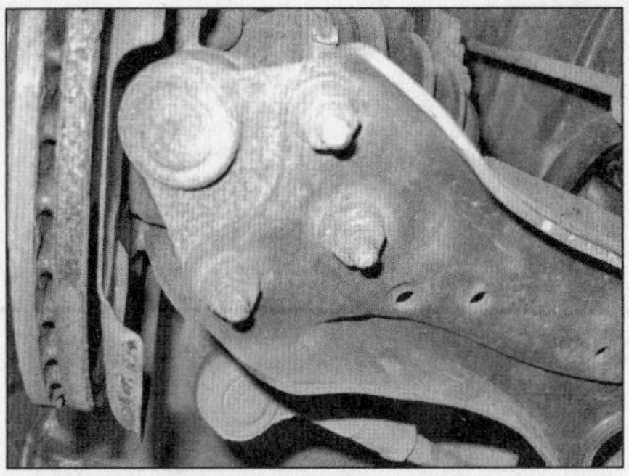

2.9a Unscrew the balljoint-to-lower arm nuts...

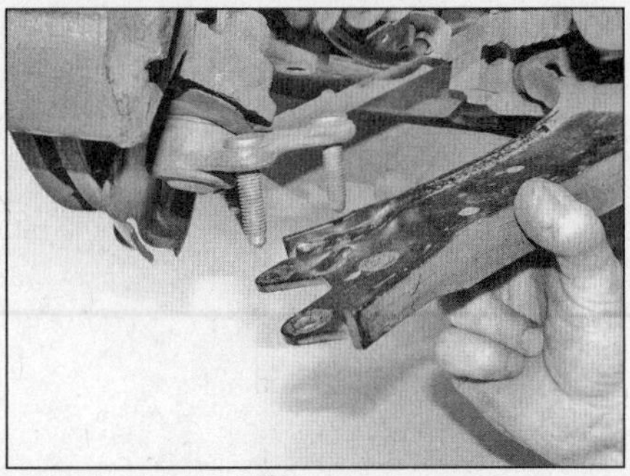

2.9b ...and detach the lower arm from the balljoint studs

also be fitted with a Traction Control System (TCS), an Electronic Differential Lock (EDL) system and an Electronic Stability Program (ESP). The ABS may also be referred to as including EBD (Electronic Brake Distribution), which means it adjusts the front and rear braking forces according to the weight being carried, and the TCS may also be referred to as ASR (Anti Slip Regulation).

7 The TCS system prevents the front wheels from losing traction during acceleration by reducing the engine output. The system is switched on automatically when the engine is started, and it utilises the ABS system sensors to monitor the rotational speeds of the front wheels.

8 The ESP system extends the ABS, TCS and EDL functions to reduce wheel spin in difficult driving conditions. It does this by using highly sensitive sensors that monitor the speed of the car, lateral movement of the car, the brake pressure, and the steering angle of the front wheels. If, for example, the car is tending to oversteer, the brake will be applied to the front outer wheel to correct the situation. If the car is tending to understeer, the brake will be applied to the rear inside wheel. The steering angle of the front wheels is monitored by an angle sensor on the top of the steering column.

9 The TCS/ESP systems are switched on automatically each time the engine is started, and should be left on except when driving with snow chains, driving in snow or driving on loose surfaces, when some wheel spin may be advantageous. The ESP switch is located in the centre of the facia.

2.11 Undo the strut lower securing bolt

10 Some models are also fitted with an Electronic Differential Lock (EDL) that reduces unequal traction from the front wheels. If one front wheel spins 100 rpm or more faster than the other, the faster wheel is slowed down by applying the brake to that wheel. The system is not the same as the traditional differential lock, where the actual differential gears are locked. Because the system applies a front brake, in the event of a brake disc overheating the system will shut down until the disc has cooled. No warning light is displayed if the system shuts down. As is the case with the TCS system, the EDL system uses the ABS sensors to monitor front wheel speeds.

2 Front wheel bearing housing – removal and refitting

Note: *All self-locking nuts and bolts disturbed on removal must be renewed as a matter of course.*

Removal

1 Remove the wheel trim/hub cap (as applicable) and loosen the driveshaft retaining nut with the car resting on its wheels. Also loosen the wheel bolts.

2 Apply the handbrake, then jack up the front of the car and support it on axle stands (see *Jacking and vehicle support*). Remove the front roadwheel and also remove the engine compartment undershield.

3 Unscrew and remove the driveshaft retaining nut **(see illustration)**. Discard, as a new one will be required for refitting.

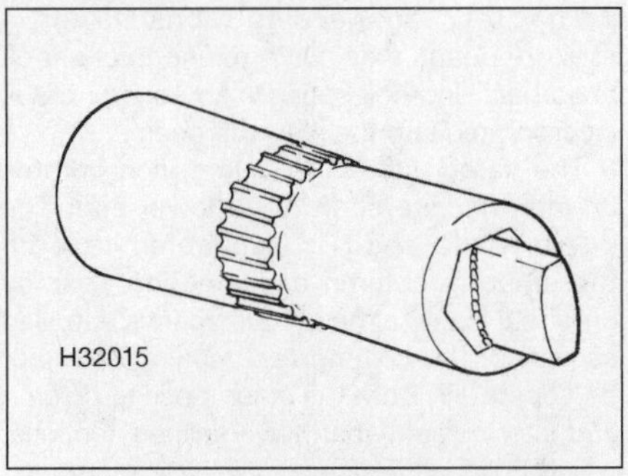

2.12a Tool used by Seat technicians to open up the split wheel bearing housing

4 Unscrew the nut securing the link to the anti-roll bar, and separate the link.

5 Remove the ABS wheel sensor as described in Chapter 9 Section 23.

6 Remove the brake disc as described in Chapter 9 Section 6. This procedure includes removing the brake caliper; however **do not** disconnect the hydraulic brake hose from the caliper. Using a piece of wire or string, tie the caliper to the front suspension coil spring, to avoid placing any strain on the hydraulic brake hose.

7 Unbolt the splash plate from the wheel bearing housing.

8 Loosen the nut securing the steering track rod balljoint to the wheel bearing housing. To do this, fit a ring spanner to the nut, then, where applicable, hold the balljoint pin stationary using an Allen key. With the nut removed, it may be possible to release the balljoint from the wheel bearing housing by turning the balljoint pin with an Allen key. If not, leave the nut on by a few turns to protect the threads, then use a universal balljoint separator to release the balljoint. Remove the nut completely once the taper has been released.

9 Unscrew the front suspension lower balljoint-to-lower arm retaining nuts **(see illustrations)**, then lever down the lower arm to release the arm from the balljoint studs.

10 Now use a soft-faced mallet to tap the driveshaft from the hub splines while pulling out the bottom end of the wheel bearing housing. If the driveshaft is tight on the splines, it may be necessary to use a puller bolted to the hub to remove it.

11 Note which way round it is fitted, then unscrew the nut and remove the clamp bolt securing the wheel bearing housing to the bottom of the strut **(see illustration)**.

12 The wheel bearing housing must now be released from the strut. To do this, Seat technicians insert a special tool into the split wheel bearing housing, and turn it through 90° to open up the clamp. A similar tool can be made out of an old screwdriver, or alternatively a suitable cold chisel can be driven into the split as a wedge. Slightly press inwards the top of the wheel bearing housing, and then push it downwards from the bottom of the strut **(see illustrations)**.

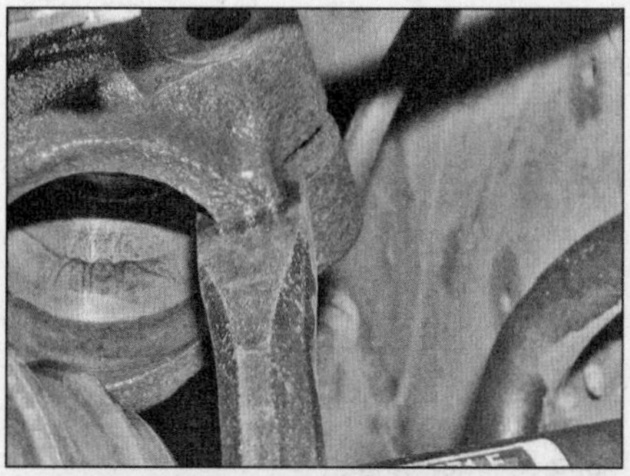

2.12b Using a cold chisel to open up the wheel bearing housing

2.12c Withdrawing the suspension strut from the wheel bearing housing

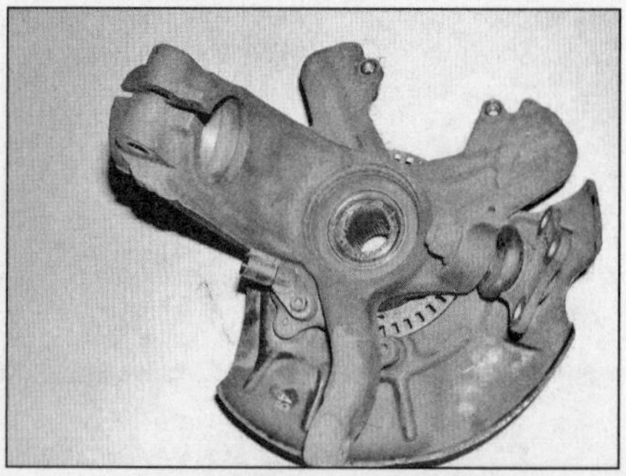

2.12d Wheel bearing housing

13 If required, unscrew the nut and remove the balljoint from the bottom of the wheel bearing housing. If it is tight, use a balljoint separator.

Refitting

14 Note that all self-locking nuts and bolts disturbed on removal must be renewed as a matter of course.

15 If removed, refit the balljoint to the wheel bearing housing and tighten the nut to the specified torque.

16 Lift the wheel bearing housing into position and engage the top of the wheel bearing housing with the bottom of the suspension strut; making sure that the hole in the side plate aligns with the holes in the split housing. Once in position, remove the tool used to open the split.

17 Ensure that the driveshaft outer joint and hub splines are clean and dry, and then engage the hub with the driveshaft. Fit the new hub nut, tightening it by hand only at this stage.

18 Insert the strut-to-wheel bearing housing clamp bolt from the front, and fit the new retaining nut. Tighten the nut to the specified torque.

19 Refit the lower arm balljoint and tighten the new nuts to the specified torque.

20 Refit the track rod balljoint to the wheel bearing housing, then fit a new retaining nut and tighten it to the specified torque. If necessary, hold the balljoint pin with an Allen key while tightening the nut.

21 Refit the splash plate and tighten the bolts.

22 Refit the brake disc and caliper.

23 Refit the ABS wheel sensor.

24 Refit the link to the anti-roll bar and tighten the nut to the specified torque.

25 Ensure that the outer joint is drawn fully into the hub, then refit the roadwheel and engine compartment undershield. Lower the car to the ground, and tighten the roadwheel bolts.

26 Tighten the new driveshaft retaining nut in the stages given in the Specifications. It is recommended that an angle gauge is used to ensure the correct tightening angle.

3 Front hub and bearings – renewal

Note: *The front hub is supplied complete with bearings, and it is not possible to renew the bearings separately. Note that the hub and bearing assembly must be assembled to the hub carrier in one single operation, by applying force to the bearing and* ***not*** *the hub. Seat technicians use special tools that locate only on the bearing, however, it is possible to fabricate spacers to insert between the hub flange and the bearing, making it possible to apply pressure to the hub itself. If these tools cannot be obtained of fabricated, it is recommended that a Seat dealer carry out the work.*

1 Remove the wheel bearing housing as described in Section 2.

2 A press will be required to remove the hub and bearing, however, if such a tool is not available, a large bench vice and spacers (such as large sockets) will serve as an adequate substitute. As a last resort, it is possible to use a lump hammer to drive out the hub and bearing **(see illustration)**.

3 Support the wheel bearing housing securely on blocks or in a vice. Using a metal tube, which bears on the inner end of the hub, press the hub and bearing out of the housing **(see illustration)**. Note that the internal circlip, retaining the bearing in the housing, will be destroyed during the removal operation.

4 Thoroughly clean the wheel bearing housing, removing all traces of dirt and grease, and polish away any burrs or raised edges, which might hinder reassembly. Check for cracks or any other signs of wear or damage, and renew if necessary. Note that the new hub and bearing is supplied with a new circlip, which locates automatically if the special Seat tool is used.

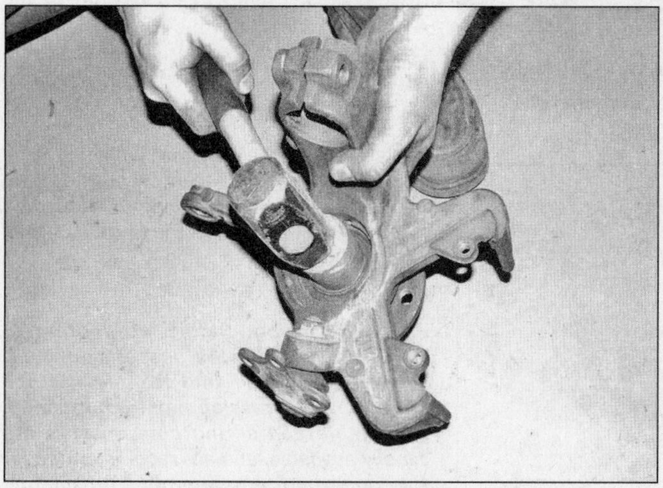

3.2 Driving out the hub and bearing with a lump hammer

3.3 Using a press to remove the hub and bearing from the wheel bearing housing

3.7a Pressing the hub and bearing into the wheel bearing housing

3.7b Make sure the circlip is fully entered in its groove

5 On reassembly, apply a light coating of molybdenum disulphide grease to the bearing outer race and bearing surface of the wheel bearing housing.

6 If using the special Seat tool fit it to the bearing, then draw the assembly into the hub carrier until the circlip is heard to click into position. **Note:** *The tools include grippers and spacers that cannot be fabricated locally.* Check that the hub rotates freely, and wipe off any excess oil or grease.

7 If not using the special tools, make up suitable spacers to fit firmly between the hub flange and the bearing, then press the hub with bearing fully into the wheel bearing housing. Using this method, it may be necessary to tap the circlip into its groove **(see illustrations)**.

8 Refit the wheel bearing housing as described in Section 2.

4 Front suspension strut – removal, overhaul and refitting

Note: *This section describes removal of the suspension strut leaving the wheel bearing housing in situ, however, if necessary it can be removed together with the wheel bearing housing, then separated on the bench. All self-locking nuts and bolts disturbed on removal must be renewed as a matter of course.*

Removal

1 Remove the wheel trim/hub cap (as applicable) and loosen the driveshaft retaining bolt (hub bolt) with the vehicle resting on its wheels. **Note:** *Do not loosen the hub bolt more than 90° at this stage, or the wheel bearing may be damaged.* Also loosen the wheel bolts.

2 Apply the handbrake, then jack up the front of the vehicle and support it on axle stands (see *Jacking and vehicle support*). Remove the appropriate roadwheel.

3 Unscrew the nut and disconnect the anti-roll bar link from the strut **(see illustration)**.

4 Disconnect the wiring plug from the ABS wheel speed sensor, then unclip the wiring and rubber brake hose from the strut.

5 Unscrew and remove the driveshaft retaining nut **(see illustration)**.

6 Note which way round it is fitted, then unscrew the nut and remove the clamp bolt securing the wheel bearing housing to the bottom of the strut **(see illustration 2.11)**.

7 In order to create sufficient clearance, it will be necessary to remove the lower arm ball joint to bearing housing nuts and separate the arm from the housing, the driveshaft outer joint should then be pushed out of the housing whilst pulling the housing outwards until clear of the shaft. Support the shaft using a suitable axle stand to prevent damage to the shaft joints.

8 Temporarily refit the housing to the lower arm, a few turns of the ball joint nuts will hold it in place.

9 The wheel bearing housing must now be released from the strut. To do this, Seat technicians insert a special tool into the split wheel bearing housing, and turn it through 90° to open up the clamp. A similar tool such as an Allen key can be used, or alternatively a suitable cold chisel can be driven into the split as a wedge. Slightly press inwards the top of the wheel bearing housing, and then push it downwards to release it from the bottom of the strut **(see illustrations 2.12a, 2.12b and 2.12c)**

10 As the wheel bearing housing is pressed downwards, use a soft-faced mallet to tap the driveshaft from the hub splines. If the driveshaft is tight on the splines, it may be necessary to use a puller bolted to the hub to remove it. Remove the bottom of the suspension strut from the top of the wheel bearing housing. Support the wheel bearing housing to one side without straining the hydraulic brake hose.

11 Remove the wiper arms (Chapter 12 Section 15) and the plenum chamber cover

12 Support the strut, then unclip the cover and unscrew the upper mounting nut and lower the strut from under the wheel arch **(see illustration)**.

Overhaul

Warning: Before attempting to dismantle the suspension strut, a suitable tool to hold the coil spring in compression must be obtained. Adjustable coil spring compressors are readily available, and are recommended for this operation. Any attempt to dismantle the strut without such a tool is likely to result in damage or personal injury.

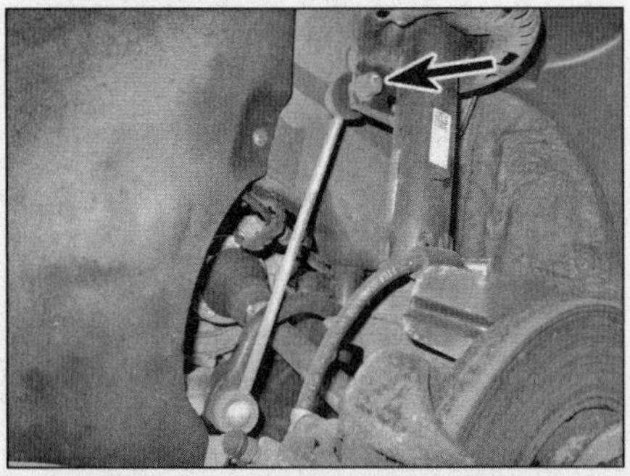

4.3 Undo the drop link upper securing nut

4.5 Remove the 12-point driveshaft retaining nut

4.12 Unclip the cover and undo the retaining nut

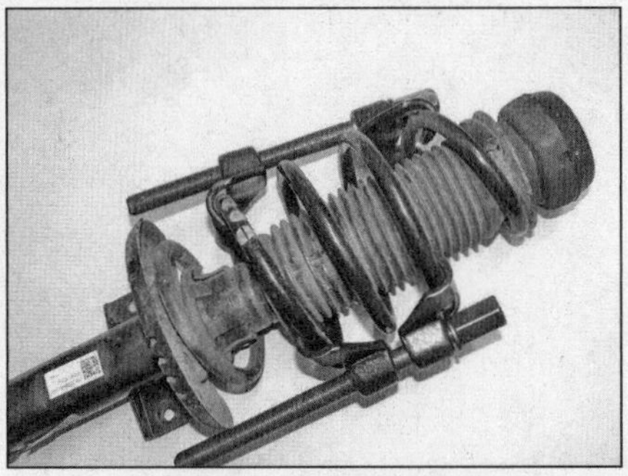

4.14 Compress the coil spring with the tool

13 With the strut removed from the car, clean away all external dirt. If necessary, mount it upright in a vice during the dismantling procedure.
14 Fit the spring compressor, and compress the coil spring until all tension is relieved from the upper spring seat **(see illustration)**.
15 Unscrew and remove the upper centre retaining nut, whilst retaining the strut piston with a suitable Allen key, then remove the rubber mounting, thrust bearing, and spring upper plate **(see illustrations)**.
16 Carefully withdraw the coil spring, still with the spring compressor attached and move it to one side. Put it in a safe place to prevent it from getting knocked, whilst still in the compressed position.
17 Remove the protective gaiter/sleeve, and then remove the bump stop from the strut piston rod **(see illustrations)**.
18 With the strut assembly now completely dismantled, examine all the components for wear, damage or deformation, and check the bearing for smoothness of operation. Renew any of the components as necessary.
19 Examine the strut for signs of fluid leakage. Check the strut piston for signs of pitting along its entire length, and check the strut body for signs of damage. While holding it in an upright position, test the operation of the strut by moving the piston through a full stroke, and then through short strokes of 50 to 100 mm. In both cases, the resistance felt should be smooth and continuous. If the resistance is jerky, or uneven, or if there is any visible sign of wear or damage to the strut, renewal is necessary.
20 If any doubt exists about the condition of the coil spring, carefully remove the spring compressors, and check the spring for distortion and signs of cracking. Renew the spring if it is damaged or distorted, or if there is any doubt as to its condition.
21 Inspect all other components for signs of damage or deterioration, and renew as necessary.
22 Assemble the bump stop and protective gaiter/sleeve to the strut piston, and then refit the coil spring (together with the compressor tool) onto the strut, making sure its lower (larger diameter) end is correctly located against the spring seat stop **(see illustration)**.
23 Fit the spring upper plate, upper bearing race and rubber mounting, making sure the rubber mounting is fitted the correct way up **(see illustration)**.
24 Refit the new upper retaining nut and tighten to the specified torque while holding the piston rod with an Allen key. The spring compressor can now be removed from the spring assembly.

Refitting

25 Manoeuvre the strut into position under the wheel arch, and locate in the suspension strut turret. Fit the stop plate on top of the strut and fit a new retaining nut. Tighten the nut to the specified torque.
26 With the outer end of the driveshaft engaged with the splines in the centre of the hub, engage the top of the wheel bearing housing with the bottom of the suspension strut.
27 Make sure the hole in the strut side plate aligns with the holes in the split housing for

4.15a Unscrew the upper centre nut...

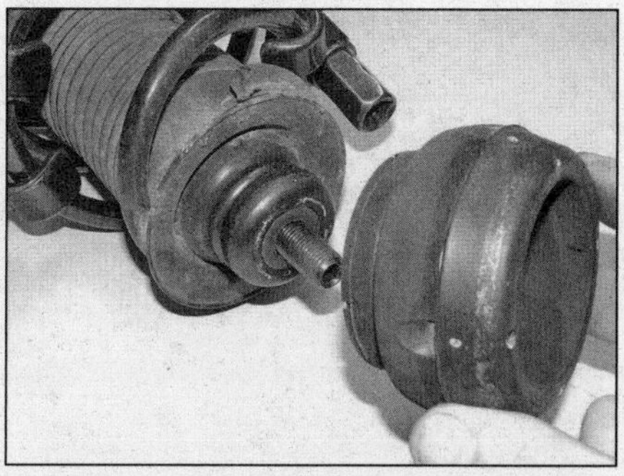
4.15b ...remove the rubber mounting...

4.15c ...thrust bearing...

4.15d ...and spring upper plate

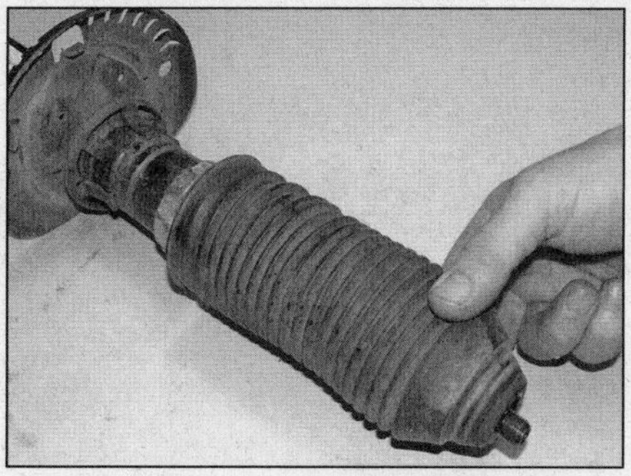
4.17a Remove the protective sleeve/ gaiter...

4.17b ...and slide the bump stop from the strut piston rod

4.22 The end of the coil springs must locate correctly in the seatings

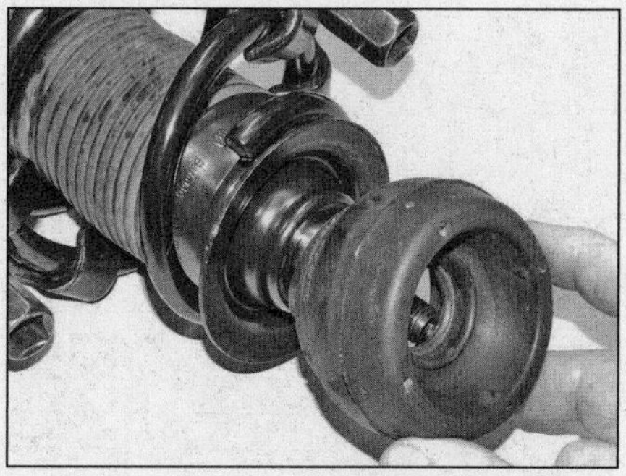
4.23 Make sure the rubber mounting is fitted the correct way up

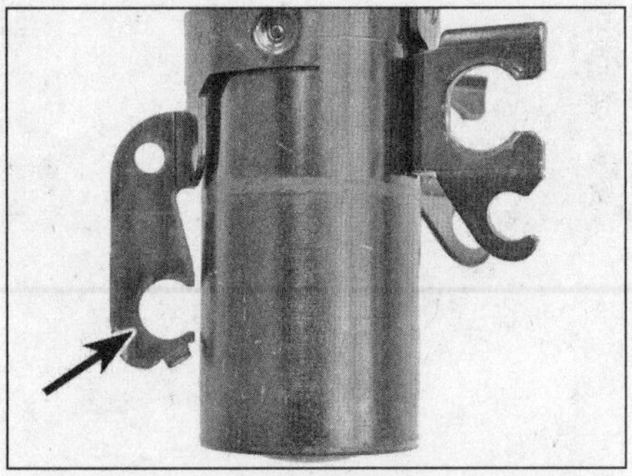

4.27 Make sure the hole in the side plate is aligned for the bolt

retaining bolt **(see illustration)**. Raise the housing, while pressing it inwards to assist entry. Use a trolley jack if necessary. When fully entered, remove the tool used to open the split.

28 Insert the new strut-to-wheel bearing housing bolt from the rear, and fit the new retaining nut. Tighten the nut to the specified torque. Also fit the new driveshaft/hub nut, tightening it by hand only at this stage.

29 Refit the ABS sensor wiring to the bracket at the base of the strut.

30 Connect the anti-roll bar link to the strut and fit a new retaining nut and tighten to the specified torque.

31 Refit the plenum chamber cover and wiper arms.

32 Ensure that the outer joint is drawn fully into the hub, and then refit the roadwheel. Have an assistant depress the brake pedal, and then tighten the driveshaft retaining nut in the stages given in the Specifications. It is recommended that an angle gauge be used to ensure the correct tightening angle. **Note:** *The car must not be standing on its wheels when tightening the nut, or the wheel bearing may be damaged.*

33 Lower the vehicle to the ground and tighten the roadwheel bolts to the specified torque.

5 Front suspension lower arm – removal, overhaul and refitting

Note: *All self-locking nuts and bolts disturbed on removal must be renewed as a matter of course.*

Removal

1 Measure the hub to wheel arch distance and note this down before starting work (see Section 23 of this Chapter). Apply the handbrake, then jack up the front of the car and support it on axle stands (see *Jacking and vehicle support*). Remove the appropriate front roadwheel and the engine compartment undershield.

2 Unscrew the front suspension lower balljoint-to-lower arm retaining nuts, then lever down the lower arm to release the arm from the balljoint studs **(see illustration 2.9a & 2.9b)**

3 Unscrew and remove the lower arm front and rear pivot bolts from the subframe **(see illustrations)**.

4 Swivel out the front of the lower arm, and withdraw it forwards to release it from the subframe.

Overhaul

5 Thoroughly clean the lower arm and bracket, then check carefully for cracks or any other signs of wear or damage, paying particular attention to the pivot and rear mounting rubber bushes.

6 The removal and fitting of new bushes is essentially the same for both front and rear bushes A range of sockets and a length of threaded bar will be required **(see illustrations)**. Where available a hydraulic press can also be used.

Refitting

7 Locate the lower arm into the subframe.

8 Insert the front and rear pivot bolts, but do not fully tighten them at this stage.

9 Refit the balljoint to the lower arm using new nuts, then tighten the nuts to the specified torque.

10 The control arm pivot bolts must only be fully tighten with the vehicle in the unladen position.

5.3a Lower arm front mounting bolt

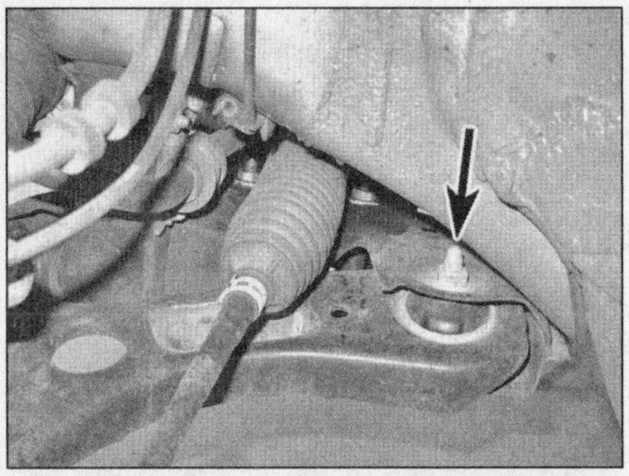

5.3b Lower arm rear mounting bolt

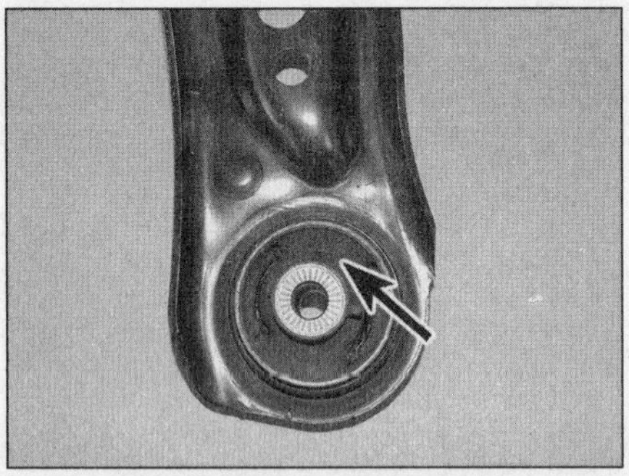

5.6a Before removing the bush, note the alignment marks on the rear bush

5.6b A suitable setup for bush removal. The old bush is pulled into the large socket

5.6c Two sockets are used to allow clearance for the lip of the bush

5.6d Adjust the position of the bush so that it protrudes equally on both sides

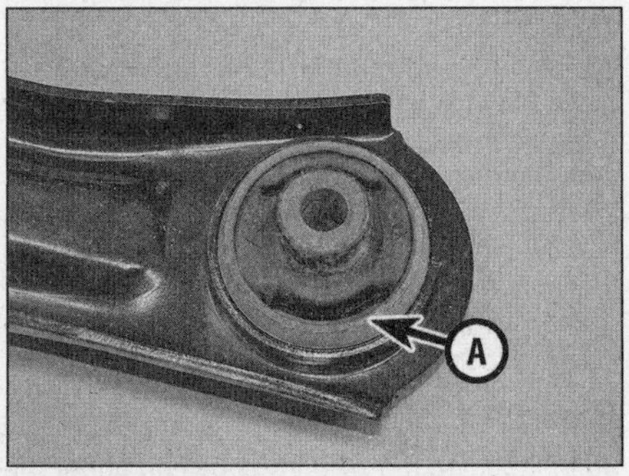

5.6e The longer slot (A) must always point to the outside of the vehicle

11 With reference to Section 23, raise the arm using a suitable jack until the suspension is in the unladen position. Measure the distance from the hub nut centre to the wheel arch and adjust the distance to the those shown in the specifications. Fully tighten the lower arm pivot bolts to the specified torque.

12 Refit the roadwheel and undershield, and then lower the car to the ground.

6 Front suspension lower arm balljoint – removal, inspection and refitting

Note: *All self-locking nuts and bolts disturbed on removal must be renewed as a matter of course.*

Removal

Method 1

1 Remove the wheel bearing housing as described in Section 2.

2 Unscrew and remove the balljoint retaining nut **(see illustrations)**, then release the balljoint from the wheel bearing housing using a universal balljoint separator. Withdraw the balljoint.

Method 2

3 Remove the wheel trim/hub cap (as applicable) and loosen the driveshaft retaining nut (hub nut) with the vehicle resting on its wheels. **Note:** *Do not loosen the hub nut more than 90° at this stage, or the wheel bearing may be damaged.* Also loosen the wheel bolts.

4 Apply the handbrake, then jack up the front of the vehicle and support it on axle stands (see *Jacking and vehicle support*). Remove the appropriate roadwheel.

5 Unscrew and remove the driveshaft retaining nut. Discard, as a new one will be required for refitting.

6 Unscrew the front suspension lower balljoint-to-lower arm retaining nuts, then lever the lower arm down to release the balljoint studs **(see illustrations 2.9a & 2.9b)**. Now use a soft-faced mallet to tap the driveshaft from the hub splines while pulling out the bottom end of the wheel bearing housing. If the driveshaft is tight on the splines, it may be necessary to use a puller bolted to the hub to remove it. It is not necessary to remove the driveshaft completely from the hub. Retain the wheel bearing housing away from the lower arm by inserting a block of wood between the strut and the inner body panel.

7 Unscrew and remove the balljoint retaining nut, then release the balljoint from the wheel bearing housing using a universal balljoint separator **(see illustration 6.2a & 6.2b)**. Withdraw the balljoint.

Inspection

8 With the balljoint removed, check that it moves freely, without any sign of roughness. Check also that the balljoint rubber gaiter shows no sign of deterioration, and is free from cracks and splits. Renew as necessary.

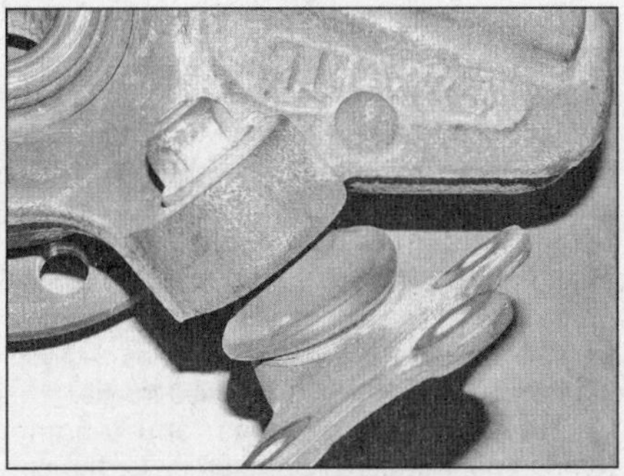

6.2a The front suspension lower balljoint on the wheel bearing housing

Refitting

Method 1

9 Fit the balljoint to the wheel bearing housing and fit the new retaining nut. Tighten the nut to the specified torque setting, noting that the balljoint shank can be retained with an Allen key if necessary to prevent it from rotating.

10 Refit the wheel bearing housing with reference to Section 2.

Method 2

11 Fit the balljoint to the wheel bearing housing and fit the new retaining nut. Tighten the nut to the specified torque setting, noting that the balljoint shank can be retained with an Allen key if necessary to prevent it from rotating.

12 Remove the wooden block and move the strut inwards, then refit the balljoint to the lower arm using new nuts, and tighten them to the specified torque.

13 Refit the driveshaft retaining nut and tighten it sufficiently to draw the driveshaft fully into the hub, and then refit the roadwheel.

14 Have an assistant depress the brake pedal, and then tighten the driveshaft retaining nut in the stages given in the Specifications. It is recommended that an angle gauge be used to ensure the correct tightening angle. **Note:** *The car must not be standing on its wheels when tightening the nut, or the wheel bearing may be damaged.*

15 Lower the vehicle to the ground and tighten the roadwheel bolts.

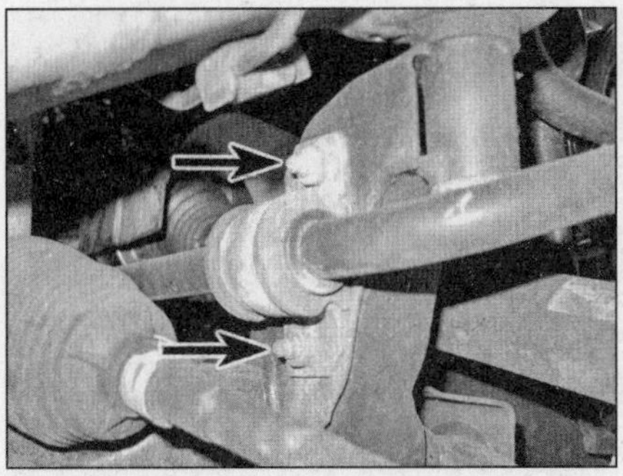

7.3 Anti-roll bar clamp securing bolts

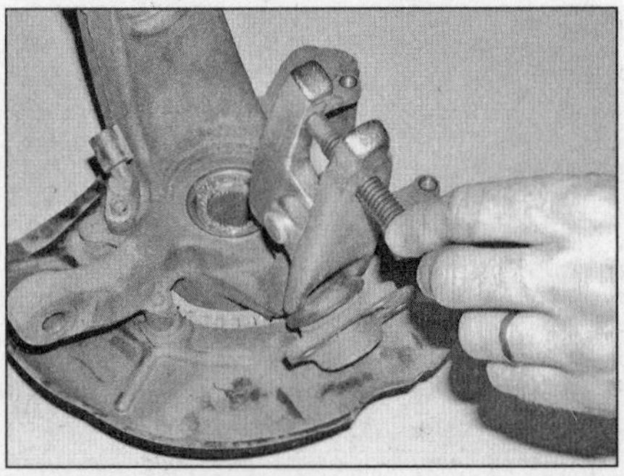

6.2b Using a universal balljoint separator tool to remove the lower balljoint

7 Front anti-roll bar – removal and refitting

Note: *All self-locking nuts and bolts disturbed on removal must be renewed as a matter of course.*

Removal

1 Apply the handbrake, then jack up the front of the car and support it on axle stands (see *Jacking and vehicle support*). Remove both front roadwheels and the engine compartment undershield.

2 Unscrew the bolts securing the engine rear mounting link to the bottom of the transmission.

3 Unscrew the bolts securing the anti-roll bar clamps to the rear of the lower arm brackets **(see illustration)**. Note that the lower right-hand bolt cannot be completely removed at this stage.

4 Unscrew the nuts and disconnect the lower part of the connecting/drop links from the ends of the anti-roll bar **(see illustration)**.

5 Unscrew the steering gear mounting bolts from the bottom of the subframe. Tie the steering gear to the underbody.

6 Mark the position of the subframe on the underbody to retain the wheel alignment. Also, mark the anti-roll bar to indicate which way round it is fitted, and the position of the rubber mounting bushes. This will aid refitting.

7 Support the subframe on a trolley jack, then unscrew the mounting bolts and lower the subframe approximately 4 cm.

7.4 Connecting link/drop link lower balljoint

8.2 The drop link upper and lower securing nuts

8 Remove the clamp, then turn the anti-roll bar upwards and withdraw towards the rear of the car. Remove the rubber mounting bushes from the bar.

9 Carefully examine the anti-roll bar components for signs of wear, damage or deterioration, paying particular attention to the rubber mounting bushes. Renew worn components as necessary.

Refitting

10 Fit the rubber mounting bushes to the anti-roll bar, aligning them with the marks made prior to removal.

11 Manoeuvre the anti-roll bar into position, then refit the mounting clamps and insert the retaining bolts. Ensure that the bush markings are still aligned with the marks on the bars, and then tighten the mounting clamp retaining bolts to the specified torque.

12 Raise the subframe and align with the previously made marks. Insert the mounting bolts and tighten to the specified torque and angle.

13 Untie the steering gear, then secure it to the subframe with the bolts tightened to the specified torque.

14 Refit the anti-roll bar side connecting links and tighten the nuts to the specified torque.

15 Refit the engine rear mounting link bolts, then push the transmission forwards as far as possible and tighten the bolts to the specified torque.

16 Refit the roadwheels and engine compartment undershield, then lower the car to the ground and tighten the wheel bolts to the specified torque.

8 Front anti-roll bar drop link – removal and refitting

Note: *All self-locking nuts and bolts disturbed on removal must be renewed as a matter of course.*

Removal

1 Apply the handbrake, then jack up the front of the car and support it on axle stands (see *Jacking and vehicle support*). Remove the relevant front roadwheel.

2 Unscrew the nuts securing the anti-roll bar drop link to the front suspension strut and anti-roll bar and remove it **(see illustration)**. A torx (or hex) key will be needed to counter hold the balljoint as the nut is removed.

3 Inspect the link rubbers for signs of damage or deterioration. If evident, renew the drop link complete.

9.3 Using a chisel to remove the rear hub dust cap

9.4 Unscrew the self-locking 12-point hub nut...

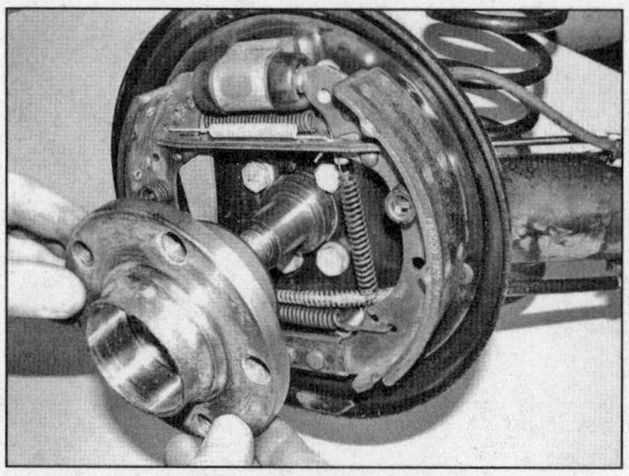

9.5 ...and remove the hub and bearings from the stub axle

9.8 Using a socket to drive the hub onto the stub axle

Refitting

4 Refitting is a reversal of removal, but delay fully tightening the bolts until the weight of the car is on the front suspension.

9 Rear hub assembly – removal and refitting

Note: *The rear wheel bearings cannot be renewed independently of the rear hub, because the outer races are formed in the hub itself. If excessive wear is evident, the rear hub must be renewed complete. The rear hub nut must always be renewed after removal.*

Removal

1 Chock the front roadwheels, then jack up the rear of the car and support on axle stands (see *Jacking and vehicle support*). Release the handbrake and remove the relevant rear roadwheel.

2 Remove the rear brake disc or drum (as applicable) with reference to Chapter 9 Section 6 for brake disc or Chapter 9 Section 10 for brake drum.

3 Remove the dust cap from the centre of the hub using a screwdriver or cold chisel **(see illustration)**.

4 Unscrew and remove the self-locking 12-point hub nut. Note that it is tightened to a high torque and a socket extension bar may be required to loosen it **(see illustration)**. It is recommended that the nut is renewed whenever removed.

5 Using a suitable puller if necessary, pull the hub and bearings from the stub axle **(see illustration)**. Take care not to damage the ABS sensor ring on the inside of the hub.

6 Examine the hub and bearings for wear, pitting and damage. If all the bearing surfaces and balls appear to be in good order upon inspection, the hub may be re-used.

Refitting

7 Wipe clean the stub axle, then check that the bearing races are adequately lubricated with suitable grease.

8 Locate the hub as far as possible onto the stub axle. Seat technicians use a special drift to drive the inner race onto the stub; however, a suitable metal tube or deep socket will do the same **(see illustration)**. Make sure that the tube is only located on the inner race.

9 Screw on the new self-locking nut and tighten it to the specified torque and angle.

10 Check the dust cap for damage and renew it if necessary. Use a hammer to carefully tap the cap into the hub. **Note:** *A badly fitting dust cap will allow moisture to enter the bearing, reducing its service life. Seat recommend replacement every time the cap is removed.*

11 Refit the brake disc or drum (as applicable).

12 Refit the roadwheel and lower the car to the ground.

10 Rear stub axle – removal and refitting

Note: *All self-locking nuts and bolts disturbed on removal must be renewed as a matter of course.*

Removal

1 Chock the front roadwheels, then jack up the rear of the car and support on axle stands (see *Jacking and vehicle support*). Release the handbrake and remove the relevant roadwheel.
2 Remove the rear hub as described in Section 9.
3 Disconnect the wiring, then unscrew the bolt and remove the ABS speed sensor from the rear axle trailing arm **(see illustration)**.
4 Unscrew the mounting bolts securing the stub axle and backplate to the rear axle trailing arm. Carefully withdraw the backplate and stub axle, taking care not to bend the brake line excessively. If necessary, remove the rear wheel cylinder or rear caliper as applicable with reference to Chapter 9.
5 Inspect the stub axle for signs of damage and renew if necessary. **Do not** attempt to straighten the stub axle.

Refitting

6 Ensure the mating surfaces of the axle; stub axle and backplate are clean and dry. Check the backplate for signs of damage.
7 Refit the stub axle together with the backplate, then insert the new bolts and progressively tighten to the specified torque.
8 If removed, refit the rear wheel cylinder or rear caliper as applicable with reference to Chapter 9.
9 Refit the speed sensor, tighten the bolt, and reconnect the wiring.
10 Refit the rear hub with reference to Section 9.
11 Refit the roadwheel and lower the car to the ground.

11 Rear suspension shock absorber and coil spring – removal, inspection and refitting

Note: *All self-locking nuts and bolts disturbed on removal must be renewed as a matter of course.*

Shock absorber

Removal

1 Before removing the shock absorber, an idea of how effective it is can be gained by depressing the rear corner of the car. If the shock absorber is in good condition, the body should rise then settle in its normal position. If the body oscillates more than this, the shock absorber is defective. **Note:** *The rear shock absorbers can be renewed individually if necessary.*

10.3 ABS rear wheel speed sensor

2 Chock the front roadwheels, then jack up the rear of the car and support on axle stands (see *Jacking and vehicle support*). Remove the relevant rear roadwheel.
3 Position a trolley jack and block of wood beneath the coil spring position on the trailing arm, and raise the arm so that the shock absorber is slightly compressed **(see illustration)**. Note that on some models, it may be necessary to remove the stone protection guard first.
4 On models with gas-discharge (Xenon) headlights, disconnect the tension rod for the rear sender.
5 Unscrew and remove the shock absorber lower mounting nut and bolt, and lever the bottom of the shock absorber from the trailing arm **(see illustration)**.
6 Support the shock absorber, then unscrew the upper mounting bolts located in the rear wheel arch. Lower the shock absorber and withdraw from under the wheel arch **(see illustration)**.
7 With the shock absorber on the bench, prise off the cover, then unscrew the nut from the top of the piston rod and remove the upper mounting bracket. The piston rod can be held stationary with a pair of grips on the raised peg on the top of the rod. Remove the rubber stop and protectors from the top of the rod.

Inspection

8 If necessary, the action of the shock absorber can be checked by mounting it upright in a vice. Fully depress the rod, and then pull it up fully. The piston rod must move smoothly over its complete length.

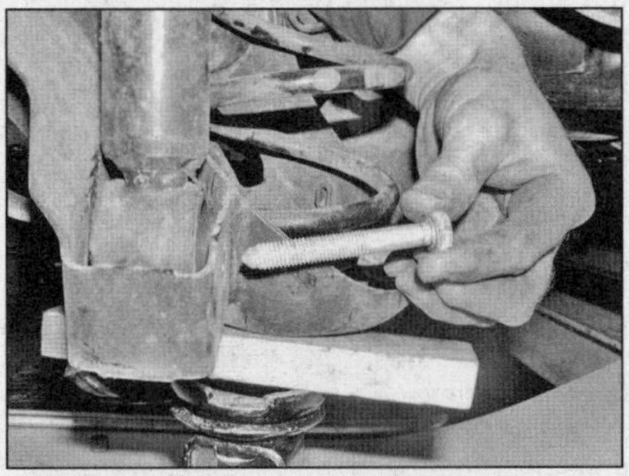
11.5 Remove the shock absorber lower mounting bolt

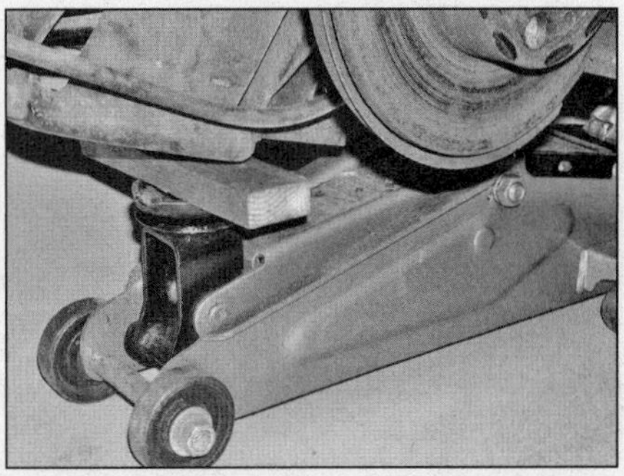
11.3 Position the trolley jack and block of wood beneath the trailing arm

Refitting

9 Locate the rubber stop and protectors on the piston rod followed by the upper mounting bracket. Fit the new nut and tighten to the specified torque while holding the piston rod as for removal, then refit the cover.
10 Locate the shock absorber in the rear wheel arch, then insert the upper mounting bolts and tighten to the specified torque.
11 Locate the bottom of the shock absorber in the trailing arm, insert the bolt from the outside, then screw on the nut. Raise the trailing arm with the jack to take the weight of the rear suspension, then tighten the lower mounting bolt to the specified torque.
12 Lower the jack, and where necessary refit the stone protection guard.
13 On models with gas-discharge (Xenon) headlights, reconnect the tension rod and adjust it so that the lever points towards the rear and not upwards when the rear suspension is flexed.
14 Refit the roadwheel and lower the car to the ground.

Coil spring

Note: *It is possible to remove the rear coil spring without the use of a coil spring compressor; both methods are described in the following paragraphs.*

Warning: Adjustable coil spring compressors are readily available, and are recommended for this operation.

15 Chock the front roadwheels, then jack up the rear of the car and support on axle stands

11.6 Unscrew the shock absorber upper mounting bolts

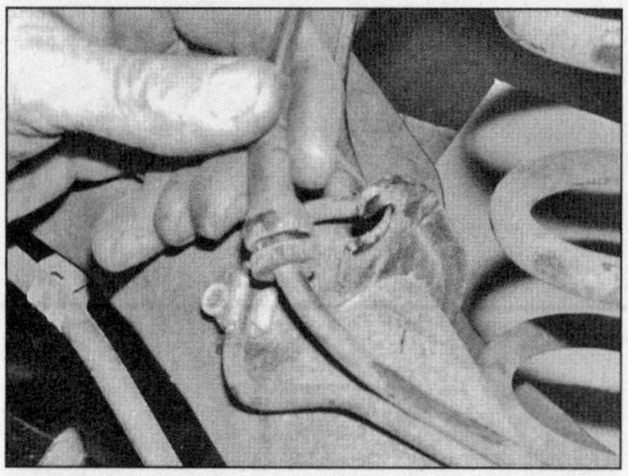
11.20 Release the ABS sensor wiring from the bracket on the trailing arm

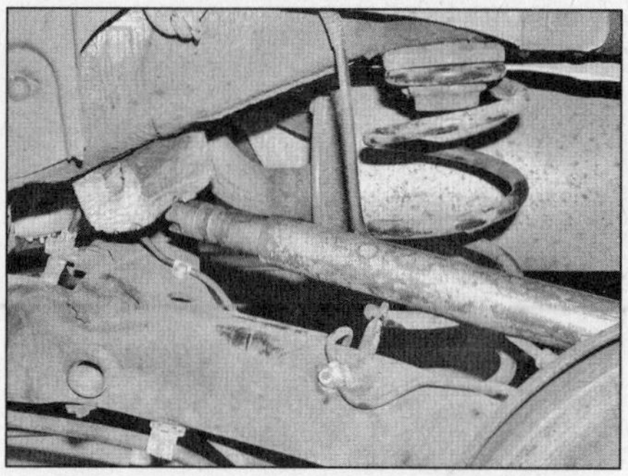
11.21a Lever down the trailing arm...

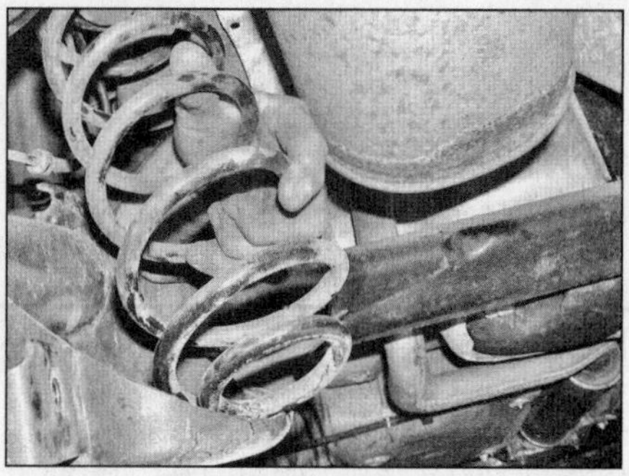
11.21b ...then release the coil spring from its lower seat...

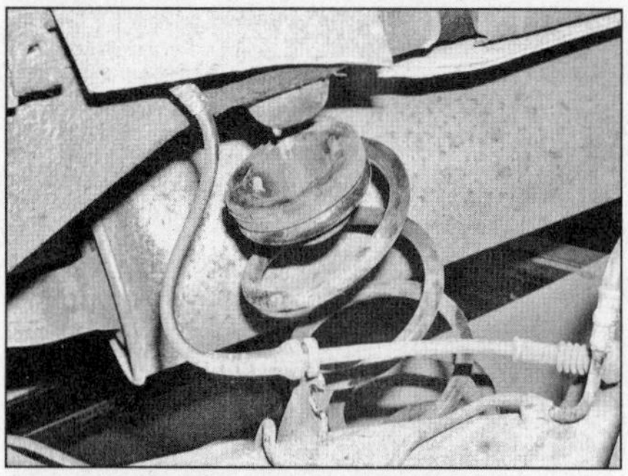
11.21c ...and underbody seat

11.22 Recover the upper and lower spring seats

(see *Jacking and vehicle support*). Remove the relevant rear roadwheel.

16 If removing the left-hand rear coil spring, it may be necessary to release the exhaust rubber mountings and move the exhaust tail pipe/silencer to one side.

With a spring compressor

17 Support the trailing arm with a trolley jack, then fit the tool to the coil spring and compress it until it can be removed from the trailing arm and underbody. With the coil spring on the bench, carefully release the tension of the tool and remove it.

Without a spring compressor

18 Position a trolley jack and block of wood beneath the coil spring position on the trailing arm, and raise the arm so that the shock absorber is slightly compressed. Note on some models, it may be necessary to remove the stone protection guard first.

13.7 Flexible brake hose on the rear axle and underbody

19 Unscrew and remove the shock absorber lower mounting nut and bolt, and lever the bottom of the shock absorber from the trailing arm.

20 Release the ABS sensor wiring from the bracket on the trailing arm **(see illustration)**.

21 Lower the trolley jack and remove it from under the trailing arm, then carefully lever the arm down until the coil spring can be removed. Lever against a block of wood to prevent damage to the underbody. Make sure that the car is adequately supported on the axle stands **(see illustrations)**.

Inspection

22 With the coil spring removed, recover the upper and lower spring seats and check them for damage **(see illustration)**. Obtain new ones if necessary. Also clean the spring locations on the underbody and trailing arm.

Refitting

23 Refitting is a reversal of removal, but make sure that the upper spring seat is located correctly on the top of the coil spring, with the spring end abutting the shoulder on the seat. The lower seat is circular and locates only in the centre of the spring. Before tightening the shock absorber lower mounting bolt to the specified torque, raise the trailing arm to its normal running position. If removed, make sure the exhaust rear tail pipe/silencer is secured in the rubber mountings.

12 Rear anti-roll bar – removal and refitting

1 The rear anti-roll bar runs along the length of the rear axle beam. It is an integral part of the axle assembly, and cannot be removed. If the anti-roll bar is damaged, which is unlikely, the complete axle assembly must be renewed.

13 Rear axle assembly – removal and refitting

Note: *All self-locking nuts and bolts disturbed on removal must be renewed as a matter of course.*

Removal

1 Chock the front roadwheels, then jack up the rear of the car and support on axle stands positioned beneath the underbody (see *Jacking and vehicle support*). Remove both rear roadwheels. Fully release the handbrake.

2 Working on each side at a time, slightly raise the trailing arm so that the shock absorber is not fully extended, then unscrew and remove the shock absorber upper mounting bolts from inside the rear wheel arch. Carefully lower the trailing arm to relieve the tension in the coil spring.

3 On models fitted with gas-discharge (Xenon) headlights, disconnect the tension rod at the rear of the vehicle level sensor. If necessary, disconnect the wiring and unbolt the sensor.

4 With both shock absorber upper mountings detached, lower the trailing arms until the coil springs and seats can be removed.

5 Remove the stone protection plates from the trailing arms where fitted, then unscrew the lower mounting bolts and remove the shock absorbers from the rear axle.

6 Release the handbrake cable from the supports/clips on the rear axle and underbody.

7 Pull out the clips and disconnect the flexible brake hoses from the supports on the rear axle and underbody bracket on both sides **(see illustration)**. **Do not** disconnect the rigid brake lines from the hoses.

8 Refer to Section 10 and remove the rear stub axles from the rear trailing arms. Release the rigid pipes from their clips and place the rear wheel cylinders or calipers (as applicable) to one side, together with the handbrake cables. Where fitted, also unbolt the rear brake load regulator.
9 Support the rear axle with a trolley jack, and then unscrew and remove the rear axle front mounting bolts from the underbody brackets **(see illustration)**.
10 Manoeuvre the rear axle down from the underbody brackets and withdraw from under the car. The help of an assistant is recommended.
11 Inspect the rear axle mountings for signs of damage or deterioration, and refer to Section 14 if renewal is necessary.

Refitting

12 Apply a little brake grease or soapy water to the kidney-shaped cavity in the front mounting rubbers, then manoeuvre the rear axle into the underbody brackets and insert the mounting bolts from the outside. Screw on the nuts finger-tight at this stage. **Note:** *Make sure that the bolts are inserted through the centres of the rubber mountings and are not located in one of the three off-centre cut-outs. If the bolts are not correctly centred, the rear wheel alignment will be incorrect causing excessive tyre wear.*
13 Refit the rear stub axles as described in Section 10. Secure the brake lines to their clips, and where applicable refit the rear brake load regulator.
14 Refit the flexible brake hoses to the supports and secure with the clips.
15 Refit the handbrake cables and locate them in the supports/clips.
16 Locate the shock absorbers on the trailing arms and insert the lower mounting bolts loosely.
17 On models with gas-discharge (Xenon) headlights, refit the vehicle level sensor if removed, then reconnect the wiring and tension rod.
18 Carefully locate the coil springs and seats on the rear axle with reference to Section 11.
19 Working on each side at a time, raise the trailing arm until the shock absorber upper mounting bolts can be inserted. Tighten the bolts to the specified torque.
20 Working on each side at a time, raise the trailing arm with a trolley jack until the weight of the car is taken on the coil spring. Fully tighten the front mounting bolts to the specified torque, and then tighten the shock absorber mounting bolts to the specified torque.
21 Refit the stone protection plates under the trailing arms.
22 Check and if necessary adjust the handbrake as described in Chapter 9 Section 17.
23 Refit the roadwheels and lower the car to the ground.

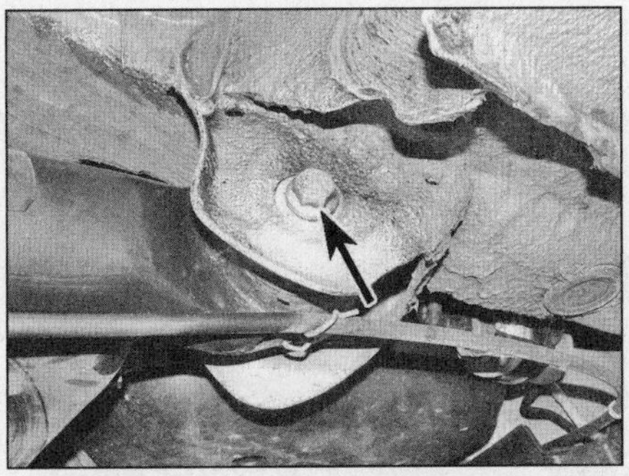

13.9 Rear axle front mounting bolt

14 Rear axle rubber mountings – renewal

Note: *It is recommended that the rubber mountings are renewed on both sides at the same time to ensure the correct rear wheel alignment.*
1 Chock the front roadwheels, and then jack up the rear of the car and support it on axle stands positioned beneath the underbody (see *Jacking and vehicle support*). Remove both rear roadwheels.
2 Release the handbrake cables from the supports/clips on the rear axle and underbody.
3 Pull out the clips and disconnect the flexible brake hoses from the supports on the rear axle and underbody brackets.
4 Unscrew and remove both rear axle front mounting bolts from the underbody brackets.
5 Working on one side at a time, pull the front end of the trailing arm down from the underbody bracket and retain it in this position by placing a block of wood between the arm and underbody.
6 When fitting a new mounting bush, make sure that it is correctly aligned with any markings on the arm. If no alignment marks are visible, then alignment marks should be made, so that correct fitting of the bushes is carried out.
7 Seat technicians use a special tool to remove the rubber mounting from the rear axle. If a similar tool is not available, use a long bolt with suitable-sized metal tubing and washers to force out the mounting.
8 The new mounting must be located correctly in the rear axle. Using a suitable tool, pull the mounting into the rear axle until it is positioned as noted on removal.
9 Renew the mounting on the other side using the same procedure described in paragraphs 5 to 8.
10 Apply a little brake grease or soapy water to the mounting rubbers, and then locate the rear axle in the underbody brackets. Insert the mounting bolts from the outside, hand-tight at this stage.
11 Refit the flexible brake hoses and handbrake cables, and secure with the clips.
12 Working on one side at a time, raise the trailing arm with a trolley jack until the weight of the car is taken on the coil spring, then fully tighten the front mounting bolt to the specified torque.
13 Refit the roadwheels and lower the car to the ground.

15 Steering wheel – removal and refitting

Removal

1 Set the front wheels in the straight-ahead position, and release the steering lock by inserting the ignition key.
2 Disconnect the battery negative lead (as described in Chapter 5A Section 3), and position it away from the terminal.
3 Remove the driver's airbag as described in Chapter 12 Section 24.
4 Using a multi-spline socket, unscrew and remove the retaining bolt, while holding the steering wheel stationary – do not use the steering lock to hold the wheel, as it may be damaged **(see illustration)**.
5 The wheel should have an alignment mark already, to indicate its correct fitted position. If necessary, use a centre-punch or dab of paint to mark the steering wheel in relation to the column in order to aid refitting **(see illustration)**.
6 Refit the steering wheel retaining bolt a couple of threads, and then ease the steering wheel from the column splines by firmly rocking it side-to-side. With the steering wheel

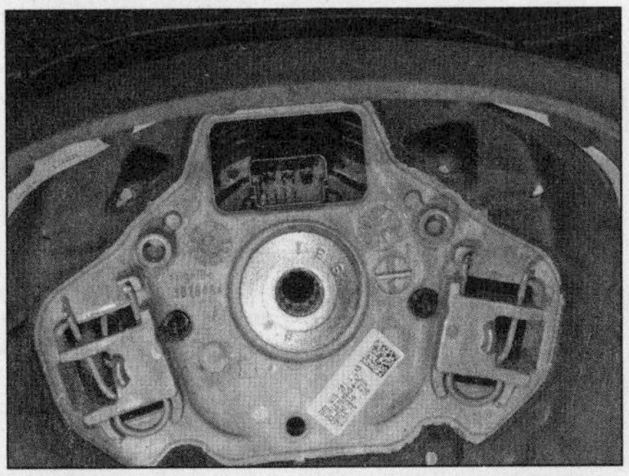

15.4 Steering wheel multi-spline retaining bolt

15.5 Alignment marks for steering wheel in relation to column

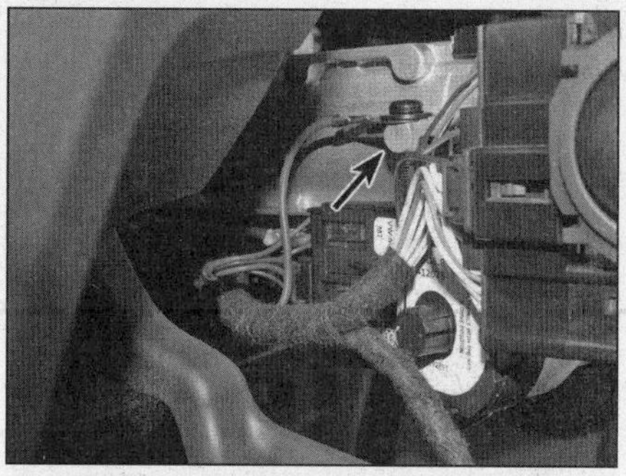

16.8a Undo the earth wire securing screw...

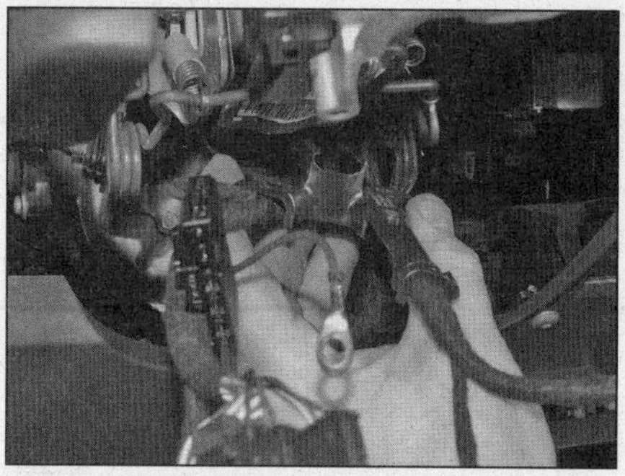

16.8b ...and unclip the wiring loom from under the column

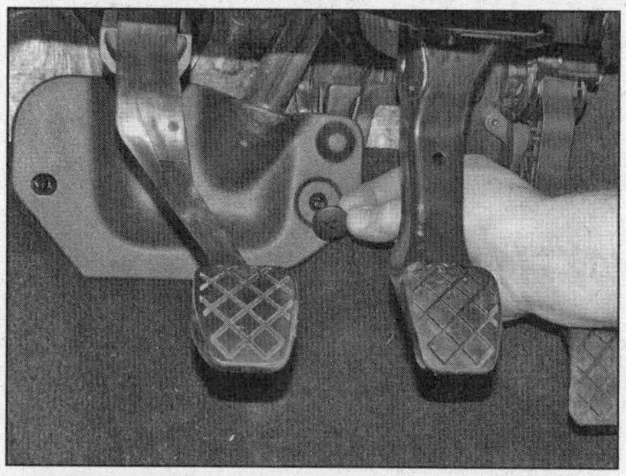

16.9 Removing the plastic cover from the steering column lower universal joint

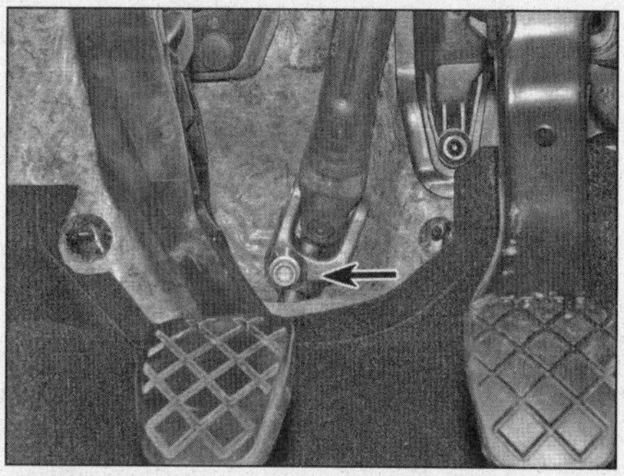

16.10 Steering column lower universal joint

loose on the column, remove the retaining bolt again and discard, as a new one must be used on refitting.

Refitting

7 Locate the steering wheel on the column splines making sure that the previously made marks are correctly aligned and the electrical connector is aligned with the opening in the steering wheel.

8 Refit the bolt. The bolt can be reused up to 5 times. Mark the bolt with a centre punch each time it is removed. If in any doubt always fit a new bolt and tighten it to the specified torque while holding the steering wheel stationary.

9 Refit the driver's airbag as described in Chapter 12 Section 24.

10 Reconnect the battery negative (earth) lead.

16 Steering column – removal, inspection and refitting

Removal

1 Disconnect the battery negative lead (as described in Chapter 5A Section 3), and position it away from the terminal.

2 Remove the steering wheel as described in Section 15.

3 Return the steering to the straight-ahead position. Adjust the steering column to its lowest position and extend it into the passenger compartment as far as possible, and then lock it in this position.

4 Unclip and remove the upper shroud from the steering column, then undo the two upper screws and single lower screw and remove the lower shroud from the steering column, as described in Chapter 11 Section 26.

5 Remove the lower facia panels located around the steering column as described in Chapter 11 Section 28.

6 Remove the switch assembly from the top of the steering column as described in Chapter 12 Section 5.

7 Disconnect the wiring connector from the transponder around the ignition switch, and then release the wiring retaining clips and earth cables from the steering column.

8 Follow the wiring loom down the length of the steering column, undo the earth cable retaining screw, release the retaining clips and remove the wiring loom from under the steering column, noting its fitted position **(see illustrations)**.

9 Working in the footwell, release the retaining clips and remove the plastic trim panel from over the steering column lower universal joint **(see illustration)**.

10 Unscrew the clamp bolt and pull the universal joint from the steering gear pinion. Note that the pinion shaft has a cut-out to enable fitting of the clamp bolt, and the splined pinion shaft incorporates a flat making it impossible to assemble the joint to the shaft in the wrong position **(see illustration)**. Discard the clamp bolt; a new one should be used on refitting.

11 Note that the inner and outer columns, and the intermediate shaft, are telescopic, to facilitate the reach adjustment. It is important to keep the splined sections of the inner steering column engaged with each other while the steering column is removed. If they become detached due to the outer column sections being separated, especially on a vehicle, which has completed a high mileage, it is possible that rattling noises may occur.

12 Remove the air distribution duct **(see illustration)**. On models fitted with electric power steering disconnect the wiring plugs from the motor.

13 Support the steering column, then unscrew and remove the mounting bolts. Withdraw the steering column from inside the car. On models with electric power steering removing the column through the facia is just possible, but because the assembly is heavy the aid of an assistant is recommended **(see illustration)**. Note that the mounting bracket on the bulkhead has locating lugs, which aligns with a slot on the top of the steering column.

Caution: Do not carry the steering column by suspending it from the universal joint or intermediate shaft, as this will damage the universal joint and steering column bushes. Also, do not bend the joints by more than 90º.

14 If necessary, remove the ignition switch/steering column lock with reference to Section 17.

16.12 Remove the duct

16.13 Remove the column (electric power steering model shown)

Inspection

15 The steering column is designed to collapse in the event of a front-end crash, to prevent the steering wheel injuring the driver. Before refitting the steering column, examine the column and mountings for signs of damage and deformation.

16 Check the inner column sections for signs of free play in the column bushes. If any damage or wear is found on the steering column bushes, the column must be renewed as an assembly.

17 The intermediate shaft is permanently attached to the inner column and cannot be renewed separately. Inspect the universal joints for excessive wear. If evident, the complete steering column must be renewed.

Refitting

18 Where removed, refit the ignition switch/ steering column lock/switch carrier with reference to Section 22.

19 Refit the steering column to the bulkhead bracket, making sure it located on the locating lug. Insert the mounting bolts, and tighten to the specified torque, starting with the upper bolts first and then the lower bolts.

20 Attach the universal joint on the steering gear pinion splines, making sure the road wheels and steering wheel are in the correct position. Insert the new clamp bolt, and tighten to the specified torque.

21 Reconnect the earth cable and tighten the retaining nut, then refit the wiring harness under the steering column.

22 Reconnect the wiring to the ignition switch transponder and secure the wiring in its retaining clips.

23 Refit the plastic trim panel over the steering column lower universal joint.

24 Refit the light switch assembly.

25 Refit the lower facia panels.

26 Refit the lower and upper shrouds.

27 Refit the steering wheel with reference to Section 15.

28 Reconnect the battery negative lead.

29 On models with ESP (electronic stability programme), the steering angle sensor basic settings must be set by a Seat dealer using specialist diagnostic equipment.

17 Ignition switch and steering column lock – removal and refitting

Ignition switch

Removal

1 Disconnect the battery negative lead (as described in Chapter 5A Section 3).

2 Remove the steering wheel as described in Section 15.

3 With the steering in the straight-ahead position, adjust the steering column to its lowest position, then extend it into the passenger compartment as far as possible, and then lock it in this position.

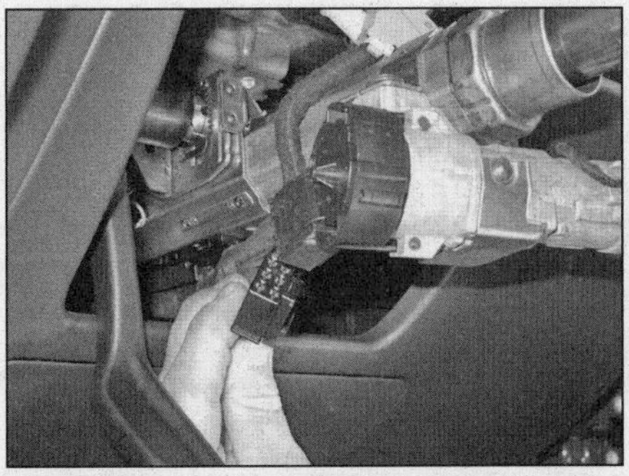

17.6 Disconnecting the ignition switch wiring plug

4 Unclip and remove the upper shroud from the steering column, then undo the two upper screws and single lower screw and remove the lower shroud from the steering column, as described in Chapter 11 Section 26.

5 Remove the switch assembly from the top of the steering column as described in Chapter 12 Section 5.

6 Release the securing clip and carefully pull the wiring plug from the ignition switch **(see illustration)**.

7 On early models, remove the locking paint from the switch retaining screw heads, then loosen them slightly and pull out the switch from the rear of the steering lock housing. On later models release the switch using two lengths of wire **(see illustrations)**.

Refitting

8 Insert the ignition key and turn it to the 'on' position. Also turn the switch in the same position.

9 Carefully insert the switch into the housing, then insert the screws and tighten securely. Lock the screws by applying some paint over their heads and onto the housing.

10 Reconnect the wiring plug to the ignition switch.

11 Refit the light switch assembly.

12 Refit the lower and upper shrouds.

13 Refit the steering wheel.

14 Reconnect the battery negative lead (as described in Chapter 5A Section 3).

Steering column lock

Removal

15 Carry out the procedures as described in paragraphs 1 to 5.

16 Release the securing clips and disconnect the wiring plug connectors from the ignition switch and ignition key immobiliser coil. Also undo the retaining screw and disconnect the earth wiring terminal from the top of the housing.

17 The lock is secured to the outer column by shear-head bolts **(see illustration)**, and the heads are broken off in the tightening procedure. To remove the old bolts, either

17.7a Switch retaining screws

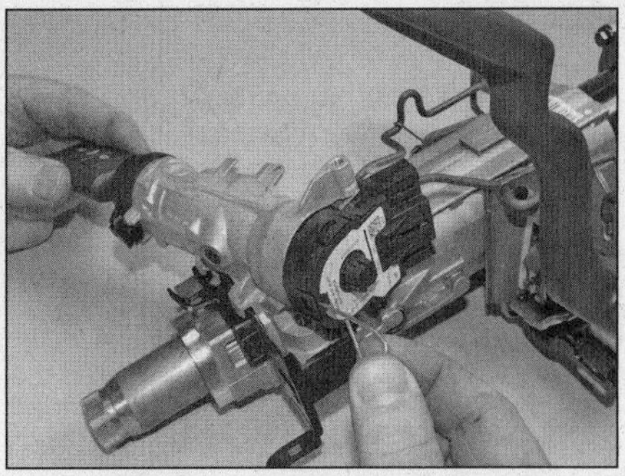

17.7b On later models release the switch with a tool made from welding rod (or similar)

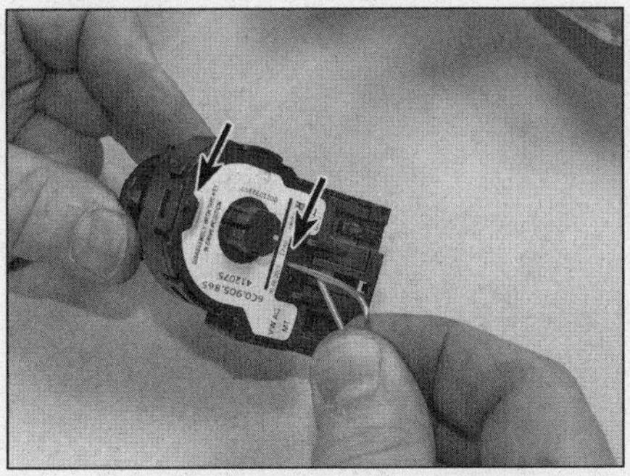

17.7c Note the two access points

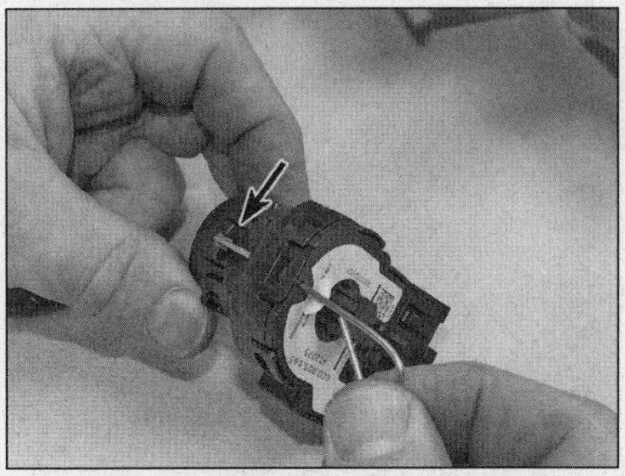

17.7d The release pin in position showing the tab that must be depressed to remove the pin

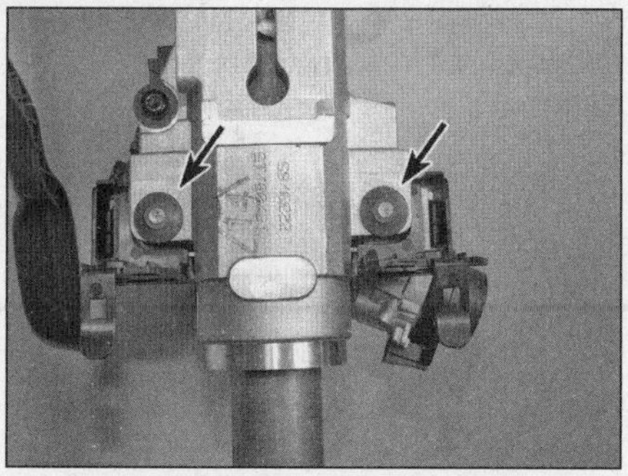

17.17 Steering column lock shear-head bolts (shown with column removed)

17.28 Disconnect the wiring connector

drill them out, or use a sharp cold chisel to cut off their heads or turn them anti-clockwise. Withdraw the lock from the steering column.

18 If necessary, the lock cylinder can be removed from the steering lock housing as described later in this section.

Refitting

19 If removed, refit the lock cylinder as described later in this section.

20 Locate the lock on the outer column and insert the new shear-head bolts. Tighten the bolts until their heads break off.

21 Reconnect the wiring plug to the ignition switch and ignition key immobiliser coil.

22 Attach the earth terminal to the housing and tighten the retaining screw.

23 Refit the light switch assembly.

24 Refit the lower and upper shrouds.

25 Refit the steering wheel as described in Section 15.

26 Reconnect the battery negative lead (as described in Chapter 5A Section 3).

Lock cylinder

Removal

27 Carry out the procedures as described in paragraphs 1 to 4.

28 Disconnect the wiring connector from the immobiliser transponder around the ignition switch **(see illustration)**.

29 Insert the ignition key and turn the lock cylinder to the drive position (which is 90° from off position).

30 Insert a piece of wire 1.2 mm in diameter in the drilling next to the ignition key, slide it in to release the locking lever, then withdraw the lock cylinder from the housing **(see illustrations)**. To make the piece of wire locate in the locking lever easier, file an angle on the end of the wire.

17.30a insert a thin rod through the hole in the Ignition switch...

17.30b ...to release the locking lever

Refitting

31 Refit the lock cylinder with the ignition key in the Drive position, then remove the wire.

32 Reconnect the wiring connector to the immobiliser/transponder.

33 Refit the upper and lower shrouds, and tighten the screws.

34 Refit the steering wheel with reference to Section 15.

35 Reconnect the battery negative lead.

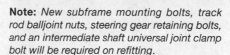

18 Steering gear assembly (EPHS) – removal, overhaul and refitting

Note: *New subframe mounting bolts, track rod balljoint nuts, steering gear retaining bolts, and an intermediate shaft universal joint clamp bolt will be required on refitting.*

Removal

1 Removal and refitting of the steering gear is essentially the same for later models fitted with electric power steering. There will of course be no hydraulic components to remove.

2 Apply the handbrake, then jack up the front of the car and support it on axle stands positioned on the underbody, leaving the subframe free (see *Jacking and vehicle support*). Position the steering straight-ahead, and then remove both front roadwheels. Also remove the engine compartment undershield. As a precaution against the steering wheel turning and damaging the airbag contact spring, use adhesive tape to secure it to the facia or steering column.

3 Beneath the pedal bracket, undo the plastic nuts and remove the cover for access to the steering column lower universal joint.

4 Unscrew and remove the clamp bolt and free the steering column universal joint from the steering gear pinion (the shaft is telescopic to enable it to be easily disconnected). Discard the clamp bolt, as a new one should be used on refitting. Note that the pinion shaft has a cut-out to enable fitting of the clamp bolt, and the splined pinion shaft incorporates a flat making it impossible to assemble the joint to the shaft in the wrong position. Some models may have a clamp ring securing the universal joint to the inner column.

5 Remove the battery and battery tray as described in Chapter 5A Section 3.

6 Remove the air filter and air ducting from the engine compartment.

7 Release the power-assisted steering sensor wiring from the holder on the inner panel above the left-hand driveshaft.

8 Unscrew the two bolts securing the rear engine/transmission mounting link to the underside of the transmission unit. Discard both bolts, new ones must be used on refitting, and leave the mounting attached to the subframe.

9 Unscrew the nuts and disconnect the links from the anti-roll bar on each side.

10 Working on each side at a time, unscrew the nuts from the track rod ends, then use a balljoint separator tool to release the ends from the steering arms on the front wheel bearing housings.

11 On models with hydraulic power steering, unscrew the filler cap from the top of the hydraulic fluid reservoir on top of the electric power steering pump, then syphon all the fluid into a suitable container. Note that there will still be fluid in the system lines. Discard the removed fluid. **Note:** *Seat specifically state that a hose clamp* **must not** *be fitted to the hydraulic fluid line.*

12 Support the weight of the subframe with a trolley jack, then mark the position of the bolts securing the subframe to the underbody, and unscrew them.

13 Position a suitable container beneath the steering gear to catch spilt fluid.

14 Lower the subframe approximately 4 cm, at the same time guiding the pinion shaft from the rubber grommet in the floor, and making sure that the hydraulic lines are not damaged.

15 Unscrew the union nut and disconnect the supply line and return lines from the steering gear, then recover the copper sealing washers. Tape over or plug the ends of the lines and the apertures in the steering gear to prevent entry of dust and dirt into the hydraulic system. The line ends can be wrapped in a plastic bag if preferred.

16 Unscrew the bolts and remove the power-assisted steering sensor from the steering gear pinion housing. Be prepared for some loss of fluid.

17 Unscrew the mounting bolts and withdraw the steering gear from the subframe to the rear. Note that the mounting on the passenger side of the gear incorporates a clamp and rubber mounting. Examine the mounting for wear and damage, and renew it if necessary. Discard the steering gear mounting bolts; new ones should be used on refitting.

Overhaul

18 Examine the steering gear assembly for signs of wear or damage, and check that the rack moves freely throughout the full length of its travel, with no signs of roughness or excessive free play between the steering gear pinion and rack. It is not possible to overhaul the steering gear assembly housing components, and if it is faulty the assembly must be renewed. The only components, which can be renewed individually, are the steering gear gaiters, the track rod end balljoints and the track rods, as described later in this Chapter.

Refitting

19 Locate the steering gear on the subframe, and insert the new mounting bolts. Make sure that the location dowel is correctly fitted. Tighten the bolts to the specified torque and Stage 2 angle.

20 Refit the power-assisted steering sensor together with a new seal to the steering gear pinion housing, and tighten the bolts.

21 Refit the hydraulic supply and return lines to the steering gear together with new copper sealing washers, and tighten to the specified torque.

22 Raise the subframe and at the same time guide the steering gear pinion shaft through the rubber grommet in the floor. Align the subframe with the previously made marks, then insert the new mounting bolts and tighten them to the specified torque and angle.

23 Align the engine/transmission rear mounting with the transmission unit and fit the new mounting bolts. Tighten the bolts to the specified torque and angle.

24 Refit the track rod ends to the steering arms, screw on the new nuts, and tighten them to the specified torque.

25 Refit the links to the anti-roll bar and tighten the nuts to the specified torque.

26 Where applicable, refit the exhaust front pipe.

27 Secure the power-assisted steering sensor to the holder on the inner panel.

28 Refit the air filter and ducting.

29 Refit the battery and battery tray with reference to Section. **Note:** *On some models access to the hydraulic fluid reservoir is restricted by the battery, therefore delay refitting the battery until the hydraulic system has been bled.*

30 Working inside the car, locate the steering column universal joint on the pinion shaft, making sure that the cut-out is aligned with the bolt holes. Insert the new bolt and tighten to the specified torque.

31 Check that the rubber grommet is located correctly in the floor, then refit the plastic cover and secure with the screws.

32 Refit the engine compartment undershield and roadwheels, and then lower the car to the ground. On completion check and, if necessary, adjust the front wheel alignment as described in Section 24.

33 Refill and bleed the hydraulic system as described in Section 20.

34 Have the system checked for fault codes by a Seat dealer at the earliest opportunity.

19 Steering gear rubber gaiters and track rods – renewal

Steering gear rubber gaiters

1 Remove the track rod end balljoint as described in Section 22.

2 Note the fitted position of the gaiter on the track rod, then release the retaining clips and slide the gaiter off the steering gear housing and track rod **(see illustration)**.

3 Wipe clean the track rod and the steering gear housing, and then apply a film of suitable grease to the surface of the rack. To do this, turn the steering wheel as necessary to fully extend the rack from the housing, then reposition it in its central position.

4 Carefully slide the new gaiter onto the track rod, and locate it on the steering gear housing. Position the gaiter as previously noted on removal, making sure that it is not twisted, then lift the outer sealing lip of the gaiter to equalise air pressure within the gaiter.

5 Secure the gaiter in position with new retaining clips. Where crimped-type clips are used, pull the clip as tight as possible, and locate the hooks in their slots. Remove any slack in the clip by carefully compressing the raised section. In the absence of the special crimping tool, a pair of side-cutters may be used, taking care not to cut the clip.

6 Refit the track rod end balljoint as described in Section 22.

Track rods

7 Remove the relevant steering gear rubber gaiter as described earlier. If there is insufficient working room with the steering gear mounted in the car, remove it as described in Section 18 and hold it in a vice while renewing the track rod.

19.2 Steering rack gaiter securing clips

8 Hold the steering rack stationary with one spanner on the flats provided, then loosen the balljoint nut with another spanner. Fully unscrew the nut and remove the track rod from the rack.

9 Locate the new track rod on the end of the steering rack and screw on the nut. Hold the rack stationary with one spanner and tighten the balljoint nut to the specified torque. A crow's foot adapter may be required since the track rod prevents access with a socket, and care must be taken to apply the exact torque in this situation.

10 Refit the steering gear or rubber gaiter with reference to the earlier paragraphs or Section 18. On completion check and, if necessary, adjust the front wheel alignment as described in Section 24.

20 Power steering system – bleeding

1 Apply the handbrake, then jack up the front of the car and support it on axle stands (see *Jacking and vehicle support*). Turn the front roadwheels to their straight-ahead position.

2 Unscrew the filler cap from the electric power steering hydraulic fluid reservoir and top-up the level to the MAX mark.

3 With the engine switched off, turn the steering from lock-to-lock ten times, then check and top-up the level again.

4 Screw on the filler cap loosely, then start the engine and allow it to idle for approximately 10 seconds.

5 Switch off the engine and top-up the fluid level.

6 Screw on the filler cap loosely, start the engine, and turn the steering from lock-to-lock ten times.

7 Switch off the engine and top-up the fluid level.

8 Repeat the procedure in paragraphs 6 and 7 until the fluid level no longer requires topping-up.

9 Refit and tighten the filler cap.

21.1 Electric power steering pump viewed with the wing liner removed

21.10 Wiring plugs on the electric power steering pump

21 Electric power steering pump – removal and refitting

Removal

1 The electric power steering hydraulic pump is located behind the front bumper in front of the left-hand front wheel **(see illustration)**.

2 On models where access to the fluid reservoir is restricted by the battery, remove the battery and battery tray as described in Chapter 5A Section 3.

3 Apply the handbrake, then jack up the front of the car and support it on axle stands (see *Jacking and vehicle support*).

4 Remove the road wheel and then remove the wing liner **(see illustration)**.

5 Unscrew the filler cap from the top of the hydraulic fluid reservoir on top of the electric

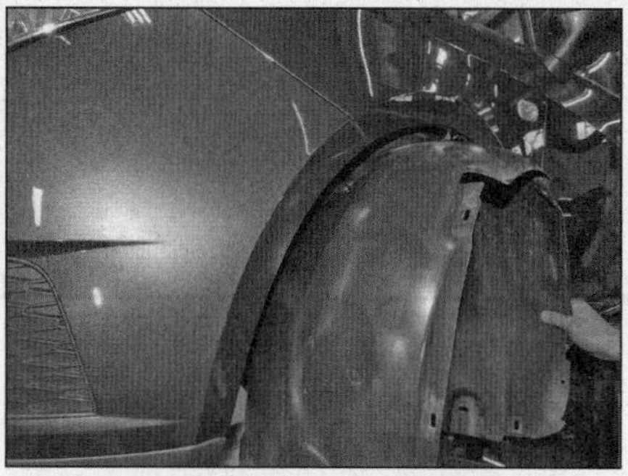
21.4 Remove the wing liner

21.12 Remove the bolts (note one bolt hidden)

power steering pump, then syphon all the fluid into a suitable container. Note that there will still be fluid in the system lines. Discard the removed fluid. **Note:** Seat *specifically state that a hose clamp***must not***be fitted to the hydraulic fluid line.*

6 On models with a radiator fan control unit **(see illustration)**, disconnect the wiring and unscrew the mounting nuts, then remove the radiator fan control unit from the left-hand front chassis leg.

7 Whilst not strictly required removing the screen washer fluid reservoir greatly improves access.

8 Release the support clip and remove the supply and return hydraulic lines from the inner body.

9 Locate a suitable container beneath the electric power steering pump to catch spilled hydraulic fluid.

10 Note their location, and then disconnect the three wiring plugs from the electric power steering pump **(see illustration)**.

21.6 Radiator fan control unit

11 Unscrew the union nut and disconnect the pressure line from the pump. Recover the O-ring seal, then loosen the clip and disconnect the return line from the pump reservoir. Tape over or plug the ends of the lines and the apertures in the steering gear to prevent entry of dust and dirt into the hydraulic system. The line ends can be wrapped in a plastic bag if preferred.

12 Unscrew the mounting bolts and lower the electric power steering pump and bracket from the underbody **(see illustration)**.

13 Unscrew the nuts/bolts and remove the mounting bracket from the pump. Where applicable, unscrew the rubber mountings from the pump.

Caution: The power steering control unit and the electric motor must not be separated.

Refitting

14 Refitting is a reversal of removal, but finally bleed the system as described in Section 20. At the earliest opportunity, have a Seat dealer or suitably equipped garage perform a system self-diagnosis and erase any fault codes.

22 Track rod end – removal and refitting

Note: *A new balljoint retaining nut will be required on refitting.*

Removal

1 Apply the handbrake, then jack up the front of the car and support it on axle stands (see *Jacking and vehicle support*). Remove the relevant roadwheel.

2 If the track rod end is to be re-used, mark its position in relation to the track rod to facilitate refitting.

3 Unscrew the track rod end locknut by a quarter of a turn. Do not move the locknut from this position, as it will serve as a handy reference mark on refitting.

4 Loosen and remove the nut securing the track rod end balljoint to the wheel bearing housing, and release the balljoint tapered shank using a universal balljoint separator. Note that the balljoint shank has a hexagon hole – hold the shank with an Allen key while loosening the nut **(see illustrations)**.

22.4a Using an Allen key to hold the balljoint shank while loosening the nut

22.4b Using a balljoint separator to release the track rod balljoint

5 Counting the exact number of turns necessary to do so, unscrew the track rod end from the track rod **(see illustration)**.
6 Carefully clean the balljoint and the threads. Renew the balljoint if its movement is sloppy or too stiff, if excessively worn, or if damaged in any way; carefully check the stud taper and threads. If the balljoint gaiter is damaged, the complete balljoint assembly must be renewed; it is not possible to obtain the gaiter separately.

Refitting

7 Screw the track rod end onto the track rod by the number of turns noted on removal. This should bring the track rod end to within a quarter of a turn of the locknut, with the alignment marks that were made on removal (if applicable) lined up. Tighten the locknut.
8 Refit the balljoint shank to the steering arm on the wheel bearing housing, then fit a new retaining nut and tighten it to the specified torque. Hold the shank with an Allen key if necessary.
9 Refit the roadwheel, then lower the car to the ground and tighten the roadwheel bolts to the specified torque.
10 Check and, if necessary, adjust the front wheel toe setting as described in Section 24.

23 Vehcle ride height – checking

1 Before undertaking any work on the suspension the vehicle ride hide should be checked and compared to the specifications.
2 The vehicle must be parked on level ground. The fuel tank must be at least three quarters full. The tyre pressures should be checked and adjusted as required. Where fitted the spare tyre must be present.
3 Check that the vehicle is level across the axle by measuring from the top of the door frame (or any other suitable datum point) to the ground.
4 Next measure from the centre of the wheel to the centre of the wheel arch **(see illustration)**. The wheel trim may require removal, depending on the model trim level. Compare the measurement to the specifications at the start of this Chapter. Note that the figures specified are for a new vehicle, some settlement of the suspension is to be expected on a used vehicle.
5 Whenever a suspension component is removed or replaced that has a bonded rubber bush fitted the component's fixings must not be fully tightened until the vehicle is at the specified ride height. Lowering the vehicle to the ground will be the obvious solution, but this may make access to the fixings (and the use of a torque wrench) difficult, if not impossible.
6 An alternative method is to raise the hub, trailing arm or control arm with a jack until the the hub to wheel arch distance meets the specifications. At this point the fixings can be tightened to the specified torque (and angle where specified). However extreme caution is required if this method is adopted as the vehicle may start to lift off the axle stands as the jack is raised. **Never crawl under a vehicle that is not fully supported on axle stands.**

24 Wheel alignment and steering angles – general information

Definitions

1 A car's steering and suspension geometry is defined in three basic settings – all angles are expressed in degrees; the steering axis is defined as an imaginary line drawn through the axis of the suspension strut, extended where necessary to contact the ground.
2 Camber is the angle between each roadwheel and a vertical line drawn through its centre and tyre contact patch, when viewed from the front or rear of the car. Positive camber is when the roadwheels are tilted outwards from the vertical at the top; negative camber is when they are tilted inwards.
3 Camber angle is only adjustable by loosening the front suspension subframe mounting bolts and moving it slightly to one side. This also alters the Castor angle. The camber angle can be checked using a camber checking gauge.
4 Castor is the angle between the steering axis and a vertical line drawn through each roadwheel's centre and tyre contact patch, when viewed from the side of the car. Positive castor is when the steering axis is tilted so that it contacts the ground ahead of the vertical; negative castor is when it contacts the ground behind the vertical. Slight castor angle adjustment is possible by loosening the front suspension subframe bolts and moving it slightly to one side. This also alters the Camber angle.
5 Castor is not easily adjustable, and is given for reference only; while it can be checked using a castor checking gauge, if the figure obtained is significantly different from that specified, the car must be taken for careful checking by a professional, as the fault can only be caused by wear or damage to the body or suspension components.
6 Toe is the difference, viewed from above, between lines drawn through the roadwheel centres and the car's centre-line. Toe-in is when the roadwheels point inwards, towards each other at the front, while toe-out is when they splay outwards from each other at the front.
7 The front wheel toe setting is adjusted by screwing the track rod(s) in/out of the outer balljoint(s) to alter the effective length of the track rod assembly.
8 Rear wheel toe setting is not adjustable, and is given for reference only. While it can be checked, if the figure obtained is significantly different from that specified, the car must be taken for careful checking by a professional, as the fault can only be caused by wear or damage to the body or suspension components.

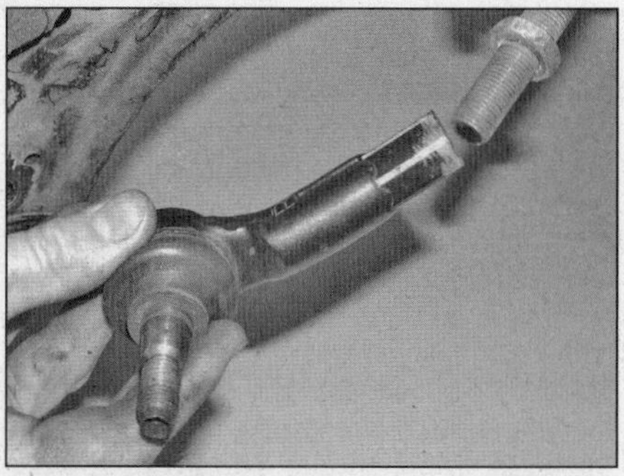

22.5 Unscrewing the track rod end from the track rod

Checking and adjustment

Front wheel toe setting

9 Due to the special measuring equipment necessary to check the wheel alignment, and the skill required to use it properly, the checking and adjustment of these settings is best left to a dealer or similar expert. Note that most tyre-fitting centres now possess sophisticated checking equipment.
10 To check the toe setting, a tracking gauge must first be obtained. Two types of gauge are available, and can be obtained from motor accessory shops. The first type measures the distance between the front and rear inside edges of the roadwheels, as previously described, with the car stationary – however, Seat do not quote settings in millimetres, so this type of gauge would not be suitable for the Ibiza. The second type, known as a 'scuff plate', measures the actual position of the contact surface of the tyre, in relation to the road surface, with the car in motion. This is achieved by pushing or driving the front tyre over a plate, which then moves slightly according to the scuff of the tyre, and shows this movement on a scale.
11 Make sure that the steering is in the straight-ahead position when making measurements.

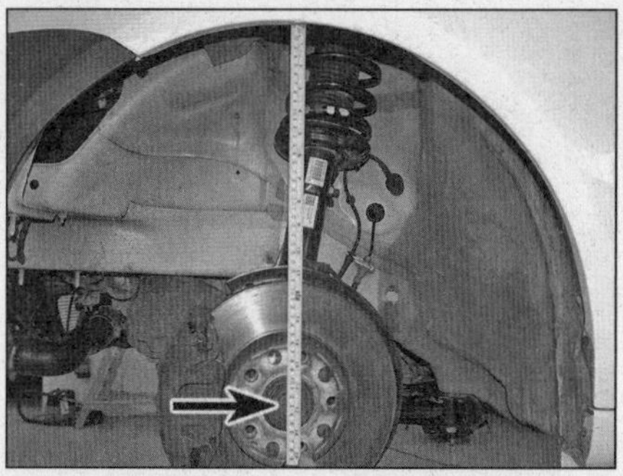

23.4 Measure the distance from the hub centre to the wheel arch centre

12 If adjustment is necessary, apply the handbrake, then jack up the front of the car and support it securely on axle stands (see *Jacking and vehicle support*). Turn the steering wheel onto full-left lock, and record the amount of exposed thread on the right-hand track rod. Now turn the steering onto full-right lock, and record the number of threads on the left-hand track rod. If there is the same amount of thread visible on both sides, then subsequent adjustment should be made equally on both sides. If there are more thread is visible on one side than the other, it will be necessary to compensate for this during adjustment.

13 First clean the track rod threads; if they are corroded, apply penetrating fluid before starting adjustment. Release the rubber gaiter outer clips, peel back the gaiters and apply a smear of grease. This will ensure that both gaiters are free and will not be twisted or strained as there respective track rods are rotated.

14 Retain the track rod with a suitable spanner, and loosen the balljoint locknut fully. Alter the length of the track rod, by screwing it into or out of the balljoint. Rotate the track rod using an open-ended spanner fitted to the track rod flats provided; shortening the track rod (screwing it onto its balljoint) will reduce toe-in/increase toe-out.

15 When the setting is correct, hold the track rod and tighten the balljoint locknut to the specified torque setting. If after adjustment, the steering wheel spokes are no longer horizontal when the wheels are in the straight-ahead position, remove the steering wheel and reposition it (see Section 15).

16 Check that the toe setting has been correctly adjusted by lowering the car to the ground and rechecking the toe setting; re-adjust if necessary. Ensure that the rubber gaiters are seated correctly and are not twisted or strained, and secure them in position with the retaining clips; where necessary, fit a new retaining clip (refer to Section 19).

Rear wheel toe setting

17 The procedure for checking the rear toe setting is the same as described for the front setting in paragraph 10. The setting is not adjustable – see paragraph 8.

Front wheel camber and castor angles

18 Checking and adjusting the front wheel camber angle should be entrusted to a Seat dealer or other suitably equipped specialist. Note that most tyre-fitting centres now possess sophisticated checking equipment. For reference, adjustments are made by loosening the front suspension subframe mounting bolts, and repositioning the subframe.

Chapter 11
Bodywork and fittings

Contents

Degrees of difficulty

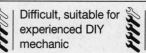

Easy, suitable for novice with little experience	Fairly easy, suitable for beginner with some experience	Fairly difficult, suitable for competent DIY mechanic	Difficult, suitable for experienced DIY mechanic	Very difficult, suitable for expert DIY or professional

Specifications

Torque wrench settings	Nm	lbf ft
Bonnet hinge retaining bolts	20	15
Bonnet lock	14	10
Door hinge bolts	20	15
Door lock retaining bolts	20	15
Door striker	20	15
Door check strap-to-pillar bolt	30	22
Door check strap-to-door bolts	10	8
Front and rear bumpers	5	4
Front bumper crossmember	30	22
Front seat belt height adjustment	23	17
Front seat belt inertia reel and anchorages	35	26
Front seat mounting retaining bolts	24	18
Rear bumper crossmember	30	22
Rear seat belt inertia reel and anchorages	35	26
Tailgate hinge retaining bolts	15	11
Tailgate lock	22	16
Tailgate strut	20	15

1 General Information

1 The body shell is made of pressed-steel sections, and is available in five-door Hatchback and Estate versions. Most components are welded together, and some use is made of structural adhesives. The front wings are bolted on.
2 The bonnet, door, and some other vulnerable panels are made of zinc-coated metal, and are further protected by being coated with an anti-chip primer before being sprayed.
3 Extensive use is made of plastic materials, mainly in the interior, but also in exterior components. The front and rear bumpers, and front grille, are injection-moulded from a synthetic material that is very strong and yet light. Plastic components such as wheel arch liners are fitted to the underside of the vehicle, to improve the body's resistance to corrosion.

2 Maintenance – bodywork and underframe

1 The general condition of a vehicle's bodywork is the one thing that significantly affects its value. Maintenance is easy, but needs to be regular. Neglect, particularly after minor damage, can lead quickly to further deterioration and costly repair bills. It is important also to keep watch on those parts of the vehicle not immediately visible, for instance the underside, inside all the wheel arches, and the lower part of the engine compartment.
2 The basic maintenance routine for the bodywork is washing – preferably with a lot of water, from a hose. This will remove all the loose solids which may have stuck to the vehicle. It is important to flush these off in such a way as to prevent grit from scratching the finish. The wheel arches and underframe need washing in the same way, to remove any accumulated mud, which will retain moisture and tend to encourage rust. Paradoxically enough, the best time to clean the underframe and wheel arches is in wet weather, when the mud is thoroughly wet and soft. In very wet weather, the underframe is usually cleaned of large accumulations automatically, and this is a good time for inspection.
3 Periodically, except on vehicles with a wax-based underbody protective coating, it is a good idea to have the whole of the underframe of the vehicle steam-cleaned, engine compartment included, so that a thorough inspection can be carried out to see what minor repairs and renovations are necessary. Steam-cleaning is available at many garages, and is necessary for the removal of the accumulation of oily grime, which sometimes is allowed to become thick in certain areas. If steam-cleaning facilities are not available, there are some excellent grease solvents available which can be brush-applied; the dirt can then be simply hosed off. Note that these methods should not be used on vehicles with wax-based underbody protective coating, or the coating will be removed. Such vehicles should be inspected annually, preferably just prior to winter, when the underbody should be washed down, and any damage to the wax coating repaired. Ideally, a completely fresh coat should be applied. It would also be worth considering the use of such wax-based protection for injection into door panels, sills, box sections, etc, as an additional safeguard against rust damage, where such protection is not provided by the vehicle manufacturer.
4 After washing paintwork, wipe off with a chamois leather to give an unspotted clear finish. A coat of clear protective wax polish will give added protection against chemical pollutants in the air. If the paintwork sheen has dulled or oxidised, use a cleaner/polisher combination to restore the brilliance of the shine. This requires a little effort, but such dulling is usually caused because regular washing has been neglected. Care needs to be taken with metallic paintwork, as special non-abrasive cleaner/polisher is required to avoid damage to the finish. Always check that the door and ventilator opening drain holes and pipes are completely clear, so that water can be drained out. Brightwork should be treated in the same way as paintwork. Windscreens and windows can be kept clear of the smeary film which often appears, by the use of proprietary glass cleaner. Never use any form of wax or other body or chromium polish on glass.

3 Maintenance – upholstery and carpets

1 Mats and carpets should be brushed or vacuum-cleaned regularly, to keep them free of grit. If they are badly stained, remove them from the vehicle for scrubbing or sponging, and make quite sure they are dry before refitting. Seats and interior trim panels can be kept clean by wiping with a damp cloth. If they do become stained (which can be more apparent on light-coloured upholstery), use a little liquid detergent and a soft nail brush to scour the grime out of the grain of the material. Do not forget to keep the headlining clean in the same way as the upholstery. When using liquid cleaners inside the vehicle, do not over-wet the surfaces being cleaned. Excessive damp could get into the seams and padded interior, causing stains, offensive odours or even rot.
2 If the inside of the vehicle gets wet accidentally, it is worthwhile taking some trouble to dry it out properly, particularly where carpets are involved. Do not leave oil or electric heaters inside the vehicle for this purpose.

4 Minor body damage – repair

Scratches

1 If the scratch is very superficial, and does not penetrate to the metal of the bodywork, repair is very simple. Lightly rub the area of the scratch with a paintwork renovator, or a very fine cutting paste, to remove loose paint from the scratch, and to clear the surrounding bodywork of wax polish. Rinse the area with clean water.
2 Apply touch-up paint to the scratch using a fine paint brush; continue to apply fine layers of paint until the surface of the paint in the scratch is level with the surrounding paintwork. Allow the new paint at least two weeks to harden, then blend it into the surrounding paintwork by rubbing the scratch area with a paintwork renovator or a very fine cutting paste. Finally, apply wax polish.
3 Where the scratch has penetrated right through to the metal of the bodywork, causing the metal to rust, a different repair technique is required. Remove any loose rust from the bottom of the scratch with a penknife, then apply rust-inhibiting paint to prevent the formation of rust in the future. Using a rubber or nylon applicator, fill the scratch with bodystopper paste. If required, this paste can be mixed with cellulose thinners to provide a very thin paste which is ideal for filling narrow scratches. Before the stopper-paste in the scratch hardens, wrap a piece of smooth cotton rag around the top of a finger. Dip the finger in cellulose thinners, and quickly sweep it across the surface of the stopper-paste in the scratch; this will ensure that the surface of the stopper-paste is slightly hollowed. The scratch can now be painted over as described earlier in this Section.

Dents

4 When deep denting of the vehicle's bodywork has taken place, the first task is to pull the dent out, until the affected bodywork almost attains its original shape. There is little point in trying to restore the original shape completely, as the metal in the damaged area will have stretched on impact, and cannot be reshaped fully to its original contour. It is better to bring the level of the dent up to a point which is about 3 mm below the level of the surrounding bodywork. In cases where the dent is very shallow anyway, it is not worth trying to pull it out at all. If the underside of the dent is accessible, it can be hammered out gently from behind, using a mallet with a wooden or plastic head. Whilst doing this, hold a suitable block of wood firmly against the outside of the panel, to absorb the impact from the hammer blows and thus prevent a large area of the bodywork from being 'belled-out'.
5 Should the dent be in a section of the

bodywork which has a double skin, or some other factor making it inaccessible from behind, a different technique is called for. Drill several small holes through the metal inside the area – particularly in the deeper section. Then screw long self-tapping screws into the holes, just sufficiently for them to gain a good purchase in the metal. Now the dent can be pulled out by pulling on the protruding heads of the screws with a pair of pliers.

6 The next stage of the repair is the removal of the paint from the damaged area, and from an inch or so of the surrounding 'sound' bodywork. This is accomplished most easily by using a wire brush or abrasive pad on a power drill, although it can be done just as effectively by hand, using sheets of abrasive paper. To complete the preparation for filling, score the surface of the bare metal with a screwdriver or the tang of a file, or alternatively, drill small holes in the affected area. This will provide a really good 'key' for the filler paste.

7 To complete the repair, see the Section on filling and respraying.

Rust holes or gashes

8 Remove all paint from the affected area, and from an inch or so of the surrounding 'sound' bodywork, using an abrasive pad or a wire brush on a power drill. If these are not available, a few sheets of abrasive paper will do the job most effectively. With the paint removed, you will be able to judge the severity of the corrosion, and therefore decide whether to renew the whole panel (if this is possible) or to repair the affected area. New body panels are not as expensive as most people think, and it is often quicker and more satisfactory to fit a new panel than to attempt to repair large areas of corrosion.

9 Remove all fittings from the affected area, except those which will act as a guide to the original shape of the damaged bodywork (eg headlight shells etc). Then, using tin snips or a hacksaw blade, remove all loose metal and any other metal badly affected by corrosion. Hammer the edges of the hole inwards, in order to create a slight depression for the filler paste.

10 Wire-brush the affected area to remove the powdery rust from the surface of the remaining metal. Paint the affected area with rust-inhibiting paint, if the back of the rusted area is accessible, treat this also.

11 Before filling can take place, it will be necessary to block the hole in some way. This can be achieved by the use of aluminium or plastic mesh, or aluminium tape.

12 Aluminium or plastic mesh, or glass-fibre matting, is probably the best material to use for a large hole. Cut a piece to the approximate size and shape of the hole to be filled, then position it in the hole so that its edges are below the level of the surrounding bodywork. It can be retained in position by several blobs of filler paste around its periphery.

13 Aluminium tape should be used for small or very narrow holes. Pull a piece off the roll, trim it to the approximate size and shape required, then pull off the backing paper (if used) and stick the tape over the hole; it can be overlapped if the thickness of one piece is insufficient. Burnish down the edges of the tape with the handle of a screwdriver or similar, to ensure that the tape is securely attached to the metal underneath.

Filling and respraying

14 Before using this Section, see the Sections on dent, deep scratch, rust holes and gash repairs.

15 Many types of bodyfiller are available, but generally speaking, those proprietary kits which contain a tin of filler paste and a tube of resin hardener are best for this type of repair. A wide, flexible plastic or nylon applicator will be found invaluable for imparting a smooth and well-contoured finish to the surface of the filler.

16 Mix up a little filler on a clean piece of card or board – measure the hardener carefully (follow the maker's instructions on the pack), otherwise the filler will set too rapidly or too slowly. Using the applicator, apply the filler paste to the prepared area; draw the applicator across the surface of the filler to achieve the correct contour and to level the surface. As soon as a contour that approximates to the correct one is achieved, stop working the paste – if you carry on too long, the paste will become sticky and begin to 'pick-up' on the applicator. Continue to add thin layers of filler paste at 20-minute intervals, until the level of the filler is just proud of the surrounding bodywork.

17 Once the filler has hardened, the excess can be removed using a metal plane or file. From then on, progressively-finer grades of abrasive paper should be used, starting with a 40-grade production paper, and finishing with a 400-grade wet-and-dry paper. Always wrap the abrasive paper around a flat rubber, cork, or wooden block – otherwise the surface of the filler will not be completely flat. During the smoothing of the filler surface, the wet-and-dry paper should be periodically rinsed in water. This will ensure that a very smooth finish is imparted to the filler at the final stage.

18 At this stage, the dent should be surrounded by a ring of bare metal, which in turn should be encircled by the finely 'feathered' edge of the good paintwork. Rinse the repair area with clean water, until all of the dust produced by the rubbing-down operation has gone.

19 Spray the whole area with a light coat of primer – this will show up any imperfections in the surface of the filler. Repair these imperfections with fresh filler paste or bodystopper, and once more smooth the surface with abrasive paper. Repeat this spray-and-repair procedure until you are satisfied that the surface of the filler, and the feathered edge of the paintwork, are perfect. Clean the repair area with clean water, and allow to dry fully.

20 The repair area is now ready for final spraying. Paint spraying must be carried out in a warm, dry, windless and dust-free atmosphere. This condition can be created artificially if you have access to a large indoor working area, but if you are forced to work in the open, you will have to pick your day very carefully. If you are working indoors, dousing the floor in the work area with water will help to settle the dust which would otherwise be in the atmosphere. If the repair area is confined to one body panel, mask off the surrounding panels; this will help to minimise the effects of a slight mis-match in paint colours. Bodywork fittings (eg chrome strips, door handles etc) will also need to be masked off. Use genuine masking tape, and several thicknesses of newspaper, for the masking operations.

21 Before commencing to spray, agitate the aerosol can thoroughly, then spray a test area (an old tin, or similar) until the technique is mastered. Cover the repair area with a thick coat of primer; the thickness should be built up using several thin layers of paint, rather than one thick one. Using 400-grade wet-and-dry paper, rub down the surface of the primer until it is really smooth. While doing this, the work area should be thoroughly doused with water, and the wet-and-dry paper periodically rinsed in water. Allow to dry before spraying on more paint.

22 Spray on the top coat, again building up the thickness by using several thin layers of paint. Start spraying at one edge of the repair area, and then, using a side-to-side motion, work until the whole repair area and about 2 inches of the surrounding original paintwork is covered. Remove all masking material 10 to 15 minutes after spraying on the final coat of paint.

23 Allow the new paint at least two weeks to harden, then, using a paintwork renovator, or a very fine cutting paste, blend the edges of the paint into the existing paintwork. Finally, apply wax polish.

Plastic components

24 With the use of more and more plastic body components by the vehicle manufacturers (eg bumpers. spoilers, and in some cases major body panels), rectification of more serious damage to such items has become a matter of either entrusting repair work to a specialist in this field, or renewing complete components. Repair of such damage by the DIY owner is not really feasible, owing to the cost of the equipment and materials required for effecting such repairs. The basic technique involves making a groove along the line of the crack in the plastic, using a rotary burr in a power drill. The damaged part is then welded back together, using a hot-air gun to heat up and fuse a plastic filler rod into the groove. Any excess plastic is then removed, and the area rubbed down to a smooth finish. It is important that a filler rod of the correct plastic

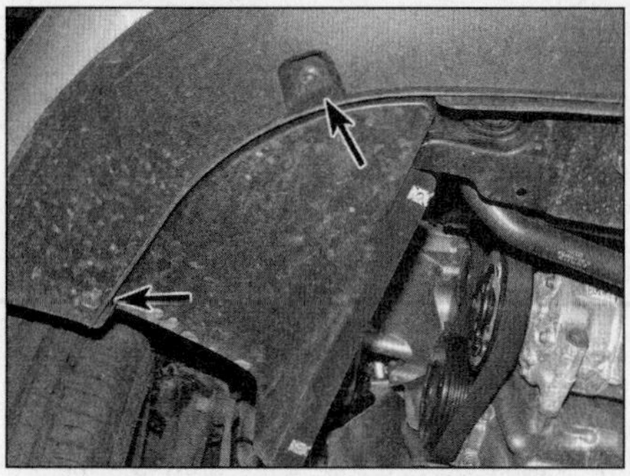

6.2 Undo the screws and bolts

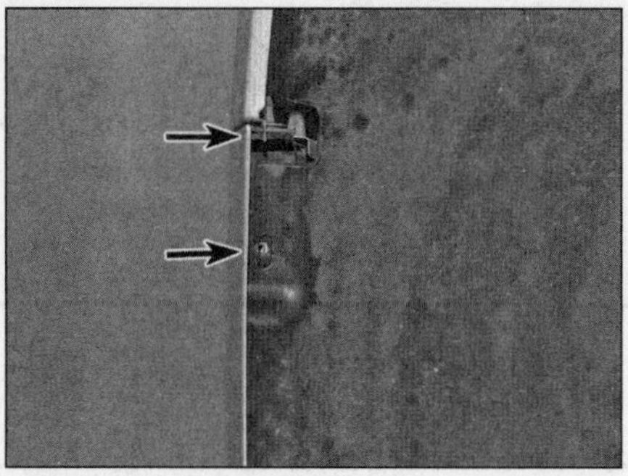

6.3 The upper bumper cover to wing liner screws

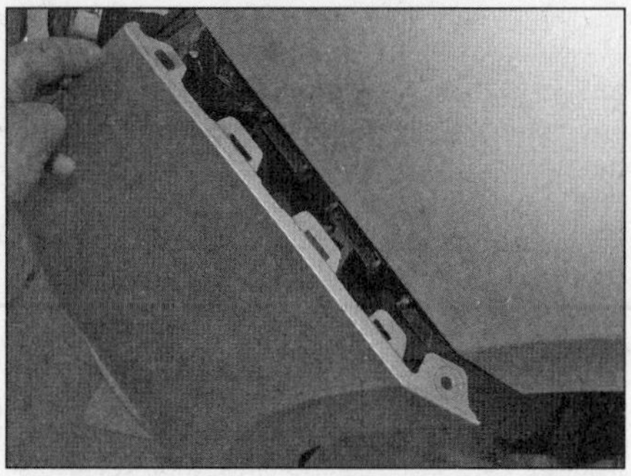

6.4 Unclip the bumper at the front of the wings

is used, as body components can be made of a variety of different types (eg polycarbonate, ABS, polypropylene).

25 Damage of a less serious nature (abrasions, minor cracks etc) can be repaired by the DIY owner using a two-part epoxy filler repair material. Once mixed in equal proportions, this is used in similar fashion to the bodywork filler used on metal panels. The filler is usually cured in twenty to thirty minutes, ready for sanding and painting.

26 If the owner is renewing a complete component himself, or if he has repaired it with epoxy filler, he will be left with the problem of finding a suitable paint for finishing which is compatible with the type of plastic used. At one time, the use of a universal paint was not possible, owing to the complex range of plastics encountered in body component applications. Standard paints, generally speaking, will not bond to plastic or rubber satisfactorily. However, it is now possible to obtain a plastic body parts finishing kit which consists of a pre-primer treatment, a primer and coloured top coat. Full instructions are normally supplied with a kit, but basically, the method of use is to first apply the pre-primer to the component concerned, and allow it to dry for up to 30 minutes. Then the primer is applied, and left to dry for about an hour before finally applying the special-coloured top coat. The result is a correctly-coloured component, where the paint will flex with the plastic or rubber, a property that standard paint does not normally possess.

5 Major body damage – repair

1 Where serious damage has occurred, or large areas need renewal due to neglect, it means that complete new panels will need welding-in, and this is best left to professionals. If the damage is due to impact, it will also be necessary to check completely the alignment of the body shell, and this can only be carried out accurately by a Seat dealer using special jigs. If the body is left misaligned, it is primarily dangerous, as the car will not handle properly, and secondly, uneven stresses will be imposed on the steering, suspension and possibly transmission, causing abnormal wear, or complete failure, particularly to such items as the tyres.

6 Front bumper – removal and refitting

Removal

1 Apply the handbrake, then jack up the front of the vehicle and support it on axle stands (see *Jacking and vehicle support*).

2 Working under the front of the vehicle, undo the retaining screws from the lower part of the bumper **(see illustration)**. **Note:** *The number varies depending on the trim level and year of manufacture.*

3 Undo the retaining screws at each side that secure the bumper to the wing liner **(see illustration)**.

4 Working at the wing pull out the edges of the bumper from the bracket that holds the bumper to the wing panel and then push the outer edges forward **(see illustration)**. The bumper will still be secured at the bonnet slam panel at this point.

5 Pivot the bumper and where fitted, reach up to disconnect the front foglights, parking sensors and the headlight washer system.

6 Have an assistant support the bumper, then remove the fixings from across the upper edge of the bumper panel **(see illustrations)**.

7 With the aid of and assistant remove the bumper and store it so that the painted finish is not damaged.

Refitting

8 Refitting is a reversal of removal.

7 Rear bumper – removal and refitting

Removal

1 Remove both rear light units as described in Chapter 12 Section 8.

2 Working in the rear wheel arches, undo the mounting screws from the ends of the rear bumper **(see illustration)**.

3 Undo the fixings from along the lower edge of the bumper, under the rear of the vehicle.

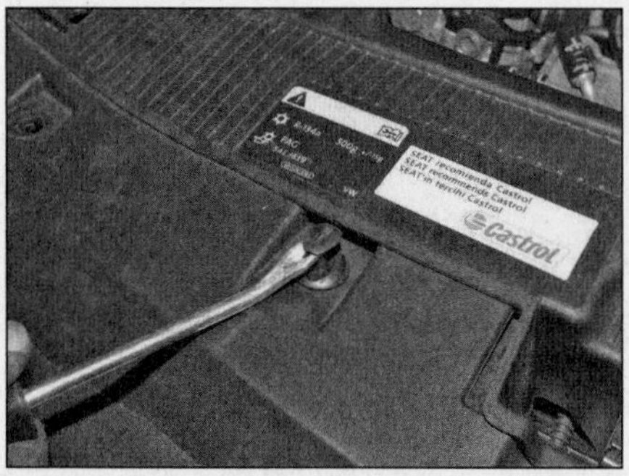

6.6a Lever up...

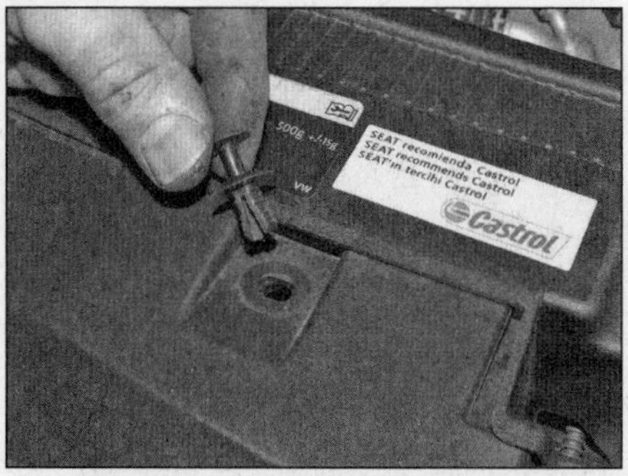

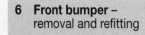

6.6b ...and remove the 'scrivets'

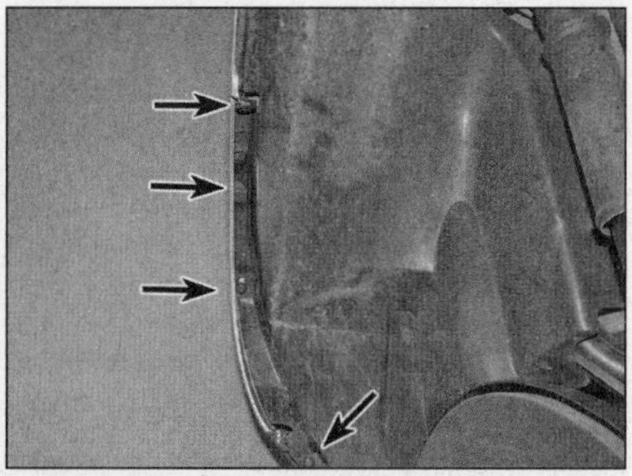

7.2 Rear bumper mounting screws in the rear wheel arch

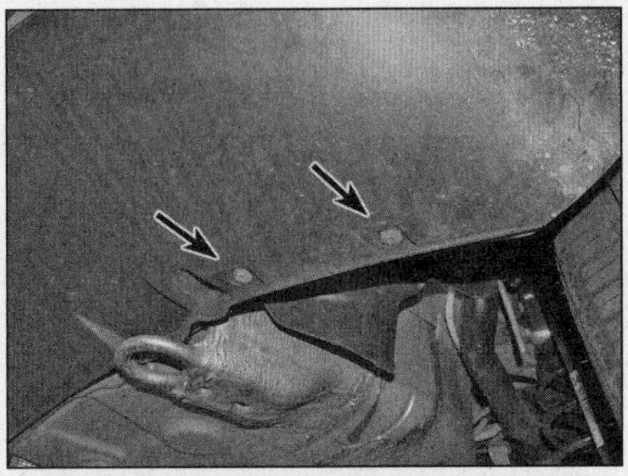

7.3 Remove the screws from the lower edge of the bumper cover

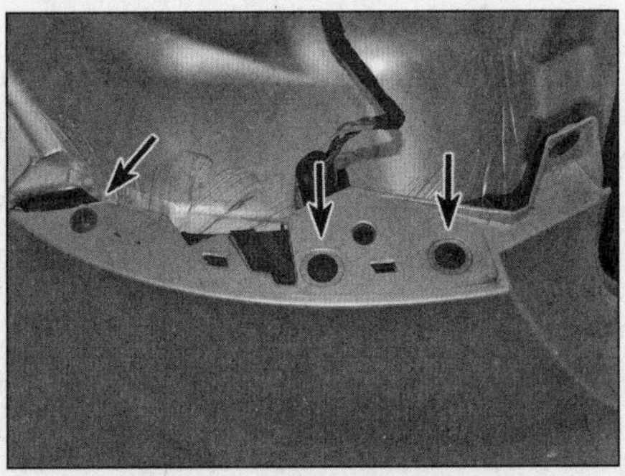

7.4 The upper retaining screws

7.5 Ease the bumper from the guides

The number of fixings will vary depending on the model **(see illustration)**.

4 Have an assistant support the bumper, then undo the retaining screws from the rear light apertures **(see illustration)**.

5 Working with an assistant, at the other side of the vehicle, carefully ease the ends of the bumper from the guides, at each side of the vehicle **(see illustration)**. along screwdriver can be used to ease the tabs of the locking pegs.

6 As the bumper is withdrawn from the rear of the vehicle, disconnect the wiring connectors from the number plate lamp and thr rear parking sensors (where fitted) Unclip the wiring from the rear of the bumper as required.

Refitting

7 Refitting is a reversal of removal.

8 Lock panel – removal and refitting

1 The lock panel is the complete front panel that holds the headlights, radiator, cooling fans, intercooler and AC condenser. Not all parts are fitted to all models. Moving the panel to the service position is essential for removal of the cooling fans and radiator on some models. Access to components at the front of the engine is greatly improved with the panel in the service position.

2 Complete removal of the panel makes removal and refitting of the engine and transmission a much simpler task for the home mechanic. On models fitted with AC the refrigerant must be drained first before removing the panel.

Moving the panel to the service position

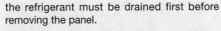

3 Seat/VAG special tools T20070 or suitable lengths of threaded bar will be required to move the lock carrier to the service position.

4 The coolant does not require draining as there is sufficient play in the coolant hoses to pull the panel forward. On some engines the coolant hoses must be unclipped from the brackets on the cooling fan shroud **(see illustration)**.

5 Open and support the bonnet and then remove the support prop from the slam panel/lock carrier. The bonnet prop can them be re-positioned in the slot provided on the left-hand strut tower **(see illustration)**.

6 Jack up and support the front of the vehicle (see *Jacking and vehicle support*)

7 Remove the front bumper as described in Section 6.

8 Remove the engine undershield (where fitted).

9 Disconnect the air intake duct from the air filter and then remove the housing from the bonnet slam panel **(see illustrations)**.

10 Mark the position of the bonnet lock and then remove the lock and bowden cable as described in Section 11 and Section 10.

11 Disconnect the wiring plugs from the bonnet contact switch and headlights **(see illustrations)**. Release the wiring loom as required.

12 The lock carrier can be moved to the service position with the headlights in position, however to avoid any possibility of damaging the headlights, removal (as described in Chapter 12 Section 8) is highly recommended at this point.

8.4 Where required unclip the coolant hoses

8.5 The mounting point for the bonnet support strut

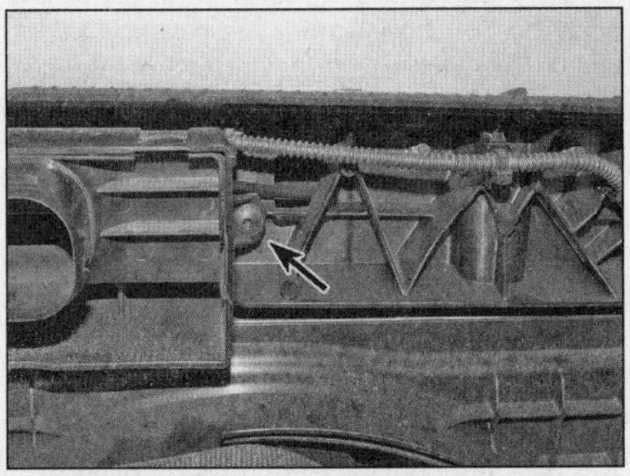

8.9a Remove the screw and...

8.9b ...lift out the housing

8.11a The bonnet open warning light wiring plug

8.11b Disconnect the headlight wiring plugs

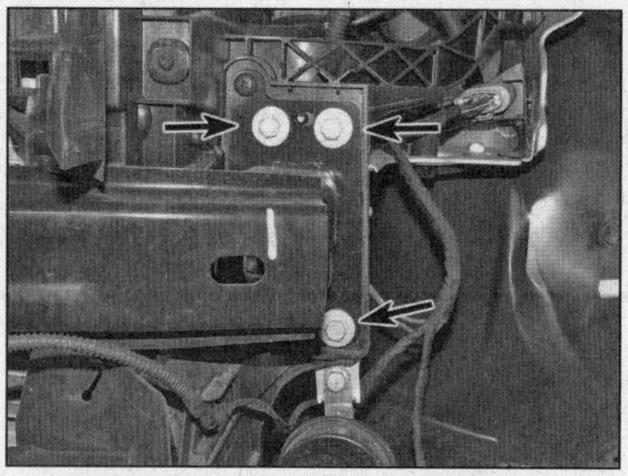
8.14a Remove one of the bolts...

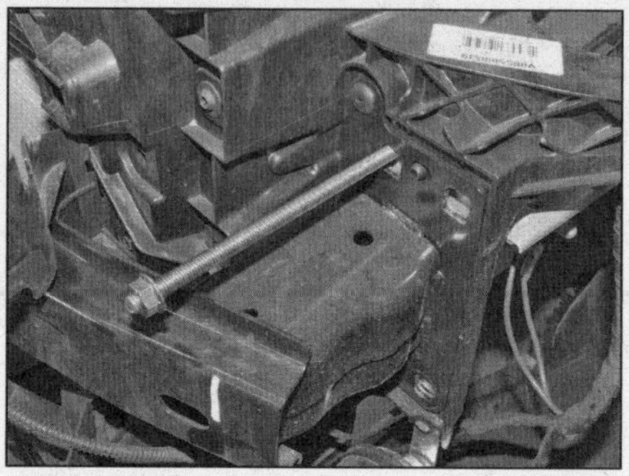
8.14b ...and install a length of threaded bar

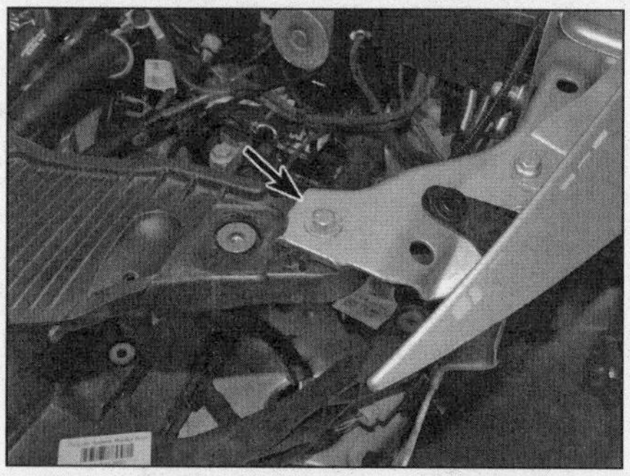
8.15a Remove the wing to panel bolts

8.15b The rear outer headlight mounting bolt

13 Disconnect the wiring plug from the ambient air temperature sensor or pull out the sensor and move it.

14 Remove one of the lock panel bolt from each side and either install the Seat special tool (T20070) or lengths of threaded bar **(see illustrations)**.

15 Remove the bolts from the upper section of the panel (at each side). If the headlights are to be left in position remove the bolts from the rear of the headlights **(see illustrations)**.

16 On models with AC unclip the refrigerant pipes from the brackets at the bottom of the lock carrier.

17 Remove the remaining bolts from the lock carrier (2 per side). Pull the panel forward and wedge a block of wood between the panel and the end of the chassis leg.

Removal

18 Drain the cooling system as described in Chapter 1A Section 32 or Chapter 1B Section 33.

Warning: It is a criminal offence to knowingly discharge refrigerant gas to the atmosphere.

19 On models fitted with AC have the refrigerant recovered by a garage equipped with an AC charge station. Most garages will have this equipment.

20 Follow the procedure detailed above for moving the lock carrier to the service position.

21 Disconnect the radiator hoses and (where fitted) the intercooler hoses. On models with AC disconnect the refrigerant lines and immediately seal both lines.

22 Remove both headlights as described in Chapter 12 Section 8.

23 Check that all connections between the panel and the body have been disconnected and then with the aid of an assistant, unscrew the support tools and lift out the lock panel.

9.3 Slide out the clip and disconnect the hose

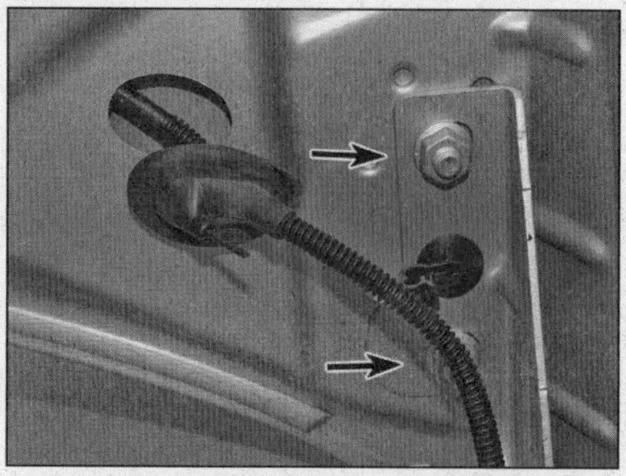
9.4 Mark the position of the hinge

Refitting

24 Refitting is a reversal of removal, noting the following:

a) Refill the cooling system and check for leaks.
b) Check that the body lock and cable work correctly before refitting the bumper cover.
c) On models with AC fit new seals. Have the system re-gassed and leak checked.

9 Bonnet – removal, refitting and adjustment

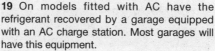

Removal

1 Open the bonnet and support with the stay, then place some cardboard or rags beneath the corners by the hinges to protect the bodywork.

2 Remove the wiper arms as described in Chapter 12 Section 15 and then remove the plenum chamber cover as described in Chapter 12 Section 16.

3 Disconnect the screen washer jet hose **(see illustration)**.

4 Using a pencil or felt tip pen, mark the outline of each bonnet hinge relative to the bonnet, to use as a guide on refitting **(see illustration)**.

5 Have an assistant support the bonnet in its open position.

6 Unscrew the bonnet retaining bolts and carefully lift the bonnet clear. Store the bonnet out of the way in a safe place.

7 Inspect the bonnet hinges for signs of wear and free play at the pivots, and if necessary renew them. Each hinge is secured to the body by two bolts; mark the position of the hinge on the body then undo the retaining bolts and remove it from the vehicle.

Refitting and adjustment

8 Where removed, refit the bonnet hinges, and align them with the previously-made marks. Tighten the bolts securely.

9 With the aid of an assistant, offer up the bonnet and loosely fit the retaining bolts. Align the hinges with the marks made on removal, then tighten the retaining bolts securely.

10 Close the bonnet, and check for alignment with the adjacent panels. If necessary, slacken the hinge bolts and re-align the bonnet. Adjust

10.3a Release the securing clip at the point shown...

the height of the bonnet so that it is level with the surrounding front wings, by turning the rubber buffer at each front corner of the bonnet. Once the bonnet is correctly aligned, tighten the hinge bolts. Check that the bonnet fastens and releases satisfactorily.

10 Bonnet release cable – removal and refitting

Removal

1 Open the bonnet and where required remove the air filter housing and inlet ducting.

2 Mark the position the lock and then undo the two securing nuts and lift out the bonnet lock from the bonnet slam panel. Disconnect the release cable from the lock, as described in the next section.

3 Working inside the vehicle, locate the release lever and pull it out slightly, then insert a small screwdriver into the gap between the release lever and its securing clip. Let the lever return to its original position, then release the clip with a screwdriver **(see illustrations)**.

4 Pull the door seal away from the door aperture, and then unclip the sill panel as described in Section 26.

5 Undo the two retaining screws and remove the release lever mechanism from the body **(see illustration)**. Then unclip the cable from the release lever mechanism.

6 Remove the wiper arms and the windscreen grille panel as described in Chapter 12 Section 16.

7 Work along the length of the cable, noting its correct routing, and free it from the retaining clips and ties. Also, prise the rubber grommet from the bulkhead.

8 Tie a length of cord (approximately 1.0 m long) to the end of the cable inside the vehicle, then withdraw the cable through into the engine compartment.

9 Once the cable is free, untie the cord and leave it in position in the vehicle; the cord can then be used to draw the new cable back into position.

Refitting

10 Tie the inner end of the cord to the end of the cable, then use the cord to draw the

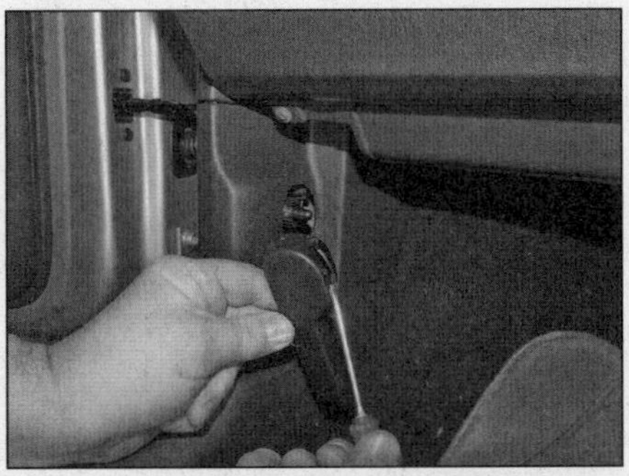

10.3b...and remove the handle

bonnet release cable back from the engine compartment. Once the cable is through, untie the cord.

11 The remaining refitting procedure is a reversal of removal. Ensure the rubber grommet in the bulkhead is fitted correctly, and the cable is correctly routed and secured to all the relevant retaining clips. Before closing the bonnet, check the operation of the release lever and cable.

11 Bonnet lock – removal and refitting

Removal

1 Open the bonnet, then using a pencil or felt tip pen, mark the outline of the bonnet lock on the slam panel, to use as a guide on refitting.

11.2 Bonnet lock mounting bolts

11.3b ...and remove the micro switch

10.5 Undo the two securing screws

2 Unscrew the mounting nuts and withdraw the lock assembly **(see illustration)**.

3 As the lock is removed, disconnect the wiring from the alarm switch micro-switch connector on the lock mechanism **(see illustrations)**. Note that the micro switch can also be removed with the lock if the wiring plug is disconnected from the connector at the left-hand end of the slam panel and the loom released from the retaining clips under the slam panel.

4 Unclip the bonnet release cable from the lock **(see illustration)**.

Refitting

5 Before refitting, remove all traces of old locking compound from the lock retaining bolts and their threads.

6 Refitting is a reversal of removal, ensuring the bolts are securely tightened using thread-locking compound. Check that the

11.3a Remove the locking peg...

11.4 Remove the release cable

12.1 Slide up the locking collar

12.2 Check strap securing bolt

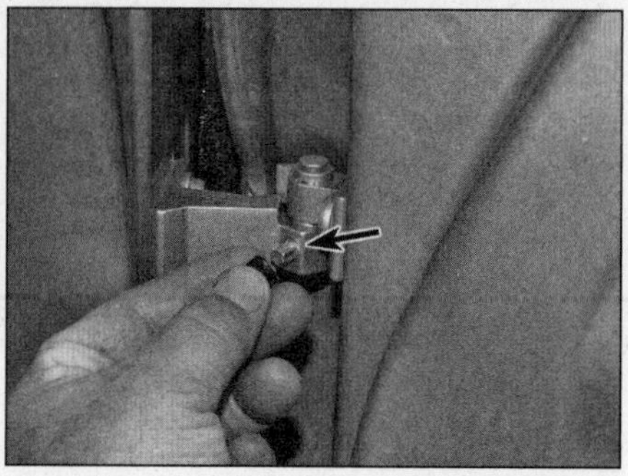

12.3 Remove the seal and then the bolt

bonnet fastens and releases satisfactorily. If adjustment is necessary, slacken the bonnet lock retaining bolts, and adjust the position of the lock. Once the lock is operating correctly, tighten the retaining bolts.

12 Door – removal, refitting and adjustment

Note: *The hinge bolts must always be renewed if loosened.*

Removal

1 Open the door then disconnect the wiring at the A- or B-pillar as applicable. To do this, slide up the locking collar and release the wiring plug from the door pillar **(see illustration)**.

2 Undo the retaining bolt and disconnect the check strap from the door pillar **(see illustration)**. With this disconnected the door can swing fully open, take care it does not go to far and damage the body panels.

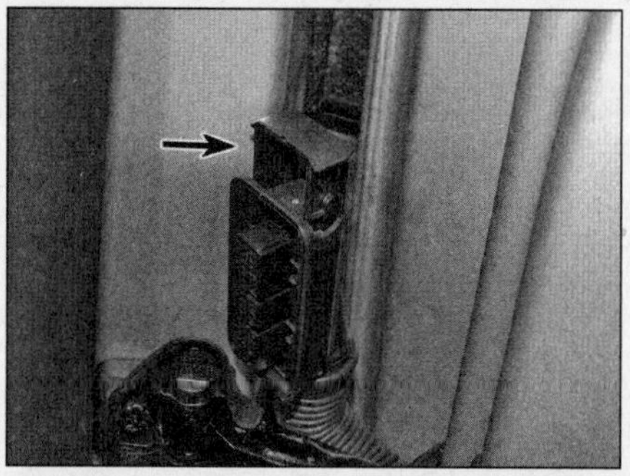

13.2 Release the wiring plug cover at the top

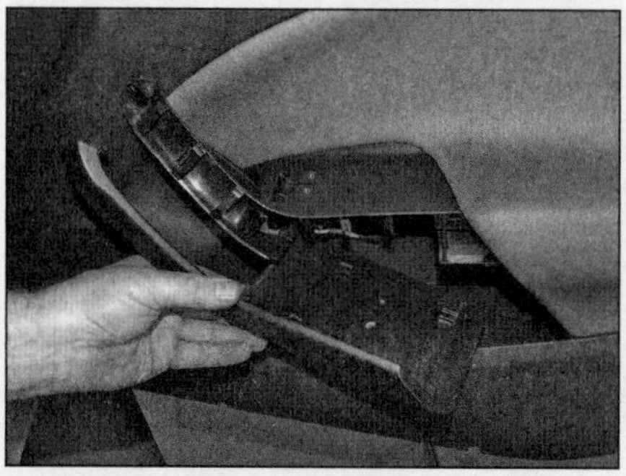

13.5b ...and unclip the trim panel

3 With the door supported by an assistant, unscrew and remove the bolts from the upper and lower hinge pin bolts **(see illustration)**. Lift the door upwards to lift it off the hinge pins. With the aid of an assistant remove the door from the vehicle.

4 Examine the hinges for signs of wear or damage. If renewal is necessary, the hinges can be unbolted from the A- or B-pillar. Note however that access to the drivers side upper hinge requires removal of the facia as described in Section 28. The hinges on the passenger side can be accessed after the glovebox is removed. Before removing them, accurately mark their position to ensure correct refitting.

Refitting

5 Where renewed, fit the hinges and tighten the bolts to the specified torque. Refit the trim.

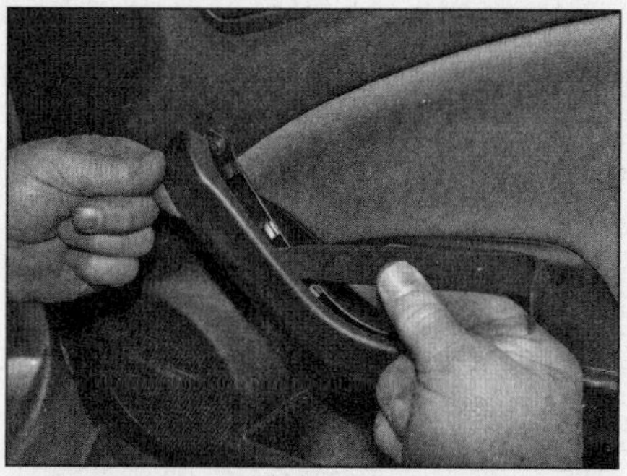

13.5a Work around the cover with a trim tool...

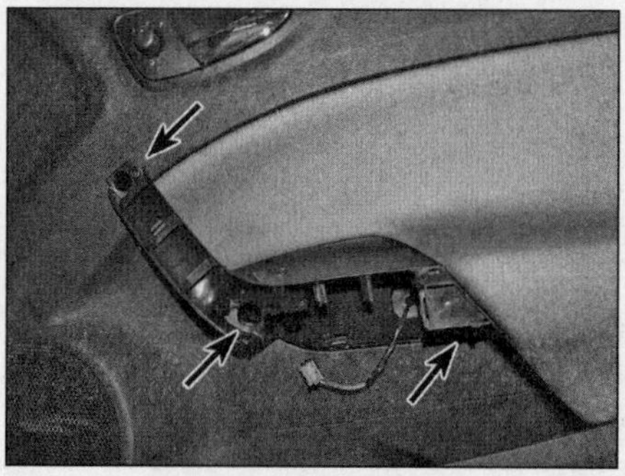

13.5c Remove the screws

6 With the aid of an assistant, offer up the door to the vehicle and locate it on the hinge pin. Fit the new hinge bolts and tighten to the specified torque.

7 Reconnect the wiring plug and secure with the locking lever, then refit the rubber bellows.

8 Reconnect the check strap to the A-pillar, and then tighten the securing bolt to the specified torque setting.

Adjustment

9 Close the door and check the door alignment with the surrounding body panels. There must be an even gap all around, and the door must be level with the surrounding body panels.

10 Check that the striker enters the door lock centrally as the door is closed, and if necessary adjust the position of the striker by loosening its mounting bolts.

13 Door inner trim panel – removal and refitting

Removal

Front door

Note: *The front door trim panel is removed complete with the door lock assembly, the window regulator and the loudspeaker. If required the lock assembly can be detached from the trim panel as the bracket that holds the lock to the panel is only a factory assembly aid.*

1 Remove the lock cylinder and the door lock bolts as described in Section 14.

2 Slide up the locking clamp and disconnect the wiring plug at the A-pillar **(see illustration)**. Push the wiring plug into the door frame.

3 On models fitted with manual door mirrors unclip the cover and release the joystick.

4 On models fitted with electric door mirrors, remove the mirror glass and the mirror cover. Disconnect the wiring plug (see Section 19).

5 Carefully unclip and remove the cover from the door grab handle. Slacken and remove the retaining screws inside the door panel **(see illustrations)**.

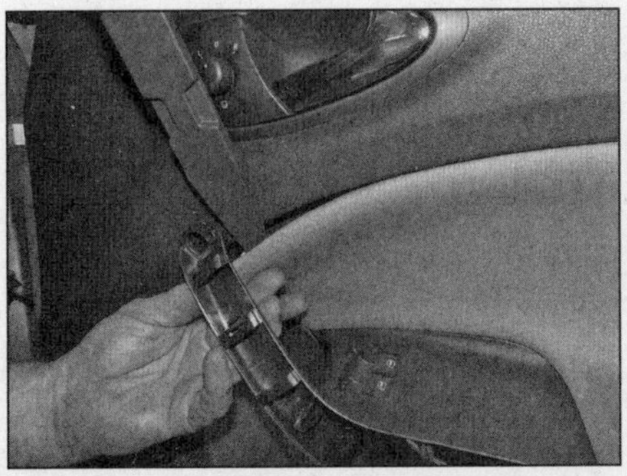
13.6a Using a trim tool...

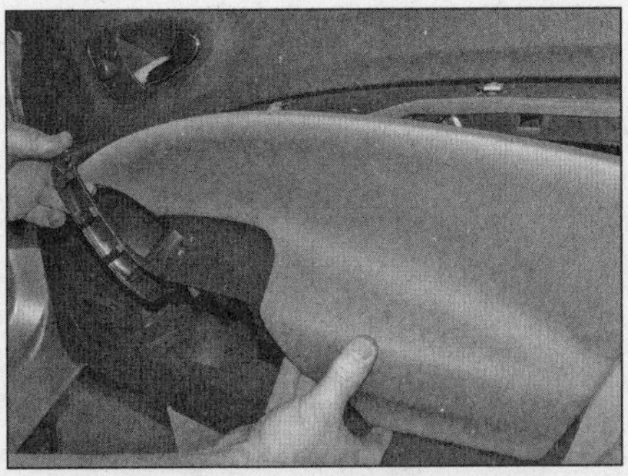
13.6b ...remove the inner trim panel

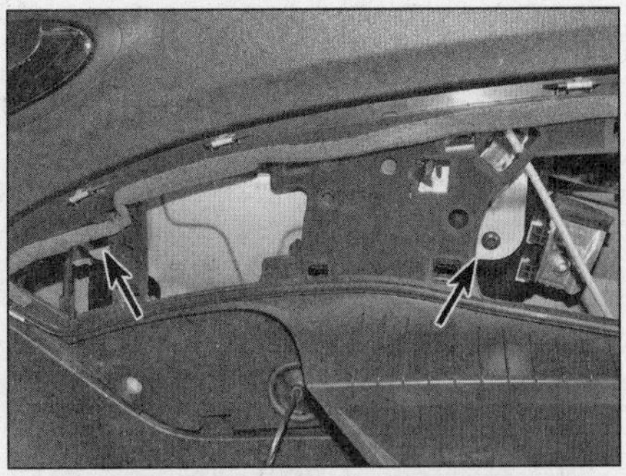
13.9a Remove the upper bolts...

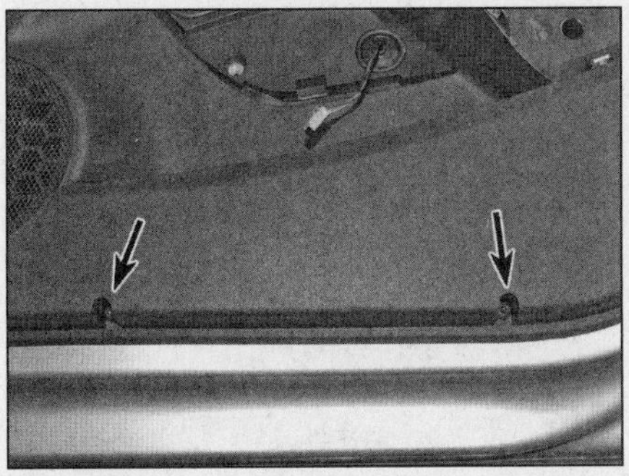
13.9b ...and slacken the lower bolts

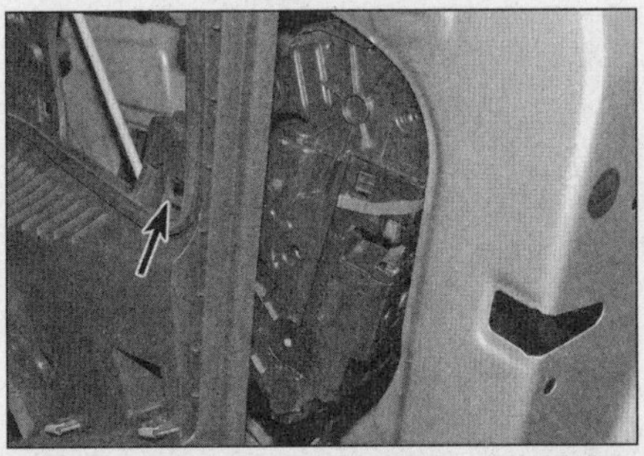
13.11 Partially remove the panel. Note the bracket that holds the door lock assembly to the trim panel

13.13 Press the spacer/clip and remove the handle

6 Disconnect the power window switch and then remove the door trim inner panel **(see illustrations)**.

7 Reconnect the power window switch and position the window so that the glass clamp screws are accessible.

8 slacken the glass clamp bolts and then remove the glass as described in Section 15.

9 Remove the window regulator upper bolts and then slacken the lower bolts **(see illustrations)**.

10 Release the trim panel by pushing it upwards (to release the regulator from the door frame) and then lower it to release the upper section of the regulator from the door frame.

11 Move the panel to the front of the door so that the lock assembly can be removed with the panel **(see illustration)**.

12 Release the wiring loom from the clips on the door frame and then remove the trim panel.

Rear door

Note: *The rear door trim panel is removed complete with the window regulator and the loudspeaker.*

13 On manual window models, with the window fully closed, note the position of the window crank handle, to ensure correct refitting. Slide the locking ring to release the internal spring, then withdraw the crank handle from the splines on the regulator **(see illustration)**. Several attempts at releasing the spacer ring in different positions may be required, in order to release the internal spring.

14 Carefully unclip and remove the trim panel from the door grab handle. Slacken and remove the retaining screws **(see illustrations)**.

15 On models with power windows unclip the control panel.

16 Using a trim tool remove the inner section of the door trim panel **(see illustrations)**.

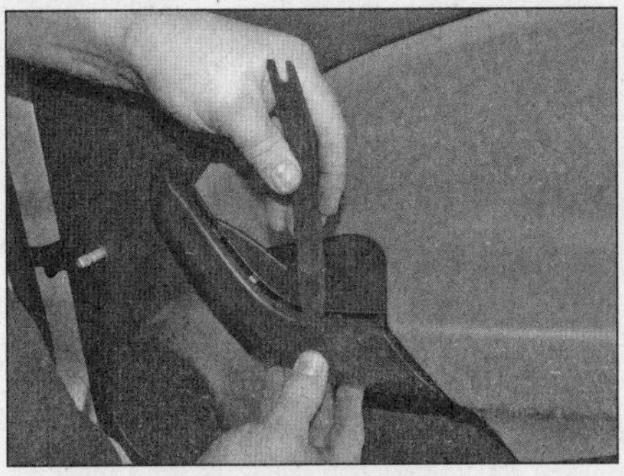
13.14a Use a trim tool...

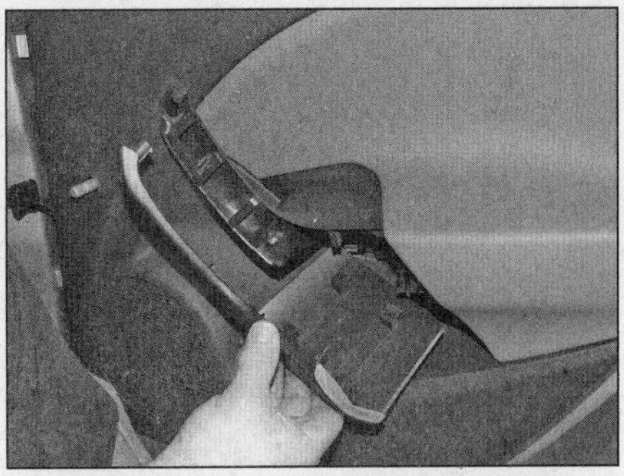
13.14b ...and remove the handle cover

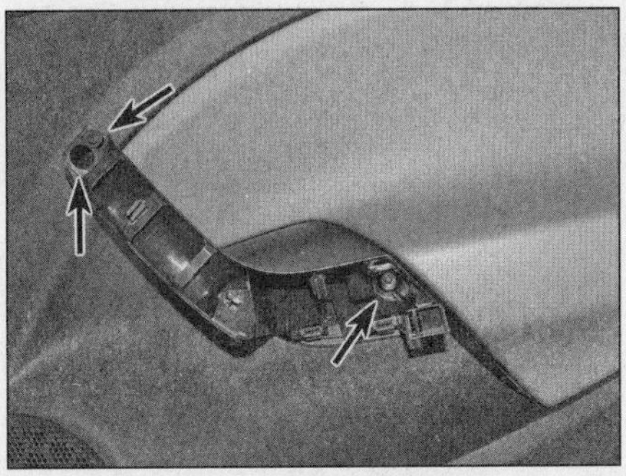
13.14c Remove the screws

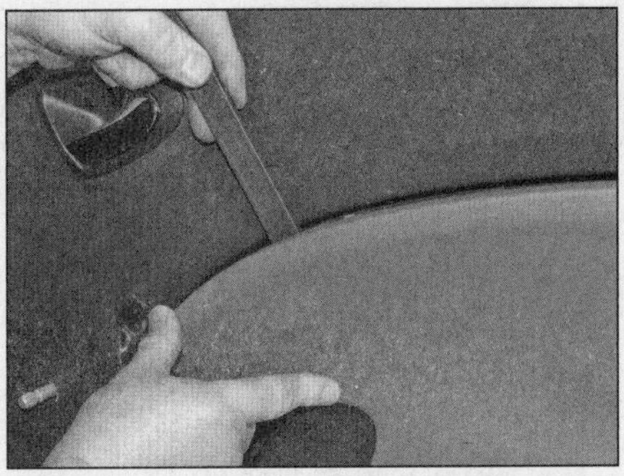
13.16a Use a trim tool to release...

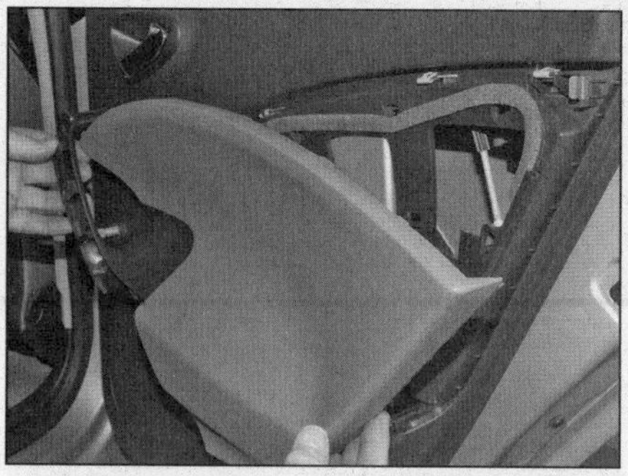

13.16b ...and then remove the inner trim panel

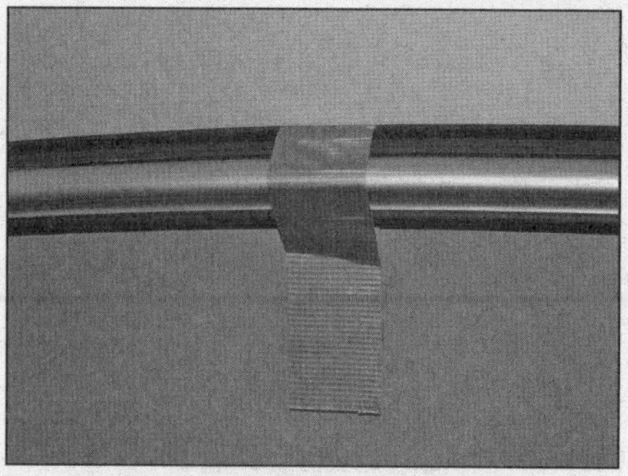

13.18 Secure the glass in the closed position

13.19 Disconnect the wiring plug at the B-pillar

13.20 Remove the 'scrivet'

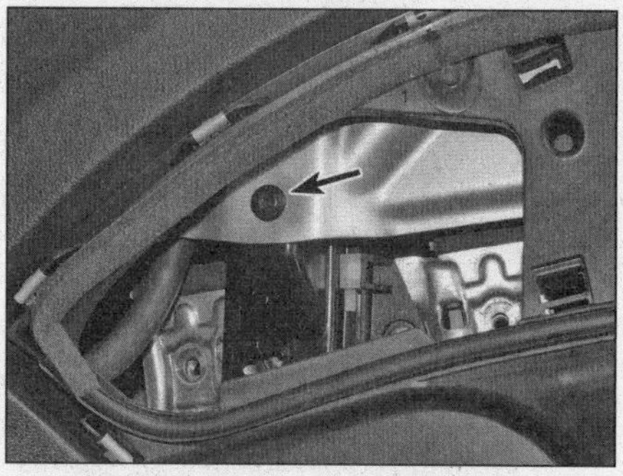

13.21a Remove the upper bolt...

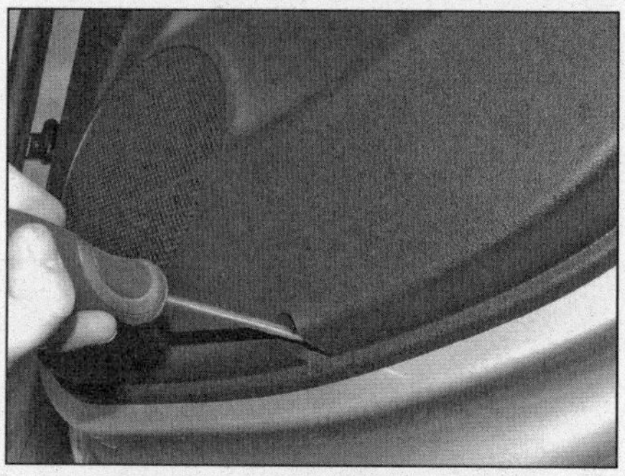

13.21b ...and slacken the lower

17 Refit the wider handle (or power window switch) and adjust the position of the glass so that the glass clamp is accessible.

18 Release the rear window glass from the regulator as described in Section 15 and tape it in the closed position **(see illustration)**.

19 Remove the wiring plug at the B-pillar and push the connector into the door frame **(see illustration)**.

20 Remove the small upper trim panel. Remove the 'scrivet' **(see illustration)**.

21 Remove the upper bolt from the regulator and then slacken the lower bolt **(see illustrations)**.

22 Remove the trim panel by first lifting up the panel to release the lower section of the regulator and then lower it to release the upper section of the regulator.

23 Support the panel and disconnect the bowden cable. Disconnect the wiring plug from the lock and then release the loom from the retaining clips on the door inner frame. Remove the panel **(see illustrations)**.

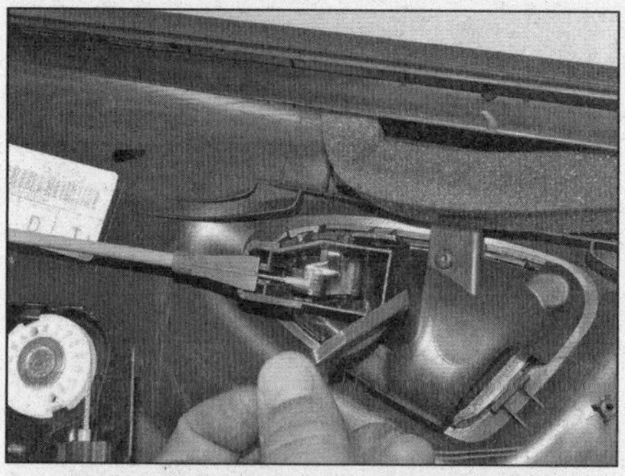

13.23a Release the bowden cable at the handle...

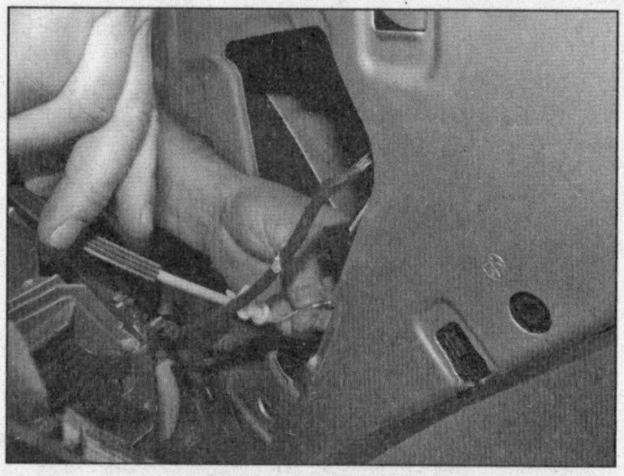

13.23b ...or the lock...

13.23c ...and then remove the trim panel

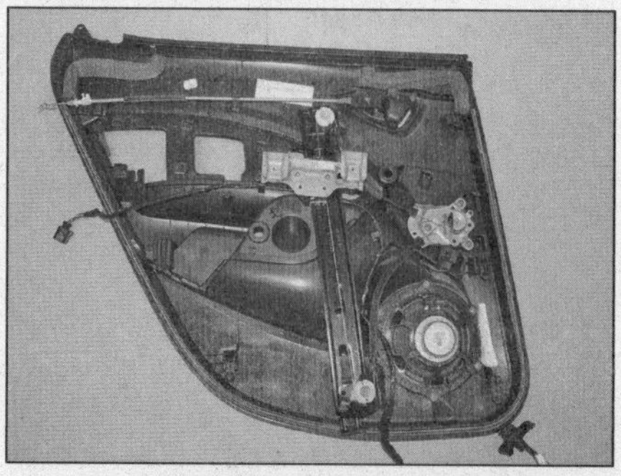

13.23d The components mounted to the rear door trim panel

Refitting

24 Refitting is a reversal of removal, but check the operation of the door electrical equipment as applicable.

14 Door handle and lock components – removal and refitting

Removal

Interior door handle

1 The interior door handle is fitted to the door trim panel. Remove the door trim panel as described in Section 13.

2 Disconnect the bowden cable, remove the fixings and remove the handle **(see illustration)**.

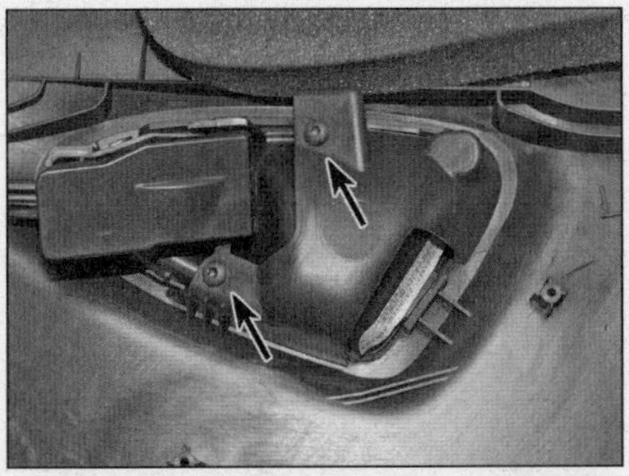

14.2 Remove the screws and unclip the handle

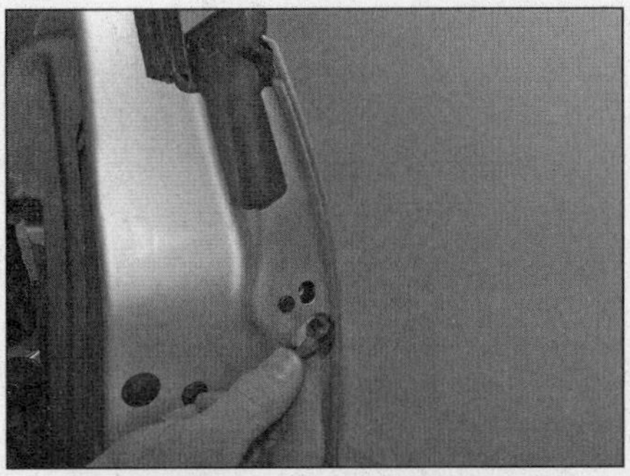

14.3 Unclip the cover from the lock cylinder securing screws

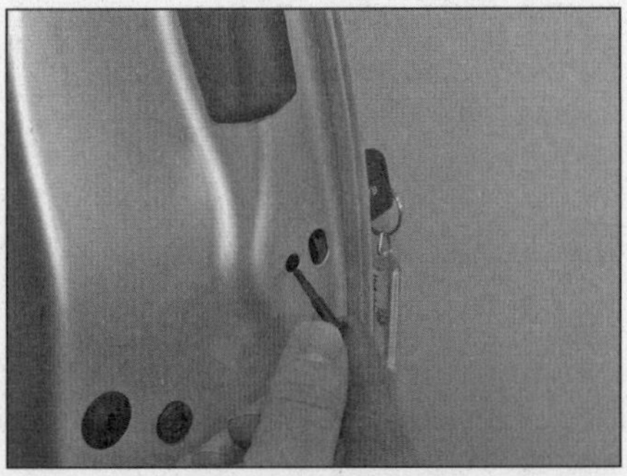

14.5a Remove the long screw

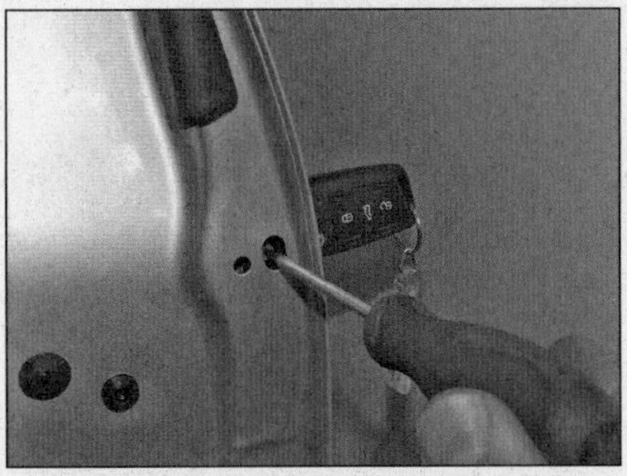

14.5b Push on the screw to release the locking clamp

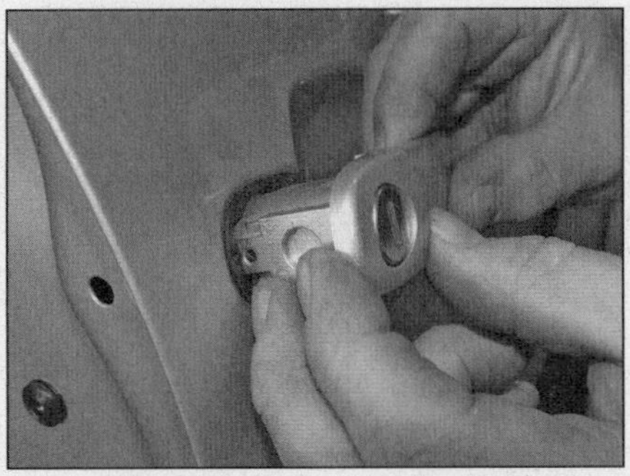

14.6 Pull out the door handle, and withdraw the door lock cylinder

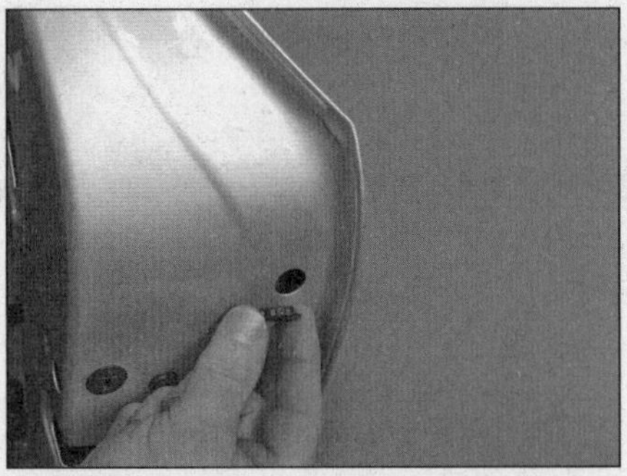

14.7 Remove the rubber grommet/seal

Front door lock cylinder/ door handle end cap

3 Open the door, then remove the plastic cap in the rear edge of the door to locate the retaining screws **(see illustration)**.

4 On the passenger door the cover/end cap is released with a hooked tool and not a screw. The removal of the cover is identical to that detailed below for the rear doors.

5 Remove the long inner screw and then unscrew the outer retaining screw (T20 torx) until the stop. Push the screw inwards to release the locking clamp **(see illustrations)**.

6 Pull out the door handle, and hold it in this position whilst withdrawing the lock cylinder/ end cap out of the door handle, then release the handle to its original position **(see illustration)**.

Rear door handle end cap

7 Open the door, then remove the blanking grommet from the rear edge of the door **(see illustration)**.

8 Seat technicians use a special tool (T10389 or 3438) to release the locking clamp. A tool can be made out of a length of metal rod with a small hook on the end. Make a mark on the tool at 40mm from the end.

9 Insert the special tool approx 40mm through the hole in the door. With the hook facing to the outside of the vehicle, hook the locking clamp and pull, to release the clamp **(see illustrations)**.

10 Pull out the door handle, and hold it in this position whilst withdrawing the end cap out of the door handle, then release the handle to its original position **(see illustration)**.

Exterior door handle

11 Depending on the door being worked on, either remove the door lock cylinder or door handle end cap, as described previously in this Section.

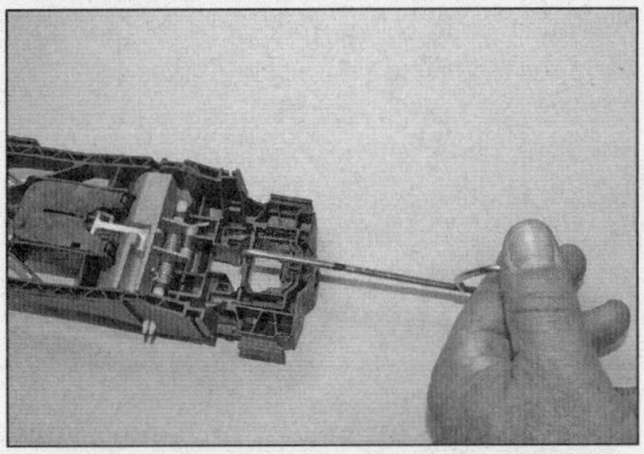

14.9a Insert the hooked rod and pull to release the locking clamp (shown with the lock removed for clarity)

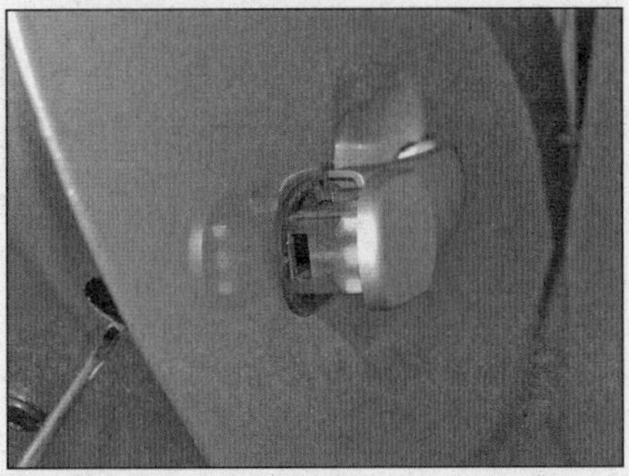

14.10 Pull out the door handle, and remove the end cap

12 Slide the handle to the rear edge of the door, to release it from the door handle mounting plate, and then pull it outwards and disengage it from the door **(see illustration)**.

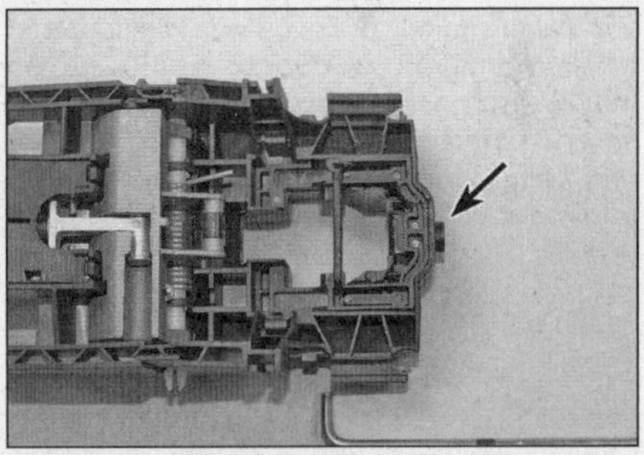

14.9b Note the position of the peg. On refitting this must be pushed home to lock the handle end cap in position

14.12 Slide the door handle to the rear of the door, then pull it out to remove

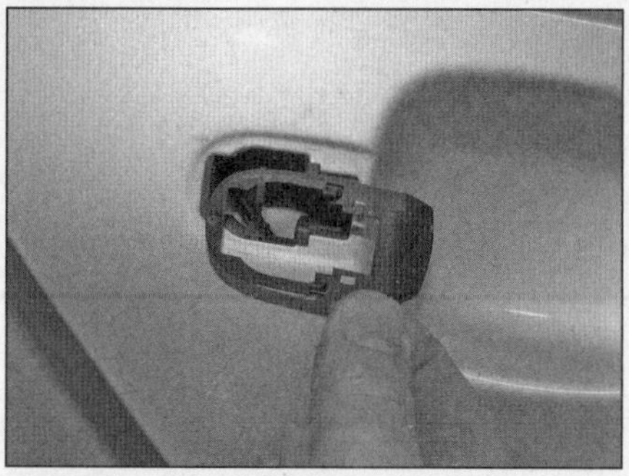

14.13 Unclip the seal from the door panel

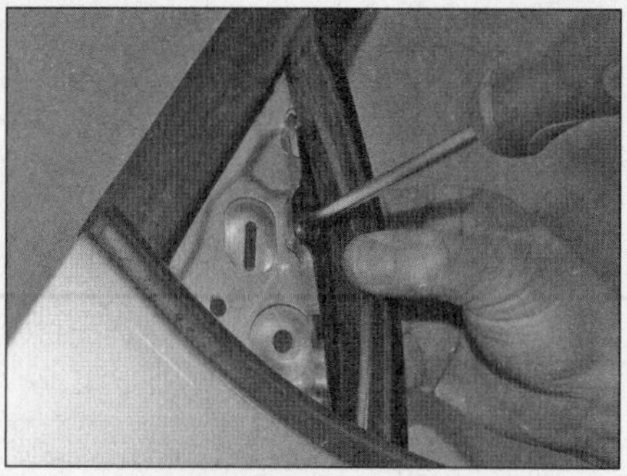

14.15a Pull back the seal and remove the guide rail upper bolt

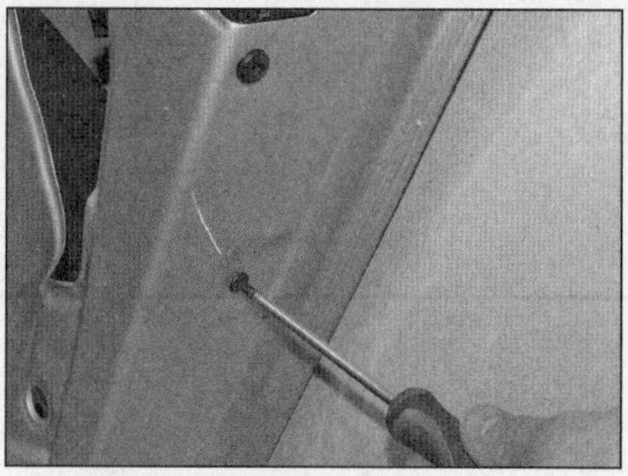

14.15b Remove the lower bolt

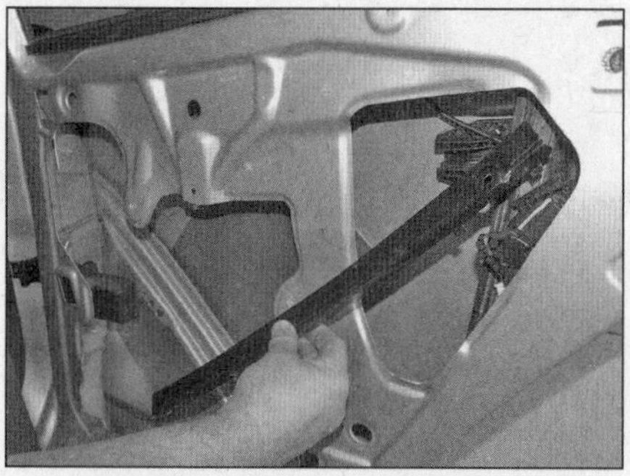

14.15c Remove the guide rail

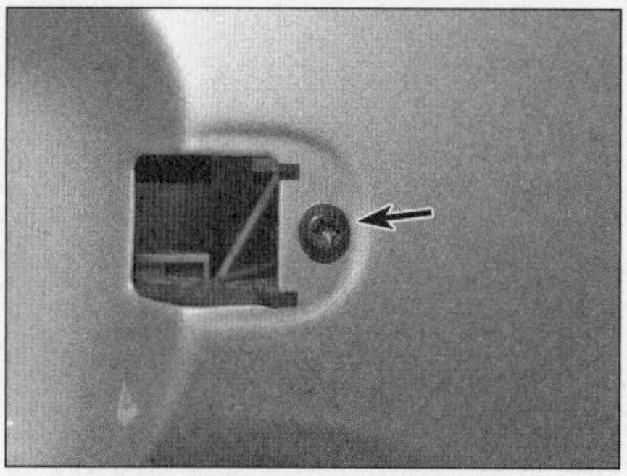

14.17 Undo the retaining screw

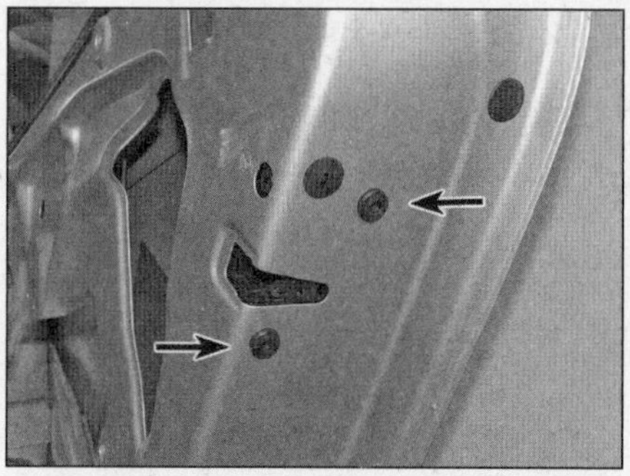

14.18 Remove the bolts (rear door shown)

13 If required recover the gasket from the handle aperture **(see illustration)**.

Exterior door handle mounting plate and door lock

Note: *On the front door, the handle mounting plate and door lock are attached to the door trim panel and are removed with the door trim panel. If required the door trim panel can be removed without the lock and door handle by unclipping the mounting plate from the door trim panel, however the trim panel is easier to remove with the lock and handle mounting plate as a complete assembly.*

14 Remove the door inner trim panel as described in Section 13.

15 On the rear door remove the outer quarter trim panel. Remove the upper and lower bolts from the window guide channel and then remove the guide channel **(see illustrations)**.

16 Remove the exterior door handle as described above.

17 On the outside of the door, undo the retaining screw from the front of the door handle aperture **(see illustration)**.

18 Remove the lock mounting bolts from the door frame **(see illustration)**.

19 Reaching up inside the door, slide the mounting plate to the rear edge of the door, and then disengage it from the outer panel.

20 On the front door the lock and handle mounting plate can now be removed with the door trm panel.

21 On the rear door, remove the styrene block and then remove the lock and handle mounting plate **(see illustrations)**.

Refitting

22 Refitting is a reversal of removal, but always check the operation of the lock and exterior handle before fitting the door trim panel.

15 Door window glass and regulator – removal and refitting

Removal

Front door window glass

1 Prise off the armrest cover, remove the now exposed bolts and disconnect the power window switch

2 Starting at the door pull/armrest remove the door trim centre panel.

3 Reconnect the power window switch and turn on the ignition. Adjust the window glass so that the bolts of the clamping jaws are accessible.

4 Turn off the ignition and disconnect the power window switch.

5 Slacken the bolts on the door glass clamps **(see illustration)**.

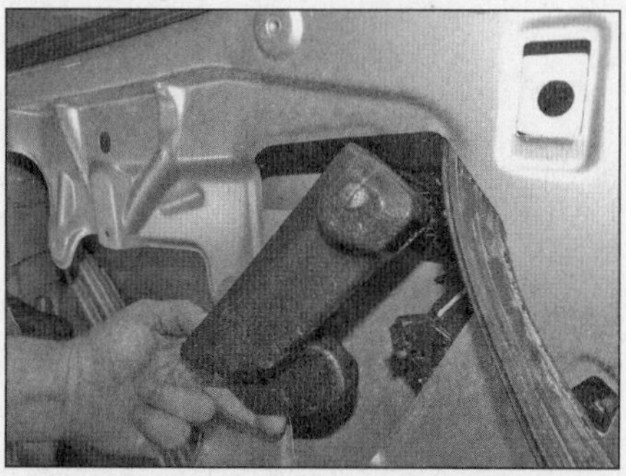

14.21a Remove the styrene block

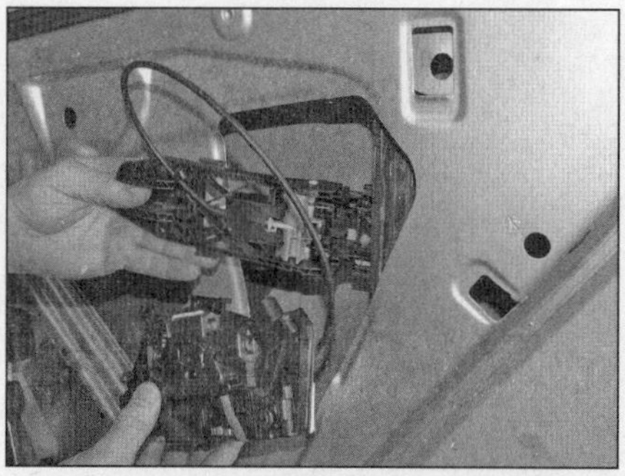

14.21b Lower the lock and handle mounting bracket from the door frame

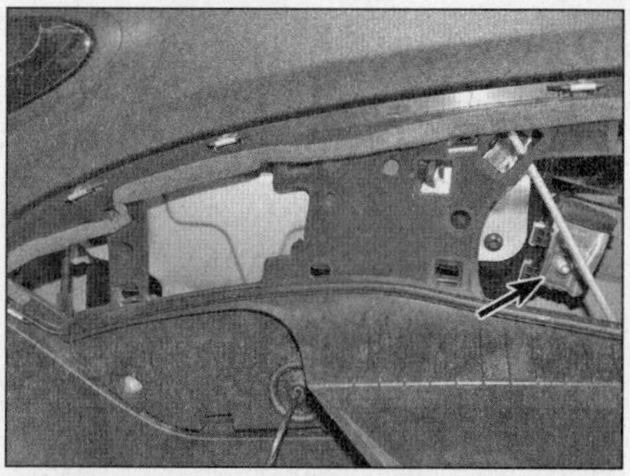

15.5 The door glass clamps (one shown, one hidden)

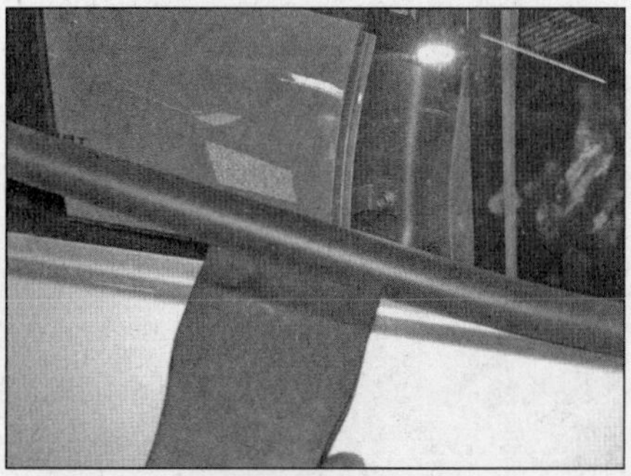

15.6a Release and then...

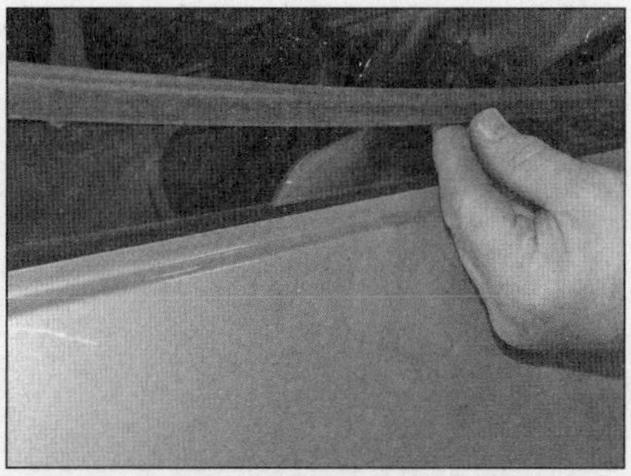

15.6b ...remove the outer weather seal

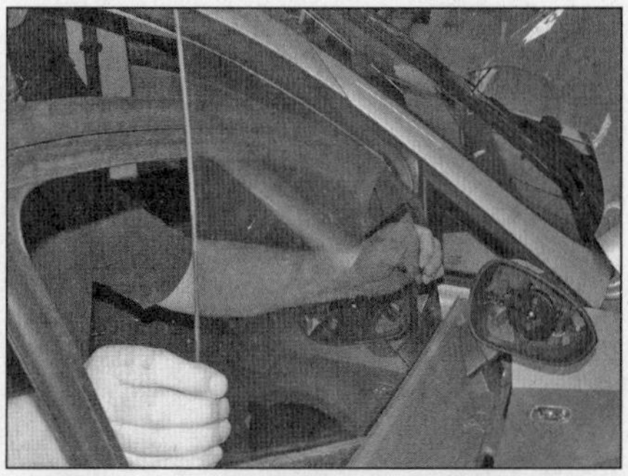

15.7 Remove the door glass

15.11 The glass clamping bolts

15.13a Remove the screw and...

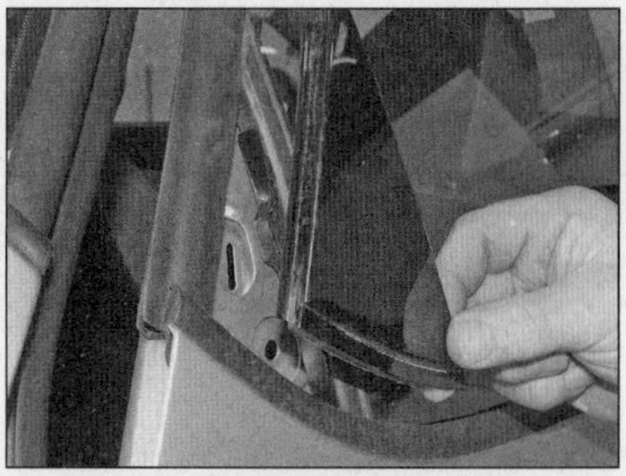

15.13b ...lift off the outer panel

6 Protect the paintwork and remove the outer weatherseal from the door frame using a broad trim tool **(see illustrations)**.

7 Pull up the glass, raise the rear section, rotate it forwards and remove it from the door frame **(see illustration)**.

Rear door window glass

8 Prise off the door pull handle trim and remove the fixings.

9 On models fitted with rear power windows disconnect the window switch.

10 Remove the inner section of the door trim panel as described in Section 13.

11 On models fitted with power windows reconnect the power window switch and turn on the ignition. On both types of rear window, adjust the window glass so that the bolts of the clamping jaws are accessible **(see illustration)**.

12 Slacken the bolts on the door glass clamps – do not remove the bolts.

13 Remove the inner quarter panel and then unbolt the outer trim panel **(see illustrations)**. This allows the guide channel rubber to be pushed back to release the glass.

14 Peel back the rear guide channel rubber and then pull the window glass straight up and and out of the door frame **(see illustration)**.

Window regulator and motor

15 The door window regulator and motor (where fitted) are removed with the door trim panel as described in Section 13.

16 Protect the work bench with and then unbolt/unclip the regulator and motor assembly from the door trim panel **(see illustration)**.

Refitting

Front and rear door window glass

17 Carefully lower the tilted window glass into the door and engage it with the regulator clamps. Apply light downwards pressure to the glass to make sure it is correctly located in the channels, then tighten the regulator clamp bolts.

18 If necessary, the window may be checked for correct operation at this stage by connecting the wiring to the switches.

19 Refit the door inner trim panel with reference to Section 13.

Window regulator and motor

20 Refitting is a reversal of removal.

16 Tailgate and support struts – removal and refitting

Tailgate

Removal

1 Disconnect the battery negative lead (as described in Chapter 5A Section 3).

2 Open the tailgate and remove the screws (hatchback models only). Use a trim tool and release the panel clips and remove the panel **(see illustrations)**.

3 Remove the high level brake light from the top of the tailgate as described in Chapter 12 Section 8.

4 Disconnect the wiring connectors from all the electrical components inside the tailgate.

15.14 Remove the glass

15.16 The regulator mounting bolts on a manual rear window

16.2a Remove the screws (one per side)

16.2b Remove the trim panel

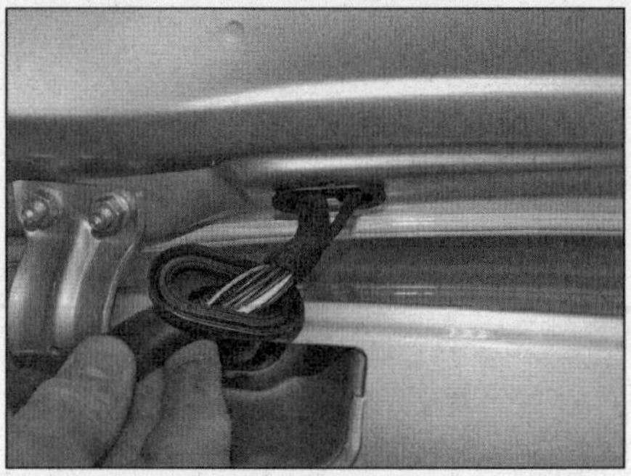
16.5 Release the harness rubber gaiter

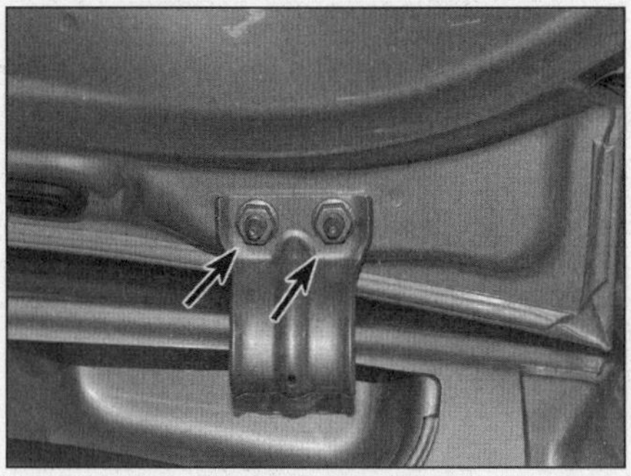
16.7 The hinge bolts

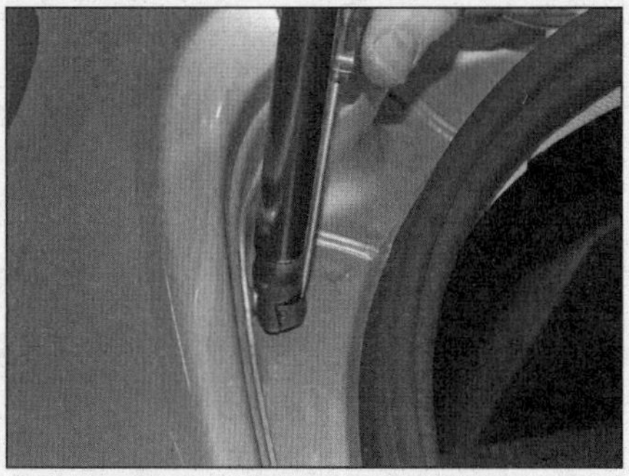
16.11 Lift the locking clips

5 Tie a piece of string to each end of the wiring/washer hose then, noting the correct routing of the wiring harness, release the harness rubber gaiter from the tailgate **(see illustration)** and withdraw the wiring. When the end of the wiring appears, untie the string and leave it in position in the tailgate; it can then be used on refitting to draw the wiring back into position.

6 With the help of an assistant to support the tailgate, remove the support struts as described below.

7 Mark the position of the hinges, using a marker pen or similar to aid refitting, then unscrew and remove the bolts securing the hinges to the tailgate. Protect the surrounding paintwork to prevent any damage **(see illustration)**. Where necessary, recover the gaskets which are fitted between the hinge and vehicle body.

8 Inspect the hinges for signs of wear or damage and renew if necessary. The hinges are secured to the vehicle by nuts or bolts (depending on model) which can be accessed once the headlining rear cover strip has been removed.

Refitting

9 Refitting is a reversal of removal but tighten the tailgate mounting bolts to the specified torque. Check the tailgate alignment with the surrounding panels. If necessary slight adjustment can be made by slackening the retaining bolts and repositioning the tailgate on its hinges.

Support struts

Warning: The support struts are filled with gas and must be disposed of safely.

Removal

10 With the help of an assistant, support the tailgate in the open position.

11 Using a small screwdriver, lift the locking clip and pull the gas support strut off its balljoint mounting on the vehicle body **(see illustration)**. Repeat the procedure on the upper strut mounting and remove the strut from the tailgate. Note: *If the gas strut is to be re-used, the locking clip must not be taken all the way out, or the clip will be damaged.*

Refitting

12 Refitting is a reversal of removal.

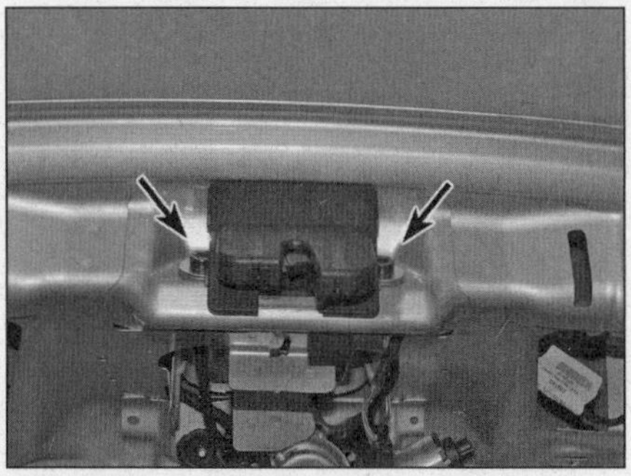
17.3 Undo the mounting bolts

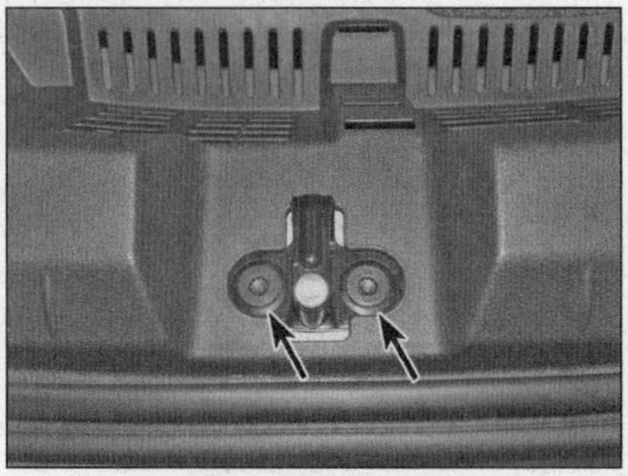
17.5 Remove the bolts

17 Tailgate lock components – removal and refitting

Removal

Lock

1 With the tailgate open, remove the tailgate inner trim panel as described in Section 16.

2 Reaching inside the lower part of the tailgate disconnect the wiring connector from the rear of the lock.

3 Slacken and remove the bolts and withdraw the lock from the tailgate **(see illustration)**.

Lock striker

4 Mark the position of the lock before removing it. This will aid refitting.

5 With the tailgate open remove the bolts. Angle the lock up slightly, rotate it and remove it from the trim panel **(see illustration)**.

Refitting

6 Refitting is a reversal of removal. Before refitting the trim panel, check the operation of the lock components and central locking system.

18 Central locking components – description, removal and refitting

Description

1 The central locking system consists of the following main components. Note that the central locking and anti-theft alarm systems share some components (see Chapter 12 Section 22):

a) Convenience system onboard supply control unit located behind next to the fusebox, behind the glovebox.
b) Door control unit fitted to the door frame.
c) Electric door lock actuators integrated in the door locks.
d) Fuel tank filler cap flap actuator located behind the rear wing liner.
e) Tailgate lock actuator located in the tailgate, together with the release button.
f) Anti-theft alarm horn located in the plenum chamber.
g) Bonnet contact switch located on the bonnet lock.
h) Remote control transmitter on the ignition key fob.

Removal

2 Before working on any electrical circuit, disconnect the battery negative lead (refer to Chapter 5A Section 3).

Convenience system control unit

Note: *The convenience control unit is often referred to as the BCM (Body Control Module) or on board control unit. It controls the vehicle secondary systems – mirrors, central locking, wipers and lights to name but a few.*

3 The control unit is located behind the passenger compartment fusebox. Remove the fusebox cover, unscrew the fusebox fixings and lower the fusebox to access the control unit.

4 Disconnect the wiring plug, unclip the module and remove it.

Electric door lock actuator

5 Remove the door lock (see Section 14).

Tailgate/boot lid lock actuator

6 Remove the tailgate handle/release unit as described in Section 17.

Bonnet contact switch

7 Remove the bonnet lock as described in Section 11.

8 On the lock, release the tab and push the switch from the slotted holes.

Remote control transmitter battery

9 Using a screwdriver or fingernail inserted in the slot, separate the transmitter unit cover from the key **(see illustrations)**.

10 Carefully prise out the battery, noting which way round it is fitted **(see illustrations)**.

18.9a Flip open the cover to...

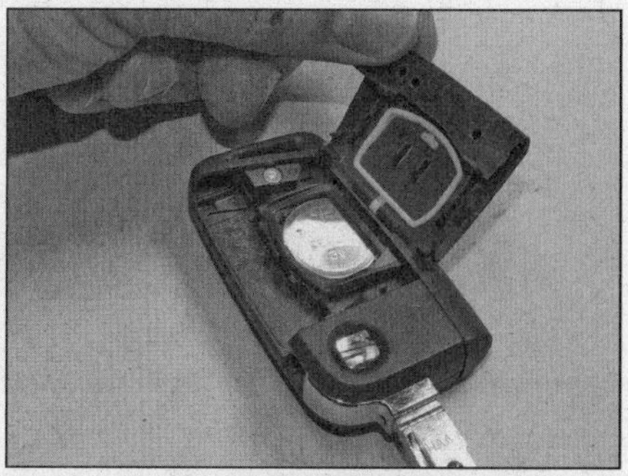

18.9b ...expose the battery

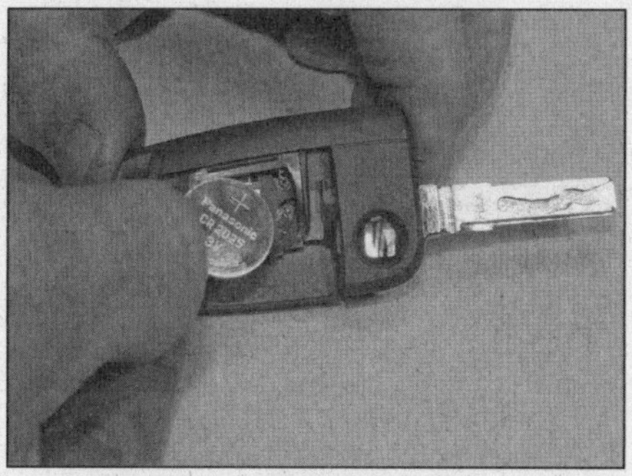

18.10a Remove the battery...

18.10b ...noting which way it is fitted

Refitting

11 Refitting is a reversal of removal.

19 Exterior mirrors and associated components – removal and refitting

Removal

Mirror glass

Caution: Wearing gloves is highly recommended.

1 Push in the lower edge of the glass. Insert a broad flat bladed trim tool into the top of the glass and whilst pushing in the lower edge pull out the glass at the top. **(see illustration)**.

2 Release the glass from the housing and (where fitted) disconnect the wiring plugs **(see illustration)**.

Mirror cover

3 Remove the glass as described above. Locate the locking tabs and release the cover from the mirror housing **(see illustrations)**.

19.1 Push the lower edge of the glass in

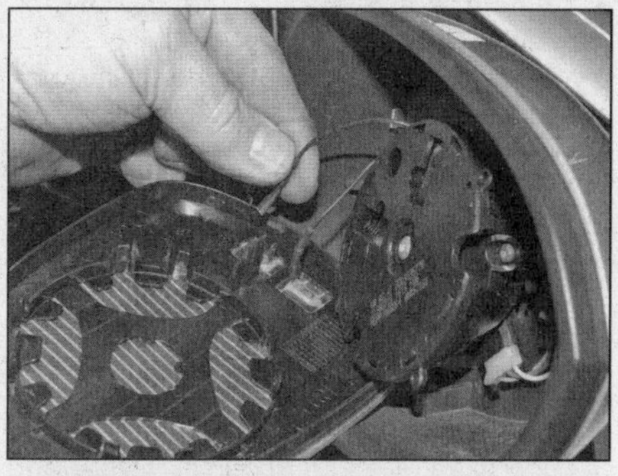

19.2 On heated glass mirrors disconnect the wiring plug

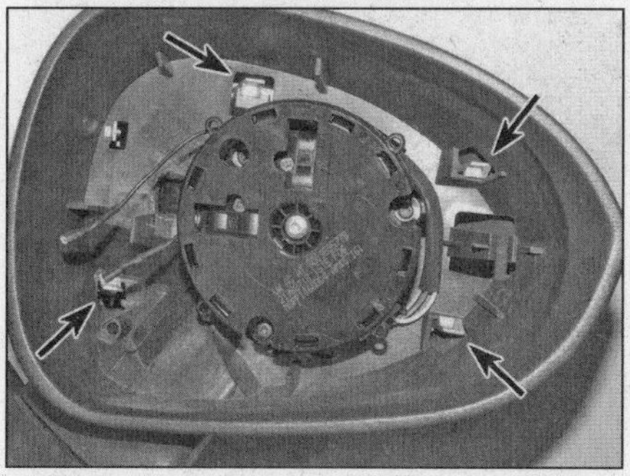

19.3a Release the locking tabs and...

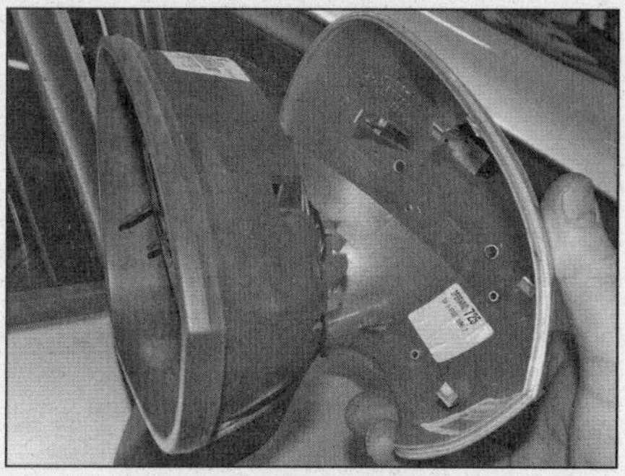

19.3b ...remove the cover

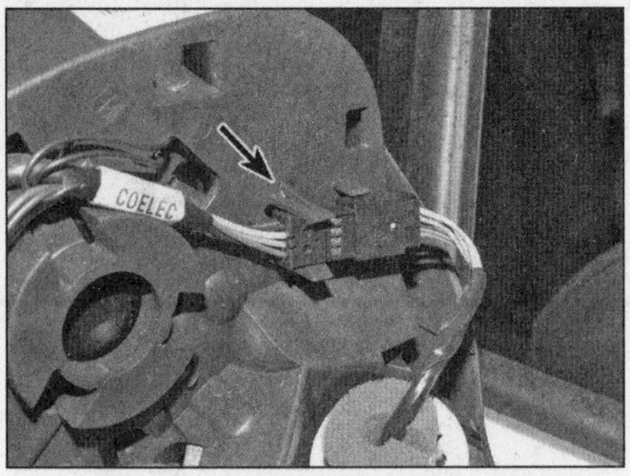

19.6 Disconnect the wiring plug

Mirror switch

4 Refer to Chapter 12 Section 5.

Mirror body

5 Remove the mirror glass and mirror cover as described above.

6 The type of mirror fitted can be identified with the cover removed. Early types have the electrical connection inside the door frame and require the removal of the door trim as described in Section 13 to access the wiring plug. Later versions have the connector at the mirror **(see illustration)**.

7 Rotate the mirror to access the mounting bolt (or bolts on some types) **(see illustration)**. On early mirrors remove the plastic nut from the spring mounting. Use locking pliers with a rag wrapped around the nut to avoid crushing the fixing.

Refitting

8 Refitting is a reversal of removal. When refitting the mirror glass, press firmly at the centre using a wad of cloth and taking care not to use excessive force, as the glass is easily broken.

20 Windscreen, tailgate and fixed rear quarter window glass – general information

1 These areas of glass are bonded in position with a special adhesive. Renewal of such fixed glass is a difficult, messy and time-consuming task, which is beyond the scope of the home mechanic. It is difficult, unless one has plenty of practice, to obtain a secure, waterproof fit. In view of this, owners are strongly advised to have this work carried out by one of the many specialist windscreen fitters.

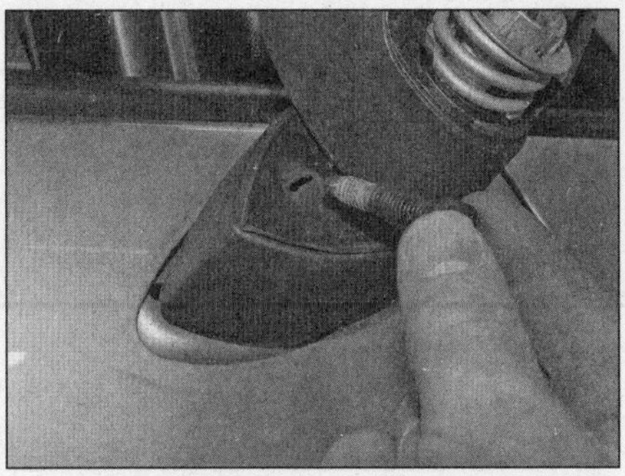

19.7 Remove the mounting bolt

21 Sunroof – general information

1 Due to the complexity of the sunroof mechanism, considerable expertise is needed to repair, renew or adjust the sunroof components successfully. Removal of the roof first requires the headlining to be removed, which is a complex and tedious operation, and not a task to be undertaken lightly. Therefore, any problems with the sunroof should be referred to a Seat dealer. On models with an electric sunroof, if the sunroof motor fails to operate, first check the relevant fuse. If the fault cannot be traced and rectified, the sunroof can be opened and closed manually using an Allen key to turn the motor spindle (a suitable key is supplied with the vehicle, and should be clipped onto the inside of the sunroof motor trim). To gain access to the motor, unclip the rear of the trim cover to open. Unclip the Allen key, then insert it fully into the motor opening (against spring pressure). Rotate the key to move the sunroof to the required position.

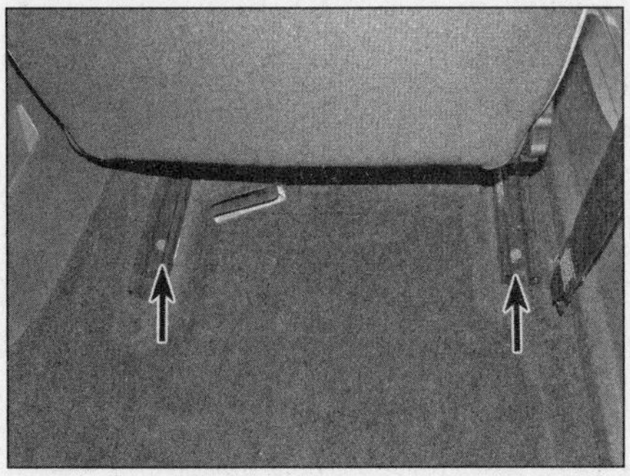

23.2 Seat rear mounting bolts

23.3 Front seat mounting bolt (one shown)

22 Body exterior fittings – removal and refitting

Wheel arch liners and body under-panels

1 The various plastic covers fitted to the underside of the vehicle are secured in position by a mixture of screws, nuts and retaining clips and removal will be fairly obvious on inspection. Work methodically around the panel removing its retaining screws and releasing its retaining clips until the panel is free and can be removed from the underside of the vehicle. Most clips used on the vehicle are simply prised out of position. Remove the wheels to ease the removal of the wheel arch liners.

2 On refitting, renew any retaining clips that may have been broken on removal, and ensure that the panel is securely retained by all the relevant clips and screws.

Body trim strips and badges

3 The various body trim strips and badges (including the door entrance plates on vRS models) are held in position with a special adhesive tape and locating lugs. Removal requires the trim/badge to be heated, to soften the adhesive, and then carefully lifted away from the surface. Due to the high risk of damage to the vehicle's paintwork during this operation, it is recommended that this task should be entrusted to a Seat dealer.

23 Seats – removal and refitting

Note: *Refer to the warnings in Chapter 12 Section 23 if side airbags are fitted to the vehicle. Also refer to 'Safety first!'.*

Removal

Front seats

1 Disconnect the battery negative lead (as described in Chapter 5A Section 3).

2 Slide the seat fully forwards, then unscrew the rear mounting bolts securing the sliding rail to the floor **(see illustration)**.

3 Slide the seat fully rearwards, and unscrew the front mounting bolts **(see illustration)**.

4 Tilt the seat backwards and disconnect the wiring for the seat heating, side airbag and seat belt buckle warning light. The number of connectors will vary according to the trim level **(see illustrations)**.

5 Carefully remove the seat from inside the car, taking care not to damage the door opening plastic trim panels and paintwork. The help of an assistant may be necessary as the seat is heavy.

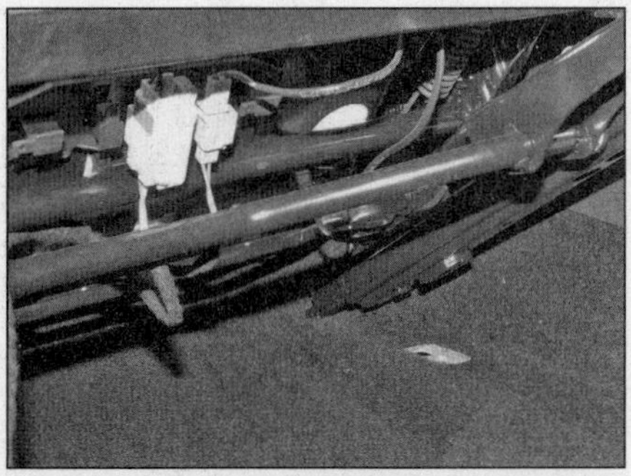

23.4a Unclip the connectors from the bracket...

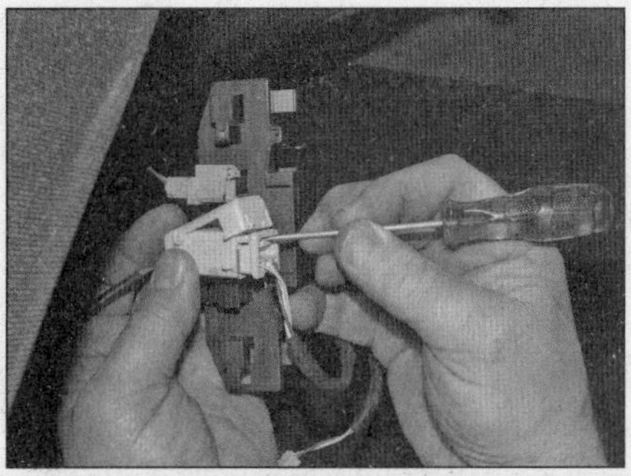

23.4b ...and disconnect the wiring connector plugs

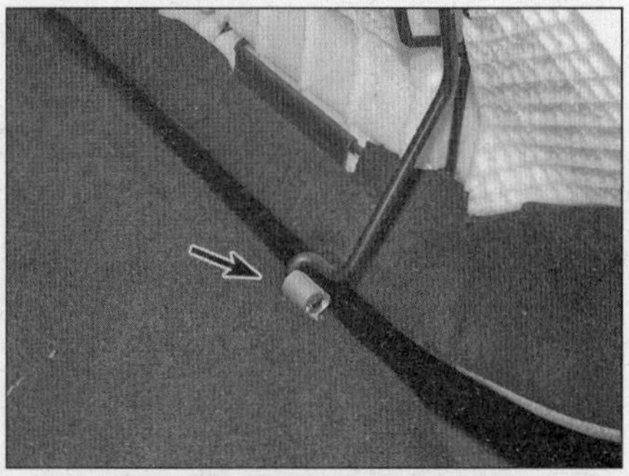

23.7 Unhook the struts

23.9 Remove the bolt

23.11 Depress the catch hook and pull the backrest pivot pin from the bracket

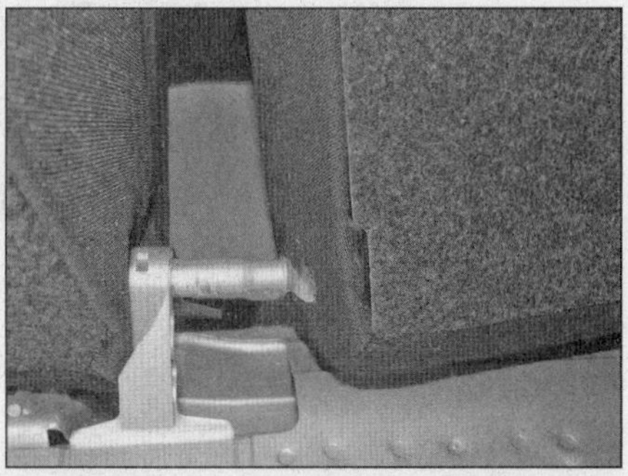

23.12 Slide the backrest from the centre pivot pin

Rear seat cushion

6 Pull up the seat cushion and hinge the seat cushion forwards.

7 Push in the hooks from the pivot brackets and remove the cushion from the car **(see illustration)**.

Rear seat backrest

8 Fold the rear seat cushion forwards.

9 Where an inertia reel centre seat belt is fitted in the backrest, unscrew the anchorage bolt from the floor **(see illustration)**.

10 Pull up the locking handle to release the relevant backrest section, and fold it forwards.

11 Using a screwdriver, depress the catch hook and pull the backrest pivot pin from the side bracket **(see illustration)**.

12 Slide the backrest from the pivot pin on the centre bracket and remove it from the car **(see illustration)**. If necessary, remove the plastic cap from the bracket.

Refitting

13 Refitting is a reversal of removal.

24 Front seat belt tensioning mechanism – general information

1 The front seat belt inertia reels are fitted with integral automatic belt tensioners. The rear seat belt inertia reels are not all fitted with automatic tensioners, (some still have the standard inertia reel seat belts fitted). The system is designed to instantaneously take up any slack in the seat belt in the case of a sudden frontal impact, therefore reducing the possibility of injury to the front seat occupants. Each front seat is fitted with its own system, the tensioner being situated behind the sill trim panel.

2 The seat belt tensioner is triggered by a frontal impact above a predetermined force. Lesser impacts, including impacts from behind, will not trigger the system.

3 When the system is triggered, the explosive gas in the tensioner mechanism retracts and locks the seat belt through a cable which acts on the inertia reel. This prevents the seat belt moving and keeps the occupant firmly in position in the seat. Once the tensioner has been triggered, the seat belt will be permanently locked and the assembly must be renewed.

4 Note the following warnings before contemplating any work on the front seat belts.

Warning: Do not expose the tensioner mechanism to temperatures in excess of 100°C (212°F).

- ***If the tensioner mechanism is dropped, it must be renewed, even it has suffered no apparent damage.***
- ***Do not allow any solvents to come into contact with the tensioner mechanism.***
- ***Do not attempt to open the tensioner mechanism as it contains explosive gas.***
- ***Tensioners must be discharged before they are disposed of, but this task should be entrusted to a Seat dealer.***
- ***If the battery is to be disconnected, refer to ' Disconnecting the battery'.***

25 Seat belt components – removal and refitting

Removal

Front inertia reel and height adjuster

Warning: The seat belt inertia reel incorporates a pyrotechnic automatic tensioner; do not subject the unit to temperatures in excess of 100°C (212°F), or allow any solvents or cleaning agents to contact the unit. The unit is sensitive to impact; if it is dropped or damaged it should be renewed.

1 Disconnect the battery negative lead (as described in Chapter 5A Section 3).

2 Remove the door sills and the B-pillar trim as described in Section 26.

3 Disconnect the wiring plug from the inertia reel **(see illustration)**.

25.3 Disconnect the wiring plug

25.4a Undo the upper seat belt bolt

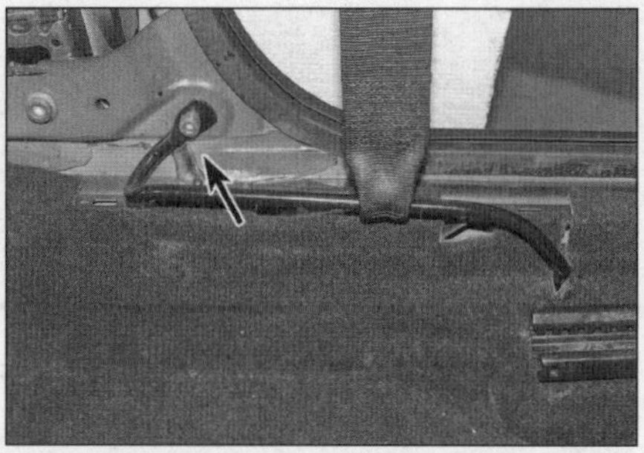
25.4b On 3 door models remove the bolt and then unhook the guide rail from the inner sill

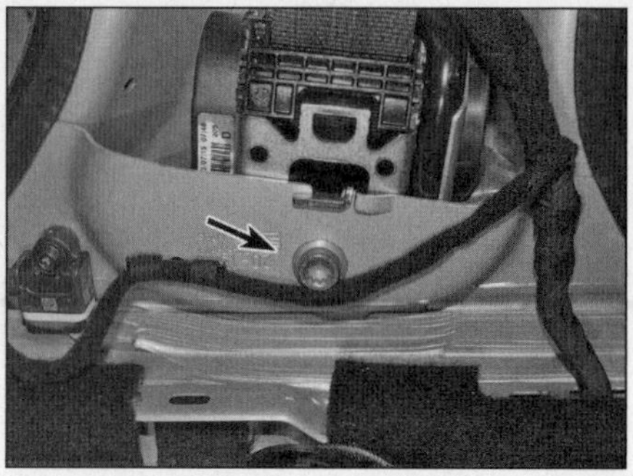
25.5 Remove the lower bolt

4 Undo the seat belt upper anchorage bolt from the B-pillar and then remove the lower bolt **(see illustrations)**.

5 Remove the inertia reel mounting bolt and pull the reel from the B-pillar **(see illustration)**.

6 To remove the belt height adjuster, remove the securing bolt and lift upwards from the pillar.

Front belt stalk

7 Remove the front seat assembly as described in Section 24.

8 Where necessary, undo the screws and remove the plastic cover from the inner side of the seat.

9 Disconnect the wiring from the seat occupancy monitor and stalk buckle indicator.

10 Unscrew the stalk mounting bolt and remove the stalk from the seat.

Rear side belt

11 Fold down the rear seat back and remove the load area shelf support panel as described in Section 26.

12 Remove the bolt and release the inertia reel **(see illustration)**.

13 To fully remove the trim panel from the vehicle, it will be necessary to undo the seat belt lower anchorage bolt and pass the seat belt through the trim panel as it is being removed **(see illustration)**. There is just enough room to remove the lower anchor bolt without removing the lower C-pillar trim, panel.

14 To remove the centre stalk, unscrew the mounting bolt **(see illustration 23.9)**. The right-hand side stalk also includes the anchorage for the centre belt.

Rear seat centre belt

15 Remove the rear seat cushion and backrest as described in Section 23.

16 To remove the inertia reel, first prise the belt guide from the top of the backrest **(see illustrations)**.

17 Carefully prise the trim moulding from around the edge of the backrest **(see illustration)**.

18 Pull back the padding from the seat back to access the inertia reel fixings **(see illustration)**.

19 Unscrew the mounting nut and remove the inertia reel, guiding it out from the backrest.

Refitting

20 Refitting is a reversal of the removal procedure, ensuring that all the seat belt units are located correctly and mounting bolts are tightened to their specified torque. Check all the trim panels are securely retained by all the relevant retaining clips. When refitting the B-pillar trim panel, ensure that the height adjustment peg engages correctly with the trim panel.

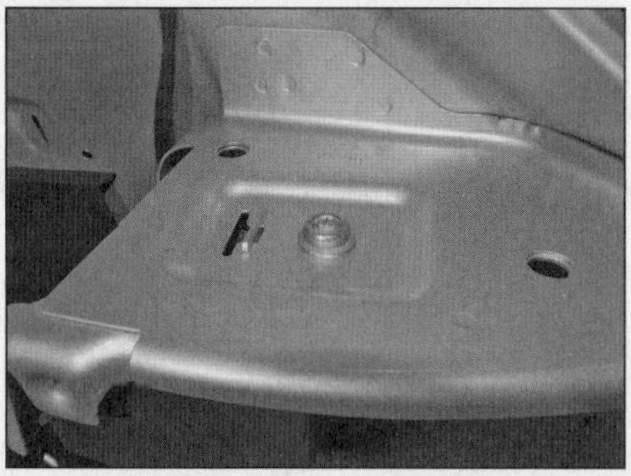
25.12 The inertia reel mounting

25.13 Undo the seat belt lower anchorage bolt

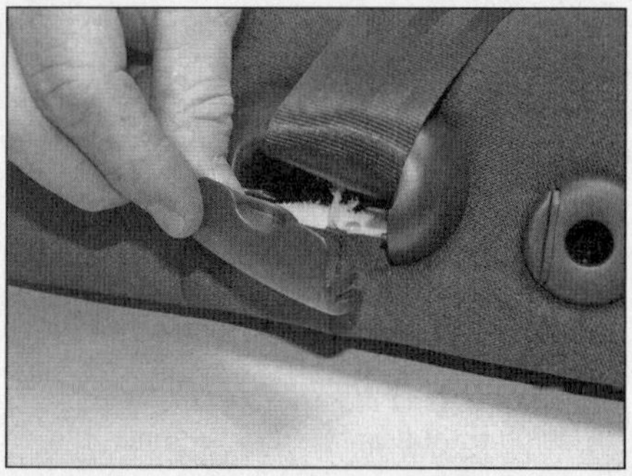
25.16a Prise out the trim clip...

25.16b...and remove the belt guide

25.17 Release the seat trim from the seat frame

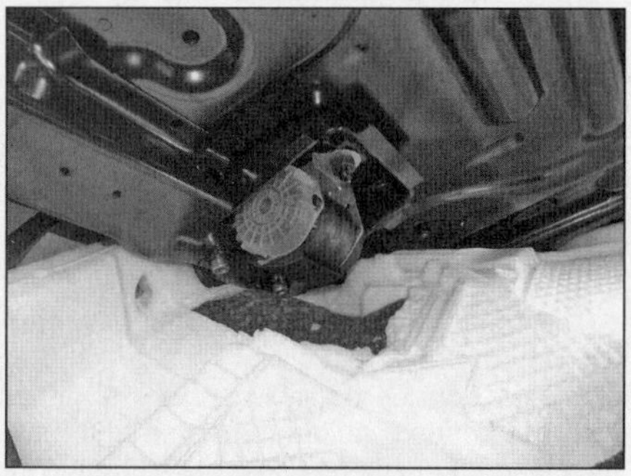
25.18 Seat belt inertia reel mounting nut

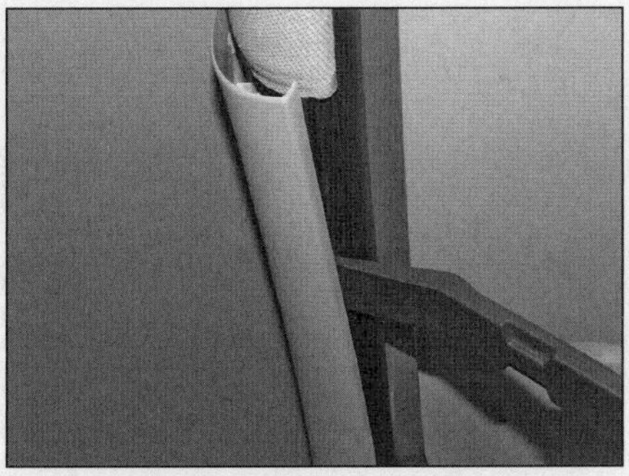

26.5 Work the upper clip free

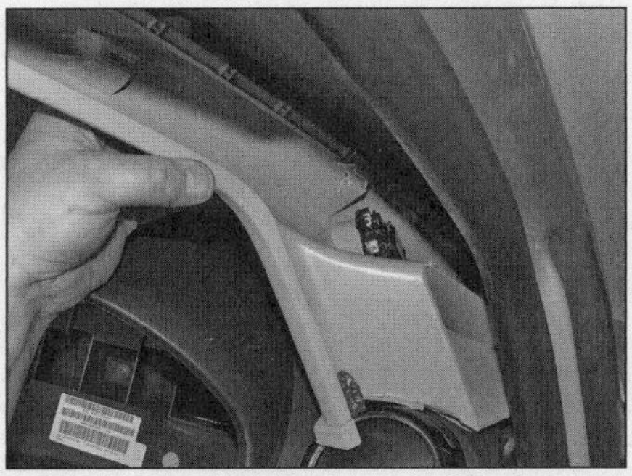

26.7a Remove the panel

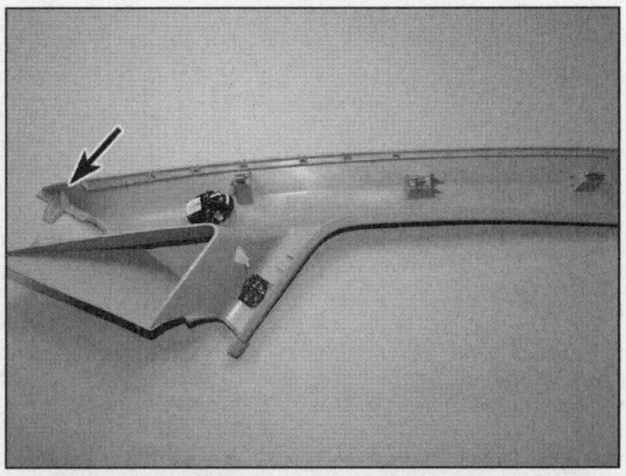

26.7b The rear of the panel showing the location of the retaining clips. Note the lower peg that must engage with the slot in the end of the facia

26 Interior trim – removal and refitting

Interior trim panels

1 The interior trim panels are secured using either screws or various types of trim fasteners, usually studs or clips. Check that there are no other panels overlapping the one to be removed; usually there is a sequence that has to be followed, and this will only become obvious on close inspection.

2 Remove all obvious fasteners, such as screws. If the panel will not come free, it is held by hidden clips or fasteners. These are usually situated around the edge of the panel and can be prised up to release them; note, however that they can break quite easily so new ones should be available. The best way of releasing such clips, without the correct type of tool, is to use a large flat-bladed screwdriver. Note in many cases that the adjacent sealing strip must be prised back to release a panel.

3 When removing a panel, never use excessive force or the panel may be damaged; always check carefully that all fasteners or other relevant components have been removed or released before attempting to withdraw a panel.

4 Refitting is the reverse of the removal procedure; secure the fasteners by pressing them firmly into place and ensure that all disturbed components are correctly secured to prevent rattles.

Interior side and pillar trim panels

A-pillar trim

5 Prise the upper end of the trim away from the door seal and locate the upper trim clip. Using a trim tool release the upper clip **(see illustration)**.

6 Slide the tool down the trim and release the lower trim clip.

7 Pull the trim up (and in at the top) to release it from the end of the facia **(see illustrations)**. Where fitted disconnect the wiring from the tweeter and remove the panel.

B-pillar trim

5-door models

8 Remove the lower seat belt mounting bolt.

9 Peel back the door seal and locate the upper retaining clips (these are just below the seat belt aperture). Release the upper clips, locate the lower clips (close to the junction with the door sill panel) and release them.

10 Pull the trim down from the head lining and remove it.

3-door models

11 On 3-door models the lower section of the B-pillar trim panel is part of the rear side door trim panel.

12 Slide the front seat fully forward, release the carpet from the sill to gain access to the seat belt lower mounting bolt.

13 Remove the seat belt lower bolt and slide it off the rail.

14 At the rear lower edge of the trim panel insert a trim tool and release the rear edge of the panel. Push the lower section of the panel forwards and then pull it downwards to release it **(see illustration)**. Feed the seat belt through the panel and remove it.

Upper C-pillar trim

3 and 5-door hatchback models

15 The upper C-pillar trim panel is the parcel shelf support panel.

16 Remove the parcel shelf, tip up (or remove) the seat cushion and fold down the seat back.

17 Where fitted prise out the load area lamp and disconnect the wiring plug.

18 Unbolt the lower seat belt mounting.

19 Remove the screws and then using a trim tool and release the panel **(see illustrations)**.

5-door estate (ST) models

20 Remove the load area upper side panel as described in this section.

21 Prise the panel from the pillar and remove it downwards.

Lower C-pillar trim

22 Remove the seat back as described in Section 23.

23 Prise up the lower and upper threaded trim clips. Prise up the trim, unhook it from the sill panel and remove it. **(see illustrations)**.

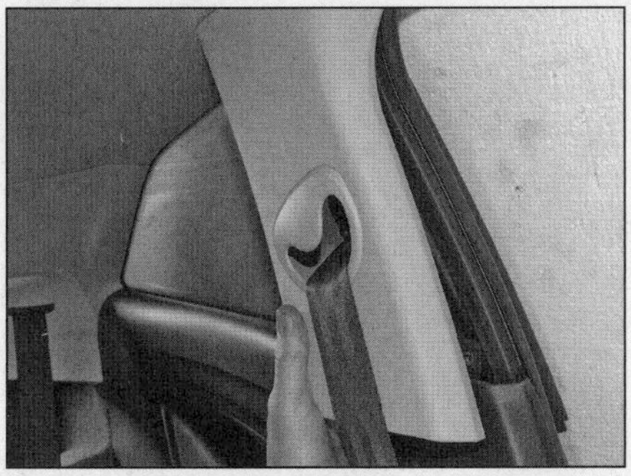

26.14 Remove the B-pillar trim panel (3 door model)

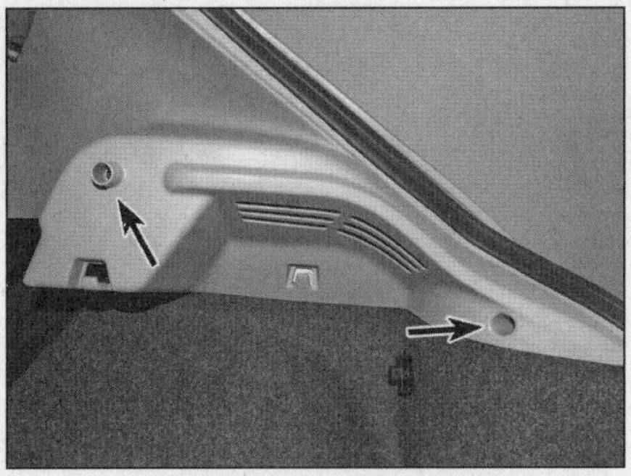

26.19a Remove the screws

26.19b Remove the panel

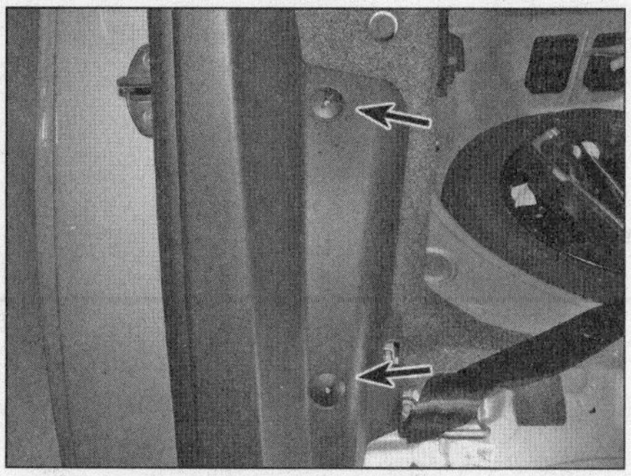

26.23a Remove the trim clips...

26.23b ...and release the panel

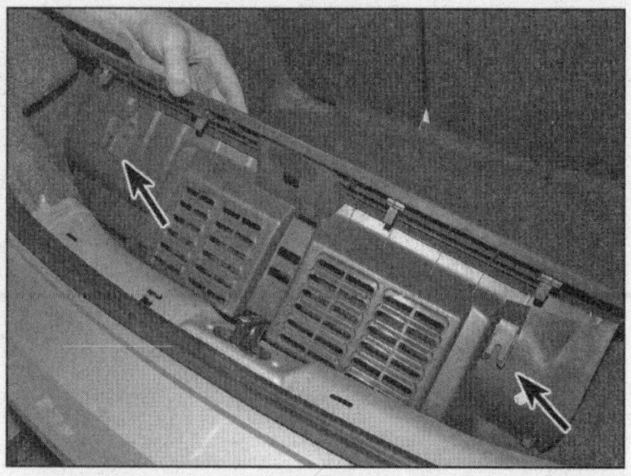

26.26 The tailgate slam panel. Note the slots that must engage correctly with the bodywork

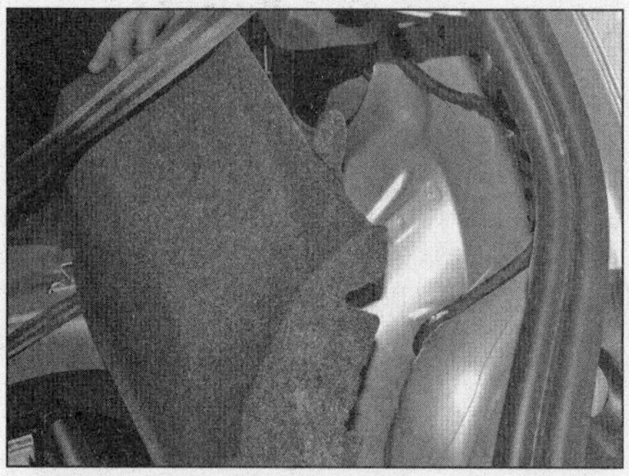

26.31 Remove the load area side panels

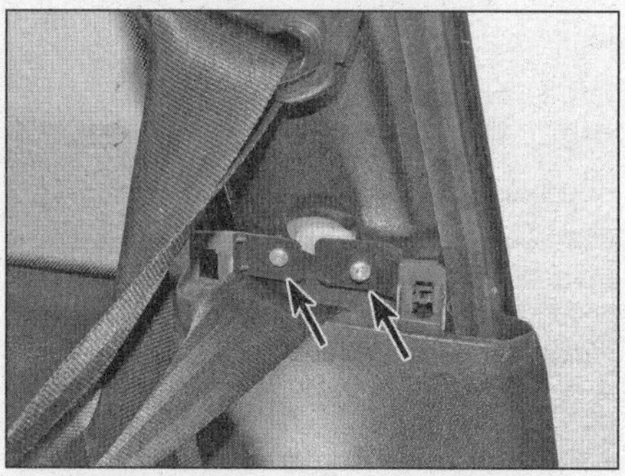

26.34a Remove the screws from the B-pillar...

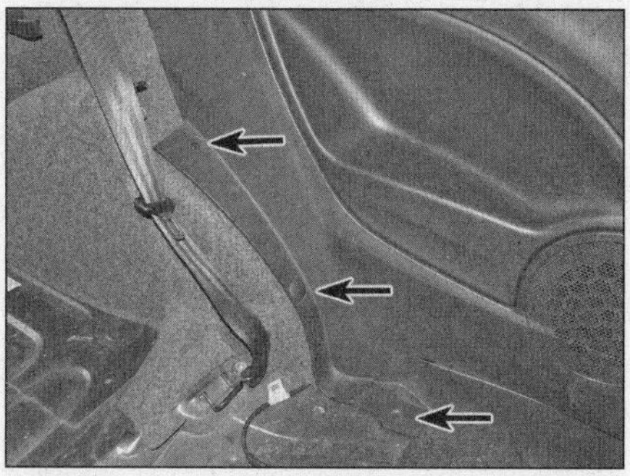

26.34b ...and the trim clips from the wheel arch

D-pillar trim (ST models only)

24 Remove the load area side panel as described below.

25 Remove the single 'scrivet' type trim clip and then using a trim tool remove the panel.

Tailgate slam panel

26 Use a trim tool and prise off the panel **(see illustration)**.

Load area side panels

27 The load side area panels are made from a flexible material. In some cases the panel can be released from the parcel shelf support panel without the need to completely remove the adjacent panels.

28 Fold down or remove the rear seat backs and then remove the parcel shelf support panel as described above.

29 Open the tailgate and remove the slam panel cover by prising it up.

30 Remove the floor covering and then unbolt the load hold down brackets.

31 Remove the trim clips and lift out the panel **(see illustration)**.

Side panels (3-door models)

32 Remove the B-pillar trim panel as described above.

33 Remove the rear seats as described in Section 23.

34 Remove the upper mounting screws and then remove the threaded trim clips from the wheel arch **(see illustrations)**.

35 Use a trim tool and release the panel from the bodywork and slide out the seat belt webbing **(see illustration)**.

Sill trim panels

36 Remove the B-pillar trim panel as described above.

37 If working on the left-hand sill, remove the bonnet release handle by levering out the retaining clip with a small screwdriver (as described in Section 10).

38 Lift up the rear seat cushion and remove the rear trim clip.

39 Working from the front of the vehicle prise free the panel and remove it **(see illustration)**.

Steering column shrouds

40 Remove the steering wheel as described in Chapter 10 Section 15.

41 Release the securing clips and lift the upper shroud from the steering column. To remove the upper shroud completely, release the securing clips and remove the surround from around the instrument panel **(see illustrations)**.

42 Undo the retaining screw from the under the lower shroud and the two from the top,

26.35 Remove the side panel

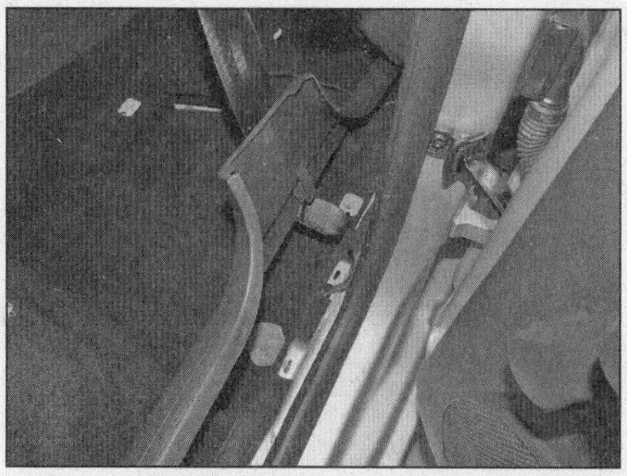

26.39 Remove the sill panel

26.41a Unclip the upper shroud from the instrument panel...

26.41b ...and then remove it

then withdraw the lower shroud from the steering column **(see illustrations)**.

Glovebox

Note: *There are slight variations, depending on the trim level and year of production. Removal and refitting is essentially the same for all versions*.

43 Open the upper storage compartment and undo the retaining screws from inside the compartment **(see illustration)**. Where fitted remove the 'scrivet' type trim clips.

44 Where fitted remove the lower outer screws **(see illustration)**.

45 Work around the edge of the glovebox and remove the remaining screws.

46 Pull the glovebox forward to release it, and then disconnect the key switch wiring, the lamp wiring plug and the AC cooling duct (all where fitted). Remove the glovebox from the facia **(see illustrations)**.

47 Refitting is the reverse of removal.

Carpets

48 The passenger compartment floor carpet is in one piece and is secured at its edges by screws or clips, usually the same fasteners used to secure the various adjoining trim panels.

49 Carpet removal and refitting is reasonably straightforward but very time-consuming because all adjoining trim panels must be removed first, as must components such as the seats, the centre console and seat belt lower anchorages.

Headlining

50 The headlining is clipped to the roof and can be withdrawn only once all fittings such as the grab handles, sun visors, sunroof (if fitted), and related upper trim panels have been removed and the door, tailgate and sunroof aperture sealing strips have been prised clear. To remove the sun visors and grab handles the plastic covers have to be unclipped first, to gain access to the securing screws.

51 Note that headlining removal requires considerable skill and experience if it is to be

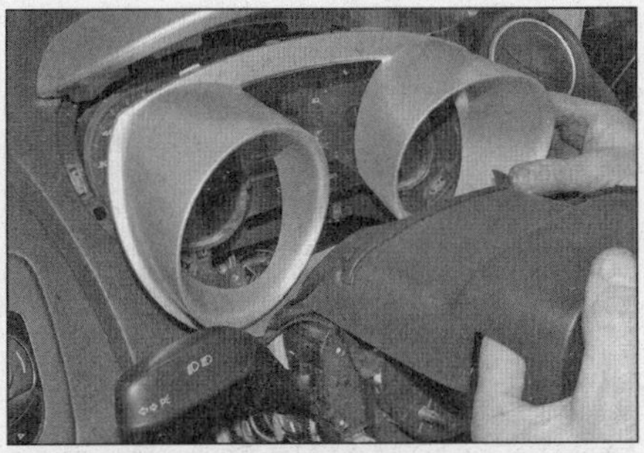

26.41c On early models the upper shroud is removed with the instrument panel surround

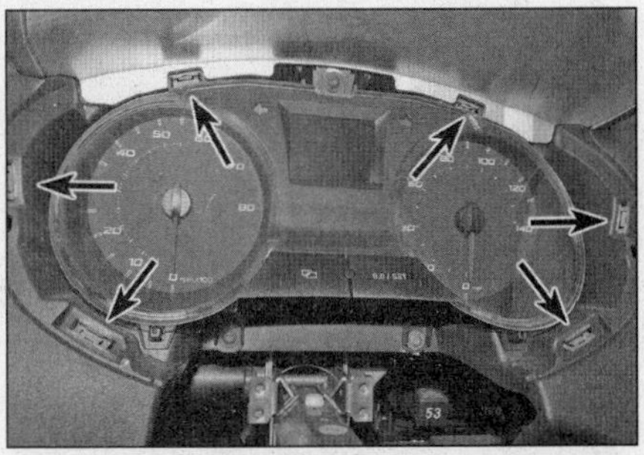

26.41d The position of the retaining clips on the instrument panel surround (early models only)

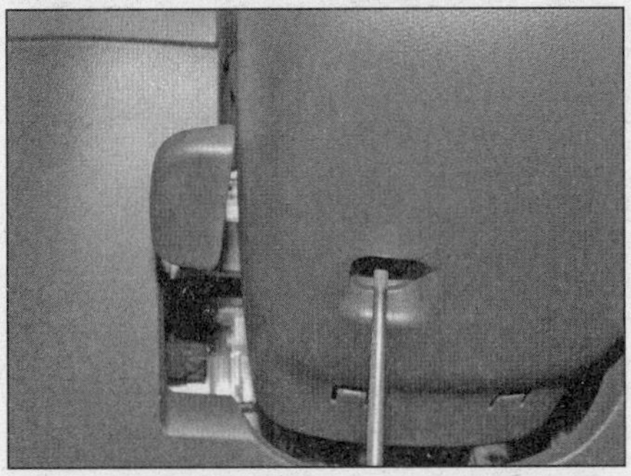

26.42a Undo the lower screw

26.42b ...and the upper screws

26.42c Unclip the lower shroud

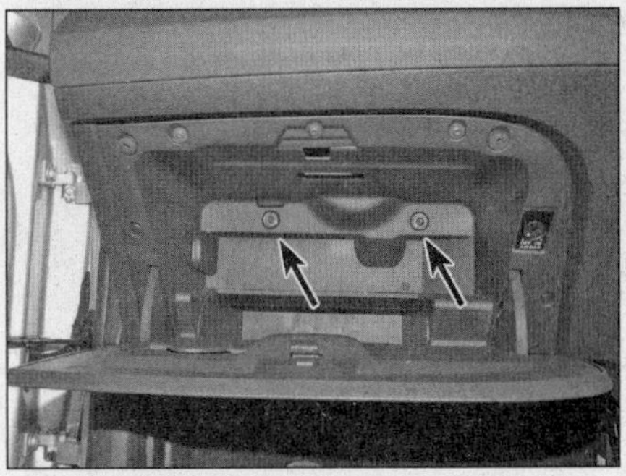

26.43 Remove the inner screws

26.44 Remove the lower screws

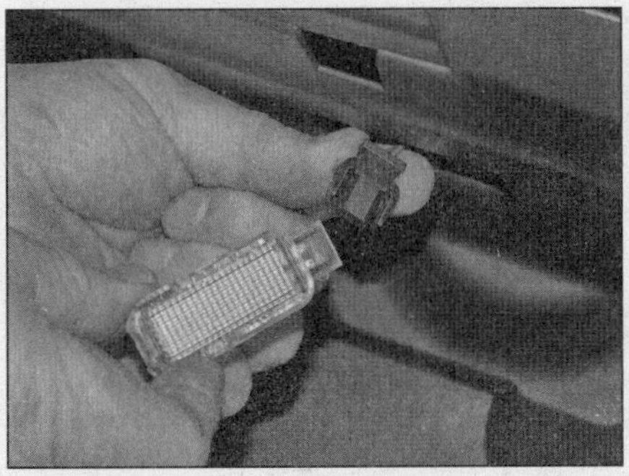

26.46a Disconnect the glovebox light...

26.46b ...and the 'PAD' switch

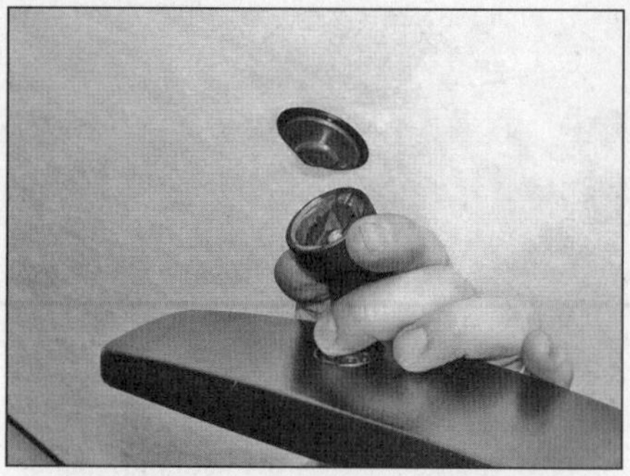
26.52 Removing the interior mirror

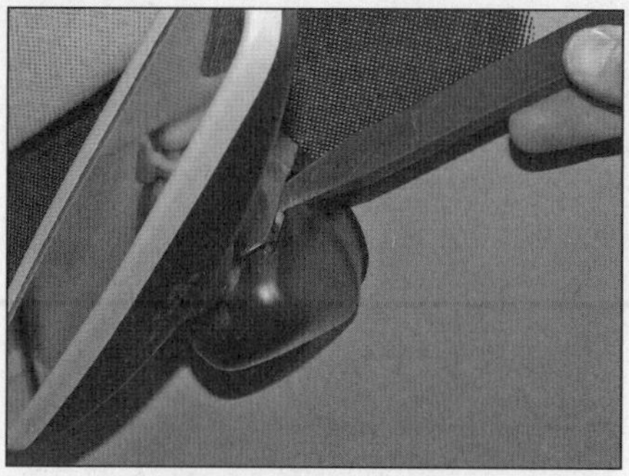
26.54a Use a trim tool to...

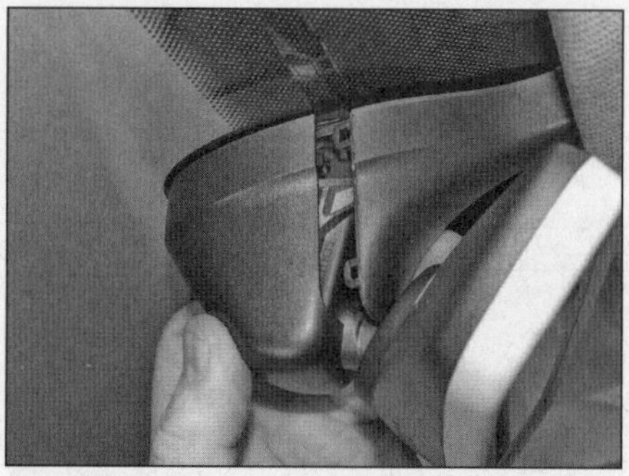
26.54b ...release the covers

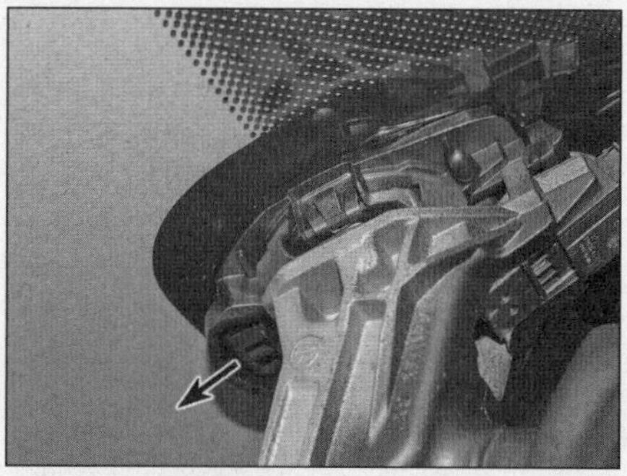
26.54c Push in the direction shown to remove the mirror

carried out without damage and is therefore best entrusted to an expert.

Interior mirror

52 On models fitted with a simple mirror, turn the mirror base 90° anti-clockwise to remove it from the retaining plate **(see illustration)**.

53 When refitting, place the mirror at 60° to 90° anti-clockwise to the mounted position; then turn clockwise until the locking clip locks into place to secure the mirror.

54 On models fitted with a rain sensor and automatic dimming function, remove the covers and then release the mirror by pulling it downwards **(see illustrations)**.

55 Refitting is a reversal of removal.

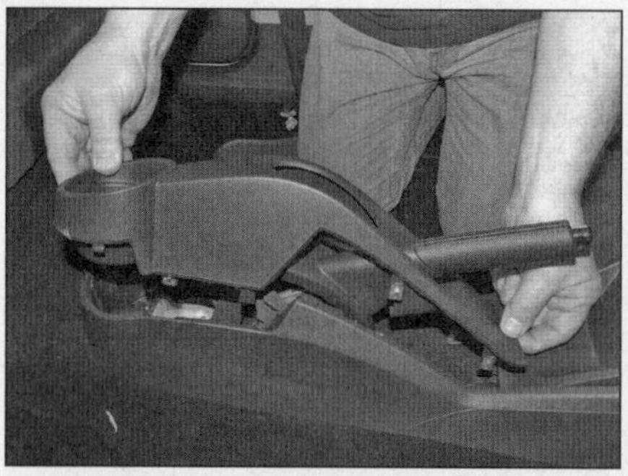
27.3 Unclip the handbrake cover panel

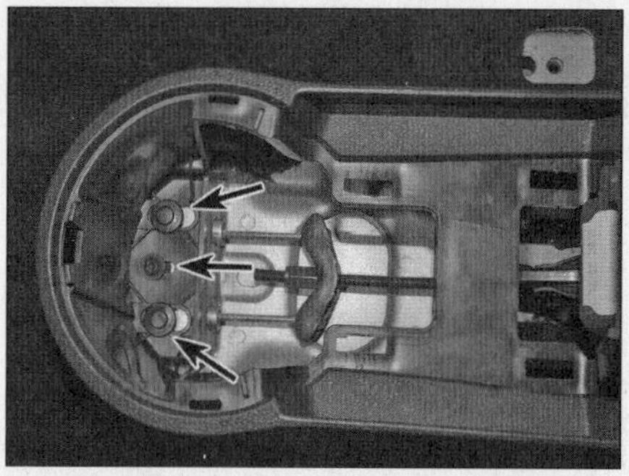
27.4 Remove the clips (where fitted)

27 Centre console – removal and refitting

Removal

Note: *Removal of the front seats is not necessary, however if the centre console is to be removed for access to the heater housing (for example) then removal of both front seats is recommended.*

1 Switch off the ignition.

2 On models fitted with an armrest move the seats forward, lift up the armrest and lever off the rear and side covers. Remove the mounting bolts and lift out the armrest.

3 Pull up the hand brake and then (with difficulty) unclip the hand brake cover **(see illustration)**.

4 Remove the screw and (where fitted) the 'scrivet' type clips from the rear of the console **(see illustration)**.

5 Unclip the trim panel and release the gear lever gaiter from the centre console. Turn over the panel and disconnect the wiring plug **(see illustrations)**.

6 Prise open the gear stick gaiter clip and remove the gaiter complete with the panel **(see illustration)**.

7 Remove the screws from the centre of the console and then from the front at both sides **(see illustrations)**.

8 Lift up the console and reach around the front to push out the media connectors (where fitted) and then disconnect the wiring plug from the 12 power outlet **(see illustration)**.

9 Lift up the centre console, ease it over the handbrake and remove it **(see illustration)**.

Refitting

10 Refitting is a reversal of removal.

27.5a Release the gaiter trim panel from the centre console

27.5b Disconnect the wiring plug

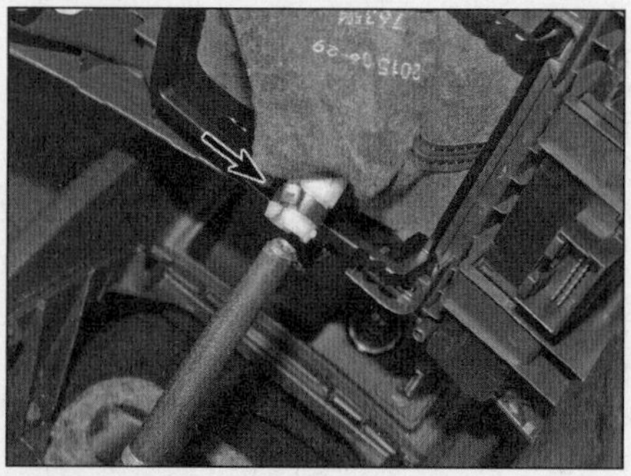
27.6 Remove the gaiter from the gear stick

28 Facia panel assembly – removal and refitting

Note: *Refer to the warnings in Chapter 12 Section 23 for airbags. Label each wiring connector as it is disconnected from its component to aid refitting. Note the exact routing of the wiring.*

Removal

1 Disconnect the battery negative lead (as described in Chapter 5A Section 3).
2 Remove the centre console as described in Section 27.
3 Remove both A-pillar trim panels as described in Section 26.
4 Remove the glovebox as described in Section 26.
5 Working through the glovebox aperture disconnect and then remove the passenger airbag as described in Chapter 12 Section 24.
6 Remove the drivers airbag form the steering wheel as described in Chapter 12 Section 24.
7 Remove the steering wheel as described in Chapter 10 Section 15.
8 Remove the steering column shrouds as described in Section 26.
9 Remove the airbag contact switch (slip-ring) and combination switch from the top of the steering column as described in Chapter 12 Section 5.
10 Remove the instrument panel as described in Chapter 12 Section 11.
11 Remove the lighting switch as described in Chapter 12 Section 5.
12 Where fitted prise up and remove the solar sensor from the centre of the facia.
13 On early models (and where fitted) open the cover of the navigation system mount and remove the screw **(see illustration)**. Use a trim tool and with care lever out the mounting. Disconnect the wiring plug as the mount is removed.
14 Remove the radio/audio unit/CD player, as described in Chapter 12 Section 19.
15 Remove the lower centre trim panel and disconnect the wiring plugs **(see illustrations)**. Note that on early models this panel is held in place with screws, on later models it is clipped in place.

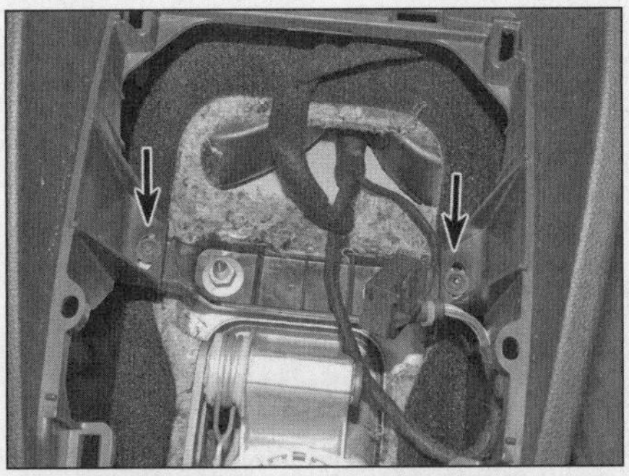

27.7a Remove the screws from the centre...

27.7b ...and at both sides

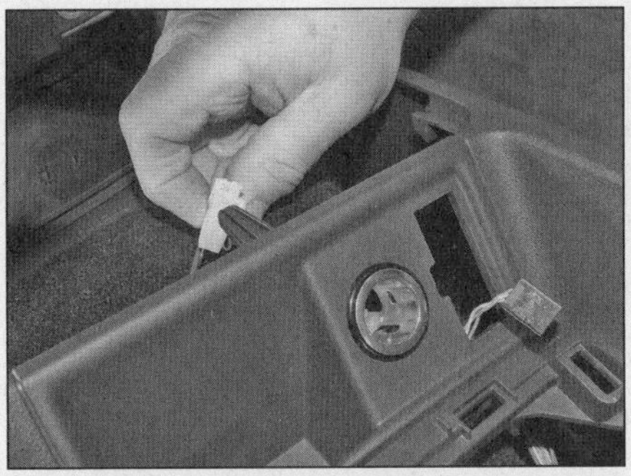

27.8 Disconnect the wiring plug from the 12 volt outlet

27.9 Remove the centre console

16 Remove the heater control panel as described in Chapter 3 Section 9.
17 Unclip the cover from each end of the facia panel **(see illustration)**.
18 Remove the cover from the fusebox.
19 There are a number of securing screws holding the facia in place and the number varies according to the trim level and year of production. Work logically from one side to the other and remove the screws **(see illustrations)**.

28.13 Remove the screw from the base of the mount

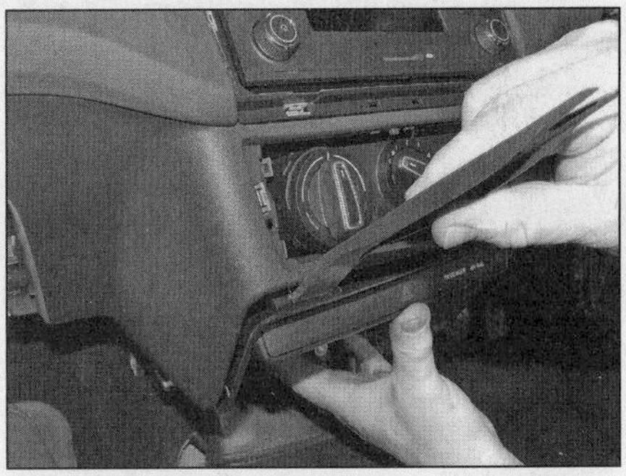

28.15a Remove the centre lower panel...

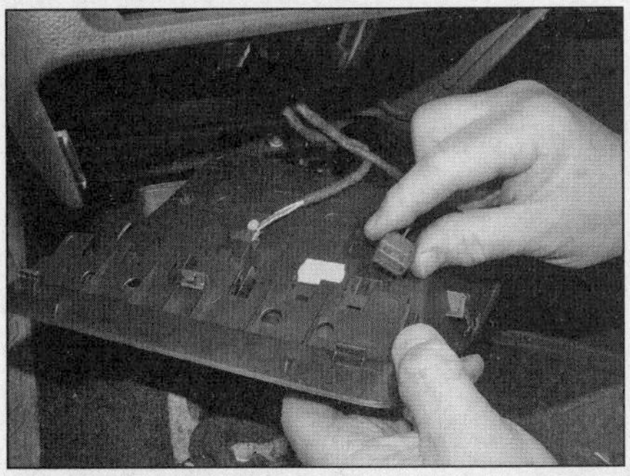

28.15b ...and disconnect the wiring pugs

28.17 Unclip the cover from each end of the facia panel

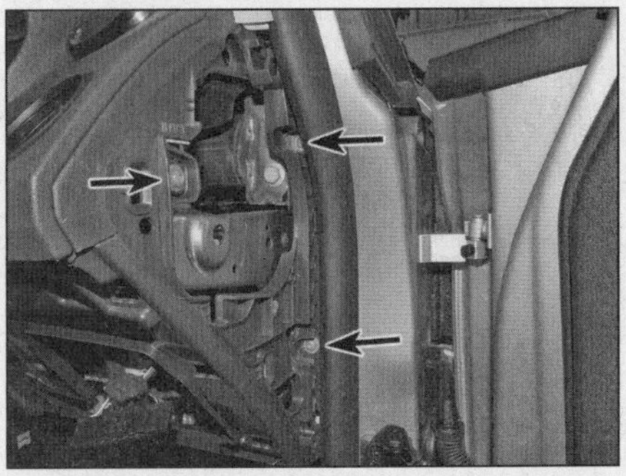

28.19a Behind the right-hand end panel

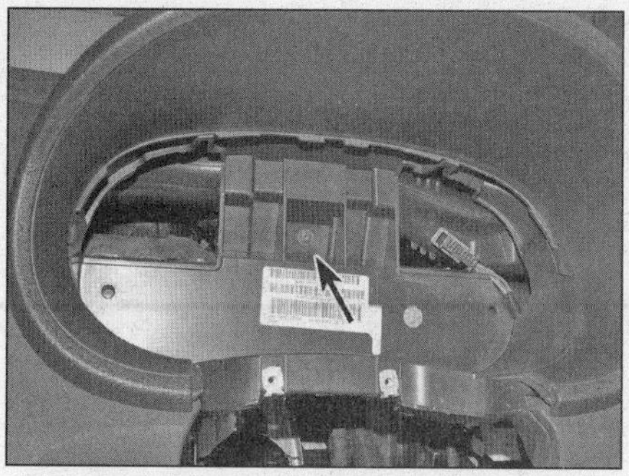

28.19b A single screw behind the instrument aperture

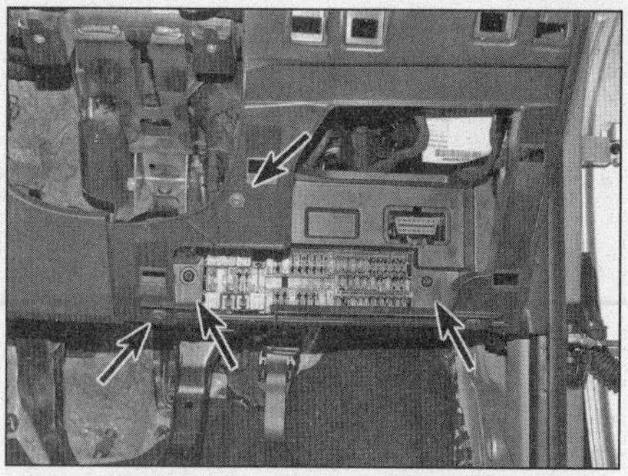

28.19c Screws behind the fuse box cover

28.19d Screws behind the heater control and audio unit housings

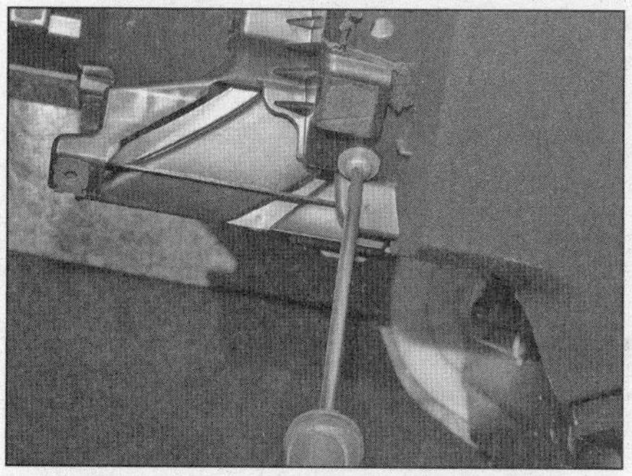

28.19e Screws by the glovebox (one shown)

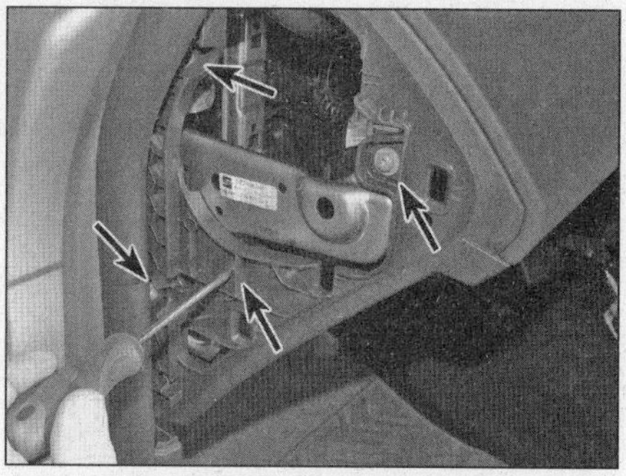

28.19f Screws behind the left-hand end panel

20 Disconnect all wiring plugs from the rear of the facia, noting their routing for correct refitting. Also, release any wiring loom retaining straps and ties.

21 Check that all the wiring and retaining screws have been removed, then, with the help of an assistant, withdraw the facia from the bulkhead and remove from one side of the car. The front of the facia may be tight on the front guides located just behind the windscreen.

Refitting

22 Refitting is a reversal of the removal procedure, noting the following points:

a) Make sure the wiring is correctly routed and connected, and secure where necessary with cable ties. Refit all the facia fasteners, and tighten them securely.

b) On completion, check that all the electrical components and switches function correctly. As a precaution against the airbags being activated, make sure no one is sitting in the vehicle as the battery is being reconnected.

29 Crossmember – removal and refitting

Removal

1 Remove the facia as described in the previous Section 28.

2 Disconnect the ignition switch and remove the steering column as described in Chapter 10 Section 16.

3 Remove the wiper arms (Chapter 12 Section 15) and the plenum chamber cover.

4 Unclip the engine management ECU and move it to the side. Note that on some models the bracket can be removed with the ECU **(see illustration)**.

5 On early models the ECU bracket is bolted to the plenum chamber front panel. Remove the bolts and remove the bracket. Where fitted remove the clips from the rear of the plenum chamber back wall.

6 Remove the clips and move the sound proofing material as required to gain access to the plenum chamber front panel mountings **(see illustration)**.

7 Unbolt and remove the plenum chamber front panel **(see illustration)** and then remove the wiper motor assembly as described in Chapter 12 Section 16.

8 Remove the cross member bolt from the rear wall of the plenum chamber **(see illustration)**.

9 Working inside the vehicle disconnect the wiring plug from the headlight height control unit – where fitted.

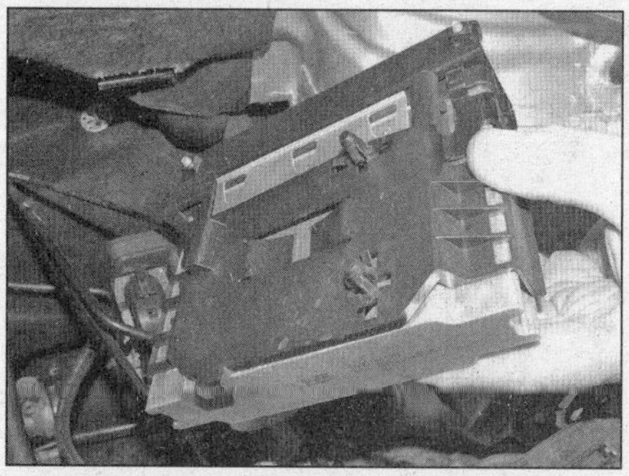

29.4 The ECU removed with mounting bracket

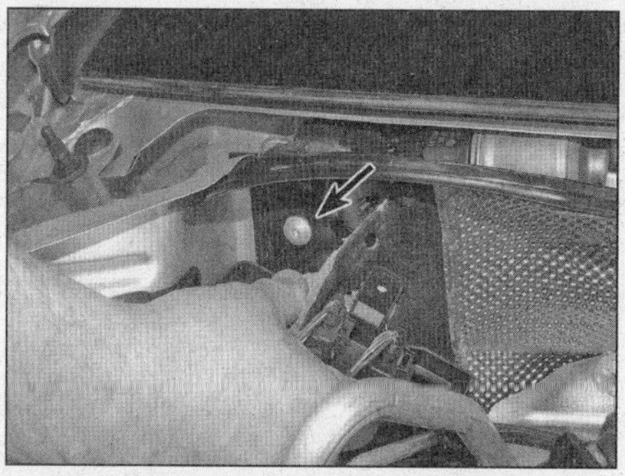

29.6 Gain access to the mounting bolts

29.7 Remove the front panel

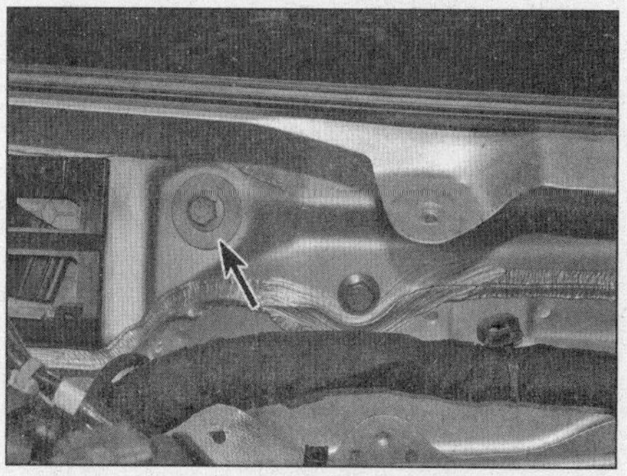

29.8 Remove the bolt. The lower bolt is for the heater housing

29.10 Remove the central support struts

10 Unbolt and remove the central support struts **(see illustration)**.

11 Unbolt the fusebox and relay panel and move it to the side.

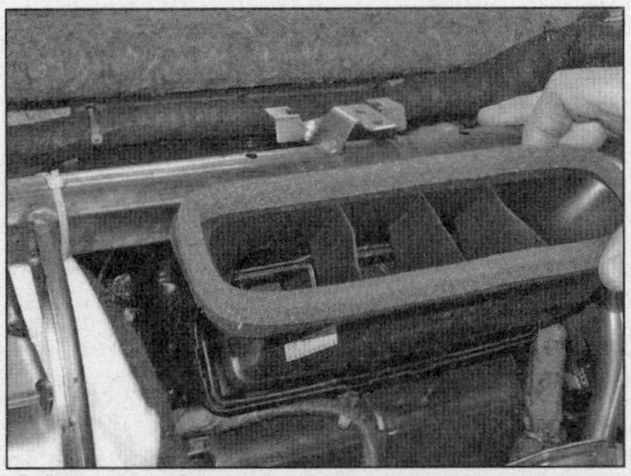

29.12 Remove the central air distribution duct

12 Remove the air distribution ducts **(see illustration)**.

29.13 Remove the heater housing bolts

13 Remove the bolts that secure the heater/air distribution housing to the crossmember **(see illustration)**.

14 Note the position and routing of the wiring loom and then release it from the crossmember as required **(see illustrations)**.

29.14a Release the wiring loom cable ties where possible...

29.14b ...or cut them as required

15 Remove the mounting bolts and then with the aid of an assistant remove the crossmember from the vehicle **(see illustrations)**.

29.15a Remove the mounting bolts...

29.15b ...and lift out the crossmember

Refitting

16 Refitting is a reversal of removal. Replace the cable ties as required.

Chapter 12
Body electrical system

Contents

Degrees of difficulty

Easy, suitable for novice with little experience	Fairly easy, suitable for beginner with some experience	Fairly difficult, suitable for competent DIY mechanic	Difficult, suitable for experienced DIY mechanic	Very difficult, suitable for expert DIY or professional

Specifications

System type ..... 12 volt negative earth

Fuses ..... See *Wiring diagrams* at the end of this Chapter

Bulbs	**Wattage**	**Type**
Front:		
Daytime running light (DRL)	21	P21W (or LED)
Direction indicators	21	PY21W
Direction indicator side repeater	5	W5W
Front foglight	35	HB4 (up to 2013) /H8 (2013 on) Halogen*
Front sidelight	5	W5W
Headlight:		
Halogen (twin bulb):		
Main beam	55	H7
Low beam	55	H7
Halogen (single bulb):		
Main/dip beam	60/55	H4
Bi-Xenon (main/dip)	35	D1S
Rear:		
Direction indicator	21	PY21W
High-level stop-light	N/A	LED
Rear foglight	21	P21W
Rear number plate light	5	W5W
Reversing light	10	R10W
Stop/tail light	21/5	P21/5W
Interior:		
Glovebox light	5	W5W
Load area light	10	C10W
Overhead light	10	C10W
Reading light	5	5W5

Torque wrench setting	**Nm**	**lbf ft**
Airbag (passenger)	10	7

1 General information and precautions

Warning: Before carrying out any work on the electrical system, read through the precautions given in 'Safety first!' at the beginning of this manual, and in Chapter 5A Section 1.

1 The electrical system is of 12 volt negative earth type. Power for the lights and all electrical accessories is supplied by a lead-acid type battery, which is charged by the alternator.

2 This Chapter covers repair and service procedures for the various electrical components not associated with the engine. Information on the battery, alternator and starter motor can be found in Chapter 5A.

3 It should be noted that prior to working on any component in the electrical system, the ignition and all electrical consumers must be switched off. Additionally, where stated, the battery negative lead must be disconnected, however, note the information given in, in the Reference section at the end of this manual, as special procedures have to be carried out when reconnecting the battery.

4 Most models are fitted with standard halogen headlights, however, some are fitted with Xenon gas discharge headlights. These vehicles are also equipped with automatic range control, to reduce the possibility of dazzling oncoming drivers. Note the special precautions which apply to these systems as given in Section 6.

2 Electrical fault finding – general information

Note: *Refer to the precautions given in 'Safety first!' and in Chapter 5A Section 1 before starting work. The following tests relate to testing of the main electrical circuits, and should not be used to test delicate electronic circuits (such as anti-lock braking systems), particularly where an electronic control module is used.*

General

1 A typical electrical circuit consists of an electrical component, any switches, relays, motors, fuses, fusible links or circuit breakers related to that component, and the wiring and connectors which link the component to both the battery and the chassis. To help to pinpoint a problem in an electrical circuit, wiring diagrams are included at the end of this Chapter.

2 Before attempting to diagnose an electrical fault, first study the appropriate wiring diagram to obtain a complete understanding of the components included in the particular circuit concerned. The possible sources of a fault can be narrowed down by noting if other components related to the circuit are operating properly. If several components or circuits fail at one time, the problem is likely to be related to a shared fuse or earth connection.

3 Electrical problems usually stem from simple causes, such as loose or corroded connections, a faulty earth connection, a blown fuse, a melted fusible link, or a faulty relay (refer to Section for details of testing relays). Visually inspect the condition of all fuses, wires and connections in a problem circuit before testing the components. Use the wiring diagrams to determine which terminal connections will need to be checked in order to pinpoint the trouble spot.

4 The basic tools required for electrical fault finding include a circuit tester or voltmeter (a 12 volt bulb with a set of test leads can also be used for certain tests); a self-powered test light (sometimes known as a continuity tester); an ohmmeter (to measure resistance); a battery and set of test leads; and a jumper wire, preferably with a circuit breaker or fuse incorporated, which can be used to bypass suspect wires or electrical components. Before attempting to locate a problem with test instruments, use the wiring diagram to determine where to make the connections.

5 To find the source of an intermittent wiring fault (usually due to a poor or dirty connection, or damaged wiring insulation), a wiggle test can be performed on the wiring. This involves wiggling the wiring by hand to see if the fault occurs as the wiring is moved. It should be possible to narrow down the source of the fault to a particular section of wiring. This method of testing can be used in conjunction with any of the tests described in the following sub-Sections.

6 Apart from problems due to poor connections, two basic types of fault can occur in an electrical circuit – open-circuit, or short-circuit.

7 Open-circuit faults are caused by a break somewhere in the circuit, which prevents current from flowing. An open-circuit fault will prevent a component from working, but will not cause the relevant circuit fuse to blow.

8 Short-circuit faults are caused by a short somewhere in the circuit, which allows the current flowing in the circuit to escape along an alternative route, usually to earth. Short-circuit faults are normally caused by a breakdown in wiring insulation, which allows a feed wire to touch either another wire, or an earthed component such as the bodyshell. A short-circuit fault will normally cause the relevant circuit fuse to blow.

Finding an open-circuit

9 To check for an open-circuit, connect one lead of a circuit tester or voltmeter to either the negative battery terminal or a known good earth.

10 Connect the other lead to a connector in the circuit being tested, preferably nearest to the battery or fuse.

11 Switch on the circuit, bearing in mind that some circuits are live only when the ignition switch is moved to a particular position.

12 If voltage is present (indicated either by the tester bulb lighting or a voltmeter reading, as applicable), this means that the section of the circuit between the relevant connector and the battery is problem-free.

13 Continue to check the remainder of the circuit in the same fashion.

14 When a point is reached at which no voltage is present, the problem must lie between that point and the previous test point with voltage. Most problems can be traced to a broken, corroded or loose connection.

Finding a short-circuit

15 To check for a short-circuit, first disconnect the load(s) from the circuit (loads are the components which draw current from a circuit, such as bulbs, motors, heating elements, etc).

16 Remove the relevant fuse from the circuit, and connect a circuit tester or voltmeter to the fuse connections.

17 Switch on the circuit, bearing in mind that some circuits are live only when the ignition switch is moved to a particular position.

18 If voltage is present (indicated either by the tester bulb lighting or a voltmeter reading, as applicable), this means that there is a short circuit.

19 If no voltage is present, but the fuse still blows with the load(s) connected, this indicates an internal fault in the load(s).

Finding an earth fault

20 The battery negative terminal is connected to earth – the metal of the engine/transmission and the car body – and most systems are wired so that they only receive a positive feed, the current returning through the metal of the car body. This means that the component mounting and the body form part of that circuit. Loose or corroded mountings can therefore cause a range of electrical faults, ranging from total failure of a circuit, to a puzzling partial fault. In particular, lights may shine dimly (especially when another circuit sharing the same earth point is in operation), motors (eg, wiper motors or the radiator cooling fan motor) may run slowly, and the operation of one circuit may have an apparently unrelated effect on another. Note that on many vehicles, earth straps are used between certain components, such as the engine/transmission and the body, usually where there is no metal-to-metal contact between components due to flexible rubber mountings, etc.

21 To check whether a component is properly earthed, disconnect the battery (refer to the warnings given in the Reference section at the rear of the manual) and connect one lead of an ohmmeter to a known good earth point. Connect the other lead to the wire or earth connection being tested. The resistance reading should be zero; if not, check the connection as follows.

22 If an earth connection is thought to be faulty, dismantle the connection and clean back to bare metal both the bodyshell and the wire terminal or the component earth connection mating surface. Be careful to remove all traces of dirt and corrosion, then use a knife to trim away any paint, so that a clean metal-to-metal joint is made. On reassembly, tighten the joint fasteners securely; if a wire terminal is being refitted, use serrated washers between the terminal and the bodyshell to ensure a clean and secure connection. When the connection is remade, prevent the onset of corrosion in the future by applying a coat of petroleum jelly or silicone-based grease or by spraying on (at regular intervals) a proprietary ignition sealer or a water dispersant lubricant.

3 Fuses and relays – general information

Fuses and fusible links

1 Fuses are designed to break a circuit when a predetermined current is reached, in order to protect the components and wiring, which could be damaged by excessive current flow. Any excessive current flow will be due to a fault in the circuit.

2 The main fuses are located in the fusebox on the driver's side of the facia; open the driver's door and unclip the fusebox cover from the lower edge of the facia to gain access to the fuses **(see illustration)**. The fuse locations are marked onto the rear of the fusebox cover.

3 To remove a fuse, first switch off the circuit concerned (or the ignition), and then pull the fuse out of its terminals.

4 The wire within the fuse should be visible; if the fuse has blown it will be broken or melted.

5 Always renew a fuse with one of the correct rating; never use a fuse with a different rating from that specified.

6 Refer to the wiring diagrams for details of the fuse ratings and the circuits protected. The fuse rating is stamped on the top of the fuse; the fuses are also colour-coded as follows.

Colour	Rating
Light brown	5A
Brown	7.5A
Red	10A
Blue	15A
Yellow	20A
White or clear	25A
Green	30A
Orange	40A

7 Never renew a fuse more than once without tracing the source of the trouble. If the new fuse blows immediately, find the cause before renewing it again; a short to earth as a result of faulty insulation is most likely. Where a fuse protects more than one circuit, try to isolate the fault by switching on each circuit in turn (where possible) until the fuse blows again.

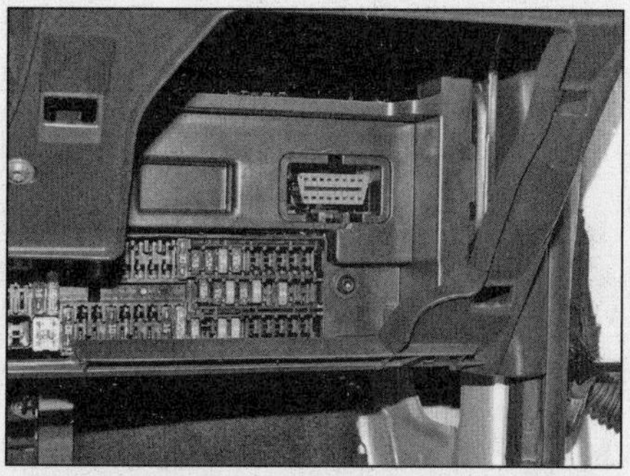

3.2 The fusebox and diagnostic socket

Always carry a supply of spare fuses of each relevant rating on the vehicle.

8 Additional fused links (or maxi fuses) are located in a bracket on top of the battery in the engine compartment or behind the battery. Release the securing clips and withdraw the cover to gain access **(see illustration)**.

9 To renew a fusible link, first disconnect the battery negative terminal. Unscrew the retaining nuts then remove the blown link. Fit the new link to its terminals and reconnect the leads. Ensure the link and leads are correctly seated then refit the retaining nuts and tighten securely. Where Maxi-fuses replace the links (or are in addition to) pull out the fuse and replace it. Clip the cover back into position then reconnect the battery.

Relays

10 A relay is an electrically operated switch, which is used for the following reasons:

a) *relay can switch a heavy current remotely from the circuit in which the current is flowing, allowing the use of lighter-gauge wiring and switch contacts.*
b) *relay can receive more than one control input, unlike a mechanical switch.*
c) *relay can have a timer function – for example, the intermittent wiper relay.*

11 Most of the relays are located on the relay plate behind the driver's side facia, however, the glowplug relay on diesel models is located in the bracket on top of the battery **(see illustration)**.

12 Access to the relays can be obtained by reaching above the interior fusebox **(see

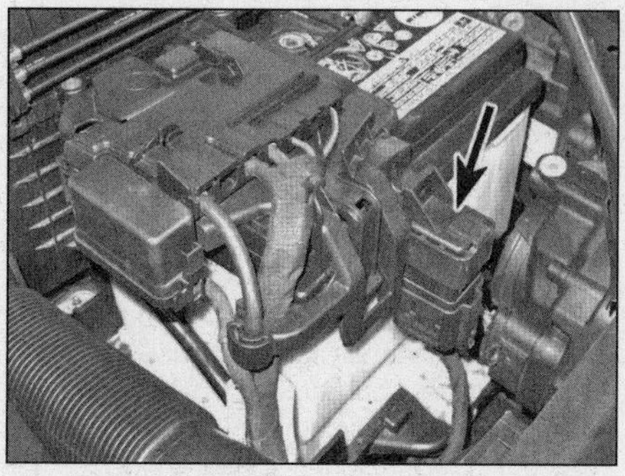

3.11 Glow plug relay

3.8 Large and small capacity fuses are fitted behind the battery on newer models

illustration)**. Removal is straight forward, but refitting may require the lowering of the fusebox to improve access. Identification details of the relays are given at the start of the wiring diagrams.

13 If a circuit or system controlled by a relay develops a fault, and the relay is suspect, operate the system. If the relay is functioning, it should be possible to hear it click as it is energised. If this is the case, the fault lies with the components or wiring of the system. If the relay is not being energised, then either the relay is not receiving a main supply or a switching voltage, or the relay itself is faulty. Testing is by the substitution of a known good unit, but be careful – while some relays are identical in appearance and in operation, others look similar but perform different functions.

14 To remove a relay, first ensure that the relevant circuit is switched off. The relay can then simply be pulled out from the socket, and pushed back into position.

15 The direction indicator/hazard flasher relay is integral with the hazard warning switch. Refer to Section 5 for the switch removal procedure.

4 Electrical connectors

1 Most electrical connections on these vehicles are made with multiwire plastic connectors. The mating halves of many

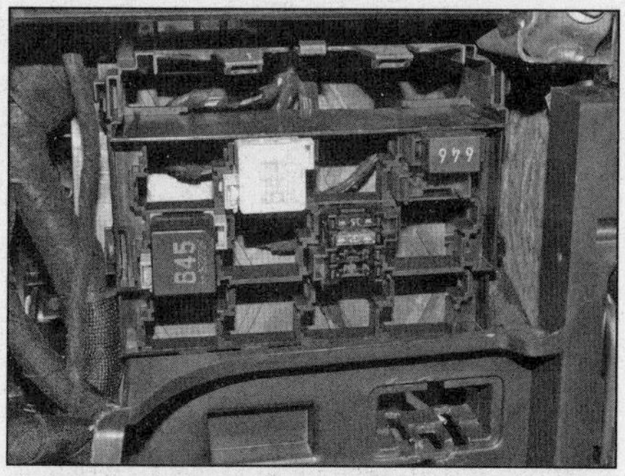

3.12 Relays located behind interior fusebox (shown with facia removed)

4.5a Most electrical connectors have a single release tab that you depress to release the connector

4.5b Some electrical connectors have a retaining tab which must be pried up to free the connector

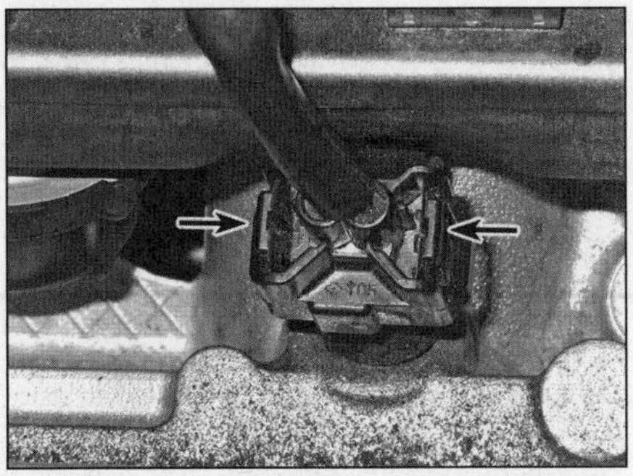

4.5c Some connectors have two release tabs that you must squeeze to release the connector

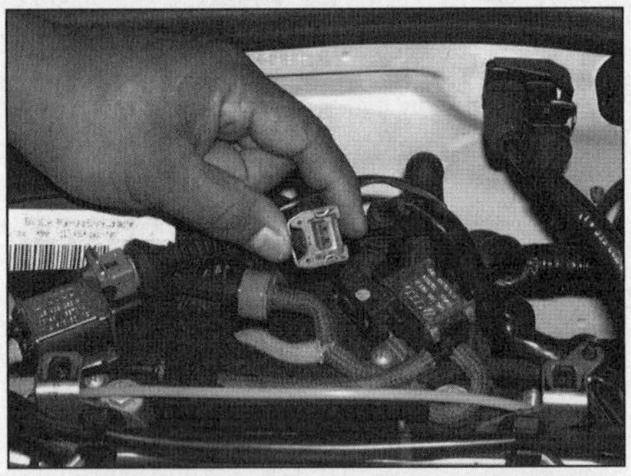

4.5d Some connectors use wire retainers that you squeeze to release the connector

4.5e Critical connectors often employ a sliding lock (1) that you must pull out before you can depress the release tab (2)

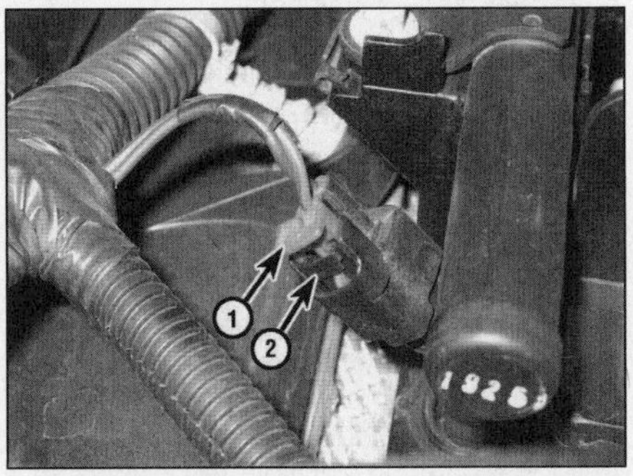

4.5f Here's another sliding-lock style connector, with the lock (1) and the release tab (2) on the side of the connector

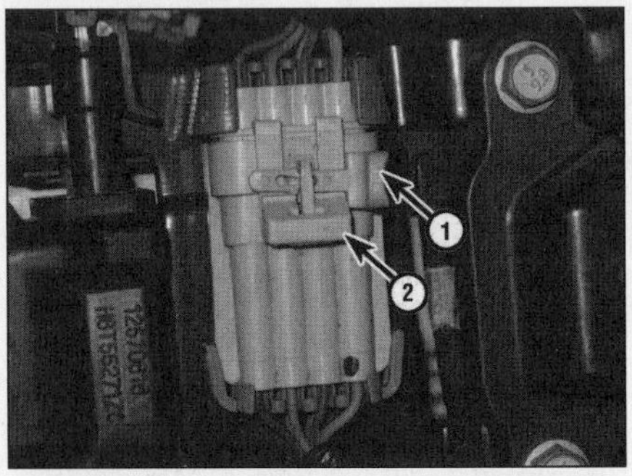

4.5g On some connectors the lock (1) must be pulled out to the side and removed before you can lift the release tab (2)

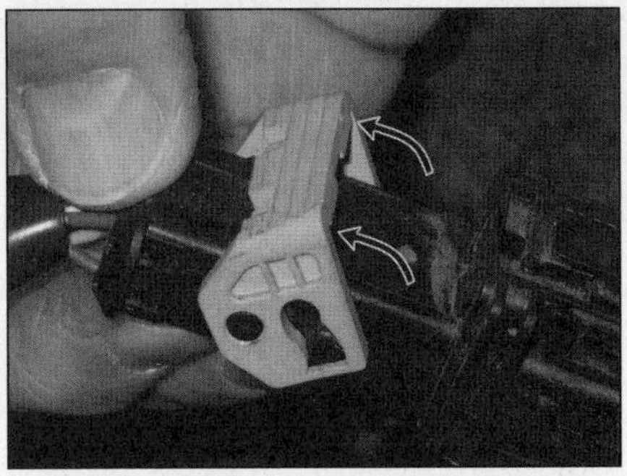

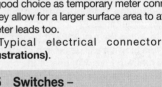

4.5h Some critical connectors, like the multi-pin connectors at the Electronic Control Module employ pivoting locks that must be flipped open

connectors are secured with locking clips molded into the plastic connector shells. The mating halves of some large connectors, such as some of those under the instrument panel, are held together by a bolt through the center of the connector.

2 To separate a connector with locking clips, use a small screwdriver to pry the clips apart carefully, then separate the connector halves. Pull only on the shell, never pull on the wiring harness, as you may damage the individual wires and terminals inside the connectors. Look at the connector closely before trying to separate the halves. Often the locking clips are engaged in a way that is not immediately clear. Additionally, many connectors have more than one set of clips.

3 Each pair of connector terminals has a male half and a female half. When you look at the end view of a connector in a diagram, be sure to understand whether the view shows the harness side or the component side of the connector. Connector halves are mirror images of each other, and a terminal shown on the right side end-view of one half will be on the left side end-view of the other half.

4 It is often necessary to take circuit voltage measurements with a connector connected. Whenever possible, carefully insert a small straight pin (not your meter probe) into the rear of the connector shell to contact the terminal inside, then clip your meter lead to the pin. This kind of connection is called "backprobing." When inserting a test probe into a terminal, be careful not to distort the terminal opening. Doing so can lead to a poor connection and corrosion at that terminal later. Using the small straight pin instead of a meter probe results in less chance of deforming the terminal connector. "T" pins are a good choice as temporary meter connections. They allow for a larger surface area to attach the meter leads too.

5 Typical electrical connectors **(see illustrations)**.

5 Switches – removal and refitting

Note: *Before working on any electrical systems switch off the ignition and all electrical consumers and remove the ignition key.*

Ignition switch

1 Refer to Chapter 10 Section 17.

Wiper and indicator/switches

Note: *The indicator and wiper switches are combined in single unit. They can not be renewed separately.*

2 Check that the front wheels are pointing straight-ahead and the steering wheel is in its centre position, then remove the steering wheel as described in Chapter 10 Section 15.

3 Remove the steering column shrouds, as described in Chapter 11 Section 26.

4 To prevent the airbag clock spring/slip ring from moving from its position use a piece

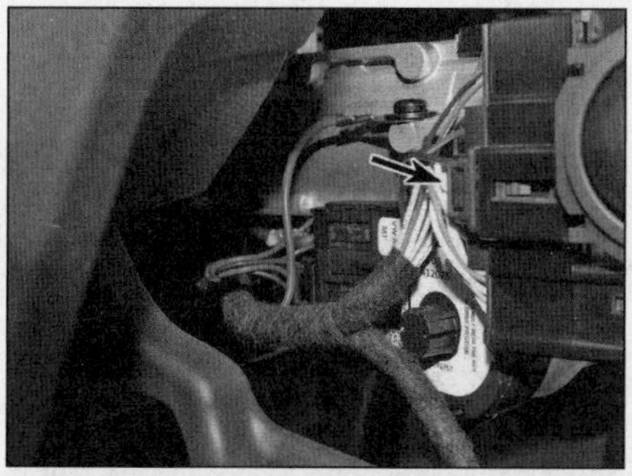

5.5a Pull out the safety lock, depress the tab and remove the wiring plugs from both sides

5.5b The lower locking tab on later models

5.5c Slide off the switch assembly

5.5d The locking tabs that hold the switch in place

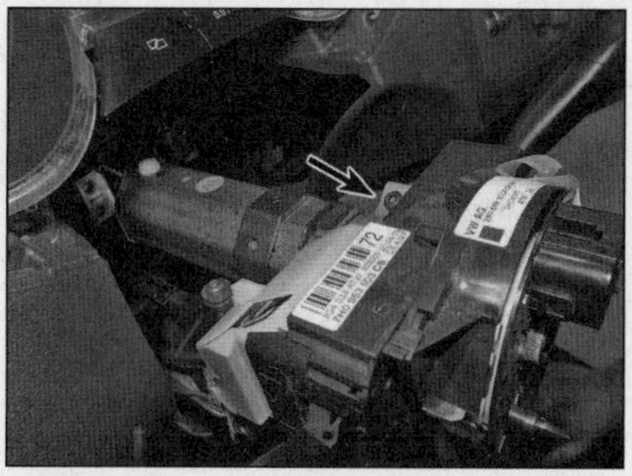

5.5e On early models slacken the screw...

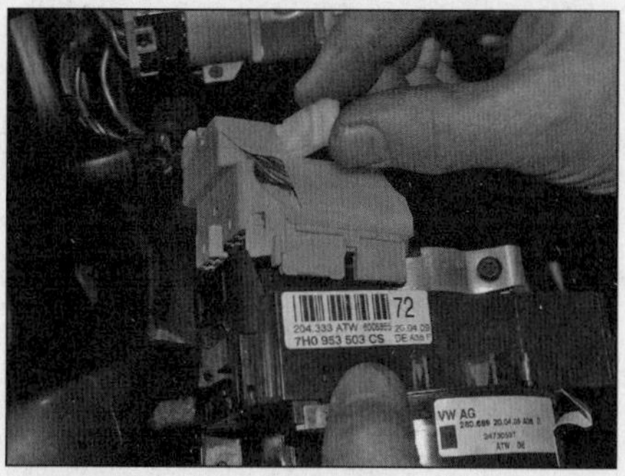

5.5f ...pull off the switch assembly and disconnect the wiring plug

of tape to secure it in position. Remove the screws, disconnect the wiring plug and slide off the clock spring (see Section 24).

5 Disconnect the wiring plugs at the rear of the switch assembly. On early models, slacken the securing screw from the mounting clamp bracket at the rear of the switch assembly. On later models unclip the switch assembly from the mounting bracket **(see illustrations)**.

6 Refitting is a reversal of removal. On models where the switch assembly is secured by a screw install the switches (and clock spring) so that the gap between the clock spring and steering wheel is 1 mm **(see illustration)**.

Lighting switch

7 With the light switch in position O, press the switch centre inwards and turn it slightly to the right. Hold this position and pull the switch from the dash **(see illustration)**.

8 As the switch is withdrawn from the dash, disconnect the wiring plug or plugs.

9 To refit the switch, first reconnect the wiring plug, then hold the switch and press the rotary part inwards and slightly to the right. Insert the switch into the dash, turn the rotary part to position O and release. Check the switch for correct operation.

Headlamp range control and instrument illumination switch

10 Remove the lighting switch as described in paragraphs 9 to 11. On early models the switches are part of the main lighting switch panel.

11 Remove the fusebox cover from the driver's side of the facia, reach up and push out the switch from the rear **(see illustrations)**. Disconnect the wiring plug as the switch is removed.

12 Refitting is a reversal of removal.

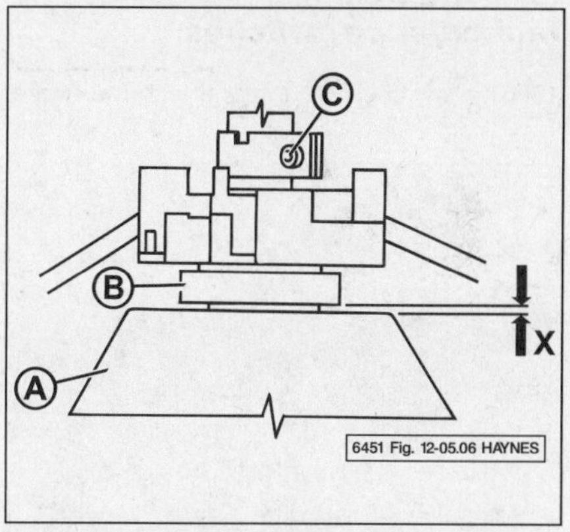

5.6 Adjust the position of the switch assembly so that the gap (X) between the steering wheel (A) and the clock spring (B) = 1 mm. Tighten the locking collar screw (C)

5.7 Press the switch centre inwards and turn it slightly to the right to remove (later model shown)

5.11a Remove the switch

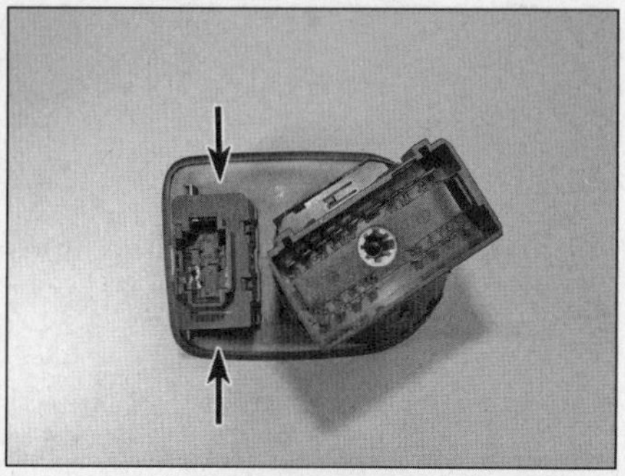

5.11b On early models unclip the switch from the panel

5.16a Prise out the panel...

5.16b ...disconnect the wiring plug...

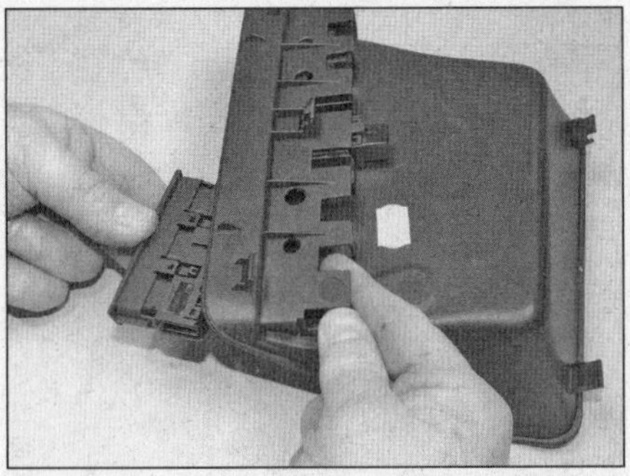
5.16c ...and push out the switches

5.18 Unclip the switch

Air conditioning/ recirculation switches

13 The switches are integral with the heater control panel, and cannot be removed separately. Refer to Chapter 3 Section 9, for details of heater control panel removal and refitting.

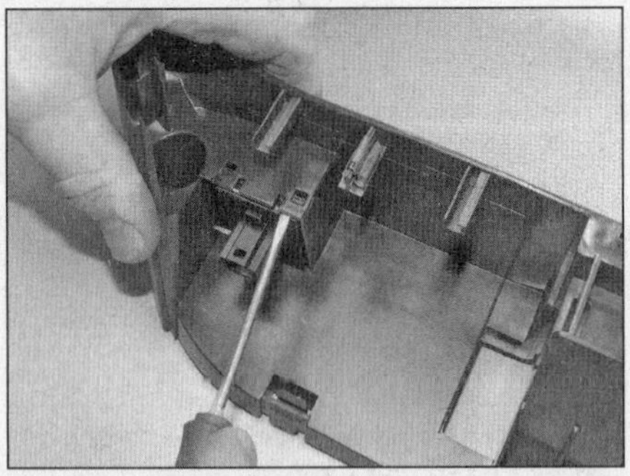
5.30a Release the switch panel...

5.30b ...and remove the switches

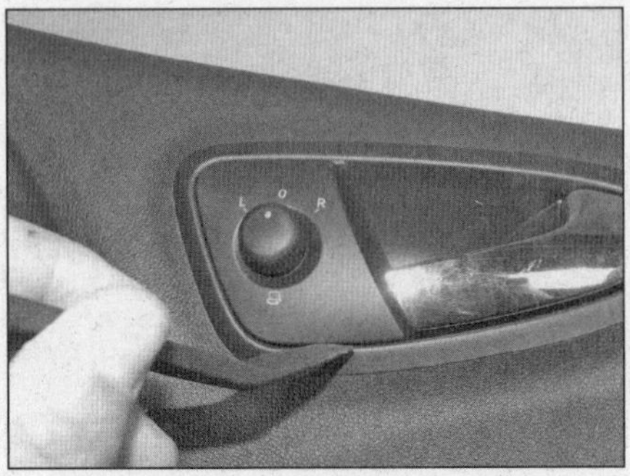
5.31a Prise out the the switch...

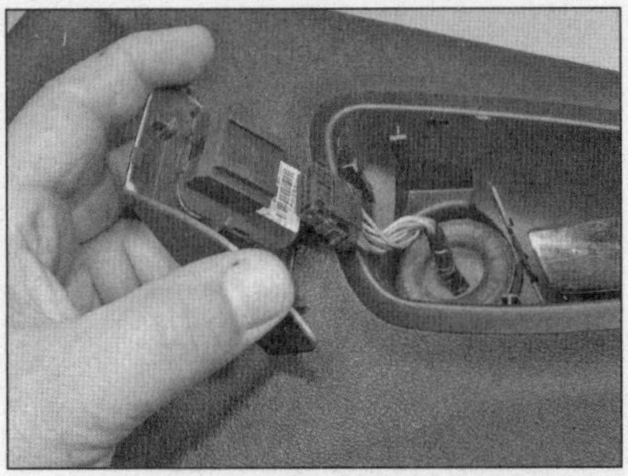
5.31b ...and disconnect the wiring plug

Heater blower motor switch

14 The switch is integral with the heater control panel, and cannot be removed separately. Refer to Chapter 3 Section 9, for details of heater control panel removal and refitting.

Hazard warning switch/Airbag warning light

15 Depending on the year of manufacture and equipment level the the switches are either located below the heater controls, below the audio unit or in front of the gear lever.

16 Prise out the panel to access the rear of the facia mounted switches **(see illustrations)**.

17 Remove the front section of the centre console as described in Chapter 11 Section 27 to access the console mounted switches.

18 Push out the switch panel and remove it **(see illustration)**. Note that the version shown is from a late model and has the Stop/Start switch where the hazard switch is fitted on earlier models. Other switches fitted here may include the heated seat controls switches and heated screen switches.

19 To access the switches mounted below the audio unit, remove the unit as described in Section 19.

20 Release the locking tabs and push the individual switch out of the panel. On some versions the switches (and warning lights) are a single panel. They can not be replaced individually.

21 Refitting is a reversal of removal.

Heated rear window (HRW) and Traction control (TCS) switches

22 Where fitted, these switches are located in either the centre console switch panel or below the audio unit. Refitting and removal is the same as described for the hazard warning and heated windscreen switches above.

23 Refitting is a reversal of removal.

Passenger air bag on/off switch

24 Disconnect the battery as described in Chapter 5A Section 3.

25 Remove the glovebox as described in Chapter 11 Section 28.

26 Push out the switch from the glovebox.

27 Refitting is a reversal of removal.

Door locking/ Heated seat switches

28 The door locking and heated seat switches (depending on model) are located at the front of the centre console. They are part of the main switch panel. Removal and refitting is described above **(see illustration 5.18)**.

Power window switch assembly

29 The window switch is located in the door trim panel. Remove the door pull handle as described in Chapter 11 Section 13.

30 Use a small screw driver to release the switch panel **(see illustrations)**.

Exterior mirror switch

31 Using a trim tool and working from

6.12a Release the spring clip...

6.12b ...and remove the cover

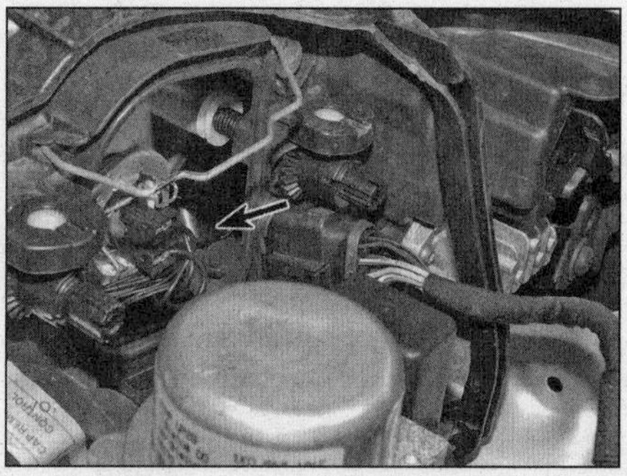

6.13 Disconnect the wiring plug...

the bottom of the switch panel unclip the panel and disconnect the wiring plug **(see illustrations)**.

32 Refitting is a reversal of removal.

Handbrake 'on' warning switch

33 Refer to Chapter 9 Section 20.

Brake light switch

34 Refer to Chapter 9 Section 21.

Reversing light switch

35 Refer to Chapter 7A Section 5.

Courtesy light switches

36 The courtesy light switch is integrated into the door lock mechanism, and cannot be renewed independently. If the courtesy light switch is faulty, renew the door lock mechanism as described in Chapter 11 Section 14.

Load area light switch

37 The luggage compartment light switch is integrated into the tailgate/boot lid lock mechanism, and cannot be renewed independently. If the luggage compartment light switch is faulty, renew the tailgate/boot lid lock mechanism as described in Chapter 11 Section 17.

6 Bulbs (exterior lights) – renewal

General

1 Whenever a bulb is renewed, note the following points:

a) Switch off the ignition and all electrical consumers before commencing work.
b) Remember that if the light has just been in use the bulb may be extremely hot.
c) Always check the bulb contacts and holder, ensuring that there is clean metal-to-metal contact. Clean off any corrosion or dirt before fitting a new bulb.
d) Wherever bayonet-type bulbs are fitted ensure that the spring-tensioned arms bear firmly against the bulb contacts.
e) Always ensure that the new bulb is of the correct rating and that it is thoroughly clean before fitting it.

Warning: The headlight bulb contains gas at very high pressure, and it is recommended that gloves and eye protection be worn to prevent potential personal injury.

Xenon headlights

Main and dip beam

Note: *Do not touch the glass envelope of the bulb if it is to be re-used.*

2 If working on the left-hand headlight with a vehicle with the air filter behind the battery, remove the battery as described in Chapter 5A Section 3

3 If working on the right-hand headlight on diesel vehicles remove the fuel filter and secure it to the side. There is no need to disconnect the fuel lines.

4 On earlier models (before 2012) disconnect the wiring plug from the daytime running and sidelights.

5 Remove the rear cover from the headlight.

6 Rotate the locking ring, pull out the bulb and disconnect the wiring plug.

7 When handling the new bulb, use a tissue or clean cloth to avoid touching the glass with the fingers; moisture and grease from the skin can cause blackening and rapid failure of this type of bulb. If the glass is accidentally touched, wipe it clean using methylated spirit.

8 Connect the wiring plug and fit the new bulb. Rotate the locking ring to secure the bulb in the headlight.

9 Refit the cover, making sure that it is secure and then refit the headlight.

Halogen headlights

Main and dip beam

Note: *Do not touch the glass envelope of the bulb if it is to be re-used.*

Note: *The Ibiza range of vehicles are fitted with separate dip and main beam bulbs or with a single combined main/dip beam bulb.*

10 If working on the left-hand headlight with a vehicle with the air filter behind the battery, remove the battery as described in Chapter 5A Section 3. Note that removing the battery greatly improves access, regardless of the engine fitted.

11 If working on the right-hand headlight on diesel vehicles remove the fuel filter and secure it to the side. There is no need to disconnect the fuel lines.

12 Release the locking wire and remove the rear cover **(see illustrations)**. If working on a model fitted with separate main and dipped beam bulbs remove the upper cover for access to the dipped beam and the inner cover for access to the main beam.

13 Disconnect the wiring plug from the rear of the bulb **(see illustration)**.

14 Unhook and release the ends of the bulb retaining clip from the light unit, then withdraw the bulb. Note that on some versions the headlight bulb the spring retainer is part of the headlight and the bulb is pulled straight out – there is no need to release a spring clip **(see illustrations)**.

15 When handling the new bulb, use a tissue or clean cloth to avoid touching the glass with the fingers; moisture and grease from the skin can cause blackening and rapid failure of

6.14a Unhook the clip...

6.14b...and withdraw the bulb

6.14c Detailed view of the headlight bulb with the headlight removed. Note the spring retainer

6.14d A close up view of the headlight bulb that clips in place. Note the position of the sidelight bulb

6.20a Compress the locking tabs and remove the bulb holder

6.20b Pull the capless style bulb from the bulb holder

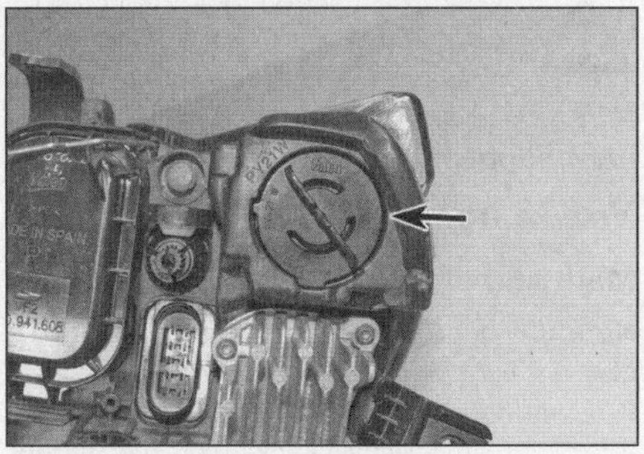

6.22 Turn the bulb holder anti-clockwise to remove (shown with the headlight removed)

6.23 Twist the bayonet type bulb anti-clockwise to remove

6.26 Remove the cover

6.27a Depress the locking tab...

6.27b ...rotate the complete lamp, pull it forward...

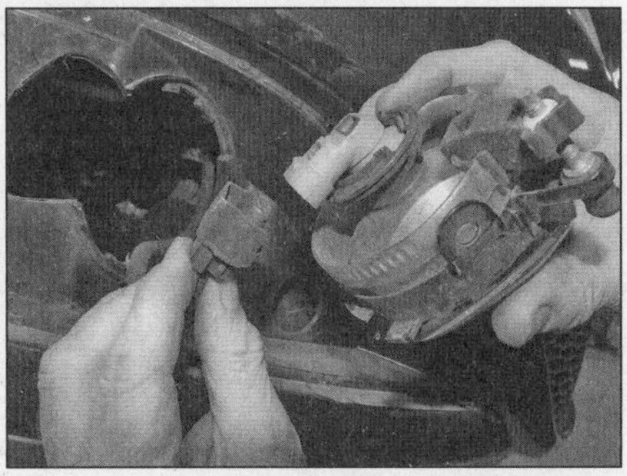

6.27c ...and disconnect the wiring plug

this type of bulb. If the glass is accidentally touched, wipe it clean using methylated spirit.

16 Install the new bulb, ensuring that its locating tabs are correctly positioned in the light cut-outs, and secure it in place with the retaining clip.

17 Reconnect the wiring plug and refit the headlight cover, making sure it is secure.

18 Refit the headlight cover, making sure that it is secure and then refit the headlight.

Front sidelight

Note: *Some later models have LED type bulbs. If these fail the complete headlight must be replaced.*

19 Raise the locking clip and remove the bulb cover.

20 Carefully pull the sidelight bulbholder from the headlight unit. The bulb is a push-fit in the holder and can be removed by grasping the end of the bulb and pulling it out **(see illustrations)**.

21 Refitting is a reversal of removal, making sure that the headlight cover is securely refitted.

Front direction indicator

22 Turn the bulb holder anti-clockwise and remove it from the headlight complete with bulb **(see illustration)**.

23 The bulb is a bayonet fit, push the bulb in slightly, then turn the bulb anti-clockwise and remove it from the holder **(see illustration)**.

24 Refit the bulb to the holder, then fit the bulbholder to the headlight and turn clockwise to secure.

25 Check the operation of the indicator bulb before closing the bonnet.

Front foglight

Note: *If the vehicle is raised and supported (see 'Jacking and vehicle support') for other work, then the foglight bulbs can be accessed by reaching up from below.*

Models built up to 01/2012

26 Remove the cover section by prising it free with a trim tool **(see illustration)**.

27 Rotate the complete lamp assembly

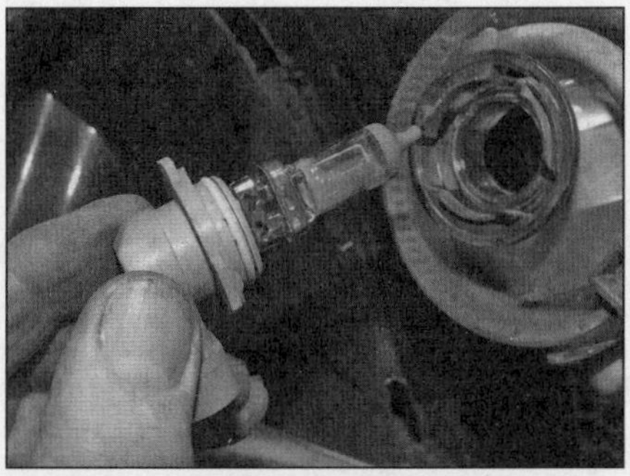
6.28 Remove the bulb

6.29a Remove the screw...

6.29b ...and release the trim

6.30 Remove the bolts

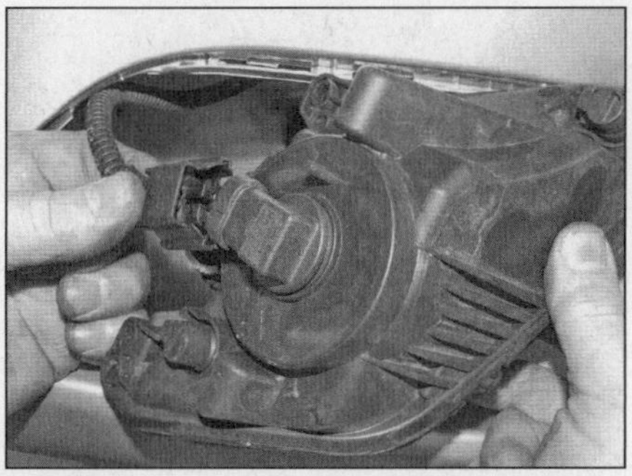
6.31a Disconnect the wiring plug and...

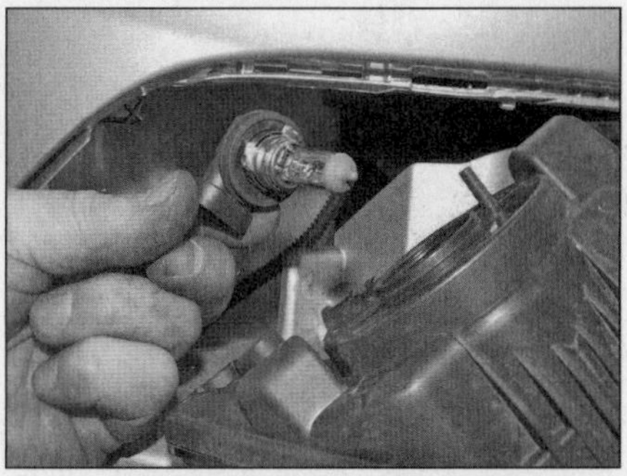
6.31b ...and remove the bulb

anti-clockwise to release it. Pull the lamp forward and disconnect the wiring plug **(see illustrations)**.

28 Rotate the bulb (complete with the bulb holder) and remove it **(see illustration)**.

Models built after 02/2012

29 Remove the single fixing screw and then (using a trim tool) prise off the trim surround **(see illustrations)**.

30 Remove the fixing bolts from the lamp and pull it forward **(see illustration)**. Disconnect the wiring plug.

31 Rotate the bulb (complete with the bulb holder) and remove it **(see illustrations)**.

FR models

32 Jack up and support the front of the vehicle (see *Jacking and vehicle support*) and then release the bumper cover from the wing liner (as described in Chapter 11 Section 6). Complete removal of the bumper is not required. Pull the corner of the bumper free from the wing to access the lamp.

33 Remove the locking bar from the lamp.

34 Disconnect the wiring plug. Rotate the bulb (complete with the bulb holder) and remove it.

Daytime running lights

35 On early models (where fitted) rotate the bulb holder to remove the bulb. Push and twist the bulb to remove the bayonet type bulb from the bulb holder. Later models have LED type lights. If faulty the complete headlight must be replaced.

Direction indicator side repeater

36 Using a plastic lever, carefully unclip the light unit from the front wing panel **(see illustration)**. Note that the lamp can only be released in one direction and it is impossible to tell at which end the spring clip is. Protect the paintwork with masking tape if required.

37 Disconnect the bulb holder from the light unit and then pull the wedge type bulb from the bulb holder **(see illustrations)**.

38 Refitting is a reversal of removal.

Rear light cluster

Note: *Some later models have LED type bulbs for the rear light and tail light. On these models the complete lamp must be replaced if either are faulty.*

Hatchback models

39 On hatchback models, remove the rear light cluster as described in Section 8.

40 Unclip the bulb holder assembly from the lamp **(see illustrations)**.

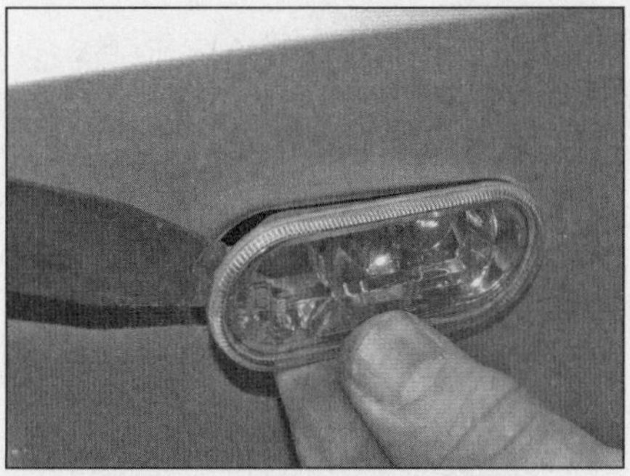
6.36 Carefully unclip the lamp

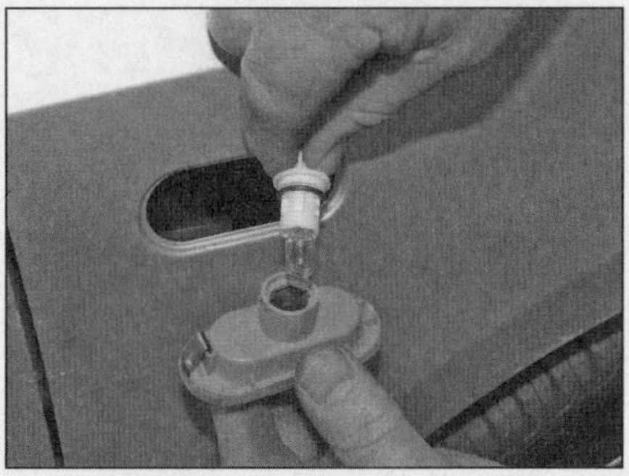
6.37a Pull out the bulb holder...

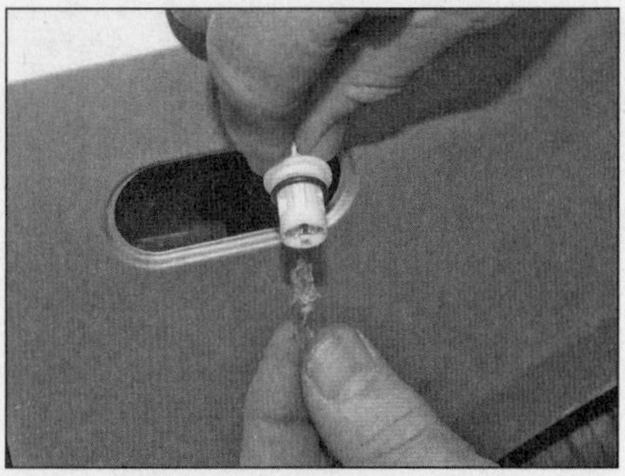
6.37b ...and pull out the bulb

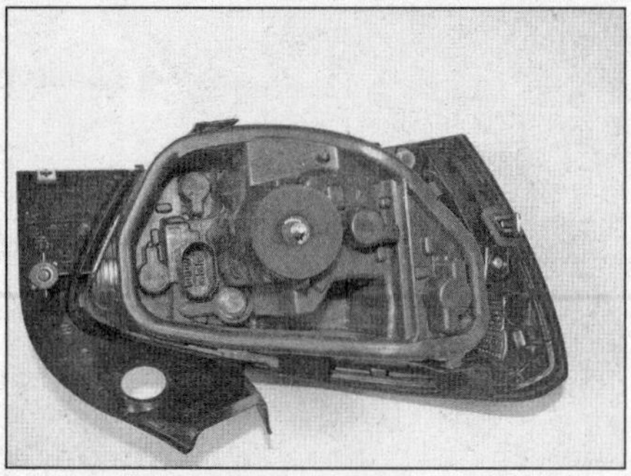
6.40a Unclip...

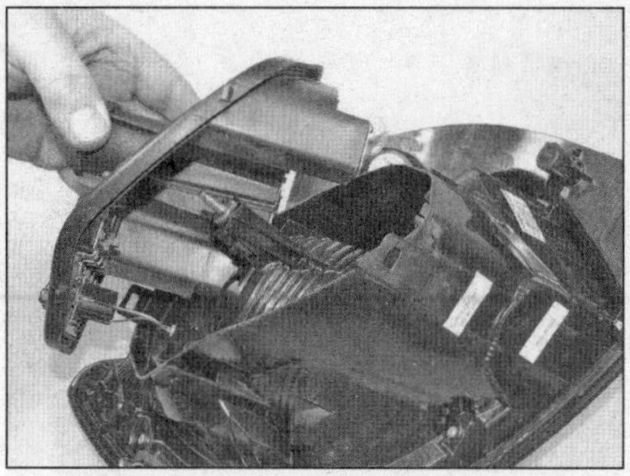
6.40b ...and remove the bulb holder

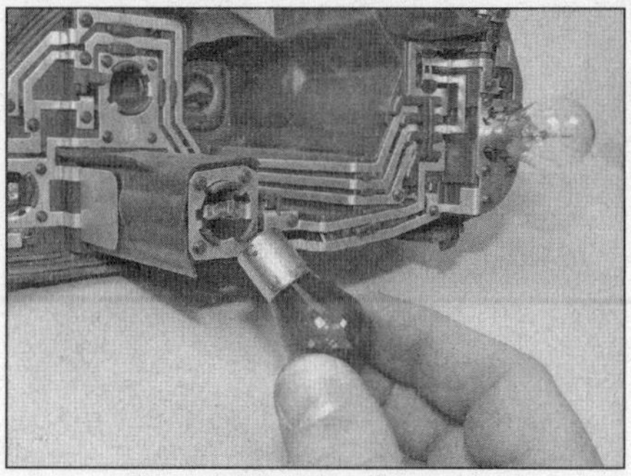
6.41 Remove the bulb

6.43 Open the cover

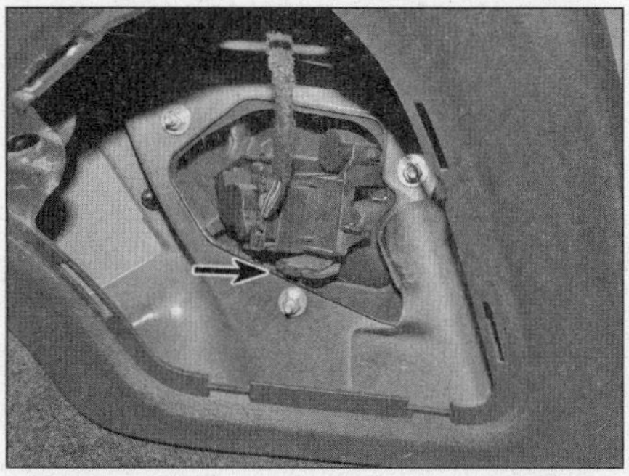
6.44a Remove the bulb holder...

6.44b ...and remove the bulb

41 Depending on bulb being replaced, it is either a bayonet type bulb (fog, reversing light, indicator and brake light) or a wedge type bulb (side/parking light). If the bulb is a bayonet-fit in the bulb holder – depress and twist the relevant bulb anti-clockwise to remove it **(see illustration)**. If the bulb is a glass wedge type – pull the relevant bulb to remove.

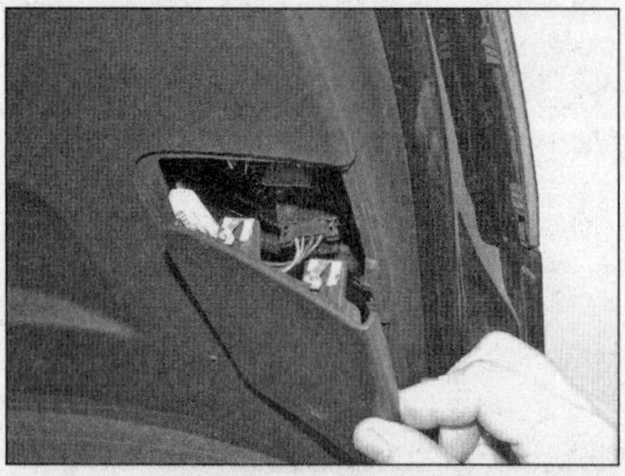
6.46 Remove the cover

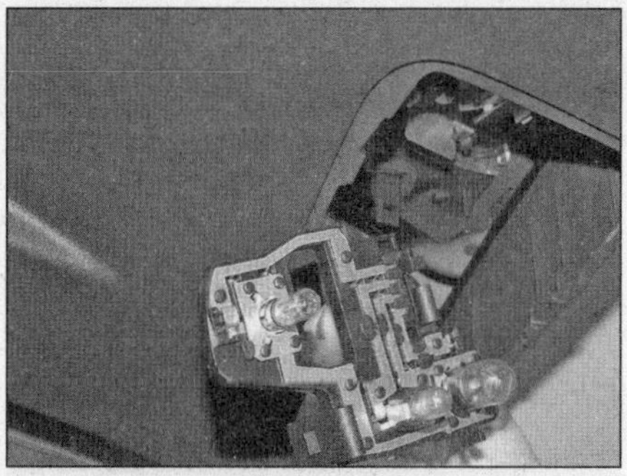
6.47 The tailgate lamp bulb holder

6.48 Remove the blown bulb

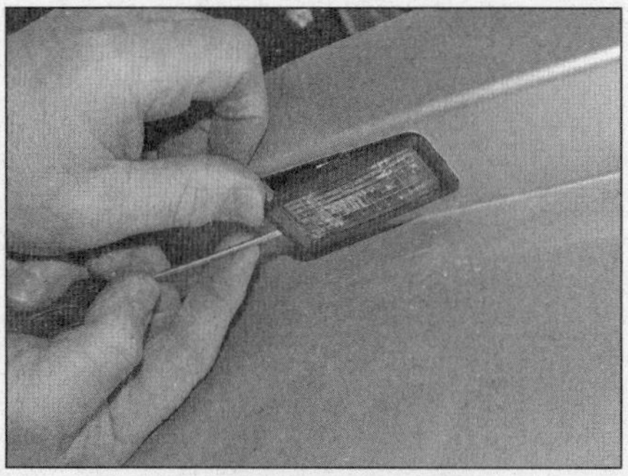
6.50 Unclip the light unit...

42 Fit the new bulb using a reversal of the removal procedure.

Estate models (ST)

43 Open the cover in the load area side panel **(see illustration)**.

44 Release the locking tab and remove the bulb holder assembly **(see illustrations)**.

45 Fit the new bulb using a reversal of the removal procedure.

Tailgate mounted rear light cluster (estate models)

46 Open the tailgate and remove the lamp cover **(see illustration)**.

47 Depress the locking tab and remove the bulb holder assembly **(see illustration)**.

48 Locate and remove the blown bulb **(see illustration)**.

High-level brake light

Note: *The light is of LED design; therefore if faulty the complete unit must be renewed.*

49 Remove the high-level light unit as described in Section 8.

Number plate light

50 Release the securing clip, and withdraw the light unit from the tailgate **(see illustration)**.

51 Remove the bulb holder from the lamp **(see illustrations)**.

52 Fit the new bulb using a reversal of the removal procedure.

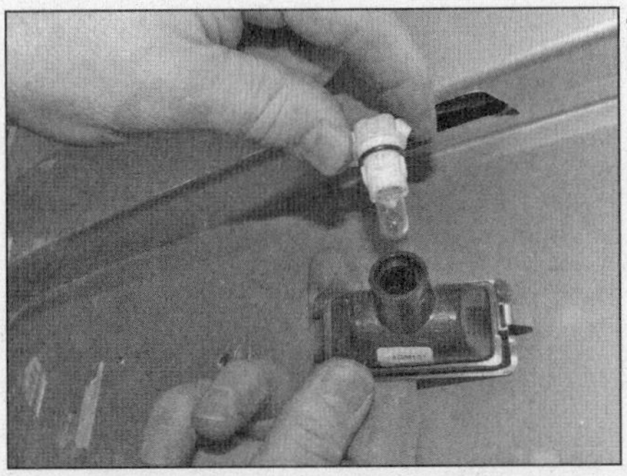

6.51a ...remove the bulb holder...

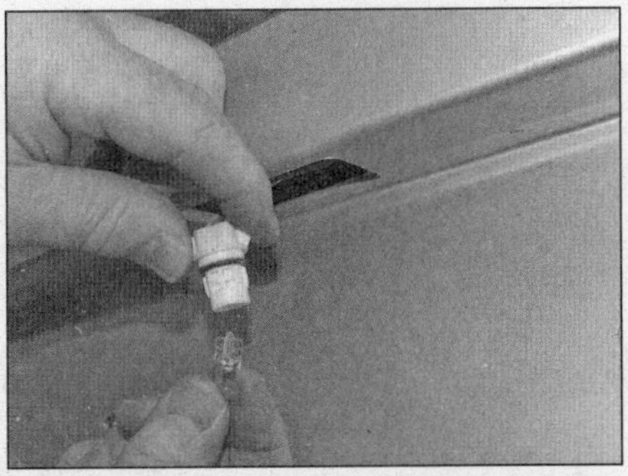

6.51b ...and pull out the wedge style bulb

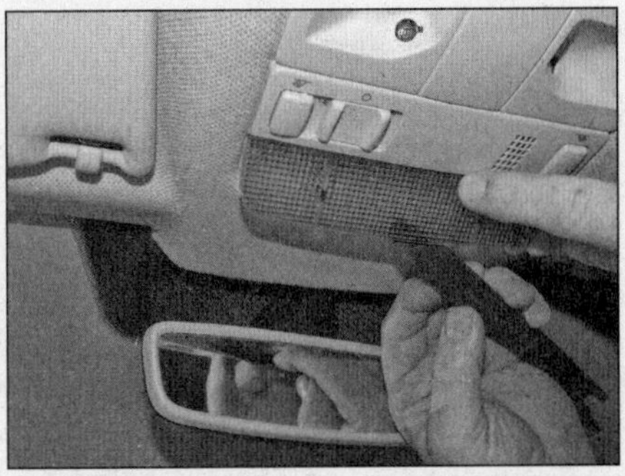

7.2 Unclip the interior light lens

7 Bulbs (interior lights) – renewal

General

1 Whenever a bulb is renewed, note the following points:

a) Switch off the ignition and all electrical consumers before commencing work.

b) Remember that if the light has just been in use the bulb may be extremely hot.

c) Always check the bulb contacts and holder, ensuring that there is clean metal-to-metal contact between them. Clean off any corrosion or dirt before fitting a new bulb.

d) Wherever bayonet-type bulbs are fitted ensure that the live contact(s) bear firmly against the bulb contact.

e) Always ensure that the new bulb is of the correct rating and that it is completely clean before fitting it.

Front courtesy/reading light

2 Using a thin screwdriver, carefully release the locking lugs and remove the lens from the light unit **(see illustration)**.

3 Depending on bulb being replaced, it is either a festoon type bulb or a wedge type bulb **(see illustrations)**.

4 Fit the new bulb using a reversal of the removal procedure.

Luggage/glovebox storage compartment light

5 Carefully prise the light unit from its location in the load area or storage compartment. Pull out the wedge-type bulb or compress the the retaining springs on the festoon type bulb to release it **(see illustrations)**.

6 Fit the new bulb using a reversal of the removal procedure.

Instrument panel illumination/ warning lights

7 The instrument panel illumination/warning lights are non-renewable LED's.

Heater/ventilation control panel illumination

8 The control panel is illuminated by LED's built into the panel. Consequently, if a fault develops, renewal of the panel is necessary.

Switch illumination

9 The switch illumination bulbs are integral with the switches. If a bulb fails, the complete switch must be renewed.

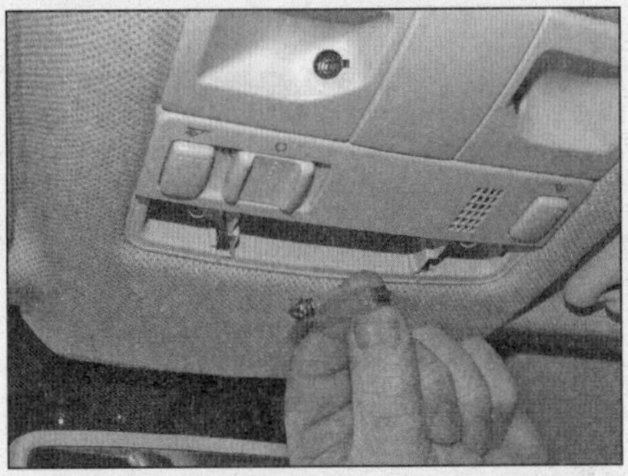

7.3a Festoon type bulb in the centre...

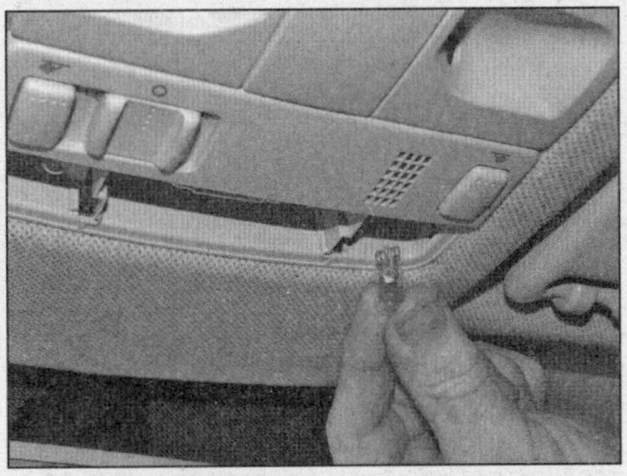

7.3b...and wedge type each side

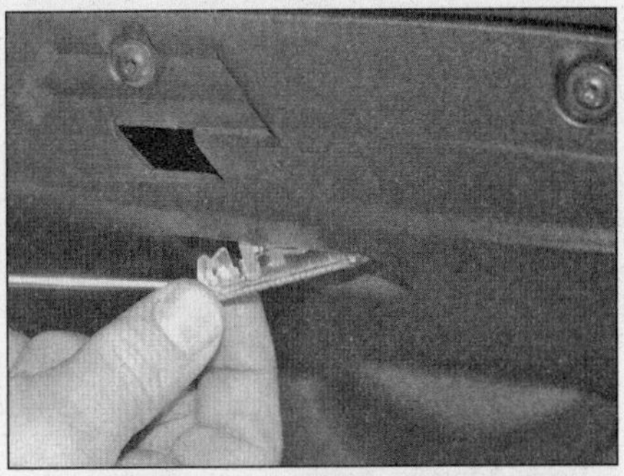

7.5a Prise out the glovebox light

7.5b Turn over the lamp and remove the bulb

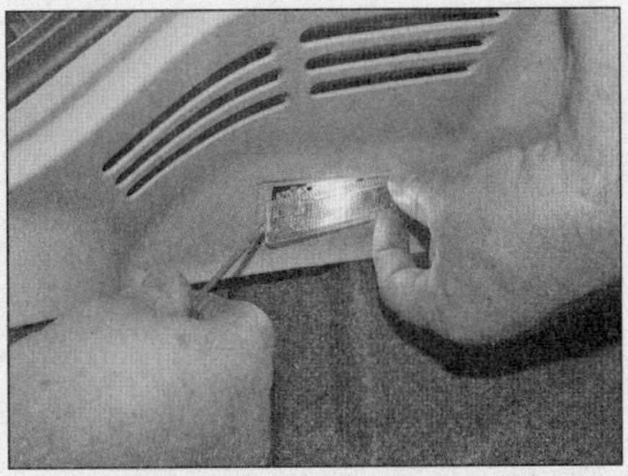

7.5c Release the load area lamp with a small screwdriver

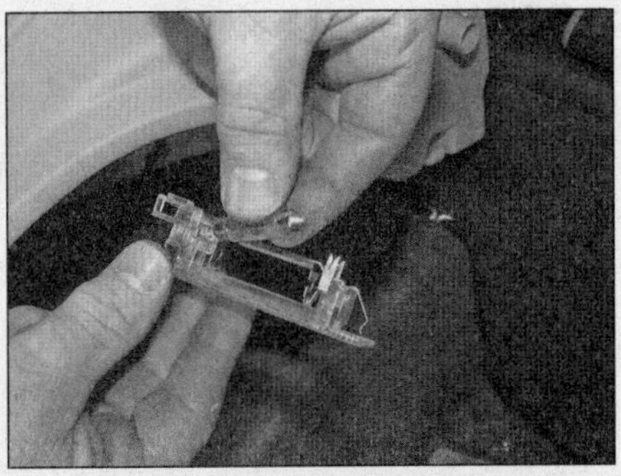

7.5d Pull out the festoon type bulb

8.3 Mark the position of the headlight

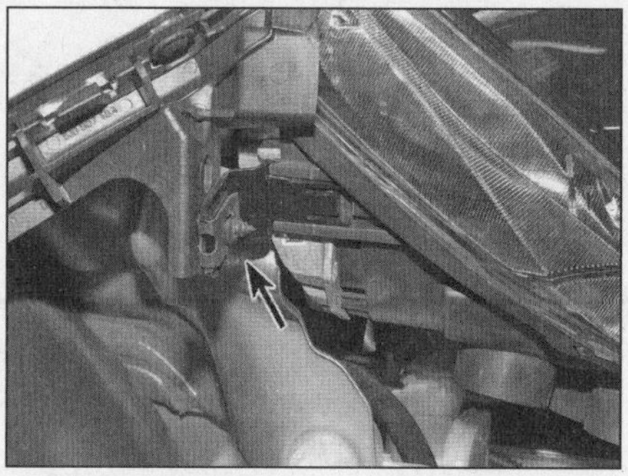

8.4a Remove the outer bolt...

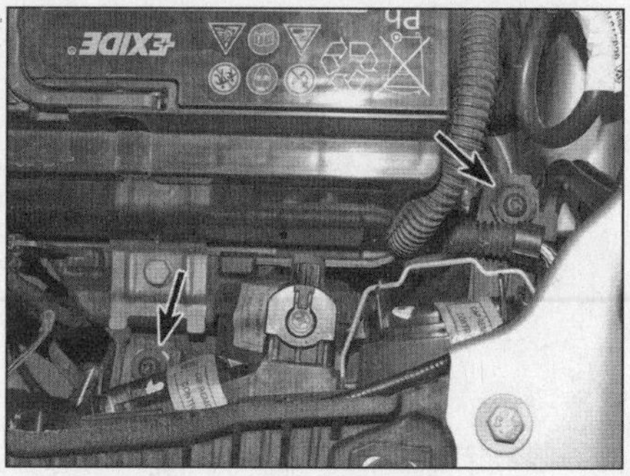

8.4b ...the inner bolts...

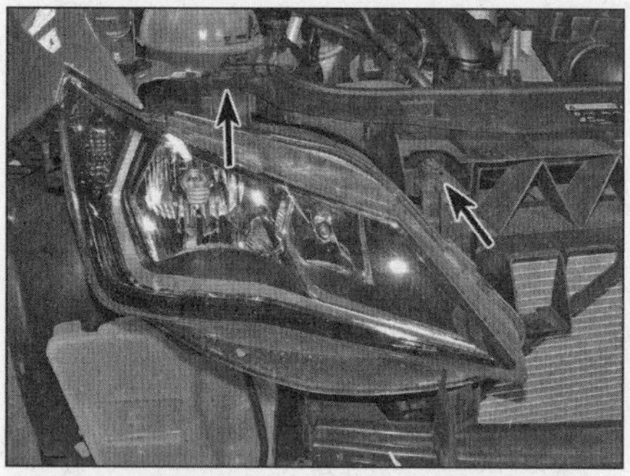

8.4c ...and the top bolts

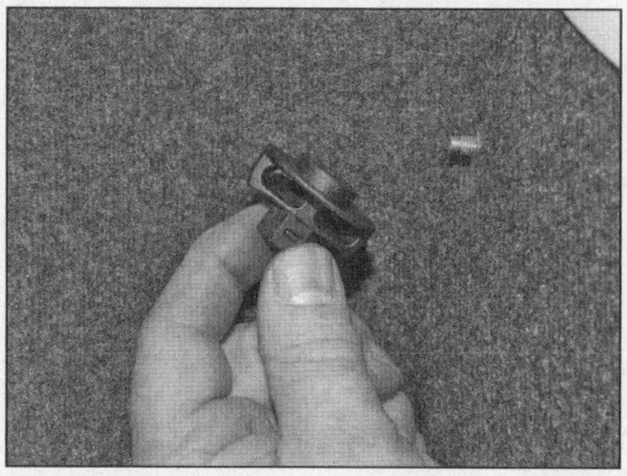

8.8a Remove the nut...

8.8b ...or open the cover

8 Exterior light units – removal and refitting

1 Before removing any light units, switch off the ignition and all electrical consumers, and then remove the ignition key.

Headlight

2 Remove the front bumper as described in Chapter 11 Section 6.

3 Mark the position of the headlight mountings on the mounting brackets, to ensure correct alignment on refitting **(see illustration)**.

4 Support the headlight unit and then undo the mounting bolts **(see illustrations)**.

5 Unplug the wiring multiplug connector as the headlight is withdrawn.

6 Refitting is a reversal of removal, but on completion, check that the headlight is aligned flush with the surrounding bodywork. If not, slacken the mounting bolts and re-align the light unit. Finally, have the headlight alignment checked at the earliest opportunity.

Caution: After refitting a gas discharge headlamp, the basic setting of the Automatic Range Control system should be checked. Because of the requirement for specialised equipment, a Seat dealer or suitably equipped specialist can only carry this out. The headlight bulb contains gas at very high pressure, and it is recommended that gloves and eye protection be worn to prevent potential personal injury.

Front foglight

7 The procedure is described as part of the front foglight bulb renewal procedure in Section 6.

Rear light cluster

8 Open the tailgate and on hatchback models unscrew the plastic securing nut on the inside rear of the light unit. On estate models remove the cover **(see illustrations)**.

9 On hatchback models pull the light from the rear wing and disconnect the wiring plug **(see illustrations)**.

10 On estate models, disconnect the wiring plug and unscrew the mounting bolts from the rear of the light unit **(see illustration)**.

11 Pull the light out from the rear wing and remove it.

12 Refitting is a reversal of removal.

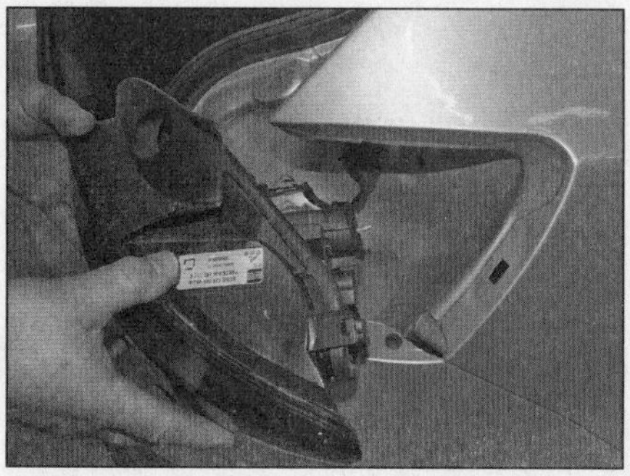

8.9a Pull out the light and...

8.9b ...and disconnect the wiring plug

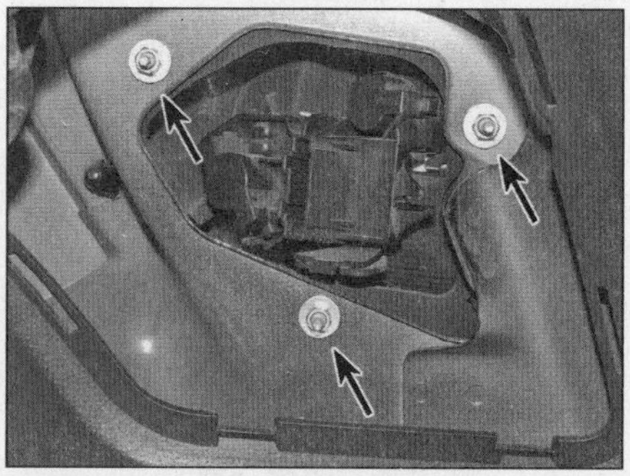

8.10 Unscrew the nuts

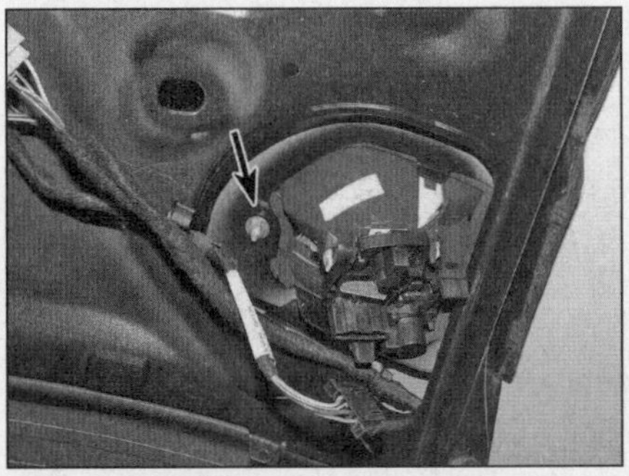

8.15a Remove the nut and...

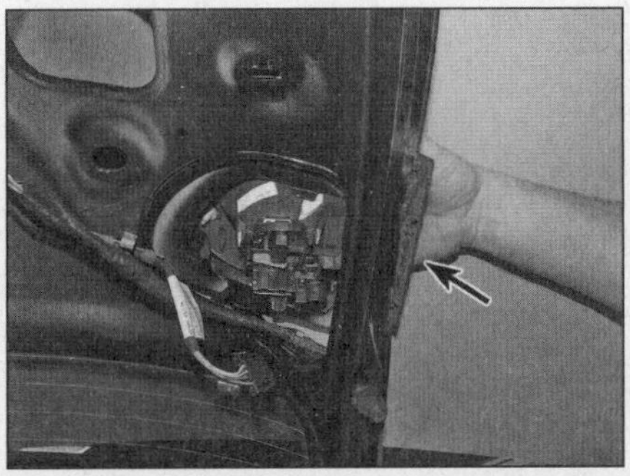

8.15b ...unhook the light from the edge of the tailgate

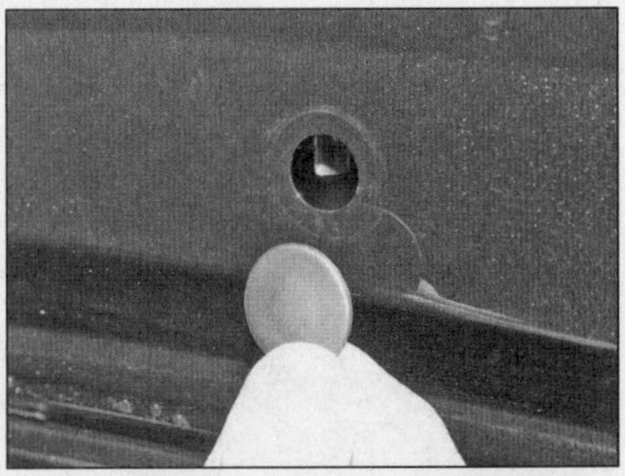

8.19 Remove the blanking plugs

8.20a Release the lamp

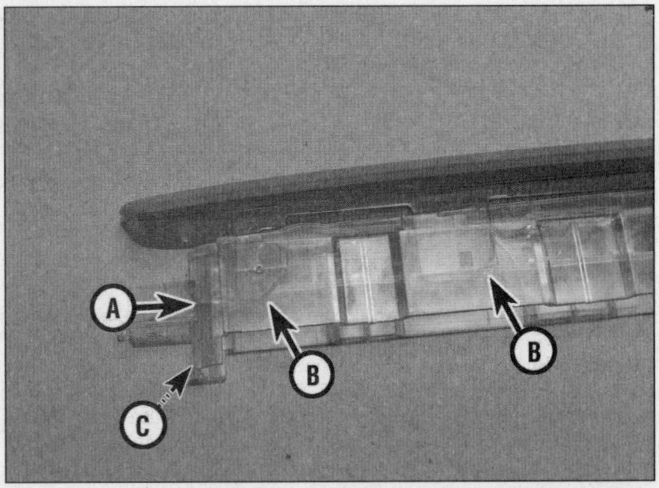

8.20b A detailed view of the locking cams on the brake light. Section A slides along the reflector and releases it from the cams (B). C is the leverage point through the tailgate

Tailgate mounted light cluster (estate models)

13 Open the tailgate and remove the light cover. The light can be removed with the tailgate trim fitted, but access is restricted (and the nut will need to be slackened with a spanner as there is no room for a socket).

14 Remove the tailgate trim as described in Chapter 11 Section 16.

15 Remove the nut and unhook the light from the tailgate **(see illustrations)**.

16 Disconnect the wiring connector as the light unit is withdrawn from the vehicle.

17 Refitting is a reversal of removal.

High level brake light

Note: *The light is of LED design; therefore if faulty the complete unit must be renewed.*

Note: *On later models with a full size spoiler the spoiler must be removed to remove the remove the brake light. As the spoiler is bonded to the tailgate glass this task is best left to a bodyshop or Seat dealer.*

18 On models built after 02/2012 the brake light is removed from the outside with a trim tool. Protect the paintwork with masking tape and lever out the brake light. Disconnect the brake light as it is removed.

19 Open the tailgate and remove the blanking plugs **(see illustration)**.

20 Use a screwdriver through the blanking plug aperture and release the locking tang by pushing it towards the centre of the tailgate **(see illustrations)**.

21 Pull out the lamp **(see illustration)** and disconnect the wiring plug.

22 Fit the new light unit using a reversal of the removal procedure, but lock the light in place by pushing the movable section home through the opposite (right-hand) hole in the tailgate. Refit the blanking grommets.

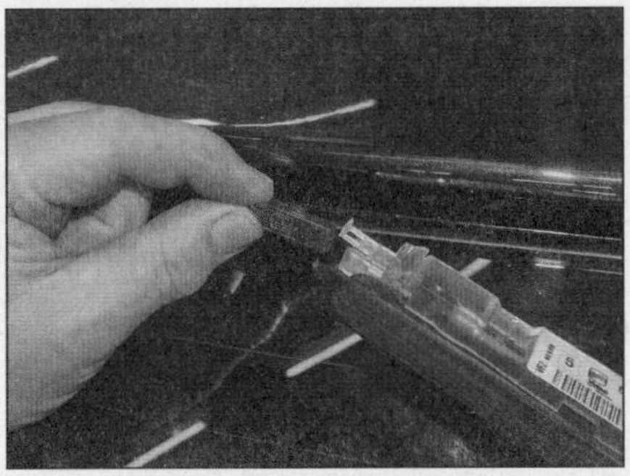

8.21 Remove the lamp

Rear number plate light

23 The procedure is described as part of the rear number plate light bulb renewal procedure in Section 6.

9 Headlight beam adjustment components – removal and refitting

Headlight adjustment switch

1 Removal of the switch is described in Section 5.

2 Removal and refitting of the switch assembly is covered in Section 5.

Headlight range adjustment motor

3 Remove the headlight as described in Section 8.

4 Remove the cover from the rear of the headlight **(see illustration)**.

5 Turn the range control motor anti-clockwise and pull it upwards and to the left slightly to disengage the ball-head from the guide on the

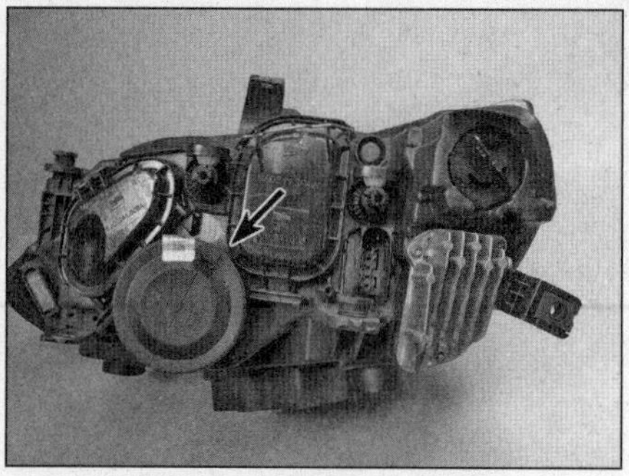

9.4 Remove the cover

9.5 Remove the range control motor

10.2 Headlight adjustment screws

reflector, then disconnect the wiring connector to remove **(see illustration)**.

6 Refitting is a reversal of removal, making sure the ball joint mounting is correctly located in the headlight reflector.

10 Headlight beam alignment – general information

1 Accurate adjustment of the headlight beam is only possible using optical beam setting equipment and this work should therefore be carried out by a Seat dealer or suitably-equipped workshop. All UK MOT stations have the required equipment.

2 For reference, the headlights can be manually adjusted using the adjuster assemblies fitted to the top of each light unit **(see illustration)**. The inner adjuster alters the lateral position of the beam whilst the outer adjuster alters the height of the beam.

11 Instrument panel – removal and refitting

Removal

1 Switch off the ignition and all electrical consumers and remove the ignition key. Release the steering wheel adjustment handle, pull the wheel out as far as possible, and set it in the lowest position.

2 Remove the steering column upper shroud and (on early models) the instrument panel surround, as described in Chapter 11 Section 26.

3 Undo the retaining screws (two on later models, three on early models) securing the instrument panel in the facia**(see illustration)**.

4 Release the instrument panel from the facia, release the locking lever and disconnect the wiring plug from the rear of the instrument panel **(see illustrations)**.

Refitting

5 Refitting is a reversal of removal.

12 12V accessory socket – removal and refitting

Removal

Note: *A special tool is available from Seat that allows the 12v socket to be removed without dismantling the centre console.*

1 Disconnect the battery negative lead as described in Chapter 5A Section 3.

2 Remove the centre console as described in Chapter 11 Section 27.

3 Release the retaining clips and push the centre element out of the outer plastic mounting, then remove the socket from the centre console.

Refitting

4 Refitting is a reversal of removal.

13 Horn – removal and refitting

Removal

1 Switch off the ignition and all electrical consumers and remove the ignition key.

2 Remove the front bumper as described in Chapter 11 Section 6. It also possible to release the front of the left-hand side inner wheel arch liner and reach up behind the front bumper to access the horn.

3 Disconnect the wiring, then unscrew the mounting bolt and withdraw the horn together with the mounting bracket **(see illustration)**.

4 If required, unscrew the nut on the top of the horn to remove the bracket.

Refitting

5 Refitting is a reversal of removal.

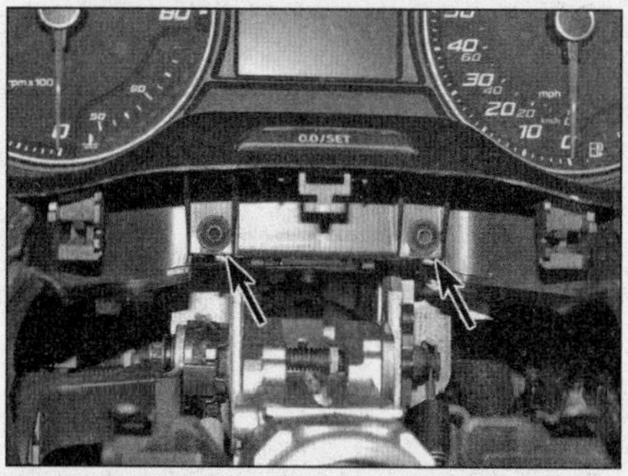

11.3 Undo the retaining screws

11.4a Withdraw it from the facia...

11.4b ...then release locking lever to disconnect the wiring connector

13.3 The horn mounted behind the front bumper cover on the left-hand side

15.2a Prise off the cover...

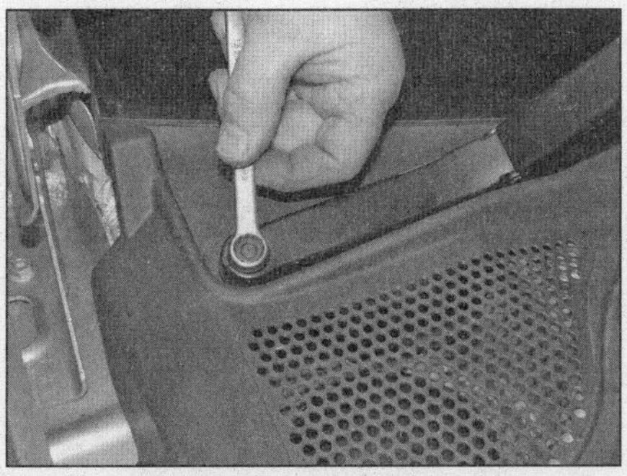
15.2b ...undo the securing nut...

15.2c ...then remove the wiper arm

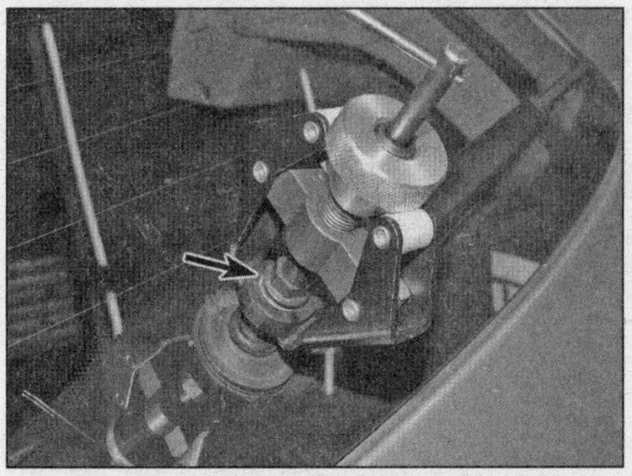
15.3 Use a small puller to remove wiper arm, if required. Note the nut refitted to the spindle to protect the threads

15.4a Unclip the cover

15.4b Remove the washer jet

14 Speedometer sensor – general information

1 Vehicle speed is determined from the ABS wheel sensor signals, and processed by the engine management ECU. This measures the rotational speed of the transmission final drive and converts the information into an electronic signal, which is then sent to the speedometer module in the instrument panel. On certain models, the signal is also used as an input by the engine management system ECU, and the trip computer.

15 Wiper arm – removal and refitting

Removal

1 Mark the parking position of the blades with masking tape.This will act as an alignment aid on refitting.

2 On front wiper arms, prise off the wiper arm spindle nut cover, then slacken but do not completely remove the spindle nut. Lift the blade off the glass and carefully rock the wiper arm from side to side, until it releases from the spindle. Remove the spindle nut and the wiper arm **(see illustrations)**. **Note:** *If both windscreen wiper arms are to be removed at the same time mark them for identification; the arms are not interchangeable.*

3 If the arm is a tight fit on the spindle, the arm can be removed from the spindle using a small puller**(see illustration)**.

4 On rear wiper arms, unclip the spindle nut cover and then carefully remove the washer jet by pulling it out with pliers **(see illustrations)**. Take care not to crush the jet.

5 Mark the position of the blade on the glass using masking tape.

6 Slacken but do not completely remove the spindle nut. Lift the blade off the glass and carefully rock the wiper arm from side to side, until it releases from the spindle. Remove the spindle nut and wiper arm **(see illustration)**.

7 Work the arm free from the spindle and remove it **(see illustration)**. Take particular care with the rear arm as the metal sleeve can be easily torn from the plastic arm. Use a puller if necessary.

15.6 Remove the securing nut

Refitting

8 Ensure that the wiper arm and spindle splines are clean and dry, and then refit the arm to the spindle, aligning the wiper blade with the tape fitted on removal. Refit the spindle nut, tightening it securely, and clip the nut cover back in position. On the rear wiper, make sure the washer jet is refitted and it is clear of any dirt.

16 Windscreen wiper motor and linkage – removal and refitting

Removal

1 Remove the wiper arms as described in Section 15.

15.7 Remove the wiper arm

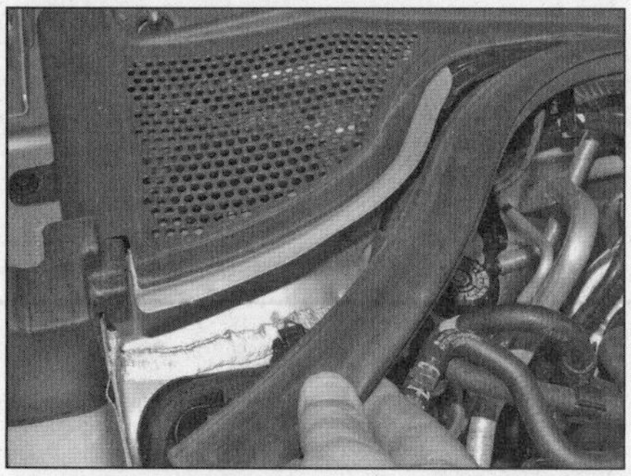
16.3 Peel back the rubber seal...

16.4 Remove the trim clips

16.5 Unclip the panel from along the windscreen seal

16.6 Remove the ECU...

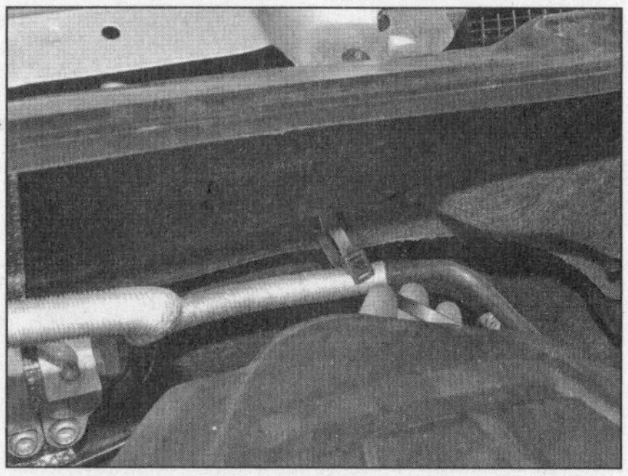
16.7a Release the vacuum line

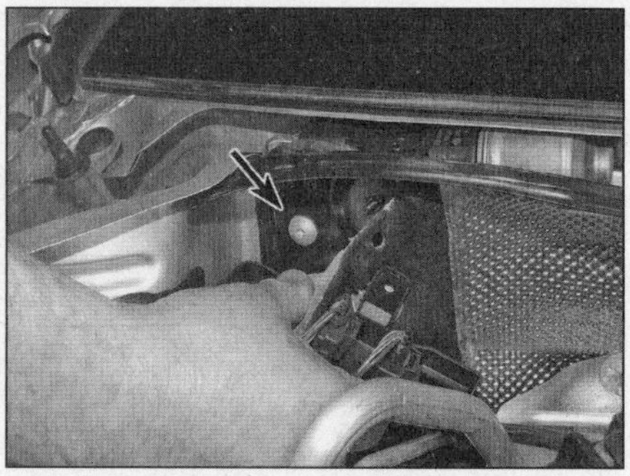
16.7b Fold back the insulation padding from the bulkhead

2 Disconnect the battery negative lead (as described in Chapter 5A Section 3).

3 Pull off the rubber sealing strip from along the top of the bulkhead **(see illustration)**.

4 Remove the 'scrivet' type trim clips from each end of the scuttle panel **(see illustration)**.

5 Working along the lower part of the windscreen, carefully pull the scuttle panel from the windscreen seal and remove the panel from the bulkhead **(see illustration)**.

Caution: Do not use a screwdriver lever between the cowling and windscreen, as this is likely to result in the windscreen cracking.

6 Remove the ECU from the left-hand rear of the bulkhead panel as described in Chapter 4A Section 4 (petrol models) or Chapter 4B Section 4, (diesel models). Remove the ECU from the mounting bracket **(see illustration)**.

7 Where required unclip the vacuum hose from the bulkhead. Working along the rear of the engine compartment, release the fasteners and remove the insulation padding from the bulkhead panel **(see illustrations)**.

8 Undo the retaining bolts and remove the bulkhead panel from the rear of the engine compartment **(see illustration)**.

9 Unscrew the mounting bolts and manoeuvre the windscreen wiper motor and linkage out from the scuttle **(see illustration)**.

10 Disconnect the wiring plug from the wiper motor **(see illustration)**.

11 Where required, recover the washers and spacers from the motor mounting rubbers, noting their locations, then inspect the rubbers for signs of damage or deterioration, and renew if necessary.

Refitting

12 Refitting is a reversal of removal, bearing in mind the following points.

a) *If the motor has been separated from the linkage, ensure that the marks made on the motor spindle and linkage before removal are aligned, and ensure that the linkage is orientated as noted before removal.*

b) *Ensure that the washers and spacers are fitted to the motor mounting rubbers as noted before removal.*

c) *Make sure the locating peg aligns with the*

16.8 Unbolt and remove the bulkhead panel

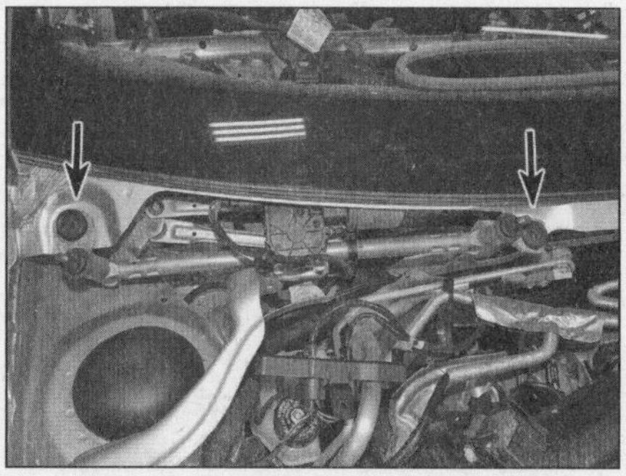
16.9 Undo the wiper motor/linkage mounting bolts

16.10 Disconnect the wiring plug

16.12 Make sure peg the peg fits in the grommet

17.3a Disconnect the washer hose...

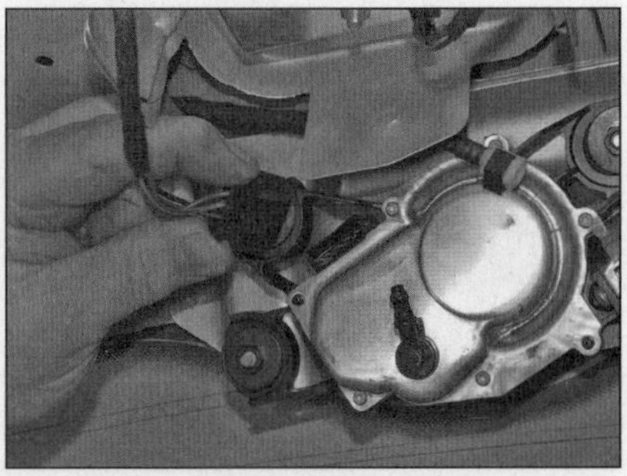

17.3b...and the wiring connector

grommet in the bulkhead, when refitting **(see illustration)**.

d) *Lubricate the windscreen cowling mounting slots with a silicone-based spray lubricant to ease installation. Do not strike the cowling to seat it in position as this could result in the windscreen cracking.*

e) *Refit the wiper arms as described in Section 15.*

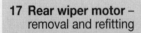

17 Rear wiper motor – removal and refitting

Removal

1 Remove the wiper arm as described in Section 15.

2 Open the tailgate, then remove the trim panel as described in Chapter 11 Section 16.

3 Release the locking collar and disconnect the washer hose from the wiper motor, then release the securing clip and unplug the wiring connector from the motor **(see illustrations)**.

4 Unscrew the three nuts securing the motor, and then withdraw the assembly. Note the position of the rubber sealing ring, renew if necessary **(see illustration)**.

Refitting

5 Refitting is a reversal of removal, but ensure that the motor shaft rubber sealing ring/ grommet is correctly refitted to prevent water leaks (the arrow mark must be at the top) **(see illustration)** and refit the wiper arm with reference to Section 15.

18 Washer system components – removal and refitting

Washer fluid reservoir and pumps

1 The reservoir is either mounted at the left-hand side of the engine bay or at the front right-hand side. Removal and refitting is essentially the same for both versions.

2 Switch off the ignition and all electrical consumers and remove the ignition key.

3 On models with the air filter behind the battery remove the air filter and battery. Remove the battery support tray as described in Chapter 5A Section 3.

4 Unclip or unbolt the filler neck **(see illustrations)**.

5 If the complete reservoir needs to be replaced, remove the front bumper and wing liner as described in Chapter 11 Section 6. Access to the pump is possible if the wing liner only is removed.

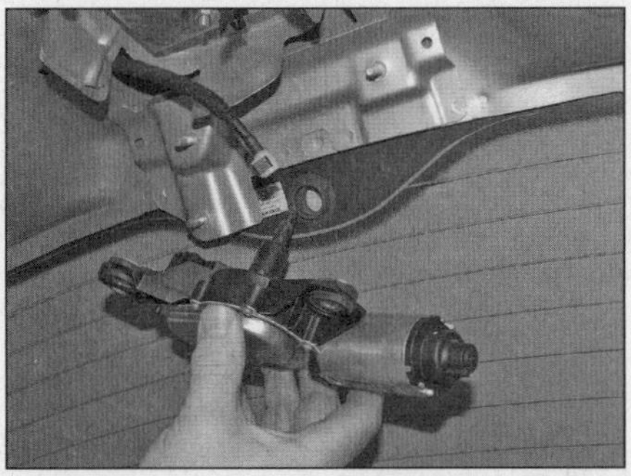

17.4 Removing the tailgate wiper motor

17.5 The arrow mark must be at the top of the sealing ring

18.4a Unclip the reservoir filler neck...

18.4b ...or unbolt it

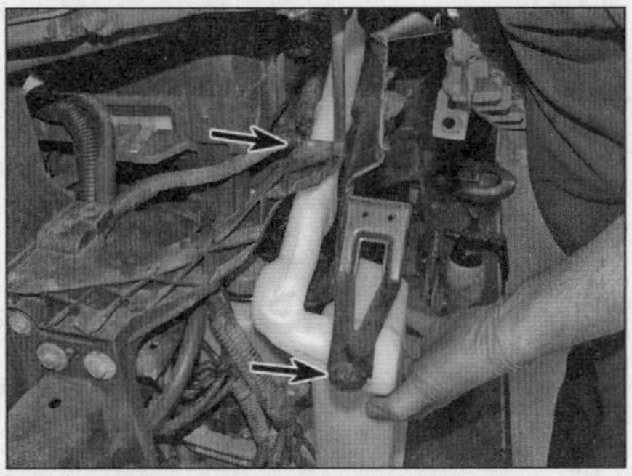

18.4c On models with the reservoir on the left, remove the nut and bolt (headlight removed for clarity)...

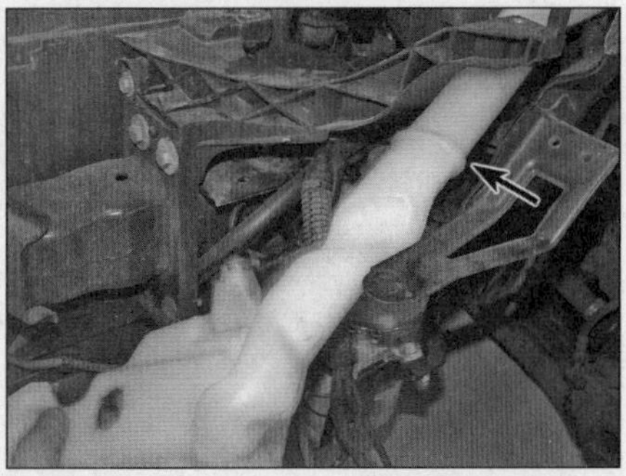

18.4d ...and manoeuvre the reservoir from the inner wing. Do not be tempted to separate the neck from the reservoir at the point show as this is a bonded joint

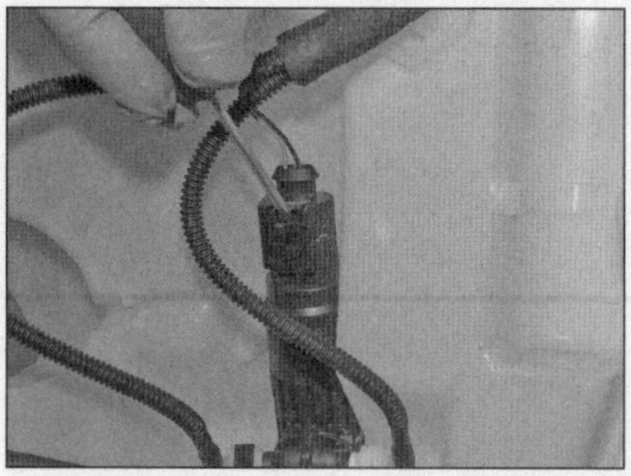

18.6 Disconnect the wiring plug

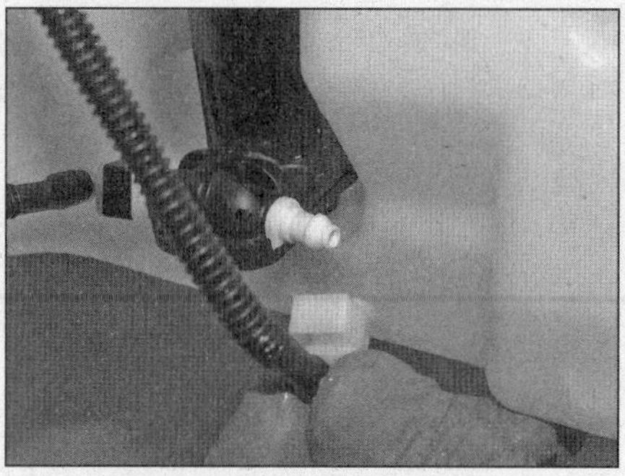

18.7 Disconnect the hoses

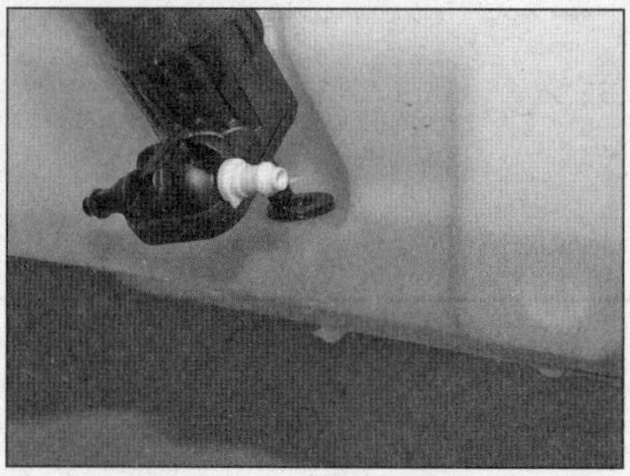

18.8 Remove the washer pump

6 Disconnect the wiring connector from the top of the washer pump **(see illustration)**.

7 Note the position of the hoses, and then disconnect them from the washer pump **(see illustration)**. Position a container beneath the reservoir to catch spilt fluid. **Note:** *Depending on model, there may be more than one washer pump.*

8 To remove the washer pump, pull it upwards from the reservoir and out from its rubber grommet **(see illustration)**. Position a container beneath the reservoir to catch spilt fluid.

9 Where fitted, disconnect the wiring plug from the sensor for the fluid level.

10 Release the retaining clip and disconnect the wiring loom from the top of the washer reservoir.

11 Unscrew the mounting nuts and then remove the reservoir from the vehicle **(see illustrations)**.

12 Refitting is a reversal of removal.

Windscreen washer jets

13 Use a trim tool and unclip the jet from the bonnet. Release the securing clip and disconnect the washer tube from the washer jet **(see illustrations)**.

14 Refitting is a reversal of removal.

Tailgate washer jet

15 The washer jet is fitted to the rear wiper arm spindle, lift up the wiper arm cover and pull the washer jet from the spindle **(see illustration)**.

16 On refitting, ensure that the jet is securely pushed into position. Check the operation of the jet. If necessary, adjust the nozzle, aiming the spray at a point slightly above the area of glass swept by the wiper blade.

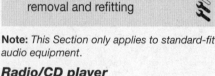

19 Audio/Multimedia control unit – removal and refitting

Note: *This Section only applies to standard-fit audio equipment.*

Radio/CD player

Removal

1 The radio/CD player is equipped with an electronic anti-theft system linked to the instrument panel. If the voltage supply to the radio is temporarily disconnected, the radio will function again when the supply is reconnected, without entering the safety code number, provided the radio is located in the original vehicle. Should the radio operation be blocked, normal operation can be restored by entering the correct anti-theft code.

2 Remove any CDs, which may be in the unit. Switch off the ignition and all electrical consumers, and remove the ignition key.

3 On early models, carefully unclip the trim panel from around the Radio/CD player **(see illustration)**.

4 Undo the radio/CD player mounting screws, and pull out the unit until the wiring plugs can be disconnected **(see illustrations)**. Pull the aerial lead from the rear of the unit, and then release the locking clip and disconnect the wiring block connector from the rear of the unit.

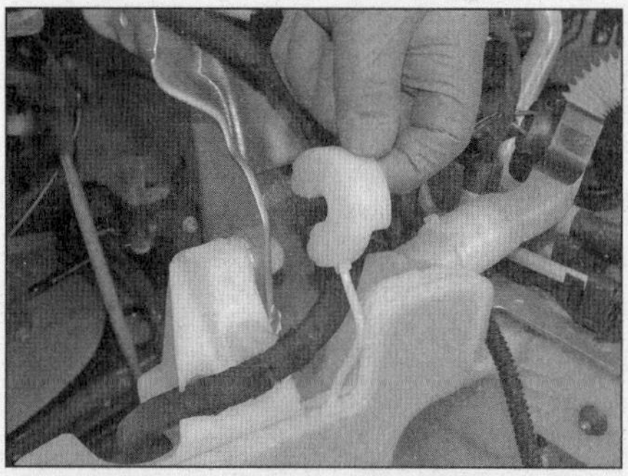

18.11a Remove the collar...

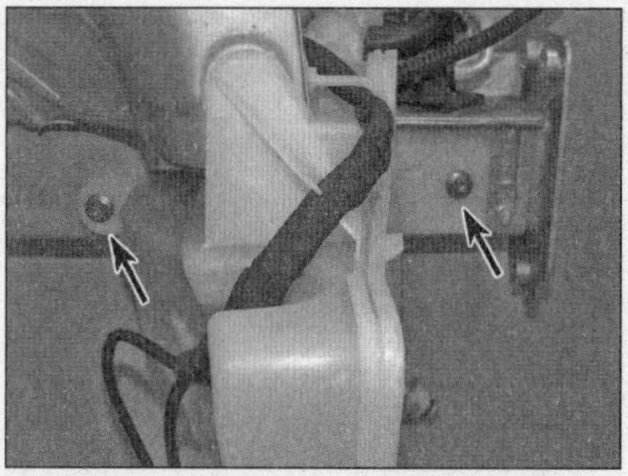

18.11b ... and the mounting nuts

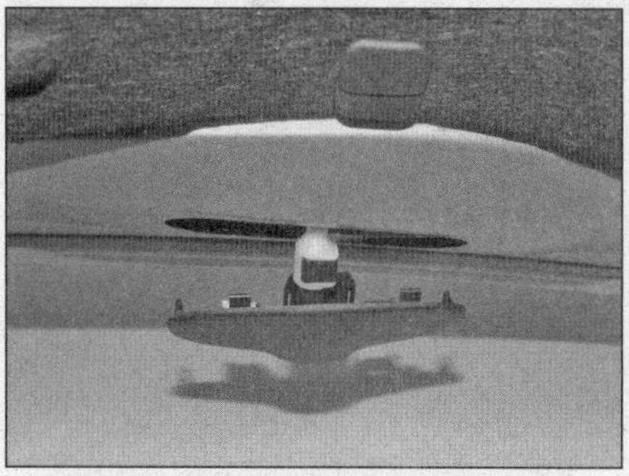

18.13a Unclip the washer jet...

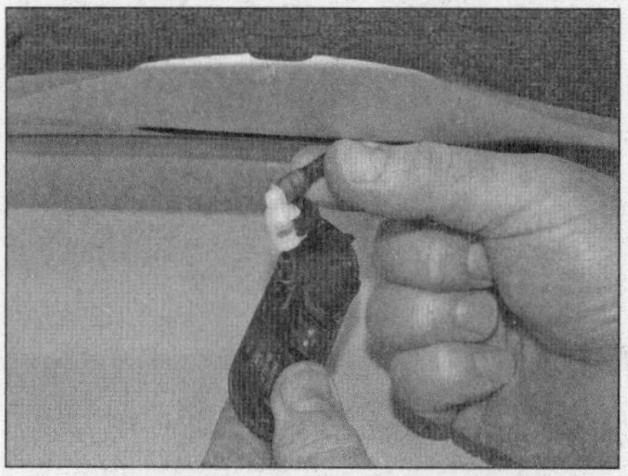

18.13b...and disconnect the washer hose

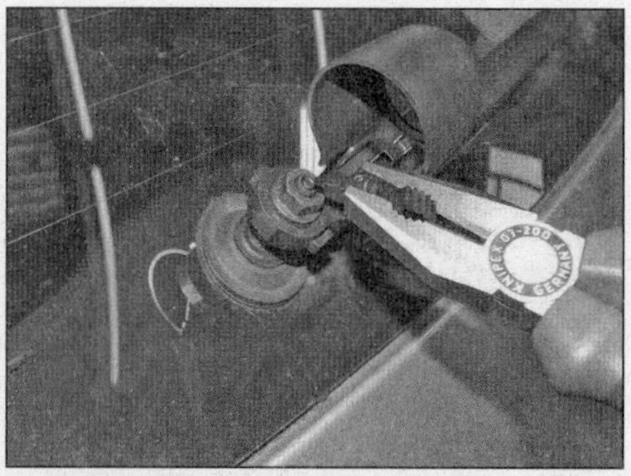

18.15 Pull the washer jet from the spindle

19.3 Carefully remove the trim by releasing the retaining clips

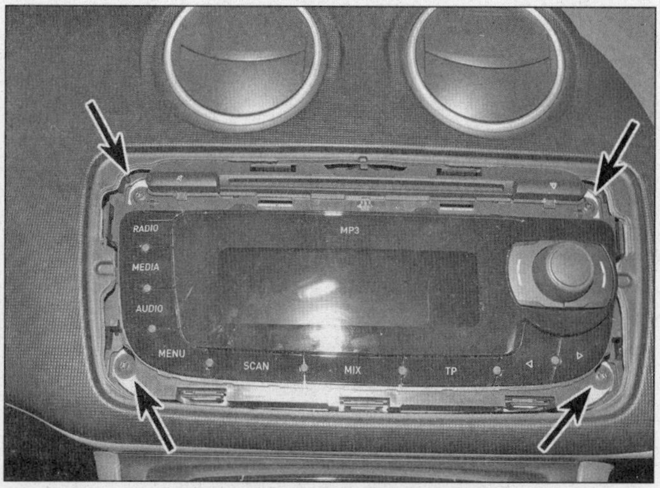

19.4a Undo the mounting screws

5 On some later models a set of four audio set removal keys will be required to remove the unit **(see illustrations)**.

Refitting

6 Refitting is a reversal of removal.

Multimedia interface

7 Switch off the ignition and all electrical consumers, and remove the ignition key.
8 The interface (where fitted) is either mounted in the front section of the centre console, or below the heater control panel.
9 On models fitted with the interface in the centre console, remove the front section of the centre console as described in Chapter 11 Section 27 and then push the interface from the front section. Disconnect the wiring plug.
10 On models with the interface below the heater control panel, remove the screws and lower the panel. Disconnect the wiring plugs and remove the panel. Unscrew the interface from the panel and remove it.
11 Refitting is a reversal of removal.

20 Loudspeakers – removal and refitting

Front treble speaker

1 Switch off the ignition and all electrical consumers, and remove the ignition key.
2 Remove the A-pillar trim panel as described in Chapter 11 Section 28.
3 The loudspeaker is integral with the A-pillar trim panel and can only be renewed as a complete unit.
4 Refitting is a reversal of removal.

Front and rear bass speakers

5 Switch off the ignition and all electrical consumers, and remove the ignition key.
6 Remove the relevant door inner trim, as described in Chapter 11 Section 13. On 3 door models remove the rear side panel as described in Chapter 11 Section 26.

19.4b Withdraw the unit...

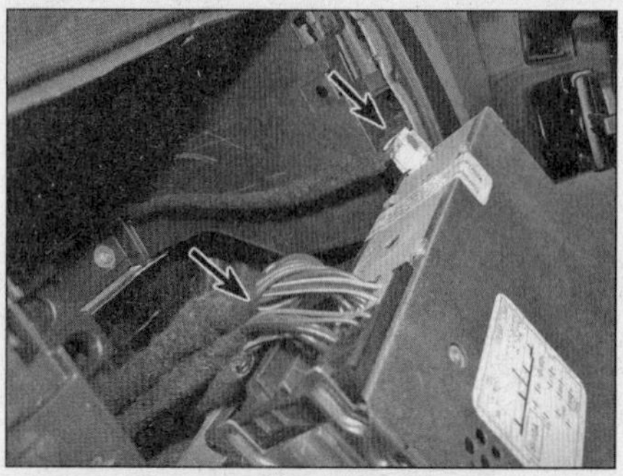

19.4c ...and disconnect the wiring and aerial plugs

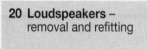

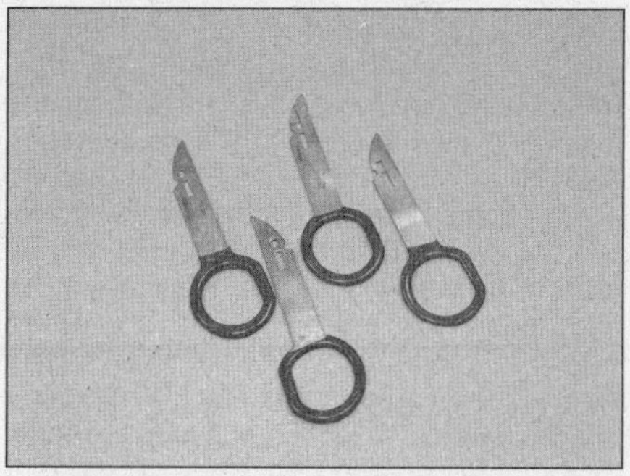

19.5a The correct type of release key

19.5b Insert the keys with the straight edge to the outside

19.5c Fit all the keys, pull out the unit...

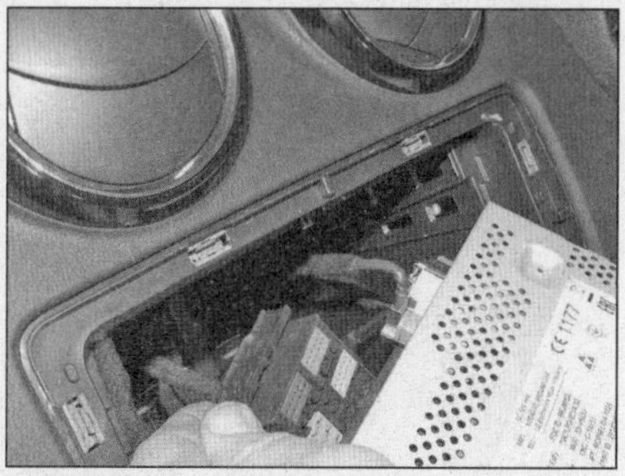

19.5d ...and disconnect the wiring plugs

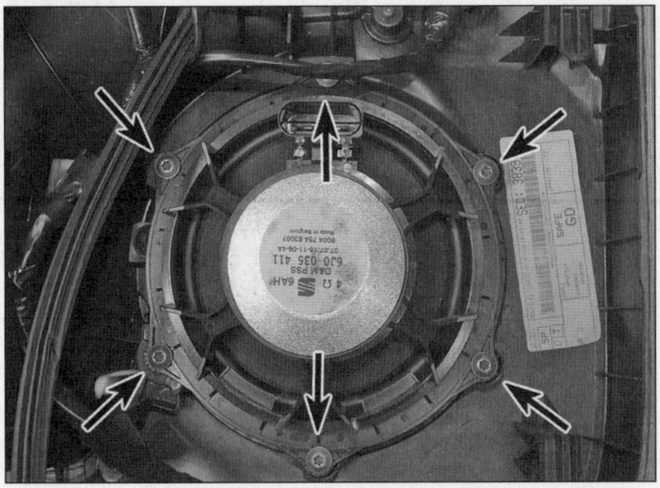

20.8a Remove the screws (door trim mounted speakers)...

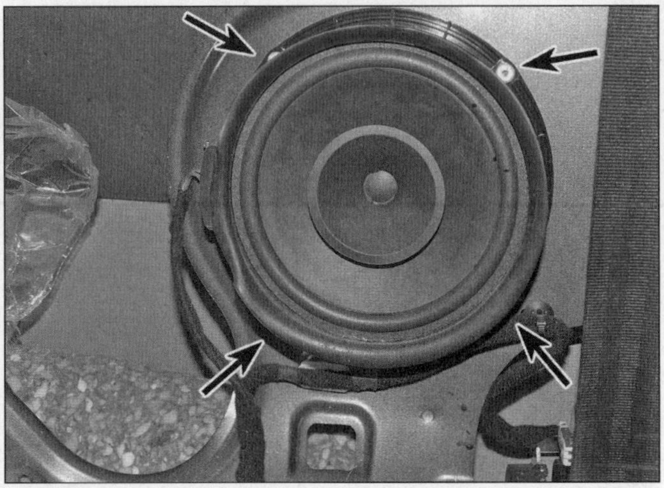
20.8b ...or drill out the rivets (3 door model rear speakers)

7 Disconnect the wiring plug from the loudspeaker.

8 Remove the torx type screws and lift out the speaker **(see illustrations)**.

9 Refitting is a reversal of removal.

21 Radio aerials, filters and modules – removal and refitting

Aerials

1 The aerial is fitted to the rear of the roof panel and the mast can be unscrewed.

2 To access the aerial the roof lining must be partially (or completely removed). Remove all the rear trim panels as described in Chapter 11 Section 25.

3 Carefully lower the rear of the headlining, taking care not to damage it. Disconnect the wiring; note the fitted position of the wiring, as there may be more than one connector (for aerial, telephone and navigation GPS), depending on model.

4 Unscrew the securing nut, remove the serrated washer and withdraw the aerial base from the roof. Hold the aerial base as the nut is being unscrewed to prevent the base from rotating and scratching the roof panel. Recover the rubber spacer.

5 Refitting is a reversal of removal, but make sure that any guide lugs on the rubber spacer are correctly located in the aerial base.

22 Anti-theft alarm system and engine immobiliser – general information

Note: *This information is applicable only to the anti-theft alarm system fitted by Seat as standard equipment.*

1 Models in the range are fitted with an anti-theft alarm system as standard equipment. The alarm has switches on all the doors (including the tailgate/boot lid), the bonnet and the ignition switch. If the tailgate/boot lid, bonnet or any of the doors are opened whilst the alarm is set, the alarm horn will sound and the hazard warning lights will flash. Some models are equipped with an internal monitoring system, which will activate the alarm system if any movement in the cabin is detected.

2 The alarm is set using the key in the driver's or passenger's front door lock, and tailgate/boot lid lock, or with the central locking remote control transmitter. The alarm system will then start to monitor its various switches approximately 30 seconds later.

3 With the alarm set, if the tailgate/boot lid is unlocked, the lock switch sensing will automatically be switched off but the door and bonnet switches will still be active. Once the tailgate/boot lid is shut and locked again, the switch sensing will be switched back on.

4 All models are fitted with an immobiliser system, which is activated by the ignition switch. A transponder reading coil on the ignition switch reads a code contained within the ignition key. The system sends a signal to the engine management electronic control unit (ECU), which allows the engine to start if the code is correct. If an incorrect ignition key is used, the engine will not start.

5 If a fault is suspected with the alarm or immobiliser systems, the vehicle should be taken to a Seat dealer for examination. They will have access to a special diagnostic tester that will quickly trace any fault present in the system.

23 Airbag system – general information and precautions

Warning: Before carrying out any operations on the airbag system, disconnect the battery negative terminal (as described in Chapter 5A Section 3). When operations are complete, make sure no one is inside the vehicle when the battery is reconnected.

- ***Note that the airbags must not be subjected to temperatures in excess of 90°C. When the airbag is removed, ensure that it is stored with the pad upwards to prevent possible inflation.***
- ***Do not allow any solvents or cleaning agents to contact the airbag assemblies. They must be cleaned using only a damp cloth.***
- ***The airbags and control unit are both sensitive to impact. If either is dropped or damaged they should be renewed.***

1 A driver's airbag and passenger's airbag are fitted as standard to the Ibiza range. Certain models may have curtain airbags (behind the headlining) and side impact airbags (in the seats) fitted. The airbag system consists of the airbag unit (complete with gas generator), which is fitted to the steering wheel (driver's side), facia (passenger's side), roof (where applicable) and front seats, an impact sensor, the control unit and a warning light in the instrument panel.

2 The airbag system is triggered in the event of a heavy frontal or side impact above a predetermined force; depending on the point of impact. The airbag is inflated within milliseconds and forms a safety cushion between the driver and the steering wheel, the passenger and the facia, and in the case of side impact, between front seat occupants and the sides of the cabin. This prevents contact between the upper body and cabin interior, and therefore greatly reduces the risk of injury. The airbag then deflates almost immediately.

3 Every time the ignition is switched on, the airbag control unit performs a self-test. The self-test takes approximately 3 seconds and during this time the airbag warning light on the facia is illuminated. After the self-test has been completed the warning light should

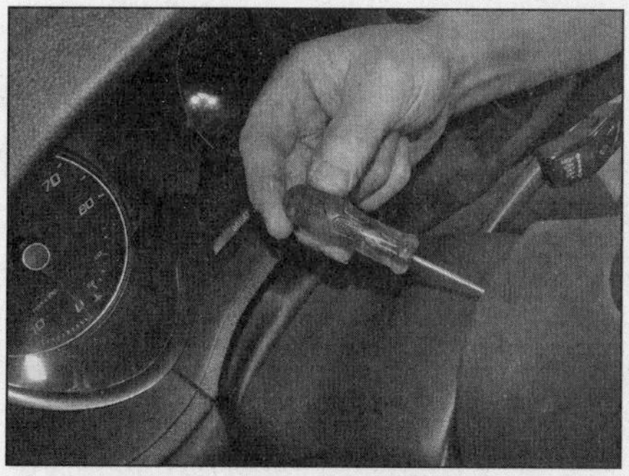

24.4a Insert a screwdriver...

24.4b ...and release the spring clips

24.4c Pull out the airbag and...

go out. If the warning light fails to come on, remains illuminated after the initial 3-second period or comes on at any time when the vehicle is being driven, there is a fault in the airbag system. The vehicle should then be taken to a Seat dealer for examination at the earliest possible opportunity.

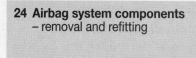

24 Airbag system components – removal and refitting

Note: *Refer to the warnings in Section 23 before carrying out the following operations.*

1 Disconnect the battery negative lead (as described in Chapter 5A Section 3) then continue as described under the relevant heading.

Caution: To prevent any discharge of static electricity into the airbag circuit, temporarily touch the vehicle bodywork before disconnecting the wiring from any airbag unit.

Driver's airbag

2 Set the front wheels to the straight-ahead position, and release the steering lock by inserting the ignition key.

3 Adjust the steering column to its highest position by releasing the adjustment handle, then extend the steering wheel as far as possible. Lock the column in this position.

4 With the spokes in the vertical position, insert a screwdriver into the hole in the upper rear of the steering wheel hub, then move it up to release the clip and free the airbag locking lug **(see illustrations)**. Now turn the steering wheel through 180° and release the remaining airbag locking lug.

5 Turn the steering wheel to its central, straight-ahead position.

Warning: Position the airbag in a safe and secure place, away from the work area.

6 When refitting make sure the steering wheel is in the straight-ahead position, then locate the airbag module in position and reconnect the wiring. Carefully press in the module until both locking lugs are heard to engage. Reconnect the battery negative lead, ensuring that nobody is inside the vehicle as the lead is connected.

24.4d ...disconnect the wiring plug

Passenger's airbag

7 Remove the glovebox with reference to Chapter 11 Section 26.

8 Working inside the upper part of the facia disconnect the wiring plug **(see illustration)**.

9 With difficulty remove the mounting bolts and lower the airbag **(see illustration)**.

Warning: Position the airbag in a safe and secure place, in an upright position, away from the work area.

10 Refitting is a reversal of removal, but tighten the mounting screws to the specified torque. Reconnect the battery negative lead, ensuring that nobody is inside the vehicle as the lead is connected.

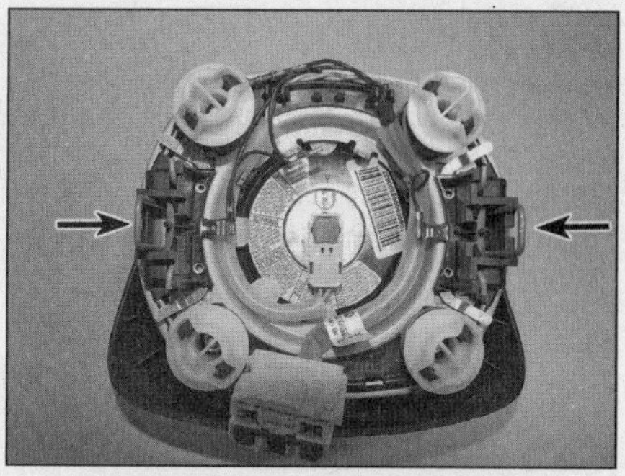

24.4e Note that on earlier models the spring clips are on the airbag, not the steering wheel

Front seat side impact airbags

11 The side impact air bags are integral with the seats. As seat upholstery removal requires considerable skill and experience, if it is to be carried out without damage, it is best entrusted to an expert.

Roof curtain and rear side airbags

12 This work involves removing the headlining and major dismantling of interior trim panels, and is best entrusted to a Seat dealer.

Airbag control unit

13 The airbag control unit is located beneath the centre of the facia, under the heater housing.

14 Remove the centre console as described in Chapter 11 Section 27.

24.8 Disconnect the wiring plug

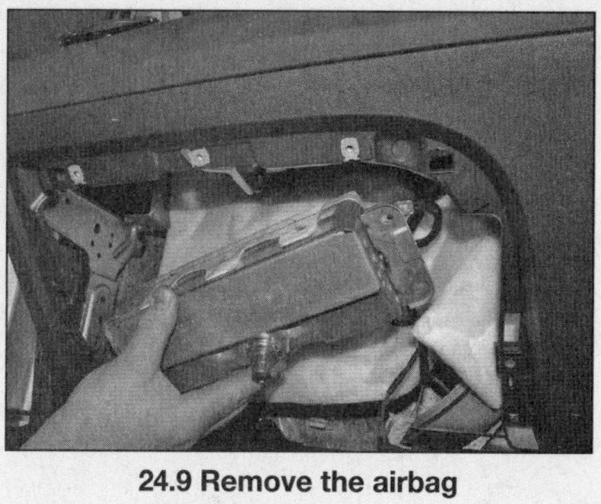

24.9 Remove the airbag

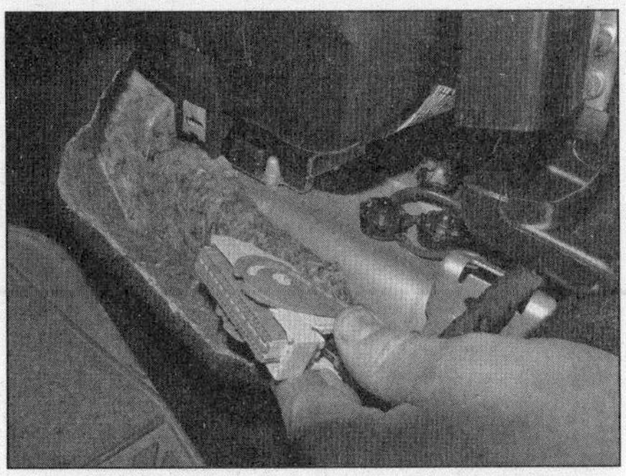

24.15 Disconnect the wiring plug

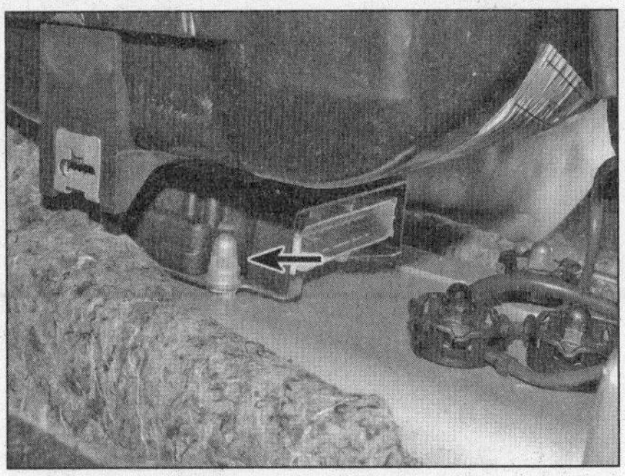

24.16a Remove the 'acorn' nuts with difficulty (one shown)

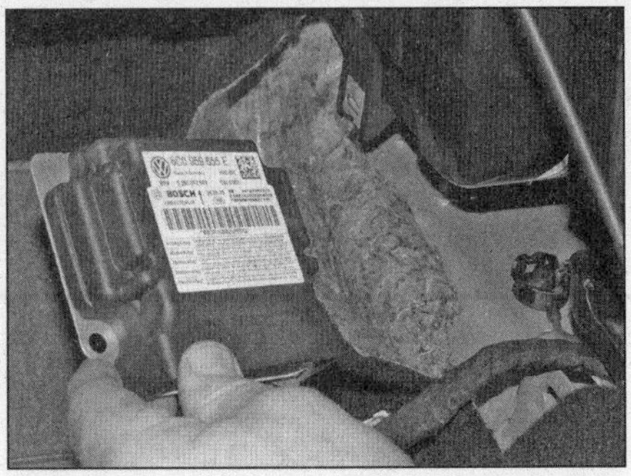

24.16b Lift the unit up and over the studs. Note that the unit is a tight fit and difficult to remove

15 Pull back the carpet/insulation, then release (with difficulty) the locking lever and disconnect the wiring from the control unit **(see illustration)**.

16 Unscrew the nuts and remove the control unit from the vehicle **(see illustrations)**.

17 Refitting is the reverse of removal making sure the wiring connector is securely reconnected. Reconnect the battery negative lead, ensuring that nobody is inside the vehicle as the lead is connected.

Airbag wiring contact unit

18 The airbag contact unit/clock spring is secured to the steering column switch assembly, remove the steering wheel as described in Chapter 10 Section 15.

19 Remove the upper and lower column shrouds as described in Chapter 11 Section 26.

20 The airbag clock spring/slip-ring must be held in its central position while it is removed, to ensure correct refitting. Secure the clock spring in position with tape **(see illustration)**.

21 Disconnect the wiring plug and either remove the screws (later models) or unclip the clock spring from the switch assembly. Withdraw the clock spring **(see illustrations)**. Note that on early models where the switch assembly is held on to the column with a screw, then removing the complete switch assembly and then separating the clock spring from the switches on the bench is an alternative method.

22 When refitting the switch assembly. Reconnect the battery negative lead, ensuring that nobody is inside the vehicle as the lead is connected.

Passenger airbag on/off switch

23 The switch is located inside the glovebox, remove the switch with reference to Section 5.

Side crash sensor

24 Remove the B-pillar trim panel, as described in Chapter 11 Section 25.

25 Disconnect the wiring from the crash sensor, then undo the retaining screw and withdraw the sensor from the door pillar **(see illustration)**.

26 Refitting is a reversal of removal. Make sure that nobody is inside the vehicle when first switching on the ignition.

24.20 Secure the clock spring with tape. Note the alignment arrow and notch (A)

24.21a Disconnect the wiring plug...

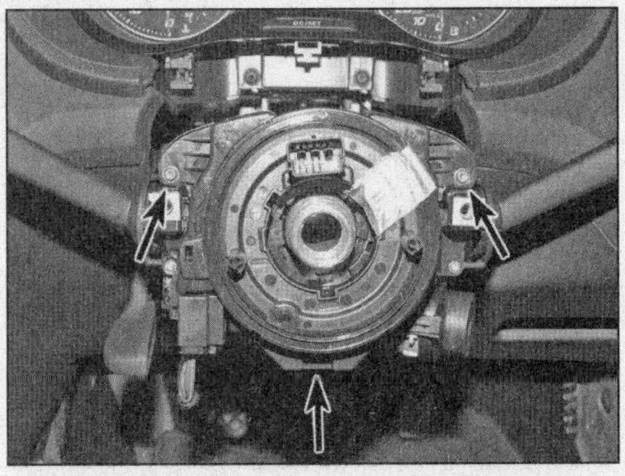

24.21b ...remove the screws and...

24.21c ...remove the clock spring

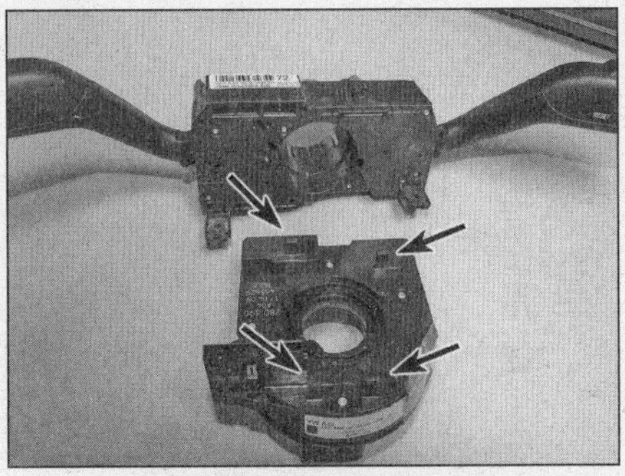

24.21d On early models unclip the clock spring on the bench

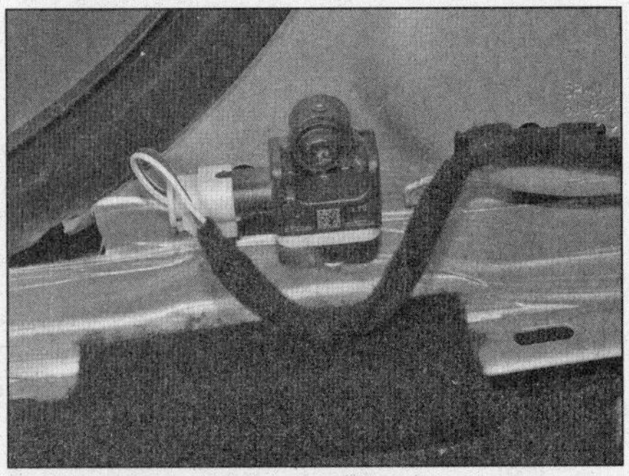

24.25 Sensor at the base of the B-pillar

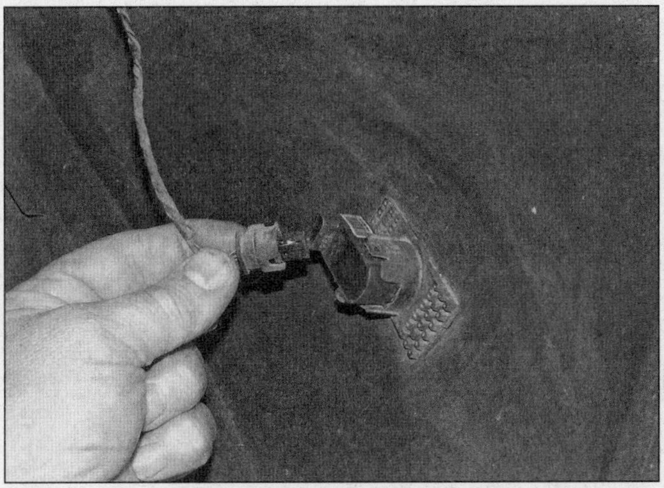

25.9 Disconnect the wiring connector...

25.10 ...and unclip the sensor from the bumper

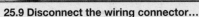

25 Parking aid components – general information, removal and refitting

General information

1 The parking aid system is available as a standard fitment on some models, and optional on other models. Four ultrasound sensors located in the front and rear bumper. These measure the distance to the closest object behind or in front of the car, and inform the driver using acoustic signals from a warning buzzer. The nearer the object, the more frequent the acoustic signals.

2 The system includes a control unit and self-diagnosis program, and therefore, in the event of a fault, the vehicle should be taken to a Seat dealer or suitably equipped garage.

3 Switch off the ignition and all electrical consumers and remove the ignition key, before removing any electrical components.

Control unit

4 The parking aid control unit is located behind the right-hand rear side trim panel in the luggage compartment. Refer to Chapter 11 Section 25 to aid removing the trim panels.

5 Withdraw the control unit complete with mounting bracket from the body panel.

6 Disconnect the wiring connectors as the control unit is removed.

7 Refitting is a reversal of removal.

Range/distance sensors

8 Remove the rear bumper as described in Chapter 11 Section 7.

9 Disconnect the wiring from the sensor **(see illustration)**.

10 Release the two retaining clips at each side and pull the sensor from the bumper **(see illustration)**.

11 Refitting is a reversal of removal. Press the sensor firmly into position until the retaining clips engage.

FUSE BOX IN ENGINE COMPARTMENT

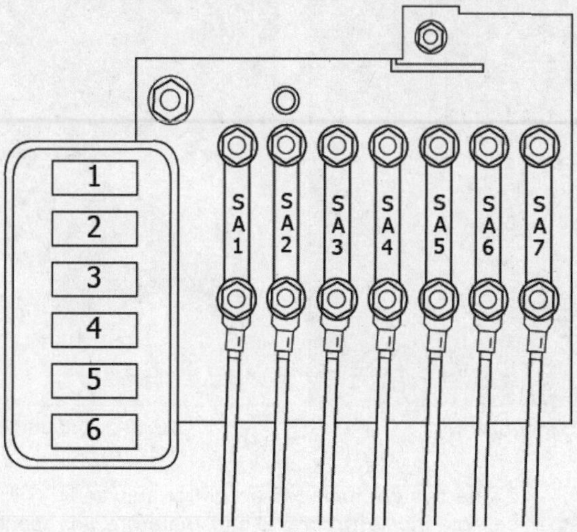

FUSE	VALUE	DESCRIPTION	OEM NAME
SA1	175 A	Alternator (150 A also used)	SA1
SA2	-	Not used	SA2
SA3	110 A	Interior	SA3
SA4	50 A	Power steering control unit	SA4
SA5	40 A	ABS control unit	SA5
SA6	40 A	Radiator fan control unit	SA6
SA7	50 A	Automatic glow period control unit or Mechatronic unit for dual clutch gearbox	SA7
1	25 A	ABS control unit	SB1
2	30 A	Radiator fan thermal switch or Radiator fan control unit	SB2
3	5 A	Radiator fan control unit (Up to May 2011)	SB3
	30 A	Mechatronic unit for dual clutch gearbox (From June 2011)	
4	10 A	ABS control unit and Voltage stabiliser 2 (If fitted) or Not used	SB4
5	5 A	Onboard supply control unit and Battery monitor control unit (If fitted)	SB5
6	30 A	Selector lever, Mechatronic unit for dual clutch gearbox or Engine control unit (5 A, 15 A also used)	SB6

Fuses and relays up to May 2015

FUSE IN LUGGAGE COMPARTMENT (ONLY MODELS WITH BATTERY IN LUGGAGE COMPARTMENT)

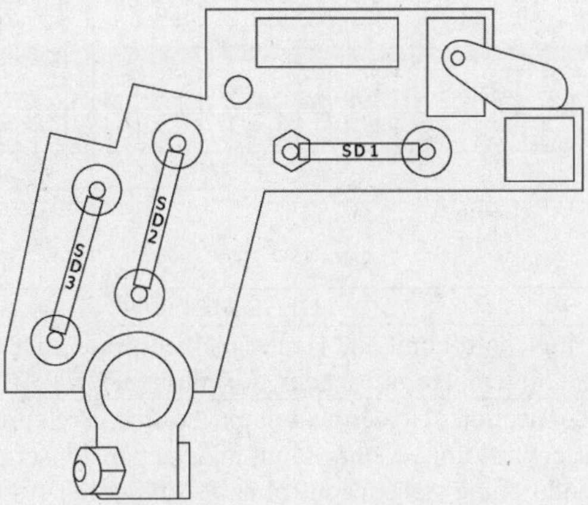

UP TO OCTOBER 2012

FUSE	VALUE	DESCRIPTION	OEM NAME
SD1	110 A	Interior	SD1
SD2	-	Not used	SD2
SD3	-	Not used	SD3

FROM NOVEMBER 2012

FUSE	VALUE	DESCRIPTION	OEM NAME
SD1	40 A	ABS control unit	SD1
SD2	110 A	Interior	SD2
SD3	30 A	ABS control unit	SD3

Fuses and relays up to May 2015 (continued)

FUSE AND RELAY IN PASSENGER COMPARTMENT UNDER LEFT DASH PANEL

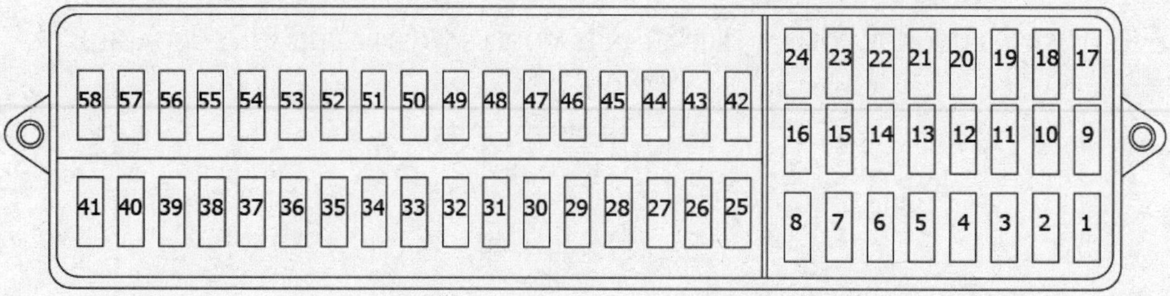

FUSE	VALUE	DESCRIPTION	OEM NAME
1	7.5 A	Power steering control unit and Heater element for crankcase breather or Oil level and oil temperature sender, Air mass meter, Power steering control unit	SC1
2	10 A	Diagnosis connection , Heater/heat output switch, High pressure sender, Climatronic control unit, Control unit in dash panel insert, Radiator fan control unit, Air conditioning system control unit, Navigation system interface, Automatic anti-dazzle interior mirror	SC2
3	5 A	Air mass meter, Fuel pump relay, Current supply relay for Simos control unit, Engine control unit	SC3
4	10 A	Steering angle sender, ABS control unit	SC4
5	10 A	Reversing light switch, Left washer jet heater element, Right washer jet heater element	SC5
6	10 A	Diagnostic connector or Control unit in dash panel insert (5 A also used)	SC6
7	7.5 A	Airbag control unit or Fog lights or Fog lights, Starter motor relay 1,2, Voltage stabiliser, Stop/start system button (If fitted), Onboard supply control unit (5 A also used)	SC7
8	10 A	Injectors or not used	SC8
9	10 A	Intermittent wiper switch, Rear wiper switch, Intermittent wiper regulator, Washer pump switch (automatic wash/wipe and headlight washer system)	SC9
10	5 A	Cruise control system switch, Clutch pedal switch, Brake pedal position sender	SC10
11	5 A	Airbag control unit or not used	SC11
12	10 A	Multifunction steering wheel control unit, Mechatronic unit for dual clutch gearbox or not used	SC12
13	15 A	Dipped headlight control unit, on/off or Mirror adjustment change-over switch (5 A also used)	SC13
14	15 A	Power output module for left headlight or not used	SC14
15	15 A	Power output module for right headlight not used	SC15
16	-	Not used	SC16
17	5 A	Illumination regulators - switches and instruments, Number plate light	SC17
18	7.5 A	Headlight range control regulator (5 A also used)	SC18
19	5 A	Onboard supply control unit	SC19
20	15 A	Onboard supply control unit - Exterior lights	SC20
21	10 A	Steering angle sender (5 A also used)	SC21
22	5 A	Onboard supply control unit	SC22
23	7.5 A	Engine control unit or Main relay (5 A also used) or not used	SC23
24	10 A	Onboard supply control unit, Luggage compartment light, Glove compartment light, Front passenger side reading light, Interior light with switch-off delay, Driver side reading light	SC24
25	5 A	Parking aid control unit	SC25

Fuses and relays up to May 2015 (continued)

26	-	Not used	SC26
27	15 A	Cigarette lighter or not used	SC27
28	10 A	Lambda probe heater, Lambda probe 1 heater after catalytic converter	SC28
29	20 A	Vacuum pump relay, Vacuum pump for brakes or not used	SC29
30	10 A	Oil level and oil temperature sender, Intake manifold preheating heater element, Charge pressure control solenoid valve, Activated charcoal filter solenoid valve 1, Exhaust gas recirculation cooler change-over valve	SC30
31	10 A	Radiator fan control unit or Injectors or not used	SC31
32	30 A	Engine control unit or not used (20 A, 15 A also used)	SC32
33	5 A	Clutch pedal switch and Low heat output relay, High heat output relay(only models for cold climate countries) or Brake pedal position sender, Clutch pedal switch, Clutch position sender, Low heat output relay, High heat output relay	SC33
34	15 A	Fuel system pressurisation pump, Fuel pressure regulating valve or not used	SC34
35	15 A	Engine control unit or Power socket or not used	SC35
36	15 A	Right main beam bulb or Control unit in dash panel insert, Light control unit, Main beam bulb (10 A also used)	SC36
37	10 A	Dipped headlight control unit, on/off, Left main beam bulb or Main beam warning lamp, Left gas discharge light control unit, Dipped headlight control unit, on/off, Left main beam bulb, Relay for headlight flasher	SC37
38	30 A	Heated driver seat switch, Heated front passenger seat switch, Heated front seats control unit or Fresh air blower switch, Fresh air blower control unit (15 A also used)	SC38
39	10 A	Rear window wiper motor or not used	SC39
40	15 A	Mirror adjustment change-over switch or Cigarette lighter or not used	SC40
41	25 A	Fresh air blower switch, Fresh air blower control unit or not used	SC41
42	20 A	Onboard supply control unit, Horn or dual tone horn	SC42
43	30 A	Diagnostic connector, Control unit in dash panel insert, Sliding sunroof adjustment control unit (5 A also used)	SC43
44	20 A	Onboard supply control unit, Windscreen wiper motor	SC44
45	30 A	Onboard supply control unit, Heated rear window (20 A also used)	SC45
46	20 A	Operating unit in steering wheel, Mobile telephone operating electronics control unit, Multimedia control unit, Radio	SC46
47	5 A	Climatronic control unit or Air conditioning system control unit	SC47
48	15 A	Onboard supply control unit	SC48
49	30 A	Driver door control unit, Front passenger door control unit or Driver door control unit (25 A also used)	SC49
50	30 A	Rear left door control unit, Rear right door control unit	SC50
51	25 A	Onboard supply control unit, Driver side heated exterior mirror, Front passenger side heated exterior mirror or Front passenger door control unit (5 A also used)	SC51
52	15 A	Interior monitoring sensor, Alarm horn	SC52
53	15 A	Fuel pump relay or not used	SC53
54	15 A	Onboard supply control unit, Left fog light bulb, Right fog light bulb, Left reversing light bulb, Right reversing light bulb	SC54
55	15 A	Ignition coils or not used	SC55
56	15 A	Fuel pump control unit or Rear window wiper motor or not used (10 A also used)	SC56
57	15 A	Right dipped beam bulb, Right headlight range control motor	SC57
58	15 A	Left dipped beam bulb, Left headlight range control motor	SC58

Fuses and relays up to May 2015 (continued)

FUSE AND RELAYS IN PASSENGER COMPARTMENT

UP TO APRIL 2009

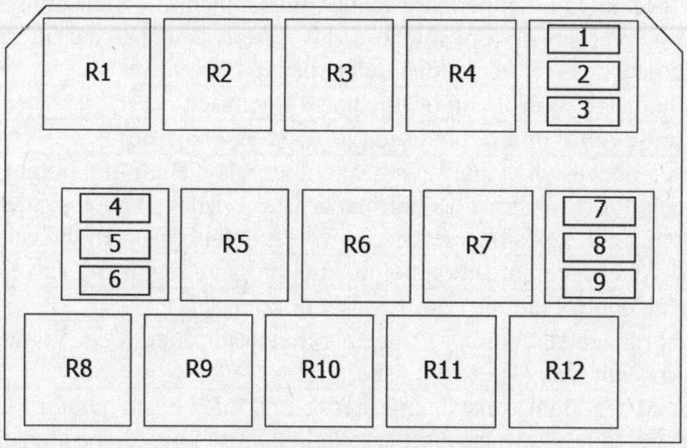

FUSE/RELAY	VALUE	DESCRIPTION	OEM NAME
1	20 A	Sliding sunroof adjustment control unit	SF13
2	25 A	Rain and light detector sensor or Heated driver seat switch, Heated front passenger seat switch, Heated front seats control unit (5 A also used)	SF14
3	20 A	Headlight washer system relay	SF15
4	15 A	Left day driving light bulb	SF16
5	15 A	Right day driving light bulb	SF17
6	-	Not used	SF18
7	40 A	Auxiliary heater element	SF28
8	40 A	Auxiliary heater element	SF29
9	40 A	Auxiliary heater element	SF30
R1	-	Fuel pump relay or not used	J17
R2	-	Starter inhibitor relay or not used	J207
R3	-	Not used	-
R4	-	Fuel supply relay or not used	J643
R5	-	Headlight washer system relay	J39
R6	-	Headlight washer system relay	J828
R7	-	Dipped headlight control unit, on/off	J665
R8	-	Terminal 30 voltage supply relay or Motronic current supply relay	J317; J271
R9	-	Low heat output relay	J359
R10	-	X-contact relief relay	J59
R11	-	High heat output relay	J360
R12	-	Not used	-

Fuses and relays up to May 2015 (continued)

FROM MAY 2009 TO MAY 2012

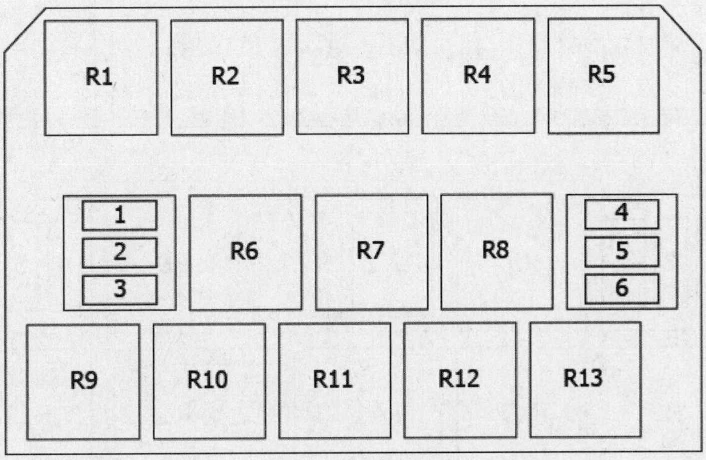

FUSE/RELAY	VALUE	DESCRIPTION	OEM NAME
1	20 A	Left day driving light bulb (15 A also used)	SF16
2	15 A	Right day driving light bulb (5 A also used)	SF17
3	20 A	Headlight washer system relay	SF18
4	40 A	Auxiliary heater element	SF28
5	40 A	Auxiliary heater element	SF29
6	40 A	Auxiliary heater element	SF30
R1	-	Fuel pump relay or not used	J17
R2	-	Starter inhibitor relay or not used	J207
R3	-	Not used	-
R4	-	Fuel supply relay or Additional coolant pump relay	J643; j496
R5	-	Headlight washer system relay	J39
R6	-	Not used	-
R7	-	Relay for headlight flasher	J828
R8	-	Dipped headlight control unit, on/off	J665
R9	-	Terminal 30 voltage supply relay or Motronic current supply relay	J317; J271
R10	-	Low heat output relay	J359
R11	-	X-contact relief relay	J59
R12	-	High heat output relay	J360
R13	-	Not used	-

Fuses and relays up to May 2015 (continued)

FROM JUNE 2012 UP TO OCTOBER 2012

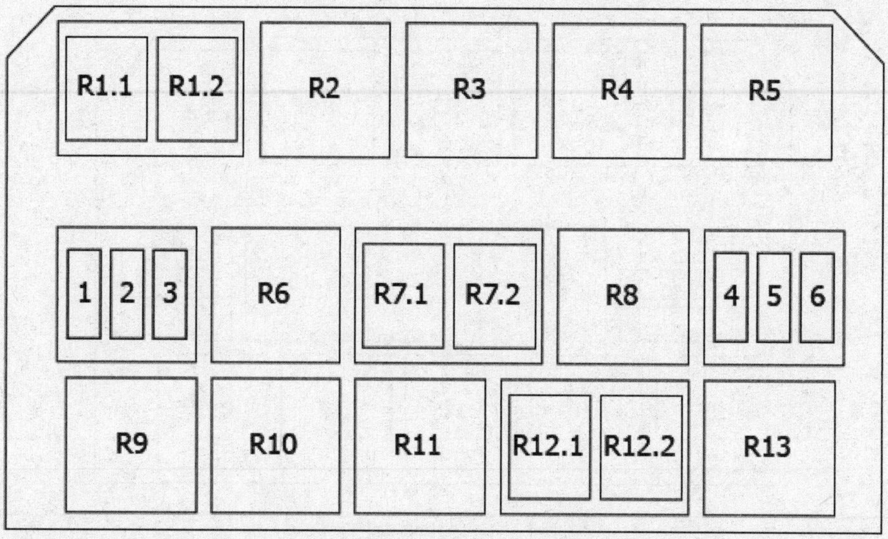

FUSE/RELAY	VALUE	DESCRIPTION	OEM NAME
1	5 A	Control unit in dash panel insert, Voltage stabiliser 2	SF16
2	20 A	Mobile telephone operating electronics control unit, Multimedia control unit, Operating unit in steering wheel	SF17
3	20 A	Headlight washer system relay	SF18
4	40 A	Auxiliary heater element	SF28
5	40 A	Auxiliary heater element	SF29
6	40 A	Auxiliary heater element	SF30
R1.1	-	Fuel pump relay	J17
R1.2	-	Fuel pump relay	J643
R2	-	X-contact relief relay	J59
R3	-	Starter motor relay 2	J907
R4	-	High heat output relay	J360
R5	-	Headlight washer system relay	J39
R6	-	Starter motor relay 1	J906
R7.1	-	Terminal 50 voltage supply relay	J682
R7.2	-	Dipped beam relay or Relay for headlight flasher	J331, J828
R8	-	Dipped headlight control unit, on/off, Voltage stabiliser 2	J665; J570
R9	-	Main relay or Terminal 30 voltage supply relay or Current supply relay for Simos control unit	J271; J317; J363
R10	-	Low heat output relay	J359
R11	-	Starter inhibitor relay or Intake manifold preheating relay	J207; J81
R12.1	-	Terminal 15 voltage supply relay	J329
R12.2	-	Not used	
R13	-	Fuel pump relay or not used	J17

Fuses and relays up to May 2015 (continued)

FROM NOVEMBER 2012 UP TO MAY 2015

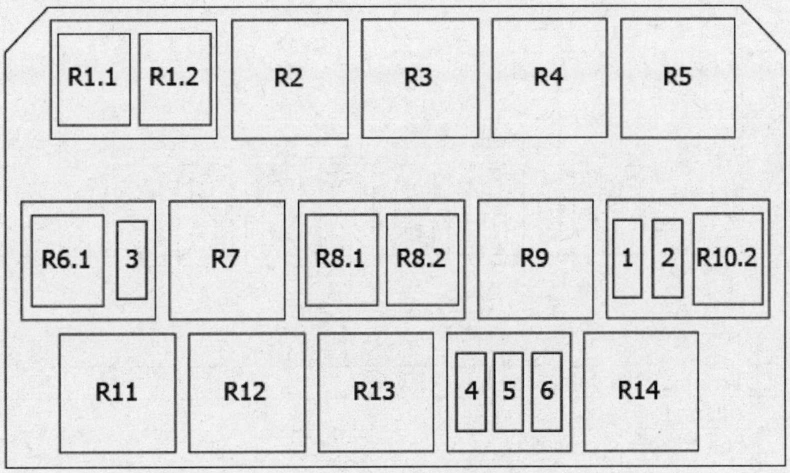

FUSE/RELAY	VALUE	DESCRIPTION	OEM NAME
1	5 A	Control unit in dash panel insert, Voltage stabiliser 2	SF16
2	20 A	Mobile telephone operating electronics control unit, Multimedia control unit, Operating unit in steering wheel	SF17
3	-	Not used	
4	40 A	Auxiliary heater element	SF28
5	40 A	Auxiliary heater element	SF29
6	40 A	Auxiliary heater element	SF30
R1.1	-	Fuel pump relay	J17
R1.2	-	Fuel pump relay	J643
R2	-	X-contact relief relay	J59
R3	-	Starter motor relay 2	J907
R4	-	High heat output relay	J360
R5	-	Headlight washer system relay	J39
R6.1	-	Terminal 15 voltage supply relay	J329
R7	-	Starter motor relay 1	J906
R8.1	-	Terminal 50 voltage supply relay	J682
R8.2	-	Dipped beam relay or Relay for headlight flasher	J331; J828
R9	-	Dipped headlight control unit	J665
R10.2	-	Not used	
R11	-	Main relay or Terminal 30 voltage supply relay or Current supply relay for Simos control unit	J271; J317; J363
R12	-	Low heat output relay	J359
R13	-	Starter inhibitor relay or Intake manifold preheating relay	J207
R14	-	Fuel pump relay or not used	J17

Fuses and relays up to May 2015 (continued)

MAIN FUSE AND RELAY BOX IN ENGINE COMPARTMENT

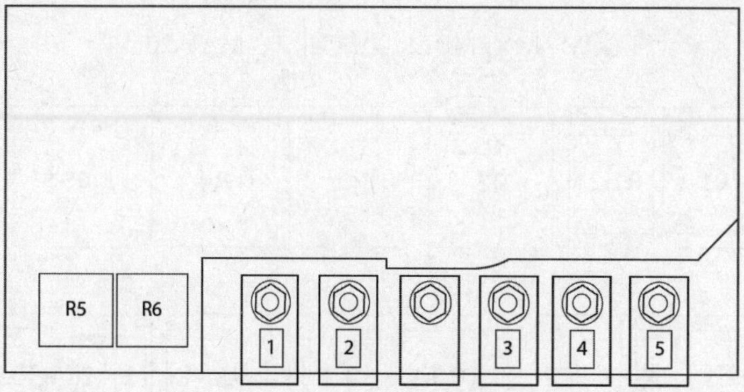

FUSE/RELAY	VALUE	DESCRIPTION	OEM NAME
1	50 A	Terminal 75x voltage supply relay	SA1
2	250 A	Alternator	SA2
3	80 A	Power steering control unit	SA3
4	80 A	Current supply for fuses: SC38-SC54	SA4
5	125 A	Current supply for fuses: SC1-SC17	SA5
R5	-	Engine component current supply relay	J757
R6	-	Not used	-

FUSE IN LUGGAGE COMPARTMENT (ONLY MODELS WITH BATTERY IN LUGGAGE COMPARTMENT)

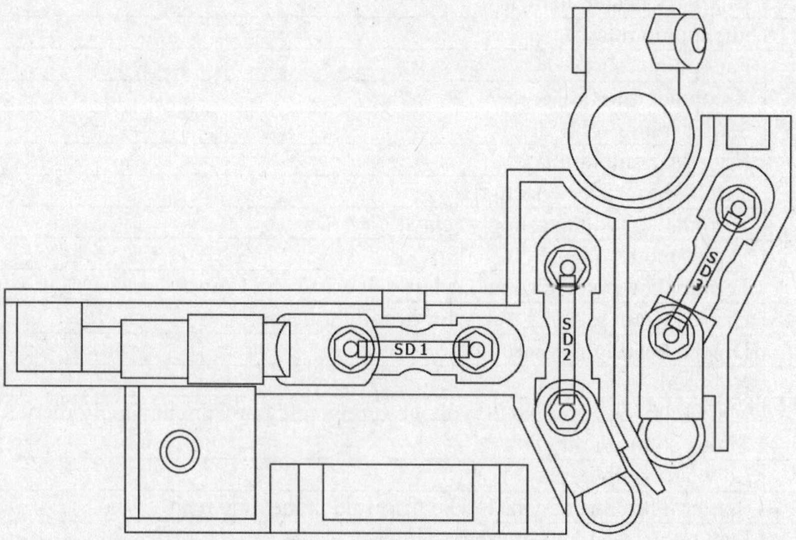

FUSE	VALUE	DESCRIPTION	OEM NAME
SD1	80 A	Power steering control unit	SD1
SD2	110 A	Fuse and relay in passenger compartment SC1	SD2
SD3	110 A	Fuse and relay in passenger compartment SC38	SD3

Fuses and relays from June 2015

FUSE AND RELAY BOX IN ENGINE COMPARTMENT

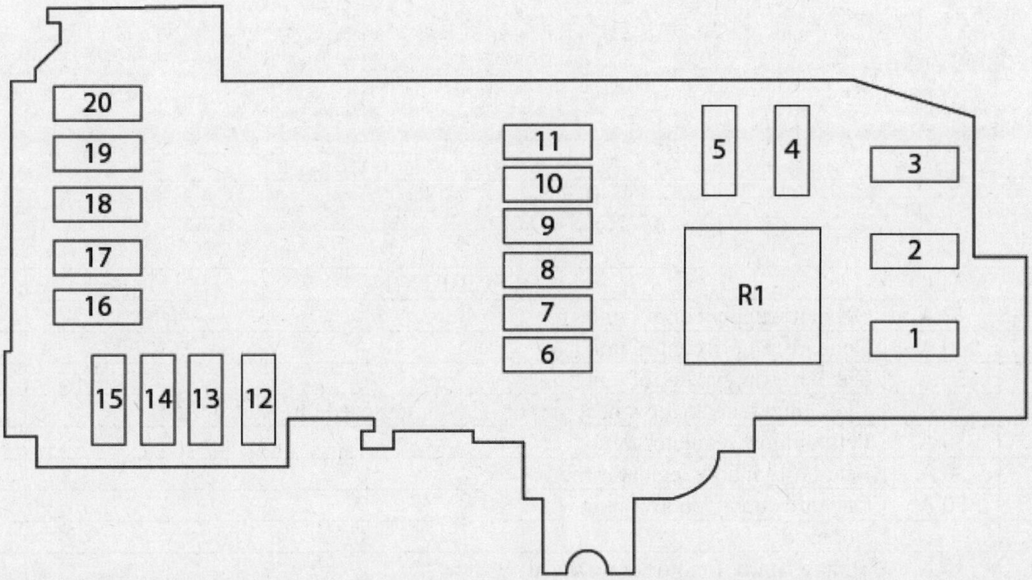

FUSE/RELAY	VALUE	DESCRIPTION	OEM NAME
1	50 A	Radiator fan thermal switch, Radiator fan control unit, Suppression filter (40 A also used)	SB1
2	50 A	Automatic glow period control unit or not used	SB2
3	40 A	ABS hydraulic pump relay	SB3
4	50 A	Engine preheating element or not used	SB4
5	50 A	Engine preheating element or not used	SB5
6	5 A	Onboard supply control unit	SB6
7	7.5 A	Engine control unit	SB7
8	30 A	Windscreen wiper motor	SB8
9	30 A	Automatic gearbox control unit or not used	SB9
10	25 A	ABS control unit, Engine component current supply relay	SB10
11	-	Not used	SB11
12	10 A	Fuel metering valve or Exhaust gas temperature sender	SB12
13	5 A	Brake light switch	SB13
14	10 A	Fuel pump relay, Charge air cooling pump, Auxiliary pump for heating, Valve for oil pressure control	SB14
15	5 A	Engine control unit	SB15
16	30 A	Starter	SB16
17	20 A	Engine control unit	SB17
18	10 A	Oil level and oil temperature sender, High heat output relay, Low heat output relay, Charge pressure positioner, Intake manifold flap valve or Activated charcoal filter solenoid valve 1, Camshaft control valve 1	SB18
19	30 A	Fuse SD1	SB19
20	20 A	Ignition coils or not used	SB20
R1	-	High heat output relay or not used	J360

Fuses and relays from June 2015 (continued)

FUSE AND RELAY IN PASSENGER COMPARTMENT

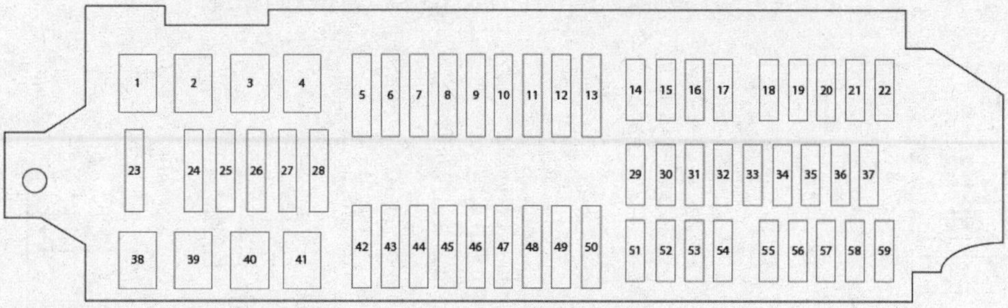

FUSE	VALUE	DESCRIPTION	OEM NAME
1	40 A	Onboard supply control unit	SC1
2	40 A	Onboard supply control unit	SC2
3	30 A	Onboard supply control unit	SC3
4	50 A	Glow plug relay or Low heat output relay or not used (40 A also used)	SC4
5	30 A	Left window regulator motor	SC5
6	30 A	Rear left window regulator motor	SC6
7	20 A	Onboard supply control unit	SC7
8	-	Not used	SC8
9	30 A	Sliding sunroof motor or not used	SC9
10	7.5 A	Electronically controlled damping control unit	SC10
11	30 A	Headlight washer system relay	SC11
12	5 A	Multimedia system operating unit	SC12
13	30 A	Terminal 15 voltage supply relay	SC13
14	7.5 A	Diagnostic connection, Ignition key withdrawal lock solenoid, Steering column combination switch, Light switch	SC14
15	7.5 A	Air conditioning system control unit, Selector lever	SC15
16	5 A	Dash panel insert	SC16
17	7.5 A	Anti-theft alarm sensor	SC17
18	-	Not used	SC18
19	-	Not used	SC19
20	-	Not used	SC20
21	-	Not used	SC21
22	-	Not used	SC22
23	7.5 A	Washer pump	SC23
24	30 A	Heater control unit, Fresh air blower switch, Fresh air blower control unit	SC24
25	-	Not used	SC25
26	5 A	Terminal 15 voltage supply relay	SC26
27	15 A	Rear window wiper motor	SC27
28	20 A	Cigarette lighter	SC28
29	7.5 A	Airbag control unit, Front passenger side airbag deactivated warning lamp	SC29
30	7.5 A	Rotary light switch, Anti-dazzle interior mirror button, Reversing light switch, Heater control unit, Mirror adjustment switch, High-pressure sender, Heated driver seat regulator, Heated front passenger seat regulator, Parking aid control unit	SC30
31	5 A	Fuel pump control unit	SC31
32	7.5 A	Right headlight range control motor, Right dynamic cornering light control motor, Headlight range control and instrument illumination regulator, Steering column combination switch	SC32
33	5 A	Clutch position sender, Start/Stop switch	SC33
34	5 A	Washer jets heater elements	SC34

Fuses and relays from June 2015 (continued)

35	5 A	Cruise control system switch, Radiator fan control unit, Control unit for structure-borne sound	SC35
36	10 A	Heated front seats control unit, Heated rear seats control unit	SC36
37	5 A	Cruise control system switch, Radiator fan control unit, Control unit for structure-borne sound or not used	SC37
38	40 A	Onboard supply control unit	SC38
39	40 A	ABS control unit or not used	SC39
40	-	Not used	SC40
41	30 A	Onboard supply control unit	SC41
42	30 A	Front right window control unit	SC42
43	30 A	Rear left window control unit	SC43
44	10 A	Reversing camera	SC44
45	10 A	Windscreen wiper switch, Diagnostic connection	SC45
46	20 A	Relay for power sockets or not used	SC46
47	25 A	Main ABS valve or not used	SC47
48	-	Not used	SC48
49	30 A	Fuel pump control unit or Fuel pump relay (15 A, 20 A also used)	SC49
50	20 A	Control unit 1 for information electronics, Operating and display unit for radio	SC50
51	10 A	Onboard supply control unit	SC51
52	-	Not used	SC52
53	5 A	Rain sensor	SC53
54	5 A	Ignition/starter switch	SC54
55	10 A	Seat heater relay	SC55
56	-	Not used	SC56
57	-	Not used	SC57
58	-	Not used	SC58
59	-	Not used	SC59

Fuses and relays from June 2015 (continued)

ADDITIONAL FUSE AND RELAY IN PASSENGER COMPARTMENT

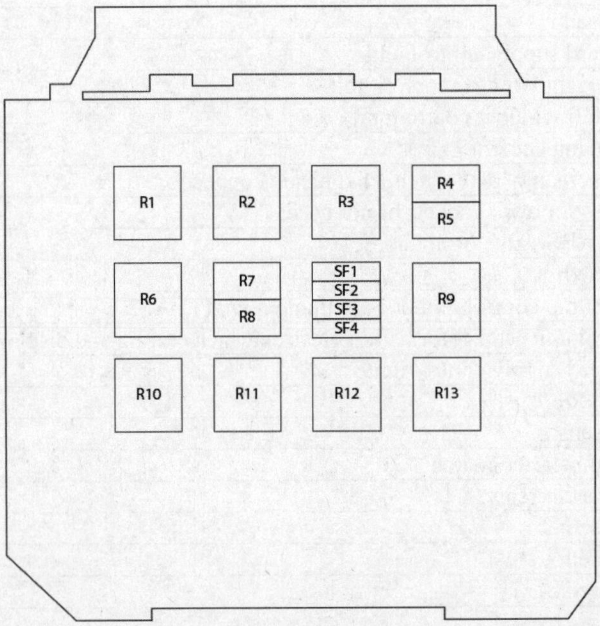

FUSE/RELAY	VALUE	DESCRIPTION	OEM NAME
SF1	15 A	Lambda probe heater, Lambda probe 1 heater after catalytic converter or not used	SF1
SF2	20 A	Vacuum pump relay or Auxiliary pump for heating, Camshaft control motor, Activated charcoal filter solenoid valve 1, Secondary air inlet valve, Main pressure valve (10 A also used)	SF2
SF3	-	Not used	SF3
SF4	-	Not used	SF4
R1	-	Low heat output relay or not used	J359
R2	-	X-contact relief relay	J59
R3	-	Not used	-
R4	-	Washer pump relay	J576
R5	-	Fuel pump relay	J17
R6	-	Terminal 15 relay	J940
R7	-	Relay for power sockets or not used	J807
R8	-	Not used	-
R9	-	Headlight washer system relay	J39
R10	-	Not used	-
R11	-	Not used	-
R12	-	Not used	-
R13	-	Not used	-

Fuses and relays from June 2015 (continued)

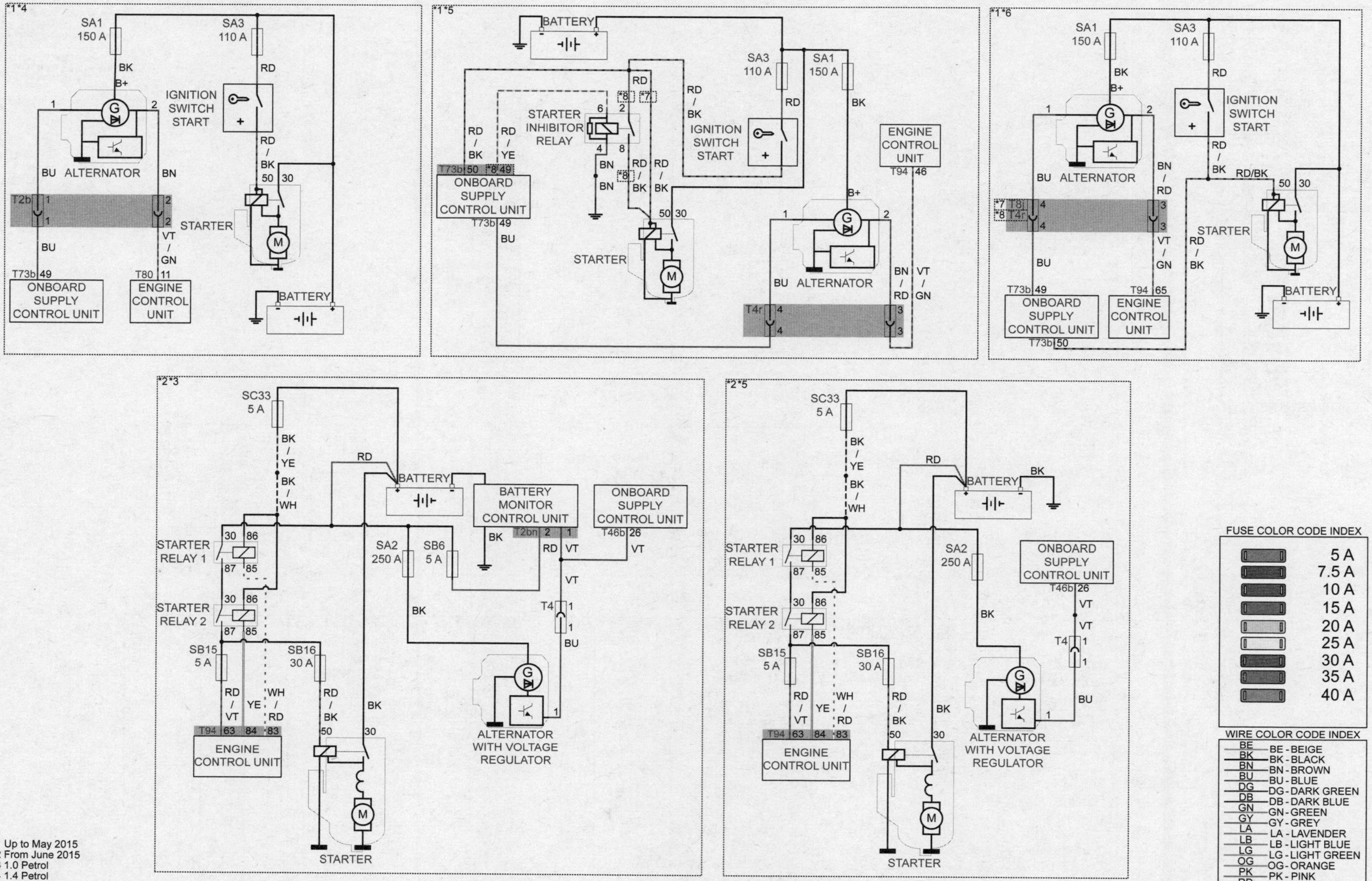

*1 Up to May 2015
*2 From June 2015
*3 1.0 Petrol
*4 1.4 Petrol
*5 1.2 Petrol
*6 1.6 Diesel
*7 Manual transmission
*8 Automatic transmission

FUSE COLOR CODE INDEX

	5 A
	7.5 A
	10 A
	15 A
	20 A
	25 A
	30 A
	35 A
	40 A

WIRE COLOR CODE INDEX

BE	BE - BEIGE
BK	BK - BLACK
BN	BN - BROWN
BU	BU - BLUE
DG	DG - DARK GREEN
DB	DB - DARK BLUE
GN	GN - GREEN
GY	GY - GREY
LA	LA - LAVENDER
LB	LB - LIGHT BLUE
LG	LG - LIGHT GREEN
OG	OG - ORANGE
PK	PK - PINK
RD	RD - RED
VT	VT - VIOLET
WH	WH - WHITE
YE	YE - YELLOW

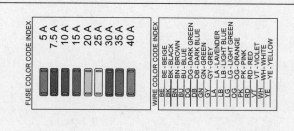

Diagram 1 – Starting and charging

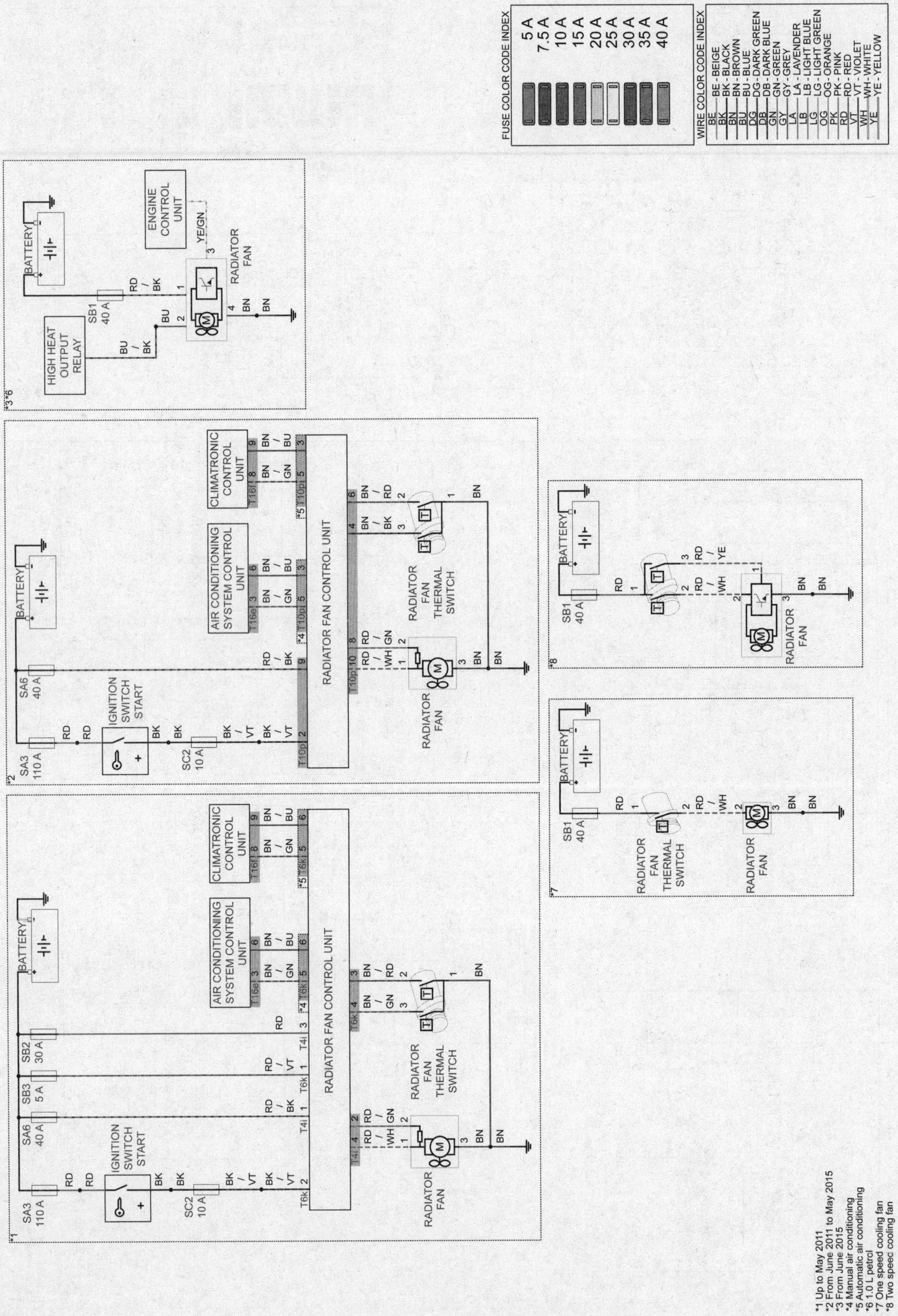

*1 Up to May 2011
*2 From June 2011 to May 2015
*3 From June 2015
*4 Manual air conditioning
*5 Automatic air conditioning
*6 1.0 L petrol
*7 One speed cooling fan
*8 Two speed cooling fan

Diagram 2 – Engine cooling

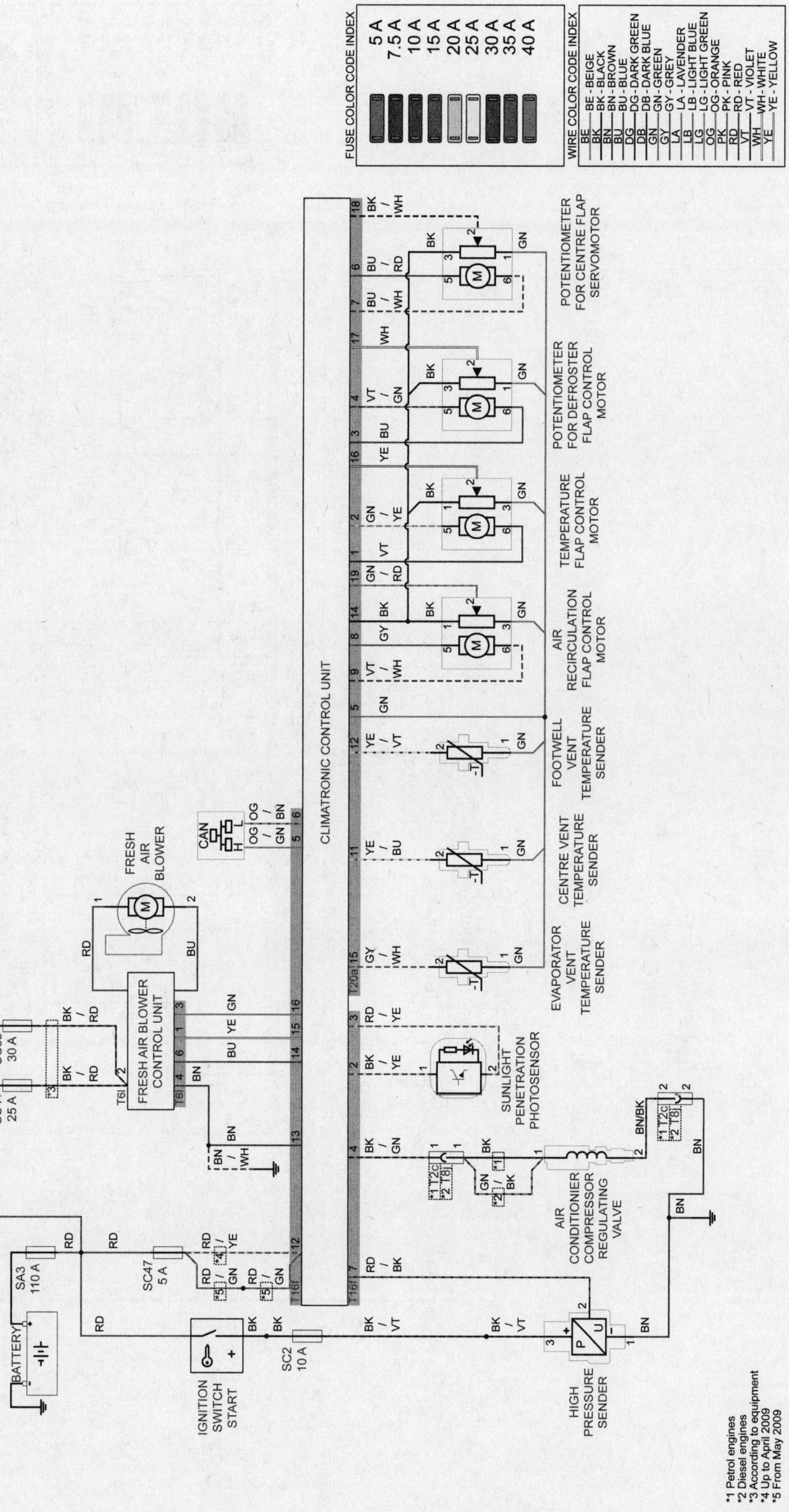

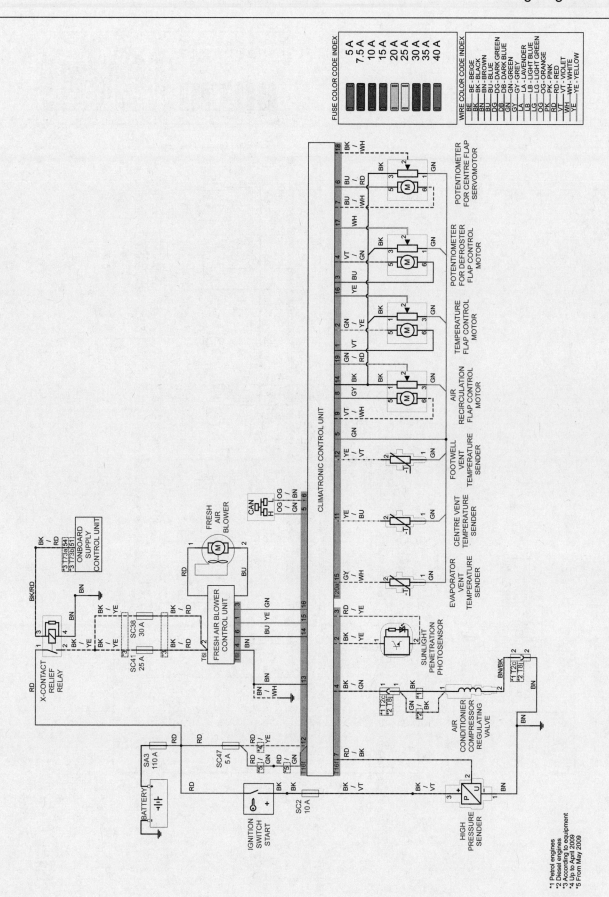

Diagram 3 – Heating and cooling – Automatic air conditioning up to May 2015

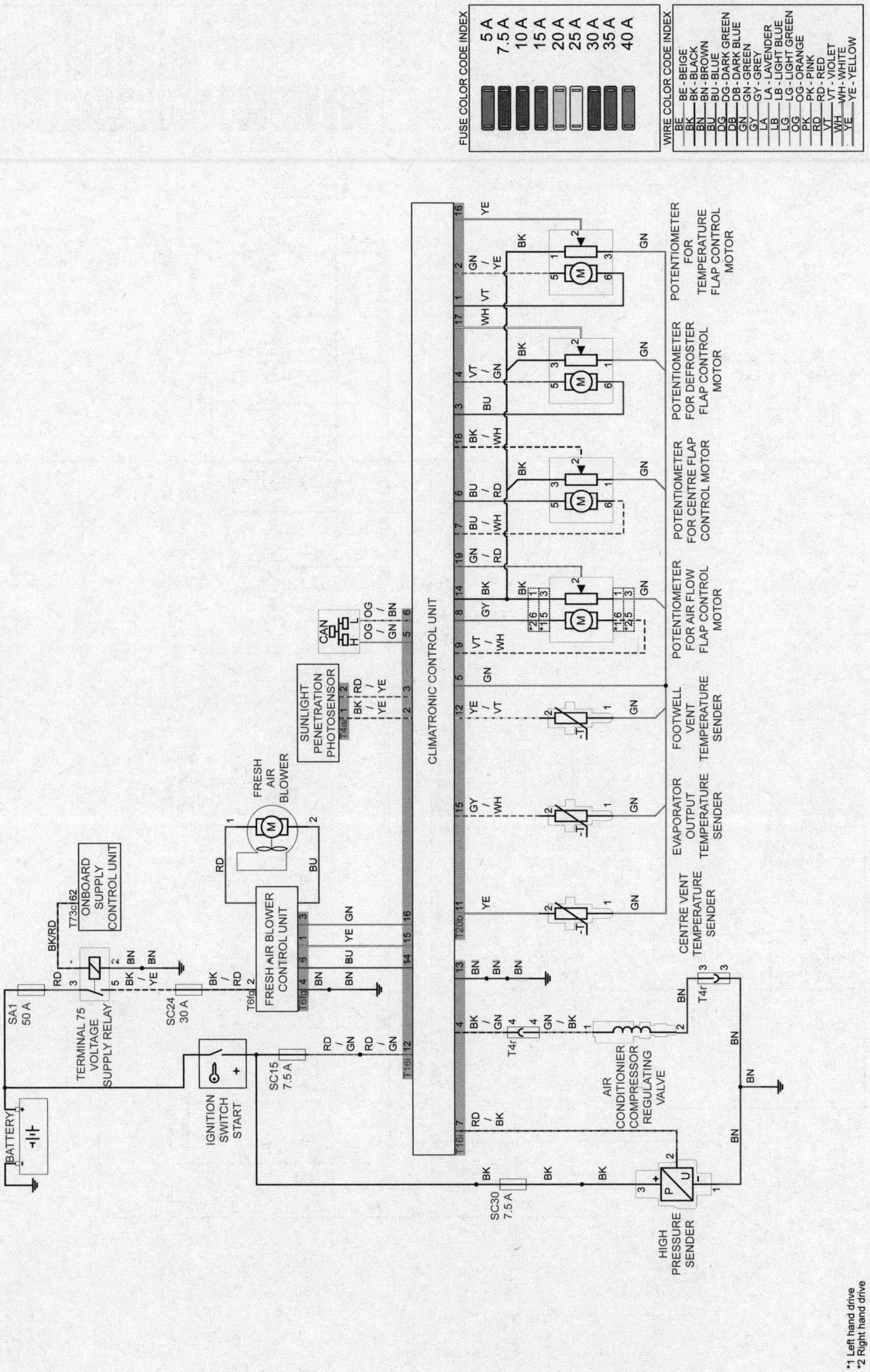

Diagram 4 – Heating and cooling – Automatic air conditioning from June 2015

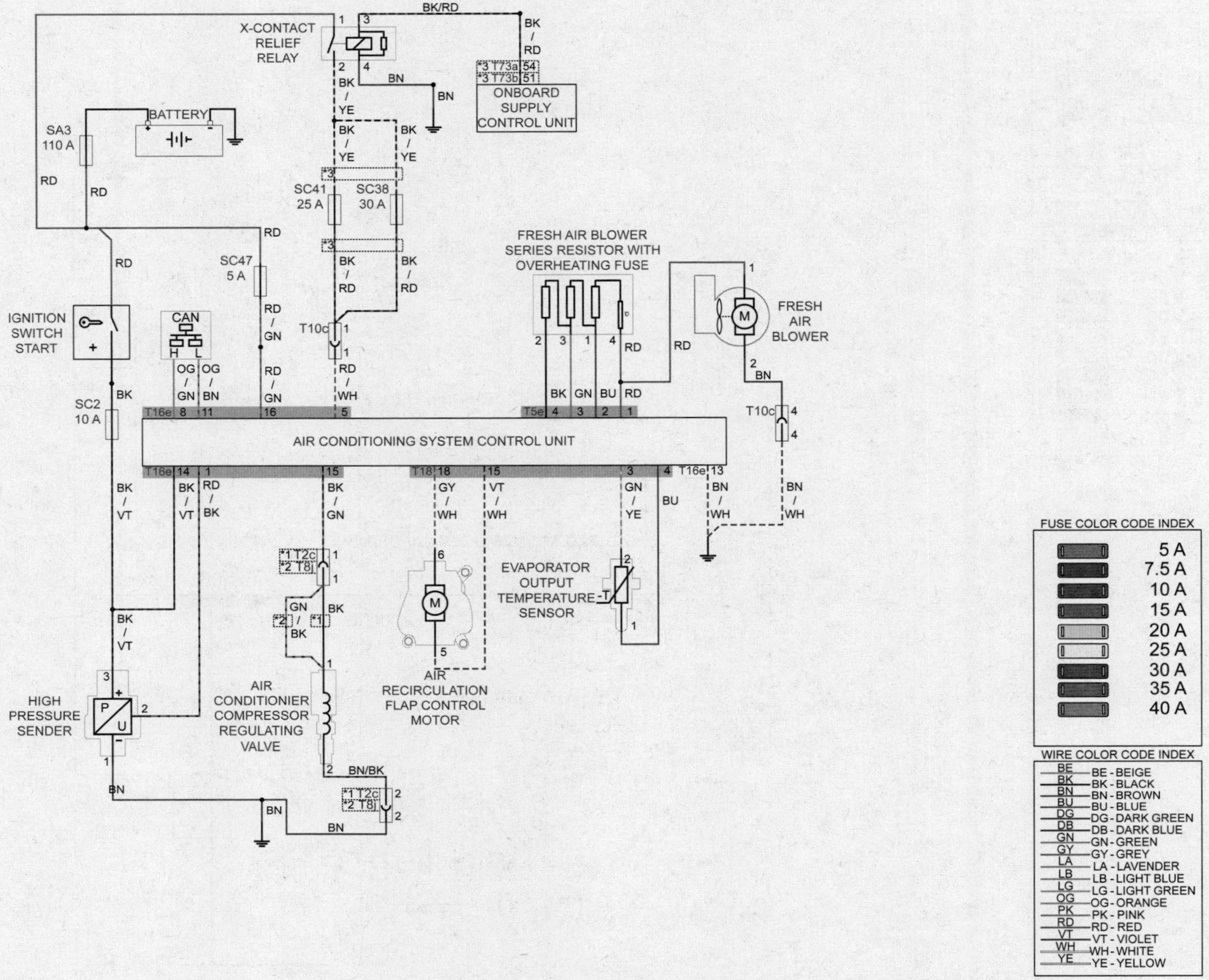

*1 Petrol engines
*2 Diesel engines
*3 According to equipment

Diagram 5 – Heating and cooling – Manual air conditioning up to May 2015

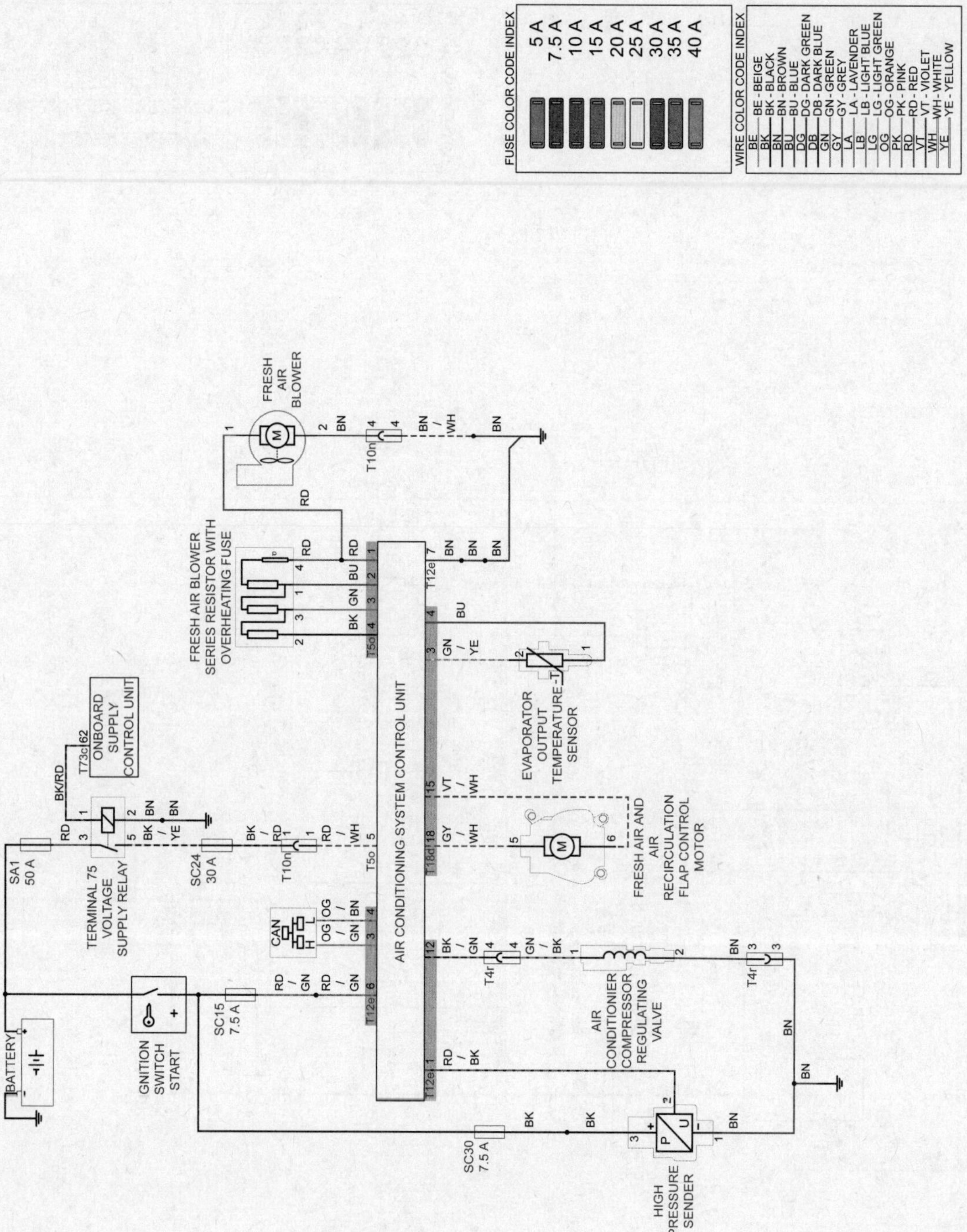

Diagram 6 – Heating and cooling – Manual air conditioning from June 2015

FUSE COLOR CODE INDEX

- 5 A
- 7.5 A
- 10 A
- 15 A
- 20 A
- 25 A
- 30 A
- 35 A
- 40 A

WIRE COLOR CODE INDEX

- BE - BEIGE
- BK - BLACK
- BN - BROWN
- BU - BLUE
- DG - DARK GREEN
- DB - DARK BLUE
- GN - GREEN
- GY - GREY
- LA - LAVENDER
- LB - LIGHT BLUE
- LG - LIGHT GREEN
- OG - ORANGE
- PK - PINK
- RD - RED
- VT - VIOLET
- WH - WHITE
- YE - YELLOW

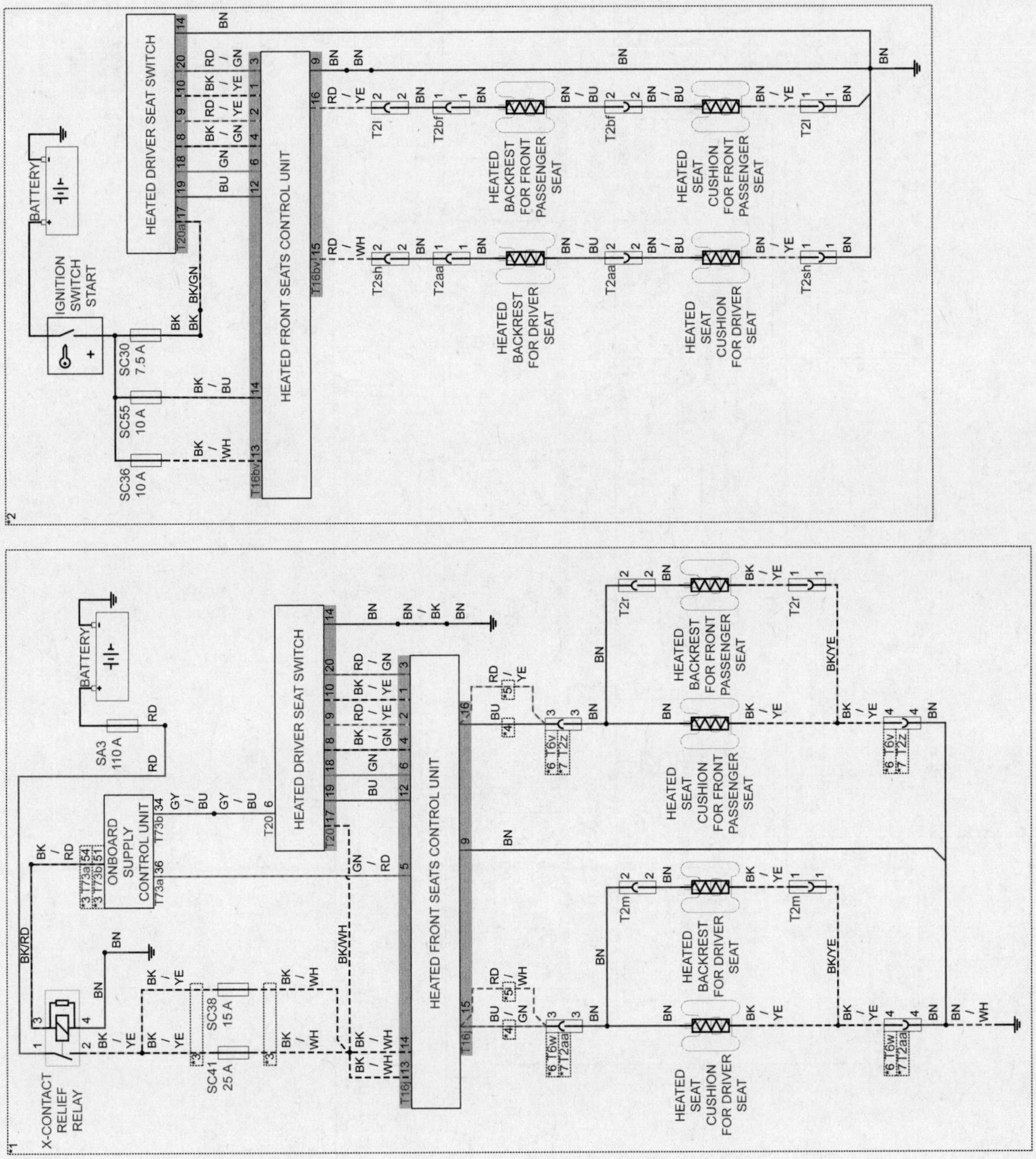

Diagram 7 – Heated seats

*1 Up to May 2015
*2 From June 2015
*3 According to equipment
*4 Up to April 2009
*5 From May 2009
*6 Up to May 2010
*7 From June 2010

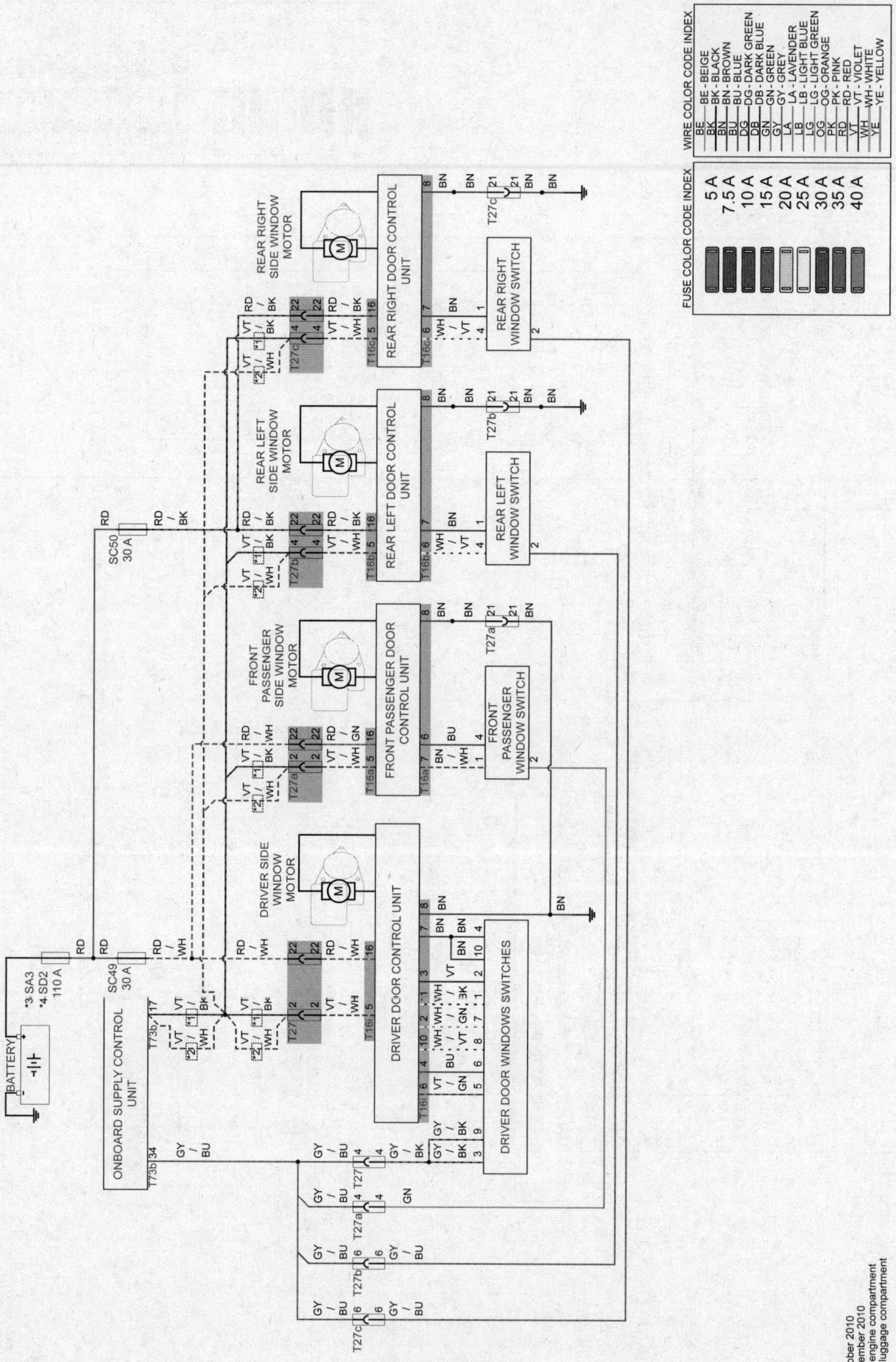

*1 Up to October 2010
*2 From November 2010
*3 Battery in engine compartment
*4 Battery in luggage compartment

Diagram 8 – Electric windows up to May 2015

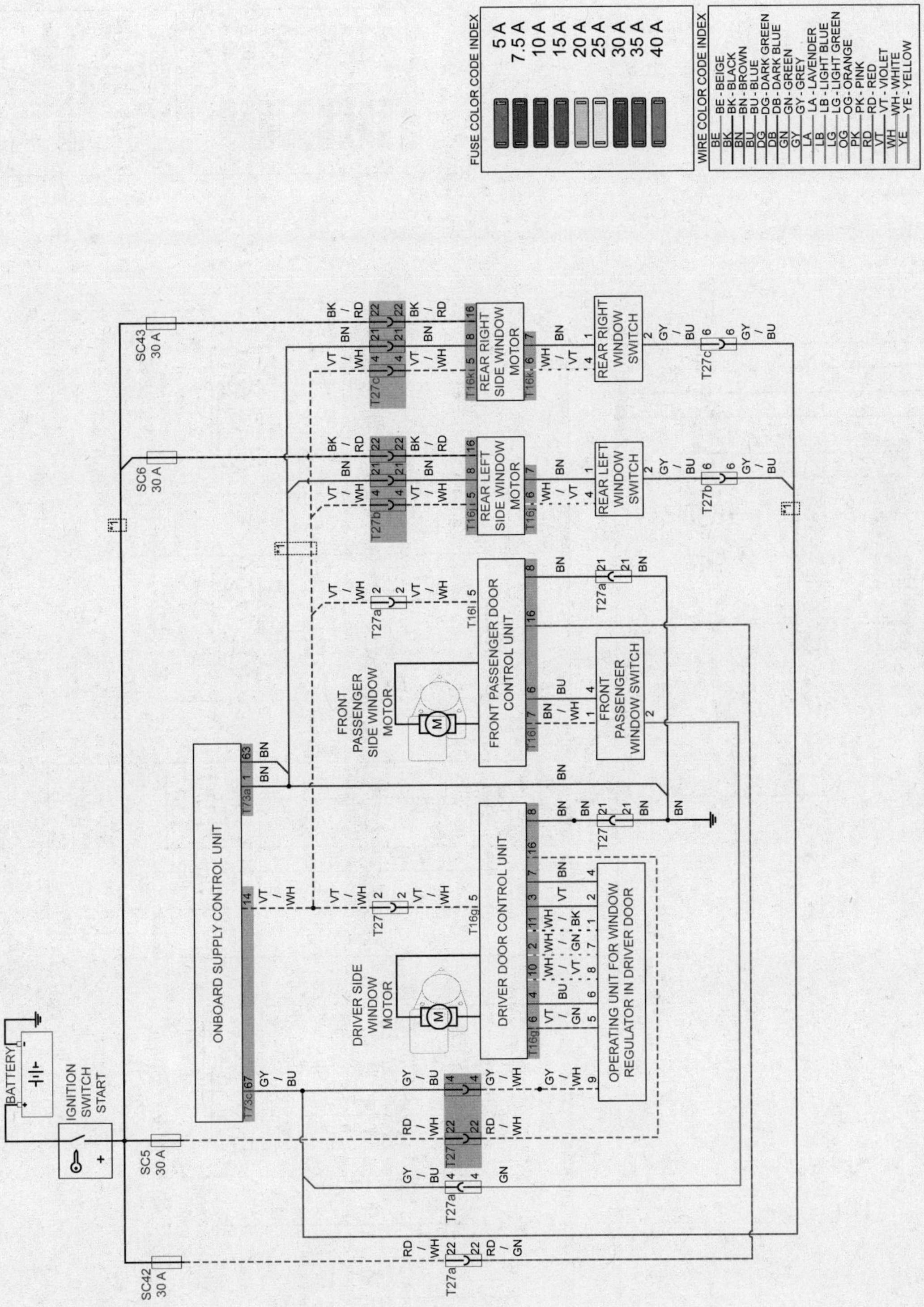

Diagram 9 – Electric windows from June 2015

*1 With rear power windows

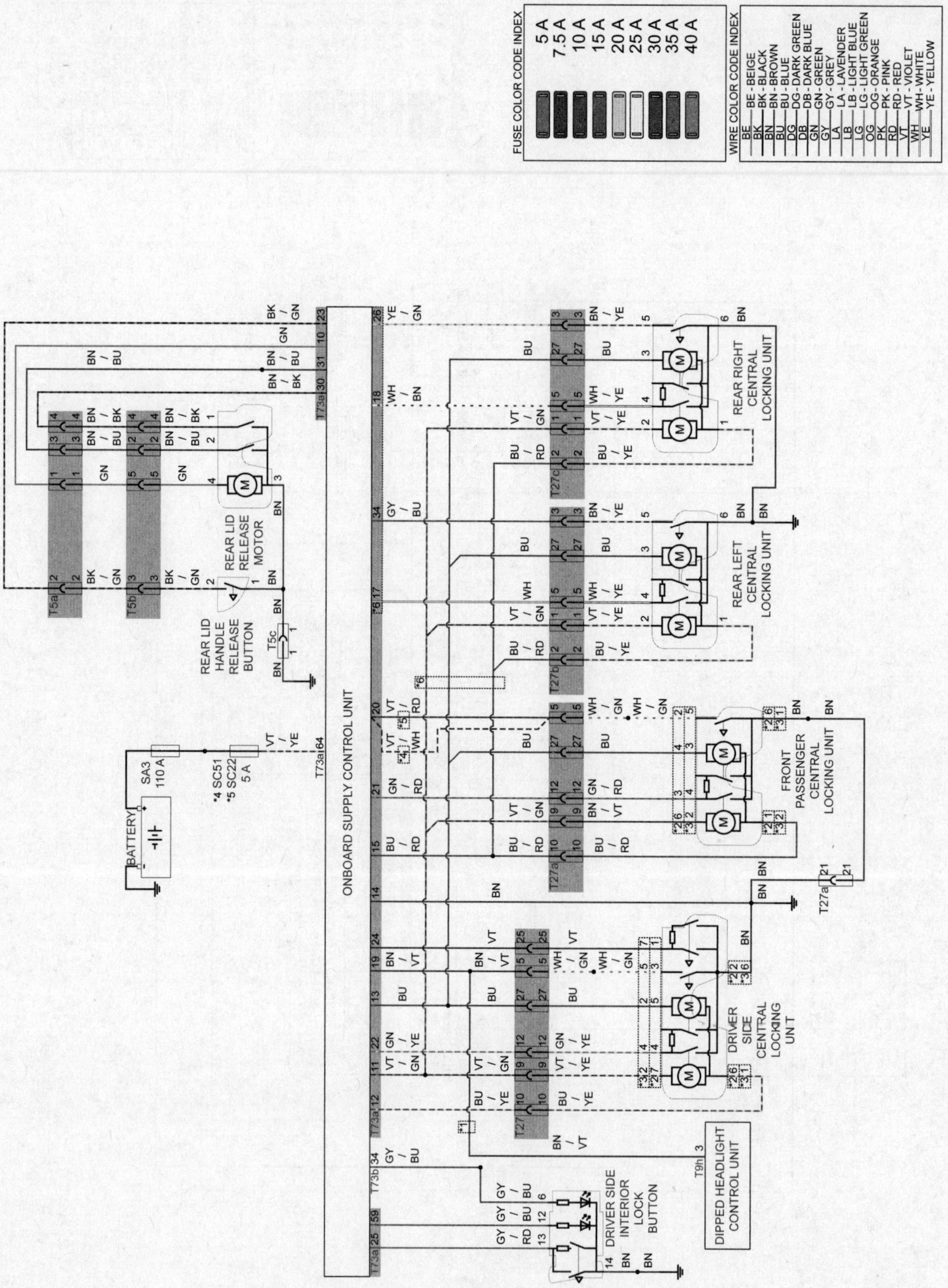

Diagram 10 – Central locking up to May 2015

*1 Only models with coming home
*2 Left hand drive
*3 Right hand drive
*4 Up to May 2012
*5 From June 2012
*6 With 4 doors

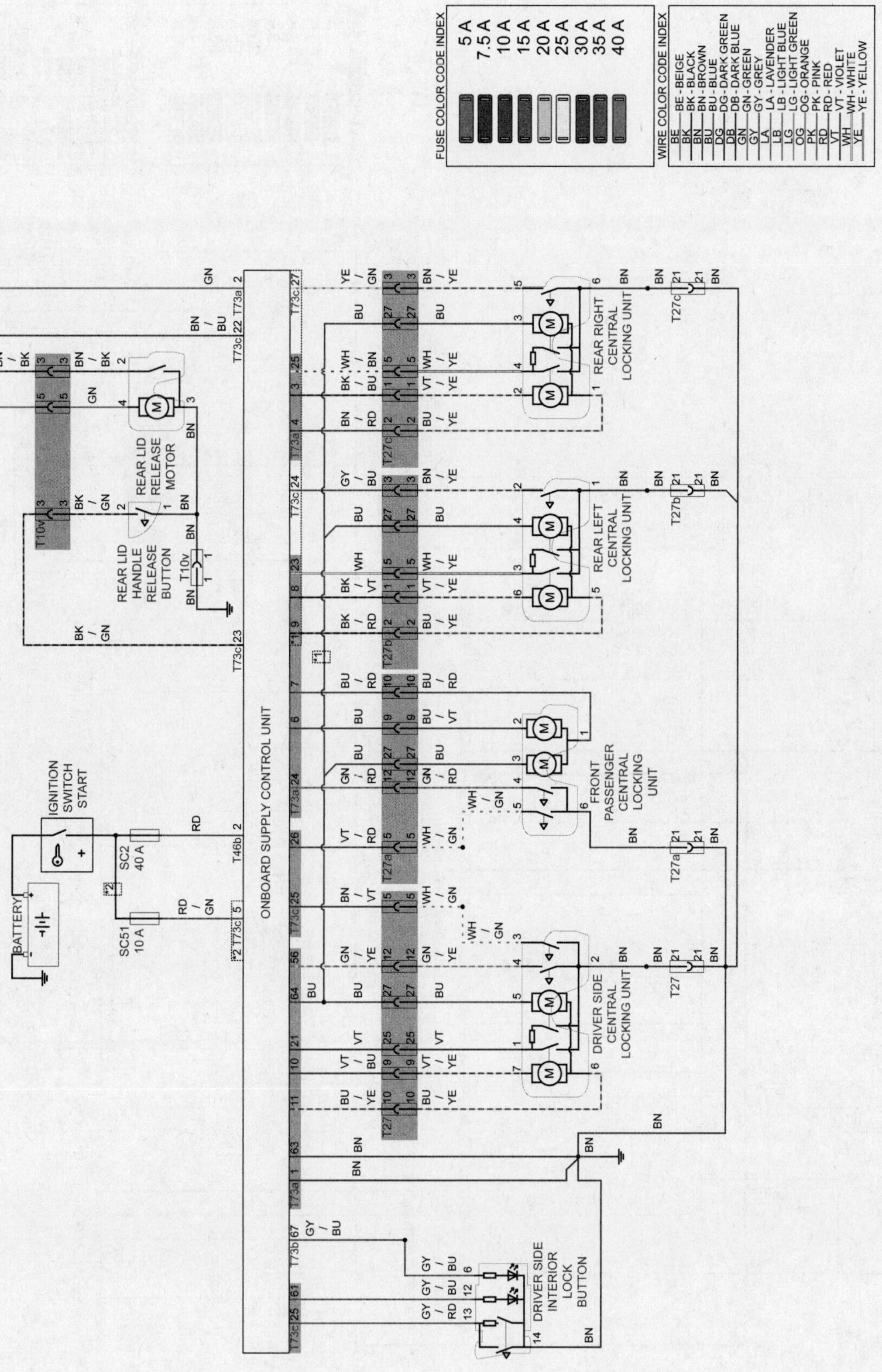

Diagram 11 – Central locking from June 2015

*1 With 4 doors
*2 If equipped

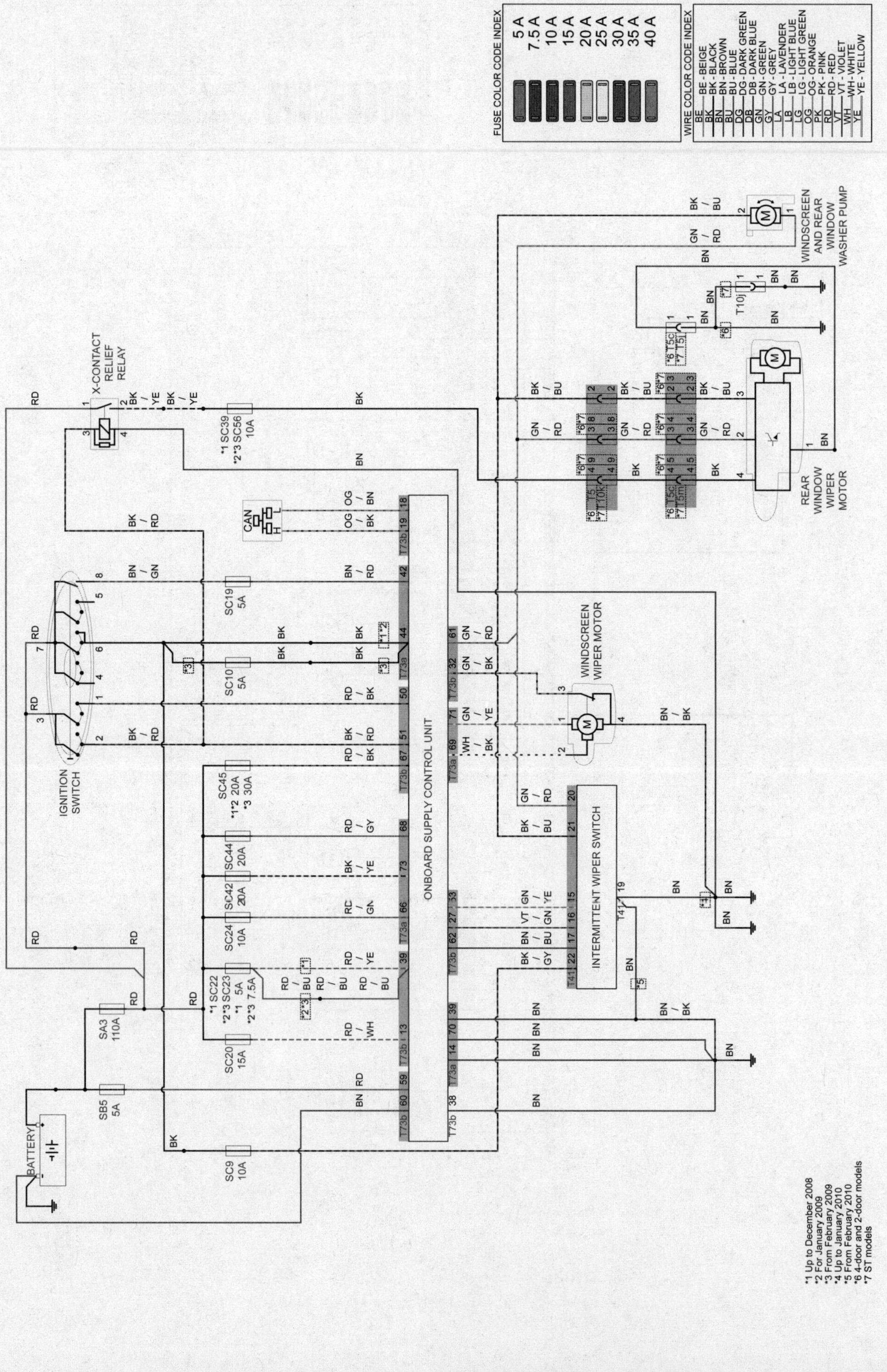

Diagram 12 – Washers and wipers up to May 2010

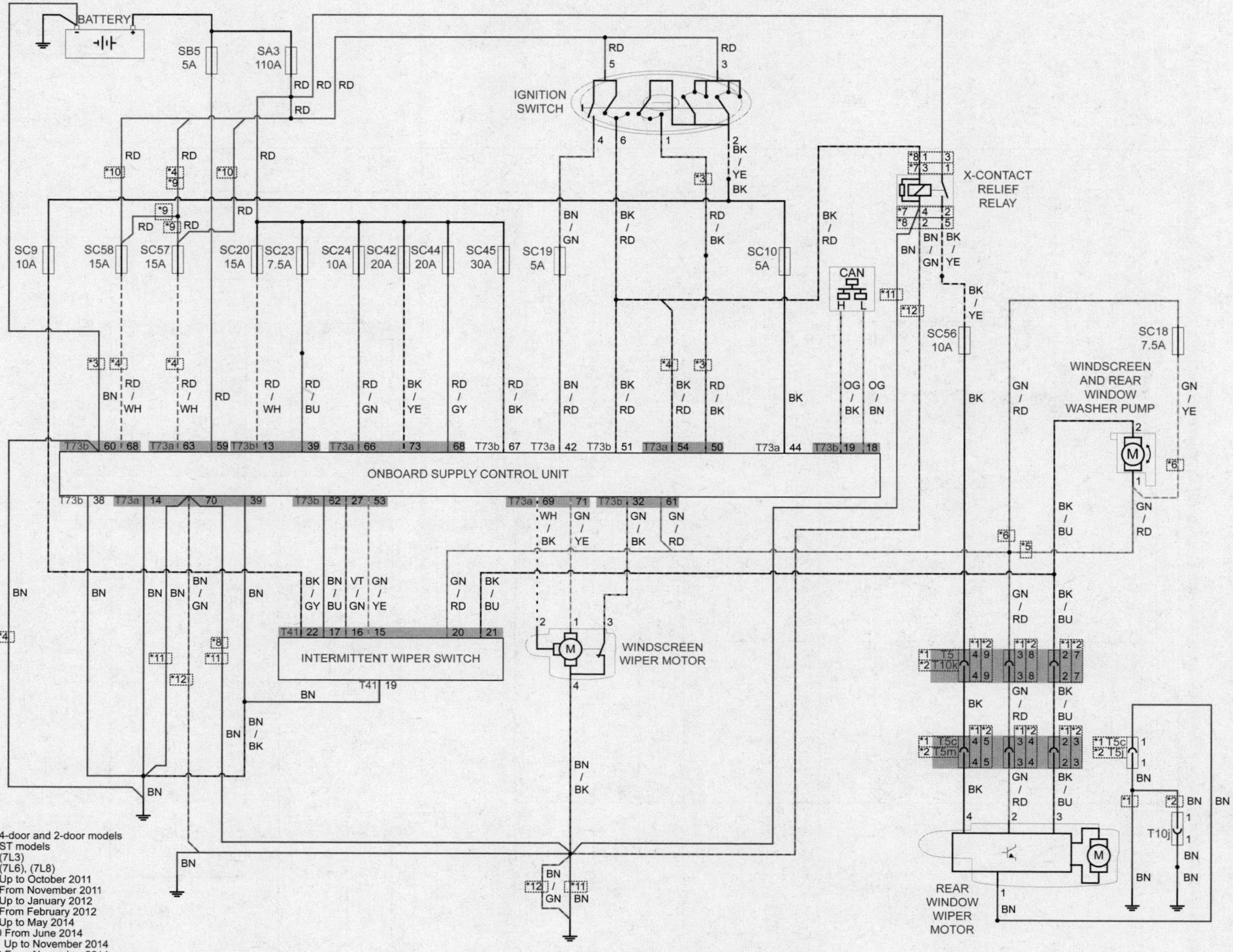

FUSE COLOR CODE INDEX

- 5 A
- 7.5 A
- 10 A
- 15 A
- 20 A
- 25 A
- 30 A
- 35 A
- 40 A

WIRE COLOR CODE INDEX

- BE - BEIGE
- BK - BLACK
- BN - BROWN
- BU - BLUE
- DG - DARK GREEN
- DB - DARK BLUE
- GN - GREEN
- GY - GREY
- LA - LAVENDER
- LB - LIGHT BLUE
- LG - LIGHT GREEN
- OG - ORANGE
- PK - PINK
- RD - RED
- VT - VIOLET
- WH - WHITE
- YE - YELLOW

*1 4-door and 2-door models
*2 ST models
*3 (7L3)
*4 (7L6), (7L8)
*5 Up to October 2011
*6 From November 2011
*7 Up to January 2012
*8 From February 2012
*9 Up to May 2014
*10 From June 2014
*11 Up to November 2014
*12 From November 2014

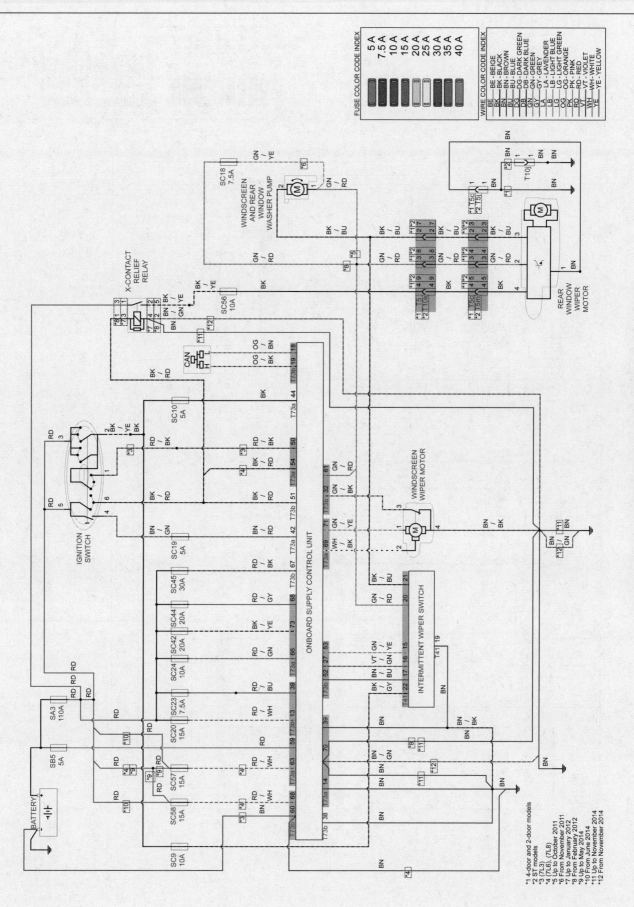

Diagram 13 – Washers and wipers from June 2010 to May 2015

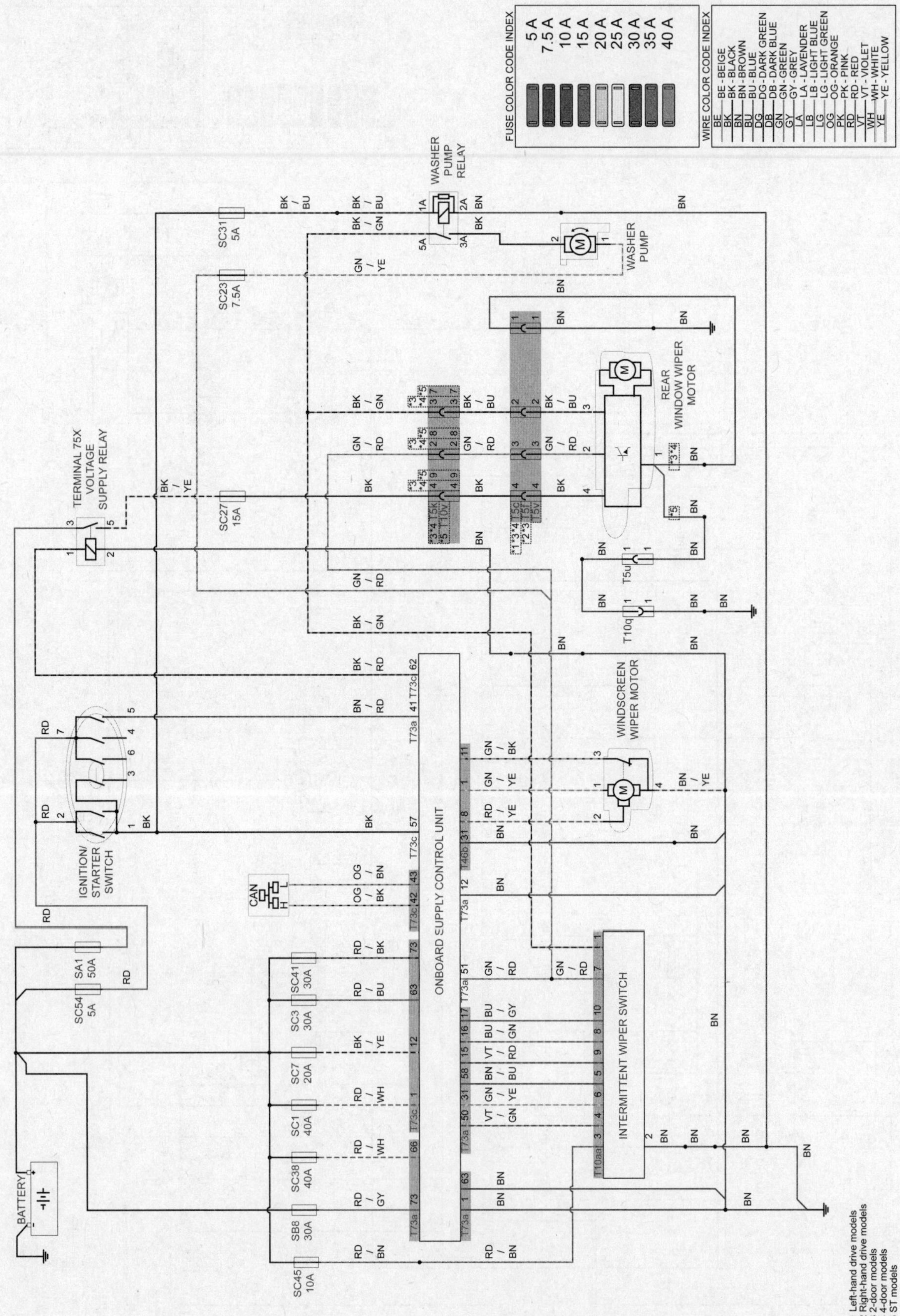

Diagram 14 – Washers and wipers from June 2015

*1 Left-hand drive models
*2 Right-hand drive models
*3 2-door models
*4 4-door models
*5 ST models

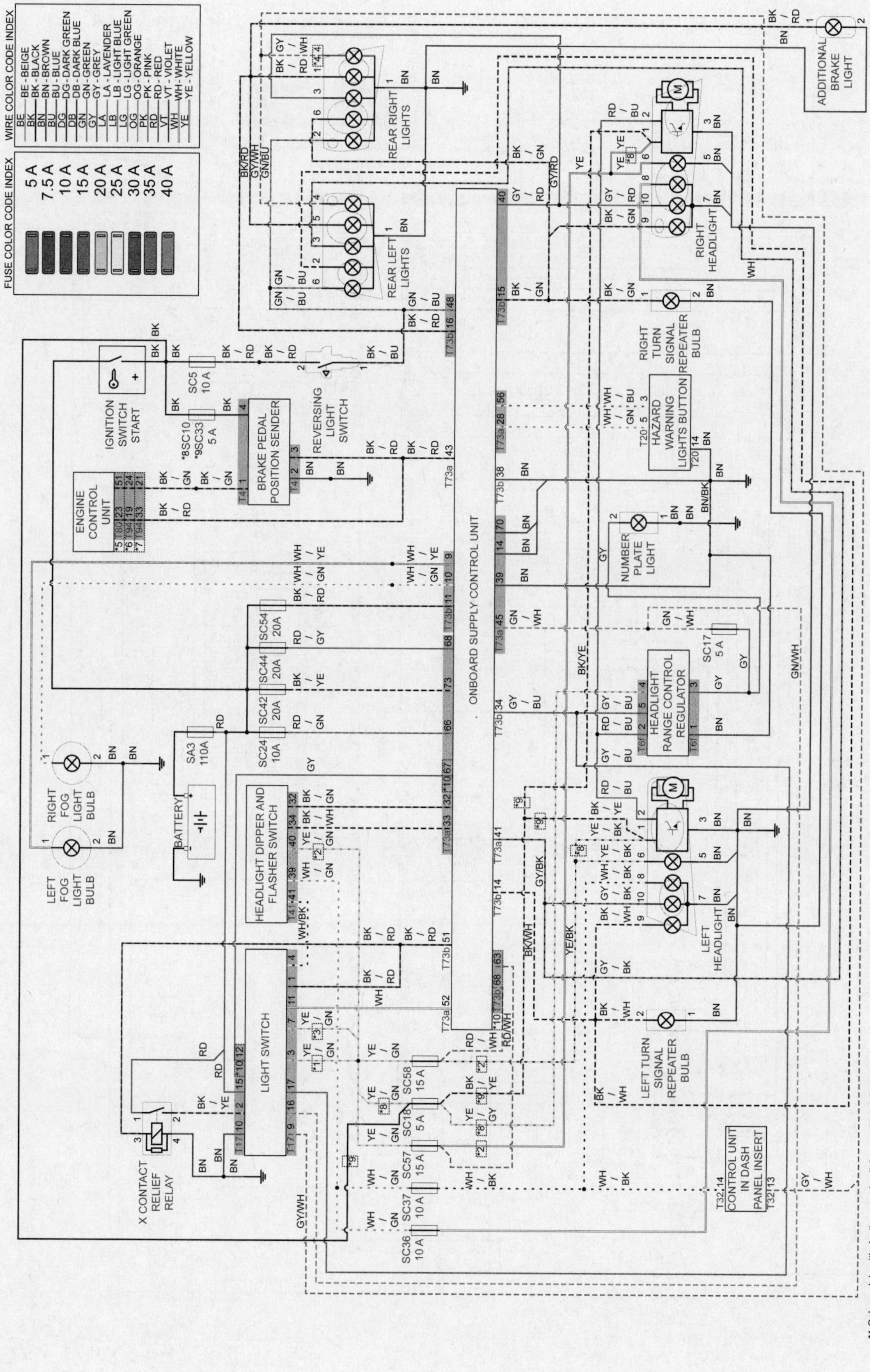

Diagram 15 – Exterior lights up to May 2015

*1 Only models with daytime running lights
*2 According to equipment
*3 Only models with dual headlights
*4 Right hand drive
*5 1.4 Petrol
*6 1.2 Petrol
*7 1.6 Diesel
*8 Up to January 2010
*9 From February 2010
*10 Only models with automatic driving lights control

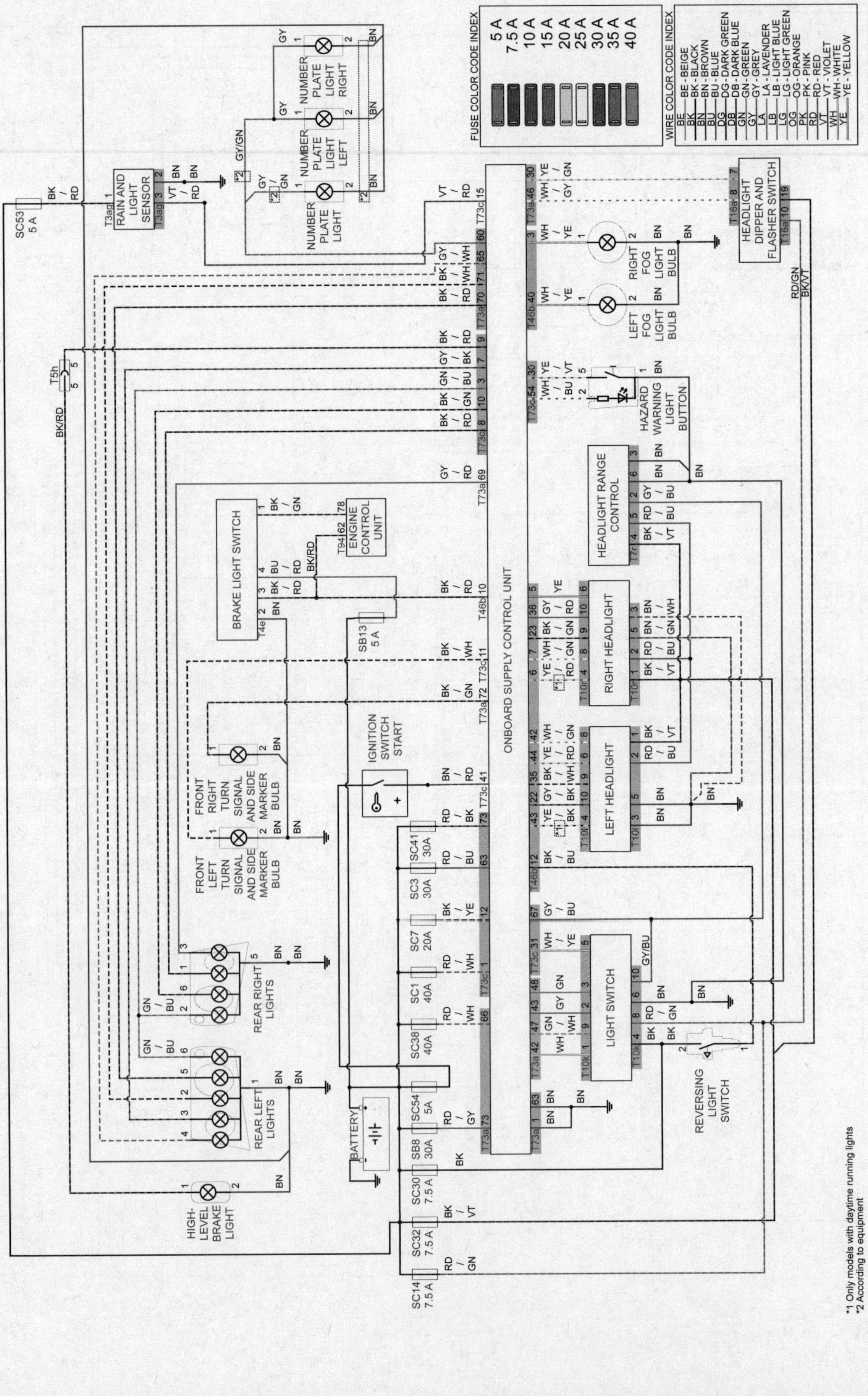

Diagram 16 – Exterior lights from June 2015

*1 Only models with daytime running lights
*2 According to equipment

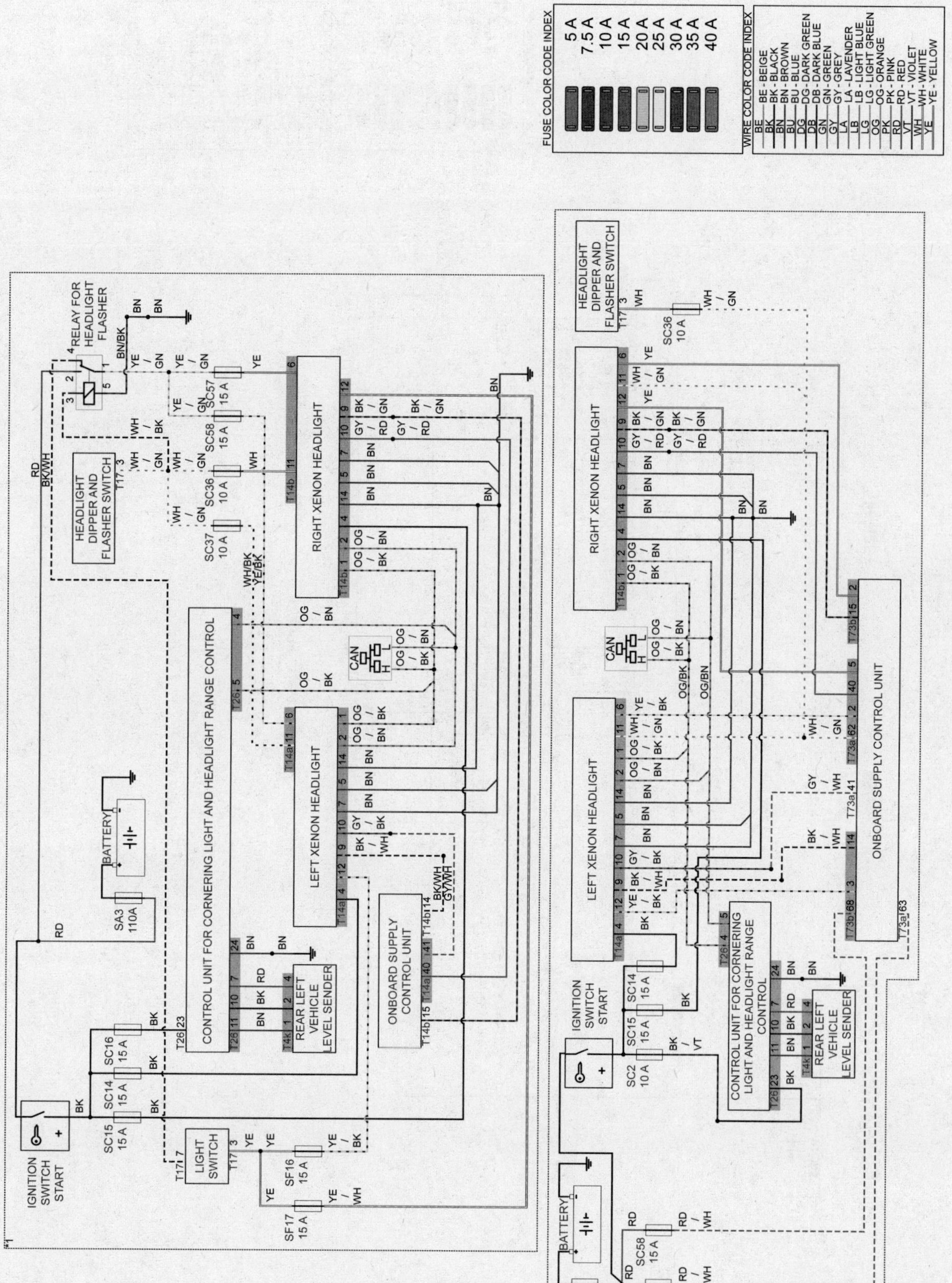

Diagram 17 – Exterior lights – Xenon up to May 2015

*1 Up to May 2010
*2 From June 2010

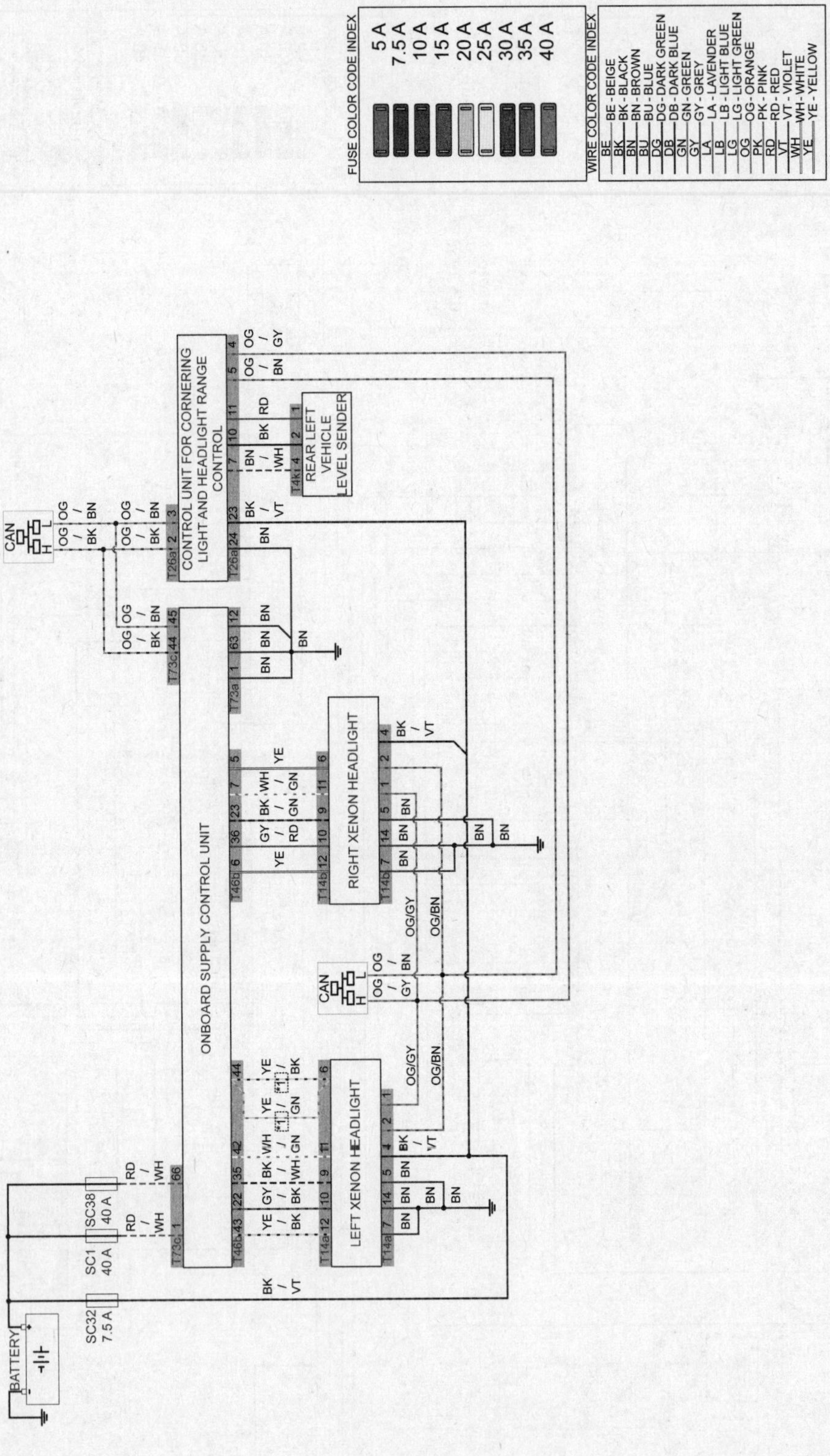

*1 According to equipment

Diagram 18 – Exterior lights – Xenon from June 2015

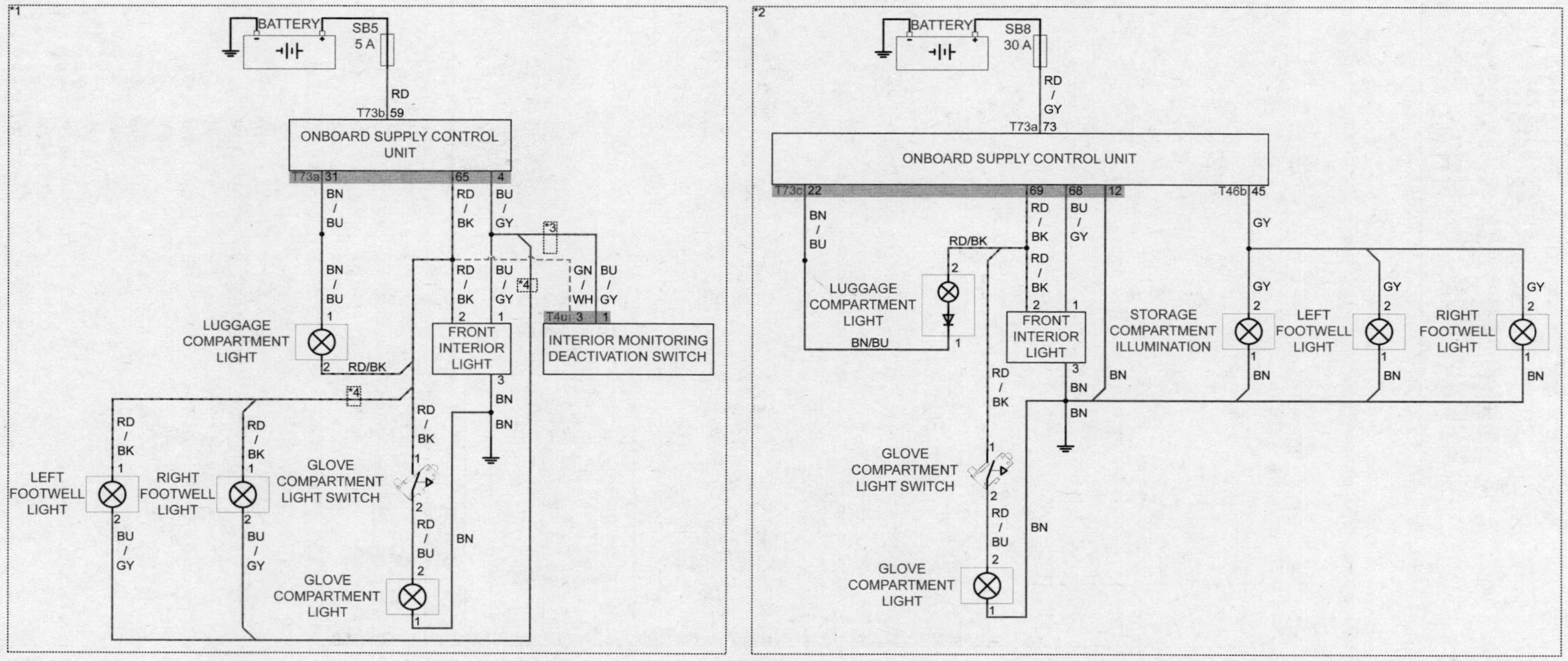

*1 Up to May 2015
*2 From June 2015
*3 With interior monitoring
*4 With footwell light

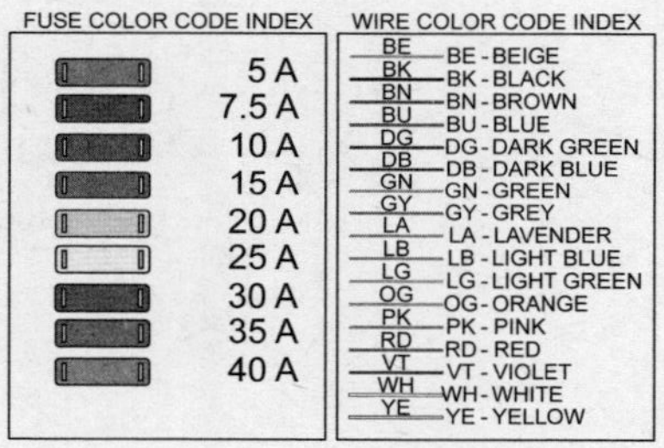

Diagram 19 – Interior lights

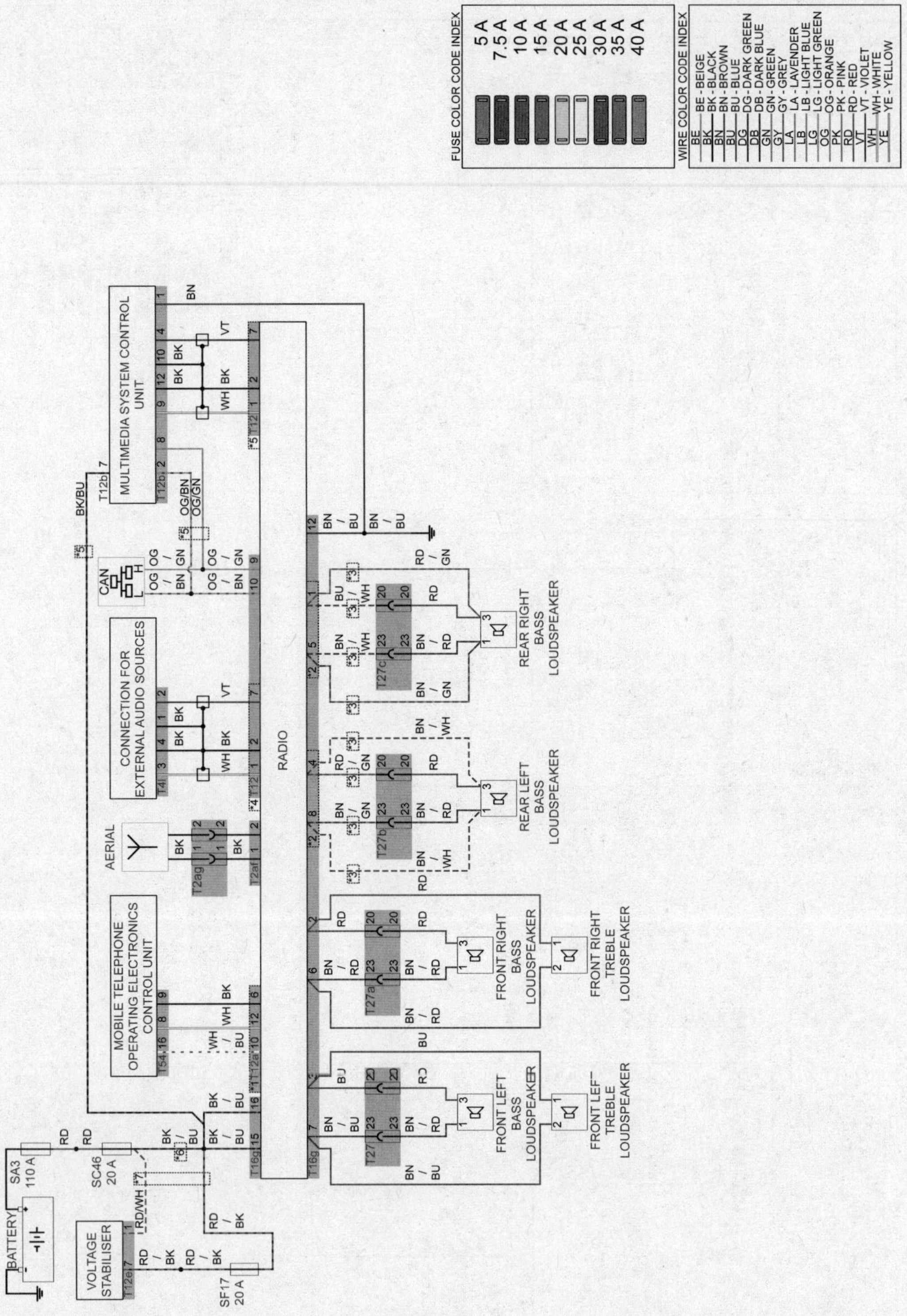

Diagram 20 – Sound system up to May 2015

*1 Only models with mobile telephone
*2 Only models with 4 doors
*3 According to equipment
*4 With AUX-IN
*5 With MEDIA-IN
*6 Without start/stop
*7 With start/stop

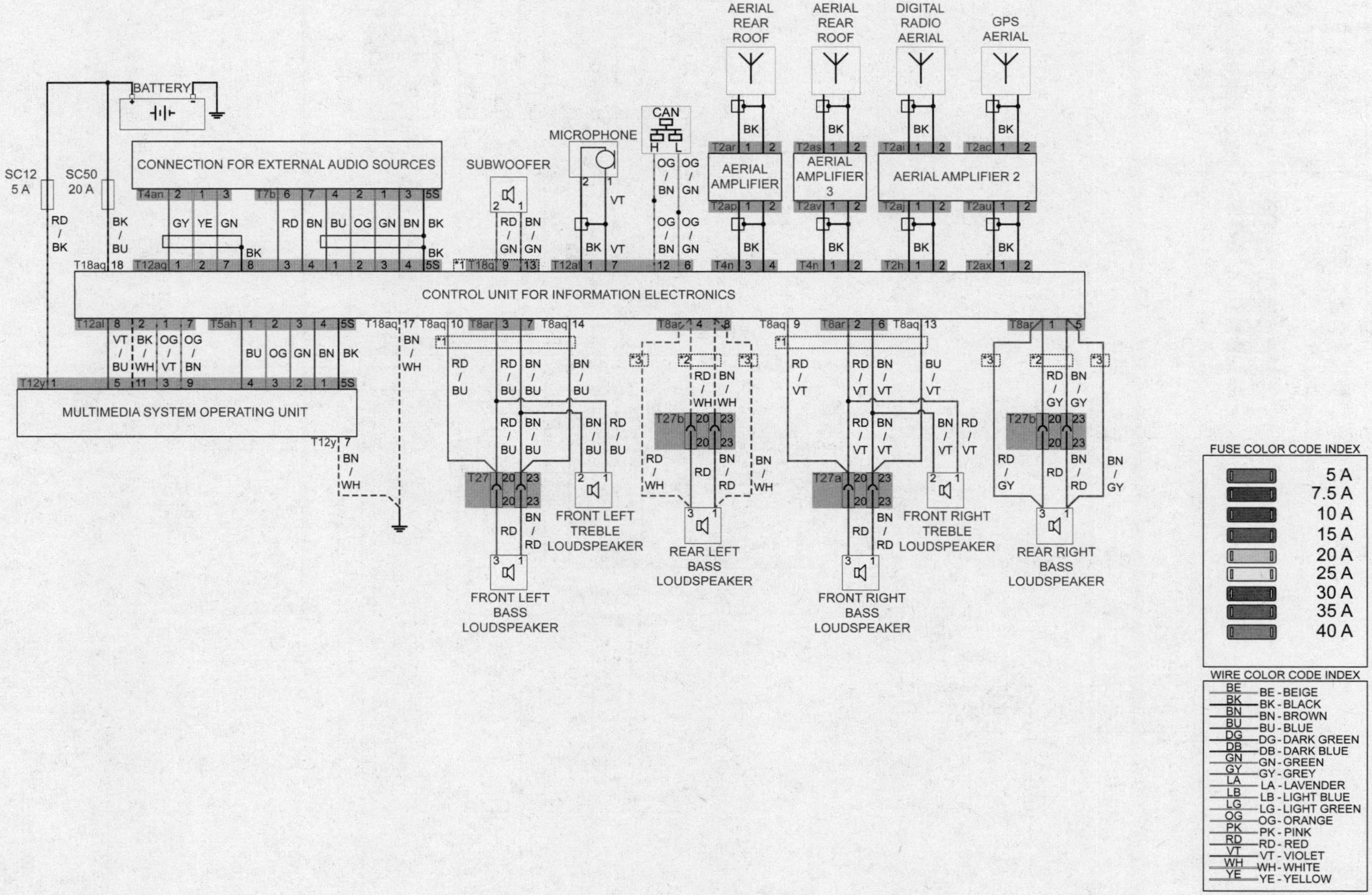

*1 According to equipment
*2 Only models with 5 doors
*3 Only models with 3 doors

Diagram 21 – Sound system from June 2015

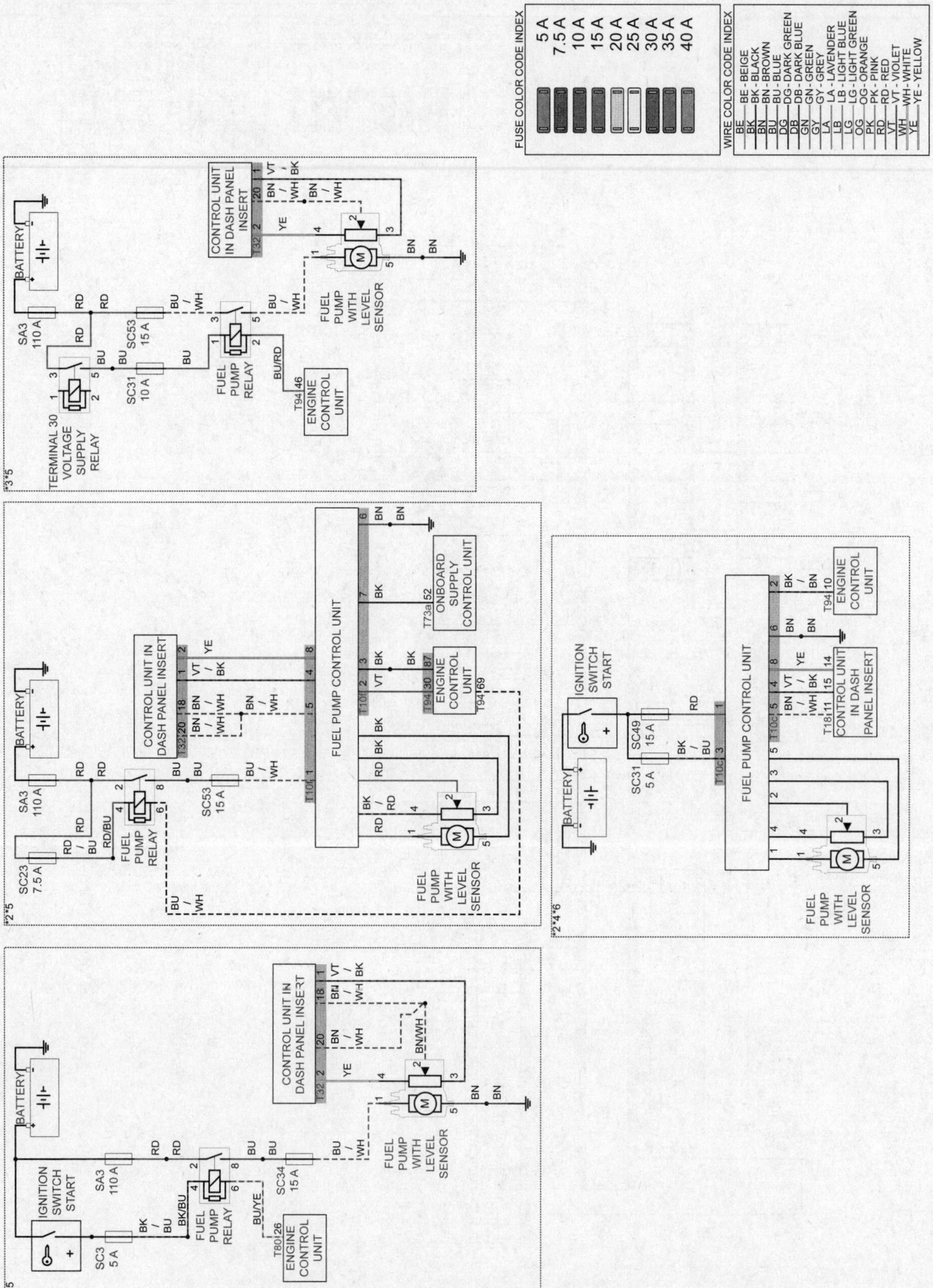

Diagram 22 – Fuel pump

*1 1.4 Petrol
*2 1.2 Petrol
*3 1.6 Diesel
*4 1.0 Petrol
*5 Up to May 2015
*6 From June 2015

Dimensions and weights

Note: *All figures and dimensions are approximate and may vary according to model. Refer to manufacturer's data for exact figures.*

Dimensions

Overall length:		
Hatchback models	4061 mm	
Estate models	4236 mm	
Overall width:		
All models (excluding mirrors)	1693 mm	
Overall height (unladen):		
Standard suspension	1445 mm	
Wheelbase:		
All models	2469 mm	

Weights

Kerb weight:*		
Hatchback	1156 to 1161 kg	
Estate	1206 to 1211 kg	
**Exact kerb weights depend upon model and specification (see VIN plate on the inner wing)*		
Maximum gross vehicle weight:**		
Hatchback	1650 kg	
Estate	1690 kg	
***Exact gross vehicle weight depends on models and specification (see VIN plate on the inner wing)*		
Maximum roof rack load:		
All models	75 kg	
Maximum towing weights:*	**Unbraked trailer**	**Braked trailer**
Hatchback	580 kg	1200 kg
Estate	600 kg	1200 kg

**Exact towing weights depend on model and specification (see VIN plate on the inner wing)*

Conversion factors

Length (distance)

Inches (in)	x 25.4	= Millimetres (mm)	x 0.0394	–	Inches (in)
Feet (ft)	x 0.305	= Metres (m)	x 3.281	=	Feet (ft)
Miles	x 1.609	= Kilometres (km)	x 0.621	=	Miles

Volume (capacity)

Cubic inches (cu in; in³)	x 16.387	= Cubic centimetres (cc; cm³)	x 0.061	=	Cubic inches (cu in; in³)
Imperial pints (Imp pt)	x 0.568	= Litres (l)	x 1.76	=	Imperial pints (Imp pt)
Imperial quarts (Imp qt)	x 1.137	= Litres (l)	x 0.88	=	Imperial quarts (Imp qt)
Imperial quarts (Imp qt)	x 1.201	= US quarts (US qt)	x 0.833	=	Imperial quarts (Imp qt)
US quarts (US qt)	x 0.946	= Litres (l)	x 1.057	=	US quarts (US qt)
Imperial gallons (Imp gal)	x 4.546	= Litres (l)	x 0.22	=	Imperial gallons (Imp gal)
Imperial gallons (Imp gal)	x 1.201	= US gallons (US gal)	x 0.833	=	Imperial gallons (Imp gal)
US gallons (US gal)	x 3.785	= Litres (l)	x 0.264	=	US gallons (US gal)

Mass (weight)

Ounces (oz)	x 28.35	= Grams (g)	x 0.035	=	Ounces (oz)
Pounds (lb)	x 0.454	= Kilograms (kg)	x 2.205	=	Pounds (lb)

Force

Ounces-force (ozf; oz)	x 0.278	= Newtons (N)	x 3.6	=	Ounces-force (ozf; oz)
Pounds-force (lbf; lb)	x 4.448	= Newtons (N)	x 0.225	=	Pounds-force (lbf; lb)
Newtons (N)	x 0.1	= Kilograms-force (kgf; kg)	x 9.81	=	Newtons (N)

Pressure

Pounds-force per square inch (psi; lbf/in²; lb/in²)	x 0.070	= Kilograms-force per square centimetre (kgf/cm²; kg/cm²)	x 14.223	=	Pounds-force per square inch (psi; lbf/in²; lb/in²)
Pounds-force per square inch (psi; lbf/in²; lb/in²)	x 0.068	= Atmospheres (atm)	x 14.696	=	Pounds-force per square inch (psi; lbf/in²; lb/in²)
Pounds-force per square inch (psi; lbf/in²; lb/in²)	x 0.069	= Bars	x 14.5	=	Pounds-force per square inch (psi; lbf/in²; lb/in²)
Pounds-force per square inch (psi; lbf/in²; lb/in²)	x 6.895	= Kilopascals (kPa)	x 0.145	=	Pounds-force per square inch (psi; lbf/in²; lb/in²)
Kilopascals (kPa)	x 0.01	= Kilograms-force per square centimetre (kgf/cm²; kg/cm²)	x 98.1	=	Kilopascals (kPa)
Millibar (mbar)	x 100	= Pascals (Pa)	x 0.01	=	Millibar (mbar)
Millibar (mbar)	x 0.0145	= Pounds-force per square inch (psi; lbf/in²; lb/in²)	x 68.947	=	Millibar (mbar)
Millibar (mbar)	x 0.75	= Millimetres of mercury (mmHg)	x 1.333	=	Millibar (mbar)
Millibar (mbar)	x 0.401	= Inches of water (inH_2O)	x 2.491	=	Millibar (mbar)
Millimetres of mercury (mmHg)	x 0.535	= Inches of water (inH_2O)	x 1.868	=	Millimetres of mercury (mmHg)
Inches of water (inH_2O)	x 0.036	= Pounds-force per square inch (psi; lbf/in²; lb/in²)	x 27.68	=	Inches of water (inH_2O)

Torque (moment of force)

Pounds-force inches (lbf in; lb in)	x 1.152	= Kilograms-force centimetre (kgf cm; kg cm)	x 0.868	=	Pounds-force inches (lbf in; lb in)
Pounds-force inches (lbf in; lb in)	x 0.113	= Newton metres (Nm)	x 8.85	=	Pounds-force inches (lbf in; lb in)
Pounds-force inches (lbf in; lb in)	x 0.083	= Pounds-force feet (lbf ft; lb ft)	x 12	=	Pounds-force inches (lbf in; lb in)
Pounds-force feet (lbf ft; lb ft)	x 0.138	= Kilograms-force metres (kgf m; kg m)	x 7.233	=	Pounds-force feet (lbf ft; lb ft)
Pounds-force feet (lbf ft; lb ft)	x 1.356	= Newton metres (Nm)	x 0.738	=	Pounds-force feet (lbf ft; lb ft)
Newton metres (Nm)	x 0.102	= Kilograms-force metres (kgf m; kg m)	x 9.804	=	Newton metres (Nm)

Power

Horsepower (hp)	x 745.7	= Watts (W)	x 0.0013	=	Horsepower (hp)

Velocity (speed)

Miles per hour (miles/hr; mph)	x 1.609	= Kilometres per hour (km/hr; kph)	x 0.621	=	Miles per hour (miles/hr; mph)

Fuel consumption*

Miles per gallon, Imperial (mpg)	x 0.354	= Kilometres per litre (km/l)	x 2.825	=	Miles per gallon, Imperial (mpg)
Miles per gallon, US (mpg)	x 0.425	= Kilometres per litre (km/l)	x 2.352	=	Miles per gallon, US (mpg)

Temperature

Degrees Fahrenheit = (°C x 1.8) + 32

Degrees Celsius (Degrees Centigrade; °C) = (°F - 32) x 0.56

* *It is common practice to convert from miles per gallon (mpg) to litres/100 kilometres (l/100km), where mpg x l/100 km = 282*

Spare parts are available from many sources, including maker's appointed garages, accessory shops, and motor factors. To be sure of obtaining the correct parts, it will sometimes be necessary to quote the vehicle identification number. If possible, it can also be useful to take the old parts along for positive identification. Items such as starter motors and alternators may be available under a service exchange scheme – any parts returned should be clean.

Our advice regarding spare parts is as follows.

Officially appointed garages

This is the best source of parts which are peculiar to your car, and which are not otherwise generally available (eg, badges, interior trim, certain body panels, etc). It is also the only place at which you should buy parts if the vehicle is still under warranty.

Accessory shops

These are very good places to buy materials and components needed for the maintenance of your car (oil, air and fuel filters, light bulbs, drivebelts, greases, brake pads, touch-up paint, etc). Components of this nature sold by a reputable shop are usually of the same standard as those used by the car manufacturer.

Besides components, these shops also sell tools and general accessories, usually have convenient opening hours, charge lower prices, and can often be found close to home. Some accessory shops have parts counters where components needed for almost any repair job can be purchased or ordered.

Motor factors

Good factors will stock all the more important components which wear out comparatively quickly, and can sometimes supply individual components needed for the overhaul of a larger assembly (eg, brake seals and hydraulic parts, bearing shells, pistons, valves). They may also handle work such as cylinder block reboring, crankshaft regrinding, etc.

Tyre and exhaust specialists

These outlets may be independent, or members of a local or national chain. They frequently offer competitive prices when compared with a main dealer or local garage, but it will pay to obtain several quotes before making a decision. When researching prices, also ask what extras may be added – for instance fitting a new valve and balancing the wheel are both commonly charged on top of the price of a new tyre.

Other sources

Beware of parts or materials obtained from market stalls, car boot sales or similar outlets. Such items are not invariably sub-standard, but there is little chance of compensation if they do prove unsatisfactory. In the case of safety-critical components such as brake pads, there is the risk not only of financial loss, but also of an accident causing injury or death.

Second-hand components or assemblies obtained from a car breaker can be a good buy in some circumstances, but this sort of purchase is best made by the experienced DIY mechanic.

Jacking and vehicle support

The jack supplied with the vehicle tool kit should only be used for changing the roadwheels – see *Wheel changing* at the front of this book. When carrying out any other kind of work, raise the vehicle using a hydraulic (or 'trolley') jack, and always supplement the jack with axle stands positioned under the vehicle jacking points.

When using a hydraulic jack or axle stands, always position the jack head or axle stand head under one of the relevant jacking points.

To raise the front and/or rear of the vehicle, use the jacking/support points at the front and rear ends of the door sills, indicated by the triangular depressions in the sill panel **(see illustration)**. Position a block of wood with a groove cut in it on the jack head to prevent the vehicle weight resting on the sill edge; align the sill edge with the groove in the wood so that the vehicle weight is spread evenly over the surface of the block. Supplement the jack with axle stands (also with slotted blocks of wood) positioned as close as possible to the jacking points **(see illustrations)**.

Do not jack the vehicle under any other part of the sill, sump, floor pan, or any of the steering or suspension components. With the vehicle raised, an axle stand should be positioned beneath the vehicle jack location point on the sill.

Warning: Never work under, around, or near a raised car, unless it is adequately supported in at least two places.

Front and rear jacking points (arrowed)

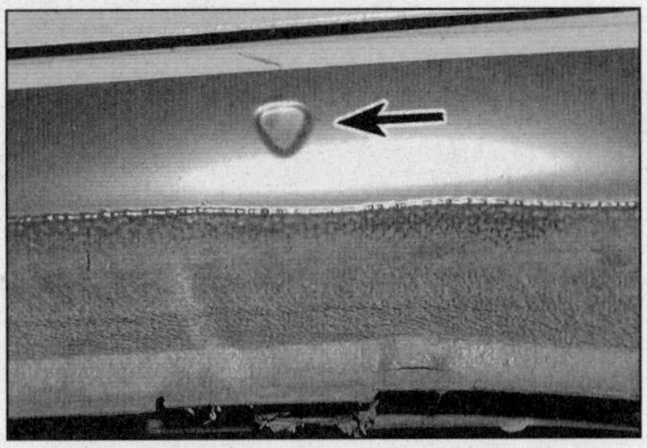

The jacking points are indicated by an arrow on the sill

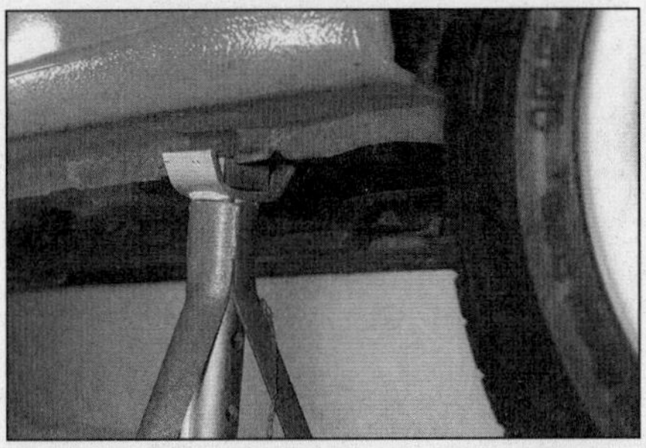

Use an axle stand with a suitable block of wood

Modifications are a continuing and unpublicised process in vehicle manufacture, quite apart from major model changes. Spare parts manuals and lists are compiled upon a numerical basis, the individual vehicle identification numbers being essential for correct identification of the part concerned.

When ordering spare parts, always give as much information as possible. Quote the car model, year of manufacture and registration, chassis and engine numbers, as appropriate.

The *Vehicle Identification Number (VIN) plate* is visible from the outside of the vehicle, through the left-hand lower corner of the windscreen **(see illustration)**.

The *Vehicle Data Sticker* is located on the luggage compartment floor panel next to the spare wheel well **(see illustration)**. It contains the VIN, vehicle type, engine power, transmission type, engine and transmission codes, paint number, interior equipment, optional extras and PR number (for maintenance schedule).

The *Type plate and factory plate* is located on the right-hand inner wing **(see illustration)**. It contains the chassis (VIN) and engine number. Also the gross vehicle weight, front axle weight and rear axle weight.

The *Engine Number* is stamped into the left-hand end of the cylinder block and on the right-hand end of the cylinder head on petrol engines. On diesel engines and some petrol engines it is stamped into the front of the cylinder block, next to the engine to transmission joint. A barcode identification sticker is located on the top of the timing cover on several engines **(see illustrations)**. If the engine number is difficult to find, check the *Vehicle Data Sticker* on the luggage compartment floor panel (see above).

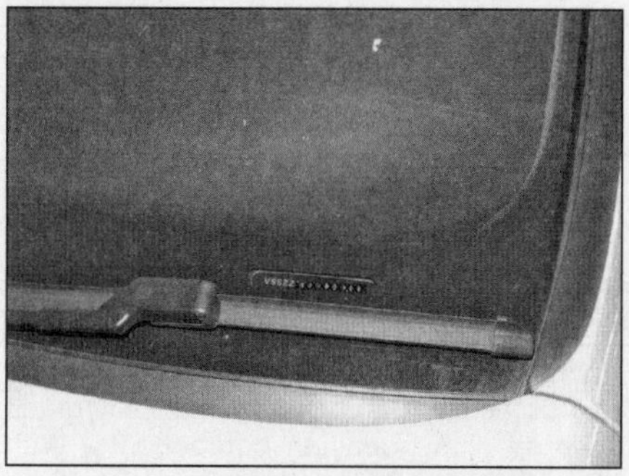

Vehicle Identification Number (VIN) located on the left-hand front edge of the windscreen

Vehicle Data Sticker close to the spare wheel well

VIN and engine number located on the right-hand inner wing

Engine code sticker on the timing belt cover on some petrol engines

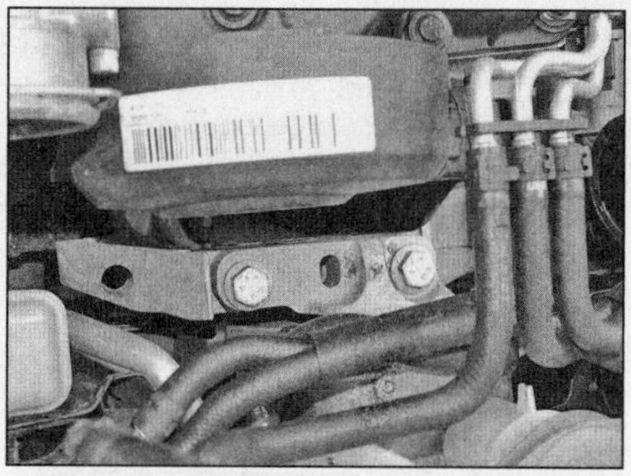

Engine code sticker on the top of the timing cover on diesel engines

Whenever servicing, repair or overhaul work is carried out on the car or its components, observe the following procedures and instructions. This will assist in carrying out the operation efficiently and to a professional standard of workmanship.

Joint mating faces and gaskets

When separating components at their mating faces, never insert screwdrivers or similar implements into the joint between the faces in order to prise them apart. This can cause severe damage which results in oil leaks, coolant leaks, etc upon reassembly. Separation is usually achieved by tapping along the joint with a soft-faced hammer in order to break the seal. However, note that this method may not be suitable where dowels are used for component location.

Where a gasket is used between the mating faces of two components, a new one must be fitted on reassembly; fit it dry unless otherwise stated in the repair procedure. Make sure that the mating faces are clean and dry, with all traces of old gasket removed. When cleaning a joint face, use a tool which is unlikely to score or damage the face, and remove any burrs or nicks with an oilstone or fine file.

Make sure that tapped holes are cleaned with a pipe cleaner, and keep them free of jointing compound, if this is being used, unless specifically instructed otherwise.

Ensure that all orifices, channels or pipes are clear, and blow through them, preferably using compressed air.

Oil seals

Oil seals can be removed by levering them out with a wide flat-bladed screwdriver or similar implement. Alternatively, a number of self-tapping screws may be screwed into the seal, and these used as a purchase for pliers or some similar device in order to pull the seal free.

Whenever an oil seal is removed from its working location, either individually or as part of an assembly, it should be renewed.

The very fine sealing lip of the seal is easily damaged, and will not seal if the surface it contacts is not completely clean and free from scratches, nicks or grooves. If the original sealing surface of the component cannot be restored, and the manufacturer has not made provision for slight relocation of the seal relative to the sealing surface, the component should be renewed.

Protect the lips of the seal from any surface which may damage them in the course of fitting. Use tape or a conical sleeve where possible. Where indicated, lubricate the seal lips with oil before fitting and, on dual-lipped seals, fill the space between the lips with grease.

Unless otherwise stated, oil seals must be fitted with their sealing lips toward the lubricant to be sealed.

Use a tubular drift or block of wood of the appropriate size to install the seal and, if the seal housing is shouldered, drive the seal down to the shoulder. If the seal housing is unshouldered, the seal should be fitted with its face flush with the housing top face (unless otherwise instructed).

Screw threads and fastenings

Seized nuts, bolts and screws are quite a common occurrence where corrosion has set in, and the use of penetrating oil or releasing fluid will often overcome this problem if the offending item is soaked for a while before attempting to release it. The use of an impact driver may also provide a means of releasing such stubborn fastening devices, when used in conjunction with the appropriate screwdriver bit or socket. If none of these methods works, it may be necessary to resort to the careful application of heat, or the use of a hacksaw or nut splitter device. Before resorting to extreme methods, check that you are not dealing with a left-hand thread!

Studs are usually removed by locking two nuts together on the threaded part, and then using a spanner on the lower nut to unscrew the stud. Studs or bolts which have broken off below the surface of the component in which they are mounted can sometimes be removed using a stud extractor.

Always ensure that a blind tapped hole is completely free from oil, grease, water or other fluid before installing the bolt or stud. Failure to do this could cause the housing to crack due to the hydraulic action of the bolt or stud as it is screwed in.

For some screw fastenings, notably cylinder head bolts or nuts, torque wrench settings are no longer specified for the latter stages of tightening, "angle-tightening" being called up instead. Typically, a fairly low torque wrench setting will be applied to the bolts/nuts in the correct sequence, followed by one or more stages of tightening through specified angles.

When checking or retightening a nut or bolt to a specified torque setting, slacken the nut or bolt by a quarter of a turn, and then retighten to the specified setting. However, this should not be attempted where angular tightening has been used.

Locknuts, locktabs and washers

Any fastening which will rotate against a component or housing during tightening should always have a washer between it and the relevant component or housing.

Spring or split washers should always be renewed when they are used to lock a critical component such as a big-end bearing retaining bolt or nut. Locktabs which are folded over to retain a nut or bolt should always be renewed.

Self-locking nuts can be re-used in non-critical areas, providing resistance can be felt when the locking portion passes over the bolt or stud thread. However, it should be noted that self-locking stiffnuts tend to lose their effectiveness after long periods of use, and should then be renewed as a matter of course.

Split pins must always be replaced with new ones of the correct size for the hole.

When thread-locking compound is found on the threads of a fastener which is to be re-used, it should be cleaned off with a wire brush and solvent, and fresh compound applied on reassembly.

Special tools

Some repair procedures in this manual entail the use of special tools such as a press, two or three-legged pullers, spring compressors, etc. Wherever possible, suitable readily-available alternatives to the manufacturer's special tools are described, and are shown in use. In some instances, where no alternative is possible, it has been necessary to resort to the use of a manufacturer's tool, and this has been done for reasons of safety as well as the efficient completion of the repair operation. Unless you are highly-skilled and have a thorough understanding of the procedures described, never attempt to bypass the use of any special tool when the procedure described specifies its use. Not only is there a very great risk of personal injury, but expensive damage could be caused to the components involved.

Environmental considerations

When disposing of used engine oil, brake fluid, antifreeze, etc, give due consideration to any detrimental environmental effects. Do not, for instance, pour any of the above liquids down drains into the general sewage system, or onto the ground to soak away, as this is likely to pollute your local environment. Many local council refuse tips provide a facility for waste oil disposal, as do some garages. You can find your nearest disposal point by calling the Environment Agency on 03708 506 506 or by visiting www.oilbankline.org.uk.

OIL CARE®

Note: It is illegal and anti-social to dump oil down the drain. To find the location of your local oil recycling bank, call 03708 506 506 or visit www.oilbankline.org.uk.

Introduction

A selection of good tools is a fundamental requirement for anyone contemplating the maintenance and repair of a motor vehicle. For the owner who does not possess any, their purchase will prove a considerable expense, offsetting some of the savings made by doing-it-yourself. However, provided that the tools purchased meet the relevant national safety standards and are of good quality, they will last for many years and prove an extremely worthwhile investment.

To help the average owner to decide which tools are needed to carry out the various tasks detailed in this manual, we have compiled three lists of tools under the following headings: *Maintenance and minor repair, Repair and overhaul*, and *Special*. Newcomers to practical mechanics should start off with the *Maintenance and minor repair* tool kit, and confine themselves to the simpler jobs around the vehicle. Then, as confidence and experience grow, more difficult tasks can be undertaken, with extra tools being purchased as, and when, they are needed. In this way, a *Maintenance and minor repair* tool kit can be built up into a *Repair and overhaul* tool kit over a considerable period of time, without any major cash outlays. The experienced do-it-yourselfer will have a tool kit good enough for most repair and overhaul procedures, and will add tools from the *Special* category when it is felt that the expense is justified by the amount of use to which these tools will be put.

Maintenance and minor repair tool kit

The tools given in this list should be considered as a minimum requirement if routine maintenance, servicing and minor repair operations are to be undertaken. We recommend the purchase of combination spanners (ring one end, open-ended the other); although more expensive than open-ended ones, they do give the advantages of both types of spanner.

☐ *Combination spanners:*
Metric - 8 to 19 mm inclusive
☐ *Adjustable spanner - 35 mm jaw (approx.)*
☐ *Spark plug spanner (with rubber insert) - petrol models*
☐ *Spark plug gap adjustment tool - petrol models*
☐ *Set of feeler gauges*
☐ *Brake bleed nipple spanner*
☐ *Screwdrivers:*
Flat blade - 100 mm long x 6 mm dia
Cross blade - 100 mm long x 6 mm dia
Torx - various sizes (not all vehicles)
☐ *Combination pliers*
☐ *Hacksaw (junior)*
☐ *Tyre pump*
☐ *Tyre pressure gauge*
☐ *Oil can*
☐ *Oil filter removal tool*
☐ *Fine emery cloth*
☐ *Wire brush (small)*
☐ *Funnel (medium size)*
☐ *Sump drain plug key (not all vehicles)*

Repair and overhaul tool kit

These tools are virtually essential for anyone undertaking any major repairs to a motor vehicle, and are additional to those given in the *Maintenance and minor repair* list. Included in this list is a comprehensive set of sockets. Although these are expensive, they will be found invaluable as they are so versatile - particularly if various drives are included in the set. We recommend the half-inch square-drive type, as this can be used with most proprietary torque wrenches.

The tools in this list will sometimes need to be supplemented by tools from the *Special* list:

☐ *Sockets (or box spanners) to cover range in previous list (including Torx sockets)*
☐ *Reversible ratchet drive (for use with sockets)*
☐ *Extension piece, 250 mm (for use with sockets)*
☐ *Universal joint (for use with sockets)*
☐ *Flexible handle or sliding T "breaker bar" (for use with sockets)*
☐ *Torque wrench (for use with sockets)*
☐ *Self-locking grips*
☐ *Ball pein hammer*
☐ *Soft-faced mallet (plastic or rubber)*
☐ *Screwdrivers:*
Flat blade - long & sturdy, short (chubby), and narrow (electrician's) types
Cross blade – long & sturdy, and short (chubby) types
☐ *Pliers:*
Long-nosed
Side cutters (electrician's)
Circlip (internal and external)
☐ *Cold chisel - 25 mm*
☐ *Scriber*
☐ *Scraper*
☐ *Centre-punch*
☐ *Pin punch*
☐ *Hacksaw*
☐ *Brake hose clamp*
☐ *Brake/clutch bleeding kit*
☐ *Selection of twist drills*
☐ *Steel rule/straight-edge*
☐ *Allen keys (inc. splined/Torx type)*
☐ *Selection of files*
☐ *Wire brush*
☐ *Axle stands*
☐ *Jack (strong trolley or hydraulic type)*
☐ *Light with extension lead*
☐ *Universal electrical multi-meter*

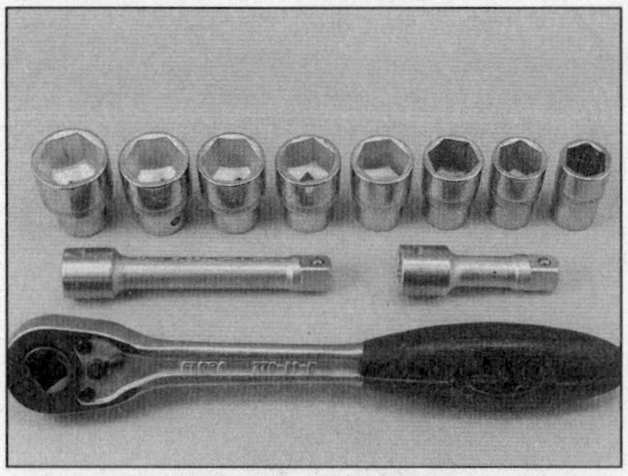

Sockets and reversible ratchet drive

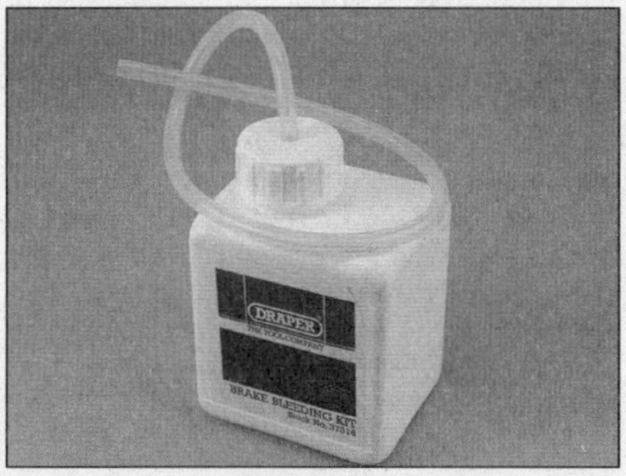

Brake bleeding kit

Torx key, socket and bit

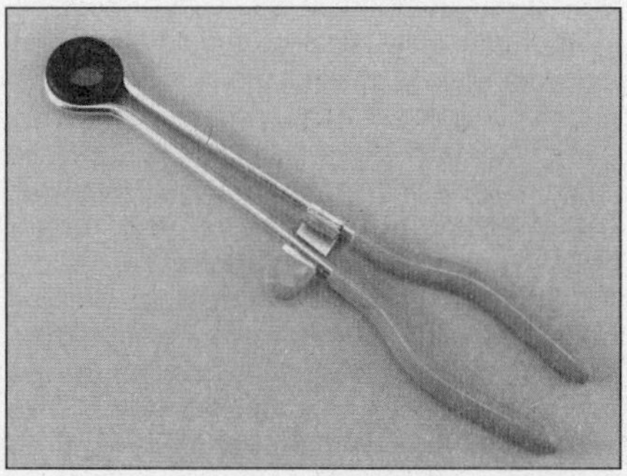

Hose clamp

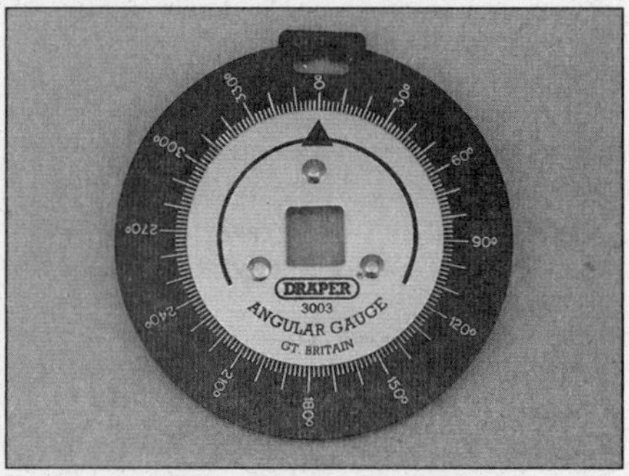

Angular-tightening gauge

Special tools

The tools in this list are those which are not used regularly, are expensive to buy, or which need to be used in accordance with their manufacturers' instructions. Unless relatively difficult mechanical jobs are undertaken frequently, it will not be economic to buy many of these tools. Where this is the case, you could consider clubbing together with friends (or joining a motorists' club) to make a joint purchase, or borrowing the tools against a deposit from a local garage or tool hire specialist. It is worth noting that many of the larger DIY superstores now carry a large range of special tools for hire at modest rates.

The following list contains only those tools and instruments freely available to the public, and not those special tools produced by the vehicle manufacturer specifically for its dealer network. You will find occasional references to these manufacturers' special tools in the text of this manual. Generally, an alternative method of doing the job without the vehicle manufacturers' special tool is given. However, sometimes there is no alternative to using them. Where this is the case and the relevant tool cannot be bought or borrowed, you will have to entrust the work to a dealer.

- ☐ *Angular-tightening gauge*
- ☐ *Valve spring compressor*
- ☐ *Valve grinding tool*
- ☐ *Piston ring compressor*
- ☐ *Piston ring removal/installation tool*
- ☐ *Cylinder bore hone*
- ☐ *Balljoint separator*
- ☐ *Coil spring compressors (where applicable)*
- ☐ *Two/three-legged hub and bearing puller*
- ☐ *Impact screwdriver*
- ☐ *Micrometer and/or vernier calipers*
- ☐ *Dial gauge*
- ☐ *Stroboscopic timing light*
- ☐ *Dwell angle meter/tachometer*
- ☐ *Fault code reader*
- ☐ *Cylinder compression gauge*
- ☐ *Hand-operated vacuum pump and gauge*
- ☐ *Clutch plate alignment set*
- ☐ *Brake shoe steady spring cup removal tool*
- ☐ *Bush and bearing removal/installation set*
- ☐ *Stud extractors*
- ☐ *Tap and die set*
- ☐ *Lifting tackle*
- ☐ *Trolley jack*

Buying tools

Reputable motor accessory shops and superstores often offer excellent quality tools at discount prices, so it pays to shop around.

Remember, you don't have to buy the most expensive items on the shelf, but it is always advisable to steer clear of the very cheap tools. Beware of 'bargains' offered on market stalls or at car boot sales. There are plenty of good tools around at reasonable prices, but always aim to purchase items which meet the relevant national safety standards. If in doubt, ask the proprietor or manager of the shop for advice before making a purchase.

Care and maintenance of tools

Having purchased a reasonable tool kit, it is necessary to keep the tools in a clean and serviceable condition. After use, always wipe off any dirt, grease and metal particles using a clean, dry cloth, before putting the tools away. Never leave them lying around after they have been used. A simple tool rack on the garage or workshop wall for items such as screwdrivers and pliers is a good idea. Store all normal spanners and sockets in a metal box. Any measuring instruments, gauges, meters, etc, must be carefully stored where they cannot be damaged or become rusty.

Take a little care when tools are used. Hammer heads inevitably become marked, and screwdrivers lose the keen edge on their blades from time to time. A little timely attention with emery cloth or a file will soon restore items like this to a good finish.

Working facilities

Not to be forgotten when discussing tools is the workshop itself. If anything more than routine maintenance is to be carried out, a suitable working area becomes essential.

It is appreciated that many an owner-mechanic is forced by circumstances to remove an engine or similar item without the benefit of a garage or workshop. Having done this, any repairs should always be done under the cover of a roof.

Wherever possible, any dismantling should be done on a clean, flat workbench or table at a suitable working height.

Any workbench needs a vice; one with a jaw opening of 100 mm is suitable for most jobs. As mentioned previously, some clean dry storage space is also required for tools, as well as for any lubricants, cleaning fluids, touch-up paints etc, which become necessary.

Another item which may be required, and which has a much more general usage, is an electric drill with a chuck capacity of at least 8 mm. This, together with a good range of twist drills, is virtually essential for fitting accessories.

Last, but not least, always keep a supply of old newspapers and clean, lint-free rags available, and try to keep any working area as clean as possible.

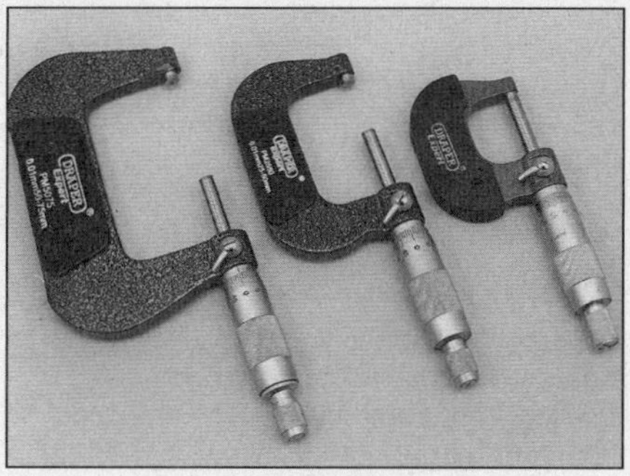

Micrometers

Dial test indicator ("dial gauge")

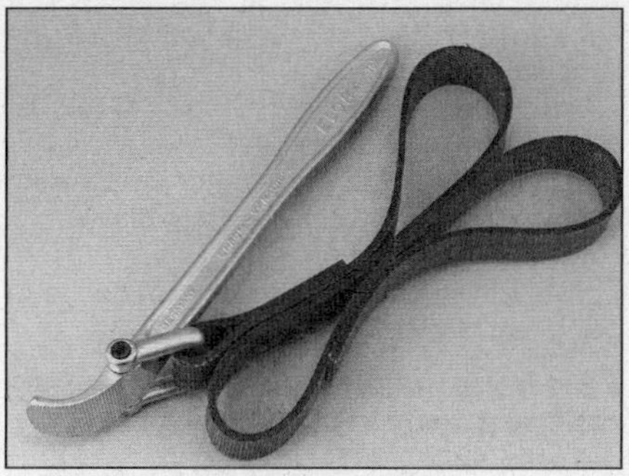

Strap wrench

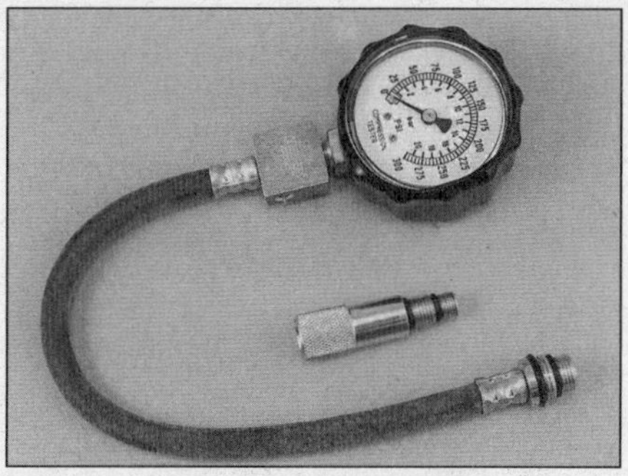

Compression tester

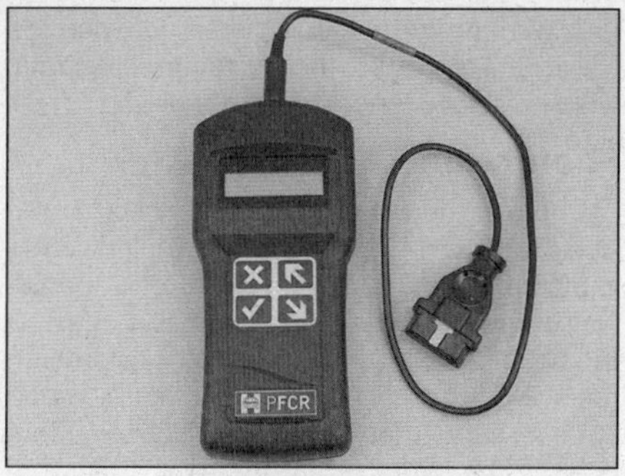

Fault code reader

This is a guide to getting your vehicle through the MOT test. Obviously it will not be possible to examine the vehicle to the same standard as the professional MOT tester. However, working through the following checks will enable you to identify any problem areas before submitting the vehicle for the test.

It has only been possible to summarise the test requirements here, based on the regulations in force at the time of printing. Test standards are becoming increasingly stringent, although there are some exemptions for older vehicles.

An assistant will be needed to help carry out some of these checks.

The checks have been sub-divided into four categories, as follows:

1 Checks carried out **FROM THE VEHICLE INTERIOR**

2 Checks carried out **WITH THE VEHICLE ON THE GROUND**

3 Checks carried out **WITH THE VEHICLE RAISED AND THE WHEELS FREE TO TURN**

4 Checks carried out on **YOUR VEHICLE'S EXHAUST EMISSION SYSTEM**

1 Checks carried out FROM THE VEHICLE INTERIOR

Handbrake (parking brake)

☐Test the operation of the handbrake. Excessive travel (too many clicks) indicates incorrect brake or cable adjustment.

☐Check that the handbrake cannot be released by tapping the lever sideways. Check the security of the lever mountings.

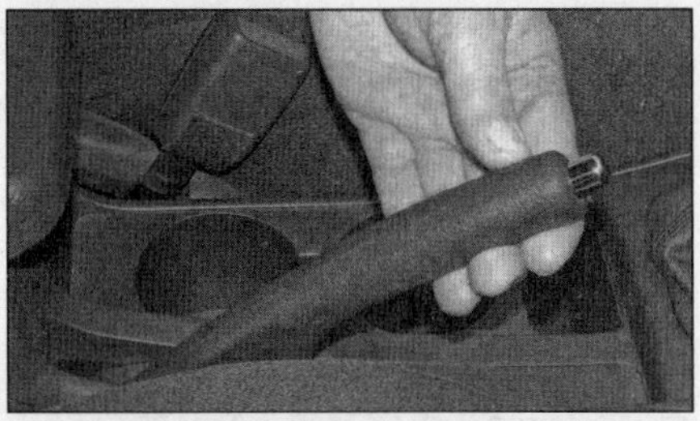

☐If the parking brake is foot-operated, check that the pedal is secure and without excessive travel, and that the release mechanism operates correctly.

☐Where applicable, test the operation of the electronic handbrake. The brake should engage and disengage without excessive delay. If the warning light does not extinguish, or a warning message is displayed when the brake is disengaged, this could indicate a fault which will need further investigation.

Footbrake

☐Depress the brake pedal and check that it does not creep down to the floor, indicating a master cylinder fault. Release the pedal, wait a few seconds, then depress it again. If the pedal travels nearly to the floor before firm resistance is felt, brake adjustment or repair is necessary. If the pedal feels spongy, there is air in the hydraulic system which must be removed by bleeding.

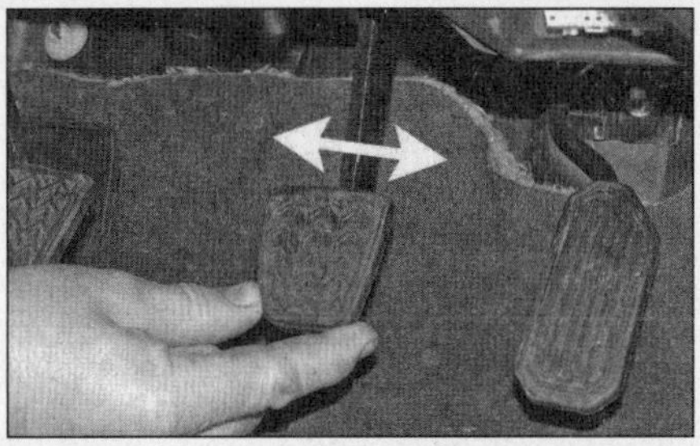

☐Check that the brake pedal is secure and in good condition. Check also for signs of fluid leaks on the pedal, floor or carpets, which would indicate failed seals in the brake master cylinder.

☐Check the servo unit (when applicable) by operating the brake pedal several times, then keeping the pedal depressed and starting the engine. As the engine starts, the pedal will move down. If not, the vacuum hose or the servo itself may be faulty.

Steering wheel and column

☐Examine the steering wheel for fractures or looseness of the hub, spokes or rim.

☐Move the steering wheel from side to side and then up and down. Check that the steering wheel is not loose on the column, indicating wear or a loose retaining nut. Continue moving the steering wheel as before, but also turn it slightly from left to right.

☐Check that the steering wheel is not loose on the column, and that there is no abnormal movement of the steering wheel, indicating wear in the column support bearings or couplings.

☐Check that the ignition lock (where fitted) engages and disengages correctly.

☐Steering column adjustment mechanisms (where fitted) must be able to lock the column securely in place with no play evident.

Windscreen, mirrors and sunvisor

☐The windscreen must be free of cracks or other significant damage within the 'swept area' of the windscreen. This is the area swept by the windscreen wipers. A second test area, known as 'Zone A', is the part of the swept area 290 mm wide, centred on the steering wheel centre line. Any damage in Zone A that cannot be contained in a 10 mm diameter circle, or any damage in the remainder of the swept area that cannot be contained in a 40 mm diameter circle, may cause the vehicle to fail the test.

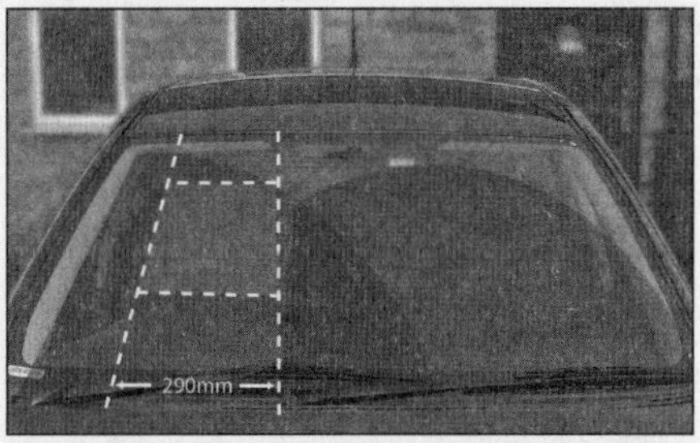

☐Any items that may obscure the drivers view, such as stickers, sat-navs, anything hanging from the interior mirror, should be removed prior to the test.

☐Vehicles registered after 1st August 1978 must have a drivers side mirror, and either an interior mirror, or a passenger's side mirror. Cameras (or indirect vision devices) may replace the mirrors, but they must function correctly.

☐ The driver's sunvisor must be capable of being stored in the "up" position.

Seat belts, seats and supplementary restraint systems (SRS)

Note: *The following checks are applicable to all seat belts, front and rear.*

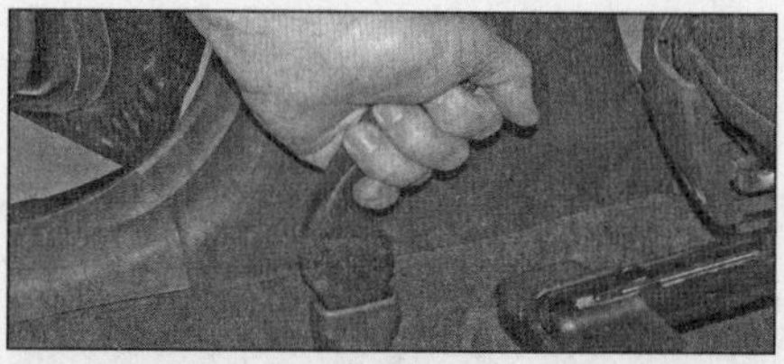

☐Examine the webbing of all the belts (including rear belts if fitted) for cuts, serious fraying or deterioration. Fasten and unfasten each belt to check the buckles. If applicable, check the retracting mechanism. Check the security of all seat belt mountings accessible from inside the vehicle, ensuring any height adjustable mountings lock securely in place.
☐Where the seat belt is attached to a seat, the frame and mountings of the seat form part of the belt mountings, and are to be inspected as such.
☐Any airbag, or SRS warning light must extinguish a few seconds after the ignition is switched on. Failure to do so indicates a fault which must be investigated.
☐Seat belts with pre-tensioners, once activated, have a "flag" or similar showing on the seat belt stalk. This, in itself, is a reason for test failure.
☐Check that the original airbag(s) is/are present, and not obviously defective.
☐The seats themselves must be securely attached and the backrests must lock in the upright position. The driver's seat must also be able to slide forwards/rearwards, and lock in several positions.

Doors

☐Both front doors must be able to be opened and closed from outside and inside, and must latch securely when closed.
☐The rear doors must open from the outside.
☐Examine all door hinges, catches and striker plates for missing, deteriorated, or insecure parts that could effect the opening and closing of the doors.

Speedometer

☐The vehicle speedometer must be present, and appear operative. The figures on the speedometer must be legible, and illuminated when the lights are switched on.

2 Checks carried out **WITH THE VEHICLE ON THE GROUND**

Vehicle identification

☐Number plates must be in good condition, secure and legible, with letters and numbers correctly spaced – spacing at (A) should be 33 mm and at (B) 11 mm. At the front, digits must be black on a white background and at the rear

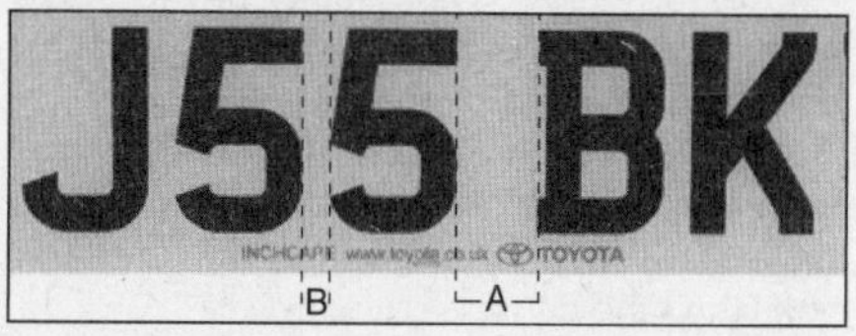

black on a yellow background. Other background designs (such as honeycomb) are not permitted.
☐The VIN plate and/or homologation plate must be permanently displayed and legible.

Electrical equipment

☐Switch on the ignition and check the operation of the horn.
☐Check the windscreen washers and wipers, examining the wiper blades; renew damaged or perished blades. The wiper blades must clear a large enough area of the windscreen to provide an 'adequate' view of the road, and be able to be parked in a position where they will not affect the drivers' view.

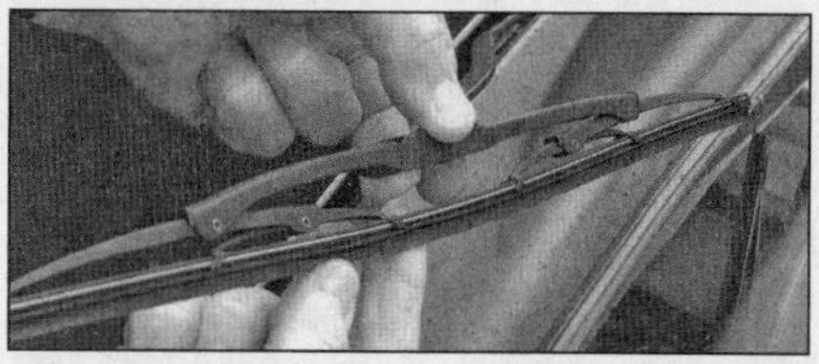

☐On vehicles first used from 1st September 2009, the headlight washers (where fitted) must operate correctly.
☐Check the operation of the stop-lights. This includes any lights that appear to be connected – Eg. high-level lights.
☐Check the operation of the sidelights and number plate lights. The lenses and reflectors must be secure, clean and undamaged.
☐Check the operation and alignment of the headlights. The headlight reflectors must not be tarnished and the lenses must be undamaged. Where plastic lenses are fitted, check they haven't deteriorated to the extent where they affect the light ouput or beam image. It's often possible to restore the plastic lens using a suitable polish or aftermarket treatment.
☐Where HID or LED headlights are fitted, check the operation of the cleaning and self-levelling functions.
☐The headlight main beam warning lamp must be functional.
☐On vehicles first used from 1st March 2018, the daytime running lights (where fitted) must operate correctly.
☐Switch on the ignition and check the operation of the direction indicators (including the instrument panel tell-tale) and the hazard warning lights. Operation of the sidelights and stop-lights must not affect the indicators – if it does, the cause is usually a bad earth at the rear light cluster. Indicators should flash at a rate of between 60 and 120 times per minute – faster or slower than this could indicate a fault with the flasher unit or a bad earth at one of the light units.
☐The hazard warning lights must operate with the ignition on and off.
☐Check the operation of the rear foglight(s), including the warning light on the instrument panel or in the switch. Note that the foglight must be positioned in the centre or driver's side of the vehicle. If only the passenger's side illuminates, the test will fail.
☐The warning lights must illuminate in accordance with the manufacturers' design (this includes any warning messages). For most vehicles, the ABS and other warning lights should illuminate when the ignition is switched on, and (if the system is operating properly) extinguish after a few seconds. Refer to the owner's handbook.
☐On vehicles first used from 1st September 2009, the reversing lights must operate correctly when reverse gear is selected.
☐Check the vehicle battery for security and leakage.
☐Check the visible/accessible vehicle wiring is adequately supported, with no evidence of damage or deterioration that could result in a short-circuit.

Footbrake

☐Examine the master cylinder, brake pipes and servo unit for leaks, loose mountings, corrosion or other damage. If ABS is fitted, this unit should also be examined for signs of leaks or corrosion.
☐The fluid reservoir must be secure and the fluid level must be between the upper (**A**) and lower (**B**) markings.

☐Check the fluid in the reservoir for signs of contamination.
☐Inspect both front brake flexible hoses for cracks or deterioration of the rubber. Turn the steering from lock to lock, and ensure that the hoses do not contact the wheel, tyre, or any part of the steering or suspension mechanism. With the brake pedal firmly depressed, check the hoses for bulges or leaks under pressure.

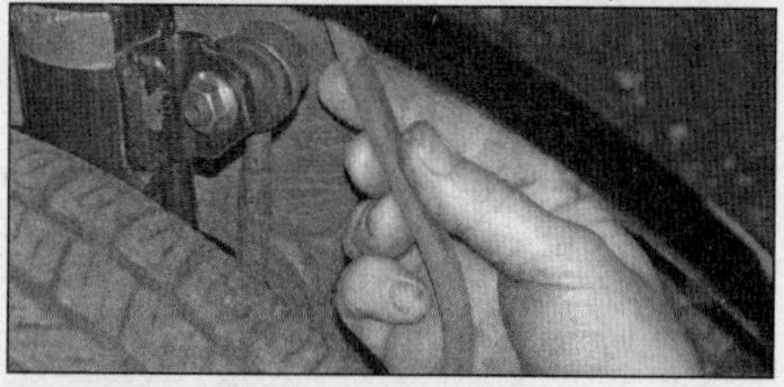

Steering and suspension

☐Have your assistant turn the steering wheel from side to side slightly, up to the point where the steering gear just begins to transmit this movement to the roadwheels. Check for excessive free play between the steering wheel and the steering gear, indicating wear or insecurity of the steering column joints, the column-to-steering gear coupling, or the steering gear itself. With a standard (380 mm diameter) steering wheel, there should be no more than 13 mm of free play for rack-and-pinion systems, and no more than 75 mm for non-rack-and-pinion designs.
☐Have your assistant turn the steering

wheel more vigorously in each direction, so that the roadwheels just begin to turn. As this is done, examine all the steering joints, linkages, fittings and attachments. Renew any component that shows signs of wear or damage. On vehicles with hydraulic power steering, check the security and condition of the steering pump, drivebelt and hoses.

□ Note that all movement checks on power steering systems are carried out with the engine running.

□ Check that the vehicle is standing level, and at approximately the correct ride height.

Exhaust system

□ Start the engine. With your assistant holding a rag over the tailpipe, check the entire system for leaks. Repair or renew leaking sections.

3 Checks carried out WITH THE VEHICLE RAISED AND THE WHEELS FREE TO TURN

Jack up the front and rear of the vehicle, and securely support it on axle stands. Position the stands clear of the suspension assemblies. Ensure that the wheels are clear of the ground and that the steering can be turned from lock to lock.

Steering mechanism

□ Have your assistant turn the steering from lock to lock. Check that the steering turns smoothly, and that no part of the steering mechanism, including a wheel or tyre, fouls any brake hose or pipe or any part of the body structure.

□ Examine the steering rack rubber gaiters for damage or insecurity of the retaining clips. If power steering is fitted, check for signs of damage or leakage of the fluid hoses, pipes or connections. Also check for excessive stiffness or binding of the steering, a missing split pin or locking device, or severe corrosion of the body structure within 30 cm of any steering component attachment point.

□ Check the track rod end ball joint dust covers. Any covers that are missing, seriously damaged, deteriorated or insecure, may fail inspection.

Front and rear suspension and wheel bearings

□ Starting at the front right-hand side, grasp the roadwheel at the 3 o'clock and 9 o'clock positions and rock gently but firmly. Check for free play or insecurity at the wheel bearings, suspension balljoints, or suspension mountings, pivots and attachments.

□ Now grasp the wheel at the 12 o'clock and 6 o'clock positions and repeat the previous inspection. Spin the wheel, and check for roughness or tightness of the front wheel bearing.

□ If excess free play is suspected at a component pivot point, this can be confirmed by using a large screwdriver or similar tool and levering between the mounting and the component attachment. This will confirm whether the wear is in the pivot bush, its retaining bolt, or in the mounting itself (the bolt holes can often become elongated).

□ Carry out all the above checks at the other front wheel, and then at both rear wheels.

Springs and shock absorbers

□ Examine the suspension struts (when applicable) for serious fluid leakage, corrosion, or damage to the casing. Also check the security of the mounting points.

□ If coil springs are fitted, check that the spring ends locate in their seats, and that the spring is not corroded, cracked or broken.

□ If leaf springs are fitted, check that all leaves are intact, that the axle is securely attached to each spring, and that there is no deterioration of the spring eye mountings, bushes, and shackles.

□ The same general checks apply to vehicles fitted with other suspension types, such as torsion bars, hydraulic displacer units, etc. Ensure that all mountings and attachments are secure, that there are no signs of excessive wear, corrosion or damage, and (on hydraulic types) that there are no fluid leaks or damaged pipes.

□ Check any suspension and anti-roll bar link ball joint dust covers. Any covers that are missing, seriously damaged, deteriorated or insecure, may fail inspection.

□ Examine each shock absorber for signs of leakage, corrosion of the casing, missing, detached or worn pivots and/or rubber bushes.

Driveshafts (fwd vehicles only)

□ Rotate each front wheel in turn and inspect the inner and outer joint gaiters for splits or damage. Also check that each driveshaft is straight and undamaged.

Braking system

□ If possible without dismantling, check brake pad wear and disc condition. Ensure that the friction lining material has not worn excessively, (A) and that the discs are not fractured, pitted, scored or badly worn (B). As a general rule, if the friction material is less than 1.5 mm thick, the inspection will fail.

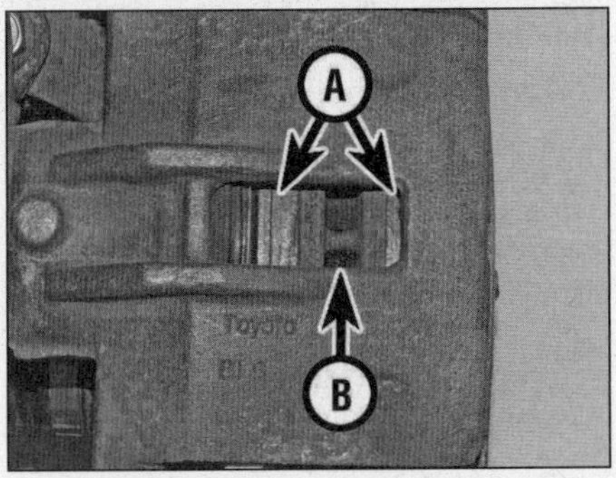

□ Examine all the rigid brake pipes underneath the vehicle, and the flexible hose(s) at the rear. Look for corrosion, chafing or insecurity of the pipes, and for signs of bulging under pressure, chafing, splits or deterioration of the flexible hoses.

□ Look for signs of fluid leaks at the brake calipers or on the brake backplates. Repair or renew leaking components.

□ Slowly spin each wheel, while your assistant depresses and releases the footbrake. Ensure that each brake is operating and does not bind when the pedal is released.

☐ Examine the handbrake mechanism, checking for frayed or broken cables, excessive corrosion, or wear or insecurity of the linkage. Check that the mechanism works on each relevant wheel, and releases fully, without binding.

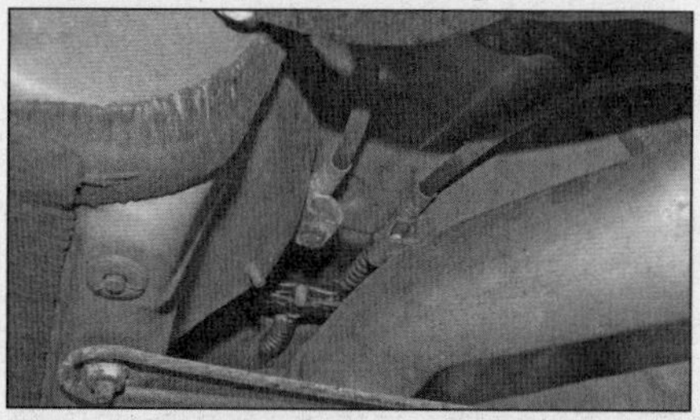

☐ Check the ABS sensors' wiring for signs of damage, deterioration or insecurity.

☐ It is not possible to test brake efficiency without special equipment, but a road test can be carried out later to check that the vehicle pulls up in a straight line.

Fuel and exhaust systems

☐ Inspect the fuel tank (including the filler cap), fuel pipes, hoses and unions. All components must be secure and free from leaks. Locking fuel caps must lock securely and the key must be provided for the MOT test.

☐ Examine the exhaust system over its entire length, checking for any damaged, broken or missing mountings, security of the retaining clamps and rust or corrosion.

☐ If the vehicle was originally equipped with a catalytic converter or particulate filter, one must be fitted.

Wheels and tyres

☐ Examine the sidewalls and tread area of each tyre in turn. Check for cuts, tears, lumps, bulges, separation of the tread, and exposure of the ply or cord due to wear or damage. Check that the tyre bead is correctly seated on the wheel rim, that the valve is sound and properly seated, and that the wheel is not distorted or damaged.

☐ Check that the tyres are of the correct size for the vehicle, that they are of the same size and type on each axle, and that the pressures are correct. The vehicle will fail the test if the tyres are obviously under-inflated.

☐ Check the tyre tread depth. The legal minimum at the time of writing is 1.6 mm over the central three-quarters of the tread width. Abnormal tread wear may indicate incorrect front wheel alignment or wear in steering or suspension components.

☐ Check that all wheel bolts/nuts are present.

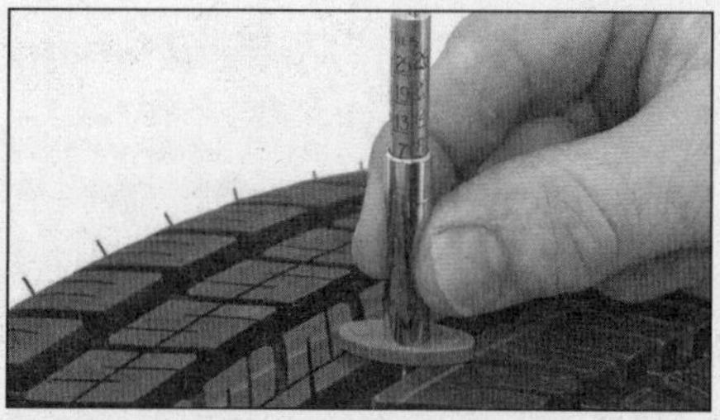

☐ If the spare wheel is fitted externally or in a separate carrier beneath the vehicle, check that mountings are secure and free of excessive corrosion.

Body corrosion

☐ Check the condition of the entire vehicle structure for signs of corrosion in load-bearing areas. (These include chassis box sections, side sills, cross-members, pillars, and all suspension, steering, braking system and seat belt mountings and anchorages.) Any corrosion which has seriously reduced the thickness of a load-bearing area (or is within 30 cm of safety-related components such as steering or suspension) is likely to cause the vehicle to fail. In this case professional repairs are likely to be needed.

☐ Damage or corrosion which causes sharp or otherwise dangerous edges to be exposed will also cause the vehicle to fail.

Towbars

☐ Check the condition of mounting points (both beneath the vehicle and within boot/hatchback areas) for signs of corrosion, ensuring that all fixings are secure and not worn or damaged. There must be no excessive play in detachable tow ball arms or quick-release mechanisms.

☐ Examine the security and condition of the towbar electrics socket. If the later 13-pin socket is fitted, the MOT tester will check its' wiring functions/connections are correct.

General leaks

☐ The vehicle will fail the test if there is a fluid leak of any kind that poses an environmental risk.

4 Checks carried out on **YOUR VEHICLE'S EXHAUST EMISSION SYSTEM**

Petrol models

☐ The engine should be warmed up, and running well (ignition system in good order, air filter element clean, etc).

☐ Before testing, run the engine at around 2500 rpm for 20 seconds. Let the engine drop to idle, and watch for smoke from the exhaust. If the idle speed is too high, or if dense blue or black smoke emerges for more than 5 seconds, the vehicle will fail. Typically, blue smoke signifies oil burning (engine wear); black smoke means unburnt fuel (dirty air cleaner element, or other fuel system fault).

☐ An exhaust gas analyser for measuring carbon monoxide (CO) and hydrocarbons (HC) is now needed. If one cannot be hired or borrowed, have a local garage perform the check.

CO emissions (mixture)

☐ The MOT tester has access to the CO limits for all vehicles from 1st August 1992. The CO level is measured at idle speed, and at 'fast idle' (2500 to 3000 rpm). The following limits are given as a general guide:

At idle speed – Less than 0.3% CO
At 'fast idle' – Less than 0.2% CO
Lambda reading – 0.97 to 1.03

☐ If the CO level is too high, this may point to poor maintenance, a fuel injection system problem, faulty lambda (oxygen) sensor or catalytic converter. Try an injector cleaning treatment, and check the vehicle's ECU for fault codes.

HC emissions

☐ The MOT tester has access to HC limits for all vehicles. The HC level is measured at 'fast idle' (2500 to 3000 rpm). The following limits are given as a general guide:

At 'fast idle' – Less than 200 ppm

☐ Excessive HC emissions are typically caused by oil being burnt (worn engine), or by a blocked crankcase ventilation system ('breather'). If the engine oil is old and thin, an oil change may help. If the engine is running badly, check the vehicle's ECU for fault codes.

Diesel models

☐ If the vehicle was fitted with a DPF (Diesel Particulate Filter) when it left the factory, it will fail the test if the MOT tester can see smoke of any colour emitting from the exhaust, or finds evidence that the filter has been tampered with.

☐ The only emission test for diesel engines is measuring exhaust smoke density, using a calibrated smoke meter.

☐ This test involves accelerating the engine to its maximum unloaded speed a minimum of once, and a maximum of 6 times. With the smoke meter connected, the engine is accelerated quickly to its maximum speed. If the smoke level is at or below the limit specified, the vehicle will pass. If the level is more than the specified limit then two further accelerations are carried out, and an average of the readings calculated. If the vehicle is still over the limit, a further three accelerations are carried out, with the average of the last three calculated after each check.

Note: *On engines with a timing belt, it is VITAL that the belt is in good condition before the test is carried out.*

Vehicles registered after 1st July 2008

Smoke level must not exceed 1.5m-1 – Turbo-charged and non-Turbocharged engines

Vehicles registered before 1st July 2008

Smoke level must not exceed 2.5m-1 – Non-turbo vehicles
Smoke level must not exceed 3.0m-1 – Turbocharged vehicles:

☐ If excess smoke is produced, try fitting a new air cleaner element, or using an injector cleaning treatment. If the engine is running badly, where applicable, check the vehicle's ECU for fault codes. Also check the vehicle's EGR system, where applicable. At high mileages, the injectors may require professional attention.

Engine

- ☐ Engine fails to rotate when attempting to start
- ☐ Engine rotates, but will not start
- ☐ Engine difficult to start when cold
- ☐ Engine difficult to start when hot
- ☐ Starter motor noisy or excessively-rough in engagement
- ☐ Engine starts, but stops immediately
- ☐ Engine idles erratically
- ☐ Engine misfires at idle speed
- ☐ Engine misfires throughout the driving speed range
- ☐ Engine hesitates on acceleration
- ☐ Engine stalls
- ☐ Engine lacks power
- ☐ Engine backfires
- ☐ Oil pressure warning light on with engine running
- ☐ Engine runs-on after switching off
- ☐ Engine noises

Cooling system

- ☐ Overheating
- ☐ Overcooling
- ☐ External coolant leakage
- ☐ Internal coolant leakage
- ☐ Corrosion

Fuel and exhaust systems

- ☐ Excessive fuel consumption
- ☐ Fuel leakage and/or fuel odour
- ☐ Excessive noise or fumes from exhaust system

Clutch

- ☐ Pedal travels to floor – no pressure or very little resistance
- ☐ Clutch fails to disengage (unable to select gears)
- ☐ Clutch slips (engine speed rises, with no increase in vehicle speed)
- ☐ Judder as clutch is engaged
- ☐ Noise when depressing or releasing clutch pedal

Manual transmission

- ☐ Noisy in neutral with engine running
- ☐ Noisy in one particular gear
- ☐ Difficulty engaging gears
- ☐ Jumps out of gear
- ☐ Vibration
- ☐ Lubricant leaks

DSG (automatic transmission)

- ☐ Fluid leakage
- ☐ General gear selection problems
- ☐ Engine won't start in any gear, or starts in gears other than Park or Neutral
- ☐ Transmission slips, shifts roughly, is noisy, or has no drive in forward or reverse gears

Driveshafts

- ☐ Clicking or knocking noise on turns (at slow speed on full-lock)
- ☐ Vibration when accelerating or decelerating

Braking system

- ☐ Vehicle pulls to one side under braking
- ☐ Noise (grinding or high-pitched squeal) when brakes applied
- ☐ Excessive brake pedal travel
- ☐ Brake pedal feels spongy when depressed
- ☐ Excessive brake pedal effort required to stop vehicle
- ☐ Judder felt through brake pedal or steering wheel when braking
- ☐ Brakes binding
- ☐ Rear wheels locking under normal braking

Suspension and steering systems

- ☐ Vehicle pulls to one side
- ☐ Wheel wobble and vibration
- ☐ Excessive pitching and/or rolling around corners, or during braking
- ☐ Wandering or general instability
- ☐ Excessively-stiff steering
- ☐ Excessive play in steering
- ☐ Lack of power assistance
- ☐ Tyre wear excessive

Electrical system

- ☐ Battery won't hold a charge for more than a few days
- ☐ Ignition/no-charge warning light stays on with engine running
- ☐ Ignition/no-charge warning light fails to come on
- ☐ Lights inoperative
- ☐ Instrument readings inaccurate or erratic
- ☐ Horn inoperative, or unsatisfactory in operation
- ☐ Windscreen/tailgate wipers failed, or unsatisfactory in operation
- ☐ Windscreen/tailgate washers failed, or unsatisfactory in operation
- ☐ Electric windows inoperative, or unsatisfactory in operation
- ☐ Central locking system inoperative, or unsatisfactory in operation

Introduction

The vehicle owner who does his or her own maintenance according to the recommended service schedules should not have to use this section of the manual very often. Modern component reliability is such that, provided those items subject to wear or deterioration are inspected or renewed at the specified intervals, sudden failure is comparatively rare. Faults do not usually just happen as a result of sudden failure, but develop over a period of time. Major mechanical failures in particular are usually preceded by characteristic symptoms over hundreds or even thousands of miles. Those components that do occasionally fail without warning are often small and easily carried in the vehicle.

With any fault-finding, the first step is to decide where to begin investigations. Sometimes this is obvious, but on other occasions, a little detective work will be necessary. The owner who makes half a dozen haphazard adjustments or replacements may be successful in curing a fault (or its symptoms), but will be none the wiser if the fault recurs, and ultimately may have spent more time and money than was necessary. A calm and logical approach will be found to be more satisfactory in the long run. Always take into account any warning signs or abnormalities that may have been noticed in the period preceding the fault – power loss, high or low gauge readings, unusual smells, etc – and remember that failure of components such as fuses or spark plugs may only be pointers to some underlying fault.

The pages that follow provide an easy-reference guide to the more common problems, which may occur during the operation of the vehicle. These problems and their possible causes are grouped under headings denoting various components or systems, such as Engine, Cooling system, etc. The general Chapter that deals with the problem is also shown in brackets; refer to the relevant part of that Chapter for system-specific information. Whatever the fault, certain basic principles apply. These are as follows:

Verify the fault. This is simply a matter of being sure that you know what the symptoms are before starting work. This is particularly important if you are investigating a fault for someone else, who may not have described it very accurately.

Don't overlook the obvious. For example, if the vehicle won't start, is there fuel in the tank? (Don't take anyone else's word on this particular point, and don't trust the fuel gauge either!) If an electrical fault is indicated, look for loose or broken wires before digging out the test gear.

Cure the disease, not the symptom. Substituting a flat battery with a fully charged one will get you off the hard shoulder, but if the underlying cause is not attended to, the new battery will go the same way. Similarly, changing oil-fouled spark plugs (petrol models) for a new set will get you moving again, but remember that the reason for the fouling (if it wasn't simply an incorrect grade of plug) will have to be found and corrected.

Don't take anything for granted. Particularly, don't forget that a 'new' component may itself be defective (especially if it's been rattling around in the boot for months), and don't leave components out of a fault diagnosis sequence just because they are new or recently fitted. When you do finally diagnose a difficult fault, you'll probably realise that all the evidence was there from the start.

Engine

Engine fails to rotate when attempting to start

- ☐ Battery terminal connections loose or corroded (*Weekly checks*).
- ☐ Battery discharged or faulty (Chapter 5A Section 2).
- ☐ Broken, loose or disconnected wiring in the starting circuit (Chapter 12 Section 2).
- ☐ Defective starter motor (Chapter 5A).
- ☐ Starter pinion or flywheel ring gear teeth loose or broken (Chapter 5A).
- ☐ Engine earth strap broken or disconnected (Chapter 12 Section 2).

Engine rotates, but will not start

- ☐ Fuel tank empty.
- ☐ Battery discharged (engine rotates slowly) (Chapter 5A Section 2).
- ☐ Battery terminal connections loose or corroded (*Weekly checks*).
- ☐ Worn, faulty or incorrectly-gapped spark plugs – petrol models (Chapter 1A).
- ☐ Preheating system faulty – diesel models (Chapter 5C).
- ☐ Engine management system fault – petrol models (Chapter 4A).
- ☐ Air in fuel system – diesel models (Chapter 4B).
- ☐ Fuel injector/injection pump fault – diesel models (Chapter 4B).
- ☐ Low cylinder compressions (Chapter 2A, 2B, 2C, 2D or 2E).
- ☐ Major mechanical failure (e.g. camshaft drive).

Engine difficult to start when cold

- ☐ Battery discharged (Chapter 5A Section 2).
- ☐ Battery terminal connections loose or corroded (*Weekly checks*).
- ☐ Worn, faulty or incorrectly-gapped spark plugs – petrol models (Chapter 1A).
- ☐ Preheating system faulty – diesel models (Chapter 5C).
- ☐ Engine management system fault – petrol models (Chapter 4A).
- ☐ Fuel injector/injection pump fault – diesel models (Chapter 4B).

Engine difficult to start when hot

- ☐ Engine management system fault – petrol models (Chapter 4A).
- ☐ Fuel injector/injection pump fault – diesel models (Chapter 4B).
- ☐ Low cylinder compressions (Chapter 2A, 2B, 2C, 2D or 2E).

Starter motor noisy or excessively rough in engagement

- ☐ Starter pinion or flywheel/driveplate ring gear teeth loose or broken (Chapter 5A).
- ☐ Starter motor mounting bolts loose or missing (Chapter 5A).
- ☐ Defective starter motor (Chapter 5A).

Engine starts, but stops immediately

- ☐ Vacuum leak at the throttle housing/inlet manifold – petrol models (Chapter 4A).
- ☐ Engine management system fault – petrol models (Chapter 4A).
- ☐ Air in fuel system – diesel models (Chapter 4B and 4C).
- ☐ Fuel injector/injection pump fault – diesel models (Chapter 4B).

Engine idles erratically

- ☐ Vacuum leak at the throttle housing/inlet manifold – petrol models (Chapter 4A).
- ☐ Worn, faulty or incorrectly-gapped spark plugs – petrol models (Chapter 1A).
- ☐ Engine management system fault – petrol models (Chapter 4A).
- ☐ Air in fuel system – diesel models (Chapter 4B).
- ☐ Fuel injector/injection pump fault – diesel models (Chapter 4B).
- ☐ Uneven or low cylinder compressions (Chapter 2A, 2B, 2C, 2D or 2E).
- ☐ Camshaft lobes worn (Chapter 2A, 2B, 2C, 2D or 2E).
- ☐ Timing belt/chain incorrectly fitted (Chapter 2A, 2B, 2C, 2D or 2E).

Engine misfires at idle speed

- ☐ Worn, faulty or incorrectly-gapped spark plugs – petrol models (Chapter 1A).
- ☐ Vacuum leak at the throttle housing/inlet manifold – petrol models (Chapter 4A).
- ☐ Engine management system fault – petrol models (Chapter 4A).
- ☐ Faulty injector(s) – diesel models (Chapter 4B).
- ☐ Uneven or low cylinder compressions (Chapter 2A, 2B, 2C, 2D or 2E).
- ☐ Disconnected, leaking, or perished crankcase ventilation hoses (Chapter 4C or 4D).

Engine misfires throughout the driving speed range

- ☐ Fuel filter blocked (Chapter 4A or 4B).
- ☐ Fuel pump faulty (Chapter 4A or 4B).
- ☐ Fuel tank vent blocked, or fuel pipes restricted (Chapter 4A or 4B).
- ☐ Worn, faulty or incorrectly-gapped spark plugs – petrol models (Chapter 1A).
- ☐ Vacuum leak at the throttle housing/inlet manifold – petrol models (Chapter 4A).
- ☐ Engine management system fault – petrol models (Chapter 4A).
- ☐ Fuel injector/injection pump fault – diesel models (Chapter 4B).
- ☐ Faulty ignition HT coil – petrol models (Chapter 5B).
- ☐ Uneven or low cylinder compressions (Chapter 2A, 2B, 2C, 2D or 2E).

Engine hesitates on acceleration

- ☐ Worn, faulty or incorrectly-gapped spark plugs – petrol models (Chapter 1A).
- ☐ Vacuum leak at the throttle housing/inlet manifold – petrol models (Chapter 4A).
- ☐ Engine management system fault – petrol models (Chapter 4A).
- ☐ Fuel injector/injection pump fault – diesel models (Chapter 4B).

Engine (continued)

Engine stalls

- ☐ Fuel filter blocked (Chapter 4A or 4B).
- ☐ Fuel pump faulty (Chapter 4A or 4B).
- ☐ Fuel tank vent blocked, or fuel pipes restricted (Chapter 4A or 4B).
- ☐ Worn, faulty or incorrectly-gapped spark plugs – petrol models (Chapter 1A).
- ☐ Vacuum leak at the throttle housing/inlet manifold – petrol models (Chapter 4A).
- ☐ Engine management system fault – petrol models (Chapter 4A).
- ☐ Fuel injector/injection pump fault – diesel models (Chapter 4B).

Engine lacks power

- ☐ Timing belt/chain incorrectly fitted (Chapter 2A, 2B, 2C, 2D or 2E).
- ☐ Fuel filter blocked (Chapter 4A or 4B).
- ☐ Fuel pump faulty (Chapter 4A or 4B).
- ☐ Uneven or low cylinder compressions (Chapter 2A, 2B, 2C, 2D or 2E).
- ☐ Worn, faulty or incorrectly-gapped spark plugs – petrol models (Chapter 1A).
- ☐ Vacuum leak at the throttle housing/inlet manifold – petrol models (Chapter 4A).
- ☐ Engine management system fault – petrol models (Chapter 4A).
- ☐ Fuel injector/injection pump fault – diesel models (Chapter 4B).
- ☐ Brakes binding (Chapter 9).
- ☐ Clutch slipping (Chapter 6A).

Engine backfires

- ☐ Timing belt/chain incorrectly fitted (Chapter 2A, 2B, 2C, 2D or 2E).
- ☐ Vacuum leak at the throttle housing/inlet manifold – petrol models (Chapter 4A).
- ☐ Engine management system fault – petrol models (Chapter 4A).

Oil pressure warning light on with engine running

- ☐ Low oil level, or incorrect oil grade (*Weekly checks*).
- ☐ Faulty oil pressure warning light switch (Chapter 2A, 2B, 2C, 2D or 2E).
- ☐ Worn engine bearings and/or oil pump (Chapter 2A, 2B, 2C, 2D or 2E).
- ☐ High engine operating temperature.
- ☐ Oil pressure relief valve defective (Chapter 2A, 2B, 2C, 2D or 2E).
- ☐ Oil pick-up strainer clogged (Chapter 2A, 2B, 2C, 2D or 2E).

Engine runs-on after switching off

- ☐ Excessive carbon build-up in engine (Chapter 2F).
- ☐ High engine operating temperature.
- ☐ Engine management system fault – petrol models (Chapter 4A).
- ☐ Fuel injection pump fault – diesel models (Chapter 4B).

Engine noises

Pre-ignition (pinking) or knocking during acceleration or under load

- ☐ Engine management system fault – petrol models (Chapter 4A).
- ☐ Incorrect grade of spark plug – petrol models (Chapter 1A).
- ☐ Vacuum leak at the throttle housing/inlet manifold – petrol models (Chapter 4A).
- ☐ Excessive carbon build-up in engine (Chapter 2F).

Whistling or wheezing noises

- ☐ Leaking inlet manifold or throttle housing gasket – petrol models (Chapter 4A).
- ☐ Leaking vacuum hose (Chapter 9).
- ☐ Blowing cylinder head gasket (Chapter 2A, 2B, 2C, 2D or 2E).

Tapping or rattling noises

- ☐ Worn valve gear or camshaft (Chapter 2F).
- ☐ Ancillary component fault (coolant pump, alternator, etc).

Knocking or thumping noises

- ☐ Worn big-end bearings (regular heavy knocking, perhaps less under load) (Chapter 2F).
- ☐ Worn main bearings (rumbling and knocking, perhaps worsening under load) (Chapter 2F).
- ☐ Piston slap (most noticeable when cold) (Chapter 2F).
- ☐ Ancillary component fault (coolant pump, alternator, etc).

Cooling system

Overheating

- ☐ Insufficient coolant in system (*Weekly checks*).
- ☐ Thermostat faulty (stuck closed) (Chapter 3).
- ☐ Radiator core blocked, or grille restricted (Chapter 3).
- ☐ Electric cooling fan or sensor faulty (Chapter 3).
- ☐ Pressure cap faulty (Chapter 1A or 1B).
- ☐ Inaccurate temperature gauge/sensor (Chapter 3).
- ☐ Airlock in cooling system (Chapter 1A or 1B).
- ☐ Engine management system fault (Chapter 4A or 4B).

Overcooling

- ☐ Thermostat faulty (stuck open) (Chapter 3).
- ☐ Inaccurate temperature gauge/sensor (Chapter 3).

External coolant leakage

- ☐ Deteriorated or damaged hoses or hose clips (Chapter 3).
- ☐ Radiator core or heater matrix leaking (Chapter 3).
- ☐ Pressure cap faulty (Chapter 1A or 1B).
- ☐ Coolant pump leaking (Chapter 3).
- ☐ Boiling due to overheating (Chapter 3).
- ☐ Core plug leaking (Chapter 2F).

Internal coolant leakage

- ☐ Leaking cylinder head gasket (Chapter 2A, 2B, 2C, 2D or 2E).
- ☐ Cracked cylinder head or cylinder bore (Chapter 2F).

Corrosion

- ☐ Infrequent draining and flushing (Chapter 1A or 1B).
- ☐ Incorrect coolant mixture or inappropriate coolant type (Chapter 1A or 1B).

Fuel and exhaust systems

Excessive fuel consumption

- ☐ Air filter element dirty or clogged (Chapter 1A or 1B).
- ☐ Engine management system fault (Chapter 4A or 4B).
- ☐ Faulty injector(s) (Chapter 4A or 4B).
- ☐ Tyres under-inflated (*Weekly checks*).
- ☐ Brakes binding (Chapter 9).

Fuel leakage and/or fuel odour

- ☐ Damaged or corroded fuel tank, pipes or connections (Chapter 4A or 4B).

Excessive noise or fumes from exhaust system

- ☐ Leaking exhaust system or manifold joints (Chapter 4C).
- ☐ Leaking, corroded or damaged silencers or pipe (Chapters 4C or 4D).
- ☐ Broken mountings causing body or suspension contact (Chapter 4C).

Clutch

Pedal travels to floor – no pressure or very little resistance

- ☐ Air in hydraulic system/faulty master or slave cylinder (Chapter 6A).
- ☐ Broken clutch release bearing or fork (Chapter 6A).
- ☐ Broken diaphragm spring in clutch pressure plate (Chapter 6A).

Clutch fails to disengage (unable to select gears)

- ☐ Air in hydraulic system/faulty master or slave cylinder (Chapter 6A).
- ☐ Clutch disc sticking on gearbox input shaft splines (Chapter 6A).
- ☐ Clutch disc sticking to flywheel or pressure plate (Chapter 6A).
- ☐ Faulty pressure plate assembly (Chapter 6A).
- ☐ Clutch release mechanism worn or incorrectly assembled (Chapter 6A).

Clutch slips (engine speed rises, with no increase in vehicle speed)

- ☐ Faulty hydraulic release system (Chapter 6A).
- ☐ Clutch disc linings excessively worn (Chapter 6A).
- ☐ Clutch disc linings contaminated with oil or grease (Chapter 6A).
- ☐ Faulty pressure plate or weak diaphragm spring (Chapter 6A).

Judder as clutch is engaged

- ☐ Clutch disc linings contaminated with oil or grease (Chapter 6A).
- ☐ Clutch disc linings excessively worn (Chapter 6A).
- ☐ Faulty or distorted pressure plate or diaphragm spring (Chapter 6A).
- ☐ Worn or loose engine or gearbox mountings (Chapter 2A, 2B, 2C, 2D or 2E).
- ☐ Clutch disc hub or gearbox input shaft splines worn (Chapter 6A).

Noise when depressing or releasing clutch pedal

- ☐ Worn clutch release bearing (Chapter 6A).
- ☐ Worn or dry clutch pedal bushes (Chapter 6)A.
- ☐ Faulty pressure plate assembly (Chapter 6A).
- ☐ Pressure plate diaphragm spring broken (Chapter 6A).
- ☐ Broken clutch disc cushioning springs (Chapter 6A).

Manual transmission

Noisy in neutral with engine running

- ☐ Input shaft bearings worn (noise apparent with clutch pedal released, but not when depressed).*
- ☐ Clutch release bearing worn (noise apparent with clutch pedal depressed, possibly less when released) (Chapter 6A).

Noisy in one particular gear

- ☐ Worn, damaged or chipped gear teeth.*

Difficulty engaging gears

- ☐ Clutch fault (Chapter 6A).
- ☐ Worn or damaged gear selection cables (Chapter 7A).
- ☐ Worn synchroniser units.*

Jumps out of gear

- ☐ Worn or damaged gear selection cables (Chapter 7A).
- ☐ Worn synchroniser units.*
- ☐ Worn selector forks.*

Vibration

- ☐ Lack of oil (Chapter 1A or 1B).
- ☐ Worn bearings.*

Lubricant leaks

- ☐ Leaking differential output oil seal (Chapter 7A).
- ☐ Leaking housing joint.*
- ☐ Leaking input shaft oil seal (Chapter 7A).

**Although the corrective action necessary to remedy the symptoms described is beyond the scope of the home mechanic, the above information should be helpful in isolating the cause of the condition, so that the owner can communicate clearly with a professional mechanic.*

DSG (automatic transmission)

Fluid leakage

Note: *Due to the complexity of the automatic transmission, it is difficult for the home mechanic to properly diagnose and service this unit. For problems other than the following, the vehicle should be taken to a Seat dealer service department or suitably equipped specialist.*

To determine the source of a leak, first remove all built-up dirt and grime from the transmission housing and surrounding areas using a degreasing agent, or by steam-cleaning. Drive the vehicle at low speed, so airflow will not blow the leak far from its source. Raise and support the vehicle, and determine where the leak is coming from.

General gear selection problems

The following are common problems, which may be caused by a poorly adjusted cable:

a) Engine starting in gears other than Park or Neutral.
b) Indicator panel showing a gear other than that being used.
c) Vehicle moves when in Park or Neutral.
d) Poor gear shift quality or erratic gear changes.

Refer to Chapter 7B, Section 4 for the selector cable adjustment procedure.

Engine won't start in any gear, or starts in gears other than Park or Neutral

- ☐ Incorrect selector cable adjustment (Chapter 7A).

Transmission slips, shifts roughly, is noisy, or has no drive in forward or reverse gears

There are many probable causes for the above problems, but the home mechanic should be concerned with only one possibility – fluid level. Before taking the vehicle to a dealer or transmission specialist, check the fluid level as described in Chapter 1A, Section 16. Correct the fluid level as necessary, or change the fluid. If the problem persists, professional help will be necessary.

Driveshafts

Clicking or knocking noise on turns (at slow speed on full-lock)

- ☐ Lack of constant velocity joint lubricant, possibly due to damaged gaiter (Chapter 8).
- ☐ Worn outer constant velocity joint (Chapter 8).

Vibration when accelerating or decelerating

- ☐ Worn inner constant velocity joint (Chapter 8).
- ☐ Bent or distorted driveshaft (Chapter 8).
- ☐ Worn intermediate bearing (Chapter 8).

Braking system

Note: *Before assuming that a brake problem exists, make sure that the tyres are in good condition and correctly inflated, that the front wheel alignment is correct, and that the vehicle is not loaded with weight in an unequal manner. Apart from checking the condition of all pipe and hose connections, any faults occurring on the anti-lock braking system should be referred to a Seat dealer or suitably equipped garage for diagnosis.*

Vehicle pulls to one side under braking

- ☐ Worn, defective, damaged or contaminated brake pads on one side (Chapter 9).
- ☐ Seized or partially-seized front brake caliper (Chapter 9).
- ☐ A mixture of brake pad materials fitted between sides (Chapter 9).
- ☐ Brake caliper mounting bolts loose (Chapter 9).
- ☐ Worn or damaged steering or suspension components (Chapters 1A or 1B and 10).

Noise (grinding or high-pitched squeal) when brakes applied

- ☐ Brake pad material worn down to metal backing (Chapter 9).
- ☐ Brake shoe material worn down to metal backing (Chapter 9).
- ☐ Excessive corrosion of brake disc. May be apparent after the vehicle has been standing for some time (Chapter 9).
- ☐ Foreign object (stone chipping, etc) trapped between brake disc and shield (Chapter 9).

Excessive brake pedal travel

- ☐ Faulty master cylinder (Chapter 9).
- ☐ Air in hydraulic system (Chapter 9).
- ☐ Faulty vacuum servo unit (Chapter 9).

Brake pedal feels spongy when depressed

- ☐ Air in hydraulic system (Chapter 9).
- ☐ Deteriorated flexible rubber brake hoses (Chapter 9).
- ☐ Master cylinder mounting nuts loose (Chapter 9).
- ☐ Faulty master cylinder (Chapter 9).

Excessive brake pedal effort required to stop vehicle

- ☐ Faulty vacuum servo unit (Chapter 9).
- ☐ Disconnected, damaged or insecure brake servo vacuum hose (Chapter 9).
- ☐ Primary or secondary hydraulic circuit failure.
- ☐ Seized brake caliper (Chapter 9).
- ☐ Brake pads incorrectly fitted (Chapter 9).
- ☐ Brake shoes incorrectly fitted (Chapter 9).
- ☐ Brake pads contaminated (Chapter 1A or 1B).

Judder felt through brake pedal or steering wheel when braking

- ☐ Excessive run-out or distortion of discs (Chapters 9).
- ☐ Brake pads worn (Chapter 9).
- ☐ Brake caliper mounting bolts loose (Chapter 9).
- ☐ Wear in suspension or steering components or mountings (Chapter 10).

Brakes binding

- ☐ Seized brake caliper (Chapter 9).
- ☐ Incorrectly-adjusted handbrake mechanism (Chapter 9).
- ☐ Faulty master cylinder (Chapter 9).

Rear wheels locking under normal braking

- ☐ Rear brake pads contaminated (Chapter 9).
- ☐ ABS system fault (Chapter 9).

Suspension and steering

Note: *Before diagnosing suspension or steering faults, be sure that the trouble is not due to incorrect tyre pressures, mixtures of tyre types, or binding brakes.*

Vehicle pulls to one side

- ☐ Defective tyre (*Weekly checks*).
- ☐ Excessive wear in suspension or steering components (Chapter 10).
- ☐ Incorrect front wheel alignment (Chapter 10).
- ☐ Damage to steering or suspension components (Chapter 10).

Wheel wobble and vibration

- ☐ Front roadwheels out of balance (vibration felt mainly through the steering wheel).
- ☐ Rear roadwheels out of balance (vibration felt throughout the vehicle).
- ☐ Roadwheels damaged or distorted.
- ☐ Faulty or damaged tyre (*Weekly checks*).
- ☐ Worn steering or suspension joints, bushes or components (Chapter 10).
- ☐ Wheel bolts loose (*Weekly checks*).

Excessive pitching and/or rolling around corners, or during braking

- ☐ Defective shock absorbers (Chapter 10).
- ☐ Broken or weak spring and/or suspension part (Chapter 10).
- ☐ Worn or damaged anti-roll bar or mountings (Chapter 10).

Wandering or general instability

- ☐ Incorrect front wheel alignment (Chapter 10).
- ☐ Worn steering or suspension joints, bushes or components (Chapter 10).
- ☐ Roadwheels out of balance.
- ☐ Faulty or damaged tyre (*Weekly checks*).
- ☐ Wheel bolts loose (*Weekly checks*).
- ☐ Defective shock absorbers (Chapter 10).

Excessively-stiff steering

- ☐ Lack of power steering fluid (*Weekly checks*).
- ☐ Seized track rod end balljoint or suspension balljoint (Chapter 10).
- ☐ Incorrect front wheel alignment (Chapter 10).
- ☐ Steering rack or column bent or damaged (Chapter 10).
- ☐ Power steering pump fault (Chapter 10).

Excessive play in steering

- ☐ Worn steering column universal joint (Chapter 10).
- ☐ Worn steering track rod end balljoints (Chapter 10).
- ☐ Worn steering rack (Chapter 10).
- ☐ Worn steering or suspension joints, bushes or components (Chapter 10).

Lack of power assistance

- ☐ Power steering motor faulty (models with electric power steering) (Chapter 10).
- ☐ Incorrect power steering fluid level (*Weekly checks*).
- ☐ Restriction in power steering fluid hoses.
- ☐ Faulty power steering pump (Chapter 10).
- ☐ Faulty steering rack (Chapter 10).

Tyre wear excessive

Tyre treads exhibit feathered edges

- ☐ Incorrect toe setting (Chapter 10).

Tyres worn in centre of tread

- ☐ Tyres over-inflated (*Weekly checks*).

Tyres worn on inside and outside edges

- ☐ Tyres under-inflated (*Weekly checks*).

Tyres worn on inside or outside edges

- ☐ Incorrect camber/castor angles (wear on one edge only) (Chapter 10).
- ☐ Worn steering or suspension joints, bushes or components (Chapters 10).
- ☐ Excessively-hard cornering.
- ☐ Accident damage.

Tyres worn unevenly

- ☐ Tyres/wheels out of balance (*Weekly checks*).
- ☐ Excessive wheel or tyre run-out.
- ☐ Worn shock absorbers (Chapter 10).
- ☐ Faulty tyre (*Weekly checks*).

Electrical system

Note: *For problems associated with the starting system, refer to the faults listed under 'Engine' earlier in this Section.*

Battery won't hold a charge for more than a few days

- ☐ Battery defective internally (Chapter 5A).
- ☐ Battery terminal connections loose or corroded (*Weekly checks*).
- ☐ Auxiliary drivebelt broken, worn or incorrectly adjusted (Chapter 1A or 1B).
- ☐ Alternator not charging at correct output (Chapter 5A).
- ☐ Alternator or voltage regulator faulty (Chapter 5A).
- ☐ Short-circuit causing continual battery drain (Chapter 12).

Ignition/no-charge warning light stays on with engine running

- ☐ Auxiliary drivebelt broken, worn, or incorrectly adjusted (Chapter 1A or 1B).
- ☐ Internal fault in alternator or voltage regulator (Chapter 5A).
- ☐ Broken, disconnected, or loose wiring in charging circuit.

Ignition/no-charge warning light fails to come on

- ☐ Instrument panel faulty (Chapter 12).
- ☐ Broken, disconnected, or loose wiring in warning light circuit (Chapter 12).
- ☐ Alternator faulty (Chapter 5A).

Electrical system (continued)

Lights inoperative

- ☐ Bulb blown (Chapter 12).
- ☐ Corrosion of bulb or bulbholder contacts (Chapter 12).
- ☐ Blown fuse (Chapter 12).
- ☐ Faulty relay (Chapter 12).
- ☐ Broken, loose, or disconnected wiring.
- ☐ Faulty switch (Chapter 12).

Instrument readings inaccurate or erratic

Fuel or temperature gauges give no reading

- ☐ Faulty gauge sensor unit (Chapter 4A or 4B).
- ☐ Wiring open-circuit.
- ☐ Faulty gauge (Chapter 12).

Fuel or temperature gauges give continuous maximum reading

- ☐ Faulty gauge sensor unit (Chapter 4A or 4B).
- ☐ Wiring short-circuit (Chapter 12).
- ☐ Faulty gauge (Chapter 12).

Horn inoperative, or unsatisfactory in operation

Horn operates all the time

- ☐ Horn push either earthed or stuck down (Chapter 12).
- ☐ Horn cable-to-horn push earthed (Chapter 12).

Horn fails to operate

- ☐ Blown fuse (Chapter 12).
- ☐ Cable or cable connections loose, broken or disconnected.
- ☐ Faulty horn (Chapter 12).

Horn emits intermittent or unsatisfactory sound

- ☐ Cable connections loose.
- ☐ Horn mountings loose.
- ☐ Faulty horn (Chapter 12).

Windscreen/tailgate wipers failed, or unsatisfactory in operation

Wipers fail to operate, or operate very slowly

- ☐ Wiper blades stuck to screen, or linkage seized or binding (Chapter 12).
- ☐ Blown fuse (Chapter 12).
- ☐ Cable or cable connections loose, broken or disconnected.
- ☐ Faulty wiper motor (Chapter 12).

Wiper blades sweep over too large or too small an area of the glass

- ☐ Wiper arms incorrectly positioned on spindles (Chapter 12).
- ☐ Excessive wear of wiper linkage (Chapter 12).
- ☐ Wiper motor or linkage mountings loose or insecure (Chapter 12).

Wiper blades fail to clean the glass effectively

- ☐ Wiper blade rubbers worn or perished (*Weekly checks*).
- ☐ Wiper arm tension springs broken, or arm pivots seized (Chapter 12).
- ☐ Insufficient windscreen washer additive to adequately remove road film (*Weekly checks*).

Windscreen/tailgate washers failed, or unsatisfactory in operation

One or more washer jets inoperative

- ☐ Blocked washer jet (Chapter 12).
- ☐ Disconnected, kinked or restricted fluid hose (Chapter 12).
- ☐ Insufficient fluid in washer reservoir (*Weekly checks*).

Washer pump fails to operate

- ☐ Broken or disconnected wiring or connections.
- ☐ Blown fuse (Chapter 12).
- ☐ Faulty washer switch (Chapter 12).
- ☐ Faulty washer pump (Chapter 12).

Electric windows inoperative, or unsatisfactory in operation

Window glass will only move in one direction

- ☐ Faulty switch (Chapter 12).

Window glass slow to move

- ☐ Regulator seized or damaged, or in need of lubricant (Chapter 11).
- ☐ Door internal components or trim fouling regulator (Chapter 11).
- ☐ Faulty motor (Chapter 11).

Window glass fails to move

- ☐ Blown fuse (Chapter 12).
- ☐ Broken or disconnected wiring or connections.
- ☐ Faulty motor (Chapter 11).

Central locking system inoperative, or unsatisfactory in operation

Complete system failure

- ☐ Blown fuse (Chapter 12).
- ☐ Broken or disconnected wiring or connections (Chapter 12).

Door/tailgate locks but will not unlock, or unlocks but will not lock

- ☐ Broken or disconnected link rod(s).
- ☐ Faulty lock motor (Chapter 11).

One lock fails to operate

- ☐ Broken or disconnected wiring or connections.
- ☐ Faulty lock motor (Chapter 11).
- ☐ Broken, binding or disconnected link rod(s).

A

ABS (Anti-lock brake system) A system, usually electronically controlled, that senses incipient wheel lockup during braking and relieves hydraulic pressure at wheels that are about to skid.

Air bag An inflatable bag hidden in the steering wheel (driver's side) or the dash or glovebox (passenger side). In a head-on collision, the bags inflate, preventing the driver and front passenger from being thrown forward into the steering wheel or windscreen.

Air cleaner A metal or plastic housing, containing a filter element, which removes dust and dirt from the air being drawn into the engine.

Air filter element The actual filter in an air cleaner system, usually manufactured from pleated paper and requiring renewal at regular intervals.

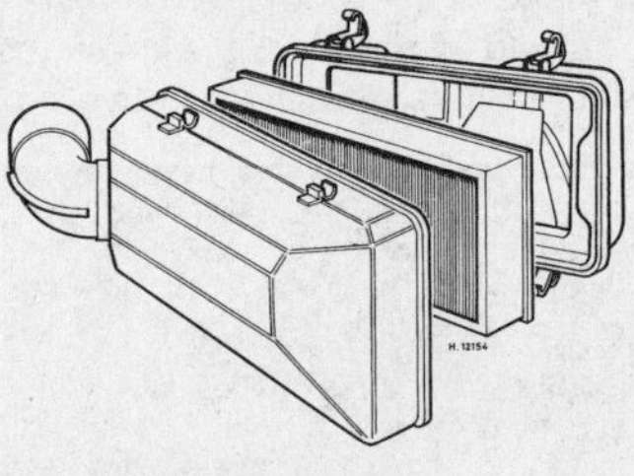

Air filter

Allen key A hexagonal wrench which fits into a recessed hexagonal hole.

Alligator clip A long-nosed spring-loaded metal clip with meshing teeth. Used to make temporary electrical connections.

Alternator A component in the electrical system which converts mechanical energy from a drivebelt into electrical energy to charge the battery and to operate the starting system, ignition system and electrical accessories.

Ampere (amp) A unit of measurement for the flow of electric current. One amp is the amount of current produced by one volt acting through a resistance of one ohm.

Anaerobic sealer A substance used to prevent bolts and screws from loosening. Anaerobic means that it does not require oxygen for activation. The Loctite brand is widely used.

Antifreeze A substance (usually ethylene glycol) mixed with water, and added to a vehicle's cooling system, to prevent freezing of the coolant in winter. Antifreeze also contains chemicals to inhibit corrosion and the formation of rust and other deposits that would tend to clog the radiator and coolant passages and reduce cooling efficiency.

Anti-seize compound A coating that reduces the risk of seizing on fasteners that are subjected to high temperatures, such as exhaust manifold bolts and nuts.

Asbestos A natural fibrous mineral with great heat resistance, commonly used in the composition of brake friction materials. Asbestos is a health hazard and the dust created by brake systems should never be inhaled or ingested.

Axle A shaft on which a wheel revolves, or which revolves with a wheel. Also, a solid beam that connects the two wheels at one end of the vehicle. An axle which also transmits power to the wheels is known as a live axle.

Axleshaft A single rotating shaft, on either side of the differential, which delivers power from the final drive assembly to the drive wheels. Also called a driveshaft or a halfshaft.

B

Ball bearing An anti-friction bearing consisting of a hardened inner and outer race with hardened steel balls between two races.

Bearing The curved surface on a shaft or in a bore, or the part assembled into either, that permits relative motion between them with minimum wear and friction.

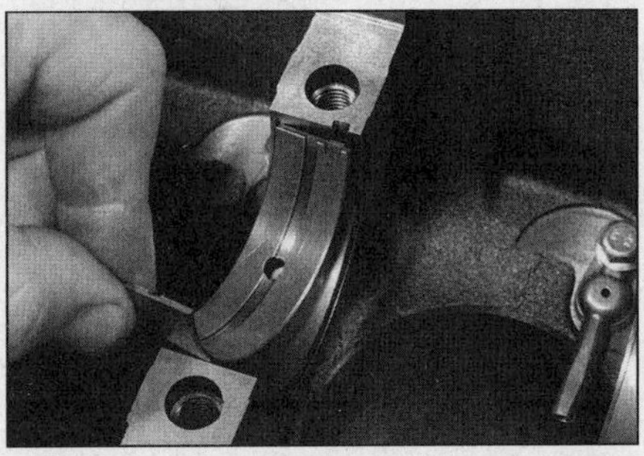

Bearing

Big-end bearing The bearing in the end of the connecting rod that's attached to the crankshaft.

Bleed nipple A valve on a brake wheel cylinder, caliper or other hydraulic component that is opened to purge the hydraulic system of air. Also called a bleed screw.

Brake bleeding Procedure for removing air from lines of a hydraulic brake system.

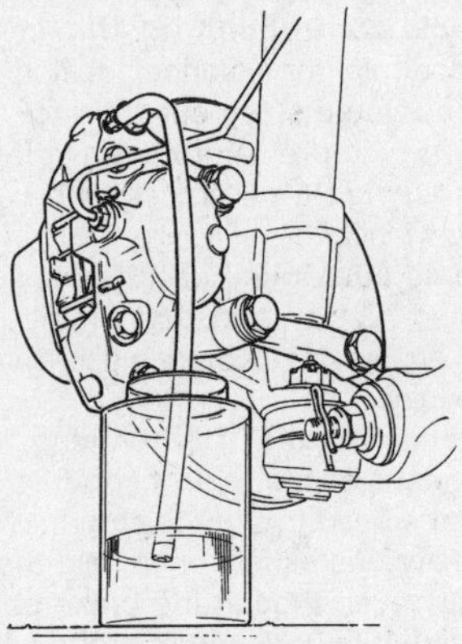

Brake bleeding

Brake disc The component of a disc brake that rotates with the wheels.

Brake drum The component of a drum brake that rotates with the wheels.

Brake linings The friction material which contacts the brake disc or drum to retard the vehicle's speed. The linings are bonded or riveted to the brake pads or shoes.

Brake pads The replaceable friction pads that pinch the brake disc when the brakes are applied. Brake pads consist of a friction material bonded or riveted to a rigid backing plate.

Brake shoe The crescent-shaped carrier to which the brake linings are mounted and which forces the lining against the rotating drum during braking.

Braking systems For more information on braking systems, consult the *Haynes Automotive Brake Manual*.

Breaker bar A long socket wrench handle providing greater leverage.

Bulkhead The insulated partition between the engine and the passenger compartment.

C

Caliper The non-rotating part of a disc-brake assembly that straddles the disc and carries the brake pads. The caliper also contains the hydraulic components that cause the pads to pinch the disc when the brakes are applied. A caliper is also a measuring tool that can be set to measure inside or outside dimensions of an object.

Camshaft A rotating shaft on which a series of cam lobes operate the valve mechanisms. The camshaft may be driven by gears, by sprockets and chain or by sprockets and a belt.

Canister A container in an evaporative emission control system; contains activated charcoal granules to trap vapours from the fuel system.

Canister

Carburettor A device which mixes fuel with air in the proper proportions to provide a desired power output from a spark ignition internal combustion engine.

Castellated Resembling the parapets along the top of a castle wall. For example, a castellated balljoint stud nut.

Castor In wheel alignment, the backward or forward tilt of the steering axis. Castor is positive when the steering axis is inclined rearward at the top.

Catalytic converter A silencer-like device in the exhaust system which converts certain pollutants in the exhaust gases into less harmful substances.

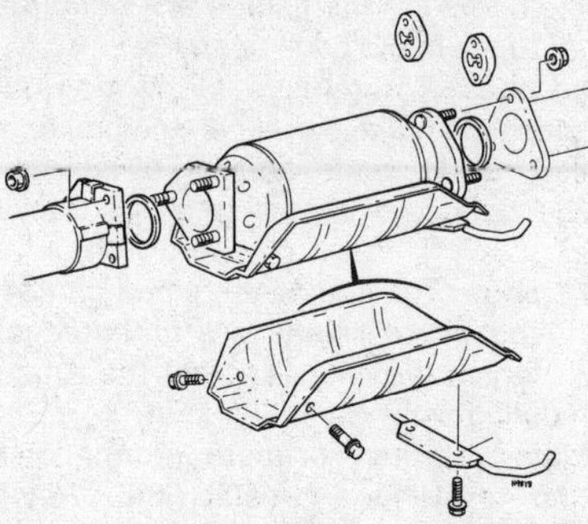

Catalytic converter

Circlip A ring-shaped clip used to prevent endwise movement of cylindrical parts and shafts. An internal circlip is installed in a groove in a housing; an external circlip fits into a groove on the outside of a cylindrical piece such as a shaft.

Clearance The amount of space between two parts. For example, between a piston and a cylinder, between a bearing and a journal, etc.

Coil spring A spiral of elastic steel found in various sizes throughout a vehicle, for example as a springing medium in the suspension and in the valve train.

Compression Reduction in volume, and increase in pressure and temperature, of a gas, caused by squeezing it into a smaller space.

Compression ratio The relationship between cylinder volume when the piston is at top dead centre and cylinder volume when the piston is at bottom dead centre.

Constant velocity (CV) joint A type of universal joint that cancels out vibrations caused by driving power being transmitted through an angle.

Core plug A disc or cup-shaped metal device inserted in a hole in a casting through which core was removed when the casting was formed. Also known as a freeze plug or expansion plug.

Crankcase The lower part of the engine block in which the crankshaft rotates.

Crankshaft The main rotating member, or shaft, running the length of the crankcase, with offset "throws" to which the connecting rods are attached.

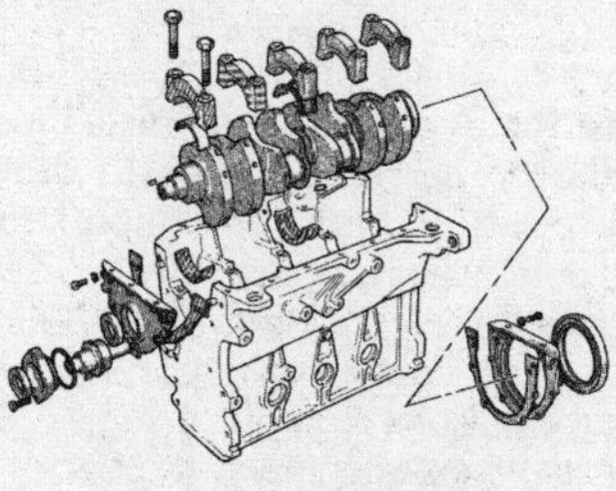

Crankshaft assembly

Crocodile clip See Alligator clip

D

Diagnostic code Code numbers obtained by accessing the diagnostic mode of an engine management computer. This code can be used to determine the area in the system where a malfunction may be located.

Disc brake A brake design incorporating a rotating disc onto which brake pads are squeezed. The resulting friction converts the energy of a moving vehicle into heat.

Double-overhead cam (DOHC) An engine that uses two overhead camshafts, usually one for the intake valves and one for the exhaust valves.

Drivebelt(s) The belt(s) used to drive accessories such as the alternator, water pump, power steering pump, air conditioning compressor, etc. off the crankshaft pulley.

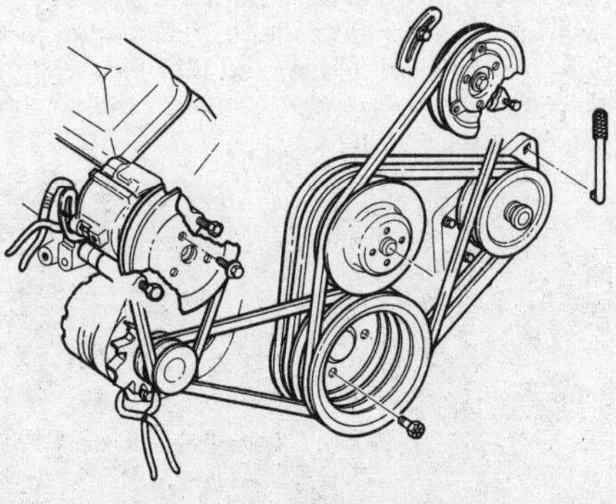

Accessory drivebelts

Driveshaft Any shaft used to transmit motion. Commonly used when referring to the axleshafts on a front wheel drive vehicle.

Drum brake A type of brake using a drum-shaped metal cylinder attached to the inner surface of the wheel. When the brake pedal is pressed, curved brake shoes with friction linings press against the inside of the drum to slow or stop the vehicle.

E

EGR valve A valve used to introduce exhaust gases into the intake air stream.

Electronic control unit (ECU) A computer which controls (for instance) ignition and fuel injection systems, or an anti-lock braking system. For more information refer to the *Haynes Automotive Electrical and Electronic Systems Manual.*

Electronic Fuel Injection (EFI) A computer controlled fuel system that distributes fuel through an injector located in each intake port of the engine.

Emergency brake A braking system, independent of the main hydraulic system, that can be used to slow or stop the vehicle if the primary brakes fail, or to hold the vehicle stationary even though the brake pedal isn't depressed. It usually consists of a hand lever that actuates either front or rear brakes mechanically through a series of cables and linkages. Also known as a handbrake or parking brake.

Endfloat The amount of lengthwise movement between two parts. As applied to a crankshaft, the distance that the crankshaft can move forward and back in the cylinder block.

Engine management system (EMS) A computer controlled system which manages the fuel injection and the ignition systems in an integrated fashion.

Exhaust manifold A part with several passages through which exhaust gases leave the engine combustion chambers and enter the exhaust pipe.

F

Fan clutch A viscous (fluid) drive coupling device which permits variable engine fan speeds in relation to engine speeds.

Feeler blade A thin strip or blade of hardened steel, ground to an exact thickness, used to check or measure clearances between parts.

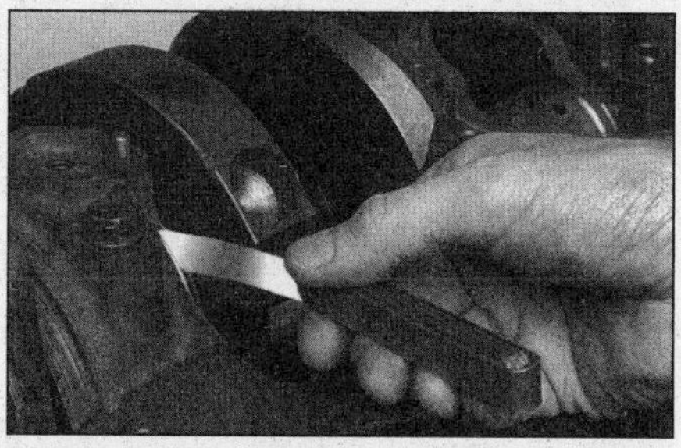

Feeler blade

Firing order The order in which the engine cylinders fire, or deliver their power strokes, beginning with the number one cylinder.

Flywheel A heavy spinning wheel in which energy is absorbed and stored by means of momentum. On cars, the flywheel is attached to the crankshaft to smooth out firing impulses.

Free play The amount of travel before any action takes place. The "looseness" in a linkage, or an assembly of parts, between the initial application of force and actual movement. For example, the distance the brake pedal moves before the pistons in the master cylinder are actuated.

Fuse An electrical device which protects a circuit against accidental overload. The typical fuse contains a soft piece of metal which is calibrated to melt at a predetermined current flow (expressed as amps) and break the circuit.

Fusible link A circuit protection device consisting of a conductor surrounded by heat-resistant insulation. The conductor is smaller than the wire it protects, so it acts as the weakest link in the circuit. Unlike a blown fuse, a failed fusible link must frequently be cut from the wire for replacement.

G

Gap The distance the spark must travel in jumping from the centre electrode to the side electrode in a spark plug. Also refers to the spacing between the points in a contact breaker assembly in a conventional points-type ignition, or to the distance between the reluctor or rotor and the pickup coil in an electronic ignition.

Adjusting spark plug gap

Gasket Any thin, soft material - usually cork, cardboard, asbestos or soft metal - installed between two metal surfaces to ensure a good seal. For instance, the cylinder head gasket seals the joint between the block and the cylinder head.

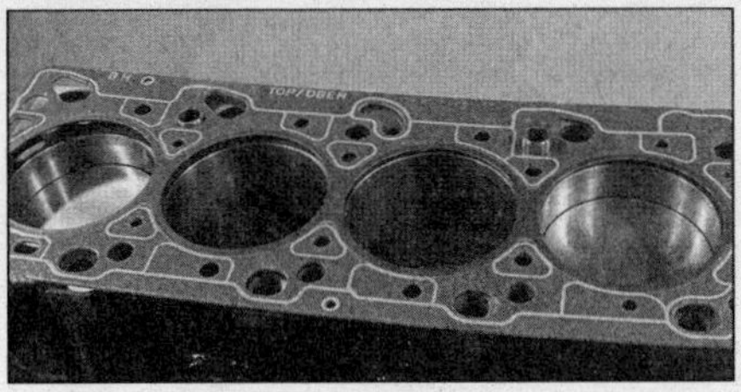

Gasket

Gauge An instrument panel display used to monitor engine conditions. A gauge with a movable pointer on a dial or a fixed scale is an analogue gauge. A gauge with a numerical readout is called a digital gauge.

H

Halfshaft A rotating shaft that transmits power from the final drive unit to a drive wheel, usually when referring to a live rear axle.

Harmonic balancer A device designed to reduce torsion or twisting vibration in the crankshaft. May be incorporated in the crankshaft pulley. Also known as a vibration damper.

Hone An abrasive tool for correcting small irregularities or differences in diameter in an engine cylinder, brake cylinder, etc.

Hydraulic tappet A tappet that utilises hydraulic pressure from the engine's lubrication system to maintain zero clearance (constant contact with both camshaft and valve stem). Automatically adjusts to variation in valve stem length. Hydraulic tappets also reduce valve noise.

I

Ignition timing The moment at which the spark plug fires, usually expressed in the number of crankshaft degrees before the piston reaches the top of its stroke.

Inlet manifold A tube or housing with passages through which flows the air-fuel mixture (carburettor vehicles and vehicles with throttle body injection) or air only (port fuel-injected vehicles) to the port openings in the cylinder head.

J

Jump start Starting the engine of a vehicle with a discharged or weak battery by attaching jump leads from the weak battery to a charged or helper battery.

L

Load Sensing Proportioning Valve (LSPV) A brake hydraulic system control valve that works like a proportioning valve, but also takes into consideration the amount of weight carried by the rear axle.

Locknut A nut used to lock an adjustment nut, or other threaded component, in place. For example, a locknut is employed to keep the adjusting nut on the rocker arm in position.

Lockwasher A form of washer designed to prevent an attaching nut from working loose.

M

MacPherson strut A type of front suspension system devised by Earle MacPherson at Ford of England. In its original form, a simple lateral link with the anti-roll bar creates the lower control arm. A long strut - an integral coil spring and shock absorber - is mounted between the body and the steering knuckle. Many modern so-called MacPherson strut systems use a conventional lower A-arm and don't rely on the anti-roll bar for location.

Multimeter An electrical test instrument with the capability to measure voltage, current and resistance.

N

NOx Oxides of Nitrogen. A common toxic pollutant emitted by petrol and diesel engines at higher temperatures.

O

Ohm The unit of electrical resistance. One volt applied to a resistance of one ohm will produce a current of one amp.

Ohmmeter An instrument for measuring electrical resistance.

O-ring A type of sealing ring made of a special rubber-like material; in use, the O-ring is compressed into a groove to provide the sealing action.

Overhead cam (ohc) engine An engine with the camshaft(s) located on top of the cylinder head(s).

Overhead valve (ohv) engine An engine with the valves located in the cylinder head, but with the camshaft located in the engine block.

Oxygen sensor A device installed in the engine exhaust manifold, which senses the oxygen content in the exhaust and converts this information into an electric current. Also called a Lambda sensor.

P

Phillips screw A type of screw head having a cross instead of a slot for a corresponding type of screwdriver.

Plastigage A thin strip of plastic thread, available in different sizes, used for measuring clearances. For example, a strip of Plastigage is laid across a bearing journal. The parts are assembled and dismantled; the width of the crushed strip indicates the clearance between journal and bearing.

Plastigage

Propeller shaft The long hollow tube with universal joints at both ends that carries power from the transmission to the differential on front-engined rear wheel drive vehicles.

Proportioning valve A hydraulic control valve which limits the amount of pressure to the rear brakes during panic stops to prevent wheel lock-up.

R

Rack-and-pinion steering A steering system with a pinion gear on the end of the steering shaft that mates with a rack (think of a geared wheel opened up and laid flat). When the steering wheel is turned, the pinion turns, moving the rack to the left or right. This movement is transmitted through the track rods to the steering arms at the wheels.

Radiator A liquid-to-air heat transfer device designed to reduce the temperature of the coolant in an internal combustion engine cooling system.

Refrigerant Any substance used as a heat transfer agent in an air-conditioning system. R-12 has been the principle refrigerant for many years; recently, however, manufacturers have begun using R-134a, a non-CFC substance that is considered less harmful to the ozone in the upper atmosphere.

Rocker arm A lever arm that rocks on a shaft or pivots on a stud. In an overhead valve engine, the rocker arm converts the upward movement of the pushrod into a downward movement to open a valve.

Rotor In a distributor, the rotating device inside the cap that connects the centre electrode and the outer terminals as it turns, distributing the high voltage from the coil secondary winding to the proper spark plug. Also, that part of an alternator which rotates inside the stator. Also, the rotating assembly of a turbocharger, including the compressor wheel, shaft and turbine wheel.

Runout The amount of wobble (in-and-out movement) of a gear or wheel as it's rotated. The amount a shaft rotates "out-of-true." The out-of-round condition of a rotating part.

S

Sealant A liquid or paste used to prevent leakage at a joint. Sometimes used in conjunction with a gasket.

Sealed beam lamp An older headlight design which integrates the reflector, lens and filaments into a hermetically-sealed one-piece unit. When a filament burns out or the lens cracks, the entire unit is simply replaced.

Serpentine drivebelt A single, long, wide accessory drivebelt that's used on some newer vehicles to drive all the accessories, instead of a series of smaller, shorter belts. Serpentine drivebelts are usually tensioned by an automatic tensioner.

Serpentine drivebelt

Shim Thin spacer, commonly used to adjust the clearance or relative positions between two parts. For example, shims inserted into or under bucket tappets control valve clearances. Clearance is adjusted by changing the thickness of the shim.

Slide hammer A special puller that screws into or hooks onto a component such as a shaft or bearing; a heavy sliding handle on the shaft bottoms against the end of the shaft to knock the component free.

Sprocket A tooth or projection on the periphery of a wheel, shaped to engage with a chain or drivebelt. Commonly used to refer to the sprocket wheel itself.

Starter inhibitor switch On vehicles with an automatic transmission, a switch that prevents starting if the vehicle is not in Neutral or Park.

Strut See MacPherson strut.

T

Tappet A cylindrical component which transmits motion from the cam to the valve stem, either directly or via a pushrod and rocker arm. Also called a cam follower.

Thermostat A heat-controlled valve that regulates the flow of coolant between the cylinder block and the radiator, so maintaining optimum engine operating temperature. A thermostat is also used in some air cleaners in which the temperature is regulated.

Thrust bearing The bearing in the clutch assembly that is moved in to the release levers by clutch pedal action to disengage the clutch. Also referred to as a release bearing.

Timing belt A toothed belt which drives the camshaft. Serious engine damage may result if it breaks in service.

Timing chain A chain which drives the camshaft.

Toe-in The amount the front wheels are closer together at the front than at the rear. On rear wheel drive vehicles, a slight amount of toe-in is usually specified to keep the front wheels running parallel on the road by offsetting other forces that tend to spread the wheels apart.

Toe-out The amount the front wheels are closer together at the rear than at the front. On front wheel drive vehicles, a slight amount of toe-out is usually specified.

Tools For full information on choosing and using tools, refer to the *Haynes Automotive Tools Manual.*

Tracer A stripe of a second colour applied to a wire insulator to distinguish that wire from another one with the same colour insulator.

Tune-up A process of accurate and careful adjustments and parts replacement to obtain the best possible engine performance.

Turbocharger A centrifugal device, driven by exhaust gases, that pressurises the intake air. Normally used to increase the power output from a given engine displacement, but can also be used primarily to reduce exhaust emissions (as on VW's "Umwelt" Diesel engine).

U

Universal joint or U-joint A double-pivoted connection for transmitting power from a driving to a driven shaft through an angle. A U-joint consists of two Y-shaped yokes and a cross-shaped member called the spider.

V

Valve A device through which the flow of liquid, gas, vacuum, or loose material in bulk may be started, stopped, or regulated by a movable part that opens, shuts, or partially obstructs one or more ports or passageways. A valve is also the movable part of such a device.

Valve clearance The clearance between the valve tip (the end of the valve stem) and the rocker arm or tappet. The valve clearance is measured when the valve is closed.

Vernier caliper A precision measuring instrument that measures inside and outside dimensions. Not quite as accurate as a micrometer, but more convenient.

Viscosity The thickness of a liquid or its resistance to flow.

Volt A unit for expressing electrical "pressure" in a circuit. One volt that will produce a current of one ampere through a resistance of one ohm.

W

Welding Various processes used to join metal items by heating the areas to be joined to a molten state and fusing them together. For more information refer to the *Haynes Automotive Welding Manual.*

Wiring diagram A drawing portraying the components and wires in a vehicle's electrical system, using standardised symbols. For more information refer to the *Haynes Automotive Electrical and Electronic Systems Manual.*

Note: *References throughout this index are in the form* **"Chapter number" • "Page number"**. *So, for example, 2C•15 refers to page 15 of Chapter 2C.*

A

B

C

Note: *References throughout this index are in the form* "**Chapter number**" • "**Page number**". *So, for example, 2C•15 refers to page 15 of Chapter 2C.*

Note: *References throughout this index are in the form* "**Chapter number**" • "**Page number**". *So, for example, 2C•15 refers to page 15 of Chapter 2C.*

Note: *References throughout this index are in the form* "**Chapter number**" • "**Page number**". *So, for example, 2C•15 refers to page 15 of Chapter 2C.*

Note: *References throughout this index are in the form* "**Chapter number**" • "**Page number**"*. So, for example, 2C•15 refers to page 15 of Chapter 2C.*

Preserving Our Motoring Heritage

< The Model J Duesenberg Derham Tourster. Only eight of these magnificent cars were ever built – this is the only example to be found outside the United States of America

Almost every car you've ever loved, loathed or desired is gathered under one roof at the Haynes Motor Museum. Over 300 immaculately presented cars and motorbikes represent every aspect of our motoring heritage, from elegant reminders of bygone days, such as the superb Model J Duesenberg to curiosities like the bug-eyed BMW Isetta. There are also many old friends and flames. Perhaps you remember the 1959 Ford Popular that you did your courting in? The magnificent 'Red Collection' is a spectacle of classic sports cars including AC, Alfa Romeo, Austin Healey, Ferrari, Lamborghini, Maserati, MG, Riley, Porsche and Triumph.

A Perfect Day Out

Each and every vehicle at the Haynes Motor Museum has played its part in the history and culture of Motoring. Today, they make a wonderful spectacle and a great day out for all the family. Bring the kids, bring Mum and Dad, but above all bring your camera to capture those golden memories for ever. You will also find an impressive array of motoring memorabilia, a comfortable 70 seat video cinema and one of the most extensive transport book shops in Britain. The Pit Stop Cafe serves everything from a cup of tea to wholesome, home-made meals or, if you prefer, you can enjoy the large picnic area nestled in the beautiful rural surroundings of Somerset.

> *John Haynes O.B.E., Founder and Chairman of the museum at the wheel of a Haynes Light 12.*

< *Graham Hill's Lola Cosworth Formula 1 car next to a 1934 Riley Sports.*

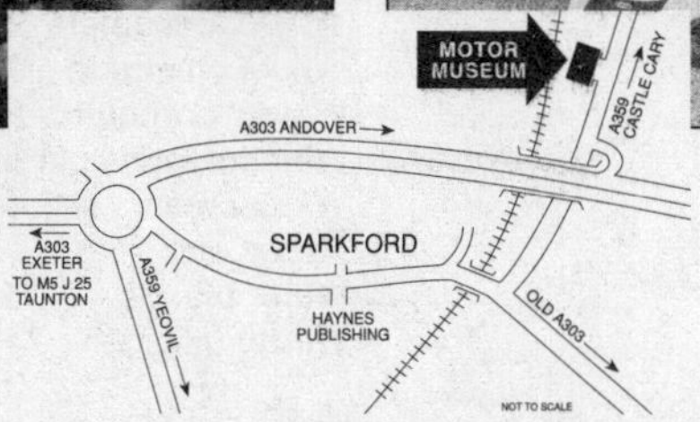

The Museum is situated on the A359 Yeovil to Frome road at Sparkford, just off the A303 in Somerset. It is about 40 miles south of Bristol, and 25 minutes drive from the M5 intersection at Taunton.

Open 9.30am - 5.30pm (10.00am - 4.00pm Winter) 7 days a week, *except Christmas Day, Boxing Day and New Years Day*

Special rates available for schools, coach parties and outings Charitable Trust No. 292048